DEDICATION

Business and Professional Ethics for Directors, Executives & Accountants *is focused on deepening the understanding of how best to incorporate ethical values into governance, strategies, and actions to the benefit of us all.*

Our preparation of the Eighth Edition has been enriched by the contributions of many, but none more than our wives and families who have supported and encouraged us and to whom we dedicate this work. It is with great pride, thankfulness, and love that we acknowledge Jean and Kathy and our growing families.

Leonard J. Brooks, FCPA, FCA

Paul Dunn, CPA, CA

Toronto, Canada
August 2016

ABOUT THE AUTHORS

Leonard J. Brooks is Professor of Business Ethics & Accounting at the Rotman School of Management of the University of Toronto. He is the Executive Director of the Rotman School's Clarkson Centre for Business Ethics & Board Effectiveness, Director of the University's Professional Accounting Centre, and Director of its Master of Forensic Accounting Program.

Professor Brooks served for fourteen years on the Editorial Board of the *Journal of Business Ethics* and continues to serve as a reviewer for that as well as other journals. He has published articles on ethics issues in the *Journal of Business Ethics, Accounting Organizations and Society*, and *Business & Society* and has authored or coauthored/edited the research monograph *Canadian Corporate Social Performance* and books or publications entitled *Business & Professional Ethics for Accountants, 2e*; *Principles of Stakeholder Management: The Clarkson Principles*; and *Ethics & Governance: Developing and Maintaining an Ethical Corporate Culture, 4e.*

Before joining the University of Toronto, Professor Brooks obtained his Chartered Accountant (C.A.) designation in Canada and subsequently became an audit manager and Director of Manpower for Touche Ross & Co. (now Deloitte LLP) in Toronto. He has served as a member, then Chairman, of the CAs' national Board of Examiners, and Chairman of their national Syllabus Committee. Professor Brooks became a Fellow of the Institute of Chartered Accountants of Ontario in 1982. He became a Chartered Professional Accountant (CPA) and a Fellow of the Chartered Professional Accountants (FCPA) of Ontario in 2012.

Paul Dunn is an Associate Professor of Business Ethics at the Goodman School of Business, Brock University. He attended the University of Toronto, graduating with a BA in philosophy and then an MA in philosophy. He worked as a Chartered Accountant (now a CPA) in downtown Toronto in accounting, finance and controllership before returning to school to receive his doctorate in accounting from Boston University. Formerly an accounting theory professor, Professor Dunn now teaches business ethics at both the graduate and undergraduate levels.

Dr. Dunn's research focuses on issues in corporate governance, corporate social responsibility, and business ethics. His work has been published in a variety of scholarly journals including the *Journal of Business Ethics*, the *Journal of Management, Business Ethics Quarterly*, and *Business & Society*. He sits on the editorial boards of the *Journal of Business Ethics* and *Business & Society*. Professor Dunn is the Treasurer for the Society of Business Ethics, and is also the Treasurer for the Social Issues in Management division of the Academy of Management. He is a frequent media commentator on corporate governance issues, especially the role and function of the board of directors.

CONTENTS

BPE DIGITAL RESOURCES: Digital Resources are available for *Business & Professional Ethics* including readings and references noted in the margin of this book, as well as cases and a chapter from earlier editions. Visit **www.cengagebrain.com** for access.

DIGITAL RESOURCES—TABLE OF CONTENTS

PREFACE

CHALLENGES & OPPORTUNITIES

Expectations for appropriate business and professional accounting behavior have changed dramatically. Corporations now face *an era of heightened accountability* beyond shareholders to stakeholders who are intently interested in how corporations achieve their objectives, not just what they achieve. The challenge is to make a profit ethically while respecting the interests of others including the environment, human rights, and contributing positively to society. Opportunities abound for those who face these challenges successfully. More is also expected of professional accountants, who are expected more than ever to serve society's best interests in increasingly complex and challenging business environments.

The era of heightened accountability has been forced by stakeholders who have recognized that errant corporate directors and managers and professional accountants have failed the public interests with catastrophic and lasting impacts. There is a broad understanding that *the last three major negative impacts on the world economy were ethical failures*, including the following:

- The *crisis of confidence in corporate governance and credibility in reporting* caused by the 2002 failures of Enron, Arthur Andersen, and WorldCom, leading to the crash of the stock market and the introduction of the *Sarbanes-Oxley Act of 2002 (SOX)*
- *The Subprime Lending Crisis of 2007–2009*, where greed and unethical behavior led to a crash of the U.S. housing market and the collapse of investment values around the world and the enactment of the U.S. *Dodd-Frank Wall Street Reform and Consumer Protection Act* in 2010.
- The *LIBOR rate manipulation scandal* of 2012 in which the underpinning basis for interest rates was knowingly manipulated for the benefit of a few banks and their traders

In addition, there have been many other ethical failures, such as the Madoff Ponzi scheme; damage to the environment and to vulnerable members of society that has caused serious damage to the reputations of individuals, organizations, or professionals; and an understanding that higher expectations were warranted and that lower levels of performance were to be penalized. Farsighted businesspeople and professional accountants took note and began to search out and manage so as to prevent serious ethics risks from damaging their reputations and their ability to reach their objectives.

This book presents an examination of how businesspeople and professional accountants can prepare themselves, their colleagues, and their organizations to identify important ethics challenges and opportunities and meet the heightened performance expectations they face. To succeed in the future, businesspeople and professional accountants will need to understand the key historical developments that have given rise to these heightened expectations and the techniques that are available and developing to shape future performance.

The demise of Enron, Arthur Andersen, and WorldCom triggered SOX. The subprime lending scandal in 2007 led to the worldwide recession that has so significantly negatively affected economies, jobs, and the lives of us all. *These events were ethical failures that could have been prevented.* Unchecked until too late, they subsequently galvanized reforms in the accountability and governance of both corporations and professional accounting that have influenced business and professional ethics around the world. Undoubtedly, they will continue to bring new challenges and opportunities for directors, executives, managers, and professional accountants.

The reforms in accountability and governance frameworks have recognized that corporations and professional accountants have become increasingly more broadly accountable than generally understood. The *crisis of corporate governance and reporting credibility* that Enron began, Arthur Andersen fostered, WorldCom capped, and SOX sought to remedy heightened the awareness that corporations and the accounting profession must have the support of many stakeholder groups to achieve their strategic objectives. Following very quickly, the subprime lending fiasco from 2007 to 2009 further exacerbated the *crisis of confidence* by sensitizing the public and adding to ethical awareness and generating higher expectations for ethical behavior in order to sustain stakeholder support.

That support requires trust. Trust is based on the expectation that the corporation—really its board, executives, employees, and agents—and professional accountant will do the right thing and that their actions will respect the interests of the stakeholder groups. Earning and maintaining that trust requires changing the strategy, risk management, planning, operations, and decision making of the corporation to take account of the interests and expectations of stakeholder groups in addition to shareholders. A new accountability framework is required that focuses on indicators of performance related to stakeholder expectations for both internal and external reporting.

Governance must focus on this new, broader accountability framework in order to ensure that stakeholder trust objectives are met. Such a change will not happen by itself, and directors are in danger of not fulfilling their expectations to shareholders for risk management and due diligence if they ignore this duty. Some directors have understood the value of an excellent reputation and have been including risks to reputation in their risk management programs. Now that the linkage among ethics, reputation, and trust is clear and better understood, it is vital for corporations to upgrade their accountability and governance frameworks to ensure continued support. Shareholders and other stakeholders have come to expect more than they did pre-SOX—and the bar continues to rise.

Professional accountants can and should provide a critical facilitating element in the trust-oriented accountability and governance system. First, professional accountants can be important agents for ensuring trust. They are expected to serve in the public interest and must do so to preserve the trust placed in them by a society that expects them to behave as professionals. This expectation, which applies to professional accountants in public practice as well as those employed by corporations, requires a rededication to their role as a trusted fiduciary. Second, professional accountants are well placed to understand the role of trust in internal control and accountability frameworks and in the governance frameworks that provide direction and oversight to corporate activities. Third, good professional accountants are expected to display a level of professional skepticism and duty that should enable them to recognize the red flags of potential problems and report or remediate them.

Perhaps most important, these new governance and ethics expectations have reached the academic launching pads for new directors, executives, and professional accountants. The interest in newly created directors' governance education programs is startling. In 2004, the accreditation body for business schools worldwide published an Ethics Education Task Force Report that called for business students to be educated about (1) the responsibility of business in society, (2) ethical leadership, (3) ethical decision making, and (4) corporate governance and ethics.[1] Moreover, many jurisdictions are requiring compulsory ethics courses for accounting students before they are considered ready to write their qualifying exams for professional accounting designation. Accordingly, ethics and governance coverage is penetrating the curricula of far more business schools than in the past—which bodes well for the future.

Understanding these trust expectations and the interrelationship to ethics and governance will resolve challenges and present opportunities for directors, executives, and professional accountants. It will facilitate the assessment of ethics risks, the protection of reputation, and the development of management safeguards such as a strong culture of integrity. More important, it will provide the essential foundation for ensuring the support of individuals—and that of corporations and firms—in the future.

PURPOSE OF THE BOOK

The crisis of corporate reporting credibility became so severe in mid-2002 that drastic measures were required to restore that credibility and relieve the gridlock that froze capital markets and dampened economies around the world. In fact, the financial disasters in 2002 accelerated and crystallized the impact of pressures for enhanced corporate accountability and a supportive governance framework that had been growing for years. As governance reform based on sound ethics takes hold around the world, there is an increasing need to understand the historical precursors involved, the responsibilities expected, and the techniques available for the satisfaction of those expectations.

Telling the story of ongoing pressures for more trusted governance and of the contributions of key financial scandals is important to the development of an appropriate understanding of the post-SOX world for directors, executives, and accountants, and of the heightened ethical expectations arising from the subprime lending crisis. Ethical failures have cost us all dearly. In response, governance has recently incorporated the need for a risk management process—a process that must now be broadened to involve awareness of factors that can erode the support of stakeholder groups.

The reputation of corporations is recognized as being connected with the degree to which stakeholders trust that corporations will do the right thing. In other words, there is now *a concern for both what a corporation does and how it is done.* At certain times in the past, the emphasis was so strongly on achieving profit that little attention was given to how the profit was earned. Now that the support of stakeholders is recognized as critical to success, an important second objective of the book is to provide an understanding how to create a corporate *culture of integrity*—one that builds stakeholders' ethical expectations into corporate behavior, accountability, and governance. Extending this discussion to the new era for professional accountants and reviewing their potential roles is a third objective.

Directors, executives, and accountants need to understand how to make ethical decisions they can defend to stakeholders. Codes of conduct cannot cover all situations, so organizational cultures need to be developed and decision processes utilized that are based on sound ethical decision-making frameworks. *Business and Professional Ethics for Directors, Executives & Accountants* covers these topics as well as the development of an *ethics risk management process*, strategies for dealing with and reporting to stakeholders, and strategies for ensuring ethical behavior in the workplace and during the management of crises.

[1]The Association to Advance Collegiate Schools of Business, *AACSB Ethics Education Task Force Report*, June 2004, available at http://www.aacsb.edu/publications/researchreports/archives/ethics-education.pdf.

In a nutshell, *Business and Professional Ethics for Directors, Executives & Accountants* examines the background and nature of the heightened stakeholder-accountability era of corporate and professional accountability and governance and provides insights into the development of sound patterns of behavior on the part of directors, executives, and accountants. Successful management of ethical risks and the development of ethical competitive advantages depend upon the mastery of the subjects discussed. Professional accountants must understand the issues covered as a foundation for the fulfillment of their role as fiduciaries and experts in accountability and governance.

APPLICABILITY

Business and Professional Ethics for Directors, Executives & Accountants is intended as a sourcebook for directors, executives, and professional accountants on accountability and governance, on appropriate decision making and behavior, and on ethics risk management in the new era of heightened corporate accountability. Blending text, readings, and cases, it can be used as or for the following:

- A stand-alone book in courses in business and/or professional ethics and/or in governance.
- An adjunct to traditional strategy, governance, or accounting texts to provide access to interesting, real-world dilemmas. The material in the book has been used very successfully with MBA and Executive MBA students as well as accounting students.
- Custom selections from the text, cases, and readings can be tailored to specific course requirements.
- Independent study.

The book has been organized into relatively freestanding chapters to facilitate custom publishing of a selection of chapters and/or cases. For example, material in Chapter 2 could be used to introduce governance and provide a historical path to current thinking on reputational issues and stakeholder support. The history of ethics and governance scandals since 2001, which appears in Chapter 2, has been well used to start off Executive MBA programs. Similarly, directors and executives or MBA students wishing to focus on conflict of interests could benefit from Chapters 2, 5, and 7, plus cases from other chapters. Chapters 1 and 4 provide a fundamental platform for understanding current business ethics expectations and defensible approaches to ethical decision making for business students beginning their studies. Chapter 8, which covers the subprime lending fiasco, provides an essential understanding of the current business challenge gripping us all worldwide. Professional accounting students should be familiar with all chapters.

The coverage provided is largely North American in orientation. Examples, readings, and cases are drawn with that perspective in mind. Basic ethical problems and principles are the same throughout North America since they are shaped by the same concerns, markets, and similar institutional structures and legal strictures. Where points of difference are noteworthy, they are dealt with specifically. It should be noted that the increasing globalization of capital markets has extended North American expectations and problems to large companies around the world. Several cases covering problems of large European companies and doing business abroad are included to provide a global perspective.

Because of the prominence of American capital markets and the significant impact of the American practices of the Big Four professional accounting firms, North American governance frameworks for both business and professional accountants around the world will serve as a benchmark for developments in other jurisdictions. In addition, domestic and foreign expectations for behavior will be increasingly intertwined because the practices of multinational corporations or firms will be increasingly scrutinized globally by stakeholders active in major consumer and capital markets and in regulatory arenas around the world.

Ethical behavior in international operations and international accountability are specifically explored because differing cultures call for somewhat different ethical behavior. In addition, the recent emergence of global ethical accounting standards under the auspices of the International Federation of Accountants (IFAC) is covered extensively to prepare readers for the global harmonization process that is occurring.

AUTHORS' APPROACH

To the greatest extent possible, *Business and Professional Ethics for Directors, Executives & Accountants* focuses on the development of a practical understanding of the ethical issues driving recent unethical events, the resulting development of emerging accountability and governance frameworks, and the practical skills required to deal with them effectively. Of necessity, this means providing a learning experience embedded with real-life cases and examples. At the same time, these real-life problems are interpreted through exposure to classic positions and articles that have had a lasting impact on business ethics in general and accounting ethics in particular. The authors' experiences as directors, executives, and professional accountants, plus substantial experience in the teaching of and consulting on business and accounting ethics, management control, and similar governance-related subjects, contribute significantly to the development of the issues and discussions offered.

ORGANIZATION OF THE BOOK, & DIGITAL RESOURCES WEBSITE

The book is arranged in eight chapters that include 139 cases, of which fifteen are new to this edition, as well as four readings and appendices. Additional cases, appendices, readings, and material on the Enron fiasco are available in the book's Digital Resources website at **www.cengagebrain.com.**

		CASES	READINGS & APPENDICES
Chapter 1	Ethics Expectations	22	1
Chapter 2	Ethics & Governance Scandals	8	
Chapter 3	Philosophers' Contributions	7	
Chapter 4	Practical Ethical Decision Making	7	
Chapter 5	Corporate Ethical Governance & Accountability	29	1
Chapter 6	Professional Accounting in the Public Interest	35	1 in Digital Resources
Chapter 7	Managing Ethics Risks & Opportunities	23	1
Chapter 8	Subprime Lending Fiasco—Ethics Issues	8	
		139	4

The first two chapters provide an understanding of concerns that have been driving the development of current ethics expectations:

- Chapter 1 provides an overview of the book as it deals with the origins of concerns traditionally felt by a range of stakeholder groups and how these concerns have produced a broadened and heightened stakeholder-oriented accountability expectation.

- Chapter 2 provides a historical perspective on the ethics and governance scandals that stimulated changes in ethics expectations for accountability and governance reform and how these changes have been crystallized in law or generally accepted standards of performance. Both chapters provide a useful foundation for the rest of the book.

The next two chapters facilitate how a director, executive, employee, or professional accountant should respond to the emerging ethical expectations by taking decisions and actions that will be considered both right and defensible particularly when codes of conduct do not precisely fit the circumstances. It presents concepts developed over the centuries by philosophers as well as practical frameworks for their application:

- Chapter 3 covers important contributions by several philosophers to provide a background from which to reason ethically.
- Chapter 4 presents several practical approaches to ethical decision making—the core of ethical behavior—that facilitate the development of strategy as well as day-to-day decisions business people must face.

Chapters 5 and 6 examine how corporations and professional accountants can develop sound ethical accountability, governance, and management systems that respond to emerging ethics expectations:

- Chapter 5 covers those issues, expectations, and ethical culture-promoting systems that directors and executives should understand in order to discharge their duties successfully in the modern era.
- Chapter 6 deals with the roles and functions of professional accountants in the new accountability system for corporations, as agents of ethical accountability, as experts in the development of ethical accountability and governance mechanisms, and as professionals who should be demonstrating professional skepticism. Chapters 5 and 6 both cover the identification, assessment, and management of *conflicts of interest* and other key elements of a modern ethics-oriented governance system.

The final two chapters deal with a set of extremely important issues that directors, executives, and professional accountants need to understand and develop a facility with in order to avoid serious pitfalls and to take unique opportunities that others will miss. The last chapters of the book provide overviews of the most pressing and formative ethical and economic problems of our lifetimes and offer guidance as to the lessons that we all should learn:

- Chapter 7 deals with the supercritical areas of ethics risk and opportunity management, effective stakeholder management, sustainability and corporate social responsibility performance and reporting, workplace ethics, whistleblower programs and ethics inquiry services, motivation and avoidance of fraud and white-collar crime, bribery and the challenges of international operations including cultural networking practices such as *guanxi*, and ethical crisis management.
- Chapter 8 reviews the subprime lending fiasco and presents an ethical analysis of this latest ethical disaster to influence the world negatively. Lessons drawn from the ethical analysis are presented to provide a platform for discussion and learning so that future problems can be avoided. In its own way, this chapter provides a summary application of the material covered in earlier chapters.

Each chapter presents an interesting selection of cases and a useful list of references. The combination of text, 139 cases, four readings and appendices provides a much richer learning experience than books that present just cases, or text plus a limited number of cases and no seminal readings.

In addition, numerous references are made in the margin where a website link/reference or a downloadable file is available on the *Business and Professional Ethics for Directors, Executives & Accountants* (*BPE*) Digital Resources website at **www.cengagebrain.com**. This website is updated continuously with new information, notes, and website links of interest. The BPE Digital Resources website also houses cases and relevant chapter material from earlier editions to provide a resource for students and instructors, including the following:

- Cases deleted from past editions (see list in the Table of Contents on page xiv).
- *Chapter 9: The Credibility CrisisEnron, WorldCom, & SOX* from the sixth edition.
- Readings:
  - The Liability Crisis in the United States: Impact on the Accounting Profession—A Statement of Position
  - A Lawyer's Perspective on an Accountant's Professional Obligations
- Additional References and Seminal Reports

IMPROVEMENTS TO THE EIGHTH EDITION

Building on the strong foundation developed in the earlier seven editions, this new edition has been thoroughly updated. Major improvements include the following:

- Helpful videos for cases and other developments are identified in the cases or on the **www.cengagebrain.com** website for students and for instructors.
- Chapter 1, "Ethics Expectations," has been updated to reflect the revisions made to the other chapters of the textbook, and six new cases have been added dealing with current ethical issues including: winning at any cost, health and environmental issues, as well as the harm caused by some business models.
- Chapter 2, "Ethics & Governance Scandals," has been extended to provide a time line, analysis, and summary of the significant ethics and governance scandals, events, and responses in three time frames: prior to 1970, 1970 to 1990, and 1990 to the present. Two key cases have been added covering GM's faulty ignition switches and VW's cheating on emissions tests.
- Chapter 3 has been updated with the revision of one case and the addition another on art forgeries.
- Chapter 4 has been updated for a recently issued international ethics standard and simplified to approach practical ethical decision making more directly and with greater clarity. A new case has been added on concussions in the NFL.
- In Chapter 5, "Corporate Ethical Governance & Accountability," updates have introduced new material covering a revised conflict-of-interest framework, B Corps and B corporations, the shareholder value myth, new public accountability standards, and inserts with key examples, as well as four new cases covering hospital/not-for-profit governance challenges, salary equity, helping the poor, and questionable decisions at Lululemon.

- Chapter 6, "Professional Accounting in the Public Interest," has been significantly revised to reflect the global shift to a new IFAC international ethics code, the merger of three professional accounting bodies in Canada, a new framework for assessing threats to compliance, adverse interest conflicts, changes in professional expectations regarding tax havens caused by the release of the Panama Papers, transfer pricing for tax advantage, and the removal of tax inversions. A new case have been added covering KPMG's tax shelters.
- Chapter 7, "Managing Ethics Risk & Opportunities," has been updated and expanded to include new frameworks for Enterprise Risk Management, sustainability (GR4), Social Responsibility Performance (ISO 31000), and Integrated Reporting. In addition, new examples have been included for Sustainability/SRI reporting and audit and for crisis management. New inserts offer information on famous briberies by Lockheed and DaimlerChrysler.
- Chapter 8 has been updated to take account of recent analyses and the prosecutions of investment banks and their officers.
- Fifteen new cases have been added to this edition, including the following:

Chapter	Title
1	Selling Only Sugary Drinks
1	Buying and Selling Blood
1	Tiger Woods: "Winning Takes Care of Everything"
1	Nestlé Bottles Water in a California Drought
1	The Right to Be Informed? The Link Between Talcum Powder and Cervical Cancer
1	Valeant Pharmaceuticals vs. Coca Cola—Which Business Model Is Worse: Price Gouging or Fostering Obesity & Diabetes?
2	General Motors Ignores Obvious Ignition Faults
2	VW Cheats on Emissions Tests
3	Art Forgeries: Is Deceiving Art Experts Unethical?
4	Concussions in the NFL
5	Hospital Governance Challenges
5	Salary Equity at Gravity Payments
5	Merck and River Blindness
5	Lululemon's Questionable Leadership
6	KPMG's Questionable Tax Shelters

Importantly, the *BPE* website, **www.cengagebrain.com**, is constantly expanding to include helpful references such as video clips of major events and brief summaries of key books on ethical matters.

As noted above, a *BPE Digital Resources website* has been created at **www.cengagebrain.com** to provide access to readings and references identified in the margin of the book, as well as cases and chapter material from past editions.

In addition, the *BPE Instructor's Manual*, which is available online, has been augmented to provide sample examinations and the discussion of successful, innovative usage of the book by satisfied instructors. PowerPoints are available for instructors through *the BPE Instructor's Manual* website.

Accessing CengageBrain

1. Use your browser to go to **www.CengageBrain.com**.
2. The first time you go to the site, you will need to register. It's free. Click on "Sign Up" in the top right corner of the page and fill out the registration information. (After you have signed in once, whenever you return to CengageBrain, you will enter the user name and password you have chosen and you will be taken directly to the companion site for your book.)
3. Once you have registered and logged in for the first time, go to the "Search for Books or Materials" bar and enter the author or ISBN for your textbook. When the title of your text appears, click on it and you will be taken to the companion site. There you can choose among the various folders provided on the Student side of the site. NOTE: If you are currently using more than one Cengage textbook, the same user name and password will give you access to all the companion sites for your Cengage titles. After you have entered the information for each title, all the titles you are using will appear listed in the pull-down menu in the "Search for Books or Materials" bar. Whenever you return to CengageBrain, you can click on the title of the site you wish to visit and go directly there.

ACKNOWLEDGMENTS

By Len Brooks

I have been fortunate to receive excellent suggestions for improving this and earlier versions of *Business & Professional Ethics* from Graham Tucker, Alex Milburn, Bill Langdon, Peter Jackson, Michael Deck, Curtis Verschoor, Lyall Work, and John Grant. But, as in the past, I want to acknowledge specifically the searching and insightful contributions by David Selley and particularly Ross Skinner. In addition, I want to thank Miguel Minutti and Lee Benson, whose research enriched many of the book's cases and discussions. These contributors should rest easy, however, as I did not accept all their suggestions and therefore take responsibility for any errors or omissions.

To my former colleague, Max Clarkson, I owe a debt of gratitude for providing the initial platform and encouragement for development and exercise of my ideas in the classroom and as a consultant and the stimulation to search for new ideas to contribute to our discipline.

To the Canadian Centre for Ethics & Corporate Policy, I owe appreciation for their willingness to agree to reciprocal use in this edition of material written for *Ethics & Governance: Developing & Maintaining an Ethical Corporate Culture,* 4th edition, which I wrote with David Selley and which the EthicsCentre published in 2012.

To my mother and my father, who was a CA, CGA, CMA, and CPA, I owe my understanding of values and my interest in pursuing them.

To my wife, Jean, for her continued support and, for their forbearance, my children, Catherine, Len, Heather, and John; their spouses or significant others Christina, Gabe, Rob, and Julia; and my grandchildren Bianca, Willow, Mya, and Owen, I owe my love and respect.

By Paul Dunn

To my colleagues who constantly help me explore the numerous aspects of business ethics.

To the many students and instructors who have provided useful comments on the text and the cases.

To my children, Megan, Heather, and Ryan, and their spouses, Todd and Katie, and my grandson Henry, who have encouraged me to explore alternative approaches and analyses to life.

Finally, to my wife, Kathy, for her constant love and support.

THE END OF THE BEGINNING

Amid the tragedy created by the Enron, Arthur Andersen, WorldCom, and subprime lending fiascos, there is a silver lining—the acceleration and crystallization of stakeholder-oriented accountability and governance frameworks for corporations and professional accountants. The subprime lending fiasco and other ethics scandals have further stimulated these processes. Awareness of these developments and what they require to generate and maintain stakeholder support provides the foundation for the roles, responsibilities, and future success of directors, executives, and professional accountants. We have entered an era wherein appropriate values upheld and applied hold the key to ethical behavior, reputation, and sustained success. *Business and Professional Ethics for Directors, Executives & Accountants* provides an orderly development of the issues and skills involved and the understanding necessary to use them effectively—hopefully for the benefit of the business community, the accounting profession, and society as a whole.

Leonard J. Brooks, FCPA, FCA
Professor of Business Ethics & Accounting
Executive Director, The Clarkson Centre for Business Ethics & Board Effectiveness
Joseph L. Rotman School of Management
University of Toronto

Paul Dunn, CPA, CA
Associate Professor of Business Ethics
Goodman School of Business
Brock University

August 2016

OVERVIEW OF THE BOOK

The disasters at Enron, Arthur Andersen, and WorldCom and more recently the subprime lending crisis have fundamentally changed expectations for the behavior of directors, executives, and professional accountants. Good risk management practices must now incorporate ethics risk management, accountability, and governance practices that ensure that the reputations of individuals, corporations, and firms are protected and that the support of stakeholders is strong enough to facilitate success. Leaving the development of ethical boundaries to trial and error—risking bad practice—is no longer acceptable.

Corporations and business professionals are now part of a new post-SOX era of broadened stakeholder-oriented accountability and governance. Directors, executives, and professional accountants now realize that this necessitates considering the impacts and risks of their decisions on their reputations and on the public interest—certainly on more than the traditional short-term set of shareholder interests. Some businesspeople and professionals will want to go beyond developing a good defensive accountability and governance system to develop a competitive advantage where customers, employees, and others will be attracted by distinctly higher levels of trust based on commonly respected values such as honesty, fairness, compassion, integrity, predictability, and responsibility.

Unless directors, executives, and professional accountants develop effective accountability, governance, and risk management processes that incorporate ethics,

- directors will be unable to fulfil their due diligence requirements,
- executives will be unable to develop sound competitive business models and protect their emerging legal liability,
- professional accountants will be unable to fulfill their role as fiduciaries and as leaders in the development of accountability and governance system, and
- corporations and the accounting profession as we know them will be further discredited and regulated.

Business and Professional Ethics for Directors, Executives & Accountants provides an understanding of why ethics has become a critical success factor, the nature and role of the Enron/SOX developments, how ethical behavior can be guided, how ethical decision making can be improved and made defensible, and how special problems—including the subprime lending crisis—facing directors, executives, and the accounting profession can be dealt with.

1

Ethics Expectations

PURPOSE OF THE CHAPTER

Business and the professions function within a framework created by the expectations of the public. Scandals have traditionally triggered a "sea change" of new expectations for business governance and the accounting profession around the world. Enron, WorldCom, Arthur Andersen, the subprime lending fiasco, the Madoff Ponzi scheme, huge bribery prosecutions, manipulation of interest rates by major banks, shocking disregard for fairness and safety, and the violation of environmental protection laws have reinforced the need for new standards and have pushed expectations to even higher levels. Not surprisingly, the newest behavioral expectations are based on an acceleration of business and professional ethics trends that have been long in the making. As a result, business and professional ethics have become key determinants of corporate and personal success and the focal points of research and corporate change.

This chapter explores the changes that the ethics trends have brought to the expectations framework as well as the developments that have arisen in response to those changes. It also begins to consider what the changes in expectations mean for the directors, executives, and professional accountants. As such, this chapter provides an introduction and overview of the book. Unless businesspeople understand the historical genesis of current expectations, they are likely to repeat the unfortunate errors of earlier executives and directors.

THE ETHICS ENVIRONMENT FOR BUSINESS: THE BATTLE FOR CREDIBILITY, REPUTATION, & COMPETITIVE ADVANTAGE

During the last thirty-five years, there has been an increasing expectation that business exists to serve the needs of both shareholders and society. Many people have a "stake" or interest in a business, its activities, and impacts. If the interests of these stakeholders are not respected, then action that is often painful to shareholders, officers, and directors usually occurs. In fact, it is unlikely that businesses or professions can achieve their long-run strategic objectives without the support of key stakeholders, such as shareholders, employees, customers, creditors, suppliers, governments, host communities, and activists.

The support for a business—and business in general—depends on the credibility that stakeholders place in corporate commitments, the company's reputation, and the strength of its competitive advantage. All of these depend on the trust that stakeholders place in a company's activities. Trust, in turn, depends on the values underlying corporate activities.

Stakeholders increasingly expect that a company's activities will respect their values and interests. To a large extent, this respect for stakeholder values and interests determines a corporation's ethical standing and success. Consequently, corporate directors are expected to govern their company ethically, meaning they are to see that their executives, employees, and agents act ethically. Moreover, the corporation is increasingly expected to be accountable to stakeholders in a transparent or ethical manner. Performance assessment now extends beyond what is achieved to encompass how ethically those results were achieved.

As a result, the governance and accountability regime for business and the professions has become far more concerned with stakeholder interests and ethical matters than in the past. Directors, executives, and professional accountants, who serve the often-conflicting interests of shareholders directly and the public indirectly, must be aware of the public's new expectations for business and other similar organizations and must manage their risks accordingly. More than just to serve intellectual curiosity, this awareness must be combined with traditional values and incorporated into a framework for ethical decision making and action. Otherwise, as was the case with the Enron and subprime lending debacles, the credibility, reputation, and competitive advantage of capital markets and the organization, the management, the professional, and the profession will suffer. What has produced this change in public expectations for business governance, behavior, and accountability? Several factors appear to share causal responsibility, as indicated in Table 1.1.

Environmental Concerns

Nothing galvanized early public opinion about the nature of good corporate behavior more than the realization that the public's physical well-being and the well-being of some

TABLE 1.1 Factors Affecting Public Expectations for Business Behavior

Unbridled greed	Subprime lending fiasco, CEO overcompensation
Physical	Quality of air and water, safety
Moral	Desire for fairness and equity at home and abroad
Bad judgments	Operating mistakes, executive compensation, cover-up of failed environmental engineering
Activist stakeholders	Ethical investors, consumers, environmentalists
Environmental reality	Environmental degeneration, need for sustainability
Economic	Weakness, pressure to survive, to falsify
Competition	Global pressures, substandard environmental engineering
Financial malfeasance	Numerous scandals, victims, greed
Governance failures	Recognition that good governance and ethics risk assessment matter
Accountability	Desire for transparency, corporate social responsibility (CSR)
Synergy	Publicity, successful changes
Institutional reinforcement	New laws-environment, whistleblowing, recalls, *U.S. Sentencing Guidelines*, OECD antibribery regime, *Sarbanes-Oxley Act* (SOX) reforms, professional accounting reform, globalization of standards (IFAC, IFRS) and principles (Caux), *Dodd-Frank Wall Street Reform and Consumer Protection Act* New enforcement standards–Foreign Corrupt Practices Act-bribery

workers was being threatened by corporate activity. Initially, concern about air pollution centered on smokestack and exhaust pipe smog, which caused respiratory irritation and disorders. These problems were, however, relatively localized so that when the neighboring population became sufficiently irate, local politicians were able and generally willing to draft controlling regulation, although effective enforcement was by no means ensured.

Two other problems associated with air pollution that were slower to be recognized were acid rain, which neutered lakes and defoliated trees, and the dissipation of the earth's ozone layer. In the first case, the sulfur in exhaust gases combined with rain and fell to the ground far away from the source, often in other legal jurisdictions. Consequently, the reaction by politicians in the source jurisdiction was predictably slow, and many arguments were raised about who was responsible and whether the damage was real or not. Ultimately, however, the level of awareness of the problem became sufficiently widespread to support international treaties and more stringent local regulations.

The dissipation of the earth's ozone layer and its role in global warming has been more recently recognized as a serious threat to our physical well-being. The release into the atmosphere of chlorofluorocarbon (CFC), once the most common residential and industrial refrigerant, allows CFC molecules to use up molecules of ozone. At the same time, cutting down rain forests in Brazil, a main source for replenishing ozone, has contributed further to the depletion of the ozone layer around our planet. This layer was our major barrier from the sun's ultraviolet rays, which cause skin cancer and damage our eyes.

The timing of the recognition of water pollution as a problem worthy of action has paralleled the concern about our depleted ozone layer, partly because of our limited ability to measure minute concentrations of toxins and our inability to understand the precise nature of the risk of waterborne metals and dioxins. Corporations asserted that they did not have the technical solutions to the elimination of air and water pollution at reasonable cost and therefore could not do so and remain competitive. However, once the short- and long-term threats to personal safety were understood, the public, led by special interest groups, began to pressure companies as well as governments directly to improve safety standards for corporate emissions.

Government reaction, often prompted by disasters, has been significant at all levels. Locally, no-smoking regulations have been enacted and local ordinances tightened. Environmental regulation has been the subject of international treaties. Environmental protection acts in the United States and Canada have been put in place that feature significant fines of up to $1 million to $2 million per day for a corporation convicted of environmental malfeasance. In addition, personal fines and/or jail terms for officers and directors have focused the attention of executives on programs to ensure compliance with environmental standards. Nothing energized executives in the United States and Canada more than the statement of a judge in regard to the promulgation of the *U.S. Sentencing Guidelines* on November 1, 1991. He said that the "demonstrated presence of an effective program of environmental protection would constitute an adequate 'due diligence' defense which could reduce the level of fine from $2 million/day to $50,000/day." Although this reaction may be viewed as defensive, the "due diligence" movement should be viewed as the *codification phase* of the movement toward corporate environmental responsibility.

More recently, the growing concern for local and global environmental sustainability has led to competitive and activist pressures for companies to report publicly on their environmental impacts using sustainability frameworks such as the Global Reporting Initiative's G4 Guidelines. In addition,[1] the huge fines, lawsuit settlements, and loss of

[1] See the Global Reporting Initiative's website at https://g4.globalreporting.org/Pages/default.aspx.

reputation and the support of the public by offending companies such as BP for its oil spill and Volkswagen for cheating on emission standards have reinforced the need for other companies to take preventive action rather than pay an astronomical price for environmental negligence.

Moral Sensitivity

Beginning in the 1980s and 1990s, there has been a significant increase in the sensitivity to the lack of fairness and to discrepancies in equitable treatment normally afforded to individuals and groups in society. Increased recognition of the plight of several groups was responsible for this heightened social conscience, including the feminist movement, the mentally and physically challenged, Native people, and minorities. To some degree, the public was prepared to entertain the concerns of these groups because unfortunate events had brought the realization that some special interest groups were worth listening to, as environmentalists, consumer advocates, and antiapartheid supporters had shown. Also, for most of the period from 1960 onward, disposable incomes and leisure time have been sufficiently high to allow members of the public to focus on issues beyond earning their livelihood. In addition, as a result of advances in satellite communications that have allowed virtually "live" coverage of worldwide problems, the thinking of the North American public has become less inner directed and parochial and more sensitive to problems featured by wide-ranging investigative reporters.

Evidence of public pressure for more fairness and equity is readily available. The desire for equity in employment has resulted in laws, regulations, compliance conditions in contracts, and affirmative action programs in corporations. Pay equity programs have begun to appear to readjust the discrepancy between the pay scales for men and women. Consumer protection legislation has tightened to the point that the old philosophy of "buyer beware," which tended to protect the large corporation, has become "vendor beware," which favors the individual consumer. Employee drug tests have been much more carefully handled to minimize the prospect of false findings. All of these are examples in which public pressure has brought about institutional changes through legislatures or courts for more fairness and equity and less discrimination and therefore will be virtually impossible to reverse. Indeed, the trend is unmistakable.

Moral sensitivity is evident to international issues as well as domestic. The campaign to boycott buying from corporations that engage in child or sweatshop labor in foreign countries provides ample testimony to this and has resulted in the creation of codes of ethical practice for suppliers and compliance mechanisms to ensure they are followed. Organizations such as the Social Accountability International and AccountAbility have developed workplace policies, standards, workplace auditor training programs, and reporting frameworks.

Bad Judgments & Activist Stakeholders

Directors, executives, and managers are human, and they make mistakes. Sometimes the public or specific groups take offense at these instances of bad judgment and take action to make the directors and management aware that they do not approve. For example, the recent Volkswagen decision to cheat on emissions tests and then cover it up stirred the anger of many consumers and environmentalists, resulting in the loss of many new and returning customers with a resulting dramatic fall in share price. In earlier times, the decision by Shell UK to scuttle the Brent Spar oil storage vessel in a deep part of the ocean rather than take it apart onshore led to demonstrations in support of

Greenpeace, which tried to stop the scuttling, and to the boycott of Shell gas stations in Europe. Nestlé products were boycotted in North America and Europe to stop the free distribution of baby formula powder to African mothers who were mixing it with contaminated water, thereby killing their babies. Nike and other companies' products were boycotted through the efforts of concerned individuals and groups to stop the use of sweatshop and child labor, particularly in foreign countries. The recall of Firestone tires was ignited by the media, beginning with a television show in Houston, Texas. North American corporations were extravagantly overpaying their executives—including several above $100 million per annum—or not reducing executive pay when profits declined, so CalPERS, the California Public Employees' Pension Fund, called for the establishment of compensation committees consisting of a majority of independent directors. Activist stakeholders were clearly able to make a difference—which most people thought was for the best.

Two other kinds of activists also made their appearance in the late 1980s and early 1990s: ethical consumers and ethical investors. Ethical consumers were interested in buying products and services that were made in ethically acceptable manners. Consequently, books such as *Shopping for a Better World*, *The Ethical Shopper's Guide*, and *Conscious Consumption* were published in the United States, Canada, and the United Kingdom. They provided ratings of companies, their affiliates, and their suppliers on different performance dimensions, such as hiring and treatment of women, environmental management and performance, charity, progressive staff policies, labor relations, consumer relations, and candor at answering questions. Ethical consumers were then able to "vote with their checkbooks."

Ethical investors took the view that their investments should not only make a reasonable return but should do so in an ethical manner as well. Originally pioneered by large pension funds such as CalPERS and the New York City Employees Pension Fund, as well as several church investment funds, the movement has been augmented since the early 1990s by several ethical mutual funds. These ethical mutual funds employ screens that are intended to knock out companies from consideration that are involved in so-called harmful activities—such as producing tobacco products, armaments, or atomic energy or misusing animals for testing. Alternatively, individuals or mutual funds can invest in companies or in indices of companies that have been screened by an ethical consulting service such as Domini Social Investments (http://www.domini.com) or MSCI (http://www.msci.com/esg-integration). Morgan Stanley Capital International (MSCI), for example, provides several indices of companies ranked high in sustainability, social responsibility, or environmental performance. A similar index, the Sustainalytics (http://www.sustainalytics.com) Jantzi Social Index (JSI), is available for the top sixty Canadian stocks as well as screening ESG (environmental, social, and governance) factors for Canadian, U.S., and European stocks. In addition, the FTSE4Good Index (http://www.ftse.com/products/indices/FTSE4Good) has been created for companies listed on the London Stock Exchange. The performance of these indices compares well to those for nonscreened stocks in each country. A current list of ethical mutual funds and an update on socially responsible investing (SRI) can be found at the websites of the Forum for Sustainable and Responsible Investment (http://charts.ussif.org/mfpc) or SocialFunds.com (http://www.socialfunds.com) in the United States and the Responsible Investment Association in Canada (http://riacanada.ca). Many consultants offer screening services to investors on a fee-for-service basis. The entire field of ethically screened investing has continued to grow.

These developments signal that business decisions are being judged against different standards than before, by groups that have billions of dollars at their disposal. For additional information, contact the Investor Responsibility Research Centre at http://www.irrcinstitute.org and similar websites.

Economic & Competitive Pressures

Although the public's expectations have been affected directly by the factors already discussed, a number of underlying or secondary factors are also at work. For example, in general, the pace of economic activity slowed during the late 1980s and early 1990s and just before and after the millennium. Corporations and the individuals in them had to wrestle with "no growth," or shrinking volume scenarios, instead of the expansion that had been the norm. In the 1990s, growing pressure from global competitors and the drive for improved, costly technology shrank profit margins. Absence of growth and shrinking margins led to downsizing to maintain overall profitability and desirability to capital markets. Whether to maintain their jobs, volume-incentive-based earnings, or their company, some people resorted to questionable ethical practices, including falsification of transactions and other records, and the exploitation of the environment or workers. The result has been part of the reason for triggering cases of environmental and/or financial malfeasance.

The development of global markets has led to the manufacture and sourcing of products throughout the world. The accompanying restructuring has been viewed as enabling greater productivity and lower costs with lower rates of domestic employment. Therefore, the pressure on employed individuals to maintain their jobs may not abate as production increases. Nor, given greater competition, will greater volume necessarily increase profit, so the pressure on corporations will not abate to levels experienced in the past. In addition, corporations will be unable to rely on a cyclical return to profitability to restore the risk of unethical behavior to former levels. Consequently, it would appear that a return to former risk levels will depend on the institution of new regimes of ethical-behavior management and governance.

Financial Scandals: The Expectations Gap & the Credibility Gap

There is no doubt that the public has been surprised, stunned, dismayed, and devastated by financial fiascos. The list of classic examples would include Enron, WorldCom, Adelphia, Tyco, HealthSouth, Parmalat, Royal Ahold, Barings Bank, Livent, Bre-X, Madoff, the U.S. subprime lending disaster, and the collusion and manipulation of financial markets by major banks as well as the slightly older U.S. savings and loan (S&L) bankruptcies and bailouts and the bankruptcies of several real estate companies.

As a result of these repeated shocks, the public has become cynical about the financial integrity of corporations, so much so that the term *expectations gap* has been coined to describe the difference between what the public thinks it is getting in audited financial statements and what it is actually getting. The public outrage over repeated financial fiascos has led, in both the United States and Canada, to tighter regulation, higher fines, and investigations into the integrity, independence, and role of the accounting and auditing profession and, more recently, of executives and directors.

On a broader basis, continuing financial malfeasance has led to a *crisis of confidence* over corporate reporting and governance. This lack of credibility has spread from financial stewardship to encompass other spheres of corporate activity and has become known as the *credibility gap*. Audit committees and ethics committees, both peopled by a majority of outside directors; the widespread creation of corporate codes of conduct; the increase of corporate reporting designed to promote the integrity of the corporation; and increasing fines and regulation all testify to the importance being assigned to this crisis.

No longer is it presumed that "whatever company 'X'[2] does is in the best interests of the country." Fiascos related to the environment or to dealings with employees, customers, shareholders, or creditors have put the onus on corporations to manage their affairs more ethically and to demonstrate that they have done so.

Devastated by the sequence of U.S. disasters in 2001 and 2002 involving Enron, Arthur Andersen, and WorldCom, public confidence evaporated in the business community, its financial reporting, and the accounting profession. In the ensuing crisis of confidence, capital markets were reeling. President George W. Bush and other business leaders strove to restore lost confidence, but their efforts were largely in vain. Finally, in record time, the U.S. Congress and Senate passed the *Sarbanes-Oxley Act of 2002* (SOX) on July 30, 2002. That act provides for the reform of both corporate governance and the accounting profession, first in the United States, then indirectly in Canada and around the world. Further details are provided in the next chapter and in the Web archive for this book at **www.cengagebrain.com**.

Governance Failures & Risk Assessment

The Enron, Arthur Andersen, and WorldCom series of disasters in 2001–2002 made it clear that current existing modes governing companies and reporting on their activities were not sufficient to protect investors' interests and, more broadly, the public interest in orderly markets and corporate activities.

Corporate directors have been expected to ensure that their corporations act in the interests of investors and within the range of activity deemed suitable by the societies in which they operate. But in the Enron, WorldCom, and other cases, the oversight by company directors failed to contain the greed of executives, managers, and other employees. These and other companies were out of control, and unacceptable practices resulted. To quote the U.S. Senate's report on the *Role of the Board of Directors in the Collapse of Enron*:

> (1) **Fiduciary Failure.** The Enron Board of Directors failed to safeguard Enron shareholders and contributed to the collapse of the seventh largest public company in the United States, by allowing Enron to engage in high-risk accounting, inappropriate conflict of interest transactions, extensive undisclosed off-the-books activities, and excessive executive compensation. The Board witnessed numerous indications of questionable practices by Enron management over several years, but chose to ignore them to the detriment of Enron shareholders, employees, and business associates.
>
> Source: U.S. Senate's Permanent Subcommittee on Investigations, *Role of the Board of Directors in the Collapse of Enron*, 2002, 3.

Clearly, the public was fed up with directors, executives, and others enriching themselves at the public's expense. It was evident that directors and executives were not identifying, assessing, and managing ethics risks in the same manner or depth that they were for other business risks. But the Enron, Arthur Andersen, and WorldCom cases resulted in the bankruptcy of two of the world's largest companies and the disappearance of one of the world's most respected professional accounting firms within a year. This sudden reversal of fortunes, caused by the failure to govern ethics risks, changed the calculus of

[2] "Whatever is good for General Motors is good for the country" was a commonly used statement before 2000.

risk management profoundly. The probability of catastrophic failure caused by unidentified and/or unmanaged ethics risks was undeniably real and much higher than anyone expected.

Governance reform was perceived as necessary to protect the public interest. Where directors had been expected to assess and make sure that the risks faced by their corporation were properly managed, ethics risks were now seen to be a key aspect of the process. Governance reform to ensure that this would happen was overdue.

Increased Accountability & Transparency Desired

The lack of trust in corporate processes and activities also spawned the desire for increased accountability and transparency on corporate matters by investors and particularly by other stakeholders. Companies around the world have responded by publishing more information on their websites and freestanding reports on their corporate social responsibility (CSR) performance, including such subjects as environmental, health and safety, philanthropic, and other social impacts. Although some information in these reports is skewed toward management objectives, the advent of external verification and the reaction to misinformation are gradually improving the information content involved. The trend is definitely toward increased nonfinancial reporting to match the public's growing expectations.

In addition, the realization that *unbridled greed* by executives and/or dominant shareholders lay behind many of the financial scandals that have damaged both investors and other stakeholders has reinforced the desire for more accountability for and transparency of corporate actions. For example, the subprime lending fiasco (see Chapter 8) spawned the *Dodd-Frank Wall Street Reform and Consumer Protection Act*, which mandated clear disclosures of risks inherent in complex financial instruments, Similarly, examples of outrageous executive compensation and bonuses, even when companies were doing poorly, resulted in a vigorous backlash leading companies to offer shareholders more information on remuneration plans and an opportunity to have a nonbinding but helpful "say-on-pay" input to the pay-setting process. Likewise, companies like General Motors and investment banks that received bailouts during the subprime lending crisis found that incredibly large bonuses paid to senior personnel were subject to monitoring, approval, and rollbacks. Contrary to the way executives are often portrayed in the movies, unbridled greed is no longer considered good.

Synergy among Factors & Institutional Reinforcement

Linkages among the factors affecting public expectations for ethical performance have already been identified but not the extent to which these linkages reinforce each other and add to the public's desire for action. Few days go by in which the daily newspapers, radio, and television do not feature a financial fiasco, a product safety issue, an environmental problem, or an article on gender equity or discrimination. On occasion, public furor and expectations are jolted by a glaring revelation of lack of personal and corporate integrity, such as in April 2016 when the Panama Papers leak of secret offshore arrangements occurred that documented tax avoidance, hidden wealth, and significant potential corruption. In the aggregate, the result is a cumulative heightening of the public's awareness of the need for controls on unethical corporate behavior. In addition, there are many examples emerging where business executives did not make the right decision and where ethical consumers or investors acted and were successful in making companies change their practices or improve their governance structures to ensure that future decision processes were more wholesome. The entire ethical consumer and SRI movement has been strengthened by the knowledge that acting on their concerns can make companies and society better, not poorer.

In turn, the public's awareness impacts politicians who react by preparing new laws or the tightening of regulations. In effect, the many issues reaching the public's consciousness result in institutional reinforcement and codification in the laws of the land. The multiplicity of ethical problems receiving exposure is focusing thought on the need for more ethical action, much like a snowball gathering speed as it goes downhill.

One of the most important examples of reactive legislation is the *U.S. Sentencing Guidelines of 1991*. As previously noted, it stimulated significant interest by directors and executives everywhere in North America in whether their companies were providing enough guidance to their personnel about proper behavior. The consequences for not doing so prior to the introduction of the guidelines had been minor since directors and senior officers had rarely been held personally accountable for the actions of their employees and their companies had been able to escape significant fines.

A second example is the antibribery regime spawned by Transparency International's influence on the Organization for Economic Cooperation and Development (OECD). By mid-2016, all thirty-four OECD member countries and seven additional countries had signed the Convention on Combatting Bribery of Foreign Public Officials in International Business Transactions[3] agreeing to enact antibribery legislation similar to that of the U.S. *Foreign Corrupt Practices Act* (FCPA), which bans bribery of foreign officials. The new antibribery regime is more advanced in that it seeks to facilitate extraterritorial legal action. One of the recent antibribery laws, the U.K. *Bribery Act* mandates British enforcement over a corporation's activities anywhere in the world as long as the company has a presence in the United Kingdom. Also, in 2010, the United States used the FCPA to charge and settle a bribery case for $185 million against Daimler AG, a German company, for bribes to foreign government officials in over twenty countries. A third and perhaps the most significant example of reactive legislation is SOX, which is driving the reform of corporate governance and professional accounting throughout the world. The rationale that generated SOX, its nature, and impact are the subject of Chapter 2.

The desire for global standards of corporate disclosure, auditing practice, and uniform ethical behavior by professional accountants has generated international accounting and auditing standards under the auspices of the International Accounting Standards Board (IASB) and the International Federation of Accountants (IFAC). Their creations, the International Financial Reporting Standards and the Code of Ethics for Professional Accountants, are the focal points for harmonization worldwide.

Since 2005, there has also been an increasing degree of interest by business leaders worldwide in the *Principles for Business* put forward by the Caux Round Table as well as in Caux conferences and recommendations for ethical management practice. The Aspen Institute is a further example of an institution providing ethical leadership insights for corporate leaders. The willingness for corporate and academic leaders to become involved with such institutions is evidence of the interest and relevance of their work.

The movement toward higher levels of corporate accountability and ethical performance is no longer characterized only by leaders who are willing to go out on a limb: it has become mainstream and international.

---

[3] OECD website at http://www.oecd.org/corruption/oecdantibriberyconvention.htm.

Outcomes

Broadly speaking, public expectations have changed to exhibit less tolerance, heightened moral consciousness, and higher expectations of business behavior. In response to this heightening of expectations, a number of watchdogs and advisors have emerged to help or harry the public and business. Organizations such as Greenpeace, Pollution Probe, and the Coalition for Environmentally Responsible Economies (CERES, formerly the Sierra Club) now maintain a watching brief on the business–environment interface. Consultants are available to advise corporations and so-called ethical investors on how to screen activities and investments for both profitability and ethical integrity. Mutual funds that specialize in ethical investments have sprung up to service the needs of small investors. Large investor activity has also become evident as many public-sector and not-for-profit pension funds have taken an active interest in the governance of their investee corporations and have presented shareholder resolutions designed to cover their concerns. In the face of all of this interest, politicians have responded by increasing regulations and the fines and penalties (both personal and corporate) involved for malfeasance. The *credibility gap* has not favored business organizations. Lack of credibility has brought increasing regulation, international standards, mainstream interest, and profound changes in governance and management practices.

NEW EXPECTATIONS FOR BUSINESS

New Mandate for Business

The changes in public expectations have triggered, in turn, an evolution in the mandate for business: the laissez-faire, profit-only world of Milton Friedman has given way to the view that business exists to serve society, not the other way around. For some, this may be stating the degree of change too strongly, but even they would concede that the relationship of business to society is one of interdependence where the long-run health of one determines that of the other.

In many forums, Milton Friedman made the following case:

> In a free-enterprise, private property system a corporate executive … has [the] responsibility to make as much money as possible while conforming to the basic rules of society, both … in law and in ethical custom. [This is] the appropriate way to determine the allocation of scarce resources to alternative uses.
>
> Source: Friedman (1970).

Although there are many arguments for and against this position (see Mulligan 1986), three critical issues deserve mention. They are (1) that the deviation from a profit-only focus does not mean that profit will fall—in fact, profit may rise; (2) profit is now recognized as an incomplete measure of corporate performance and therefore an inaccurate measure for resource allocation; and (3) Friedman explicitly expected that performance would be within the law and ethical custom.

First, there is the myth that business could not afford to be ethical because too many opportunities would be given up for profit to be maximized or that executives could not afford to divert their attention from profit or else profit would fall. In fact, research studies exist that show short-term profits increasing as well as decreasing when social objectives are taken into account by executives.[4] However, two long-term perspectives also

[4] See, for example, the study by Curtis Verschoor, "A Study of the Link between a Corporation's Financial Performance and Its Commitment to Ethics," *Journal of Business Ethics* 17 (1998): 1509–16.

strengthen the case that social and profit goals can mix profitably. The first is a study by Clarkson (1988), which ranked the social performance of sixty-plus companies on a modified Wartick and Cochran (1985) scale and found that above-average social performance is positively correlated with profits. The second is that the performance of some ethical mutual funds, such as the Parnassus Fund (U.S.), have surpassed that of the New York Stock Exchange as measured by the Standard & Poor's (S&P) Index. Other funds based on SRI often outperform the S&P 500. This assertion is supported by a comprehensive review undertaken by RBC Global Asset Management[5] of whether SRI hurts investment returns. These perspectives do not demonstrate causality, but they should give some comfort to executives who hear the theoretical argument that the health of society and the businesses in it are interdependent but who waver on the profitability of implementing a multiple-objective structure that respects stakeholder interests.

The second aspect of the Friedman argument that has eroded since it was first proposed is the accuracy with which profit guides the allocation of resources to their best use for society. In 1970, when Friedman began to articulate the profit–resource linkage, there was virtually no cost ascribed to the air and water used in the manufacturing process, nor was a significant cost ascribed to the disposal or treatment of wastes. Since the 1980s, the costs of these so-called externalities have skyrocketed, and yet they are still not fully included in calculating the profit for the year for the polluting company under generally accepted accounting principles (GAAP). Often, pollution costs are born by and charged against the profits of other companies, towns, or governments, so the original-company profit–maximum-resource-use-for-society linkage is far less direct than Friedman originally envisaged. As the cost associated with these and other externalities rises, the profit–resource use linkage promises to become less and less useful unless the framework of traditional profit computations is modified or supplemented. Perhaps environmental accounting, or schemes by which companies buy pollution credits, will yield some relief from this dilemma in the future.

Finally, Milton Friedman himself expressed the view that profit should *be* sought within the laws and ethical customs of society. This is not appreciated by many who argue for profit-only in its strongest, laissez-faire, bare-knuckled form. Obviously, chaos would result if business were carried out in an absolutely no-holds-barred environment. A minimum framework of rules is essential for the effective, low-cost working of our markets and the protection of all participants. Increased regulation is one response to outrageous behavior or to the increasing ethical needs of society. What most profit-only advocates fail to see is that the alternative to increasing regulation by government is an increasing self-emphasis on better ethical governance and behavior. Interestingly, many U.S. states have already altered their corporate governance statutes to permit the consideration by directors of both shareholder and stakeholder interests, and some noted legal scholars, Lynn Stout and Margaret Blair, have argued that incorporation statutes do not restrict corporate objectives to a profit-only focus.[6]

Those who focus on profit-only often make short-term opportunistic decisions that jeopardize sustainable long-run profits. They often lose sight of the fact that sustained profit is the consequence of providing high-quality goods and services, within the law

---

[5] RBC Global Management, *Does Socially Responsible Investing Hurt Investment Returns?* July 22, 2016, http://funds.rbcgam.com/_assets-custom/pdf/RBC-GAM-does-SRI-hurt-investment-returns.pdf.

[6] For example, Lynn A. Stout, *The Shareholder Value Myth*, Berrett-Koehler Publishers, Inc. San Francisco, 2012. However, for an analysis for recent court cases, see also Margaret M. Blair, "Of Corporations, Courts, Personhood, and Morality," *Business Ethics Quarterly* 25 (2015): 415–31, doi:10.1017/beq.2015.32.

and ethical norms in an efficient and effective manner. It is far more effective to focus on providing goods and services required by society efficiently, effectively, legally, and ethically than to adopt the high-risk goal of making profit any way possible.

For these reasons, the profit-only mandate of corporations is evolving to one recognizing the interdependence of business and society. Future success will depend on the degree to which business can balance both profit and other stakeholders' interests. This, in turn, will be impossible to manage unless new governance and reporting structures emerge. If ethical and economic objectives cannot be integrated or balanced successfully and shareholders' interests continue to unreasonably dominate those of other stakeholders, the tension between business and society's stakeholders will continue to grow. Fortunately, the mandate for business is changing; the focus is shifting from a narrow shareholder-oriented view of what business is achieving to include what and how a broader stakeholder-oriented set of achievements is achieved. *Judgments of the future success of corporations will be made within the broader stakeholder-oriented framework, taking into account corporate objectives, achievements, and how those are achieved.*

New Governance & Accountability Frameworks

Based on this analysis, successful corporations are best served by governance and accountability mechanisms that focus on a different and broader set of fiduciary relationships than in the past. The allegiances of directors and executives must reflect stakeholder interests in terms of goals, processes, and outcomes. Governance objectives and processes must direct attention to these new perspectives, and modern accountability frameworks should include reports that focus on them. If not, the public's expectations will not be met, and regulations may be created to ensure such attention and focus.

To provide greater clarity about their objectives, some for-profit companies have chosen, during the last ten years, to apply for certification as a Benefit or B Corp. This requires the company to agree to a declaration that the company will, among other things, purposely create benefits for all stakeholders, not just stakeholders, and aspire to do no harm. In addition, the certified company agrees to report on its progress annually.[7] In a related development, not-for-profit companies can be incorporated under laws that specifically authorize pursuing benefits for a broad range of stakeholders. These are referred to as B corporations.

Reinforced Fiduciary Role for Professional Accountants

The public's expectations for trustworthy reports on corporate performance cannot be met unless the professional accountants who prepare or audit those reports focus their primary loyalty on the public interest and adopt principles such as independence of judgment, objectivity, and integrity that protect the public interest. Loyalty by auditors to management and/or directors can be misguided because management and directors have frequently proven to be so self-interested that they cannot be trusted to protect other stakeholder's interest. Moreover, directors who are supposed to govern management often rely extensively on professional accountants, such as by reporting to the audit subcommittee of the board, to fulfill the directors' own fiduciary responsibilities. Consequently, the primary fiduciary responsibility of professional accountants should be to the public or to the public interest. Otherwise, the expectations of stakeholders in

[7] See the B Corps website at https://www.bcorporation.net/what-are-b-corps.

society will not be met, and the credibility of corporations will erode, as will the credibility and reputation of the accounting profession.

This is not a new assignment. However, as shown in the Enron, Arthur Andersen, and WorldCom cases, professional accountants have, on occasion, lost track of to whom they should ultimately be responsible. Failure to understand this expectation and the underpinning values of independence, integrity, and objective judgment and reporting caused the collapse of the entire Arthur Andersen firm, which once employed over 80,000 people worldwide.

In addition, these corporate failures have brought the realization that loyalty to the public means more than just loyalty to current investors. Future investors rely on financial reports, and their interests need to be protected, as do those of other stakeholders in the corporation's broadened fiduciary model.

Reform of the accounting profession is under way in order to reinforce the public's expectations. The impetus for recent reform, while begun with SOX, the U.S. Securities and Exchange Commission (SEC), and the Public Company Accounting Oversight Board in the United States, has shifted to harmonization with the global standards worked out under the auspices of the IASB and IFAC. As discussed in later chapters, these global standards have returned professional accountants to a focus on serving the public interest.

RESPONSES & DEVELOPMENTS

Emerging Governance & Stakeholder Accountability Models

The reaction by business to the evolution from a profit-only mandate to one recognizing the interdependence of business and society became more readily observable as the 1990s progressed. In addition, several other important trends developed as a result of economic and competitive pressures that had and that continue to have an effect on the ethics of business and therefore on the professional accountant. These trends included the following:

- Expanding legal liability for corporate directors and, ultimately, the CEO and the CFO
- Management assertions to shareholders on the adequacy of internal controls
- A stated intention to manage risk and protect reputation, even though significant changes were also occurring in how organizations operate, including delayering, employee empowerment, and the use of electronic data interfaces and increasing the reliance by management on nonfinancial performance indicators used on a real-time basis

As a result of these trends and changes, corporations began to take a much greater interest in how ethical their activities were and how to ensure that ethical problems did not arise. It became evident that the traditional command-and-control (top-down) approach was not sufficient and that organizations needed to create an environment favorable to ethical behavior to foster it, not to impose it. Boards and management were becoming more interested in ethical issues in spite of the larger size, quicker pace, and complexity of business entities and dealings that were decreasing the ability to check and inspect the decisions of others. Consequently, it has become increasingly important that each employee has a personal code of behavior that is compatible with that of the employer. The pathway to these realizations took the following steps.

The initial corporate reaction to a more demanding ethical environment was the desire to know how ethical their activities have been, then to attempt to manage their employees' actions by developing a code of ethics/conduct. After implementing the code, the desire was to monitor activities in relation to it and to report on that behavior, first internally and then externally.

The desire to know about the appropriateness of their activities led many corporations to undertake an inventory of significant impacts on various aspects of society. Often organized by program and by stakeholder group, these listings could be used to identify specific issues, policies, products, or programs that were the most problematic and therefore needed earliest remedial attention.

It quickly became clear that the "inventory and fix" approach led to a "patched-up" system for governing employee behavior: one that was incomplete and did not offer ethical guidance on all or even most issues to be faced. Employees who had committed a malfeasance, whether voluntarily or not, could still frequently claim that "nobody told me not to do it." In order to reduce this vulnerability and provide adequate guidance, corporations began to develop and implement comprehensive codes of conduct/ethics.

Neither easy to develop nor universally accepted, codes usually had to be refined through a number of revisions. Implementation processes also had to be improved. Even today, some executives are uncertain of their role and how to play it most successfully to facilitate strong commitment by employees to the ethical principles involved. More detailed information on the role, nature, content, and monitoring of performance relative to codes is provided in Chapter 5. It is evident that codes of conduct will continue to be the touchstone for the ethical guidance of employees for the foreseeable future.

Although codes of conduct offer an essential framework for employee decision making and control, those corporations, in highly vulnerable positions due to their products or productive processes, found it in their interest to develop early warning information systems to facilitate fast remedial action in the event of a problem. For example, Occidental Petroleum recognized its capacity to damage the environment and created a three-tier, notification-to-head-office requirement to provide timely information to senior management and experts in cleanup procedures. Depending on the seriousness of the environmental problem, a "significant matter" had to be reported by computer immediately, an "excursion" within twelve hours (the next business day in New York), or a "reportable incident" within the next reporting cycle (Friedman 1988). This type of notification system is essential to facilitate crisis management activities and to mobilize response resources on a worldwide basis in an effort to reduce the impact of the problem on the environment and the corporation.

Not satisfied to encourage the use of ethics just through a code of conduct, leading-edge corporations sought ways to inculcate ethics into their corporate culture—the system of shared values that drive action—to foster specific consideration of ethical conduct in operating decisions, in strategic decision making, and in crisis management practices. Mechanisms were developed to ensure that ethical principles were understood, reinforced, and not lost sight of. These include general training and training to instill decision frameworks designed to produce sound ethical decisions; compliance checkoff lists; the encouragement of internal whistleblowing to ombudspersons; mind-focusing scorecards and categorizations for operations and strategies; inclusion of ethical performance as a factor in the determination of remuneration and in continuing internal and external reports; the creation of specific ethical operating goals, such as for equity employment levels; and the creation of whistleblowing programs and executive positions, such as chief ethics or compliance officer, ombudsperson, vice president for environmental affairs, and of specific subcommittees of the Board of Directors to oversee the ethical performance of the corporation.

Although the commitment to these mechanisms grew during the 1980s and early 1990s, nothing galvanized the corporate community more than (1) the promulgation of the *U.S. Sentencing Guidelines* for environmental offenses on November 1, 1991, which led to widespread concern about "due diligence" procedures, and (2) the realization in the summer of 1992 that General Electric had been sued under the *False Claims Act* in the United States for $70 million by a whistleblower too fearful of retribution to report internally to the company (Singer 1992, 19). The fact that the whistleblower could receive up to 25% of the outcome was considered shocking, just as the size of the fines in the *U.S. Sentencing Guidelines* had been a year earlier. In combination, these events matured the realization that corporations ought to create an ethical operating environment in order to protect their interests and those of others with a stake in the activities of the corporation.

As a result of the *U.S. Sentencing Guidelines*, many U.S. directors and executives suddenly became very interested in the governance mechanism that was to convey appropriate guidance to their personnel; U.S.-owned foreign subsidiaries were also involved, as were foreign-owned multinational companies operating in the United States. Consequently, and with the additional stiffening of penalties for environmental malfeasance in Canada, the governance structures of major companies that had been focused primarily on making a profit now began to include a serious focus on how that profit was made.

Early in 1994, Lynn Sharp Paine[8] published an excellent seminal article in the *Harvard Business Review* titled "Managing for Integrity," in which she made the case for integrating ethics and management. At about the same time, pronouncements from the Toronto Stock Exchange[9] (1994) and the Canadian Institute of Chartered Accountants[10] (1995) (renamed CPA Canada in 2012) specified that directors were to provide the "social conscience" of their companies and that directors were responsible for developing and maintaining an ethical culture at their companies, sufficient to support an adequate system of internal control. Without adequate ethical grounds for systems of internal control, the financial statements of the enterprise would be of varying accuracy, and the actions of employees might or might not correspond with what the directors and senior executives hoped. Many examples are available that attest to the fact that without adequate ethical underpinning, companies can get into difficulty.

Later, in 1996, the *Caremark National Case*, which was decided in the Chancery Court of Delaware, added to directors' responsibilities the requirement of proactively seeking out ethical problems. Until this case was decided, directors could claim "hear no evil, see no evil" to avoid prosecution for some corporate wrongdoing, so there were times that directors "didn't want to hear about" for their own protection. Unfortunately, that left the corporation rudderless. The bottom line is that the expectations for proper corporate governance have changed, and directors are responding—some more quickly than others.

---

[8] Lynn Sharp Paine, "Managing for Organizational Integrity," *Harvard Business Review* 72, no. 2 (1994): 106–17.

[9] Stock Exchange, *Report of the Toronto Stock Exchange Committee on Corporate Governance in Canada* (Toronto: Toronto Stock Exchange, 1994), p. 17, paras. 4.3 and 4.4.

[10] Canadian Institute of Chartered Accountants, *Guidance for Directors-Governance Processes for Control* (Toronto: Canadian Institute of Chartered Accountants), p. 2, para. 8; see also pp. 8 and 9 for a discussion of approving and monitoring the organization's ethical values.

Law Case Summary: Caremark National Inc.

L. J. Brooks

Late in 1996, the Chancery Court of the State of Delaware—a very influential court in corporate matters—handed down a decision that changed the expectations of directors for monitoring the affairs of the organizations they direct. The change held in the Caremark National Inc. case was to require directors to monitor organizational activities even when there is no cause for suspicion of wrongdoing.

Until the Caremark decision, the guiding case was the Delaware Supreme Court's 1963 decision in *Graham v. Allis-Chalmers Manufacturing Co.* In *Allis-Chalmers*, a case involving director's liability for violations of U.S. antitrust laws, the court had found that, "absent cause for suspicion," a Board of Directors had no legal duty to create a system for monitoring of or compliance with organizational activities. This allowed directors to argue an "ostrich" defense in the event of wrongdoing to the effect that they had "seen no evil nor heard no evil" and had made their decisions in good faith and to the best of their ability. As a result, the fiduciary duties of directors and the duty of care were somewhat circumscribed from the level of responsibility that some stakeholders felt reasonable.

The *Chancery Court* took the view, in the Caremark case, a derivative lawsuit to one involving kickbacks to health care providers in violation of the *Federal Anti-Referral Payments Law*, that the directors could be liable for recovery of some of the company's $250 million in fines from its directors for breach of their duty of care by failing to take good-faith measures to prevent or remedy the violations. The court noted, since employee actions could prevent a corporation from achieving its strategic goals, "that a director's obligation includes a duty to assure in good faith that [an] information reporting system, which the Board concludes is adequate, exists, and that failure to do so under some circumstances may, in theory at least, render a director liable for losses caused by non-compliance with applicable legal standards." Moreover, due to the issuance of the *U.S. Sentencing Guidelines* on November 1, 1991, and their subsequent integration into expectations, directors must now consider the "due diligence defense" criteria that those guidelines have spawned when advancing their "good-faith" defense. This means that the Chancery Court no longer considers a corporate compliance and monitoring program to be optional.

For further information, the reader is referred to an article by Frank M. Placenti in *The National Law Journal* on Monday, June 23, 1997 (pages B5, B6). Further insights are possible if higher courts modify the Chancery Court's Caremark decision, but, until then, directors are well advised to be ethically proactive in the development of strategic plans and operating policies and in the monitoring of performance.

Additionally, during the 1990s, it became understood that management approaches must reflect accountability to stakeholders, not just shareholders. Companies have a wide range of stakeholders—employees, customers, shareholders, suppliers, lenders, environmentalists, governments, and so on—who have a stake in the activities or impacts of the corporation. Even though these stakeholders may not have a legal claim on the corporation, they can influence its fortunes in the short and long runs. Consequently, if a corporation wants to achieve its strategic objectives optimally, the interests of its stakeholders should be taken into account when management makes decisions. The best way to do this is to build the recognition of stakeholder interests into strategic planning and other functional areas of management. Further insight can be found in the *Principles of Stakeholder Management* that can be downloaded from the Clarkson Centre for Business Ethics and Board Effectiveness website at https://www.rotman.utoronto.ca/FacultyAndResearch/ResearchCentres/ClarksonCentreforBoardEffectiveness/CCBEpublications. Schematically, the emerging stakeholder accountability and governance frameworks are represented in Figures 1.1 and 1.2. It is now recognized that *although corporations are legally responsible to shareholders, they are strategically responsible to stakeholders.*

FIGURE 1.1 Map of Corporate Stakeholder Accountability

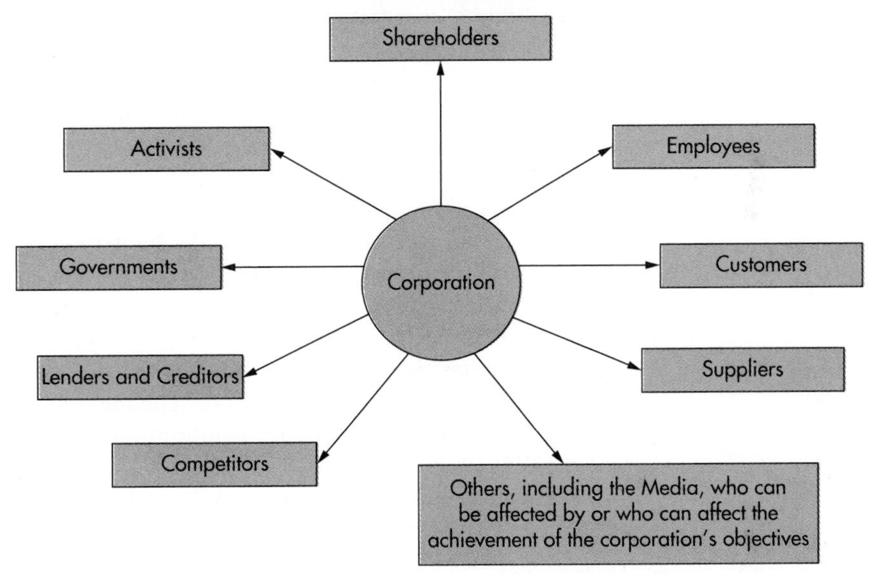

FIGURE 1.2 Corporate Governance Framework

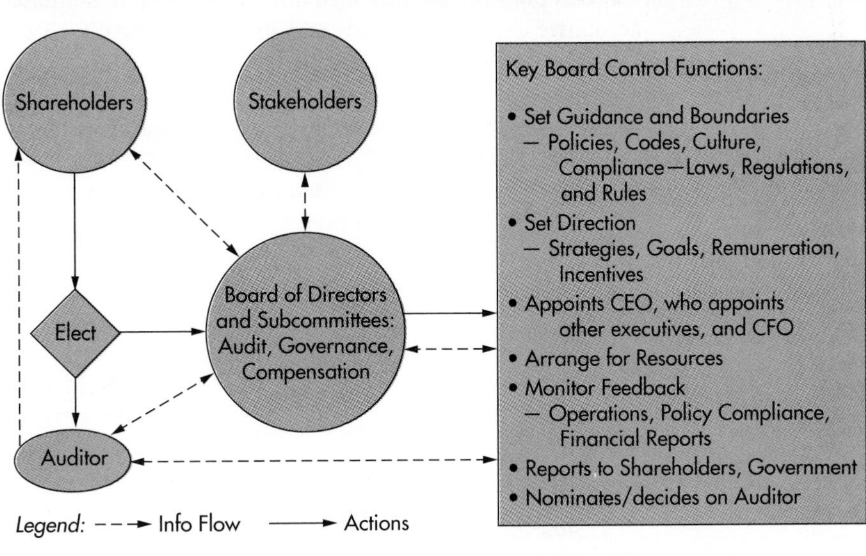

Management Based on Values, Reputation, & Risks

In order to incorporate the interests of stakeholders into the policies, strategies, and operations of their corporation, directors, executives, managers, and other employees must understand the nature of their stakeholders' interests and the values that underpin them. The reputation of the company and the degree of support garnered from stakeholders will depend on this understanding and on the ability of the company to manage the risks facing the company directly as well as those impacting its stakeholders.

Numerous approaches have been developed for examining the interests of stakeholders, such as surveys, focus groups, and mapping according to stereotypes. These are developed more extensively in Chapter 5.

In addition, investigation is under way on the values that lie behind stakeholder interests so that a corporation's policies, strategies, and procedures can take them into account. These values differ somewhat depending on the stakeholder group as well as regional differences. However, progress has been made toward a set of *hypernorms*—values that are respected by most groups or cultures around the world. According to researchers, the six values known to come closest to universal application around the world are those noted in Table 1.2.

The relevance of these six hypernorms is very significant to the future success of corporations. Consequently, they should be built into a corporation's code of conduct, policies, strategies, and activities in an attempt to make sure that the interests of many stakeholder groups are respected and that the corporation's reputation will generate maximum support.

Reputation has also been a subject of considerable recent study. Not surprisingly, the factors seen as important determinants of reputation are closely aligned with the hypernorms previously identified. Charles Fombrun, of the Reputation Institute, has specified four determinants as identified in Figure 1.3.

Both management and auditors have become increasingly risk management oriented since the mid-1990s. Risk management techniques and a risk management standard (*ISO 31000*)[11] have been developed, as directors, executives, and professional accountants recognize the value in identifying risks early and in planning to avoid or mitigate the unfortunate consequences inherent in the risks. Professional accountants have also shifted their audit approach to the examination of the risks facing a corporation, how the corporation has provided for these risks operationally, and how they have been accounted for in the records and financial reports.

TABLE 1.2 Hypernorms (Basic Values) Underlying Stakeholder Interests

A hypernorm is a value that is almost universally respected by stakeholder groups. Therefore, if a company's activities respect a hypernorm, the company is likely to be respected by stakeholder groups and will encourage stakeholder support for the company activities.

Hypernorms involve the demonstration of the following basic values:

Honesty	Fairness
Compassion	Integrity
Predictability	Responsibility

Source: R. Berenbeim, director, Working Croup on Global Ethics Principles, The Conference Board, Inc., 1999.

[11] *ISO 31000* Principles and Guidelines on Implementation was issued in 2009 by the International Organization for Standardization, http://www.iso.org/iso/home/standards/iso31000.htm.

FIGURE 1.3 Determinants of Reputation

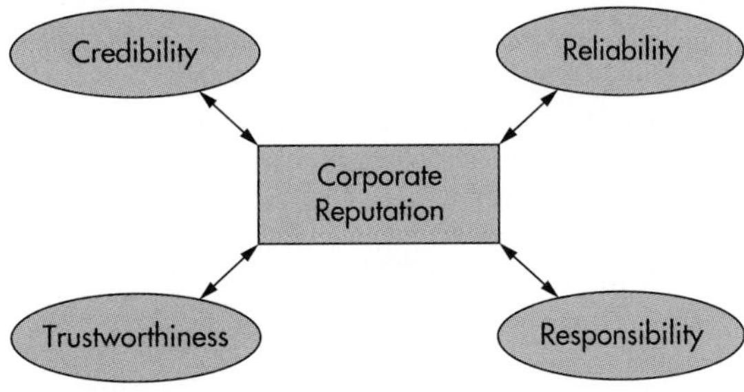

TABLE 1.3 Risk Events Causing Drops of Over 25% Share Value, Percentage of Companies, 1993–1998

Strategic (58%)	Customer demand shortfall (24%)
	Competitive pressure (12%)
	M & A integration problems (7%)
	Misaligned products (6%)
	Others (9%)
Operational (31%)	Cost overruns (11%)
	Accounting irregularities (7%)
	Management ineffectiveness (7%)
	Supply chain pressures (6%)
Financial (6%)	Foreign, macroeconomic, interest rates
Hazard and other (5%)	Lawsuits, natural disasters

Source: Mercer Management Consulting/Institute of Internal Auditors, 2001.

An early study by Mercer Management Consulting identifies some of the risk events that were important in companies that experienced very large stock price drops between 1993 and 1998. These findings are shown in Table 1.3.

Companies had not been looking systematically for such risks, but as the 1990s came to a conclusion, risk identification and assessment were becoming important parts of strategic and operational management processes, and the oversight of the risk management process was becoming an important part of directors' due diligence activities. Several studies have been published that provide insights on the subject, including those by the Institute of Internal Auditors (2001), the American Institute of Certified Public Accountants, and the Canadian Institute of Chartered Accountants (2001). Important risk management terms are reproduced in Table 1.4.

During late 2001 and into 2002, the financial world was rocked by the Enron, Arthur Andersen, and WorldCom scandals, and the resulting outrage triggered the creation of corporate governance reform through the enactment of SOX. This act and the resulting SEC regulations have transformed corporate governance expectations significantly, including the requirement that directors are now expected to ensure that

TABLE 1.4 Important Risk Management Terms

Risk is the chance of something happening that will have an impact on objectives.

Risk Management includes the culture, processes, and structures that are directed towards the effective management of potential opportunities and adverse effects.

Risk Management Process includes the systematic application of management policies, procedures, and practices to the tasks of establishing the context, identifying, analyzing, assessing, managing, monitoring, and communicating risk.

Source: Institute of Certified Public Accountants and Canadian Institute of Chartered Accountants (2001), 4.

their corporation has, among many other governance mechanisms, an effective risk management process. Many jurisdictions around the world have responded by following suit.

Although most large corporations have put in place some form of risk management process, most do not specifically consider their ethics risks—*the risks of failing to meet the expectations of stakeholders*—in a broad and comprehensive way. However, since these ethics risks have proven to be so important to reputation and corporate sustainability—such as the Volkswagen emissions debacle in 2015 and the investment banks' contribution to the 2008 financial crisis—it would be a serious mistake not to include them in the risk management process. A representative list of ethics risks is provided in Table 1.5.

In summary, particularly in view of the Volkswagen, Valeant and Turing Pharmaceuticals, and other cases, directors, executives, and professional accountants will find that meeting the expectations of stakeholders is increasingly important. This will involve delving into the values that determine a corporation's reputation and managing those values so that potential risks are avoided and/or effectively mitigated. To ignore these ethics risks is to risk the fates evident in earlier corporate debacles.

TABLE 1.5 Ethics Risks—A Representative List

STAKEHOLDER EXPECTATIONS NOT MET	ETHICS RISK
Shareholders	
Stealing, misuse of funds or assets	Honesty, integrity
Conflict of interests with officers	Predictability, responsibility
Performance level	Responsibility, honesty
Reporting transparency, accuracy	Honesty, integrity
Employees	
Safety	Fairness
Diversity	Fairness
Child and/or sweatshop labor	Compassion, fairness
Customers	
Safety	Fairness
Performance	Fairness, integrity
Environmentalists	
Sustainability, pollution	Integrity, responsibility

Accountability

The rise of stakeholder interest and accountability and the stunning financial debacles in 2001 and then again in 2008 have raised the desire for reports that are more relevant to the various interests of stakeholders, more transparent, and more accurate than in the past. In general, it is recognized that corporate reports frequently lack *integrity* because they do not cover some important issues, nor is there always a clear, balanced presentation of how the interests of stakeholders will be affected. Sometimes issues will be mentioned but in such an obtuse or unclear manner that the lack of *transparency* will cloud the understanding of the reader. *Accuracy*, or faithful representation, is, of course, fundamental to an understanding of the underlying facts.

The needed improvement in integrity, transparency, and accuracy has motivated the discussion among accountants about the nature of the guidelines they should use for preparation of financial reports—rules or principles. Enron's financial reports clearly lacked integrity, transparency, and accuracy, but they may have been in accord with a very narrow, rules-based interpretation of generally accepted accounting standards and legal definitions. Chapter 2 identifies how accounting rules and legal interpretations with regard to special purpose entities allowed Enron's board and executives to mislead the public and allowed professional accountants to rationalize their participation in the process and even provide a clean audit certification of the misleading reports. The fact that the reports were probably technically compliant with the rules was taken as satisfactory, even though they did not show the whole story transparently or accurately, and many people were misled. The misuse of rules allowed fraud-intent Enron executives to take advantage of the reporting system. However, principles based on integrity, transparency, and accuracy are considered by many to provide more robust guidance than rules against such misuse.

The desire for relevancy has spawned a surge in reports that are principally nonfinancial in nature and are tailored to the needs of specific stakeholders. These stakeholder-oriented CSR reports, which are discussed more fully in Chapter 7, cover topics such as those identified in Table 1.6. They appear in hard copy and on corporate websites. Broadly applicable reporting frameworks are being developed to guide corporations by Global Reporting Initiative[12] for comprehensive sustainability reports and by the International Integrated Reporting Council[13] integrated reports. In addition, the International Organization for Standardization has recently introduced a standard, *ISO 26000*,[14] designed to assist corporations in dealing with their social responsibility.

TABLE 1.6 Stakeholder Report Topics

Health and safety	Environmental performance/impact
Sustainability	CSR
Philanthropy	Workplace responsibility

[12] GRI G4 Guidelines, https://g4.globalreporting.org/Pages/default.aspx.

[13] The International Integrated Reporting Council website is http://integratedreporting.org/the-iirc-2.

[14] International Organization for Standardization, *ISO 26000 Guidance on Social Responsibility*, 2010, accessed December 31, 2010, at http://www.iso.org/iso/home/standards/iso26000.htm.

Ethical Behavior & Developments in Business Ethics

In response to the changes previously described, there is a renewed interest in how philosophers defined ethical behavior and the lessons that have been learned over the centuries. In addition, on a more applied level, several concepts and terms have been developed that facilitate an understanding of the evolution taking place in the accountability of business and in the making of ethical decisions.

PHILOSOPHICAL APPROACHES TO ETHICAL BEHAVIOR Commerce and economics are as old as prehistoric times when business was based on trade and barter. The ethical theories concerning acceptable and unacceptable business behaviors are just as old, although their articulation, in a Western philosophical tradition, dates primarily from the Socratic era. Although these theories were developed at an earlier time, the logic underpinning them and the lessons involved are readily applicable to current business dilemmas, as the following examples indicate.

The Greek philosopher Aristotle argued that the goal of life is happiness, and happiness is achieved by leading a virtuous life in accordance with reason. Some of these virtues include integrity, honor, loyalty, courage, and forthrightness. In a business sense, this means that directors, executives, and accountants should demonstrate *integrity* in all their business dealings; they should *honor* the terms of contracts rather than look for loopholes; they should be *loyal* to their employees, customers, and suppliers; they should have the *courage* to be candid and transparent in their dealings with relevant stakeholders; and they should be *forthright* when providing explanations of good and bad business behavior.

The German philosopher Immanuel Kant held the position that people are ethical when they do not use other people opportunistically and when they do not act in a hypocritical manner demanding a high level of conduct for everyone else while making exceptions for themselves. Unfortunately, there are many instances of organizations that do not live up to this standard. Some treat employees, customers, and suppliers merely as a means, exploiting them for some short-term goal. Often businesses are rightly accused of hypocrisy when they fail to live up to their own internally generated codes of conduct.

The English philosopher John Stuart Mill argued that the goal of life is to maximize happiness and/or to minimize unhappiness or pain, and the goal of society is to maximize the net social benefits to all people. Degrees of happiness can be both physical and psychological. So, this theory implies that the goal of business is to contribute to increasing the physical and/or psychological benefits of society. This does not mean that the goal of business is to maximize its profits; rather, the goal of business is to contribute to the overall good of society. Business does so by providing goods and services required by society.

The American philosopher John Rawls contends that society should be structured so that there is a fair distribution of rights and benefits and that any inequalities should be to everyone's advantage. This implies that businesses act in an ethical manner when they do not have discriminatory prices and hiring systems. Nor should businesses provide goods and services to one segment of society at the expense of other segments of society. Polluting and exploiting developing countries so that developed nations can have an opulent lifestyle is not to everyone's advantage.

These are but four examples of Western philosophic approaches to business ethics. They are more fully explained in Chapter 3. Suffice to say that these theories set a high standard for acceptable business behavior. Studying these theories should help directors, executives, and accountants to better understand the ethical foundations of business and provide a basis for conducting business in a socially responsible manner.

BUSINESS ETHICS CONCEPTS & TERMS Two developments are particularly useful in understanding business ethics and how business and the professions can benefit from its application. They are the *stakeholder concept* and the concept of a *corporate social contract.*

As the ethical environment for business changed, observers and executives realized that many more people than just shareholders had an interest in the corporation or its activities. As previously noted, although some of these had no statutory claim on the corporation, they had a very real capacity to influence the corporation favorably or unfavorably. Moreover, as time went by, the claims of some of these interested parties became codified through statute or regulation. It became evident that the interests of this set of people with a stake in the business or its impacts—who are affected by or can affect the achievement of the organization's objectives[15]—ought to be considered in corporate plans and decisions. For ease of reference, these people have come to be known as *stakeholders* and their interests as *stakeholders' rights.* Examples of stakeholder groups would include employees, customers, suppliers, lenders, creditors, borrowers, host communities, governments, environmentalists, media, and, of course, shareholders. A corporation's normal set of stakeholders was mapped in Figure 1.1.

The relationship between a corporation and its stakeholders has slowly but steadily broadened over the years. Initially, the corporation was established as a means of gathering large amounts of capital from shareholders. It was accountable only to those shareholders, and its goal was to generate profits. Later, when larger factories appeared, times were such that child labor was prevalent and no cost was ascribed to environmental practices that today would not be condoned. However, as previously described, corporate accountability has broadened to go beyond just shareholders to embrace the reality of stakeholders, and the corporate mandate has evolved to respect stakeholders' interests and thereby engender their support. Profits are to be generated but not at any cost to society and preferably in a way that supports society. This evolving relationship between corporations and society has come to be known, in concept, as the *corporate social contract.*

APPROACHES TO ETHICAL DECISION MAKING The evolving accountability to stakeholders within the newer versions of the corporate social contract have made it incumbent on executives to ensure that their decisions reflect the ethical values established for the corporation and do not leave out of consideration any significant stakeholder's rights. This has led to the development of ethical decision-making approaches that combine both philosophical and practical techniques, such as *stakeholder impact analysis.*

The ethical principles developed by philosophers provide insights into the key dimensions of ethical reasoning. Decision makers should understand three basic philosophical approaches: *consequentialism*, *deontology*, and *virtue ethics*. Consequentialism requires that an ethical decision have good consequences; deontology holds that an ethical act depends on the duty, rights, and justice involved; and virtue ethics considers an act ethical if it demonstrates the virtues expected by stakeholders of the participants. These approaches are expanded on in Chapter 3 and

[15] R. E. Freeman, *Strategic Management: A Stakeholder Approach* (Boston: Pitman, 1984).

are incorporated into three practical ethical decision-making approaches and a comprehensive approach in Chapter 4.

All approaches begin with the identification of significant stakeholders, an investigation of their interests, and a ranking of those interests to ensure that the most important are given adequate attention during the remaining analysis and more consideration at the decision stage. Chapter 4 provides insights into the saliency of the various stakeholder interests, which are very important to the making of ethical decisions.

The first practical analytical approach, known as the *Modified Five Question Approach*, involves challenging any proposed policy or action with five questions designed to rate the proposal on the following scales: profitability, legality, fairness, impact on the rights of each individual stakeholder and on the environment specifically, and the demonstration of virtues expected by stakeholders. The questions are asked and options for action are discarded depending on the degree to which corporate ethical values and stakeholder interests are offended. Often, action options can be modified to be made more ethical as a result of these challenges (Tucker 1990).

The *Modified Moral Standards Approach*, originally developed by Velasquez (1992), focuses on four dimensions of the impact of the proposed action: (1) whether it provides a net benefit to society, (2) whether it is fair to all stakeholders, (3) whether it is right, and (4) whether it demonstrates the virtues expected by stakeholders. Although there is some overlap with the first approach, Velasquez's focus is less company centered and is therefore better suited to the evaluation of decisions in which the impact on stakeholders outside the corporation is likely to be very severe. Longer-term impacts are also more readily incorporated.

The last approach to stakeholder impact analysis presented in Chapter 4 is the *Modified Pastin Approach*, which extends the Moral Standards Approach by specifically taking account of the culture within the corporation and of so-called commons problems. Pastin (1986) suggests that any proposed decision be evaluated in comparison to the company's ground rules (he calls this "ground rule ethics"), the net benefit it produces ("end-point ethics"), whether it impinges on any stakeholder's rights and requires rules to resolve the conflict ("rule ethics"), and, finally, whether it abuses rights apparently belonging to everyone ("problems of the commons"). The addition of the "virtues demonstrated" question (whether it demonstrates the virtues expected by stakeholders) produces the Modified Pastin Approach, which is quite practical and is best suited to decisions with impacts primarily on stakeholders directly attached to the corporation, such as employees or customers.

Chapters 4 and 7 provide frameworks for the management of issues using the stakeholder impact analysis.

The use of stakeholder impact analysis in management decision making and in the management of contentious issues will contribute significantly to the development of an ethical corporate culture (also known as a culture of integrity), which is now regarded as a precursor to the development of the ethically defensible positions that are necessary to the development and maintenance of stakeholder support for corporate activities.

THE ETHICS ENVIRONMENT FOR PROFESSIONAL ACCOUNTANTS

Role & Conduct

The aftermath of the Enron, Arthur Andersen, and WorldCom debacles brought fundamental changes in the role and conduct of those professional accountants who forgot where their primary duty is owed. Professional accountants owe their primary loyalty to the public interest, not just to their own financial interests, company directors or management, or current shareholders at the expense of future shareholders. The reasons for these changes are made clear in Chapters 2 to 6, but just as in the case of corporate governance, cracks that had been apparent for some time in the governance framework for professional accountants became so serious that the public credibility of the profession was virtually destroyed. Reforms, through new regulations and supervisory structures, and internationally harmonized standards of disclosure and revised codes of conduct that rededicate the accounting profession to its original fiduciary roots became a necessary restorative that has influenced professional accounting behavior around the world.

The need for additional changes in the role and conduct of professional accountants predates the recent debacles. Whether they are involved in the audit or assurance service functions, in management, in consulting, or as directors, professional accountants have been looked on historically as the arbiters of organizational accountability and experts in the science of decision making. Because we are witnessing a sea change in corporate accountability, with a broadening beyond just shareholders to stakeholders, it is incumbent on accountants to understand this evolution and how it can impact on their function. If they do not do so, substandard advice may be given, and the legal and nonlegal consequences for ethical shortfalls can be severe.

There is also a very real possibility that the *expectations gap* between what users of audits and financial statements thought they had been getting and what they are receiving will be exacerbated if accountants are seen to be out of step with emerging standards of ethical behavior. Studies have been undertaken, such as those by the Treadway Commission in the United States, the Macdonald Commission in Canada, and the Cadbury Report in the United Kingdom, that have called for recognition of new levels of ethical behavior in revisions to professional codes of conduct. Some professional codes were revised in response, but Enron and the other debacles have put the spotlight on the need for further revisions. A thorough understanding of the reasons for these revisions and the underlying principles involved are essential for their proper application and the protection of professionals, the profession, and the public.

An appreciation of the sea change under way in the ethics environment for business is essential to an informed understanding of how professional accountants ought to interpret their profession's code as employees of corporations. Although the public expects all professional accountants to respect the professional values of objectivity, integrity, and confidentiality, which are designed to protect the fundamental rights of the public, an employee-accountant must respond to the direction of management and the needs of current shareholders. Trade-offs are difficult. In the future, there will be less escape from the glare of public scrutiny and greater danger in greeting problems with a wink and a nod or by sweeping them under the rug. Professional accountants will have to ensure that their ethical values are current and that they are prepared to act on them to best exercise their role and to maintain the credibility of and support for the profession.

Governance

Globalization and internationalization have come to the corporate world, the capital markets, and corporate accountability. Stakeholders are global in their reach, and events that were kept secret in far-off jungles are now featured worldwide each evening on CNN or BBC World News, in revealing environmental protection or human rights documentaries, or in Internet blogs created by special interest authors or groups. Corporations with dealings around the world are conscious that they are increasingly accountable for each of their operations and are looking for effective ways to manage, account for, and disclose their activities. These approaches are discussed in Chapter 5 and include the development and maintenance of ethics programs, ethical corporate cultures (or cultures of integrity), codes of conduct, and particularly ethical leadership.

In the accounting profession, there is a movement to a globally harmonized set of generally accepted accounting and auditing principles (GAAP and GAAS) to provide analytical efficiencies for the providers of capital to the world's markets and computational and audit efficiencies around the world. There is a plan in place to harmonize, where possible, the set of GAAP developed by the IASB in London, England, and those developed by the U.S. Financial Accounting Standards Board.

Concurrently, IFAC has developed an international *Code of Ethics for Professional Accountants*,[16] and all IFAC-member countries have agreed to standardize their country's code on the same or a similar basis to the new international code. The details of this international code are reviewed in Chapter 6.

The principles inherent in the new international code *are becoming* the basis for future behavior and education of professional accountants. Difficult areas of professional behavior, such as the identification and management of conflicts of interest, have received a fresh set of guidelines. These are also discussed in Chapter 6.

Globalization has also come to audit firms. They are developing global audit standards to serve their major clients and supportive behavior standards to ensure that their judgments are independent, objective, and accurate. The rulings of the SEC, motivated by SOX and the Enron, Arthur Andersen, and WorldCom fiascos, will inform these global standards. Consequently, the IFAC-SOX-SEC intention to reinforce the professional accountant's focus on the public interest will be extended worldwide even if disclosure and audit standards ultimately differ between publicly traded and privately held corporations.

Services Offered

In this redefined global environment, the offering of nonaudit services to audit clients, which was a contentious issue for Arthur Andersen in the Enron debacle, has been curtailed so that tighter conflict-of-interest expectations can be met. The advent and growth of multidisciplinary firms in the late 1990s, which included professionals such as lawyers and engineers to provide a broader range of assurance and other services to their audit clients, has also been curtailed by revised SEC and other standards. Several major audit firms initially sold off part of their consulting units but subsequently have redeveloped specifically directed consulting services. Professional accountants should be particularly alert to conflicts in which the values and codes of other professionals in their employ differ from those of the accounting profession. Chapters 5 and 6 provide insights into these conflicts of interest.

MANAGING ETHICS RISKS & OPPORTUNITIES

Developing a Culture of Integrity

According to recent evidence,[17] the most effective way to manage ethics risks and opportunities is to ensure that integrity is part of the decision making culture of the firm. This occurs when ethical behavior becomes taken for granted as the normal expectation for

---

[16] International Federation for Accountants Ethics Committee, *IFAC Code of Ethics for Professional Accountants* (New York: International Federation for Accountants Ethics Committee, July 5, 2008), http://www.ifac.org/Store/Category.tmpl?Category=Ethics&Cart=1215563035160178.

[17] See Chapters 4 to 6.

employees, the firm, and its agents. It is worth noting that Lynn Sharp Paine[18] has suggested five essential elements required to develop an organizational culture of integrity and ethical behavior, including the following:

- *Clear communication.* Ethical values and standards must be clearly and unambiguously disseminated to all employees so that everyone knows that the firm is committed to integrity.
- *Personal commitment by senior management.* The firm cannot merely espouse that ethics is important; that causes cynicism. Instead, senior management must be willing to make difficult ethical decisions and then assume personal responsibility for their decisions.
- *Integration.* Ethical values, norms, and standards must become part of the normal everyday activities and routines of the firm.
- *Ethics must be reinforced.* Information systems and compensation structures should be designed to ensure that ethical behavior becomes the norm rather than the exception to the rule.
- *Education.* Continuous learning programs, such as ethics training, help employees to develop the competencies required to make ethical decisions on a daily basis.

A firm can more easily manage ethics risks and opportunities when integrity becomes so firmly ingrained into the decision-making structures and routines of the firm that it becomes institutionalized as part of the normal decision-making process. Practical suggestions for how a culture of integrity and ethics can become part of the firm's DNA are discussed in more detail in Chapters 4 to 6.

Two of the fundamental ingredients for a successful culture of integrity that were identified in recent studies are *ethical leadership* and effective *whistleblower encouragement programs.* Without ethical leaders—those who actively and vocally support the desired culture—*very few* employees will assume that profits are to be earned ethically. Instead, they will assume that profits are to be earned at any cost. Similarly, whistleblowers—who are essential in bringing ethical lapses to light—not only monitor ethical performance but also, by the way in which reports are followed up and made public, provide employees with the sense that management is serious or not about the company's stated ethical objectives and the degree of integrity of top management. These topics are covered in Chapters 5 to 7.

Corporate Governance

The impact of increasing expectations for business in general and for directors, executives, and accountants in particular has brought demands for governance reform, ethical decision making, and management that would benefit from leading-edge thinking on how to manage ethics risks and opportunities. Several important topics in this regard are discussed in Chapters 5 and 7.

Guidance is provided for the process of ethics risk identification, caution is advised against overreliance on external auditors for this purpose, and insights are offered for the management and reporting of ethics risks.

Next, effective strategies and mechanisms for influencing stakeholders are discussed with the view of developing and maintaining their support. Linkages are made between ethics risk management and traditional environmental scanning or issues management

[18] Lynn Sharp Paine, "Managing for Organizational Integrity," *Harvard Business Review* 72, no. 2 (1994): 106–17.

and also to the field of business–government relations. Both of these can benefit significantly from a broadened, modern stakeholder accountability perspective.

Business and professional accounting inevitably depend on people—both as external and, perhaps more important, internal stakeholders, such as employees. Understanding expectations for workplace ethics is extremely important to the success of all organizations and their executives. Employee rights are changing, as are expectations for privacy, dignity, fair treatment, health and safety, and exercising one's conscience. Development of trust, which depends on ethical values and is so important to communications, cooperation, the sharing of ideas, the excellence of innovation, and the exercise of modern leadership, is also a critical success factor. So important are these dimensions of workplace ethics that expert observers believe *the way employees view their own treatment by the company determines what the employees think about their company's ethics program.* A company cannot have an effective ethical corporate culture without laudable workplace ethics.

Similarly, a company cannot develop an effective culture of integrity if its personnel engage in improper behavior, such as sexual abuse, fraud, or white-collar crime, or belong to a group known as *corporate psychopaths* who have no sense of right and wrong. Recent high-profile sexual abuse tragedies within the Catholic Church and at Pennsylvania State University (see these two ethics cases at the end of this chapter) are stark reminders of the personal and financial problems that unresolved continuing abuse can cause. To some degree, the actions of employees at investment banks during the subprime lending crisis, which were evidently facilitated by unethical corporate cultures, could have been the result of corporate psychopaths who enjoyed taking advantage of their unsuspecting clients and without regard to the impact on society. Subsequent scandals (see the ethics case on the LIBOR rate scandal at the end of chapter 2) involving the manipulation of interest rates by some bank traders suggest that systemic changes may be required before an enterprise's culture can become ethical. Preventive measures should be put in place to avoid serious losses. These must be based on an understanding of the motivations and rationalizations used by these individuals. Discussion of how to identify and deal with these risks is very important and is covered in Chapter 7.

Most companies deal with different cultures in their hiring and management of personnel, even if their operations are within one country. Modern corporations, particularly those that deal internationally, should understand how their impacts are regarded as well as the sensitivities they arouse. Handling these ethically is a growing expectation and will contribute significantly to the achievement of strategic objectives. Many corporations are taking steps to develop a *global mind-set*[19] in their personnel. At the heart of this is an understanding of, respect for, and ethical treatment of different cultures.

Part of the ethical puzzle for modern corporations to sort out is the giving and receiving of gifts, bribes, and facilitating payments. All of these create conflicts of interest, but they are expected in many cultures. Insights are provided, including comment on using moral imagination, into how to handle these challenges ethically, respect the interest of different cultures, and protect the corporation. In the light of the new push by several countries to enforce antibribery statutes worldwide and to collect huge fines, not only in the United States also but much more broadly than contemplated by the U.S. *FCPA*, it is imperative for directors, management, employees, and agents to understand

[19] See, for example, the Najafi Global Mindset Institute at http://globalmindset.thunderbird.edu.

and apply the discussions on bribery, whistleblowing, and white-collar crime that are included in Chapter 7.

CSR, also known as corporate citizenship, and telling the company's story through CSR, sustainability, or citizenship reporting are important parts of strategic planning and the achievement of strategic objectives. Developing the kind of corporate citizenship that the leaders and stakeholders of the company want is necessarily an extension of the ethical values that are fundamental to the organization's ethical culture. Exciting new frameworks discussed in Chapter 7 are emerging that directors, executives, and professional accountants would be well advised to watch in order to take advantage of new opportunities as they arise. Reports on CSR programs and assurance thereon are growing rapidly.

Finally, businesspeople with experience know that crises are inevitable and that crisis management approaches have been developed to ensure that corporations and executives do not suffer more damage to their prospects and reputation than necessary. In fact, if the ethical aspects of crises are properly managed, reputation can be enhanced. Incorporating ethics into crisis management can clearly turn a risk into an opportunity.

Looking forward, directors, executives, and accountants would do well to understand the relevance of ethical behavior and do their best to incorporate ethics into all their plans and actions. Indeed, they should direct their efforts toward developing and maintaining an ethical culture—a culture of integrity—in their corporation or firm in order to best reach their strategic objectives.

The next chapter examines the debacles that triggered the new era of governance and accountability for corporations and the accounting profession.

Questions

1. Why have concerns over pollution become so important for management and directors?
2. Why are we more concerned now than our parents were about fair treatment of employees?
3. What could professional accountants have done to prevent the development of the *credibility gap* and the *expectations gap*?
4. Why might ethical corporate behavior lead to higher profitability?
5. Why is it important for the clients of professional accountants to be ethical?
6. How can corporations ensure that their employees behave ethically?
7. Should executives and directors be sent to jail for the acts of their corporation's employees?
8. Why are the expectations of a corporation's stakeholders important to the reputation of the corporation and to its profitability?
9. How can a corporation show respect for its stakeholders?
10. How can conflicts between the interests of stakeholders be resolved by a corporation's management?
11. Why are philosophical approaches to ethical decision making relevant to modern corporations and professional accountants?

12. What are the common elements of the three practical approaches to ethical decision making that are briefly outlined in this chapter?
13. Is a professional accountant a businessperson pursuing profit or a fiduciary that is to act in the public interest?
14. Why is it important for a professional accountant to understand the ethical trends discussed in this chapter?
15. Why should a professional accountant be aware of the Ethics Code of the International Federation of Accountants?
16. Why is an ethical corporate culture important?

Reading Insight

The article by Andrew Singer reveals the significance of whistleblowing and the impact it may have on corporations. This impact is one of the catalysts that will lead companies to want to develop ethical corporate cultures in the future.

References

Achar, R., D. Nitkin, K. Otto, P. Pellizzari, and EthicScan Canada. 1996. *Shopping with a Conscience: The Informed Shopper's Guide to Retailers, Suppliers, and Service Providers in Canada.* Toronto: Wiley.

American Institute of Certified Public Accountants and Canadian Institute of Chartered Accountants. 2001. *Managing Risk in the New Economy.* New York: American Institute of Certified Public Accountants and Canadian Institute of Chartered Accountants.

Canadian Institute of Chartered Accountants. 1995. *Guidance for Directors—Governance Processes for Control.* Toronto: Canadian Institute of Chartered Accountants. (See p. 2, para. 8, and also pp. 8 and 9 for a discussion of approving and monitoring the organization's ethical values.)

Clarkson, Max B. E. 1988. "Corporate Social Performance in Canada, 1976–86." *Research in Social Performance and Policy* 10: 241–65.

Fombrun, C. J. 1996. *Reputation: Realizing Value from the Corporate Image.* Boston: Harvard Business School Press.

Freeman, R. E. *Strategic Management: A Stakeholder Approach.* Boston: Pitman, 1984.

Friedman, F. B. 1988. *Practical Guide to Environmental Management.* Washington, DC: Environmental Law Institute.

Friedman, M. 1970. "The Social Responsibility of Business to Increase Profits." *New York Times Magazine,* September 13.

GRI G4 Guidelines. https://g4.globalreporting.org/Pages/default.aspx.

Helson, J., K. Green, D. Nitkin, and A. Stein. 1992. *The Ethical Shopper's Guide to Canadian Supermarket Products.* Toronto: Broadview Press.

Institute of Internal Auditors Research Foundation. 1995. *Guidance for Directors—Governance Processes for Control.* Toronto: Canadian Institute of Chartered Accountants. (See p. 2, para. 8, and also pp. 8 and 9 for a discussion of approving and monitoring the organization's ethical values.)

Institute of Social and Ethical Accountability. *AccountAbility.* London: Institute of Social and Ethical Accountability. http://www.accountability.org.uk.

International Federation for Accountants Ethics Committee. 2005. *IFAC Code of Ethics for Professional Accountants.* New York: International Federation for Accountants Ethics Committee, June. http://www.ifac.org/Store/Category.tmpl?Category=Ethics&Cart=1215563035160178.

International Organization for Standardization. 2010. *ISO 26000 Guidance on Social Responsibility.* 1st ed. 2010-11-01. http://www.iso.org.

Macdonald Commission. 1988. See *The Report of the Commission to Study the Public's Expectations of Audits* (Toronto: Canadian Institute of Chartered Accountants).

Mulligan, T. 1986. "A Critique of Milton Friedman's Essay 'The Social Responsibility of Business Is to

Increase Its Profits.'" *Journal of Business Ethics* 5, no. 4: 265–69.

Organization for Economic Cooperation and Development. http://www.oecd.org.

Paine, L. S. 1994. "Managing for Organizational Integrity." *Harvard Business Review* 72, no. 2, March–April: 106–17.

Pastin, M. 1986. *The Hard Problems of Management: Gaining the Ethics Edge*. San Francisco: Jossey-Bass.

Pellizzari, P. 2002. *Conscious Consumption: Corporate Social Responsibility and Canada's Grocery Giants.* Toronto: EthicScan Canada.

Placenti, F. M. 1997. "Caremark National Case." *National Law Journal*, B5, B6.

Sarbanes-Oxley Act of 2002. http://www.thomsonedu.com/accounting/brooks.

Singer, A. W. 1992. "The Whistle-Blower: Patriot or Bounty Hunter." *Across the Board*, 16–22.

Toronto Stock Exchange. 1994. *Report of the Toronto Stock Exchange Committee on Corporate Governance in Canada*. Toronto: Toronto Stock Exchange.

Treadway Commission. 1987. See American Institute of Certified Public Accountants, *Report of the National Commission on Fraudulent Public Reporting* (Washington, DC: American Institute of Certified Public Accountants).

Tucker, G. 1990. "Ethical Analysis for Environmental Problem Solving." In *Agenda for Action Conference Proceedings*, 53–57. Toronto: Canadian Centre for Ethics and Corporate Policy.

U.S. Senate Permanent Subcommittee on Investigations. 2002. *Role of the Board of Directors in the Collapse of Enron*, 3. Washington, DC: U.S. Government Printing Office. http://www.thomsonedu.com/accounting/brooks.

U.S. Sentencing Guidelines of 1991. November 1, 1991.

Velasquez, M. G. 1992. *Business Ethics: Concepts and Cases*. 3rd ed. Englewood Cliffs, NJ: Prentice Hall.

Verschoor, Curtis, C. 1998. "A Study of the Link between a Corporation's Financial Performance and Its Commitment to Ethics." *Journal of Business Ethics* 17, no. 13: 1509–16.

Wartick, S. L., and P. L. Cochran. 1985. "The Evolution of the Corporate Social Performance Model." *Academy of Management Review* 10, no. 4: 758–69.

Case Insights

The cases that follow are designed to stimulate an awareness of ethical issues currently facing directors, executives, managers, and accountants. Specifically, the scenarios covered are as follows:

Cases Involving Improper Behavior

- *Selling Only Sugary Drinks* tells the story of a doughnut chain on a university campus that refuses to sell diet soft drinks or diet juices even though many patrons are adversely affected by that decision and by the very high sugar content of popular beverages.
- *Buying and Selling Blood* examines whether is it ethical to buy and sell blood that is essential to life.
- *Pedophile Priests in the Catholic Church* provides an understanding of recent instances of continued unchecked sexual abuse that resulted in an outraged church and public.
- *Sexual Abuse by a Penn State Football Coach* continued over many years even though it was reported to officials who turned a blind eye to preserve the reputation of the university and its extremely popular football program. Failing to deal with the problem resulted in disaster for the victims, the university, Coach Paterno, university officials, and current students and alumni.
- *LIBOR Manipulations Cause Widespread Impacts* reviews the huge impacts on those banks and their executives whose employees were found to have manipulated the information on which the LIBOR benchmark rate was based—see discussion in Chapter 2 and the case beginning on page 138.

Advertising & Sales Promotion Cases

- *Tiger Woods: "Winning Takes Care of Everything"* raises the question of whether winning is all that matters and relieves people of their ethical responsibilities.
- *Pepsi's iPhone App Stereotypes Women* describes a promotional campaign that was targeted at males between the ages of eighteen and twenty-four that many women and the media considered to be sexist.
- *Should Porn Be Sold by Cell Phone Companies?* addresses whether companies that supply goods and services to the public need to take ethical responsibility into account.

Cases Involving Financial Transactions

- *Goldman Sachs and the Greek Veil* deals with the ethicality of Goldman Sachs's role in arranging transactions that hid some of the borrowing by Greece at the time when Greece wanted admission to the European Monetary Union (EMU). Greece subsequently borrowed even more with EMU backing and then needed a bailout from EMU members.
- *Martha Stewart's Lost Reputation* offers an opportunity to see how Martha lost her reputation and, with investors, a lot of money, based on allegations of selling a personal investment after receiving a tip from the CEO, who was a personal friend. What constitutes reputation? How do stakeholders fit into reputation and brand image development? What constitutes insider trading, and why is it a conflict-of-interest situation? Should insider trading be encouraged or banned? These are issues raised by the case.

Cases Involving the Control of Information

- *Google versus China* recounts Google's reaction to a cyberattack, which probably originated in China, to obtain confidential software codes. Should Google permit the Chinese government to monitor the information that is available on the Internet?
- *China's Tainted Baby Milk Powder: Rumored Control of Online News* reveals the excessive pursuit of profit, lax attention to content, and flawed health regulation that caused deaths and illness of babies in China and pets in North America. In addition, the case identifies unexpected problems associated with rumored control of online news to manage reputation risks.

Cases Concerning the Environment

- *Nestlé Bottles Water in a California Drought* presents the dilemma of whether it is ethical to reduce the water table level during a drought in order to bottle spring water.
- *Bhopal–Union Carbide* is intended to raise the reader's awareness of ethical issues facing modern corporations. It presents the reader with an event that, although improbable, happens repeatedly in different scenarios and offers the reader an opportunity to explore what they and others believe to be appropriate levels of corporate responsibility and ethical behavior.
- *Texaco in Ecuador* outlines the environmental difficulties Texaco faced in their oil operations in Ecuador. Even after leaving the country, Texaco was sued in U.S. courts by South Americans. Did Texaco act responsibly? Could this have been prevented?

Product Safety Cases

- *The Right to be Informed? The Link between Talcum Powder and Cervical Cancer* indicates that Johnson & Johnson knew for many years that their talcum powder was associated with higher levels of cervical cancer but never disclosed this to its customers. Was this ethical? Was it legal?
- *Valeant Pharmaceuticals vs. Coca Cola—Which Business Model Is Worse: Price Gouging or Fostering Obesity & Diabetes?* Two opposing business titans were concerned about investing in organizations with flawed business models. This case causes readers to consider the problem and which of two "successful" business model is worse.
- *Betaseron (A)* discusses the real dilemmas that were faced by a pharmaceutical management team when they faced difficult choices affecting customers' quality of life. The ethical implications of such decisions can be ignored but not without cost.
- *Magnetic Toys Can Hurt* explains how a Mega Brands's product was potentially harmful to children if they swallowed powerful magnets contained in the toys. The product was recalled only after the company was pressured by the government and the public.

Accounting & Auditing Cases

- *Where Were the Accountants?* presents a brief series of scandals and ethical problems on which management accountants, academic accountants, and auditors could have commented on in time to significantly mitigate the outcome. Why didn't they? Should they have?
- *Resign or Serve?* introduces the problem of balancing ethical trade-offs in a modern, creative economic world. How far should an auditor go to protect a fellow professional, the profession, or the public?

Cases Involving Improper Behavior

ETHICS CASE

Selling Only Sugary Drinks

It's legal, but is it ethical?

For years, a nationally known doughnut chain only sold sugary drinks at its retail outlets on a prominent university campus. Sugar consumption is known to contribute to diseases such as heart disease, tooth decay, diabetes, kidney stones, and obesity. Although these health concerns were brought to the attention of the chain several times, patrons were told that if they wanted diet drinks, they had to purchase them from coin-operated machines or from other food operations on the campus. Since speed of service is important, many consumers were unwilling to make a second stop to buy their diet beverages. The chain continued to sell only sugary drinks, even though they had been banned as health risks from elementary schools, hospitals, and some retail establishments.

The amount of sugar in well-known sugary drinks is incredibly high:

- 38 grams (10 sugar cubes) in a 12 oz. can of Coca Cola;
- 91 grams (23.5 sugar cubes) in a 32 oz. fountain drink of Coca Cola;
- 77 grams (19.5 sugar cubes) in a 20 oz. bottle of Mountain Dew;
- 46 grams (14.5 sugar cubes) in a 16 oz. bottle of Snapple Iced Tea; and
- 48 grams (12 sugar cubes) in a 16 oz. bottle of Minute Maid orange juice.

In March 2013, the situation was of such concern that Michael Bloomberg, then mayor of New York City, proposed banning the sale of nondiet soft drinks of larger than 16 oz. in New York City but was stopped by the decision of a New York State judge.

Questions

1. Why do you think that the doughnut chain continued to sell only sugary soft drinks even though it was under pressure to sell diet soft drinks as well?
2. Was selling only sugary soft drinks ethical?
3. Should the university campus officials have forced the doughnut chain to carry diet soft drinks?

Sources: Sugar Stacks, "How Much Sugar in Beverages?" accessed July 19, 2016 at http://www.sugarstacks.com/beverages.htm.

Steven Nelson, "New York Soda Ban Struck Down, Bloomberg Promises Appeal-US News and World Report," March 3, 2013, accessed July 19, 2013, at http://www.usnews.com/news/articles/2013/03/11/new-york-soda-ban-struck-down-bloomberg-promises-appeal.

ETHICS CASE

Buying and Selling Blood

In Canada, selling body parts, such as organs, sperm and eggs, is illegal. Selling blood is not. Canadian Blood Services, which manages the blood supply for Canadians, neither pays for nor sells blood. It is freely available to whoever needs it. A similar system operates in the United Kingdom, where the National Health Service Blood and Transplant Authority also relies on voluntary blood donations from the public. In most countries in the world, donors freely give their blood to help others. That is not the case in the United States, where blood is bought and sold like any other commodity.

In the 1980s, about 30,000 Canadians were infected with HIV and hepatitis C from tainted blood and plasma that had been imported from the United States. The Krever Commission, which investigated the tainted blood scandal, found that the American donors, who had been paid, had not been adequately screened and often came from high-risk populations. One of the recommendations of the commission was that blood donations in Canada should be from unpaid donors. The findings of the Krever Commission resulted in the formation of Canadian Blood Services, a not-for-profit organization that oversees the blood supply in Canada.

The plasma industry is highly competitive and international. Plasma is used not only for blood transfusion but also for the production of various pharmaceutical products. In various parts of the world, blood can be bought for as little as a dollar a pint and can be sold to hospitals for up to $150 per pint.

On March 18, 2014, a start-up company called Canadian Plasma Resources opened its first blood donation clinic. The company hired forty people and spent $7 million on two clinics in Toronto and a third in Hamilton. The clinics were located near homeless shelters and in poor neighborhoods. The purpose of these clinics was to buy blood. It would pay donors $25 for each donation, and regular donors could donate up to once a week. The company said that it would follow all Heath Canada guidelines. Barzin Bahardoust, the CEO of Canadian Plasma Resources, said that his company will meet market demand and create local jobs. Bahardoust's long-term goal was to establish a plasma manufacturing facility in Canada. "This is our hope. But it is a huge investment. Not comparable to setting up a few plasma centres."[1]

Questions

1. Is it unethical to pay donors for making blood donations?
2. Is blood a commodity that can be bought and sold like any other commodity?

[1] Kelly Crowe, "Paying for Blood Plasma Raises New Questions," *CBC News*, April 25, 2013.

3. Is there a difference between selling blood that can be used in transfusions and selling blood that will be used to make pharmaceutical products?
4. Do companies, such as Canadian Plasma Resources, contribute to drug addiction and alcoholism by locating their clinics in poorer neighborhoods?

Sources: Ian Merringer, "Proposal for Paid Blood Plasma Donations Prompts Concerns," *The Globe and Mail*, January 31, 2014

Kelly Grant, "Ontario Tries to Ban Blood-Buying before Clinics Open," *The Globe and Mail*, March 14, 2014.

ETHICS CASE

Pedophile Priests in the Catholic Church

In January 2002, the *Boston Globe* began a series of articles reporting that Fr. John Geoghan had been transferred from one parish to another in the Archdiocese of Boston, even though senior church officials knew that he was a pedophile. There was outrage among parishioners that archdiocesan administrators, including Cardinal Bernard Law, could be complacent about Fr. Geoghan's behavior while he was being relocated to various parishes. The message being sent was that "abusive priests mattered more than innocent children." Anger among Boston Catholics led to the formation of Voice of the Faithful, a grassroots movement among concerned Catholics in the Boston area that quickly spread to becoming an international movement. Their call was simple: Keep the Faith, Change the Church. Their plea was eventually heard. Cardinal Law resigned, and Fr. Geoghan was sent to prison, where he died.

But the problem of sexual abuse by the clergy became a worldwide scandal. Abuses were reported in various countries around the world. In Canada, it concerned children who were at the Mount Cashel Orphanage in Newfoundland. In Ireland, the allegations were so severe that Pope Benedict XVI had a special team of cardinals investigate the matter. In March 2010, the pope issued an apology to the Catholics of Ireland. He acknowledged that serious mistakes had been made by the clergy and recommended that "no effort should be spared in improving and updating existing procedures" so that this would not reoccur. For some the apology was enough, while other Catholics called for the pope's resignation.

Questions

1. What are the responsibilities of employees who become aware of unethical behavior by their superiors?
2. What actions should be taken by corporate leaders when they receive reports of sexual abuse? Why?
3. If unethical or illegal behavior occurs within a business enterprise, how can employees bring about change when initial reports are ignored?
4. Why do you think that senior managers want to cover up scandals that occur within their organizations?
5. What actions can senior managers take to repair the damaged reputations of their organizations after scandals become publicly known? Do you think that apologies are worthwhile?

Sources: Benedict XVI, "Pastoral Letter of the Holy Father Pope Benedict XVI to the Catholics of Ireland," 2010, http://w2.vatican.va/content/benedict-xvi/en/letters/2010/documents/hf_ben-xvi_let_20100319_church-ireland.html

B. Gutierrez, J. Howard-Grenville, and M. A. Scully, "The Faithful Rise Up: Split Identification and an Unlikely Change Effort," *Academy of Management Journal* 53, no. 4 (2010): 673–99

James E. Post, *Voice of the Faithful—A Decade of Catholic Activism*, http://www.votf.org/2012Conference/VOTFADecadeof CatholicActivism.pdf.

ETHICS CASE

Sexual Abuse by a Penn State Football Coach

In June 2012, Jerry Sandusky was convicted of sexually abusing ten boys while he was an assistant football coach at Pennsylvania State University. His abuse of children went back almost fourteen years and was known by his superior, Joe Paterno, the head football coach. In 1998, there was an investigation by Penn State campus police after an allegation that Sandusky had molested a boy in the football shower room. It was later revealed that Paterno lied when he said that he was not aware of the 1998 investigation. In 2001, there was a report that Sandusky had abused a ten-year-old boy in the showers at Penn State. Paterno convinced the university's senior administrators, including President Graham Spanier, that they should simply issue a warning letter to Sandusky. Finally, in November 2011, Sandusky was arrested on charges of sexually abusing ten boys. That same month, both Paterno, who held the record for the largest number of victories in American college football history, and Spanier, who was one of the longest serving of U.S. university presidents, were fired.

In July 2012, Louis Freeh, a former director of the Federal Bureau of Investigation (FBI) who had been hired by Penn State University, issued a 250-page report to the university and turned his evidence over to the Pennsylvania state attorney general. As a result, Tim Curley, the athletic director, and Garry Schultz, of campus police, are now facing criminal charges for their role in the 2001 cover-up.

Why would so many senior administrators protect a known pedophile and engage in such a cover-up? According to Freeh, there was a pervasive fear of bad publicity. "That publicity, Mr. Freeh said Thursday, would have hurt the nationally ranked football program, Mr. Paterno's reputation as a coach of high principles, the Penn State 'brand' and the university's ability to raise money as one of the most respected public institutions in the country."

Questions

1. Football is big business, raising millions and millions of dollars for American universities. Numerous administrators and officials at Penn State University put a higher value on college football than on the welfare of children. How would an organization develop such a misguided culture?
2. Louis Freeh discovered that a janitor saw Jerry Sandusky abusing a boy in the showers in 2000 but said nothing because he was afraid to "take on the football program." Why do you think that certain organizational departments and programs develop a mystique such that their activities and behaviors cannot be challenged or questioned? What can organizations do to prevent this from happening?

Sources: K. Belson, "Abuse Scandal Inquiry Damns Paterno and Penn State," *New York Times*, July 12, 2012.

L. J. Freeh, *The Freeh Report on Pennsylvania State University*, 2012, https://www.documentcloud.org/documents/396512-report-final-071212.html.

Advertising & Sales Promotion Cases

ETHICS CASE

Tiger Woods: "Winning Takes Care of Everything"

Tiger Woods, once probably the world's greatest golfer, lost his number one ranking in October 2010, the same year that his marriage to Lin Nordegren blew up when she chased him out of the house and broke the windows of his vehicle with a 9 iron. His popularity sagged as the stories of his infidelity with strippers became common in national news and his back injuries prevented him from competing at his best.

Nike severed its relationship with Lance Armstrong after he revealed using performance enhancing drugs and with Oscar Pistorius after he shot his girlfriend. But Nike kept its sponsorship arrangement with Tiger, generating huge revenues for both. However, there was immediate and critical reaction from many when Nike posted an online ad in May 2013 that carried a picture of Tiger superimposed by the quote "Winning Takes Care of Everything." Others did not seem to mind the double-edged inference projected by the ad: that it does not matter how you play the game of golf or the game of life—it matters only if you win.

If you win, can you get away with anything?

Questions

1. Does winning take care of everything? In golf? In life? In business?
2. Does how you play the game or run your business ever matter?
3. Is the reputational impact of unethical behavior different for a sports star than for a business or for yourself?

Sources: "Nike's Tiger Woods Ad Draws Critics," ESPN.com News Services, May 29, 2013, accessed July 19, 2016, at http://espn.go.com/golf/story/_/id/9100497/nike-winning-takes-care-everything-tiger-woods-ad-draws-critics.

The Nike ad is shown in the story "Does Winning Take Care of Everything?" Global News on YouTube, March 28, 2013, accessed July 19, 2016, at https://www.youtube.com/watch?v=RgGixKWOv1w.

ETHICS CASE

Pepsi's iPhone App Stereotypes Women

In October 2009, PepsiCo Inc. launched, apologized, and then pulled an iPhone application called "AMP Up Before You Score," designed to promote its Amp Energy drink. The drink's target market is males between the ages of eighteen and twenty-four. Released on October 8, the app stereotyped women into two dozen groups, including "rebound girl," "sorority girl," "cougar," and "foreign exchange student." Users could flip through a series of digital cards that provided background information on each type of woman, including how to calculate a carbon footprint to score with a "treehugger" as well as strategies on how to seduce a "married" girl. It also provided some pickup lines: "Wasn't I in Space Academy with you?" for the "nerd," and for the "artist" it suggested "You know the Mona Lisa has no eyebrows. I wonder what else she shaves." The app included a "Brag List" so that guys who "scored" could post a name, the date, and any other information on their Facebook or Twitter accounts.

Pepsi was inundated with criticism from blogs, emails, and the media. The app was accused of being sexist because it degraded and objectified women. On October 12, Pepsi apologized through its Twitter page: "Our app tried 2 show the humorous lengths guys go 2 pick up women. We apologize if it's in bad taste & appreciate your feedback."[1] But not all the feedback was negative. Many males said that they considered it to be funny. Nevertheless, on October 22, Pepsi announced that it was withdrawing the app. "We have decided to discontinue the AMP iPhone application. We've listened to a variety of audiences and determined this was the most appropriate course of action."[2]

[1] Valerie Bauerlein and Suzanne Vranica, "Drink's iPhone 'App' Gets Anger Flowing," *Wall Street Journal*, October 14, 2009.

[2] Brian Morrissey, "Pepsi Pulls Amp iPhone App," *Adweek*, October 22, 2009.

Questions

1. Do you find it interesting that most of the critics were women and the media but those who considered the app to be funny were young men?
2. The target market of Amp Energy is males between the ages of eighteen and twenty-four. If this group of consumers found the iPhone amp to be funny and acceptable, then why did Pepsi withdraw the app?
3. Are advertising campaigns that are in bad taste also unethical?

Sources: The factual information in this case has been drawn from various publications, including the following:

Alienate Female Customers? Pepsi Has an App for That," *The Globe and Mail*, October 15, 2009, B10; Brian Morrissey.

Pepsi Brand App Comes with NC-17 Rating," *Brandweek*, October 9, 2009; Marisa Taylor.

Pepsi Apologizes for Before You Score iPhone App," *Wall Street Journal*, October 13, 2009.

ETHICS CASE

Should Porn Be Sold by Cell Phone Companies?

Telus Corp., the second-largest wireless company in Canada, introduced an "adult content" service to their cell phone customers in 2007. Customers were charged $3 to $4 for downloads, and the company expected to make very large amounts of money based on observable Internet trends.

Fairly quickly, however, Telus was under pressure from customers rather than the government to discontinue the service, even though the service was apparently legal. In response, Telus's company spokespeople argued about the following:

- The service consisted of photographs and videos featuring "full and partial nudity, but no sex."
- Customers would be age verified very rigorously to prove they were adults.
- The service was already universally available, although Telus was the first wireless carrier in North America to offer such a service.[1]

There were many complaints in the form of calls from cell phone users and the Roman Catholic Church threatening to discontinue their contracts with Telus. According to Archbishop Roussin, the service "takes the accessibility of pornographic material further into the public realm."[2]

At the same time, Telus was developing a community support program involving community investment boards and ambassadors in an effort to improve its reputation and acceptance. On its website at the time, Telus stated:

> At Telus, we aspire to be Canada's premier corporate citizen. We are committed to building a corporate culture of giving, and engaging the hearts and minds of our team members and retirees to improve the quality of life in our communities. We recognize that leading the way in corporate social responsibility is as important as our financial performance. We have made a commitment to our customers, shareholders and all stakeholders to stay ahead or our competitors in all aspects of business—economically, environmentally and socially. Corporate social responsibility remains an integral part of what we do—it defines our business practices and culture as we strive to achieve long-term sustainable growth.[3]

---

[1] Virginia Galt, "Telus Hangs Up on Mobile Porn Service," *The Globe and Mail*, February 21, 2007.

[2] Gudrun Schultz, "BC Archbishop Considers Cancelling Telus Contract over Porn Sales," LifeSiteNews.com, February 12, 2007.

[3] Telus's website at http://wwwr.telns.com at the community investment page. The message has changed somewhat on the current website.

Questions

1. If selling pornography is legal, profitable, and readily available elsewhere, should Telus shut down its adult service? Why or why not?
2. Telus said that it wanted to be Canada's premier corporate citizen. Should companies such as Telus feel obligated to give back to society?

ETHICS CASE

Virgin Mobile's Strip2Clothe Campaign: Exploitive, Risqué, and Worthwhile?

In July 2008, Virgin Mobile USA began a "Strip2Clothe" advertising campaign. There are millions of homeless teenagers in the United States, and Virgin Mobile's website said that "someone out there needs clothes more than you." Virgin Mobile invited teenagers to upload videos of themselves disrobing. For every uploaded striptease video, Virgin Mobile would donate a new piece of clothing. For every five times the video was viewed, an additional piece of clothing would be donated. Virgin Mobile said that they would screen all the videos. The strippers had to be eighteen or older, and there was to be no full nudity. By July 12, there were twenty videos on the site that had generated 51,291 pieces of donated clothing.

The campaign sparked immediate criticism. Rebecca Lentz of the Catholic Charities of St. Paul and Minneapolis called the advertising campaign "distasteful and inappropriate and exploitative." Parents were concerned that their under-eighteen-year-old children would strip, zip the video, and not reveal their real age. On Tuesday July 15, the National Network for Youth (NN4Y) said that it would decline to partner with Virgin Mobile. Some of the 150 charities represented by NN4Y objected to the campaign, saying that it was inappropriate given that many homeless teenagers are sexually exploited. NN4Y said that any member organizations that wished to receive clothing donations through the Strip2Clothe campaign would have to contact Virgin Mobile directly.

In response to the public outcry, Virgin Mobile altered its campaign. On July 21, it launched "Blank2Clothe," in which the company would accept any kind of talent video, such as walking, juggling, singing, riding, and so on. All of the striptease videos were removed, and the strippers were asked to send in new, fully clothed videos.

The arguments against the campaign were that it targeted youth, many homeless teenagers are sexually exploited, the homeless normally need shelter and safety rather than clothes, and the campaign was in poor taste. But there were some supporters. Rick Koca, founder of StandUp for Kids in San Diego, said that the campaign was not hurting anyone and was raising public awareness. In the one week ending July 19, the controversy and the campaign had resulted in a further 15,000 clothing donations.

Questions

1. The Strip2Clothe campaign may have been in questionable taste, but it did raise tens of thousands of pieces of clothing for the homeless. Does the end justify the means?
2. Virgin Mobile has a history of using cutting-edge advertisements. It poked fun at religion in its 2004 holiday commercial "Christmas-hanukwanzakah," and it had the company's founder, Sir Richard Branson, stand in a nude suit in New York's Times Square as part of a "Nothing to Hide" campaign. Are marketing tactics that are tasteless and risqué also unethical?
3. Some years before, the Benetton Group S.p.A. developed the United Colors of Benetton Campaign, originally to draw attention to prejudice against black people. The campaign broadened over

time to include other prejudices and consist of a series of shocking pictures published in unexpected venues. For example, there were pictures of a nun kissing a priest, a bombed car in a street, a white dog kissing a black lamb, an AIDS activist on his death bed in front of a picture of a crucified Christ, and a white girl portrayed with an angelic halo and a black boy with hair like horns. Is the Virgin campaign substantively different that the Benetton campaign of 1992?

4. What rule would you put forward that would differentiate ethical from unethical advertising campaigns?

Sources: "Charities Can't Bare 'Strip2Clothe' Blitz," McClatchy News Services, July 14, 2008, http://www.wsj.com/articles/SB121660673649869421

Andrew LaVallee, "Virgin Mobile Pulls Back Racy Campaign," *Wall Street Journal,* July 21, 2008, http://online.wsj.com/article/SB121660673649869421.html

Abby Simons, "Homeless Youth Network Ditches 'Strip2Clothe' Campaign," *Minneapolis-St. Paul Star Tribune*, July 15, 2008, http://www.startribune.com/local/25489799.html.

Cases Involving Financial Transactions

Goldman Sachs and The Greek Veil

ETHICS CASE

On February 11, 2010, the leaders of the European Union (EU) agreed on a plan to bail out Greece, a country that had joined the EU in 1981 and was admitted to the European Monetary Union (EMU), allowing Greece to adopt the euro as its currency in 2001. Greece had been unable to pay its bills or to borrow more money to do so because it had overspent its income on its social programs and other projects. In the aftermath of providing Greece with bailout credit ultimately totaling €100 billion ($147 billion),[1] questions were asked about how this could have happened. A spotlight was brought to bear on how Goldman Sachs (GS) had enabled Greece to qualify for adopting the euro in the first place[2] and for providing the means to hide some transactions in which Greece pledged its future revenues in return for instant cash to spend. In a sense, GS helped Greece draw a veil over its finances with arrangements that were not transparent.

In 2001, Greece wanted to join the EMU but faced a requirement that its ratio of debt to gross domestic product (GDP) ratio be less than 60%.[3] Unfortunately, Greece had some debt that was payable in U.S. dollars (USD) and other debt in Japanese yen. Both currencies had grown in value relative to the euro in 1999 and 2000. Under EU rules, such unhedged debt had to be valued and reported at the year-end exchange rates, so Greece faced the prospect reporting increased debt liabilities.

In late 2000 and 2001, GS proposed and arranged two types of hedges that reduced reported Greek debt by €2.367 billion and allowed Greece to access unreported, off-balance-sheet financing:

- Currency hedges that turned the USD and yen debt payments into euro payments and subsequently the Greek swap portfolio into new cross-currency swaps valued using a historical implied foreign exchange rate rather than market value exchange rate. Since the historical exchange rate was lower than the market rate at the time, the resulting valuation

[1] Lefteris Papadimas and Jan Strupczewski, "EU, IMF Agree $147 Billion Bailout for Greece," Reuters, May 2, 2010, http://www.reuters.com/article/2010/05/02/us-eurozone-idUSTRE6400PJ20100502.

[2] See, for example, the interview "Is Goldman Responsible for Greek Crisis?," RussiaToday Commentary, February 11, 2010, https://www.youtube.com/watch?v=tCe80hsx-ig.

[3] Goldman Sachs, "Goldman Sachs Transactions in Greece," accessed November 27, 2010, at http://www2.goldmansachs.com/our-firm/on-the-issues/viewpoint/viewpoint-articles/greece.html.

of the debt was reduced by almost €2.4 billion ($3.2 billion).

- Interest rate swaps that, when coupled with a bond, provided Greece with instant cash in 2001 in return for pledging future landing fees at its airports. GS was reportedly paid $300 million for this transaction. A similar deal in 2000 saw Greece pledge the future revenue from its national lottery in return for cash. Greece was obligated to pay GS substantial amounts until 2019 under these agreements but chose to sell these interest rate swaps to the National Bank of Greece in 2005 after criticism in the Greek Parliament.[4]

In essence, through these so-called interest rate swaps, Greece was converting a stream of variable future cash flows into instant cash. But, although there was a fierce debate among EU finance ministers, these obligations to pay out future cash flows were not required to be disclosed in 2001 and were therefore a type of "off-balance-sheet financing." In 2002, the requirements changed, and these obligations did require disclosure. Humorously, the 2000 deal related to a legal entity called Aeolos that was created for the purpose—Aeolos is the Greek goddess of wind.[5]

In response to public criticism, GS argues on its website that "these transactions [both currency and interest rate hedges] were consistent with the Eurostat principles governing their use and disclosure at the time."[6] In addition, GS argues that the reduction of €2.367 billion had "minimal effect on the country's overall fiscal situation in 2001" since its GDP was approximately $131 billion and its debt was 103.7% of GDP.[7] However, it is not clear how much cash was provided by the so-called interest rate swaps that allowed Greece to report lower debt obligations in total.

Questions

1. Did GS do anything wrong legally or ethically? Explain your answer.
2. Would it make a difference if other investment bankers were also providing such services?
3. What subsequent impacts could the transactions described above have on GS?

[4] Louise Story, Landon Thomas Jr., and Nelson D. Schwartz, "Wall St. Helped to Mask Debt Fueling Europe's Crisis," February 13, 2010, http://www.nytimes.com/2010/02/14/business/global/14debt.html?pagewanted=all&_r=0.

[5] Ibid.

[6] Ibid.

[7] Ibid.

ETHICS CASE

Martha Stewart's Lost Reputation

In June 2002, Martha Stewart began to wrestle with allegations that she had improperly used inside information to sell a stock investment to an unsuspecting investing public. That was when her personal friend Sam Waksal was defending himself against SEC allegations that he had tipped off his family members so that they could sell their shares of ImClone Systems Inc. (ImClone) just before other investors learned that ImClone's fortunes were about to take a dive. Observers presumed that Stewart was also tipped off, and even though she proclaimed her innocence, the rumors would not go away.

On TV daily as the reigning guru of homemaking, Stewart is the multimillionaire proprietor, president, and driving force of Martha Stewart Living Omnimedia Inc.

(MSO), of which, on March 18, 2002, she owned 30,713,475 (62.6%[1]) of the class A and 30,619,375 (100%) of the class B shares. On December 27, 2001, Stewart's class A and class B shares were worth approximately $17 each, so on paper the MSO class A shares alone were worth over $500 million. Class B shares are convertible into class A shares on a one-to-one basis.

Stewart's personal life became public. The world did not know that she had sold 3,928 shares of ImClone for $58 each on December 27, 2001,[2] until it surfaced in June 2002.[3] The sale generated only $227,824 for Stewart, and she avoided losing $45,673 when the stock price dropped the next day,[4] but it has caused her endless personal grief and humiliation and the loss of reputation as well as a significant drop to $5.26 in the MSO share price.

What Happened?

Stewart had made an investment in ImClone, a company that was trying to get the approval of the U.S. Food and Drug Administration (FDA) to bring to market an anti-colon cancer drug called Erbitux. Waksal, then the CEO of ImClone and a personal friend of Stewart's, was apparently warned on or close to December 25, 2001, that the FDA was going to refuse[5] to review Erbitux.[6] According to SEC allegations, Waksal relayed the information to his family so that they could dump their ImClone shares on an unsuspecting public before the official announcement. Stewart claims that she did not get any inside information early from Waksal, but regulators believe that she may have, or from her broker or her broker's aide. The activities of several of Waksal's friends, including Waksal, are under investigation by the SEC.

Waksal was arrested on June 12, 2002, and charged with "nine criminal counts of conspiracy, securities fraud and perjury, and then freed on $10 million bail."[7] In a related civil complaint, the SEC alleged that Waksal "tried to sell ImClone stock and tipped family members before ImClone's official FDA announcement on Dec. 28."[8]

According to the SEC, two unidentified members of Waksal's family sold about $10 million worth of ImClone stock in a two-day interval just before the announcement. Moreover, Waksal also tried for two days to sell nearly 80,000 ImClone shares for about $5 million, but two different brokers refused to process the trades.[9]

Stewart has denied any wrongdoing. She was quoted as saying, "In placing my trade I had no improper information.... My transaction was entirely lawful."[10] She admitted calling Waksal after selling her shares but claimed, "I did not reach Mr. Waksal, and he did not return my call."[11] She maintained that she had an agreement with her broker to sell her remaining

---

[1] *Proxy Statement for 2002 Annual Meeting of Stockholders of Martha Stewart Living Omnimedia, Inc.*, held May 9, 2002, SEC Edgar Filing, http://www.sec.gov/Archives/edgar/data/1091801/000095012302003236/y58395def14a.txt

[2] "Martha Scrutiny Heats Up: Shares of Decorator's Company End Tough Week as Martha Stewart's ImClone Links Prove Troubling," *CNN/Money*, June 14, 2002.

[3] "Martha Stewart Resigns as NYSE Board Member," Reuters per *The Financial Express*, January 5, 2003, http://www.financialexpress.com/archive/martha-stewart-resigns-as-nyse-board-member/59960/.

[4] "Broker's Aide Pleads Guilty in Martha Stewart Matter," *Washington Post*, October 2, 2002.

[5] "ImClone Ex-CEO Takes the 5th: Sam Waksal Declines to Testify; His Brother Harlan Says His Sales Were Not Improper," *CNN/Money*, June 13, 2001.

[6] Later it became known that the application for review had "multiple deficiencies" and provided insufficient information that the drug would work on its own. Ibid.

[7] Ibid.

[8] Ibid.

[9] Ibid.

[10] "Martha Scrutiny Heats Up."

[11] Ibid.

ImClone shares "if the stock dropped below $60 per share."[12]

Stewart's public, however, was skeptical. She was asked embarrassing questions when she appeared on TV for a cooking segment, and she declined to answer, saying, "I am here to make my salad." Stewart's interactions with her broker, Peter Bacanovic, and his assistant, Douglas Faneuil, are also being scrutinized. Merrill Lynch & Co. suspended Bacanovic (who was also Waksal's broker[13]) and Faneuil, with pay, in late June. Later, since all phone calls to brokerages are taped and emails kept, it appeared to be damning when Bacanovic initially refused to provide his cell phone records to the House Energy and Commerce Commission for their investigation.[14] Moreover, on October 4, 2001, Faneuil "pleaded guilty to a charge that he accepted gifts from his superior in return for keeping quiet about circumstances surrounding Stewart's controversial stock sale."[15] Faneuil admitted that he received extra vacation time, including a free airline ticket from a Merrill Lynch employee in exchange for withholding information from SEC and FBI investigators.[16]

According to the *Washington Post* report of Faneuil's appearance in court:

> On the morning of Dec. 27, Faneuil received a telephone call from a Waksal family member who asked to sell 39,472 shares for almost $2.5 million, according to court records. Waksal's accountant also called Faneuil in an unsuccessful attempt to sell a large bloc of shares, the records show.
>
> Prosecutors allege that those orders "constituted material non-public information." But they alleged that Faneuil violated his duty to Merrill Lynch by calling a "tippee" to relate that Waksal family members were attempting to liquidate their holdings in ImClone.
>
> That person then sold "all the Tip-pee's shares of ImClone stock, approximately 3,928 shares, yielding proceeds of approximately $228,000" the court papers said.[17]

One day later, on October 5, it was announced that Stewart resigned from her post as a director of the New York Stock Exchange (NYSE)—a post she held only four months—and the price of MSO shares declined more than 7% to $6.32 in afternoon trading.[18] From June 12 to October 12, the share price of MSO had declined by approximately 61%.[19]

Stewart's future took a further interesting turn on October 15, when Waksal pleaded guilty to six counts of his indictment, including bank fraud, securities fraud, conspiracy to obstruct justice, and perjury. But he did not agree to cooperate with prosecutors and did not incriminate Stewart.[20] Waksal's sentencing was postponed until 2003 so that his lawyers could exchange information with U.S. District Judge William Pauley concerning Waksal's financial records.[21]

---

[12] Ibid.

[13] "Aide to Martha Stewart's Broker Admits He Withheld Information from Investigators," *CBC News*, October 2, 2002, http://cbc.ca/news.

[14] "Martha's Broker under Microscope," CBSNews.com, July 9, 2001, http://www.cbsnews.com/news/marthas-broker-under-microscope/.

[15] "Martha Stewart Resigns as NYSE Board Member."

[16] "Broker's Aide Pleads Guilty in Martha Stewart Matter."

[17] Ibid.

[18] Ibid.

[19] Assuming a value per share of $13.50 on June 12, the decline to a low of $5.26 in early October amounted to a decline of 61%.

[20] "ImClone Founder Pleads Guilty," CBSNews.com, October 15, 2002, http://www.cbsnews.com/news/imclone-founder-pleads-guilty/.

[21] Ultimately, on June 10, 2003, Waksal was "sentenced to 87 months in prison for insider trading, bank fraud, perjury and obstruction of justice. He also was ordered to pay more than US$4 million in fines and restitution for illegally tipping off his daughter in December 2001, that shares in the company he founded were about to fall sharply." Peter Morton, "Waksal Jailed for 7 Years," *Financial Post*, June 11, 2003, FP3.

After October 15, the price of MSO shares rose, perhaps as the prospect of Stewart's going to jail appeared to become more remote and/or people began to consider MSO to be more than just Stewart and her reputation. The gain from the low point of the MSO share price in October to December 9, 2002, was about 40%.[22]

Stewart still had a lot to think about, however. Apparently the SEC gave her notice in September of its intent to file civil securities fraud charges against her. Stewart's lawyers responded, and the SEC deliberated. Even if Stewart were to get off with a fine, prosecutors could still bring a criminal case against her in the future. It is an interesting legal question, how, if Stewart were to plead guilty to the civil charges, she could avoid criminal liability.[23]

On June 4, 2003, Stewart was indicted on charges of obstructing justice and securities fraud. She then quit as chairman and CEO of her company but stayed on the board and served as chief creative officer. She appeared in court on January 20, 2004, and watched the proceedings throughout her trial. In addition to the testimony of Faneuil, Stewart's personal friend Mariana Pasternak testified that Stewart told her that Waksal was trying to dump his shares shortly after selling her ImClone stock.[24] Ultimately, the jury did not believe the counterclaim by Bacanovic, Stewart's broker, that he and Stewart had a prior agreement to sell ImClone if it went below $60. Although Judge Cedarbaum dismissed the charge of securities fraud for insider trading, on March 5, 2004, the jury found Stewart guilty on one charge of conspiracy, one of obstruction of justice, and two of making false statements to investigators.[25] The announcement caused the share price of her company to sink by $2.77 to $11.26 on the NYSE.[26]

Source: Reprinted courtesy of StatPro Canada, Inc.

Stewart immediately posted the following on her website:

> I am obviously distressed by the jury's verdict, but I continue to take comfort in knowing that I have done nothing wrong and that I have the enduring support of my family and friends. I will appeal the verdict and continue to fight to clear my name. I believe in the fairness of the judicial system and remain confident that I will ultimately prevail.[27]

Stewart was subsequently sentenced to five months in prison and five months of home detention—a lower-than-maximum sentence under the *U.S. Sentencing Guidelines*—and she did appeal. Although she could have remained free during the

[22] "Market Betting Martha Won't Go to Jail: Shares Up 40 Percent in 6 Weeks," *Financial Post*, December 10, 2001, IN1, 3.

[23] "SEC Knocking on Martha's Door," CBSNEWS.com, October 22, 2002.

[24] "TIMELINE: Martha Stewart," *CNN/Money*, downloaded March 5, 2004, http://money.cnn.com/pf/features/popups/martha_timeline/.

[25] "Martha Stewart Found Guilty on All Charges; Vows to Appeal," *CBC.CA News*, March 5, 2005.

[26] Ibid.

[27] "Martha Stewart: I Will Appeal," CNN.com, March 5, 2004, http://www.cnn.com/2004/LAW/03/05/martha.responds/.

appeal, on September 15, 2004, she asked for her sentence to start[28] so that she could be at home in time for the spring planting season. Stewart's appeal cited "prosecutorial misconduct, extraneous influences on the jury and erroneous evidentiary rulings and jury instructions," but on January 6, 2006, her conviction was upheld.[29]

Impact on Reputation

Stewart may still disagree with the verdict. But there is little doubt that the allegations and her convictions had a major impact on her personally and on the fortunes of MSO and the other shareholders that had faith in her and her company. Assuming a value per share of $13.50 on June 12, the decline to a low of $5.26 in early October 2003 represents a loss of market capitalization (i.e., reputation capital as defined by Charles Fombrun[30]) of approximately $250 million, or 61%. The value of MSO's shares did return to close at $35.51 on February 7, 2005,[31] but fell off to under $20 in early 2006. According to a New York brand-rating company, Brand-Keys, the Martha Stewart brand reached a peak of 120 (the baseline is 100) in May 2002 and sank to a low of 63 in March 2004.[32]

What will the future hold? Stewart has returned to TV with a version of *The Apprentice* as well as her usual homemaking and design shows, and her products and magazines continue to be sold. Will she regain her earlier distinction? Would she do it again to avoid losing $45,673?

Questions

1. What was the basis of Stewart's reputation?
2. Why did MSO's stock price decline due to Stewart's loss of reputation?
3. Who is Stewart's target market?
4. What qualities were associated with the Martha Stewart brand before the controversy? Which of these were affected by the accusations of insider trading, and how? How would you find out for sure?
5. What level of sales and profits would MSO have reached if Stewart's reputation had not been harmed? Refer to the SEC or MSO websites for information on financial trends.
6. What range would the stock price have been in at the end of 2002, based on your estimates?
7. Stewart's overall net worth was huge relative to her investment in ImClone. Assuming she did not have inside information, was there any way she could have avoided the appearance of having it?
8. How could Stewart have handled this crisis better?
9. Why is insider trading considered harmful? Should insider trading be banned if it assists in moving a stock price to a new equilibrium quickly so that noninsiders are trading at appropriate prices sooner?
10. If you wished to sell an investment in a company where one of your friends is an insider or even a significant employee, should you call your friend to advise him that you are about to sell? Why or why not?

---

[28] Drew Hasselback, "Martha to Judge: Jail Me Now," *Financial Post*, September 16, 2004, FP1.

[29] Larry Neumeister, "Conviction Stands, Court Tells Celebrity Homemaker Stewart," *Toronto Star*, January 7, 2006, D3.

[30] Charles J. Fombrun, *Reputation: Realizing Value from the Corporate Image* (Boston: Harvard Business School Press, 1996).

[31] Michael Santoli, "Martha's Comeback May Be Brief," *Financial Post*, February 8, 2005, IN3.

[32] Peter Morton, "Omnimedia Eyes Life without Martha," *Financial Post*, March 9, 2004, FP1, FP4.

Cases Involving the Control of Information

Google versus China

ETHICS CASE

Google is the world's largest search engine. In 2009, it had approximately 400 million Web users, of which 200 million are located in the United States. Its global revenue from advertising amounted to $23.6 billion. China is the world's third-largest economy. China has a potential 384 million Internet users, and advertising revenue from China is estimated to be $15 billion to $20 billion annually. In 2006, Google began operations in China as Google.cn. Part of the agreement with the Chinese government was that the Google.cn search engine would censor information from topics that had been banned by the Chinese government.

In January 2010, Google threatened to pull out of China after it claimed that Google and some twenty other large companies had been subjected, in December 2009, to "a highly sophisticated and targeted attack"[1] designed to steal software codes. The alleged purpose of the attack was so that the Chinese government could break into the Gmail accounts of Chinese human rights activists. Although the attack was unsuccessful, Google decided it should review its operations in China. "We have decided that we are no longer willing to continue censoring our results on Google.cn, and so over the next few weeks we will be discussing with the Chinese government the basis on which we could operate an unfiltered search engine within the law, if at all. We recognize that this may well mean having to shut down Google.cn, and potentially our offices in China."[2]

Three months later, in March 2010, Google closed Google.cn and began directing its Chinese customers to a search engine in Hong Kong, Google.com.hk. Hong Kong is a special administrative region, so the Google.com.hk search engine is not subject to Chinese government censorship. The Chinese government complained that this was a violation of the written promise Google had made when it began operations in China in 2006.

The license for Google to operate in China was up for renewal on June 30, 2010. Without the license, "Google would effectively go dark in China."[3] Then, in July, a compromise was reached. The Chinese government renewed Google's license to operate in China, and Google said that it would not automatically redirect its Chinese users to the uncensored Hong Kong site. Instead, users would go to a landing page on Google.cn that is linked to Google.com.hk. In other words, users would have to double-click in order to get to the Hong Kong site. This solution saved face. Google agreed to obey Chinese laws while at the same time, by providing access to the Hong Kong site, the company could say that it was maintaining its anticensorship policies. "As a company we aspire to make information available to users everywhere, including China. It's why we have worked so hard to keep Google.cn alive, as well as to continue our research and development work in China. This new approach is consistent with our commitment not to self censor [*sic*] and, we believe, with local law."[4] After the announcement that Google's Chinese license had been renewed, the company's stock rose 2.8%.

---

[1] David Drummond, "A New Approach to China," *The Official Google Blog* (blog), January 12, 2010, http://googleblog.blogspot.com/2010/01/new-approach-to-china.html.

[2] Ibid.

[3] Ibid.

[4] David Drummond, "An Update on China," *The Official Google Blog* (blog), July 9, 2010, http://googleblog.blogspot.com/2010/06/update-on-china.html.

Questions

1. When it began operations in China in 2006, Google had agreed to have the search engine Google.cn censor information. Did Google have an ethical right to renege on its agreement in 2010 by directing its Chinese users to the uncensored search engine Google.com.hk?
2. Google derives its revenue by selling advertising. Should Google be concerned about the type of information that users access through the various Google search engines?
3. Do for-profit businesses, such as Google, have an ethical responsibility to lobby for human rights and against censorship in the various countries in which they have commercial operations?
4. After the December 2009 attack, Google enhanced the security for all of its users. Does Google have any additional ethical responsibility to human rights activists to provide them with even more sophisticated architectural and infrastructure improvements so that their specific Gmail accounts cannot be compromised?

Sources: The factual information in this case has been drawn from various newspapers, including the following:

Google And China Work It Out, For Now", Carl Gutierrez, Forbes, July 9, 2010, http://www.forbes.com/2010/07/09/google-china-baidu-markets-equities-technology-censorship.html accessed Nov. 11, 2016

Google Says China Licence Renewed by Government," *BBC News Business*, July 9, 2010, http://www.bbc.co.uk/news/10566318 accessed Dec. 28, 2010

Google vs. China," *Washington Post*, January 14, 2010, http://www.washington post.com/wp-dyn/content/article/2010/01/13/AR2010011302908.html; Miguel Helft and David Barboza

Google Shuts China Site in Dispute over Censorship," *New York Times*, March 22, 2010, http://www.nytimes.com/2010/03/ 23/technology/23google.html

ETHICS CASE

China's Tainted Baby Milk Powder: Rumored Control of Online News

On July 16, 2008, it was announced that several Chinese producers of baby milk powder had been adding melamine, a chemical usually used in countertops, to increase the "richness" of their milk powder and to increase the protein count. Shockingly, the melamine-tainted milk powder was responsible for the deaths of four infants and the sickening of an additional 6,200.[1] Milk manufacturers had been using melamine as a low-cost way of "enriching" their product in both taste and protein count.

Melamine, a toxic chemical that makes countertops very durable, damages kidneys.[2] This fact came to world attention on March 16, 2007, when Menu Foods of Streetsville, Ontario, Canada, recalled dog and cat foods that it had mixed in Canada from Chinese ingredients that were found to include melamine.[3] Very quickly thereafter, pet owners' claims and class action lawsuits threatened to put the company into bankruptcy until settlements were worked out.[4] A subsequent investigation

[1] Sky Canaves, "Baidu Caught in Backlash over Tainted Milk Powder," WSJ.com, September 19, 2008, http://www.wsj.com/articles/SB122176870268453547, accessed November 18, 2008.

[2] See technical report prepared by the University of Guelph Laboratory Services at http://www.labservices.uoguelph.ca/urgent.cfm.

[3] Menu Foods, "Menu Foods Income Fund Announces Precautionary Dog and Cat Food Recall," press release, accessed November 24, 2008, at http://www.menufoods.com/recall/Press_Recall_03162007.htm

[4] Dana Flavelle, "Menu Foods Settling Pet Food Suits," Thestar.com, April 2, 2008, accessed November 24, 2008, at http://www.thestar.com/Business/article/408926

by the U.S. Food and Drug Administration (FDA) led to the recall of pet food by major manufacturers, including Del Monte, Nestlé Purina, Menu Foods, and many others.[5] On February 6, 2008, "the FDA announced that that two Chinese nationals and the businesses they operate, along with a U.S. company and its president and chief executive officer, were indicted by a federal grand jury for their roles in a scheme to import products purported to be wheat gluten into the United States that were contaminated with melamine."[6] It will be interesting to follow what penalties are ultimately paid by the Chinese manufacturers.

Although the story of melamine-tainted ingredients broke in mid-March 2007, the similarly tainted milk powder link did not come to light in China until sixteen months later. Governmental follow-up has not been speedy even though unmarked bags of "protein powder" had probably been added to several other products, including baking powder and feed for chickens, thus contaminating eggs and meat.[7] On October 8, 2008, the Chinese government stopped reporting updated figures of infant milk powder sufferers "because it is not an infectious disease, so it's not necessary to announce it to the public."[8] Knowledgeable members of the Chinese public, however, have been using the suitcases of their visiting relatives to import U.S.- and Canadian-made milk formula for their children.

It is also fascinating to consider another aspect of life in China—rumored control of online news. Although there is no proof of the rumors, which might have been started by competitors, the *Wall Street Journal*'s online service has reported that Baidu.com Inc., the company referred to as the "Google of China," is under attack for accepting payments to keep stories containing a specific milk manufacturing company's name from online searches about the tainted milk scandal even when the manufacturer was recalling the product. Local government officials also declined to confirm the milk manufacturer's problem during the same period.

Baidu.com "said it had been approached this week by several dairy producers but said that it 'flat out refused' to screen out unfavorable news and accused rivals of fanning the flames."[9] In a statement, it said, "Baidu respects the truth, and our search results reflect that commitment."

Currently, there is no evidence that Baidu.com did accept the screen-out payments as rumored, but it does face some challenges of its own making in trying to restore it reputation. For example, unlike Google, which separates or distinguishes paid advertisements from nonpaid search results, Baidu.com integrated paid advertisements into its search listing until critics recently complained. In addition, companies could pay more and get a higher ranking for their ads. According to the *Wall Street Journal* article, a search for "mobile phone" generates a list where almost the entire first page consists of paid advertisements. Also, competitors fearing increased competition and new products from Baidu.com, which recently increased its market share to 64.4%, have begun to restrict Baidu's search software (spiders) from penetrating websites that the competitors control.

Baidu.com's profit growth had been strong, but for how long? Baidu.com Inc. is traded on the U.S. NASDAQ under the symbol BIDU. Since the rumors surfaced in late August to early September 2008, BIDU's share price has declined from $308 to almost $110 on November 20, 2008.

---

[5] FDA, "Pet Food Recall (Melamine)/Tainted Animal Feed," accessed November 24, 2008, at http://www.fda.gov/oc/opacom/hot-topics/petfood.html.

[6] Ibid.

[7] *Wikipedia*, accessed November 24, 2008, at http://en.wikipedia.org/wiki/2008_Chinese_milk_scandal#Source_of_contamination

[8] Ibid.

[9] Sky Canaves, "Baidu Caught in Backlash over Tainted Milk Powder," WSJ.com, September 19, 2008, http://www.wsj.com/articles/SB122176870268453547, accessed November 18, 2008.

Questions

1. Given strong profit growth, has there been any damage to Baidu.com's reputation?
2. What would future reputational damage affect, and how could it be measured?
3. What steps could Baidu.com take to restore its reputation, and what challenges will it have to overcome?
4. Governments throughout the world have been slow to react publicly to serious problems such as SARS, mad cow disease, and now melamine contamination. Who benefits and who loses because of these delays?
5. In some cultures, a "culture of secrecy" or manipulation of the news is tolerated more than others. How can this be remedied by other governments, corporations, investors, and members of the public?
6. Many other companies with long supply chains, including subcontractors in far-off lands, have found themselves in difficulty. For example, in 1995, Nike was accused of employing child labor in Pakistan and Cambodia through its subcontractors and subsequently changed its policy and practices with respect to the minimum age of employees working in contract factories. However, it is very difficult to verify age when people do not have birth certificates or when they can be bought cheaply on the black market.
7. Under such conditions, what are a firm's responsibilities with respect to checking that each stage in the supply chain is complying with company policy?
8. Are there organizations that can help companies set standards and confirm adherence to them? If so, what are the organizations' mandates and website addresses?
9. Should Menu Foods be held responsible for the melamine found in its products?
10. Would your response be different if it were the lives of people that were at stake rather than the lives of animals?
11. How and why does Nike disclose its policies and practices with regard to supply chain responsibility, and what are the major factors covered?

Cases Concerning the Environment

ETHICS CASE

Nestlé Bottles Water in a California Drought

The bottled water industry is lucrative and expanding, especially in the United States, where it has been growing steadily since 2010, reaching 11 billion gallons in 2014.[1] This upward trend is likely to continue as health conscious consumers opt for water over sweetened beverages.

The Swiss multinational beverage company Nestlé operates five facilities in California that bottle approximately 700 million gallons of water. One of these bottling facilities is located in the Millard Canyon, about eighty-five miles east of Los Angeles. For over ten years, the Millard Canyon operation has been bottling spring water for export outside of California. In 2013, it pumped out 200 million gallons of groundwater, enough water for about 400 California homes for one year.

The state of California has been in a drought since 2011. In April 2015, Governor Jerry Brown enacted an emergency

[1] John Rodwan, "Bottled Water 2014: Reinvigoration," International Bottled Water Association, http://www.desertsun.com/story/news/environment/2014/07/12/nestle-arrowhead-tapping-water/12589267/

regulation that requires a mandatory 25% reduction in water use throughout the state. The Millard Canyon spring, however, is located on land that is owned by the Morongo Band of Mission Indians. Because this is an Indian reservation, the land is considered a sovereign nation and therefore is not required to comply with California laws and regulations.

The Millard Canyon spring is located in a Mojave Desert oasis, where only three inches of rain fall annually. Any reduction in the groundwater that is extracted from the Millard Canyon spring prevents water from seeping downhill to fill the aquifers of the nearby towns. These towns have been struggling for water during the drought.

Protesters object to the Millard Canyon bottling facility. "If you had the same bottling plant in a water-rich area, then the amount of water bottled and diverted would be a small fraction of the total water available. But this is a desert ecosystem. Surface water in the desert is exceedingly rare and has a much higher environmental value than the same amount of water somewhere else."[2]

Local residents say that the bottling plant provides badly needed jobs in the area and is helping the local economy. The Morongo Band of Mission Indians contends that they are "responsible stewards of the environment" and that they are monitoring the bottling plant's operation "to ensure that these water resources remain healthy and reliable for future generations."[3]

Critics, however, note that neither the Morongo Band nor Nestlé has provided reports on exactly how much water has been extracted from the Millard Canyon spring since 2009. Because this land is considered a sovereign nation, the Morongo Indians are not required to report water consumption information. As such, critics contend that it is difficult to assess the impact of this operation on the areas water supply.

For its part, Nestlé maintains that it complies with regulations and operates its business in a transparent manner. In a 2015 interview, the CEO, Tim Brown, noted that "people need to drink water.... If I stop bottling water tomorrow, people would buy a different brand of bottled water.... In fact, if I could increase [bottling], I would."[4] In contrast, Starbucks, which sells bottled water branded as Ethos, moved its plant out of California due to the historic drought.

Questions

1. Do you think that it is ethical or unethical for Nestlé to drain the groundwater in the Millard Canyon spring during a drought?
2. Does Nestlé have an ethical obligation to disclose proprietary information, such as the amount of groundwater extracted and the water levels in the Millard Canyon spring? Or does Nestlé have the right to privacy and therefore need not disclose water consumption information?
3. From a marketing perspective, what, if anything, is required of companies in order to sell bottled water in an ethical manner?

[2] Ian James, "Little Oversight as Nestlé Taps Morongo Reservation Water," *The Desert Sun*, March 31, 2014.
[3] Ibid.
[4] Alex Lockie, "Nestlé Waters' CEO Will 'Absolutely Not' Stop Bottling Water in California—'In Fact, If I Could I'd Increase It,'" *Business Insider UK*, May 14, 2015.

Bhopal–Union Carbide

ETHICS CASE

On April 24, 1985, Warren M. Anderson, the sixty-three-year-old chairman of Union Carbide Corporation, had to make a disappointing announcement to angry stockholders at their annual meeting in Danbury, Connecticut. Anderson, who had been jailed briefly by the government of India on charges of "negligence and criminal corporate liability," had been devoting all his attention to the company's mushrooming problems. His announcement concerned the complete breakdown of negotiations with officials in the Indian government: they had rejected as inadequate an estimated $200 million in compensation for the deaths of 2,000 people and the injuries of 200,000 others, which had been caused in December 1984 by a poisonous leak of methyl isocyanate gas from a Union Carbide pesticide plant located in Bhopal, India.[1] In the wake of more than $35 billion in suits filed against the company's liability coverage, reported to total only about $200 million, the company's stock tumbled. Angry stockholders filed suit, charging that they had suffered losses of more than $1 billion because the company's managers had failed to warn them of the risks at the Indian plant. Analysts predicted the company would be forced into bankruptcy. Ironically, the Union Carbide plant in Bhopal had been losing money for several years, and Anderson had considered closing it.

The deadly methyl isocyanate gas that leaked from the Union Carbide plant is a volatile and highly toxic chemical used to make pesticides. It is 500 times more poisonous than cyanide, and it reacts explosively with almost any substance, including water. Late on the night of December 2, 1984, the methyl isocyanate stored in a tank at the Bhopal factory started boiling violently when water or some other agent accidentally entered the tank. A cooling unit that should have switched on automatically had been disabled for at least a year. Both Shakil Qureshi, a manager on duty at the time, and Suman Dey, the senior operator on duty, distrusted the initial readings on their gauges in the control room. "Instruments often didn't work," Qureshi said later. "They got corroded, and crystals would form on them."

By 11:30 p.m., the plant workers' eyes were burning. But the workers remained unconcerned because, as they later reported, minor leaks were common at the plant and were often first detected in this way. Many of the illiterate workers were unaware of the deadly properties of the chemical. Not until 12:40 a.m., as workers began choking on the fumes, did they realize something was drastically wrong. Five minutes later, emergency valves on the storage tank exploded, and white toxic gas began shooting out of a pipestack and drifting toward the shantytowns downwind from the plant. An alarm sounded as manager Dey shouted into the factory loudspeaker that a massive leak had erupted and the workers should flee the area. Meanwhile, Qureshi ordered company fire trucks to spray the escaping gas with water to neutralize the chemical. But water pressure was too low to reach the top of the 120-foot-high pipestack. Dey then rushed to turn on a vent scrubber that should have neutralized the escaping gas with caustic soda. Unfortunately, the scrubber had been shut down for maintenance fifteen days earlier. As white clouds continued to pour out of the pipestack, Qureshi shouted to workers to turn on a nearby flare tower to burn off the gas. The flare, however, would not go on because its pipes had corroded and were still being repaired.

Panicked workers poured out of the plant, and the lethal cloud settled over the neighboring shantytowns of Jaipraksh and Chola. Hundreds died in their beds, choking helplessly in violent spasms as their burning lungs filled with fluid. Thousands were blinded by the caustic gas, and thousands of others suffered burns and lesions

[1] All material concerning Union Carbide and the Bhopal plant, including all quotations and all allegations, is drawn directly from the following sources: *New York Times*: December 9, 1984, IE; December 16, 1984, 1, 8; January 28, 1985, 6, 7; January 30, 1985, 6; April 25, 1985, 34; *San Jose Mercury News*: December 6, 1984, 16A; December 12, 1984, 1, 1H; December 13, 1984, 1; *Time*: December 17, 1985, 22–31.

in their nasal and bronchial passages. When it was over, at least 2,000 lay dead, and 200,000 were injured. The majority of the dead were squatters who had illegally built huts next to the factory. Surviving residents of the slums, most of them illiterate, declared afterward that they had built their shacks there because they did not understand the danger and thought the factory made healthy "medicine for plants."

Union Carbide managers from the United States built the Bhopal plant in 1969 with the blessing of the Indian government, which was anxious to increase production of the pesticides it desperately needed to raise food for India's huge population. Over the next fifteen years, pesticides enabled India to cut its annual grain losses from 25% to 15%, a saving of 15 million tons of grain, or enough to feed 70 million people for a full year. Indian officials willingly accepted the technology, skills, and equipment that Union Carbide provided, and Indian workers were thankful for the company jobs, without which they would have had to beg or starve, as India has no welfare system. In return, India offered the company cheap labor, low taxes, and few laws requiring expensive environmental equipment or costly workplace protections. In comparison with other factories in India, the Union Carbide plant was considered a model, law-abiding citizen with a good safety record. Said a government official, "They never refused to install what we asked."

At the time of the disaster, the pesticide plant in Bhopal was operated by Union Carbide India Ltd, a subsidiary of the Union Carbide Corporation of Danbury, Connecticut, which had a controlling interest of 50.9% in the Indian company. The Board of Directors of Union Carbide India Ltd included one top manager from the parent Union Carbide Corporation in the United States and four managers from another Union Carbide subsidiary based in Hong Kong. Reports from the Indian company were regularly reviewed by the managers in Danbury, who had the authority to exercise financial and technical control over Union Carbide India Ltd. Although day-to-day details were left to the Indian managers, the American managers controlled budgets, set major policies, and issued technical directives for operating and maintaining the plant.

Before the tragedy, the Indian subsidiary had been doing poorly. In an effort to contain annual losses of $4 million from the unprofitable plant, local company managers had initiated several cost-cutting programs. Only a year before, the number of equipment operators on each shift had been reduced from twelve to five; morale dropped, and many of the best operators quit and were replaced with workers whose education was below that required by company manuals. Although Warren Anderson and other Union Carbide Corporation (U.S.) managers insisted that responsibility for the plant's operations rested with the local Indian managers, they hastened to say that all cost-cutting measures had been justified.

Two years before the disaster, the American managers had sent three engineers from the United States to survey the plant and, as a result, had told the Indian managers to remedy ten major flaws in safety equipment and procedures. The Indian managers had written back that the problems were corrected. "We have no reason to believe that what was represented to us by Union Carbide India Ltd. did not in fact occur," said the U.S. managers. The U.S. managers had considered closing the failing plant a year earlier, but Indian city and state officials had asked that the company remain open to preserve the jobs of thousands of workers in the plant and in dependent local industries.

Questions

1. What are the ethical issues raised by this case?
2. Did the legal doctrine of "limited liability" apply to protect the shareholders of Union Carbide Corporation (U.S.)?

3. Were the Indian operations, which were being overseen by the managers of Union Carbide Corporation (U.S.), in compliance with legal, moral, or ethical standards?

ETHICS CASE

Texaco: The Ecuador Issue

In 1964, at the[1] invitation of the Ecuadorian government, Texaco Inc. began operations through a subsidiary, TexPet, in the Amazon region of Ecuador. The purpose of the project was to "develop Ecuador's natural resources and encourage the *colonization* of the area." TexPet was a minority owner of the project, and its partner was Petroecuador, the government-owned oil company. Over the years from 1968 to 1992, the consortium extracted 1.4 billion barrels of oil from the Ecuadorian operations.

Ecuador benefited greatly during this period. Ecuador received approximately 98% of all moneys generated by the consortium in the form of royalties, taxes, and revenues. Altogether, this amount represented more than 50% of Ecuador's gross national product during that period. TexPet's operations over the years provided jobs for 840 employees and approximately 2,000 contract workers, thereby benefiting almost 3,000 Ecuadorian families directly, in addition to the thousands of Ecuadorian nationals who supplied the company's needs for goods and services. Also, TexPet made substantial contributions to the Quito, Guayaquil, and Loja Polytechnics and other institutions of higher education. Oil is Ecuador's lifeblood—a $1 billion-per-year industry that accounts for 50% of the export earnings and 62% of its fiscal budget.

Unfortunately, problems also arose. Although Petroecuador acquired 100% of the ownership of the Transecuadorian pipeline in 1986, TexPet still accounted for 88% of all oil production and operated the pipeline in 1987 when it ruptured and was buried by a landslide. A spill of 16.8 million gallons (4.4 million barrels) occurred, which Texaco attributed to a major earthquake that devastated Ecuador.

Other spills apparently occurred as well. Although Texaco pulled out of the consortium in 1992 entirely (having retreated to be a silent minority partner in 1990), three lawsuits were filed against it in the United States—the Aquinda (November 1993), the Sequihua (August 1993), and the Jota (1994). The indigenous people who launched the lawsuits charged that, during two decades of oil drilling in the Amazon, Texaco dumped more than 3,000 gallons of crude oil a day—millions of gallons in total—into the environment. The indigenous people say that their rivers, streams, and lakes are now contaminated and that the fish and wild game that once made up their food supply are now decimated. They asked in the lawsuit that Texaco compensate them and clean up their land and waters.

Maria Aquinda, for whom the suit is named, says that contaminated water from nearby oil wells drilled by the Texaco subsidiary caused her to suffer chronic stomach ailments and rashes and that she lost scores of pigs and chickens. Aquinda and seventy-six other Amazonian residents filed a $1.5 billion lawsuit in New York against Texaco. The class action suit, representing 30,000 people, further alleges that Texaco acted "with callous disregard for the health, wellbeing, and safety of the plaintiffs" and that "large-scale disposal of inadequately treated hazardous wastes and destruction of tropical rain forest habitats, caused harm to indigenous peoples and their property." According to the Ecuadorian

[1] By Professor Timothy Rowley of the Rotman School of Management.

environmental group Ecological Action, Texaco destroyed more than 1 million hectares of tropical forest, spilled 74 million liters of oil, and used obsolete technology that led to the dumping of 18 million liters of toxic waste. Rainforest Action Network, a San Francisco–based organization, says effects include poor crop production in the affected areas, invasion of tribal lands, sexual assaults committed by oil workers, and loss of game animals (which would be food supply for the indigenous peoples).

Audits were conducted to address the impact of operations on the soil, water, and air and to assess compliance with environmental laws, regulations, and generally accepted operating practices. Two internationally recognized and independent consulting firms, AGRA Earth & Environmental Ltd and Fugro-McClelland, conducted audits in Ecuador. Each independently concluded that TexPet acted responsibly and that no lasting or significant environmental impact exists from its former operations. Nonetheless, TexPet agreed to remedy the limited and localized impacts attributable to its operations. On May 4, 1995, Ecuador's minister of energy and mines, the president of Petroecuador, and TexPet signed the *Contract for Implementing of Environmental Remedial Work and Release from Obligations, Liability, and Claims* following negotiations with Ecuadorian government officials representing the interests of indigenous groups in the Amazon. In this remediation effort, producing wells and pits formerly utilized by TexPet were closed, producing water systems were modified, cleared lands were replanted, and contaminated soil was remediated. All actions taken were inspected and certified by the Ecuadorian government. Additionally, TexPet funded social and health programs throughout the region of operations, such as medical dispensaries and sewage and potable water systems. That contract settled all claims by Petroecuador and the Republic of Ecuador against TexPet, Texaco, and their affiliates for all matters arising out of the consortium's operations.

In the summer of 1998, the $40 million remediation project was completed. On September 30, 1998, Ecuador's minister of energy and mines, the president of Petroecuador, and the general manager of Petroproduccion signed the *Final Release of Claims and Delivery of Equipment*. This document finalized the government of Ecuador's approval of TexPet's environmental remediation work and further stated that TexPet fully complied with all obligations established in the remediation agreement signed in 1995.

Meanwhile, in the United States, Texaco made the following arguments against the three lawsuits:

- Activities were in compliance with Ecuadorian laws and international oil industry standards.
- Activities were undertaken by a largely Ecuadorian workforce—which Texaco believed would always act in the interest of its community/country.
- All investments/operations were approved and monitored by the Ecuadorian government and Petroecuador.
- All activities were conducted with the oversight and approval of the Ecuadorian government.
- Environmentally friendly measures were used, such as helicopters instead of roads.
- The health of Ecuadorians increased during the years Texaco was in Ecuador.
- Ninety-eight percent of the money generated stayed in Ecuador—50% of gross domestic product during that period.
- Jobs were provided for 2,800.
- Money was provided for schools.
- Independent engineering firms found no lasting damage.
- A $40 million remediation program was started per an agreement with the Ecuadorian government.

- U.S. courts should not govern activities in a foreign country.

The three lawsuits were dismissed for similar reasons—the Sequihua in 1994, the Aquinda in 1996, and the Jota in 1997. The Aquinda lawsuit, for example, was launched in New York (where Texaco has its corporate headquarters) because Texaco no longer had business in Ecuador and could not be sued there. The case was dismissed by a New York court in November 1996 on the basis that it should be heard in Ecuador. Failing that, the Ecuadorian government should have been involved in the case as well, or the case should have been filed against the government and the state-owned Petroecuador as well as Texaco. At that point, the Ecuadorian government did get involved and filed an appeal of the decision. This was the first time a foreign government had sued a U.S. oil company in the United States for environmental damage. In addition, in 1997, the plaintiffs in the Aquinda and Jota cases also appealed the district court's decisions.

On October 5, 1998, a U.S. court of appeals remanded both cases to the district court for further consideration as to whether they should proceed in Ecuador or the United States. Written submissions were filed on February 1, 1999. Texaco has long argued that the appropriate venue for these cases is Ecuador because the oil-producing operations took place in Ecuador under the control and supervision of Ecuador's government, and the Ecuadorian courts have heard similar cases against other companies. It is Texaco's position that U.S. courts should not govern the activities of a sovereign foreign nation, just as foreign courts should not govern the activities of the United States. In fact, Texaco claimed that the ambassador of Ecuador, the official representative of the government of Ecuador, noted in a letter to the district court that Ecuador would not waive its sovereign immunity.

Notwithstanding Texaco's arguments, the case was sent back to the court that threw it out on the basis that the government of Ecuador does have the right to intervene. The question of whether the case can and will finally be tried in the United States or Ecuador under these circumstances will now take many years to be decided. Texaco claims that it has done enough to repair any damage and disputes the scientific validity of the claims—the Amazonians (or their supporters) seem to have the resources to continue fighting this suit in the U.S. courts. Ultimately, the company may prefer the fairness of U.S. and/or Canadian courts.[2]

Questions

1. Should Ecuadorians be able to sue Texaco in U.S. courts?
2. If an oil spill was caused by an act of God, an earthquake, should Texaco be held responsible?
3. Do you find Texaco's arguments against the lawsuits convincing? Why and why not?

Source: Texaco and Chevron websites: http://www.texaco.com/sitelets/ecuador/en/default.aspx and http://www.chevron.com/ecuador.

[2] For an interesting update of the progress of the Ecuadorian lawsuit in the Canadian and U.S. courts, see Nicole Hong and Kim Mackrael, "Canada's Top Court Rules in Favor of Ecuador Villagers in Chevron Case," *Wall Street Journal*, September 4, 2015, http://www.wsj.com/articles/canadas-top-court-rules-in-favor-of-ecuador-villagers-in-chevron-case-1441384265, and "Judge Rules in RICO Trial: U.S. Federal Court Finds the Judgment in Ecuador a Product of Fraud and Racketeering," Chevron website, https://www.chevron.com/ecuador.

Product Safety Cases

ETHICS CASE

The Right to Be Informed? The Link between Talcum Powder and Cervical Cancer

Decades after the event, Johnson & Johnson (J&J), the 130-year-old American multinational, is still praised for swiftly recalling nearly 31 million bottles of Tylenol in 1982 when in-store tampering resulted in several cyanide poisoning-related deaths. The company indicated that its response was based on the expectations set forth in the Credo, its moral compass.[1] The Credo, which begins with the sentence "We believe our first responsibility is to the doctors, nurses and patients, to mothers and fathers and all others who use our products and services," spells out the company's responsibilities to its various stakeholders, including consumers, employees, and shareholders.[2]

Currently, J&J is facing more than 1,200 lawsuits in the United States based on the claim that the company ignored the link between ovarian cancer and its baby powder and Shower-to-Shower talcum products. In early 2016, two U.S. juries decided against J&J as follows:

- The family of Jacqueline Fox received $72 million in February 2016. Fox died of ovarian cancer after using J&J's talcum powder products for feminine hygiene for several decades.
- Gloria Ristesund received $55 million in damages in May 2016 because she developed ovarian cancer and had to have a hysterectomy after using J&J talcum powder for over forty years. A jury member involved in Ristesund's case told *Bloomberg News*, "We felt like they knew for decades that they should have put a warning on this product."[3]

The science on the matter is not definitive. The World Health Organization's International Agency for Research on Cancer (IARC) reported that there is "limited evidence in humans" for a connection between ovarian cancer and the genital use of talcum-based body powders.[4] However, as early as 1982, Dr. Daniel Cramer, an obstetrician-gynecologist with the Epidemiology Center at Brigham and Women's Hospital in Boston, reported talcum being found in the lymph nodes of ovarian cancer patients. Paul Demers of Cancer Care Ontario, a member of the IARC committee, evaluated the evidence of talcum being a possible carcinogen. He noted, "We have some evidence to be concerned about … it is not definitive enough to say probably carcinogenic."[5]

An internal J&J memo from 1987 indicates the company was aware of the potential risks of talcum powder. In it, a medical consultant wrote, "Anybody who denies [the] risks" between ovarian cancer and hygienic talcum powder use will be publicly perceived in the same light as those who denied a link between cancer and smoking cigarettes. "Denying the obvious in the face of all evidence to the contrary."[6]

---

[1] "Tylenol and the Legacy of J&J's James Burke," TIME.com, 2016, accessed July 25, 2016, at http://business.time.com/2012/10/05/tylenol-and-the-legacy-of-jjs-james-burke.

[2] Johnson & Johnson, "Our Credo Values," 2016, accessed July 25, 2016, at http://www.jnj.com/about-jnj/jnj-credo.

[3] M. Fisk, T. Bross, and J. Feeley, "J&J Faces 1,000 More Talc-Cancer Suits after Verdict Loss," Bloomberg.com, 2016, accessed May 22, 2016, at http://www.bloomberg.com/news/articles/2016-05-02/j-j-ordered-to-pay-55-million-over-cancer-linked-to-talc.

[4] "Jury Awards $72M US to Family of Woman Who Died of Ovarian Cancer after Talcum Powder Use," *CBC News*, 2016, accessed May 22, 2016, at http://www.cbc.ca/news/business/talcum-powder-ovarian-cancer-1.3461632.

[5] Ibid.

[6] Ibid.

While some of this research indicates that the extended use of talcum powder increases the risk of ovarian cancer by approximately one-third, Ovacome, a U.K.-based ovarian cancer support charity, notes that some perspective is needed in interpreting this figure. The organization wrote, "Although this may sound frightening, to put it into context, smoking and drinking increases the risk of esophageal cancer by 30 times."[7]

Questions

1. Was J&J's decision to not inform its customers of the potential risks of extended use of talcum powder products acceptable?
2. If J&J knew about the potential risks of talcum powder products in 1987, should the company have withdrawn all its talcum products in the same way that it recalled all of its Tylenol products in 1982?
3. Do you think that Credos are effective at encouraging ethical business behavior?

Source: Written by B. Y. Perera, Goodman School of Business, Brock University. Permission has been granted by the author for publication in this and future editions of *Business and Professional Ethics* and in derivative formats and publications.

[7] Ibid.

ETHICS CASE

Valeant Pharmaceuticals vs. Coca Cola—Which Business Model Is Worse: Price Gouging or Fostering Obesity & Diabetes?

It was a battle of titans. Warren Buffet, long considered the world's most successful value investor through his Berkshire Hathaway Inc. and a major shareholder in Coca Cola Co., claimed that Valeant Pharmaceuticals business model was "enormously flawed." In response, billionaire investor, Bill Ackman, who was a major shareholder in Valeant, through his investment company Pershing Square Capital Management, criticized Buffet saying that Coca Cola has "probably done more to create obesity, [and] diabetes on a global basis than any other company in the world."[1] Which one of these titans was correct? Does it matter?

Valeant Pharmaceuticals had become extremely profitable by buying drugs developed by other companies and then raising their prices astronomically.[2] For example, in February 2015, Valeant "bought the rights to a pair of life-saving heart drugs [Isuprel and Nitropress]. The same day, their list prices rose by 525% and 212%."[3] The negative impact of these price increases on heart patients and similar increases on drugs by other pharmaceutical companies, especially Turing Pharmaceuticals in 2015, raised a public outcry. U.S. politicians summoned company officials to a public hearing on why they were price gouging vulnerable members of society. This brought significant pressure on Valeant's CEO and Board of Directors, and they subsequently lowered the prices on these drugs.[4]

[1] All quotations are drawn from Margaret Collins, Noah Buhayar, and Cynthia Koons, "Valeant Pharmaceuticals International Inc.'s Business Model 'Enormously Flawed,' Warren Buffett Tells Investors," *Bloomberg News*, May 2, 2016, accessed August 5, 2016, at http://business.financialpost.com/investing/market-moves/valeant-pharmaceuticals-international-inc-s-business-model-enormously-flawed-warren-buffett-tells-investors?__lsa=5d91-bb28.

[2] Jonathan D. Rockoff and Ed Silverman, "Pharmaceutical Companies Buy Rivals' Drugs, Then Jack Up the Prices," April 26, 2015, http://www.wsj.com/articles/pharmaceutical-companies-buy-rivals-drugs-then-jack-up-the-prices-1430096431, accessed August 5, 2016.

[3] Ibid.

[4] Damon van der Linde, "U.S. Senate Unmoved by Valeant Pharmaceuticals Presenting Itself as a Changed Company," April 27, 2016, accessed August 5, 2016, at http://business.financialpost.com/investing/market-moves/u-s-senate-unmoved-by-valeant-pharmaceutical-presenting-itself-as-a-changed-company?__lsa=c64b-14d2.

At the same time, questions were raised about the relationship between Valeant and a specialty online pharmacy retailer, Philidor, which supplied Valeant's products to the U.S. market and accounted for approximately 10% of Valeant's revenue. Valeant had an arrangement that compensated Philidor handsomely if Valeant's revenue reached a specific level, and Philidor worked very hard, possibly fraudulently, to "persuade" insurers and doctors to choose Valeant's products and achieve the desired sales level.[5] Under public pressure, Valeant terminated its relationship with Philidor and subsequently switched its sales to Walgreen's.[6] Philidor closed its doors as a result.[7]

Valeant's CEO, Michael Pearson, resigned on March 21, 2016, but remained one of its largest shareholders.[8] He had benefited significantly from earlier incentive remuneration allocations of stock options. Although the price of Valeant's shares had declined almost 80% since the beginning of the 2016, he proceeded to sell some of his share to settle his debts: June 30: 288,441 shares for $5.8 million; July 5: 411,601 shares for $8.2 million; and July 1: 4,144,687 shares for $82.9 million. Afterward, he stated that he had no intention to sell further shares (estimated at 3.5 million) until the company recovered.[9]

Questions

1. Compare the ethicality of the two business models—(a) price gouging and questionable practices by Valeant to (b) contributing to obesity and diabetes by Coca Cola. Which is worse?
2. From a business standpoint, what is the most significant loss that could occur to each of Valeant and Coca Cola as a result of their business models?
3. Based on your assessment of the two business models, what would you do if you owned shares in each company: Continue to hold? Sell? Something else? What was your reasoning for the action chosen?
4. Review the incentive remuneration disclosures in Valeant's Securities Exchange Commission (SEC) 10-K filings for 2012, 2013, and 2014. Were the incentive arrangements with Valeant's CEO, Michael Pearson, appropriate?
5. How much of a price increase for Isuprel and Nitropress would have been considered reasonable and would not have attracted negative attention?

[5] Caroline Chen and Ben Elgin, "Philidor Said to Modify Prescriptions to Boost Valeant Sales," Bloomberg.com, October 29, 2015, accessed August 5, 2016, at http://www.bloomberg.com/news/articles/2015-10-29/philidor-said-to-modify-prescriptions-to-boost-valeant-sales; Robert Langreth and Neil Weinberg, "Valeant Pharmaceuticals Offered Philidor Millions of Dollars to Hit Sales Targets on Its Drugs, Contracts Show," *Bloomberg News*, May 9, 2016, accessed August 5, 2016, at http://business.financialpost.com/investing/market-moves/valeant-pharmaceuticals-offered-philidor-millions-of-dollars-to-hit-sales-targets-on-its-drugs-contracts-show?__lsa=e61c-8abe.

[6] Meg Tirrell, "Valeant Strikes Distribution Deal with Walgreens," CNBC, December 1, 2015, accessed August 11, 2016, at http://www.cnbc.com/2015/12/15/valeant-strikes-distribution-deal-with-walgreens.html.

[7] "Philidor to Close Up Shop as Valeant Cuts Ties with Specialty Pharmacy," Associated Press, October 30, 2015, accessed August 11, 2016, at http://www.cbc.ca/news/business/valeant-philidor-drug-1.3295947.

[8] Rupert Neate and agencies, "Valeant CEO Resigns over Drug Company's 'Improper' Financial Conduct," *The Guardian*, March 21, 2016, accessed August 11, 2016, at https://www.theguardian.com/business/2016/mar/21/valeant-ceo-michael-pearson-resigns-financial-conduct; Ross Marowits, "Valeant Pharmaceuticals CEO Stepping Down, Board Director Refuses to Resign," The Canadian Press, March 21, 2016, http://www.haidagwaiiobserver.com/national/372960661.html.

[9] Jacquie McNish and Charley Grant, "Valeant's Ex-CEO Michael Pearson Sells Nearly $100 Million in Company Stock," *Wall Street Journal*, July 14, 2016, accessed July 25, 2016, at http://www.wsj.com/articles/valeants-ex-ceo-michael-pearson-sells-nearly-100-million-in-company-stock-1468446524.

ETHICS CASE

The Betaseron Decision (A)

On July 23, 1993, the United States Food and Drug Administration (FDA) approved interferon beta-1b (brand name Betaseron), making it the first treatment for multiple sclerosis to get FDA approval in twenty-five years. Betaseron was developed by Berlex Laboratories, a U.S. unit of Schering AG, the German pharmaceutical company. Berlex handled the clinical development, trials, and marketing of the drug, while Chiron, a biotechnology firm based in California, manufactured it. The groundbreaking approval of Betaseron represented not only a great opportunity for Berlex but also a difficult dilemma. Available supplies were insufficient to meet initial demand, and shortages were forecasted until 1996. With insufficient supplies and staggering development costs, how would Berlex allocate and price the drug?

The Challenge of Multiple Sclerosis

Multiple sclerosis (MS) is a disease of the central nervous system that interferes with the brain's ability to control such functions as seeing, walking, and talking. The nerve fibers within the brain and spinal cord are surrounded by myelin, a fatty substance that protects the nerve fibers in the same way that insulation protects electrical wires. When the myelin insulation becomes damaged, the ability of the central nervous system to transmit nerve impulses to and from the brain becomes impaired. With multiple sclerosis, there are *sclerosed* (i.e., scarred or hardened) areas in *multiple* parts of the brain and spinal cord when the immune system mistakenly attacks the myelin sheath.

The symptoms of MS depend to some extent on the location and size of the sclerosis. Symptoms include numbness, slurred speech, blurred vision, poor coordination, muscle weakness, bladder dysfunction, extreme fatigue, and paralysis. There is no way to know how the disease will progress for any individual because the nature of the course it takes can change over time. Some people will have a relatively benign course of MS, with only one or two mild attacks, nearly complete remission, and no permanent disability. Others will have a chronic, progressive course resulting in severe disability. A third group displays the most typical pattern, with periods of *exacerbations*, when the disease is active, and periods of *remission*, when the symptoms recede while generally leaving some damage. People with MS live with an exceptionally high degree of uncertainty because the course of their disease can change from one day to the next. Dramatic downturns as well as dramatic recoveries are not uncommon.

The Promise of Betaseron

Interferon beta is a protein that occurs naturally and regulates the body's immune system. Betaseron is composed of interferon beta-1b, which has been genetically engineered and laboratory manufactured as a recombinant product. Although other interferons (i.e., alpha and gamma) had been tested, only beta interferon had been shown, through large-scale trials, to affect MS. Because it is an immunoregulatory agent, it was believed to combat the immune problems that make MS worse. However, the exact way in which it works was yet to be determined.

In clinical studies, Betaseron was shown to reduce the frequency and severity of exacerbations in ambulatory MS patients with a relapsing-remitting form of the disease. It did not reverse damage already done, nor did it completely prevent exacerbations from occurring. However, Betaseron could dramatically improve the quality of life for the person with MS; for example, people taking Betaseron were shown to have fewer and shorter hospitalizations. Betaseron represented the first and only drug to have an effect on the frequency of exacerbations.

Betaseron is administered subcutaneously (under the skin) every other day by self-injection. In order to derive the most benefits from the therapy, it was important that the MS patient maintain a regular schedule of the injections. Some flu-like side effects, as well as swelling and irritation around the injection, had been noted; however, they tended to decrease with time on treatment. In addition, one person who received Betaseron committed suicide, while three others attempted to kill themselves. Because MS often leads to depression, there was no way to know whether the administration of Betaseron was a factor. Finally, Betaseron was not recommended for use during pregnancy.

The Betaseron Dilemma

In July 1993, the FDA approval for Betaseron allowed physicians to prescribe the drug to MS patients who were ambulatory and had a relapsing-remitting course of MS. An estimated one-third of the 300,000 people with MS in the United States fell into that category, resulting in a potential client base of 100,000. However, the expedited FDA approval process took only one year instead of the customary three years taken to review new drug applications. As a result, Berlex was unprepared for its manufacture and distribution in the anticipated amount needed. Chiron Corporation had been making the drug in small quantities for experimental use and did not have the manufacturing facilities to handle the expected explosion in demand. Chiron estimated that it would have enough of the drug for about 12,000 to 20,000 people by the end of 1993. By the end of 1994, Chiron expected to be able to provide the drug to 40,000 patients. Depending on demand, it might take until about 1996 to provide the drug to all patients who requested it. Chiron's expanded manufacturing represented the only option for Berlex because the process required for another company to get FDA approval to manufacture the drug would take even longer.

In addition to availability, price was a concern because successes must fund the failures that precede them. Betaseron represented the results of years of expensive, risky research by highly trained scientists in modern research facilities. Furthermore, genetically engineered drugs were extremely expensive to manufacture. In the case of Betaseron, a human interferon gene was inserted into bacteria, resulting in a genetically engineered molecule. The stringent quality controls on the procedure take time and are expensive. As a result, the price of Betaseron was expected to be about $10,000 per year for each patient.

Betaseron brought great hope to people with MS and a great quandary to Berlex. How should Berlex handle the supply limitations, the distribution, and the price of this drug?

Source: By Ann K. Buchholtz, University of Georgia. This case was written from public sources, solely for the purpose of stimulating class discussion. All events are real. The author thanks Dr. Stephen Reingold, vice president, Research and Medical Programs of the National Multiple Sclerosis Society; Avery Rockwell, chapter services associate of the Greater Connecticut Chapter of the Multiple Sclerosis Society; and two anonymous reviewers for their helpful comments.

ETHICS CASE

Magnetic Toys Can Hurt

Mega Brands has been selling Magnetix toys for many years. It also sells Mega Bloks, construction toys based on Spider-Man, Pirates of the Caribbean, as well as other products in over 100 countries. In 2006, Mega Brands had over $547 million in revenue, including over $100 from magnetic toys, but its share price fell approximately $27 to $20.30 in mid-July 2007. One reason for the fall was that a child, who had swallowed a magnet that had fallen out of a toy, had died in the late fall of 2005. The U.S. Consumer Products Safety Commission (CPSC) had issued a product recall in March 2006.

Subsequently, a number of lawsuits appeared involving other children who had suffered bowel complications. The symptoms resulting from a child swallowing a magnet are similar to those of a stomachache, cold, or flu, so the problem is sometimes misdiagnosed. The consequences can be much worse if a child swallows more than one magnet, particularly if they are the super-powerful magnets like those in Magnetix toys. They are so strong that they do not pass through the child's digestive system; instead, the magnets rip through tissue as they are attracted to each other. Complex surgery is required for extraction, and complications can continue afterward.

After refusing twice, Mega Brands engaged in two voluntary recalls at the request of the CPSC in March 2006 and April 2007. Defective merchandise was still found on store shelves by CPSC investigators in April. Even then, at a hearing on June 18, 2007, Senator Robert Durban stated, "The company did everything in its power to derail the commission's effort to take the product off the shelf." In frustration, Senator Durban commented, "When a company is selling dangerous products in America and refuses to co-operate with the CPSC, we have few laws and few tools to use to protect consumers."

In addition, the company did not quickly comply with CPSC requests for information and violated the terms of one recall. Finally, on December 1, 2007, after failing to respond on time to a subpoena, data were submitted covering 1,500 complaint reports made to Mega Brands or to Rose Art Industries, the toy's manufacturer. Mega Brands asserted that they had to search through warehouses to gather the data because they lacked an organized comprehensive reporting system.

A new product, supposedly improved, has been introduced with new labeling that indicates the suitable minimum age to be six instead of three.

Questions

1. If you were an executive of Mega Brands, what concerns would you express to the CEO about the Magnetix toy issues noted above?
2. If the CEO did not pay any attention, what would you do?
3. Should the CPSC have more powers to deal with such hazards and companies? If so, what would they be? If not, why not?

Source: Gretchen Morgenson, "Magnetic Toys Attract Suits," *Financial Post*, July 17, 2007, FP3.

Bausch & Lomb's Hazardous Contact Lens Cleaner

ETHICS CASE

On April 13, 2006, Bausch & Lomb (B&L) CEO Ron Zarrella indicated that B&L would not be recalling their soft contact lens cleaner Renu with MoistureLoc. Drugstores in the United States were, however, removing the product from their shelves due to a concern over reported infections related to *Fusarium keratitis*, a fungus frequently found in drains and sinks. Zarrella went on to say that Renu kills the fungus that causes the infection, and he was considering how to rebuild the brand and mitigate the "ripple effect" caused to other B&L products. Up to April 12, B&L's shares had fallen by 7% due to these health concerns.

On May 31, 2006, B&L indicated that it was halting worldwide sales of Renu because tests showed that misuse could cause blindness due to Fusarium fungal infection. "B&L said it appeared common, if frowned-upon, lens care practices—like topping off solution in storage instead of replacing it—could leave a film on lenses that shielded Fusarium from the sterilizing agent in MoistureLoc." The company also found unacceptable manufacturing practices in the company's Greenville, South Carolina, factory but said they did not relate to the infection problem.

When Zarrella was first questioned, he knew that there had been a number of incidents of infection in Hong Kong, which B&L had reported to the U.S. Centers for Disease Control and Prevention in

December 2005, as well as other reports in the United States. However, another product from the Greenville plant was also implicated. Although the incidence of infection were five times higher for Renu than for any other cleaner, the evidence was not enough to halt production and sales.

At the time, lens care contributed 20% of the company's revenue, which had amounted to $1.75 billion in the first nine months of 2006. When the recall was announced, the company's stock rose 12.7% but was $10 below its early April level. Lawsuits subsequently occurred.

Questions

1. What lessons should be taken from B&L's Renu experience?
2. What should Zarrella have done, and when?

Sources: Juliann Walsh and Duncan Moore, "Bausch & Lomb Refuses to Recall Suspect Lens Cleaner," *Toronto Star*, April 13, 2006, C4

Barnaby J. Feder, "Bausch & Lomb Halting Lens Cleaner Sales Worldwide," *International Herald Tribune*, May 31, 2006.

Accounting & Auditing Cases

Where Were the Accountants?

ETHICS CASE

"Sam, I'm really in trouble. I've always wanted to be an accountant. But here I am just about to apply to the accounting firms for a job after graduation from the university, and I'm not sure I want to be an accountant after all."

"Why, Norm? In all those accounting courses we took together, you worked super hard because you were really interested. What's your problem now?"

"Well, I've been reading the business newspapers, reports, and accounting journals lately, and things just don't add up. For instance, you know how we have always been told that accountants have expertise in measurement and disclosure, that they are supposed to prepare reports with integrity, and that they ought to root out fraud if they suspect it? Well, it doesn't look like they have been doing a good job. At least, they haven't been doing what I would have expected."

"Remember, Norm, we're still students with a lot to learn. Maybe you are missing something. What have you been reading about?"

"OK, Sam, here are a few stories for you to think about:

1. In this article, 'Accountants and the S&L Crisis,' which was in *Management Accounting* in February 1993, I found the argument that the $200 million fiasco was due to the regulators and to a downturn in the real estate market, not to accounting fraud … but I don't buy it entirely. According to this article, rising interest rates and fixed lending rates resulted in negative cash flow at the same time as a decline in value of the real estate market reduced the value underlying S&L loan assets. As a result, the net worth of many S&Ls fell, and regulators decided to change some accounting practices to make it appear that the S&Ls were still above the minimum capital requirements mandated to protect depositors' funds. Just look at this list of the seven accounting practices or problems that were cited:
   - write-off of losses on loans sold over the life of the loan rather than when the loss occurred,
   - use of government-issued *Net Worth Certificates* to be counted as S&L capital,
   - use of deals involving up-front money and near-term cash flow, which would bolster current earnings at the expense of later,

- inadequate loan loss provisions due to poor loan monitoring,
- write-off of goodwill created on the merger of sound S&Ls with bankrupt S&Ls over a forty-year period,
- write-ups of owned property based on appraisal values, and
- lack of market-based reporting to reflect economic reality.

2. The problem, for me, is that many of these practices are not in accord with generally accepted accounting principles [GAAP] and yet the accountants went along—at least they didn't object or improve their practices enough to change the outcome. Why not? Where were the accountants?"
3. "I am also concerned about the expertise the accounting profession claims to have in terms of measurement and disclosure. For example, recently there have been many articles on the health costs created by smoking, yet there are no accountants involved. For instance, a May 1994 report by the Center on Addiction and Substance Abuse at Columbia University estimates that 'in 1994 dollars, substance abuse will cost Medicare $20 billion in inpatient hospital costs alone' and that tobacco accounts for 80 percent of those hospitalizations. Over the next twenty years, substance abuse will cost the Medicare program $1 trillion. No wonder the trustees of the Medicare Trust Fund released a report on April 21 'predicting that the Fund would run out of money in seven years.' These are important issues. Why do we have to wait for economists and special interest groups to make these calculations? Shouldn't accountants be able to make them and lend credibility and balance in the process? Wouldn't society benefit? Where were the accountants?"
4. "What about the finding of fraud? Are auditors doing enough to prevent and catch fraudulent behavior? I know what our professors say: auditors can't be expected to catch everything; their job is not to search for fraud unless suspicions are aroused during other activities; and their primary task is to audit the financial statements. But aren't the auditors just reacting to discovered problems, when they could be proactive? Couldn't they stress the importance of using codes of conduct and the encouragement of employees to bring forward their concerns over unethical acts? Why is proactive management appropriate in some other areas, such as ironing out personnel problems, but reactive behavior is appropriate when dealing with fraud? Reactive behavior will just close the barn door after the horse has been stolen. In the case of the Bank of Credit & Commerce International (BCCI), for example, at least $1.7 billion was missing."

"I guess I'm having second thoughts about becoming a professional accountant. Can you help me out, Sam?"

Question

1. What would you tell Norm?

ETHICS CASE

To Resign or Serve?

The Prairieland Bank was a medium-sized midwestern financial institution. The management had a good reputation for backing successful deals, but the CEO (and significant shareholder) had recently moved to San Francisco to be "close to the big-bank center of activity." He commuted into the Prairieland head office for two or three days each week to oversee major deals.

Lately, the bank's profitability had decreased, and the management had begun to renegotiate many loans on which payments had fallen behind. By doing so, the bank was able to disclose them as current rather than nonperforming, as the unpaid interest was simply added to the principal to arrive at the new principal amount. Discussions were also under way on changing some accounting policies to make them less conservative.

Ben Hunt, the audit partner on the Prairieland Bank account, was becoming concerned about the risk associated with giving an opinion on the fairness of the financial statements. During the early days of the audit, it became evident that the provision for doubtful loans was far too low, and he made an appointment to discuss the problem with the CEO and his vice president of finance. At the interview, Ben was told that the executives knew the provision was too low, but they did not want to increase it because that would decrease their reported profits. Instead, they had approached a company that provided insurance to protect leased equipment, such as earthmovers, against damage during the lease and arranged for insurance against nonpayment on the maturity of their loans. As a result, they said, any defaults on their loans would be made up from the insurance company, so they did not see any point to increasing the provision for loan losses or disclosing the insurance arrangement.

When he heard of this, Ben expressed concern to the Prairieland management, but they were adamant. Because Prairieland was such a large account, he sought the counsel of James London, the senior partner in his firm who was in charge of assessing such accounting treatments and the related risk to the auditing firm. James flew out to confer with Ben, and they decided that the best course of action was to visit the client and indicate their intent to resign, which they did.

After dinner, James was waiting at the airport for his plane home. By coincidence, he met Jack Lane, who held responsibilities similar to his own at one of the competing firms. Jack was returning home as well and was in good spirits. On the flight, Jack let it slip that he had just picked up an old client of James's firm, Prairieland Bank.

Questions

1. Which decision was right: to resign or to serve?
2. What should James do?

READING

The WhistleBlower: Patriot or Bounty Hunter?

Andrew W. Singer

The False Claims Act provides financial incentives for employees to report their companies' transgressions to the government. Does that debase their motives?

While serving in Vietnam, Emil Stache had the misfortune to stumble onto a booby-trapped Viet Cong bomb. The explosion killed several of his fellow soldiers, and Stache himself suffered severe shrapnel wounds to his left arm and shoulder. He later learned that the trap had been made from a defective U.S. bomb—one that never exploded.

Years later, Stache was manager of quality engineering and reliability at Teledyne Relays, a subsidiary of Teledyne, Inc. He suspected that Teledyne Relays falsified tests on the electromagnetic relays (electronic components used in missiles, planes, rockets and other military hardware) the company manufactured for the U.S. government.

Stache felt it his ethical duty to report the matter: He knew only too well the price of defective hardware. "It was the only thing he could do," explains his lawyer, John R. Phillips. "He complained about it. He got fired."

Stache brought a lawsuit against Teledyne Relays under the federal False Claims Act: he was later joined in the action by the Department of Justice. The suit claims that

Teledyne Relays' failure to properly test the relay components defrauded the government of as much as $250 million. If found guilty, the Los Angeles–based company could be liable for as much as $750 million in damages, treble the amount that the government claims it was defrauded.

Who is Emil Stache? A patriot who just did his duty? That certainly is how Phillips and others see him. But if Stache's lawsuit succeeds, he stands to become a very rich patriot, indeed. According to provisions of the amended *False Claims Act*, Stache and his co-plaintiffs in the suit—another Teledyne Relays employee named Almon Muehlhausen and Taxpayers Against Fraud, a nonprofit organization founded by Phillips—could get 15 percent to 25 percent of any money recovered by the government. Stache himself theoretically could receive as much as $62 million.

(Contacted for comment on the case, Teledyne spokesperson Berkley Baker said, "We have no comment to make. It's in the legal system now.")

Creating Market Incentives

The amended False Claims Act grew out of public outrage in the mid-1980s over reports of fraud and abuse on the part of military contractors—of $600 toilet seats and country club memberships billed to the government. Congress decided to put some teeth into its efforts to reduce contracting fraud. In 1986, it passed the False Claims Act amendments, whose *qui tam* provisions allow employees who bring forward information about contractor fraud to share with the government in any financial recovery realized by their efforts. (*Qui tam* is Latin shorthand for, "He who sues for the king as well as himself.")

Those market incentives are now bearing fruit. In July, the government recovered $50 million in a case brought by a whistleblower against a former division of Singer Co. And a week later, the government recovered the largest amount ever in such an action: a $59.5 million settlement with General Electric Co. (GE). That case, a scandal involving the sale of military-jet engines in Israel, was brought initially by the manager of a GE unit.

U.S. Rep. Howard L. Berman of California, a cosponsor of the 1986 amendment, expects recoveries from *qui tam* actions, most of which are against defense contractors, to reach $1 billion in the next two to three years. The Teledyne Relays suit looms as one of the largest cases, but Phillips speaks of two others in the pipeline, one against Litton Industries Inc. and another that is under court seal that could bring the government "staggering" amounts.

Undermining Voluntary Efforts?

Not surprisingly, many of the defense industry are aghast at the new False Claims Act—and, specifically, its *qui tam* provisions. The law has created "enormous concern in the defense industry," says Alan R. Yuspeh, a government-contracts attorney and partner in Howrey & Simon in Washington, D.C. Some fear that cases may proliferate and people with essentially technical disagreements may bring suits in the hope of reaping payoffs from an out-of-court settlement.

The *qui tam* provisions encourage "bounty hunting" and undermine voluntary ethics efforts, add critics. Why should an employee report wrongdoing to his company when he can hold out and earn millions from the government? And from the larger ethical perspective: Shouldn't people report fraud because it's the right thing to do, and not because they hope to reap a windfall profit?

"I think personally that the provision of bounties is misguided," said Gary Edwards, president of the Ethics Resource Center, a nonprofit education and consulting organization based in Washington, D.C. "It creates an incentive for individuals in companies that are trying to do a better job—not to report wrongdoing, but to gather data so as to participate in the reward."

"Encouraging tittle-tattles is destructive," declares Charles Barber, former chairman and CEO of Asarco, Inc., a *Fortune* 500 company that produces nonferrous metals. "The integrity of the organization has to be built another way," such as with corporate ombudsman offices. "You can't run a defense company if everyone is being watched."

"I deplore the way we have developed into such a litigious society in which everyone is jumping on the bandwagon to sue about anything that comes up," says Sanford N. McDonnell, chairman emeritus of McDonnell Douglas Corp., the nation's largest defense contractor.

"If We All Lived in an Ideal World..."

Phillips, who is generally credited with drafting the amended *False Claims Act*, responds: "If we all lived in an ideal world, where all did the right thing on principle, we would have no need for such a law. But we don't live in such a world." People who bring charges against their companies take great risks—to their jobs, their families, and their careers, he says.

Most agree that the plight of the corporate whistle-blower has historically been a bleak one. A survey of 85 whistle-blowers by the Association of Mental Health Specialties (now Integrity International) in College Park, Md., in the late-1980s found that 82 percent experienced harassment after blowing the whistle, 60 percent got fired, 17 percent lost their homes, and 10 percent reported having attempted suicide. "You can't expect them to [report fraud] when there is nothing but risk and heartache down the road," says Phillips. Sharing in the recovery of damages is one way to right the balance.

Yuspeh, for one, isn't convinced. It is an "unsound piece of legislation. It almost invites disgruntled former employees who may have had some technical disagreement to go out and file a lawsuit." (It should be added that in recent years, large contractors have increasingly reported instances of wrongdoing or fraud to the government voluntarily, before evidence came to public light.)

Congressman Berman says the law works precisely as intended: By providing marketplace incentives, it encourages people to protect the government and the public from waste, fraud and abuse. "I'm not only happy with the law, I'm proud of it," he tells *Across the Board.*

Morally problematic? "You mean like: If you have any information about a wanted criminal, we'll pay a reward?" asks Berman, rhetorically.

Those companies that commit fraud don't like the Act, suggests Berman, while those in compliance with the law aren't troubled by it. And he is skeptical of detractors who claim that these are merely technical disputes. "The test here is commission of fraud," he says.

Harks Back to the Civil War

The original False Claims Act dates back to the Civil War, where it was used to prosecute manufacturers who substituted sawdust for gunpowder in Union army supplies. Employees who exposed contractors who overcharged the government could, theoretically, earn 10 percent of the amount recovered. But under the old law, federal prosecutors who took over cases had the option of removing private plaintiffs, leaving whistle-blowers high and dry.

"Very few people were willing to do it under the old system," either through fear of losing their jobs, being black-balled within their industry, or shunned by their friends, says Phillips, a partner in the Los Angeles law firm of Hall & Phillips. It took a kind of heroic figure to blow the whistle, he says.

The amended False Claims Act aimed to fix some of those problems, "We tried to rebuild the law, to give it some teeth," explains Berman. "Where the government is not privy to information about fraud, the taxpayers are represented by private parties."

Even more important than the sheer amounts of money recovered, says Phillips, is the preventive effect of the statute on corporations. "The law has shaken up their internal practices. People who were previously inclined to go along with questionable practices are now doing the right thing," he says.

But companies say the statute undermines their voluntary ethics efforts. "I know their argument," replies Phillips. "But there's no basis to it. They're saying, 'We have a whole system set up. You should come to us first.' With fraud, he says, the government has an interest in being the first to know. The government is saying, 'We want information to come directly to us in cases of fraud.'"

"It will enhance corporate efforts, because companies can get socked with treble damages for fraud," says Berman. "Companies will become more vigilant."

Does he know of any contractors who support the amendments? "The goal of the act is not to please government contractors," snaps Berman. "The goal is to protect the government and the public."

Portrait of a Whistle-Blower

Corporate whistle-blowers have traditionally been treated as malcontents, troublemakers, and misfits. And many have paid a steep price for their actions.

A 1987 survey of 87 whistle-blowers by Dr. Donald Soeken, president of Integrity International in College Park, Md., noted: "All but one respondent reported experiencing retaliation which they attributed to their whistle-blowing. And that one individual merely indicated that 'nothing could be proved.'"

Soeken, who was a government whistle-blower himself, compares the whistle-blower to a cross between a bloodhound and a bulldog. "He will track it down [i.e., the wrongdoing] and stand his ground.... His conscience is very strong, unwavering. He's the first one to feel guilty when something happens.

That certainly applies to Richard Walker, a whistle-blower in the era before the amended False Claims Act. A scientist with a Ph.D. in physics, Walker worked for 27 years at American Telephone & Telegraph Co.'s (AT&T) prestigious Bell Laboratories.

In 1971, as head of a team of scientists working on a high-level military project for the U.S. Navy, he discovered serious errors in Bell Labs' computer projections. He informed his superior of the errors, and said they had better report them to the Navy. When his boss refused, Walker took matters into his own hands.

He decided to give a corporate seminar within Bell Labs, which was his prerogative as a manager. Walker spent an hour exposing the errors he had found and explaining how the company had overestimated the effectiveness of the project. "The way to avoid corruption is to get it out in the open," he told Ethikos in a 1987 interview, recalling his thinking at the time.

The immediate response within the company to his seminar seemed positive. "I thought, in view of his feedback, that I had gotten through to these people," said Walker.

He was mistaken. Several months later, Walker's boss wrote a letter to a high Bell Labs officer questioning Walker's technical competence. "On the basis of that criticism, I was moved out of that area and put into a totally inappropriate assignment. It was just a way of getting rid of me."

There was a succession of increasingly demeaning and meaningless assignments. He spent three-and-a-half years in a marine-cable engineering department, followed by a supervisory appointment at a "planning" center in which "for three-and-a-half years, they wouldn't tell me what my responsibilities were." In 1979, Bell Labs fired Walker for allegedly not taking an active interest in his assigned work. In 1982, Walker brought suit against AT&T, charging that he had been fired without good cause. Walker devoted himself full time to his case. He had an entire room in his apartment set aside to store depositions and other evidence relevant to his case. He spent $50,000 of his own money pressing the litigation. During this time, his wife divorced him and he was forced to sell the house he designed in affluent Mendham, N.J., where he raised his four children.

On March 23, 1987, Walker vs. Bell came to trial. Eight days later, the New Jersey judge dismissed the case that Walker had brought.

According to AT&T, justice was served. "Dr. Walker had ample opportunity to prove his allegations before the court, and the court rejected those allegations as being totally unfounded," the AT&T attorney who tried the case commented.

Walker took the defeat hard. Despite the advice of people like Soeken and others, he refused to let the matter rest. For years he tried to interest journalists, government officials and employee-rights organizations in this case. He barraged AT&T officers and directors with letters seeking redress for the wrong he felt he had suffered. All to no avail.

Eventually, Walker moved back to his home state of Michigan, where he remarried and is now working to establish a retreat for whistle-blowers.

Walker may have been ahead of his time. New Jersey has since passed legislation to protect whistle-blowers. AT&T now has an excessive network of corporate ombudsman to handle cases like his. And the amended False Claims Act has since been enacted.

John Phillips, an attorney who has represented other whistle-blowers and a principal author of the amended False Claims Act says that one key effect of the amended Act is that it no longer requires a "heroic" figure to blow the whistle. The Act could also bring forth a higher order of whistle-blower, he suggests. In the past, whistle-blowers "were not always the most stable people," noted Phillips in a 1989 interview with Ethikos. Many, he said, had a "need to confess" or to "point the finger at someone."

The people whom Phillips sees coming forward now to report wrongdoing by government contractors are still idealistic in some ways, but in many ways they are "far more credible, substantial, senior people than whistle-blowers, from the pre-[*False Claims Act*] amendment era."

The GE Case

The case involving General Electric's aircraft-engine division is one of the more interesting *False Claims Act* actions to arise. Employees in the division conspired with an Israeli general, Rami Dotan, to submit fraudulent claims for work done for the Israeli Air Force. General Electric eventually pleaded guilty to four federal criminal-fraud charges. It agreed to pay the Justice Department $9.5 million in fines for the criminal charges and $59.5 million for the civil case brought under the False Claims Act.

The Justice Department said the company's employees helped divert as much as $40 million to Dotan and others, money that ultimately came from the U.S. government. The scheme became known through a lawsuit filed by Chester Walsh, who served as general manager of the aircraft-engine division's Israeli unit from 1984 to 1988.

What irks General Electric is that Walsh reported the matter first to the government instead of the company, despite the fact that Walsh, like others at GE, signed an ethics statement each year affirming that he would report wrongdoing to the company if and when it was discovered.

"The man involved decided not to report wrongdoing," says Bruce Bunch, a

False Claims Suits Growing

How does the government view the False Claims Act? "It is hardly a secret that the Act is critical to the government's anti-fraud effort," Stuart Gerson, assistant attorney general, acknowledged last year, Gerson added, however, that the statute's *qui tam* provisions, which allow private citizens to bring actions on behalf of the government, have been controversial, affecting as they do "the climate of government contracting and the dynamics of a corporation's relationship with its employees."

As of April 1, six years since the amendments passed, 407 *qui tam* suits had been filed. The government took over 66 of these cases; it is currently litigating 29 cases and has settled or obtained judgments in 37 others. The total recoveries of $147 million from *qui tam* suits under the Act comprise about 13.5 percent of the government's total fraud recoveries for the six-year period. Individuals who brought suits had won $14.5 million as of April, but 75 cases were still under investigation. (The dollar amount doesn't include the large recoveries in July from the General Electric Co. case reported in the main story.)

The number of *qui tam* suits has grown steadily since 1986, notes Gerson, and it is expected to rise further. Thirty-three were filed in all of fiscal-year 1987, for example, while 78 were filed in the first eight months of fiscal-year 1991 alone. Cases involving the Department of Defense are by far the most numerous, but now action is being taken in other areas, including health care, agriculture, and the Department of Housing and Urban Development.

"In short, as attention is focused on the whistle-blower suits, and significant recoveries have been reported, this form of action is proliferating," said Gerson.

However, some government officials recently have expressed second thoughts about the potentially large awards to individual whistle-blowers. In the GE fraud case, Gerson said he had reservations about just how much credit and money the whistle-blower and his lawyers should receive. It remains to be seen whether attempts will be made to curb such awards.

GE spokesman. "He took no steps to stop it. "He participated in it, and all the time he signed our written statement each year that he would report any improprieties to management." It is General Electric's position that Walsh gathered information from 1986 to 1990 and then filed his lawsuit, from which he hoped to gain personally. Walsh could receive 25 percent of the nearly $60 million recovered by the government as a result of the civil suit. (A hearing that will determine the exact amount is set to begin in November in Cincinnati.)

If he had reported the corruption immediately, the case would have come to light, continues Bunch. "We had an ombudsman telephone number at the corporate office, outside of the business loop. Additionally, he could have called the Department of Defense ombudsman."

A case of bounty hunting? "That clearly appears to be what happened here," says Bunch.

Phillips, who represents Walsh, claims that General Electric has smeared his client. "They claim Walsh is a money grubber. That's their party line." (GE Chairman John F. Welch, Jr. had been quoted in the *Corporate Crime Reporter*, a weekly legal publication, labeling Walsh as "a money-grubbing guy who sat back and waited in the weeds so the damages would mount." Bunch declines to comment on the accuracy of that quote.) Phillips tells a different story: "It was his dream job. It was very painful for him to do this."

Walsh feared for his job and even his life, Phillips says. He worried that anything he told GE would get back to Dotan, whom Phillips characterizes as a ruthless, violence-prone individual. His superiors at the aircraft-engine division were all aware of the arrangement with Dotan, Walsh believed, "He says that Dotan had people removed from their jobs at GE. The idea that he would go back and write a letter to Cincinnati [where the aircraft-engine division is based] about what he had seen was simply not credible," says Phillips.

As proof that Walsh's suspicions were well-founded, Phillips points to the fact that Dotan is now serving 13 years in prison in Israel. The general was charged by the Israeli government with kickbacks, theft, fraud, obstruction of justice and conspiring to kidnap and harm a fellow Israeli Ministry of Defense official.

Couldn't Walsh have gone to General Electric's corporate ombudsman, who is based in Fairfield, Conn., and is presumably outside the aircraft-engine division loop? "He doesn't know who's on the other end," answers Phillips. For all Walsh knew, Phillips says, the ombudsman might just get on the phone with Cincinnati to find out what was going on.

But couldn't he have called anonymously? "It's an 800 number. They can find out where it came from. There was no way he could protect his anonymity." Or so Walsh believed, Phillips says.

"The idea that people will call up blindly some number is ludicrous," Phillips says. "I don't think people have confidence in the GE program." (Subsequent to this interview, the *Wall Street Journal* ran a front-page story on the company headlined: "GE's Drive to Purge Fraud Is Hampered by Workers' Mistrust," which appeared to support many of Phillips' assertions.)

"A Detrimental Effect"

Whatever the whys and wherefores of the GE case, it seems clear that the *qui tam* provisions are causing havoc among those in charge of compliance at some defense companies. "Pandemonium" was how the ombudsman at one large defense company characterized the provisions and the large suits now being filed.

"I've heard from some company representatives who believe the availability of the *qui tam* rewards have had a detrimental effect, that they have caused people not to use their internal systems," says the Ethics Resource Center's Edwards.

"No company can be happy with *qui tam* procedures," says John Impert, director of corporate ethics policy and assistant general counsel at The Boeing Co., even though his company has been virtually untouched by the False Claims Act. "It provides incentives to employees to take an adverse position. This is illustrated graphically in the GE case."

It's important that people report matters of ethical concern, says McDonnell of McDonnell Douglas, "But I don't think they should receive remuneration for that," he says.

"Won't this help eliminate the steep price whistle-blowers have paid for coming forward?" "I'm sure it will stimulate more action, more people coming forward, but I'd rather see it come from individuals who take it to the company ombudsman, and report it without attribution," says McDonnell.

Deputizing Citizens

Attorney Yuspeh and others are fundamentally at odds with the notion that individuals should bring lawsuits on the part of the U.S. government. "The role of initiating [lawsuits] on the part of the government is a role for the officer of the U.S. government. I have a big problem with individuals who have a personal profit motive, who have inside information, and who may be disgruntled because of downsizing, having the power of the government to advance a personal agenda."

Yuspeh notes that plaintiffs' lawyers tend to profit from the amended False Claims Act and its controversial *qui tam* provisions: "There's a lot of money for them to make." He would prefer an arrangement where informants would get some money from the government, but would not bring suit themselves. "At least the government is then deciding whether to bring a suit." This would also cut out the plaintiffs' legal fees.

"The problem with *qui tam* suits is that someone who would otherwise do this as part of their normal duties might now wait until they are no longer employed, or until they have an opportunity to enrich themselves," says LeRoy J. Haugh, who is vice president for procurement and finance of the Aerospace Industries Association, an organization based in Washington, D.C.

"Our biggest concern with *qui tam* proceedings is that someone who wants to bring a suit is at no risk at all," Haugh says. "If they can get a lawyer to handle it on a contingency basis and they win, they stand to win a great deal of money. And if they lose, they haven't lost anything, except the lawyer's time." Answers Congressman Berman: "The situation here is that no one gets anything unless fraud is committed. Lawyers won't take cases if they're not legitimate."

Still, Haugh says, the negative publicity generated from such suits—even if the company accused of wrongdoing is eventually found to be not guilty—"often overshadows efforts over the last seven or eight years on the part of many companies to comply with Defense Industry Initiative guidelines [a set of voluntary guidelines developed by the nation's largest defense contractors to promote ethical business conduct] and to put into place adequate checks and balances."

Importance of Building Trust

"I'm not saying that every suit that is brought is a frivolous suit," says Yuspeh, who served as coordinator of the Defense Industry Initiative (DII) steering committee. (He makes clear that he is speaking only for himself in making these comments, not the DII companies.) "Clearly some cases are meritorious. But it makes more sense to have officials of the U.S. government handle them."

Ethics Resource Center's Edwards doesn't quarrel with the notion that whistle-blowers have historically been treated very badly. But he points out that today they have protection under the law against retaliation, and that many excellent voluntary corporate programs have been initiated since the amendments were passed. Many companies today have ethics hotlines, ombudsman offices, extensive ethics-training programs and ethics committees. "Maybe several years ago it was necessary to entice them to blow the whistle," he says. But that isn't the case in many major American corporations today. "A well-developed ethics program should obviate the need for that," he adds.

Even Phillips concedes that voluntary corporate ethics efforts could be effective. "But you've got to convince people that the corporation wants you to do this, and that the corporation will reward you," he says.

Phillips may have hit on something there. Or to put the problem in quasi-dialectical terms: If the *thesis* back in the 1980s was egregious defense-industry waste and abuse, and the *antithesis* was the punitive (at least, from the industry perspective) bounty-hunting provisions of the False Claims Act, the *synthesis* could well be voluntary corporate ethics efforts that enjoy the full confidence of employees—and that really work.

"It takes time, no doubt about it," says McDonnell, referring to building trust within a company. "You can't just mandate it. It has to be built up by actual cases, and it's difficult to advertise it, because that [confidentiality] is the sort of thing you're trying to protect. But when it's done right, it gets the desired result."

Source: *Across the Board*, November 1992, pp. 16–22. Reprinted with permission of the author, Andrew Singer.

2

Ethics & Governance Scandals

PURPOSE OF THE CHAPTER

Corporate personnel are expected to behave within applicable laws, regulations, and ethical custom. They are also to adhere to the ethics and governance guidelines laid down by boards of directors whose role is to supervise the corporate governance process. Over the years, governance expectations have become more stringent, usually in response to ethics and governance scandals that catch the attention of the public sufficiently to cause lawmakers, directors, professional bodies, and securities market regulators and stock exchange officials to make changes that further protect investors, consumers, employees, lenders, and other stakeholders.

This chapter provides a time line and summary of some of the most notorious corporate ethics and governance scandals and failures, as well as an analysis of the governance changes and trends these scandals produced. Throughout the period covered, the pattern of change has remained the same:

- Each scandal has outraged the public and made people aware that the specific behavior of corporate personnel or professionals needs to be improved.
- With each additional scandal, the awareness and sensitivity of the public to substandard behavior has grown, and the public's tolerance level has diminished.
- The credibility of corporate promises and financial statements has been eroded.
- Lawmakers, regulators, directors, and professional bodies have responded to restore confidence in the corporate governance system.

The failure of boards of directors, management, and accountants to ensure that business and the accounting profession are acting in the best interests of shareholders, stakeholders, and society is traced through the following scandals and reactions:

- Enron Corporation—the board of directors failed to provide the oversight needed to prevent the largest bankruptcy in American history, at the time.
- Arthur Anderson—as a result of shifting its focus from providing audit services to selling high-profit-margin consulting services, Arthur Anderson lost its perceived independence when conducting the Enron audit.
- WorldCom—at $11 billion, it eclipsed the $2.6 billion Enron fraud. There was no one in the organization to challenge and question the authority of Bernard Ebbers, CEO of WorldCom.

- *Sarbanes–Oxley Act* (SOX)—as result of the business, audit, and corporate governance failures, the U.S. government passed SOX in 2002 to enhance corporate accountability and responsibility.
- Tax Shelters—Ernst & Young (now EY) and KPMG were no longer protecting the public interest when they began to sell highly lucrative tax shelters to the super-rich. The government was so incensed with their egregious behavior that the firms were fined and *Circular 230* was issued.
- *Circular 230*—in 2007, the Internal Revenue Service (IRS) imposed new professional standards on tax preparers and tax advisors.
- Subprime Mortgage Meltdown—there was a lot of money to be made in speculating on mortgage-backed securities. But the risks had not been carefully assessed, so when the U.S. housing market collapsed in 2008, the value of the associated securities fell, and governments around the world had to provide bailouts to avert a global financial crisis.
- *Dodd-Frank Wall Street Reform and Consumer Protection Act*—in July 2010, as a result of the subprime mortgage crisis, the U.S. Congress enacted new regulations over the financial services marketplace in order to provide enhanced consumer protection.
- Bernard Madoff—in 2009, Madoff was sent to prison for cheating investors out of billions of dollars. Investors should remember that if they are offered returns that are too good to be true, they probably are.
- LIBOR Benchmark Interest Rate Manipulation—many of the world's largest banks colluded to manipulate a determinant of the interest rates of house mortgages and other borrowings in order to maximize the profits of banks and their traders at the expense of the borrowers throughout the world.

Many of the world's largest corporations are subject to the U.S. governance framework, even those that are not incorporated in the United States. For example, the largest 250 Canadian companies raise capital in the United States and are therefore subject to U.S. Securities and Exchange Commission (SEC) regulations. This pattern is repeated to a lesser extent in many other countries, such as Britain or Australia. Moreover, since U.S. governance developments have been emulated in other parts of the world, the study of the important drivers of governance change in the United States is well warranted. Even with the realization that capital and consumer markets are now interrelated on a global scale and international standards are likely to be developed, the steering effect of U.S. governance developments will continue. Unfortunately, instances of greed and corruption will also continue, so the lessons to date—that directors, executives, and accountants must remain aware of their professional and business responsibilities and conduct their dealings in an ethical manner with honesty and integrity—are well worth learning.

ETHICS & GOVERNANCE: A TIME LINE OF IMPORTANT EVENTS

Figure 2.1 provides a graphic time line of important events, beginning in 1929, that have contributed to the rise in awareness of the need for enhanced ethics and governance.

FIGURE 2.1 Ethics & Governance: A Time Line of Important Events

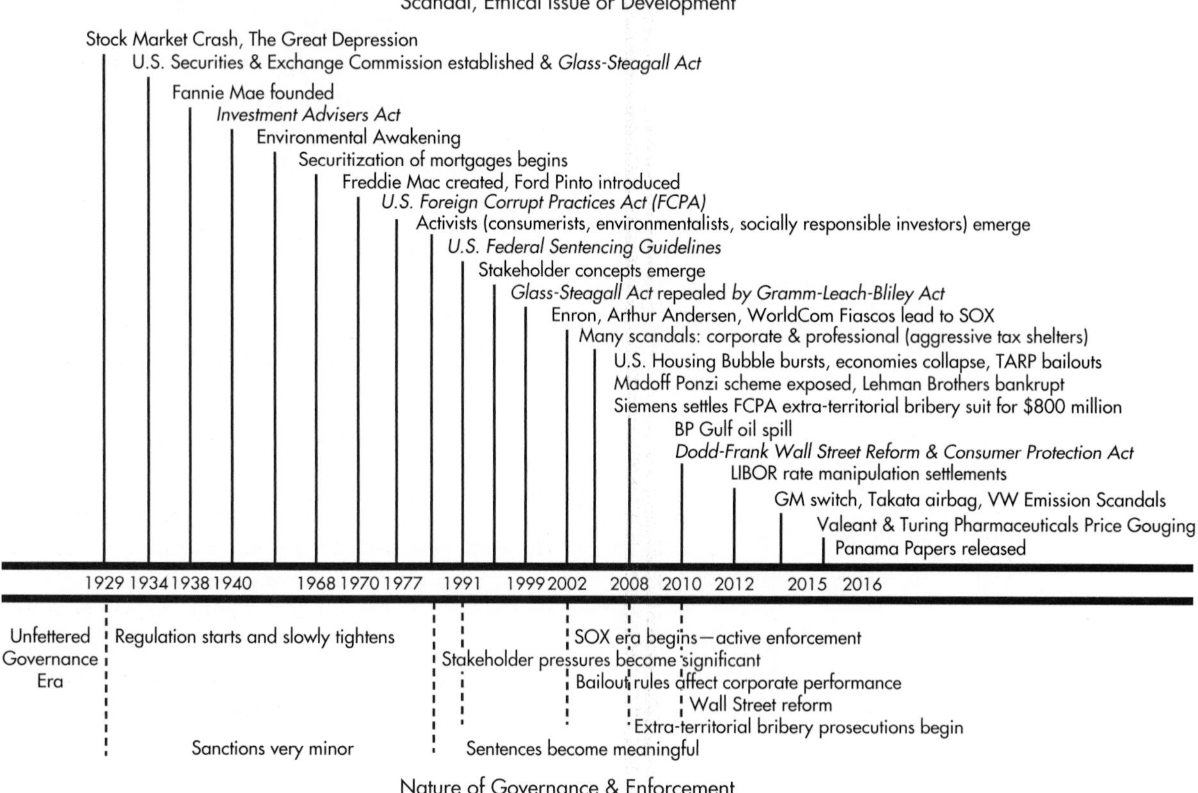

ETHICS & GOVERNANCE: THE EARLY DEVELOPMENTS PRIOR TO 1970

Until Black Tuesday on October 29, 1929, economies around the world had been enjoying the "Roaring Twenties," a period of high profitability, full employment, a booming housing market, and boundless optimism. Corporations appeared to be doing the job expected of them, so corporate governance also appeared to be doing its job. Then the stock market crashed, signaling that the corporate world was incredibly speculative, secretive, and rife with conflicts of interest. It seemed to be dedicated to the service of those executives or owners who controlled it, and not to other stakeholders, including consumers, employees, and minority or distant shareholders. Manipulation and inflation of financial reports were widespread, so investors did not know the financial condition of their investments. Banks which should have been protecting their depositors' money failed because they, too, had invested in speculative investments to make a quick buck.

Governments were stunned by the widespread elimination of wealth as the stock market crashed and unemployment soared. People could not pay their mortgages and lost their homes. They did not have enough money to buy goods or even groceries. The world's economies did not recover until the gearing up of production and employment brought on in 1939 to supply armies in World War II.

During the Great Depression from 1929 to 1939, the U.S. government did recognize some of the ethics and governance flaws that had contributed to the debacle and enacted laws designed to remedy them, including, among others, the following:

- *Securities Act of 1933* (otherwise known as the *Truth in Securities Act*)—creating the SEC and requiring companies raising money from the public in the United States to register with the SEC and follow its regulations governing the original issue of some corporate securities, investor information, audit certification by an independent accountant, and civil liability for the issuer and underwriters
- *Securities Act of 1934*—creating the regulatory framework for the secondary trading (on stock exchanges) of securities (stock, bonds, and debentures) of registered companies
- *Glass-Steagall Act of 1933* (otherwise known as *The Banking Act of 1933*)—mandating banking reforms designed to separate investment and commercial banking functions to safeguard against commercial bank failures from speculative investment mistakes
- *Investment Advisers Act of 1940*—creating a framework for registration and regulation of investment advisers

But as history shows, these laws have been insufficient to curb the greed and conflicts of interest of management, investors, and the investment community who have been responsible for the many scandals that subsequently have occurred. In response, the U.S. Congress and Senate enacted *Sarbanes-Oxley Act of 2002* (SOX) to bring about more stringent governance reform. Even then, further governance reform for banks has proven necessary. Most recently, the repeal of the *Glass-Steagall Act in 1999* by the passage of the *Gramm-Leach-Bliley Act* contributed directly—but not solely—to the subprime lending crisis of 2008 that once again devastated the economies of the world. This has led to the new international banking regulations of 2010.

ETHICS & GOVERNANCE: 1970–1990

As the 1950s and 1960s wore on, the awareness that our environment was a finite resource became clearer, as did the realization that corporations could make changes to protect the environment. An activist group known as environmentalists began to do what they could to raise the general awareness of the public to environmental issues and sensitize the public to bad practices. Their objective was to put pressure on boards of directors, executives, and managers to realize that bad environmental practices would not only harm our environment but in turn also harm the reputation of the individuals and the companies involved and ultimately their profitability.

Environmentalism was not the only "-ism" or development to emerge in the 1970s under pressure from interested activists. Other problems outraged the public and gave rise to the following:

- Consumerism—unsafe cars galvanized the public and led to the opportunity for Ralph Nader to sensitize the public over car safety and the need to protect consumers.
- Socially responsible investing.
- Regulation concerning fair trade, child labor, fair wage, and sweatshop production.
- *Foreign Corrupt Practices Act* (FCPA)—contained antibribery provisions in reaction to Lockheed executives bribing Japanese officials to buy the company's airplanes.

In so doing, the *expectations* for corporate actions were beginning to be changed by interested activists without the passage of new laws, although new laws did crystallize these expectations when new statutes and regulations, such as the 1991 *U.S. Federal Sentencing Guidelines*, were enacted.

In addition, the rise of activism raised awareness of the power of activists who became known as *corporate stakeholders*. In 1984, Edward Freeman published his seminal work on stakeholder theory, putting these developments into a framework useful for those interested in governance and in understanding the relevance of stakeholder support to enhancing firm reputation and achieving corporate strategic objectives. This understanding has proven to be instrumental in framing how directors, shareholders, and managers now think about the role of corporations and how they earn their profits. Of course, the contribution of stakeholder theory took years to mature.

ETHICS & GOVERNANCE: THE MODERN ERA—1990 TO THE PRESENT

In November 1991, just before the introduction of the *U.S. Federal Sentencing Guidelines*, a judge commented that if a company could prove that all reasonable efforts had been made to avoid environmental harm (i.e., a due diligence program had been in place), then the proposed penalties of up to $2 million per day and jail time for responsible executives could be reduced to $50,000 per day. Immediately, many major companies began to develop environmental due diligence and compliance programs that generated greater awareness of environmental problems and the desire of those corporations to avoid environmental damage as well as some assurance of compliance.

Essentially, corporations, under the direction of their boards of directors, developed governance programs that shaped their behavior and benefited society. In response to pressure from other activist stakeholders, corporations have instituted governance programs devoted to the following:

- Encourage and protect whistleblowers
- Improve health and safety
- Ensure fair dealing
- Reduce conflicts of interest
- Ensure reasonable employment practices

Despite these favorable developments, greed and conflicts of interest did not vanish. They accounted for many of the scandals that have triggered further governance reform in the form of SOX and internationally generated bank reform regulations in 2010. The significant scandals triggering these two reforms are identified in Figure 2.2 and are discussed below.

SIGNIFICANT ETHICS & GOVERNANCE SCANDALS & EVENTS

Enron—A Failure of the Board of Directors

Enron Corporation was formed by Ken Lay in 1985 as a result of the merger of two natural gas pipeline companies. As the demand for natural gas grew, the stock price of Enron rose steadily through the 1990s, trading in the $20 to $40 range. At the beginning of 2000, the stock price began to soar, trading in the $60 to $90 range. At that time, Enron was the seventh-largest public company in the United States. However, in 2001, the stock began to fall, and on December 2, 2001, the company filed for bankruptcy

FIGURE 2.2 Notable Business Failures & Fiascos Since 2000

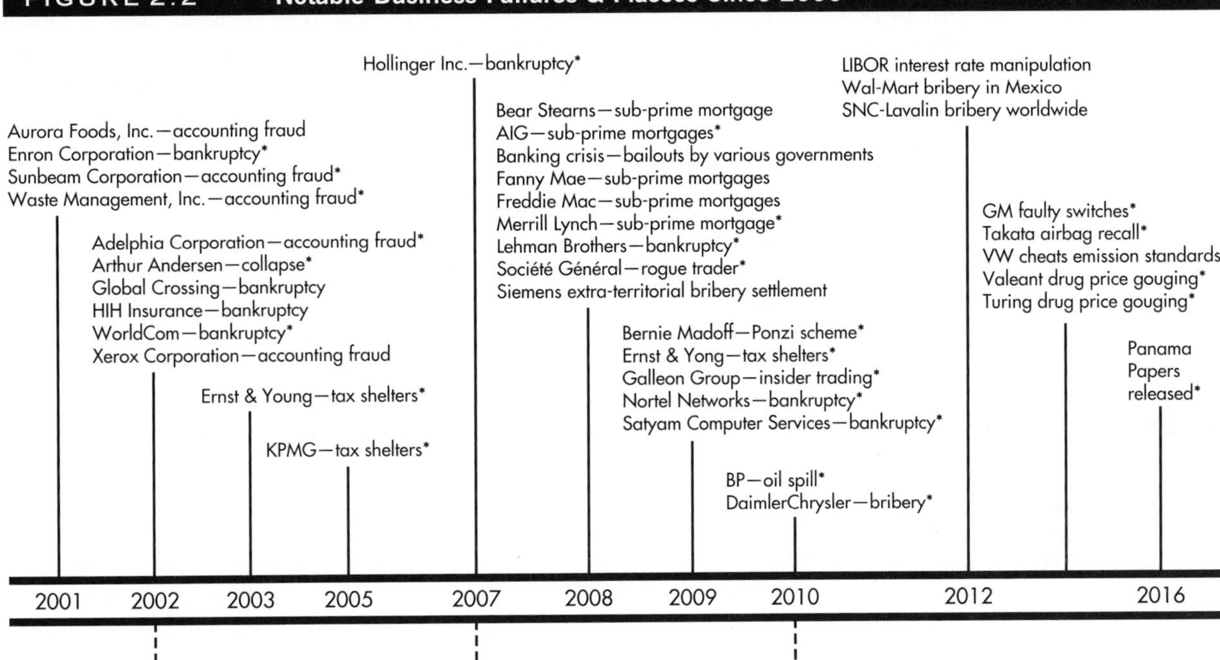

protection. Four months later, as shown in Figure 2.3, on April 2, 2002, Enron stock was trading for 24 cents.

Headquartered in Houston, Texas, Enron's core business was selling natural gas. But it moved into the business of selling energy futures. A futures contract is an agreement

FIGURE 2.3 Enron Stock Chart, Weekly Prices, 1997–2002

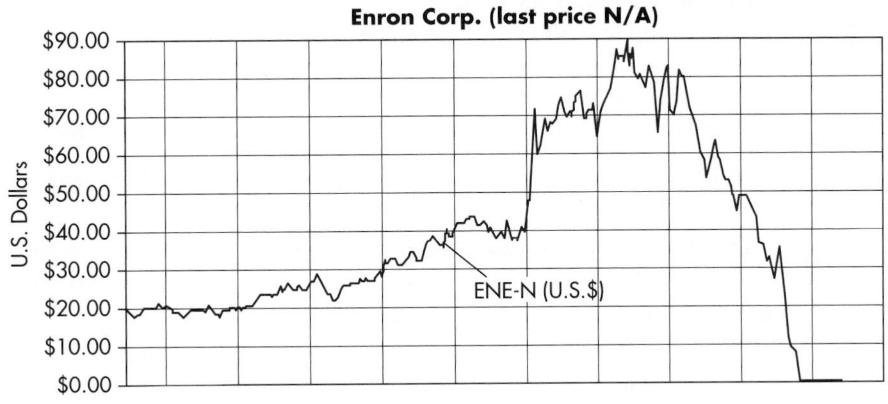

Source: Reprinted courtesy of StatPro Canada, Inc.

whereby one party agrees to sell energy to another party at a specified date in the future at a price agreed to today. From the seller's point of view, revenue is normally recorded when the energy is delivered to the customer. In Enron's case, it began to record income using an estimate of future sales. Called "prepays," Enron recorded revenue in the current period, when the cash was received, in advance of delivering the natural gas over a period of years in the future.

Another ploy was to artificially sell, or syndicate, Enron's long-life assets, such as its capital-intensive energy projects. Unfortunately, Enron was unable to find real independent buyers to invest in these syndicates. So, when Enron created unconsolidated affiliates or special purpose enterprises/entities (SPEs) to serve as investment vehicles, an Enron employee masqueraded as an independent outside investor to falsely permit transfers from Enron to be recorded as sales and generate profit. However, *since these SPEs were not independent from Enron, in reality Enron was selling assets to itself.* Since there was no independent investor voice, Enron could manipulate profit as much as they wanted by selling at any price—which they did. Most investors and lenders were misled into thinking that Enron sales and profits were growing superbly and were stunned when the company was declared bankrupt.

Through these sorts of transactions, Enron managed to artificially overstate its revenue while understating its liabilities. But because Enron was selling assets to itself, the transactions did not generate any real profit or any significant external cash flow. However, the SPEs were used to attract loans (i.e., new cash) from banks interested in dealing with Enron, and this new cash was transferred to Enron in settlement of the false sales transactions. Consequently, Enron's financial results showed false increases in sales, cash, and profit and did not reflect the borrowing from banks (i.e., liabilities incurred) that produced the increase in cash. The borrowings from banks were shown on the statements of the SPEs, but these were not consolidated into the Enron statements because the SPEs were falsely represented to have external investors who contributed at least 3% of the capital and who were making all of the SPE decisions, including those related to the asset purchases from Enron.

On November 19, 2001, the company announced that it could not meet its next debt payment. On December 2, it declared bankruptcy. When the financial statements were eventually restated, Enron's revenue was reduced by over $2.6 billion for the four-year period from 1997 to 2000. Overall debt was increased by a similar amount. Almost one-half of its reported profits, which had driven up its stock price so dramatically through the late 1990s, were shown to be false. At the time, this was the largest fraud ever reported in the United States.

According to both an internal investigation (Powers Report) and an external investigation (Senate Subcommittee Report), the failure of Enron was attributed, in large part, to the failure of the board of directors to provide oversight and governance. The board members knew of and permitted the Enron executives to do the following:

- Engage in high-risk accounting transactions, such as recording revenue early through the use of "prepays"
- Engage in inappropriate conflicts of interest, such as permitting Jeffrey Skilling, Enron's CEO, to also operate private equity funds that were dealing with Enron
- Not record material off-the-book liabilities through the use of SPEs
- Pay excessive compensation to its senior executives, often without proper approval, including almost $1 billion in stock options to 12 senior executives

Furthermore, the members of the board of directors engaged in a number of financial transactions with Enron, thus compromising their own independence.

The board failed to ensure the independence of Enron's auditor, Arthur Andersen. It also appears that it chose to ignore the complaints of various whistleblowers and instead placed its faith in the company's senior executives, Ken Lay (chairman and sometimes CEO), Jeffrey Skilling (CEO), and Andrew Fastow (CFO). These were the men who were orchestrating the fraud.

The ethics case "Enron's Questionable Transactions" is provided at the end of this chapter to provide insights into how flaws in corporate governance and accounting made possible the massive Enron fraud. Additional background information on Enron is available in the digital archive at **www.cengagebrain.com**.

As a consequence of Enron's failure, tens of thousands of employees lost their jobs; millions of investors, either directly or indirectly through their pension funds, lost millions of dollars. Ten key employees were indicted and sent to prison, although Ken Lay died before sentencing. Within one year, Arthur Andersen, Enron's auditor, would be convicted of obstruction of justice; WorldCom would announce that its financial statements were inaccurate by $11 billion; and the U.S. Congress would enact SOX. The world of corporate governance changed dramatically.

Arthur Andersen—An Organizational Culture Gone Awry

At the turn of the 21st century, there were five large accounting firms: Arthur Andersen, Deloitte Touche Tohmatsu (now Deloitte), Ernst & Young, KPMG, and PricewaterhouseCoopers. Each of these represented a network of firms that were spread throughout the world, with offices in almost every major city. Called the Big 5, they were an oligopoly when it came to providing audit services to large publicly traded companies.

Arthur Andersen (hereafter simply Andersen) was founded in 1913 in Chicago.[1] It had a reputation for integrity and technical competence. In 1954, it expanded from providing accounting and audit services to providing consulting services to the managers of the firms to whom it was also providing audit services. By 1984, consulting services revenue was greater than audit services revenue. In 1989, the consulting arm was spun off into a separate organization that eventually changed its name to Accenture.

During the 1980s, the culture at Andersen was altered:

- Revenue generation became the key to promotion.
- The focus was on providing nonaudit services to management, including providing advice on how to structure transactions so that they would be disclosed in a manner favorable to management.
- Pressure to reduce audit costs increased, and audit partners were allowed to override the rulings of the quality control partners.

The potential conflict of interest between fair reporting to shareholders and serving the interest of management was not addressed. The partnership was interested only in revenue generation.

Andersen was providing both audit and consulting services to Enron. In 2000, it was deriving more of its revenue from providing management services; audit fees charged to Enron were $25 million while consulting fees were $27 million.[2] David Duncan, the partner in charge of the Enron audit, did not challenge the accounting policies of Enron.

[1] A more detailed description of the collapse of Arthur Andersen is provided in the digital archive for this book at **www.cengagebrain.com**, as Chapter 9, "The Credibility Crisis—Enron, WorldCom, & SOX."

[2] Paul Healy and Krishna Palepu, "The Fall of Enron," *Journal of Economic Perspectives* 17, no. 2 (March 2003): 3–26.

He even ignored three internal e-mails from Carl Bass, a quality control partner, who was questioning some of Enron's accounting policies and possible conflicts of interest between Enron, Fastow (Enron's CFO), and the SPEs that Fastow was managing. Eventually, Bass was removed from providing Enron audit oversight.

In March 2002, the SEC announced that it was investigating Andersen for audit deficiencies with respect to the Enron audit. This came after Andersen had been found guilty of similar audit deficiencies with respect to the audits of Waste Management, Inc., and Sunbeam Corporation. Meanwhile, many companies were switching auditors; they did not want their reputations damaged by being associated with Andersen.[3]

On October 10, Andersen's lawyer, Nancy Temple, sent an e-mail to the Houston office reminding the Enron audit team of the Andersen policy, "which calls for destruction of extraneous and redundant material." Tons of documents were shredded. When this became known, the perception was that Anderson staff was destroying any evidence that might indicate that they had been complicit in the Enron fraud.

Andersen was charged with obstruction of justice and was found guilty on June 15, 2002. Andersen agreed to cease auditing all publicly traded companies while it appealed the conviction. Almost three years later, on May 31, 2005, the U.S. Supreme Court overturned the Andersen conviction. But it was too late. The partnership had no clients; it had voluntarily surrendered its license to practice, and its personnel had already joined other accounting firms in the United States and around the world. A firm that once had 85,000 employees worldwide was no more. The Big 5 had become the Big 4 accounting firms.

The ethics case "Arthur Andersen's Troubles" is available at the end of this chapter.

WorldCom—Power in the Hands of One Man

Prior to cellular telephones, phone calls were sent through fixed fiber-optic telephone cables. Because it was expensive for each company to build and operate its own telephone line network, the telephone companies would share the existing landlines. The company that owned the landline would charge the telephone company that was using that line a service fee. The telephone company would then pass the landline charge to the telephone user. From a reporting perspective, the telephone company would record an expense for the cost of using the third-party landline and record revenue for the amount that it charged the long-distance telephone caller.[4]

WorldCom, headquartered in Clinton, Mississippi, was started in 1983 by Bernard Ebbers as a long-distance discount service.[5] The company experienced spectacular growth in the 1990s through a series of takeovers. Eventually WorldCom became the second-largest telecommunications company after AT&T, and Ebbers became known as the Telecom Cowboy. In 1999, WorldCom planned a $115 billion takeover of Sprint Corporation. However, the takeover was vetoed by U.S. and European regulators. This put downward pressure on WorldCom's stock, which had been propped up by using takeovers rather than normal operating growth to increase earnings.

In order to artificially increase its net income, WorldCom adopted a simple accounting policy: it would capitalize expenses. Rather than record an expense for third-party

[3] Paul Chaney and Kirk Philipich, "Shredded Reputation: The Cost of Audit Failure," *Journal of Accounting Research* 40, no. 4 (May 2002): 1221–45.

[4] See also the ethics case "Manipulation of MCI's Allowance for Doubtful Accounts" in Chapter 5.

[5] A more detailed discussion of the WorldCom fraud and bankruptcy is provided in Chapter 9, "The Credibility Crisis—Enron, WorldCom, & SOX," which is available in the digital archive at **www.cengagebrain.com**.

line costs, the company recorded these costs as assets. These capitalized costs reduced operating expenses and artificially inflated net income by over $7.6 billion for the years 1999 to 2002. WorldCom also had Andersen as its auditor.

The fraud was perpetrated by Ebbers; Scott Sullivan, the company's CFO; and four of Sullivan's staff. In 2000, Ebbers and Sullivan each received retention bonuses of $10 million. By 2001, they had each been allocated millions of stock options. In addition, Ebbers had been lent $408 million by the company to buy or pay margin calls on his WorldCom stock. The security on his margin account was his WorldCom stock. Ebbers had a strong financial motivation to keep WorldCom's stock strong, especially after the failed Sprint takeover. To keep the stock price up and to meet analysts' forecasts, Ebbers directed Sullivan to engage in a straightforward financial statement fraud. The company would record expenses as assets, thereby increasing net income. The company also created fictitious reserves of $2 billion. The fraud eventually totaled $11 billion, dwarfing the $2.6 billion Enron fraud.

Despite the aggressive overstatement of income from 1999 to 2002, the stock price began to fall. After Ebbers was fired as CEO in April, an internal investigation revealed the extent of the fraud. But it was too late. In July 2002, WorldCom declared bankruptcy. It was later merged with MCI and its name changed to Verizon Business in 2006. The perpetrators of the fraud—Ebbers, Sullivan, and their assistants—were fined and sent to prison.

During the court case, the jury chose to believe the prosecution's claim that the fraud had been orchestrated by Ebbers. They accepted Sullivan's testimony when he said that Ebbers had ordered him to "hit his numbers." They needed to falsify the accounting records in order to meet Wall Street's expectation, thereby keeping the stock price high and the stock options in the money. There appeared to be no control over Ebbers, the man who had created the company and oversaw its growth through takeovers and false financial reporting. Sullivan was not in a position to challenge him. No one was. And so, with almost unlimited power, Ebbers could engineer the largest fraud in American history. He was out of control.

The ethics case "WorldCom: The Final Catalyst" is located at the end of this chapter.

WorldCom had developed an unhealthy corporate environment and culture. Senior executives were overcompensated, and they had too many stock options. There was insufficient oversight, and power was concentrated in the hands of one person. A similar situation occurred in Australia. HIH Insurance was autocratically ruled by one individual whose poor management decisions bankrupted the company in 2001. It had developed a culture, similar to WorldCom, where executive decisions were neither challenged nor questioned.[6] Without an adequate balance of power between the board and management, the chances of a business failure increase.

Crisis of Confidence

Prior to the collapse of WorldCom in July 2002, the demise of Andersen a month earlier, and the bankruptcy of Enron in December of 2001, *investors and regulators had become extremely concerned about the lack of integrity of business leaders, and stock markets plunged, as did the confidence in financial reports.* Furthermore, there were obvious flaws in the governance structures designed to ensure that management was not

---

[6] "Report of the Royal Commission into HIH Insurance," *Department of the Parliamentary Library* 32 (May 13, 2003), http://www.aph.gov.au/library/pubs/rn/2002-03/03rn32.pdf.

operating the businesses to further their own personal self-interests. There had been a number of spectacular corporate governance failures:

- Adelphia Corporation—founded by John Rigas, the company filed for bankruptcy in 2002 as result of internal corruption by Rigas and his family, who were convicted of a $2.3 billion fraud and looting the company of more than $100 million.[7]
- Aurora Foods, Inc.—in 2001, the company was found guilty of underreporting expenses by $43.7 million in order to meet analysts' earnings expectations.[8]
- Global Crossing—when it declared bankruptcy in 2002, it was the fourth-largest business failure in American history. The fiber-optics company's market capitalization had fallen from $47.6 billion in February 2000 to $273 million on January 28, 2002.[9]
- HIH Insurance—with losses estimated at A$5.3 billion, this was the largest corporate failure in Australia's history. The subsequent Royal Commission found that the failure was due to gross mismanagement and an organizational culture that did not question leadership decisions.[10]
- Sunbeam Corporation—turnaround artist Albert "Chainsaw" Dunlap increased net income by fraudulently recording $62 million of sales. The company went into bankruptcy protection in 2001.[11]
- Waste Management, Inc.—in March 2001, the SEC laid charges against the senior officers of the company for fraudulently overstating pretax income by $3.5 billion from 1992 to 1996. Andersen, the company's auditor, paid a $7 million fine as a result of this audit failure.[12]
- Xerox Corporation—in April 2002, the company was fined $10 million (the largest fine the SEC had ever levied) for fraudulently recognizing over $3 billion of equipment revenue over the four-year period 1997–2000.[13]

This is only a partial list of the accounting and business debacles that occurred in the year prior to the WorldCom fiasco. But WorldCom, an $11 billion fraud, was the last straw. *Business and business people faced a crisis of confidence because their integrity, financial reports, and activities lacked credibility.* As the news of each debacle came to the attention of the public, stock markets plummeted, as noted in Figure 2.4. President George W. Bush, recognizing the developing crisis of confidence, delivered a television appeal for the public to trust that the government[14] would be able to fix the flawed governance and reporting systems, but further fiascos caused stock prices sink further. In response, Congress quickly passed SOX, which became law on July 30, 2002.

[7] See also the ethics case "Adelphia—Really the Rigas' Family Piggy Bank" in Chapter 5.

[8] "Former Aurora Foods Executives Plead Guilty to Securities Fraud," *St. Louis Business Journal*, September 4, 2001, http://www.bizjournals.com/stlouis/stories/2001/09/03/daily8.html.

[9] "Global Files for Bankruptcy," *CNN Money*, January 28, 2002, http://money.cnn.com/2002/01/28/companies/globalcrossing/.

[10] "Report of the Royal Commission into HIH Insurance," *Department of the Parliamentary Library* 32 (May 13, 2003), http://www.aph.gov.au/library/pubs/rn/2002–03/03rn32.pdf.

[11] See also the ethics case "Sunbeam Corporation and Chainsaw Al" in the digital archive at **www.cengagebrain.com**.

[12] See also the ethics case "Waste Management, Inc." in the digital achieve at **www.cengagebrain.com**.

[13] "Xerox Charged with Fraud," *CNN Money*, April 11, 2002, http://money.cnn.com/2002/04/11/technology/xerox_fraud/.

[14] On March 7, 2002, he called for governance reforms and advanced a 10-point plan for legislative action.

FIGURE 2.4 Impact of Financial Debacles on NYSE Share Prices per Dow Jones Industrial Index Average (DJI), November 1, 2001–August 31, 2002

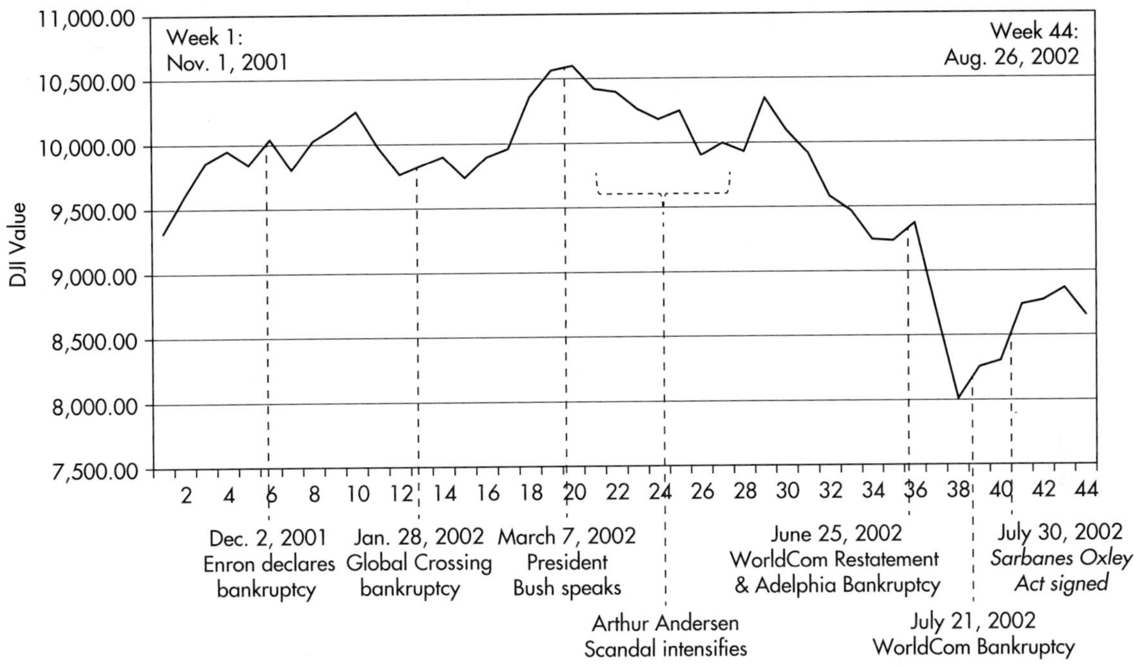

Source: DJI weekly close values were downloaded on December 11, 2013 from http://ca.finance.yahoo.com/q/hp?s=%5EDJI&a=10&b=1&c=2001&d=07&e=31&f=2002&g=w

Sarbanes-Oxley Act—Closing the Barn Door

SOX provided direction in three main areas: the responsibilities of management, conflicts of interest, and the responsibilities of the auditors and the audit committee. A primary responsibility of management is to implement a proper internal control system to ensure that the company's financial reports are accurate, complete, understandable, and transparent. Furthermore, the quarterly and annual financial reports must include a management certification, signed by the CEO and CFO, attesting to the scope, adequacy, and effectiveness of the company's internal controls concerning financial reporting.

Several sections of SOX are designed to reduce conflicts of interest. These include requiring the following:

- The disclosure of management stock trades and any dealings that management has with major investors
- That all publicly traded companies have a corporate code of ethics

Numerous sections of SOX address the responsibilities of auditors and the audit committee. Some of these require that:

- the directors who sit on the audit committee be independent of management,
- the audit committee have at least one member who is a financial expert and the others be financially literate,
- the audit committee have a sufficient budget of time and money to complete its work,

- the auditor report to the audit committee without management being present, and
- the auditor not provide any management services, other than tax and information technology, to its audit clients.

Furthermore, SOX required the establishment of the Public Company Accounting Oversight Board (PCAOB). Composed of five members appointed by the SEC, the PCAOB is charged with establishing auditing and attestation standards. It is also responsible for inspecting and disciplining accounting firms. As a result of the numerous audit failures and the collapse of Arthur Andersen, the U.S. government decided that the accounting firms could no longer be left to discipline themselves. Hence, the PCAOB is designed to audit the auditors.

SOX was designed to strengthen corporate governance. When the board is not independent of management, it becomes harder for the board to control management. Non-arm's-length transactions between management and major investors may not be priced at fair values, so there is an opportunity for managerial opportunism. Stock options had been generously granted to senior executives of public companies, often because many people thought, wrongly, that stock options were of no cost to the company. SOX helps ensure that there is greater transparency, which should minimize the possible adverse effects of conflicts of interests.

The audit committee is a key governance control. The committee is to oversee the financial reporting system and the financial reports of the company. The committee must have the expertise to objectively and independently assess the audit and the veracity of the financial statements. The auditor must also be independent in order to objectively assess the financial statements that are prepared by management. SOX provided guidelines in that regard.

Overall, SOX forced directors, especially those who are also audit committee members, to realize that they could no longer take the assertions of management at face value. Directors were now required to be knowledgeable and vigilant. They were to ask tough questions of management. Directors have the ultimate responsibility to oversee management and to set strategic policy. Therefore, they must act with integrity and honesty.

Another consequence of SOX is that auditors are now acquiring a greater knowledge of their clients' internal control systems and are adjusting their audit procedures to take advantage of this enhanced knowledge.[15] This has resulted in an improvement in the quality of financial reporting by listed companies.[16] However, the increased restrictions of SOX have meant that many local and regional accounting firms in the United States have ceased to conduct audits of publicly traded companies.[17]

Tax Shelters—Not in the Public Interest

Tax practitioners are hired to provide advice to clients on how to pay the minimum amount of tax. Sometimes, accountants become too aggressive in designing tax strategies. This happened to both Ernst & Young (now EY) and KPMG. They recommended that their clients invest in tax shelters later judged to be illegal. Both accounting partnerships were fined, and the IRS implemented *Circular 230*.

---

[15] Greg Trompeter and Arnold Wright, "The World Has Changed—Have Analytical Procedures Practices?" *Contemporary Accounting Research* 27, no. 2 (Summer 2010): 669–700.

[16] Daniel Cohen, Dey Aiyesha, and Thomas Lys, "Real and Accruals-Based Earnings Management in the Pre- and Post-*Sarbanes-Oxley* Periods," *The Accounting Review* 83, no. 3 (May 2008): 757–87.

[17] Williams Read, Dasaratha Raghunandan, and K. Rama, "Local and Regional Audit Firms and the Market for SEC Audits," *Accounting Horizons* 18, no. 4 (December 2004): 241–54.

In the 1990s, E&Y designed and marketed a variety of tax shelters that would delay paying taxes on stock options for up to thirty years. They were aggressively marketing these shelters to their wealthy clients, including two senior executives at Sprint Corporation, an E&Y audit client. The IRS deemed the tax shelters to be a sham and disallowed the tax deductions. The executives were reassessed and had to pay millions of dollars in taxes and fines. E&Y reached a settlement with the government and paid a fine of $15 million.

From 1996 to 2003, KPMG designed, implemented, and aggressively marketed a variety of tax shelters targeted at wealthy taxpayers, those who paid taxes of $10 million to $20 million. These abusive tax shelters generated at least $11 billion of artificial tax losses that cost the U.S. government $2.5 billion of evaded taxes. The government rejected the tax shelters on the basis that they had no economic purpose other than to reduce taxes. The taxpayers were reassessed, the tax deductions were disallowed, and they had to pay the taxes otherwise payable along with fines and penalties. The KPMG tax shelters were considered so egregious that some wanted to see KPMG put out of business. However, this would have meant that, with the recent collapse of Andersen, the Big 4 would have become the Big 3, which would have been an unacceptably small oligarchy. Instead, the U.S. government fined KMPG $456 million.

Then, in May 2009, four E&Y tax partners were found guilty for their role in marketing illegal tax shelters to wealthy clients. From 1998 to 2006, the four had sold tax shelters that resulted in fictitious tax losses of approximately $2 billion. E&Y was not charged, but the firm's reputation was damaged. See the ethics case "Marketing Aggressive Tax Shelters" contained in Chapter 6.

In the wake of the E&Y and KPMG tax debacles, the IRS issued *Circular 230* on September 26, 2007.[18] It provides rules and suggested best practices for tax professionals. The basic rules are know your client, serve the client's needs, explain and disclose fully, and propose strategies likely to succeed. *Circular 230* requires tax professionals to do the following:

- Practitioners need to understand the facts of the situation as well as the goals, needs, and expectations of the client.
- Any advice or tax planning strategies have to be consistent with the objectives of the client and the current applicable tax rules and regulations.
- Any written opinions, including emails, called "covered opinions," need to clearly explain all the facts and assumptions, the proposed strategy, and the probable consequences of the strategy.
- Any proposed tax strategy must have a better than 50% chance of success if there is the possibility that it will be challenged by the IRS.
- If no opinion can be reached, then the tax practitioner must explain why a conclusion cannot be drawn.
- Opinions must also disclose the compensation method.

Overall, the tax professional needs to know the client and make tax planning suggestions that are reasonable and consistent with the law and the requirements of the client.

Critics argued that the regulations requiring new opinions would preclude most tax practitioners from providing any meaningful tax advice to their clients. Opinions would include a disclaimer that the client should not rely on the advice to be protected against prosecution, fines, and/or penalties. If they wanted a higher level of assurance, clients

---

[18] A more detailed analysis of *Circular 230* is provided in Chapter 6.

would have to pay more for a "covered opinion." Contrary to the critics' wishes, the counterargument prevailed. Tax practitioners had shown such a disregard for the law and professional standards that the government had to impose new standards of professional conduct on tax preparers and tax advisors.

Subprime Mortgage Meltdown[19]—Greed without Due Diligence

The subprime lending crisis was years in the making but came to crisis proportions in 2008 with the bankruptcy of Lehman Brothers, an old and respected investment firm headquartered in New York with operations around the world. Before the crisis could be remedied, governments in the United States and Europe had to bail out or provide funds to many banks and major companies to prevent their bankruptcy and also had to increase the liquidity in their own economies to provide economic stimulation. The crisis spread around the world because investors buy and sell securities on a global basis, and many held securities that were undermined by the failure of mortgages from the U.S. housing market.

Traditionally, commercial banks borrowed money from depositors and then lent that money to home owners, secured by a mortgage on the property. Investment banks, on the other hand, assisted clients, normally corporations, in the raising of capital funds through underwriting, mergers and acquisitions, and trading in financial instruments. In 1999, the *Gramm-Leach-Bliley Act* repealed the *Glass-Steagall Act of 1933*. Commercial banks were permitted to engage in investing activities. One such activity was to borrow money at a low rate by issuing short- to medium-term commercial paper and then lending that money through mortgage investments at a higher interest rate. Called *structured investment vehicles* (SIVs), these deals permitted banks to earn money through the spread between the two interest rates.

Banks then began to issue collateralized debt obligations (CDOs), which were a specific type of SIV. The bank would issue a CDO, basically a bond that was secured by a portfolio of mortgages. The portfolio of mortgages involved were then said to have been securitized, and the whole process was referred to as securitization. The cash receipts from the mortgagors were used to pay the interest on the CDO. The riskiness of the CDO was a function of the riskiness of the mortgages in the portfolio. Large CDO bond offerings often contained different risk classes, called *tranches*, that were sold to investors. Interest and principal payments to the CDO holders were made in order of "seniority" where senior tranches were the safest; junior tranches were the riskiest. Because they were the riskiest, junior tranches paid a higher interest or coupon rate. Because of their different risk levels, CDOs became popular investment vehicles.[20]

If the owner of an investment or a nonowner/speculator becomes concerned about the risk that the value of an investment will decline, he or she can buy a promise from another investor or speculator to pay for whatever value loss occurs. For example, a credit default swap (CDS) permits an investor who buys a security, such as a CDO, to contract with a third party to buy protection in the event the issuer of the security defaults on the contract. A CDS is similar to an insurance policy; it acts as a hedge against the risk of default. The investor makes periodic payments, normally quarterly, to the seller of the CDS. In the event of default on the security, the investor sells the

[19] This section presents a summary. Extensive coverage is included in Chapter 8, "The Subprime Lending Fiasco—Ethics Issues."

[20] An example of a CDO, "Goldman Sachs' GSAMP Trust 2006-S3," is included in Chapter 8.

security to the CDS issuer for the par value of the security. The CDS issuer then sells the security for whatever it will fetch in the secondary bond market.

A CDS is dissimilar to an insurance policy in that anyone can buy a CDS, even if the purchaser of the CDS does not own the underlying security. Referred to as a naked credit default swap, it can be bought by an investor who is speculating on the creditworthiness and default risk of a particular security, such as a specific CDO. It is analogous to betting on a horse that you do not own as to whether the horse will win a race at the racetrack. A naked CDS is a derivative instrument that obtains its value from the value of the corresponding CDO. In 2007, most of the CDS market consisted of naked credit default swaps. One of the most informative movies about the subprime lending scandal, *The Big Short*,[21] describes how a small number of people realized that the scandal was likely to occur and used CDSs to profit significantly as the value of CDOs fell dramatically.

Prior to 2007, housing prices in the United States were constantly climbing. Banks were encouraging people to buy houses and take out short- to medium-term mortgages by offering very low interest rates. The sales pitch was that when the mortgage came due, the borrower's salary would have increased sufficiently to cover a higher renewal interest rate or, if the home owner did not want to renew the mortgage, the value of the house would have risen such that the home owner could sell the house, pay off the mortgage, and make money on the transaction. What a great deal!

Securitization permitted financial institutions to issue mortgages to home owners and then to sell those mortgages to another financial institution or investor. In addition to transferring the risk of mortgage default, this generated sufficient cash flow for the initial financial institution to make more mortgage loans. The financial institution would also collect more transaction fees. This system encouraged financial institutions to make high-risk mortgage loans as long as the mortgages could then be sold quickly to a third party.

Lenders were encouraging property owners to take out second and third mortgages. Houses were now being viewed as investments rather than as homes. Money was lent to high-risk clients—clients with lower-than-prime creditworthiness, hence the term *subprime*. The competition to make loans became so intense that loans were even made to borrowers who had no assets and in some cases no income or job.[22] Often documents covering creditworthiness were not even requested. An added bonus for the home owner was that the interest paid on these mortgages was deductible for tax purposes.

The CDOs associated with these subprime mortgages also yielded a high rate of return, so they were attractive investments. The banks were selling them to all their clients. They promised high yields and were considered low risk because the housing market was booming. At the same time, credit rating agencies were classifying high-risk SIVs and CDOs as low risk. Often these rating agencies were not performing the required due diligence to assess the inherent risk thoroughly. Furthermore, prospectuses were often quite lengthy, with technical jargon that many could not understand. As such, investors were often relying on the good reputations of the underwriters, the credit rating agencies, and the banks. The CDOs were being bought on faith and by many financial institutions that should have known better.

Like all investments, there is the risk that the investment may drop in value. That began to occur in 2006. House prices began to fall, and home owners who had been

[21] *The Big Short* was a movie released in late 2015 that presents an excellent explanation and portrayal of the causes, players, and roles involved in the subprime lending scandal.

[22] See further discussion in Chapter 8, "The Subprime Lending Fiasco—Ethics Issues," particularly the discussion on "Liar" loans, "Ninja" loans, and "Teaser" loans.

encouraged to take out huge mortgages relative to the value of their property found that the value of the mortgage exceeded the value of the property. Home owners began to default on their mortgages. Banks were foreclosing and selling off the houses quickly, depressing the market even further. The American economy was slowing down. An economic crisis was looming. By the end of 2006, 12.5% of all subprime mortgages were in default. Over 1.5 million Americans had lost their homes. As the housing market soared, the value of the CDOs that were backed by subprime mortgages began to fall rapidly. Because a CDS is a derivative instrument whose value is a function of the corresponding CDO, as the value of the CDOs decreased, so too did the value of the CDSs.

The CDOs and CDSs had been bought and sold, often on faith, by investors who had not properly assessed the associated risks. When the market collapsed, financial institutions that had never previously recorded a loss began to go bankrupt:

- In the third quarter of 2007, Merrill Lynch reported an operating loss of $2.3 billion and announced that it had set up a $7.9 billion loss provision for mortgage-related investments. It avoided bankruptcy by being sold to the Bank of America for $1 per share.[23]
- On July 16, 2007, Bear Stearns announced that two of its subprime mortgage hedge funds had lost nearly all of their value. On September 21, it reported a 61% drop in its third-quarter profits resulting, in part, from an $800 million loss as it liquidated its CDO portfolio.[24]
- Lehman Brothers held substantial amounts of CDOs and was extremely active in the selling of securitized mortgages. On June 9, 2008, it reported a quarterly loss of $2.8 billion. The investment bank sought financial assistance. But none arrived. It declared bankruptcy on September 15, 2008, making it the largest bankruptcy in American history.[25]
- American International Group, Inc. (AIG), had been a principal seller of credit default swaps, but when the financial crisis hit, the company began to report extensive losses: in February 2008, they were $4.8 billion; they rose to $11 billion a month later; for the half-year ending June 30, losses had reached $13.2 billion. Although the government let Lehman Brothers fail, it stepped in with emergency funding for AIG. The argument was that AIG was too big to let fail.[26]
- Both the Federal National Mortgage Association (Fanny Mae) and the Federal Home Loan Mortgage Corporation (Freddie Mac) were extensively involved in buying securitized mortgages. Their subprime mortgage losses were so huge that the U.S. government took over both companies in September 2008.

The financial crisis was harming the entire U.S. economy. The banks and other financial institutions were considered too important to the economy to let them go bankrupt. So, after the sale of Merrill Lynch and the bankruptcy of Lehman Brothers, the government stepped in. It reduced interest rates, created new lending facilities, and made

[23] See also the ethics case "Subprime Lending—Greed, Faith, & Disaster" in Chapter 8.

[24] Shanny Basar and Vivek Ahuja, "Bear Downgraded in Face of First Loss in 83 Years," *Financial Times*, November 15, 2007, http://www.efinancialnews.com/story/2007-11-15/bear-downgraded-in-face-of-first-loss-in-83-years.

[25] Abigail Field, "Lehman Report: The Business Decisions That Brought Lehman Down," *Daily Finance*, March 14, 2010, http://www.dailyfinance.com/story/investing/lehman-report-the-business-decisions-that-brought-lehman-down/19398397/.

[26] See also the ethics cases "Market-to-Market Accounting and the Demise of AIG" and "The Ethics of AIG's Commission Sales," both of which are provided in Chapter 8.

money available through the enactment in October 2008 of the *Troubled Asset Relief Program* (TARP), a $700 billion stimulus package.

But this was becoming a worldwide crisis. Banks and investors in other countries had also bought the American mortgage-backed securities and credit default swaps. These companies were failing, too:

- In October 2008, UBS, Switzerland's largest bank, received a $59.2 billion bailout from the Swiss government. The bank had over $60 billion of "toxic" assets.[27]
- In Iceland, the economic crisis was so severe that within a week in October 2008, the country's three main banks—Glitnir, Kaupthing, and Landsbanki—collapsed, and the krona, the country's currency, plummeted.[28]
- On October 13, 2008, the British government announced that it was injecting £37 billion into the Royal Bank of Scotland, Lloyds TSB, and HBOS. The nationalization scheme resulted in the government owning about 60% of the Royal Bank of Scotland and 40% of the merged Lloyds TSB and HBOS banks.[29]

This was a global crisis that was plunging the world into an economic downturn. All governments were acknowledging the need for global cooperation and commitment to addressing the financial crisis. At their meeting in Toronto in June 2010, the G-20 (leaders from the twenty largest economies) reiterated their pledge for continued support to work together to reform international financial markets and to strengthen their economic cooperation.

Most of the subprime mortgage disaster can be summarized in one word: *greed*. Home owners began greedily viewing their residences as investments rather than as homes. The tax rules that allow the deductibility of mortgage interest but not of rent further encouraged people to take out large mortgages. Mortgage companies were selling as many mortgages as they could regardless of the risks so that they could collect mortgage commissions and then sell the mortgages to another investor, thereby avoiding any default risks. Issuers of CDOs saw high profits in selling mortgage-backed securities as long as the housing market kept rising. Prudent risk management through the purchase of CDSs actually became a highly speculative strategy, betting on which way the market would go. Credit advisors collected fees without properly analyzing the risks associated with the CDOs. Happy days existed as long as no one asked what would happen if the housing bubble burst.[30] When it did burst, even those who were on the sidelines watching the parade were adversely affected in the resulting economic downturn.

Further discussion of the subprime lending crisis is provided in Chapter 8.

Dodd-Frank Wall Street Reform and Consumer Protection Act

In July 2010 as a result of the subprime mortgage crisis, the U.S. Congress passed the *Dodd-Frank Wall Street Reform and Consumer Protection Act*.[31] Its overall objective

---

[27] Warren Giles, "UBS Gets $59.2 Billion Bailout: Credit Suisse Raises Capital," *Bloomberg*, October 16, 2008, http://www.bloomberg.com/apps/news?pid=newsarchive&sid=ah0AFa2SEHhw.

[28] "Iceland Expected to Turn Down Bank Failure Repay," *Washington Times*, March 6, 2010, http://www.washingtontimes.com/news/2010/mar/06/iceland-expected-turn-down-bank-failure-repay/.

[29] "UK Banks Receive £37bn Bail-Out," *BBC News*, October 13, 2008, http://news.bbc.co.uk/2/hi/business/7666570.stm.

[30] See also the ethics case "Moral Courage: Toronto-Dominion Bank CEO Refuses to Invest in High-Risk Asset-Backed Commercial Paper" in Chapter 8.

[31] A summary of the *Dodd-Frank Wall Street Reform and Consumer Protection Act* (H.R. 4173) can be found at http://www.govtrack.us/congress/bill.xpd?bill=h111-4173&tab=summary.

was to provide financial stability and increased consumer protection by imposing more regulation on the investment marketplace, including the following:

- New federal agencies were created that would identify the risks associated with complex financial instrument and packages. These agencies are to provide consumer protection from deceptive financial service practices associated with mortgages, credit cards, and other financial products.
- New regulations concerning risky financial products, such as financial derivatives.
- Tighter rules over the activities of financial intermediaries, such as mortgage brokers, hedge funds, and credit rating agencies.
- The U.S. government is no longer allowed to bail out financially troubled organizations.
- Shareholders now have a greater say on the levels of executive compensation.

Overall, these new rules and regulations were intended to provide consumer protection by imposing more restrictions on the activities of organizations that operate in the financial services marketplace.

Only time will tell if this will help to forestall a similar economic crisis in the future. While there is a continuing debate over whether the *Dodd-Frank Act* should be repealed, there is evidence that it is working effectively. For example, on July 13, 2016, Michael Coscia, a commodities trader,[32] was sentenced[33] to three years in prison plus two years of supervised release for six convictions for commodities fraud and six for "spoofing ... where orders—bids to buy and offers to sell—are placed with the intent of cancelling the trade before execution. So the markets get spoofed. Fooled. Manipulated."

Bernard Madoff—If It's Too Good to Be True

Carlo Ponzi (1882–1949) invented a clever scheme of defrauding investors that now bears his name. In 1920, Ponzi established a company in Boston to buy foreign postage coupons and convert them into cash. Such a business was legal. The way he operated the business was not. He promised phenomenal returns to investors: 50% in six weeks. He did this by using the money of subsequent investors to pay off the early investors. Referred to as a "pyramid scheme," its success depends on having a large number of subsequent people invest in the plan. In Ponzi's case, many reinvested rather than take their profits. The fraud cheated thousands of investors out of millions of dollars. Ponzi was convicted of eighty-six counts of mail fraud and sent to prison.

In the subsequent years, there have been hundreds of other Ponzi schemes around the world. Although there are many variations, the basic design is always the same. Investors are duped into believing that they can make above-normal returns by investing their money with the fraudster.[34] However, the man who perfected the Ponzi scam was Bernard Madoff, who defrauded investors of billions of dollars.[35]

Madoff was an important and influential Wall Street stockbroker and financial advisor. He ran a successful investment firm, was a governor of the National Association of

---

[32] Jennifer Wells, "A Part of the Dodd-Frank Worth Saving," *Toronto Star*, December 30, 2015, S8.

[33] Michael Hirtzer and Tom Polansek, "First U.S. trader convicted of spoofing sentenced to three years in jail," Reuters, July 13, 2016, http://www.reuters.com/article/us-court-spoofing-sentence-idUSKCN0ZT232

[34] For a variation on this form of swindle, see Hans Christian Anderson, "The Emperor's New Clothes," in *Fairy Tales*, trans. Tiina Nummally (New York: Viking, 2004).

[35] See also the ethics case "Bernie Madoff Scandal—The King of the Ponzi Schemes" at the end of this chapter.

Securities Dealers (NASD), and made substantial donations to worthwhile charities and political campaigns. His investment business promised and delivered (to some) above-normal returns, as high as 1% a month. But it was an exclusive club. People would petition to have him handle their money, and he would often decline. Those whom he did accept as clients were honored and pleased and did not question Madoff. His list of clients included A-level Hollywood stars, universities, charitable organizations, hedge funds, and even some international banks.

The first warning of a fraud occurred in 1999 with a report to the SEC by Harry Markopolos, a finance expert. His analysis revealed that it was mathematically impossible for Madoff to have paid the returns he claimed to have paid. However, the SEC ignored Markopolos's report. In 2004, the SEC began to investigate some anomalies in some of the reports Madoff had filed with the commission. But this investigation was subsequently dropped. The end came as a consequence of the 2007 financial collapse. Investors were seeking their money, but there was none available. Madoff owed clients over $7 billion. On December 11, 2008, Madoff was arrested and charged with fraud. The extent of the fraud was still not known; estimates varied from $10 billion to $65 billion. But in 2009, the seventy-one-year-old Madoff was convicted and sent to jail for 150 years. Five years later, in 2013, the Madoff Ponzi fraud was estimated to have cost $17 billion, in total, of which $9 billion had been recovered.[36]

See the ethics case "Bernie Madoff Scandal: The King of the Ponzi Schemes" at the end of this chapter.

Ponzi schemes work because many people are looking for something for nothing, and the fraudster gives them nothing for something. Even investors who should have known better were deceived. They should have known that the "clothes" that were being offered for sale did not exist. The old adage—if it's too good to be true, it probably is—is advice that all investors should follow. Otherwise, they will discover that they too are walking naked beside the Emperor in his new clothes.

Public Disillusionment: The Occupy Movement

Most corporate directors, executives, and shareholders understand that corporate interests can be influenced directly by members of the public or indirectly by public pressure on political processes and regulators. Events in 2010 and 2011 provided new evidence of the success of these pressures, which should give members of the corporate world cause to reflect carefully on those practices considered by many to be questionable or unethical. In many ways, these pressures are likely to be harbingers of future developments.

The Occupy Movement began on September 17, 2011, in New York City when protestors massed in Zuccotti Park and declared an occupation of Wall Street in a demonstration against economic disparities and lack of corporate accountability. Within three weeks, the Occupy Movement protests had spread worldwide to over 1,500 cities, towns, and communities in over eighty countries and involving thousands of people.

Some observers have claimed that the impetus for the Occupy Movement came from the success of the Arab Spring movement in the Middle East and North Africa. In December 2010, the Tunisian people rose in protest against the longtime presidency of Zine El Abidine Ben Ali, who subsequently fled to Saudi Arabia in January 2011. Throughout 2011, there were protests and riots that led to the overthrow of governments

[36] Jordan Maglich,"Madoff Ponzi Scheme, Five Years Later," *Forbes*, December 9, 2013, accessed August 8, 2016, at http://www.forbes.com/sites/jordanmaglich/2013/12/09/madoff-ponzi-scheme-five-years-later/#3c7766ac789f.

in Tunisia, Libya, Egypt, and Yemen; civil war in Syria; and civil unrest in more than a dozen other Arab countries. The protests were both political and economic, and, as in so much of the world, these two are very closely related. The protestors, mainly the young and unemployed, were angry about social, political, and economic injustices. Government corruption, high unemployment, poor living conditions, and the lack of social and political freedoms are endemic in these countries. Vast inequalities of income had been created by business elites and supported by the government. Arab Spring protests were about both political and economic injustices and the lack of accountability by politicians and the rich.[37]

Then, on September 17, 2011, in New York City, a similar protest occurred. Called the Occupy Movement, it was a protest against "Wall Street banks, big corporations, and others among the 1% [who] are claiming the world's wealth for themselves at the expense of the 99% and having their way with our governments."[38] Within three weeks, the Occupy Movement had spread like wildfire. Surveys revealed that tens of millions of people supported the movement and their general contention that most people were not to blame for the subprime mortgage meltdown, the ensuing poor economy, and the financial bankruptcy of governments around the world.[39] It was the small percentage, the 1%, who were to blame. These were the business leaders who had shirked their ethical responsibilities by focusing on their own personal prosperity at the expense of their companies and society as a whole. Business was seen not to be creating wealth for society. It was seen to be creating wealth for the few.

Prime examples of economic injustice were the excessive compensation packages that senior executives were taking while their companies' financial performance deteriorated. These pay packages indicated short-term self-interest by executives who were being paid disproportionately large sums relative to the average worker. In 1980, CEOs on average were paid forty-two times more than the average worker, but by 2012, CEOs were receiving 354 times more than the average worker.[40] The greed of business leaders was typified by Richard Fuld, the CEO of Lehman Brothers. His one-year compensation in 2007, the year before Lehman Brothers declared bankruptcy, was $22 million. (See the ethics case "Lehman Brothers Repo 105 Manipulations" at the end of Chapter 8.) Business leaders were not showing the leadership that was expected, and the general public knew that executives were concerned more with their own financial welfare than with the financial welfare of the organizations that they oversaw. Business was seen to be letting down society, and many in society wanted better.

Shareholder Disillusionment: Shareholder Resolutions

The disenchantment with business was not restricted to students, the unemployed, the disenfranchised, and the disillusioned. Shareholders were also angry at the levels of compensation that was being drawn by senior executives, especially as the profits of those companies were flagging. This gave rise to the so-called say-on-pay shareholder resolution movement.

Shareholders who disapprove of management, the board, and/or the firm's performance have two options. They can vote with their feet by selling their shares, or they

[37] Anya Schiffrin and Eamon Kircher-Allen, eds., *From Cairo to Wall Street: Voices from the Global Spring* (New York: New Press, 2012).

[38] Sarah van Gelder, ed., *This Changes Everything: Occupy Wall Street and the 99% Movement* (San Francisco: Berrett-Koehler, 2011), 1.

[39] Ibid.

[40] Melanie Trottman, Melanie, "Corporate Pay = 354 Workers," *Wall Street Journal*, April 13, 2013.

can fight for change by putting forward shareholder resolutions that will be voted on at annual general meetings. Shareholder resolutions are attempts by dissident shareholders to correct the perceived incorrect behavior of management with respect to running the firm.

Shareholders have raised many issues through shareholder resolutions, but they can be classified into five basic areas:

- *Environmental issues* address such topics as climate change, renewable energy, pollution, and hazardous waste.
- *Social issues* include human rights, worker safety, codes of ethical conduct, and philanthropy.
- *Governance issues* include the role and function of the board directors, including how they are elected and remunerated.
- *Transparency resolutions* call for greater stakeholder engagement and communication, especially with respect to risk disclosures.
- *Compensation issues* involve the composition and amount of pay given to senior managers.

In 2010, the U.S. Congress passed the *Dodd-Frank Wall Street Reform and Consumer Protection Act.* Part of the act permitted greater shareholder involvement by allowing shareholders to vote on whether they approve of the pay packages of senior executives. Called "say-on-pay," they are nonbinding shareholder resolutions concerning executive compensation. Similar say-on-pay legislation was passed in the United Kingdom and Australia. No such legislation exists in Canada, although many Canadian firms accept say-on-pay shareholder resolutions.

The LIBOR Scandal: How Banks Manipulated a Benchmark Interest Rate

The LIBOR rate scandal of 2012 is a story of systematic manipulation of a benchmark interest rate, supported by a culture of fraud in the world's biggest banks, in an environment where little or no regulation prevailed. After decades of abuse that enriched the big banks, their shareholders, executives, and traders at the expense of others, investigations and lawsuits were initiated, and huge penalties have been assessed.

The London Interbank Offered Rate (LIBOR) is a rate of interest, first computed in 1985 by the British Banking Association (BBA), the Bank of England, and others, to serve as a readily available reference or benchmark rate for many financial contracts and arrangements. Prior to its creation, contracts utilized many privately negotiated rates that were difficult to verify and not necessarily related to the market rate for the security in question. The LIBOR rate, which is the average interest rate estimated by leading banks that they would be charged if they were to borrow from other banks, provided a simple alternative that came to be widely used. For example, in the United States in 2008, when the subprime lending crisis began, around 60% of prime adjustable-rate mortgages and nearly all subprime mortgages were indexed to the U.S. dollar LIBOR.[41,42] In 2012, around 45% of prime adjustable rate mortgages, and over 80% of

[41] Mark Schweitzer and Guhan Venkatu, "Adjustable-Rate Mortgages and the Libor Surprise," Federal Reserve Bank of Cleveland, January 21, 2009, archived from the original on January 24, 2009.

[42] Dylan Matthews, "Ezra Klein's WonkBlog: Explainer: Why the LIBOR Scandal Is a Bigger Deal Than JPMorgan." *Washington Post*, July 5, 2012.

subprime mortgages were indexed to the LIBOR.[43,44] American municipalities also borrowed around 75% of their money through financial products that were linked to the LIBOR.[45]

At the time of the LIBOR scandal, eighteen of the largest banks in the world provided their estimates of the costs they would have had to pay for a variety of interbank loans (loans from other banks) just prior to 11:00 a.m. on the submission day. These estimates were submitted to the Reuters news agency (which acted for the BBA) for calculation of the average and its publication, and dissemination. Reuters set aside the four highest and four lowest estimates and averaged the remaining ten. The banks[46] submitting their estimates in 2012 included the following:

- Bank of America
- Bank of Tokyo-Mitsubishi UFJ
- Barclays Bank
- BNP Paribas
- Citibank NA
- Credit Agricole CIB
- Credit Suisse
- Deutsche Bank
- HSBC
- JP Morgan Chase
- Lloyds Bank
- Rabobank
- Royal Bank of Canada
- Société Générale
- Sumitomo Mitsui Bank
- Norinchukin Bank
- Royal Bank of Scotland
- UBS AG

So huge were the investments affected[47] that a small manipulation in the LIBOR rate had a very significant impact on the profit of the banks and of the traders involved in the manipulation. For example, in 2012, the total of derivatives priced relative to the LIBOR rate has been estimated at from $300 trillion to $600 trillion, so a manipulation of 0.1% in the LIBOR rate would generate an error of $300 million to 600 million per annum. Consequently, it is not surprising that once the manipulations came to light, the settlements and fines assessed were huge. By June 30, 2016, ten of the eighteen submitting banks have been charged with manipulation and have paid the fines and settlements indicated in Table 2.1. In addition, the European Commission gave immunity for revealing wrongdoing to the following banks, thereby allowing them to avoid fines: Barclays, €690 million; UBS, €2.5 billion; and Citigroup, €55 million.

HOW THE LIBOR SCANDAL CAME TO LIGHT Insiders to the banking system knew about the manipulation of LIBOR rate submissions for decades, but changes were not made until the public became aware of the problem and until the U.S. Department of Justice forced the U.K. government to act.

Timothy Geithner, president of the New York Federal Reserve Bank, emailed Mervyn King, governor of the Bank of England, on June 1, 2008, suggesting ways to "enhance" LIBOR.[48] Although ensuing emails report agreement on the suggestions and

---

[43] Schweitzer and Venkatu, "Adjustable-Rate Mortgages and the Libor Surprise."

[44] Guhan Venkatu, "How Many U.S. Mortgages Are Linked to Libor?" Federal Reserve Bank of Cleveland, accessed June 30, 2013, at http://www.clevelandfed.org/research/trends/2012/0712/01banfin.cfm.

[45] Nathaniel Popper, "Rate Scandal Stirs Scramble for Damages," *New York Times*, July 10, 2012, accessed June 30, 2013, at http://dealbook.nytimes.com/2012/07/10/Libor-rate-rigging-scandal-sets-off-legal-fights-for-restitution/?_r=0.

[46] Edward V. Murphy, *LIBOR: Frequently Asked Questions*, July 16, 2012, accessed June 30, 2013, at http://www.fas.org/sgp/crs/misc/R42608.pdf.

[47] Liam Vaughan and Gavin Finch, "Libor Lies Revealed in Rigging of $300 Trillion Benchmark," *Bloomberg Markets Magazine*, January 28, 2013, accessed June 30, 2013, at http://www.bloomberg.com/news/2013-01-28/Libor-lies-revealed-in-rigging-of-300-trillion-benchmark.html.

[48] "Libor Email from Timothy Geithner to Bank of England," *The Guardian*, July 13, 2012, accessed June 30, 2013, at http://www.guardian.co.uk/business/interactive/2012/jul/13/Libor-email-timothy-geithner-bank-england.

TABLE 2.1 LIBOR Charges & Settlements* to June 30, 2016

	DEUTSCHE BANK	LLOYD'S BANKING GROUP	BARCLAY'S	RABO-BANK	ROYAL BANK OF SCOTLAND	UBS AG	SOCIÉTÉ GÉNÉRALE	J.P. MORGAN	CITI-GROUP
Fine Total US/£/€	$2,500 €725	$370	$453.6	$1,000	$612 £391	$1.5	€446	€80 €62	€70
No. Charged	6		4			1			
No. Convicted			4			1			
US Dept. of Justice	$775	$86	$160	$325	$475 shared	$500			
US Commodity Futures Trading Commission	$800	$105	$200	$475	$475 shared	$700			
UK Fin. Conduct Authority	£227	£105	$93.6	£105	£87.5	$260			
European Commission	€725 2013				£391		£446	€142	€70
Other Agencies	NY Dept. of Fin. Services $600		UK Serious Fraud Office 2016	Dutch Authorities $96		Swiss Fin. Markets $65			
Year(s)	2013, 2015	2014	2012, 2016	2013	2013	2012	2013	2013,14	2013
Sources	e, f	l	a, b, n, o, p	l, j	a, c, e	a, d	e	e, m	e

Sources: (*Over $10 Million – All figures in Millions)

[a]"Banks in Libor rigging case face huge EU fines: Official sends a warning signal that it is seeking settlements," Neil Behrmann, *The Business Times*, February 23, 2013, accessed August 20, 2013, at http://search.proquest.com/docview/1305030162?accountid=44262.

[b]"The Libor Settlements", Margot Patrick, The Wall Street Journal, February 13, 2013, accessed July 11, 2013, at http://online.wsj.com/article/SB10001424127887324616604578302321485831886.html.

[c]"RBS and Libor: The wrong stuff: A widening scandal threatens to suck in more banks, and ruin more careers," *The Economist*, February 9, 2013, accessed July 14, 2013, at http://www.economist.com/news/finance-and-economics/21571446-widening-scandal-threatens-suck-more-banks-and-ruin-more-careers-wrong/print.

[d]"As Unit Pleads Guilty, UBS Pays $1.5 Billion Over Rate Rigging," Mark Scott and Ben Protess, Dealbook, *New York Times*, December 19, 2012, accessed July 14, 2013, at http://dealbook.nytimes.com/2012/12/19/as-unit-pleads-guilty-ubs-pays-1-5-billion-in-fines-over-rate-rigging

[e]"Antitrust: Commission fines banks € 1.71 billion for participating in cartels in the interest rate derivatives industry" (Press release). Brussels: European Commission, December 4, 2013), accessed February 13, 2014, at http://europa.eu/rapid/press-release_IP-13-1208_en.htm.

[f]"Deutsche Bank pays record fine for Libor manipulation," FT Reporters, *The Financial Times*, April 23, 2015, accessed February 15, 2016, at http://www.ft.com/cms/s/0/ccf7af08-e904-11e4-a71a-00144feab7de.html#axzz40HhuYOeH.

[g]"U.S. and British Officials Fine ICAP in Libor Case," Mark Scott and Julia Werdigier, Dealbook, *New York Times*, September 25, 2013, accessed February 18, 2016, at http://dealbook.nytimes.com/2013/09/25/icap-to-pay-87-million-fine-in-libor-fixing-case/.

[h]"These are the Brokers Cleared of Helping Tom Hayes Rig Libor: Six ex-brokers accused of helping convicted trader Tom Hayes fix the benchmark Libor interest rate have been acquitted by a London court," Liam Vaughan, *Bloomberg Business*, January 28, 2016, accessed February 18, 2016, at http://www.bloomberg.com/features/2016-libor-trial-brokers/.

[i]"Dutch Bank Settles Case Over Libor Deceptions," Chad Bray, Dealbook, *New York Times*, October 29, 2013, accessed February 18, 2016, at http://dealbook.nytimes.com/2013/10/29/rabobank-to-pay-more-than-1-billion-in-libor-settlement-chairman-resigns/.

[j]"Rabobank fined $1bn over Libor," *BBC News*, October 29, 2013, accessed February 18, 2016 at http://www.bbc.com/news/business-24730242

[k]"RP Martin Fined $2.2 Million in Libor Rigging," Chad Bray, Dealbook, *New York Times*, May 15, 2014, accessed February 18, 2016 at http://dealbook.nytimes.com/2014/05/15/rp-martin-fined-more-than-2-million-in-libor-inquiry/.

[l]"Lloyds Banking Group Admits Wrongdoing in LIBOR Investigation, Agrees to Pay $86 Million Criminal Penalty," U.S. Dept. of Justice, *Justice News*, July 28, 2014, accessed February 18, 2016, at http://www.justice.gov/opa/pr/lloyds-banking-group-admits-wrongdoing-libor-investigation-agrees-pay-86-million-criminal.

[m]"Antitrust: Commission settles RBS-JPMorgan cartel in derivatives based on Swiss franc LIBOR; imposes € 61.6 million fine on JPMorgan" (Press release). Brussels: European Commission., October 21, 2014), accessed February 18, 2016, at http://europa.eu/rapid/press-release_IP-14-1189_en.htm.

[n]"Ten Ex-Deutsche Bank, Barclays Traders Charged in Euribor Probe," Suzi Ring, November 13, 2015, *Bloomberg Business*, http://www.bloomberg.com/news/articles/2015-11-13/ten-ex-deutsche-bank-barclays-euribor-traders-charged-in-u-k-

[o]"Libor-rigging trial: jury finds no defence in 'just doing my job,'" Simon Bowers, July 4, 2016, *The Guardian*, https://www.theguardian.com/business/2016/jul/04/barclays-libor-convictions-a-major-victory-for-sfo.

[p]"Convicted LIBOR manipulators sentenced," Serious Fraud Office, July 7, 2016, *News Releases*, https://www.sfo.gov.uk/2016/07/07/convicted-libor-manipulators-sentenced/

articles appeared, for example, in the *Wall Street Journal* from 2008 to 2011, serious changes were not applied until October 2012, when the U.K. government accepted the recommendations of the *Wheatley Review of LIBOR*.[49] This review by Martin Wheatley, Managing Director of the British Financial Services Authority, was commissioned in June 2012 in view of investigations, charges, and settlements that were raising public awareness of LIBOR deficiencies.[50]

One of the motivations for creating the *Wheatley Review* involved the prosecution of former UBS and later Citigroup Inc. trader Tom Hayes for criminal fraud charges for manipulating the LIBOR rates. But it appears that the United States may have forced the United Kingdom to act. In December 2012, the U.S. Department of Justice charged Hayes and a colleague, but on the day before, he was arrested near London by the U.K. Serious Fraud Office, which seized his passport and then released him on bail. This meant that the Department of Justice would likely be unable to extradite Hayes to the United States to face charges, and department officials complained to the press, thus alerting the public.[51] Ultimately, on June 18, 2013, the *Wall Street Journal* announced that the U.K. Serious Fraud Office in London was about to charge Hayes.[52] Hayes, known to insiders as the "Rain Man" for his abilities and demeanor, allegedly sought his superiors' approval before attempting to influence the LIBOR rates—an act that some observers thought might provide a strong defense against conviction. Others believed that if Hayes pleaded guilty to some U.K. charges, he would avoid deportation to the United States, where possible penalties are much stiffer than in the United Kingdom.[53] In fact, Hayes was arrested in the United Kingdom in December 2012, convicted in August 2015, and sentenced to fourteen years in prison. In late 2015, on appeal, his sentence was reduced to eleven years in prison. He also faces a clawback of the proceeds of his crime.[54]

Insiders who knew of LIBOR manipulations were generally reluctant to take a public stand for earlier change. However, on July 27, 2012, Douglas Keenan, a former trader for Morgan Stanley in London, published an article that told of his earlier attempts to bring LIBOR rate manipulations to the attention of authorities, but without success.[55] In his article, he indicated how he learned as a new trader in 1991 that the banks manipulated their rate submissions to make profit on specific contracts and to mask liquidity problems, such as during the subprime lending crisis of 2008. For example, if the LIBOR rate submissions were misstated to be low, the discounted valuation of related assets would be raised, thus providing misleadingly higher levels of short-term, near-cash assets than should have been reported.

---

[49] "Government Accepts Recommendation from the *Wheatley Review of LIBOR* in Full," October 17, 2012, accessed June 30, 2012, at https://www.gov.uk/government/news/government-accepts-recommendations-from-the-wheatley-review-of-Libor-in-full.

[50] "Wheatley Review May Mean Big Changes for LIBOR," accessed June 30, 2013, at http://www.blakes.com/English/Resources/Bulletins/Pages/Details.aspx?BulletinID=1516.

[51] Ibid.

[52] David Enrich, "U.K. to File Fraud Charges in Libor Probe," *Wall Street Journal* as published in *The Globe and Mail*, June 18, 2013, B10.

[53] Ibid.

[54] Reuters, "Libor Trader Tom Hayes Loses Appeal but Has Jail Sentence Cut to 11 Years," December 21, 2015, http://www.theguardian.com/business/2015/dec/21/libor-trader-tom-hayes-loses-appeal-but-has-jail-sentence-cut-to-11-years. Sean Farrell and Reuters, *The Guardian*, "Jailed Libor trader Tom Hayes must pay more than £878,000," https://www.theguardian.com/uk-news/2016/mar/23/jailed-libor-trader-tom-hayes-must-pay-878000-pounds.

[55] Douglas Keenan, "My Thwarted Attempt to Tell of Libor Shenanigans,", *Financial Times*, July 27, 2012, accessed June 30, 2013, at http://www.informath.org/media/a72/b1.pdf.

EXAMPLES OF LOSSES CAUSED BY LIBOR MANIPULATIONS *Manipulation of home mortgage rates:* Many home owners borrow their mortgage loans on a variable- or adjustable-rate basis rather than a fixed-rate basis. Consequently, many of these borrowers receive a new rate at the first of every month based on the LIBOR rate. A study prepared for a class action lawsuit has shown that on the first of each month for 2007–2009, the LIBOR rate rose more than 7.5 basis points on average.[56] One observer estimated that each LIBOR submitting bank may be liable for as much as $2.3 billion.[57]

Municipalities lose on interest rate swaps: Municipalities raise funds through the issue of bonds, and many were encouraged to issue variable-rate rather than fixed-rate bonds to take advantage of lower interest payments. For example, the saving could be as much as $1 million on a $100 million bond.[58] After issue, the municipalities were encouraged to buy interest rate swaps from their investment banks to hedge their risk of volatility in the variable rates by converting or swapping into a fixed-rate arrangement. The seller of the swap agrees to pay the municipality for any requirement to pay interest at more than the fixed rate agreed on if interest rates rise, but if interest rates fall, the swap seller buys the bonds at the lower variable interest rate. However, the variable rate was linked to the LIBOR rate, which was artificially depressed, thus costing U.S. municipalities as much as $10 billion.[59] A class action suit has been launched to recover these losses,[60] which "may have cost municipalities, hospitals, and other non-profits as much as $600 million a year,"[61] and although many of the claims were initially rejected by the courts, on May 23, 2106 a New York Appeals Court reversed that decision.[62] Regardless of the final court determination, the remaining liability is expected to assist the municipalities in further settlement negotiations.[63]

Freddie Mac losses: On March 27, 2013, Freddie Mac sued fifteen banks for their losses of up to $3 billion due to LIBOR rate manipulations. Freddie Mac accused the banks of

> fraud, violations of antitrust law and breach of contract, and is seeking unspecified damages for the financial harm, as well as punitive damages and treble damages for violations of the *Sherman Act*. To the extent that defendants used false and dishonest USD LIBOR submissions to bolster their respective

[56] "Banks Rigged Libor to Inflate Adjustable-Rate Mortgages: Lawsuit, Halah Touryala," *Forbes*, October 15, 2012, accessed June 30, 2013, at http://www.forbes.com/sites/halahtouryalai/2012/10/15/banks-rigged-Libor-to-inflate-adjustable-rate-mortgages-lawsuit/.

[57] Ibid.

[58] Stephen Gandel, "Wall Street's Latest Sucker: Your Hometown," *Fortune*, July 11, 2012, accessed June 30, 2013, at http://finance.fortune.cnn.com/2012/07/11/Libor-sucker-hometowns/.

[59] Darrell Preston, "Rigged LIBOR Hits Sates-Localities with $6 Billion: Muni Credit," *Bloomberg*, October 9, 2012, accessed June 30, 2013, at http://www.bloomberg.com/news/2012-10-09/rigged-Libor-hits-states-localities-with-6-billion-muni-credit.html.

[60] Michael A Fletcher, "Baltimore Takes Lead in Suit against Banks over Alleged Libor Manipulation," *Washington Post*, July 11, 2012, accessed June 30, 2013, at http://articles.washingtonpost.com/2012-07-11/business/35488816_1_Libor-interest-rates-deutsche-bank.

[61] Gandel, "Wall Street's Latest Sucker."

[62] Jonathan Stempel, "Big Banks Lose as U.S. Appeals Court Revives Libor Lawsuits," Reuters, May 23, 2106, accessed August 2, 2016, at http://www.reuters.com/article/us-libor-banks-decision-idUSKCN0YE212.

[63] Reuters, "Judge Rejects Much of Libor Lawsuit against Banks," Reuters, *New York Times*, March 29, 2013, accessed June 30, 2013, at http://www.nytimes.com/2013/03/30/business/global/judge-rejects-much-of-Libor-lawsuit-against-banks.html.

reputations, they artificially increased their ability to charge higher underwriting fees and obtain higher offering prices for financial products to the detriment of Freddie Mac and other consumers.[64]

Liability claims/antitrust cases (commodities-manipulations claims): Other organizations have also sued the LIBOR rate submitting banks for anticompetitive behavior, partly because of the possibility of treble damages, but they must demonstrate related damages to be successful. Nonetheless, credible plaintiffs include the Regents of the University of California, who have filed a suit claiming fraud, deceit, and unjust enrichment.[65] Time will tell the extent and value of these losses.

Bribery Attracts Prosecutions and Huge Fines

Bribery has been a common practice for centuries. What has changed dramatically since 2008 is the increase in level of prosecution by U.S., British, and German governments and the increase in the size of the fines and settlements corporations are facing. These two developments have made combating bribery a very important priority for corporations, executives, and their boards of directors and a key element in risk management programs. *Corporations are extremely reluctant to face the large fines that follow conviction and are wary of the loss of reputation that a conviction can bring as well as the possibility of being barred from seeking government contracts for a period of time.* For many executives, being involved in bribery is more likely than it was in the past to result in dismissal or jail. Whistleblowers are being encouraged to come forward, and in some cases amnesty has been offered to employees if they come forward and admit instances of bribery.

Increased scrutiny for bribery is not only within the borders of the prosecuting country; the major countries—the United States, the United Kingdom, and Germany—are now prosecuting for acts of bribery beyond their borders. Due to the urging of Transparency International, the member countries of the Organization for Economic Cooperation and Development created legislation similar to the *U.S. Foreign Corrupt Practices Act* and have now begun to pursue violators. Influenced by aggressive prosecutions by the United States, the United Kingdom designed its *Bribery Act* to assert its jurisdiction over any act anywhere by any company that had presence in the United Kingdom. In Germany, where bribery by German companies had long been legal and tax deductible outside of its borders but illegal and not tax deductible in Germany, German companies were suddenly prosecuted for worldwide bribery. See further discussion of bribery in Chapter 7.

High-profile cases have frequently been in the news, including those noted in Table 2.2.

Automaker's Sins Come Home to Roost

In 2013–2014, three significant examples of incredibly scandalous behavior by automakers came to light, providing evidence that automakers or parts manufacturers knew

---

[64] Tom Schoenberg and Andrew Zajac, "Freddie Mac Sues Multiple Banks over Libor Manipulations," *Bloomberg*, March 20, 2013, accessed June 30, 2013, at http://www.bloomberg.com/news/2013-03-19/freddie-mac-sues-multiple-banks-over-Libor-manipulation.html.

[65] Keri Geiger, "Economists Tackle Puzzle of Libor Losses for Investors," *Bloomberg*, June 26, 2013, accessed July 1, 2013, at http://www.bloomberg.com/news/2013-06-27/economists-build-Libor-time-machines-as-losses-puzzle-investors.html.

TABLE 2.2 High Profile Bribery Prosecutions

DATE	COMPANY–BRIBERY IN	FINE/ SETTLEMENT	JURISDICTION	CASE AT PAGE
2007-8	Siemens—worldwide	€418 million	European Commission	xx
2016		€201 million	European Commission	
		$800 million	U.S.	
		$43 million	Israel (7)	
2010	DaimlerChrysler—worldwide	$185 million	U.S.	xx
2012	Wal-Mart—Mexico	$4.5 billion, est.(1)	U.S.	xx
2012	SNC-Lavalin—worldwide	Unknown (2)	Canada	Xx
2014	Alstom—global	$772 million (3)	U.S. (4)	
2014	Petrobas—Brazil	To be determined (5)	U.S.(4)	
2014	GlazoSmithKline (GSK)—China	$490 million (3)	China [UK co. in China]	
2015-6	Electrobras—Brazil	To be determined (6)	Brazil (6)	

Source: Source notes are located in www.cengage.com/brooks.

[1]Still under investigation; estimated fine could be as high as $4.5 billion per "Mexican Bribery Scandal Could Cost Wal-Mart $4.5 Billion; Shares Down 4.7%," Abram Brown, *Forbes*, April 23, 2012, accessed December 11, 2013, at http://www.forbes.com/sites/abrambrown/2012/04/23/spooked-investors-sink-wal-mart-nearly-5-after-bribery-revelations-at-least-4-5b-penalty-likely/.

[2]At February 19, 2016, investigations are still underway. Proceedings are expected to resume February 26, 2016. See "SNC-Lavalin fraud case with links to Libya put off until February [2016]," October 16, 2015, *Canadian Press*, *The Globe and Mail*, accessed February 19, 2016 at http://www.theglobeandmail.com/report-on-business/industry-news/the-law-page/snc-lavalin-fraud-case-with-links-to-libya-put-off-until-february/article26842703/.

[3]See "The anti-bribery business: As the enforcement of laws against corporate bribery increases, there are risks that it may go too far," May 9, 2015, *The Economist*, accessed February 19, 2016, at http://www.economist.com/news/business/21650557-enforcement-laws-against-corporate-bribery-increases-there-are-risks-it-may-go.

[4]French company with a U.S. presence fined under the U.S. Foreign Corrupt Practices Act (FCPA) for an alleged $72 million of bribes to obtain power-plant contracts in the Middle East, Indonesia, Taiwan and other countries. See "Alstom to Pay Record $772 Million in U.S. Bribery Settlement," December 22, 2014, Tom Schoenberg and David McLaughlin, *Bloomberg Business*, accessed February 19, 2016, at http://www.bloomberg.com/news/articles/2014-12-22/alstom-to-pay-record-772-million-in-u-s-bribery-settlement.

[5]At February 19, 2016, investigations are still underway. Trading on the New York Stock Exchange, Petrobras can be fined under the FCPA.

[6]At February 19, 2016, investigations of several Electrobras dam projects are still underway. Report expected March, 2016. Trading on the New York Stock Exchange, Electrobras can be fined under the FCPA. See "Internal investigation of Brazil's Eletrobras expands—source," January 7, 2015, Caroline Stauffer and Phil Berlowitz [editor], Reuters, accessed February 19, 2016, at http://af.reuters.com/article/commoditiesNews/idAFL1N13W21720160107.

[7]In a ten-year old case, Siemens pays fine in Israel. See "Corruption Currents: Siemens to Pay $43 Million Fine in Israel", May 4, 2016, Samuel Rubenfeld, *Wall Street Journal*, accessed July 26, 2016, at http://blogs.wsj.com/riskandcompliance/2016/05/03/corruption-currents-siemens-to-pay-43-million-fine-in-israel/.

that they were endangering lives or breaking laws long before they informed the public or regulators and took meaningful action on the problems to protect the public. As a result, the impact on victims and the ultimate impact on the companies themselves were increased dramatically in the following instances:

- *General Motors (GM) installed faulty ignition switches:* On February 7, 2014, GM recalled over 800,000 Chevrolet Cobalts and Pontiac G5s and in June 2014 recalled a further 8.45 million cars for correction of faulty ignition switches. The fault in the ignition switches was serious in that jiggling the keys with a knee or something similar could cause the engine to shut off, thereby disabling the power steering and causing drivers to lose control of the vehicle. *The problem was known by GM before the switch went into production in 2005 and would have cost 57 cents per switch to fix*—instead, over 150 people died. GM paid a fine of $900 million in 2015, and settled some civil lawsuits with aggrieved family members and angry investors for approximately $575 million. The recall cost GM over $3 billion in shareholder value over four weeks. Sales lost due to disenchanted GM customers are not known. The Ethics Case *General Motors Ignores Obvious Faults* at the end of this chapter expands on the GM's ignition switch difficulties.[66]

- *Takata air bags explode, injuring passengers with metal shrapnel:* By mid-February 2016, faulty Takata air bags had been installed in 34 million vehicles in the United States and in an additional 7 million worldwide. When deployed, the resulting air bag explosion could project metal pieces like shrapnel from a bomb that could kill or severely harm those in the car. *According to a potential whistleblowing engineer, he warned the company in 1999 that it was using too volatile and risky a propellant for cost reasons. Tests in 2004 confirmed the problems, but the company reportedly delayed reporting them to regulators for four years and put off serious recalls until 2013.* Initially, the company delayed by arguing that only air bags in hot, high-humidity climates were likely to be affected, and the propellant was changed to a less volatile alternative in 2008. As of September 2015, faulty Takata air bags had caused at least 139 injuries, including two deaths, and Honda dropped Takata as a supplier. Ultimately, U.S. fines could top more than $200 million. Civil lawsuits are certain to be significant.[67]
- *Volkswagen (VW) software defeats environmental exhaust emissions testing:* Faced with competitors such as Mercedes-Benz that had developed environmentally friendly diesel engines, VW needed to come up with a competitive response or else face repudiation in the marketplace. VW developed a new "clean diesel" system in 2009, but it could not operate in compliance with U.S. environmental limits except with very poor gas mileage and poor performance characteristics. VW's solution was to install a computer software switch that, when government emission tests were started, would alter the engine performance characteristics during the tests from high performance/high emission to low emission/low performance. VW "clean diesels" actually won several environmental awards, even though they were polluting at up to forty times the allowable limits. However, this software deception was discovered in 2014 by scientists at West Virginia University who disclosed their results at a public forum that came to the attention of the U.S. Environmental Protection Agency, which repeated the tests, questioned VW, and triggered VW's halt of sales of some diesels and the production of others, an internal investigation, and the resignation of the CEO as well as a recall of many autos. In September 2015, VW stock sank by 20% and then another 17%, and $7.3 billion was allocated to cover the recalls, refits, and other costs of the scandal. The amount of fines and the cost of settling civil lawsuits will not be known for some time. *It is evident that many VW employees and managers knew of this illegal deception of cheating on emissions standards*

---

[66] David Ingram, Nate Raymond, and Joseph White, "GM to Pay $900 Million, Settle U.S. Criminal Case over Ignition Switches—Sources," September 17, 2015, https://ca.finance.yahoo.com/news/gm-pay-900-million-settle-004103824.html; Jessica Dye, "GM Also Resolves Civil Lawsuits over Ignition-Switch Defect," September 17, 2015, https://ca.finance.yahoo.com/news/gm-resolves-civil-lawsuits-over-192504285.html.

[67] Clifford Atiyeh, "Takata Engineer Who Warned of "Catastrophic Failures" Willing to Testify against Company," February 5, 2015, http://blog.caranddriver.com/takata-engineer-who-warned-of-catastrophic-failures-willing-to-testify-against-company; Clifford Atiyeh and Rusty Blackwell, "Massive Takata Airbag Recall: Everything You Need to Know, Including Full List of Affected Vehicles," February 16, 2016, http://blog.caranddriver.com/massive-takata-airbag-recall-everything-you-need-to-know-including-full-list-of-affected-vehicles.

from before 2009 to 2014, thus putting the company at great financial and reputation risk. VW's difficulties with their software defeat of emission testing are expanded on in the Ethics Case *VW Cheats on Emissions Tests* at the end of this chapter.[68]

Such cavalier behavior by auto manufacturers that endangers lives and the interests of families, the environment, investors, workers, and others is hard to understand. That management kept such behavior secret for long periods of time, harming many more than need be, is also hard to fathom. But these decisions were clearly due to the failure of VW's governance processes to create an ethical culture that set out ethics standards and encouraged them to be met, proper monitoring and remuneration procedures, and adequate penalties for failure to comply.

Drugmakers Raise Prices, Gouging Patients

The year 2015 brought two startling cases to light where extremely important drugs were acquired by companies that subsequently raised prices to stunning levels, making the medications involved extremely difficult for patients or insurance companies to afford them:

- *Valeant Pharmaceuticals and Turing Pharmaceuticals bought drugs and jumped prices:* "On February 10, Valeant Pharmaceuticals International Inc. bought the rights to a pair of life-saving heart drugs [Isuprel and Nitropress]. The same day, their list prices rose by 525% and 212%."[69] Turing Pharmaceuticals did almost the same in September 2015 after it bought the U.S. rights to market Daraprim and Vecamyl in August 2015. The price of Daraprim was raised 5555% from $13.50 to $750 per tablet. After a public outcry, both companies moderated their prices somewhat and/or made it more possible that hospitals and those without insurance could buy the products. The CEOs of both companies were called on to testify before congressional fact-finding committees, and the fortunes of both companies sank.[70] Martin Shkeli, the thirty-two-year-old entrepreneur and CEO of Turing, pleaded the Fifth Amendment four times during his hearing and on leaving his hearing tweeted, "Hard to accept that these imbeciles represent the people in our government."[71] His lawyer later argued that he had been provoked by incorrect and unfair comments that he had had to listen to without responding.

---

[68] Guilbert Gates, Josh Keller, Karl Russell, and Derek Watkins, "How Volkswagen Got Away with Diesel Deception," *New York Times*, October 2, 2015, http://www.nytimes.com/interactive/2015/09/22/business/international/vw-volkswagen-emissions-explainer.html; Jack Ewing, "VW's New Chief Says Scandal Will Cost It More Than Expected," *New York Times*, October 6, 2015, http://www.nytimes.com/2015/10/07/business/international/vw-diesel-emissions-job-cuts.html?_r=0.

[69] Jonathan D. Rockoff and Ed Silverman, "Pharmaceutical Companies Buy Rivals' Drugs, Then Jack Up the Prices," *Wall Street Journal*, April 26, 2015, http://www.wsj.com/articles/pharmaceutical-companies-buy-rivals-drugs-then-jack-up-the-prices-1430096431.

[70] Valeant's share price fell from $347 in August 2015 to $135 by September 29, 2015; Richard Blackwell, "Drugs Targeted in Valeant Pricing Controversy Acquired in February," *The Globe and Mail*, September 29, 2016, http://www.theglobeandmail.com/report-on-business/drugs-targeted-in-valeant-pricing-controversy-acquired-in-february/article26590603.

[71] Marcy Gordon, "Pharma Bad Boy Thumbs Nose at U.S. Congress," *Toronto Star*, February 5, 2016, S1.

In hindsight, it would appear that these individuals and their companies failed to anticipate the reaction to their gouging tactics. Why was this? Did they take the view that just because they could do something, it was okay to do it? What a shortsighted view that turned out to be. It is also worth wondering why the board of directors of either company did not stop the move to gouge prices before it happened. Was it due to CEOs who were too dominant, insensitivity to ethical issues, greed, or all of these? Once again, the companies lacked a culture of integrity that provided guidance that would have challenged such actions before they were taken.

New Emphasis on Individual Accountability for Corporate Wrongdoing

On September 9, 2015, the Deputy Attorney General of the United States, Sally Quillian Yates issued a memorandum[72] to the Department of Justice (DOJ), the Director of the FBI, and all U.S. Attorney's, providing policy guidance that efforts should be made to identify the individuals responsible for corporate wrongdoing, and to hold them accountable. This initiative was stimulated by the public's concern that very few individuals were being charged in regard to significant fiascos such as the subprime lending and LIBOR manipulation debacles.

The memorandum acknowledges that individual "accountability is important for several reasons: it deters future illegal activity, it incentivizes changes in corporate behavior, it ensures that the proper parties are held responsible for their actions, and it promotes the public's confidence in our justice system." The memorandum applies to criminal and civil matters, and it puts forward six policies to strengthen the pursuit of individual accountability. This signals the DOJ's intention to aggressively pursue individuals responsible for corporate wrongdoing. Going forward, this intention to pursue a broader accountability model including individuals *could make future patterns of fines and prosecutions significantly different from those of the past.* Time will tell.

Panama Papers Released

In April 2016, there was a huge leak of 11.5 million private records detailing the hidden wealth and income of thousands of the world's leaders, drug lords, criminals, and richest people. Over 214,000 entities were identified, that were created to allow the clients of the law firm, Mossack Fonseca, headquartered in Panama, to use tax havens to hide their wealth and income from tax and criminal authorities and others such as partners and spouses.[73] Now that the building blocks of their deception have become public, the tax authorities in many countries are prosecuting the offenders and recovering significant amounts. For example, although some countries are slower to act than others, as at

[72] The Yates Memorandum: "Individual Accountability for Corporate Wrongdoing", Sally Quillian Yates, Deputy Attorney General, U.S. Department of Justice, Washington D.C., September 9, 2015, https://www.justice.gov/dag/file/769036/download

[73] "Giant Leak of Offshore Financial Records Exposes Global Array of Crime and Corruption," *International Consortium of Investigative Journalists*, April 3, 2016, accessed August 1, 2016, at http://www.webcitation.org/6gVXG3LvI.

August 1, 2016, the U.K. had recovered $3.5 billion from offshore tax havens.[74] More prosecutions and loss of reputation are sure to follow—the disillusioned public will demand it, and the practice of secretly hiding wealth, although sometimes legal, will change forever.

SIGNS OF ETHICAL COLLAPSE

In her book *The Seven Signs of Ethical Collapse: How to Spot Moral Meltdowns in Companies*,[75] Marianne Jennings outlines seven causes of ethical problems within organizations:

1. Pressure to meet goals, especially financial ones, at any cost
2. A culture that does not foster open and candid conversation and discussion
3. A CEO who is surrounded with people who will agree and flatter the CEO as well as a CEO whose reputation is beyond criticism
4. Weak boards that do not exercise their fiduciary responsibilities with diligence
5. An organization that promotes people on the basis of nepotism and favoritism
6. Hubris—the arrogant belief that rules are for other people but not for us
7. A flawed cost/benefit attitude that suggests that poor ethical behavior in one area can be offset by good ethical behavior in another area

Almost all of the business scandals detailed in this book exhibit at least one of these ethical problems. Many of them have several of these signs of an ethical collapsed culture. Certainly, that is the case with Enron and WorldCom. So pervasive are these seven failings that they make an excellent framework for the analysis and diagnosis of companies before they fail so that remedial actions can be taken. They provide a set of red flags that directors, executives, and professional accountants should enshrine in their anticipatory routines.

ETHICS & GOVERNANCE: TRENDS

A constant theme and trend has been evident since the 1920s. The judgment and moral character of executives, owners, boards of directors, and auditors has been insufficient, on their own, to prevent corporate, ethical, and governance scandals. Governments and regulators have been required to increasingly tighten guidelines and governance regulations to ensure the protection of the public. The self-interested lure of greed has proven to be too strong for many to resist, and they have succumbed to conflicts of interest when left too much on their own. Corporations that were once able to shift jurisdictions to avoid new regulations now are facing global measures designed to expose and control bad ethics and governance practices. Accountants and auditors are also facing international standards of behavior.

[74] Marco Chown Oved, "CRA Convicts a Fraction Of Offshore Tax Evaders," *Toronto Star*, August 1, 2016, accessed August 1, 2016, at https://www.thestar.com/news/world/2016/08/01/cra-convicts-a-fraction-of-offshore-tax-evaders-exclusive.html.

[75] Marianne Jennings, *Seven Signs of Ethical Collapse: How to Spot Moral Meltdowns in Companies* (New York: St. Martin's Press, 2006).

These changes have come about because of the pressures brought to bear by activist stakeholders and the outraged public. But changes in laws, regulations, and standards are only part of what stakeholders have contributed. In modern times, the expectations for good ethical behavior and good governance practices have changed. Failure to comply with these expectations now impacts reputations, profits, and careers even if the behavior is within legal boundaries.

It is now evident to most executives, owners, and auditors that their success is directly related to their ability to develop and maintain a corporate culture of integrity. They cannot afford the loss of reputation, revenue, reliability, and credibility as a result of a loss of integrity. It is no longer an effective, sustainable, risk-minimizing medium- or long-term strategy to practice questionable ethics.

ETHICS & GOVERNANCE: TIMETABLES OF IMPORTANT EVENTS, 1929–2016

Tables 2.3 and 2.4 are offered for reference purposes.

TABLE 2.3 Ethics and Governance: A Timetable of Important Events, 1929–1990

Prior to 1929	Unfettered and individualistic governance.
1929	Stock market crash—the bubble and crash on Black Tuesday, October 29, leads to the Great Depression, which lasted twelve years, until World War II.
1933, 1934	SEC is established to set and enforce corporate governance and accountability regulations.
1933	*Glass-Steagall Act*—to control bank speculation and protect investor deposits.
1938	Federal National Mortgage Association, known as Fannie Mae, founded to provide support for the U.S. housing and mortgage markets.
1940	*Investment Advisers Act*—regulation of investment advisors.
1957	Discovery of carbon dioxide buildup in the atmosphere.
1962	*Silent Spring* by Rachel Carson catalyzes environmentalism.
1965	*Unsafe at Any Speed* by Ralph Nader catalyzes car safety and consumerism.
1968	Fannie Mae expands the U.S. mortgage securities market by securitizing mortgage-backed securities so they could be sold, thus allowing lenders to reinvest their capital.
1970	Federal Home Loan Mortgage Corporation, known as Freddie Mac, created to buy mortgages, pool them into mortgage-backed securities, and resell them to investors.
1970	Ford Pinto introduced.
1974	Ozone depletion hole discovered.
1977	*Foreign Corrupt Practices Act*—enacts penalties for U.S. companies and subsidiaries caught bribing foreign officials.
1977	Activist investors launch socially responsible investing.
1984	*Strategic Management: A Stakeholder Approach* by R. E. Freedman articulates a stakeholder theory of corporate governance responsive to the interests of those stakeholders who have an interest in the outcomes or who can influence the achievement of the company's strategic objectives.
1988	Nestlé boycott—powered baby food used with tainted water.
1989	*Exxon Valdez* runs aground on Bligh Reef off Alaska.

TABLE 2.4 Ethics & Governance: A Timetable of Important Events, 1991–2016

Year	Event
1991	*U.S.Federal Sentencing Guidelines*—created common sentences for the same crime, thus avoiding incredibly low penalties for such as environmental harm in some states.
1997	Nike boycott—sweatshop labor and low wages
1999	*Glass-Steagall Act* repealed by the *Gramm-Leach-Bliley Act.*
2001	Enron bankruptcy
2002	Arthur Andersen suspended by SEC and implodes, WorldCom bankruptcy, Crisis of Confidence
2002	*Sarbanes-Oxley Act* reforms U.S. governance framework and the accounting profession
2002	New York Stock Exchange Governance Guidelines updated, Other scandals—see Figure 2.2
2005	KPMG fined $456 million for role in aggressive tax schemes
2007	Four E&Y tax partners are fined for marketing aggressive tax schemes
2007	U.S. Tax *Circular 230* issues to control aggressive tax practices
2008	Bear Stearns investment bank and brokerage firm collapses and is sold to J.P. Morgan Chase
2008	Subprime lending crisis begins, Lehman Brothers bankruptcy
2008	*Troubled Asset Relief Program* (TARP)—U.S. Government bail-out begins
2008	Bernie Madoff—arrested for $50 billion Ponzi scheme
2008	Siemens prosecuted for international bribery under U.S. FCPA—$800 million settlement
2010	BP oil well disaster in Gulf of Mexico
2010	International banking regulations created
2010	*Dodd-Frank Wall Street Reform and Consumer Protection Act*—responds to subprime lending problems
2010	Mercedes Benz prosecuted for international bribery under U.S. FCPA—$185 million settlement
2012	Bribery scandals surface: SNC-Lavalin worldwide, Wal-Mart in Mexico
2012	LIBOR Interest Rate Scandal emerges, prosecutions and massive fines follow for major banks
2013-4	Automaker scandals—GM Faulty Ignition Switches, Takata's Faulty Airbags, VW Cheats on Emissions Tests
2015	Drug Price Gouging—Valeant Pharmaceuticals, Turing Pharmaceutical
2016	Panama Papers released

USEFUL VIDEOS & FILMS

- *The Big Short* (2015) portrays the story of how a few individuals foresaw the 2008 burst of the subprime lending housing investment bubble and profited sensationally by their insight while the rest of the world lost mightily.
- *Too Big to Fail* (2011) shows how the subprime lending scandal developed to such a crisis that U.S. officials decided that many investment firms, banks, and other financial institutions needed to be bailed out by TARP because their bankruptcies would cause too great harm to the U.S. and worldwide economies. They were simply too big to fail.
- *Margin Call* (2011) is a film that depicts the first thirty-six hours of the subprime lending crisis as experienced by individuals of a large Wall Street investment house. It focuses on greed and investment fraud.
- *Inside Job* (2010) is a documentary, directed by Charles Ferguson, that provides a comprehensive analysis of the financial crisis of 2008.
- *The Love of Money* is a three-part PBS series that first showed on July 12, 2010; website: http://www.tvo.org/TVOsites/WebObjects/TvoMicrosite.woa?political_literacy_the_love_of_money.

- *Wall Street: Money Never Sleeps* (2010) is a fictional but realistic portrayal of the crisis meetings that led to TARP and the bankruptcy of a firm such as Lehman Brothers.
- *Enron: The Smartest Guys in the Room* (2005) provides valuable insights into Enron's activities and the personalities that presided over Enron's rise and demise. See http://www.amazon.com/exec/obidos/ASIN/B000C3L2IO/ethics.
- *The Emerging LIBOR Scandal*, The Big Picture RT video, July 6, 2012, first six minutes of http://www.youtube.com/watch?v=FN5BKra4ebM.

Questions

1. Do you think that the events recorded in this chapter are isolated instances of business malfeasance, or are they systemic throughout the business world?
2. The events recorded in this chapter have given rise to legislative reforms concerning how business executives, directors, and accountants are to behave. There is a recurring pattern of questionable actions followed by more stringent legislation, regulation, and enforcement. Is this a case of too little legislation being enacted too late to prevent additional business fiascos?
3. Is there anything else that can be done to curtail this sort of egregious business behavior other than legislation?
4. Many cases of financial malfeasance involve misrepresentation to mislead boards of directors and/or investors. Identify the instances of misrepresentation in the Enron, Arthur Andersen, and WorldCom cases discussed in this chapter. Who was to benefit, and who was being misled?
5. Use the Jennings "Seven Signs" framework to analyze the Enron and WorldCom cases in this chapter.
6. Rank the worst three villains in the film *Wall Street: Money Never Sleeps* (2010). Explain your ranking.
7. In each case discussed at some length in this chapter—Enron, Arthur Andersen, WorldCom, and Bernie Madoff—the problems were known to whistleblowers. Should those whistleblowers each have made more effort to be heard? How?
8. The lack of corporate accountability and an increased awareness of inequities and other questionable practices by corporations led to the Occupy Movement. Identify and comment on additional recent instances that have led to concerns over the legitimacy of corporate activities.
9. It seems likely that the top executives of the major banks involved in the manipulation of the LIBOR rate were aware of the manipulations and of the massive profits and losses caused by those manipulations. Why did they think that such manipulations could continue to be undetected and/or unpunished?
10. The new antibribery prosecution regime involves serious charges and penalties for bribery in foreign countries during past times when many people were bribing in the normal course of international business and penalties were not levied. Is it unreasonable to levy extremely high fines at the beginning of the new regime and/or not to limit the period over which bribery can trigger those fines? Why and why not?

11. At GM and Takata, whose improper actions finally came to light, a whistle-blower raised objections to the actions before or very early in the production process. Why were their concerns ignored and risks taken? In VW's case, why didn't a whistle-blower come forward? What aspects of governance were lacking in each company?
12. The CEOs of Valeant Pharmaceuticals and Turing Pharmaceuticals took the view that they could jack up the price of their drugs by huge percentages because they could, and they failed to consider seriously enough whether they should. Whose fault was this? In a well-functioning corporate governance system, what measures should be in place to control such actions?
13. What are the reactions and outcomes that can be attributed to the leaked Panama Papers?

Sources: William Cohan, *House of Cards: A Tale of Hubris and Wretched Excess on Wall Street* (New York: Doubleday, 2009); Michael Lewis, *Liar's Poker: Rising through the Wreckage of Wall Street* (New York: Penguin, 1989); Michael Lewis, *The Big Short: Inside the Doomsday Machine* (New York: Norton, 2010); Roger Lowenstein, *When Genius Failed: The Rise and Fall of Long-Term Capital Management* (New York: Random House, 2000); Andrew Sorkin, *Too Big to Fail: The Inside Story of How Wall Street and Washington Fought to Save the Financial System—and Themselves* (New York: Viking, 2009); Tom Wolfe, *Bonfire of the Vanities* (New York: Farrar, Straus and Giroux, 1987).

Case Insights

- *Enron's Questionable Transactions* is an account of the questionable transactions underlying the massive fraud made possible by flaws in corporate governance and professional accounting. A more detailed analysis is available in the digital archive for this book at **www.cengagebrain.com**.
- *Arthur Andersen's Troubles* is the story of the once-revered but systematically flawed auditor of all the companies that forgot to whom fiduciary duty was owed.
- *WorldCom: The Final Catalyst* explains the massive fraud that triggered meaningful reform of corporate governance and professional accounting standards.
- *Bernie Madoff Scandal—The King of the Ponzi Schemes* describes how the subprime lending crisis destroyed Bernie Madoff's ability to attract new investors and use their money to pay off those who had invested earlier. As a result, in late 2009, his $65 billion fraud was exposed, and he was arrested, although the SEC had been alerted ten years earlier.
- *Wal-Mart Bribery in Mexico* describes how a company that wanted to improve its reputation for integrity was sabotaged by self-interested executives who were erroneously supported at the head office by misguided executives and an unaware board of directors.
- *LIBOR Manipulations Cause Widespread Impacts* reviews the huge impacts on those banks and their executives whose employees were found to have manipulated the information on which the LIBOR benchmark rate was based.
- *General Motors Ignores Obvious Ignition Faults* explores how GM made millions of cars with faulty ignition switches that malfunctioned, killing some people and injuring others, even though the fault was known before production began.
- *VW Cheats on Emissions Tests* describes the almost incredible gamble VW engineers took to cheat on emission tests by using built-in software to defeat the test equipment and win awards when, in fact, their "clean diesels" were emitting forty times the allowable limits.

ETHICS CASE

Enron's Questionable Transactions

An understanding of the nature of Enron's questionable transactions is fundamental to understanding why Enron failed. What follows is an abbreviated overview of the essence of the major important transactions with the SPEs, including Chewco, LJM1, LJM2, and the Raptors. A much more detailed but still abbreviated summary of these transactions is included in the *Enron's Questionable Transactions Detailed Case* in the digital archive for this book at **www.cengagebrain.com**.

Enron had been using specially created companies called SPEs for joint ventures, partnerships, and the syndication of assets for some time. But a series of happenstance events led to the realization by Enron personnel that SPEs could be used unethically and illegally to do the following:

- Overstate revenue and profits
- Raise cash and hide the related debt or obligations to repay
- Offset losses in Enron's stock investments in other companies
- Circumvent accounting rules for valuation of Enron's Treasury shares
- Improperly enrich several participating executives
- Manipulate Enron's stock price, thus misleading investors and enriching Enron executives who held stock options

In November 1997, Enron created an SPE called Chewco to raise funds or attract an investor to take over the interest of Enron's joint venture investment partner, CalPERS,[1] in an SPE called Joint Energy Development Investment Partnership (JEDI). Using Chewco, Enron had bought out CalPERS interest in JEDI with Enron-guaranteed bridge financing and tried to find another investor.

Enron's objective was to find another investor, called a *counterparty*, which would do the following:

- Be independent of Enron
- Invest at least 3% of the assets at risk
- Serve as the controlling shareholder in making decisions for Chewco

Enron wanted a 3%, independent, controlling investor because U.S. accounting rules would allow Chewco to be considered an independent company, and any transactions between Enron and Chewco would be considered at arm's length. This would allow "profit" made on asset sales from Enron to Chewco to be included in Enron's profit even though Enron would own up to 97% of Chewco.

Unfortunately, Enron was unable to find an independent investor willing to invest the required 3% before its December 31, 1997, year end. Because there was no outside investor in the JEDI-Chewco chain, Enron was considered to be dealing with itself, and U.S. accounting rules required that Enron's financial statements be restated to remove any profits made on transactions between Enron and JEDI. Otherwise, Enron would be able to report profit on deals with itself, which, of course, would undermine the integrity of Enron's audited financial statements because there would be no external, independent validation of transfer prices. *Enron could set the prices to make whatever profit it desired and manipulate its financial statements at will.*

That, in fact, was exactly what happened. When no outside investor was found, Enron's CFO, Andrew Fastow, proposed that he be appointed to serve as Chewco's outside investor. Enron's lawyers pointed out that such involvement by a high-ranking Enron officer would need to be disclosed publicly, and one of Fastow's financial staff—a fact not shared with the board—Michael Kopper, who continued to be an Enron employee, was appointed as Chewco's 3%, independent, controlling investor, and the chicanery began.

Enron was able to "sell" (transfer really) assets to Chewco at a manipulatively high profit. *This allowed Enron to show profits*

[1] The California Public Employees' Retirement System.

on these asset sales and draw cash into Enron accounts without showing in Enron's financial statements that the cash stemmed from Chewco borrowings and would have to be repaid. Enron's obligations were understated—they were "hidden" and not disclosed to investors.

Duplicity is also evident in the way that Chewco's funding was arranged. CalPERS's interest in JEDI was valued at $383 million; of that amount, Kopper and/or outside investors needed to be seen to provide 3%, or $11.5 million. The $383 million was arranged as follows[2]:

$240.0	Barclays Bank PLC—Enron would later guarantee this
132.0	JEDI to Chewco under a revolving credit agreement
0.1	Kopper and his friend Dodson ($125,000)
11.4	Barclays Bank PLC "loaned" to Dodson/Kopper companies
$383.5	

These financing arrangements are diagrammed in Figure 2.5.

Essentially, Enron as majority owner put no cash into the SPE. A bank provided virtually all of the cash, and in reality the so-called 3%, independent, controlling investor had very little invested—not even close to the required 3% threshold. Nonetheless, Chewco was considered to qualify for treatment as an arm's-length entity for accounting purposes by Enron and its auditors, Arthur Andersen. Enron's board—and presumably Arthur Andersen—was kept in the dark.

A number of other issues in regard to Chewco transactions were noted in the Powers Report, including the following:

- Excessive management fees were paid to Kopper for little work.[3]
- Excessive valuations were used on winding up, thus transferring $10.5 million to Kopper.

FIGURE 2.5 Chewco Financing, in Millions

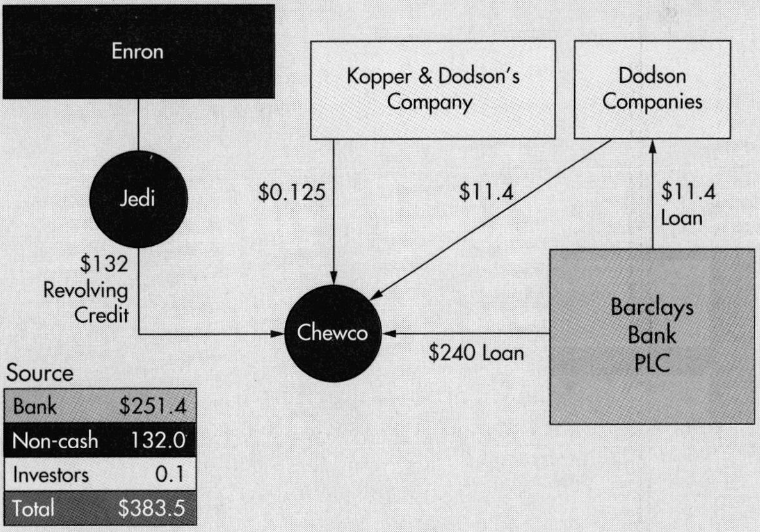

[2] "Loaned" through shell companies and for "certificates" that would generate a yield.

[3] Fastow's wife did most of the work.

- Kopper sought and received $2.6 million as indemnification from tax liability on the $10.5 million.
- Unsecured, nonrecourse loans totaling $15 million were made to Kopper and not recovered.
- Enron advance-booked revenues from Chewco.

This pattern of financing—no or low Enron cash invested, banks providing most of the funding, and Enron employees masquerading as 3%, independent, controlling investors—continued in other SPEs. Some of these SPEs, such as the LJM partnerships, were used to create buyers for Enron assets over which Enron could keep control but convert fixed assets into cash for growth at inflated prices, thus overstating cash and profits. Other SPEs, such as LJM1 and LJM2, provided illusionary hedge arrangements to protect Enron against losses in its merchant[4] investment portfolio, thereby falsely protecting Enron's reported profits.

In March 1998, Enron invested in Rhythms NetCommunications, Inc. (Rhythms), a business Internet service provider. Between March 1998 and May 1999, Enron's investment of $10 million in Rhythms stock soared to approximately $300 million. Enron recorded the increase in value as profit by increasing the value of its investment on its books. But Jeffrey K. Skilling, Enron's CEO, realized that the mark-to-market accounting procedure used would require continuous updating, and the change could have a significant negative effect on Enron's profits due to the volatility of Rhythms stock price. He also correctly foresaw that Rhythms stock price could plummet when the Internet bubble burst due to overcapacity.

LJM1 (LJM Cayman LP) was created to hedge against future volatility and losses on Enron's investment in Rhythms. If Rhythms stock price fell, Enron would have to record a loss in its investment. However, LJM1 was expected to pay Enron to offset the loss, so no net reduction would appear in overall Enron profit. As with Chewco, the company was funded with cash from other investors and banks based partly on promises of large guaranteed returns and yields. Enron invested its own shares but no cash.

In fact, LJM1 did have to pay cash to Enron as the price of Rhythms stock fell. This created a loss for LJM1 and reduced its equity. Moreover, at the same time as LJM1's cash was being paid to Enron, the market value of Enron's shares was also declining, thus reducing LJM1's equity even further. Ultimately, LJM1's effective equity eroded, as did the equity of the SPE (Swap Sub) Enron created as a 3% investment conduit. Swap Sub's equity actually became negative. *These erosions of cash and equity exposed the fact that the economic underpinning of the hedge of Rhythms stock was based on Enron's shares—in effect, Enron's profit was being hedged by Enron's own shares. Ultimately, hedging yourself against loss provides no economic security against loss at all.* Enron's shareholders had been misled by $95 million profit in 1999 and $8 million in 2000. These were the restatements announced in November 2001, just before Enron's bankruptcy on December 2, 2001.

Unfortunately for Enron, there were other flaws in the creation of LJM1 that ultimately rendered the arrangement useless, but by that time investors had been misled for many years. For example, there was no 3%, independent, controlling investor—Andrew Fastow sought special approval from Enron's chairman to suspend the conflict of interest provisions of Enron's *Code of Conduct* to become the sole managing/general partner of LJM1 and Swap Sub; and Swap Sub's equity

[4] A merchant investment is an investment in a company's shares that are held for speculative purposes, not for control purposes.

became negative and could not qualify for the 3% test unless Enron advanced more shares, which it did. Ultimately, as Enron's stock price fell, Fastow decided the whole arrangement was not sustainable, and it was wound up on March 22, 2000. Once again, the windup arrangements were not properly valued; $70 million more than required was transferred from Enron, and LJM1 was also allowed to retain Enron shares worth $251 million.

Enron's shareholders were also misled by Enron's recording of profit on the Treasury shares used to capitalize the LJM1 arrangement. Enron provided the initial capital for LJM1 arrangements in the form of Enron's own Treasury stock, for which it received a promissory note. Enron recorded this transfer of shares at the existing market value, which was higher than the original value in its Treasury, and therefore recorded a profit on the transaction. Since no cash had changed hands, the price of transfer was not validated, and accounting rules should not have allowed the recording of any profit.

Initially, the LJM1 arrangements were thought to be so successful at generating profits on Treasury shares, hedging against investment losses, and generating cash, that LJM2 Co-Investment LP (LJM2) was created in October 1999 to provide hedges for further Enron merchant investments in Enron's investment portfolio. LJM2 in turn created four SPEs, called "Raptors," to carry out this strategy using similar methods of capitalization based on its own Treasury stock or options thereon.

For a while, the Raptors looked like they would work. In October 2000, Fastow reported to LJM2 investors that the Raptors had brought returns of 193%, 278%, 2,500%, and 125%, which was far in excess of the 30% annualized return described to the finance committee in May 2000. Of course, as we know now, Enron retained the economic risks.

Although nontransparent arrangements were used again, the flaws found in the LJM1 arrangements ultimately became apparent in the LJM2 arrangements, including the following:

- Enron was hedging itself, so no external economic hedges were created.
- Enron's falling stock price ultimately eroded the underlying equity and creditworthiness involved, and Enron had to advance more Treasury shares or options to buy them at preferential rates[5] or use them in "costless collar"[6] arrangements, all of which were further dilutive to Enron earnings per share.
- Profits were improperly recorded on Treasury shares used or sheltered by nonexistent hedges.
- Enron officers and their helpers benefited.

In August 2001, matters became critical. Declining Enron share values and the resulting reduction in Raptor creditworthiness called for the delivery of so many Enron shares that the resulting dilution of Enron's earnings per share was realized to be too great to be sustainable. In September 2001, accountants at Arthur Andersen and Enron realized that the profits generated by recording Enron shares used for financing at market values was incorrect because no cash was received, and shareholders' equity was overstated by at least $1 billion.

The overall effect of the Raptors was to misleadingly inflate Enron's earnings during the middle period of 2000 to the end of the third quarter of 2001 (September 30) by

---

[5] Raptors III and IV were not fully utilized and/or used to shore up the equity of Raptors I and II.

[6] A "costless collar" is a two-step arrangement wherein Enron offered to contain LJM2's risk of Enron's stock price falling below a lower limit using its own Treasury shares while at the same time making an offsetting arrangement for LJM2 to pay Enron if Enron's share price were to rise above a threshold. Since the arrangements offset one another in risk premium and Treasury stock was to be used, the transaction was considered to be an equity transaction, which did not affect the income statement of Enron. See page 110 of the Powers Report.

TABLE 2.5 Enron's Key Special Purpose Entities (SPEs)

SPE SCHEME	PURPOSE	IMPACT
Chewco/JEDI	Syndicated investment	Off-balance-sheet liabilities hidden ($628 million) Revenues recognized early Profits on own shares
LJM	Provided market for assets	Artificial profits Off-balance-sheet liabilities hidden Equity overstated ($1.2 billion)
LJM1/Rhythms	Investment "hedge"	Unrecognized losses ($508 million)
LJM2/Raptors	Investment "hedge"	Unrecognized losses ($544 million)

$1,077 million, not including a September Raptor winding-up charge of $710 million.

On December 2, 2001, Enron became the largest bankruptcy in the world, leaving investors ruined, stunned, and outraged—and quite skeptical of the credibility of the corporate governance and accountability process. By that time, the Enron SPEs and related financial dealings had misled investors greatly. Almost 50% of the reported profits driving Enron stock up so dramatically were false. Table 2.5 summarizes the impacts of Enron's questionable transactions through key Enron SPEs.

Questions

1. Enron's directors realized that Enron's conflict of interests policy would be violated by Fastow's proposed SPE management and operating arrangements, and they instructed the CFO, Andrew Fastow, as an alternative oversight measure, endure that he kept the company out of trouble. What was wrong with their alternatives?
2. Ken Lay was the chair of the board and the CEO for much of the time. How did this probably contribute to the lack of proper governance?
3. What aspects of the Enron governance system failed to work properly, and why?
4. Why didn't more whistle-blowers come forward, and why did some not make a significant difference? How could whistle-blowers have been encouraged?
5. What should the internal auditors have done that might have assisted the directors?
6. What conflict-of-interest situations can you identify in the following?
   - SPE activities
   - Executive activities
7. Why do you think that Arthur Andersen, Enron's auditors, did not identify the misuse of SPEs earlier and make the board of directors aware of the dilemma?
8. How would you characterize Enron's corporate culture? How did it contribute to the disaster?

ETHICS CASE

Arthur Andersen's Troubles

Once the largest professional services firm in the world and arguably the most respected, Arthur Andersen LLP (AA) has disappeared. The Big 5 accounting firms are now the Big 4. Why did this happen? How did it happen? What are the lessons to be learned?

Arthur Andersen, a twenty-eight-year-old Northwestern University accounting professor, cofounded the firm in 1913. Tales of his integrity are legendary, and the culture of the firm was very much in his image. For example, "Just months after [Andersen] set up shop in

Chicago, the president of a local railroad insisted that he approve a transaction that would have inflated earnings. Andersen told the executive there was "not enough money in the City of Chicago" to make him do it."[1] In 1954, consulting services began with the installation of the first mainframe computer at General Electric to automate its payroll systems. By 1978, AA became the largest professional services firm in the world with revenues of $546 million, and by 1984, consulting brought in more profit than auditing. In 1989, the consulting operation, wanting more control and a larger share of profit, became a separate part of a Swiss partnership from the audit operation. In 2000, following an arbitrator's ruling that a break fee of $1 billion be paid, Andersen Consulting split completely and changed its name to Accenture. AA, the audit practice, continued to offer a limited set of related services, such as tax advice.[2]

Changing Personalities and Culture

Throughout most of its history, AA stood for integrity and technical competence. The firm invested heavily in training programs and a training facility in St. Charles, a small town south of Chicago, and developed it until it had over 3,000 residence beds and outstanding computer and classroom facilities. AA personnel from all over the world were brought to St. Charles for training sessions on an ongoing basis. Even after the consulting and audit operations split, both continued to use the facility.

Ironically, AA was the first firm to recognize the need for professional accountants to study business and professional accounting formally. In the late 1980s, AA undertook a number of programs to stimulate that formal education, including the development of ethics cases, the creation of an approach to the resolution of professional ethical problems, and the hosting of groups of 100 accounting academics to get them started in the area. Most had no formal ethics training and were uncertain how to begin ethics teaching or even if they should. It is likely that AA's farsighted policies are responsible for the genesis of much of the professional ethics education and research in accounting that is going on today.

What happened to the AA culture that focused on integrity and technical competence? What changed that would account for AA's involvement in the major scandals noted in Table 2.6 as the audit firm that failed to discover the underlying problems?

TABLE 2.6 Arthur Andersen's Problem Audits

CLIENT	PROBLEM MISSED, DATE	LOSSES TO SHAREHOLDERS	JOB LOSSES	AA FINE
WorldCom	$4.3 billion overstatement of earnings announced, June 25, 2002	$179.3 billion	17,000	N.A.
Enron	Inflation of income, assets, etc., bankrupt December 2, 2001	$66.4 billion	6,100	$.5 million (for shredding)
Global Crossing	Candidate for bankruptcy	$26.6 billion	8,700	
Waste Management[1]	Overstatement of income by $1.1 billion, 1992–1996	$20.5 billion	11,000	$7 million
Sunbeam*	Overstatement of 1997 income by $71.1 million, then bankruptcy	$4.4 billion	1,700	
Baptist Foundation of Arizona	Books cooked, largest nonprofit bankruptcy ever	$570 million	165	

1. Cases are in the digital archive for this book at **www.cengagebrain.com**.

Source: "Fall from Grace," *Business Week*, August 12, 2002, 54.

[1] "Fall from Grace," *Business Week*, August 12, 2002, 54.

[2] Ibid.; see table on page 53.

Some observers have argued that a change in AA's culture was responsible. Over the period when the consulting practice was surpassing the audit practice as the most profitable aspect of the firm, a natural competitiveness grew up between the two rivals. The generation of revenue became more and more desirable and the key to merit and promotion decisions. The retention of audit clients took on an increasingly greater significance as part of this program, and since clients were so large, auditors tended to become identified with them. Many audit personnel even looked forward to joining their clients. In any event, the loss of a major client would sideline the career of the auditors involved at least temporarily if not permanently. For many reasons, taking a stand against the management of a major client requires a keen understanding of the auditor's role, the backing of senior partners in your firm, and courage.

The pressure for profit was felt throughout the rest of the audit profession, not only at Arthur Andersen. Audit techniques were modified to require higher levels of analysis and lower investment of time. Judgment sampling gave way to statistical sampling and then to strategic risk auditing. While each was considered better than its predecessor, the trend was toward tighter time budgets, and the focus of the audit broadened to include development of value-added nonaudit outcomes, suggestions, or services for clients. Such nonaudit services could include advice on the structuring of transactions for desired disclosure outcomes and other work on which the auditor would later have to give an audit opinion.

According to discussions in the business and professional press, many audit professionals did not see the conflicts of interest involved as a problem. The conflict between maximizing audit profit for the firm and providing adequate audit quality so that the investing public would be protected was considered to be manageable so that no one would be harmed. The conflict between auditing in the public interest with integrity and objectivity that could lead to the need to roundly criticize mistakes that your firm or you had made in earlier advice was considered not to present a worry. In addition, the conflict between the growing complexity of transactions, particularly those involving derivative financial instruments, hedges, swaps, and so on, and the desire to restrain audit time in the interest of profit was thought to be within the capacity of auditors and firms to resolve. The growing conflict for auditors between serving the interests of the management team that was often instrumental in making the appointment of auditors and the interests of shareholders was recognized but did not draw reinforcing statements from firms or professional accounting bodies. Some professional accountants did not understand whether they should be serving the interests of current shareholders or future shareholders or what serving the public interest had to do with serving their client. They did not understand the difference between a profession and a business.

Ethical behavior in an organization is guided by the ethical culture of that organization, by any relevant professional norms and codes, and particularly by the "tone at the top"[3] and the example set by the top executives. Also, presumably, the selection of the CEO is based partly on the choice of the values that an organization should be led toward. Joe Berardino was elected AA's CEO on January 10, 2001, but he had been partner in charge of the AA's U.S. audit practice for almost three years before. He was the leader whose values drove the firm from 1998 onward and probably continued those of his predecessor. What were his values? Barbara Ley Toffler, a former Andersen partner during this period and before, has provided the following insight:

> When Berardino would get up at a partners meeting, all that was ever

[3] This is a concept emerging in new governance standards that boards of directors are to monitor.

> reported in terms of success was dollars. Quality wasn't discussed. Content wasn't discussed. Everything was measured in terms of the buck.... Joe was blind to the conflict. He was the most aggressive pursuer of revenue that I ever met.[4]

Arthur Andersen's Internal Control Flaw

Given this "tone at the top," it is reasonable to assume that AA partners were going to be motivated by revenue generation. But if too many risks are taken in the pursuit of revenue, the probability of a series of audit problems leading to increasingly unfavorable consequences becomes greater. That is exactly what happened. Unfortunately, the leaders of AA failed to recognize the cumulative degree to which the public, the politicians, and the SEC were angered by the progression of AA audit failures.

If they had recognized the precarious position they were in, the AA leadership might have corrected the flaw in the AA internal control that allowed the Enron audit failures to happen. *AA was the only one of the Big 5 to allow the partner in charge of the audit to override a ruling of the quality control partner.* This meant that at AA, the most sensitive decisions were taken by the person who was most concerned with the potential loss of revenue from the client in question and who was most likely to be subject to the influence of the client. In all of the other Big 5 firms, the most sensitive decisions are taken by the person whose primary interest is the compliance with generally accepted accounting principles (GAAP), the protection of the public interest, and the reputation of the firm.

On April 2, 2002, the U.S. House Energy and Commerce Committee[5] released a memo dated December 18, 1999, from Carl Bass, a partner in AA's Professional Services Group in Chicago, to David Duncan, the AA partner in charge of the Enron account. That memo asked for an accounting change (believed to be in regard to SPE transactions) that would have resulted in a $30 million to $50 million charge to Enron's earnings. In February 2000, Bass e-mailed Duncan to object to the setting up of an LJM partnership because he indicated that "this whole deal looks like there is no substance."[6] On March 4, 2001, Bass wrote that "then-chief financial officer Andrew Fastow's role as manager of special partnerships compromised deals Enron made with the entities."[7] Duncan overruled Bass on the first issue, and Bass was removed from Enron audit oversight on March 17, 2001, less than two weeks after he questioned Fastow's role in Enron's SPEs. In any other Big 5 firm, Duncan would not have been able to overrule a quality control partner on his own. History might have been different if a quality-focused internal control procedure had been in place at AA rather than one that was revenue focused.

Arthur Andersen's Apparent Enron Mistakes

The previously presented "Enron Debacle" discussion covers in detail many of the questionable accounting transactions, legal structures, and related disclosures that AA reviewed as auditors of and consultants to Enron. Without repeating these in detail, it is possible to provide the following summary of significant issues that AA could be questioned about in court proceedings:

- AA apparently approved as auditors and consultants (and collected fees for the consulting advice) the structure of many SPEs that were used to generate false profits, hide losses, and keep financing off Enron's consolidated financial statements and that failed to

[4] "Fall from Grace," 55, 56.

[5] "Andersen under Fire over Memos: Carl Bass Documents," *Financial Post*, April 4, 2002, FP1, FP10.

[6] "Andersen Partner Warned on Enron in '99: Questioned Partnerships," *Financial Post*, April 3, 2002, FP9.

[7] "Andersen under Fire over Memos," FP1.

meet the required outsider 3% equity at risk and decision control criteria for nonconsolidation.

- AA failed to recognize the GAAP that prohibits the recording of shares issued as an increase in shareholders equity unless they are issued for cash (not for notes receivable).
- AA did not advise Enron's audit committee that Andrew Fastow, Enron's CFO, and his helpers were involved in significant conflict-of-interest situations without adequate alternative means of managing these conflicts.
- AA did not advise the Enron Audit Committee that Enron's policies and internal control were not adequate to protect the shareholders' interests even though AA had assumed Enron's internal audit function.
- Many transactions between Enron and the SPEs were not in the interest of Enron shareholders because:
  - Enron profits and cash flow were manipulated and grossly inflated, misleading investors and falsely boosting management bonus arrangements.
  - Extraordinarily overgenerous deals, fees, and liquidation arrangements were made by Fastow (or under his influence) with SPEs owned by Fastow, his family, and Kopper, who was also an employee of Enron.
- AA apparently did not adequately consider the advice of its quality control partner, Carl Bass.
- AA apparently did not find significant audit evidence or did not act on evidence found, related to the following:
  - Erroneous valuation of shares or share rights transferred to SPEs
  - Side deals between Enron and banks removing the banks' risk from transactions such as the following:
    - Chewco SPE Rhythms hedge
  - Numerous prepay deals for energy futures even though AA made a presentation to Enron on the GAAP and AA requirements that precluded such arrangements[8]

Why Did Arthur Andersen Make These Apparent Mistakes?

The term "apparent" is used because AA's side of the story has not been heard. The so-called mistakes may have logical, reasonable explanations and may be supportable by other accounting and auditing experts. That stated, these apparent mistakes may have been made for several reasons, including the following:

- Incompetence, as displayed and admitted in the Rhythms case
- Judgment errors as to the significance of each of the audit findings or of the aggregate impact in any fiscal year
- Lack of information caused by Enron staff not providing critical information or failure on the part of AA personnel to ferret it out
- Time pressures related to revenue generation and budget pressures that prevented adequate audit work and the full consideration of complex SPE and prepay financial arrangements
- A desire not to confront Enron management or advise the Enron board in order not to upset management, particularly Fastow, Skilling, and Lay
- A failure of AA's internal policies whereby the concerns of a quality control or practice standards partner were overruled by the audit partner in charge of the Enron account. AA was the only one of the Big 5 accounting firms to have this flaw, and it left the entire firm vulnerable to the decision of the person with the most to lose by saying no to a client
- A misunderstanding of the fiduciary role required by auditors

[8] Testimony of Robert Roach to the Senate Permanent Subcommittee on Investigations, July 23, 2002, Appendix A, A-6.

Because AA has now disintegrated, it is unlikely that the cause of specific audit deficiencies will ever be known. However, it is reasonable to assume that all of the causes listed played some part in the apparent mistakes that were made.

A review of additional cases of failure where AA was the auditor, such as the Waste Management and Sunbeam failures that may be found in the digital archive at **www.cengagebrain.com**, reveal that AA's behavior was strikingly similar to that in the Enron debacle. In each case, AA appears to have been so interested in revenue generation that they were willing not to take a hard line with their clients. AA personnel apparently believed that there was no serious risk of default and that, over time, accounting problems could be worked out. At the very least, AA's risk assessment process was seriously flawed. Also, when AA's client had a combined chairman of the board and CEO who intimidated or was willingly helped by his CFO, neither additional professional accountants working for the corporations nor other nonaccounting personnel who knew of the accounting manipulations raised their concerns sufficiently with AA or the Audit Committee of their board of directors to stimulate corrective action. This lack of courage and understanding of the need and means to stimulate action left AA, the board, and the public vulnerable.

Shredding Enron Audit Documents: Obstruction of Justice

The final disintegration of AA was not caused directly by the Enron audit deficiencies but rather by a related decision to shred Enron audit documents and the conviction on the charge of obstruction of justice that resulted. This charge, filed on March 7, 2002, raised the prospect that if AA were convicted, the SEC would withdraw AA's certification to audit SEC registrant companies.[9] That would preclude those large public companies that needed to be registered with the SEC to have their shares traded on U.S. stock exchanges (the New York Stock Exchange [NYSE] and NASDAQ) or raise significant amounts of capital in the United States.

Since these clients represented the bulk of AA's U.S. and foreign accounting practices, if convicted, AA would be effectively reduced to insignificance unless a waiver could be arranged from the SEC. The SEC, however, was very angry about the Enron audit deficiencies, particularly in view of the earlier similar cases involving the AA audits of Waste Management and Sunbeam. In regard to the Waste Management debacle, "The commission argued that not only did Andersen knowingly and recklessly issue materially false and misleading statements, it failed to enforce its own guidelines to bring the company in line with minimally accepted accounting standards."[10] As a condition of the $7 million fine paid in June 2001 settling AA's Waste Management audit deficiencies, AA had agreed to rectify its audit inadequacies, and the SEC believed that AA had not honored this undertaking. Consequently, since AA's behavior in the Enron debacle was so similar, the SEC provided only a temporary and conditional waiver,[11] pending the outcome of the trial.

The conviction was announced on Saturday, June 15, 2002, but many large clients had already transferred their work to other large audit firms. Some boards of directors and CEOs thought that AA's reputation was so damaged by the Enron fiasco that they no longer wanted to be associated with

[9] AA could also face probation for up to five years and a $500,000 fine as well as fines for up to twice any gains or damages the court determines were caused by the firm's action.

[10] "'Back Time' May Catch Andersen," *Toronto Star*, March 21, 2002, D11.

[11] "SEC Announces Actions for Issuers in Light of Indictment of Arthur Andersen LLP," SEC Release 2002-37.

AA or that such an association might weaken their company's ability to attract financing at the lowest rates. The outrage of the public was so intense that other boards could not face the lack of credibility that continuing with AA would have produced with their shareholders. Still other boards realized that if AA were convicted, there would be a stampede to other firms, and their company might not be able to make a smooth transition to another SEC-certified audit firm if they waited to switch. By the time the conviction was announced, only a small percentage of AA's largest clients remained. Even though AA's chances of acquittal on appeal were considered by some observers to be good, AA was a shell of its former self and was essentially finished as a firm in the United States and ultimately around the world.

The chain of events that led to the shredding of some of AA's Enron audit documents begins before Enron decided to announce a $618 million restatement of earnings and a $1.2 billion reduction of equity on October 16, 2001. An SEC investigation was launched into Enron's accounting on October 17, and AA was advised on October 19. However, AA had advised Enron that such an announcement was necessary to correct its accounting for SPEs and, on October 9 as the eight-page indictment states, "retained an experienced New York law firm to handle further Enron-related litigation."[12] Eleven days later, the subject of shredding was discussed as part of an emergency conference call to AA partners, and shredding began three days after that.[13]

Shredding was undertaken in AA's Houston office, as well as in London, Chicago, and Portland. "According to the U.S. government,... the destruction was 'wholesale,' with workers putting in overtime in order to get the job done." "Tonnes of paper relating to the Enron audit were promptly shredded as part of the orchestrated document destruction. The shredder at the Andersen office at the Enron building was used virtually constantly and to handle the overload, dozens of large trunks filled with Enron documents were sent to Andersen's Houston office to be shredded."[14]

At the trial, AA argued differently. AA's lawyer attempted to clarify the purpose of Chicago-based AA lawyer Nancy Temple's e-mail of October 10 to Michael Odom of AA's Houston office. In that e-mail, she wrote that "it might be useful to consider reminding the [Enron audit] team that it would be helpful to make sure that we have complied with the policy[15] which calls for destruction of extraneous and redundant material."[16] This lack of relevance, of course, was difficult to prove after the documents in question had been destroyed. Essentially, AA contended that "the order to follow the document retention policy was an innocent effort to organize papers, emails and computer files and eliminate extraneous material."[17]

David Duncan, however, testified against AA. He had been fired from AA (where he had been the partner in charge of the Enron audit) on January 15, one day after he met with the U.S. Justice Department. He said, "I obstructed justice... I instructed people on the [Enron audit] team to follow the document retention policy, which I knew would result in the destruction of documents."[18]

The jury deliberated for many days, emerged, and was sent back for additional

---

[12] *Grand Jury Indictment on the Charge of Obstruction of Justice, United States of America against Arthur Andersen, LLP*, filed in the United States District Court Southern District of Texas on March 7, 2002, 5.

[13] "Back Time May Catch Andersen," D11.

[14] Ibid.

[15] "Auditor Evidence Attacked," *Toronto Star*, May 22, 2002, E12.

[16] Ibid.

[17] Ibid.

[18] "Andersen Partner Admits Wrongdoing," *Toronto Star*, May 14, 2002, D3.

deliberations. Ultimately, AA was declared guilty. Although AA planned to appeal, it agreed to cease all audits of public companies by the end of August. Ironically, AA's conviction turned on the jury's view that the shredding was part of a broad conspiracy, and that rested on testimony that was reread to the jury, indicating that an AA memo (or memos) was altered. The acts of shredding alone were not enough for conviction. The jury was reported as concluding that

> Duncan eventually pleaded guilty to one count of obstruction and testified on the government's behalf, but jurors said afterwards that they didn't believe his testimony. Instead, the jury agreed that Andersen in-house attorney Nancy Temple had acted corruptly in order to impede the SEC's pending investigation. One of Temple's memos was a response to an email from Duncan about Enron's third quarter earnings statement. Enron wanted to describe a massive earnings loss as "non-recurring," but Duncan advised Enron against using that phrase. Temple's memo advised Duncan to delete any language that might suggest that Andersen disagreed with Enron, and further advised Duncan to remove her own name from his correspondence, since she did not want to be called as a witness in any future litigation stemming from Enron's earnings announcements.[19]

On October 16, 2002, AA was fined the maximum of $500,000 and placed on five years' probation. AA appealed out of principle, even though only 1,000 employees remained. Interestingly, on May 31, 2005, the U.S. Supreme Court overturned the conviction on the grounds that the "jury instructions failed to convey the requisite consciousness of wrong-doing"[20]—that AA personnel needed to think they were doing wrong rather than right to be convicted. The U.S. government must decide whether to retry the case. Unfortunately, the Supreme Court's ruling came too late for AA.

Lingering Questions

Within a few months, arrangements had been made for the AA units around the world to join other firms, but not before many staff had left, and not all those remaining were hired by the new employers. A firm of 85,000 people worldwide, including 24,000 in the United States, was virtually gone.

Was this an appropriate outcome? Perhaps only 100 AA people were responsible for the Enron tragedy, but 85,000 paid a price. Will the reduced selection of large accounting firms, the Big 4, be able to serve the public interest better than the Big 5? What if another Big 4 firm has difficulty? Will we have the Big 3, or are we now facing the Final Four? Will fate await other individual AA partners and personnel beyond David Duncan or by the American Institute of Certified Public Accountants through the exercise of its code of conduct? Will a similar tragedy occur again?

Emerging Research

These questions and others have stimulated the accounting research community to investigate them. Conferences are being held, and research articles are appearing.

One of the early studies, by Paul R. Chaney and Kirk L. Philipich, titled "Shredded Reputation: The Cost of Audit Failure,"[21] provided insights into the impact of AA's problems on its other corporate clients and

---

[19] Greg Farrell, "Arthur Andersen Convicted of Obstruction of Justice," *USA Today*, June 15, 2002.

[20] Barry McKenna, "Supreme Court Overrules Jury—But Too Late to Save Andersen," *The Globe and Mail*, June 1, 2005, B1, B11.

[21] Paul R. Chaney and Kirk L. Philipich, "Shredded Reputation: The Cost of Audit Failure," *Journal of Accounting Research*, 40, no. 4 (September 2002): 1235–40.

their investors. On January 10, 2002, AA admitted shredding Enron's documents, and in the ensuing three days, the stock prices of most of AA's 284 other large clients that were part of the Standard & Poor's 1,500 Index fell. Over that time, these stocks dropped an average of 2.05% and lost more than $37 million in market value. This was the largest movement observed for the four critical information events tested. The other events were November 8, 2001, when Enron announced its restatements; December 12, 2001, when AA's CEO admitted AA made an error; and February 3, 2002, the day following the release of the Powers Report, when AA hired former Federal Reserve Chairman Paul Volcker to chair an independent oversight board to shore up AA's credibility. Volcker later resigned when it became evident that AA was unwilling to embrace significant changes.

Additional research studies have examined many aspects of the conduct of the directors, executives, lawyers, and accountants involved in the Enron, AA, and WorldCom tragedies. In addition, the roles of regulators, of directors, and of professional independence have come under scrutiny. These studies are to be found in many academic and professional journals as well as the popular business press. In particular, useful articles can be found in the *Journal of Business Ethics, Business Ethics Quarterly, Journal of Accounting Research, Contemporary Accounting Research, Journal of Research in Accounting Ethics*, and *Business Week*.

Questions

1. What did Arthur Andersen contribute to the Enron disaster?
2. Which Arthur Andersen decisions were faulty?
3. What was the prime motivation behind the decisions of Arthur Andersen's audit partners on the Enron, WorldCom, Waste Management, and Sunbeam audits: the public interest or something else? Cite examples that reveal this motivation.
4. Why should an auditor make decisions in the public interest rather than in the interest of management or current shareholders?
5. Why didn't the Arthur Andersen partners responsible for quality control stop the flawed decisions of the audit partners?
6. Should all of Arthur Andersen have suffered for the actions or inactions of fewer than 100 people? Which of Arthur Andersen's personnel should have been prosecuted?
7. Under what circumstances should audit firms shred or destroy audit working papers?
8. Answer the "Lingering Questions" on page 119.

ETHICS CASE

WorldCom: The Final Catalyst

This case presents, with additional information, the WorldCom saga included in this chapter. Questions specific to WorldCom activities are located at the end of the case.

WorldCom Lights the Fire

WorldCom, Inc., the second-largest U.S. telecommunications giant and almost 70% larger than Enron in assets, announced on June 25, 2002, that it had overstated its cash flow by $3.8 billion.[1] This came as a staggering blow to the credibility of capital markets. It occurred in the middle of the furor caused by: the following:

- The Enron bankruptcy on December 2, 2001, and the related Congress and

[1] Simon Romero and Alex Berenson, "WorldCom Says It Hid Expenses, Inflating Cash Flow $3.8 Billion," *New York Times*, June 26, 2002.

Senate hearings and Fifth Amendment testimony by Enron executives

- The depression of the stock markets
- The pleas by business leaders and President Bush for restoration of credibility and trust to corporate governance, reporting, and the financial markets
- Responsive introduction of governance guidelines by stock exchanges and the SEC
- Debate by the U.S. Congress and Senate of separate bills to improve governance and accountability
- The conviction of Arthur Andersen, auditor of both Enron and WorldCom, for obstruction of justice on June 15, 2002

WorldCom's Accounting Manipulations

WorldCom's accounting manipulations involved very basic, easy-to-spot types of fraud.[2] Overstatements of cash flow and income were created because one of WorldCom's major expenses, line costs, or "fees paid to third party telecommunication network providers for the right to access the third parties networks"[3] were accounted for improperly. Essentially, line costs that should have been expensed, thus lowering reporting income, were offset by capital transfers or charged against capital accounts, thus placing their impact on the balance sheet rather than the income statement. In addition, WorldCom created excess reserves or provisions for future expenses that they later released or reduced, thereby adding to profits. The manipulation of profit through reserves or provisions is known as "cookie jar" accounting.

The aggregate overstatement of income quickly rose to more than $9 billion[4] by September 19, 2002, for the following reasons:

- $3.85 billion for improperly capitalized expenses, announced June 25, 2002[5]
- $3.83 billion for more improperly capitalized expenses in 1999, 2000, 2001, and the first quarter of 2002, announced on August 8, 2002[6]
- $2.0 billion for manipulations of profit through previously established reserves, dating back to 1999

Ultimately, the WorldCom fraud totaled $11 billion.

Key senior personnel involved in the manipulations at WorldCom included the following:

- Bernard J. Ebbers, CEO
- Scott D. Sullivan, CFO
- Buford Yates Jr., Director of General Accounting
- David F. Myers, Controller
- Betty L. Vinson, Director of Management Reporting, from January 2002
- Troy M. Normand, Director of Legal Entity Accounting, from January 2002

According to the SEC's complaint against Vinson and Normand,[7]

> 4. WorldCom fraudulently manipulated its financial results in a number of respects, including by improperly reducing its operating expenses in at least two ways. First, WorldCom

---

[2] Bruce Myerson, "A WorldCom Primer," *Associated Press*, June 26, 2001.

[3] *Complaint: SEC v. WorldCom, Inc.*, U.S. Securities and Exchange Commission, June 26, 2002, para. 5, http://www.sec.gov/litigation/complaints/complr17588.htm.

[4] "WorldCom to Reveal More Bogus Accounting," *Associated Press*, September 19, 2002; David E. Royella, "WorldCom Faces Two New Charges, Misstatement Grows," *Financial Post*, November 6, 2002, FP4.

[5] WorldCom Inc., *Form 8-K, Current Report Pursuant to Section 13 or 15(D) of the Securities Exchange Act of 1934*, August 14, 2002, para. 2, http://www.sec.gov/archives/edgar/.

[6] Ibid., para. 3.

[7] *Complaint: SEC v. Betty L. Vinson, and Troy M. Normand*, U.S. Securities and Exchange Commission, modified October 31, 2002, paras. 4, 5, 6, http://www.sec.gov/litigation/complaints/comp17783.htm.

improperly released certain reserves held against operating expenses. Second, WorldCom improperly recharacterized certain operating costs as capital assets. Neither practice was in conformity with generally accepted accounting principles ("GAAP"). Neither practice was disclosed to WorldCom's investors, despite the fact that both practices constituted changes from WorldCom's previous accounting practices. Both practices artificially and materially inflated the income WorldCom reported to the public in its financial statements from 1999 through the first quarter of 2002.

5. Many of the improper accounting entries related to WorldCom's expenses for accessing the networks of other telecommunications companies ("line costs"), which were among WorldCom's major operating expenses. From at least the third quarter of 2000 through the first quarter of 2002, in a scheme directed and approved by senior management, and participated in by VINSON, NORMAND and others, including Yates and Myers, WorldCom concealed the true magnitude of its line costs. By improperly reducing reserves held against line costs, and then—after effectively exhausting its reserves—by recharacterizing certain line costs as capital assets, WorldCom falsely portrayed itself as a profitable business when it was not, and concealed the large losses it suffered. WorldCom's fraudulent accounting practices with respect to line costs were designed to and did falsely and fraudulently inflate its income to correspond with estimates by Wall Street analysts and to support the price of WorldCom's common stock and other securities.

6. More specifically, in the third and fourth quarters of 2000, at the direction and with the knowledge of WorldCom's senior management, VINSON, NORMAND and others, by making and causing to be made entries in WorldCom's books which improperly decreased certain reserves to reduce WorldCom's line costs, caused WorldCom to overstate pretax earnings by $828 million and at least $407 million respectively. Then, after WorldCom had drawn down WorldCom's reserves so far that the reserves could not be drawn down further without taking what senior management believed was an unacceptable risk of discovery, VINSON, NORMAND and others, again at the direction and with the knowledge of senior management, made and caused to be made entries in WorldCom's books which improperly capitalized certain line costs for the next five quarters, from the first quarter 2001 through the first quarter 2002. This accounting gimmick resulted in an overstatement of WorldCom's pretax earnings by approximately $3.8 billion for those five quarters.

The motivation and mechanism for these manipulations is evident from the SEC's description of what happened at the end of each quarter, after the draft quarterly statements were reviewed. Steps were taken by top management to hide WorldCom's problems and boost or protect the company's stock price in order to profit from stock options, maintain collateral requirements for personal loans, and keep their jobs. These steps were required, in part, to offset the downward pressure on WorldCom's share price caused by U.S. and European regulators' rejection of WorldCom's U.S.$115 billion bid for Sprint Communications.[8] Ebbers's company had been using takeovers rather than organic

[8] "Ebbers Became Symbol of Scandals," *Financial Post*, July 14, 2005, FP1, FP3.

growth to prop up earnings, and the financial markets began to realize this would be increasingly difficult.

According to the SEC,

> 27. In or around October 2000, at the direction and with the knowledge of WorldCom senior management, VINSON, NORMAND and others, including Yates and Myers, caused the making of certain improper entries in the company's general ledger for the third quarter of 2000. Specifically, after reviewing the consolidated financial statements for the third quarter of 2000, WorldCom senior management determined that WorldCom had failed to meet analysts' expectations. WorldCom's senior management then instructed Myers, and his subordinates, including Yates, VINSON and NORMAND, to make improper and false entries in WorldCom's general ledger reducing its line cost expense accounts, and reducing—in amounts corresponding to the improper and false line cost expense amounts—various reserve accounts. After receiving instructions through Yates, VINSON and NORMAND ensured that these entries were made. There was no documentation supporting these entries, and no proper business rationale for them, and they were not in conformity with GAAP. These entries had the effect of reducing third quarter 2000 line costs by approximately $828 million, thereby increasing WorldCom's publicly reported pretax income by that amount for the third quarter of 2000.[9]

Manipulations followed the same pattern for the fourth quarter of 2000, but a change was required for the first quarter of 2001 for fear of discovery:

> 29. In or around April 2001, after reviewing the preliminary consolidated financial statements for the first quarter of 2001, WorldCom's senior management determined that WorldCom had again failed to meet analysts' expectations. Because WorldCom's senior management determined that the company could not continue to draw down its reserve accounts to offset line costs without taking what they believed to be unacceptable risks of discovery by the company's auditors, WorldCom changed its method of fraudulently inflating its income. WorldCom's senior management then instructed Myers, and his subordinates, including Yates, VINSON and NORMAND, to make entries in WorldCom's general ledger for the first quarter of 2001, which fraudulently reclassified line cost expenses to a variety of capital asset accounts without any supporting documentation or proper business rationale and in a manner that did not conform with GAAP.
>
> 30. Specifically, in or around April 2001, at the direction and with the knowledge of WorldCom's senior management, defendants VINSON, NORMAND and others, including Yates and Myers, fraudulently reduced first quarter 2001 line cost expenses by approximately $771 million and correspondingly increased capital asset accounts, thereby fraudulently increasing publicly reported pretax income for the first quarter of 2001 by the same amount. In particular, in or about April 2001, NORMAND telephoned WorldCom's Director of Property Accounting (the "DPA") and instructed him to adjust the schedules he maintained for certain

[9] *Complaint: SEC v. Betty L. Vinson, and Troy M. Normand*, U.S. Securities and Exchange Commission, modified October 31, 2002, http://www.sec.gov/litigation/complaints/comp17783.htm.

> Property, Plant & Equipment capital expenditure accounts (the "PP&E Roll-Forward") by increasing certain capital accounts for "prepaid capacity." NORMAND advised the DPA that these entries had been ordered by WorldCom's senior management. Correspondingly, a subordinate of NORMAND made journal entries in WorldCom's general ledger, transferring approximately $771 million from certain line cost expense accounts to certain PP&E capital expenditure accounts.[10]

In future periods, the increase of certain accounts for "prepaid capacity" remained the manipulation of choice.

WorldCom's Other Revelations

It should be noted that Ebbers was not an accountant—he began as a milkman and bouncer and became a basketball coach and then a Best Western Hotel owner before he entered the telecommunications business,[11] where his 60 acquisitions and style earned him the nickname "the Telecom Cowboy." However, he was ably assisted in these manipulations by Scott Sullivan, his CFO, and David Myers, his Controller. Both Sullivan and Myers had worked for Arthur Andersen before joining WorldCom.

Other spectacular revelations offer a glimpse behind the scenes at WorldCom. The company, which applied for bankruptcy protection in July 21, 2002, also announced that it might write off $50.6 billion in goodwill or other intangible assets when restating for the accounting errors previously noted. Apparently, other WorldCom decisions had been faulty.

The revelations were not yet complete. Investigation revealed that Bernard Ebbers, the CEO, had been loaned $408.2 million. He was supposed to use the loans to buy WorldCom stock or for margin calls as the stock price fell. Instead, he used it partly for the purchase of the largest cattle ranch in Canada, construction of a new home, personal expenses of a family member, and loans to family and friends.[12]

Finally, it is noteworthy that

> at the time of its scandal, WorldCom did not possess a code of ethics. According to WorldCom's Board of Director's Investigative Report, the only mention of "ethics" was contained in a section in WorldCom's Employee Handbook that simply stated that "… fraud and dishonesty would not be tolerated" (WorldCom 2003, p. 289). When a draft version of a formal code was presented to Bernie Ebbers … for his approval before the fraud was discovered in 2001, his response was reportedly that the code of ethics was a ". . . colossal waste of time" (WorldCom 2003, 289).[13]

Why Did They Do It?

According to U.S. Attorney General John Ashcroft,

> The alleged Sullivan-Myers scheme was designed to conceal five straight quarterly net losses and create the illusion that the company was profitable.[14]

In view of Ebbers's $408.2 million in loans, which were largely to buy or pay margin calls on WorldCom stock and

[10] *Complaint: SEC v. Betty L. Vinson, and Troy M. Normand,* U.S. Securities and Exchange Commission, modified October 31, 2002, http://www.sec.gov/litigation/complaints/comp17783.htm.

[11] Krysten Crawford, "Ex-WorldCom CEO Ebbers Guilty," *CNN Money,* March 15, 2005, http://money.cnn.com/2005/03/15/news/newsmakers/ebbers/?cnn=yes.

[12] Royella. "WorldCom Faces Two New Charges, Misstatement Grows," FP4.

[13] Mark S. Schwartz, "Effective Corporate Codes of Ethics: Perceptions of Code Users," *Journal of Business Ethics* 55 (2004): 324; WorldCom 2003, "Report of the Investigation by the Special Investigative Committee of the Board of Directors," June 9, 2003.

[14] "WorldCom Accounting Fraud Rises to $7 Billion," *Baltimore Sun,* August 9, 2002.

which were secured by WorldCom stock, he would be loath to see further deterioration of the WorldCom stock price. In short, he could not afford the price decline that would follow from lower WorldCom earnings.

In addition, according to WorldCom's *2002 Annual Meeting Proxy Statement*,[15] on December 31, 2001, Ebbers had been allocated exercisable stock options on 8,616,365 shares and Sullivan on 2,811,927. In order to capitalize on the options, Ebbers and Sullivan (and other senior employees) needed the stock price to rise. A rising or at least stable stock price was also essential if WorldCom stock was to be used to acquire more companies.

Finally, if the reported results became losses rather than profits, the tenure of senior management would have been shortened significantly. In that event, the personal loans outstanding would be called, and stock option gravy train would stop. In 2000, Ebbers and Sullivan had each received retention bonuses of $10 million, so they would stay for two years after September 2000. In 1999, Ebbers received a performance bonus allocation of $11,539,387, but he accepted only $7,500,000 of the award.[16]

An Expert's Insights

Former Attorney General Richard Thornburgh was appointed by the U.S. Justice Department to investigate the collapse and bankruptcy of WorldCom. In his *Report to the U.S. Bankruptcy Court* in Manhattan on November 5, 2002, he said,

> One person, Bernard Ebbers, appears to have dominated the company's growth, as well as the agenda, discussions and decisions of the board of directors,...
>
> A picture is clearly emerging of a company that had a number of troubling and serious issues ... [relating to] culture, internal controls, management, integrity, disclosure and financial statements.
>
> While Mr. Ebbers received more than US $77 million in cash and benefits from the company, shareholders lost in excess of US $140 billion in value.[17]

The Continuing Saga

The WorldCom saga continues as the company's new management try to restore trust it its activities. As part of this effort, the company changed its name to MCI. "On August 26, 2003, Richard Breeden, the Corporate Monitor appointed by the U.S. District Court for the Southern District of New York, issued a report outlining the steps the Company will take to rebuild itself into a model of strong corporate governance, ethics and integrity ... (to) foster MCI's new company culture of 'integrity in everything we do.'"[18] The company is moving deliberately to reestablish the trust and integrity it requires to compete effectively for resources, capital, and personnel in the future.

The SEC has filed complaints, which are on its website, against the company and its executives. The court has granted the injunctive relief the SEC sought. The executives have been enjoined from further such fraudulent actions and subsequently banned by the SEC from practicing before it, and some have been banned by the court from acting as officers or directors in the future.

---

[15] WorldCom, *2002 Annual Meeting Proxy Statement*, SEC Edgar File, April 22, 2002, http://www.sec.gov /Archives/edgar/data/723527/000091205702015985/0000912057-02-015985.txt.

[16] Ibid.

[17] Don Stancavish, "WorldCom Dominated by Ebbers," *Financial Post*, November 5, 2002, FP13.

[18] MCI, *Governance: Restoring the Trust*, accessed January 3, 2006, at http://global.mci.com/about/governance /restoring-trust/.

WorldCom, as a company, consented to a judgment:

> imposing the full injunctive relief sought by the Commission; ordering an extensive review of the company's corporate governance systems, policies, plans, and practices; ordering a review of WorldCom's internal accounting control structure and policies; ordering that WorldCom provide reasonable training and education to certain officers and employees to minimize the possibility of future violations of the federal securities laws; and providing that civil money penalties, if any, will be decided by the Court at a later date.[19]

Bernie Ebbers and Scott Sullivan were each indicted on nine charges: one count of conspiracy, one count of securities fraud, and seven counts of false regulatory findings.[20] Sullivan pleaded guilty on the same day he was indicted and later cooperated with prosecutors and testified against Bernie Ebbers "in the hopes of receiving a lighter sentence."[21]

Early in 2002, Ebbers stood up in church to address the congregation, saying, "I just want you to know that you're not going to church with a crook."[22] Ebbers took the stand and argued "that he didn't know anything about WorldCom's shady accounting, that he left much of the minutiae of running the company to underlings."[23] But after eight days of deliberations, on March 15, 2005, a federal jury in Manhattan did not buy his "aw shucks," "hands-off," or "ostrich-in-the-sand" defense.

The jury believed Sullivan, who told the jury that Ebbers repeatedly told him to "'hit his numbers'—a command … to falsify the books to meet Wall Street expectations."[24] They did not buy Ebbers' "I know what I don't know" argument, "especially after the prosecutor portrayed a man who obsessed over detail and went ballistic over a US $18,000 cost overrun in a US $3-billion budget item while failing to pick up on the bookkeeping claim that telephone line costs often fluctuated—fraudulently—by up to US $900-million a month. At other times, he replaced bottled water with tap water at WorldCom's offices, saying employees would not know the difference."[25]

On July 13, 2005, Ebbers was sentenced to 25 years in a federal prison.[26] Once a billionaire, he also lost his house, property, yacht, and fortune. At 63 years of age, he is appealing his sentence. Sullivan's reduced sentence was for five years in a federal prison, forfeiture of his house, ill-gotten gains, and a fine.

Investors lost over $180 million in WorldCom's collapse[27] and more in other companies as the confidence in the credibility of the financial markets, governance mechanisms, and financial statements continued to deteriorate.

Questions

1. Describe the mechanisms that WorldCom's management used to transfer profit from other time periods to inflate the current period.

---

[19] *SEC Litigation Release No. 17883*, December 6, 2002, http://www.sec.gov/litigation/litreleases/lr17883.htm.

[20] "Jury Convicts Ebbers on All Counts in Fraud Case," *MSNBC*, March 15, 2005, http://www.msnbc.msn.com/id/7139448/.

[21] Crawford, "Ex-WorldCom CEO Ebbers Guilty."

[22] "Ebbers Became Symbol of Scandals," FP1, FP3.

[23] Crawford, "Ex-WorldCom CEO Ebbers Guilty."

[24] "Jury Convicts Ebbers on All Counts in Fraud Case."

[25] "Ebbers Became Symbol of Scandals."

[26] Ibid.

[27] Ibid.

2. Why did Arthur Andersen go along with each of these mechanisms?
3. How should WorldCom's board of directors have prevented the manipulations that management used?
4. Bernie Ebbers was not an accountant, so he needed the cooperation of accountants to make his manipulations work. Why did WorldCom's accountants go along?
5. Why would a board of directors approve giving its Chair and CEO loans of over $408 million?
6. How can a board ensure that whistleblowers will come forward to tell them about questionable activities?

ETHICS CASE

Bernie Madoff Scandal—The King of Ponzi Schemes

Bernie Madoff perpetrated the world's largest Ponzi scheme,[1] in which investors were initially estimated to have lost up to $65 billion. Essentially, investors were promised—and some received—returns of at least 1% per month. However, beginning in the early 1990s, these payments came from funds invested by new investors, not from returns on invested funds. Consequently, when new investor contributions slowed due to the subprime lending crisis in 2008, Madoff ran out of funds to pay redemptions and returns, and the entire scheme unraveled.

As Warren Buffet has said, "You only learn who has been swimming naked when the tide goes out."[2]

Bernie Madoff certainly was, much to the chagrin of some supposedly very savvy investors who were attracted by seemingly constant returns of about 1% per month in up as well as down markets. Among those who invested sizable sums[3] were the actors Kevin Bacon and Kyra Sedgwick as well as Jeffrey Katzenberg, the CEO of DreamWorks Animation. Others are listed here.

LOSS BY	BILLIONS
Hedge Funds	
Fairfield Greenwich Advisers	$7.5
Tremont Group Holdings	3.3
Ascot Partners	1.8
International Banks	
Banco Santander	2.9
Bank Medici, Austria	2.1
Fortis, the Netherlands	1.4
	MILLIONS
Charities	
Jewish Community Foundation of Los Angeles	$18
The Elie Wiesel Foundation For Humanity	15.2
Yeshiva University	14.5
Celebrity	
Zsa Zsa Gabor	10

Ultimately, Madoff pleaded guilty to 11 charges by the SEC, confessed, and was sentenced to 150 years in the penitentiary. The story of how Madoff began his scheme, what he actually did, who suspected he was a fraudster and warned the SEC, why the

[1] Named after Charles Ponzi (March 3, 1882–January 18, 1949), who was born in Italy, lived in the United States, and became famous for his swindle of unsuspecting investors wherein early investors are paid returns from funds invested by later investors.

[2] W. Buffet, 2008 Annual Letter to the shareholders of Berkshire Hathaway Inc.

[3] Doug Steiner, "Bernie, I Hardly Knew Ya," *The Globe and Mail*, March 2009, 50–53.

SEC failed to find wrongdoing, who knew, and who did nothing is a fascinating story of ethical misbehavior, greed, innocence, incompetence, and misunderstanding of duty.

How Did Madoff Do It?

In his plea elocution[4] on March 12, 2009, Madoff told the court,

> The essence of my scheme was that I represented to clients and prospective clients who wished to open investment advisory and investment trading accounts with me that I would invest their money in shares of common stock, options and other securities of large well-known corporations, and upon request, would return to them their profits and principal.... [F]or many years up until I was arrested ... I never invested those funds in the securities, as I had promised. Instead, those funds were deposited in a bank account at Chase Manhattan Bank. When clients wished to receive the profits they believed they had earned with me or to redeem their principal, I used the money in the Chase Manhattan bank account that belonged to them or other clients to pay the requested funds.[5]

Of course, in reality, Madoff's scheme was more complex and went undiscovered for a very long time.

Over the years, Madoff became involved in two major activities as (1) a market maker or broker and (2) an investment adviser or manager. The first, which he began in 1960 as Bernard L. Madoff Securities, matched, by phone, buyers and sellers of stocks of smaller companies that were not traded on large recognized stock exchanges, such as the NYSE. Initially, he made a commission on each over-the-counter trade, but soon he was buying or selling on his own account, thereby taking the risk of not being able to find a matched buyer or seller and not making a profit on the spread. In time, this form of trading became more regulated, and the spread between the buying and selling prices for shares became restricted to one-eighth of a dollar, or 12.5 cents, per share. In order to maximize his volume of orders, Madoff would "pay for order flow" a sum of 1 to 2 cents per share of the 12.5\-cent spread to the referring broker. Later, computerized trading[6] allowed share prices to be denominated in cents rather than one-eighth of a dollar, and the spreads shrunk to 1 cent or so by 2001.[7] Consequently, Madoff's profit on this type of trading activity dwindled, and he had to be creative to make any significant profit. It is speculated[8] that he did so by "front running," a variation on insider trading. Using advance knowledge of a large buy transaction garnered through his "pay for order flow" process, Madoff could buy the stock for his own account at the current price and then sell the stock moments later to fulfill the large buy order at an increased price.

The trading part of Madoff's activity was properly registered with authorities and was not the source of Madoff's Ponzi scheme. The second activity—that of investment advisor—which Madoff began as early as 1962, was the source. Interestingly, he did not register as an investment advisor until he was forced to do so by the SEC in 2006 in reaction to a very public and now famous whistle-blower's report

---

[4] A plea allocution is a confession in court required at a sentencing hearing before the judge sentences the accused.

[5] http://www.pbs.org/wgbh/pages/frontline/madoff/cron/.

[6] Computerized trading began in 1971, initially mirroring the pricing of stocks in intervals of 12.5 cents, or one-eighth of a dollar.

[7] Steiner, "Bernie, I Hardly Knew Ya," 53.

[8] See Harry Markopolos, 2005 Letter to the SEC.

by Harry Markopolos.[9] In fact, Madoff is said to have asked his clients not to divulge his investment services to them, perhaps in an effort to keep the service below the level of recognition by authorities. In any event, as Madoff states in his plea elocution, his fraud began in the early 1990s:

> Your Honor, for many years up until my arrest on December 11, 2008, I operated a Ponzi scheme through the investment advisory side of my business, Bernard L. Madoff Securities LLC, which was located here in Manhattan, New York at 885 Third Avenue.
>
> To the best of my recollection, my fraud began in the early 1990s. At that time, the country was in a recession and this posed a problem for investments in the securities markets. Nevertheless, I had received investment commitments from certain institutional clients and understood that those clients, like all professional investors, expected to see their investments out-perform the market. While I never promised a specific rate of return to any client, I felt compelled to satisfy my clients' expectations, at any cost. I therefore claimed that I employed an investment strategy I had developed, called a "split strike conversion strategy," to falsely give the appearance to clients that I had achieved the results I believed they expected.
>
> Through the split-strike conversion strategy, I promised to clients and prospective clients that client funds would be invested in a basket of common stocks within the Standard & Poor's 100 Index, a collection of the 100 largest publicly traded companies in terms of their market capitalization. I promised that I would select a basket of stocks that would closely mimic the price movements of the Standard & Poor's 100 Index. I promised that I would opportunistically time these purchases and would be out of the market intermittently, investing client funds during these periods in United States Government-issued securities such as United States Treasury bills. In addition, I promised that as part of the split strike conversion strategy, I would hedge the investments I made in the basket of common stocks by using client funds to buy and sell option contracts related to those stocks, thereby limiting potential client losses caused by unpredictable changes in stock prices. In fact, I never made the investments I promised clients, who believed they were invested with me in the split strike conversion strategy.
>
> To conceal my fraud, I misrepresented to clients, employees and others, that I purchased securities for clients in overseas markets. Indeed, when the United States Securities and Exchange Commission asked me to testify as part of an investigation they were conducting about my investment advisory business, I knowingly gave false testimony under oath to the staff of the SEC on May 19, 2006 that I executed trades of common stock on behalf of my investment advisory clients and that I purchased and sold the equities that were part of my investment strategy in European markets. In that session with the SEC, which took place here in Manhattan, New York, I also knowingly gave false testimony under oath that I had executed options contracts on behalf of my investment advisory clients and that my firm had custody of the assets managed on behalf of my investment advisory clients.
>
> To further cover-up the fact that I had not executed trades on behalf of my investment advisory clients, I

[9] Ibid.

knowingly caused false trading confirmations and client account statements that reflected the bogus transactions and positions to be created and sent to clients purportedly involved in the split strike conversion strategy, as well as other individual clients I defrauded who believed they had invested in securities through me. The clients receiving trade confirmations and account statements had no way of knowing by reviewing these documents that I had never engaged in the transactions represented on the statements and confirmations. I knew those false confirmations and account statements would be and were sent to clients through the U.S. mails from my office here in Manhattan.

Another way that I concealed my fraud was through the filing of false and misleading certified audit reports and financial statements with the SEC. I knew that these audit reports and financial statements were false and that they would also be sent to clients. These reports, which were prepared here in the Southern District of New York, among things, falsely reflected my firm's liabilities as a result of my intentional failure to purchase securities on behalf of my advisory clients.

Similarly, when I recently caused my firm in 2006 to register as an investment advisor with the SEC, I subsequently filed with the SEC a document called a Form ADV Uniform Application for Investment Adviser Registration. On this form, I intentionally and falsely certified under penalty of perjury that Bernard L. Madoff Investment and Securities had custody of my advisory clients' securities. That was not true and I knew it when I completed and filed the form with the SEC, which I did from my office on the 17th floor of 855 Third Avenue, here in Manhattan.

In more recent years, I used yet another method to conceal my fraud. I wired money between the United States and the United Kingdom to make it appear as though there were actual securities transactions executed on behalf of my investment advisory clients. Specifically, I had money transferred from the U.S. bank account of my investment advisory business to the London bank account of Madoff Securities International Ltd., a United Kingdom corporation that was an affiliate of my business in New York. Madoff Securities International Ltd. was principally engaged in proprietary trading and was a legitimate, honestly run and operated business.

Nevertheless, to support my false claim that I purchased and sold securities for my investment advisory clients in European markets, I caused money from the bank account of my fraudulent advisory business, located here in Manhattan, to be wire transferred to the London bank account of Madoff Securities International Limited.

There were also times in recent years when I had money, which had originated in the New York Chase Manhattan bank account of my investment advisory business, transferred from the London bank account of Madoff Securities International Ltd. to the Bank of New York operating bank account of my firm's legitimate proprietary and market making business. That Bank of New York account was located in New York. I did this as a way of ensuring that the expenses associated with the operation of the fraudulent investment advisory business would not be paid from the operations of the legitimate proprietary trading and market making businesses.

In connection with the purported trades, I caused the fraudulent investment advisory side of my business to charge the investment clients

> $0.04 per share as a commission. At times in the last few years, these commissions were transferred from Chase Manhattan bank account of the fraudulent advisory side of my firm to the account at the Bank of New York, which was the operating account for the legitimate side of Bernard L. Madoff Investment Securities—the proprietary trading and market making side of my firm. I did this to ensure that the expenses associated with the operation of my fraudulent investment advisory business would not be paid from the operations of the legitimate proprietary trading and market making businesses. It is my belief that the salaries and bonuses of the personnel involved in the operation of the legitimate side of Bernard L. Madoff Investment Securities were funded by the operations of the firm's successful proprietary trading and market making businesses.[10]

Who Knew or Suspected the Fraud, and What Did They Do?

According to Madoff, his family—his sons, his wife, and his brother—knew nothing of his fraudulent behavior until he revealed it to them—first to his brother on December 9, 2009, and a day later to his sons and wife. On December 10, his sons wanted to know why he would pay out millions of dollars in bonuses several months early and how he would do so when he was complaining that he was having difficulty paying off investment withdrawals and returns. After shifting the meeting to his apartment, he confessed to his sons

> that he is "finished," that he has "absolutely nothing," and that the operation was basically a giant Ponzi scheme.... Madoff also tells his sons that he plans to surrender to authorities in a week but he wants to use the $200–300 million he has left to make payments to selected employees, family and friends.
>
> After speaking to his sons, the FBI knocks on Madoff's door on the morning of Dec. 11 and asks if there is an innocent explanation. Madoff says no, it was "one big lie."[11]

According to many reports, several senior members of the financial community questioned how Madoff's investment business could earn such consistent, positive returns. Some thought he had to be running some type of fraudulent scheme and refused to deal with him. Others thought he was a genius, but they failed to look very deeply into his investment strategy and how he made his money.

In 1999, Harry Markopolos, a finance expert, was asked by his employer, who was a competitor of Madoff, to investigate Madoff's strategy. After four hours of analysis, Markopolos appeared in his boss's office to declare that it was *extremely* unlikely that Madoff could generate the consistent positive returns he paid by legal means. In his opinion, it was much more likely that Madoff was operating a Ponzi scheme or that he was front running orders through his broker/dealer operation with "the split-strike conversion strategy" as mere "front" or "cover."[12] Markopolos even went so far as to contact the SEC with an eight-page submission in 2000 with his concerns, but no investigation was launched, and no significant action was taken. Later, the alleged front running operation was proven to be "unworkable."

Markopolos, however, did not give up. He resubmitted his information several times between 2000 and 2008, usually

[10] Madoff's plea allocution was extracted from "Madoff Speaks: The Plea Allocution," WSJ Law Blog (blog), March 12, 2009, by Ashby Jones at http://blogs.wsj.com/law/2009/03/12/madoff-speaks-the-plea-allocution/.

[11] http://www.pbs.org/wgbh/pages/frontline/madoff/cron/.

[12] Testimony of Harry Markopolos before the U.S. House of Representatives Committee on Financial Services, Wednesday, February 4, 2009, 10, digital copy at BPE website.

with little effect. He attributed this to the fact that some of the key SEC representatives had insufficient financial background in derivatives to understand his submissions until he met Mike Garrity, the branch chief of the SEC's Boston Regional Office in late October 2005. Garrity understood the significance of Markopolos's analysis and referred it on to the SEC's New York Region Branch Office. Markopolos quickly submitted a 21-page report to Meaghan Cheung, the branch chief, on November 7, 2005, but she failed to understand it or its significance and concentrated on the Adelphia case that she was handling.

In his November 7, 2005, letter,[13] Markopolos identifies a series of 29 red flags and provides analyses supporting the following (greatly distilled) summary of the salient points he made at the time about Bernard Madoff's (BM's) activities:

- BM chose an unusual broker-dealer structure that costs 4% of annual fee revenue more than necessary. Why would he do this unless it was a Ponzi scheme?
- BM pays an average of 16% to fund its operations although cheaper money is readily available.
- Third-party hedge funds and funds of funds are not allowed to name BM as the actual fund manager. Shouldn't he want publicity for his wonderful returns?
- The split-strike conversion investment strategy is incapable of generating returns that beat the U.S. Treasury Bill rates and are nowhere near the rates required to sustain the rates of return paid to BM's clients.
- The total OEX options[14] outstanding are not enough to generate BM's stated split-strike strategy returns of 1% per month or 12% per year. Actually BM would have to earn 16% to net 12%.
- Over the last 14 years, BM has had only 7 monthly losses, and a 4% loss percentage is too unbelievably good to be true.
- There are not enough OEX index put option contracts *in existence* to hedge the way BM says he is hedging.
- The counter-party credit exposures for UBS and Merrill Lynch are too large for these firm's credit departments to approve.
- The customization and secrecy required for BM's options is beyond market volume limits and would be too costly to permit a profit.
- The paperwork would be voluminous to keep track of all required Over-The-Counter (OTC) trades.
- It is mathematically impossible to use a strategy involving index options (i.e., baskets of stocks representative of the market), and not produce returns that track the overall market. Hence, the consistency of positive returns (96% of the time) is much too good to be true.
- Over a comparable period, a fund using a strategy more sound than the split-strike approach had losses 30% of the time. Return percentages were similarly worse.
- Articles have appeared that question BM's legitimacy and raise numerous red flags.
- BM's returns could only be real if he uses the knowledge of trades from his trading arm to front-run customer orders, which is a form of insider trading and illegal. In addition, it is not the strategy he is telling hedge fund investors he is using.

[13] Markopolos's letter to the SEC, November 2005, http://finances.unanimocracy.com/money/2009/01/07/harry-markopolous-markopolos-letter-to-the-sec-2005-against-madoff/.

[14] According to the Chicago Board Options Exchange's website (http://www.cboe.com), the Standard & Poor's (S&P) 100 Index is a capitalization-weighted index of 100 blue-chip, large-cap stocks from the U.S. equities marketplace from diverse industry sector groups. It is a broad market index; together, these 100 stocks represent over 50% of the market capitalization of the S&P 500 Index. The impact of a price change in any component stock on the level of the overall index is proportional to the issue's total market value. Options on the S&P 100 are used primarily by hedgers and speculators in conjunction with bullish or bearish opinions on large-cap U.S. stocks.

- However, this access to inside knowledge only became available in 1998, so front running could not have generated the high profits BM reported before that date.
- If BM is front running, he could earn very high profits and therefore would not need to pay 16% to fund his operations. Since he is paying 16%, he is probably not front running, but is very probably involved in a Ponzi scheme.
- To achieve the 4% loss rate, BM must be subsidizing returns during down-market months, which is a misstatement of results or the volatility of those results and therefore constitutes securities fraud.
- BM reportedly has perfect market-timing ability. Why not check this to trading slips?
- BM does not allow outside performance audits.
- BM is suspected of being a fraud by several senior finance people including:
    - a managing director at Goldman, Sachs; so they don't deal with him
    - an official from a Top 5 money center bank; so they don't deal with him
    - several equity derivatives professionals believe that the split-strike conversion strategy that BM runs is an outright fraud and cannot achieve the consistent levels of returns declared, including:
        - Leon Gross, Managing Director of Citigroup's equity derivatives unit
        - Walter Haslett, Write Capital Management, LLC
        - Joanne Hill, V.P., Goldman, Sachs
- Why does BM allow third-party hedge funds and funds of funds to pocket excess returns of up to 10% beyond what is needed?
- Why are only Madoff family members privy to the investment strategy?
- BM's Sharpe Ratio[15] is at 2.55. This is too outstanding to be true.
- BM has announced that he has too much money under management and is closing his strategy to new investments. Why wouldn't he want to continue to grow?
- BM is really running the world's largest hedge fund. But it is an unregistered hedge fund for other funds that are registered with the SEC. Even though the SEC is slated to begin oversight of hedge funds in 2006, BM operates behind third-party shields and so the chances of BM escaping scrutiny are very high.

Although Markopolos continued to call, Ms. Cheung was not responsive. As a result, he pursued other avenues, and when he uncovered leads to people who suspected that Madoff was a fraudster, he passed the names on to the SEC. Unfortunately, no action was taken. If it had been, Markopolos believes that Madoff "could have been stopped in 2006."[16]

Markopolos continued to try to influence the SEC orally and in writing as late as March or early April 2008 with no apparent response. On February 4, 2009, he testified before the U.S. House of Representatives Committee on Financial Services about his concerns. During that testimony, he was asked why he and three other concerned associates had not turned Madoff in to the Federal Bureau of Investigation (FBI) or the Federal Industry Regulatory Authority (FINRA)[17] and responded as follows:

> For those who ask why we did not go to FINRA and turn in Madoff, the answer

[15] The Sharpe Ratio is a measure that relates investment return over the risk-free rate of return to volatility, so a higher ratio gives more return for the risk than investments with lower ratios.

[16] Testimony of Harry Markopolos before the U.S. House of Representatives Committee on Financial Services, 17.

[17] FINRA, according to its website (http://www.finra.org), "is the largest non-governmental regulator for securities firms doing business in the United States." Created in July 2007 through the consolidation of NASD and the member regulation, enforcement, and arbitration functions of the NYSE, FINRA is dedicated to investor protection and market integrity through effective and efficient regulation and complementary compliance and technology-based services.

is simple: Bernie Madoff was Chairman of their predecessor organization and his brother Peter was former Vice-Chairman. We were concerned we would have tipped off the target too directly and exposed ourselves to great harm. To those who ask why we did not turn in Madoff to the FBI, we believed the FBI would have rejected us because they would have expected the SEC to bring the case as subject matter expert on securities fraud. Given our treatment at the hands of the SEC, we doubted we would have been credible to the FBI.[18]

Markopolos goes on to lament that

> dozens of highly knowledgeable men and women also knew that BM was a fraud and walked away silently, saying nothing and doing nothing.... How can we go forward without assurance that others will not shirk their civic duty? We can ask ourselves would the result have been different if those others had raised their voices and what does that say about self-regulated markets?[19]

Harry Markopolos is tough on the SEC in his February 2009 oral testimony. The YouTube video of his testimony is available at http://www.youtube.com/watch?v=uw_Tgu0txS0 and is well worth viewing. For example, he states the following:

- "I gift wrapped and delivered to the SEC the largest Ponzi scheme in history, and they were too busy to investigate."
- "I handed them ... on a silver platter."
- "The SEC roars like a mouse and bites like a flea."

During, and at the end of his verbal testimony, Markopolos points out why the SEC has a lot to answer for, repeatedly letting down investors, U.S. taxpayers, and citizens around the world.

Why Didn't the SEC Catch Madoff Earlier?

According to Markopolos, SEC investigators and their bosses were both incompetent and unwilling to believe that people as well respected in the investment community as Madoff and his brother Peter Madoff could be involved in illicit activities. According to the Madoff's own website,[20]

> Bernard L. Madoff was one of the five broker-dealers most closely involved in developing the NASDAQ Stock Market. He has been chairman of the board of directors of the NASDAQ Stock Market as well as a member of the board of governors of the NASD and a member of numerous NASD committees. Bernard Madoff was also a founding member of the International Securities Clearing Corporation in London.
>
> His brother, Peter B. Madoff has served as vice chairman of the NASD, a member of its board of governors, and chairman of its New York region. He also has been actively involved in the NASDAQ Stock Market as a member of its board of governors and its executive committee and as chairman of its trading committee. He also has been a member of the board of directors of the Security Traders Association of New York. He is a member of the board of directors of the Depository Trust Corporation.

In order to find out why the SEC did not catch Madoff earlier, an internal review was undertaken by the SEC's Office of Inspector General. The resulting report by H. David Kotz, the inspector general, on the *Investigation of the Failure of the SEC to Uncover Bernard Madoff's Ponzi Scheme—Public Version* (OIG-509),[21] dated August 31, 2009, is a ringing condemnation of SEC

[18] Ibid., 24.

[19] Ibid., 24, 25.

[20] http://www.madoff.com, Quote taken from Markopolos, November 7, 2005, to the SEC; also referenced in Kotz Report, http://www.sec.gov/news/studies/2009/oig-509.pdf, 175.

[21] Kotz Report, http://www.sec.gov/news/studies/2009/oig-509.pdf.

investigative and decision-making activities. Although the SEC was approached by several individuals with concerns, tips, and/or analyses, including Markopolos several times, the red flags raised were ignored or not understood, or, when investigated the so-called investigations failed to identify the Ponzi scheme. According to the report, the investigations failed for the following reasons:

- Investigators were inexperienced, usually fresh from law school.
- Investigators were untrained in forensic work:
  - Their practice during the few investigations undertaken was usually to interview Madoff himself and then write their report without further action even though Madoff had been caught in contradictions during the interview.
  - Their work was poorly planned at best and poorly led, although work ratings were exemplary and promotion followed for some.
- Investigators did not have sufficient knowledge of capital markets, derivatives, and investment strategies to understand the following:
  - The fundamentals underlying the marketplace and the fraud.
  - What was a red flag or a red flag worthy of following up?
  - How to check the red flags raised by others.
  - That external third-party verification of Madoff's verbal or fabricated written claims was necessary and would have revealed the Ponzi scheme.
  - What the correct scope of the investigation should have been.
- Investigators were biased in favor of Madoff and against Markopolos.
- Investigators were frequently delayed by other SEC priorities or by inter-SEC rivalry and bureaucratic practices.

H. David Kotz is to be commended for his report and his related recommendations for the improvement of SEC personnel and practices. Anyone who reads the Kotz Report will conclude that the SEC's performance in the Madoff scandal was serially and ridiculously incompetent.

It is interesting to note that although there were repeated indications to the SEC that Madoff's company auditor was allegedly a related party to Madoff, SEC agents never checked. It was finally checked by the New York Division of Enforcement after Madoff confessed. "Within a few hours of obtaining the working papers, the New York Staff Attorney determined that no audit work had been done."[22] Apparently, there had been no external or independent verification of trades or of securities held. The so-called auditor was David Friehling, Madoff's brother-in-law,[23] who headed up a sole practitioner, three-person accounting firm known as Friehling & Horowitz. Friehling has since been charged with fraud.[24] He had been Madoff's auditor from 1991 through 2008.

A Happy Ending?

Fortunately, Madoff confessed on December 11, 2008, and the SEC subsequently charged him with 11 counts of fraud. In fact, Madoff thought that the jig was up in 2006[25] when he had fabricated a story to support his claim of placing orders to hedge his portfolio, but the SEC investigators failed to check the trades *externally*. If they had, they would have found that there were essentially *no trades* even though his claim placed him as running the world's largest hedge fund.

On March 12, 2009, Madoff appeared in court and pleaded guilty to 11 charges.[26]

---

[22] Ibid., 95.

[23] Ibid., 146.

[24] Larry Neumeister, "Prosecutors Charge Madoff's Accountant with Fraud," *The Associated Press*, Yahoo! Canada Finance website, March 18, 2009.

[25] Kotz Report, 23.

[26] Sinclair Stewart, "Madoff Goes to Jail on 11 Guilty Pleas," *The Globe and Mail*, March 13, 2009, B1.

On June 29, 2009, he returned to court. where he was sentenced for "extraordinary evil" to the maximum sentence of 150 years in penitentiary[27] for the following:

TYPE OF FRAUD	SENTENCE (YEARS)—ALL AT THE MAXIMUM
Securities	20
Investment advisor	5
Mail	20
Wire	20
International money laundering related to transfer of funds	20
International money laundering	20
Money laundering	10
False statements	5
Perjury	5
Making a false filing to the SEC	20
Theft from an employee benefit plan	5

Madoff was 71 years old when he was sentenced, so he will spend the rest of his life in prison. His friends did not make out well either. Over the years, however, some friends who were also investors made considerable profits on their investments with Madoff. One of these, Jeffry Picower—a sophisticated investor and friend of Madoff's and a noted philanthropist—was found drowned at the bottom of his Palm Beach pool when a trustee attempted to claw back the $7 million Jeffry and his wife made in Madoff-related profit.[28] It remains to be seen how much will be recovered by court-appointed trustees to be ultimately distributed to investors who lost money investing with Madoff.

Questions

1. Was Madoff's sentence too long?
2. Some SEC personnel were derelict in their duty. What should happen to them?
3. Are the reforms undertaken by the SEC (see http://www.sec.gov/spotlight/sec-postmadoffreforms.htm) tough enough and sufficiently encompassing?
4. Does it matter that Madoff's auditor, Friehling, was his brother-in-law?
5. Does it matter that Friehling did no audit work?
6. Comment on the efficacy of self-regulation in the form of FINRA and in respect to the audit profession. What are the possible solutions to this?
7. Answer Markopolos' questions: "How can we go forward without assurance that others will not shirk their civic duty? We can ask ourselves would the result have been different if those others had raised their voices and what does that say about self-regulated markets?"
8. How could Markopolos and the other whistle-blowers have gotten action on their concerns earlier than they did?
9. Did Markopolos act ethically at all times?
10. What were the most surprising aspects of Markopolos' verbal testimony on YouTube at http://www.youtube.com/watch?v=uw_Tgu0txS0?
11. Did those who invested with Madoff have a responsibility to ensure that he was a legitimate and registered investment advisor? If not, what did they base their investment decision on?
12. Should investors who make a lot of money (1% per month while markets are falling) say, "Thank you very much," or should they query the unusually large rate of return they are receiving?
13. Should investors who made money from "investing" with Madoff be forced to give up their gains to compensate those who lost monies?
14. Is this simply a case of "buyer beware"?

[27] Aaron Smith, "Madoff Sentenced to 150 Years," CNNMoney.com, June 29, 2009.

[28] Diana B. Henriques, "Investor with Madoff Is Found Dead in His Pool," *New York Times*, October 25, 2009.

Wal-Mart Bribery in Mexico

ETHICS CASE

Wal-Mart has a brand image that triggers strong reactions in North America, particularly from people whose businesses have been damaged by the company's overpowering competition with low prices and vast selection and by those who value the small-business/small-town culture that has been supplanted. The company does not need any more controversy and has taken on causes such as environmental sustainability and rushing aid to hurricane victims, partly to build brand support. Consequently, according to the *New York Times*,[1] from September 2005 when a report of significant bribery in Wal-Mart de Mexico was received, senior officers in Mexico and then the United States sought to keep the matter quiet, impede company investigations, blunt the efforts of qualified investigators, refer the matter to senior company lawyers implicated in the scandal for investigation and resolution, weaken company protocols for investigation and reporting, and promote executives involved. As is often the case today, the bribery scandal could not be hushed up, and now the company faces prosecution under the *U.S. Foreign Corrupt Practices Act* (FCPA) as well as significantly more damage to Wal-Mart's image and credibility. Wal-Mart issued an immediate response[2] to the *New York Times* article indicating nontolerance for bribery and committing to get to the bottom of the allegations. The company also stated that it had met, at its request, with the U.S. Department of Justice and the SEC about the matters raised and had disclosed the investigation in the company's 10-Q filing in December 2011. Unfortunately, dealing partially with the matter six years after it was first raised did little to appease the company's critics.

In September 2005, a senior Wal-Mart lawyer received an e-mail from a former Mexican executive, Mr. Cicero, a lawyer, who had been in charge of the bribery payments process, using *gestores* (trusted fixers) to speed up permits for store construction, obtain confidential information, and eliminate fines. "Bribes, he [Cicero] explained, accelerated growth. They got zoning maps changed. They made environmental objections vanish. Permits that typically took months to process magically materialized in days." According to Cicero, the Mexican operations of Wal-Mart had a culture of "very aggressive growth goals" in which doing "whatever was necessary" to obtain building and construction permits facilitated the opening of new stores "in record times." Wal-Mart was the largest private employer in Mexico, employing 209,000 people.[3]

Wal-Mart investigators were sent immediately from the United States and established the veracity of a paper trail for $24 million in bribery payments. When they wanted to expand their investigation, the U.S. executives of Wal-Mart shut it down. According to the *New York Times* article, senior executives were "under fire from labor critics, worried about press leaks, and facing sagging stock prices … recognized that the allegations could have devastating consequences." No one was disciplined, an executive involved was promoted to a senior post at Wal-Mart headquarters, and investigators were criticized for being overly aggressive by H. Lee Scott, Wal-Mart's chief executive. Responsibility for the investigations was shifted,

[1] David Barstow, "Vast Mexico Bribery Case Hushed-Up by Wal-Mart after Top-Level Struggle," *New York Times*, April 21, 2012, accessed April 23, 2012, at http://www.nytimes.com/2012/04/22/business/at-wal-mart-in-mexico-a-bribe-inquiry-silenced.html?pagewanted=all.

[2] Wal-Mart, "Wal-Mart Statement in Response to Recent New York Times Article about Compliance with the U.S. Foreign Corrupt Practices Act," April 21, 2012, accessed April 23, 2012, at http://www.walmartstores.com/pressroom/news/10879.aspx.

[3] Barstow, "Vast Mexico Bribery Case Hushed-Up by Wal-Mart after Top-Level Struggle."

investigators were confined only to "significant" matters, and administrative oversight and approvals were increased. In time, a law firm was hired, and a full investigation was recommended. This was rejected by senior Wal-Mart executives, and a special in-house, major corruption investigations unit was created. But the unit was under-resourced, and senior executives were allowed to transfer some sensitive cases involving themselves or their people to other units and individuals. The Mexican bribery investigation was reassigned. Ms. Munich, the general counsel of Wal-Mart International, who had received the original e-mail and had triggered the initial investigation, complained about these changes and ultimately resigned in 2006.

In an interesting twist, the bribery investigation was ultimately assigned to a lawyer, José Luis Rodríguezmacedo Rivera, the general counsel of Wal-Mart de Mexico, who had been identified as a person who had redacted a 2003 report on the company's FCPA compliance by an auditor who had red-flagged *gestores* payments. The auditor was fired. Rodríguezmacedo dealt with the matter in 2006 as follows: he asked his colleagues if they had bribed anyone, and they denied doing so, and he cast aspersions on the whistle-blower, Mr. Cicero, inferring that the bribes were actually to enrich Cicero, who had been passed over for promotion and whose wife was a partner at the law firm where one of the *gestores* was also a partner. Rodríguezmacedo further claimed that Cicero had been fired for failing to report his wife's potential conflict of interest, although he had personally negotiated with Cicero for his resignation bonus package. He also claimed that because Cicero had triggered the payments to enrich himself, the money was therefore stolen, and bribes were not attributable to Wal-Mart—it was a case of employee theft, not company bribery. Rodríguezmacedo, it should be noted, was an instructor at Wal-Mart's in-house seminar on FCPA compliance.

Questions

1. Where were Wal-Mart's questionable payments made, and where did this result in serious damage to the company and its executives? Why?
2. The *gestores* payments were made to third parties who then bribed local officials. How would a company ensure that its third-party vendors are operating within the law?
3. Some of Wal-Mart's senior executives knew about the bribes but did not take any effective actions to curtail this activity. What steps should the board of directors take to ensure that systems and internal controls are in place so that they are informed about questionable managerial activities and actions?
4. Wal-Mart Mexico seemed to have a culture of the goal justifying the means. How can the board of directors ensure that the operational activities of the company do not subvert proper governance objectives?

ETHICS CASE

LIBOR Manipulations Cause Widespread Impacts

On any given day, a bank may have either a surplus or a deficiency of cash. When this occurs, banks tend to lend to and borrow from other banks at a negotiated rate of interest. These interbank loans could be as short as one day and as long as several months.

The interest rate charged on these interbank loans is estimated by various banks and averaged every day by the British Banking Association (BBA) to create a benchmark interest rate called LIBOR. Eighteen of the world's largest banks submit information about their borrowing costs. The BBA then determines the LIBOR rates based on those submissions. LIBOR in turn is used as a benchmark rate to price more than $800 trillion of securities and loans around the word, including swaps, derivatives, mortgages, and corporate and consumer loans. In September 2012, the United Kingdom's Financial Securities Authority (FSA) announced that the BBA would no longer be administering LIBOR because of a scandal. This LIBOR scandal has had a significant impact on several banks.

Barclays Bank

In June 2012, Barclays Bank PLC admitted to wrongdoing and was fined £290 million ($453 million) for artificially manipulating the LIBOR rate from 2005 to 2009. The bank paid £59.5 million to the FSA, £102 million to the U.S. Department of Justice, and £128 million to the Commodity Futures Trading Commission. The next month, Marcus Agius, chairman of the bank; Robert Diamond, CEO; and Jerry del Missier, COO, all resigned. Diamond agreed to forgo his £20 million bonus for 2012, but he was still entitled to his £2 million pension.

Barclays admitted that it reported artificially high (or low) borrowing costs when it wanted the LIBOR rate to be high (or low). For example, in 2007, it made submissions indicating high borrowing costs, while in 2008, during the credit crisis, the bank began to underreport its costs of borrowing. Part of the reason for these incorrect submissions was to create the false impression that the bank was financially healthier than it really was. In October 2008, the Royal Bank of Scotland and Lloyds Banking Group were partially nationalized through bailout money provided by the U.K. government. There was widespread concern at Barclays that it would be next. The bank wanted to indicate that it was financially viable to forestall a government takeover.

During this period, there was media speculation concerning the true position of the bank, although a Barclays compliance officer assured the BBA that its submissions were "within a reasonable range." There was also widespread concern that LIBOR was being manipulated.

Later, when the FSA report on the scandal was released, it stated that Barclays' derivative traders (who could make profitable trades based on a manipulated LIBOR) made 257 requests of other banks to misstate LIBOR submissions between January 2005 and June 2009. In addition, in November 2008, the BBA issued a draft report on the guidelines for LIBOR submissions that included a recommendation that submissions be audited as part of compliance. Barclays ignored the guidelines until June 2010, when the bank implemented new policies, one of which required the reporting of any attempt to influence LIBOR by either internal or external parties.

UBS

In December, the Swiss bank UBS paid £940 million ($1.5 billion) in penalties for its role in the LIBOR scandal. This was more than twice the fine paid by Barclays Bank. UBS also admitted to manipulating LIBOR, EURIBOR (the Eurozone rate), and TIBOR (the Tokyo rate) from 2005 to 2010. The bank said that all the employees involved in the manipulations were no longer with UBS, including 35 who left in 2012. In February 2013, the bank announced that it was reducing investment bankers' bonuses by a third in order to recoup some of the fine.

At UBS, brokers were allowed to make the LIBOR submissions, creating direct conflicts of interests. Derivate traders could make a lot of money if they knew what LIBOR would be in advance of it being published. Traders boasted in chat forums and through e-mail about how successful they were at manipulating the rate. "Think of me when yur on yur yacht in Monaco," one broker wrote. Another said that he was "getting bloody good" at rate rigging. Another allegedly said that LIBOR "is too high (be)cause I have kept it artificially high."

There were at least 2,000 manipulations designed to simply enrich the brokers themselves. This was collusion on a grand scale. According to the FSA, the manipulations involved at least 45 people, including UBS employees as well as external brokers. In one case, the bank paid £15,000 every three months to outside brokers to assist in the manipulations.

UBS also admitted that management had asked staff to submit artificially low LIBOR borrowing costs during the final days of the subprime mortgage crisis in order to give the false impression that the bank was financially more secure than it actually was. Barclays had similarly used LIBOR submissions to artificially maintain market confidence.

Other Banks

In January 2013, the Deutsche Bank of Germany announced that it was recording a €1 billion provision to cover the cost of potential lawsuits concerning LIBOR manipulations. In February 2013, the Royal Bank of Scotland agreed to pay £390 million for its role in the LIBOR scandal.

Subsequent Event and Additional Information

As a result of this scandal, perpetrated by various banks designed to manipulate the LIBOR rate and the valuation of many security prices, the NYSE Euronext will take over the setting of LIBOR beginning in early 2014. A detailed analysis and description of LIBOR and the scandal is contained on pages 93 to 98.

Questions

1. Which groups were most at fault for the LIBOR manipulations: brokers, traders, bank executives, bank boards of directors, or regulators? Why?
2. What should the regulatory bodies do with the fines paid by these banks? Reduce tax rates for the general public? Use the funds to reeducate investment bankers?
3. Robert Diamond continues to receive his £2 million pension annually. Should he suffer financially by having to forfeit this pension because the LIBOR scandal occurred while he was CEO of Barclays?
4. Both Barclays and UBS reduced the bonuses of current employees to help pay part of the fines that occurred because of the actions of former employees. Is this fair?
5. The rate manipulations seemed to be systemic to the industry because so many banks were involved. What can be done to curtail such widespread unethical practices within an industry?
6. Why weren't the directors of the banks that had caused the scandal fined or jailed? Should they have been?
7. Why should members of the public trust the banks that were involved in manipulating the LIBOR rate?

Sources: D. Cimilluca, M. Colchester, and S. S. Munoz, "No Bonus for Barclay's Ex-CEO," *The Globe and Mail*, July 11, 2012; D. Enrich, and Eaglesham, "UBS Admits Rigging Rates in 'Epic' Plot," *Wall Street Journal*, December 20, 2012; "Timeline: Libor-Fixing Scandal," *BBC News Business*, February 6, 2013; "UBS Fined $1.5bn for Libor Rigging," *BBC News Business*, December 19, 2012.

ETHICS CASE

General Motors Ignores Obvious Ignition Faults

On a fateful day in 2001, a GM engineer realized during preproduction testing of the Saturn Ion that there was a defect that caused the small car's engine to stall without warning.[1] This switch was approved in 2002 by an engineer, Raymond DiGeorgio, who said he knew the switch was substandard, but "he did not think it could endanger

[1] Interestingly, the ignition switch for the Cadillac Catera, a high-quality GM small car, was redesigned at the time to avoid these ignition faults. The Catera design was not implemented on other cars until 2008 and was later found to be below GM standards. See footnote 9.

lives."[2] The defect—that would allow the switch to disengage when a heavy key-chain was jiggled by a knee or a pothole—was discovered again when the Chevrolet Cobalt replaced the Chevrolet Cavalier in 2004,[3] but GM apparently did not realize the full significance of the problem until late 2013[4]—*that the defect would disable the car's power-assisted steering, brakes, and airbags, and over 150 people would die as a result.* How could this happen at one of the world's largest carmakers?

When the engine stops in a car equipped with power steering and brakes, the driver suddenly has to exert almost superhuman strength to turn the car or to stop it, and the airbags may not work. When a moving car stalls without warning, the driver instantly finds that she or he is driving the equivalent of a block of concrete on wheels. Even if the driver is not stunned by the transition, the direction of the car and its speed often cannot be controlled by a person of normal strength. Even abnormal strength cannot activate airbags if they are electronically enabled, which GM's were. The driver and passengers usually just have to go wherever the car is headed without the protection of brakes and airbags. No wonder many people died or were injured.

In March 2005, GM rejected fixing the ignition switch because "it would be too costly and take too long."[5] Instead, GM sent a bulletin to its dealers warning that the ignition switch could fail when "the driver is short and has a large and/or heavy key chain … the customer should be advised of this potential and should … [remove] unessential items from their key chain."[6] Later estimates would place the cost of the fix at 57 cents per switch.[7]

However, a GM engineer, Raymond DiGeorgio, did redesign the switch in 2006, but did not change the part number, which was "very unusual"[8] and against GM policy.[9] Nor did he tell anyone.[10] The redesigned switch apparently solved the problem in some cars built after 2006, but since the part number was not changed, National Highway Traffic Safety Association (NHTSA) investigators in 2007 and 2010 did not discover the link between the faulty switch and the crashes and deaths.[11] Later, in 2016, GM admitted that these redesigned switches still didn't meet their minimum standards so cars produced between 2008-2011 were also defective.[12]

By the time the subprime lending crisis became a reality in 2007-2008, GM was in financial difficulty and was in need of a bailout, as were some other auto makers, to preserve the jobs of their employees as

---

[2] Jessica Dye, "Ex-GM Engineer Acknowledges 'Mistakes' Made over Ignition Switch," Reuters, January 15, 2016, accessed February 27, 2016, at http://www.reuters.com/article/us-gm-recall-trial-idUSKCN0UT2DF.

[3] Tanya Basu, "Timeline: A History of GM's Ignition Switch Defect," June 18, 2014, published March 31, 2014, accessed February 27, 2016, at http://www.npr.org/2014/03/31/297158876/timeline-a-history-of-gms-ignition-switch-defect.

[4] Ibid.

[5] Ibid

[6] Ibid.

[7] "GM Recall Linked to 57-Cent Ignition Switch Component," *Associated Press*, April 1, 2014, updated April 2, 2014, accessed February 28, 2016, at http://www.cbc.ca/news/business/gm-recall-linked-to-57-cent-ignition-switch-component-1.2593930.

[8] Dye, "Ex-GM Engineer Acknowledges 'Mistakes' Made over Ignition Switch."

[9] Todd Wasserman, "How One GM Engineer's Decisions Helped Lead to 5.8 Million Recalls," June 17, 2014, accessed February 27, 2016, at http://mashable.com/2014/06/17/gm-engineer-ray-degiorgio/#eOywuU1kDqq8.

[10] Ibid.

[11] Basu, "Timeline."

[12] Nick Bunkley "Lawmakers ID Engineer behind '06 GM Switch Redesign," *Automotive News*, March 31, 2014, accessed February 27, 2016, at http://www.autonews.com/article/20140331/OEM11/140339971/lawmakers-id-engineer-behind-06-gm-switch-redesign.

well as those of their suppliers. Part of GM's recovery plan involved it going into bankruptcy, and emerging as a "new" GM to allow it to shed it liabilities as at June 1, 2009, including some of the liabilities to people injured due to the faulty ignition switches.[13]

When the full fury of the public and outraged lawmakers surfaced in 2014, the GM Board of Directors commissioned a report by Anton R. Valukas, who had earlier been called upon to investigate the Enron scandal. His 325 page report, dated May 29, 2014, provides many details about the individuals and processes involved in this tragedy.[14] One of the observations made concerned GM's method for dealing with difficult issues like the faulty ignition switch. He reported:

> While GM heard over and over from various quarters including customers, dealers, the press, and their own employees—that the car's ignition switch led to moving stalls, group after group, committee after committee with GM that reviewed the issue failed to take action, or acted too slowly. Although everyone had responsibility to fix the problem, nobody took responsibility. It was an example of what one top executive described as the "GM nod," when everyone nods in agreement to a proposed plan of action, but then leaves the room and does nothing.

In January 2014, Mary Barra became the CEO of GM. She learned of the faulty ignition switch on January 31, 2014. Since that time, she has had to steer GM through the crisis, the lawsuits, the public hearings, and the recall of millions of cars. Even with the 2008 bankruptcy, GM faced lawsuits of approximately $1 billion[15] and refit costs of hundreds of millions of dollars, not to mention dealing with the loss of reputation and future sales. For her role in leading the company in 2014, Mary was paid a "base salary of $1.6m, and granted stock awards worth more than $13.7m that she cannot cash in for several years."[16]

Questions

1. Why didn't GM act effectively on suspicions that their ignition switches were faulty?
2. Who was at fault for the deaths and injuries involved, and why?
3. Should a company be able to escape liability for harming individuals by declaring bankruptcy?
4. Should any GM personnel go to jail over the ignition switch failures? If so, whom.
5. Would you trust GM enough to buy one of their cars in the future?
6. Was Mary Barra paid enough for the job she was required to do?

---

[13] Basu, "Timeline."

[14] Anton R. Valukas, "General Motors Report regarding Ignition Switch Recall," *Washington Post*, May 29, 2014, accessed February 28, 2016, at https://www.washingtonpost.com/apps/g/page/business/general-motors-report-regarding-ignition-switch-recall/1085. See also, for a copy of the report: http://www.npr.org/news/documents/2014/valukas-report-on-gm-redacted.pdf at p. 2.

[15] David Ingram, Nate Raymond, and Joseph White, "GM to Pay $900 Million, Settle U.S. Criminal Case over Ignition Switches—Sources," Reuters, September 17, 2015, https://ca.finance.yahoo.com/news/gm-pay-900-million-settle-004103824.html; Jessica Dye, "GM Also Resolves Civil Lawsuits over Ignition-Switch Defect," Reuters, September 17, 2015, https://ca.finance.yahoo.com/news/gm-resolves-civil-lawsuits-over-192504285.html.

[16] Rupert Neate, "General Motors CEO Mary Barra Paid 80% More Than Predecessor in First Year," *The Guardian*, April 24, 2015, accessed February 28, 2016, at http://www.theguardian.com/business/2015/apr/24/general-motors-mary-barra-first-year-pay.

ETHICS CASE

VW Cheats on Emissions Tests

In 2006, Mercedes-Benz introduced BlueTEC, an advanced system to trap and neutralize harmful emissions and particulates that allowed Mercedes to market "clean diesel" cars. VW and Audi made agreements to share the technology to enable all three companies to market clean diesels in an attempt to expand the market for diesel car. If VW and Audi had not joined Mercedes, they would probably have been at a significant competitive disadvantage.

VW, however, being a company of proud employees, started work on their own "clean diesel" system and introduced one in 2009. Unfortunately, VWs new system could operate in compliance with U.S. emission standards only if their engines were adjusted to run at very poor performance and gas usage levels, which were not competitive with the BlueTEC systems already on the market. Motivated by pride and enabled by arrogance and complacency,[1] VW engineers decided to install a computer software switch that, when government emission tests were started, would alter the engine performance characteristics during the tests from a normal high-performance/high-emission setting to a low-emission/low-performance setting. This computer software defeat device allowed VW vehicles to pass the California emission tests, which were the toughest in the United States. In fact, the VW engines produced up to thirty-eight times the allowed pollution levels.[2] Hypocritically, VW's Super Bowl ad showed their engineers sprouting white wings like angels.

Essentially, VW engineers decided to cheat—to defeat the emission tests—with a technical "fix." They *gambled* that no one would find out and/or that there would be little negative reaction. Apparently, top management were unaware of the plan to cheat. Interestingly, this was not the first time that a defeat device had been used. In 1973, VW was fined $120,000 in the United States for using an earlier defeat device, and in 1998, truck engine makers agreed to a $1 billion settlement for a similar instance. But VW tried it again, and when high test results came to light in 2014.

VWs software deception was discovered in 2014 by scientists at West Virginia University who disclosed their results at a public forum. VW's reaction was that the testers did not conduct the tests properly.[3] The U.S. Environmental Protection Agency repeated the tests and questioned VW personnel. This triggered VW's halt of sales of some diesels and the production of others, an internal investigation, and the resignation of the CEO, Martin Winterkorn, as well as a recall of 11 million cars.[4]

In September 2015, VW stock sank by 20% and then another 17%, and $7.3 billion was allocated to cover the recalls, refits, and other costs of the scandal.[5] The amount of fines and the cost of settling civil lawsuits will not be known for some time, although the U.S. Justice Department has sued VW

---

[1] Armin Mahler, "VW Scandal: Time for German Industry to Abandon Its Arrogance," *Spiegel Online International*, September 30, 2015, http://www.spiegel.de/international/business/vw-scandal-shows-german-companies-are-no-longer-big-league-a-1055098.html.

[2] Guilbert Gates, Josh Keller, Karl Russell, and Derek Watkins, "How Volkswagen Got Away with Diesel Deception," updated October 2, 2015, *New York Times*, http://www.nytimes.com/interactive/2015/09/22/business/international/vw-volkswagen-emissions-explainer.html.

[3] Danny Hakim, Aaron M. Kessler, and Jack Ewing, "As Volkswagen Pushed to Be No. 1, Ambitions Fueled a Scandal," *New York Times*, September 26, 2015, http://www.nytimes.com/2015/09/27/business/as-vw-pushed-to-be-no-1-ambitions-fueled-a-scandal.html.

[4] Ibid.

[5] Jack Ewing, "VW's New Chief Says Scandal Will Cost It More Than Expected," *New York Times*, October 6, 2015, http://www.nytimes.com/2015/10/07/business/international/vw-diesel-emissions-job-cuts.html?_r=0.

for up to $48 billion.[6] *It is evident that many VW employees and managers knew of this illegal deception of cheating on emissions standards from before 2009 to 2014, thus putting the company at great financial and reputation risk.*

Concern has been expressed that the VW emissions cheating scandal has undermined the vaunted reputation of German engineering, calling into question the traditionally respected Mercedes, BMW, and other brands that employ so many in Germany and abroad. Also, VW's cheating has deeply offended the environmental/sustainability movement, which is very strong in Europe, and the governments that backed the "clean diesel" program there. As David Bach has pointed out, "'Clean diesel,' it turns out, is as much a lie as 'clean coal.' Volkswagen's abhorrent behaviour therefore threatens to delegitimise the countless and essential efforts by companies around the world to develop scalable environmental solutions."[7]

Questions

1. Why would VW engineers think they could get away with a defeat device when the technique had been caught twice before?
2. If they thought they would be caught, why did they try the defeat device?
3. Why didn't one of the several design engineers and test engineers and technicians involved blow the whistle to top management and/or the regulators?
4. VW has a governance system, where the Supervisory Board[8] is different from North American boards of directors. How is it different from North American governance models? The VW governance system does not appear to have a whistleblower encouragement and reporting system. Could the differences in governance have contributed to the decision to cheat, and to keeping it a secret? If so, how?
5. Describe how VW would have to change to institute a culture of integrity.
6. How would VW ensure that their policy on environmental protection be upheld?
7. Should VW engineers, managers, and the CEO be sent to jail? Why or why not?
8. Would you buy a VW? Why or why not?

---

[6] Julia Edwards and Georgina Prodhan, "VW Faces Billions in Fines as U.S. Sues for Environmental Violations," *Reuters*, January 5, 2016, accessed January 5, 2016, at https://ca.finance.yahoo.com/news/volkswagen-faces-billions-fines-u-113033762.html.

[7] David Bach, "Seven Reasons Volkswagen Is Worse Than Enron," *FT Confidential Research*, September 27, 2015; see paper copy at http://www.ft.com/cms/s/0/cf9f73e8-62d6-11e5-9846-de406ccb37f2.html#axzz41V16gCCh. Also available from the *Irish Times* at http://www.irishtimes.com/business/transport-and-tourism/seven-reasons-volkswagen-is-worse-than-enron-1.2369683.

[8] The VW Supervisory Board membership is described at http://annualreport2014.volkswagenag.com/group-management-report/executive-bodies/supervisory-board.html. VW complies with the German Corporate Governance Code in that it is governed by a Management Board and a Supervisory Board instead of a single Board of Directors as is normal in North American corporations. For more information, see http://www.dcgk.de/en/code//foreword.html.

3 Ethical Behavior—Philosophers' Contributions

PURPOSE OF THE CHAPTER

Philosophers have been dedicated to the study of ethical behavior for millennia. The ideas, concepts, and principles they have developed have long been recognized as important touchstones for the assessment of corporate and personal activities. The ethicality of the strategies and actions of corporations and individuals cannot be left to chance. Consequently, directors, executives, and professional accountants need to be aware of ethical parameters and need to build these into the cultures of their organizations. Given the diverse nature of individuals making up our corporations and the global challenges they face, it is no longer defensible to leave the principles of ethical behavior up to the individual employee. Organizations must hire individuals who are ethically aware and provide them with an understanding of which ethical principles drive action. The philosopher's contributions discussed in this chapter and made practical in Chapter 4 provide a helpful basic background to enable directors, executives, and professional accountants to make ethical plans and decisions. To ignore the wisdom in this chapter and Chapter 4 would be irresponsible and would leave important gaps of ethical understanding and vulnerability.

Ethics is a branch of philosophy that investigates normative judgments about what behavior is right or what ought to be done. The need for ethics arises from the desire to avoid real-life problems. It does not address issues of what you should or should not believe; those are contained in religious codes. Instead, ethics deals with the principles that guide human behavior. It is the study of norms and values concerning ideas of right and wrong, good and bad, as well as what we ought to do and what we should eschew doing. The ethical theories described in this chapter will not provide boilerplate solutions to practical problems. Instead, the theories and frameworks provide guidance to assist decision makers in determining acceptable and unacceptable business behavior and actions.

Decisions spring from beliefs about what norms, values, and achievements are expected and what the rewards and sanctions are for certain actions. Ethical dilemmas arise when norms and values are in conflict and there are alternative courses of action available. This means that the decision maker must make a choice. Unlike many other business decisions that have clear decision-making criteria, with ethical dilemmas there are no objective standards. Therefore, we need to use subjective moral codes. The ethical theories described in this chapter explain how to understand, implement, and act in accordance with moral codes concerning appropriate business behavior.

Although the fundamental principles and ideals of all of the ethical theories described in this chapter have application to business, each theory is not without its critics. So we need to demonstrate tolerance as we work though the strengths and weaknesses of the theories. Remember, they provide guidance about factors to consider, not decision tools that will always yield the same answer. It is still up to the decision maker to consider the issues, make the final decision, act accordingly, and live with the consequences.

ETHICS & MORAL CODES

The *Encyclopedia of Philosophy* defines ethics in three ways as follows:

1. A general pattern or "way of life"
2. A set of rules of conduct or "moral code"
3. Inquiry *about* ways of life and rules of conduct

In the first sense, we speak of Buddhist or Christian ethics; in the second, we speak of professional ethics and unethical behavior. In the third sense, ethics is a branch of philosophy that is frequently given the special name of metaethics.[1]

This book is interested in the second sense of ethics, as it relates to moral codes concerning human conduct and behavior in a business setting. We do not address religious beliefs about how humans should live their lives and the proper way of achieving the various goals of a religious life. Nor are we interested in metaethics, the theory about ethics. Instead, we are interested in studying the moral codes that relate to business behavior.

Morality and moral codes are defined in the *Encyclopedia of Philosophy* as containing four characteristics:

1. Beliefs about the nature of man
2. Beliefs about ideals, about what is good or desirable or worthy of pursuit for its own sake
3. Rules laying down what ought to be done and what ought not to be done
4. Motives that incline us to choose the right or the wrong course[2]

Each of these four aspects is explored using the four major ethical theories that apply to people making ethical decisions in a business environment: utilitarianism, deontology, justice and fairness, and virtue ethics.[3]

Each of these theories places a different emphasis on these four characteristics. For example, utilitarianism stresses the importance of rules in pursuing what is good or desirable, whereas deontology examines the motives of the ethical decision maker. Virtue ethics tends to examine humans in a more holistic fashion, looking at the nature of humanity. Although each theory emphasizes different aspects of moral codes, they all have many common features, especially a concern of what should and should not be done. But, as Rawls notes, no theory is complete, so we must be tolerant of their various

[1] Paul Edwards, ed., *The Encyclopedia of Philosophy*, vol. 3 (New York: Macmillan 1967), 81–82.

[2] Ibid., vol. 7, 150.

[3] These four were identified in the Association to Advance Collegiate Schools of Business (AACSB) Ethics Education Committee Report (2004) as essential for business students and accountants to understand. The AACSB accredits business schools and programs worldwide. See http://www.aacsb.edu. The 2004 Ethics Education Report is available at http://www.aacsb.edu/publications/researchreports/archives/ethics-education.pdf.

weaknesses and deficiencies. "The real question at any given time is which of the views [theories] already proposed is the best approximation overall [of what we should do]."[4] The goal is to be able to use these theories to help in our ethical decision making.

Most people, most of the time, know the difference between right and wrong. Ethical dilemmas rarely involve choosing between these two stark alternatives. Instead, ethical dilemmas normally arise because there is no entirely right option. Instead, there are compelling reasons for each of the alternatives, so it is up to the individual to decide which alternative to choose. An ethical decision maker should not choose what others have chosen simply to be consistent with other people, to follow the crowd. Instead, to act as an ethical person means that you are capable of taking a stand on an important and difficult problem of human life and be able to explain and justify your stance. You must be able to clearly articulate and defend why you selected that course of action, using ethical theories and reasons.

As indicated in Figure 3.1, the ethical theories that are explained in this chapter provide guidance in making ethical decisions. Although there are many other ethical theories, these are the ones that are particularly useful in making ethical decisions in a business context. But we are not naïve. We are aware that sometimes we do not do what we decide we should do. Even though you should not have that chocolate éclair because you are on a diet, sometimes you eat it anyways. In business, there are many constraints that influence whether a decision maker actually does the right thing. These mitigating factors can be broadly grouped into organizational constraints and personal characteristics. Organizational constraints include reward systems, organizational culture, and the tone at the top of the firm. For example, people do what they are paid to do, and if the reward system encourages questionable behaviors or discourages ethical discussion of a proposed course of action, then employees will not factor ethics into their

FIGURE 3.1 The Ethical Reasoning Process

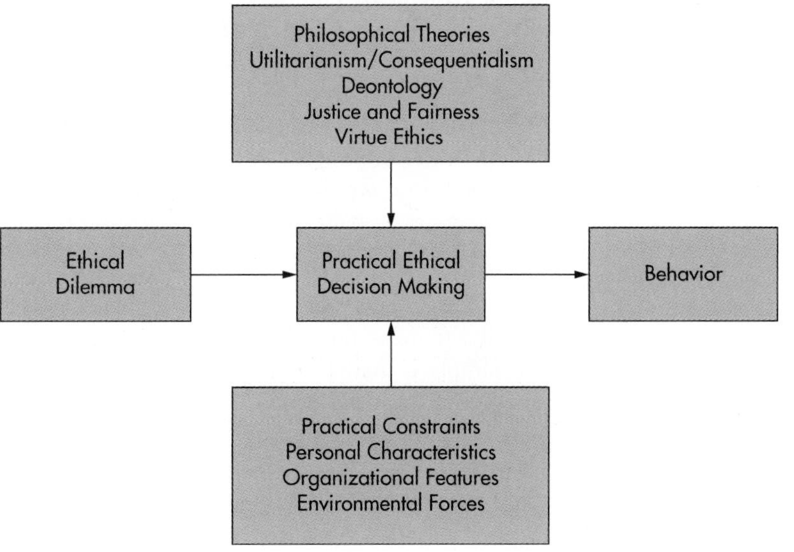

[4] John Rawls, *A Theory of Justice* (Cambridge, MA: Harvard University Press, 1971), 52.

decision-making process. The values of the organization also influence employee behavior, as well as the behavior of senior managers. If employees see that the firm tacitly encourages misleading customers and that the board of directors flaunts the corporate code of conduct, then junior employees will think that ethics and doing the right thing are unimportant in business. These organizational constraints are discussed in more detail in the discussion of corporate culture in Chapter 5.

Personal characteristics that influence actually doing what the individual knows is correct include a misguided understanding of business, an overcommitment to the firm, and ethical immaturity. Some employees mistakenly think that the goal of business is only to make a profit. As long as the business succeeds, the techniques (i.e., means) used are erroneously thought to be irrelevant. This is an example of the mistaken belief that the end justifies the means. An overcommitment to the firm can cloud ethical judgment. John DeLorean, the founder of the DeLorean Motor Company, was so committed to his firm that he attempted to illegally sell cocaine in order to forestall the bankruptcy of his company.[5] There are numerous other acts of misguided loyalty to the firm. However, the most important personal constraint may very well be ethical immaturity. Like physical maturity, ethical maturity comes with age and experience. It is easy to speculate what you would do in a hypothetical situation. Many of the cases in this book present hypothetical problems for you to solve. The choices that you make will help to develop and reinforce your judgment, values, and moral code.[6] But you will not really know what you will do until you are confronted with an actual ethical problem and have to make a decision.

John DeLorean's Overcommitment to His Company

In 1972, the flamboyant business executive John DeLorean was poised to become the next president of General Motors, at the time, one of the largest corporations in the world. DeLorean had a stellar career with the company, first in the Pontiac division designing the GTO, the first muscle car, and then as the head of Chevrolet, the flagship division of GM. On April 3, 1973, he suddenly resigned to form his own car company. Under his leadership, the DeLorean Motor Company designed and built a fiberglass and stainless-steel two-seater sports car with gull wings. About 9,000 cars were manufactured prior to 1983, one of which was used as the time machine in the trilogy of Back to the Future *movies. Unfortunately, the company was not profitable, and so, in 1982 he attempted to illegally sell cocaine in order to obtain the cash necessary to keep his company afloat. When captured in a sting operation by the government, he said that he would do anything to forestall the bankruptcy of his company.*

Usually, there is no single right answer in resolving ethical problems. Nor is the decision simply a matter of a leap of faith. Instead, it requires careful and thoughtful analysis. Then, once the decision is made and the course of action is decided on, the decision maker must take an action or decide not to act. Frameworks are provided in this chapter and the next to help you to make an ethical decision. What you actually do is up to you, and you will have to live with the consequences.

[5] Hillel Levin, *Grand Delusions: The Cosmic Career of John De Lorean* (New York: Viking Press, 1983).

[6] For further discussion of the development of judgment (e.g., Kohlberg's Six Stages of Moral Reasoning), values, and moral codes, see Chapters 5 and 6.

ETHICS & BUSINESS

Archie Carroll astutely observes that you can talk meaningfully about business ethics only if the business is economically viable.[7] If it is not profitable, then it goes out of business, and the question of what is appropriate and inappropriate business behavior is moot. Consequently, a primary goal of a for-profit firm is to remain in business. It does this by providing goods and services that are required by society in an efficient and effective manner. This is a fundamental goal of business, but it is not the only goal and should not be pursued at any cost. Profit is the consequence of doing business well. But business must also adhere to the applicable laws and regulations as a bare minimum. Applicable laws provide the base level of acceptable business behavior. Importing cocaine may be profitable, but it is illegal. The third and fourth responsibilities of business, according to Carroll, are to be ethical and socially responsible. Business operates within society and must adhere to the norms of society and should contribute to the betterment of society.

On the other hand, some people will argue that being economically viable and obeying the law are the only two responsibilities of business and that ethics has nothing to do with business. Why, then, should businesspeople be ethical?

Three of the most common explanations for why individuals should be ethical are grounded on views about religion, our relationships with other people, and our perception about ourselves. As was mentioned, some define ethics as having to do with the pattern of how we should live our lives based on religious principles. In the Judeo-Christian tradition, this would include the principles of "do unto others as you would have them do unto you," "do not bear false witness," and "love your neighbor as yourself." Similar principles and laws are proscribed by other religions. For many people, it is respect for such laws and religious codes that govern behavior. We should be ethical because that is God's law.

Others believe that ethics has nothing to do with religion per se. Instead, it has to do with our regard for other people, demonstrated through love, sympathy, beneficence, and the like. We are social animals who live in society with other people. We naturally develop strong emotional attachments to other people that we often show through acts of love and self-sacrifice. Through our interactions, we become sympathetic to their emotions and feelings. We reproduce in ourselves the pleasures, pains, and satisfactions that we recognize are being felt by others based on our own experiences of pleasure, pain, and satisfaction. Ethics represents our sympathetic identification with others and is often manifested in acts of beneficence, friendship, and love.

Still others believe that we behave ethically because of enlightened self-interest. This last view is compelling for many businesspeople. The first characteristic of morality, as defined above, has to do with beliefs about the nature of people. A fundamental aspect of human nature is that we are self-interested. Although we live with others in society, each of us is living our unique individual life. This perspective takes the following pattern: It is my life; I am interested in myself. Factors that influence me are important to me, so I am interested in the things that will have an impact on my life. However, there is a difference between self-interest and selfishness. Selfishness concerns only the individual and places the individual's needs and concerns above those of other people. Self-interest, on the other hand, is an interest *concerning* the self, not an interest *in* the self. Self-interest is not narrowly defined as being about only me. Instead, it is an interest in

[7] Archie Carroll, "The Pyramid of Corporate Social Responsibility: Toward the Moral Management of Organizational Stakeholders," *Business Horizons* 34 (1991): 39–48.

all matters that relate to me, my family, my friends, and the society in which I live. Self-interest has an intimate connection with economic behavior.

SELF-INTEREST & ECONOMICS

In the 1987 movie *Wall Street*, the principal character, Gordon Gekko, played by Michael Douglas, argues in his presentation to the board of directors of Teldar Paper that business is grounded on greed. "The point is, ladies and gentlemen, that greed, for lack of a better word, is good. Greed is right, greed works. Greed clarifies, cuts through, and captures the essence of the evolutionary spirit. Greed, in all its forms; greed for life, for money, for love, knowledge has marked the upward surge of mankind." The better word that Gordon Gekko is looking for is *self-interest* rather than *greed*. It is self-interest, not greed, that moves the economy. In social and economic theory, self-interest works and is good; selfishness, avarice, and greed do not. In case after case, unbalanced greed has created vulnerabilities and has proved to be a highly risky strategy for the individuals and corporations that pursue it—usually ending in disaster.

The concept of self-interest has a long tradition in English empirical philosophy to explain both social harmony and economic cooperation. Thomas Hobbes (1588–1679) argued that self-interest motivates people to form peaceful civil societies. Writing after the English civil war (1642–1651), he was comparing factors that contributed to a stable society and those that led to a state of war. He observed that people have multiple natural desires, a fundamental one being self-preservation. People are also driven by their short-term interests. Some may want a particular good or to achieve a particular goal and are willing to acquire it by any means. But this can lead to war and conflict as people compete for the same things. When people are driven by their base desires, by unbridled self-interest, anarchy occurs. There is no economic prosperity, no social infrastructures, and no civilized social order. Peace, on the other hand, is probably in everyone's best long-term interests. It avoids the uncertainties and dangers of what Hobbes calls a state of nature, where life is "solitary, poore [*sic*], nasty, brutish, and short."[8] But peace means accepting rules that limit individual freedom. People will no longer be able to pursue their personal goals when those goals would have a negative effect on other people.

From this perspective, civil society can be seen as a voluntary contract among individuals in which some individual freedoms and rights are given up in exchange for peace and self-preservation. This is enlightened self-interest. The desire for personal security means that individuals voluntarily limit their personal freedoms in order to secure social harmony. As such, society can be seen as a Leviathan, a commonwealth that guarantees peace and security to its citizens. Although this may have some negative short-term consequences, most will realize that voluntarily refraining from exploiting others will ensure their personal security. For Hobbes, self-interest leads to cooperation and the formation of a civil society.

Following in this tradition, Adam Smith (1723–1790) argued that self-interest leads to economic cooperation. In his opus *An Inquiry into the Nature and Causes of the Wealth of Nations*, he observes that both buyers and sellers are interested in satisfying their individual needs and desires. Buyers want to derive the most relative satisfaction or utility from their consumer purchases. Sellers want to earn the maximum profit they can from the transaction. In a perfect market, buyers and sellers negotiate to Pareto-optimum equilibrium, what Smith calls the natural price. If the seller sets the price too

[8] Thomas Hobbes, *Leviathan*, ed. C. B. Macpherson (Middlesex: Penguin, 1968), 186.

high, no one will buy the product. If the price is very low, consumers will be more than willing to buy the product. As the demand for the product increases, either the seller will increase the price or new sellers will enter the market in an attempt to satisfy consumer demands for the product. If the price then rises too high, the buyers will leave the market. This is what Smith meant by a free market; both buyers and sellers can freely and without compulsion enter and exit the marketplace. As a result, competition among vendors and consumers pushes prices to the point where markets clear, where all the goods available for sale sell at prices that consumers are willing to pay for those products and vendors are willing to accept for their products.

Profits occur when goods and services are provided in an efficient and effective manner. Smith uses the example of a pin factory. Ten men working independently can produce fewer than twenty pins per day. However, these same ten men, working cooperatively with each man doing one part of the pin-making process, can produce almost 48,000 pins per day. Utilizing the available labor in an efficient and effective manner results in the maximum number of pins of a uniform quality being produced in a given amount of time. Higher production through a cooperative division of labor is in everyone's best interests.

The invisible hand of the marketplace results in a Pareto-optimum position where it is impossible to improve anyone's condition without worsening the condition of someone else. This means that society as a whole is better off. Self-interested individuals unintentionally increase the wealth of their nation. "He generally, indeed, neither intends to promote the publick [*sic*] interest, nor knows how much he is promoting it. By preferring the support of domestick [*sic*] to that of foreign industry, he intends only his own security; and by directing that industry in such a manner as its produce may be of the greatest value, he intends only his own gain, and he is in this, as in many other cases, lead by an invisible hand to promote an end which was no part of his intention."[9]

Smith is often, mistakenly, seen as the advocate of unfettered capitalism. This is not the case. He did advocate minimal governmental interference in the marketplace. The government should be responsible only for establishing and paying for the infrastructures of society, including such things as the transportation system, public education, and the justice system. Business should be able to handle all other matters. However, it is important to note that selfishness, avarice, and greed are not part of Smith's model. Smith was both an economist and an ethicist. He held the chair in moral philosophy at the University of Glasgow. In 1790, he published his *Theory of Moral Sentiments*, a treatise in which he developed an ethics based on sympathy. Sympathy is our feeling the passions of others. It is being affected by the sentiments of other people with a corresponding feeling within us. Because we identify with the emotions of others, we strive to establish good relations with other people. We desire their approbation and shun their disapproval. This provides the basis for benevolent acts and social justice. *For Smith, individuals do not act out of narrow selfishness but rather out of sympathy both for oneself and for others. In other words, ethical behavior is grounded on the sentiment of sympathy, which in turn constrains unbridled self-interest.*

How does this relate to his economic theory? The key features of Smith's economic model are, first, that business is a cooperative social activity. Firms provide goods and services that are required by society. Sellers and buyers work toward a common objective by satisfying their needs at mutually agreeable prices. These are not atomistic transactions but rather are socially constructed events. Business is a social activity, and society

[9] Adam Smith, *An Inquiry into the Nature and Causes of the Wealth of Nations*, ed. Kathryn Sutherland (Oxford: Oxford University Press, 1993), 291–292.

operates on ethical principles. Second, markets are competitive, not adversarial. Trade is dependent on fair play, honoring contracts, and mutual cooperation. Healthy competition ensures that the highest quality goods and services are provided at the lowest prices. Competition also means that firms strive to operate as efficiently and effectively as possible in order to maximize their long-term profits. Finally, ethics constrains economic opportunism. Ethics keeps narrow selfishness and unbridled greed in check. According to Smith, individuals follow ethical guidelines for the good of society. By analogy, they should also follow ethical guidelines for the good of the economy. So, in answer to Gordon Gekko, it is self-interest, not greed, that moves the marketplace, and self-interest has the unintended consequence of improving the social welfare of everyone.

Smith's insight is that self-interest leads to economic cooperation. Self-interest is the motivation for a division of labor, and a cooperative division of labor means that more and better products can be provided to society in an efficient and effective manner. The marketplace will price these products based on consumer needs, their availability, their quality, and other qualitative aspects of the products. The profits that ensue to the vendor are a result of providing goods and services. So, the goal of the marketplace is not for a firm to make a profit. Rather, the purpose is for firms to provide goods and services in an efficient and effective manner, that is, by being profitable. Profit is the consequence, not the end. In a competitive environment, the wants and desires of both buyers and sellers are satisfied through self-interested contracting. Cooperative contracting results in the buying and selling of goods and services at Pareto-optimum prices. Such a system promotes the economic well-being of all and the nation as a whole.

ETHICS, BUSINESS & THE LAW

Schwartz and Carroll[10] argue that business, ethics, and the law can be seen as three intersecting circles in a Venn diagram as per Figure 3.2. Area 1 represents the aspects of business activity that are not covered by the law or ethics. For example, in the United States, a set of financial statements consists of a balance sheet, an income statement, a statement of change in equity, and a statement of cash flows. Under International Financial Reporting, they are referred to as a statement of financial position, a statement of comprehensive income, a statement of changes in equity, and a statement of cash flows. These conventions have nothing to do with ethics or the law." In Area 2 are laws that have nothing to do with ethics or business. Driving on the right-hand side of the road is a convenience law so that people do not bump into one another. In Australia and the United Kingdom, the law is reversed. Area 3 represents ethical prohibitions that do not concern business and are not illegal. Lying or cheating on a spouse would be an example.

There are many overlaps among the law, ethics, and business. Area 4 represents the myriad of rules and regulations that firms must follow—laws that are passed by governments, regulatory agencies, professional associations, and the like. There are also many overlaps between the law and ethics (Area 6), a primary one being the prohibition against killing. Area 5 is the focus of this book, the overlap between business activity and ethical norms. This is also the area where some deny that there is an overlap. Their argument is that Area 4 exists and that as long as firms do not violate the law, they are behaving ethically. That is, the law and ethics are one and the same when it comes to business. The main message of this book is that ethics should guide behavior beyond the law. The law is usually the minimum standard of acceptable behavior, but

[10] Mark Schwartz and Archie Carroll, "Corporate Social responsibility: A Three Domain Approach," *Business Ethics Quarterly* 13, no. 4 (2003), 503–530.

FIGURE 3.2 Intersection of Business, Law, & Ethics

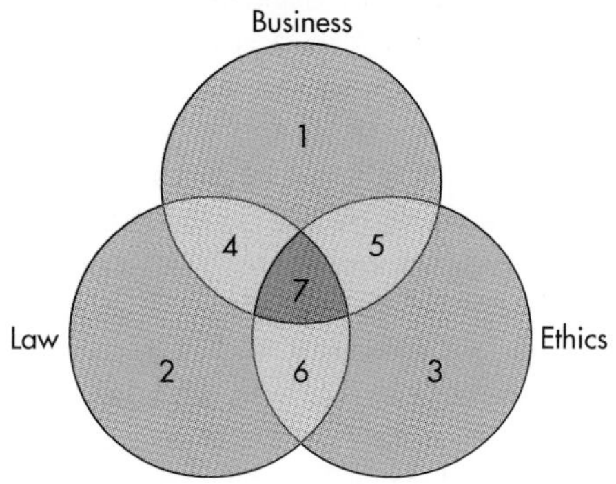

sometimes laws conflict (as in different countries) or are out of date or do not exist in one locale but should. In such cases, ethics requires performance beyond the bare legal minimum.

Area 7, the intersection of law, ethics, and business, normally becomes a problem only if the law says one thing while ethics says the opposite. In Nazi Germany during World War II, the law was prejudicial against Jews. What should an ethical businessperson do when (1) the law encourages the exploitation of Jews, (2) the law is beneficial to the businessperson since the Jewish employees do not have to be paid, and yet (3) the businessperson knows that the exploitation of these people is wrong? The story of *Schindler's List* vividly portrays the ethical dilemma when law, business, and ethics intersect but are incompatible.

The remainder of this chapter outlines some of the major ethical theories that are used by businesspeople to help resolve ethical dilemmas. This is not an exhaustive list, but it does cover the major philosophies that are used in the area of business ethics.

MAJOR ETHICAL THEORIES USEFUL IN RESOLVING ETHICAL DILEMMAS

Teleology: Utilitarianism & Consequentialism—Impact Analysis

Teleology has a long history among English empirical philosophies. John Locke (1632–1704), Jeremy Bentham (1748–1832), and James Mill (1773–1836) and his son John Stuart Mill (1806–1873) all examined ethics from a teleological perspective. Teleology is derived from the Greek word *telos*, which means "ends," "consequences," or "results." *Teleological theories study ethical behavior in terms of the results or consequences of ethical decisions.* Teleology resonates with many results-oriented businesspeople because it focuses on the impact of decision making. It evaluates decisions as good or bad, acceptable or unacceptable, in terms of the consequences of the decision.

Investors judge an investment as good or bad, worthwhile or not, based on its expected return. If the actual return is below the investor's expectation, it is deemed to be a bad investment decision; if the return is greater than expected, it is considered a good or worthwhile investment decision. Ethical decision making follows a similar pattern. In the same way that the goodness and badness of an investment is assessed on the basis of results of the financial decision, ethical goodness or badness is based on the consequences of the ethical decision. Ethical decisions are right or wrong if they lead to either positive or negative results. Ethically good decisions result in positive outcomes, while ethically bad decisions lead to either less positive outcomes or negative consequences. However, the consequences of an ethical decision are not themselves ethical. The consequence is simply what happens.

The ethicality of the decision maker and the decision are determined on the basis of the value of the action or consequence. If the decision brings about a positive result, such as helping an individual to achieve self-realization, then the decision is said to be an ethically correct one. Other positive results would include such things as happiness, enjoyment, health, beauty, and knowledge, while negative results would include unhappiness, misery, illness, ugliness, and ignorance. In other words, judgments about right and wrong, or ethical correctness, are based solely on whether good or bad results occur.

Teleology has its clearest articulation in utilitarianism, most noticeably in the writings of Bentham and J. S. Mill. In *Utilitarianism*, Mill wrote, "The creed which accepts as the foundation of morals, Utility, or the Greatest Happiness Principle, holds that actions are right in proportion as they tend to promote happiness, wrong as they tend to produce the reverse of happiness. By happiness is intended pleasure, and the absence of pain; by unhappiness, pain, and the privation of pleasure."[11]

Utilitarianism defines good and evil in terms of pleasure and pain. The ethically correct action is the one that produces the greatest amount of pleasure or the least amount of pain. This is a very simple theory. The goal of life is to be happy, and all those things that promote happiness are ethically good, as they tend to produce pleasure or alleviate pain and suffering. For utilitarians, pleasure and pain may be both physical and mental. The alleviation of stress, anguish, and mental suffering is as important as reducing physical pain and discomfort. For example, the stress level of an employee may increase when her supervisor asks her to complete an assignment but then provides her with little information and insufficient time to produce the report and makes unrealistic demands in terms of the quality of the report. The increased stress does not contribute to her general happiness or to the pleasure of completing the assignment. For a utilitarian, the only things worth having are pleasurable experiences, and these experiences are good simply because they are pleasurable. However, in this case, completing the assignment is neither pleasurable nor, from the employee's perspective, good. It does not contribute to her utility or to her general happiness.

Mill was quick to point out that pleasure and pain have both quantitative and qualitative aspects. Bentham developed a calculus of pleasure and pain based on intensity, duration, certainty, propinquity, fecundity, purity, and extent.[12] Mill added that the nature of the pleasure or pain is also important. Some pleasures are more desirable than others and worth the effort of achieving. An athlete, for example, trains daily to compete in the Olympics. The training may be very painful, but the athlete keeps his eye on the prize, winning the gold medal. The qualitative pleasure of standing on the podium exceeds the quantitatively grueling road to becoming an Olympic champion.

Hedonism focuses on the individual and seeks the greatest amount of personal pleasure or happiness. Epicurus (341–270 B.C.) argued that the goal of life is secure and lasting pleasure, a life in which pains are accepted only if they lead to greater pleasures and pleasures are rejected if they lead to greater pains. Utilitarianism, on the other hand,

---

[11] John Stuart Mill, *Utilitarianism*, ed. Roger Crisp (Oxford: Oxford University Press, 1998), 55.

[12] Jeremy Bentham, *An Introduction to the Principles of Morals and Legislation* (Garden City, NY: Dolphin Books, 1961), 37–40.

measures pleasure and pain not at the individual level but rather at the level of society. The pleasure of the decision maker, as well as everyone who could possibly be affected by the decision, needs to be considered. But additional weight should not be given to the decision maker. The "happiness that forms the utilitarian standard of what is right in conduct, is not the agent's own happiness, but that of all concerned. As between his own happiness and that of the others, utilitarianism requires him to be as strictly impartial as a disinterested and benevolent spectator."[13] A CEO who talks the board of directors into giving the CEO a $100 million bonus may derive great happiness from the bonus, but if he does not consider the effects that the bonus might have on all the other employees in his firm, his peer group of other executives, and society as a whole, then he is ignoring the ethical aspects of his decision.

Google's Tax Minimization Strategy: Utilitarian Consequences

When using utilitarianism, the decision maker must take a broad perspective concerning who in society might be affected by the decision. Consider the case of tax minimization by multinational organizations that set up subsidiaries in tax-haven countries in order to reduce their tax liabilities. From management's point of view, good tax planning reduces the monies that are paid to governments, thereby having more money to reinvest in the company or pay out as dividends. In 2014, Google generated approximately 10% of its profits in the United Kingdom but paid taxes at less than 3%. How? Google recorded the revenue in Ireland, where the tax rate was only 12%, and then had its Netherlands subsidiary, in another low-tax-rate country, charge a huge royalty to the Irish subsidiary, which was then paid to a Google subsidiary located in Bermuda, which has no corporate taxation. Referred to as the "double Irish," it was a scheme whose only purpose was to reduce incomes taxes. In 2016, at the end of a six-year tax audit, Google agreed to pay the British government £130 million. Other multinationals, such as Starbucks, Apple Computers, and Facebook, that have come under similar scrutiny have had their reputations tarnished and labeled as "tax cheaters." These tax-minimization decisions have had serious consequences for the multinationals, the British government, and the British public who provided profits to these companies by purchasing their goods and services but have not received the social benefits through an increase in the taxes collected by the British government from these multinationals.

There are several key aspects to utilitarianism. First, ethicality is assessed on the basis of consequences. Next, ethical decisions should be oriented toward increasing happiness and/or reducing pain, where happiness and pain can be either physical or psychological. Furthermore, happiness and pain relate to all of society and not only to the personal happiness or pain of the decision maker. Finally, the ethical decision maker must be impartial and not give extra weight to personal feelings when calculating the overall net probable consequences of a decision.

ACT & RULE UTILITARIANISM Over time, utilitarianism has evolved along two main lines, called act utilitarianism and rule utilitarianism. The former, sometimes referred to

[13] Mill, *Utilitarianism*, 64.

as *consequentialism,*[14] *deems an action to be ethically good or correct if it will probably produce a greater balance of good over evil.* An action is ethically bad or incorrect if it will probably produce the opposite. *Rule utilitarianism, on the other hand, says that we should follow the rule that will probably produce a greater balance of good over evil and avoid the rule that will probably produce the reverse.*

The presumption is that it is possible, in principle, to calculate the net pleasure or pain associated with a decision. For Mill, "the truths of arithmetic are applicable to the valuation of happiness, as of all other measurable quantities."[15] Returns on investments can be measured; so too happiness, according to Mill. This means that the decision maker must calculate, for each alternative course of action, the corresponding amounts of pleasure for each person who will probably be affected by the decision. Similarly, the amount of displeasure or pain for each person under each of the alternatives needs to be measured. The two sums are then netted, and the ethically correct action is the one that produces the greatest net positive balance or the least negative balance of pleasure over pain. Furthermore, in the same way that an investor is indifferent between two investments that each has the same level of risk and return, two alternatives would each be ethically correct if they both have the same net arithmetic score and each of these scores is higher than the scores of any of the other alternatives that are available to the decision maker.

Rule utilitarianism is somewhat simpler. It recognizes that human decision making is often guided by rules. For example, most people believe that it is better to tell the truth than to lie. Although exceptions are acknowledged, truth telling is the standard of normal ethical human behavior. So, the guiding principle for a rule utilitarian is, follow the rule that tends to produce the greatest amount of pleasure over pain for the greatest number of people who will probably be affected by the action. Truth telling normally produces the greatest pleasure for most people most of the time. Similarly, accurate, reliable financial statements are extremely useful to investors and creditors in making investment and credit decisions. False financial statements are not useful since they lead to incorrect financial decisions. The rule "financial statements should fairly reflect the financial position of the firm" should produce the greater happiness for investors than the alternative rule "financial statements should be falsified." Truth telling and candor normally produce the best consequences, so these are the principles that should be followed.

MEANS & ENDS Before identifying some of the problems with utilitarianism, we must understand what the theory is not. The principle "promote the greatest amount of happiness for the largest number of people" does not imply that the end justifies the means. The latter is a political theory, not an ethical principle. The foremost proponent of this political philosophy was Niccolò Machiavelli (1469–1527), who wrote the *Prince* for Lorenzo Medici as a primer on how to maintain political power. In it, he advised that "in the actions of men, and especially of princes, from which there is no appeal, the end justifies the means."[16] The state, as sovereign power, can do whatever it wishes, and the prince, as ruler of the state, can use any political strategy in order to maintain power. Machiavelli was quite clear that duplicity, subterfuge, and deception are acceptable means for a prince to maintain control over the populous and his rivals. A "prince,

---

[14] Consequentialism is the version of utilitarianism that the AACSB advocates as being useful for business decisions. See the next chapter for the reasons.

[15] Mill, *Utilitarianism*, 105.

[16] Niccolò Machiavelli, *The Prince and the Discourses*, intro. Max Lerner (New York: Modern Library, 1950), 66.

and especially a new prince, cannot observe all those things which are considered good in men, being often obligated, in order to maintain the state, to act against faith, against charity, against humanity, and against religion."[17] Clearly, this is a political theory—and a questionable one at that—but it is not an ethical theory.

Unfortunately, "the end justifies the means" is often taken out of context and incorrectly used as an ethical theory. In the 2001 movie *Swordfish*, Gabriel, played by John Travolta, poses the following to Stanley, played by Hugh Jackman: "Here's a scenario. You have the power to cure all the world's diseases, but the price for this is that you must kill a single innocent child. Could you kill that child, Stanley?" The decision that is being forced on Stanley is unethical because it offends significant rights of one or more individuals. By phrasing the question this way, Gabriel is trying to give ethical justification to a political statement. He is attempting to lead Stanley into saying that the action is justified because more are saved with the sacrifice of one. This may be an extreme example, but the decisions of CEOs often have profound impacts on the lives of other people. Toxic waste, hazardous products and working conditions, and pollution and other environmental problems are often defended on the basis that the end justifies the means. This principle is also used to defend cheating by university students, abuses of power by some CEOs, and the betrayal of their corporate responsibilities by some boards of directors.

However, a rule utilitarian would say that there are some classes of actions that are manifestly right and wrong regardless of their consequences as either good or bad. Pollution and hazardous products do not increase the overall long-term well-being of society. The killings of innocent children, the extraction of excessive perquisites by opportunistic CEOs, and boards that ignore their firm's corporate codes of conduct are never ethically correct behaviors, regardless of the consequences. Each of these actions is wrong because these sorts of actions have an obvious negative effect on the general happiness of society as a whole.

The political principle "the end justifies the means" is not an ethical theory. First, it incorrectly assumes that means and ends are ethically equivalent, and, second, it incorrectly assumes that there is only one means to achieving the end. Take the case of two executives who collude to falsify a set of financial statements. One does so because she will receive a bonus based on the firm's reported net income. The other executive conducts the fraud in order to forestall bankruptcy, believing that if the firm continues in business, then the staff will have employment, customers will have the firm's products, and suppliers will still be able to make sales to the firm. Their means are both the same; they perpetrate a financial statement fraud. But their ends are different: the former is from pure economic selfishness; the other is from a misguided sense of loyalty to the firm's various stakeholders. Most would view these two individuals as dissimilar despite the similar means to obtaining their different ends. The two motivations or ends—economic selfishness and misguided altruism—and the one means—fraud—are not ethically equivalent. Most would view the means as wrong and have antipathy for the one executive and perhaps some sympathy for the latter executive.

More important, "the end justifies the means" often implies either that there is only one means to achieving the end or that, if there are a variety of means to achieving the end, all the means are ethically equivalent. But this is not the case. There are many ways of traveling across the country, but the costs vary with the mode of transportation. They are not equivalent. Similarly, there are various ways of temporally forestalling bankruptcy, one of which is to perpetrate a financial statement fraud. But there are other

[17] Ibid., 65.

alternatives, including refinancing. Although refinancing and fraud may lead to the same end, the two means are ethically quite different. The one is ethically correct, and the other is not. It is the job of the manager to be able to see this difference and then to use moral imagination to identify an alternative means to achieving the same end.

Some people misuse utilitarianism by saying that the end justifies the means. But this is an inappropriate application of an ethical theory. For a utilitarian, the end never justifies the means. Instead, the moral agent must consider the consequences of the decision in terms of producing happiness or in terms of the rule that, if followed, will probably produce the most happiness for all. The overall appeal of utilitarianism is that it appears to be quite simple, whereas the full consideration of all consequences is challenging if a comprehensive result is desired. It uses a simple standard: the goal of ethical behavior is to promote happiness. It is also forward looking; it concentrates on the future happiness of those who will be affected by the decision. It also acknowledges the uncertainty of the future, so it focuses on probable consequences. Finally, the theory is expansive and unselfish; the best ethical alternative is the one that promotes the greatest pleasure for all concerned. This may be why the theory resonates with businesspeople. Managers are accustomed to making decisions under conditions of uncertainty, assessing the probable consequences to identifiable stakeholders and then choosing the alternative that probably will have the best net results for all concerned parties. However, the theory is not without its problems.

WEAKNESS IN UTILITARIANISM Utilitarianism presupposes that such things as happiness, utility, pleasure, pain, and anguish can be quantified. Accountants are very good at measuring economic transactions because money is a uniform standard of measurement. Almost all economic transactions can be measured in a currency, such as euros, and everyone knows what one euro will purchase. However, there is no common unit of measurement for happiness, nor is one person's happiness the equivalent of another person's happiness, whereas one euro means the same to both. And money is an inadequate proxy for happiness. Not only does money not buy happiness, but it cannot capture the degree of happiness felt when sitting on the shores of a favorite lake watching the sunset on a warm summer evening or the pleasure in seeing the smile on the face of a mother holding her newborn.

Another problem concerns the distribution and intensity of happiness. The utilitarian principle is to produce as much happiness as is possible and to distribute that happiness to as many as is possible. Raphael uses the example of alms giving.[18] One option is for you to give $50 each to two old-age pensioners, who would then buy two warm sweaters. Or you could give fifty pensioners enough money for a cup of coffee each. The intensity of the happiness is surely greater for the two pensioners who receive warm sweaters. But more people are positively affected by distributing $2 so that they can all buy a cup of coffee. Which alternative should you choose? The utilitarian principle is too vague to be useful in this instance. Should a CEO increase wages by 0.05% across the board, which would make all the employees slightly better off and presumably a bit happier, or should the CEO double the salaries of the top management team, thereby greatly increasing the general happiness of seven vice presidents? Assuming that the net arithmetic happiness of both options is the same (regardless of how the happiness and unhappiness of the employees are measured), are both options equivalent? Is there not the perception of injustice in the latter? Utilitarianism can often appear to be as cold and unfeeling as Machiavelli's advice on the use of naked political power.

[18] D. D. Raphael, *Moral Philosophy* (Oxford: Oxford University Press, 1981), 47.

Another measurement problem concerns scope. How many people are to be included? Only those who are alive? If not, then for how many future generations? Consider the problems of global warming and pollution. The short-term happiness of current generations may come at the pain of future generations. If future generations are to be included, then the overall amount of happiness must increase greatly to accommodate enough happiness being available to be allocated to both this and subsequent generations. Furthermore, is the timing of the happiness important? Assuming that the net scores are the same regardless of the ordering, is happiness today and pain tomorrow the same as pain today and happiness tomorrow? Are we willing to have exorbitant fuel costs today and the associated economic pain so that there will be adequate fuel supplies for future generations?

This point is clearly illustrated by Al Gore in his book and video *An Inconvenient Truth*, in which he identifies how pollution is leading to global warming and that we are reaching a point where rejuvenation of our environment may not be possible. This conclusion is the same as that developed by a UN study[19] in the late 1980s and reiterated at the 2015 UN Climate Change Conference in Paris.

Minority rights may be violated under utilitarianism. In a democracy, the will of the majority rules on Election Day. People are comfortable with this because those who lose in one election always have the chance of having their party come into power in the next election. It is not as simple with ethical decision making. Consider the following example. There are two options available that will affect only four people. The one action will create two units of happiness for each of the four people. The other option will create three units of happiness for three people and no happiness or unhappiness for the fourth person. The second option generates more happiness (nine units) versus eight units under the first option. However, under the second option, one individual receives no happiness. In this case, unlike the election example, there is no possibility of waiting for a subsequent opportunity for another distribution of happiness in which that person might share. Is it fair that one individual does not get to share in any happiness? Ethical decision making under utilitarianism may be perceived as unfairly benefiting some stakeholder groups at the expense of other stakeholder groups.

Utilitarianism ignores motivation and focuses only on consequences. This leaves many people unsatisfied. Consider the previous example of the two executives who fraudulently issue a set of financial statements. The motivation of the two executives is quite different. Many would consider that they have different degrees of ethical culpability, with the bonus-based executive acting worse than the misguided altruist. However, utilitarianism would judge both as equally ethically remiss since the consequence of their decision is the same, a financial statement fraud. This is an example of the saying, "The road to hell is paved with good intentions." Utilitarianism, by itself, is insufficient to produce a comprehensive ethical decision. To overcome this problem, an alternative ethical theory, deontology, assesses ethicality on the motivation of the decision maker rather than on the consequences of the decision.

Deontological Ethics—Motivation for Behavior

Deontology, a term that is derived from the Greek word *deon*, meaning "duty" or "obligation," is the theory that concerns one's ethical duties and responsibilities. It evaluates the ethicality of behavior based on the motivation of the decision maker. According to a

[19] The Brundtland Report, *Our Common Future*, New York, UN World Commission on Environment and Development, 1987, http://www.un-documents.net/wced-ocf.htm.

deontologist, an action can be ethically correct even if it does not produce a net balance of good over evil for the decision maker or for society as a whole. This makes it a useful complement to utilitarianism because an action that satisfies both theories can be said to have a good chance of being ethical.

Immanuel Kant (1724–1804) provided the clearest articulation of this theory in his treatise *Groundwork of the Metaphysics of Morals*. For Kant, the only unqualified good is a good will, the will to follow what reason dictates regardless of the consequences to oneself. He argued that all our moral concepts are derived from reason rather than from experience. A good will manifest itself when it acts for the sake of duty, where duty implies a recognition and adherence to a law or precept. The precept might be "in this situation I ought to do such and such," or it might be "in this situation I should refrain from doing such and such." These assertions—that this is what I ought to do or that this is what I ought not to do—are absolutely binding and permit no exceptions. This sense of acting out of duty is unique to humankind. Everything in nature acts according to the laws of nature, but only humans can act according to the idea of a law, that is, in accordance with rational principles.

For Kant, duty is the standard by which ethical behavior is judged. Moral worth exists only when a person acts from a sense of duty. You are acting correctly when you follow your ethical duties and obligations, not because they might lead to good consequences and not because they might increase your pleasure or happiness; rather, you do them for duty's sake. It is the motive of duty that gives moral worth to your action. Other actions may be based on self-interest or on a consideration for others. When you deal honestly with your customers because you want their repeat business, you are acting out of self-interest rather than from duty. Acting in this way may be praiseworthy, but it lacks moral worth. According to deontologists, it is only when you act out a sense of duty that you are acting ethically.

Kant developed two laws for assessing ethicality. The first is the *categorical imperative*: "I ought never to act except in such a way that I can also will that my maxim should become a universal law."[20] This is the supreme principle of morality. It demands that you should act only in such manner that you would be prepared to have anyone else who is in a similar situation act in a similar way. It is an imperative because it must be obeyed and is categorical because it is unconditional and absolute. It must be followed even if obedience is contrary to what you would prefer to do. A rational principle or moral law is being laid down for everyone to follow, including you.

There are two aspects to this categorical imperative. First, Kant assumes that a law entails an obligation, and this implies that an ethical law entails an ethical obligation. So, any ethical action that an individual is obligated to perform must be in accordance with an ethical law or maxim. This means that all ethical decisions and behavior can be explained in terms of ethical maxims, that is, in terms of laws that must be obeyed. The second part of the imperative is that an action is ethically correct if and only if the maxim that corresponds to the action can be consistently universalized. You must be willing to have your maxim be followed by anyone else who is in a similar kind of situation, even if you would be adversely affected personally because that other individual followed and obeyed your maxim. You are not allowed to make yourself an exception to the rule.

Kant uses the example of breaking promises. Assume that you want to break a promise. If you do so, then you are making that a maxim that can be followed by other

---

[20] Immanuel Kant, *Groundwork of the Metaphysic of Morals*, trans. H. J. Paton (New York: Harper Torchbooks, 1964), 17.

people. But if others follow that maxim, then you may be taken advantage of when they break their promises to you. So, it would be illogical to say that everyone else should keep their promises except for you. You cannot say that it is acceptable for you to lie to your investors about the quality of your firm's financial statements while also saying that it is unacceptable for others to falsify their financial statements because you might lose your investment if you unwittingly rely on their false financial reports.

Kant's second rule is a *practical imperative* for dealing with other people: "Act in a way that you always treat humanity, whether in your own person or in the person of any other, never simply as a means, but always at the same time as an end."[21] For Kant, laws have universal application, so the moral law applies without distinction to everybody. This means that everyone must be treated equally under the moral law. In the same way that you are an end, an individual with moral worth, so also is everyone else. They too must be treated as ends in themselves, as individuals of moral worth. Hence, you cannot use them in a way that ignores their moral worth in the same way that you cannot ignore your personal moral worthiness.

The practical imperative suggests not that you cannot use people but simply that if you treat them as means, then you must simultaneously treat them as ends. If you treat people solely as a means, it could lead to their exploitation. An old-time master–slave relationship treated the slave as a means and not as an end. The slave is considered to have no moral worth and no desires and to be unable to make choices. On the other hand, a healthy employer–employee relationship treats the employee with respect and dignity as both a means and an end. A professional accountant, for example, employs accounting students. The hourly billing rate that is charged to clients for the students' work is considerably more than the rate paid to the students. The professional accountant reaps the benefits of the students' labor, and those accounting students are a means to the professional accountant's financial prosperity. Is this an unethical relationship? No, because the relationship recognizes that the employee has the power to make choices and decisions, including ethical ones, and that these decisions have the potential to influence the well-being of the employee, as well as others, such as the client, the client's personnel, and the employer.

Everyone is entitled to pursue their own personal goals as long as they do not violate the practical imperative. This is the *Kantian principle*. Treating others as ends requires that we acknowledge that we are all part of society, part of a moral community. In the same way that I am to act positively toward my own ends, I also have a duty to act positively toward their ends. So, I treat my employees as ends when I help them fulfill their desires (to learn accounting and have employment) while accepting that they are as able as me to make ethical decisions that may have an impact on society, our moral community.

WEAKNESSES IN DEONTOLOGY Just like other ethical theories, deontology has its problems and weaknesses. A fundamental problem is that the categorical imperative does not provide clear guidelines for deciding which principle to follow when two or moral laws conflict and only one can be chosen. Which moral law takes precedence? In this regard, utilitarianism may be a better theory since it can evaluate alternatives based on their consequences. Unfortunately, with deontology, consequences are irrelevant. The only thing that matters is the intention of the decision maker and the decision maker's adherence to obey the categorical imperative while treating people as ends rather than as a means to an end.

---

[21] Ibid., 66–67.

The categorical imperative sets a very high standard. For many, it is a hard ethic to follow. There is no shortage of examples where people are not treated with respect and dignity, where they are seen as merely tools in the production cycle to be used and then discarded after their usefulness is gone. Firms have suffered customer boycotts for using sweatshop labor or underage workers, for failing to provide a living wage, or for sourcing inputs in support of repressive regimes. In 2013, the Rana Plaza outside of Dhaka, Bangladesh, collapsed, killing over 1,000 garment workers and injuring another 2,500. There was worldwide criticism of clothing manufacturers, accused of using sweatshop labor in unsafe working conditions. In response to this tragedy, global brands such as Benetton, Joe Fresh, H&M, and others, set up a fund to compensate the victims and their families. Then these companies developed an accord to improve fire and building safety in garment factories in Bangladesh.[22] Living up to the Kantian ideal means acknowledging that we are all part of a moral community that places duty above happiness and economic well-being. Business might very well be better off if more managers follow their ethical duties and follow them simply because they are their ethical duties. However, following one's duty may result in adverse consequences, such as an unjust allocation of resources. As such, many argue that instead of focusing on consequences and intentions or motivations, ethics should instead be grounded in the principles of justice and fairness.

Justice & Fairness—Examining the Balance

The English philosopher David Hume (1711–1776) argued that the need for justice occurs for two reasons: people are not always beneficent, and there are scarce resources. In keeping with the English empiricist tradition, Hume believed that society was formed through self-interest. Since we are not self-sufficient, we need to cooperate with others for our mutual survival and prosperity (i.e., to engender the support of other stakeholders). However, given a limited number of resources and the fact that some people can benefit at the expense of others, there needs to be a mechanism for fairly allocating the benefits and burdens of society. Justice is that mechanism. It presupposes that people have legitimate claims on scarce resources and that they can explain or justify their claims. This, then, is the meaning of justice, to render or allocate benefits and burdens based on rational reasons. There are also two aspects to justice: procedural justice (the process for determining the allocation) and distributive justice (the actual allocations).

PROCEDURAL JUSTICE Procedural justice concerns how justice is administered. Key aspects of a just legal system are that the procedures are fair and transparent. This means that everyone is treated equally before the law and that rules are impartially applied. Preference is not given to one person based on physical characteristics (ethnicity, gender, height, or hair color) or on social or economic status (the law is applied in the same way to both the rich and the poor). There should be a consistent application of the law both within the legal jurisdiction and over time. Also, justice is to be assessed based on the facts of the case. This means that the information used to assess the various claims needs to be relevant, reliable, and validly obtained. Finally, there must be the right of appeal; the one who loses the claim should be able to ask a higher authority to review the case so that any potential miscarriage is corrected. Both the assessment of the information used for the allocation and the ability to appeal depend on the transparency of

[22] The Canadian Press, "Bangladesh Factory Collapse: Joe Fresh Owner Loblaws Signs Up to Safety Pact," May 14, 2013, http://www.huffingtonpost.ca/2013/05/15/bangladesh-factory-joe-fresh-loblaws-safety-pact_n_3275213.html.

the process. These are the characteristic of blind justice, where all are treated fairly before the law. Both sides present their claims and reasons, and the judge decides.

How does this apply to business ethics? In a business setting, procedural justice is not normally an important issue. Most organizations have standard operating procedures that are clearly understood by all employees. The procedures may be right or wrong, but because they are the standards, they are normally consistently applied. As such, most employees are willing to present their case to an ombudsperson or senior official or even a subcommittee of the board of directors and let that person or persons rule on the matter. Once a decision is taken or a new policy is established, most employees are willing to adhere to it because they feel that their alternative position was given a fair hearing. (See the ethics case "Team Player Problems" at the end of Chapter 6 for a dilemma concerning procedural justice.)

DISTRIBUTIVE JUSTICE Aristotle (384–322 B.C.) may very well have been the first to argue that equals should be treated equally and that unequals should be treated unequally in proportion to their relevant differences. "This, then, is what the just is—the proportional; the unjust is what violates the proportion."[23] The presumption is that everyone is equal. If someone wants to argue that two people are not equal, then the burden of proof is on demonstrating that, in this particular situation, they are unequal based on relevant criteria. For example, if a prospective employee is confined to a wheelchair but otherwise able to perform normal duties, would it be ethical (fair) not to hire the worker, or would it be more ethical to provide wheelchair access to the workstation? Another example involves equal pay for equal work. After years of blatant discrimination, pay equity legislation has now guaranteed that both men and women are paid the same wage for the same job. Recently, there has been pressure on banks and public accounting firms to pay their employees for overtime. The argument is that unpaid overtime is unjust since employees in other service organizations are paid for their overtime but these employees are not. All service employees are not being treated equally.

On the other hand, if people are not equal, then they should not be treated equally. Pay differentials are just if they are based on real differences, such as training and experience, education, and differing levels of responsibility. A new lawyer is not paid as much as the more experienced senior partner of the firm. Although they both have the same formal law school training, the older partner has a deeper well of experience to draw on and so should be able to make quicker, better, and more accurate decisions than the less experienced junior.

Under distributive justice, there are three main criteria for determining the just distribution: need, arithmetic equality, and merit. In most developed countries, the taxation systems are based on need. The rich, who can afford to pay, are taxed so that funds can be distributed to the less fortunate in society—from those who have to those who have not. Distributive justice can occur in a business setting. For example, a company's budget process might be based on the fair allocation of scarce resources. Such a system could be used to motivate executives and employees in each unit to utilize their limited resources in the most efficient and effective manner. Another instance would involve the consideration of what might be a fair profit to leave in the country where it is earned rather than use transfer pricing techniques to redistribute it to a tax haven to minimize overall enterprise tax paid. (See the ethics case "Multinationals and Tax Planning" at the end of Chapter 6.)

---

[23] Aristotle, *The Nicomachean Ethics*, trans. David Ross, rev. J. L. Ackrill and J. O. Urmson (Oxford: Oxford University Press, 1925), 114.

Another distribution method is based on arithmetic equality. For example, in order to ensure an equal distribution of a cake, have the person who cuts the cake get the last piece. Assuming that everyone is just as eager to share in the cake, and that everyone would prefer to get a larger than a smaller piece, then the person cutting will make sure that all pieces are of an equal size so that the first piece is no different than the last, the one that goes to the cake cutter. Unequal distributions are deemed to be unjust.

In a business setting, the principle of arithmetic equality can be considered violated when a firm has two classes of shares that have equal rights to dividends (cash flow rights) but unequal voting rights (control rights) and therefore unequal rights to control the destiny of their cash flow rights. Many companies in Germany, Canada, Italy, Korea, and Brazil have dual class shares for which cash flow rights do not equal control rights. In Canada, for example, the Class A shares often may have ten votes each and the Class B shares only one vote each. In this way, a shareholder can have, say, 54% of the control rights through ownership of the Class A shares while having only 14% of the cash flow rights based on the total number of Class A and Class B shares outstanding. Such a Class A shareholder is called a minority controlling shareholder and may unjustly take advantage of the other shareholders. The minority (controlling) shareholder can always out vote any objection of the majority shareholders. (For an example of an opportunistic minority controlling shareholder, see the ethics case "Lord Conrad Black's Fiduciary Duty?" at the end of Chapter 5.)

New York Times Dual Class Share Structure: Distributive Injustice?

In 1896, Aloph O. Ochs bought a controlling interest in the New York Times. *His descendants continue to own a controlling interest in the newspaper chain through a dual class share structure. The Ochs and Sulzberger families own 19% of the Class A shares and 88% of the Class B shares of the New York Times Company. The Class A shares, which trade on the New York Stock Exchange, can vote on a limited number of matters and are restricted to electing four of the thirteen members to the board of directors. The Class B shares, which are thinly traded, can vote on all company matters and are entitled to elect the remaining nine members to the board of directors. This ownership structure means that the Ochs and Sulzberger families are minority controlling shareholders. The families have a minority equity interest in the company (through the Class A shares) but a controlling voting interest (through the Class B shares). By June 2005, the investment firm Morgan Stanley had acquired 7.2% of the Class A shares of the New York Times Company. Unfortunately, the New York Times Company had not been performing well, and Morgan Stanley blamed the governance structure of the company. In 2006, Morgan Stanley proposed two shareholder resolutions that would require the company to change its dual class ownership structure and to separate the duties of the publisher from those of the chair of the board of directors. Neither resolution was successful. At the 2007 annual general meeting, 47% of the Class A shareholders withheld their votes for the election of the four directors. Although a rebuff to the Ochs and Sulzberger families, it was only a symbolic gesture since the two families continued to elect the other nine directors to the board. In October 2007, Morgan Stanley sold its 7.2% interest in the company.*

Another distribution method is based on merit. This means that if one individual contributes more to a project, then that individual should receive a greater proportion of the benefits from the project. Shareholders who own more shares are entitled to receive more dividends in proportion to their larger shareholdings. Merit pay is another example. Employees who contribute more to the financial prosperity of the firm should share in that prosperity, often in the form of a bonus. Bonuses based on financial performance are quite common. Unfortunately, such merit-based plans can also encourage directors, executives, and employees to artificially increase net income in order to receive a bonus.

In terms of distributed justice, perceptions are critical. For example, if an employee feels that he is being underpaid, then he might begin to shirk his duties and not put in his full effort. The perception that an employee is not receiving his just deserts may have adverse consequences for the firm. People who steal company assets will often justify their illegal behavior on the basis that they deserve the money that they defraud from their employers. (See Chapter 4 for a discussion of the rationalizations used by people to justify unethical behavior.) Employees might feel that they have been unjustly treated when favoritism is shown. When the brother-in-law of the owner of the company is made a vice president even though he lacks the requisite qualifications, employees often feel that the appointment was unfair or unjust. Transfer pricing may also be perceived to be unfair. One divisional manager, for example, may not consider it fair that she has to pay a high internal price for an overhead item when the same item can be bought outside the corporate entity at a lower cost. She may be loath to have her highly profitable division subsidize an overhead division that generates no revenue for the firm. Although this internal redistribution of profits may be just, the manager may not consider it fair, especially if she has a merit-pay bonus based on the reported net income of her division.

JUSTICE AS FAIRNESS One of the problems with distribute justice is that the allocations may not be fair. The American philosopher John Rawls (1921–2002) addressed this issue by developing a theory of justice as fairness. In *A Theory of Justice*, he presents an argument grounded in the classical position of self-interest and self-reliance. No one can ever get all the things one wants because there are other people who will prevent this from happening, for they too may want the same things. Therefore, there is a need for everyone to cooperate because that is everyone's best interest. As such, society can be seen as a cooperative arrangement for mutual benefit; it is a venture that balances conflicts of interests with identity of interests. There is an identity of interests since cooperation makes for a better life for everyone. However, human nature, being that each person would prefer to receive a larger share of the benefits and a small share of the burdens, creates a conflict of interest on how the benefits and burdens of society should be allocated. The principles that determine a fair allocation among the members of society are the principles of justice. "The concept of justice I take to be defined, then, by the role of its principles in assigning rights and duties and in defining the appropriate division of social advantages."[24]

Using the philosophical device of a hypothetical social contract, Rawls asks, What principles of justice would free and rational people choose under a veil of ignorance? The veil of ignorance means that the people setting these principles do not know in advance their place in society (class, social status, economic and political situation, gender, ethnicity, or which generation they belong to), their primary goods (rights, liberties,

[24] Rawls, *A Theory of Justice*, 10.

powers, and opportunities), or their natural goods (health, vigor, intelligence, imagination, and the like). "It is a state of affairs in which the parties are equally represented as moral persons and the outcome is not conditioned by arbitrary contingencies or the relative balance of social forces."[25] Justice as fairness means that whatever principles they agree to in this initial state would be considered fair by all. Otherwise, there would be no agreement on the terms of the social contract.

Rawls believes that in this hypothetical initial state, people would agree on two principles: that there should be equality in the assignment of basic rights and duties and that social and economic inequalities should be of benefit to the least advantaged members of society (the *difference principle*) and that access to these inequalities should be open to all (*fair equality of opportunity*). "First: each person is to have an equal right to the most extensive basic liberty compatible with a similar liberty for others. Second: social and economic inequalities are to be arranged so that they are both (a) reasonably expected to be to everyone's advantage, and (b) attached to positions and offices open to all."[26]

The difference principle recognizes that natural endowments are undeserved. Some people live in areas that have many natural resources, others are born into rich and privileged families, and some are endowed with natural gifts or talents that are in high demand. No one person deserves or merits more than another simply because of these accidents of birth. That would be unjust. On the other hand, it is just for these people to use their natural gifts, talents, and advantages not only for their own benefit but also for the benefit of the less endowed. Under the principle of justice as fairness, what is right and fair is that everyone should benefit from social and economic inequalities.

Ben and Jerry's Application of the Rawlsian Difference Principle

When applied to the business world, John Rawls's difference principle means that the diffusion of benefits should be to everyone's benefit and that offices and positions within a firm should be open to everyone if they have the requisite talents and skill set. Started as a boutique manufacturer of ice cream in Vermont in 1978, Ben & Jerry's Homemade, Inc., found a niche in the super-premium ice cream market in the 1980s. The company's founders, Ben Cohen and Jerry Greenfield, developed a managerial philosophy that embodied much of Rawls' difference principle. The company used only socially responsible suppliers, and 7.5% of pretax profits were distributed annually to projects of social change. They also imposed a five-to-one salary ratio, which was raised to seven to one in 1990. This meant that the highest-paid employee could only receive a salary that was five times (later, seven times) greater than the lowest-paid employee. There was also a salary floor; no employee's salary could fall below a fixed amount. It was initially set at $20,000 when the average per capita income in Vermont was $17,000. These corporate policies were an embodiment of the difference principle. Inequalities are acknowledged and recognized, but they are also used for the betterment of all, in this case for suppliers and employees living in Vermont. Positions of increasing responsibility within the firm are open to all. (The salary ratio was finally raised to seventeen to one before the company was sold to the multinational conglomerate Unilever in 2000.[27])

---

[25] Ibid., 120.

[26] Ibid., 60.

[27] Michael Weiss, "A Sweet Solution to the Sticky Wage Disparity Problem," *ABC News*, August 10, 2013, http://abcnews.go.com/Business/companies-follow-ben-jerrys-lead-wages/story?id=19920634.

Compare Ben & Jerry's salary ratio with the huge salaries paid to most CEOs. In 1982, the pay of the average CEO in the United States was forty-two times that of the average worker. By 2014, it had risen to 373 times that of the average worker.[28] Rawls would say that such discrepancy is just only if paying an executive 373 times more helps the lowest-paid employee within the firm. If not, then the high executive salary is unjust. "Thus it seems probable that if the privileges and powers of legislators and judges, say, improve the situation of the less favored, they improve that of citizens generally."[29] This means that remuneration structures as well as the privileges and powers of current CEOs should be designed to improve the welfare of all employees within the organization and should be of benefit to society as a whole. (See the ethics case "Salary Equality at Gravity Payments" at the end of Chapter 5 for an example of a CEO who arbitrarily lowered the pay gap differential.)

A criticism of utilitarianism is that it may deem unfair situations to be acceptable. Rawls gives the example of slavery. A slave owner might argue that, given the structure of his society, slavery is a necessary institution since the net pain to the slave might not outweigh the utility derived from the slave owner from owing the slave. But slavery is wrong not because it is unjust but rather because it is unfair. It is not a situation where, under a veil of ignorance, both parties would agree that the practice is acceptable since the system is not of benefit to the slave, the least advantaged person in the social contract. Multinationals operating in Third World countries need to bear this in mind. Is the wage that they are paying fair? Are salaries to the benefit of everyone in society, including those who are not employed by the multinational? Is the wage structure a system that both parties would agree to if they were in the initial state? If not, the wage is not fair or just.

Merck and River Blindness: Justice as Fairness

River blindness (onchocerciasis) is a disease that is carried by parasite worms that can enter a person's body through the bites of black flies that breed in many of the rivers in Africa. The parasites can cause severe discomfort, often resulting in blindness. In 1979, scientists at the pharmaceutical company Merck & Co. discovered a drug, Mectizan, that cures river blindness. The company offered the drug for sale to the World Health Organization (WHO), the U.S. government, and various African nations. None stepped forward to buy the drug. So, Merck & Co. said that they give the drug away for free. But these impoverished nations said that they did not have a distribution system for getting the drug to the affected people, often because they lived in remote areas. So, with the assistance of WHO, the company set up their own distribution system for getting the drugs to the people who needed them. This meant that Merck was incurring costs to manufacture and distribute a product that was generating no income for the company. Why would Merck do this? The company said the decision was consistent with the core values of the organization. In 1950, George W. Merck, said, "We try never to forget that medicine is for the people. It is not for the profits. The profits follow, and if we have remembered that, they have never failed to appear. How can we bring the best of medicine to each and every person? We cannot rest until the way has been found with our help to bring our finest achievements to everyone." The decision to give away Mectizan may not have been economically prudent, but it was certainly just. The company was helping some of the least advantaged. This is justice as fairness.

---

[28] Tim Mullaney, "Why Corporate CEO Pay Is So High, and Going Higher," CNBC, May 18, 2015.

[29] Rawls, *A Theory of Justice*, 82.

Virtue Ethics—Analysis of the Virtue Expected

Virtue ethics draws its inspiration from the Greek philosopher Aristotle (384–322 B.C.). In *The Nicomachean Ethics*, he explored the nature of a good life. He thought that the goal of life is happiness. This is not happiness in a hedonistic sense. Instead, happiness, for Aristotle, is an activity of the soul. We fulfill our goal of being happy by living a virtuous life, a life in accordance with reason. Virtue is a character of the soul that is demonstrated only in voluntary actions, that is, in acts that are freely chosen after deliberation. So, we become virtuous by regularly performing virtuous acts. But Aristotle also felt that there is a need for ethical education so that people will know what acts are virtuous.

Aristotle thought that we can understand and identify virtues by arranging human characteristics in triads, with the two extremes being vices and the middle one being a virtue. For Aristotle, courage is the mean between cowardice and rashness; temperance is between self-indulgence and insensibility. The other virtues of pride, ambition, good temper, friendliness, truthfulness, ready wit, shame, and justice can similarly be seen as the middle way between two vices. Virtue is the golden mean. This is not an arithmetic mean but rather a path between extreme positions that would vary depending on the circumstances. You need to use your reason to identify the mean in each ethical situation, and you become better at doing this with experience, by acting virtuously. Practice makes perfect.

Virtue ethics focuses on the moral character of the decision maker rather than the consequences of the action (utilitarianism) or the motivation of the decision maker (deontology). It adopts a more holistic approach to understanding human ethical behavior. It recognizes that there are many aspects to our personalities. Each of us has a variety of character traits that are developed as we mature emotionally and ethically. Once these character traits are formed, they tend to remain fairly stable. Our personalities are many faceted, and our behavior is reasonably consistent. Although we all have numerous and often similar virtues, we demonstrate them in varying degrees despite similar situations.

By focusing on the whole person, who has a unique combination of virtues, this theory avoids false dichotomies. It denies that the consequences of actions are either right or wrong or that the motivation of the decision maker was either good or bad. In a business setting, virtue ethics eschews the notion that executives wear two hats—one hat representing personal values and the other corporate values, believing that an executive can wear only one hat at a time. This was the attitude of the two executives at Beech-Nut Nutrition Corporation who were model citizens (socially responsible when not at work) while at the same time they sold diluted apple juice to infants (tough businessmen while at work). How many executives erroneously see themselves as wearing two hats—one for corporate values and the other for personal values? They forget that it is the same head under each of the hats. Virtue ethics denies false dichotomies such as that it is either business related or ethics related, that you can do good or be profitable, and that you need to check your personal values at the door when you show up for work. The advantage of virtue ethics is that it takes a broader view, recognizing that the decision maker has a variety of character traits.

Beech-Nut Nutrition Corporation and Blind Corporate Loyalty

The Beach-Nut Nutrition Corporation, formed in 1891, was bought by the Swiss food conglomerate Nestlé in 1979. Neils Hoyvald, the CEO, promised the Nestlé executives that Beech-Nut, which had been losing money, would become profitable by 1982. Beech-Nut had earned a reputation for using high-quality natural ingredients in its baby food products. Its apple juice was advertised as 100% pure fruit juice, with no artificial flavoring, preservatives, or coloring. However, the company and two of its executives, Hoyvald and John Lavery, who were responsible for manufacturing, were convicted of selling millions of bottles of apple juice for babies that they knew contained little or no apples. At their trials, Hoyvald and Lavery argued that they were being loyal corporate executives, making decisions that were necessary for the survival of the firm, which was under intense financial and competitive pressures. Their crime, they contended, was at worst an error in judgment. At the same time as they were orchestrating a cynical and reckless fraud against babies who were the consumers of the bogus apple juice, they were model citizens with impeccable records. The lawyer for Hoyvald described him as "a person we would be proud to have in our family."[30]

WEAKNESSES WITH VIRTUE ETHICS There are two interrelated problems with virtue ethics. What are the virtues that businesspeople should have, and how is virtue demonstrated in the workplace? A key virtue in business is integrity. A 2014 global survey by the Conference Board asked CEOs, presidents, and chairs of boards of directors to identify the leadership attributes and behaviors they believed were critical to future success. The top attribute was integrity.[31] Integrity is an essential leadership quality and is fundamental in business behavior.

Integrity involves being honest and upstanding. For a business, it means that the firm's actions are consistent with its principles. It is demonstrated by not compromising on core values even when there is strong pressure to do so. Consider the case of fundraising by nonprofit organizations. Most organizations in the not-for-profit sector have very clear objectives: universities teach and conduct research, a hospice provides solace to the dying, and a choir society trains children to sing. The driving force for many nonprofits is their core values as described in the organization's mission statement. A nonprofit demonstrates integrity by not accepting donations from individuals and organizations that have values that are opposed to the core values of the nonprofit. For example, the American Cancer Society does not usually accept money from tobacco companies, and Mothers Against Drunk Driving declined a donation from the Anheuser-Busch brewery. Although they often need the funds, many nonprofits are not willing to compromise their core values and principles for money.

Companies demonstrate consistency when they adhere to their core ethical values, often articulated in their mission statements. The pharmaceutical company Johnson & Johnson engaged in the first major product recall in 1982 when bottles of its best-selling product Tylenol were found to contain cyanide. Harming customers was a violation of the core values and principles of Johnson & Johnson, so the product was recalled. Similarly, in 2008, Maple Leaf Foods withdrew its meat products when twenty-two people died after eating cold cuts that contained listeria. The company's mission statement said, "Maple Leaf Foods is a strong, values-based company where we take pride in doing what's right for our consumers, customers, our people and the communities where we

[30] James Traub, "Into the Mouths of Babes," *New York Times Magazine*, July 24, 1988, http://www.nytimes.com/1988/07/24/magazine/into-the-mouths-of-babes.html?pagewanted=all.

[31] The Conference Board, *CEO Challenge* 2014, https://www.conference-board.org/retrievefile.cfm?filename=TCB_R-1537-14-RR1.pdf&type=subsite.

live and work." Withdrawing the product was consistent with the company's values. How many other companies would demonstrate this level of integrity by voluntarily removing a profitable product promptly, thereby causing the stock price to fall, simply because the product violated the company's core values?

Johnson & Johnson's Worldwide Recall of Tylenol: Virtue Ethics

In 1982, the pharmaceutical company Johnson & Johnson withdrew Tylenol from the market after a number of people in the Chicago area who had taken Extra Strength Tylenol died. At the time of the crisis, Tylenol had 37% of the analgesic market, contributing 7.4% to the company's gross revenues and 17% to 18% of its net income. Five bottles had been tampered with and the capsules injected with cyanide by a still unknown person. An internal investigation revealed that the problem had not occurred in the manufacturing process; the Federal Bureau of Investigation (FBI) looked into the deaths and recommended that the product not be withdrawn because Johnson & Johnson was not at fault in the poisoning; and legal counsel advised against withdrawing the product lest it indicate culpability on the part of the firm. At the time, a product recall was an extremely rare event. Nevertheless, the CEO, James Burke, withdrew the product because it violated the company's Credo or mission statement, called Credo. Written by Robert Woods Johnson in the 1940s, it outlines, in four short paragraphs, the company's responsibilities to the medical community, customers, suppliers, employees, local and worldwide communities, and stockholders. The first two sentences of the Credo are these: "We believe our first responsibility is to the doctors, nurses, and patients, to mothers and all others who use our products and services. In meeting their needs everything we do must be of the highest quality." For Burke this was an easy decision that was consistent with the company's core values. Johnson & Johnson had an obligation to maintain the safety of its customers. Tylenol was an unsafe product. Therefore, it had to be recalled—and not only in the Chicago area but also worldwide.

At the individual level, what are the important virtues that businesspeople should have? Bertrand Russell thought that Aristotle's list was applicable only to respectable middle-aged people since it lacked ardor and enthusiasm and seemed to be grounded on the principles of prudence and moderation. He may be right. The list may also represent the values of middle-class accountants. Libby and Thorne identified the virtues that public accountants hold dear. They came up with an Aristotelian-type list that included honesty, sincerity, truthfulness, reliability, dependability, and trustworthiness.[32] However, the problem with virtue ethics is that we are unable to compile an exhaustive list of virtues. Furthermore, virtues may be situation specific. A public accountant may need courage when telling a CFO that her accounting policy does not result in the fair presentation of her company's financial statements. A CEO requires candor and truthfulness when explaining a potential downsizing to company employees and those who live in the community who will be adversely affected by a plant closing.

[32] Theresa Libby and Linda Thorne, "Auditors' Virtue: A Qualitative Analysis and Categorization," *Business Ethics Quarterly* 14, no. 3 (2004).

Many items on the list may be self-contradictory in certain circumstances. Should you tell the truth or be compassionate when dealing with a dying relative? Assume that you know that, due to adverse economic factors, your employer is going to lay off three employees at the end of next week. One of those employees tells you that she has just bought a new condominium and that, although it is expensive, she can afford the mortgage payments because she has this good job. Do you tell her that she should not sign the agreement because she will be laid off next week (compassion), or do you remain silent because your boss told you the names of the employees in confidence (not betraying a trust)?

MORAL IMAGINATION

Business students are trained to become business managers, and business managers are expected to be able to make hard decisions. Managers are to be creative and innovative in the solutions that they come up with to solve practical business problems. They should be no less creative when it comes to ethical problems. Managers should use their moral imagination to determine win-win ethical alternatives. That is, the decisions need to be good for the individual, good for the firm, and good for society.

This chapter has provided a background on the theoretical foundations to make ethical decisions. Chapter 4 provides an ethical decision-making framework. Together, these two chapters should help in allowing you to be creative and imaginative in solving and resolving ethical problems and dilemmas.

Questions

1. How would you respond when someone makes a decision that adversely affects you while saying, "It's nothing personal, it's just business"? Is business impersonal?
2. Is someone who makes an ethical decision based on enlightened self-interest worthy of more or less praise than someone who makes a similar decision based solely on economic considerations?
3. Since happiness is extremely subjective, how would you objectively measure and assess happiness? Do you agree with J. S. Mill that arithmetic can be used to calculate happiness? Is money a good proxy for happiness?
4. Is there any categorical imperative that you can think of that would have universal application? Isn't there an exception to every rule?
5. Assume that Firm A is a publicly traded company that puts its financial statements on the Web. This information can be accessed and read by anyone, even those who do not own shares of Firm A. This a free-rider situation, where an investor can use Firm A as a means to making an investment decision about another company. Is this ethical? Does free riding treat another individual as a means and not also as an end?
6. How does a business executive demonstrate virtue when dealing with a disgruntled shareholder at the annual meeting?
7. Commuters who have more than one passenger in the car are permitted to drive in a special lane on the highway while all the other motorists have to contend with stop-and-go traffic. What does this have to do with ethics? Assess this situation using each of the following ethical theories: utilitarianism, deontology, justice, fairness, and virtue ethics.

Case Insights

- *Dealing with Disappointed Apple iPhone Customers* is an illustrative application of the problem Apple Corporation encountered when it suddenly and dramatically decreased the price of its iPhone within months of introducing the product. The customers who bought the iPhone at the earlier and higher price were not pleased. (An analysis of this case is provided in this chapter under the heading "An Illustration of Ethical Decision Making.")
- *Art Forgeries: Is Deceiving Art Experts Unethical?* asks whether it is unethical to freely donate forgeries to an art gallery even if doing so, technically, is not illegal.
- *Gender Discrimination at IKEA* describes the ethical problems that IKEA encountered when it deleted all the photographs of women and children from the furniture catalog that was distributed in Saudi Arabia.
- *Deciding Who Receives the Swine Flu Vaccine* requires students to decide who should be the first to receive a limited supply of medicine using two different theories: utilitarianism and justice as fairness.
- *Insurance and Genetically Inherited Diseases* asks whether it is unethical for insurance companies to deny insurance coverage to people who have a genetically inherited disease.
- *Terrorist Payments* presents the dilemma a CEO faces when a terrorist group "offers" to protect the company's South American personnel and operations. Should the payments continue to be made even if they are immaterial in amount.
- *The Case of Cesar Correia* tells the story of two entrepreneurs who start a business and then lose customers when the customers learn that one of the entrepreneurs has a criminal past. If it is not a business-related crime, should it be disclosed? Does the other entrepreneur have the right to know about his partner's criminal past?

Useful Video & Film

- *Basic Frameworks in Business Ethics* by Thomas Donaldson and Mark O. Winkelman, professor, Wharton School at the University of Pennsylvania. Video is from the 2010 Conference on Teaching Ethics at the Wheatley Institution at Brigham Young University; see http://teachingethics.byu.edu/.
- *Margin Call*, the 2011 award-winning movie, presents a moral dilemma during the 2007–2008 subprime mortgage crisis. Should an investment dealer knowingly sell toxic assets to an unsuspecting buyer in order to avoid having to record a write-down on those assets that might result in the selling firm going bankrupt?

References

Aristotle. 1925. *The Nicomachean Ethics.* Translated with an introduction by David Ross, revised by J. L. Ackrill and J. O. Urmson. Oxford: Oxford University Press.

Bentham, J. 1961. "An Introduction to the Principles of Morals and Legislation." In *The Utilitarians.* Garden City, NY, Dolphin Books.

Carroll, A. "The Pyramid of Corporate Social Responsibility: Towards the Moral Management of Organizational Stakeholders." *Business Horizons* 42 (1991): 39–48.

Edwards, P., ed. 1967. *Encyclopedia of Philosophy.* New York: Macmillan.

Frankena, W. K. 1963. *Ethics*. Englewood Cliffs, NJ: Prentice Hall.

Gore, Al. 2006. *An Inconvenient Truth: The Planetary Emergency of Global Warming and What We Can Do about It*. New York: Rodale.

Hobbes, Thomas. 1968. *Leviathan*. Edited with an introduction by C. B. Macpherson. Middlesex: Penguin.

Hume, D. 1969. *A Treatise of Human Nature*. Edited with an introduction by Ernest C. Mossner. Middlesex: Penguin.

Kant, I. 1964. *Groundwork of the Metaphysic of Morals*. Translated with an introduction by H. J. Paton. New York: Harper Torchbooks.

Levin, H. 1983. *Grand Delusions: The Cosmic Career of John De Lorean*. New York: Viking.

Libby, Theresa, and Linda Thorne. 2004. "Auditors' Virtue: A Qualitative Analysis and Categorization." *Business Ethics Quarterly* 14, no. 3.

Machiavelli, N. 1950. *The Prince and the Discourses*. Introduction by Max Lerner. New York: Modern Library.

MacIntyre, A. 1981. *After Virtue*. Notre Dame, IN: University of Notre Dame Press.

Mackie, J. L. 1977. *Ethics: Inventing Right and Wrong*. Middlesex: Penguin.

Mill, J. S. 1998. *Utilitarianism*. Edited by Roger Crisp. Oxford: Oxford University Press.

Raphael, D. D. 1981. *Moral Philosophy*. Oxford: Oxford University Press.

Rawls, J. 1971. *A Theory of Justice*. Cambridge, MA: Harvard University Press.

Russell, B. 1945. *A History of Western Philosophy*. New York: Simon and Schuster.

Schwartz, M, and Archie Carroll. 2003. "Corporate Social Responsibility: A Three Domain Approach." *Business Ethics Quarterly* 13, no. 4: 503–530.

Smith, A. 1993. *An Inquiry into the Nature and Causes of the Wealth of Nations*. Edited with an introduction and notes by Kathryn Sutherland. Oxford: Oxford University Press.

Smith, A. 1997. *The Theory of Moral Sentiments*. Washington, DC: Regency Publishing.

Cases Involving Improper Behavior

An Illustration of Ethical Decision Making

ETHICS CASE

Dealing with Disappointed Apple iPhone Customers

On September 5, 2007, Steve Jobs, the CEO of Apple Inc., announced that the spectacularly successful iPhone would be reduced in price by $200 from $599, its introductory price of roughly two months earlier.[1] Needless to say, he received hundreds of e-mails from irate customers. Two days later, he offered early customers who paid full price a $100 credit good at Apple's retail and online stores. Was this decision to mitigate the $200 price decrease and the manner of doing so appropriate from an ethical perspective?

iPhone Analysis

The ethicality of this iPhone marketing decision can be analyzed using different ethical theories, and, interestingly, the conclusions are not the same. Ethical theories help to frame a question, and they help in highlighting aspects of the case that might be overlooked if the case were analyzed in purely economic terms. The theories can also help in explaining and defending the option you ultimately choose. But, in the end, you must have the courage of your convictions and make a choice.

Utilitarianism

Utilitarianism argues that the best ethical alternative is the one that will produce the greatest amount of net pleasure to the widest audience of relevant stakeholders. In this case, pleasure can be measured in terms of customer satisfaction. Presumably, the customers who bought the iPhone at both the higher and the lower prices are satisfied with the product function, so

[1] David Ho, "Apple CEO Apologizes to Customers," *Toronto Star*, September 7, 2007, B4.

there is no product dissatisfaction. The only dissatisfaction is the effect among the customers who paid $599. They were upset that they paid $200 more than the current customers, who were purchasing the identical product at $399. Steve Jobs received over a hundred e-mails in the two days after the price was dropped.

Does the dissatisfaction of the $599 group outweigh the satisfaction of the $399 group? Presumably, there are a larger number of customers purchasing the iPhone at the lower price, so, all other things being equal, there will be a greater number of satisfied customers at the $399 price than the number of dissatisfied customers at the $599 price. So, the conclusion would be to do nothing.

However, utilitarianism requires that you examine the consequences to all stakeholders. The dissatisfied customers voiced their displeasure to Steve Jobs through their e-mails to him. This presumably lowered his feeling of satisfaction. These dissatisfied customers might also take their anger out at the sales representatives at the Apple stores. More important, they may show their dissatisfaction by not purchasing any additional Apple products. To mitigate this, Steve Jobs should offer rebates to the $599 customers that are equal to their level of dissatisfaction. That is, the rebates should be sufficient enough to ensure that these customers return to buy other Apple products rather than take their business to the competition.

Deontology

Deontology looks at the motivation of the decision maker rather than the consequences of the decision. Are you willing to make it a universal rule that whenever prices fall, all previous customers should be subsidized? The iPhone was launched in June 2007 at a price of $599 per unit. Customers willingly paid $599 for the product. Nevertheless, two months later, on September 5, the price was dropped to $399. Presumably, the costs of production had not decreased during the summer, so the $200 price reduction was because the iPhone was initially overpriced, even though customers were purchasing the product at $599 per unit.

Thus, the deontological question becomes, Should rebates be given whenever products are incorrectly priced too high and the price is shortly thereafter lowered and the price reduction is not due to product efficiencies? That is, is it ethically correct to compensate those who have been overcharged? It would appear that Apple thinks so, and as result, the company was willing to give an in-store rebate to anyone who bought the iPhone at the higher price. If the company did not offer a rebate, then it would be treating its initial customers merely as a means of generating abnormal rents (i.e., profits). From a deontological perspective, a rebate should be offered because otherwise you are treating the first group of customers opportunistically, as a means to the company's end.

However, by offering a rebate, has the company set a bad precedent for itself? Every time the price of a product falls, should all the customers who paid the higher price receive a rebate? Technological advances are so rapid that the manufacturing costs of electronics are constantly decreasing. As a consequence, the price of electronics tends to decrease over time. The iPhone version 2.0, launched in June 2008, one year after the original iPhone, has more features than the original phone and is priced at $199 per unit. Should all those who paid $399 for the original iPhone be given a rebate too?

It is clear that the 2008 model is different from the original 2007 model. But what if the differences were not readily apparent to the consumer? Assume that the selling price decreases because of production efficiencies. Are you prepared to make a rebate every time the current price falls because the current costs of production have decreased? This may be the perception of Apple customers if the company begins to pay rebates.

Remember, from a deontological perspective, the consequences are unimportant. What is important is that the decision was made for the right reasons. The fact that customers cannot differentiate between overcharging and production efficiencies is irrelevant. The only relevant aspect is that the decision maker knows the difference between overcharging and production efficiencies and that the decision maker makes a rebate in the former case but not in the latter. The fact that the presence or absence of a rebate may influence future sales is irrelevant.

Justice & Fairness

Distributive justice argues that equals should be treated equally and that unequals should be treated unequally in relationship to their relevant inequalities and differences. Are all customers equal? This would depend on your time frame. If you assume that there will be no repeat business from any customer, then they are not equal. A fair price is defined as one that a willing buyer and a willing seller would accept in a noncoercive arm's-length transaction. Assuming there was no undue sales pressure, then the customers who bought the iPhone at $599 thought that that was a fair price. The ones who bought the iPhone at $399 also, presumably, considered that to be a fair price. So, both groups were willing to pay fair value for the product at the time of purchase. There is no ethical reason to reverse those transactions. Both were fair albeit different prices.

On the other hand, if a business is attempting to establish an ongoing relationship with its customers who will be buying numerous products over a long period of time, then all customers are equal. As such, they need to be treated equally. This means that a business does not want to alienate any of its customer base, so it will offer a rebate to make everyone equal.

Rawls argues that social and economic inequalities are just if these inequalities are to everyone's benefit. This means that a price differentiation is just if it relates to production cost differences. Assume that the cash flow from the $599 sales were used to fund production efficiencies that permitted the company to maintain the same profit margin while reducing the price of the product to $399. If this had been the case, then the price inequality would be to everyone's advantage. The higher price permitted the lower price to occur. However, the actual price decrease occurred two months after the launch of the product. Presumably, there were no production changes during the summer. So, this price differentiation is not to everyone's advantage and as such would not be considered just.

Virtue Ethics

Virtue ethics focuses on the moral character of the decision maker. What values does Steve Jobs want his company to project? The website of Apple Inc. has separate pages concerning responsible supplier management and Apple's commitment to the environment. The company projects an image of high quality with high ethical standards. The last thing this company wants is criticism that it is not behaving responsibly.

Two days after the price of the iPhone was dropped to $399, Steve Jobs publicly apologized for the pricing error and offered a $100 in-store rebate to those customers who had paid $599 for the product. What values is Steve Jobs demonstrating by making a public apology? By admitting his pricing error and atoning for the error by offering a rebate, he is demonstrating rectitude. By being honest and straightforward in his apology, he is taking personal responsibility for the mistake.

On the other hand, you might say that he is not demonstrating integrity because he is recanting under pressure. This was not a free decision. He was reacting to public pressure. He had received hundreds of e-mails from irate customers. Furthermore, he waited two days before succumbing to the pressure. Instead, he should have demonstrated courage by not offering a rebate. He could have said that the $599 was a fair price at that time and that $399 is a fair price at this time. No one was coerced into buying the product at either price.

Moral Imagination or Marketing Ploy?

Moral imagination means coming up with a creative and innovative solution to an ethical dilemma. The price of the iPhone was dropped to $399 in order to better market the product during the holiday season. Was offering a $100 rebate an example of moral imagination, or was it simply another marketing ploy?

Both sets of customers paid fair value for their iPhones, which implies that no rebate should be offered. But if a rebate should be offered, then presumably it should be for $200, thereby making the sales price to both sets of customers equal. So, the two options are to provide either no rebate or a $200 rebate. However, Apple chose a third alternative: not to give a rebate but instead to give a partial credit. The $599 customers were given a $100 in-store credit toward future purchases. Such a credit costs Apple far less than a cash rebate of $100. Furthermore, the $100 is half of the price decrease. So, if the $599 price was incorrectly set too high and Jobs was truly contrite about his pricing error, then why did he not offer a full cash rebate of $200?

An argument can be made that Steve Jobs was willing to admit his pricing mistake, but he was not willing to suffer the full financial consequences of his error. By adopting this compromise position, he managed to deflect customer criticism without having to make an actual cash settlement. Cynics may say that this third option was mostly motivated by marketing concerns and very little by ethical concerns—that it was a marketing ploy to appease irate customers and that Apple is appearing to be ethically responsible without having to bear the full economic consequences of its decision.

In conclusion, a decision maker would be wise to consider how consumers, employees, and others will react to a proposed decision. Will it fulfill their ethical expectations of what is right or wrong? Ethical theories can provide useful perspectives that should be weighed when arriving at an overall conclusion about the ethicality of the decision.

ETHICS CASE

Art Forgeries: Is Deceiving Art Experts Unethical?

Eric Hebborn (1934–1996) was an English painter and art forger. Hebborn attended the Royal Academy of Arts and then the British School at Rome, two of the most prestigious fine arts schools at the time. Underappreciated as an artist, he turned his hand to copying old masters. His forgeries were detected when an art curator noticed that two of the Gallery's drawings, by two different artists, were sketched on identical paper.

In his autobiography, *Drawn to Trouble: Confessions of a Master Forger*, Hebborn admitted to selling thousands of forged paintings, drawings, and sculptures. He boasted how easy it was to fool art experts who, he contended, should have been able to detect that they were fakes. "Only the experts are worth fooling. The greater the expert, the greater the satisfaction in deceiving them." However, his personal moral code would not allow him to sell his forgeries to amateur collectors. Hebborn was never sued because embarrassed art experts refused to admit in court that they had been deceived.

Mark Landis (born 1955) is an American art forger. He attended the Art Institute of Chicago, where he learned to restore damaged paintings. Then he began to forge lesser-known artists and donated his fake paintings to more than fifty art galleries and museums in twenty states. His forgeries were detected when a gallery curator noticed that a Paul Signac watercolor of two boats was similar to a Signac watercolor that had been donated to another art gallery.

Landis donated the paintings under various aliases, saying that the paintings were in memory of a deceased parent. Landis has not been prosecuted because he never profited from his forgeries. He never accepted any money from the art galleries and museums, nor did he claim any tax deductions for his donations. "We couldn't identify a federal crime violation," said Robert Withman, senior FBI investigator. "Basically, you have a guy going around the country on his own nickel giving stuff to museums."

Questions

1. Is it ethically acceptable to sell forgeries to art experts who should be able to differentiate a fake from an authentic work of art?
2. Comment on Hebborn's personal moral code.
3. Was anyone harmed when Landis donated his forged paintings to various art galleries and museums?
4. Does the fact that Landis did not profit from his donations mean that it was ethically acceptable to give forgeries to art galleries and museums?

Sources: Eric Hebborn, *Drawn to Trouble: Confessions of a Master Forger* (Mainstream Publishing, 1991); Alec Wilkinson, "The Giveaway." *New Yorker Magazine*, August 26, 2013.

ETHICS CASE

Gender Discrimination at IKEA

On October 1, 2012, IKEA apologized for removing women from the photographs in the IKEA catalogs that were shipped to Saudi Arabia. IKEA is a Swedish company that was founded in 1943. It is now the world's largest furniture retailer with stores in over forty-one countries. IKEA has been in the forefront of environmental and social responsibility. It generously contributes to charitable organizations. It is a world leader in producing eco-friendly furniture. For three years in a row, it was on the Fortune's 100 Best Companies to Work For and has been named four times as one of the 100 Best Companies for Working Mothers by *Working Mothers* magazine.

Since 1951, IKEA has been publishing an annual catalog. In 2012, it printed 212 million catalogs in twenty-nine languages. The images in the catalog were identical across the world—until recently. In the 2012 Saudi Arabian catalog, the images of all women were deleted. In one bathroom picture, a mother is with her son, and the father is with a younger boy. In the Saudi version, there is no woman; she has been airbrushed out of the photograph. There is only the father and the two boys. In another photo, there are two women smiling at each other with four pieces of furniture in the background; in the Saudi Arabian catalog, there are only the four pieces of furniture. In other pictures, women have been digitally removed or else have been altered to become men.

A spokeswoman for IKEA admitted that the error occurred at the head office and was not done by the Saudi Arabian franchisee. She said that excluding women from the catalog was in conflict with the values of IKEA. "We encourage fair treatment and equal employment opportunities without regard to race, ethnicity, religion, gender, disability, age, or sexual orientation."

Questions

1. Discuss the pros and cons of altering the catalog using the following:
   - Deontology
   - Utilitarianism
   - Virtue ethics
2. Should a company alter its marketing campaigns to reflect biases that might be prevalent in various countries in which the company does business?

Sources: CSR, "IKEA Named for Fortune's 2007 '100 Best Companies to Work For' List for Third Consecutive Year," 2009, http://www.csrwire.com/press_releases/16621-IKEA-Named-To-Fortune-s-2007

-100-Best-Companies-To-Work-For-List-For-Third-Consecutive-Year.

"IKEA Group Sustainability Report FY12," http://www.ikea.com/ms/en_GB/pdf/annual_report/ikea_group_sustainability_report_2012.pdf.

Anna Molin, "IKEA Regrets Cutting Women from Saudi Ad," *Wall Street Journal*, October 1, 2012.

ETHICS CASE

Deciding Who Receives the Swine Flu Vaccine

Throughout 2009, the world was plagued with the H1N1 swine flu epidemic. The H1N1 influenza virus, which began in Mexico, spread rapidly. In June, the World Health Organization (WHO) declared it to be a global pandemic.

Those who caught the virus suffered from chills, fever, headaches, coughing, pain, weakness, and general discomfort. At the extreme, it could kill, and thousands around the world died from the disease. In order to minimize the chances of catching swine flu, WHO recommended that everyone be inoculated against the disease. However, there was not enough vaccine available, so a priority system had to be established. The Centers for Disease Control and Prevention (CDC) in Atlanta recommended that those who were at greater risk be inoculated first. Priority would be given to pregnant women, caregivers of young children, health care and emergency medical service personnel, and people from six months to twenty-four years of age. The elderly were excluded because the risks of contracting the disease for people over age sixty-five were less than for the younger age-groups.

Although many people chose not to receive the vaccine, the line ups of those who wanted to be inoculated were often hours long. Sometimes people waited all day, only to be told at the end of the day that the supply of the vaccine had run out. On November 2, 2009, *BusinessWeek* reported that Goldman Sachs, Citigroup, and a number of other large employers in New York City were given the vaccine to distribute. Although these companies were to follow the CDC priority group guidelines, there was the appearance that these employees were line jumping, especially after it was revealed that Goldman Sachs received as many doses as the Lennox Hill Hospital in New York City.

At the same time, in Canada, it was reported that many of the Calgary Flames hockey players, along with their families, the coaching staff, and management, had received the swine flu vaccine. None of these people were in the priority group.

Questions

1. From a utilitarian point of view, who do you think should be in the priority group?
2. From a justice as fairness perspective, who should be in the priority group?
3. Should people who make society flourish through their economic productivity, such as the employees of Goldman Sachs, be put into the priority group?
4. Should people who contribute to making life enjoyable, such as entertainers and athletes, be put into the priority group?
5. If you were the CEO of the company that manufactured the swine flu vaccine, would you ensure that all your employees were inoculated first, or would you recommend that they too wait in line?

Sources: Esmé E. Deprez, "New York Businesses Get H1N1 Vaccine," *Business Week*, November 2, 2009, http://www.businessweek.com/bwdaily/dnflash/content/nov2009/db2009112_606442.htm.

Tony Seskus, "Flames Skipped Queue for H1N1 Flu Vaccine," *National Post*, November 2, 2009, http://www.nationalpost.com/sports/story.html?id=2179790.

Joe Weisenthal, "Goldman Sachs Received H1N1 Vaccine before Several Hospitals," *Business Insider*, November 5, 2009, http://www.businessinsider.com/goldman-sachs-received-h1n1-vaccine-before-several-hospitals-2009-11.

ETHICS CASE

Insurance and Genetically Inherited Diseases

Adverse selection occurs when one party has an information advantage over the other party. In the case of insurance, people taking out insurance know more about their health and lifestyle than the insurance company. Therefore, in order to reduce information asymmetry, the insurance company asks prospective customers to complete a medical questionnaire and/or submit to a medical examination. Knowing the health risks associated with the people taking out insurance allows the insurance company to better adjust the premiums that it charges. For example, the premium for smokers is higher than for nonsmokers.

Some people are subject to genetically inherited health problems, such as Alzheimer's disease, ALS, and Huntington's disease. Huntington's, for example, is an incurable degenerative brain disorder that affects about 1 in 10,000 people. Children of a parent who has Huntington's have a 50% chance of inheriting the disease.

Legislation in Belgium, Denmark, Finland, France, Norway, and Sweden make it illegal to discriminate against people who may have inherited diseases. Similar legislation was enacted in the United States in 2008, where the *Genetic Information Nondiscrimination Act* prohibits employment and insurance discrimination simply on the basis that a person has a genetic predisposition to developing a disease in the future.

There is no such legislation in Canada. But in February 2010, Member of Parliament Judy Wasylycia-Leis tabled a private member's bill against genetic discrimination. She was opposed to genetic discrimination for three reasons. "One is that people who carry genes that code for particular diseases may or may not eventually develop them. The second is that some people may not want to be forced to take a test because they don't want to know what their eventual fate in life may be. Finally, the third is that people who do want to take a test for health reasons may not do so because they fear having the results used against them." Her bill did not get beyond first reading. In April 2013, Liberal Senator James Cowan tabled a similar bill that would stop insurance companies from discriminating on the basis of genetic testing.

Questions

1. Do you consider it to be unethical for insurance companies to charge high-risk people a higher premium than low-risk people?
2. Are insurance companies acting responsibly when they require customers to disclose medical information and/or submit to a medical examination?
3. Argue either in favor of or opposed to 'Senator Cowan's proposed legislation.

Sources: Paul Turenne, "MP Fights 'Genetic Discrimination,'" *Winnipeg Sun*, February 25, 2010, http://www.winnipegsun.com/news/winnipeg/2010/02/25/13023676.html.

ETHICS CASE

Terrorist Payments

Alex McAdams, the recently retired CEO of Athletic Shoes, was honored to be asked to join the Board of Consolidated Mines International Inc. Alex continues to sit on the Board of Athletic Shoes, as well as the Board of Pharma-Advantage, another publicly traded company on the New York Stock Exchange. However, CMI, as it is known, is a major step up for Alex.

CMI was formed as the United Mines Company in the 1870s by an American railway magnate, and in 1985, it became Consolidated Mines International Inc. It operates mines in Central America and northern South America. In 2004, its revenues were approximately $4.5 billion, and it employed about 25,000 people worldwide.

In deciding whether to accept the board seat, Alex conducted his own due diligence. As a result, there were two issues that he wanted to raise with Cameron Derry, the CEO of CMI. One concerned the allegations of questionable business practices. The other concerned the political instability in several of the Latin American countries in which the CMI mines are located. Today, Alex was meeting with Cameron at the Long Bar Lounge.

During lunch, Cameron candidly talked about the history of the company and the bad press that it often received. "In the 1920s we were accused of bribing government officials and using our political connections to have unions outlawed. In the 1950s we were accused of participating in the overthrow of a Latin American government. In the 1990s there were charges that we were exploiting our employees, polluting the environment, and facilitating the importation of cocaine into the U.S. But, none of these allegations has ever been proven in a court of law," said Cameron. "And we've even successfully sued one newspaper chain that published a series of these unproven stories about us.

"As for the political environment, Alex, you're right. There is no effective government in many of the countries in which we operate. In fact it is often the paramilitary that are in control of the countryside where we have our mines. These are very unsavory organizations, Alex. They have their own death squads. They have been involved in the massacre, assassination, kidnapping, and torture of tens of thousands of Latin Americans, most of them peasants and workers, as well as trade unionists and left-wing political figures."

"Do they interfere with CMI's operations?" asked Alex.

"No, and that's because we've been paying them off. It's now 2007 and we've been paying them since 1997. To date we've given them about $1.7 million in total. Don't look so shocked, Alex. Occasionally, we have to do business with some very unsavory characters. And the United Peoples Liberation Front that controls much of the region around our mines is probably the worst of the lot. They are involved in disappearances, murder, rape, and drug trafficking. The payments we make to them are for our protection. If we don't make these payments it could result in harm to our personnel and property."

"That's extortion!"

"We don't call it that. We list these payments as being for 'security services,' but we have no invoices to support the payments, and beginning in 2002 we began making direct cash payments to them.

"But, we now have an additional problem. The United States government has declared the United Peoples Liberation Front to be a terrorist organization, and our outside legal counsel has advised us to stop making the payments. But if we stop I'm afraid of what might happen to our employees. I don't want to support drug trafficking and terrorism, but I need our mines to stay open.

"I'm telling you this, Alex, because if you join the Board, the first item on next month's agenda is these payments. I want the Board to approve that we continue to make these payments in order to ensure the safety of our Latin American employees and operations."

Questions

1. Should Alex join the Board of Directors of Consolidated Mines International Inc.?
2. If Alex joins the Board, should he vote in favor of continuing to make the payments to the United Peoples Liberation Front?
3. What other options are available to Alex?

ETHICS CASE

The Case of Cesar Correia

In 1984, when he was eighteen years old, Cesar Correia murdered his father, killing him with a baseball bat. Cesar then dumped the body in the Assiniboine River. The body was eventually found, and Cesar confessed to the crime. He pleaded guilty to manslaughter and was sentenced to prison for five years.

Background

His father, Joachim, was abusive to Cesar, to Cesar's brother, and to Cesar's mother. The judge said that Joachim was a cruel and abusive man whose home "was a living hell." The judge said, "I have no difficulty in concluding it instilled in the heart and mind of the accused a sense of devastation, desperation and frustration, which was consumed in a burning hatred for his father."

Cesar argued that he was protecting his mother and younger brother.

The Murder

Cesar and his father got into an argument while working on the family car. Cesar went and got a baseball and clubbed his father from behind, hitting him three or four times. He then got a smaller bat and hit him once or twice more. Cesar then wrapped the body in a blanket and put it and his bicycle in the family car. He drove to the Assiniboine River, where he dumped the body in the river, left the car, and returned home on the bicycle. Both Cesar and his mother claimed that they did not know what happened to Joachim. Cesar helped in the search for his missing father. A few weeks later, the body was found by some children, and Cesar quickly confessed to the police when questioned by them. He was initially charged with murder but later pleaded guilty to manslaughter.

Afterward

While at prison, he completed his university education, graduating from the University of Manitoba in 1989 with a bachelor of science degree in computer sciences and statistics. After he was released from jail, he moved to Toronto and began working in the information technology industry.

In Canada, people can apply for a pardon five years after the expiration of their sentence. They must have completed their sentence and demonstrated that they are law-abiding citizens. In 1996, twelve years after the murder and conviction, Cesar applied for and received a pardon that expunged his criminal record.

Infolink Technologies Ltd

In 1999, Cesar formed an information dissemination company, Infolink Technologies Ltd, with George Theodore. Infolink, of which Cesar was president, traded on the Toronto Stock Exchange until 2007, when it went private. The Ontario Securities Commission, which oversees the Toronto Stock Exchange, requires that all directors and officers of public companies disclose any criminal convictions and "any other penalties or sanctions imposed by a court or regulatory body that would likely be considered important to a reasonable investor in making an investment decision."

The Lawsuit

In 2003, George resigned from the company and then sued Cesar for lost profits on two transactions. George contended that two customers backed out of deals when they found out about Cesar's conviction.

Questions

1. Ignoring any legal issues, was Cesar ethically obligated to inform his partner, George, of his criminal past?
2. Did George have a right to know about Cesar's criminal past?

4

Practical Ethical Decision Making

PURPOSE OF THE CHAPTER

A businessperson or professional accountant facing a decision has traditionally referred to the normal expectations in the industry or profession for guidance as well as their own personal ethical values. However, recent corporate scandals have led to the 2002 crisis of credibility over corporate governance and accountability, the subprime lending crisis of 2008, and the LIBOR rate fiasco of 2012—all of which are ethical failures with worldwide impacts and which make it clear that decision making based only on profit and legality, motivated only by self-interest, is no longer adequate.

In the future, business and professional decisions will be expected to be ethically defensible from a stakeholder perspective. As a first step, they will be expected to conform to corporate and professional codes of conduct. But these *often* do not apply specifically to the problems faced and require interpretation to fit the circumstances. When this is required, to make practical defensible ethical decisions, the decision maker should be able to use the principles, approaches, and frameworks discussed in this chapter. Even when established codes and practices appear to cover the ethical aspects of a decision, decision makers should be considering whether they fulfill current ethical expectations of relevant stakeholders. In either case, understanding the principles, approaches, and frameworks covered in this chapter will always be relevant to making defensible ethical decisions.

INTRODUCTION

Traditional business decision making based only on profit, legality, and self-interest has repeatedly led to significant ethical failures, including those in 2002 and 2008, which have had far-reaching, worldwide financial, and human consequences. While profit, legality, and self-interest provide useful and necessary core criteria, history has shown that they need to be supplemented by ethical considerations to be ethically defensible and to afford protection for directors, executives, professional accountants, investors, and other stakeholders. In the future, decision makers will be well advised to make sure that their decisions are in accordance with reasonable ethical principles and standards.

What are these general ethical principles, and how should they be applied? Building on the philosophers' contributions discussed in Chapter 3, this chapter explores these ethical principles and develops a practical, comprehensive decision framework based on how a proposed action would impact on the stakeholders to the decision. The chapter concludes by proposing a comprehensive framework for making ethical decisions.

MOTIVATING DEVELOPMENTS FOR ETHICAL LEARNING

The Enron, Arthur Andersen, and WorldCom scandals gave rise to public outrage, the collapse of capital markets, and ultimately the *Sarbanes-Oxley Act of 2002*, which brought about widespread governance reform. Subsequent corporate scandals and the subprime lending fiasco served to further heighten public awareness that corporate executives can make better decisions, and should do so to preserve the profitability and viability of their corporations. Ensuing court cases as well as related fines, imprisonments, and settlements have underscored the need for those decisions to reduce vulnerability to legal actions as well. The court of public opinion has also been harsh to companies and individuals who have behaved unethically. Loss of reputation due to unethical and/or illegal acts has proven to be revenue and profit reducing, damaging to share prices, and career ending for many executives even before the acts are fully investigated and responsibility for them is fully proven. These developments have been so important that corporate executives and directors now must give increased attention to corporate governance and the guidance it provides, in addition to their own role. Additionally, business schools that want worldwide accreditation by the Association to Advance Collegiate Schools of Business (AACSB)[1] are to incorporate ethics education into their policies, practices, and curricula. Specifically, according to the AACSB's Ethics Education Task Force,[2] business school curricula should deal with several ethical matters, including corporate social responsibility, governance, ethical corporate culture, and ethical decision making (AACSB, 2004).

Beginning in 2003, the International Federation of Accountants (IFAC) issued International Education Standards (IES) for accountants. Standard IES 4 (2015),[3] for example, details the professional values, ethics, and attitudes required for professional accountants to understand and discharge their duties under the IFAC Code of Ethics for Professional Accountants.[4]

The lesson is clear. It is no longer enough to make decisions and take actions that are only profitable and legal—actions must also be ethically defensible.

ETHICAL DECISION MAKING FRAMEWORK—AN OVERVIEW

In response to the need for ethically defensible decisions, this chapter presents a practical, comprehensive, multifaceted framework for ethical decision making (EDM). This EDM framework incorporates traditional requirements for profitability and legality as well as requirements shown to be philosophically important and those recently demanded by stakeholders. It is designed to enhance ethical reasoning by providing the following:

- Insights into the identification and analysis of key issues to be considered and questions or challenges to be raised.
- Approaches to combining and applying decision-relevant factors into practical action.

[1] The Association to Advance Collegiate Schools of Business (AACSB) International accredits business schools and programs worldwide. See http://www.aacsb.edu.

[2] The AACSB's Ethics Education Task Force is at http://www.aacsb.edu/~/media/AACSB/Publications/research-reports/ethics-education.ashx.

[3] See "IES 4, Initial Professional Development—Professional Values, Ethics, and Attitudes (2015)," in International Accounting Education Standards Board, *Handbook of International Education Pronouncements* (2015 ed.) *[International Education Standards]* (New York: International Federation of Accountants, 2015). (Download available at https://www.ifac.org/publications-resources/2015-handbook-international-education-pronouncements.) Standards IES 1 (2015) to IES 6 (2015), inclusive, are reproduced at www.cengage.com/accounting/brooks for further reference.

[4] International Accounting Education Standards Board, *Handbook of the Code of Ethics for Professional Accountants* (2015 ed.) (New York: International Federation of Accountants, 2015). (Download available at https://www.ifac.org/ethics/iesba-code.)

In general, *a decision or action is considered ethical or "right" if it conforms to certain standards.* Philosophers have been studying which standards are important for millennia, and business ethicists have recently been building on their work. Both groups have found that *one standard alone is insufficient to ensure an ethical decision. Consequently, the EDM framework proposes that decisions or actions be compared against three standards for a comprehensive assessment of ethical behavior.*

The EDM framework assesses the ethicality of a proposed decision or action by examining the following:

- Consequences or well-offness created in terms of profit, net benefit, or net cost
- Rights and duties affected, including fairness and those protected by law
- Motivation or virtues expected

The first two of these considerations involve practical application of the philosophical principles of *consequentialism*, *deontology*, and *justice* and are examined by focusing on the impacts of a decision on shareholders and other affected stakeholders—an approach known as *stakeholder impact analysis.* The third consideration—the *motivation* of the decision maker—involves applying what philosophers know as *virtue ethics.* It provides insights likely to be helpful when assessing current and future governance problems as part of a normal risk management exercise. It is vital to note that all three EDM considerations must be examined thoroughly and that appropriate ethical values must be applied in the decision and its implementation if a decision or action is to be defensible ethically.

Figure 4.1 provides an overview of the EDM framework developed in the remainder of the chapter.

Practical EDM—the overriding focus of this chapter—involves the use of practical questions and approaches based on concepts developed by philosophers and are the

FIGURE 4.1 **EDM Framework—An Overview**

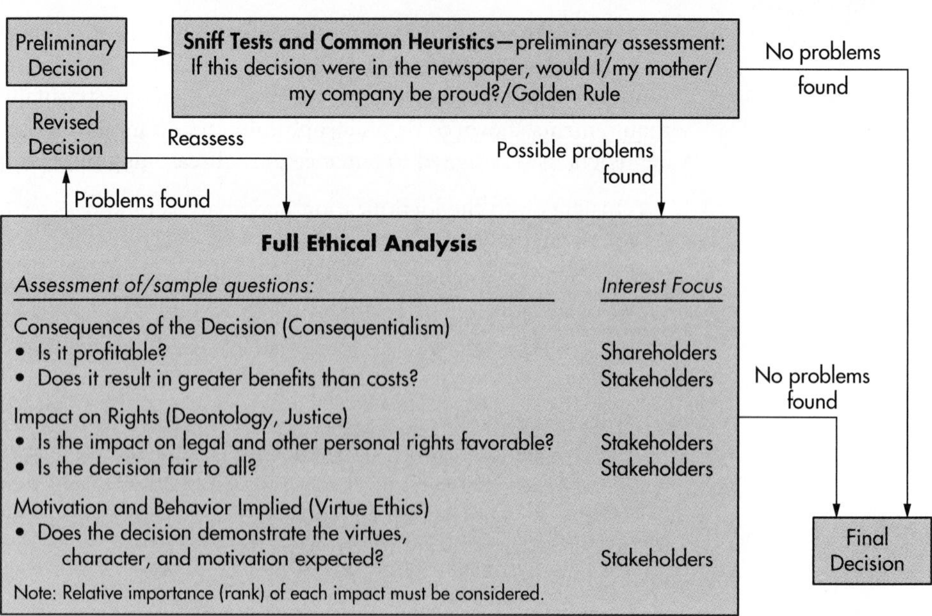

TABLE 4.1 **EDM Considerations: Philosophical Underpinnings**

EDM CONSIDERATIONS	PHILOSOPHICAL THEORIES
Well-offness or well-being	Consequentialism, utilitarianism, teleology[1]
Respect for the rights of stakeholders	Deontology (rights and duties)[2]
Fairness among stakeholders	Kant's categorical imperative,[3] justice as impartiality[4]
Expectations for character traits, virtues	Virtue[5]
Specific EDM Issues	
Different behavior in different cultures (bribery)	Relativism,[6] subjectivism[7]
Conflicts of interest and limits to self-interested behavior	Deontology, subjectivism, egoism[8]

[1]See John Stuart Mill (1861/1998).
[2]See, for example, https://en.wikipedia.org/wiki/Deontological_ethics or http://www.sophia-project.org/uploads/1/3/9/5/13955288/russo_deontology1.pdf.
[3]See Immanuel Kant (Stumpf, 1988).
[4]See Rawls (1971).
[5]See Cafaro (1998) at http://www.bu.edu/wcp/Papers/TEth/TEthCafa.htm.
[6]See, for example, http://plato.stanford.edu/entries/relativism/.
[7]See, for example, section 2.3 of http://plato.stanford.edu/entries/heidegger-aesthetics/#SymSub.
[8]See, for example, http://www.iep.utm.edu/egoism/ or http://plato.stanford.edu/entries/egoism/.

subject of in-depth discussions in Chapter 3. Developing an understanding of the decision-making approaches that philosophers pioneered is essential. Table 4.1 provides a cross-reference of EDM considerations and relevant philosophical theories.

The following section summarizes the extensive treatment of philosophical approaches provided in Chapter 3 and relates them to the EDM framework.

PHILOSOPHICAL APPROACHES—AN OVERVIEW: CONSEQUENTIALISM (UTILITARIANISM), DEONTOLOGY, & VIRTUE ETHICS

Philosophers have long been focused on making the best decision from a societal as well as individual perspective, but the salience of their philosophies has not been well appreciated or understood in business and the professions.

Stimulated to improve ethics education and EDM by the Enron, Arthur Andersen, and WorldCom scandals and the ensuing governance reform, the AACSB Ethics Education Task Force (2004) has called for business students to be familiar with three philosophical approaches to ethical decision making: *consequentialism (utilitarianism)*, *deontology*, and *virtue ethics*. Each of the three approaches contributes differently to a useful and defensible approach for ethical decision making in business or personal life. However, because some philosophical principles and theories conflict with others and appear to clash with acceptable business practice, particularly in some cultures around the world, it is best to use a multifaceted set of considerations drawn from all three approaches to determine the ethicality of actions and to guide choices to be made.

The basic question that interests philosophers is, What makes a decision or action or person more or less good or ethical? Each of the three philosophical approaches to ethical decision making—consequentialism, deontology, and virtue ethics—focuses on a different conception of a right action. These will be reviewed in turn. Bear in mind, however, since philosophers have been studying what makes an act good or morally right for thousands of years, it is not possible to provide a complete understanding of philosophical concepts in a few pages.

Consequentialism, Utilitarianism, or Teleology

Consequentialists are intent on maximizing the utility produced by a decision. For them, the rightness of an act depends on its consequences. This approach is essential to a good ethical decision and an understanding of it will be part of AACSB-accredited business school education in the future. According to the AACSB,

> The consequentialist approach requires students to analyze a decision in terms of the harms and benefits to multiple stakeholders and to arrive at a decision that produces the greatest good for the greatest number.[5]

Consequentialism holds that an act is morally right if and only if that act maximizes the net good.[6] In other words, an act (and therefore a decision) is ethical if its favorable consequences outweigh its negative consequences. Moreover, some believe that only the act that maximizes the net benefit of favorable minus negative consequences is morally right or ethical. Philosophers also debate the following:

- Which consequences should be counted?
- How should they be counted?
- Who deserves to be included in the set of affected stakeholders that should be considered?

For example, should the consequences to be considered be actual rather than foreseen, foreseeable, intended, or likely? Should the consequences to be considered depend on the values involved, such as the impact on life, health, pleasure, pain, privacy rights, or property rights, and with what weighting? How should the overall assessment be developed?

- Based only on the best consequences or based on all of the outcomes or only a subset thereof?
- Based on total net good rather than average per person?
- Based on the impacts on all persons or only a select set?
- Based on the assumption that all consequences are considered of equal impact or that some are more important?
- Should the impact of the act on the decision maker or agent involved be considered?

An excellent overview of these variations and useful references can be found in the work of Walter Sinnott-Armstrong (2015).

Classic *utilitarianism*—concerned with overall utility—embraces all of these variants, and therefore it is only of partial usefulness in making ethical decisions in a business, professional, or organizational context. *Consequentialism*, however, refers to a subset of these variants that may be defined to avoid problematic measurements or other issues or to make the process more relevant to the act, decision, or context involved. Because utilitarianism and consequentialism focus on the results or "ends" of an action, they are sometimes referred to as *teleological*.[7] In the development of the practical EDM approaches that follow, this chapter adopts a consequentialist approach involving the impact analysis of decisions and actions on a comprehensive set of stakeholders and their interests based on foreseeable likely impacts, which are value weighted in

---

[5] AACSB (2004), 12.

[6] Alternatively, an ethical choice could be the one that minimizes the net negative impact of choices where one *must* be made.

[7] *Teleos* in Greek means "end," and the study of "ends" is known as teleology.

importance. The total net benefit of alternative decisions and actions is considered to identify the best and/or most defensible choices.

Deontology

Deontology[8] is different from consequentialism in that deontologists focus on the obligations or duties motivating a decision or actions rather than on the consequences of the action. Deontological ethics takes the position that rightness depends on the respect shown for duty and the rights and fairness that those duties reflect. Consequently,

> A deontological approach raises issues related to duties, rights, and justice considerations and teaches students to use moral standards, principles, and rules as a guide to making the best ethical decision.[9]

Deontological reasoning is based largely on the thinking of Immanuel Kant (1964). He argued that a rational person making a decision about what would be good to do would consider what action would be good for all members of society to do. Such an act would improve the well-being of the decision maker and the well-being of society as well.

Kant began to search for an overriding principle that would guide all action—an imperative that everyone should follow without exception and that could therefore be considered universal or categorical. His search led to what is known as Kant's Categorical Imperative, which is a dominant principle or rule for deontologists. Kant's principle indicates that there is a duty or imperative to

> Always act in such a way that you can also will that the maxim of your action should become a universal law.[10]

This means that "if you cannot will[11] that everyone follow the same decision rule, your rule is not a moral one" (Kay, 1997).

As a universal principle, everyone should follow it. Suppose a person is considering whether to lie or tell the truth. Kant would argue that lying would not be a good rule because others following the same rule would lie to you—an eventuality you would not want. Honesty would, however, qualify as a good rule. Similarly, impartiality would also qualify rather than favoritism. Moreover, the Golden Rule—do unto others as you would have them do unto you—would readily[12] qualify as a universal principle.

Using the same approach could yield a universal respect for human rights and for fair treatment for all. This can be best achieved by adopting the position that one must fulfill obligations or duties that respect moral or human rights and legal or contract[13] rights. Furthermore, it can be achieved only if individuals act with "enlightened self-interest" rather than pure self-interest. Under enlightened self-interest, the interests of individuals are taken into account in decisions—they are not simply ignored or overridden. Individuals are considered "ends" rather than used as "means" to achieve an end or objective.

---

[8] *Deon* in Greek means "obligation."

[9] AACSB (2004), 12.

[10] Charles D. Kay, "Notes on Deontology," 1997, http://sites.wofford.edu/kaycd/deontology/.

[11] "Will" can be taken to mean "wish, want, desire, or intend."

[12] Kant foresaw, however, that an individual might "will" bad consequences on others such as by willing euthanasia on everyone. He sought to avoid such ill will effects by further specifying that individuals be always considered "ends" rather than "means" and that an individual's freedom and one's ability to choose freely should be respected.

[13] Legal and contract rights are those protected by law, regulation, and/or contract.

The concepts of fair treatment and impartiality are fundamental to the development of the concepts of distributive, retributive, or compensatory justice. John Rawls developed a set of principles of justice involving expectations for equal civil liberty, maximization of benefits to the least advantaged, and the provision of fair opportunities (Rawls, 1971). His approach utilized the concept of a "veil of ignorance" to simulate conditions of uncertainty to enable decision makers to evaluate the impact of their actions on themselves. Decision makers were to decide on the best action without knowing if they would be the ones benefiting or losing by it.

Action based on duty, rights, and justice considerations are particularly important to professionals, directors, and executives who are expected to fulfill the obligations of a fiduciary. These would include actions that maintain the trust of a client of someone reliant on the more knowledgeable, expert professional to act in the client's best interest with regard to matters of considerable value. The professional accountant, for example, has a duty to act in the client's best interest provided that such action does not contravene the law and/or the codes and guidelines of related professional and regulatory bodies, such as generally accepted accounting principles (GAAP), generally accepted auditing standards, Securities and Exchange Commission (SEC), and securities commission regulations. Directors and executives must observe governance laws in order to protect shareholders and other stakeholders as noted in Chapter 5. These duties must supersede self-interest, bias, and favoritism.

Unfortunately, utilitarianism and consequentialism focus on utility and may lead to decisions or acts that ignore, downplay, or circumscribe the justice or fairness of a decision and its respect for the duties owed to and rights expected by those involved. However, *augmenting the consequentialist approach with a deontological analysis specifically including fair treatment will guard against the situation where the desire for what some consider to be beneficial consequences (or ends) will be allowed to justify the use of illegal or unethical actions (means) to achieve those ends.* For example, a deontological analysis could avoid endangering the health of workers and/or the public in order to minimize the costs of hazardous waste disposal. From a philosophical perspective as well as from the perspective of damaged investors, workers, and other stakeholders who have suffered from recent financial scandals, unfettered pursuit of self-interest and short-term profit has led to illegal and unethical acts that are regrettable.

For society, protecting some individual rights—to life and health—is usually more important than maximizing the net benefit to all. However, occasionally, such as in times of war or dire emergency, a choice justified by consequential analysis is considered ethically preferential to a choice justified by deontological considerations.

Virtue Ethics

Consequentialism emphasizes the consequences of actions, and deontology uses duties, rights, and principles as guides to correct moral behavior, whereas virtue ethics is concerned with the motivating aspects of moral character demonstrated by decision makers. Responsibility—especially culpability or blameworthiness—in both morality and law has two dimensions: the *actus reus* (guilty act) and the *mens rea* (guilty mind).[14] Consequentialism, which examines the former, is said to be "act centered" rather than "agent centered," as deontology and virtue ethics are.

According to the AACSB,

> Virtue ethics focuses on the character or integrity of the moral actor and looks to moral communities, such as professional communities, to help identify ethical issues and guide ethical action.[15]

---

[14] Prof. Jack T. Stevenson, personal correspondence, December 2005.

[15] AACSB (2004), 12.

Aristotle's central question was, What is the good life and how can I live it (Cafaro 1998)? The answer evolved to mean that flourishing, excellence, and happiness were criteria for the good life, but there was a continuing debate over whether the focus should be our communities' interests, our own, or both. Moreover, excellence was said to involve "intellectual, moral and physical excellence, the excellence of human beings and their creations and achievements," which again could be taken individually or in regard to broader communities. The focus of modern[16] virtue ethics is, however, on character virtues that lead to "enlightened self-interest"; it is not focused only on self-serving fulfillment.

Virtues are those character traits that dispose a person to act ethically and thereby make that person a morally good human being. For Aristotle, a virtue allowed a person to make reasonable decisions. Prudence was his key virtue in determining the proper choice between extremes. His other three important or Cardinal virtues were courage, temperance, and justice. For Christian philosophers, these virtues were not sufficient,[17] and they added the theological or Christian virtues of faith, hope, and charity. Other dispositions that are often cited as virtues include honesty, integrity, enlightened self-interest, compassion, fairness, impartiality, generosity, humility, and modesty.

Virtues need to be cultivated over time so that they become embedded and are therefore a consistent reference point. "If you possess a virtue, it is part of your character, a trait or disposition that you typically show in action. It is not just something that you are *able* to exhibit, but something that you usually or *dependably* exhibit."[18]

For virtue ethicists, possessing a virtue is a matter of degree. For example, being honest can mean that one tells the truth. But a person's honesty can be considered stronger or of a higher order if he or she deals only with honest people or causes, works for honest companies, has honest friends, raises his or her children to be honest, and so on. Similarly, the reason a person acts virtuously is important. For example, an honest act undertaken to gain a greedy end result is considered to be less virtuous than one taken because it is believed to be the right thing to do to improve society and/or to discharge a duty to another person or organization. A further problem in reaching the fullest levels of virtue is lack of moral or practical wisdom, such as is evident in some acts of overgenerosity or too much compassion or courage, which can sometimes be harmful.

Although the lack of a "right" reason for virtuous action may seem academic, without such a reason, some businesspeople or professionals are prone to act for greedy self-interest rather than modern enlightened self-interest and are likely to commit unethical and/or illegal acts. They represent higher risks of ultimate deception and malpractice because they lack a basic commitment to virtue or professionalism unless it suits their own purpose. Conversely, overvirtuosity may result in emotional acts by executives or employees before seeking and receiving full information, in taking too much risk, or in harming others unnecessarily. Both the lack of virtue and the lack of what Aristotle would call "prudence" constitute ethics risks to good governance.

There are a number of reservations about the strength of virtue ethics as an approach to EDM. For example, virtue ethics has to do with the process of decision making incorporating moral sensitivity, perception, imagination, and judgment, and

[16] Note that Aristotle's early formulations referred more to personal happiness and pleasure than to enlightened self-interest.

[17] To ensure a union with God on death.

[18] Prof. Jack T. Stevenson, personal correspondence, December 2005.

some claim that this does not lead to easily useful EDM principles. Other criticisms are relevant, however, including the following:

- The interpretation of a virtue is culture sensitive.
- The interpretation of what is justifiable or right is culture sensitive.
- One's perception of what is right is to some degree influenced by ego or self-interest.

A fuller discussion of virtue ethics and the points raised may be found in Chapter 3 and in the work of Rosalind Hursthouse (2003) and Nafsika Athanassoulis (2004) as well as through the readings noted on this title's website.

SNIFF TESTS & COMMON HEURISTICS—PRELIMINARY TESTS OF ETHICALITY

Philosophical theories provide the bases for useful practical decision approaches and aids, although most executives and professional accountants are unaware of how and why this is so. Directors, executives, and professional accountants, however, have developed tests and commonly used rules that can be used to assess the ethicality of decisions on a preliminary basis. *If these preliminary tests give rise to concerns, a more thorough analysis should be performed using the stakeholder impact analysis techniques discussed later in this chapter.*

It is often appropriate for managers and other employees to be asked to check a proposed decision in a quick, preliminary manner to see if an additional full-blown ethical analysis is required. These quick tests are often referred to as *sniff tests.* Commonly applied sniff tests are noted in Table 4.2.

If any of these quick tests are negative, employees are asked to seek out an ethics officer for consultation or perform a full-blown analysis of the proposed action. This analysis should be retained and perhaps reviewed by the ethics officer. A reading on sniff tests is available on the website for this book.[19]

Many executives have developed their own rules[20] for deciding whether an action is ethical or not. Common examples would include the following:

- The Golden Rule: Do unto others as you would have them do unto you.
- The Intuition Ethic: Do what your "gut feeling" tells you to do.

TABLE 4.2 Sniff Tests for Ethical Decision Making
Would I be comfortable if this action or decision were to appear on the front page of a national newspaper tomorrow morning?
Will I be proud of this decision?
Will my mother be proud of this decision?
Is this action or decision in accord with the corporation's mission and code?
Does this feel right to me?

[19] Leonard J. Brooks, "Sniff Tests," *Corporate Ethics Monitor* 7, no. 5 (1995): 65. Reproduced at www.cengage.com/accounting/.

[20] A. B. Carroll, "Principles of Business Ethics: Their Role in Decision Making and Initial Consensus," *Management Decision* 28, no. 8 (1990): 20–24.

FIGURE 4.2 Ethical Decision-Making Approaches & Criteria

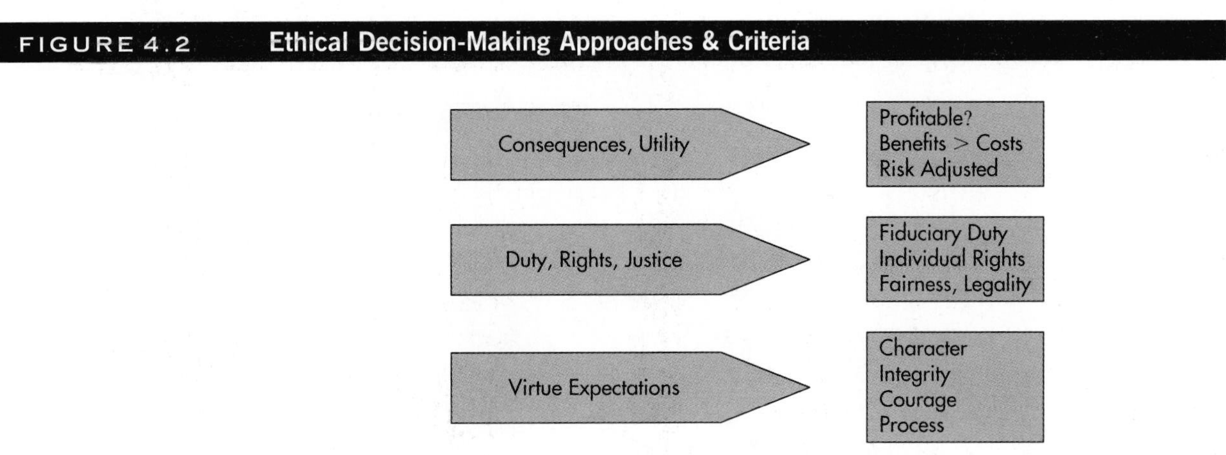

Unfortunately, although sniff tests and commonly used rules are based on ethical principles and are often very useful, they rarely, by themselves, represent a comprehensive examination of the decision and therefore leave the individuals and corporation involved vulnerable to making an unethical decision. For this reason, more comprehensive techniques of stakeholder impact analysis should be employed whenever a proposed decision is questionable or likely to have significant consequences.

Figure 4.2 is provided to link philosophers' principles and the criteria assessed by practical sniff tests, commonly used rules, and stakeholder impact analysis. Comparison of specific sniff tests and heuristics reveals that they usually focus on a fraction of the comprehensive set of criteria that stakeholder impact analysis examines.

STAKEHOLDER IMPACT ANALYSIS—COMPREHENSIVE TOOL FOR ASSESSING DECISIONS & ACTIONS

Overview

Since John Stuart Mill developed the concept of *utilitarianism* in 1861, an accepted approach to the assessment of a decision and the resulting action has been to evaluate the end results or consequences of the action. To most businesspeople, this evaluation has traditionally been based on the decision's impact on the interests of the company's owners or shareholders. Usually, these impacts have been measured in terms of the profit or loss involved because profit has been the measure of well-offness that shareholders have wanted to maximize.

This traditional view of corporate accountability has recently been modified in two ways. First, the assumption that *all* shareholders want to maximize *only* short-term profit appears to represent too narrow a focus. Second, the rights and claims of many nonshareholder groups, such as employees, consumers/clients, suppliers, lenders, environmentalists, host communities, and governments that have a stake or interest in the outcome of the decision or in the company itself, are being accorded status in corporate decision making. *Modern corporations are now accountable to shareholders and to nonshareholder groups*, both of which form the set of *stakeholders*[21] to which a company responds (see Figure 4.3). It has become evident that a company cannot reach its full potential

[21] A stakeholder is anyone who is affected by or can affect the objectives of the organization (Freeman 1984, 25).

FIGURE 4.3 **Map of Corporate Stakeholder Accountability**

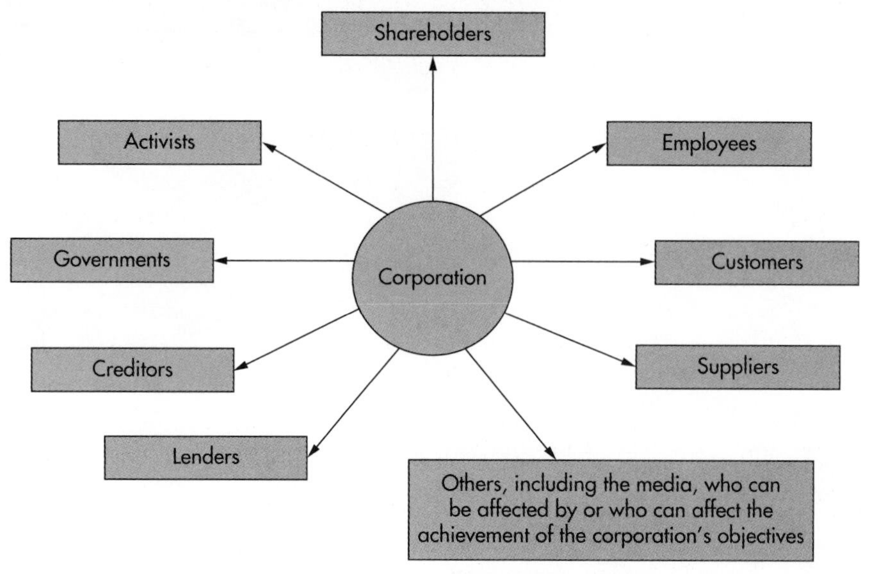

Source: AACSB EETF Report, June 2004.

(and may even perish) if it loses the support of one of a select set of its stakeholders known as *primary stakeholders*. These ideas on stakeholders and their emerging role are fully developed in Chapter 1.

The assumption of a monolithic shareholder group interested only in short-term profit is undergoing modification because modern corporations are finding that their shareholders are also made up of persons and institutional investors who are interested in longer-term time horizons and in how ethically business is conducted. The latter, who are referred to as *ethical investors*, apply two screens to investments: Do the investee companies make a profit in excess of appropriate hurdle rates, and do they earn that profit in an ethical manner? Because of the size of shareholdings of mutual and pension funds and other institutional investors involved, corporate directors and executives have found that the wishes of ethical investors can be ignored only at their peril. Ethical investors have developed informal and formal networks through which they inform themselves about corporate activity, decide how to vote proxies, and how to approach boards of directors to get them to pay attention to their concerns in such areas as environmental protection, excessive executive compensation, and human rights activities in specific countries, such as South Africa.

Ethical investors and many other investors, as well as other stakeholder groups, tend to be unwilling to squeeze the last ounce of profit out of the current year if it means damaging the environment or the rights of other stakeholders. They believe in managing the corporation on a broader basis than short-term profit only. *Usually, the maximization of profit in a longer than one-year time frame requires harmonious relationships with most stakeholder groups based on the recognition of their interests.* A negative public relations experience can be a significant and embarrassing price to pay for a decision-making process that fails to take the wishes of stakeholder groups into account. Whether or not special interest groups are also shareholders, their capacity to make corporations accountable through the media is evident and growing. The farsighted executive and director will want these concerns taken into account before offended stakeholders have to remind them. *Corporations are finding that in the past, they have been legally and pragmatically accountable to shareholders, but they are also becoming increasingly accountable to stakeholders.*

Fundamental Interests of Stakeholders

Taking the concerns or interests of stakeholders into account when making decisions by considering the potential impact of decisions on each stakeholder is therefore a wise practice if executives want to maintain stakeholder support. However, the multiplicity of stakeholders and stakeholder groups makes this a complex task. To simplify the process, it is desirable to identify and consider a set of commonly held or fundamental stakeholder interests to be used to focus analyses and decision making on ethical dimensions, such as the following:

1. Their interest(s) should be better off as a result of the decision.
2. The decision should result in a fair distribution of benefits and burdens.
3. The decision *should* not offend any of the rights of any stakeholder, including the decision maker.
4. The resulting behavior should demonstrate duties owed as virtuously as expected.

The first springs from consequentialism and the second, third, and fourth from deontology and virtue ethics. To some extent, these fundamental interests have to be tempered by the realities facing decision makers. For example, although a proposed decision should maximize the betterment of all stakeholders, trade-offs often have to be made between stakeholders' interests. Consequently, the incurrence of pollution control costs may be counter to the interests of short-term profits that are of interest to some current shareholders and managers. Similarly, there are times when all stakeholders will find a decision acceptable even though one or more of them or the groups they represent may be worse off as a result. In recognition of the requirement for trade-offs and for the understanding that a decision can advance the well-offness of all stakeholders as a group, even if some individuals are personally worse off, this fundamental interest should be modified to focus on the *well-offness* of stakeholders rather than only on their betterment. *This modification represents a shift from utilitarianism to consequentialism.*

Once the focus on betterment is relaxed to shift to well-offness, the need to analyze the impact of a decision in terms of all four fundamental interests becomes apparent. It is possible, for example, to find that a proposed decision may produce an overall benefit, but the distribution of the burden of producing that decision may be so debilitating to the interests of one or more stakeholder groups that it may be considered grossly unfair. Alternatively, a decision may result in an overall net benefit and be fair but may offend the rights of a stakeholder and therefore be considered not right. For example, deciding not to recall a marginally flawed product may be cost effective but would not be considered to be "right" if users could be seriously injured. Similarly, a decision that does not demonstrate the character, integrity, or courage expected will be considered ethically suspect by stakeholders. Consequently, *a proposed decision can be declared unethical if it fails to provide a net benefit,*[22] *or is unfair, or offends the rights of a stakeholder, including reasonable expectations for virtuous behavior* (see Table 4.3). Testing a proposed decision against only one principle is definitely short sighted and usually results in a faulty diagnosis.

[22] Unless it is a choice of the least worst of a net negative set of options.

TABLE 4.3 Fundamental Interests of Stakeholders

Well-offness	The proposed decision should result in more benefits than costs.
Fairness	The distribution of benefits and burdens should be fair.
Right	The proposed decision should not offend the rights of the stakeholders and the decision maker.
Virtuosity	The proposed decision should demonstrate virtues reasonably expected.

All four interests must be satisfied for a decision to be considered ethical.

Measurement of Quantifiable Impacts

PROFIT Profit is fundamental to the interests of shareholders and is essential to the survival and health of our corporations. In inflationary times, profit is essential simply to replace inventory at the higher prices required. Fortunately, the measurement of profit is well developed and needs few comments about its use in ethical decision making. It is true, however, that profit is a short-term measure and that several important impacts are not captured in the determination of profit. Both of these conditions can be rectified as discussed in the following sections.

ITEMS NOT INCLUDED IN PROFIT: MEASURABLE DIRECTLY There are impacts of corporate decisions and activities that are not included in the determination of the profit of the company that caused the impact. For example, when a company pollutes, the cost of cleanup is usually absorbed by individuals, companies, or municipalities that are downstream or downwind. These costs are referred to as *externalities*, and their impact can often be measured directly by the costs of cleanup incurred by others.

In order to see a complete picture of the impacts of a decision, the profit or loss from a transaction should be modified by the externalities it creates. Frequently, corporations that ignore their externalities over time will find that they have underestimated the true cost of the decision when fines and cleanup costs are incurred or bad publicity emerges.

ITEMS NOT INCLUDED IN PROFIT: NOT MEASURABLE DIRECTLY Other externalities exist where the cost is included in the determination of the company's profit but where the benefit is enjoyed by persons outside of the company. Donations and scholarships are examples of this kind of externality, and obviously it would be attractive to include an estimate of the benefits involved in the overall evaluation of the proposed decision. The problem is that neither the benefit nor the cost of some negative impacts, such as the loss of health suffered by people absorbing pollution, can be measured directly, but they should be included in an overall assessment.

Although it is impossible to measure these externalities directly, it is possible to measure these impacts indirectly through the use of *surrogates* or mirror-image alternatives. In the case of the scholarship, a surrogate for the benefit could be the increase in earnings gained by the recipient. The value of the loss of health could be estimated as the income lost plus the cost of medical treatment plus the loss of productivity in the workplace involved as measured by the cost of fill-in workers.

The accuracy of these estimates will depend on the closeness of the mirror image measure. It is likely, however, that the estimates arrived at will understate the impact involved; in the previous example, no estimate was made for the intellectual gain of the education permitted by the scholarship or the pain and suffering involved as a result of the loss of health. Nevertheless, it is far better to make use of estimates that are generally accurate rather than make decisions on the basis of direct measures that measure precisely only a fraction of the impact of a proposed decision.

The measurement and use of surrogates to estimate external impacts of corporate decisions is discussed further in the article by Brooks (1979),[23] which appears as a reading on the companion resource site for this title at **www.cengagebrain.com**.

BRINGING THE FUTURE TO THE PRESENT The technique for bringing future impacts of a decision into an analysis is not difficult. It is handled in a parallel manner to capital budgeting analysis, where future values are discounted at an interest rate that reflects the expected interest rates in future years. This approach is demonstrated as part of *cost–benefit analysis* in Brooks (1979). Using the net present value approach of capital budgeting analysis, the benefits and costs of a proposed action can be assessed as follows:

$$\text{Net Present Value} = \text{Present Value of Benefits} - \text{Present Value of Costs of Proposed Action}$$

where *benefits* include revenues and good externalities and *costs* include costs plus bad externalities.

Frequently, executives who have learned the hard way to keep their focus on short-term profit will reject the idea of including externalities in their analyses. However, *what is being advocated here is not that they abandon short-term profit as a yardstick but that they also consider impacts that are now externalities that have an excellent chance of affecting the company's bottom line in the future*. It is likely, for example, that pollution costs will be turned into fines and/or cleanup will be required. Moreover, the advantages bestowed through donations will strengthen society and allow the corporation to reach its full potential in the future. What cost–benefit analysis allows a decision maker to do is to bring these future benefits and costs into the present for a fuller analysis of a proposed decision. For example, Table 2 of the Cost–Benefit Analysis reading on the book website (Brooks, 1979) could be reformatted as Table 4.4 to give the decision maker a clearer view of present and possible future impacts on profit.

DEALING WITH UNCERTAIN OUTCOMES Just as in capital budgeting analysis, there are estimates that are uncertain. However, a full range of techniques has been developed to factor this uncertainty into the analysis of proposed decisions. For example, the analysis can be based on best estimates, on three possibilities (most optimistic, pessimistic, and best estimate), or on expected values developed from a computer simulation. All of these are *expected values*, which are combinations of a value and a probability of its occurrence. This is normally expressed as follows:

$$\text{Expected Value of an Outcome} = \text{Value of Outcome} \times \text{Probability of Outcome Occurring}$$

The advantage of this expected value formulation is that the cost–benefit analysis framework can be modified to include the risk associated with outcomes to be included. This

[23] L. J. Brooks, "Cost–Benefit Analysis," *CAmagazine*, October 1979, 53–57. Reproduced at www.cengage.com/accounting/brooks.

TABLE 4.4 Cost-Benefit Analysis: Short-Term & Long-Term Profit Impact

	POLLUTION CONTROL EQUIPMENT *IMPACT ON PROFIT*			UNIVERSITY ADMISSION SCHOLARSHIPS *IMPACT ON PROFIT*		
	SHORT TERM	**LONG TERM**	**TOTAL**	**SHORT TERM**	**LONG TERM**	**TOTAL**
Benefits (Present valued at 10%)						
Reduction in worker health costs		$500,000	$500,000			
Increase in worker productivity	$200,000		$200,000			
Improvement in level of earnings of scholarship recipients					$600,000	$600,000
Total benefits	$200,000	$500,000	$700,000		$600,000	$600,000
Costs (present valued at 10%)						
Pollution equipment	$350,000		$350,000			
Scholarships paid				$400,000		$400,000
Total costs	$350,000		$350,000	$400,000		$400,000
Net benefit-costs	($150,000)	$500,000	$350,000	($400,000)	$600,000	$200,000

new approach is referred to as *risk–benefit analysis*, and it can be applied where risky outcomes are prevalent in the following framework:

$$\text{Risk-Adjusted or Expected Value of Net Benefits} = \text{Expected Present Value of Future Benefits} - \text{Expected Present Value of Future Costs}$$

IDENTIFYING STAKEHOLDERS & RANKING THEIR INTERESTS The measurement of profit, augmented by externalities discounted to the present and factored by riskiness of outcome, is more useful in assessing proposed decisions than profit alone. However, the usefulness of a stakeholder impact analysis depends on the full identification of all stakeholders and their interests and on a full appreciation of the significance of the impacts on the position of each.

There are occasions, for example, when the simple adding up of benefits and costs does not fully reflect the importance of a stakeholder or of the impact involved, such as when the capacity of a stakeholder to withstand the impact is low. For example, if a stakeholder is poor, he will not be able to buy remedial treatment, or, alternatively, his reserves may be so low that other family members—perhaps children—will suffer. On the other hand, a scholarship to a poor recipient could create a benefit for that person and others of significantly greater impact than to a person who is well off. In these situations, the values included in the cost–benefit analysis or risk–benefit analysis can be weighted, or the net present values created can be ranked according to the impact created on the stakeholders involved. The ranking of stakeholders and the impacts on them based on their situational capacity to withstand is also used when nonmeasurable impacts are being considered.

Relative financial strength does not provide the only rationale for ranking the interests of stakeholders. In fact, several more compelling reasons exist, including the impact of the proposed action on the life or health of a stakeholder or on some aspect of our flora, fauna, or environment that is near a threshold of endangerment or extinction. Usually, the public takes a very dim view of companies that put profits ahead of life, health, or the preservation of our habitat. In addition, making these issues a high priority will often trigger a rethinking of an offending action so as to improve it by removing its offensiveness.

The illustrative case, *Castle Manufacturing Inc.*, analyzed at the end of this chapter, extends the concept of ranking stakeholders to correlate legal rights, financial and psychological capacity to withstand the impact, and the resulting probable public impact of the action. It is interesting that an item may not be "material" to a lay investor in an accounting sense but may be quite significant to stakeholders. In the long run, such sensitivity to corporate decisions may rebound on the shareholders through the bottom line. In time, the *accounting concept of materiality* as we know it may be inadequate and need to be expanded.

Two research thrusts can prove quite useful in identifying and understanding stakeholder groups and their interactions. Mitchell, Agle, and Wood (1997) suggest that stakeholders and their interests be evaluated on three dimensions: *legitimacy*, or legal and/or moral right to influence the organization; *power* to influence the organization through the media, government, or other means; and perceived and real *urgency* of the issues arising. Such an analysis forces the consideration of impacts thought to be very damaging (particularly to external stakeholders) to the fore, so that if an executive decides to go ahead with a suboptimal plan, at least the potential downside will be known. The three sets of claims are identified in Figure 4.4.

Logic suggests that claims where the three circles overlap in Figure 4.4 (i.e., legitimate and/or viewed as legitimate, urgent, and held by the powerful) will always be the most important. However, this is not necessarily the case. Other urgent stakeholder claims can become the most important if they garner more support of the powerful and those with legitimate claims and are ultimately seen to have legitimacy.

Many executives forget that an organization's stakeholders change over time, as does the power they wield depending on the urgency they feel about issues brought to their attention. In real life, stakeholders without legitimacy or power will try to influence those with clout, and they succeed. Another researcher, Tim Rowley (1997), has suggested that a set of stakeholders be considered to be a *dynamic network* and that projections be made

FIGURE 4.4 Stakeholder Identification & Interests

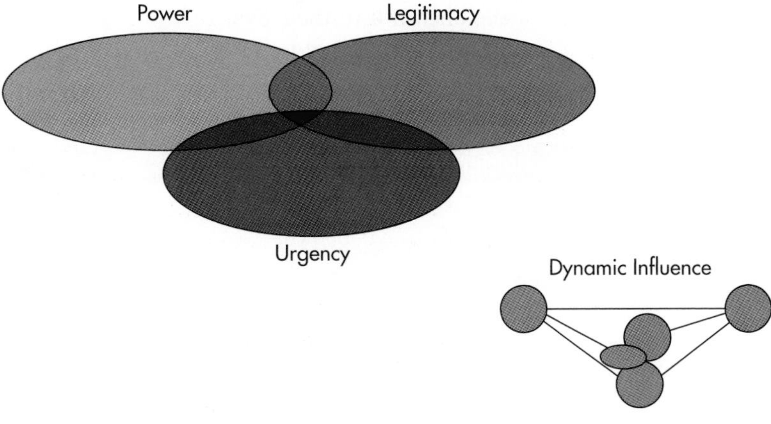

Source: Mitchell, Agle and Wood (1997); Rowley (1997).

TABLE 4.5 Approaches to The Measurement of Quantifiable Impacts of Proposed Decisions*

A.	Profit or loss only
B.	A. plus externalities, (i.e., cost–benefit analysis)
C.	B. plus probabilities of outcomes, (i.e., risk–benefit analysis)
D.	Cost–benefit analysis or risk–benefit analysis plus ranking of stakeholders

*Optimal decisions usually result from the most thorough approach.

about who in the network will influence whom to forecast which issues and interests will become more important. These concepts are developed in the analysis of the illustrative case *Bribery or Opportunity in China*, located at the end of the chapter.

SUMMARY OF APPROACHES TO THE MEASUREMENT OF QUANTIFIABLE IMPACTS The previously discussed approaches to the measurement of impacts of proposed decisions are summarized in Table 4.5.

Assessment of Nonquantifiable Impacts

FAIRNESS AMONG STAKEHOLDERS Although the expectation of fair treatment is a right that individuals and groups can properly expect to receive, it is treated here on its own because of its importance to ethical decision making. The concern for fair treatment has been evident in society's recent preoccupation with such issues as discrimination against women and other matters of hiring, promotion, and pay. Consequently, a decision will be considered unethical unless it is seen to be fair to all stakeholders.

Fairness is not an absolute concept. It is evidenced by a relatively even distribution of the benefits and burdens springing from a decision. For example, it is possible that a decision to increase taxes may weigh more heavily on high-income earners but be seen as relatively fair in terms of their capacity to pay those taxes. Reasonability and perspective are required to judge fairness accurately.

RIGHTS OF STAKEHOLDERS A decision will be considered ethical only if its impacts do not offend the rights of the stakeholders impacted on and the rights of the person(s) making the decision. This latter point can be seen in the case of a decision being made by executives who subscribe to values that make them offended by child labor or by low standards of worker safety in developing countries. The executives making the decision are stakeholders to it in their own right.

An individual stakeholder or a stakeholder group in North America[24] may generally expect to enjoy the rights listed in Table 4.6.

TABLE 4.6 Stakeholder Rights

- Life
- Health and safety
- Fair treatment
- Exercise of conscience
- Dignity and privacy
- Freedom of speech

[24] The importance attached to these rights varies somewhat in different cultures around the world.

Some of these rights have been accorded with protection under laws and legal regulations, while others are enforced through common law or through public sanction of offenders. For example, employees and consumers are protected under statute for health and safety, whereas dignity and privacy tend to be subject to common law, and the exercise of conscience is subject to public sanction.

In many cases, even where protection is afforded through statute, considerable judgment is required to know when an individual's rights are being violated. Drug testing in the form of urinalysis, for example, appears to be warranted when the health of the worker and fellow workers is at stake, but the degree of jeopardy has to be severe. Airline pilots are considered worthy of urinalysis, but, at the moment, drivers of transport trucks are not. There are many reasons for this, including the lack of accuracy and timeliness of the tests and the stigma that attaches to a false accusation. However, it appears to be reasonable to test a truck driver's reflexes and hand–eye coordination using computer games just prior to his or her shift, so evidently the stigma of failing a computer game related closely to the task to be performed is acceptable in today's society. This complex interplay of statute, regulation, common law, and judgment based on values makes it advisable to give any apparent infringement of a stakeholder's rights very careful scrutiny.

ASSESSMENT OF MOTIVATION & BEHAVIOR Unfortunately, as recent scandals indicate, in the past decision makers have not recognized the importance of stakeholder's expectations of virtue. If they had, the decisions made by corporate executives, accountants, and lawyers involved in the Enron, Arthur Andersen, and WorldCom fiascos, the 2008 subprime mortgage crisis, and the LIBOR scandal in 2012 might have been avoided, along with the personal and organizational tragedies that ensued. Some executives were motivated by greed rather than by enlightened self-interest focused on the good of all. Others went along with unethical decisions because they did not recognize that they were expected to behave differently and had a duty to do so. Some reasoned that because everyone else was doing something similar, how could it be wrong? *The point is that they forgot to consider sufficiently the virtues (and duties) they were expected to demonstrate.* Where a fiduciary duty was owed to future shareholders and other stakeholders, the virtues expected—character traits such as integrity, professionalism, courage, and so on—were not taken into account sufficiently. *In retrospect, it would have been wise to include the assessment of virtue ethics expectations as a separate step in any EDM process to strengthen governance and risk management systems and guard against unethical, short-sighted decisions.*

It is also evident that employees who continually make decisions for the wrong reasons—even if the right consequences result—can represent a high governance risk. Many examples exist where executives motivated solely by greed have slipped into unethical practices and others have been misled by faulty incentive systems. Sears Auto Center managers were selling repair services that customers did not need to raise their personal commission remuneration and ultimately caused the company to lose reputation and future revenue.[25] Many of the recent financial scandals were caused by executives who sought to manipulate company profits to support or inflate the company's share price in order to boost their own stock option gains. *Motivation based too narrowly on self-interest can result in unethical decisions when proper self-guidance and/or external monitoring is lacking.* Because external monitoring is unlikely to capture all decisions

[25] See Mike Harden, "Learn from Sears: Don't Make This Monumental Mistake," *Huffington Post*, The Blog, July 8, 2014; updated August 19, 2014.

TABLE 4.7 Motivation, Virtue, Character Trait & Process Expectations

Motivations expected:

- Self-control rather than greed
- Fairness or justice considerations
- Kindness, caring, compassion, and benevolence

Virtues expected:

- Dutiful loyalty
- Integrity and transparency
- Sincerity rather than duplicity

Character traits expected:

- Courage to do the right thing per personal and/or professional standards
- Trustworthiness
- Objectivity, impartiality
- Honesty, truthfulness
- Selflessness rather that selfishness
- Balanced choices between extremes

Processes that reflect the motivations, virtues and character traits expected

before implementation, it is important for all employees to clearly understand the broad motivation that will lead to their own and their organization's best interest from a stakeholder perspective. Consequently, decision makers should take motivations and behavior expected by stakeholders into account specifically in any comprehensive EDM approach, and organizations should require accountability by employees for those expectations through governance mechanisms.

During the earlier discussion of virtue ethics, several aspects of ethical behavior were identified as being indicative of *mens rea* (a guilty mind), which is one of the two dimensions of responsibility, culpability, or blameworthiness. Although some of the virtues named by philosophers may not resonate with modern stakeholders, those listed in Table 4.7 do play a role in framing current expectations for ethical business behavior. If personal or corporate behavior does not meet these expectations, there will probably be a negative impact on reputation and the ability to reach strategic objectives on a sustained basis in the medium and long term.

The stakeholder impact assessment process will offer an opportunity to assess the motivations that underlie the proposed decision or action. Although it is unlikely that an observer will be able to know with precision the real motivations that go through a decision maker's mind, it is quite possible to project the perceptions that stakeholders will have of the action. In the minds of stakeholders, perceptions will determine reputational impacts whether those perceptions are correct or not. Moreover, it is possible to infer from remuneration and other motivational systems in place whether the decision maker's motivation is likely to be ethical or not.

In order to ensure a comprehensive EDM approach, in addition to projecting perceptions and evaluating motivational systems, the decisions or actions should be challenged by asking questions about each of the items listed in Table 4.8. For example,

> *Does the decision or action involve and exhibit the integrity, fairness, and courage expected?*

Alternatively,

TABLE 4.8 Modified 5-Question Approach* to Ethical Decision Making

The following 5 questions are asked about a proposed decision:

IS THE DECISION	STAKEHOLDER INTERESTS EXAMINED
1. profitable?	Shareholders'—usually short term
2. legal?	Society at large—legally enforceable rights
3. fair?	Fairness for all
4. right?	Other rights of all
5. demonstrating expected motivation, virtues and character?	Motivation, virtues, character traits, and process expectations

Optional questions can be added designed to focus the decision-making process on a particular issue of relevance to the organization(s) or decision maker involved.

*This approach is based on that proposed by Graham Tucker (1990), modified with the addition of specific examination of motivation, virtues, and character.

> *Does the decision or action involve and exhibit the motivation, virtues, and character expected?*

The objective of these techniques should be to construct a profile about the motivations, virtues, character traits, and processes involved with and exhibited by the decision or action that can be compared to those expected.

STAKEHOLDER IMPACT ANALYSIS—MODIFIED TRADITIONAL DECISION-MAKING APPROACHES

Several approaches have been developed that utilize stakeholder impact analysis to provide guidance about the ethicality of proposed actions to decision makers. Discussions of three traditional approaches follow. *Each approach has been modified to include tests of virtues expected.* Choosing the most useful approach depends on whether decision impacts are short rather than long run, involve externalities and/or probabilities, or take place within a corporate setting. The approaches may be blended into a tailored hybrid approach to best cope with a specific situation.

MODIFIED 5-QUESTION APPROACH—DECISIONS WITH SHORT-TERM IMPACTS & NO EXTERNALITIES The 5-question approach, or 5-box approach, as Graham Tucker (1990) has called it, involves the examination or challenge of a proposed decision through the five questions in Table 4.8. The proposed decision is to be challenged by asking all of the questions. If a negative response is forthcoming (or more than one) when all five questions are asked, the decision maker can iteratively attempt to revise the proposed action to remove the negative and/or offset it. If the revision process is successful, the proposal will be ethical. If not, the proposal should be abandoned as unethical. Even if no negative response is forthcoming when the questions are first asked, an effort should be made to improve the proposed action using the five questions as a guide.

The order of asking the questions is not important, but all of the questions must be asked to ensure that the decision maker is not overlooking an important area of impact. Some ethical problems are not as susceptible to examination by the 5-question approach as to the other approaches described in following sections. For example, the first question focuses on profit, which is a substantially shorter-term, less comprehensive measurement tool than cost–benefit analysis and/or risk–benefit analysis, with or without the ranking of stakeholders depending on their ability to withstand the impact of the decision. As it stands, however, the 5-question framework is a useful approach to the orderly consideration of problems without externalities and where a specific focus is desired by the decision-process designer.

MODIFIED MORAL STANDARDS APPROACH—MEDIUM- & LONG-TERM DECISIONS INVOLVING EXTERNALITIES The moral standards approach to stakeholder impact analysis builds directly on the fundamental interests of stakeholders that are identified in Table 4.3. It is somewhat more general in focus than the 5-question approach and leads the decision maker to a more broadly based analysis of net benefit rather than only profitability as a first challenge of proposed decisions. As a result, it offers a framework that is more suited to the consideration of decisions that have significant impacts outside the corporation, including externalities, than the 5-question framework.

The standards making up the moral standards approach are listed in Table 4.9. Questions that sprang from each standard and that ought to be applied to each decision are also offered. If the result of a challenge is unfavorable, the proposed action can be changed on an iterative basis, and the revised proposal can be challenged anew until it is as ethical as possible.

As shown in Table 4.9, the satisfaction of the utilitarian principle is examined through a question that focuses on cost–benefit analysis or risk–benefit analysis rather than only profit. Consequently, the full range of options discussed in Table 4.6 can be employed as befits the need.

In addition, as explained in Velasquez (1992), the examination of how the proposed decision respects individual rights looks at the impact of the decision on each stakeholder's rights, as noted in Table 4.6, as well as at the process involved. For example, has deception or manipulation been used (or some type of force, such as coercion), or has there been some other limit placed on information made available to the individuals impacted on them or on their freedom to choose a response or limit their

TABLE 4.9 Modified Moral Standards Approach* to Ethical Decision Making

MORAL STANDARD	QUESTION OF PROPOSED DECISION
Utilitarian:	
Maximize net benefit to society as a whole	Does the action maximize social benefits and minimize social injuries?
Individual rights:	
Respect and protect	Is the action consistent with each person's rights?
Justice:	
Fair distribution of benefits and burdens	Will the action lead to a just distribution of benefits and burdens?
Virtues:	
Motivation, virtues, and character expected	Does the action demonstrate the motivation, virtues, and character expected? See Table 4.7 for specifics.

All four moral standards must be applied; none is a sufficient test by itself.

*The Moral Standards Approach, which was created by Manuel G. Velasquez (1992), is modified here with the addition of specific examination of motivation, virtue, and character.

redress? If so, their rights have not been respected. One of the interesting questions raised in this connection is whether notification of the intent to undertake an action implies the consent of those individuals impacted on. Usually, notification does not imply consent unless the notification provides full information, allows time for consideration, and reasonable options are at hand to avoid the impact.

The question focusing on distributive justice, or fairness, is handled in the same way as in the 5-question approach. For a full treatment of the moral standards approach, see Velasquez (1992).

The recent recognition of the importance of assessing the virtues inherent in a decision as an effective risk management technique has led to a comparison of the motivation, virtues, and character traits demonstrated by a proposed action with those expected by the corporation's stakeholders. Each corporation should identify what its stakeholders expect for each of the items identified on Table 4.7 and should communicate to employees why and how those expectations should be taken into account when decisions are being made, monitored, and rewarded. At a minimum, when assessing a proposed action, the following questions should be asked with reference to the items noted on Table 4.7:

> *Does the decision or action involve and exhibit the motivation, virtues, and character expected?*

When a proposed action has been assessed against all four moral standards, and the relative importance of the impacts on stakeholders have been taken into account, an overall decision on the ethicality of the proposal can be taken. *All four moral standards must be considered to ensure a comprehensive decision.*

MODIFIED PASTIN'S APPROACH—DECISIONS WITHIN COMPANIES; INNOVATIVE TECHNIQUES In his book *The Hard Problems of Management: Gaining the Ethical Edge*, Mark Pastin (1986) presents his ideas on the appropriate approach to ethical analysis, which involves examining the first four key aspects of ethics noted in Table 4.10. The last aspect—the examination of motivation, virtue and character—has been added to ensure the review of these items.

Pastin uses the concept of *ground rule ethics* to capture the idea that individuals and organizations have ground rules or fundamental values that govern their behavior or their desired behavior. If a decision is seen to offend these values, it is likely that disenchantment or retaliation will occur. Unfortunately, this could lead to the dismissal of an employee who acts without a good understanding of the ethical ground rules of the

TABLE 4.10 Modified Pastin's Approach* to Stakeholder Impact Analysis

KEY ASPECT	PURPOSE FOR EXAMINATION
Ground rule ethics	To illuminate an organization's and/or an individual's rules and values
End-point ethics	To determine the greatest net good for all concerned
Rule ethics	To determine what boundaries a person or organization should take into account according to ethical principles
Social contract ethics	To determine how to move the boundaries to remove concerns or conflicts
Virtue ethics	To determine if the motivations, virtues, and character traits demonstrated in the decision are ethical

*Technique proposed by Mark Pastin, *The Hard Problems of Management: Gaining the Ethical Edge* (San Francisco: Jossey-Bass, 1986), has been modified with the addition of specific examination of virtue ethics expected.

employer organization involved. In order to understand the prevailing ground rules, to correctly gauge the organization's commitment to proposals and to protect the decision maker, Pastin suggests that an examination of past decisions or actions be made. He calls this approach *reverse engineering* a decision because an attempt is made to take past decisions apart to see how and why they were made. Pastin suggests that individuals are often guarded (voluntarily or involuntarily) about expressing their values and that reverse engineering offers a way to see, through past actions, what their values are.

In his concept of *end-point ethics*, Pastin suggests employing the full extent of the measurement techniques—profit, cost–benefit analysis, risk–benefit analysis, and ranking of stakeholder impacts—summarized in Table 4.5. The application of these techniques to the Ford Pinto Case (which appears at the end of this chapter) should illuminate the concept of utilitarianism and illustrate the pitfalls of focusing an analysis on only short-term profit.

The concept of *rule ethics* is used to indicate the value of rules that spring from the application of valid ethical principles to an ethical dilemma. In this case, these principles involve respect for and protection of the rights of individuals noted in Table 4.6 and derivative principles, such as the Golden Rule of "Do unto others as you would have them do unto you." The establishment of rules based on respect for individual rights can prove helpful when an interpretation is particularly difficult or when senior executives want to remove ambiguity about what they believe should be done in certain situations. For example, Pastin suggests that rules, formulated by senior executives to assist their employees, can divide possible actions into those that are obligatory, prohibited, or permissible. Similarly, rules can be crafted so as to make them categorical (i.e., no exceptions allowed) or prima facie (exceptions are allowed in certain circumstances) or to trigger consultation with senior executives. As such, rule ethics represent Pastin's examination of the impact of proposed decisions on the rights of the individuals involved.

The concept of fairness is incorporated by Pastin into his idea of *social contract ethics*. Here he suggests that formulating the proposed decision into an imaginary contract would be helpful because it would allow the decision maker to change places with the stakeholder to be impacted on. As a result, the decision maker could see if the impact was fair enough to enter freely into the contract. If the decision maker found that he or she was not prepared to enter into the contract with the roles reversed, then the terms (or boundaries) of the contract should be changed in the interests of fairness. This technique of role reversal can prove to be quite helpful, particularly in the case of strong-willed executives who are often surrounded by yes-men" or "yes-women". In the case of a real contract, this approach can be useful in projecting how proposed actions will affect the contract or whether a contract change (such as in a union contract) will be resisted.

For the reasons noted above, as with the other two approaches, the assessment of the motivations, virtues, and character inherent in a decision has been added to the set of considerations originally proposed by Pastin. Each corporation should identify what its stakeholders expect for each of the items identified in Table 4.7 and should communicate to employees why and how those expectations should be taken into account when decisions are being made, monitored, and rewarded. At a minimum, when assessing a proposed action, the following questions should be asked with reference to the items noted on Table 4.7:

Does the decision or action involve and exhibit the motivation, virtues, and character expected?

When a proposed action has been assessed against all five aspects listed on Table 4.10 and the relative importance of the impacts on stakeholders have been taken into account, an overall decision on the ethicality of the proposal can be taken. *All five aspects must be considered to ensure a comprehensive decision.* If the proposed action is considered to be unethical, it can be changed and iteratively reassessed until it is considered to be ethical before being acted on.

EXTENDING & BLENDING THE TRADITIONAL DECISION-MAKING APPROACHES From time to time, an ethical problem will arise that does not fit perfectly into one of the approaches described. For example, the issues raised by an ethical problem may be examined by the 5-question approach, except that there are significant long-term impacts or externalities that call for cost–benefit analysis rather than profitability as a first-level question. Fortunately, cost–benefit analysis can be substituted or added to the approach to enrich it. Similarly, the concept of ground rule ethics can be grafted onto a non-Pastin approach if needed in a decision that deals with an in-company setting. Care should be taken when extending and blending the approaches, however, to ensure that each of well-offness, fairness, impact on individual rights, and virtues expected are examined to provide a comprehensive analysis—otherwise, the final decision may be faulty.

INTEGRATING PHILOSOPHICAL & STAKEHOLDER IMPACT ANALYSIS APPROACHES

The philosophical approaches—consequentialism, deontology, and virtue ethics—that were developed early in this chapter and in Chapter 3 underlay the three stakeholder impact analysis approaches and should be kept in mind to inform and enrich the analysis. In turn, the stakeholder impact analysis approach used should provide an understanding of the facts, rights, duties, and fairness involved in the decision or act that are essential to a proper ethical analysis of the motivations, virtues, and character traits expected. Consequently, in an effective, comprehensive analysis of the ethicality of a decision or proposed action, the traditional philosophical approaches should augment the stakeholder models (and vice versa), as shown in Figure 4.5.

FIGURE 4.5 Ethical Decision-Making Approaches

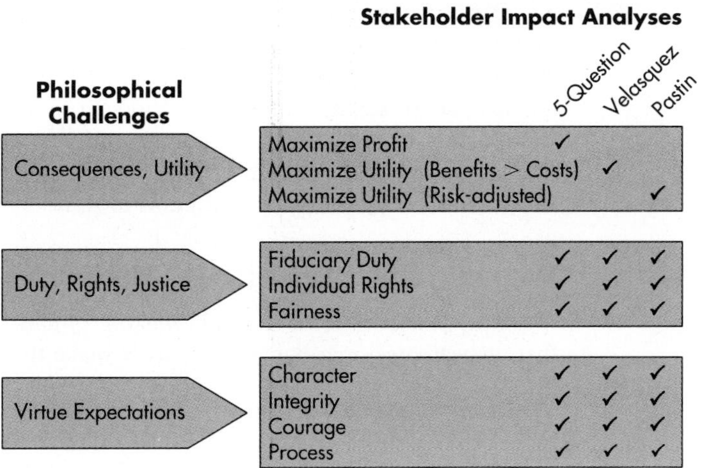

Source: See AACSB EETF Report, June 2004.

OTHER ETHICS DECISION-MAKING ISSUES

Commons Problems

The term *commons problem* refers to the inadvertent or knowing overuse of jointly owned assets or resources. The concept first arose when villagers in old England overgrazed their livestock on land that was owned in common or jointly with everyone else in the village, and the term *commons* was used to identify this type of pasture.

The problem of overgrazing could not be stopped because everyone had a right to use the pasture and thus could not be prevented from doing so. Only when the majority of villagers agreed to regulate the commons did the overgrazing stop. Sometimes, when they could not agree, outside authority was called on to settle the matter. Outdated though these issues seem, the problem of the commons is still with us in modern times. For example, pollution represents the misuse of the environment, a commons we all share. Similarly, if everyone in a business attempts to draw on limited capital funds, a tight expense budget, or a busy service department, the result will be akin to overgrazing.

The lesson to be learned from this is that frequently the decision maker, who is not sensitized to the problem of the commons, will not attribute a high enough value to the use of an asset or resource and therefore make the wrong decision. Awareness of the problem should correct this and improve decision making. If an executive is confronted by the overuse of an asset or resource, she or he will do well to employ the solutions applied in olden times.

Developing a More Ethical Action

Iterative improvement is one of the advantages of using the proposed EDM framework. If the ethical analysis reveals unethical aspects of a decision, the decision can be iteratively improved to enhance the overall impact of the decision. For example, if a decision is expected to be unfair to a particular stakeholder group, perhaps the decision can be altered by increasing the compensation to that group or by eliminating or replacing the offending words, image, or specific action. At the end of every EDM approach, there should be a specific search for a better or a win-win outcome. This process involves the exercise of *moral imagination*.

Occasionally, directors, executives, or professional accountants will suffer from *decision paralysis* as a result of the complexities of analysis or the inability to determine the maximal choice for reasons of uncertainty, time constraints, or other causes. Herbert Simon[26] proposed the concept of *satisficing* to solve this problem. He argued that one "should not let perfection be the enemy of the good"—iterative improvement until no further progress can be made should yield a solution that should be considered good enough and even optimal at that point in time.

Common Ethics Decision-Making Pitfalls

Avoiding common ethical decision-making pitfalls is imperative. Experience has shown that unaware decision makers repeatedly make the following mistakes:

- *Conforming to an unethical corporate culture.* There are many examples where corporate cultures that are not based on ethical values have influenced or motivated executives and employees to make unethical decisions. As noted in Chapters 2 and 5,

[26] Herbert Simon coined the term *satisficing* in 1957. See http://en.wikipedia.org/wiki/Satisficing.

the *unethical cultures* at Enron, WorldCom, Arthur Andersen, and the banks in 2008 led executives and employees to make tragically wrong decisions. In many instances, an *absence of ethical leadership*—the wrong "tone at the top"—was responsible. In others, companies were silent or *insufficiently clear on core values*, or these were misinterpreted, to allow unethical and illegal actions. On other occasions, *unethical reward systems* motivated employees to manipulate financial results or focus on activities not in the organization's best interest. Frequently, decision makers have been subject to *unreasonable pressures* to meet unrealistic expectations or deadlines and have made decisions that bring short-term relief at a significant cost to longer-term performance or objectives. Sometimes, employees simply *lack sufficient awareness of ethical issues and expectations* to be able to appreciate the need for ethical actions, and the organization's screening, monitoring, training, and reinforcement programs are inadequate to prevent unethical decisions.

- *Misinterpreting public expectations.* Many executives erroneously think unethical actions are acceptable because for the following reasons:
  - "It's a dog eat dog world out there."
  - "Everyone's doing it."
  - "If I don't do it someone else will."
  - "I'm off the hook because my boss ordered me to do it."
  - It's a story or practice mentioned in the popular press, media, or movies.

  In today's world, these justifications for unethical decisions are very questionable. Each action contemplated must be rigorously considered against the ethical standards discussed in Chapters 3 and 4.
- *Focusing on short-term profit and shareholder only impacts.* Often, the most significant impacts (for nonshareholder stakeholders) of a proposed action are those that surface in the future and those that befall nonshareholder stakeholders first. Only after these groups react do shareholders bear the cost for misdeeds. The remedy for this myopia is to ensure an adequate medium- or long-term time horizon for the analysis and to take into account externalities on a cost–benefit basis even though the impact measured is felt initially by a nonshareholder group.
- *Focusing only on legalities.* Many managers are concerned only with whether an action is legal. They argue, "If it's legal, it's ethical." Unfortunately, many find their corporation unnecessarily subject to consumer boycotts, employee slowdowns, increasing government regulation to cover loopholes, and fines. Some do not care because they are only intending to stay at this corporation for a short while. The fact is that laws and regulations lag behind what society wants, but reaction does come and sometimes well before new laws and regulations are promulgated. One reason is that corporations lobby against such rule changes. Just because a proposed action is legal does not make it ethical.
- *Limits to fairness.* Sometimes decision makers are biased or want to be fair only to groups they like. Unfortunately for them, they do not have the ability to control public opinion and usually end up paying for their ethical oversight. Many executives have been put off by activist organizations such as Greenpeace but have learned that environmental issues are ignored at their peril. A full review of fairness to all stakeholders is the only way to ensure an ethical decision.
- *Limits to rights canvassed.* Bias is not restricted to fairness. Decision makers should canvass the impact on all rights for all stakeholder groups. Also, decision makers should be encouraged to take their own values into account when making a

decision. Courts in North America no longer react favorably to the defense that "I was ordered to do it by my boss." Employees are expected to use their own judgment, and many jurisdictions have set up protective whistleblowing and "right to refuse" statutes to encourage employees to do so. Often, managers who force unfortunate actions on subordinates are really not speaking in the best interests of shareholders anyway.

- *Conflicts of interest.* Bias based on prejudice is not the only reason for faulty assessments of proposed actions. Judgment can be clouded by conflicting interests—the decision maker's personal interest versus the corporation's best interest or that the interests of a group the decision maker is partial to versus the corporation's best interest can both account for erroneous assessments and decisions. Sometimes employees get caught on what is called a *slippery slope* where they begin with a minor decision that conflicts with the interest of their employer, which is followed by another and another of growing significance, and it becomes extremely difficult to correct or admit to their earlier decisions. Often, an employee will be caught by doing a minor favor that leads to a greater favor and so on, but when the employee wants to stop granting further favors, they are told that they cannot stop, or their boss will hear of their earlier actions, and they are caught on a slippery slope.
- *Interconnectedness of stakeholders.* Often decision makers fail to anticipate that what they do to one group will trigger action by another. For example, spoiling the environment in a far-off country can cause negative reactions by domestic customers and capital markets.
- *Failure to identify all stakeholder groups.* The need to identify all stakeholder groups and interests before assessing the impacts on each is self-evident. However, this is a step that is repeatedly taken for granted, with the result that important issues go unnoticed. A useful approach to assist with this problem is to speculate on the downside that might happen from the proposed action and try to assess how the media will react. This often leads to the identification of the most vulnerable stakeholder groups.
- *Failure to rank the specific interests of stakeholders.* The common tendency is to treat all stakeholder interests as equal in importance. However, those that are urgent usually become the most important. Ignoring this is truly short sighted and may result in a suboptimal and unethical decision.
- *Failing to assess well-offness, fairness, or other rights.* As previously pointed out, a comprehensive ethical decision cannot be made if one of these aspects is overlooked. Repeatedly, however, decision makers short-circuit their assessments and suffer the consequences.
- *Failure to consider the motivation for the decision.* For many years, businesspeople and professionals were not concerned about the motivation for an action as long as the consequences were acceptable. Unfortunately, many decision makers lost sight of the need to increase overall net benefits for all (or as many as possible) and made decisions that benefited themselves or only a select few in the short run and disadvantaged others in the longer run. These short sighted, purely self-interested decision makers represent high governance risks for organizations.
- *Failure to consider the virtues that are expected to be demonstrated.* Board members, executives, and professional accountants are expected to act in good faith and discharge the duties of a fiduciary for people relying on them. Ignoring the virtues

expected of them can lead to dishonesty, lack of integrity in the preparation of reports, failure to act on behalf of stakeholders, and failure to discharge courage in confronting others who are involved in unethical acts or in whistleblowing when needed. Professional accountants who ignore virtues expected of them are prone to forget that they are expected to protect the public interest.

A COMPREHENSIVE ETHICAL DECISION-MAKING FRAMEWORK

A comprehensive EDM analysis should include all of the considerations outlined in Table 4.11. But this can be achieved within a philosophical analysis, a stakeholder impact analysis, or a hybrid analysis. Which one should a decision maker choose?

The best EDM approach will depend on the nature of the proposed action or ethical dilemma and the stakeholders involved. For example, as noted above, a problem involving short-term impacts and no externalities may be best suited to a modified 5-question analysis. A problem with longer-term impacts and/or externalities is probably better suited to a modified moral standards approach, or modified Pastin approach. A problem with significance for society rather than a corporation would likely be best analyzed using a philosophical approach, or the modified moral standards approach. Whatever the EDM approach used, the decision maker must consider all of the fundamental interests raised in Table 4.3 and articulated in Table 4.11.

Summary of Steps for an Ethical Decision

The approaches and issues previously discussed can be used independently or in hybrid combination to assist in producing an ethical decision. Experience has shown that completing the following three steps provides a sound basis for challenging a proposed decision:

1. *Identify* the facts and all stakeholder groups and interests likely to be affected.
2. *Rank* the stakeholders and their interests, identifying the most important and weighting them more than other issues in the analysis.
3. *Assess the impact* of the proposed action on each stakeholder group interests with regard to their well-offness, fairness of treatment, and other rights, including motivation, virtues, and character traits expected, using a comprehensive framework of questions and making sure that the common pitfalls discussed later do not enter into the analysis.

TABLE 4.11 A Comprehensive Approach to EDM

CONSIDERATION	DESCRIPTION
Well-offness or *Consequentialism*	The proposed decision should result in more benefits than costs.
Rights, duty, or *Deontology*	The proposed decision should not offend the rights of the stakeholders, including the decision maker.
Fairness or *Justice*	The distribution of benefits and burdens should be fair.
Virtue expectations or *Virtue Ethics*	The motivation for the decision should reflect stakeholders' expectations of virtue.

All four considerations must be satisfied for a decision to be considered ethical.

FIGURE 4.6 Steps toward an Ethical Decision

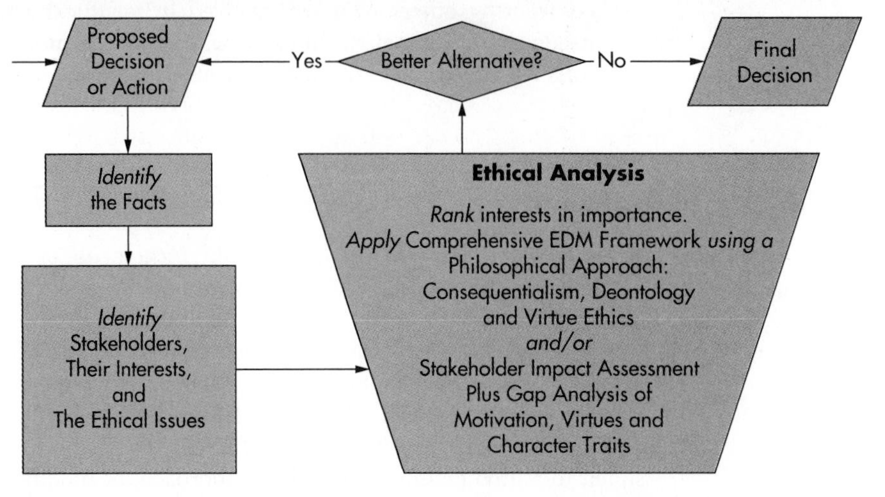

It may be helpful to organize an ethical decision analysis using the seven steps outlined by the American Accounting Association (1993) as follows:

1. Determine the facts—what, who, where, when, and how.
2. Define the ethical issue(s).
3. Identify major principles, rules, and values.
4. Specify the alternatives.
5. Compare values and alternatives and see if a clear decision emerges.
6. Assess the consequences.
7. Make your decision.

Steps toward an ethical decision are summarized in Figure 4.6.

CONCLUSION

Stakeholder impact analysis offers a formal way of bringing into a decision the needs of an organization and its individual constituents (society). Trade-offs are difficult to make and can benefit from such advances in technique. It is important not to lose sight of the fact that the concepts of stakeholder impact analysis that are reviewed in this chapter need to be applied together as a set, not as stand-alone techniques. Only then will a comprehensive analysis be achieved and an ethical decision made. Depending on the nature of the decision to be faced and the range of stakeholders to be affected, a proper analysis could be based on (1) consequentialism, deontology, and virtue ethics as a set or (2) one (or a hybrid) of the modified 5-question, moral standards, or Pastin approaches, taking into account the possible existence of commons problems that might arise.

A professional accountant can use stakeholder analysis in making decisions about accounting, auditing, and practice matters and should be ready to prepare or assist in such analyses for employers or clients just as is currently the case in other areas. Although many hard-numbers-oriented executives and accountants will be wary of becoming involved with the "soft" subjective analysis that typifies stakeholder and virtue expectations analysis, they should bear in mind that the world is changing to put a much higher value on nonnumerical information. They should be wary of placing too much weight on numerical analysis lest they fall into the trap of the economist, who, as Oscar Wilde put it, "knew the price of everything and the value of nothing."

Directors, executives, and accountants should also understand that the techniques discussed in this chapter offer a means of better understanding the interplay between their organization and/or profession and its potential supporters. The assessment of impacts on stakeholders when combined with the ranking of each stakeholder's ability to withstand the action will lead to the better achievement of strategic objectives based on satisfied stakeholders. Operating successfully in an increasingly demanding global network of stakeholders will require that future actions are not only legal but also ethically defensible.

Questions

1. Why should directors, executives, and accountants understand consequentialism, deontology, and virtue ethics?
2. Before the recent financial scandals and governance reforms, few corporate leaders were selected for their "virtues" other than their ability to make profits. Has this changed, and if so, why?
3. Is it wise for a decision maker to take into account more than profit when making decisions that have a significant social impact? Why?
4. If a framework for ethical decision making is to be employed, why is it essential to incorporate all four considerations of well-offness, fairness, individual rights and duties, and virtues expected?
5. Is the modified 5-question approach to ethical decision making superior to the modified versions of the moral standards or Pastin approach?
6. Under what circumstances would it be best to use each of the following frameworks: (1) the philosophical set of consequentialism, deontology, and virtue ethics; (2) the modified 5-question approach; (3) the modified moral standards approach; and (4) the modified Pastin approach?
7. How would you convince a CEO not to treat the environment as a cost-free commons?
8. How can a decision to downsize be made as ethically as possible by treating everyone equally?
9. From a virtue ethics perspective, why would it be logical to put in place a manufacturing process beyond legal requirements?
10. List the companies that have faced ethical tragedies due to the following failings in their ethical culture:
    a. Lack of ethical leadership
    b. Lack of clarity about important values
    c. Lack of ethical awareness and expectations by employees
    d. Lack of monitoring of ethicality of actions
    e. Unethical reward systems
    f. Unreasonable pressures for unrealistic performance
11. Give an example of behavior that might be unethical even though "everyone is doing it."

References

AACSB International (Association to Advance Collegiate Schools of Business). 2004. *Ethics Education in Business Schools: Report of the Ethics Education Task*, St. Louis, MO: AACSB International. http://www.aacsb.edu/publications/researchreports/archives/ethics-education.pdf.

American Accounting Association. 1993. *Ethics in the Accounting Curriculum: Cases & Readings*. Updated ed. Sarasota, FL: American Accounting Association. See Introduction by William May.

Aristotle. 1925. *The Nicomachean Ethics*. Translated with an introduction by David Ross, revised by J. L. Ackrill and J. O. Urmson. Oxford: Oxford University Press.

Athanassoulis, N. 2004. "Virtue Ethics." In *The Internet Encyclopedia of Philosophy*. http://www.iep.utm.edu/v/virtue.htm.

Brooks, L. J. 1979. "Cost–Benefit Analysis." *CAmagazine*, October, 53–57.

Brooks, L. J. 1995. "Sniff Tests." *Corporate Ethics Monitor* 7, no. 5: 65.

Cafaro, P. 1998. "Virtue Ethics (Not Too) Simplified." Paper presented at the Twentieth World Congress of Philosophy, Boston, August 10–15. See http://www.bu.edu/wcp/Papers/TEth/TEth Cafa.htm.

Carroll, A. B. 1990. "Principles of Business Ethics: Their Role in Decision Making and Initial Consensus." *Management Decision* 28, no. 8: 20–24.

Freeman, R. E. 1984. *Strategic Management: A Stakeholder Approach*. Boston: Pitman.

Hursthouse, R. 2003. "Virtue Ethics." In *The Stanford Encyclopedia of Philosophy*, fall 2003 ed., edited by Edward N. Zalta. http://plato.stanford.edu/archives/fall2003/entries/ethics-virtue/.

International Federation of Accountants. 2003. *International Standards for the Education of Professional Accountants* (IES 1–6) including *IES 4: Professional Values, Skills and Attitudes*, New York: IES 4: 59–65.

Kant, I. 1964. *Groundwork of the Metaphysic of Morals*. Translated with an introduction by H. J. Paton New York: Harper Torchbooks.

Kay, C. D. 1997. "Notes on Deontology." http://webs.wofford.edu/kaycd/ethics/deon.htm.

Mill, J. S. 1998. *Utilitarianism*. Edited with an introduction by Roger Crisp. New York: Oxford University Press, 1998. First published in 1861.

Mitchell, R. K., B. R. Agle, and D. J. Wood. 1997. "Toward a Theory of Stakeholder Identification and Salience: Defining the Principle of Who and What Really Counts." *Academy of Management Review* 22, no. 4: 853–86.

Pastin, M. 1986. *The Hard Problems of Management: Gaining the Ethics Edge*. San Francisco: Jossey-Bass.

Rawls, J. 1971. *A Theory of Justice*. Cambridge, MA: Harvard University Press.

Roty, A. O., ed. 1980. *Essays on Aristotle's Ethics*. Berkeley: University of California Press.

Rowley, T. 1997. "Moving beyond Dyadic Ties: A Network Theory of Stakeholder Influences." *Academy of Management Review* 22, no. 4: 887–910.

Sinnott-Armstrong, W. 2015. "Consequentialism." In *Stanford Encyclopedia of Philosophy*. http://plato.stanford.edu/entries/consequentialism/.

Stumpf, S. E. 1988. *Socrates to Sartre: A History of Philosophy*. New York: McGraw-Hill.

Tucker, G. 1990. "Ethical Analysis for Environmental Problem Solving." In *Agenda for Action Conference Proceedings*. Toronto: Canadian Centre for Ethics & Corporate Policy, 53–57.

Velasquez, M. G. 1992. *Business Ethics: Concepts and Cases*, Englewood Cliffs, NJ: Prentice Hall.

Illustrative Applications & Case Insights

Illustrative Applications

- *Dealing with Disappointed Apple iPhone Customers Case*—a comprehensive ethical analysis of the decision Apple made to reprice the iPhone soon after its introduction—an extension of the illustration from Chapter 3.
- *Bribery or Opportunity in China*—a real-life example of how a young executive faced the realities of business abroad and how he came to an innovative solution.
- *Proposed Audit Adjustment—Castle Manufacturing, Inc.*—describes the thinking involved in proposing an adjustment to year-end audited financial statements.

- *When Does an "Aggressive Accounting" Choice Become Fraudulent?*—indicates how the fundamental interests of stakeholders described in Table 4.3 ought to generate issues to be considered in a stakeholder impact analysis on the topic of accounting choices.

Cases

- *Concussions in the NFL* are imperiling NFL players and the game of football as we know it. The ethicality of the NFL's actions have become the subject of a sensational movie and possibly a guide to future resolution. This case explores how techniques of ethical analysis may help.
- *BP's Gulf Oil Spill Costs* could reach $80 billion according to a Reuters estimate, or it could be closer to $40 billion. Which estimate covers all the costs including loss of life, health, environment, economic livelihood, and reputation? How should uncertainties be estimated and built into the analysis?
- *Tylenol Recalls (2010): It's Still About Reputation* reviews how Johnson & Johnson—once revered for its iconic Tylenol recalls in 1982 (see page 274)—found itself facing mandatory shutdowns of Tylenol manufacturing plants and recalls of children's and other medications in 2010. How could such a reversal happen, and what are the costs involved?
- *Vioxx Decisions—Were They Ethical?*—provides an opportunity for students to research a serious dilemma that is currently in the news and develop a comprehensive, practical ethical analysis of the decisions faced by Merck, the manufacturer, which, by 2007, faced nearly 60,000 plaintiffs and 26,600 lawsuits. Students will also consider how the current dilemma could have been avoided.
- *Just Do It—Make the Numbers!* CFOs are often influenced, ordered, or coerced to bend the rules to make financial results better and often equal to prior projections released to the public. It is not an easy decision when your demanding boss is standing over you. What should a professional accountant consider before doing so?
- *Smokers Are Good for the Economy—Really* presents an argument that is counterintuitive in that cigarette smoking can be good. Does this actuarial/economics-based argument take into account all that a comprehensive ethical analysis should?
- The *Ford Pinto* case is a classic that shows in stark relief the danger of ignoring the social impacts of a decision in favor of maximizing short-run profit. The original cost–benefit analysis was quite faulty, and our appreciation of safety has changed a lot since the Pinto was created, but the same problems continue to recur.
- *Kardell Paper* involves the possible pollution of a river with potentially life-threatening consequences. In addition to dealing with uncertainty, the reader learns to appreciate issues such as whistleblowing, corporate governance representative of stakeholders (or responsive to their interests) at the board level, and due diligence requirements on the part of executives and board members.

Dealing with Disappointed Apple iPhone Customers Case

AN ILLUSTRATION OF COMPREHENSIVE ETHICAL DECISION MAKING

On September 5, 2007, Steve Jobs, the CEO of Apple Inc., announced that the spectacularly successful iPhone would be reduced in price by $200 from $599, its introductory price of roughly two months earlier.[1] Needless to say, he received hundreds of e-mails from irate customers. Two days later, he offered early customers who paid full price a $100 credit good at Apple's retail and online stores. Was this decision to mitigate the $200 price

[1] David Ho, "Apple CEO Apologizes to Customers," *Toronto Star*, September 7, 2007, B4.

decrease, and the manner of doing so appropriate from an ethical perspective?

If Apple management had used a *sniff test* before the decision, they might have come to the conclusion that their mothers wouldn't have been proud of or comfortable with it. Similarly, they might have discovered that the price reduction may have offended the Apple Code of Conduct for treatment of customers.

If Apple had considered the *stakeholder impacts* that the decision involved, they would have realized that, while past consumers would be most affected, the reputation of Apple would also be tarnished, and that could affect future consumers who they were trying to encourage. In addition, Apple employees—many of whom had been attracted by the strong Apple reputation for providing innovative solution of high quality—would question the company's motives, which could weaken their loyalty and commitment.

If Apple personnel had applied *traditional philosophers' ethical tests*, they would have found the following:

Consequentialism

From a profit perspective, Apple was expecting to more than offset the $200 per unit drop in margin with a gain in volume of sales. For the iPhone alone, this may have been correct, but Apple has many products that are to be bought by other customers who could be affected negatively and who would see the decision as an opportunistic price decrease from an extraordinarily high starting price. Gouging behavior could be suspected, which would undermine Apple's wholesome value proposition and non-iPhone sales would suffer as a result. Overall, management might not be certain of making a combined net profit on sales of iPhones and other products.

Duty, Rights, and Justice Issues

Apple executives have a duty to make profits, as long as doing so doesn't violate any laws. In this case, early customers of the iPhone might have a legally enforceable right to sue for unfair practices, but individual actions would be far less likely than a class action. While the outcome is a matter of speculation, the prospect of further bad press that tarnishes Apple's image is of considerable concern due to the ripple effects noted above. The impact of unfairness of the price reduction could be magnified significantly by bad press. It is unlikely, although the early purchasers had the notoriety of having the newest technology available, that Apple management would have thought the $200 price reduction was fair if they had been personally affected.

Virtues Expected

In the minds of Apple's customers and employees, Jobs has an image of a far-sighted technical genius who has been driven to provide great value for his stakeholders, and this image has been transferred to Apple itself. For many stakeholders, the $200 price decrease doesn't match up to the expectations they have come to expect of Jobs or of Apple.

Apple might also have used the questions developed in the modified *Tucker Framework* to test the proposed $200 price decrease. If so, the answers could have been as follows:

1. Is it profitable?—Outcome is not clear as discussed earlier.
2. Is it legal?—Probably, unless a consumer protection act is offended.
3. Is it fair?—Not accordingly to some customers and employees.
4. Is it right?—No, according to some executives, employees, and potential customers.
5. Does it demonstrate the expected virtues?—No, as discussed earlier.
6. Optional question: Is it sustainable (environmentally or over time)? The environmental impact issue is not involved in this decision, but the medium and longer-term impacts are likely to be negative and may be significant. It would be unwise to repeat such a decision or to ignore the

possible future negative impacts to reputation.

On balance, Apple should consider the $200 price decrease to be unfair and unwise without some mitigation for early purchasers of the iPhone. Is the credit of $100 adequate, and its restricted use appropriate? Another analysis could be run, and a sound solution arrived at in an iterative fashion, applying moral imagination where possible. In this case it is probable that judgment will have to be applied. Time will tell. In any event, Jobs could have avoided the initial negative press and damage to his and Apple's reputation, if Apple had used the ethical decision making tools to analyze the decision before putting it into action.

It should be noted that, although price discounts of the type described in this case are not uncommon and are not generally regarded as serious ethical problems, they have an ethical aspect that can be assessed using the ethical decision making approaches discussed in this chapter. They certainly represent risks that could weaken the reputation of executives and the company involved.

Source: Reprinted with permission from L. J. Brooks & David Selley, *Ethics & Governance: Developing & Maintaining An Ethical Corporate Culture* (Toronto: Canadian Centre for Ethics & Corporate Policy, 2012), 122–124.

ILLUSTRATIVE APPLICATION OF STAKEHOLDER IMPACT ANALYSIS

Bribery or Opportunity in China Case

Note: Names have been changed

John Low, a North American born of Chinese descent, was given the opportunity of his lifetime. He was asked to go to China and set up a manufacturing subsidiary in a medium-sized city in the middle of the country. He had arrived in the city and had attempted to set up a new building and manufacturing facility that would employ thirty people but had run into many delays in dealings with the local authorities. Ultimately, John met with the three senior officials and asked what the problem was. They indicated that things would go a lot faster if John's company would make them a payment of $100,000 each. This, they said, was quite reasonable in view of what other companies had been paying.

John was in a quandary. When he had been sent to China, his boss had told him that under no circumstances were any bribes to be paid. It was against company policy, and it would not be tolerated. On the other hand, John was expected to get his job done, and his boss had told him that unless he did so, another manager would be sent to take over John's position. John knew that his budget contained a provision for payments to agents, but the total allowed was only $150,000. He knew that if the facility were delayed, every month of delay would cost his company a contribution of approximately $25,000. John told the senior officials repeatedly that there was no way his company would pay them, but they were insistent.

Questions

1. Should John pay the bribes?
2. Is there something else he could do instead?

Illustrative Solution

The first step in a stakeholder impact analysis is to identify all stakeholder groups affected by the proposed action and their interests. At the end of the identification process, the stakeholders and their interests are to be ranked in importance. These two steps can be facilitated by means of a tabular analysis as follows:

Analysis of Stakeholders and Their Interests

STAKEHOLDER	INTEREST	LEGITIMACY/ LEGAL INFLUENCE	POWER TO AFFECT COMPANY	URGENCY OF CLAIM	PRIMARY OR SECONDARY	RANK IN IMPORTANCE: 1 IS HIGHEST, 3 IS LOWEST
John	Potential success or dismissal, unless a new idea can be found. Probability of discovery estimated at 60%.	Yes	Yes	High	Primary	1
Local employees	Delay in job, or no job.	No	Not yet	Low	Secondary for now	3
John's boss	John's success is his own, but he runs the risk of sanction if John is found to have bribed.	Yes	Yes	High, but less than John's	Primary	2
Other managers Elsewhere	Company policy will be eroded, so observance will be difficult since employees will know of breach.	Yes	Yes	Medium	Primary	2
Shareholders	Financial success earlier, but costs of bribes will raise costs and will be called for in many situations. Possible fines and bad publicity if caught, and *Foreign Corrupt Practices Act* or similar applies, so profits down, Probability of 40%.	Yes	Yes	High	Primary	1
Chinese officials	$300,000 richer if not caught, then? Probability of 10%.	Yes	Yes	Medium/high	Primary	1
Directors and senior executives	Directors same as shareholders. Executives—no bonuses and could be dismissed.	Yes	Yes	High, but less than John's	Primary	1
Elderly Chinese in town (leaders in society)	No benefit until local employment starts or other benefit created.	No	Yes, very Influential	Low	Appears secondary, but could be primary	1
Chinese government	Bribes raise cost of doing business in China.	Yes	Yes, but Distant	Low	Secondary for now	3
John's family	Unknown if he has any.					Not applicable

In this situation, with the proposed action being to pay the bribes or not, there are not many externalities, but there are legalities and company ground rules. Consequently, John could use a hybrid ethical decision framework based on the 5-question framework but with the use of net benefit in addition to profit and ground rule ethics. The questions or challenges for the proposed action are therefore as shown in the table below, with responses noted.

Based on this analysis, John found several responses that were negative or not clearly positive, indicating an unethical—and in this case illegal—decision. Yet he had to bribe or admit failure unless he could find an ethical alternative.

John also asked himself whether the decision to bribe would involve and exhibit the motivations, virtues, and character traits expected. His answers appear in the table above.

Bribery was not in accord with expected motivations, virtues, or character traits, so John began to look for other alternatives. He began to consider the primary

Challenges to Proposed Action: Payment of Bribes

QUESTION OR CHALLENGE	RESPONSE
1. Is it profitable?	Maybe for company. $25,000 per month × 40% (i.e., the probability of being caught)—cost of fines and additional bribes elsewhere. John, probably not, as probability of being caught is 60%.
2. Is it legal?	Not really, but maybe if creative arrangement with an agent is successful and/or this is considered a facilitating payment, not a bribe.
3. Is it fair?	Not to John, his boss, top management, China, or elderly Chinese.
4. Is it right? Generally? Per company ground rules? Per John?	Everyone is doing it, so maybe. Not per company ground rules and code. Not known.
5. Does it provide the highest net benefit for all?	Maybe, unless a better idea is found.

stakeholders to the company's long-run success in the area. He realized that the company's relationship with the Chinese elderly was going to be of high long-run significance because the elderly are very influential in Chinese culture. What could he do to satisfy the elderly and perhaps bring the local officials onside as well? At the same time, he did not want to offend his company's ground rules which were to observe the code and not to bribe.

He had noticed that there was not really a good place for the elderly to gather, like his own parents had back home. In the end, he asked his boss if his company ever supported community centers, and the answer was yes. The company's donations budget would provide the funds, and company officials were quite interested in paying for a senior citizens' center and park in the Chinese town as part of the company's good corporate citizen program of supporting the communities that they operated in. John proposed this to the senior Chinese officials who wanted the bribes, indicating that his company would not make such payments directly to anyone. The officials, however, would get credit by association with the park and center and would, of course, serve on the Board of Directors of the center when it was finished.

John's plant was ready in record time, and he was awarded a citation by his company's CEO, who was also the person in charge of the company's ethics program. It seemed apparent that he had found a solution that provided the highest net benefit to all—a true win-win-win arrangement—that matched well to expected motivations, virtues, and character traits.

Expected Motivations, Virtues, & Character Traits

QUESTION: DOES THE DECISION OR ACTION (TO BRIBE) INVOLVE OR EXHIBIT THE EXPECTED	RESPONSE
Motivations	Possibly, but higher levels of self-control, fairness, and/or caring may be possible with other alternatives.
Virtues	No. John would be breaching his CEO/company's expectations. Dutiful loyalty, integrity, and sincerity would be below expectations. Duplicity would be required, rather than transparency, to appear to comply with company codes and Chinese law.
Character traits	No. It is doubtful that John would be considered trustworthy, honest, or truthful if he bribes and is found out.

ILLUSTRATIVE APPLICATION OF STAKEHOLDER IMPACT ANALYSIS

Proposed Audit Adjustment Case—Castle Manufacturing Inc.

Larry Plant, the CFO of Castle Manufacturing Inc., was involved in a lengthy discussion with Joyce Tang of the company's auditing firm, Bennett & Sange, at the conclusion of the audit fieldwork.

"Look Joyce, we just can't afford to show that much profit this year. If we do record the \$1.5 million after-tax adjustment you propose, our profit will be 20% higher than we had two years ago and 5% higher than we reported last year. On the other hand, without the adjustment, we would be close to last year's level. We are just about to enter negotiations with our labor unions, and we have been complaining about our ability to compete. If we show that much profit improvement, they will ask for a huge raise in rates. Our company will become noncompetitive due to higher labor rates than our offshore competition. Do you really want that to happen?"

"But Larry, you really earned the profit. You can't just ignore it!"

"No, I'm not suggesting that, Joyce. But virtually all of the goods making up the profit adjustment were in transit at our year end—so let's just record them as next year's sales and profits."

"But, Larry, they were all sold FOB your plant, so title passed to the buyer when they were shipped."

"I know that, Joyce, but that was an unusual move by our overzealous sales staff, who were trying to look good and get a high commission on year-end numbers. Anyway, the customer hadn't inspected them yet. Just this once, Joyce, let's put it into next year. It's not really a significant amount for our shareholders, but it will trigger a much bigger problem for them if the unions get a hold of the higher profit numbers. As you know, about 40% of our shares were willed to the United Charities Appeal here in town, and they could sure benefit by higher profits and dividends in the future. I bet the difference in their dividends could be up to \$400,000 per year over the life of the next five-year contract."

Question

1. What should Joyce do?

Illustrative Solution

Several approaches to ethical decision making are presented in the chapter: the philosophical, or those to be used with an assessment of the motivations, virtues, and character traits; the 5-question approach; the moral standards approach; and the Pastin approach. In this illustrative solution, the 5-question framework will be used, with expansions, where necessary, drawn from other approaches.

The 5-question approach calls for the identification of the stakeholders impacted by the decision and then poses five questions or challenges to assess whether these impacts are ethical. If some aspect of the decision is considered not to be ethical, the proposed decision/action may be altered to mitigate or remove the unethical element.

In this case, the auditor has proposed that a \$1.5 million adjustment be made to increase the profitability of the client Castle Manufacturing Inc. The CFO is resisting, proposing instead that the impact on profit be put into the next year so as to gain a bargaining advantage over the company's unions, who will use the profit figures to negotiate a new five-year agreement. Joyce Tang, the auditor, must decide whether the proposal to shift the adjustment to the next year is ethical: if not, she must convince the CFO to record the adjustment or qualify her audit report. It is not immediately apparent whether the adjustment is material: if it was, the correct action would be to qualify the audit report if the CFO were to hold fast to his proposal.

Identification of Stakeholders and Their Interests

The CFO's proposal would impact on the following stakeholders:

STAKEHOLDERS	INTERESTS
Directly Impacted:	
Current shareholders wishing to sell their shares in the short run	They would want the adjustment recorded in the current year to boost profit and share values.
Current shareholders wishing to hold on to their shares	They would want the adjustment deferred to minimize the labor settlement and maximize future profits and dividends.
Future shareholders	They would want an accurate assessment of profitability to properly assess whether to buy into the company. If profits are depressed, they might not buy in, so the increased future profits may not be relevant.
Employees	They would want profits accurately stated to provide a higher basis for negotiation assuming this would not jeopardize the long-run viability of the enterprise.
Company management	Depending on their bonus arrangements and their altruism, they would want short- or longer-term recognition of the adjustment.
Directors	They would want the long-run profit improvement, provided they would not be sued for sanctioning something illegal.
Creditors, suppliers, and lenders	If the labor negotiations result in higher profitability and liquidity, these stakeholders would want the adjustment deferred.
Governments and regulators	They would want profits accurately stated because this would result in higher taxes and fewer potential complaints from other stakeholders (e.g., unions).
Joyce and her audit firm	They would want to minimize the chance of legal and professional challenges arising from the audit that would result in fines and/or loss of reputation, but they also would wish to continue auditing a healthy client.
Indirectly Impacted:	
Recipients of the funds generated by the United Charities Appeal	They would want the adjustment deferred.
Altruistic management of the United Charities Appeal	They would want the adjustment properly dealt with, which would probably mean that they would side with the employees.
Host communities	They would want the highest labor rate settlement possible without jeopardizing the long-run health of the enterprise.
The auditing profession	It would want to avoid loss of reputation for the profession.

Ranking of Stakeholder's Interests

The stakeholder's interests in the decision identified above can be ranked as to their importance on "possessing legal rights," "ability to withstand both financially and psychologically" (a rank of "1" is worst), and "probable public reaction on behalf of" scales, as follows:

STAKEHOLDERS IMPACTED	POSSESS LEGAL RIGHTS	RANK OF ABILITY TO WITHSTAND	PROBABLE PUBLIC REACTION
Current shareholders—wishing to sell	Yes—first	3	Low
Current shareholders—wishing to hold	Yes—tie	3	Low
Future shareholders	Yes	3	Low
Employees:	No—none	2	Strong
— if contract is GAAP based	Yes	2	Strong
— if financial statement is used in negotiation	Yes—possibly	2	Strong
Company management—dependent on contract	Yes or no	3	Low
Directors	Yes	2	Low

(continued)

STAKEHOLDERS IMPACTED	POSSESS LEGAL RIGHTS	RANK OF ABILITY TO WITHSTAND	PROBABLE PUBLIC REACTION
Creditors, suppliers	No	4	Low
Lenders—dependent on contract	No or yes	4	Low
Governments and regulators	Yes	4	Moderate
Joyce and her audit firm	Yes	2	Strong
Recipients of charity funds	No	1	Strong
Altruistic management of charity	No	3 or 2	Strong
Host communities	No	4	Moderate
Auditing profession	No	3	Strong

It is evident from these rankings that the strength of legal rights does not correspond to the rankings of a stakeholder's ability to withstand the decision or to the probable public reaction on behalf of each stakeholder if the decision to defer the adjustment becomes public. Moreover, the legal rights of stakeholders with differing interests are equal. The "probable public reaction" scale, which corresponds strongly to the "ability to withstand" scale, offers a good idea of how politicians, governments, and regulators will react. Consequently, decision makers would be unwise to focus only on the legality of stakeholder positions.

Of course, the likelihood of the deferment becoming public has to be estimated. Unfortunately, most decision makers overlook the possibility of an altruistic or disgruntled whistleblower making the disclosure public or, alternatively, revealing it to the union bargaining team. As a result, the valid probability of revelation is usually far higher than the decision maker's assessment.

Application of the Modified 5-Question Approach

Question 1: Profitability

There is no doubt that the deferment of an upward adjustment of $1.5 million to profit will decrease profit this year and increase it the next. In addition, there is some possibility, if the decision does not become public or known to the union, that the company's profits over the life of the contract will rise substantially if total dividends will rise by $1.0 million per year ($400,000/40%). However, if the decision becomes known, the union may retaliate and bargain harder, lawsuits may be launched against the company, and the executives, auditors, and governments may levy tax penalties and fines. Consequently, the outcome on the profitability question is uncertain for the company and therefore for its shareholders and their dependents (and for the auditor, for that matter).

Question 2: Legality

Given that the decision to defer the adjustment is in the gray area of GAAP (it is not clearly material—although it is suspiciously significant—nor is it contravening usual company practice; the customers have not inspected the goods at year end, and it is a conservative treatment), it might be declared reasonable in a court of law. However, the legal process, which usually covers the company, its management and directors, and the auditor as being joint and severally liable, will involve legal fees, expert witness's testimony, commitment of time (which soaks up billable time), and the potential of having to pursue other codefendants for restitution if they are found to be culpable rather than the auditor. Of course, the auditor could mitigate these legal consequences by qualifying her report, but that would obviate the exercise and could create ill will with the CFO and possibly the rest of the management and directors. Because the legal interests do not coincide and a lawsuit is likely if the deferment is known, the decision maker may not be able to take comfort from the fact that the deferment is probably within the boundaries of GAAP and therefore legal.

Question 3: Fairness

While the decision to defer the $1.5 million adjustment may not be considered material to an investor making the decision to invest or divest, it may be very significant to the employees and their union and to the charity and its dependents. Consequently, not to disclose the $1.5 million this year may be unfair to these interest groups. If the decision becomes public, this unfair treatment may result in lawsuits and may bring the company, its auditors, and the auditing profession into disrepute with the public. The claim would be that these parties were not acting in the public interest—that the auditors failed to lend credibility to the financial statements and thereby failed to protect the public.

Question 4: Impact on Rights

To the extent that the proposed decision impacted negatively on the rights of stakeholders, in terms of life, health, privacy, dignity, and so on (i.e., rights other than fairness and legal rights, which are canvassed in questions 2 and 3), the decision would be considered unethical. In this case, there are no lives at stake, but conceivably the health and well-being of the employees and particularly the ultimate recipients of the charity are at stake. The extent of this infringement would be revealed by further investigation. Given the information in the case, the degree of infringement of stakeholder rights is unclear.

Question 5: Demonstration of Expected Motivations, Virtues, & Character Traits?

All of the stakeholder impact assessment approaches or any hybrid approach should be augmented by an assessment of motivations, virtues, and character traits involved in and exhibited by the decision or action compared to what is expected. In this case, for Joyce Tang, the decision maker, this assessment would be as shown below.

In this decision, there does not appear to be much room for reengineering to make its impact more ethical, so it must be faced as it is.

Summary of Findings of 5-Question Approach

This analysis has shown that the proposed deferment is probably legal but may not be profitable, fair, or respectful of stakeholder's rights. Certainly, the examination

Expected Motivations, Virtues, & Character Traits

QUESTION: DOES THE DECISION OR ACTION INVOLVE OR EXHIBIT THE EXPECTED RESPONSE?

Motivations	Possibly not. As a professional accountant, Joyce is supposed to use her unbiased, fair judgment to protect the public interest by following GAAP and her professional accounting code. This protects future shareholders from harmful actions that would benefit existing shareholders.
Virtues	If Joyce's action of lowering profit by $1.5 million becomes known, future shareholders, some current shareholders, and the employees will consider it unethical because Joyce will appear: — to be disloyal to her profession and those shareholders, — to be lacking in integrity and the desire to support transparency, and — duplicitous.
Character Traits	The disenchanted stakeholders will take the view that Joyce is untrustworthy, partial to some stakeholders, and lacking the courage to stand up for the rights of all stakeholders.

Suggested Format: Decision Impact on Mulitple Bases

PROJECTED	SHORT-TERM PROFIT	FIVE-YEAR PROFIT	COST–BENEFIT ANALYSIS	RISK–BENEFIT ANALYSIS
Revenues/cost savings/benefits				
Costs/opportunity costs	______	______	______	______
Net profit/net benefits				

of only a one-year time frame would have proven to be misleading. Further analysis appears needed to reach a conclusive decision on many issues, and even then reflection will be needed to weigh the trade-offs between interests.

Extensions of the 5-Question Approach

The stakeholder impact challenges inherent in the 5-question approach, the moral standards approach, and Pastin's approach can be grouped into three areas: well-offness, fairness, and rights.

On the dimension of well-offness, it is evident that looking only at the profitability of the decision focuses discussion of the interests of shareholders rather than stakeholders. The way to broaden the focus is to prepare an analysis over a longer rather than shorter time frame so that some of the externalities are included: to use cost–benefit analysis to bring in intangibles, such as the loss of quality of life, and to use risk–benefit analysis to include probabilities of occurrences. These enhancements have been included intuitively in the previous analysis but could be sharpened with further investigation and presented formally to the decision maker to assist in his or her decision, perhaps in the following format.

This presentation would allow the decision maker to see what the short-term and longer-term impact on profits was and what the overall net benefits were likely to be for all stakeholders. Frequently, the benefits and costs accruing to stakeholders ultimately accrue to shareholders, so this presentation will allow a decision maker to project what may result from the decision. In this case, we do not have enough information to develop estimates for the costs and benefits associated with the positions of many stakeholders.

With regard to fairness, the concept of ranking stakeholders on several dimensions has already been employed. If the fairness of an impact is ever in doubt, one way to assess it is to put yourself in the position of the stakeholder being assessed. If you would be willing to change places with the other party, then the decision is probably fair. If not, the decision may be made fair by altering or reengineering its impact in some way.

The consideration of impacts on stakeholder rights can be enhanced beyond the level employed in this analysis by a heightened awareness of commons problems. Sometimes rights shared with others are taken for granted, but they should not be. The environment is one example of this, but there may be others on which specific decisions impact.

Conclusion

Although the proposed decision appears to hold some promise of profitability and could be within GAAP and legal, it does not appear to be fair or right to several stakeholders. *Although the proposed action's impact may not be material for investors, it is significant to several stakeholders*. The proposed action does not match expectations for ethical motivations, virtues, or character traits. Consequently, it is somewhat unethical and may result in significant negative reaction for the directors, auditor, and auditing profession. These matters and their consequences should be fully explained to the Audit Committee of the Board of Directors. In the post–Sarbanes-Oxley regime, the Audit Committee should be informed by the auditor of such disputes with management and what the auditor's opinion was. If the Audit Committee agrees with management (whose mandate includes the preparation of the financial statements) to exclude the $1.5 million profit, the full board should be advised, and the auditor should consult within her firm to arrive at a consensus position on whether to qualify the audit report. In this way, the decision can be shared among those who would be held responsible.

ILLUSTRATIVE APPLICATION OF STAKEHOLDER IMPACT ANALYSIS

When Does an "Aggressive Accounting" Choice Become Fraudulent?

Fraudulent choices of accounting treatment are those that contain such an element of deception that a reasonably informed and careful investor or other financial report user would be misled to his or her detriment as a result. For example, revenue or expenses may be misstated to improperly increase current profit (thus diminishing future profits) to raise share prices or increase management bonuses. This would put future shareholders at a disadvantage, as they would be buying shares at inflated prices while the company's assets would be reduced by the bonus money paid out.

There are, however, times when GAAP allow a choice among alternative treatments, where some are more aggressive than others that are considered conservative usually because of their tendency not to inflate current profits. For example, a company's management may choose different approaches to depreciate its fixed assets, and this would give rise to different depreciation charges against profit. Similarly, a range of choices is available for accounting for goodwill, the recognition of warrantee expense, or the recognition of revenue from construction contracts. If these accounting choices are made without consideration of all possible accounting practices, current and future shareholders may not be properly served. However, unless there is an effective ethical framework for deciding which of these choices to make, accounting choices may become too aggressive and fraudulent.

FUNDAMENTAL STAKEHOLDER INTEREST	ISSUES TO BE CONSIDERED
Well-offness	Are current and future shareholders' interests reported clearly and accurately, and as the related economic reality warrants?
Fairness	Are the interests of current shareholders, future shareholders, management, or other stakeholders unfairly disadvantaged with the benefit being transferred to another stakeholder?

Right(s)	Are the rights of stakeholders observed, including adherence to the following?
	• Professional fiduciary focus on duty to the public
	• Professional standards—objectivity, accuracy, integrity, competency, fair presentation
	• GAAP
	• Securities Commissions guidelines for
	  • full, true and plain disclosure and
	  • specific disclosures
	• Company policies such as for clarity and completeness?

Virtue expectation	Motivations, virtues, character traits (see Table 4.8)

ETHICS CASE

Concussions in the NFL

The NFL has known for some time that serious brain damage could be caused by the head trauma that is part of a normal football game. The sudden serious jarring of a football player's head in normal tackling and blocking has been suspected for decades of causing lasting health problems. But it took the sensational film, *Concussion* (2015), about Dr. Bennet Omalu's discovery that this head trauma was linked to chronic traumatic encephalopathy (CTE) and that the NFL was covering it up for many years to raise the public's awareness to the full extent of the problem.

Dr. Omalu, a medical examiner in Pittsburgh, began his studies in 2002. Although the NFL began studying the problem in 1994, the NFL initially denied or downplayed the risks and began to introduce preventive measures only in 2009. By 2013, the NFL required players suspected of suffering concussions during a game to submit to specific sideline tests conducted by an independent neurologist before returning to play. The NFL has committed $130 million to research and has agreed to a payment of $765 million to settle a lawsuit from retired players.

Many NFL players have reportedly committed suicide because of the depression and dementia associated with the head trauma they suffered while playing the game they loved. Others have reportedly suffered CTE and other brain disorders, such as Parkinson's disease. According to Boston University,

> Chronic traumatic encephalopathy (CTE) is a progressive degenerative disease of the brain found in athletes (and others) with a history of repetitive brain trauma, including symptomatic concussions as well as asymptomatic sub concussive hits to the head.... This trauma triggers progressive degeneration of the brain tissue, including the build-up of an abnormal protein called tau. These changes in the brain can begin months, years, or even decades after the last brain trauma or end of active athletic involvement. The brain degeneration is associated with memory loss, confusion, impaired judgment, impulse control problems, aggression, depression, and, eventually, progressive dementia.

Although questions are continually raised about the efficacy of the NFL's measures to protect players from head injuries, the NFL continues to play. Many owners, management, players and fans consider CTE to be just an occupational hazard.

Questions

1. Is the NFL's stance on controlling the harm of concussions ethical?
2. Should the NFL have moved earlier on the concussion problem? If so, when and how?
3. If the concussion problem had been analysed using virtue ethics, what would the analysis have included and concluded?
4. Should the NFL continue to play football? Consider consequences, impacts on rights, and virtue ethics in your answer.

Sources: *Concussion*, 2015, a movie starring Will Smith, http://www.sonypictures.com/movies/concussion/; NFL Concussion Litigation, see http://nflconcussionlitigation.com/

PBS Frontline. "League of Denial: The NFL's Concussion Crisis", October 8, 2013, accessed April 17, 2016, from http://www.pbs.org/wgbh/frontline/film/league-of-denial/

PBS Frontline, "Timeline: The NFL's Concussion Crisis," accessed April 17, 2016, from http://www.pbs.org/wgbh/frontline/article/timeline-the-nfls-concussion-crisis/

PBS Frontline, "The NFL's Concussion Problem Still Has Not Gone Away," by Jason M. Breslow, September 19, 2014, accessed April 17, 2016, from http://www.pbs.org/wgbh/frontline/article/the-nfls-concussion-problem-still-has-not-gone-away/

"What Is CTE?," Boston University, accessed April 17, 2016, from http://www.bu.edu/cte/about/what-is-cte/.

ETHICS CASE

BP's Gulf Oil Spill Costs

One of the world's largest oil spills began on April 20, 2010, in BP's Deepwater Horizon/Macondo well in the Gulf of Mexico. Although the world did not take significant notice until the next day, an estimated 62,000 barrels of oil and gas escaped into the Gulf for most of the next 95 days until the well was capped on July 27. Damage to the Gulf Coast fishery, tourism, and quality of life was catastrophic.

At first, BP estimated that the cost of cleanup alone would be $3 billion to $6 billion[1] and set aside a claims fund of $20 billion.[2] On July 27, BP set aside $32.2 billion[3] to settle claims for loss of income and cleanup and other costs. Later BP decided to raise their estimate to $40 billion, but even that may prove not to be enough.

On December 1, 2010, Reuters published a "Special Report" that suggested BP's costs could rise to twice BP's final estimate—all the way to $80 billion.[4] Their estimates are noted in Table 1.

Estimates by Reuters included several uncertainties. For some, Reuters included a range of outcomes; for others, they simply stated their existence.

TABLE 1 **Reuters' Estimates of BP's Gulf Oil Spill Costs (U.S. Billions)**

Item	Estimate
Economic damages—claims of lost income from fishermen, tourist operators, and other businesses	$20.0
Fine for oil spilled under the U.S. Clean Water Act: $4,300 per barrel if found "grossly negligent," $1,100 per barrel if not, plus recoveries from partners, suppliers, and consultants	21.1–5.4 (range explained below)
Punitive damages based on $1 for each $1 of economic damages, the same as Exxon had to pay for the Exxon Valdez oil spill	20.0
Added regulatory scrutiny—10% of operating costs ($280 million per year) discounted at 10%	2.5
Capping the Macondo well—labor, materials, etc.	Specific Estimate Not Disclosed (✓)
Cleanup of oil—BP Gulf of Mexico Response website	✓
Cleanup of ships fouled	✓
Lost production of 30,000 barrels per day discounted at 10%	✓
Ban from future drilling site auctions—lost new oil	✓
	$80 billion

Source: BP, "Claims," in *Gulf Commitment*, 2016, http://www.bp.com/en_us/bp-us/commitment-to-the-gulf-of-mexico/claims.html.

[1] Tom Bergin, "Special Report: How BP's Oil Spill Costs Could Double," December 1, 2010, accessed December 10, 2010, from http://www.reuters.com/article/idUSTRE6B02PA20101201?pageNumber=1.

[2] BP, "BP Establishes $20 Billion Claims Fund for Deepwater Horizon Oil Spill and Outlines Dividend Decisions," June 16, 2010, http://www.bp.com/en/global/corporate/press/press-releases/bp-establishes-20-billion-claims-fund-for-deepwater-horizon-spill-and-outlines-dividend-decisions.html.

[3] BP, "BP Sets Out Gulf of Mexico Costs, Further Asset Sales and Strong Operating Performance," July 27, 2010, accessed December 12, 2010, from http://www.bp.com/extendedgenericarticle.do?categoryId=2012968&contentId=7063921.

[4] Bergin, "Special Report."

Some uncertainties will take time to clarify, such as (1) how many of the claimants of lost revenue or income can prove the basis of their claim since they may not have paid taxes on all the revenue they earned or (2) the future price of a barrel of oil. However, reasonable estimates or assumptions can be made that can contribute to a useful overall estimate.

Some matters require ultimate clarification by court judgment or political decision because current opinions conflict. For example, if BP, the project operator, is judged as "grossly negligent," then BP would be liable for a fine of $4,300 per barrel spilled rather than $1,100 per barrel, and BP's partners—Anadarko Petroleum (25%) and Japan's Mitsui (10%)—would not have to pay any fines and cleanup costs. In addition, companies such as those hired to drill (Transocean) and provide consulting advice (Halliburton) could also be off the hook. It would appear, however, that the White House Oil Spill Commission[5] did not find direct evidence that BP's senior management had been reckless and therefore grossly negligent. They found no direct evidence of a "conscious decision to favor dollars over safety," which suggested instead that the tragedy could be characterized as "a mistake by a low-level worker." On the other hand, the commission's cochairmen indicated that BP had "a culture that did not promote safety" and that their report "did not mean anyone was off the hook." Rumors were also reported of a potential political deal to lower the fine from $4,300 per barrel.

Biological uncertainties also need clarification. Various reports indicate the disappearance of the oil spilled, perhaps due to the actions of microbes in the warm water. Not surprisingly, there are opposing reports of finding oil spilled that has sunk deep into the ocean.

Time will make all uncertainties clearer, but estimates of potential costs are needed long before perfectly certain figures are available. In this regard, the estimate by Reuters of the out-of-pocket impact on BP of the Deepwater Horizon/Macondo well disaster is quite useful for investors, employees, and auditors. But Reuters would be quite ready to admit that there are costs borne by other stakeholders that they have not included. Not until the end of 2015 were penalties determined, but liabilities continued (see Table 2).

Oil Spill Videos

- "2010: First 100 Days of BP Oil Disaster" (video file). July 27, 2010. *CNN U.S.* http://www.cnn.com/videos/us/2010/07 27/natpkg.100.days.stopping.the.leak .cnn/video/playlists/bp-deepwater-horizon -oil-spill/
- "Gulf Oil Spill by the Numbers" (video file). 2010. *Time.* http://content.time.com /time/video/player/0,32068,91101495001 _1995883,00.html
- Revisit the BP Oil Spill, 5 Years Later" (video file). April 10, 2015. *CNN U.S.* http://www.cnn.com/videos/bestoftv/2014 /01/11/ac-wv-water-chemicals.cnn/video /playlists/toxic-pollution/
- Paul Hunter, "BP Deepwater Horizon Oil Spill, 5 Years Later: Louisiana Residents Say Effects of Massive 2010 Gulf of Mexico Spill Still Being Felt" (video file). April 19, 2015. *CBC News.* http:// www.cbc.ca/news/world/bp-deepwater -horizon-oil-spill-5-years-later-1.3037641

Subsequent Events

In September 2014, after four years of legal wrangling to apportion blame for the spill, BP was found "grossly negligent" and 67% responsible, while Transocean was found 30% responsible and Halliburton 3%.

Source: Margaret Cronin Fisk, Laurel Brubaker Calkins, and Jef Feeley, "BP Found Grossly Negligent in 2010 Gulf of Mexico Spill," *Bloomberg Business*, September 4, 2014, http://www.bloomberg.com/news /articles/2014-09-04/bp-found-grossly-negligent-in-2010 -gulf-of-mexico-spill.

[5] "Factbox: Oil Spill Commission Findings," November 8, 2010, accessed December 12, 2010, from http://www .reuters.com/article/idUSTRE6A74FH20101108.

TABLE 2 Spill and Post-Spill Trial Time Line

April–July 2010—Deepwater Horizon oil rig explodes; eleven killed. Millions of barrels of oil pollute the Gulf of Mexico. BP reserves $42 billion for cleanup costs, damages, and penalties (David Gregorio, Howard Goller, and Jeffrey Benkoe, "Timeline: BP Oil Spill, Litigation at a Glance," *Reuters (Edition U.S.)*, July 2, 2015), http://www.reuters.com/article/us-bp-gulfmexico-settlement-timeline-idUSKCN0PC1OD20150702?mod=related&channelName=domesticNews).

November 2012—Criminal case settlement: BP agrees to $4.5 billion in fines and penalties and pleads guilty to fourteen criminal charges (Gregorio et al., July 2, 2015). BP banned from bidding on U.S. contracts. Criminal charges laid against three employees.

December 2012—Class action settlement: judge approves BP's settlement with businesses and individuals affected by the oil spill. BP estimates $7.8 billion to settle more than 100,000 claims, but the amount is not capped (Gregorio et al., July 2, 2015).

February 2013—First phase of three-phase civil trial begins to apportion blame to BP, Halliburton, and Transocean (Gregorio et al., July 2, 2015).

September 2014—Halliburton Co. reaches $1.1 billion settlement, including legal fees, for claims against it (Dominic Rushe, "Halliburton Reaches $1.1bn Settlement over Deepwater Horizon Oil Spill," *The Guardian*, September 2, 2016, http://www.theguardian.com/environment/2014/sep/02/halliburton-11bn-settlement-deepwater-horizon-spill).

September 2014—Second phase of civil trial begins to determine amount of oil spilled for calculation of fines and damages (Gregorio et al., July 2, 2015).

September 2014—Phase 1 ruling: judge determines BP was grossly negligent. BP found 67% responsible, Transocean 30% responsible, and Halliburton 3% responsible for the spill (Gregorio et al., July 2, 2015).

January 2015—Phase 2 ruling: judge determines that 3.19 million barrels of oil were spilled (Gregorio et al., July 2, 2015)—less than the 4.2 million claimed by the federal government but more than BP's claimed 2.4 million barrels. Thus, Clean Water Act fines are capped at $13.8 billion ($4,300 per barrel) (Terry Macalister, January 16, 2015).

January 2015—Phase 3 begins to determine fines for pollution.

February 2015—BP appeals size of spill ruling. (Terry Macalister, "BP Deepwater Horizon Fine Capped at $13.8bn," *The Guardian*, January 16, 2015). Retrieved from http://www.theguardian.com/business/2015/jan/16/bp-deepwater-horizon-spill-fine-cap-14bn.

June 2015—Former BP executive acquitted (Associated Press, "BP Engineer Is Not Guilty in Case from 2010 Gulf Oil Spill," *New York Times*, February 25, 2016, http://www.nytimes.com/2016/02/26/business/energy-environment/bp-engineer-is-not-guilty-in-case-from-2010-gulf-oil-spill.html?_r=0).

July 2015—Phase 3 settlement reached: BP agrees to pay $5.5 billion in Clean Water Act fines as part of $20.8 billion settlement with federal government and five Gulf states, raising its budget for the spill to $55 billion from $42 billion (Margaret Cronin Fisk and Laurel Brubaker Calkins, "Anadarko Ordered to Pay $159.5 Million for 2010 Gulf Spill," *Bloomberg Business*, November 30, 2015, http://www.bloomberg.com/news/articles/2015-11-30/anadarko-ordered-to-pay-159-5-million-for-2010-gulf-spill).

November 2015—Anadarko Petroleum fined $160 million as part owner not directly responsible for the spill (Fisk et al., November 30, 2015).

December 2015—BP faces Mexican class action lawsuit over Deepwater Horizon oil spill (Nina Lakhani, "BP Faces Mexican Class Action Lawsuit over Deepwater Horizon Oil Spill," *The Guardian*, December 11, 2015, http://www.theguardian.com/environment/2015/dec/11/bp-gulf-oil-spill-mexico-lawsuit-deepwater-horizon.

January 2016—BP engineer sentenced to six months of probation. Another BP engineer to be sentenced in April 2016, probably with several months' probation (Associated Press, February 25, 2016).

February 2016—BP announces plans to sell $8 billion in assets and shed 7,000 jobs over two years because of low oil prices and liabilities ($4.4 million over three months for Gulf oil spill, bringing amount spent to date at $55 billion). Crude oil sits at $44 per barrel, compared to $77 per barrel in early 2015 (Macalister, February 2, 2016).

February 2016—Last of three BP employees tried on criminal charges is acquitted (Associated Press, February 25, 2016).

March 2016—BP CEO Bob Dudley (CEO since October 2010) receives 20% pay hike despite record-high loss of $6.5 billion in 2015, planned loss of 7,000 jobs, and ongoing liabilities from Gulf oil spill (Terry Macalister, "BP Chief Receives 20% Pay Hike despite Record Loss and 7,000 Axed Jobs," *The Guardian*, March 4, 2016, http://www.theguardian.com/business/2016/mar/04/bp-chief-executive-20-percent-pay-package-hike-record-loss-axed-jobs.

April 2016—Engineer, Donald Vidrine, was sentenced to 10 months probation ("BP engineer gets 10 months probation on pollution charge", Associated Press, April 6, 2016, accessed on August 23, 2016 at http://www.nola.com/politics/index.ssf/2016/04/bp_donald_vidrine_oil_spill.html.

Questions

1. What are the costs to other stakeholders in society beyond those that Reuters included? How would these costs be estimated?
2. Has the cost of lost reputation been included by Reuters? If not, how could it be estimated?
3. Since there are so many uncertainties involved in analyses such as Reuters presented, are analyses like this useful? Why or why not?
4. Calculate the discounted value of BP's estimated lost production for an appropriate time horizon using reasonable assumptions for discount rate and price of a barrel of oil. Justify your assumptions.
5. Why were BP's early estimates so low? After all, as Reuters reports, BP had experience with two other recent cases.

ETHICS CASE

Tylenol Recalls (2010): It's Still About Reputation

Johnson & Johnson (J & J) enjoyed a halo effect for many decades after their iconic precautionary recall of Tylenol capsules in 1982, which was greatly facilitated by the famous Johnson & Johnson Credo[1] that stipulated patient well-being to be paramount in importance. But that halo has now been lost due to the events that led to the company's recall of children's Tylenol and other children's medicines in 2009 and 2010.

On April 30, 2010, J & J's McNeil Consumer Healthcare, LLC (McNeil Division), "recalled some 50 children's versions of non-prescription drugs, including Tylenol, Motrin and Benadryl."[2] In total, 136 million bottles of liquid were involved.[3] This was the fourth recall in seven months. Earlier recalls included the following:

- November 2009—five lots of Tylenol Arthritis Pain 100 count with the EZ-open cap due to reports of an unusual moldy, musty, or mildew-like odor that led to some cases of nausea, stomach pain, vomiting, and diarrhea.
- December 2009—November recall expanded to all lots of the product.
- January 2010—an undisclosed number of containers of Tylenol, Motrin, and over-the-counter drugs after consumers complained of feeling sick from an unusual odor.[4]

The McNeil Division had four plants including those at Fort Washington, Pennsylvania (operated as a joint venture with Merck & Co.), and Las Piedras, Puerto Rico. J & J shut down the Fort Washington plant in April 2010 just before an unannounced inspection from the U.S. Food and Drug Administration (FDA). But according to the FDA Statement to the Committee of Oversight and Government Reform of the U.S. House of Representatives on May 21, 2010,[5] FDA concerns over the company's manufacturing processes began several years earlier.

The FDA is responsible for ensuring that companies manufacture and distribute drugs that are safe for consumers in accordance with current Good Manufacturing

---

[1] See Johnson & Johnson's Credo in Chapter 5, page 274.

[2] Parija Kavilanz, "'Shocking' Conditions at Tylenol Plant," CNNMoney.com, May 14, 2010, accessed May 14, 2010, from http://money.cnn.com/2010/05/14/news/companies/tylenol_recall_plant_conditions.

[3] "Johnson and Johnson's Recall of Children's Tylenol and Other Children's Medicines." Statement of Joshua M. Sharfstein, principal deputy commissioner, U.S. FDA, before the Committee of Oversight and Government Reform, U.S. House of Representatives, May, 27, 2010, http://www.fda.gov/NewsEvents/Testimony/ucm213640.htm.

[4] Kavilanz, "'Shocking' Conditions at Tylenol Plant."

[5] "Johnson and Johnson's Recall of Children's Tylenol and Other Children's Medicines."

Processes (cGMP) that cover minimum requirements for methods, facilities, and controls used in the manufacturing and packaging of the products. According to the FDA Report,

> Under the cGMP regulations, each manufacturer sets specifications for its own products for such factors as potency, stability and purity, and puts in place a quality system that ensures those specifications are met. Critical to the cGMP process is that a company must meet its own standards.
>
> A violation of cGMP does not necessarily mean that a product is hazardous to the public. It does indicate, however, a breakdown in a manufacturer's quality system and is an indication that a company needs to take effective steps to fix the problem promptly.
>
> FDA inspects facilities to ensure compliance with cGMP standards. These inspections occur on average for domestic facilities every two to three years. We increase the frequency of inspections for facilities when warranted by past problems or by products that are difficult to manufacture or are especially high risk.[6]

Prior to 2009, the statement says, the FDA inspections had noted several problems with "laboratory controls, equipment cleaning processes, and a failure to investigate identified problems," but these were "generally fixed." During 2009, the FDA identified several more problems including the following:

- At the Fort Washington plant—failure of McNeil to meet its own standards for an ingredient, microcrystalline cellulose, that required it to use input with no Gram-negative bacteria. The supplier found that some partial lots of a master batch did contain a Gram-negative bacteria known as *B. cepacia*, and although the lots McNeil used did not test positive, none of the partial lots from this batch should have been used. Although the FDA concluded the risk to the public was remote, 8 million bottles of finished product were recalled in August.
- At the Las Piedras, Puerto Rico plant—FDA urging resulted in McNeil investigating year-old complaints about products from the plant having a musty odor and finding that it was attributable to a pesticide (2, 4, 6-tribromoanisole [TBA]) used on wooden storage pallets for empty medication bottles. Again the risk to the public was thought not to be serious for long-term health problems because of the small quantities transferred, although exposure could include nausea, stomach pain, vomiting, and diarrhea. In this case, McNeil should have reported the problem to the FDA within three days of the first reports. The FDA also reported that little is really known about the chemical TBA.

These incidents led the FDA to send a warning letter on January 15, 2010, to McNeil, but upper management at neither McNeil nor J & J responded to ensure timely investigation and resolution of the issues raised. At about the same time, the FDA investigated a report of the death of a six-year-old girl but could not relate her death to any of the company's medications. On February 19, 2010, the FDA called senior officials from McNeill and its parent company J & J to a meeting to give them notice about the patterns of violation of cGMP standards, recent recalls and warning letters, and failure to report information to the FDA in a timely manner. At the meeting, the FDA were told that structural changes, new management, and a new consultant were to be put in place to deal with these problems.

[6] Ibid.

The FDA investigators returned to the Fort Washington plant in April 2010 to find that just days before, it had been shut down because particulates, including acetaminophen, cellulose, nickel, and chromium, had been found in several liquid medications. Moreover, bacteria and particulate counts exceeded the company's cGMP standards, and Tylenol in too high a strength had been manufactured but not sold. Although the particulates were small enough to pass out through the intestinal tract without harm, there was justifiable concern over the lack of appropriate safety-conscious culture and safeguards in place.

The FDA report concluded by indicating that they did not think the public had been subject to any serious health risk, but they were concerned and would be working with management to rectify this issue raised. They were also considering such enforcement actions as seizure, injunction, or criminal penalties. In addition, the FDA stated that they had learned several lessons that would factor into a revision of FDA inspection procedures, linkage of findings at on company site to another such site, and recall procedures.

On July 21, 2010, the FDA released a report on its investigations at another of J & J's plants—this one located in Lancaster, Pennsylvania—that indicated

> a pattern of ignoring rules for manufacturing and quality, failure to investigate problems that could affect the composition of products, carelessness in cleaning and maintaining equipment, and shoddy record-keeping.[7]

The report listed 12 types of violations, including the following:

- "Laboratory controls do not include the establishment of scientifically sound and appropriate test procedures to assure that drug products conform to appropriate standards of identity, strength, quality and purity."
- Procedures to prevent "objectionable microorganisms" from getting into medicines appear not to have been followed.
- "Deviations from written test procedures are not justified."
- Staff were not following up "to determine the causes for repeated mix-up of tablets."
- Written procedures for cleaning and maintenance did not have enough detail about the methods, equipment and materials to be used.
- The plant did not have recent drug production and quality control records readily available to the inspectors, as is required.
- Samples of drug products taken to determine if they met written specifications were not properly identified.
- There was no preventive maintenance program for at least five types of complex manufacturing or testing equipment.[8]

On the day the report was released, J & J's stock dropped 2.5% to $57.12. Estimates of the cost of recalls and the shutdown of the Fort Washington plant were $600 million in 2010. The Fort Washington plant manager had been fired, and 300 to 400 workers had lost their jobs.[9]

Questions

1. Who was really to blame for the lax procedures found?
2. How should this situation be remedied?
3. How could the job done by the FDA be improved?

---

[7] "New FDA Report Shows Multiple Lapses at J & J Plant," Associated Press, CLEVELAND.COM, July 21, 2010, accessed November 16, 2010, from http://www.cleveland.com/business/index.ssf/2010/07/new_fda_report_shows_multiple.html.

[8] Ibid.

[9] Ibid.

4. J & J had lived under a positive halo due to their earlier recall of tainted capsules of Tylenol. Why did J & J people behave differently almost thirty years later?
5. How would the total cost of this debacle be estimated?

ETHICS CASE

Vioxx Decisions—Were They Ethical?[1]

On September 30, 2004, Merck voluntarily withdrew its rheumatoid arthritis drug (Vioxx) from the market due to severe adverse effects observed in many of its users (Exhibit 1). As a result, Merck's share price fell $11.48 (27%) in one day, translating to a market-cap loss of $25.6 billion. On August 19, 2005, the day a Texas jury found Merck liable for the death of a Vioxx user, the company's market cap fell another $5 billion. During this trial, it became apparent that Merck had been profiting from Vioxx during the time it knew Vioxx had serious adverse effects.

Merck had obtained approval from the U.S. Food and Drug Administration (FDA) for its drug Vioxx on May 20, 1999. By 2003, Vioxx was available in more than eighty countries, and sales had soared to over $2.5 billion per year. Concurrently, increasing evidence (including data from Merck's own studies) suggested that those taking Vioxx were at an increased risk of cardiac arrest and stroke. Yet the drug remained on the market until September 2004.

The impact of the withdrawal on Merck's shareholders, management, patients, the FDA, and other stakeholders was dramatic. Public confidence and trust in Merck and other pharmaceutical companies were eroded. In 2005, Merck set aside $970 million to deal with 9,600 lawsuits from more than 18,200 plaintiffs, though some estimated then that Vioxx could cost Merck more than $20 billion to $25 billion. By 2007, there were more than 26,600 lawsuits against Merck from nearly 60,000 plaintiffs. In November of that year, Merck agreed to pay $4.85 billion to families of just under 3,500 people who had died of heart attack or stroke and nearly 33,000 for lesser injuries. Nearly 25,000 of the 59,365 claims resulted in no payment.[2] While the initial settlement was less than the amount some had predicted in 2007, litigation continued, and in 2012 a settlement of nearly $37 million was announced for Canadian individuals or their estates[3] and in 2016 to investors who claimed that Merck's practices had caused them lost income. By 2016, Merck had paid out more than $8.5 billion in lawsuits, including nearly $1 billion in government penalties.[4,5]

In 2004, the FDA followed the Vioxx case with interest and created a website page to provide information and updates at http://www.fda.gov/cder/drug/infopage/COX2/default.htm. On September 30, 2004, when Merck voluntarily withdrew the product, the FDA issued the public health advisory that is reproduced below as Exhibit 1 (http://www.fda.gov/NewsEvents

[1] This case is based on an assignment submitted by Rahbar Rahimpour, one of the author's executive MBA students at the Rotman School of Management. Rahbar gave permission for this use.

[2] David Voreacos and Allen Johnson, "Merck Paid 3,468 Death Claims to Resolve Vioxx Suits," *Bloomberg Business*, July 27, 2010, http://www.bloomberg.com/news/articles/2010-07-27/merck-paid-3-468-death-claims-to-resolve-vioxx-suits.

[3] "Vioxx National Class Action Canada," April 20, 2013, http://vioxxnationalclassaction.ca.

[4] Sophia Pearson and David Voreacos, "Merck to Pay $830 Million to Settle Vioxx Securities Claims." Bloomberg Business, January 15, 2016, http://www.bloomberg.com/news/articles/2016-01-15/merck-to-pay-830-million-to-settle-vioxx-securities-claims; Ed Silverman, "Merck Seeks Sanctions against Expert Witness for Talking to a Journalist," *Wall Street Journal*, June 16, 2014, http://blogs.wsj.com/pharmalot/2014/06/16/merck-seeks-sanctions-against-expert-witness-for-talking-to-a-journalist.

[5] Duff Wilson, "Merck to Pay $950 Million Over Vioxx," *New York Times*, November 22, 2011, http://www.nytimes.com/2011/11/23/business/merck-agrees-to-pay-950-million-in-vioxx-case.html.

/Newsroom/PressAnnouncements/2004/ucm108361.htm) and Vioxx Questions and Answers that can still be found at http://www.fda.gov/drugs/drugsafety/postmarketdrugsafetyinformationforpatientsandproviders/ucm106290.htm.

Two journal references from the period are provided that outline medical issues associated with Vioxx as well as a sample of articles to 2016 that illustrate that Vioxx issues did not end with its withdrawal.

Questions

1. Utilizing the information provided and available on from Web sources, use the ethical decision-making techniques discussed in the chapter to form an opinion about whether Merck's decisions regarding Vioxx were ethical. Show your analysis.
2. In order to protect the public more fully, what should the FDA do given the Vioxx lessons?

Sources: "Cardiovascular Events Associated with Rofecoxib in a Colorectal Adenoma Chemoprevention Trial," *New England Journal of Medicine* 17 (2005): 1092–102, Epub February 15, 2005.

"Comparison of Upper Gastrointestinal Toxicity of Rofecoxib and Naproxen in Patients with Rheumatoid Arthritis," *New England Journal of Medicine* 23 (2000): 1520–28, 2 pp. following 1528.

Jef Feeley, "Merck Pays $23 Million to End Vioxx Drug-Purchase Suits," *Bloomberg Business*, July 19, 2013, http://www.bloomberg.com/news/articles/2013-07-18/merck-pays-23-million-to-end-vioxx-drug-purchase-suits.

EXHIBIT 1 Letter from the FDA Acknowledging Merck's Voluntary Withdrawal of Vioxx

FDA Home Page | Search FDA Site | FDA A-Z Index | Contact FDA

FDA News

FOR IMMEDIATE RELEASE
P04-95
September 30, 2004

Media Inquiries: 301-827-6242
Consumer Inquiries: 888-INFO-FDA

FDA Issues Public Health Advisory on Vioxx as its Manufacturer Voluntarily Withdraws the Product

The Food and Drug Administration (FDA) today acknowledged the voluntary withdrawal from the market of Vioxx (chemical name rofecoxib), a non-steroidal anti-inflammatory drug (NSAID) manufactured by Merck & Co. FDA today also issued a Public Health Advisory to inform patients of this action and to advise them to consult with a physician about alternative medications.

Merck is withdrawing Vioxx from the market after the data safety monitoring board overseeing a long-term study of the drug recommended that the study be halted because of an increased risk of serious cardiovascular events, including heart attacks and strokes, among study patients taking Vioxx compared to patients receiving placebo. The study was being done in patients at risk of developing recurrent colon polyps.

"Merck did the right thing by promptly reporting these findings to FDA and voluntarily withdrawing the product from the market," said Acting FDA Commissioner Dr. Lester M. Crawford. "Although the risk that an individual patient would have a heart attack or stroke related to Vioxx is very small, the study that was halted suggests that, overall, patients taking the drug chronically face twice the risk of a heart attack compared to patients receiving a placebo."

Dr. Crawford added that FDA will closely monitor other drugs in this class for similar side effects. "All of the NSAID drugs have risks when taken chronically, especially of gastrointestinal bleeding, but also liver and kidney toxicity. They should only be used continuously under the supervision of a physician."

FDA approved Vioxx in 1999 for the reduction of pain and inflammation caused by osteoarthritis, as well as for acute pain in adults and for the treatment of menstrual pain. It was the second of a new kind of NSAID (Cox-2 selective) approved by FDA. Subsequently, FDA approved Vioxx to treat the signs and symptoms of rheumatoid arthritis in adults and children.

At the time that Vioxx and other Cox-2 selective NSAIDs were approved, it was hoped that they would have a lower risk of gastrointestinal ulcers and bleeding than other NSAIDs (such as ibuprofen and naproxen). Vioxx is the only NSAID demonstrated to have a lower rate of these side effects.

Merck contacted FDA on September 27, 2004, to request a meeting and to advise the agency that the long-term study of Vioxx in patients at increased risk of colon polyps had been halted. Merck and FDA officials met the next day, September 28, and during that meeting the company informed FDA of its decision to remove Vioxx from the market voluntarily.

In June 2000, Merck submitted to FDA a safety study called VIGOR (Vioxx Gastrointestinal Outcomes Research) that found an increased risk of serious cardiovascular events, including heart attacks and strokes, in patients taking Vioxx compared to patients taking naproxen. After reviewing the results of the VIGOR study and other available data from controlled clinical trials, FDA consulted with its Arthritis Advisory Committee in February 2001 regarding the clinical interpretation of this new safety information. In April 2002, FDA implemented labeling changes to reflect the findings from the VIGOR study. The labeling changes included information about the increase in risk of cardiovascular events, including heart attack and stroke.

Recently other studies in patients taking Vioxx have also suggested an increased risk of cardiovascular events. FDA was in the process of carefully reviewing these results, to determine whether further labeling changes were warranted, when Merck informed the agency of the results of the new trial and its decision to withdraw Vioxx from the market.

Additional information about this withdrawal of Vioxx, as well as questions and answers for patients, is available online at http://www.fda.gov/drugs/drugsafety/postmarketdrugsafetyinformationforpatientsandproviders/ucm106290.htm.

Just Make the Numbers!

ETHICS CASE

The discussion between Don Chambers, the CEO, and Ron Smith, the CFO, was getting heated. Sales and margins were below expectations, and the stock market analysts had been behaving like sharks when other companies' published quarterly or annual financial results failed to reach analysts' expectations. Executives of companies whose performance numbers failed to meet the levels projected by the executives or the analysts were being savaged. Finally, in frustration, Don exclaimed,

> We must make our quarterly numbers! Find a way, change some assumptions, capitalize some line expenses—just do it! You know things will turn around next year.

And he stormed out of Ron's office.

Question

1. What should Ron consider when making his decision?

ETHICS CASE

Smokers Are Good for the Economy—Really[1]

Antismoking advocates cheered in the summer of 1997 when the U.S. tobacco industry agreed to pay out more than U.S. $368.5 billion to settle lawsuits brought by forty states seeking compensation for cigarette-related Medicaid costs. Mississippi Attorney General Mike Moore, who helped organize the states' legal campaign, called the pact "the most historic public health achievement in history." But were the states right to do what they did?

The fundamental premise of lawsuits and other antitobacco initiatives is that smokers—and, hence, tobacco companies —place an added tax on all of us by heaping extra costs onto public health care systems. The argument is that those and other social costs outweigh the billions in duty and tax revenue that our governments collect from cigarette distribution.

But a basic actuarial analysis of that premise suggests that quite the opposite is true. As ghoulish as it may sound, smokers save the rest of us money because they die sooner and consume far less in health care and in benefits such as pensions. The extra costs they do generate are far outweighed by the subsidies they pay each time they plunk down their money for a pack of cigarettes.

First of all, let's look at life expectancy consistently over the past decade. In 1994, testimony before the U.S. Senate Finance Committee of the U.S. Office of Technology Assessment showed that the average smoker dies fifteen years earlier than a nonsmoker, so smokers cost society less in health care bills than nonsmokers because they die about a decade earlier. The longer a person lives, the more it costs to treat him or her, especially since the vast majority of health care costs occur in the last few years of life.

One of the paradoxes of modern medicine is that advances in treatments that extend lives have actually increased lifetime health care costs. People who would have died from an acute illness during their working life in the past are now enjoying lengthy retirements and suffering various debilitating diseases that require high-cost medical intervention. According to an expert, former Colorado governor Richard Lamm, director of the Center for Public Policy and Contemporary Issues at the University of Denver, the average nonsmoker is treated for seven major illnesses during his or her lifetime. The average smoker survives only two major illnesses.

So how much more do nonsmokers add to the national health care bill than smokers? One of the best studies is by Duke University economist Kip Viscusi,[2] who conducted an exhaustive comparative analysis in 1994 for a conference on tax policy

[1] This case was taken substantially, with permission, from an article written by John Woolsey, a prominent actuary who has been involved in the study of the costs of health care. The article, "Society's Windfall Profit from Smokers," was published in the *Ottawa Citizen* on August 4, 1998.

[2] W. Kip. Viscusi, "Cigarette Taxation and the Social Consequences of Smoking," *Tax Policy and the Economy* 1995: 51–101.

hosted by the National Bureau of Economic Research in Washington, D.C.

Viscusi concluded that smokers, in essence, subsidize the health care costs of nonsmokers. Using government statistics, Viscusi calculated the medical costs of tobacco by adding up things like the percentage of patient days for lung cancer treatment in hospitals that can be attributed to smoking and burn injuries and deaths from fires started by mislaid cigarettes. Viscusi then took into account other costs—by dying younger, smokers deprive society of income tax. Viscusi even added a charge for costs related to secondhand smoke. Viscusi then calculated how much tobacco saves society. Because they receive considerably fewer payments from government and employer pension plans and other retirement benefits and consume fewer drug benefits, nursing home, and hospital dollars, he estimates that the average American smoker saves society on each pack of cigarettes sold in the United States, leaving a net surplus of 31 cents over the costs attributable to smoking (see 3% discount column below). Adding the 80 cents per package in taxes that American smokers pay brings the total surplus to $1.11 for every pack of smokes.

Other experts have argued that there is a loss of productivity to society because smokers take more sick days than nonsmokers. But is this cost borne by the economy as a whole or by individual smokers whose absences mean that they will not reach their full earnings potential due to missed job promotions and merit pay? The bottom line in all this is that an actuarial approach shows that the facts do not support current political claims about the cost of smoking. Smokers actually leave the economy better off and should be encouraged, not discouraged through taxes, restrictions, and lawsuits.

Questions

1. What can an ethical analysis add to Viscusi's actuarial analysis?
2. Would an ethical analysis change the conclusion reached? Why?

External Insurance Costs per Pack of Cigarettes

	1993 COST ESTIMATE DISCOUNT RATE			1993 COST ESTIMATE WITH TAR ADJUSTMENT DISCOUNT RATE		
	0%	**3%**	**5%**	**0%**	**3%**	**5%**
Costs						
Medical care <65	0.288	0.326	0.357	0.330	0.373	0.410
Medical care ≥65	0.375	0.172	0.093	0.384	0.177	0.096
Total medical care	0.663	0.498	0.451	0.715	0.550	0.505
Sick leave	0.003	0.012	0.019	0.000	0.013	0.020
Group life insurance	0.222	0.126	0.084	0.241	0.136	0.091
Nursing home care	20.584	20.221	20.074	20.599	20.226	20.076
Retirement pension	22.660	21.099	20.337	22.886	21.193	20.365
Fires	0.014	0.016	0.018	0.014	0.016	0.018
Taxes on earnings	0.771	0.351	0.107	0.883	0.402	0.122
Total net costs	21.571	20.317	0.268	21.633	20.302	0.315

Source: W. Kip Viscusi, "Cigarette Taxation and the Social Consequences of Smoking," *Tax Policy and the Economy*, National Bureau of Economic Research (1995): 74.

ETHICS CASE

Ford Pinto[1]

In order to meet strong competition from Volkswagen as well as other foreign domestic subcompacts, Lee Iacocca, then president of Ford Motor Co., decided to introduce a new vehicle by 1970, to be known as the Pinto. The overall objective was to produce a car at or below 2,000 pounds with a price tag of $2,000 or less. Although preproduction design and testing normally requires about three and a half years and the arrangement of actual production somewhat longer, design was started in 1968 and production commenced in 1970.

The Pinto project was overseen by Robert Alexander, vice president of car engineering, and was approved by Ford's Product Planning Committee, consisting of Iacocca, Alexander, and Ford's group vice president of car engineering, Harold MacDonald. The engineers throughout Ford who worked on the project "signed off" to their immediate supervisors, who did likewise in turn to their superiors, and so on to Alexander and MacDonald and, finally, Iacocca.

Many reports were passed up the chain of command during the design and approval process, including several outlining the results of crash tests and a proposal to remedy the tendency for the car to burst into flames when rear-ended at twenty-one miles per hour. This tendency was caused by the placement of the car's gas tank between the rear axle and the rear bumper such that a rear-end collision was likely to drive the gas tank forward to rupture on a flange and bolts on a rear axle housing for the differential. The ruptured tank would then spew gas into the passenger compartment to be ignited immediately by sparks or a hot exhaust.

Ford's Cost–Benefit Analysis

SAVINGS	UNIT COST	TOTAL
Benefits:		
180 burn deaths	$200,000	$36,000,000
180 serious burn injuries	67,000	12,060,000
2,100 burned vehicles	700	1,470,000
Total benefits		$49,530,000
Costs:		
Number of units		
11 million cars	11	$121,000,000
1.5 million light trucks	11	16,500,000
Total costs		$137,500,000

Fatality Payment Component

FATALITY PAYMENT COMPONENT	1971 COSTS
Future productivity losses	
Direct	$132,000
Indirect	41,300
Medical costs	
Hospital	700
Other	425
Property damage	1,500
Insurance administration	4,700
Legal and court	3,000
Employer losses	1,000
Victim's pain and suffering	10,000
Funeral	900
Assets (lost consumption)	5,000
Miscellaneous	200
Total per fatality	$200,725

[1] More comprehensive cases on the Pinto problem can be found in T. Donaldson and A. R. Gini, *Case Studies in Business Ethics* (Englewood Cliffs, NJ: Prentice Hall, 1992), 174–83 (original case by W. M. Hoffman), and M. G. Valasquez, *Business Ethics: Concepts and Cases* (Englewood Cliffs, NJ: Prentice Hall, 1988), 119–123.

The remedies available to Ford included mounting the gas tank above the rear axle, which would cut down on trunk space, or installing a rubber bladder in the gas tank. Ford experimented with the installation of rubber bladders but apparently decided they were not cost effective. Later, as part of a successful lobby effort against government regulations for mandatory crash tests (crash tests were delayed eight years, until 1977), Ford's cost–benefit analysis came to light in a company study titled "Fatalities Associated with Crash-Induced Fuel Leakage and Fires." As the details previously outlined show, the costs of installing the rubber bladder vastly exceeded the benefits.

Ford took the $200,000 figure for the cost of a death from a study of the National Highway Traffic Safety Administration, which used the estimates in the table on the previous page.

Questions

1. Was the decision not to install the rubber bladder appropriate? Use the 5-question framework to support your analysis.
2. What faults can you identify in Ford's cost–benefit analysis?
3. Should Ford have given its Pinto customers the option to have the rubber bladder installed during production for, say, $20?

ETHICS CASE

The Kardell Paper Co.

Background

The Kardell paper mill was established at the turn of the century on the Cherokee River in southeastern Ontario by the Kardell family. By 1985, the Kardell Paper Co. had outgrown its original mill and had encompassed several facilities in different locations, generating total revenues of $1.7 billion per year. The original mill continued to function and was the firm's largest profit center. The Kardell family no longer owned shares in the firm, which had become a publicly traded company whose shares were widely held.

Kardell Paper Co. was a firm with a record of reporting good profits and had a policy of paying generous bonuses to the chief executive officer and other senior executives.

Kardell's original mill was located near Riverside, a community of 22,000. Riverside was largely dependent on the mill, which employed 500 people. The plant, while somewhat outdated, was still reasonably efficient and profitable. It was not designed with environmental protection in mind, and the waste water that discharged into the Cherokee River was screened only to remove the level of contaminants required by provincial regulation. There were other industrial plants upstream from the Kardell plant.

The residential community of Riverside, five miles downstream from the plant, was home to many of the Kardell plant's management, including Jack Green, a young engineer with two children, ages one and four.

Jack, who was assistant production manager at the Kardell plant, was sensitive to environmental issues and made a point of keeping up on the latest paper mill technology. Jack monitored activity at the plant's laboratory, which in 1985 employed a summer student to conduct tests on water quality in the Cherokee River immediately downstream from the plant.

These tests were taken across the entire width of the river. The tests conducted nearest the plant's discharge pipe showed high readings of an industrial chemical called sonox. Farther away from the plant and on the opposite shore of the river, the water showed only small trace amounts of sonox. Sonox was used in the manufacture of a line of bleached kraft paper that Kardell had begun to make at its plant in recent years.

The Issue

The student researcher discovered that the plant lab was not including the high readings of sonox in its monthly reports to management, so the student showed the complete records to Jack. In the summer of 1985, Jack made a report to the CEO with a recommendation that in-depth studies be conducted into the situation and its implications for public health and long-term effects on the ecology.

In recommending that Kardell carry out an "environmental audit" of its operations, Jack pointed out that local doctors in Riverside had been expressing concern over what appeared to be an unusually high rate of miscarriages and respiratory disorders in the community. Jack told the CEO there were data suggesting a possible link between health problems and sonox but no definite proof. Medical research into sonox's possible effects on humans was continuing.

In bringing his concerns to the CEO's attention, Jack offered as a possible solution the option of Kardell adopting a new processing technology which used recycling techniques for waste water. This technology, already employed by a handful of plants in Europe, enabled a plant to operate in a "closed cycle" that not only protected the environment but reclaimed waste material, which was then sold to chemical producers. Thus, in the long term the new process was cost-effective. In the short run, however, refitting the existing Kardell plant to incorporate the new technology would cost about $70 million, and, during the retrofit, the plant would have to operate at reduced capacity levels for about a year and possibly be closed down altogether for an additional year to make the change-over.

The Response

Kardell's traditional response to environmental concerns was reactive. The company took its cues from the regulatory climate. That is, the provincial environment ministry would apply control orders on the plant as new limits on emissions of various compounds came into effect, and Kardell would then comply with these orders.

In raising his concerns in 1985, Jack pointed out that the Ministry of Environment, responding to the serious nature of concerns raised by the sonox issue, was considering internal proposals from its staff that additional research be done into the sources and implications of sonox. Given the early stage of work in this area, Jack could offer no indication of when, if ever, the Ministry would enact new regulations to do with sonox. He argued, however, that the ground rules might change, as they had with previous compounds, and that Kardell should give some thought to the worst-case scenario of how the sonox issue could turn out down the road.

Kardell's CEO was sympathetic to the concerns raised by Jack, a valued employee of the company who had proved himself in the past by identifying many cost-efficiency measures. The CEO felt obliged, however, to match Jack's concerns about sonox against the substantial cost of refitting the plant. The CEO felt there simply was not enough data upon which to base such an important decision, and he was wary of any external force that attempted to influence the company's affairs. The CEO told Jack, "We simply can't let these 'greens' tell us how to run our business."

While the CEO did not feel it would be appropriate for Kardell to adopt the recommendations in Jack's report, the CEO did take the step of presenting the report to the board of directors, for discussion in the fall of 1985.

Kardell's board of directors represented a cross-section of interest groups. Everyone on the board felt a responsibility toward the shareholders, but, in addition, some members of the board also paid special attention to community and labor concerns. The board was composed of the CEO and president of the firm, along with several "outside" directors: two local businesspeople from Riverside, a representative of the paperworkers' union at the plant, a mutual fund manager whose firm held a large block of Kardell shares on behalf of the fund's investors, an economist, a Riverside city councillor, and the corporation's legal counsel.

Each member of the board spoke to Jack's report from his or her perspective. The Riverside representatives—the city councillor and the two businesspeople—wanted assurances that the community was not in any danger. But they also said, in the absence of any firm proof of danger, that they were satisfied Kardell probably was not a source of harmful emissions.

The lawyer pointed out that legally Kardell was in the clear: it was properly observing all existing regulations on emission levels; in any case, there was no clear indication that the Kardell mill was the only source of sonox emissions into the Cherokee River. While acknowledging the health concerns that had recently arisen over sonox, the lawyer thought it prudent to wait for the government to establish an acceptable limit for sonox emissions. Besides, the lawyer added, while liability actions had been initiated against two or three other mills producing sonox, these claims had been denied through successful defense actions in court on the grounds of lack of clear evidence of a significant health hazard.

The labor representative expressed concern about any compound that might affect the health of Kardell employees living in the area. But the labor official also had to think about the short-term consideration of job loss at the plant and the fact that, with the plant shut down, there were few other employment opportunities in the area to fill the gap. The board representatives from Riverside pointed out that, obviously, the local economy would be severely affected by the shutdown to refit the plant. And the mutual fund manager agreed with the CEO that, at least in the short term, Kardell's profitability and share price would suffer from a decision to undertake a costly overhaul of the facility.

The Decision

After much debate, the board decided to defer consideration of Jack's proposals pending the results of government research into this issue. It also asked Jack to continue monitoring the regulatory climate so that the plant would always be in basic compliance with provincial emission standards.

During the next two years, Jack presented similar warnings to the board regarding sonox and continued to meet with the same response. As a precautionary measure, he kept copies of his reports in his own files so there could never be any question of the timing or substance of his warnings to the board. During this same period, an above-average incidence of miscarriages, birth defects, and respiratory ailments was reported in the Riverside area.

Questions

1. Who are the stakeholders involved, and what are their interests?
2. Which stakeholders and interests are the most important? Why?
3. What was wrong with the quality of the board of directors' debate?
4. What is the downside if the right decision is not made? Consider economic factors and also what Jack might do.

Source: The Kardell Case was prepared by David Olive, Graham H. Tucker, Tim J. Leech, and David Sparling, *Agenda for Action Conference Proceedings* (Toronto: Canadian Center for Ethics & Corporate Policy, 1990), 20–21. Reprinted with the permission of the Canadian Center for Ethics & Corporate Policy.

5

Corporate Ethical Governance & Accountability

PURPOSE OF THE CHAPTER

Businesses, directors, executives, and professional accountants are facing increasingly demanding expectations from shareholders and other stakeholders for what organizations are doing and how they are doing it. At the same time, the environments that organizations operate in are increasingly complex, as are their ethical challenges. Organizational governance and accountability mechanisms are therefore under considerable strain, and improvement is highly desirable. It is in the best long-run interest of all concerned that they focus on the development of a culture of integrity.

Trial-and-error decision making involves too high a risk of unfortunate consequences for the reputation and achievement of strategic objectives of the organization, the profession, the employees, and the professional accountants. Consequently, the leaders of organizations, the accounting profession, and firms are expected to put in place governance programs that provide adequate ethical guidance and accountability programs that satisfy expectations. Even though the introduction of ethical governance and accountability programs is voluntary, and some organizations will never do so, those directors, executives, and professional accountants who wish to reduce the risks involved in ethical malfeasance and enjoy the benefits of continuing stakeholder support will.

Directors, executives, and professional accountants all have essential roles to play in the emerging framework for ethical governance and accountability. They are all serving mostly the same set of expectations but have different levels of duty and responsibility. This chapter deals with both the common and the distinct aspects related to each role. First, the emerging framework is developed, and then common threats to good governance are discussed, followed by matters related to the corporation and those relating to professional accountants.

MODERN GOVERNANCE & ACCOUNTABILITY FRAMEWORK—TO SHAREHOLDERS & OTHER STAKEHOLDERS

New Expectations—New Framework to Restore Credibility

Chapter 1 explained the concerns that organizations, and particularly corporations, are facing with regard to what they are doing and how they are doing it. Even before the credibility crisis in 2002 and the 2008 financial crisis, the public was pressing corporations over misleading financial reports and scandals; protection of the environment, worker, customer, and human rights; instances of bribery, undue influence, and incredible greed; and failure to govern within the bounds expected by stakeholders and to be accountable to them.

Stakeholders found that they could have significant impacts on a corporation's consumer markets, capital markets, and on the support offered to the corporation by other stakeholder groups, such as employees and lenders. A corporation's reputation could be significantly affected by irate stakeholders. Directors and executives watching boycotts, reduced revenue and profit streams, or turn-downs by outstanding recruits or employees found that the support of stakeholders was essential to the optimal achievement of medium- and long-term corporate objectives. Some directors and executives wanted that support, and with the help of academics and others, a new governance and accountability framework was developed, complete with new tools and techniques.

At the beginning of the century were the Enron, Arthur Andersen, and WorldCom debacles. They showed the world the faults and vulnerabilities inherent in the old-style shareholder-only governance and accountability model. The credibility of North American corporations, professional accountants, and capital markets was so severely eroded in the minds of the public that President George W. Bush and business leaders had to call repeatedly for reforms. Finally, as described in Chapter 2, the U.S. Congress and Senate were galvanized to rise above partisan politics to amalgamate two proposals and pass the *Sarbanes-Oxley Act of 2002* (SOX), within one month and a few days after WorldCom's declaration of bankruptcy.

SOX has reformed the governance and accountability framework for corporations wishing to raise funds from the U.S. public and/or have their shares traded on U.S. stock markets. The framework laid out in SOX has been put in place by the Securities and Exchange Commission (SEC). It applies to SEC registrants and to the professional accountants and outside lawyers who serve them. This means, for example, that all U.S. companies, plus those from other countries (including over 250 of Canada's largest) whose securities are traded on U.S. markets, have to comply, as do their professional accountants and outside lawyers. The SOX framework also applies to other foreign corporations and their auditors and legal advisors. Over time, it has become the standard on which governance and accountability frameworks around the world are based.

Expectations from decades of stakeholder concerns and about the immediate need to restore credibility have given rise to the new framework of governance and accountability. SOX represented a response to an acceleration of stakeholder concerns brought on by the scandals that affected the lives of investors, and particularly pensioners, employees and their dependents, and many others. In the end, the shortfall in expected behavior was so egregious that only quick reform—a new framework—could restore the necessary trust in corporate governance and accountability.

The continuing pattern of scandals after 2002 that are described in Chapter 2, such as the Madoff fraud and the subprime lending fiasco, have served to further strengthen the desire for better and more ethical governance and accountability. This has reinforced the commitment of leading-edge firms around the world to appreciate, develop, and maintain *a culture of integrity* as a necessary foundation of good governance and accountability.[1]

An appreciation of why and how public pressures have changed governance expectations should be based on a broad understanding of what governance means and how it is put into practice. A general overview of corporate governance is provided for that purpose.

[1] The *Dodd-Frank Wall Street Reform and Consumer Protection Act* was enacted in 2010 to bring better integrity, accountability, and governance to the U.S. bank and near-bank industry following the subprime lending scandal.

Corporate Governance Overview

Corporations are usually created to serve specific purposes as: *for-profit corporations, not-for-profit corporations*, or other entities such as trusts. They are created as legal "persons" under the incorporating statutes of jurisdictions, such as a state or province or federally, and they are evidenced by a charter or letters patent that describe the legal name, rights granted (i.e., to do business or pursue other objectives), and duties expected of the company (i.e., have an annual general meeting of shareholders, provide annual financial statements and auditor's report to the meeting, explain shareholder voting rights, elect directors, hold bank accounts, negotiate loans, and so on).

In the United States, in thirty states and in the District of Columbia, it is possible for a for-profit corporation to be created as a *benefit*, or *B, corporation.*[2] At incorporation, these companies include as their legal goals the creation of a positive impact on society, workers, the community, and the environment in addition to profit. The intent is to make clear to any shareholder, or other stakeholder, that they are not simply pursuing maximum profit in the traditional sense. Alternatively, it should be noted that it is possible for any for-profit company to apply for a designation as a Certified B Corporation (B Corp) at any time after incorporation from the nonprofit organization B Lab if the company agrees to declare that it will strive for "rigorous standards of social and environmental performance, accountability, and transparency."[3] An example of B Corp activity for CarShare Atlantic can be found at http://www.bcorporation.net/community/carshare-atlantic on the www.bcorporation.net website.

Regardless of the nature of the corporation, all have a governance process with many of the characteristics and requirements noted below.

Governance of shareholder-controlled corporations refers to the oversight, monitoring, and controlling of a company's activities and personnel to ensure support of the shareholders' interests, in accordance with laws and the expectations of stakeholders. Governance has been more formally defined by the Organisation for Economic Cooperation and Development (OECD) as follows:

> a set of relationships between a company's management, its board, its shareholders, and other stakeholders. Corporate governance also provides the structure through which the objectives of the company are set, and the means of attaining those objectives and monitoring performance are determined. Good corporate governance should provide proper incentives for the board and management to pursue objectives that are in the interests of the company and its shareholders and should facilitate effective monitoring.[4]

The typical framework for governance relationships for shareholder-owned corporations is presented in Figure 5.1.

The role and mandate of the board of directors is of paramount importance in the governance framework. Typically, the directors are elected by the shareholders at their annual meeting, which is held to receive the company's audited annual financial statements and the audit report thereon, as well as the comments of the chairman of the board, the senior company officers, and the company auditor.

The company directors have traditionally been charged with representing and protecting the interests of the shareholders. Prior to the serial U.S. bankruptcies of Enron

[2] For further information, see BenefitCorp.net, http://benefitcorp.net/, and the Benefit Corporation Gateway at DePaul University, http://driehaus.depaul.edu/about/centers-and-institutes/institute-for-business-and-professional-ethics/Pages/Benefit-Corporations.aspx.

[3] See the website of the B Lab at https://www.bcorporation.net/what-are-b-corps.

[4] *OECD Principles of Corporate Governance*, April 2004, Preamble, accessed February 4, 2013, at http://www.oecd.org/daf/corporateaffairs/corporategovernanceprinciples/31557724.pdf.)

FIGURE 5.1 **Governance Structures & Relationships**

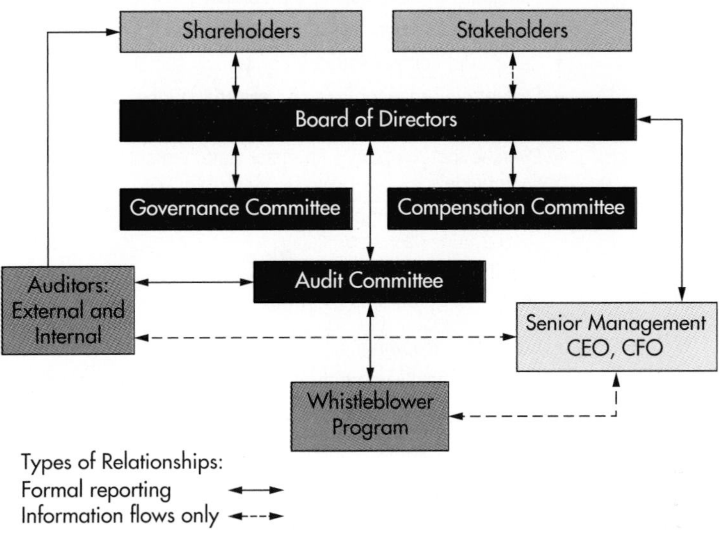

Corporation and WorldCom that led to the stock market collapse in 2002, boards of directors were expected to fulfill the functional responsibilities noted on the first line of Table 5.1. The ensuing governance and accountability credibility crisis was caused primarily by these bankruptcies. In turn, it triggered the enactment of SOX, which proposed several improvements in the governance framework. The ensuing discussion and analysis of ethical aspects involved in these and later cases of governance failure, including the subprime lending fiasco of 2008, have generated the additional governance responsibilities noted in Table 5.1 that directors are expected to ensure are effective.

In addition, however, it is important to note that in a growing number of jurisdictions, directors are legally required or permitted to take stakeholders interests into account. As subsequent discussion will show, this has always been an excellent business strategy. In summary, *directors are now understood to have legal responsibility to shareholders but are also expected to be responsive to stakeholder needs in a strategic sense while discharging these legal responsibilities.*

A board of directors often divides itself into subcommittees that concentrate more deeply in specific areas than time would allow the whole board to pursue. These subcommittees are charged with certain actions and/or reviews on behalf of the whole board, with the proviso that the whole board must be briefed on major matters and must vote on major decisions. Usually, at least three subcommittees are created to review matters related to (1) governance, (2) compensation, and (3) audit and to present their recommendations to the full board. The Governance Committee deals with codes of conduct and company policy, as well as the allocation of duties among the subcommittees of the board. The Compensation Committee reviews the performance of senior officers and makes recommendations on the nature and size of salaries, bonuses, and related remuneration plans. The Audit Committee reviews internal controls and systems that generate financial reports prepared by management, the appropriateness of those financial reports, the effectiveness of the company's internal and external auditors, its whistleblowing systems, and their findings and recommends the reelection (or not) of the company's external auditors. The board must approve the selection of a CEO, and many boards

TABLE 5.1 Directors' Functional Responsibilities

- Safeguard the interests of the company's shareholders.
- Review overall business strategy, and in some jurisdictions take stakeholder interests into account.
- Select and compensate the company's senior executives.
- Evaluate internal controls and external auditor and recommend the company's outside auditor for election by the shareholders.
- Oversee the company's financial statements and recommend them to the board for transmission to the shareholders.
- Monitor overall company performance.

Adapted from the Report on the Role of the Board of Directors in the Collapse of Enron, U.S. Senate Permanent Subcommittee on Investigations, July 8, 2002.

- Ensure the following:
  - An effective system of internal controls and internal audit
  - An effective whistleblower system reporting to the audit committee
  - Effectiveness of the company's risk management program
  - Efficacy of the company's ethical corporate culture

SOX and Recent Governance Expectations

Summary: Legal accountability to shareholders; strategic accountability also to stakeholders

are now approving the appointment of the CFO because of the important of that position. Generally, the CEO appoints other senior executives, and they, in turn, appoint the executives who report to them.

Members of these committees are selected for their expertise, interest, and character, with *the expectation that the independent judgment of each director will be exercised in the best interest of the company as a whole.* For example, members of the Audit Committee must be financially literate and have sufficient expertise to understand audit and financial matters. They must be of independent mind (i.e., not be part of management or be relying on management for a significant portion of their annual revenue) and must be prepared to exercise that independence by voting for the interest of all shareholders, not only those of management or of specific limited shareholder groups.

Several behavioral expectations are noted in Table 5.2, and these extend to all directors.

All directors are expected to demonstrate certain fiduciary[5] duties. Shareholders are relying on directors to serve shareholders' interests, not the directors' own interests, nor those of management or a third party. This means that directors must exercise their own independent judgment in the best interest of the company, which includes the interests of shareholders as well as other stakeholders. The directors must do so in good faith (with true purpose, not deceit) on all occasions. They must exercise appropriate skill, diligence, and an expected level of care in all their actions.

Obviously, there will be times when directors will be able to make significant sums of money by misusing the trust with which they have been bestowed and at the expense of the other shareholders of the company. At these times, a director's interests may conflict with those of the other shareholders. Therefore, care must be taken to ensure that such conflicts are disclosed and that they are managed so that no harm comes to the

[5] A fiduciary is a person who has undertaken to act on behalf of another person who must trust and have confidence in the fiduciary to act in their best interest due to a personal lack of knowledge or other vulnerability.

TABLE 5.2 Directors' Behavioral Expectations

Fiduciary Duties

- Acting in the best interest of the company (shareholders and stakeholders)
- Loyalty to be demonstrated by independent judgment
- Actions to be in good faith, obedient to the interests of all
- Actions demonstrate due care, diligence, and skill (i.e., financial literacy)

Adapted from Statement of Corporate Governance, The Business Roundtable (September 1997).

Conflicts

- Require disclosure, and actions to manage effectively

Liability Issues

- Business Judgment Rule
- Oppression remedy
- Personal liability for Tort Claims

Responsibilities of Directors in Canada, Torys LLP, 2009.

other shareholders. For example, if a director has an interest in some property or a company that is being purchased, he or she should disclose this to the other directors and refrain from voting on the acquisition. These actions should alert other directors to the potential self-dealing of the conflicted director and thereby avoid the nonconflicted directors from being misled into thinking that the conflicted director was acting only with the corporation's interests in mind.

From time to time, directors may be sued by shareholders or third parties who believe that the directors have failed to live up to appropriate expectations. However, courts will not second-guess reasonable decisions by nonconflicted directors that have been taken prudently and on a reasonably informed basis. This is known as the *Business Judgment Rule*,[6] and it protects directors charged with breach of their duty of care if they have acted honestly and reasonably.

Even if no breach of legal rights has occurred, shareholders may charge that their interests have been oppressed (i.e., prejudiced unfairly or unfairly disregarded) by a corporation or a director's actions, and courts may grant what is referred to as an *oppression remedy* of financial compensation of other sanctions against the corporation or the director personally. If, however, the director has not been self-dealing or misappropriating the company's opportunities,[7] he or she will likely be protected from personal liability by the *Business Judgment Rule*.

Some shareholders or third parties have chosen to sue directors "personally in tort[8] for their conduct as directors, even when they have acted in good faith and within the scope of their duties, and when they believed they were acting in the best interests of the corporations they serve."[9] Recently, courts have held that directors cannot escape such personal liability by claiming that they did the action when performing their corporate

[6] Business Judgment Rule; see http://www.law.cornell.edu/wex/business_judgment_rule (accessed February 4, 2013).

[7] Torys LLP, *Responsibilities of Directors in Canada*, 2009, 19.

[8] Tort includes, for example, negligence or negligent misrepresentation; see http://www.law.cornell.edu/wex/tort (accessed February 4, 2013).

[9] Torys LLP, *Responsibilities of Directors in Canada*, 2009, 20.

responsibilities. Consequently, directors or officers must take care when making all decisions that they meet normal standards of behavior.

The impact of recent corporate scandals on the public has been to change governance expectations dramatically. Recognition that most of these fiascos resulted from ethical failures has focused attention on how well a corporation can develop a culture of integrity. The following sections illuminate why this occurred and how a corporation can develop the needed aspects of a culture of integrity, including recognition of stakeholders' interests, identification and management of risks and conflicts of interest, implementation issues, development of codes and guidelines, monitoring ethical performance, and the development ethical leaders.

Accountability to Shareholders or Stakeholders?

The growing capacity of nonshareholder stakeholders to influence the achievement of corporate objectives and their increasing sensitivity made it very attractive for corporations to encourage stakeholder support. The business scandals detailed in Chapter 2 show that corporate activities designed to favor *current* executives, directors, and some shareholders were not necessarily in the interest of future shareholders or current shareholders who wished for long-term success, such as pensioners-investors, employees, lenders, and other stakeholders. So damaging were the actions intended to benefit executives, directors, and investors in the short term that the credibility of the entire corporate governance and accountability process was jeopardized.

The SOX reforms were designed to refocus the governance model on responsibility of directors on their fiduciary duty beyond their own self-interest to that of shareholders as a whole and to the public interest. To quote the Senate Subcommittee[10] that investigated the Enron fiasco:

> **Fiduciary Obligations of Boards of Directors.** In the United States, the Board of Directors sits at the apex of a company's governing structure. A typical Board's duties include reviewing the company's overall business strategy; selecting and compensating the company's senior executives; evaluating the company's outside auditor; overseeing the company's financial statements; and monitoring overall company performance. According to the Business Roundtable, the Board's 'paramount duty' is to safeguard the interests of the company's shareholders.[11]

Directors operate under state laws that impose fiduciary duties on them to act in good faith, with reasonable care, and in the best interest of the corporation and its shareholders. Courts generally discuss three types of fiduciary obligations. As one court put it,

> Three broad duties stem from the fiduciary status of corporate directors: namely, the duties of obedience, loyalty, and due care. The duty of obedience requires a director to avoid committing … acts beyond the scope of the powers of a corporation as defined by its charter or the laws of the state of incorporation.… The duty of loyalty dictates that a director must act in good faith and must not allow his personal interest to prevail over the interests of the corporation.… [T]he duty of care requires a director to be diligent and prudent in managing the corporation's affairs.[12]

---

[10] *Report on the Role of the Board of Directors in the Collapse of Enron*, U.S. Senate Permanent Subcommittee on Investigations, July 8, 2002.

[11] *Statement of Corporate Governance*, The Business Roundtable, September 1997, 3.

[12] *Gearheart Industries v. Smith International*, 741 F.2d 707, 719 (5th Cir. 1984), para. 42.

Given the recurring corporate scandals and the documented capacity of stakeholders to influence the achievement of corporate objectives, it would be well within the directors' duty to safeguard the interests of shareholders and prudent to take into account the interests of stakeholders when creating their governance structure.

Because stakeholder interests can potentially conflict with some shareholder interests, many states have formally modified the statutes by which corporations are created to allow directors to take stakeholder interests into account when appropriate. Directors will have to examine the trade-offs between shareholders and stakeholders and choose one or the other or a blended solution.[13] Fortunately, a longer-term shareholder perspective frequently coincides with stakeholder interests.

Based on the reality of stakeholder pressures and the desire to encourage stakeholder support, corporations realize that they are strategically accountable to stakeholders (if not legally in all jurisdictions) and are governing themselves to minimize the risks and maximize the opportunities inherent in the stakeholder accountability framework. De facto, corporations are increasingly realizing that they are accountable to all of the stakeholders shown in Figure 5.2.

The Shareholder Value Myth[14]

The debate about whether directors and management should serve the interests of shareholders before other those of other stakeholders changed dramatically when Lynn Stout, the Distinguished Professor of Corporate and Business Law at the Cornell Law School, published her book *The Shareholder Value Myth* in 2012. In it, she builds on her ideas and those of Margaret Blair[15] to argue that putting shareholders first harms investors, corporations, and the public.

To support her view, Stout provides documentation that when managers focus on shareholder value, it causes

> managers to focus myopically on short-term earnings reports at the expense of long-term performance, discourages investment and innovation, harms employees, customers, and communities, and causes companies to indulge in reckless, sociopathic, and socially irresponsible behaviors. It threatens the welfare of consumers, employees, communities, and investors, alike.[16]

[13] This is not the case in some jurisdictions. A recent Supreme Court of Canada decision placed the interest of shareholders ahead of the interest of bondholders. BCE Inc. was involved in a $52 billion takeover. The bondholders went to court arguing that the takeover would unreasonably increase the debt load of the company, thereby making their bonds riskier. In a unanimous decision, the Supreme Court reversed a lower-court ruling that threatened to stop the largest leveraged buyout in Canadian history on the basis that the Board of Directors had failed to adequately consider the rights of the bondholders. In reversing the lower-court decision, the Supreme Court implied that bondholders are entitled to receive only what is in the bondholder agreement. According to PoonamPuri, "It seems as through the court is saying that in this context of the sale of the company, the directors have a clear duty to maximize value for the shareholders, and they don't have to consider the interest, rights or expectations of creditors beyond those that have been negotiated." In the case of the BCE takeover, the directors have chosen to support the interest of shareholders over all other stakeholders, and this decision has the approval of the courts (see Sean Silcoff and Carrie Tait, *Financial Post*, June 20, 2008, http://www.financialpost.com/story.html?id5602600). Interestingly, the deal later failed because it failed to meet a key condition of viability in that the increased debt load was forecast by KPMG to be too heavy for BCE to carry (see Theresa Tedesco, "BCE Deal Dead, Telecom Giant Seeks Compensation," Canwest News Service, December 11, 2008, http://www.canada.com/topics/news/story.html?id51061692).

[14] Lynn Stout, *The Shareholder Value Myth* (San Francisco: Berrett-Koehler, 2012).

[15] Margaret Blair is the Milton R. Underwood Chair in Free Enterprise at Vanderbilt Law School.

[16] Stout, *The Shareholder Value Myth*, vi.

FIGURE 5.2 **Map of Corporate Stakeholder Accountability**

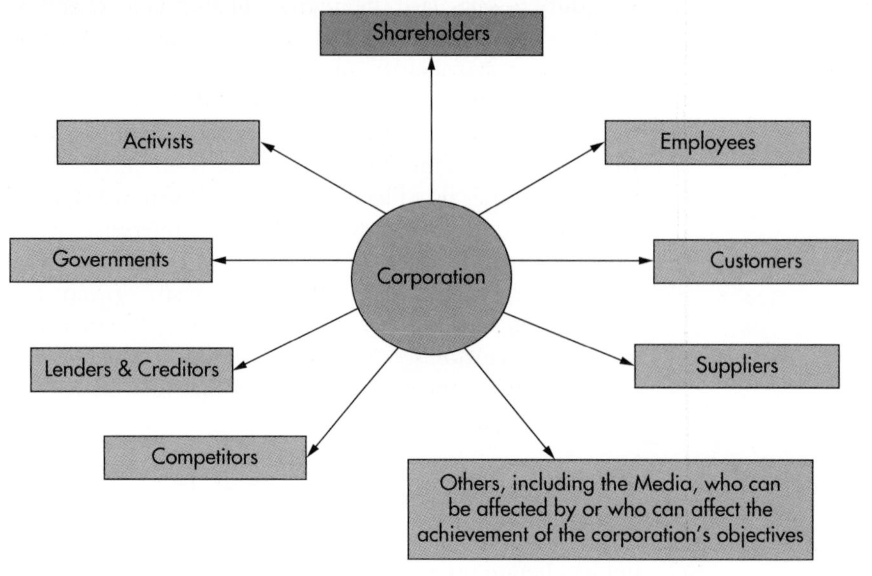

Moreover, based on her review of U.S. law cases, she asserts that "U.S. corporate law does not, in fact, require corporations to maximize either share price or shareholder wealth,"[17] and she concludes that "U.S. corporate law does not, and never has, required public corporations to "maximize shareholder value."[18] In chapter 2 of her book, she reviews several aspects of U.S. corporate law, finally advancing the position that "the *Business Judgment Rule* rules out shareholder primacy":

> In brief, the business judgment rule holds that, so long as a board of directors is not tainted by personal conflicts of interest and makes a reasonable effort to become informed, courts will not second-guess the board's decisions about what is best for the company—even when those decisions seem to harm shareholder value.[19]

Given her analysis, Stout argues that the important question for the future, is how management and directors should take into account and balance the differing interests of company stakeholders when attempting to act in the best interest of the company.

Stout's position fits well with the rationale of this book—that directors and management need to factor the interests of stakeholders into their decisions because they are ultimately accountable to stakeholders in a strategic sense. It is also true that in many jurisdictions, directors are expected to act in the best interests of the company. However, until recently, decisions about corporate actions have turned on whether they serve the interests of shareholders for two reasons: first, because current shareholders, exercising their ownership interest, can vote out and replace the directors, who will then replace the management, and, second, because legal challenges to the actions of directors have been thought to be best based on shareholder value issues.

Thinking has changed, however, and many jurisdictions have altered their statutes under which corporations are created to specifically allow directors to consider interests

[17] Ibid., v.
[18] Ibid., 23.
[19] Ibid., 29.

other than profit when making decisions *in the company's interest.* As this movement grows and logical strategic significance of taking the interests of stakeholders into account becomes better recognized, and ideas of Stout and Blair gain credence, the practice of governance will move more strongly toward the inclusion and balancing of stakeholder interests using the techniques described below.

Governance for Broad Stakeholder Accountability

GOVERNANCE PROCESS BASED ON STAKEHOLDER INTERESTS Once a corporation's directors and/or executives realize that *the corporation is accountable legally to shareholders and strategically to additional stakeholders* who can significantly affect the achievement of its objectives, it becomes logical and desirable that they govern the corporation with the interests of all important stakeholders in mind. Shareholders are, in fact, a stakeholder group—and probably the most important on a continuing basis—but they are no longer the only stakeholder group whose interests should influence corporate actions.

In order to minimize harmful stakeholder reactions and optimize opportunities in the future, corporations should assess how their actions impact on the interests of their important stakeholder groups. This has been the underlying focus for environmental scanning and issues management for decades. What has changed is that *stakeholder impact analysis* has become significantly more developed, as have the tools employed in examining, ranking, and assessing stakeholder interests—to the point that incorporating them into the governance process is now both feasible and desirable.

A schematic of the stakeholder accountability-oriented governance process is shown in Figure 5.3.

In a *stakeholder accountability-oriented governance process,* the board of directors must take all stakeholder interests into account and make sure that they are built into the company's vision, mission, strategy, policies, codes, practices, compliance mechanisms, and feedback arrangements. If this is not done, the company's actions may fail to take important interests into account, and the company may lose the support of one or more stakeholder groups. For example, not enough emphasis on customer value or safety or too much on short-term profit may cost the support of customers. The ethics case *Ford/Firestone Tire Recall* (located at the end of this chapter) or the product safety cases in Chapters 1 and 2 illustrate this problem.

Appropriate guidance reinforced by feedback mechanisms must be given to management and reinforced by an ethical corporate culture, or else management can honestly say that no one told them what boundaries they should be operating within. This guidance will influence the preparation of financial reports and other sources of feedback and also the behavior exhibited in dealings with customers, employees, and other stakeholders.

The board of directors may be advised by several employees, professionals, and professional agents if the behavior of management is questionable. Shareholders elect the external auditors to provide an expert opinion on whether the financial statements prepared by management present fairly the results of operations and financial position of the company and are in accordance with generally accepted accounting principles (GAAP). As Chapter 2 pointed out, Enron and other governance scandals have rededicated the audit profession to protecting the public interest when applying GAAP, not the interests of the senior management or current directors. External auditors are required to meet with the Audit Committee of the board and discuss the financial statements, as well as their work and opinions, and the state of the company's internal control measures.

In addition, a company's internal auditors' role is to assess whether its policies are comprehensive and are being observed. They should regularly report directly and in person, without management being present, to the Audit Committee, even though they may report on a day-to-day basis to the CEO or CFO.

FIGURE 5.3 **Stakeholder Accountability–Oriented Governance Process**

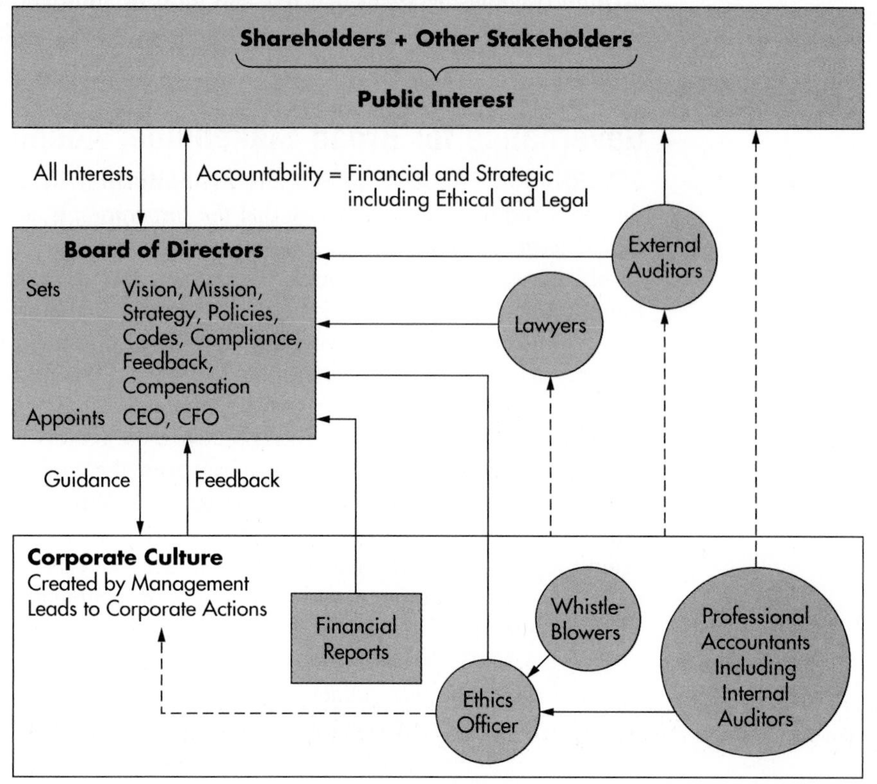

Due to the SOX proposals, the company's lawyers are expected to make the board of directors aware of problems if management does not respond appropriately when told of improprieties.[20]

Another element of modern stakeholder accountability–oriented systems should be an ethics officer or ombudsperson who watches over the ethical culture and serves as the person to whom whistleblowers report anonymously. The ethics officer should report to the Audit Committee of the board and be the conduit through which a generic report of whistleblowers reaches the board. Similar to the internal auditors, the ethics officer may report on a day-to-day basis to the CEO but should report regularly to the Audit Committee in person without other management being present. It should be noted that while SOX regulations require the Audit Committee to establish a whistleblower mechanism that brings them information on financial matters, the board also needs to monitor nonfinancial whistleblower concerns because these often influence company reputation significantly and thereby affect the company's ability to reach its strategic objectives effectively. From a governance perspective, it is extremely shortsighted not to establish a whistleblower program providing information to the board of directors on both financial and nonfinancial matters.

Professional accountants in the company's employ are called on by their professional codes of conduct to serve the public interest. Consequently, they should report financial wrongdoing to the CFO and, if appropriate action is not taken, to the ethics

[20] This point is illustrated in the ethics case *Terrorist Payments* in Chapter 3.

officer, CEO, and auditors. They are not allowed to be involved with misrepresentation and should therefore be ready to report or whistleblow inside their corporation and, per the SOX reforms, specifically to the Audit Committee of the board.

IDENTIFYING ORGANIZATIONAL VALUES—THE FOUNDATION OF BEHAVIOR & INTEGRITY

The new framework for accountability is based on responding to shareholder and other stakeholder interests, and the modern governance framework should direct corporate personnel to the integration of those interests into their strategies, planning, and decision making. Chapters 1 and 2 show that *the public has expectations not only about what is done but also how it is accomplished.* Consequently, discovering what those interests are, which are the most important, and where the risks are that should be managed is a necessary sequence that should precede the establishment of an organization's vision, mission, strategies, policies, and procedures.

This process is represented as a diagram in Figure 5.4. The specific measures used to identify, assess, and rank the stakeholder interests faced by a specific organization were discussed in Chapter 4.

In essence, what is required is an exploration of the stakeholder interests and expectations for the organization so that respect for these can be built into the values that drive behavior. This will lessen the chance that personnel will be motivated to take decisions and actions that are not in the interests of stakeholders but that are important to the achievement of company objectives.

This linkage between motivation and action is reflected in Figure 5.5. Individuals hold beliefs about what is right or improper. Those beliefs stem from many sources but

FIGURE 5.4 Stakeholder Interests Ranking, Risk Assessment, and Usage

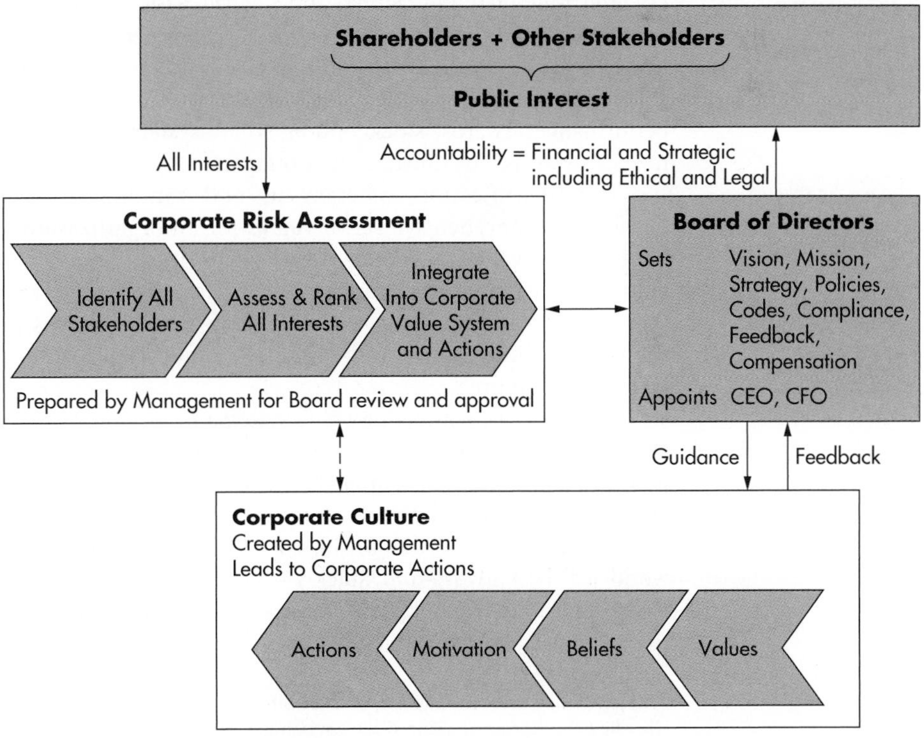

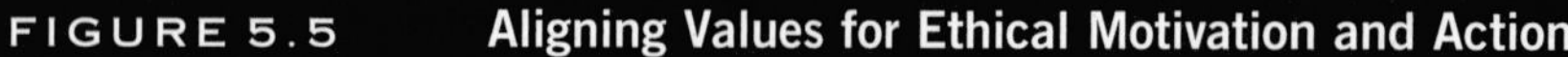

FIGURE 5.5 Aligning Values for Ethical Motivation and Action

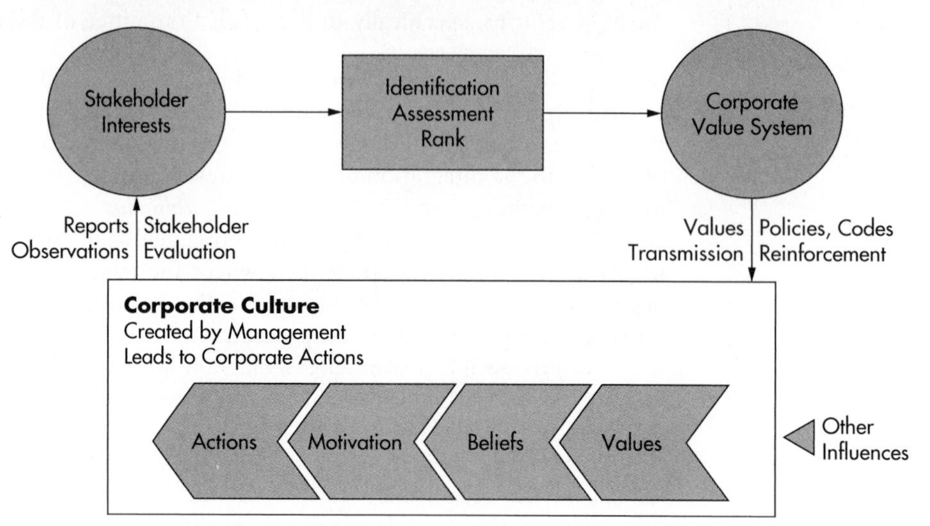

principally from the values that individuals hold. Some values were taught directly or through example by their parents, respected individuals, their bosses, friends, and so on, but other beliefs spring from the rules and motivational systems in place (or absent) at the organization. Beliefs motivate people to act.

The actions of individual personnel are understood collectively to be the "corporation's behavior." The corporation per se is inanimate. *People make things happen, so it is essential that their motivations are aligned with stakeholder expectations, which can be reliably accomplished only by ensuring that the values underlying corporate motivational elements (i.e., corporate culture, codes, policies, etc.) are similarly aligned.* Ensuring this alignment is a vital responsibility for directors, whether they are considering merit or performance rewards, stock option bonus systems, penalties for malfeasance, or paper medals (awards) for outstanding exemplars.

The identification, assessment, and ranking of stakeholder interests should develop a comprehensive set of values for an organization. However, it should be recognized that values and their priority vary in different national, regional, or religious cultures. This presents increasing complexities as the number of different cultures that an organization deals with increases. Some cultures place a high importance on the rights of individuals. Others place primacy on duty to family, company, religious beliefs, and so on.

In the face of competing value systems for the motivation of personnel, corporations should consider which set of values most aligns with those of their shareholders and of their most important stakeholders—those that can most influence their largest consumer and capital markets and their ability to achieve their strategic objectives. Modern media coverage is shrinking the world, so activities that take place on the other side of the world will be known—and quickly—by interested stakeholders everywhere. Greenpeace, CNN, and other organizations will see that pollution incidents, for example, are brought to everyone's attention quickly.[21]

[21] See the ethics case *The Brent Spar Decommissioning Disaster* in Chapter 7 for the dilemma faced by Shell UK when Greenpeace challenged the environmental impact of a management decision.

TABLE 5.3 **Cultural Values and Hypernorms**

SPHERE/CULTURE	BASIS OF VALUE SYSTEM
North American	Rights based: rights, justice, utility
Sino-Confucian	Duty based: obligation to family
Japan	Duty based: obligation to company
Middle East	Duty based: obligation to savior
Europe	Personal rights
South America	Duty based: obligation to family, religious values
Impact Evident On:	Dealing with people: hiring, gender
	Bribery
	Motivation for doing business
	Short- or long-term time horizons
	Importance of quality-of-life issues
Hypernorm Values:	Honesty, fairness, compassion, integrity, predictability, responsibility

Researchers are intent on understanding better and simplifying this multicultural diversity of values. They are working to identify a set of universal values or *hypernorms* that could be embedded in corporate values systems. Although their strict interpretation differs somewhat depending on the culture, six relatively universal respected values have been identified. These universal values are *honesty*, *fairness*, *compassion*, *integrity*, *predictability*, and *responsibility* (Table 5.3).

Directors should consider embedding these hypernorms in their corporate values systems in order to ensure that all important values are included and that maximum acceptance and respect is ensured in dealings with many cultures.

It is significant that scandals such as Enron, the subprime lending fiasco, and Madoff have strengthened the resolve of stakeholders to expect organizations to behave with integrity. That is the overall objective of identifying and embedding corporate values to guide behavior in an organization—*to produce and maintain a culture of integrity.*

Guidance Mechanisms—Ethical Culture & Code of Conduct

The values that a corporation's directors wish to instill in order to motivate the beliefs and actions of its personnel need to be conveyed to provide the required guidance. Usually, such guidance takes the form of a code of conduct that states the values selected, the principles that flow from those values, and any rules that are to be followed to ensure that appropriate values are respected. As noted in a later section, some research has been done into the improvement of the effectiveness of a code. For example, principles are more useful than only rules because principles facilitate interpretation when the precise circumstances encountered do not exactly fit the rule prescribed. A blend of principles and rules is often optimal.

Unfortunately, a code on its own may be nothing more than "ethical art" that hangs on the wall but is rarely studied or followed. *Experience has revealed that, to be effective, a code must be reinforced by a comprehensive ethical culture.* Developing an ethical culture involves continually applying significant effort over several dimensions. A code should be the subject of a training session for new recruits on joining an organization, with yearly update sessions. Moreover, the ethical behavior expected must be referred to in speeches and newsletters by top management, as often as they refer to their health and safety program or their antipollution program, for example, or else it will be seen as less important by employees. If personnel never or rarely hear about ethical expectations, they will know that they are not a serious priority. Similarly, there should be an ethical behavior–reporting mechanism linked to feedback, recognition, and promotion systems. Whistleblowers are also part of a needed monitoring, risk management, and remediation system. More often than not, a corporation that has a code of conduct without supporting it in an ethical culture is simply engaging in window dressing—not in providing effective ethical guidance.

The development of effective codes of conduct and of the necessary supportive ethical culture is discussed later in this chapter.

THREATS TO GOOD GOVERNANCE & ACCOUNTABILITY

The assumption that personnel will automatically be motivated to behave as the owners want is no longer valid. People are motivated more by self-interest than in the past and are likely to come from different cultures that emphasize different priorities of duty. As a result, there is greater need for clear guidance and for identifying and effectively managing threats to good governance and accountability. Discussion of three significant threats follows.

Misunderstanding Objectives & Fiduciary Duty

Even when different cultures are not an issue, personnel can misunderstand the organization's objectives and their own role and fiduciary duty. For example, as was mentioned in Chapter 2, many directors and employees of Enron evidently believed that the company's objectives were best served by actions that brought short-term profit:

- Through ethical dishonesty—manipulation of energy markets in California or sham displays of trading floors
- That was illusory—special purpose entity (SPE) transactions
- That benefited themselves at the expense of other stakeholders—payment of extraordinary fees and commissions to SPEs

Frequently, employees are tempted to cut ethical corners, and they have done so because they believed that their top management wanted them to, they were ordered to do so, or they were encouraged to do so by misguided or manipulative incentive programs. These actions occurred although the board of directors would have preferred (sometimes with hindsight) that they had not. Personnel simply misunderstood what was expected by the board because guidance was unclear, or they were led astray and did not understand that they were to report the problem for appropriate corrective action or to whom or how.

Lack of proper guidance or reporting mechanisms may have been the result of directors and others not understanding their duties as fiduciaries. As noted earlier, directors owe shareholders and regulators several duties, including obedience, loyalty, and due care; safeguarding of assets; accurate, comprehensive, and transparent reports; and so on. Many directors have been looking out for their own interests, and they have spent little time protecting shareholders, other stakeholders, and the public interest from top management. Even where good guidance was in place, compliance mechanisms were nonexistent, rusty, or neglected because most directors concentrated on moving the company forward, not on protecting it from ethical downsides.

Fortunately, SOX has clarified much of this lack of understanding of fiduciary relationships for directors, executives, and also professional accountants. Professional accountants at Arthur Andersen forgot they should have been serving the public interest when giving their opinion that Enron's financial statements were in accordance with GAAP. Instead, by failing to contradict the initiatives of management, Arthur Andersen allowed unreported variations that disadvantaged the interest of shareholders wanting to hold their stock and those wishing to buy in the future, as well as the interests of employees, long-term lenders, and others.

Fortunately, the ensuing investigation and SOX have clarified the primacy of the public interest as the foremost concern of professional accountants. This clarification is not only for external auditors but also for professional accountants employed by organizations. As employees, they owe a loyalty to their employer, but that does not supersede their duty to the public interest, their profession, or themselves. When acting as executives or managers, professional accountants must observe their professional code of conduct and, for example, cannot be associated with misrepresentations. These priorities of duty will be discussed more fully later.

Similarly, as discussed in Chapter 2, external lawyers who discover serious illegalities that are not rectified by management may be expected by the SEC to reveal these matters to the board through a "noisy departure" process. Amazingly, many law firms have argued against the imposition of this process, asserting that such disclosure may not be in the company's interest. A silent departure would certainly favor the interests of management who know what is going on rather than the directors, investors, and other stakeholders who do not.

Failure to Identify & Manage Ethics Risks

Recognition of the increasing complexity, volatility, and risk inherent in modern corporate interests and operations, particularly as their scope expands to different countries and cultures, has led to the requirement for risk identification, assessment, and management systems. In the late 1990s, it became a requirement that boards of directors ensure that their companies' risk management processes were effective,[22] and a number of studies were published illustrating how such a system might be developed and what types of risk might be targeted.[23]

However, *the systematic search for ethics risks—those where the expectations of stakeholders may not be met—has not been targeted* and should be, now that the need for stakeholder-oriented accountability and governance is emerging. Table 5.4 illustrates the aspects of risk that are usually investigated by corporate examiners.

Usually, there is an examination designed to safeguard assets by internal auditors who will also ensure compliance with policies. External auditors examine the financial statements and see that internal controls are in place that will ensure accurate financial reports. But given the accounting and auditing failures mentioned in Chapter 2, *both types of auditor are now expected to spend more time searching for fraudulent activities*—those where there is intent to deceive.[24] External auditors have resisted being charged with full responsibility for this in the past because fraud is very difficult to discover and the costs of doing so are much greater than boards of directors have been willing to authorize and management has been willing to incur.

---

[22] The Toronto Stock Exchange, for example, identified risk management as a matter requiring oversight by directors in 1995.

[23] See, for example, AICPA/CICA and the Institute for Internal Auditors publications on risk management identified in Chapter 1.

[24] Per the following pronouncements, for example, CICA Handbook Section 5135 (2002); AICPA: SAS 99 (2002); and International Auditing and Assurance Standards Board (IAASB) ISA 240 (2001, rev. 2004).

TABLE 5.4 Areas of Corporate Risk Assessment

Governance and objectives

Areas of impact
- Reputation
- Assets, revenues, costs
- Performance
- Stakeholders

Sources of risk
- Environmental
- Strategic
- Operational
- Informational

Specific hazards

Degree of control over risk—little, some, a great deal

Documentation

Historically, relatively few companies have had a systematic annual process designed to assess where the company's actions may not meet the expectations of stakeholders, and focus the attention of directors, executives, and advisors on those areas. To some extent, however, environmental and sustainability impact assessments do involve stakeholder engagement, but not usually on a broad or continuous basis. Stakeholder engagement programs for sustainability programs are discussed in Chapter 7.

Dow Corning has had an "ethics audit process," but based on the silicone breast implant episode,[25] its orientation was apparently toward avoiding scientifically justified, legal liability rather than making sure the interests of customers and other stakeholders are met. The Tylenol recall is an example of where planning ahead for customer interests made Johnson & Johnson famous. (See the vignette *Johnson & Johnson's Worldwide Recall of Tylenol: Virtue Ethics* in Chapter 3.) Dow Corning, by contrast, resorted to bankruptcy protection, and their parent companies made a public plea that the legal liability did not reach upward to them. As usual in product liability cases, the fine paid by Dow Corning was small relative to the damage to reputation, ongoing business relationships, and the ongoing support of stakeholders.

All of Dow Corning's stakeholders would have benefited by a broader definition of ethics risk—one that identified where the expectations of stakeholders may not have been met. The Dow Corning audit process, which was also somewhat flawed, can be readily repaired to serve as one approach to the discovery of ethical risks. Other approaches could involve making an annual reflection routine part of annual ethics sign-off and/or training processes. Charging internal audit with responsibility for identification and assessment and the ethics officer with ongoing responsibility for discovery, assessment, and reporting to the CEO and Audit Committee of the board are logical steps to take as well. Reward recognition should be accorded to personnel who bring issues forward. Prevention is the most important aspect of crisis management, and ethics risks have a nasty way of becoming crises if not diagnosed early enough.

The principles of ethics risk management are summarized in Table 5.5. The importance of maintaining the support of stakeholders is becoming more apparent and widely accepted,

[25] See the ethics case *Dow Corning Silicone Breast Implants.*

TABLE 5.5 Ethics Risk Management Principles

Normal definitions of risk are too narrow for stakeholder-oriented accountability and governance.
An ethics risk exists where the expectations of a stakeholder may not be met.
Discovery and remediation are essential in order to avoid a crisis or losing the support of stakeholders.
Assign responsibility, develop annual processes, and conduct board review.

as ethics risk management becomes a normal element of the due diligence requirements for a board of directors and a significant part of management's responsibility.

Conflicts of Interest

Conflicts of interest have been a subject of extreme importance in recent scandals in which employees, agents, and professionals failed to exercise proper judgment on behalf of their principals. In the Enron fiasco, senior officers, lawyers, and professional accountants acted in their own self-interest rather than for the benefit of the shareholders of Enron. The conflict between the self-interest of the decision makers and the interest of the shareholders interfered with the judgment being applied, causing the interests of the shareholders to be subjugated to the self-interest of the decision makers. As a result, Enron declared bankruptcy, investors lost their savings, and capital markets lost credibility and fell into turmoil. Because of this, the governance frameworks for corporations and professional accounting have been changed forever.

Stated simply, *a conflict of interests occurs when the independent judgment of a person is swayed, or might be swayed, from making decisions in the best interest of others who are relying on that judgment.* An executive or employee is expected to make judgments in the best interest of the company. A director is legally expected to make judgments in the best interest of the company and its shareholders and to do so strategically so that no harm and perhaps some benefit will come to other stakeholders and the public interest. A professional accountant is expected to make judgments that are in the public interest.

Decision makers usually have a priority of duties that they are expected to fulfill, and a conflict of interests confuses and distracts the decision maker from that duty, resulting in harm to those legitimate expectations that are not fulfilled. This situation is pictured in Figure 5.6, where a decision maker (D) "has a conflict of interest if, and only if, (1) D is in a relationship with another (P) requiring D to exercise judgment in P's behalf and (2) D has a special interest tending to interfere with the proper exercise of judgment in that relationship."[26]

A conflict of interest must to be recognized and dealt with *immediately* whether it is real or apparent, whether there is a potential for harm, or whether harm has occurred. An *apparent conflict of interest* is one where the potential for harm can be seen. In some instances, because of unseen safeguards, harm is not likely to occur. Even so, that type of apparent conflict of interest needs to be avoided or managed so that the appearance of a conflict of interest does not damage the reputation of the decision maker or company involved. In other apparent conflicts of interest where there are insufficient safeguards to prevent harm or where a conflict of interest is real but *not apparent* and actual harm can occur as a result of biased decisions, action must be taken to avoid or manage the actual or potential harm involved, *and* action should be undertaken to ensure that actions taken are seen as ethically responsible. Figure 5.7 illustrates these concepts.

[26] Michael Davis and Andrew Stark, eds., *Conflict of Interest in the Professions* (Oxford: Oxford University Press, 2001), 8. Note that D and P can be a person or a corporate body. Davis uses only P.

FIGURE 5.6 **Conflict of Interest for a Decision Maker**

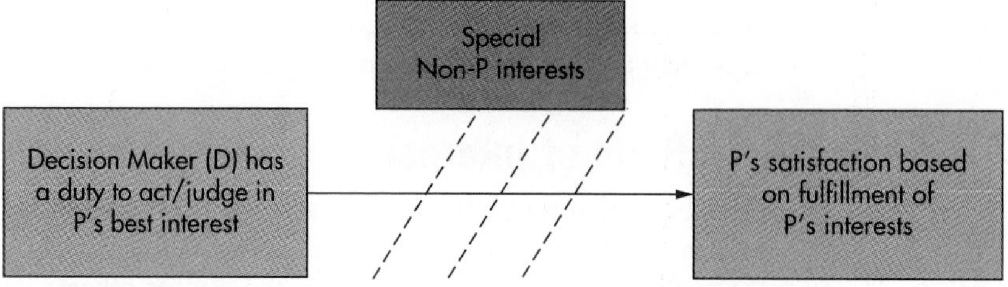

FIGURE 5.7 **Types of Conflict of Interest and Actions Required**

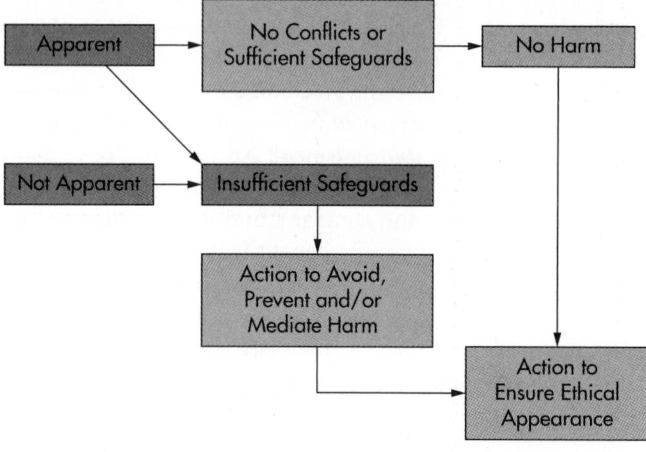

A special or conflicting interest could include "any interest, loyalty, concern, emotion, or other feature of a situation tending to make D's judgment (in that situation) less reliable than it would normally be, without rendering D incompetent. Financial interests and family connections are the most common sources of conflict of interest, but love, prior statements, gratitude, and other subjective tugs on judgment can also be an interest (in this sense)."[27] Table 5.6 provides a list of causes of conflicting interests.

Concern over a conflict of interest stems from the following:

- The fact that people who are relying on D's decision may be harmed if D does not respond or compensate.
- If D knows or should have known but does not tell P, then D is perpetrating a deception.
- If D's judgment will be less reliable than it ordinarily is.

[27] Ibid., 9.

TABLE 5.6 Conflicting Interests—Causes of Judgment Bias

How Might Judgment Be Swayed...

- Any interest, influence, loyalty, concern, emotion, or other feature tending to make judgment less reliable than normal

Self-Interest...

- Bribes, kickbacks—payments or property to decide, family, designees
- Gifts, free travel, favors
- Special advantages—nonmarket discounts on goods
- Special treatment—flattery, social involvement
- Dealings with family, relatives, or relations

Fraud...

- Misappropriation of funds or property
- Cheating on expense accounts
- Falsifying documents
- Stealing cash, assets, or resources
- Falsifying results to obtain bonuses, merit pay, or promotion

Misunderstanding...

- Confused signals or incentives
- Boss/everybody's doing it
- Cultural differences

Slippery Slope...

- Where a small favor leads to ever-larger demands

A conflict of interest is more than just bias, which can be measured for and adjusted. However, because of the unknown nature and therefore extent of the influences, *concern should be for any tendency toward bias.*[28]

MANAGEMENT TO AVOID & MINIMIZE CONSEQUENCES To remedy the concerns over a conflict of interest, three general approaches should be considered: (1) avoidance, (2) disclosure to those stakeholders relying on the decision, and (3) management of the conflict of interest so that the benefits of the judgment made outweigh the costs.

Avoidance is the preferred approach if the appearance of having a conflict of interests can be avoided as well as the reality. The appearance of having a conflict can often be as harmful to the decision maker's reputation as having a real conflict because it is almost impossible to recover lost credibility and reputation without extreme effort and cost—and then only with luck. Consequently, for example, it is advisable to provide rules against giving or receiving kickbacks because it is incredible to argue later that they really did not matter.

Management of potential conflicts is a potentially useful approach if avoidance is not possible and the cost–benefit trade-off of management measures is favorable. The probability that reputation will be lost—and the related cost—must be taken into account in the trade-off analysis. The important aspects related to the management of conflicts of interest are identified in Table 5.7.

The first step in the process of managing to defend against these influences is to ensure that all employees are *aware* of their existence and consequences. This can be

[28] Ibid., 11, 12.

TABLE 5.7 Management of Conflicting Interests

Steps to Be Taken

Ensure awareness through:

- Codes of conduct and
- Related initial and ongoing training

Create a program and an understanding of:

- Employer's concerns regarding conflict of interests
- Major issues:
  - Avoidance is preferable
  - Slippery slope
  - Management techniques:
    - Annual sign-off, confirmation review, and compliance
    - Guidelines for gifts, behavior
    - Counseling, reporting, reinforcement
    - Information barriers, firewalls, and scrutiny

done through codes of conduct[29] and related training. One of the items that should be covered in the training is the "slippery slope" problem, in which an individual can be enticed into a relationship by a seemingly innocuous request for a small favor, then a larger one, and then find that they are told that unless they go along with a serious infraction, their past secrets will be revealed. The start of the slope is too gentle for some to notice, but the slope becomes steeper and more slippery very quickly.

The second step is to *create an understanding* of the reasons: why the employer cannot afford unmanaged conflict of interests situations and why guidelines have been developed to prevent their occurrence, their exploration though counseling if recognized, their reporting if they have occurred, and penalties for their occurrence and nonreporting. Annual written confirmations of ethical behavior and adherence to the employer's code of conduct should include reference to conflicts of interest encountered by the signatory and those identified involving others.

Guidelines that can prove helpful are those that specify when it may be acceptable to give or accept a gift or preferential treatment. Useful questions to ask in this regard are shown in Table 5.8. They are intended to assess whether the offering is likely to sway the independent judgment of the professional. Obviously, something worth a very modest amount, perhaps under $100, that is offered to a group of people as a publicity venture is much less of a problem than a large-value item offered to one person who has considerable influence over the fortunes of the giver.

Additional reinforcement of problems and good examples through publicity will also serve to keep the awareness and understanding fresh. Compliance systems must be in place to provide another type of reinforcement, with appropriate penalties for significant wrongdoings.

[29] Codes of ethics and excellent guidance are available for professionals. For example, the International Federation of Accountants (IFAC) has developed a code of ethics to guide professional accountants that is analyzed in more detail in Chapter 6. It acknowledges that occasionally situations arise that threaten the accountant's ability to comply with the ethics code. These situations include self-interest, self-review, advocacy, familiarity, and intimidation. The nature and significance of the threat is situation specific. Nevertheless, the IFAC code has outlined some broad principles or safeguards that may reduce or eliminate the threat. But when all else fails, the public accountant should remove him- or herself from the situation. In other words, even if there is an adverse economic consequence from doing so, the public accountant must avoid the conflict by walking away.

TABLE 5.8 Guidelines for Acceptance of Gifts or Preferential Treatment

1. Is it nominal or substantial?
2. What is the intended purpose?
3. What are the circumstances?
4. What is the position of sensitivity of the recipient?
5. What is the accepted practice?
6. What is the firm/company policy?
7. Is it legal?

AGENCY THEORY & ETHICS Directors, executives, and professional accountants should appreciate that incentive systems that they use to motivate employees can provide appropriate or inappropriate reinforcement, depending on the way in which they are designed. In many ways, the stock option plans available to executives have been responsible for motivating them to act in ways that are detrimental to all stakeholders. See the ethics case *The Ethics of Repricing and Backdating Employee Stock Options* at the end of this chapter.

According to agency theorists, shareholders expect and hope that managers and, in turn, nonmanagerial employees will behave in line with the goals set for the corporation (see Appendix A). The principals or shareholders hope that their agents will be motivated to act as the principals wish. Incentive systems and punishment systems are created to try to influence the agents to stay on the right path. Clearly, as the public's expectations for corporate performance now include ethical standards, the reward and punishment systems set up should also reflect ethical dimensions, or shareholders are going to be disappointed. In fact, the corporation's strategic plans should include ethical dimensions to ensure that their agents, both inside and outside the corporation, are properly influenced and that conflicts of interest are avoided. The *Sears Compensation Plan Backfires* vignette provides a helpful example of where damage control was required after reward system design mistakes had been made.

Sears Compensation Plan Backfires

Performance-based compensation plans are not always the best means of motivating employees. "In 1991, Sears, Roebuck & Company—faced with severe financial pressure—decided to revamp its compensation plan for mechanics in its Sears Auto Centers. Previously, mechanics were simply paid an hourly wage. Sears' management wanted to increase productivity and profits, so it devised an incentive system that would supposedly pay mechanics a smaller hourly wage, but provide them with a performance bonus using quotas and commissions. Also, so much pressure was applied to the workforce, that many were directly or indirectly told they would lose their jobs if they did not achieve their repair sales quotas. Soon, mechanics found out that the only way to achieve their goals and make money was to concentrate on selling more work rather than servicing the customer. The new program resulted in mechanics and service managers over-billing customers, charging for work that wasn't performed and charging for work that wasn't needed." Afterward, Sears apologized for creating a misleading incentive system.

Source: *Mike Harden, "Learn from Sears: Don't Make This Monumental Mistake,"* Huffington Post, *July 8, 2014.*

INFORMATION BARRIERS & FIREWALLS An important system for preventing ethical malfeasance is an information barrier or "firewall." This practice utilizes the analogy to an impervious wall to describe those measures and methods that would prevent the transmission of client information from one part of an organization or consortium to another. Such firewalls or information barriers are not tangible in a three-dimensional sense but refer to a multidimensional set of measures, such as the following:

- Instructions to keep information confidential
- Instructions not to read, listen to, or act on specific types of information
- Educational programs and reinforcements by top management
- Monitoring and compliance sign-off procedures
- Scrutiny of insider or key-person trading of securities
- Physical barriers to information transmission, such as
  - separate computer- or physical-storage systems,
  - segregation of duties to different employees,
  - segregation of information in a different location or building etc., and
  - different lock systems
- Appointment of a compliance officer who would monitor the effectiveness of the wall
- Disciplinary sanctions for breach of the wall

Information barriers or firewalls have been a normal part of business and professional operations for many years. For example, when a client is involved in the preparation of a public offering of securities, those members of the offering team (lawyers, professional accountants, and underwriters) are expected not to divulge advance details of the underwriting to the other members of their respective firms or to anyone else. The public issuance of securities, as presently known, would be impossible without the firewall construct. Fortunately, even though in the final analysis a firewall relies on the integrity of the personnel involved for its effectiveness, such arrangements are considered effective to protect the public interest and to safeguard the interest of current clients as well as former clients.

FORENSIC EXPERTS & EVIDENCE: THE 20/60/20 RULE The time may come when a director, executive, or professional accountant must consider whether a conflict of interests has led to serious breach of duty, a fraudulent act, or a loss that must be recovered pursuant to an insurance policy. In such instances, an investigative and forensic expert may be called on if existing company personnel would benefit from assistance. The expert will employ appropriate techniques based on an understanding of the situation.

Many managers may believe that their associates and employees would rarely engage in unethical behavior. However, forensic experts indicate that their experience suggests that the general population can be divided into three groups:

- 20% would never commit a fraud.
- 60% would commit a fraud if the chance of getting caught is considered low.
- 20% would seek to commit a fraud regardless of the circumstances.

Although the precision of the percentages may be debated, the real contribution of this forensic insight is that the behavior of the largest portion of employees can be influenced by a strong ethical corporate culture, that is, a *culture of integrity*, since they will know what behavior is expected and that there will be consequences for acting contrary to the organization's values. Figure 5.8 shows that, with excellent governance, up to 80% of a company's employees could be influenced to support and comply with company values and objectives, and if the percentages rose to 5/90/5, then 95% of the company's employees might comply. Which company would you prefer to work for, invest in, or buy

FIGURE 5.8 Governance Determines Extent of Compliance or Deviance

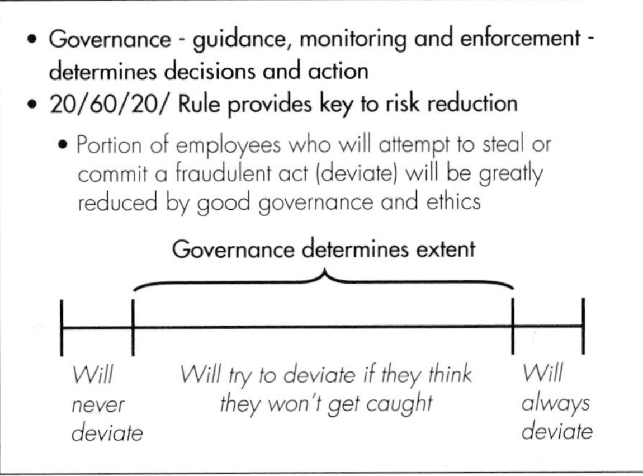

from—one where there was a good culture of integrity, where 80% to 95% of employees were likely to follow company guidance, or one where there was a poor culture of integrity and unethical acts were common? Effective guidance is extremely important.

Discussion of the development and maintenance of a culture of integrity follows.

THE GONE THEORY: IDENTIFYING POTENTIALLY HARMFUL SITUATIONS & LIKELY PERPETRATORS Forensic experts also have insights into who would commit a fraud and what the circumstances are that could come into play in the decision. They point out that in most instances of fraud or opportunistic behavior, they can begin to identify prospective perpetrators through the use of the GONE Theory. The acronym GONE stands for circumstances that account for motivation of illicit behavior, in which the letters represent the following:

- G—Greed
- O—Opportunity to take advantage
- N—Need for whatever is taken
- E—Expectation of being caught is low

The experts point out that identifying personnel who have or exhibit these characteristics can head off problems if adequate precautions are taken. These would include additional review and diligence on the part of supervisors, transfer to less vulnerable areas, signaling that extra review or audit procedures were in place, and so on. For example, if an employee exhibited signs of a lifestyle well beyond his or her means, then extra scrutiny might be warranted.

DUTY DEPENDS ON A PERSON'S ROLE Although this analysis of conflict of interests has focused on the individual, it should be noted that the analysis is similar for groups of individuals within a corporation, organization, or profession. But either as individuals or as groups of individuals, it is often the roles taken on—and therefore the duties assumed and expected by those relying on the actions to be taken—that define the nature of conflicts of interest. For example, it is unlikely that a professional accountant auditing or judging financial statements can audit objectively his or her own work without bias or maintain objectivity if asked to assume an advocacy role by a client. In order to ensure sufficient objectivity to maintain their duty to serve the public interest, professional accountants have developed standards designed to ensure independence.[30] These will be discussed in the next chapter.

KEY ELEMENTS OF CORPORATE GOVERNANCE & ACCOUNTABILITY

Compelling Evidence for the Development of an Ethical Corporate Culture

Directors, owners, and senior management are in the process of realizing that they and their employees need to understand (1) that their organizations would be wise to consider the interests of stakeholders, not just shareholders, and (2) that appropriate ethical values are to be considered when decisions are being made. *Because organizational, professional, and personal values provide the framework to decision making, it is vital that organizations create an environment or culture where appropriate shared values are created, understood, fostered, and committed to by all concerned.*

Recent evidence has underscored how important an ethics program, leading to the development and maintenance of an ethical corporate culture, is to the ongoing success and reputation of a corporation and its executives. The following extracts and comments provide compelling evidence that an ethical corporate culture, which considers the interests of stakeholders, not only short-term profitability, is relevant to success and that corporations are responding:

- *KPMG's Integrity Survey, 2013*[31] compared corporations with and without an ethics program and found evidence that an ethics program significantly improved perceptions of behavior as well as actual business behavior:
  - 13–17% reduction in observed misconduct or violation of values and principles in the prior 12 months
  - 6–13% improvement in prevention of misconduct
  - 36–46% improvement in comfort in reporting misconduct to a supervisor
  - 37–41% improvement in belief that appropriate action will follow reporting of misconduct
  - 32–43% improvement in perception that CEO and other top executives set the right "tone at the top"
  - 43–47% improvement in motivation to "do the right thing"
- The *2009 National Business Ethics Survey* of the Ethics Resource Center[32] reports that a strong ethical culture reduces the following:
  - Pressure to compromise standards
  - Observed misconduct
  - Failure to report observed misconduct
  - Experienced retaliation for reporting

---

[30] See, for example, the International Federation of Accountants (IFAC) *Code of Ethics for Professional Accountants*, November 2001, or the *IFAC Code of Ethics for Professional Accountants*, International Federation for Accountants Ethics Committee, New York, 2005, http://www.ifac.org/Store/Category.tmpl?Category5Ethics&Cart51215563035160178. Both versions of the IFAC are from downloadable from **http://www.cengagebrain.com.**

[31] KPMG Forensic, *Integrity Survey 2013* (KPMG LLP, 2013), http://www.kpmginstitutes.com/advisory-institute/insights/2013/pdf/integrity-survey-2013.pdf.

[32] Ethics Resource Center, *2009 National Business Ethics Survey*, http://www.ethics.org/resource/2009-national-business-ethics-survey.

- The PricewaterhouseCoopers's report *Building a Risk-Aware Culture for Success*[33] states the following:
  - No matter how clearly you define your risk-appetite and controls, the people who work for you won't consistently make the right decisions unless corporate culture reinforces "doing the right thing" naturally.
- The KPMG International Survey of Corporate Responsibility Reporting 201[34] states the following:
  - Corporate responsibility (CR) reporting [which demonstrates sensitivity to the interests of stakeholders] has become the *de facto* law for business.
  - CR reporting enhances financial value.
  - 95% of the 250 largest companies in the world (G250 companies) now report on their corporate responsibility (CR) activities, with two-thirds of the reporters based in the United States
  - Almost 60% of China's largest companies already report CR metrics.
- Another example, from research that focuses on the leadership role of the CEO, executives, and managers[35] finds that to be perceived to be an ethical leader an individual must speak out about, and demonstrate, the ethical values the corporation or organization expects. If this is not done, employees will take the view that the only value that matters is making a profit. If the executives or leaders are silent on ethical matters, even if they are personally ethical, their reputation will be at considerable risk, as will be the corporation's.

There are still some executives and directors, as well as shareholders, who prefer to focus on making profits without making efforts to determine whether they are made ethically or even legally. Such decision makers do not appreciate or care about the potential damage that may be caused in the long run by failing to consider the strategic significance of consistently making ethical decisions. With the increasing complexity and rising pace of operations in business, an even greater reliance will be placed on building relationships and managing risks ethically. This will require increasing attention on developing an additional point of reference for decision making—an ethical corporate culture to guide employees to behave ethically.

Wells Fargo Suffers from an Unethical Culture

On September 9, 2016, Wells Fargo was fined $185 million for illegal banking practices caused by a faulty corporate culture where employee incentives motivated bank employees to cross-sell existing customers so that they would use at least 8 Wells Fargo products. This incentive pressure caused employees to open roughly 1.5 million bank accounts and create 565,000 credit cards that were not authorized by bank customers. *When customers complained, the bank investigated, discovered the sham accounts, and fired 5,300 employees, but not the executives in charge. They were scheduled to retire or continue working with significant stock options intact. Ultimately, pressure from regulators and the public forced the bank to refund about $2.6 million of inappropriately collected fees,*[1] *and two senior executives forfeited over $70 million in retirement allowances.*[2]

---

[33] PricewaterhouseCoopers, *Building a Risk-Aware Culture for Success,* http://www.pwc.com/gx/en/risk-regulation/risk-aware-culture.jhtml.

[34] KPMG Forensic, *KPMG International Survey of Corporate Responsibility Reporting 2011,* http://www.kpmg.com/Global/en/IssuesAndInsights/ArticlesPublications/corporate-responsibility/Pages/2011-survey.aspx.

[35] Linda Klebe Treviño, Laura Pincus Hartman, and Michael Brown, "Moral Person and Moral Manager: How Executives Develop a Reputation for Ethical Leadership," *California Management Review* 42 (2000): 128–42.

But that was not the full extent of what Wells Fargo ended up losing from its faulty corporate culture. The bank, which had sailed through the subprime lending crisis in 2008 without needing a bailout because it had shown restraint in not participating in questionable practices, ended up:

- *Losing its reputation for clean, ethical dealing.*
- *Losing the trust of its customers because it had to notify all 40 million of its customers when a much smaller number had been negatively affected.*[3]
- *Losing the business of the State of California*[4]
- *Losing the services of a formerly well-regarded CEO. John Stumpf, who was berated in government hearings, and who decided to resign as CEO because he had become a distraction.*[5]
- *Losing the support of government regulators. On December 7, 2016, it was reported that the U.S. regulator for the Community Reinvestment Act was considering reducing Wells Fargo's outstanding ranking, held since 2008, by two notches, which "could limit near-term expansion for the bank."*[6]

In the ensuing firestorm, other unsavory aspects of Wells Fargo's culture came to light, including:

- *Employees who resisted illegal marketing tactics and/or reported them to an ethics hotline were fired for tardiness – even if they were only 2 minutes late.*[7]
- *John Stumpf was allegedly sent a letter in 2007 referring to the illegal, fraudulent sales practices and warning "of professional and reputational damage, consumer fraud and shareholder lawsuits, coupled with regulator sanction". That employee "later won a federal whistleblower retaliation case against Wells Fargo." A second letter was allegedly sent to the Wells Fargo Board. Although "CNNMoney hasn't been able to determine whether the letters were actually sent, nor whether Stumpf or the board members read or received them"*[8]*, the company's reputation for integrity continues to be eroded.*

However long the Wells Fargo saga takes to unfold, it is clear that the bank, regardless of its proud heritage, has become the iconic example of a company that had an unethical culture, and paid dearly for it.[9] *There is little doubt that the Board, senior executives, and investors would have preferred that the bank maintained its reputation as a company with a culture of integrity.*

---

[1]"A case of unchecked incentives. Wells Fargo Fined $185 Million for Fraudulently Opening Accounts", *New York Times*, Sept. 9, 2016, http://www.nytimes.com/2016/09/09/business/dealbook/wells-fargo-fined-for-years-of-harm-to-customers.html?emc=edit_th_20160909&nl=todaysheadlines&nlid=34879348&_r=0

[2]"Wells Fargo CEO Gives Up $41 Million in Stock After Probe", The Presidential Daily Brief, Ozy.com, September 28, 2016, http://www.ozy.com/presidential-daily-brief/pdb-72153/payback-72160. J. Stumpf gave up $41 million and Carrie Tolstedt, former head of community baking gave up $19 million.

[3]"5,300 Wells Fargo employees fired over 2 million phony accounts", Matt Egan, CNN Money, September 9, 2016, http://money.cnn.com/2016/09/08/investing/wells-fargo-created-phony-accounts-bank-fees/index.html

[4]"Despite Stumpf's departure, California not ready to do business with Wells Fargo", Michelle Fox, @MFoxCNBC , October 13, 2016, http://www.cnbc.com/2016/10/13/despite-stumpfs-departure-california-not-ready-to-do-business-with-wells-fargo.html

[5]"Wells Fargo Chief Abruptly Steps Down", Michal Corkery and Stacy Cowley, The New York Times DealB%k, Oct. 12, 2016, http://www.nytimes.com/2016/10/13/business/dealbook/wells-fargo-ceo.html?hp&action=click&pgtype=Homepage&clickSource=story-heading&module=second-column-region®ion=top-news&WT.nav=top-news&_r=0

[6]"Exclusive: U.S. regulator set to fail Wells Fargo on community lending test – sources", Patrick Rucker, *Reuters*, Dec. 7, 2016, http://www.reuters.com/article/us-wells-fargo-accounts-idUSKBN13-W2HA?feedType=RSS&feedName=businessNews

[7]"I called the Wells Fargo ethics line and was fired", Matt Egan, Sept. 21, 2016, http://money.cnn.com/2016/09/21/investing/wells-fargo-fired-workers-retaliation-fake-accounts/index.html

[8]"Letter warned Wells Fargo of 'widespread' fraud in 2007 – exclusive", Matt Egan, CNN Money, Oct. 18, 2016, http://money.cnn.com/2016/10/18/investing/wells-fargo-warned-fake-accounts-2007/index.html

[9]"Early Lessons From Wells Fargo: Three Ways To Prevent Ethical Failure", Ron Carucci, Sept. 13, 2016, http://www.forbes.com/sites/roncarucci/2016/09/13/early-lessons-from-wells-fargo-3-ways-to-prevent-ethical-failure/#a4318372d6a9

Developing, Implementing, & Managing an Ethical Corporate Culture

The development of an ethical corporate culture to guide decision making depends on the identification, sharing, fostering, and commitment to appropriate corporate values that are to be incorporated into the corporation's decision making. Reliable, risk-controlled decisions, however, cannot be reliably achieved by simply leaving ethics solely to the judgment of individuals in a workforce of divergent experiences and backgrounds to work out by trial and error. Nor can it be achieved simply by sending a letter urging employees to be on their best behavior or by publishing a code of conduct. In order to ensure commitment to the ethical principles or values considered appropriate for the organization, it must be evident to the members of the organization that top management is fully supportive and that such support is evident throughout the organization's governance systems.

Experts in organizational behavior who have been studying organizational culture, such as Edgar Schein, believe that developing the right shared values in an organization and a commitment to them can lead to many benefits. He takes the view that the organization's culture is a cognitive framework, consisting of attitudes, values, behavioral norms, and expectations shared by organization members (Schein 1985). Wayne Reschke and Ray Aldag have brought together in a model (see Figure 5.9) those elements generally thought to make up an organization's culture and the mechanisms available to reinforce that culture. They have identified aspects of individual, team, and organizational performance that might benefit from appropriate development of that culture. Others have developed ways of assessing and profiling an organization's culture[36] in order to improve the culture, provide motivation toward a goal, or assess cultures of merging organizations and manage the change to a new, shared culture. Usually, the place to start assessments is with the organization's strategic core—its philosophy and mission, its vision, what it believes drives its value added, and how it treats its stakeholders. All of these elements and "reinforcers" of organizational culture will be increasingly more dependent on their ethical aspects, as will the resulting behavior. In order to ensure an effective understanding and ongoing commitment to the organization's ethical principles, many companies create an ethics program.

Perhaps the most important aspect of an ethics program designed to ensure an effective understanding and commitment to the organization's ethical principles is the choice of program orientation. According to researchers, there are five orientations for the design and operation of ethics programs. These are described in Table 5.9.

The researchers went on to evaluate the effectiveness of the impact of these orientations on several dimensions by administering over 10,000 surveys to randomly selected

[36] See, for example, J. A. Chatman and K. A. Jehn, "Assessing the Relationship between Industry Characteristics and Organizational Culture: How Different Can You Be?," *Academy of Management Journal* 37 (1994): 522–33.

FIGURE 5.9 Organizational Culture, Individual/Team Outcomes, and Organizational Effectiveness

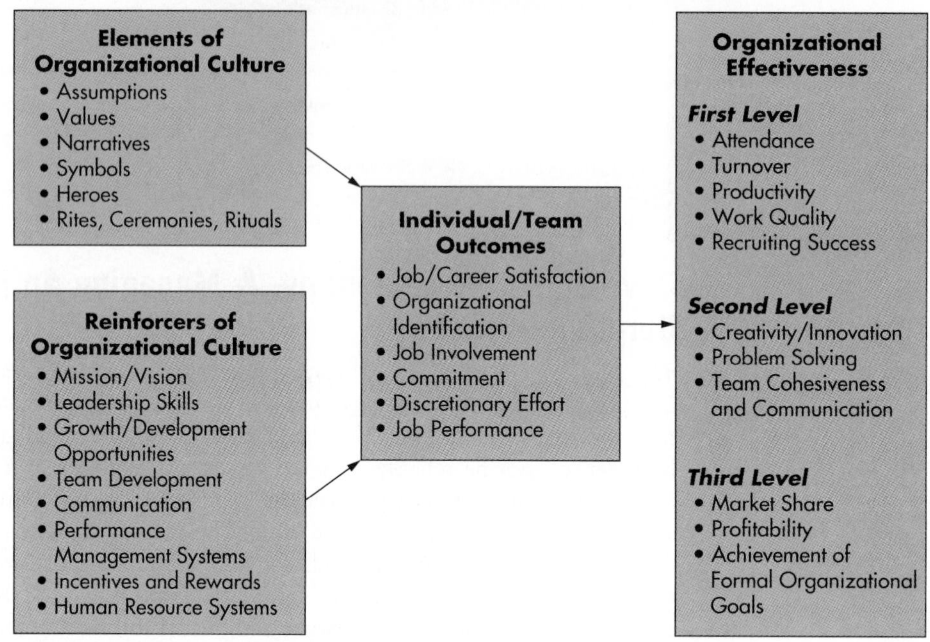

Source: A Model of the Impact of Organizational Culture on Individual/Team Outcomes and Organizational Effectiveness, *The Business Case for Culture Change*, W. Reschke & R. Aldag, Center for Organizational Effectiveness, August 2000.

TABLE 5.9 Ethics Program Orientation Types

ORIENTATION	PRIMARY FOCUS
Compliance based	Preventing, detecting, and punishing violations of the law
Integrity or values based	Defines organizational values and encourages employee commitment
Satisfaction of external stakeholders	Improvement of image with and relationships with external stakeholders (customers, the community, suppliers)
Protect top management from blame	Defensive "CYA," or cover your ———
Combinations of the above	Values and compliance based, for example

Sources: Badaracco and Webb (1995), 15; Paine (1994), 111; Treviño et al. (1999), 135–39.

employees in six large American companies from a variety of industries. The seven dimensions on which the impact was evaluated were the following:

1. Unethical/illegal behavior
2. Employee awareness of ethical issues that arise at work
3. Looking for ethics/compliance advice within the company
4. Delivering bad news to management
5. Ethics/compliance violations are reported in the organization
6. Better decision making in the company because of the ethics/compliance program
7. Employee commitment to the organization

TABLE 5.10 Ethical Culture: Important Aspects

An ethical culture combines formal and informal elements to guide employee thought and action, including the following:

- Ethical leadership by executives and supervisors*
- Reward systems incorporate ethical considerations*
- Perceived fairness, fair treatment of employees*
- Open discussion of ethics in the organization*
- Authority structure that emphasizes an employee's accountability and responsibility to question his or her own actions and an obligation to question authority when something seems wrong*
- Organizational focus that communicates care for employees and the community rather than self-interest
- Official policies and procedures (code of ethics, practice, conduct)
- Supporting offices (e.g., ethics officer, ombudsperson)
- Supporting structures (e.g., telephone hotline, whistleblower protection, code sign-off, training, etc.)

Note: Asterisks indicate the most influential factors as found by Treviño et al. (1999).
Source: Treviño et al. (1999).

According to their research, confirmed by consulting experience on the design of corporate ethics programs, *the most important factor in encouraging employee observance is that the employees perceive that the ethics program is values based.* This produced significantly more positive outcomes on all seven dimensions. Compliance and external orientations also produced favorable outcomes on the seven dimensions but not as positive as for the values-based approach. The external orientation outcomes were less than the compliance-based approach. A purely defensive, CYA approach was considered "harmful," as it resulted in negative outcomes across all dimensions. It was suggested the combined approaches could be effective, such as if a values orientation were "backed up with accountability systems and discipline for violators" where "values can include concern for customers, suppliers, and the community as well as shareholders and internal stakeholders such as employees" (Treviño et al. 1999, 139).

The study also provides some useful insights into the important aspects of an ethical culture. These, which are noted in Table 5.10, can be particularly useful for a company that is assessing what it might do to institute a new ethics program or improve its current ethical culture. According to a study by Weaver, Treviño, and Cochran (1999b), formal ethics programs usually include the dimensions listed in Table 5.11.

SOX and related changes in governance guidelines from stock exchanges and other sources have resulted in the expectation that respectable corporations will have at least the basic elements of an ethics program. Recently, the emphasis has shifted to making ethics programs effective.

KPMG Forensic Advisory's *Integrity Survey 2013* presents interesting data that are instructive, including data shown in Table 5.12 that was gleaned from over 3,500 survey responses from U.S. employees (KPMG 2013). The responses summarized above reveal that there is considerable room for improvement in the effectiveness of ethics programs even though respondents indicated increased application of virtually all program elements. Based on a comparison of survey results in 2013 and 2006, respondents indicated significant increases in formal introduction of senior level ethics compliance officers (up 11%), hotlines (up 25%), monitoring systems (up 12%), and incentives to uphold the code of conduct (up 18%).

Further data in the KPMG studies show just how important the existence of an ethics program can be. Respondents were separated into "with program" and "without program" groups, and their answers to further questions are summarized in Table 5.13. The table shows, for example, that CEOs and other top executives are considered to be setting the "right tone at the top" by 41% *more* respondents where an ethics program is

TABLE 5.11 Ethical Programs' Usual Dimensions

1. Formal ethics codes
2. Ethics committees developing policies, evaluating actions, investigating, and adjudicating policy violations
3. Ethics communications systems
4. Ethics officers or ombudspersons coordinating policies, providing education, or investigating allegations
5. Ethics training programs to raise awareness and help employees respond to ethical problems
6. Disciplinary processes for unethical behavior

TABLE 5.12 Presence of Ethics & Compliance Program Elements per *KPMG Forensic Integrity Survey 2013*

	FORMALLY	INFORMALLY	UNSURE	NOT AT ALL
RESPONSE TO: *MY ORGANIZATION...*	%	%	%	%
Has a code of conduct that articulates the values and standards of the organization	80	8	10	2
Has a senior-level ethics compliance officer	62	10	23	6
Performs background investigations on prospective employees	66	10	20	4
Provides communication and training to employees on its code of conduct	73	12	11	3
Has a confidential and anonymous hotline that employees can use to report misconduct or seek advice.	61	10	19	10
Audits and monitors employees and managers compliance with its code	56	17	21	6
Has policies to hold employees and managers accountable for code of conduct violations	68	12	17	4
Provides incentives for employees to uphold the code of conduct	41	11	23	26
Has policies to investigate and take corrective action if misconduct is alleged	69	10	17	4

Source: KPMG Forensic Integrity Survey 2013, p. 21.

present than when it is not. The gains revealed across the board in Table 5.13 are so striking that it is apparent that *the existence of an ethics program improves perceptions and potentially the related behaviors on all dimensions.*[37] KPMG Forensic's *Integrity Survey 2013* also provides interesting information on the prevalence and nature of misconduct and on understanding how organizations are preventing, detecting, and responding to misconduct, making it a most valuable benchmark source.

Once an ethics program is established, the next step is to make it as effective as possible. In a general sense, higher effectiveness results from the comprehensiveness with which a program sets the corporation's culture and employs the reinforcers of culture that are identified in Figure 5.8. Based on a study of *Fortune 500* companies, Weaver et al. (1999b) argue that the degree to which a values or compliance orientation

[37] Article reprinted from KPMG *Integrity Survey* 2013 and 2005–2006. Copyright © 2013, 2006 KPMG International. KPMG International is a Swiss cooperative of which all KPMG firms are members. KPMG International provides no services to clients. Each member firm is a separate and independent legal entity and each describes itself as such. All rights reserved. Printed in Canada. Reprinted with permission of KPMG International. All Rights Reserved.

TABLE 5.13 **Ethics and Compliance Program Effects on Behaviors & Perceptions, per KPMG Forensic Integrity Surveys**

	IMPROVEMENT WITH PROGRAM		
	2013	2009	2005
PERCEPTION OR BEHAVIOR	%	%	%
Observed—Misconduct in prior 12 months	13	17	6
• Violations of organizational values and principles in the prior 12 months	17	23	12
Causes of Misconduct—Feel pressure to do whatever it takes to meet targets	11	9	10
• Lack understanding of standards that apply to their jobs	6	6	9
• Believe policies and procedures are easy to bypass or override	12	16	16
• Believe rewards are based on results, not the means used to achieve them	13	10	16
Detecting Misconduct—Would feel comfortable reporting misconduct to a supervisor	36	37	40
• Would feel comfortable reporting misconduct to legal department	46	51	48
• Would feel comfortable reporting misconduct to internal audit	43	47	44
• Would feel comfortable reporting misconduct to board of directors	38	43	39
Responding to Misconduct—Believe appropriate action would be taken	39	45	43
• Believe they would be protected from retaliation	40	43	46
• Believe they would be satisfied with the outcome	37	38	44
• Believe they would be doing the right thing	41	29	27
Perceived Tone & Culture—CEO and other top execs set the right "tone at the top"	41	48	55
• Are approachable with ethical concerns	36	35	43
• Value ethics and integrity over short-term business goals	43	49	54
• Would respond appropriately if became aware of misconduct	42	44	50
• Know what type of behavior goes on within the organization	32	41	N.A.
• Set targets that are achievable without violating the code of conduct	42	50	N.A.
Team Culture & Environment—People feel motivated to "do the right thing"	43	47	39
• People feel comfortable raising and addressing ethics concerns	46	48	49
• People apply the right values to their decisions and behaviors	45	45	37
• People share a high commitment to integrity	43	41	41
• The opportunity to engage in misconduct is minimal	46	37	42
• The ability to conceal misconduct is minimal	43	38	N.A.
• The willingness to tolerate misconduct is minimal	43	40	49
• Adequate checks are carried out to detect misconduct	47	53	N.A.

Sources: *KPMG Forensic Integrity Survey 2005–2006*, 14–19, and *KMPG Forensic Integrity Survey 2013*, 22–26. All information provided is of a general nature and is not intended to address the circumstances of any particular individual or entity. Although we endeavor to provide accurate and timely information, there can be no guarantee that such information is accurate as of the date it is received or that it will continue to be accurate in the future. No one should act upon such information without appropriate professional advice after a thorough examination of the facts of a particular situation. For additional news and information, please access KPMG's global website on the Internet at http://www.us.kpmg.com.

characterizes an ethics program's mode of control can be seen in the program's emphasis on encouraging shared values, supporting employee aspirations, communicating values, and building trust and confidence. They conclude that the dominant influence of the U.S. Sentencing Guidelines has been to orient top management commitment and corporate ethics programs toward compliance rather than integrity or values. This orientation—according to the earlier Treviño et al. (1999) study—will not provide the best adherence to desired ethics values. Over time, it is hoped that top management will learn that a values orientation that involves encouraging shared values, supporting employee aspirations, communicating values, and building trust and confidence will produce significant benefits and that ethics programs will move in that direction.

It is worth noting that current research suggests that the values-oriented ethics program can have other benefits in addition to those described above or noted in Table 5.13. In particular, *building trust within an organization* can have favorable impacts on employees' willingness to share information and ideas, thereby enhancing the innovation quotient of the enterprise and its ability to adapt and take advantage of its opportunities. This process is called *ethical renewal.* Properly cultivated trust can also create commitment to organizational goals and enhance productivity, all of which will raise the ability of the enterprise to profit and compete. This can all be fostered with appropriate attention in the design of the code of conduct (Brooks 2000).

In the development of ethical cultures, most companies have embraced the concept of written ethical guidance, but they have fallen far short of embracing many of the supportive mechanisms that are important to the development and maintenance of a healthy ethical culture. Among the omissions of most concern are lack of strong CEO involvement, lack of training, failure to renew employee commitment to the code annually, and lack of communications and meetings dealing with ethics. From other sources, we find concerns raised about the lack of formal program follow-through; failure to create a credible investigation follow-up and sanction process; employing "quick fix" approaches rather than building a long-term solution; training by people who do not have a commitment to live with the result—in other words, top management should be more prominent; and telephone answering by distant outsiders, which makes callers have difficulty believing that the company cares and is taking their calls seriously (Treviño et al. 1999). In addition, ironically, when the current evidence is compared to what ethical cultures could be as control systems, they were found to be suboptimal.

The discussion to this point has provided an understanding of why organizations—be they corporations, not-for-profit organizations, or professional firms—should develop an ethical culture, what shape that culture should take, and why. Table 5.14 puts these ideas together in an orderly sequence, with additional ideas found in later chapters that a manager, ethics officer, or professional accountant can use to develop and maintain an ethical corporate culture. Information obtained from the Ethics Officer Association and the Center for Business Ethics at Bentley College would be helpful in keeping abreast of current developments.

The design and introduction of an ethics program is well within the capacity of professional accountants because of their exposure to the nature, purpose, and workings of internal control systems that are essential underpinnings to credible financial statements and reporting. Professional accounting bodies have developed pronouncements and guidelines related to ethics programs and antifraud programs, such as the AICPA's Statement on Auditing Standards, No. 99,[38] which contains material on management antifraud programs and controls. The large professional accounting bodies and many consulting firms have developed ethics and integrity services and forensic or governance services that may be accessed at **www.cengagebrain.com**.

Corporate Codes of Conduct

PURPOSE, FOCUS, & ORIENTATION According to The Conference Board,

> The foundation of most corporate ethics programs is the company code or business conduct statement. Company business ethics principles statements stress two objectives: (1) improving employee capability for making decisions that are in accord with policy and legal requirements; and (2) giving concrete

[38] The AICPA's SAS 99 is downloadable from the AICPA website at http://www.aicpa.org.

TABLE 5.14 Development & Maintenance of an Ethical Corporate Culture

STEP	PURPOSE
Assign responsibility:	Successful initiatives usually involve:
Chairman or CEO	• top level accountability and adequate budget
Ethics officer	• champions, arbiters
Ethics committee	• monitoring, feedback, advice, and cheerleading
Ethics audit	To understand the organization's ethical practices and its network of stakeholders and interests
Ethics risk assessment	To identify important ethics problems that could arise (Chapter 6)
Top management support	Absolutely vital to successful adherence
Develop consensus on key ethical values	Necessary to frame policies and procedures
Develop code of conduct, ethical decision-making criteria, and protocols, including sniff tests	Provide guidance for employees and all other stakeholders
Develop ethics program:	To successfully present and provide supporting mechanisms for the guidance process
Leaders involvement	
Launch	
Training	
Reinforcement policies:	
Compliance sign-off	
Measurements of performance	
Include in strategic objectives and managers' objectives	
Include in monitoring and reward structures	
Communications programs	
Exemplar award system	
Ethics inquiry service	Information, investigation, and whistleblower protection
Crisis management	To ensure that ethics are part of survival reactions
Establish a review mechanism	

expression to the company's sense of mission and its view of the duties and responsibilities that corporate citizenship entails.[39]

An effective code is the embodiment of an organization's values. It represents the major organizational structure in which to implement ethical policy[40] and to signal, communicate, and guide behavioral expectations and culture, as well as to provide strategic and legal positioning for the organization. It is an essential part of a modern system of internal control. Unless employees are told in writing how they are expected to behave, managers, executives, and directors are vulnerable to charges that they failed to provide adequate guidance to their workers. If so, the company and its officers and directors can be fined heavily, and, in some jurisdictions, the officers and directors can go to jail. More important, it has been suggested that the fines and court costs involved in ethical dilemmas are usually smaller than the lost future profit margin because of the disenchantment of customers. Whistleblowing outside the corporation may also be

[39] *Global Corporate Ethics Practices: A Developing Consensus* (New York: The Conference Board, 1999), 16.

[40] See, for example, Patrick E. Murphy, "Creating Ethical Corporate Structures," *Sloan Management Review*, Winter, 1989, 81–87.

TABLE 5.15 Depths of Code Coverage

Credo	Inspirational short statement on key values
Code of Ethics	Deals with ethics principles (short)
Code of Conduct	Deals with principles plus additional examples etc.
Code of Practice	Detailed rules of practice

prevented by effective ethical codes because they can help to create an ethical culture in which employees believe doing what is right is expected and bringing forward concerns over unethical behavior will not result in ethical martyrdom.

Codes can be drafted to fulfill different rationales and to provide different depths of coverage. Table 5.15 describes four common levels of coverage.

The rationales[41] for developing codes that were discovered by The Conference Board's survey were the following:

1. ***Instrumental***—to make employees aware that "employee adherence to the company's ethical principles is critical to bottom-line success"
2. ***Compliance***—to provide a "statement of do's and don'ts to govern employee conduct"
3. ***Stakeholder Commitment***—to offer a discussion of what is expected behavior in stakeholder relationships
4. ***Values/Mission***—to establish "certain ethics principles, modes of behavior, and habits of mind as essential to what it means to be an employee or representative of the company" (see Johnson & Johnson's famous Credo in the inset box below, which was credited with facilitating the first Tylenol product recall; see also the vignette in Chapter 2 titled *Johnson & Johnson's Worldwide Recall of Tylenol: Virtue Ethics*)
5. None or a composite of the above

Johnson & Johnson Credo

We believe our first responsibility is to the doctors, nurses, and patients, to mothers and all others who use our products and services. In meeting their needs everything we do must be of high quality. We must constantly strive to reduce our costs in order to maintain reasonable prices. Customers' orders must be serviced promptly and accurately. Our suppliers and distributors must have an opportunity to make a fair profit.

We are responsible to our employees, the men and women who work with us throughout the world. Everyone must be considered as an individual. We must respect their dignity and recognize their merit. They must have a sense of security in their jobs. Compensation must be fair and adequate and working conditions clean, orderly, and safe. Employees must feel free to make suggestions and complaints. There must be equal opportunity for employment, development, and advancement for those qualified. We must provide competent management, and their actions must be just and ethical.

We are responsible to the communities in which we live and work and to the world community as well. We must be good citizens—support good works and charities and bear our fair share of taxes. We must encourage civic improvements and better health and education. We must maintain in good order the property we are privileged to use, protecting the environment and natural resources.

Our final responsibility is to our stockholders. Business must make a sound profit. We must experiment with new ideas. Research must be carried on,

[41] Ibid., 24–27.

> *innovative programs developed and mistakes paid for. New equipment must be purchased, new facilities provided, and new products launched. Reserves must be created to provide for adverse times. When we operate according to these principles, the stockholders should realize a fair return.*

In its survey of global ethics practices, The Conference Board found that these rationales were chosen with different frequencies, depending on the country or region involved. In the United States, the dominant "instrumental" choice reflects the pressures from stakeholders and the legalistic environment faced. Potentially heavy sanctions have been created for misdeeds due to the advent of the U.S. Foreign Corrupt Practices Act and the U.S. Sentencing Guidelines. Elsewhere, except in Latin America, the values/mission approach was most popular. The choices of rationale, by region,[42] are noted in Table 5.16.

Corporate codes of conduct should encourage employees' behavior at the higher levels of Kohlberg's (1981, 1984) stages of moral development. Kohlberg argues that people develop and move through six stages in their moral maturity. At the first stage, people are ethical because they fear being punished if they are not; small children are normally at this stage. At the next stage, individuals are ethical because they realize that it is in their best interest to be so; an example would be children playing with one another's toys. At the third stage, people acknowledge that ethical behavior is what others expect; people are ethical because of peer pressure. The fourth stage is where individuals accept obedience to moral and ethical laws. At the fifth stage, individuals develop a concern for the social welfare of society, and at the final stage, individuals develop a principled conscience, adhering to moral and social codes because they are the moral principles that guide society. Each stage has a broader perspective than the one before regarding the role, duties, and obligations of the individual in society. Although few individuals may achieve the sixth stage, organizational structures should be established to encourage and facilitate individuals moving to higher levels of moral reasoning. Corporate codes of conduct can help.[43]

The research findings of Weaver et al. (1999b), Treviño et al. (1999), and others noted earlier indicate that a corporate code that adopts an integrity or values orientation will be more effective in engendering adherence to desired ethical standards than other alternatives. The most successful will be a code that is a combination that focuses on the important values that the corporation wants to apply in its stakeholder relationships but where this is reinforced by sanctions inherent in the compliance approach. Such a composite orientation

TABLE 5.16 Dominant Rationales for Codes by Region

	UNITED STATES	CANADA	EUROPE	LATIN AMERICA	JAPAN
Instrumental	64%	30%	—	50%	17%
Stakeholder	5	10	30	—	17
Legal Compliance	14	—	—	25	33
Values/Mission	14	40	60	25	33
None	2	20	10	—	—
$N = 72$					

Source: The Conference Board, *Global Corporate Ethics Practices: A Developing Consensus*\ (New York: The Conference Board, 1999), 28.

[42] Ibid., 28.

[43] Kohlberg's six stages of moral development are more fully discussed in Chapter 6.

TABLE 5.17 Code Guidance Alternatives & the Control/Motivation Signaled

GUIDANCE PROVIDED	CONTROL/MOTIVATION SIGNALED
Obey these rules	Imposed Control
Seek advice before acting	↑
Act on your best judgment but disclose what you have done	↓
Guiding principles that indicate "this is what we are and what we stand for"	Self-control

Sources: Clarkson and Deck (1992); Clarkson, Deck, and Leblanc (1997).

code would encourage shared values, support employee aspirations, communicate values, and build trust and confidence while indicating that processes were in place to monitor and judge ethical performance. In this form, the composite orientation code would provide motivation to employees on all of Kohlberg's six stages of moral reasoning.

The form and nature in which guidance is given and action expected can also limit or foster optimal motivation for moral reasoning. Four alternatives are possible for the nature of the guidance provided. The alternative chosen will provide a signal to employees about the way the organization thinks about its control structure, ranging from an autocratic, imposed control structure on one end of the spectrum to self-imposed control on the other end. Table 5.17 identifies the four alternatives and the nature of control they signal.

In view of the findings of Abraham Maslow (1954) and Douglas McGregor (1960) and subsequently others who argued that an autocratic management style was less effective than a democratic or participative approach, it is likely that using only imposed control techniques could be similarly suboptimal. Maslow argued that autocratic management techniques involved influence attempts directed at the lower level of his hierarchy of human needs (physiological and safety), whereas a democratic or participative approach was directed at higher-level needs (affiliation, esteem, and self-actualization) and therefore was more likely to provide a sustainable and more engaging level of motivation. In a world that has since moved toward employee empowerment rather than imposed control (Simons 1995), a code that employs only imposed control is likely to be less effective than one that encourages self-control. A code that successfully encourages self-control would appeal to individuals on all of Kohlberg's six stages of moral reasoning, whereas the imposed control code would motivate for the lower four stages. In keeping with the reasoning in favor of a composite-oriented, values-based, and compliance-based code, consulting experience has shown that the most successful codes encourage self-control or empowerment, with absolute rules being introduced where necessary. These codes usually provide a set of principles with explanations or rationales being given for each. These principles and their rationales are to be used by employees to reason how to deal with the decisions they face or to determine whom to contact if they need counsel.

CODE CONTENT & SCOPE Numerous readings are available that outline the topics that are covered in different codes.[44] Examples of different codes are available on the websites of major corporations.

[44] Clarkson and Deck (1992); White and Montgomery (1980); Mathews (1987); Berenbeim (1987); Brooks (1989); Institute of Chartered Accountants in England and Wales, "Developing and Implementing Organisational Codes of Conduct: An Overview of Implementing and Developing Codes of Conduct," http://www.icaew.com/en/technical/ethics/practice-business-ethics/practice/developing-and-implementing-organisational-codes-of-conduct; International Federation of Accountants, 2007, "Defining and Developing an Effective Code of Conduct for Organizations," 2007, http://www.ifac.org/sites/default/files/publications/files/Defining-and-Developing-an-Effective-Code-of-Conduct-for-Orgs_0.pdf. The last two were accessed August 30, 2013.

The choice of orientation of the code and its topics depends somewhat on the scope of the code. Is the code intended to provide guidance to the company's own employees, its suppliers and vendors, and/or its joint venture partners? Geographic locale, union contracts, legal restrictions, competitive practices, and the degree of ownership and/or partner support inherent in the scope decision are critical to the orientation and choice of topics to be included. If a company cannot be comfortable about the guidance to be given, then it should consider whether the arrangement is too high a risk to be undertaken. For example, to do business in a repressive regime that does not respect human rights or with a partner that does not do so should give rise to consideration of noninvolvement.

In the late 1990s, Nike found that its suppliers used sweatshops and child labor, producing low-cost products; this triggered boycotts and necessitated the development of monitoring and reporting mechanisms. Recently, stakeholder activists have become much more aggressive in making companies accountable for the actions of suppliers and joint ventures. Four organizations are leading the development of supplier/workplace standards and codes of conduct—Social Accountability International (SAI) and the Fair Labor Association, Maquila Solidarity, and the International Labor Office. SAI has developed the SA 8000, which is a standard designed to improve working conditions globally, and is engaged in the training of auditors for the certification of companies adhering to SA 8000. It is modeled after the ISO standards.

Table 5.18 presents a representative list of topics a company might consider including in its codes for its own employees, suppliers, and joint ventures.

Each company should undertake a review of its code when issues and risks emerge that require adjustment of the coverage. For example, codes have been modified in reaction to the external shocks identified in Table 5.19.

Looking ahead, it is likely that codes will be modified to encompass the following:

- Antibribery statutes enacted as early as 1999 by about 30 countries in the OECD who have responded to the call of Transparency International for standards that will outlaw bribery of foreign officials and allow cross-border investigation and

TABLE 5.18 Subjects Found in Codes

Ethical principles—honesty, fairness, compassion, integrity, predictability, responsibility

Respect for stakeholder rights, and duties owed to each stakeholder

Vision, mission, and key policies tied into the above

Ethical decision-making frameworks, sniff tests, rules of thumb, and guidance on making tradeoffs between competing objectives

When to seek counsel, and whom to seek it from

Specific topics found in over 5% of employee, supplier, and joint venture codes:

- Bribery/improper payments or influences
- Conflict of interest
- Security of proprietary information
- Receiving gifts
- Discrimination/equal opportunity
- Giving gifts
- Environmental protection
- Sexual harassment
- Antitrust
- Workplace safety
- Community relations
- Confidentiality of personal information
- Human rights
- Employee privacy
- Whistleblowing and protection programs
- Substance abuse
- Nepotism
- Child labor
- Political activities

Source: The Conference Board Research Report, *Global Corporate Ethics Practices*, 1999, 29.

TABLE 5.19 External Shocks & Influences Triggering Code Modification

Antibribery legislation—*U.S. Foreign Corrupt Practices Act of 1977*
  This act provided an early motivation for codes

U.S. Sentencing Guidelines of 1991
  Brought provision for "Due Diligence" defense

Environmental responsibility:
  Acid rain, air pollution, ozone depletion
  (UN Brundtland Commission Report of 1987)
  New Environmental Protection statutes
  Exxon Valdez oil tanker spill triggers Valdez (now CERES) Principles

Fair treatment for:
  Employees:
    Feminism: sexual harassment, equal opportunity for pay and promotion
    Minorities: discrimination*
    Health, safety, and well-being
      Supplier employees—no sweatshop or child labor
    Drug problems—privacy vs. safety
    Whistleblowers**
Customers—buyer beware slowly becomes seller beware
    Health and safety concerns—auto recalls (see Ford, Firestone case)
    Ethical consumerism, and quality
Shareholders:
    Misuse of inside information
    Conflict of interests
    Mandate and operations are ethical—Enron's banks engage in transactions without economic substance designed to mislead

*See ethics case *Texaco's Jelly Beans* in Chapter 7.
**See GE case described in reading by Andrew Singer in Chapter 1.

litigation by competitors (see **www.cengagebrain.com**). In addition, guidance should cover the 2010 global application of the U.S. *Foreign Corrupt Practices Act* (see the Daimler's Settles U.S. Bribery Case for $185 million in Chapter 5) and the broader U.K. *Bribery Act (2010)* that are discussed in Chapter 7.

- Adherence to company principles by suppliers, particularly in foreign operations with respect to child labor, fair wages, no forced labor, and so on.
- Integrity or values orientation.
- Self-control instead of only imposed control.
- Security of information.
- Environmental management and performance.
- Sustainability objectives and management.
- Governance principles—clarification of accountability to the board of directors and stakeholders, transparency, and risk management for regular and ethics risks.
- Ethicality of objectives and competitive practices.

These modifications will also be guided by the application of measures of the effectiveness of codes. Codes can be scored or reviewed for comprehensiveness of coverage and for the nature of control signaled. Other measures have been identified, such as surveys of employee awareness and understanding of key aspects covered in the code and in training programs, and their ability to apply these to the ethical dilemmas has been proposed.

Benchmarking of codes is done by many consultants. Company employees can also do so by comparing their code against the subjects that information services report on or that are included in the Global Reporting Initiative (GRI) discussed in Chapter 7.

Helpful advice on the preparation of codes can be obtained from several organizations, including the following:

- Institute of Business Ethics: http://www.ibe.org.uk
- Creating a Code of Ethics for Your Organization: http://www.ethicsweb.ca/codes/

EFFECTIVE IMPLEMENTATION Because a code of conduct is critical to organizational success for several reasons, it is important to ensure that a code is both effectively drafted *and implemented.* A properly functioning code is essential to the following:

- The development and maintenance of an ethical corporate culture—a culture of integrity
- An effective internal control system.
- A "due diligence defense" for directors and officers.
- Effective empowerment for employees to make ethical decisions.
- Sending proper signals to external stakeholders.

In order to avoid implementation problems, the following issues should be kept in mind. *Top management must endorse and support the code* and be seen to act in accord with it, or it will be given only lip service by management and workers. It is critical that management "walk the talk," or the entire program will be a waste of time and money.

The orientation, tone, and content of the code must be such that *general principles are favored instead of only specific rules*, or else employees will find the code oppressive and hard to interpret, and *background reasons must be given* to permit understanding sufficient for useful interpretation when specifics are not available. Experience has shown that codes designed as extensive rulebooks are rarely useful because they are too difficult to consult. If the underlying reason for a specific pattern of behavior is given, employees find it easier to understand and they buy-in rather than fight the code or dismiss it. Getting the buy-in is essential.

Guidance should be provided for trade-offs between short-term profit and social objectives. If employees believe profit is to be earned at all costs, then unethical behavior based on short-term thinking can get the company into trouble.

A complete "due diligence" defense should be in place for environmental matters, including the items noted in Table 5.20.

Employees should be empowered to make ethical decisions. This should involve setting up *decision protocols* that will require employees to use and be able to defend their decisions against a set of criteria or questions that are outlined further in Chapter 6. Part of the decision process should involve the use of *sniff tests*—quick, simple questions that will alert the decision maker when to undertake an in-depth ethical analysis or to seek counsel. When in doubt over the proper conduct, *employees should be encouraged to seek counsel.* Rather than have them act inappropriately or waste time needlessly, a company should encourage employees to consult their superior or an ethics officer or use a hotline.

A *fair and confidential hearing process should be ensured*, or whistleblowers will not come forward. They do not want to risk paying the price for snitching, even though it is in the best interests of the company. Nor do they want a person accused to be dealt with in a cavalier way—they want a speedy, fair hearing process with protection for both parties. *Whistleblowing should be legitimized*, and whistleblowers who come forward should be protected.

Someone should be charged with the *ongoing responsibility for updating the code* so that issues can be referred as they come up. Otherwise, many issues will be lost in the

TABLE 5.20 Essential Features to Demonstrate a Due Diligence Defense in Respect of Environmental Matters

1. A written environmental policy, made known to appropriate employees
2. Operating practices that guard against environmental malfeasance, including contingency plans to cover mishaps to ensure full scale, timely cleanup
3. Employees briefed on their duties and responsibilities under the policy, as well as their potential personal liability and the liability of others
4. Employees informed of legal requirements, including notice to government complete with a contact list
5. A person who is primarily responsible for environmental matters and monitoring compliance
6. Consideration of an environmental audit or consultation with an expert to start the protection process and monitor progress
7. Monitor pollution control systems and report mishaps on a timely basis
8. Regularly review reports on compliance, potential problems environmental charges, conviction, and employee training
9. Management that keeps abreast of new legislation, makes an internal review of compliance, and advises directors of the results and allocates a real and satisfactory budget to achieve these features

pressures of day-to-day activity or because people will not know where to send their suggestions.

Distribution of the code should be to all employees so that none will be able to claim they were not told how to behave. It is surprising that some companies believe their line workers do not have responsibility for environmental acts or for actions toward fellow workers and so on. Not only do excellent suggestions come from the plant, but bad actions are also noticed, and support for the company's general activities is enhanced by bringing these employees into the distribution, in addition to management personnel.

Training in support of the code is essential. This training should focus on the awareness of issues, interpretation of the code in accord with top management wishes, approaches to ethical analysis to enable decisions beyond the code, realistic cases for discussion, and legitimizing the discussion of ethical issues and of whistleblowing. Codes are written by committees who spend long hours over each paragraph, so how is each employee supposed to know all the thought that went into its construction simply by quickly reading the passage? Training is essential to help understand what is meant and how the code applies to new problems.

Reinforcement of and compliance with the code should be furthered by mechanisms of encouragement, monitoring, and facilitation of the reporting of wrongdoing. These issues should not be left to chance; otherwise, the organization might miss an opportunity to head off a disaster or to accomplish an ethical performance objective. These methods are summarized in Table 5.21.

Reinforcement of the code should be undertaken through measurement of the code's effectiveness, reporting of ethical performance for management purposes, featuring ethical performance in company publications, and ensuring that other company policies are supportive, including a linkage with the remuneration systems. If you cannot measure performance (techniques are discussed in Chapters 4, 6, and 7), it is very hard to manage it. Reporting performance has the impact of producing scorecards that people are induced to improve for their next reports. Publicity of good results can have a salutary effect on subsequent performance as well, and including that performance in

TABLE 5.21 Mechanisms for Compliance Encouragement, Monitoring, & Reporting Wrongdoing

Compliance encouragement
- Awards, bonuses
- Inclusion in performance reviews, remuneration decisions, and promotion
- Reprimands, suspension, demotion, fines, dismissal

Monitoring
- Ethics audit or internal audit procedures
- Reviews by legal department
- Annual sign-off by all or some employees
- Employee surveys

Facilitation of reporting of wrongdoing
- Assurance of a fair hearing process
- Protection: absolute confidentiality, whistleblower protection plan
- Counseling/information: ombudsperson program, hotline, human resources
- Committee oversight assured: Ethics Committee of board, Audit Committee

the corporation's reward systems will go a long way toward underscoring how important ethical issues are to top management.

The board of directors should actively review and monitor whistleblower concerns on financial and nonfinancial matters and ethics program activities and feedback. This will ensure that the board is aware of problems and can take appropriate action before the company's reputation, activities, or stakeholders are compromised.

To have an effective corporate culture, not only do codes need constant upgrading under the watchful eye of an ethics officer, but constant attention must also be given to improving training programs, measures and reports of performance, compliance, and whistleblowing mechanisms. In addition, it is essential to have a formal external or internal review of the corporation's culture, code, and other mechanisms on a periodic basis. This is often referred to as an *ethical audit*, and although it may be undertaken by the internal audit staff or a team of budding managers, such as in the Dow Corning case at the end of this chapter, an outside consulting service provides useful feedback.

Finally, it should be understood that it is unlikely that employees will see the merit of ethical behavior in regard to one area of the company's operations if they believe management wants or is prepared to tolerate questionable behavior in other areas. Whistleblowers will not come forward, for example, unless there is a feeling of trust that they and the parties they accuse will be dealt with fairly and confidentially. Consequently, the development of a broadly based ethical culture within the company is an essential precursor for an effective code of conduct and vice versa.

Helpful comprehensive references for the rationale for contents, development, and implementation of code of conduct may be found at the following websites:

- Institute of Chartered Accountants in England and Wales, "Developing and Implementing Organisational Codes of Conduct: An Overview of Implementing and Developing Codes of Conduct," http://www.icaew.com/en/technical/ethics/practice-business-ethics/practice/developing-and-implementing-organisational-codes-of-conduct
- International Federation of Accountants, 2007, "Defining and Developing an Effective Code of Conduct for Organizations": http://www.ifac.org/publications-resources/defining-and-developing-effective-code-conduct-organizations

Ethical Leadership

The values that underlay an ethical corporate culture or culture of integrity cannot be effectively shared, implemented, nurtured, and monitored without effective ethical leadership. Without the right "tone at the top," managers and employees will not subscribe to the organization's ethical values, believing instead that only short-term profit maximization matters.

Leaving employees to their own assumptions about a corporation's values is a very high-risk strategy for both the corporation and the personnel involved. Consequently, effective ethical leadership is becoming increasingly important to both corporations and executives, managers, and supervisors who wish to contribute successfully and to enhance their careers. They need to understand what ethical leadership is, what it involves, and how to achieve it. It must also be understood that, although ethical leadership should come from all persons in leadership positions, an ethical corporate culture cannot be created or sustained without strong, visible ethical leadership from the CEO and the board chair.

Ethical leaders have definite, important responsibilities in regard to the development and maintenance of a corporation's ethical culture. But there is an overarching role to be understood if their leadership is to be ethically effective. Essentially, *an ethical leader must embody the organization's vision and values and influence others to follow his or her lead.*[45] Functionally, an ethical leader must do the following:

- Ensure that the vision and values of the organization are ethically sound.
- Identify with and support them.
- Communicate them.
- Ensure that the organization's ethical culture (code, training, decision making, performance indicators, reward systems, and monitoring system) supports its vision and values.
- Motivate other leaders and employees to adhere to them.
- Monitor and reward or penalize performance.

In order to best achieve these goals, a leader must be able to successfully influence other executives and supervisors as well as employees. Long-lasting influence is based on respect. Research has shown that effective ethical leaders are respected for their character: for their care for others and their interests; for principled, fair, and balanced decisions; and for practicing what they preach.[46]

Since their purpose is to influence ethical behavior, ethical leaders cannot develop the necessary respect unless they present an ethical role model to be emulated. This requires consideration of a leader's personality characteristics, motivation, interpersonal style, moral judgment, and moral utilization level.

Research has shown that the following personality characteristics can have a direct effect on effective ethical leadership:

- Agreeableness—Are they altruistic, trusting, kind and cooperative?
- Openness—Are they imaginative, curious, artistic, and insightful?
- Extraversion—Are they active, assertive, energetic, and outgoing?

---

[45] R. Edward Freeman and Lisa Stewart, *Developing Ethical Leadership* (Business Roundtable Institute for Corporate Ethics, 2006), 3, http://www.corporate-ethics.org. See also insert box.

[46] Michael E. Brown and Linda K. Treviño, "Ethical Leadership: A Review and Future Directions," *The Leadership Quarterly* 17 (2006): 595–616.

- Conscientiousness—Are they dependable, responsible, dutiful, and determined?
- Neuroticism—Are they anxious, hostile, impulsive, or stressed? They should not be.[47]

These characteristics, which can be summarized as *integrity*, *trustworthiness*, *honesty*, *sincerity*, and *forthrightness* or *candor*,[48] identify ethical values or character traits an ethical leader should possess in order to be considered nonhypocritical. They are key to building trust with other leaders and employees, which is essential to their willingness to become followers and supporters of the organization's vision and values. Trust is vital in overcoming the natural cynicism that pervades organizations and reinforces the belief that a corporation's purpose is to make profit at any cost.

Organizational cynicism is also the reason why ethical leaders must visibly and audibly support their organization's ethical vision and values. If they stay silent, their silence will likely be interpreted to mean that they are supporters of the "profit at any cost" approach. If ethical leaders use guile, deceit, or opportunism in their interpersonal relations, followers are likely to view any message about an ethical vision and values as nonsense. To be most effective, an ethical leader's use of power should not be egotistically focused but should recognize and incorporate the interests of employees and show concern for them.

Another aspect of ethical leadership that engenders trust is in the level of moral judgment[49] used. For example, if a leader wishes to convey an ethical message, it is more effective to appeal to followers based on ethical principles that are of value to everyone and positive social interaction rather than threats to their livelihood. Even if leaders think ethical thoughts, they must evidence this in their actions, such as by using fair practices, or their thoughts will not be correctly understood due to misperceived assumptions about how followers can best be developed and motivated and to organizational cynicism.

It is helpful to recognize, as has been pointed out by Linda Treviño[50] and her colleagues, truly effective ethical leaders must be moral people as well as moral managers, or else their followers will come to recognize them as hypocrites when their true natures show. Treviño et al. proposed the two-dimensional schema shown in Figure 5.10 to represent where executives rank on each dimension and how each contributes to the reputation of the leader as an ethical leader.

The *character traits associated with ethical leadership (integrity, trustworthiness, honesty, sincerity, and forthrightness or candor)* are surprisingly similar to the dimensions in Fombrun's Reputation Model (Figure 1.3) that was developed in Chapter 1. Character traits form the basis for behaviors that exhibit the following:

- Doing the right thing
- Concern for people
- Being open and approachable for discussion of concerns
- Personal morality

---

[47] Ibid.

[48] Treviño et al., "Moral Person and Moral Manager."

[49] Lawrence Kohlberg's model of Moral Development identified six levels of what motivated moral reasoning, with the lowest level related to threats and the highest levels related to high moral principles. He and others have theorized and found that the higher the level of moral reasoning used, the more powerful the motivating potential. See L. Kohlberg, *Essays on Moral Development*, vols. 1 and 2 (New York: Harper & Row, 1981, 1984).

[50] Ibid., 130.

FIGURE 5.10 Executive Reputation and Ethical Leadership

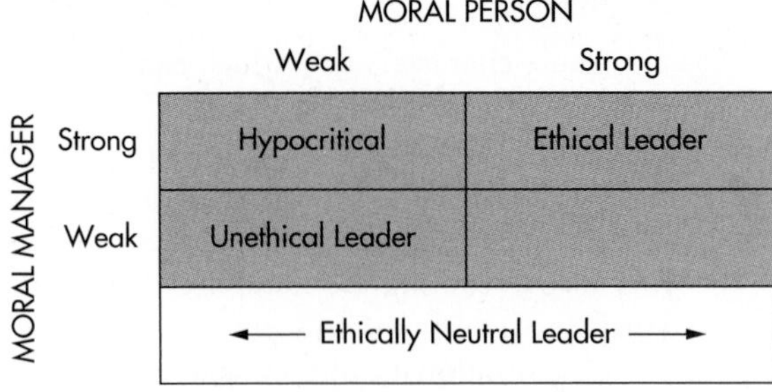

Source: L. K. Treviño et al., "Moral Person and Moral Manager: How Executives Develop a Reputation for Ethical Leadership," *California Management Review* 42, no. 4 (Summer 2000_. Reprinted with permission.)

Similarly, executive *decision making*, to be considered sound, should correspond by doing the following:

- Holding to desired values
- Being objective and fair
- Exhibiting concern for society
- Following reasonable ethical decision rules[51]

These traits, behaviors, and decision-making characteristics should be transparently evident, or else they may be misinterpreted, and the executive may not be viewed as a moral or ethical person.

Achievement of the reputation of a moral or ethical person does not, however, guarantee a reputation as a moral manager or leader—that depends on how well and extensively an executive promotes his or her support for the corporation's ethics and values agenda. Treviño et al. (2000) found that this could be done effectively through the following:

- Serving as a visible role model
- Communicating regularly and persuasively about ethical standards, principles, and values
- Using the rewards system to hold all employees accountable to ethical standards[52]

As reflected in Figure 5.10, being an ethical leader requires strong performance as both a moral person and a moral manager. To attempt ethical leadership from a weak base as a moral person is highly risky, as the likelihood of being discovered to be a hypocrite is high. An unethical leader is low on both dimensions, and a person who does not practice overt ethical guidance will be seen as an ethically neutral leader even if the individual is a highly moral or ethical person.

The key to ethical leadership is visible effective action stemming from an ethical base. This kind of leadership will greatly reinforce the corporation's ethics program and its attempts to develop and maintain an ethical corporate culture. Without strong ethical leadership from executives and supervisors, attempts to develop and maintain an ethical

[51] Ibid., 131.

[52] Ibid., 134.

corporate culture are doomed to mediocrity and probably failure. In summary, if ethical leaders genuinely want followers to learn appropriate behavior and to avoid counterproductive or unethical behavior, they must fully embody the intended vision and values and must not only believe in them but also communicate those beliefs in actions and exhortations. Only then can they provide the right "tone at the top."

Summary of a Very Helpful Publication:
The Business Roundtable's View of Developing Ethical Leadership

According to Ed Freeman and Lisa Stewart,

> *Ethical leaders embody the purpose, vision, and values of the organization and of the constituents, within an understanding of ethical ideals. They connect the goals of the organization with those of the internal employees and external stakeholders.*
>
> *Leaders see their constituents as not just followers, but rather as stakeholders striving to achieve that same common purpose, vision, and values. These follower and stakeholder constituents have their own individuality and autonomy which must be respected to maintain a moral community.*
>
> *Leaders work to create an open, two-way conversation, thereby maintaining a charitable understanding of different views, values, and constituents' opinions. They are open to others' opinions and ideas because they know those ideas make the organization they are leading better.*[53]

Freeman and Stewart suggest that ethical leaders should have the following characteristics:

1. *Articulate and embody the purpose and values of the organization.*
2. *Focus on organizational success rather than on personal ego.*
3. *Find the best people and develop them.*
4. *Create a living conversation about ethics, values, and the creation of value for stakeholders.*
5. *Create mechanisms of dissent.*
6. *Take a charitable understanding of others' values.*
7. *Make tough calls while being imaginative.*
8. *Know the limits of the values*[54] *and ethical principles they live.*
9. *Frame actions in ethical terms.*
10. *Connect the basic value proposition to stakeholder support and societal legitimacy.*[55]

Corporate Psychopaths

Not everyone can be an ethical leader. Recently, observers[56] have begun to speculate that there is a set of businesspeople who are simply incapable of being ethical leaders and that it is extremely important that care be taken to identify such people and to endure

[53] R. Edward Freeman and Lisa Stewart, *Developing Ethical Leadership* (Business Roundtable Institute for Corporate Ethics, 2006), 14, http://www.corporate-ethics.org.

[54] Values are rarely absolute, and their application needs to be tempered by judgment depending on circumstances.

[55] Freeman and Stewart, *Developing Ethical Leadership*, 3–7.

[56] See, for example, the works of Clive R. Boddy in the *Journal of Business Ethics*, 2005, 2006, 2010, and 2011.

that they do not find their way into corporate leadership positions. The term *corporate psychopaths* has been created to capture the essence of people characterized as follows:

- "Lack a conscience, have few emotions, and display an inability to have feelings, sympathy or empathy for other people."[57]
- "Ruthlessly manipulate others, without, conscience, to further their own aims and objectives."[58]
- "Although they may look smooth, charming, sophisticated, and successful … should theoretically be almost wholly destructive to the organization they work for."[59]
- "Are callously disregarding of the needs and wishes of others, prepared to lie, bully and cheat and to disregard or cause harm to the welfare of others."[60]

Needless to say, corporate psychopaths are likely to be extremely destructive within an organization and cannot be effective role models in the development and maintenance of an ethical corporate culture.

There is further concern that corporate psychopaths are drawn to specific industries, such as those in the investment and banking sector, and may have been a significant causal factor in the unethical excessive bonus, securitization, and loan practices that gave rise to the subprime lending crisis of 2008. These concerns are discussed in Chapter 8.

Given the emerging recognition of the damage corporate psychopaths can produce, it is particularly important to ensure that such people do not get into positions of power where they can hijack or divert the healthy development of an ethical corporate culture and prevent the corporation from achieving a culture of integrity.

Director & Officer Liability

Corporate ethical governance and accountability is no longer just good business—it's the law. SOX triggered governance reform for SEC registrant companies around the world and spawned similar governance reform regulation in many other national jurisdictions. Section 404 of SOX requires companies to examine the effectiveness of their internal control systems with regard to financial reporting. The CEO, CFO, and auditors must report on and certify that effectiveness. Conscious miscertification by the CEO and CFO can lead to criminal as well as civil charges.

The mandatory review of internal control involves comparison of the corporation's systems with an accepted internal control framework, such as that developed for Enterprise Risk Management (ERM) by the Committee of Sponsoring Organizations (COSO) of the Treadway Commission. Further information on the COSO approach[61] is available in auditing texts or on the COSO website. The COSO ERM framework, introduced in 2004, covers how an entity achieves its objectives on four dimensions: strategic, operations, reporting, and compliance. Within each of these dimensions or categories, the

---

[57] Clive R. Boddy, "The Corporate Psychopaths Theory of the Global Financial Crisis," *Journal of Business Ethics* 102 (Spring 2011): 256.

[58] P. Babiak and R. D. Hare, 2006, *Snakes in Suits When Psychopaths Go to Work* (New York: HarperCollins, 2006).

[59] Boddy, "The Corporate Psychopaths Theory of the Global Financial Crisis," 256.

[60] S. E. Perkel, "Book Review: Bad Leadership: What It Is, How It Happens, Why It Matters," in B. Kellerman, ed., *Consulting to Management* 16, 59–61 (an e-journal published by the Journal of Management Consulting, Inc.).

[61] See, for example, Committee of Sponsoring Organizations of the Treadway Commission, *Enterprise Risk Management—Integrated Framework: Executive Summary*, September 2004, http://www.coso.org/guidance.htm.

ERM framework involves eight interrelated components concerning the way management runs an enterprise and how they are integrated with the management process: internal environment, objective setting, event identification, risk assessment, risk response, control activities, information and communication, and monitoring. An updated ERM framework that expands on the importance of the links between enterprise risk management with organizational strategy and firm performance was released for discussion via the COSO website in June 2016, and is discussed further in Chapter 7.

Ethics and an ethical corporate culture are seen to play a vital role in setting the control environment and thereby in creating an effective ERM-oriented internal control system and the behavior that results. Consequently, a COS ERM-oriented review will examine the tone at the top, codes of conduct, employee awareness, pressures to meet unrealistic or inappropriate goals, management's willingness to override established controls, code adherence in performance appraisals, monitoring of internal control system effectiveness, whistleblowing programs, and remedial actions in response to code violations.[62]

Not surprisingly, some of these new governance requirements—tone at the top, existence of codes, adherence to policies, adequate disclosure, and so on—have been endorsed by stock exchanges that have required compliance of companies whose shares are listed. The governance requirements of the New York Stock Exchange, the Toronto Stock Exchange, and others can be accessed at **www.cengagebrain.com.**

What happens if these new governance expectations are not met? Noncompliance with stock exchange regulations can result in fines, suspension, or delisting of the stock being traded, in addition to limitations being placed on offending directors or management. Noncompliance with SOX requirements laid down in SEC regulations or in similar securities commission regulations around the world can lead to civil and also criminal prosecution. The former can result in fines and personal limitations, while the latter can add *significant jail terms* for executives. A recent development is the requirement that executives and directors may be required to pay the fines *personally* rather than with company funds or through insurance plans. This frightening prospect was responsible for an article in the January 13, 2005, issue of the *Wall Street Journal*, titled "Some Outside Directors Consider Quitting in Wake of Settlements,"[63] which related that ten Enron and ten WorldCom directors had agreed to pay a total of $31 million of their own money to settle lawsuits.

When deciding whether to prosecute, the U.S. Department of Justice uses factors identified in guidance that it has published.[64] For example, important factors examined include the following:

- Whether the compliance program is substantive or just a paper sham
- Whether management is enforcing the program or encouraging misconduct
- Whether here is staff sufficient to monitor and audit the compliance program
- Whether employees are aware of the program and convinced of the corporation's commitment to it[65]

If convicted, management and directors will have to face penalties in the United States that meet the provision of the U.S. Sentencing Guidelines as amended on November 1, 2004. Penalties for SOX violations for misconduct in the preparation of financial statements and their reporting (Section 304) could include reimbursement of the issuer for any bonus or incentive payments or equity-based compensation received by the CEO

[62] Principal source: KPMG Forensic, *Integrity Survey 2005–2006*, 2005.

[63] J. S. Lublin, T. Francis, and J. Weil, "Some Outside Directors Consider Quitting in Wake of Settlements," *Wall Street Journal*, January 13, 2005, B13.

[64] Ibid., KMPG *Integrity Survey 2005–2006*, 21.

[65] KPMG Forensic, *Integrity Survey.*

TABLE 5.22 U.S. Sentencing Guidelines Ethics Criteria per KPMG 2005–2006

CRITERIA FOR DETERMINING DEGREE OF CULPABILITY & MITIGATION OF PENALTY

Specifically, the amended guidelines call on organizations to do the following:

- Promote a culture that encourages ethical conduct and a commitment to compliance with the law.
- Establish standards and procedures to prevent and detect criminal conduct.
- Ensure the board of directors and senior executives are knowledgeable and exercise reasonable oversight of the compliance/ethics program.
- Assign a high-level individual within the organization to ensure the organization has an effective compliance and ethics program, and delegate day-to-day operational responsibility to individuals with adequate resources authority, and direct access to the board.
- Use reasonable efforts and exercise due diligence to exclude individuals from positions of substantial authority who have engaged in illegal activities or other conduct inconsistent with an effective compliance and ethics program.
- Conduct effective training programs for directors, officers, employees, and other agents and provide such individuals with periodic information appropriate to their respective roles and responsibilities relative to the compliance and ethics program.
- Ensure that the compliance and ethics program is followed, including monitoring and auditing to detect criminal conduct.
- Publicize a system, which may include mechanisms for anonymity and confidentiality, whereby the organization's employees and agents may report to seek guidance regarding potential or actual misconduct without fear of retaliation.
- Evaluate periodically the effectiveness of the compliance and ethics program.
- Promote and enforce consistently the compliance and ethics program through incentives and disciplinary measures.
- Take reasonable steps to respond appropriately to misconduct, including making necessary modification to the compliance/ethics program.

Source: Reprinted from KPMG *Integrity Survey* 2005–2006. Copyright © 2006 KPMG International. All information provided is of a general nature and is not intended to address the circumstances of any particular individual or entity. Although we endeavor to provide accurate and timely information, there can be no guarantee that such information is accurate as of the date it is received or that it will continue to be accurate in the future. No one should act upon such information without appropriate professional advice after a thorough examination of the facts of a particular situation For additional news and information, please access KPMG LLP's website on the Internet at http://www.us.kpmg.com.

and/or CFO in the year following, plus any profit on sale of stock during that period. Also, consciously certifying a statement knowing noncompliance is subject to a fine of $1 million and imprisonment up to ten years, and purposely certifying such a statement increases the penalties to $5 million and imprisonment for up to twenty years (Section 906). SOX also lowered the threshold for barring individuals from acting as a director or officer of an issuer from "substantial unfitness" to "unfitness" (Section 305).[66] As indicated in the study by KPMG Forensics, "*These guidelines now make more explicit the expectation that organizations promote a culture of ethical conduct, tailor each program element based on compliance risk, and periodically evaluate program effectiveness.*"[67]

These penalties are so significant that misunderstanding and/or failing to mitigate them is unattractive. Table 5.22 provides a list of specific ethics expectation guidelines that are to be considered in regard to the application of penalties per the *U.S. Sentencing Guidelines*, as amended on November 1, 2004.

Public Accountability Benchmarks

One of the recent developments that a board of directors and management need to consider when developing the values, policies, and principles that underpin their corporation's culture and the actions of their employees is the recent surge in stakeholder

[66] Principal source: *CEO and CFO Certification: Improving Transparency and Accountability, a Canadian Performance Reporting Board Discussion Brief*, Canadian Institute of Chartered Accountants, 2004, 41. Canadian penalties for securities act violations are fines up to $5 million or prison terms up to five years less a day, and for insider trading, the fine would be up to the greater of triple the "profit" made (or loss avoided) and $5 million. Other fines involving disgorgement of ill-gotten gains are also possible.

[67] KPMG Forensic, *Integrity Survey*.

TABLE 5.23 Emerging Public Accountability Standards and Initiatives

GRI	Global Reporting Initiative
	A framework for economic, social, and environmental reporting. Thousands of reports available
ISO 26000	Guidance on Social Responsibility
	Principles, topics, and approaches for the development and implementation of CSR programs and reports.
SASB	Sustainability Accounting Board
	Standards for the measurement, accounting for, and disclosure of sustainability issues and performance.
AA1000	AccountAbility
	An assurance standard designed to provide assurance on the quality of an organization's public reporting and the quality of its underlying systems and processes.
FTSE4Good	
	FTSE4Good is an index made up of companies judged acceptable using an objective global standard for socially responsible investment. The FTSE4Good Selection Criteria cover 3 areas: (1) Working toward environmental sustainability, (2) Developing positive relationships with stakeholders, (3) Upholding and supporting universal human rights
Domini 400 Social index	
	400 predominantly U.S. corporations are ethically screened on 11 criteria and included in the index for use by ethical investors.
The Jantzi Social Index	
	Similar to the Domini and FTS4Good indices for 400 Canadian companies that are socially and environmentally screened.
SA 8000	Social Accountability International (SAI)
	SAI is developing the SA 8000 standard to provide guidance with regard to workplace conduct and specifically with regard to sweatshops. Auditors are also trained.

Information on these is downloadable from **http://www.cengagebrain.com**

scrutiny and need for transparency and public accountability. Never before has there been such interest in what a corporation is doing and how it is doing it.

In the United States, Canada, and the United Kingdom, rating services exist that examine and score corporate governance systems and performance against competitors and external benchmarks. New visibility is being given U.S., U.K., and Canadian companies through social rating services linked to the London Stock Exchange, such as the FTSE4Good service. New standards for corporate social performance (CSR) and disclosure are emerging that will provide comparisons that corporations will watch and build into their mechanisms, performance assessments, and public disclosures. It is doubtful that corporations will be regarded as responsible corporate citizens if their operations are seen not to compare well based on these new comparators. Therefore, at the very least, corporations should maintain a watching brief over developments identified in Table 5.23. CSR and corporate citizenship are discussed further in Chapter 7.

CONCLUSION—TOWARD A CULTURE OF INTEGRITY

The need for ethical corporate governance is not just good for business—it is the law. Recent changes in governance regulation are shifting expectations significantly. In an era of increasing scrutiny, where ethical misbehavior can influence the achievement of corporate objectives profoundly, it is very much in the interest of shareholders, directors, and executives that their company's governance system provides appropriate guidance and accountability.

Directors must demonstrate due diligence in the management of the company's business and ethics risks. They need to ensure that an effective ethical culture prevails in their company. This requires the development of a code of conduct and the essential means of creating an awareness of appropriate behavior, reinforcing that behavior, and making sure that the underlying values are embedded in corporate strategy and operations. The company's positions on conflicts of interest, sexual harassment, and similar topics need to be worked out in advance, with watchful updating to keep the company's culture abreast of current expectations.

If directors are able to recognize and prepare their company for the new era of stakeholder accountability through an effective, ethical governance system, they will not only reduce risks but also produce a competitive advantage among customers, employees, partners, environmentalists, and other stakeholders—which will surely be attractive to shareholders.

In summary, *directors, executives, and professional accountants should now be fully focused on developing and maintaining a culture of integrity if they wish to satisfy the expectations of their stakeholders.*

Questions

1. Must a company be incorporated as a benefit corporation in order to legally consider actions other than those in pursuit of profit?
2. If Lynn Stout is correct, that the drive for shareholder value is a myth, why do so many companies continue to use it as a goal?
3. What is the role of a board of directors from an ethical governance standpoint?
4. Explain why corporations are legally responsible to shareholders but are strategically responsible to other stakeholders as well.
5. What should an employee consider when considering whether to give or receive a gift?
6. When should an employee satisfy his or her self-interest rather than the interest of his or her employer?
7. Can an apparent conflict of interest where there are adequate safeguards to prevent harm be as important to an executive or a company as one where safeguards are not adequate?
8. How can a company control and manage conflicts of interest?
9. What is the role of an ethical culture, and who is responsible for it?
10. What is the most important contribution of a corporate code of conduct?
11. Are one or more of the fundamental principles found in codes of conduct more important than the rest? Why?
12. Why should codes focus on principles rather than specific detailed rules?
13. How could you monitor compliance with a code of conduct in a corporation?
14. How can a corporation integrate ethical behavior into its reward and remuneration schemes?
15. Other than a code of conduct, what aspects of a corporate culture are most important and why?
16. Is the SOX-driven effort being made to check on the effectiveness of internal control systems worth the cost? Why and why not?

17. Why should an effective whistleblower mechanism be considered a "failsafe mechanism" in SOX Section 404 compliance programs?
18. If you were asked to evaluate the quality of an organization's ethical leadership, what would the five most important aspects be that you would wish to evaluate, and how would you do so?
19. Why is it suspected that corporate psychopaths gravitate to certain industries, and what should corporations within those industries do about it?
20. Descriptive commentary about corporate social performance is sometimes included in annual reports. Is this indicative of good performance, or is it just window dressing? How can the credibility of such commentary be enhanced?
21. Should professional accountants push for the development of a comprehensive framework for the reporting of corporate social performance? Why?
22. Do professional accountants have the expertise to audit corporate social performance reports?

Case Insights

Cases on Ethical Corporate Culture

- *LIBOR Manipulations Cause Widespread Impacts* describes the aberrant organizational cultures at Barclay's Bank and UBS that encouraged bank employees to artificially manipulate the information on which the LIBOR benchmark rate was based. This case in located in Chapter 2.
- *Siemens' Bribery Scandal* describes how one of Germany's oldest multinationals developed a perverse organizational culture that condoned making bribery payments in foreign jurisdictions and the adverse consequence to both the company and many of its senior executives. The total cost to Siemens of fines and expenses was estimated at $2.5 billion, not including the original payments for bribery.

Cases on Ethical Leadership

- *Salary Equity at Gravity Payments* explains how the founder and CEO of the company raised the minimum wage for all employees to $70,000 and the positive and negative reactions to his arbitrary decision.
- *Merck and River Blindness* concerns a company that follows its values and provides a life-enhancing drug for free to those who cannot afford the drug.
- *Lululemon's Questionable Leadership* describes what happened to the founder and to the CEO after they made several gaffs and the company unintentionally manufactured transparent yoga pants.

Cases on Bribery

- *Wal-Mart Bribery in Mexico* describes how a company that wanted to improve its reputation for integrity was sabotaged by self-interested executives who were erroneously supported at the head office by misguided executives and an unaware board of directors. This case is located in Chapter 2.
- *SNC-Lavalin Missing Funds Topples CEO & Triggers Investigation* describes the fallout for the officers, board, and company that used bribery and support to obtain contracts in a country with a repressive regime.

- *Rio Tinto's Bribes in China* describes how Chinese steel companies' officials bribed Rio Tinto managers in order to obtain a key raw material in the production of steel.
- *Daimler Settles U.S. Bribery Case for $185 Million* describes how the *U.S. Foreign Corrupt Practices Act* can be used to prosecute companies that are not headquartered in the United States.
- *Bribery for Russian Contract with Anti-Bribery Prosecutor's Office* describes how Hewlett Packard bribed officials at the government office that is responsible for prosecuting bribery cases in Russia.
- *Siemens' Bribery Scandal*—see description above.

Cases on Corporate Governance & Managerial Opportunism

- *Spying on HP Directors* explains how Patricia Dunn, chair of the Board of Directors at Hewlett Packard, hired investigators to determine who had leaked sensitive information to the media and the questionable techniques the investigators employed in order to identify the culprit.
- *Lord Conrad Black's Fiduciary Duty?* is a classic case of a domineering CEO/chairman who believes he did no wrong in managing his conflicts of interest, whereas many other shareholders and federal prosecutor Patrick J. Fitzgerald believe he ran a "corporate kleptography." With hindsight, his famous board of directors may agree.
- *Manipulation of MCI's Allowance for Doubtful Accountants* is the story of how Walt Pavlo, a junior manager at the telecommunications giant, hid $88 million of bad debts and reported only an allowance for doubtful accounts of $15 million.
- *Stock Options and Gifts of Publicly Traded Shares* explains how a CEO can strategically time the release of bad news so that he maximizes the tax benefit of donating shares of his company to his favorite charity.
- *The Ethics of Repricing and Backdating of Employee Stock Options* addresses several issues concerning employee stock options. Do they actually motivate employees? Do they encourage earnings management? Is manipulating the timing of the granting of stock options in the best interest of the shareholders?

Cases on Fraudulent & Questionable Financial Reporting

- *Satyam Computer Services, the Enron of India* describes how small discrepancies grew to become the largest fraud and bankruptcy in India's history. CEO dominance, combined with poor oversight by the board of directors and the external auditor, contributed to debacle.
- *Nortel Networks' Audit Committee Was in the Dark* reveals the nature of manipulations spawned by a flawed incentive scheme and carried out under the noses of an unsuspecting Audit Committee.
- *Adelphia—Really the Rigas Family Piggy Bank* presents the story of how Mr. Rigas formed a small cable company and grew it into a giant, while he and his sons used it as their own "piggy bank."
- *Tyco—Looting Executive Style* reveals how the CEO lived in style with million-dollar parties, $6,000 shower curtains, and a need to keep the money flowing.
- *HealthSouth—Can Five CFOs Be Wrong?* presents the strange case of Richard Scrushy, who was the first CEO to be charged under the governance-reforming SOX. Although

five HealthSouth CFOs testified that Scrushy had knowingly directed the fraud, the Alabama jury acquitted him of all thirty-six criminal charges. In contrast, the five CFOs were sentenced to receive a total of 115 years in prison and $11.2 million in fines. How did this come about, and what will the impact be on future prosecutions?

- *Royal Ahold—A Dutch Company with U.S.-Style Incentives* requires restructuring after several senior executives conspired with leading executives of U.S. and other suppliers to fraudulently boost profits and increase their personal wealth and position. Ahold's shares were traded on a U.S. stock exchange when disaster struck in later 2002 and early 2003. At the time, Ahold was the third-largest food retail and food service group in the world.
- *The Ethics of Bankruptcy: Jetsgo Corporation* explores how the CEO of Jetsgo misled his pilots and his passengers on the day before he voluntarily had his company declare bankruptcy.

Stock Market Cases

- *Société Générale Rogue Trader* explains how poor internal controls allowed Jerôme Kerviel, a derivate trader at one of the largest French banks, to engage in unauthorized transactions that cost the bank €4.9 billion.
- *Galleon's Insider Trading Network* describes how the billionaire stock market trader, Raj Rajaratnam, made his fortune not by being an astute investor but rather through the use of insider information.
- *KPMG Partner Shares Confidential Information with a Friend* describes why a senior professional, thinking he was helping a friend in a small way, ruined his own career, damaged his firm's reputation, and caused it have to resign from two major audits. See case at pages 454–455 of Chapter 6.
- *Conflicts of Interest on Wall Street* captures New York Attorney General Elliot Spitzer's challenge of the traditional conflicted ways that brokers have been doing business on Wall Street. While purporting to act for their investing clients, they have been profiting by misleading investors with overhyped investment analyses.
- *Loyalty, but to Whom?* Many people—particularly in the securities industry—have great difficulty understanding to whom they owe duty and in what order of priority. This is a real case that offers a chance to explore the results of tough loyalty decisions in a modern governance framework.
- *Bankers Trust: Learning from Derivatives* is the story of how the competitive culture of an enterprise got out of control and affected the company's clients, personnel, and fortunes.
- *Barings Bank: Rogue Trader* reveals why Barings is no longer the oldest family owned bank in Britain. Was it the fault of a rogue trader in derivatives, or was it that the corporate culture sabotaged a greedy management?

Cases on Product Safety

- *Dow Corning Silicone Breast Implants* illustrates the pitfalls of a company with an excellent code and a world-class, follow-up monitoring procedure—yet they still had problems with effectiveness.
- *Ford/Firestone Tire Recall* presents how two companies, with a history of earlier recalls, failed to learn from them, or use what they learned. Information was available but not used. Risks were not assessed properly, nor were crises effectively dealt with. The tension between doing what is right to maintain the confidence of consumers and following advice to minimize legal liability is explored.

Reading Insights

Appendix A discusses Agency Theory, which is frequently used to explain executive behavior and underpin governance frameworks to control the conflict between owners' and executives' interests.

References

AICPA, 2003. *Statement of Auditing Standards* (SAS) No. 99.

Badaracco, J. L., and A. P. Webb. 1995. "Business Ethics: A View from the Trenches," *California Management Review* 60, no. 2 (Winter): 8–28.

Berenbeim, R. E. 1987. *Corporate Ethics*. New York: The Conference Board, Inc.

Brooks, L. J. 1989. "Ethical Codes of Conduct: Deficient in Guidance for the Canadian Accounting Profession." *Journal of Business Ethics* 8, no. 5 (May): 325–36.

Brooks, L. J. 1990. "A Survey on the Effectiveness/ Compliance of Corporate Codes of Conduct in Canada." Unpublished manuscript.

Brooks, L. J. 1993. "No More Trial and Error: It's Time We Moved Ethics Out of the Clouds and into the Classroom." *CAmagazine*, March, 43–45.

Brooks, L. J. 2000. "Codes of Conduct: Trust, Innovation, Commitment and Productivity: A Strategic-Cultural Perspective." *Global Outlook: An International Journal of Business, Economics, and Social Policy* 12, no. 2: 1–11.

Brooks, L. J., and V. Fortunato. 1991. "Discipline at the Institute of Chartered Accountants of Ontario." *CAmagazine*, May, 40–43.

Canadian Institute of Chartered Accountants. 1995. *Guidance for Directors—Governance Processes for Control*. Toronto: Canadian Institute of Chartered Accountants.

Canadian Institute of Chartered Accountants. 2004. *CEO and CFO Certification: Improving Transparency and Accountability, A Canadian Performance Reporting Board Discussion Brief*. Toronto: Canadian Institute of Chartered Accountants.

Centre for Applied Ethics, University of British Columbia. Now transferred to the EthicsWeb Bookstore at http://www.ethicsweb.ca/resources/business/codes .html.

Chatman, J. A.. and K. A. Jehn. 1994. "Assessing the Relationship between Industry Characteristics and Organizational Culture: How Different Can You Be?" *Academy of Management Journal* 37: 522–33.

CICA Handbook Section 5135. 2002. *The Auditor's Responsibility to Consider Fraud and Error in an Audit of Financial Statements*.

Clarkson, Max B. E., and M. Deck. 1989. "Towards CSR_4: Defining Economic and Moral Responsibilities." Unpublished manuscript.

Clarkson, Max B. E., and M. Deck. 1992. "Applying the Stakeholder Management Model to the Analysis and Evaluation of Corporate Codes," Clarkson Centre for Business Ethics, University of Toronto.

Clarkson, Max, M. Deck, and R. Leblanc. 1997. *Codes of Ethics, Practice and Conduct*. Toronto: Society of Management Accountants of Canada, 1997. (An excellent practical guide that incorporates part of the material in Clarkson and Deck 1992.)

Council on Economic Priorities. Updated continuously. *SA8000: Guideline for Social Accountability*. New York: Council on Economic Priorities., http://www .cepaa.org.

Davis, Michael, and Andrew Stark, eds. *Conflict of Interest in the Professions*. New York: Oxford University Press, 2001.

Enterprise Risk Management—Integrated Framework: Executive Summary. 2004. Committee of Sponsoring Organizations (COSO) of the Treadway Commission, September, downloadable from http://www .coso.org/guidance.htm. See also 2013 update on the COSO website.

EthicScan Canada. *Corporate Ethics Monitor* (A bimonthly publication published by EthicScan Canada, Toronto.)

Institute of Business Ethics. http://www.ibe.org.uk.

Institute of Internal Auditors Research Foundation. 2001. *Enterprise Risk Management: Trends and Emerging Practices*. Altamonte Springs, FL: Institute of Internal Auditors Research Foundation.

International Federation of Accountants. 2001. *IFAC Code of Ethics for Professional Accountants.* London: International Federation of Accountants. http://www.ifac.org/Ethics/index.tmpl.

International Accounting and Audit Standards Board. 2001. *ISA 240: The Auditor's Responsibility to Consider Fraud and Error in an Audit of Financial Statements* (rev. 2004). International Accounting and Audit Standards Board.

KMPG Forensic Advisory Service. 2005. *Integrity Survey 2005–2006.* New York: KMPG Forensic Advisory Service, http://www.kpmg.com.

2001. *Managing Risk in the New Economy.* New York and Toronto: AICPA and CICA.

Maslow, A. 1954. *Motivation and Personality.* New York: Harper and Brothers.

Mathews, M. C. 1987. "Codes of Ethics: Organizational Behaviour and Misbehaviour." In *Research in Corporate Social Behaviour*, 107–30. Stamford, CT: JAI Press.

McGregor, D. D. 1960. *The Human Side of Enterprise.* New York: McGraw-Hill.

Paine, L. S. 1994. "Managing for Integrity." *Harvard Business Review,* March–April, 106–17. (Reproduced as a reading in Chapter 1.)

Reschke, W., and R. Aldag. 2000. "A Model of the Impact of Organizational Culture on Individual/Team Outcomes and Organizational Effectiveness." In *The Business Case for Culture Change*, 14. Center for Organizational Effectiveness.

Schien, E. H. 1985. *Organizational Culture and Leadership.* San Francisco: Jossey-Bass.

Stout, Lynn. 2012. *The Shareholder Value Myth.* San Francisco: Berrett-Koehler.

The Business Roundtable. 1997. *Statement of Corporate Governance.* The Business Roundtable.

The Conference Board.1999. *Global Corporate Ethics Practices: A Developing Consensus.* New York: The Conference Board,

Toronto Stock Exchange. 1994. *Report of the Toronto Stock Exchange Committee on Corporate Governance in Canada*, December. Toronto: Toronto Stock Exchange, paras. 4.3 and 4.4, p. 17.

Treviño, L. K., G. Weaver, D. G. Gibson, and B. L. Toffler. 1999. "Managing Ethics and Legal Compliance: What Works and What Hurts." *California Management Review* 41, no. 2 (Winter): 131–51.

Treviño, Linda Klebe, Laura Pincus Hartman, and Michael Brown. 2000. "Moral Person and Moral Manager: How Executives Develop a Reputation for Ethical Leadership." *California Management Review* 42, no. 4 (Summer): 128–42.

UN Brundtland Commission Report. 1987. *Our Common Future.* Oxford: World Commission on Environment and Development, Oxford University Press.

U.S. Senate Permanent Subcommittee on Investigations. 2002. *Report on the Role of the Board of Directors in the Collapse of Enron*, July 8. See **http://www.cengagebrain.com**.

U.S. Sentencing Commission 1991. *U.S. Sentencing Guidelines*, November 1. Washington, DC: U.S. Sentencing Commission.

Valdez (CERES) Principles. (Environmental management principles created by a coalition of environmental interest groups [hence CERES], including the Sierra Club, shortly after the Exxon Valdez went aground.)

Weaver, G. R., L. K. Treviño, and P. L. Cochran. 1999. "Corporate Ethics Practices in the Mid-1990's: An Empirical Study of the Fortune 1000." *Journal of Business Ethics* 18: 283–94.

Weaver, G. R., L. K. Treviño, and P. L. Cochran. 1999. "Corporate Ethics Programs as Control Systems: Influences of Executive Commitment and Environmental Factors." *Academy of Management Journal* 42, no. 1 (February): 41–57.

White, B. J., and R. Montgomery. 1980. "Corporate Codes of Conduct." *California Management Review*, Winter, 80–87.

Case on Ethical Corporate Culture

ETHICS CASE

Siemens' Bribery Scandal

Siemens AG is a 160-year-old German engineering and electronics giant. It is one of Europe's largest conglomerates, with profits in 2007 of €3.9 billion on revenue of €72.4 billion, up €6 billion from its 2006 revenue. It has over 475,000 employees and operations worldwide. It had also developed a corrupt organizational culture in which hundreds of millions of euros were put into slush funds that were then used to pay bribes in order to obtain lucrative contracts. The following details have come to light:

- In November 2006 Siemens' auditors, KPMG, completed a confidential report that detailed a number of payments that were impossible to verify. They could not identify who received the money or what services were provided. The suspicious payments, made from 2000 to 2006, totaled €1.3 billion (U.S.$1.88 billion). At the time, the company said that senior executives were unaware of these payments.
- In January 2007, the company paid a €418 million fine to the European Commission because the company was accused of heading a cartel that was dividing up the market for power station equipment. Siemens is challenging the fine.
- In October 2007, the company paid a €201 million fine related to bribery in its communication equipment business.

A number of senior executives were also accused and subsequently convicted of making bribery payments, including the following:

- Andreas Kley, CFO of the power-generating unit, was convicted (in May 2007) of channeling €6 million, from 1999 to 2002, to an Italian energy company to win gas turbine contracts. The judge also fined Siemens €38 million and required the company to forfeit the profit it made on the contract.
- Johannes Feldmayer, an executive board member, was convicted (in July 2008) of authorizing bribes to a labor union, the Association of Independent Employees, that was considered friendly to Siemens' management. The payments, made between 2001 and 2005, were intended to offset the power of IG Metall, the German union that controls almost half of the seats on Siemens' board of directors.
- Reinhard Siekaczek, a sales manager in the telecom division, was convicted (in July 2008) of building a slush fund system designed to make bribery payments. The judge said that Siekaczek acted at the behest of his superiors and that he "was part of a system of organized irresponsibility that was implicitly condoned."

Although they were never accused of any wrongdoing, in April 2007, both Klaus Kleinfeld, CEO, and Heinrich von Pierer, supervisory board chairman, resigned. They were replaced, in July 2007, by an outsider, Peter Löscher, who came from drugmaker Merck & Company. As the new CEO, Löscher began to change the organizational structure and culture. Formerly, each line of business had a managing director and a separate managing board. This structure inhibited accountability and allowed corruption to spread. Löscher reorganized the company into three sectors—industry, energy, and health care—with each of these three managers sitting on the central managing board in Munich. He also adopted a zero-tolerance policy, delivering a message that corruption must end.

Questions

1. The senior executives at Siemens spent most of their working life in an environment that condoned bribery outside of Germany but not inside. However, they failed to take notice of the changes that Transparency International—championed by a German who was embarrassed by the double standard of his countrymen—was proposing, and that ultimately resulted in a new worldwide antibribery regime. Why did they ignore the change?
2. If you were Löscher, the new CEO, how would you show the employees and external stakeholders that you actually have a zero-tolerance policy concerning corruption?

Sources: Beat Balzil, Dinah Deckstein, and Jorg Schmitt, "New Report Details Far-Reaching Corruption," *Spiegel Online*, January 29, 2007, http://www.spiegel.de/international/0,1518,462954,00.html

Carter Dougherty, "Siemens's Prosperity Doesn't Obscure Bribery Scandal," *New York Times*, January 22, 2008, http://www.nytimes.com/2008/01/22/business/worldbusiness/22siemens.html

Jens Hack, "Former Siemens Manager Convicted in Bribery Case," *International Herald Tribune*, July 28, 2008, http://www.iht.com/articles/reuters/2008/07/28/business/OUKBS-UK-SIEMENS-TRIAL.php

Karin Matussek, "Ex-Siemens Executive Feldmayer Charged over Bribery (Update 1)," *Bloomberg.com*, July 2, 2008, http://www.bloomberg.com/apps/news?pid520601100&sid5an9FWLdc0pWs&refer5germany

G. Thomas Sims, "2 Former Siemens Officials Convicted for Bribery," *New York Times*, May 15, 2007, http://www.nytimes.com/2007/05/15/business/worldbusiness/15siemens.html.

Cases on Ethical Leadership

ETHICS CASE

Salary Equality at Gravity Payments

Dan Price is the owner of Gravity Payments, a Seattle-based credit card company that he founded in 2004. In 2014, the company processed more than $65 billion of credit card transactions for more than 12,000 small and medium-sized businesses. In April 2015, thirty-year-old Price announced to his staff that everyone's salary would rise to a minimum of $70,000, even the lowest-paid employee. Furthermore, his own salary of $1 million would be reduced to $70,000.

Price said that he was motivated because of research by Deaton and Kahneman,[1] the Nobel Prize–winning psychologist, who found that a $75,000 salary made an enormous difference to an employee's emotional well-being. Furthermore, he felt that that "income inequality has been racing in the wrong direction. I want to fight for the idea that if someone is intelligent, hard-working and does a good job, then they are entitled to live a middle-class lifestyle."[2]

In 2015, the average wage at Gravity was $48,000 per year for its 120 employees. Under the salary floor plan, which would be phased in over a three-year period, seventy employees would have their pay increased, and thirty would have their pay doubled. The plan was met with enthusiasm by the employees when it was announced.

There was mixed reaction by customers. A few left because they thought that this was political posturing by Price. Despite assurances to the contrary, others left over fears that fees would rise. On the other hand, Mario Zahariev, the owner of Pop's Pizza & Pasta, switched to Gravity after he saw Price on the news. His monthly credit card processing fees dropped from $1,700 to $900. He said, "I was not going to keep the difference for myself."[3] Instead, he increased the salaries of his eight employees.

Stephanie Brooks, age twenty-three, an administrative assistant who had been at Gravity for only two months, was pleased to have her salary increased. But she now felt pressure because she did not think that she had earned it. "Am I doing my job well enough to deserve this?"[4]

---

[1] D. Kahneman and A. Deaton, "High Income Improves Evaluation of Life but Not Emotional Well-Being," *Proceedings of the National Academy of Sciences* 107, no. 38 (2010): 16489–93, http://scholar.princeton.edu/deaton/publications/high-Income-Improves-Evaluation-Life-Not-Emotional-Well-Being.

[2] P. Cohen, "A Company Copes with Backlash against the Raise That Roared," *CNBC*, July 31, 2015.

[3] Ibid.

[4] Ibid.

Two employees quit. Grant Moran, age twenty-nine, a Web developer, had his salary move from $41,000 to $50,000 in the first round of increases. He left because he thought that these raises did not support a strong work ethic. "Now the people who were clocking in and out were making the same as me. It shackles high performers to less motivated team members."[5] Maisey McMaster, age twenty-six, was the financial manager who ensured that the plan was financially viable. A five-year employee, she said that there was a special corporate culture at Gravity where people worked hard and played hard. "I love everyone there." However, she quit because "he gave raises to people who have the least skills and are the least equipped to do the job, and the ones who were taking on the most didn't get much of a bump."[6]

[5] Ibid.
[6] Ibid.

Questions

1. Do you think that Dan Price's decision to raise the minimum salary to $70,000 represented ethical leadership?
2. Do you think that Price should have arbitrarily increased the minimum salary to $70,000?
3. Should he have increased everyone's salary, even those who were earning more than $70,000?
4. Do you think that this plan will motivate the Gravity employees to work harder?
5. Should Price have consulted with his customers and his employees before he made the decision to increase the minimum salary to $70,000?

Other Source: P. Cohen, "One Company's New Minimum Wage: $70,000 a Year," *New York Times*, August 13, 2015.

ETHICS CASE

Merck and River Blindness

In 2015, Dr. William Campbell was awarded the Nobel Prize in Medicine for his work in discovering ivermectins while employed with Merck & Co. in the 1970s. The drug prevents onchocerciasis, called river blindness. In 1987, the World Health Organization (WHO) estimated that 18 million people in more than thirty countries in the Middle East, West and Central Africa, and Central and South America were infected with the river blindness disease.

The disease is spread by black flies that breed in fast-flowing rivers. A bite from one of these flies can transmit a worm that lives within the human body and can grow to over half a meter in length. The worm produces millions of larvae that can cause itching, skin nodules, eye lesions, and, in extreme cases, blindness. Through Dr. Campbell's work, Merck developed Mectizan, an easily administered wonder drug that required only one annual dose with very minor side effects. The drug would not restore the sight of a blind person, but it would prevent others from becoming blind because the drug kills the worm's larvae and prevents additional larvae from being produced.

However, Merck had a problem. The people who needed the drug often lived in remote areas of poor countries that were plagued with political and civil unrest. These countries did not have drug distribution systems, nor did they have health care infrastructures. There were importation laws, and the citizens and nations that needed Mectizan could not afford North American–developed drugs.

On October 21, 1987, Merck announced that it would distribute Mectizan for free and for as long as necessary. Dr. Roy Vagelos, CEO and chairman of Merck, said that the company would make the drug "available without charge because those who need it the most could not afford it."[1] The company formed the Merck Mectizan Donation program, a private–private partnership. It collaborated with WHO, the World Bank, UNICEF, and various public and private stakeholders as well as local and village health care workers to coordinate the distribution of the drug. By 2015, the company had donated more than 2 billion treatments to an estimated 98 million people in thirty-one countries. Because of its success, the program was expanded to address lymphatic filariasis, known as elephantiasis.

Why would a for-profit pharmaceutical company donate a drug for free? Merck said that this was consistent with the company's "medicine is for the people" philosophy. In 1950, George W. Merck said, "We try never to forget that medicine is for the people. It is not for the profits. The profits follow, and if we have remembered that, they have never failed to appear. How can we bring the best medicine to each and every person? We cannot rest until the way has been found with our help to bring our finest achievements to everyone."[2] When asked, in 2015, about the free distribution of Mectizan, Dr. Campbell said, "I think it was done because it was the right thing to do, and I think the employees [at Merck] applauded it, because they thought it was the right thing to do."[3]

Questions

1. Pharmaceutical companies have to spend millions of dollars and years of research to find just one successful drug. Merck spent time and money developing and then distributing Mectizan for free. Is it possible for Merck to justify, to its shareholders, making a sizable investment in a product and incurring ongoing costs in the distribution of that product when the product generates no revenue for the company?
2. Did Merck have an ethical obligation to develop and distribute Mectizan for free?
3. Do you think that Roy Vagelos, Merck's CEO and chairman, demonstrated ethical leadership? What value did it have/create?
4. Based on the river blindness example, how would you describe the organizational culture of Merck in the 1980s?

Other Source: Jeffrey L. Sturchio, "The Case for Ivermectin: Lessons and Implications for Improving Access to Care Treatment in Developing Countries," *Community Eye Health Journal* 14, no. 38 (2001): 22–23.

[1] "Merck Offers Free Distribution of New River Blindness Drug," *New York Times*, October 21, 1987.

[2] Merck & Co. *Our Values and Standards: The Basis of Our Success*, Edition III, http://www.merck.com/about/code_of_conduct.pdf.

[3] Darragh Murphy, "Meet Ireland's New Nobel Laureate, William C Campbell," *Irish Times*, October 9, 2015.

ETHICS CASE

Lululemon's Questionable Leadership

Lululemon Athletica, Inc., was founded by Chip Wilson in 1998 to sell yoga-inspired athletic clothing. The company's target market was women who wanted stylish exercise apparel. In 2012, the Vancouver-based company, whose shares traded on both the Toronto Stock Exchange in Canada and NASDAQ in the United States, had sales of $1.4 billion and a net income of $270 million. Its 211 stores were located in Canada, the United States, Australia, and New Zealand.

Chip Wilson, who served as chair of the board of directors and CEO, was known to make controversial statements. For example, he said that birth control pills contributed to high divorce rates and that the pill was linked to breast cancer. In 2005, he told the *Calgary Herald* that his company did not make plus-sized clothing because it cost 30% more to manufacture.

In 2008, Wilson hired Christine Day away from Starbucks to become the CEO of Lululemon. In 2011, Day was named "CEO of the Year" by the Toronto *Globe and Mail* and "Marketer of the Year" by the Canadian Marketing Association.

In response to a public outcry, on March 18, 2013, the company announced that it was recalling its black Luon yoga pants because the lightweight material used in their production made the pants too thin, too sheer, and unintentionally transparent. Christine Day candidly admitted, "The truth of the matter is, the only way to test for the problem is to put the pants on and bend over."[1] The company offered full refunds to anyone who bought the Luon pants. It was estimated that the product recall, which represented 17% of the company's inventory, cost Lululemon approximately $60 million, or 27 cents per share. The company's stock price fell more than 6% after the recall was announced. Three months later, Day stepped down as CEO of Lululemon.

Later in 2013, on November 5, Chip Wilson was asked about the product recall during a Blomberg TV interview. He said that his yoga pants were not suitable for all women: "quite frankly, some women's bodies just don't actually work.… It's really about the rubbing through the thighs, how much pressure is there over a period of time, how much they use it."[2] Wilson was immediately ridiculed in the social media for "fat-shaming" and later apologized for his comments. A month later, on December 10, 2013, Wilson stepped down as chair of the board of directors of Lululemon.

Questions

1. Do you think that the executives at Lululemon demonstrated ethical leadership? Could it have been improved?
2. Does a CEO have an ethical responsibility to step down as CEO when there is a production and marketing disaster that requires a product recall?
3. Does the chair of the board of directors have an ethical responsibility to step down as chair of the board when there is a production and marketing disaster that requires a product recall?
4. Does the board of directors have an ethical responsibility to reprimand the chair of the board if the chair makes controversial statements and comments to the press?

[1] Holloe Shaw, "Lululemon at Loss to Explain Sheer-Pants Debacle That Could Shave 27¢ a Share Off Earnings for Year," *Financial Post*, March 21, 2013.

[2] Anonymous, "Chip Wilson, Lululemon Founder: 'Some Women's Bodies' Not Right for Our Pants,'" *Huffington Post Canada*, November 6, 2013.

Cases on Bribery

SNC-Lavalin Missing Funds Topples CEO & Triggers Bribery Investigation

ETHICS CASE

Pierre Duhaime "retired" as CEO of SNC-Lavalin on March 26, 2012, a post that he had held since 2009 following over 20 years of employment at the company. He did so, because of his role in approving $56 million in payments in contravention of the company's policies.[1] Police were called in to help trace and recover the payments following an Independent Review by Stikeman Elliott LLP, a prominent law firm. The story originated at a news conference by Board Chair, Gwyn

[1] Paul Waldie and Sean Silcoff, "Mystery Funds Put CEO Out, Police In," *The Globe and Mail*, March 27, 2012, accessed March 27, 2012, at https://secure.globeadvisor.com/servlet/ArticleNews/story/gam/20120327/RBSNCLAVALINPAPER0327ATL.

Morgan, and a Press Release[2] by the company on March 26.

According to the Press Release, two payments were initiated by Riadh Ben Aissa, the Executive VP of Construction, for which "the nature of the services or actions undertaken by, or the true identity of any presumed agent" could not be established. One payment made in 2011 was for $33.5 million. When the required signatories (the Chairman of SNC-Lavalin International and the CFO) refused to authorize the payment, the CEO, Mr. Duhaime, was approached and he signed the authorization based upon the understanding that "it would help secure work in respect of Project A." Project A was not identified in the Independent Review. For the second payment incident regarding Project B, the story is much the same except that is was initiated in 2009 for $30 million, with payments aggregating $22.5 million being made in 2010 and 2011. Mr. Aissa and someone in his division improperly approved these expenditures. "In 2010, the CFO was told at a meeting with the CEO and Mr. Aissa that an agent had been hired on Project B and that its fees would be charged to other projects. The CFO objected to this at the meeting." These payments were detected as anomalous in an analysis in February 2012, and were then "reported to the Senior Vice-President and Controller of the Company" who objected to the payments.

The Independent Review concluded that the company's Code of Ethics and Business Conduct and its Agent's Code had been breached, but neither code required reporting of a breach or suspected breach, nor did it find the failure to report a breach of the code. The company's Whistleblower Policy also did not impose any obligation to report. Not surprisingly, the Independent Review recommended changes to these codes, and increased attention to management override and improvement and enforcement of controls.

In addition to the questionable payments reported above, there is evidence that SNC-Lavalin was involved with the Gadhafi regime and family in Libya. The company reportedly[3] hired Cyndy Vanier to go on a fact-finding mission to Libya and bring Gadhafi's son Saadi to Mexico, where she was incarcerated. On March 28, 2012, it became known that, when the company left Libya before the revolution of 2011, it left $22.9 million in cash in Libyan banks, and it hopes the money will be available if and when it returns to Libya.[4]

From a governance perspective, the Board failed to ensure that company policies were adequate to ensure ethical and legal conduct, and that the actions of Mr. Aissa and Mr. Duhaime speak to a lack of ethical tone at the top.

SNC-Lavalin faced legal action under the *Canadian Corruption of Foreign Public Officials Act*.

Questions

1. From a governance perspective, what can the Board of Directors do to make sure that the company's policies and procedure are adequate to ensure ethical and legal conduct by its employees?
2. Mr. Aissa and Mr. Duhaime were not demonstrating strong ethical

[2] SNC-Lavalin, "SNC-Lavalin Reports on Results of Voluntary Independent Review," press release, March 26, 2012, accessed March 27, 2012, at http://www.snclavalin.com/news.php?lang=en&id=1707&action=press_release_ details&paging=1&start=6.

[3] See Alyshah Hasham, "SNC-Lavalin Players: Who's Who as CEO Steps Down amid Ethics Probe," *thestar.com*, March 26, 2012, accessed March 27, 2012, at http://www.thestar.com/business/article/1151980--snc-lavalin-players-who-s-who-as-ceo-steps-down-amid-ethics-probe.

[4] Paul Waldie, "SNC's Libyan Mystery Deepens: It Left $23-Million Behind," *The Globe and Mail*, March 28, 2012, B1, B4.

leadership. What can a firm do to improve its ethical tone at the top?

3. Is it appropriate for a company to do business in a country with an oppressive regime? Why and why not?
4. If the decision is made to do business in a country with an oppressive regime, what limitations that should be put in place by the company to guide its employees against unethical involvement?

ETHICS CASE

Rio Tinto's Bribes in China

Bribery charges often involve a company making illegal payments to government officials in order to land lucrative contracts. For example, in April 2010, German auto manufacturer Daimler AG made a $185 million settlement with the Securities Exchange Commission (SEC) because it had violated American antibribery laws. The car company, which is now Daimler-Chrysler Corp., had made at least 200 payments in over twenty-two countries over a ten-year period totaling $56 million in bribes to foreign officials in order to earn $1.9 billion in sales and $91.4 million in illegal net income. Sometimes, however, bribery can be between two or more companies, as was the case in 2010 with Rio Tinto, the Anglo-Australian mineral company, and several Chinese steel companies.

China is one of the world's largest producers of steel, accounting for almost 40% of the 2009 global output of steel. But China lacks iron ore, an essential ingredient in the production of steel. As such, China is one of the world's largest importers of iron ore, spending almost $50.1 billion in 2009 on iron ore imports. The three largest Chinese suppliers are Rio Tinto; BHP Billiton Ltd, an Australian mining company; and Brazil's Vale SA. They are among the world's four largest mineral companies, and together they sell to China approximately 20% of the world's total sales of iron ore.

In 2007, the price of iron ore rose substantially. Many of China's steel manufacturers were concerned that foreign suppliers would be forming cartels to manipulate the price of the mineral. As a result, many Chinese steel companies began to deal directly with sellers in order to obtain a better price. Rio Tinto adopted the policy that it would give priority to the large state-run Chinese steel companies. Consequently, the smaller private steel companies resorted to bribery to increase their allocation.

In July 2009, China arrested Stern Hu, the general manager of Rio Tinto's Chinese operations, and three other Rio Tinto employees, Wang Yong, Ge Minqiang, and Liu Caikui, who are Chinese citizens. The fact that Rio Tinto was a major Australian company and Stern Hu was an Australian citizen triggered strong public comment by Rio Tinto officials and the Australian government.

Rio Tinto and China have a checkered history, including Chinese frustration over Australia's resistance to huge investments that China wanted to make in Australian mining and resource companies, Chinese frustration over negotiations for price reductions in Australian iron ore, and Chinese opposition to a joint venture between Rio Tinto and BHP Billiton that would give near-monopoly power over some resources. Interestingly, just days before the trial, Rio Tinto agreed to a large joint venture with Chinalco, the Aluminum Company of China, to develop a very large iron ore deposit in Africa, and Rio Tinto's CEO spoke at the China Development Forum pledging further assistance in finding new ore bodies.

The four Rio Tinto employees were initially charged with stealing China's state secrets and industrial espionage by bribing Chinese steel company executives for information that led to the foreign mining companies increasing the price of iron ore. However, at the trial in March 2010, the four pleaded guilty to the theft of commercial secrets and accepting about $13.5 million in bribes from more than a dozen Chinese steelmakers from 2003 to 2009. They were also found guilty of commercial espionage. In July 2009, the China Iron and Steel Association, which represents the Chinese steel industry, was in pricing and contract talks with Rio Tinto, BHP Billiton, and Vale. Rio Tinto was acting as the lead negotiator for the mining companies. During the negotiation process, the four Rio Tinto executives obtained confidential information through bribery about the association's intended strategy. The judge alleged a "direct cause-and-effect relationship" that the stolen confidential information cost Chinese steel mills an additional 1 billion yuan ($150 million). "They used illegal means to obtain commercial secrets that put the Chinese steel industry in a powerless position," the judge said.

After a two-and-a-half-day trial Messrs. Wang, Hu, Ge, and Liu were fined millions of yuan and sentenced to fourteen, ten, eight, and seven years, respectively. The court said that it had shown leniency because the four men had pleaded guilty. Australia's foreign minister, Stephen Smith, admitted that the sentences were consistent with Chinese sentencing practices but said that they were "very tough" by Australian standards. On March 29, 2010, just after the convictions were announced, the four executives were fired by Rio Tinto. "Receiving bribes is a clear violation of Chinese law and Rio Tinto's code of conduct," said Sam Walsh, a senior executive with Rio Tinto.

That same day, on March 29, two Chinese steel executives, Tan Yixin and Wang Hongjiu, who had been with Shougang Steel Group and Laigang Steel Group, respectively, were found guilty of handing over the secret business documents to the four former Rio Tinto executives. But, according to a Chinese steel industry analyst, the sentiment in China is more for the men who gave the bribes than for those who accepted them. "As a matter of fact, there is popular sympathy for the managers who are charged. People believe they were acting on behalf of their companies. Giving bribes was not for their personal interest."

The Chinese government never charged Rio Tinto with any criminal offense, although the court indicated that the company had used "stolen information to harm China's economic interests." An internal investigation by Rio Tinto found no evidence of wrongdoing by the company but said that the four former employees had engaged in "deplorable behavior" by accepting the bribes. Furthermore, such conduct was clearly at odds with the company's ethical culture and "wholly outside our systems."

Questions

1. The culture of giving and receiving payments is ingrained in China. On the other hand, accepting and paying bribes is a violation of Rio Tinto's code of conduct. When does a payment stop being a gift and turn into a bribe?
2. The smaller Chinese steel companies bribed the Rio Tinto executives because of Rio Tinto's policy of dealing only with large state-run steel companies. Can a business policy, such as giving priority to only one set of firms, be unethical? Is Rio Tinto ethically responsible for the bribes that were given to its employees because of its policy?
3. Why were these bribes prosecuted?
4. What lessons should be taken from these convictions:
   a. For foreign governments?
   b. For corporations trading in and with China?
   c. For individual employees?
   d. For possible investors in China?
5. Should Rio Tinto have been charged?

Sources: James T. Areddy, "Rio Tinto China Employees Get Prison Terms," *Wall Street Journal*, March 30, 2010.

David Barboza, "China Sentences Rio Tinto Employees in Bribe Case," *New York Times*, March 29, 2010.

Elaine Kurtenbach, "Rio Tinto Exec Admits to Some Bribery Charges," *The Globe and Mail*, March 23, 2010, B12.

Jane Macartney, "Rio Tinto Sacks Four Executives Jailed in China for Bribery," *The Times*, March 30, 2010.

Jeremy Pelofsky, "U.S. Judge OKs Settlement in Daimler Bribery Case," *Thomson Reuters*, April 1, 2010.

Michael Sainsbury, "Jailing of Two Chinese Steel Executives Ends Rio Tinto's Bribery Saga." *The Australian*, August 9, 2010.

ETHICS CASE

Daimler's Settles U.S. Bribery Case for $185 Million

David Bazzetta learned in July 2001 at a corporate audit executive committee meeting in Stuttgart Germany that DaimlerChrysler "business units 'continued to maintain secret bank accounts to bribe foreign government officials,' though the company kn[e]w the practice violated U.S. laws."[1] As a result, he filed a whistleblower complaint under the *U.S. Foreign Corrupt Practices Act* (FCPA) that ultimately led to a multiyear investigation of surprising scope and U.S. charges against a company headquartered in Germany for bribes made to foreign officials around the world.

On April 1, 2010, the German and Russian business units of Daimler AG[2] pleaded guilty to charges laid under the FCPA for bribing foreign officials and for failing to maintain books and records and internal controls as required under the FCPA. As a result, Judge Richard J. Leon of the U.S. District Court for the District of Columbia approved an arrange settlement that included the following:

- Payment of $91.4 million to the Securities Exchange Commission (SEC) for disgorgement of profits earned as a result of bribery. Daimler was subject to the U.S. law since it was a registrant with the SEC in order to raise capital (issue shares and debt) in the United States.
- Payment of $93.6 million to the U.S. Department of Justice for related criminal charges.
- Deferred prosecution and independent monitoring for two years by former Federal Bureau of Investigation Director Louis Freeh.[3]

The scope of Daimler's bribery operation was staggering. From 1998 to 2008, payments for bribes, kickbacks, gifts of armored Mercedes, a golden box, 10,000 copies of an official's personal manifesto translated into German, and lavish travel[4] had been given to officials in at least twenty-two countries, including Russia, China, Vietnam, Nigeria, Hungary, Latvia, Croatia, Bosnia, Egypt, Greece, Hungary, North Korea, and Indonesia.[5] Focusing on just fifty-one transactions out of a much higher total, the U.S. investigation found the following:

- Tens of millions of dollars "were made through the use of U.S. mails or the means or instrumentality of U.S. interstate commerce."[6]
- "Daimler also violated the FCPA's books and records and internal controls provisions in connection with the 51 transactions and at least an additional 154 transactions, in which it made improper payments totaling at least $56 million to secure business in 22 countries.... [Through these transactions that] involved at least 6,300 commercial vehicles and 500 passenger cars, Daimler

---

[1] Jeremy Pelofsky, "U.S. Judge OKs Settlement in Daimler Bribery Case," accessed November 11, 2010, at http://www.reuters.com/article/idUSTRE6303WY20100401.

[2] Daimler AG is the successor company to DiamlerChrysler following the sale of Chrysler in 2007.

[3] Ibid.

[4] Ibid.

[5] *United States Securities and Exchange Commission v. Daimler AG*, United States District Court for the District of Columbia, Case: 1:10-cv-00473, accessed November 26, 2010, at http://www.sec.gov/litigation/complaints/2010/comp-pr2010–51.pdf.

[6] Ibid., 2.

earned $1.9 billion in revenue and at least $91.4 million in illegal profits."[7]

- "Nineteen of these transactions … involved direct and indirect sales of motor vehicles and spare parts under the United Nations Oil for Food Program."[8]

In addition, the investigators found that many of the personnel and systems that should have provided safeguards against such illegal activities were actively supporting them. The SEC *Complaint* indicated the following:

> 5. A number of Daimler's former senior executives, who operated in a decentralized corporate structure, permitted or were directly involved in the Company's bribery practices, including the head of its overseas sales department, who reported directly to the Company's most senior officers. The Company's internal audit, legal, and finance and accounting departments, which should have provided checks on the activities of the sales force, instead played important roles in the subversion of internal controls and obfuscation of corporate records.
>
> 6. The improper payments were made possible in part as a result of the falsification of corporate records and a lax system of internal controls.
>
> 7. In this environment, Daimler developed several organized procedures and mechanisms through which improper payments could be made. Daimler's books and records contained over 200 ledger accounts, known internally as "*interne Fremdkonten*," or, "internal third party accounts," which reflected credit balances controlled by Daimler subsidiaries or outside third parties. Certain Daimler employees used numerous such accounts to make or facilitate improper payments to foreign government officials. Bribes were also made through the use of "corporate cash desks" where sales executives would obtain cash in amounts as high as 400,000 Deutsche Marks for making improper payments), deceptive pricing and commission arrangements, phony sales intermediaries, rogue business partners and misuse of inter-company and debtor accounts.[9]

The SEC *Complaint* indicates that, although Germany outlawed bribery in 1999 when it ratified the OECD Anti-Bribery Convention, Daimler had become an SEC registrant in 1993 and became subject to the FCPA at that time.[10] Also in 1999, Daimler created an Integrity Code that included antibribery provisions but these were essentially ignored.[11]

Prior to 1999, under German law, bribery of foreign officials was legal and tax deductible in Germany, but bribery of German officials was not—and it seems that Daimler continued to hold and act on this outdated perspective. In summary form, Daimler continued to bribe foreign officials with the knowledge and approval of very senior company officials using

> hundreds of ledger accounts on Daimler's own books, corporate "cash desks" (where sales personnel would obtain cash), deceptive pricing and commission arrangements, offshore bank accounts, inflated service fees, and nominees for government officials improperly described as "sales intermediaries" and "consultants."[12]

These arrangements are detailed in the SEC *Complaint*, as is the company's

[7] Ibid.
[8] Ibid.
[9] Ibid., 2, 3.
[10] Ibid., 4.
[11] Ibid., 5.
[12] Ibid.

reaction when its internal audit staff advised top management in 1986 that these practices could be illegal and in 1999 that internal controls were too weak to prevent misuse. Essentially, in 1986, Daimler made the practices subject to "absolute confidentiality"[13] and known to only a few employees but took no action in 1999 to improve the internal controls. However, an internal review of all special ledger account transactions outside of Germany was undertaken in 2000 and a report made to top management with recommendations, but once again, no actions were taken, and no further audit work was ordered.[14] Investigators found that the special ledger accounts were finally closed after their investigation began in 2004 and 2005. Bribes,[15] however, continued to be funded through other general ledger accounts, both directly and indirectly through agents and other means. These are detailed in the SEC *Complaint*.

On hearing the judge's verdict approving the settlement, Dieter Zetsche, chairman of Daimler's board, said in a statement, "We have learned a lot from past experience.... Today, we are a better and stronger company, and we will continue to do everything we can to maintain the highest compliance standards."[16]

Questions

1. Apparently, Daimler executives were not concerned enough with personal sanctions to change the company's bribery practices to comply with German and U.S. statutes. How can these attitudes be changed?
2. What internal controls could have been usefully introduced to prevent bribery at Daimler?
3. What should Dieter Zetsche do to ensure the highest compliance standards?
4. Whistleblowers on FCPA matters are eligible for up to 25% of the settlement and/or fine that results depending on a hearing by a tribunal on the import of their evidence (see page 68 for a discussion of this). How much of the $91.4 million restitution payment would you award David Bazzetta if you could make the decision? Provide your reasons for the choice you advocate.
5. Did David Bazzetta do what was expected of him as a professional accountant?

[13] Ibid., 13.
[14] Ibid., 15, 16.
[15] Pelofsky, "U.S. Judge OKs Settlement in Daimler Bribery Case."
[16] Ibid.

ETHICS CASE

HP Bribery for Russian Contract with Antibribery Prosecutor's Office

On April 14, 2010, Russian investigators raided the Moscow offices of Hewlett Packard (HP). They did so at the request of German prosecutors who were examining whether HP had paid bribes totaling $10.9 million (€8 million) in bribes to win a $44.5 million (€35 million) contract to supply computer hardware and IT systems to the Chief Public Prosecutor's Office of the Russian Federation—the very office responsible for prosecuting bribery cases in Russia.

In December 2009, HP received search warrants that outlined allegations against ten people for bribery in regard to a contract signed on August 1, 2003, for hardware, systems, and advice provided from 2001 to 2006. Also in December, German authorities arrested "three suspects, including one current H-P executive and two former company officials.… None of the three [was] formally charged and all [were] released on bail."[1]

Among the allegations was that bribery payments were flowed through accounts in various countries throughout Europe. German and Swiss authorities subsequently received assistance to trace transfers through the United Kingdom, the United States, the British Virgin Islands, and New Zealand as well.

Under German law, HP cannot be charged (only individuals can), but illicit profits made as a result if a bribe can be seized by a court although subsequent prosecutions could follow from the United States through its *Foreign Corrupt Practices Act* as well as other countries. Interestingly, according to HP, none of the ten individuals were still employed by HP in 2010, and the signature of the Russian official on the contract was illegible. The HP official who signed the contract has so far remained silent on the matter.

HP did not initially report the allegations on their SEC filings and subsequently, in their March 11, 2010, filing, referred only indirectly to them saying that "in many foreign countries illegal practices are 'common'" and "in violation of our policies … could have a material adverse effect on our business and reputation."[2]

In September 2010, HP announced that the investigation had been widened to additional transactions and that the U.S. Department of Justice and the SEC have been probing the Russia deal and possible violations of the *Foreign Corrupt Practices Act*. HP's share price declined 1.5% to $38.22 at that time.[3]

Questions

1. Why would HP personnel think they could get away with bribing an employee in the Russian antibribery prosecutor's office?
2. Why was it done through a series of companies in different countries?
3. What has changed to now allow investigators to unravel such a series of events, whereas in the past they would have found it almost impossible?
4. If a company decides to bribe, how many years need to go by so that they are safe from prosecution?
5. Even though German law does not allow companies to be charged, what are the possible consequences of the alleged bribery for HP?

---

[1] David Crawford, "H-P Executives Face Bribery Probes," *Wall Street Journal*, April 15, 2010, http://online.wsj.com/article/SB10001424052702303348504575184302111110966.html.

[2] Ibid.

[3] Gabriel Madway "HP Russia Bribery Probe Expands," September 10, 2010, http://www.reuters.com/article/idUSN1027122220100910.

Cases on Corporate Governance & Managerial Opportunism

ETHICS CASE

Spying on HP Directors

In January 2006, the chair of Hewlett-Packard (HP), Patricia Dunn, hired a team of independent electronic-security experts to determine the source of leaked confidential details regarding HP's long-term strategy. In September 2006, the press revealed that the independent experts spied on HP board members and several journalists. They obtained phone call records of HP board members and nine journalists, including reporters for CNET, the *New York Times*, and the *Wall Street Journal*, using an unethical and possibly illegal practice known as pretexting. Patricia Dunn claimed she did not know the methods the investigators used to determine the source of the leak but resigned after the scandal. Ten days earlier, George Keyworth, the director responsible for the leak, had resigned from HP's board after twenty-one years of service.

Company Profile

HP, founded in 1939, operates in more than 170 countries and is the world's largest seller of personal computers, offering a wide range of products and services, such as digital photography, digital entertainment, computing, and home printing. In addition, HP provides infrastructure and business offerings that span from handheld devices to some of the world's most powerful supercomputer installations. HP is among the world's largest IT companies, with revenue totaling $107.7 billion for the four fiscal quarters ended January 31, 2008. In 2007, HP was ranked 14th in the Forbes 500 list. The company's corporate headquarters is in Palo Alto, California.

Leak of Confidential Information and HP's Investigation

Patricia Dunn joined HP's board in 1998, and was elected nonexecutive chair in February 2005. She was CEO of Barclays Global Investors from 1995 to 2002. In January 2006, the online technology site CNET published an article about the long-term strategy at HP. The article quoted an anonymous source inside HP and contained information known only by the company's directors. Following the CNET article, Dunn, with the assistance of HP security personnel and the company's counsel's office, authorized a team of independent electronic-security experts to investigate the origin of the leak. The investigation targeted the January 2006 communications of HP's directors, including not only the records of phone calls and e-mails from HP but also the records from their personal accounts.

The consultants were not actually listening on the calls. They were just looking for a pattern of contacts. The investigation employed tactics that ranged from the controversial to the not necessarily legal. These tactics included using private investigators to impersonate HP's board members and then to trick phone companies into handing over the calling records of those board members' personal phone accounts. The records of nine journalists were similarly obtained. This technique is known as pretexting. With no more than a home address, an account number, or other pieces of personal information, an investigator or pretexter may obtain personal information from phone companies pretending be somebody else.

Resignation of Tom Perkins

The consultants discovered the origin of the leak, and in a board meeting held in May 2006, Patricia Dunn identified director George Keyworth, the longest-serving HP director, as the alleged leaker. He apologized and said to his fellow directors, "I would have told you all about this. Why didn't you just ask?" On September 12, 2006, Keyworth's public resignation letter apologizes and states his reasons for leaking information to CNET:

> I acknowledge that I was a source for a CNET article that appeared in January 2006. I was frequently asked by HP corporate communications officials to speak with reporters—both on the record and on background—in an effort to provide the perspective of a longstanding board member with continuity over much of the company's history. My comments were always praised by senior company officials as helpful to the company—which has always been my intention. The comments I made to the CNET reporter were, I believed, in the best interest of the company and also did not involve the disclosure of confidential or damaging information.

Immediately following the accusations, Keyworth left the board room, and another director, Tom Perkins, a renowned Silicon Valley venture capitalist and friend of the company founders, protested against the secret internal investigation, which he considered illegal, unethical, and a misplaced corporate priority on Dunn's part. Perkins was chair of the board's nominating and governance committee but had not been informed by Dunn of the surveillance, even though he knew that Dunn was attempting to discover the source of the leak.

After the board passed a motion asking Keyworth to resign, Perkins announced his own resignation. The next day, the company publicly announced Perkins's resignation without disclosing the reasons for his departure. HP reported Perkins's resignation to the SEC four days later, again giving no reason for his resignation.

In early August, after HP ignored his requests to take action, Perkins formally asked the SEC and prosecutors in California and New York to force HP to publicly file his written explanation for resigning. By early September, HP could not delay disclosing the scandal and made a filing to the SEC, laying out the pretexting story. At the same time, the story was released to the press by Perkins. On September 12, 2006, Keyworth publicly resigned from the board, and HP announced that Mark Hurd, HP chief executive officer and president, would replace Dunn as chair after the HP board meeting on January 18, 2007.

Congressional Hearings and Charges

On September 21, 2006, Mark Hurd, in an official HP press release, explained that "what began as an effort to prevent the leaks of confidential information from HP's boardroom ended up heading in directions that were never anticipated." A day later, Patricia Dunn resigned as an HP director, stating in her resignation letter the reasons for her departure and her involvement in the internal investigation:

> I have resigned today at the request of the board. The unauthorized disclosure of confidential information was a serious violation of our code of conduct. I followed the proper processes by seeking the assistance of HP security personnel. I did not select the people who conducted the investigation, which was undertaken after consultation with board members. I accepted the responsibility to identify the sources of those leaks, but I did not propose the specific methods of the investigation. I was a full subject of the investigation myself and my phone records were examined along with others. Unfortunately, the people HP relied upon to conduct this type of investigation let me and the company down.

A week later, on September 28, the parties involved appeared at the U.S. House of Representatives Energy and Commerce Committee Subcommittee on Oversight and Investigations. Ann Baskins, HP's general counsel, resigned hours before she was to appear as a witness and refused to answer questions, invoking the Fifth Amendment, due to the ongoing criminal investigations. In the hearing, Dunn and Hurd testified extensively about the internal investigation. Dunn testified she never approved the use of questionable tactics, saying she was not aware that pretexting could involve the misrepresentation of someone's identity to obtain phone records until late June or July (2006).

In October 2006, the California attorney general filed civil and criminal charges against the company, Patricia Dunn, and other HP employees. HP settled the lawsuit in December 2006, paying $14.5 million in fines and promising to improve its corporate governance practices. In June 2007, a California judge dismissed fraud charges against Patricia Dunn and other employees involved in the scandal.

At the same time, the journalists whose records were obtained by HP's external consultants filed a lawsuit against the company. Two years later, in February 2008, HP agreed to a financial settlement with the *New York Times* and three *BusinessWeek* magazine journalists. The amount of the settlement was not disclosed, and the proceeds were donated to charity.

Questions

1. Should the chair of the board of directors be allowed to initiate investigations into weaknesses in a company's internal control system?
2. Is the strategy of pretexting an acceptable means in order to obtain critical information that will strengthen a company's internal control system? The following legal advice was obtained on the subject by HP:

   > The committee was then advised by the committee's outside counsel that the use of pretexting at the time of the investigation was not generally unlawful (except with respect to financial institutions), but such counsel could not confirm that the techniques employed by the outside consulting firm and the party retained by that firm complied in all respects with applicable law.[1]

3. Should the reasons for resignations from a board of directors always be made public?

Sources: Hewlett-Packard, September 2006–July 2008, CNN Archive, http://money.cnn.com.

Hewlett-Packard, September 2006–July 2008, Newsweek Archive, http://www.newsweek.com.

Hewlett-Packard, September 2006–July 2008, New York Times Archive, http://www.nytimes.com.

Hewlett-Packard, 2006, press releases, http://www.hp.com/hpinfo/newsroom/press/2006/index.html.

The authors thank Miguel Minutti for his contributions to this case.

[1] Floyd Norris, "Euphemisms and Crimes at Hewlett-Packard," *New York Times*, September 7, 2006.

ETHICS CASE

Lord Conrad Black's Fiduciary Duty?

On November 17, 2005, Conrad Black and three other executives[1] of Hollinger International, Inc., were charged with eleven counts of fraud with regard to payments allegedly disguised as "noncompete fees" or, in one case, a "management agreement breakup fee" and the misuse of corporate perks. The payments were alleged to be a self-dealing "series of either secret or misleading transactions involving sales of a series of various newspaper publishing groups in the United States and Canada."[2] The sales involved several hundred newspapers and the alleged misdirection of over $80 million of the proceeds.

Hollinger International, Inc. (International), a U.S. holding company traded on the New York Stock Exchange, had been built up by Black over the years to own hundreds of newspapers, including the *Chicago Sun-Times*, the *Daily Telegraph* in London, the *National Post* in Toronto, and the *Jerusalem Post* in Israel. Partly in recognition of his business acumen, in 2000, Black was knighted by Britain's Queen Elizabeth and accorded the title of Lord Black of Crossharbour and the right to sit in the British House of Lords. Prevented from receiving the lordship by Jean Chrétien, then Prime Minister of Canada, Black resigned his Canadian

[1] U.S. Department of Justice, United States Attorney, Northern District of Illinois, press release, November 17, 2005, http://www.usdoj.gov/usao/iln/pr/chicago/2005/pr1117_01.pdf; John A. Boultbee, Peter Y. Atkinson, and Mark S. Kipnis are the other three executives. Another colleague, F. David Radler, pleaded guilty to a fraud count on September 20, 2005, and thereafter cooperated with the further investigation (4).
[2] Ibid.

citizenship to become a British citizen in order to accept the honor.

Black did not own the majority of Class A shares of International held by the public, but he (as CEO and principal owner) and his associates controlled it through their majority of ownership of the Class B shares that carried a 10–1 voting preference over the Class A shares. He and his associates owned 98.5% of Ravelston Corporation Limited, a private Canadian company with headquarters in Toronto, which in turn owned at least 70% of Hollinger, Inc., a Canadian holding company traded on the Toronto Stock Exchange. Hollinger, Inc. (Inc.), owned 30.3% of the equity (Class A and B) of International, which gave it and Black 72.8% of the voting power at International.[3] This type of arrangement, which allows the control of a corporation with the ownership of less than a majority of the corporation's equity, is known as "multiple-voting rights," or "super-voting rights."

The directors of International—who should have been standing up to Black on behalf of the investing public—were hand-picked by Black, probably for reasons other than their business acumen. Henry Kissinger, former U.S. secretary of state and a "trophy director," was probably selected for his fame and knowledge of history, defense, and politics—all passions of Black. The same can be said about other directors, including Richard Perle, former assistant secretary of defense and chair of the Pentagon advisory board; Robert Strauss, former chairman of the Democratic National Committee and ambassador to the Soviet Union; Richard Burt, former ambassador to Germany; and James R. Thompson, a former governor of Illinois. These directors, who were "expected to act as corporate watchdogs," and particularly the Audit Committee "seemed to behave like an old basset hound."[4] Cardinal Capital Management, which sued International's board in 2004, "described the directors … as 'supine' and 'quiescent' and accused them of 'rubber-stamping' tens of millions of dollars in pay-outs to company executives."[5]

Black was no stranger to the public spotlight or to public scrutiny. Earlier in his career, he had achieved notoriety for being spectacularly and arrogantly outspoken, for authoring acclaimed biographies of historically significant individuals, for preemptively engineering the recovery of employee surplus pension funds when their legal status was in doubt, and, most recently, for running a corporate kleptocracy.[6] The allegation of running a corporate kleptocracy was made when Black sued for peace from aggrieved minority shareholders who were blocking his ability to sell the *Daily Telegraph* to the Barclay brothers. On that occasion, Judge Strine of the Chancery Court of Delaware found that Black was not credible, saying,

> Black also vigorously defended his failure to inform the International board of his discussions with the Barclays. But then again, he could hardly deny these facts. On more debatable points, I found Black evasive and unreliable. His explanations of key events and of his own motivations do not have the ring of truth.[7]

The evidence provided to Judge Strine was ultimately responsible for the fraud charges that are the subject of this case.

[3] Opinion of Judge Strine, Vice Chancellor of the Chancery Court of the State of Delaware, in C.A. No. 183-N (February 26, 2004), 6, **http://www.cengagebrain.com.**

[4] Sinclair Stewart and Jacquie McNish, "Lord Black's Cautionary Lessons for Executives," November 21, 2005, accessed August 16, 2016, at http://www.ft.com/cms/s/0/16b5915c-5a33-11da-b023-0000779e2340.html#axzz4HW97yozW.

[5] Ibid.

[6] The charge of running a corporate kleptocracy (thiefdom) was made on August 30, 2004, to which Richard C. Breeden, former chair of the SEC, served as special investigator. See p. 4. This report is available at **http://www.cengagebrain.com.**

[7] C.A. No. 183-N, 59.

It is not unusual for a company selling a business unit to agree not to compete with that unit for a period of years. It is unusual, however, for an executive of the selling company to agree not to compete personally and to be paid to do so. It is extremely unusual for that executive to decide how much of the selling price he should be paid—as Black did—and how much should be paid to the selling company. Making such a decision places the decision maker in the position of self-dealing—a conflict of interest that, at the very least, requires disclosure to the selling company and the receipt of its approval. In this case, Black should have disclosed his related-party, self-dealing to the board of International and obtained their approval. Black claimed he did, but the district attorney claimed he did not because he failed to provide sufficient information and/or misled the board on numerous occasions.

According to the indictment press release in one case—the sale of 50% interest in the *National Post* to CanWest Global Communications Corp. for approximately $2.1 billion,

> Black negotiated the deal, … while Boultbee, Atkinson and Kipnis participated in reviewing and finalizing the transaction, which allocated approximately $51.8 million to non-competition agreements. This was allegedly done as a mechanism to pay Boultbee and Atkinson a bonus to take advantage of tax benefits that legitimate non-competition payments receive under Canadian tax laws.
>
> Between May 2000 and May 2002, Black, Boultbee, and Atkinson allegedly fraudulently inserted Boultbee and Atkinson as promissors not to compete and fraudulently caused approximately $51.8 million of the sale proceeds to be allocated to the non-competition agreements. Black, Boultbee, Atkinson and Kipnis failed to disclose this self-dealing to International's Audit Committee, the indictment alleges, and caused false and misleading statements to be made to International's independent directors about the non-competition payments. Although International was the seller and signed a non-competition agreement, all $51.8 million, plus interest, was diverted from International and, instead, was distributed to Black, Radler, Boultbee, Atkinson and Ravelston.
>
> After an outside attorney for a bank discovered and questioned these payments during the course of a due diligence inquiry, Black, Boultbee, Atkinson and Kipnis returned to International's Audit Committee and sought ratification of the payments on different grounds, claiming that the information previously provided to the directors misdescribed the transaction in a number of "inadvertent" respects. In fact, the previous submission's falsehoods were not inadvertent, and the second submission was also false and misleading. After International's independent directors ratified these payments, Black then lied to International's shareholders about the payments at International's 2002 annual shareholder meeting, according to the indictment.

The information, first submitted to the Audit Committee on September 1, 2000, was allegedly false for the following reasons:

- Only $32.4 million, not $51.8 million, was allocated to noncompetition agreements.
- CanWest had requested Boultbee and Atkinson to sign noncompetition agreements when it had not done so.
- International would be paid $2.6 million when it actually received nothing;
- It proposed that Ravelston be paid $19.4 million as a breakup fee to end a long-term management agreement with International. In fact, Ravelston had no

right to any payment if International terminated its management agreement with Ravelston.

- It failed to disclose that although approximately $647 million of the CanWest consideration would go to HCNLP, Black, Boultbee and Atkinson had unilaterally decided that International would pay 100% of the noncompetition consideration.

The first submission also failed to disclose that this decision was made to avoid having to raise the noncompetition payments with the HCNLP Audit Committee, which Black and the other two executives feared would ask more questions than the International Audit Committee. As a result, International bore 100% of the noncompete allocation attributable to the assets sold by HCNLP rather than its 87% pro rata share, a difference of approximately $2.1 million.

When the CanWest transaction closed, Ravelston, Black, Radler, Boultbee, and Atkinson caused approximately $52.8 million to be disbursed to themselves—approximately $11.9 million each to Black and Radler, approximately $1.3 million each to Boultbee and Atkinson, and approximately $26.4 million to Ravelston. (The extra $1 million was interest from July 30 to November 16, 2000.) Although the Audit Committee was told that International would receive $2.6 million for its noncompetition agreement, in fact, International received nothing.[8]

In addition to allegations of fraud with regard to noncompete and other fee arrangements, Black has been charged with repeated breaches of fiduciary duty and abuse of power in the misuse of corporate assets between May 1998 and August 2002 at the expense of the corporation and its public majority shareholders, including the following:

- In the summer of 2001, Black fraudulently caused International to pay for his use of its corporate jet to fly himself and his wife on a personal vacation to Bora Bora in French Polynesia. The couple left Seattle for Bora Bora on July 30, 2001, and returned to Seattle on August 8, 2001, logging a total of 23.1 hours in flight. There was little, if any, business purpose to this vacation. Leasing and operating the jet for Black's personal vacation cost International tens of thousands of dollars. When International's accountants sought to have Black reimburse International for this cost, Black refused, stating in an e-mail to Atkinson that "needless to say, no such outcome is acceptable."
- In December 2000, Black fraudulently caused International to pay more than $40,000 for his wife's surprise birthday party on December 4, 2000, at La Grenouille restaurant in New York City. The party cost approximately $62,000; related expenses included eighty dinners at $195 per person and $13,935 for wine and champagne. The party was a social occasion with little, if any, business purpose. Yet Black, without any disclosure or consultation with International's Audit Committee, determined that International would pay approximately $42,000 for the party and that he would pay only $20,000.
- Black and Boultbee defrauded International of millions of dollars in connection with International's renovation of the ground-floor apartment and Black's purchase from International of the second-floor apartment at 635 Park Avenue, which Black used when he was in New York City and which provided proximate quarters for his servants. Last month, the government seized approximately $8.9 million in proceeds from Black's sale of the two apartments, and the indictment alleges that those funds are now subject to criminal forfeiture.[9]

[8] U.S. Department of Justice, 6–8.

[9] C.A. No. 183-N, 11.

Time will tell if the court finds the case is as Lord Black has indicated:

> Absolute nonsense, … There's no truth or substance whatsoever to these charges. This has been one massive smear job from A to Z, and it will have a surprise ending … a complete vindication of the defendants, and exposure of their persecutors.[10]

Or will it be as Patrick Fitzgerald, the U.S. district attorney has said?

> Officers and directors of publicly traded companies who steer shareholders' money into their pockets should not lie to the board of directors to get permission to do so.… The indictment charges that the insiders at Hollinger—all the way to the top of the corporate ladder—whose job it was to safeguard the shareholders, made it their job to steal and conceal.[11]

Questions

1. What conflicts of interest may have been involved in Black's activities?
2. Were Black's noncompete agreements and payments unethical and/or illegal?
3. What questions should have been asked by International's directors?
4. If the boards of directors of his various companies approved these noncompete agreements, are the board members on the hook and Black off?
5. Black controlled key companies through multiple voting rights attached to less than a majority of shares. Was this illegal and/or unethical?
6. What risk management techniques would have prevented Black's potential conflicts from becoming harmful?

[10] Lauren La Rose, "Conrad Black Calls Charges of Fraud 'One Massive Smear Job' against Him," November 24, 2005, http://www.cbc.ca.

[11] U.S. Department of Justice, 5.

ETHICS CASE

Manipulation of MCI's Allowance for Doubtful Accounts

Walt Pavlo joined MCI in the spring of 1992. At that time, MCI was a growth company in the booming long-distance telecommunications industry that had 15% of the long-distance market, with revenues of $11 billion.

In the 1990s, the major telecommunications companies all shared their fiber-optic networks. This was more efficient than having each company lay its own network to every corner of the country. Each company would use the others' networks in places where the former did not have cable and vice versa. The cost of routing a call through these fiber-optic networks was measured in pennies per minute. However, MCI and the other telecommunication companies sold the right to use the network to their customers for dimes per minute. It was a lucrative business based on volume. The more the network was used, the greater the revenue for the telecommunication company. MCI's stellar revenue growth was due to its sales, and sales personnel were awarded lucrative commissions. Senior management was given generous stock options. It was heady times.

MCI had a wide array of clients that varied from major corporations, such as American Express, General Electric, and IBM, to small newly formed long-distance discount services (LDDS). These were primarily marketing firms that bought MCI long-distance capacity and that they resold to individuals and small businesses. Although these LDDS customers represented only 5% of MCI's annual sales, the profit margins for both MCI and the LDDS companies were quite substantial. For example, in 1992, Telephone Publishing

Corp. (TCP) paid $600,000 to MCI for long-distance calls that TCP was charging its customers approximately $5 million per month. After paying its overhead, TCP was netting, before taxes, about $20 million per year. Meanwhile, MCI was often charging a LDDS as much as 28 cents a minute for services that cost about 5 cents. Everyone was making money.

However, many of these LDDS companies were slow in paying MCI for the use of the long-distance service. Collections were a problem because these companies normally had no hard assets. Their offices were rented, the communication switch was leased, and they had no other assets other than cash. Without assets, they were somewhat bulletproof. They could be threatened, but there was nothing to collect in the event the LDDS was successfully sued by MCI. If MCI cut off access to the network, then the LDDS would fold its operations and disappear, often reappearing under a new name as a client of one of the other telecommunication companies.

Walt Pavlo was in charge of the finance unit, responsible for LDDS collections. Walt was also given some clear guidelines with respect to accounts receivable and bad debts. Accounts that were ninety or more days old should not exceed 7% of total receivables, and bad debt write-offs should be under 2% of total account receivables. For 1994, the bad debt ceiling was set at $12 million and then reduced to $10 million in 1995 even though 1995 revenues had increased. Unfortunately, both delinquent accounts and bad debts exceed these guidelines. So, Walt gathered a small group of bright MBAs, and he tasked them to be creative. How could they stay within the MCI guidelines?

One strategy was to get delinquent accounts to sign promissory notes, thereby moving their balances out of accounts receivable. These customers were also required to pay interest on the note, but because they often had no intention of paying the principal, the interest charge was irrelevant. For example, Voicecom had its account converted to a $3.5 million promissory note. It paid $100,000 per month for ten months and then defaulted on the balance. Another strategy was to accept the customer's common stock instead of cash.

They lapped payments, posting one customer's payment to another's account in order to show activity in the latter's account. They amortized bad debts, writing off a portion and pretending that the balance would be collected. They also convinced the accounting department to accept a check in the mail. This consisted of a fax of a check and a FedEx tracking number of the check to prove that the check was on its way. When the check arrived, the previous entry would be reversed. None of these procedures was identified and/or challenged by internal audit or the external auditors.

However, these strategies were merely disguising rather than solving the problem. So, in January 1996, Walt sent a note to his new boss saying that MCI's bad debts for 1995 were approaching $88 million. A month later, he was told that his budget for 1996 was $15 million. He was also reminded that there was speculation that MCI would be taken over, so it was everyone's responsibility to make their targets and budgets. At the time, Walt was being well paid for running an efficient department and staying within budget. He had a stay-at-home wife and two small children. If MCI were taken over, he would profit handsomely from his stock options.

Questions

1. After being told that the guideline for bad debts for 1996 was to be $15 million, what should Walt do?
2. What are the risks for MCI in setting an unrealistic allowance for doubtful accounts?

Source: Walter Pavlo Jr. and Neil Weinberg, Etika Books LLC, "Stolen without a Gun: Confessions from Inside History's Biggest Accounting Fraud—The Collapse of MCI WorldCom," 2007.

ETHICS CASE

Stock Options and Gifts of Publicly Traded Shares

Pierre Garvey, the CEO of Revel Information Technology, sat back in his chair and looked at his assistants. He frowned. "My son has been diagnosed with MLD," he said.

They all looked at him with shock. "Its proper name is metachromatic leukodystrophy, and it's caused by an enzyme deficiency that will eventually destroy his nervous system."

"I'm so sorry, Pierre." "That's awful." "Oh, my God! Is there anything that can be done?" They all spoke at once.

"It's an extremely rare disease. There's no known cure and no standard form of treatment," he went on. "But there has been research into bone marrow and stem cell transplant therapies. So, what I would like you to do, Gloria, is have 50% of our corporate charitable contributions redirected to organizations that are working on stem cell research."

She stared straight at her boss and said, "There is a formal procedure for how we allocate our charity."

Before she could say anything further, Pierre stopped her. "You're in charge of that committee! Fill out all the necessary forms and paperwork, but I want 50% of our corporate contributions to go to stem cell research. Do I make myself clear?" She nodded and remained silent throughout the rest of the meeting.

"I've decided to exercise some of my stock options and then donate the stock to the Lascelles Institute, which is working on bone marrow therapy." As CEO, Pierre had been given multiple stock options that varied in price from $17.51 to $29.87. Shares of Revel Information Technology have been trading in the $19 range for the last month. The current share price is $19.25. "I'm going to exercise 50,000 at $17.51 and then donate the stock to the Lascelles Institute. They'll then give me a tax receipt for the fair market value of the shares."

"Wouldn't it be easier for you to exercise the options, sell the shares, and then donate the cash proceeds to the charity?" asked Carol, the executive vice president.

"No," said Lin, the controller. "If Pierre exercises the options and sells the stock, he has to pay capital gains. But because of the recent changes to the Income Tax Act, there are no capital gains if shares are donated to a charity."

"But isn't this subject to insider trading rules?"

"That's right," said Pierre, "but, because I'm donating the shares, there are no proceeds to me, and so the securities commission is not interested because I'm not receiving any cash and there's no capital gain."

"This is all quite legal," added Lin. "However, I'm concerned about this quarter's financial results and what it will do to our stock price. Our earnings and net income are down substantially from the analysts' forecasts. I think that our stock will take a beating after we release our results and my stock options may no longer be in the money."

"That's right, Pierre," said Carol. "We lost sales to cheap imports from China, our competitors lowered their prices and stole some of our customers, our obsolete machinery finally broke down and had to be replaced, and we got hammered on those security-backed investments we bought with our surplus funds."

"Once we release this quarter's results, we should expect out stock to fall to about $17. Maybe a bit more," said Lin.

"Okay, this is what you do. Gloria, I want you to arrange that our corporate donations go to stem cell research. I also want you to contact the Lascelles Institute and let them know that I'm going to be donating 50,000 shares of Revel Information Technology to them tomorrow, on Thursday. I also want a tax receipt at whatever price our shares are trading at tomorrow, probably at about $19 per share.

"Carol, I want you to get in touch with legal and arrange for me to exercise 50,000 options at $17.51. I then want them to change the ownership on the certificates to the Lascelles Institute.

"Finally, Lin, I don't want you to release this quarter's financial statements tomorrow. Wait until Monday morning of next week.

"Everybody clear? Good. Off you go."

Questions

1. Is it right that a CEO can direct the charitable donations of his or her company to the charity of his or her choice?
2. Comment on the ethical aspects of Pierre's stock option/stock donation strategy.
3. If you were Gloria, what should you do? Would this change if you were a donations specialist, a lawyer, or a professional accountant?

Source: Michael Walker, "Publicly Traded Gifts," *CA Magazine*, June 2008, 38–40.

ETHICS CASE

The Ethics of Repricing and Backdating Employee Stock Options

Employee stock options allow company executives to buy shares of their company at a specified price during a specified time period. They are given to executives as a form of noncash compensation. The option or "strike price" is normally equal to the market price of the stock on the day that the option is granted to the employee. The stock option is intended to motivate the executive to increase the stock price of the firm. If the stock rises, the investor is pleased. If the stock rises, the executive exercises the option, buys the stock from the company at the strike price, and then immediately sells those shares on the stock exchange at the current (higher) market price to obtain a capital gain. This is considered to be a win-win situation. Both the investor and the employee gain from the increase in the market price of the company's stock.

However, sometimes the stock price falls, and the current price is less than the strike price. Such stock options are referred to as "underwater" or "out of the money." In such cases, companies will sometimes reprice the stock options to a price that is less than the current market price or cancel the underwater options and issue new options that are priced at the new current market price. Both repricing and backdating of stock options have effectively been curtailed as a result of SOX disclosure requirements. As a result, two new strategies are available. One is to "spring-load" the options by issuing them to employees just before good news is announced to investors. The other is to "bullet-dodge" by delaying the granting of stock options until after bad news has been released.

An analysis of the ethics of repricing, backdating, spring-loading, and bullet-dodging is contained in the article "Ethics of Options Repricing and Backdating: Banishing Greed from Corporate Governance and Management." In their article, which was published in the October 2007 issue of *The CPA Journal*, Raiborn, Massoud, Morris, and Pier present four ethical arguments.

The *theory of justice* says that equals should be treated equally and unequals treated unequally in proportion to their inequalities. All investors are equal, and executive investors should be treated no differently from all other investors in the company. As such, preferential treatment through the backdating of stock options is inappropriate and unethical. Spring-loading and bullet-dodging are grounded on management's inside knowledge of good and bad news that will have an impact on the company's stock price. Their inside knowledge discriminates against all the other shareholders who do not know the good or bad news.

Utilitarianism or consequentialism argues that the ethically correct decision must be of benefit to most shareholders in the long term. Backdating stock options benefits the executive at the expense of the other shareholders. It is not in the best interest of the majority of the shareholders of the company. Spring-loading and bullet-dodging are only in the short-term interests of a minority of the shareholders (i.e., executive shareholders) and not in the best long-term interests of all the other (majority) shareholders.

From a *deontological* perspective, backdating and repricing are akin to lies because the intention is to manipulate and deceive the other shareholders. Deontology does not accept that the end justifies the means. Furthermore, it does not allow exceptions to a rule. Spring-loading and backdating treat one category of shareholders (management) differently than the other category of shareholders (all the current and future shareholders). As such, it is unlikely that everyone in society would accept as a universal rule that management should be given preferential treatment.

It is difficult to say that manipulating stock options, through any of these four tactics, is the sign of a virtuous person. *Virtue ethics* does not accept discrimination and prudential treatment of insiders as the mark of an ethical businessperson.

The conclusion of the article by Raiborn et al. is that the repricing of stock options may be legal but it is certainly unethical. Their concluding paragraph reads,

> Stock options were designed as a way to provide pay for performance, not to reward poor performance by backward-looking repricing or backdating. Such activities undermine the incentive justification for use of stock option plans. Executives deserve compensation packages that provide both short-run benefits and a long-run motivation to increase organizational value for all stakeholders. Compensation methods that cause the tone at the top to be perceived as a cacophony of greed should be banished from the orchestra.

Questions

1. Do you think that stock options actually motivate employees to work for the long-term good of the company?
2. Do you think that stock options inadvertently encourage managers to engage in questionable accounting activities, such as earnings management, to artificially increase the company's net income and thereby the value of the executives stock options?
3. Do you agree or disagree with the four ethical arguments summarized above and contained in more detail in the article by Raiborn et al.? Explain why.
4. Should a board of directors approve repricing or backdating stock options for outstanding executives whose current stock options are underwater due to uncontrollable economic factors and who will be lured away unless some incentives to stay are created? What other incentives might work?

Cases on Fraudulent & Questionable Financial Reporting

ETHICS CASE

Satyam Computer Services—The Enron of India

Satyam Computer Services Ltd was founded in 1987 by B. Ramalinga Raju. By 2009, it was India's fourth-largest information technology company with 53,000 employees, operating in sixty-six countries. It provided a variety of services, including computer systems, customer services, and the outsourcing of accounting and finance. It had 185 of the Fortune 500 as customers and acted as a back office to such companies as Nestlé, General Motors, and General Electric.

On January 7, 2009, Raju sent a letter of resignation to the Board of Directors and to SEBI (the Securities and Exchange Board of India). In his letter, he outlined how he systematically falsified Satyam's financial reports. The following was found respect to the September 2008 quarterly financial statements:

- The reported cash and bank balance of 5.36 billion rupees was overstated by 5.04 billion rupees (approximately $1 billion).
- The accrued interest of 376 million rupees was fictitious.
- There was an unrecorded liability of 1.2 billion rupees that Raju had with the company.

- The quarterly revenue of 2.7 billion rupee was overstated by 22%, and the operating margin of 649 million rupees was overstated by 91%.

He revealed in his letter that what started as small discrepancies grew and, over time, reached unimaginable proportions. "It was like riding a tiger, not knowing how to get off without being eaten." He said that he alone had perpetrated the fraud and that no one on the Board of Directors knew about it. Raju concluded his letter by apologizing for what he had done and announced that he was prepared to accept the legal consequences of his actions.

In his resignation letter, Raju said that neither he nor any of his family had profited personally from the scam; none had sold their shares or taken any money out of the company. However, it was later revealed that 13,000 of the 53,000 Satyam employees were fictitious and that Raju was siphoning off approximately $4 million monthly from the company. Furthermore, it is alleged that Raju improperly transferred large numbers of Satyam shares to his mother and younger brother.

After the announcement of Raju's resignation and the details of the fraud, the price of Satyam's stock fell 78%, bringing down the Bombay stock exchange, the Sensex index, by 7.3%. In April 2010, the company was sold to Tech Mahindra and renamed Mahindra Satyam.

There had been signs of problems at Satyam's prior to Raju's resignation. In October 2008, the World Bank said that it was refusing to conduct any further business with Satyam after a Satyam employee had hacked into the World Bank's computer system. In the fall of 2008, Raju was concerned that his company was being targeted for a takeover, in which case the fraud would be detected. So, on December 16, he announced that Satyam would spend $1.6 billion to buy two construction companies, Maytas Property and Maytas Infra, each of which was run by two of his sons. ("Maytas" is "Satyam" spelled backward.) His intention was to replace the fictitious assets with real ones. However, his offer was quickly retracted under shareholder pressure. The next day, in New York, the price of Satyam's ADRs lost 50% of their value. Also, in December, Forrester Research warned customers about continuing to do business with Satyam. The day before Raju's resignation, DSP Merrill Lynch, which had been hired to consider strategic operations for the company, suddenly resigned after it learned about "material accounting irregularities."

Following the collapse of the company, people began to ask questions about the role of Satyam's auditor, Price Waterhouse (PW), the Indian branch of Pricewaterhouse-Coopers (PwC). People were wondering how PW could not detect, for example, that cash was overstated by 94%. The Indian exchange commission, SEBI, began an investigation into PW; PW had provided Satyam with clean audit opinions. The accusation is that by certifying the false financial statements as true, Price Waterhouse had misled investors. The investigation by SEBI has not yet concluded, nor has there been a court case on the Satyam Computer Services Ltd fraud.

Questions

1. Will the Satyam fraud damage India's reputation as a reliable provider of information technology outsourcing?
2. How long will it take to restore Satyam Computer's reputation, and how would you recommend that the restoration be facilitated?
3. Raju did not commit this fraud on his own. What types of individuals probably assisted him either actively or by keeping quiet about what they knew he was doing?
4. To whom should potential whistle-blowers have complained?
5. Raju likened his fraud experience to "riding a tiger, not knowing how to get off without being eaten." This is an aspect experienced by some people trapped on a slippery slope from small to ever-larger fraudulent acts. If Raju had come to you for advice during the tiger ride, what would you have advised him?
6. Should PwC worldwide have to pay any investors for their losses caused by faulty audit work of personnel in PW India?

Sources: Manjeet Kripalani, "India's Madoff? Satyam Scandal Rocks Outsourcing Industry," *Bloomberg Business Week*, January 7, 2009.

"Merrill Lynch Snaps Ties with Satyam," *Indian Express.com*, January 7, 2009.

"Satyam: B Ramalinga Raju's Resignation Letter," *The Times Online*, January 7, 2009.

"Satyam Fudged FDs, Has 40,000 Employees: Public Prosecutor," *The Economic Times*, January 22, 2009.

"Satyam Founder Ramalinga Raju Surrenders in Fraud Case," *International Business News*, November 10, 2010.

Heather Timmons and Bettina Wassener, "Satyam Chief Admits Huge Fraud," *New York Times*, January 8, 2009.

ETHICS CASE

Nortel Networks' Audit Committee Was in the Dark

By the late 1990s, Nortel Networks Corporation, headquartered in Brampton, Ontario, Canada, was one of the giants of the telecommunications industry. Seventy-five percent of North America's Internet traffic was carried by Nortel equipment,[1] which was manufactured by 73,000 employees around the world.[2] The company's shares were listed on both the New York Stock Exchange (NYSE) and the Toronto Stock Exchange (TSE). By July 2000, the company had issued over 3.8 billion shares worth C$473.1 billion in market capitalization at a peak price of C$124.50. So dominant was Nortel that it accounted for more than one-third the value of the S & P/TSE 300 Composite Index.[3]

Then the infamous dot-com bubble burst, and by September 2002, Nortel stock closed at C$0.63.[4] John Roth, named Canada's "business leader of the year" in 2000, indicated that he would step down as CEO in April 2001.[5] This may have been partly because he had not foreseen a coming slump in sales and as a result appeared to have misled the investing public. Until Roth's departure, Nortel was considered to have had an exemplary corporate culture and code of conduct.

Frank Dunn, a CMA who had been head of public affairs and then CFO, was named as replacement CEO in November 2001. He led Nortel through a radical restructuring that saw a reduction in its workforce by 50% to 45,000 in 2001 and a further 10,000 in 2002. Apparently as a result, Nortel's financial picture showed a profit of U.S.$54 million in the first quarter of fiscal 2003, which ended on March 31, 2003. Profits were also reported in the second quarter.

However, on October 23, 2003, when Nortel reported profits in the third quarter, restatements affecting 2000, 2001, and 2002 financial statements were also announced. Concern over these restatements, delays in financial reports, and concerns over bonuses paid to executives triggered the Audit Committee of Nortel Networks Corporation to authorize an independent review (IR) of the company's financial affairs by the Washington, D.C., law firm of Wilmer Cutler Pickering Hale and Dorr LLP.

The IR findings resulted in the need for a second restatement of Nortel's financial statements and the termination for cause of ten senior employees, including the CEO, CFO, and controller. All were asked to repay bonuses received. A further twelve senior employees were required to repay bonuses received and did so. They were not terminated.

Summary of Findings and of Recommended Remedial Measures of the Independent Review[6]

The following excerpts provide an overview of the IR and its findings:

> In late October 2003, Nortel Networks Corporation ("Nortel" or the

[1] *CBC.CA News*, "Nortel: Canada's Tech Giant," May 2, 2005.

[2] *CBC.CA News*, "Northern Telecom Buys American Firm," November 13, 1998.

[3] *CBC.CA News*, "Nortel: The Wild Ride of Canada's Most Watched Stock," May 2, 2005.

[4] Ibid.

[5] Nortel news release, "Nortel Networks Announces Frank Dunn as President and CEO," October 2, 2001, http://www.nortelnetworks.com/corporate/news/newsreleases/2001d/10_02_01_ceo.html.

[6] Released January 11, 2005, as part of the MD&A to the 2003 Annual Report. This can also be found at http://www.nortelnetworks.com/corporate/news/newsreleases/collateral/independent_review_summary.pdf.

"Company") announced that it intended to restate approximately $900M of liabilities carried on its previously reported balance sheet as of June 30, 2003, following a comprehensive internal review of these liabilities ("First Restatement"). The Company stated that the principal effects of the restatement would be a reduction in previously reported net losses for 2000, 2001, and 2002 and an increase in shareholders' equity and net assets previously reported on its balance sheet. Concurrent with this announcement, the Audit Committees of the Boards of Directors of Nortel Networks Corporation and Nortel Networks Limited (collectively, the "Audit Committee" and the "Board of Directors" or "Board," respectively) initiated an independent review of the facts and circumstances leading to the First Restatement. The Audit Committee wanted to gain a full understanding of the events that caused significant excess liabilities to be maintained on the balance sheet that needed to be restated, and to recommend that the Board of Directors adopt, and direct management to implement, necessary remedial measures to address personnel, controls, compliance, and discipline. The Audit Committee engaged Wilmer Cutler Pickering Hale and Dorr LLP ("WCPHD") to advise it in connection with its independent review. Because of the significant accounting issues involved in the inquiry, WCPHD retained Huron Consulting Services LLC ("Huron") to provide expert accounting assistance. Huron has been involved in all phases of WCPHD's work.

The investigation necessarily focused on the financial picture of the Company at the time that decisions were made and actions were taken regarding provisioning activity. Because of significant changes to financial results reflected in the Second Restatement, the restated financial results differ from the historical results that formed the backdrop for this inquiry.

In summary, former corporate management (now terminated for cause) and former finance management (now terminated for cause) in the Company's finance organization endorsed, and employees carried out, accounting practices relating to the recording and release of provisions that were not in compliance with U.S. generally accepted accounting principles ("U.S. GAAP") in at least four quarters, including the third and fourth quarters of 2002 and the first and second quarters of 2003. In three of those four quarters—when Nortel was at, or close to, break even—these practices were undertaken to meet internally imposed pro-forma earnings before taxes ("EBT") targets. While the dollar value of most of the individual provisions was relatively small, the aggregate value of the provisions made the difference between a profit and a reported loss, on a pro forma basis, in the fourth quarter of 2002 and the difference between a loss and a reported profit, on a pro forma basis, in the first and second quarters of 2003. This conduct caused Nortel to report a loss in the fourth quarter of 2002 and to pay no employee bonuses, and to achieve and maintain profitability in the first and second quarters of 2003, which, in turn, caused it to pay bonuses to all Nortel employees and significant bonuses to senior management under bonus plans tied to a pro forma profitability metric.

The failure to follow U.S. GAAP with respect to provisioning can be understood in light of the management, organizational structure, and internal controls that characterized Nortel's finance organization. These characteristics, discussed below, include:

- Management "tone at the top" that conveyed the strong leadership message that earnings targets could be met through application of accounting practices that finance managers knew or ought to have known were not in compliance with U.S. GAAP and that questioning these practices was not acceptable;

- Lack of technical accounting expertise which fostered accounting practices not in compliance with U.S. GAAP;
- Weak or ineffective internal controls which, in turn, provided little or no check on inaccurate financial reporting;
- Operation of a complicated "matrix" structure which contributed to a lack of clear responsibility and accountability by business units and by regions; and
- Lack of integration between the business units and corporate management that led to a lack of transparency regarding provisioning activity to achieve internal EBT targets.

Nortel posted significant losses in 2001 and 2002 and downsized its work force by nearly two-thirds. The remaining employees were asked to undertake significant additional responsibilities with no increase in pay and no bonuses. The Company's former senior corporate management asserted, at the start of the inquiry, that the Company's downturn, and concomitant downsizing of operations and workforce, led to a loss of documentation and a decline in financial discipline. Those factors, in their view, were primarily responsible for the significant excess provisions on the balance sheet as of June 30, 2003, which resulted in the First Restatement. While that downturn surely played a part in the circumstances leading to the First Restatement, the root causes ran far deeper.

When Frank Dunn became CFO in 1999, and then CEO in 2001, he drove senior management in his finance organization to achieve EBT targets that he set with his senior management team. The provisioning practices adopted by Dunn and other finance employees to achieve internal EBT targets were not in compliance with U.S. GAAP, particularly Statement of Financial Accounting Standards Number 5 ("SFAS 5"). SFAS 5, which governs accounting for contingencies, requires, among other things, a probability analysis for each risk before a provision can be recorded. It also requires that a triggering event—such as resolution of the exposure or a change in estimate—occur in the quarter to warrant the release of a provision. Dunn and other finance employees recognized that provisioning activity—how much to reserve for a particular exposure and when that reserve should be released—inherently involved application of significant judgment under U.S. GAAP. Dunn and others stretched the judgment inherent in the provisioning process to create a flexible tool to achieve EBT targets. They viewed provisioning as "a gray area." They became comfortable with the concept that the value of a provision could be reasonably set at virtually any number within a wide range and that a provision release could be justified in a number of quarters after the quarter in which the exposure, which formed the basis for the provision, was resolved. Dunn and others exercised their judgment strategically to achieve EBT targets.

Third quarter, 2002. At the direction of then-CFO Doug Beatty, a company-wide analysis of accrued liabilities on the balance sheet was launched in early August 2002. The CFO and the Controller, Michael Gollogly, learned that this analysis showed approximately \$303M in provisions that were no longer required and were available for release. The CFO and the Controller, each a corporate officer, knew, or ought to have known, that excess provisions, if retained on the balance sheet, would cause the Company's financial statements to be inaccurate and that U.S. GAAP would have required either that such provisions be released in that period and properly disclosed, or that prior period financial statements be restated. Instead, they permitted finance employees in the business units and in the regions to release excess accruals into income over the following several quarters. They acted in contravention of U.S. GAAP by failing to correct the Company's financial statements to account for the significant excess accrued liabilities. Neither the CFO nor the Controller advised the Audit Committee and/or the Board of Directors that significant excess provisions on the balance sheet had been identified and that the Company's financial statements might be inaccurate, nor did either suggest such information should be disclosed in the Company's financial statements.

As a result of this company-wide review, senior finance employees recognized that their respective business unit or region had excess provisions on Nortel's balance sheet, and directed other finance employees to track these excess provisions. Nortel finance employees had their own distinct term for a provision on the balance sheet that was no longer needed—it was "hard." Each business unit developed, in varying levels of detail and over varying periods of time, internal "hardness" schedules that identified provisions that were no longer required and were available for release. Finance employees treated provisions identified on these schedules as a pool from which releases could be made to "close the gap" between actual EBT and EBT targets in subsequent quarters.

Fourth quarter, 2002. By mid-2002, employees throughout the Company were being recruited by other companies and morale was low. Corporate management sought to retain these employees but recognized that other public companies had come under criticism for awarding "stay" bonuses in the face of enormous losses. At management's recommendation, the Board determined to reward employees with bonuses under bonus plans tied to profitability. One plan, the Return to Profitability ("RTP") bonus, contemplated a one-time bonus payment to every employee, save 43 top executives, in the first quarter in which the Company achieved pro forma profitability. The 43 executives were eligible to receive 20% of their share of the RTP bonus in the first quarter in which the Company attained profitability, 40% after the second consecutive quarter of cumulative profitability, and the remaining 40% upon four quarters of cumulative profitability. In order for the RTP bonuses to be paid, pro forma profits had to exceed, by at least one dollar, the total cost of the bonus for that quarter. Another plan, the Restricted Stock Unit ("RSU") plan, made a significant number of share units available for award by the Board to the same 43 executives in four instalments tied to profitability milestones. Once a milestone was met, the Board had discretion whether to make the award.

Through the first three quarters of 2002, Nortel experienced significant losses, and management reported to the Board that it expected losses would continue in the fourth quarter. After the initial results for the business units and regions were consolidated, they showed that Nortel unexpectedly would achieve pro forma profitability in the fourth quarter. Frank Dunn, who had been promoted to CEO in 2001, understood that profitability had been attained from an operational standpoint but determined that it was unwise to report profitability and pay bonuses in the fourth quarter because performance for the rest of the year had been poor. He determined that provisions should be taken to cause a loss for the quarter. Over a two day period late in the closing process, the CFO and the Controller worked with employees in the finance organizations in the business units, the regions, and in global operations, to identify and record additional provisions totaling more than $175 million. All of these provisions were recorded "topside"—that is, by employees in the office of the Controller based on information provided by the business units, regions and global operations—because of the late date in the closing process on which they were made. Nortel's results for the fourth quarter of 2002 turned from an unexpected profit into the loss previously forecasted by management to the Board of Directors. Neither the CEO, the CFO, nor the Controller advised the Audit Committee and/or the Board of Directors of this concerted provisioning activity to improperly turn a profit into a loss. Nortel has since determined that many of these provisions were not recorded in compliance with U.S. GAAP, and has reversed those provisions in the Second Restatement. The loss then reported by Nortel in the fourth quarter meant that no employee bonuses were paid for that quarter.

First quarter, 2003. While Nortel had announced publicly that it expected to achieve pro forma profitability in the second quarter of 2003, Dunn told a number of employees that he intended to achieve profitability one quarter earlier, and he established internal EBT targets for each business unit and for corporate to reach that goal. At Dunn's direction, "roadmaps" were developed to show how the targets could be achieved. These roadmaps made clear that the internal EBT targets for the quarter could only be met through release from the balance sheet of excess provisions that lacked an accounting trigger in the quarter. At the request of finance management in each business unit, finance employees identified excess, or "hard," provisions from the balance sheet, and, together, they determined which provisions to release to close the gap and meet the internal EBT targets. That release activity was supplemented by releases, directed by the CFO and by the Controller, of excess corporate provisions that had been identified in the third quarter of 2002 as available for release. Releases of provisions by corporate and by each business unit and region, including excess provisions, totaling $361M, enabled Nortel to show a consolidated pro forma profit in the first quarter, notwithstanding that its operations were running at a loss. The Finance Vice Presidents of the business units and two of the three regions, the Asia Controller, the CFO, the Controller, and the CEO knew, or ought to have known, that U.S. GAAP did not permit the release, without proper justification, of excess provisions into the income statement. Nortel has since determined that many of these releases in this quarter were not in accordance with U.S. GAAP, and has reversed those releases in the First and Second Restatements and restated the releases into proper quarters. When presenting the preliminary results for the quarter to the Audit Committee, the Controller inaccurately represented that the vast majority of these releases were "business as usual" and in compliance with U.S. GAAP, and that the remaining releases were one time, non-recurring events and in compliance with U.S. GAAP. Further, the CFO and the Controller failed to advise the Audit Committee and/or the Board of Directors that release of excess corporate provisions was required to achieve profitability and make up for the shortfall in operational results; that such releases were needed to cover the cost of the bonus compensation; that no event in the quarter triggered the releases (as required by U.S. GAAP); that the releases implicated Staff Accounting Bulletin 99 (relating to materiality) because they turned a loss for the quarter into a profit; and that they retained a significant amount of excess provisions on the balance sheet to be used, when needed, in a subsequent quarter. In separate executive sessions held by the Audit Committee with the CFO and the Controller, neither the CFO nor the Controller raised quality of earnings issues nor questioned the payment of the RTP bonus. Based on management's representations, the Audit Committee approved the quarterly results, and the Board approved the award of the RTP bonus.

Second quarter, 2003. Seeking to continue to show profitability in the second quarter and meet the first RSU milestone and the second tranche of the RTP bonus, senior corporate management developed internal EBT targets to achieve pro forma profitability. As was the case in the first quarter, it became clear during the quarter that operational results would be a loss. At the request of finance management in each business unit, finance employees again identified "hard" provisions from the balance sheet, and, together, they determined which provisions to release to close the gap and achieve the internal EBT targets. Nortel has since determined that many of these releases were not in accordance with U.S. GAAP, and has reversed those releases in the First and Second Restatements and restated the releases into proper quarters. In both the first and second quarters of 2003, the dollar value of many individual releases was relatively small, but the aggregate value of the releases made the difference between a pro forma loss and profit in each quarter.

The CEO, the CFO and the Controller failed to advise the Audit Committee or the Board of Directors that operations of the business units were running at a loss during the second quarter and that the validity of many of the numerous provision releases, totaling more than $370 million, could be questionable. Based on management's representations, the Audit Committee approved the quarterly results, and the Board approved payment of the second tranche of the RTP bonus and awarded restricted stock under the RSU plan.

Third and fourth quarters, 2003. In light of concerns raised by the inappropriate accounting judgments outlined above, the Audit Committee expanded its investigation to determine whether excess provisions were released to meet internal EBT targets in each of these two quarters. No evidence emerged to suggest an intent to release provisions strategically in those quarters to meet EBT targets. Given the significant volume of provision releases in these two quarters, the Audit Committee directed management to review provision releases, down to a low threshold, using the same methods used to evaluate the releases made in the first half of the year. This review has resulted in additional adjustments for these quarters, which are reflected in the Second Restatement.

Governing Principles for Remedial Measures

The Audit Committee asked WCPHD to recommend governing principles, based on its independent inquiry, to prevent recurrence of the inappropriate accounting conduct, to rebuild a finance environment based on transparency and integrity, and to ensure sound financial reporting and comprehensive disclosure. The recommendations developed by WCPHD and provided to the Audit Committee were directed at the following:

- Establishing standards of conduct to be enforced through appropriate discipline
- Infusing strong technical skills and experience into the finance organization
- Requiring comprehensive, ongoing training on increasingly complex accounting standards
- Strengthening and improving internal controls and processes
- Establishing a compliance program throughout the company which is appropriately staffed and funded
- Requiring management to provide clear and concise information, in a timely manner, to the board to facilitate its decision making
- Implementing an information technology platform that improves the reliability of financial reporting and reduces the opportunities for manipulation of results.

> These recommendations were grouped into three categories—people, processes and technology ... [which] [a]fter thorough consideration, the Audit Committee has recommended and the Board of Directors has approved, adoption of each.
>
> In summary form, these recommendations included the following:
>
> People:
>
> - Creation of an effective "tone at the top" through effective policies, procedures, and an awareness and commitment to fiduciary duty, accountability, and accuracy, particularly in financial reporting.
> - Termination for cause of the CEO, CFO, controller, and seven additional senior officers.
> - Return of RTP and RSU bonus payments.
> - Clarification through training and other means (appropriate experience) that failure to adhere to U.S. GAAP will not be tolerated.
> - External recruiting of individuals with strong accounting and reporting skills and expertise and proven records of integrity and ethical behavior, particularly in key finance positions.
> - Enhancement and bolstering of often bypassed internal "technical accounting group."
> - Review and improve the training function. Clarify through training the accounting issues that lead to restatement, confirm knowledge and understanding of the company code, and secure sign-offs testifying to reading and adherence. Introduce ongoing training requirements.
>
> Processes:
>
> - Remedial improvements to the control structure to permit sound corporate oversight—internal controls noted included financial policies, organizational structure, systems, processes, employees, leadership, and culture focused to foster accurate financial reporting and disclosure in a timely manner.
> - Reexamination of the matrix structure and the specification of key responsibility for liability provisions that has been unclear.
> - Confirmation of the role of the controller and the control structure—who should have the sole authority to release liability provisions—and the development of transparency of reporting standards.
> - Reexamination and rewriting of Nortel's accounting policies.
> - Strengthen internal audit function and standards to provide a check on the integrity of financial reporting.
> - Recruitment of a chief ethics and compliance officer; active, overt commitment to the new Nortel Code of Conduct; and the direction of management to reinforce and enhance the compliance program carrying this message to all employees.
> - The Board and Audit Committee should regularly review the activities of the

compliance officer and the related policies and performance involved.

- The board is to receive all necessary information for adequate review of policies and activities in a timely manner. Reports should be received from more than just the CFO, and meetings should be included with the chief operations and finance employees for each business unit.

Technology:

- The announced installation of a SAP information technology platform should be implemented such that the necessary and needed control elements are incorporated.

Board of Directors and Audit Committee

Guylaine Saucier, who sat on the board and its Audit Committee, has since stated that "directors were shocked to learn after an internal review in 2004"[7] of the alleged manipulations that triggered the RTP bonus. She went on to say,

> "What was the board's reaction? First of all, it's emotional. You feel betrayed," Ms. Saucier said. "You trusted your management…"
>
> Since then, Ms. Saucier said she has reflected on how a board can scrutinize a CEO to decide whether he or she has the right standards for the job, but said it is difficult because it comes down to many small elements that occur outside the boardroom.
>
> "If the board had known that Frank Dunn was building a $12-million house for himself while we were letting go 60,000 people, would that be an element in our overall judgment? These are anecdotes. It's very difficult to say somebody is ethical or unethical."
>
> Ms. Saucier also rejected the criticism that the company's compensation plan created too much temptation for manipulation. She said most companies have bonuses based on performance.
>
> "It depends on the people. If you have people with good ethical values, you won't have any problems having a performance bonus."
>
> She said she has begun to question whether chief financial officers should be paid bonuses based on corporate performance, given that they are responsible for preparing financial statements.[8]

The directors did not bail out on Nortel. They hired a former U.S. admiral and member of the Joint Chiefs of Staff, Bill Owens, to be the new CEO and preside over the recovery of their company. This process was not without challenges since the directors were sued by aggrieved shareholders and by the company's insurer, Chubb Insurance Co. Chubb wanted to rescind $40 million insurance coverage for the legal costs of defending Nortel and twenty of its officials because Nortel's CEO (Frank Dunn), CFO (Douglas Beatty), and controller (Michael Gollogly) "made material misrepresentations with stock market regulators with the intent to deceive Chubb."[9]

One of the new hires, as chief ethics and compliance officer, was Susan E. Shepard, a former commissioner for the New York State Ethics Commission and, earlier, assistant U.S. district attorney for the Eastern District of New York. Interestingly, the company announced on January 13, 2005, that "Ms. Shepard will receive a base salary of U.S.$375,000 (per annum) and will be eligible for a target annual bonus of 60% of base

---

[7] Janet McFarland, "Ex-Nortel Director Didn't See It Coming," *The Globe and Mail*, November 15, 2005.

[8] Ibid.

[9] Rick Westhead and Tyler Hamilton, "Insurer Seeks to Rescind Nortel Coverage," *Toronto Star*, February 24, 2005, D1.

salary under the annual bonus plan of NNL (known as the SUCCESS Incentive Plan), based on the generally applicable performance criteria under such plan."[10]

"Susan Shepard is not the first Nortel ethics guru. That distinction belongs to Megan Barry, who served as Nortel's senior ethics advisor between 1994 and 1999."[11] As Megan noted, Nortel was once a world leader in ethics. "By the time she left, however, Nortel wasn't really a trailblazer in ethics anymore." When John Roth took over as CEO in 1997, her department grew increasingly invisible within the organization. "When the senior leadership changed, you definitely saw a de-emphasis of ethics," she says. "Roth's legacy is what Nortel has to deal with today."[12]

On February 8, 2006, Nortel announced that it had settled two shareholder lawsuits in relation to this accounting scandal for a maximum total of U.S.$2.47 billion.[13]

Questions

1. Why would Nortel Networks, a Canadian company, hire a U.S. law firm to undertake an independent review of factors that led to restatement of accounting reports?
2. Why did the independent review focus on the "establishment and release of contractual liability and other related provisions" (also called accruals, reserves, or accrued liabilities)?[14]
3. How did the failure to follow U.S. GAAP permit the manipulation of Earnings Before Taxes (EBT) and lead to fraudulent behavior?
4. Describe the Nortel Return to Profitability (RTP) and Restricted Stock Units (RSU) bonus plans. What did the board of directors expect these plans to achieve?
5. Were the misstatements of EBT and bonuses paid material in an accounting sense?
6. Why did Nortel's auditor not discover the misstatements?
7. Why did the Audit Committee (or board as a whole_ not anticipate the manipulation?
8. What questions should the Audit Committee or board have asked?
9. What internal control flaws permitted the fraudulent manipulation to occur without detection?
10. Would the new requirements spawned by SOX and its SEC regulations have prevented the manipulation per se? Why or why not?
11. How have the expectations of the Audit Committee changed since SOX with regard to corporate culture, why is this so, and how can the Audit Committee ensure that these are met?
12. Should the Audit Committee or the whole board be held legally liable for the weaknesses noted in the review? Why and why not?
13. In February 2005, Nortel hired a new chief ethics and compliance officer using an incentive compensation scheme based on profits. Is this a sound arrangement?
14. Nortel has issued a new code of conduct with striking similarity to their previous version. Why might this new code be more effective than the last?
15. In retrospect, what were the major failings of the Nortel Audit Committee? Were they the same as those for the board as a whole?

---

[10] "Change in Directors or Principal Officers," *SEC Form 8-K*, January 13, 2005.

[11] Steve Maich, "Selling Ethics at Nortel," January 24, 2005, http://www.macleans.ca.

[12] Ibid.

[13] "Nortel Settles Lawsuits for $2.5 Billion US," *CBC News*, February 8, 2006.

[14] Wilmer Cutler Pickering Hale and Dorr LLP, *Summary of Findings and of Recommended Remedial Measures of the Independent Review* (Washington, DC, 2005), 2. See copy released January 11, 2005, at http://www.nortelnetworks.com/corporate/news/newsreleases/collateral/independent_review_summary.pdf.

NORTEL CASE POSTSCRIPT—2013

Criminal Charges for Fraud Dismissed

On January 14, 2013, Justice Frank Marrocco of the Ontario Superior Court dismissed charges of two counts of fraud against Frank Dunn (CEO), Douglas Beatty (CFO), and Michael Gollogly (controller) for deliberately misrepresenting Nortel's financial results to the investing public and to their employer during the period between January 1, 2000, and April 28, 2004. In his judgment, the judge indicated that the prosecution led by Crown Attorney Robert Hubbard had not made their case beyond a reasonable doubt that the financial reports were false in the quarter(s) in question and that the degree of falsehood was so material as to affect investors decisions or the employer's decision to pay a performance bonus. Throughout the case, the judge had asked for comment on materiality as it applied to the case, but the prosecution provided none, and in their handling of their expert witness, they never asked for his opinion on materiality. Moreover, their expert did not support the Crown's position on various points. In the end, the judge came to his own conclusions on materiality and the application of GAAP and took the view that the company would have had to pay a bonus regardless of the alleged management of earnings. Because of discussions held within management, he concluded that many executives were aware of the decisions lying behind the release of so-called cookie jar reserves and that he could not establish beyond any doubt that Dunn, Beatty, and Gollogly had demonstrated an intention to deceive (deliberately misrepresented), which is required for a finding of fraud. Without someone or some compelling evidence pointing directly to deliberate deception, the Crown had "no smoking gun," and the case was lost.[1]

[1] Theresa Tedesko, "Without a Smoking Gun, Nortel Fraud Cases Was Legal Suicide," *Financial Post*, January 14, 2013, accessed September 1, 2013, at http://business.financialpost.com/2013/01/14/without-a-smoking-gun-nortel-fraud-case-was-legal-suicide/?__lsa=fb98-8bcb.

ETHICS CASE

Adelphia—Really the Rigas Family Piggy Bank

On June 20, 2005, "John Rigas, the 80-year old founder of Adelphia Communications Corp., was … sentenced to 15 years in prison and his son Timothy, the ex-finance chief, got 20 years for looting the company and lying about its finances."[1] These were the largest sentences handed out to CEOs and CFOs after SOX and before the sentencing of Bernard J. Ebbers, CEO of WorldCom, and Dennis Kozlowski, CEO of Tyco, and before the trial of Richard Scrushy, CEO of HealthSouth.

John and Timothy Rigas had faced a maximum sentence of up to 215 years each, but John's age, bladder cancer, and heart condition were taken into account. His lawyer argued as well that John had been very generous with Coudersport, his hometown, but Judge Sand responded, stating that what Rigas had done, "he had done with assets and by means that were not appropriately his.… To be a great philanthropist with other people's money is really not very persuasive."[2]

Adelphia was founded by John Rigas in 1952 in Coudersport, Pennsylvania, and incorporated in 1972. The company started as a cinema business that transformed into a cable television provider. By 1988, Adelphia had more than 2 million customers in the cable television service. The company also expanded rapidly into a new line of telecommunications products and services (e.g., high-definition television,

[1] David Glovin and David Voreacos. "Rigas Duo Gets 35 Years," *Financial Post*, June 21, 2005, FP8.

[2] Ibid.

video on demand, high-speed Internet, and home security). By 1989, Adelphia more than doubled its reach through acquisitions, extending into forty-one states and serving more than 5 million customers. At its peak, Adelphia employed 14,000 people in the United States.

Members of the Rigas family held four seats on the firm's seven-member board. John Rigas (chairman and CEO), his son Timothy Rigas (CFO), and Michael Rigas (vice president of operations) had control of the firm and access to its resources beyond the oversight mechanisms of its Board of Directors. In essence, they used Adelphia as their own family piggy bank, withdrawing funds when they needed for their own purposes, such as golf club construction, property purchases, and stock dealings, as noted in following sections.

Unfortunately, these cash withdrawals and other improper use of company resources, as well as rapid expansion, poor management, and improper use of company's resources to pay management's personal expenses, led Adelphia into a tight financial position. Faced with the needs for meeting earnings and cash targets and to keep the company's debt levels within market averages, the Rigas family members began to commit fraud, and those frauds finally came to light.

On March 27, 2002, the company announced $2.3 billion in off-balance-sheet debt previously undisclosed in the company's financial statements. Adelphia guaranteed as coborrower $2.3 billion loans given to the Rigas family and entities controlled by them. On April 1, the company delayed filing Form 10-K, required under the SEC rules for public companies in the U.S. markets. The delay was followed by a formal inquiry by the SEC. On April 15, the company announced that continuing review of its financial statements would not result in material changes to historical filings.

However, on May 2, Adelphia changed its position, announcing a possible restatement. Two weeks later, John Rigas and his son Timothy resigned, and the company's auditors, Deloitte & Touche, suspended the 2001 financial statements audit. The trade of the company's shares in NASDAQ was suspended after the stock price went from $20.39 on March 26 to $0.79 on June 3.

On May 23, other members of the Rigas family resigned their positions in management and the Board of Directors. The Rigas family also agreed to transfer $1 billion in assets back to the company. Nevertheless, Adelphia filed for bankruptcy in June 2002 and operated subsequently under bankruptcy protection.

The SEC charged Adelphia and the Rigas family with massive financial fraud on July 24, 2002. Its complaint alleged (1) understatement of debt, (2) overstatement of financial performance, and (3) extensive self-dealing, which are summarized from the SEC press release[3] and complaint[4] documents as follows:

1. Between 1999 and the end of 2001, the Rigas family (John, Timothy, Michael, and James), with other executives, caused Adelphia to fraudulently exclude over $2 billion in its bank debt by systematically recording liabilities on the books of unconsolidated affiliates. Some of those operations where backed by the company's management with fictitious documents. False documents showed that Adelphia repaid debts while those debts were just transferred to related companies.

[3] U.S. Securities and Exchange Commission, "SEC Charges Adelphia and Rigas Family with Massive Financial Fraud," *Press Release 2002-110*, July 24, 2002.

[4] United States District Court, Southern District of New York, *Complaint: SEC against Adelphia Communications Corporation, John Rigas, Timothy J. Rigas, Michael J. Rigas, James P. Rigas, James R. Brown and Michael C. Mulcahey*, July 24, 2002.

2. From 1999, the company relied heavily on commercial credit issuance of notes and access to equity markets. As of June 1, 2002 Adelphia and its consolidated Subsidiaries owed $6.8 billion in credit facilities, $6.9 billion in senior or convertible notes, and $1.6 billion in convertible preferred stock. Certain Adelphia subsidiaries also issued separately notes of which $2.6 billion was outstanding on June 1, 2002. The company's true liabilities increased from $4.4 billion in the second quarter of 1999 to $20.4 billion in the third quarter of 2001.
3. Funds obtained from borrowing and from a series of public offerings since 1999 were deposited and disbursed from a cash management subsidiary Adelphia CMS. This third company was used to set up schemes to transfer and hide debt in related companies (i.e., special purpose entities).
4. In the same period, the Rigas family with other executives caused Adelphia to regularly misstate press releases, including earnings reports. The company reported inflated figures for the number of cable subscribers, the extent of its cable plant, and earnings before interest, taxes, depreciation, and amortization (EBITDA).
5. Specifically, the company overstated its number of customers by 142,000 by including in basic cable subscribers 43,000 customers from unconsolidated subsidiaries, 39,000 Internet service customers, and 60,000 home security customers. Adelphia also included in these statistics subscribers from the months after the quarter end and false counts of new subscribers for affiliated companies.
6. Adelphia added to reported EBITDA management fees paid by the Rigas family entities that owned cable operations. But since Adelphia did not provide any services to earn those payments, the only purpose for recording them on Adelphia's books was to inflate the company's earnings.
7. Adelphia entered into agreements with suppliers of digital converter boxes, asking the suppliers for a $26 per box advance to market a new digital service. The money would be repaid later when the boxes were sold to customers. Adelphia recorded those payments (totaling $91 million) as income. The suppliers lost the advanced payments when the company filed for bankruptcy.
8. Adelphia also shifted expenses improperly to unconsolidated related entities to decrease the company's operating expenses.
9. From at least 1998, Adelphia used fraudulent misrepresentations and omissions of material facts to conceal self-dealing by the Rigas family.
10. The Rigas Family used company funds to finance open stock purchases, purchase timber rights to land in Pennsylvania, construct a golf club for $12.8 million on a family property, pay off personal margin loans and other debts, and purchase luxury condominiums in Colorado, Mexico, and New York City.
11. The fraud continued even after Adelphia acknowledged, on March 27, that the $2.3 billion excluded liabilities from its balance sheet. In the following months, the Rigas family diverted $174 million to pay personal margin loans.

Not only were the Rigas among the first to face post-SOX justice for their financial frauds, but John, who was seventy-seven years old when arrested, and his sons were among the first to endure the famous "perp walk"—to be handcuffed and marched to a waiting car in front of reporters who were only too glad to spread the embarrassing photos over the media immediately. The perp walk came to be dreaded by executives who faced charges for perpetrating financial crimes.

The SEC charges were not the only ones leveled against the Rigas family. In August 2004, Adelphia, their own company, sued them in a civil action for the return of $3.2 billion that the family misappropriated. In the earlier SEC-sponsored criminal trial, the family had argued that "any debt or funds used from the company were 'borrowed' not stolen, 'and they intended to full repay the amounts.'"[5] Adelphia had not received the funds, nor had the Rigases assumed the debt involved, so Adelphia sued the Rigas to force them to keep their word.

This action was not surprising since Adelphia had shored up its governance processes after the Rigases left. For example, new executives were appointed to remove members of the Rigas family and related parties, and six of the seven members of the new Board of Directors were independent of Adelphia and Rigas family interests. The company developed a new code of ethics and changed its mission to the following:

> We will leverage our historical strengths of customer focus, community involvement, and employee dedication; address issues that limit profitability and growth; and act with a sense of urgency, accountability and teamwork to emerge from bankruptcy and to succeed as a broadband industry leader. We will develop a reputation as a company with outstanding corporate governance.

In November 2002, Adelphia sued its former auditor, Deloitte & Touche (D&T), accusing D&T of professional negligence, breach of contract, fraud, and other wrongful conduct "for failing to spot the problems that brought the company down … For its part, Deloitte said it was the victim of deception just as much as Adelphia's shareholders and that it would be able to answer any accusations more fully once it had examined the lawsuit. It also said that it would seek damages from whichever members of Adelphia's management proved to be complicit in any wrongdoing. At the moment, [Adelphia's] bankruptcy protects it from such action, however."[6]

Adelphia's bondholders also launched a U.S.$5 billion lawsuit in July 2003 against 450 banks and other financial institutions that had "fuelled the massive fraud by lending billions of dollars to the company's founders."[7] The lawsuit stated, "This action seeks to redress defendant's knowing participation, substantial assistance and complicity in one of the most serious cases of systematic corporate looting and breach of fiduciary duty in American history…. Aware of the obvious red flags, many of the co-borrowing lenders merely rubber-stamped the co-borrowing facilities so that their affiliated investment banks could earn hundreds of millions of dollars in fees."[8] While the Rigas family was busy using Adelphia as their own piggy bank, it appears they were not alone.

Questions

1. What breaches of fiduciary duty does the Adelphia case raise?
2. Why do you think the Rigas family thought they could get away with using Adelphia as their own piggy bank?

---

[5] Marc Hopkins, "Rigas Family Owes Adelphia US$3.2 B," *Financial Post*, August 24, 2004, FP8.

[6] "Cable Flop Sues Former Auditor," *BBC News*, November 7, 2002, http://news.bbc.co.uk/l/hi/business/2415145.stm.

[7] Keith Kalawsky, "US$5B Lawsuit Names Big Five," *Financial Post*, July 8, 2003, FP3.

[8] Ibid.

3. What allowed the Rigas family to get away with their fraudulent behavior for so long?
4. What concerns should have been raised in the following areas of risk assessment in Adelphia's control environment: integrity and ethics, commitment, Audit Committee participation, management philosophy, structure, and authority?
5. What concerns should have been raised in the following areas of risk assessment in Adelphia's strategy: changes in operating environment, new people and systems, growth, technology, new business, restructurings, and foreign operations?
6. What is your opinion on the importance of independence in corporate governance? What are the most recent rules on corporate governance for public firms?
7. Discuss which changes could be done to the Adelphia's control system and corporate governance structure to mitigate the risk of accounting fraud in future years.
8. What is the auditor's responsibility in case of fraud?
9. What is the proper audit procedure to ensure the following?
   a. Completeness of liabilities in the financial statements
   b. That all the related parties have been included or disclosed in the consolidated financial statements
10. Do you think analytical procedures would aid the detection of fraud? What is the responsibility of the auditor applying analytical procedures?
11. What should the 450 lending institutions have done to protect themselves from subsequent lawsuit?

Sources: Adelphia website, http://www.adelphia.com.

BBC News, January 2002–December 2002, "Adelphia," BBC News Archive, http://www.bbcnews.com.

Ronald Grover, "Adelphia's Fall Will Bruise a Crowd." *Businessweek*, July 8, 2002, http://www.businessweek.commagazine/content/02_27/b3790025.htm.

New York Times, January 2002–December 2002, "Adelphia," New York Times News Archive, http://www.nytimes.com.

U.S. Securities and Exchange Commission, *SEC Press Release 2002–110*, http://www.sec.gov/news/press.

U.S. Securities and Exchange Commission, *SEC Complaint 17627*, http://www.sec.gov/litigation/complaints.

ETHICS CASE

Tyco—Looting Executive Style

Dennis Kozlowski was a dominant, larger-than-life CEO of Tyco International, Ltd, a multi-billion-dollar company whose shares are still traded on the New York Stock Exchange (Symbol: TYC). His stature was huge, and his appetite for excess knew no bounds. Noted author Tom Wolfe, who wrote *Bonfire of the Vanities*, which profiled such men, says that "if you feel you are a master of the universe, then a lot of rules just don't apply,"[1] and this quote seems to apply well to Kozlowski.

Kozlowski was rolling along—often using company money—having lavish parties, planes, and cars and enjoying multiple homes with fittings such as a $6,000 shower curtain and a $15,000 umbrella stand, a yacht, and an impressive art collection. It was his interest in art that triggered the first investigation in January 2002 by New York State officials who asked about the sales tax on several multi-million-dollar paintings.[2] Kozlowski had evaded the payment of sales tax on them and was subsequently first charged in a New York court.

For Dennis, this was most unfortunate because on conviction, he would serve time in the New York prison system instead of a federal prison in which white-collar criminals often are assigned to facilities known as "Club Feds" or, for women such as Martha Stewart, "Camp Cupcake." The

[1] Brian Ross, "Greed on Wall Street: The Rise and Fall of Dennis Kozlowski," November 11, 2005, accessed March 21, 2006, at http://abcnews.go.com/2020/story? id51305010.

[2] Ibid.

New York prison system is very harsh. According to former New York prosecutor David Gourevitch, "The fed system is unpleasant, but at least you're physically safe there.… In the state system, nobody would say you are physically safe."[3] For Kozlowski and his associate Mark Swartz, his Tyco CFO who faced up to thirty years in prison, this prospect was surely daunting.

On the other hand, Kozlowski had certainly enjoyed high living, so many observers would argue he got what he deserved. Take the $2 million 40th birthday party for his new wife on the Mediterranean island of Sardinia, more than half of which was paid for by Tyco. Jurors were shown an edited twenty-one-minute version of a four-hour videotape covering the whole week with seventy-five guests. The short version did not show inflammatory scenes, such as "an anatomically correct ice sculpture of Michelangelo's David spurting vodka,"[4] scantily clad and unclad dancers, and so on. Music was provided by Jimmy Buffet and his group at a cost of $250,000 and a rock band at a cost of $20,000.[5] No wonder Kozlowski was charged with looting the company.

The SEC also took an interest, and charges for civil fraud regarding looting of the company and other misdeeds were laid on September 12, 2002. By the time of the trial in October 2003, Tyco was estimated to have about 270,000 employees and $36 billion in annual revenue derived from many sources, including electronic and medical supplies and the ADT home security business.[6] A full list of the charges against Kozlowski and CFO Mark Swartz as well against chief legal officer Mark Belnick is outlined in the SEC complaint, which is available at http://www.sec.gov/litigation/complaints/complr17722.htm.

An abbreviated version of the improper conduct of management was published by Tyco in their SEC 8-K information filing with the SEC on September 17, 2002. The Tyco press release[7] states,

> The Company said that this pattern of improper and illegal activity occurred for at least five years prior to June 3, 2002, when former CEO L. Dennis Kozlowski resigned, and that this activity was concealed from the Board and its relevant committees. The nature of such conduct, to the extent it is now known by Tyco, is described in the filing. The areas covered in this filing include:
>
> - **Relocation programs,** under which certain executive officers, including Mr. Kozlowski, former CFO Mark Swartz and former Chief Corporate Counsel Mark Belnick used the Company's relocation program to take non-qualifying interest-free loans and unauthorized benefits that were not generally available to all salaried employees affected by relocations. Under the program, Mr. Kozlowski improperly borrowed approximately $61,690,628 in non-qualifying relocation loans to purchase real estate and other properties, Mr. Swartz borrowed approximately $33,097,925 and Mr. Belnick borrowed approximately $14,635,597.
> - **The "TyCom Bonus" misappropriation,** in which Mr. Kozlowski caused Tyco to pay a special, unapproved bonus to 51 employees who had relocation loans with the Company. The bonus was

[3] Krysten Crawford, "For Kozlowski, an Especially Grim Future," June 21, 2005, accessed June 6, 2005, at http://money.cnn.com/2005/06/21/news/newsmakers/prisons_state/index.htm.

[4] Samuel Maull, Associated Press, "Tyco Jurors View Birthday Video," October 29, 2003, B7.

[5] Ibid.

[6] Ibid.

[7] Tyco press release, "Tyco Files Form 8-K Report on Improper Conduct of Former Management," accessed March 22, 2006, at http://www.tyco.com/livesite/Page/Tyco/Who+We+Are/Press+Center/Press+Releases+Details/??&DCRID51185862359.

calculated to forgive the relocation loans of 51 executives and employees, totaling $56,415,037, and to pay compensation sufficient to discharge all of the tax liability due as a result of the forgiveness of those loans. This action was purportedly related to the successful completion of the TyCom Initial Public Offering. The total gross wages paid by the Company in this mortgage forgiveness program were $95,962,000, of which amount Mr. Kozlowski received $32,976,000 and Mr. Swartz received $16,611,000. These benefits were not approved by, or disclosed to, the Compensation Committee or the Board of Directors. However, the employees who received these bonuses were led by Mr. Kozlowski to believe that they were part of a Board-approved program.

- **The "ADT Automotive Bonus" misappropriations,** in which Mr. Kozlowski authorized Tyco to pay cash, award restricted shares of Tyco common stock, and purportedly forgive additional loans and make related tax payments to approximately 17 Tyco officers and employees—even though the relocation loans of each of these 17 persons had already been paid in full. Mr. Kozlowski and Mr. Swartz received cash bonuses, restricted shares and "relocation" benefits valued approximately $25,566,610 and $12,844,632 respectively. These benefits were not approved by or disclosed to the Compensation Committee or the Board of Directors. As with the TyCom unauthorized bonus, other senior executives were misled by Mr. Kozlowski to believe that the ADT Automotive award of restricted shares was a Board-approved program.
- **The Key Employee Loan (KEL) Program,** in which certain executive officers borrowed money for purposes other than the payment of taxes due upon the vesting of restricted shares, or borrowed in excess of the maximum amount they were permitted under the program. Mr. Kozlowski was, by a large margin, the greatest abuser of this program. By the end of 2001, Mr. Kozlowski had taken over 200 KEL loans—some for millions of dollars and some as small as $100—and his total borrowings over that time exceeded $250 million. Approximately 90% of Mr. Kozlowski's KEL loans were non-program loans, which he used to fund his personal lifestyle, including speculating in real estate, acquisition of antiques and furnishings for his properties (including properties purchased with unauthorized "relocation loans") and the purchase and maintenance of his yacht. Mr. Swartz also borrowed millions in non-program loans. Like Mr. Kozlowski, Mr. Swartz used those unauthorized loans to purchase, develop and speculate in real estate; to fund investments in various business ventures and partnerships; and for miscellaneous personal uses having nothing to do with the ownership of Tyco stock. Tyco is currently evaluating the KEL program in light of recent enactment of a prohibition upon loans by public companies to directors and executive officers.
- **Attempted Unauthorized Credits to Key Employee Loan Accounts,** in which Mr. Kozlowski and Mr. Swartz attempted to erase an outstanding $25 million KEL indebtedness to Mr. Kozlowski and $12.5 million in KEL indebtedness to Mr. Swartz without the knowledge or approval of the

Compensation Committee. Mr. Kozlowski, through his attorneys, has acknowledged to Tyco that he sought no approvals for these credits and that, if they were entered as a credit to his KEL account, it was done so improperly, and that he is therefore obligated to repay these amounts to Tyco. Mr. Swartz has also agreed to repay his forgiven indebtedness with interest and has repaid most of the amounts. Tyco has reversed these entries and a related unauthorized entry, thereby increasing the outstanding balances for the key employee loan accounts of each individual involved.

- **Executive compensation,** including authorized and unauthorized compensation to Mr. Belnick, which totaled $34,331,679 for the years 1999–2001. Belnick's compensation resulted from a secret agreement that tied Mr. Belnick's compensation to Mr. Kozlowski's compensation, thereby giving Mr. Belnick an undisclosed incentive to aid and facilitate Mr. Kozlowski's improper diversion of Company funds to Mr. Kozlowski's personal benefit. The undisclosed terms of Messrs. Kozlowski's and Belnick's agreement were incorporated in a letter dated August 19, 1998 and signed by Mr. Kozlowski. Mr. Kozlowski and Mr. Belnick agreed that the letter would not be disclosed to the Tyco Board, the Board's Compensation Committee or the Tyco Human Resources department. Mr. Belnick did, however, keep a copy of the undisclosed agreement in his personal office.
- **Perquisites** in excess of $50,000 per year for Mr. Kozlowski and Mr. Swartz. These perquisites were required to be reported in a proxy to the extent they exceeded $50,000. However, these amounts were not reported in the proxy because Mr. Kozlowski and Mr. Swartz represented that they would reimburse the Company for amounts in excess of $50,000. However, in most cases Messrs. Kozlowski and Swartz failed to reimburse the Company for all perquisites in excess of $50,000. Mr. Kozlowski also caused Tyco to make available to him various properties that the Company owned for his purported business use. Tyco has now discovered that Mr. Kozlowski periodically made personal use of properties in North Hampton, NH, Boca Raton, FL, New York City and New Castle, NH.
- **Self-Dealing Transactions and Other Misuses of Corporate Trust,** including Tyco properties purchased by or from Mr. Kozlowski without disclosure to or authorization by the Compensation Committee. For example, Mr. Kozlowski and others caused a Tyco subsidiary to purchase property in Rye, New Hampshire from Mr. Kozlowski on July 6, 2000 for $4,500,000. After an appraisal in March 2002 valued the property at $1,500,000, Tyco wrote down the carrying value of the property to the appraised value and charged Mr. Kozlowski's $3,049,576 overpayment to expense. Mr. Kozlowski also used millions of dollars of Company funds to pay for his other personal interests and activities, including a $700,000 investment in the film "Endurance"; more than $1 million for an extravagant birthday party celebration for his wife in Sardinia; over $1 million in undocumented business expenses, including a private venture; jewelry, clothing, flowers, club membership dues and wine; and an

> undocumented $110,000 charge for the purported corporate use of Mr. Kozlowski's personal yacht, "Endeavour." Mr. Kozlowski also tampered with evidence under subpoena, purchased a New York City apartment at its depreciated rather than its market value, and took personal credit for at least $43 million in donations from Tyco to charitable organizations.

Not surprisingly, Tyco announced that it had launched a civil lawsuit against Kozlowski for breach of fiduciary duties and fraud and other wrongful conduct and other lawsuits against executives considered complicit in these schemes. This brings to three the major suits faced by Kozlowski launched by New York, the SEC, and Tyco but does not include class action suits by aggrieved investors. Tyco also began to replace its board members.

On June 17, 2005, fifty-eight-year old Kozlowski and forty-four-year old Swartz were each convicted of twenty-two of twenty-three counts, including grand larceny, conspiracy, and securities fraud, and eight of nine counts of falsifying business records.[8] On September 21, 2005, Kozlowski and Swartz were sentenced to up to twenty-five years in prison. Many observers thought that was about right, but others, including business leaders, thought it to be too much. In comparison, it was pointed out that some violent crimes, such as rape and manslaughter, carried a sentence of twenty years in jail.[9]

In a related announcement, the SEC and the lead auditor of Tyco, Richard Scalzo, a partner with PricewaterhouseCoopers (PwC), agreed that Scalzo was permanently barred from preparing financial statements of publicly traded companies. The Tyco account was reportedly worth $100 million per year to PwC, and they retained the audit. The SEC found that Scalzo "was 'reckless' and stood idle as the conglomerates leading figures manipulated accounting entries to conceal their lavish spending and pay."[10]

Questions

1. The pattern of illegal and improper conduct described above took place for at least five years prior to June 3, 2002. What red flags or governance mechanisms should have alerted the following people to this pattern?
   a. Tyco management accountants
   b. Tyco internal auditors
   c. Tyco external auditors
   d. Tyco board of directors
2. Identify and discuss the most important weaknesses in Tyco's internal controls and its governance systems.
3. Would a post-SOX whistleblowing program to the Audit Committee of the board have eliminated the improper and illegal actions? Why or why not?
4. If you have been a professional accountant employed by Tyco during this time and you wanted to blow the whistle, who would you have gone to with your story?
5. Why were so many Tyco employees willing to go along quietly with the looting by senior executives?
6. How many years in jail do you think Kozlowski should have received for his white-collar crimes?

[8] Chad Bray and Dow Jones Newswires, "Tyco's Ousted Top Officers Face Fines and Jail Terms," June 18, 2005, D1, D9.

[9] Daniel Kadlec, "Does Kozlowski's Sentence Fit the Crime?," September 20, 2005, accessed March 22, 2006, at http://www.time.com/time/business/printout/0,8816,1106932,00.html.

[10] Tim McLaughlin and Reuters, "Tyco Auditor Barred for Life by Regulator," August 14, 2005, D3.

ETHICS CASE

HealthSouth—Can Five CFOs Be Wrong?

On March 19, 2003, the SEC filed accounting fraud charges in the Northern District of Alabama against HealthSouth Corporation and its CEO, Richard Scrushy. Scrushy was also charged with knowingly miscertifying the accuracy and completeness of the company's financial statements. Consequently, Scrushy became the first CEO to be charged under the governance-reforming SOX. Although five HealthSouth CFOs testified that Scrushy had knowingly directed the fraud, on June 28, 2005, the Alabama jury acquitted him of all thirty-six criminal charges, and later some civil charges were initially dismissed. In contrast, the five CFOs were initially sentenced to receive a total of 115 years in prison and $11.2 million in fines. One of the CFOs, Weston Smith, had become a whistleblower who had launched a *qui tam*[1] lawsuit under the *False Claims Act* against HealthSouth and first told prosecutors about the financial statement falsification process. He was sentenced to twenty-five years and a $2.2 million fine. How did all this happen?

According to the SEC complaint,[2] HealthSouth was founded in 1984 and grew to become the largest provider of outpatient surgery, diagnostic, and rehabilitative health care services in the United States. By 2003, it owned or operated over 1,800 different facilities with worldwide revenues and earnings of $4 billion and $76 million, respectively, in 2001. HealthSouth's stock was listed on the New York Stock Exchange (NYSE), trading under the symbol HRC. Scrushy, who founded HRC, served as its chairman and CEO from 1994 to 2002. He relinquished the CEO title on August 27, 2002, but reassumed it on January 6, 2003.

The SEC claim states that Scrushy instructed that HRC earnings be inflated as early as just after the company's stock was listed on the NYSE in 1986. Specifically, during the forty-two-month period between 1999 and the six months ended on June 30, 2002, HRC's income (loss) before income taxes and minority interests was inflated by at least $1.4 billion.

Each quarter, HRC's senior officers would meet with Scrushy and compare HRC's actual results with those expected by Wall Street analysts. If there was a shortfall, "Scrushy would tell HRC's management to 'fix it' by recording false entries on HRC's accounting records."[3] HRC's senior accounting personnel then convened a meeting—referred to as "family meetings"—to "fix" the earnings. How this was done and how the auditors were deceived is outlined in the SEC complaint as follows:

> At these meetings, HRC's senior accounting personnel discussed what false entries could be made and recorded to inflate reported earnings to match Wall Street analyst's expectations. These entries primarily consisted of reducing a contra revenue account, called "contractual adjustment," and/or decreasing expenses, (either of which increased earnings),

[1] "*Qui tam* is a statute under the False Claims Act (31 U.S.C. § 3729 et seq.), which allows for a private individual, or whistleblower with knowledge of past or present fraud on the federal government to bring suit on behalf of the government. Its name is an abbreviation of the phrase "qui tam pro domino rege quam pro seipse," meaning "he who sues for the king as well as for himself." This provision allows a private person, known as a "relator," to bring a lawsuit on behalf of the United States, where the private person has information that the named defendant has knowingly submitted or caused the submission of false or fraudulent claims to the United States. The relator need not have been personally harmed by the defendant's conduct." "Qui tam," http://en.wikipedia.org/wiki/Qui_tam.

[2] *Securities and Exchange Commission v. HealthSouth Corporation and Richard M. Scrushy*, Complaint for Injunctive and Other Relief, Civil Action No. CV-03-J-0615-S (March 19, 2003), http://www.sec.gov/litigation/complaints/comphealths.htm.

[3] Ibid.

and correspondingly increasing assets or decreasing liabilities.

The contractual adjustment account is a revenue allowance account that estimates the difference between the gross amount billed to the patient and the amount that various healthcare insurers will pay for a specific treatment. [This difference was, in reality, never to be received by HealthSouth.]

. . . HRC falsified its fixed asset accounts [at numerous of its facilities] to match the fictitious adjustments to the income statement. The fictitious fixed asset line item at each facility was listed as "AP Summary."

HRC's accounting personnel designed the false journal entries to the income statement and balance sheet accounts in a manner calculated to avoid detection by the outside auditors. For example, instead of increasing the revenue account directly, HRC inflated earnings by decreasing the "contractual adjustment" account. Because the amounts booked to this account are estimated, there is a limited paper trail and the individual entries to this account are more difficult to verify than other revenue entries.

Additionally, each inflation of earnings and corresponding increase in fixed assets were recorded through several intermediary journal entries in order to make the false inflation more difficult to trace.

Furthermore, HRC increased the "AP Summary" line item at various facilities by different amounts because it knew that across the board increases of equal dollar amounts would raise suspicion.

HRC also knew that its outside auditors only questioned additions to fixed assets at any particular facility if the additions exceeded a certain dollar threshold. Thus, when artificially increasing the "AP Summary" at a particular facility, HRC was careful not to exceed the threshold.

HRC also created false documents to support its fictitious accounting entries. For example, during the audit of HRC's 2000 financial statements, the auditors questioned an addition to fixed assets at one particular HRC facility. HRC accounting personnel, knowing that this addition was fictitious, altered an existing invoice (that reflected an actual purchase of an asset at another facility that approximated the dollar amount of the fictitious addition) to fraudulently indicate that the facility in question had actually purchased that asset. This altered invoice was then given to the auditors to support the recording of the fictitious asset in question. Also, when the auditors asked HRC for a fixed assets ledger for various facilities, HRC accounting personnel would re-generate the

HealthSouth's Five CFOs Qualifications and Penalties

PERIOD AS CFO	NAME	CPA/OR	YEARS IN PRISON	FINE ($U.S. MILLION)
Jan. 1984–Oct. 1997	Aaron Beam	CPA	0.25	1.00
Oct. 1997–Feb. 2000	Michael Martin		15	1.25
Feb. 2000–Aug. 2001	Bill Owens	CPA	30	5.50
Aug. 2001–Aug. 2002	Weston Smith	CPA	25	2.20
Aug. 2002–Jan. 2003	Malcolm "Tadd" McVay	MBA	15	1.25
				$11.20

Source: Principal source: http://www/al.com.specialreport/birminghamnews/healthsouth/.

> fixed asset ledger, replacing the "AP Summary" line item with the name of a specific fixed asset that did not exist at the facility, while leaving the dollar amount of the line item unchanged.
>
> While the scheme was ongoing, HRC's senior officers and accounting personnel periodically discussed with Scrushy the burgeoning false financial statements, trying to persuade him to abandon the scheme. Scrushy insisted that the scheme continue because he did not want HRC's stock price to suffer. Indeed, in the fall of 1997, when HRC's accounting personnel advised Scrushy to abandon the earnings manipulation scheme, Scrushy refused, stating in substance, "not until I sell my stock."[4]

These manipulations were testified to during the trial by the five men who served as CFO during the interval under review, all of whom pled guilty to charges such as conspiracy to commit securities and wire fraud and falsification of financial records. On "August 14, 2002, Scrushy and HRC's CFO certified under oath that HRC's 2001 Form 10-K contained no 'untrue statement of material fact'" even though "this report overstated HRC's earnings … by at least 4,700%."[5]

The SEC complaint did not detail all of the fraud at HealthSouth, estimated to total $3.8 billion to $4.6 billion, which was reportedly made up of the following:

Fraudulent entries	$2.5 billion
Acquisition accounting/goodwill	0.5 billion
Improper (non-GAAP) accounting	0.8 billion to 1.6 billion
Total	$3.8 billion to 4.6 billion[6]

The same special report[7] stated that HRC profit was overstated by $2.74 billion from 1996 to 2002 inclusive and that Scrushy received $265 million in remuneration, consisting of $21.9 million in salary, $34.5 million in bonuses, and $208.9 million from the sale of shares. In 2002, Scrushy's remuneration totaled $112.3 million, including $99.3 million from sale of shares.

The timing of Scrushy's 2002 stock sales is of interest. In May 2002, the U.S. Justice Department joined the *qui tam* whistleblower lawsuit of Bill Owens, which accused HealthSouth of fraudulently seeking payments for services provided by unlicensed employees, including interns and students. On the same day, Scrushy exercised 5.3 million stock options at $3.78 and sold them for $14.05 for a gain of over $54 million.

The major Scrushy-directed HealthSouth fraud is not the first or only one to take place in Scrushy's companies. Earlier frauds, bankruptcies, or questionable business dealings are part of the history of several companies owned at least in part by Scrushy and/or HealthSouth and controlled by Scrushy with interlocking Boards of Directors to HealthSouth. These companies include MedPartners, Caremark National, Integrated Health Services, Capstone Capital, and HealthSouth for Medicare frauds ($1 million paid in 2000; $8.2 million in 2001).[8] It is alleged, however, that Scrushy began to "fix" earnings in the early 1990s, and it is evident that he became involved in questionable business dealings during the same time frame. Significantly, the people involved with Scrushy in these and other questionable business dealings were often current and/or former HealthSouth employees or members of the HealthSouth Board of Directors.[9] Scrushy, however,

[4] *Securities and Exchange Commission v. HealthSouth Corporations and Richard M Scrushy*, paras. 19–30, inclusive.

[5] Ibid., para. 38

[6] Everything Alabama website, "HealthSouth's Fraud," http://www/al.com.specialreport/birminghamnews/healthsouth.

[7] Ibid.

[8] These misadventures are well chronicled on the HealthSouth Web pages of the University of Wollongong at http://www.uow.edu.au/arts/sts/bmartin/dissent/documents/health/map_usa.html and in Russell Hubbard, "Rocket-Like Ascent Tumbles Back with Crushed Investors," *Birmingham News*, April 13, 2003.

[9] Ibid.

appears to have been the common link among the corporations involved.

In spite of the SEC's evidence on HealthSouth manipulations, which was supported by the testimony of five CFOs and ten other employees (all of whom pled guilty to the fraud), the jury of seven black and five white jurors voted to acquit Scrushy. Why was this?

According to the *Report on Fraud*, the reasons were multifaceted,[10] as follows:

> Surrounded by reporters as he left the courtroom, an elated Scrushy said: "Thank God for this." It was not a throwaway line, for his acquittal was partly due to a defence strategy that focussed on Scrushy's religious devotion (in fuller flourish during the trial), an unusual racism tactic, smear campaigns against key witnesses, an overabundance of prosecution documents (six million) but no smoking gun, and a victory for southern charm over northern sophistication.
>
> More than any contributing factor to Scrushy's acquittal, however, was location.... "New York juries, like those in other metropolitan areas, often include people who have worked in the financial field and are more skeptical of CEOs who claim ignorance." "One of the questions in a very complex case like this is: 'How much did they understand?'"
>
> Another was: who did they believe?... Scrushy was a prominent and respected figure in Birmingham, where HealthSouth employed thousands of residents. Perceived as "local boy made good," as he was often described, he donated lavishly to community causes ...
>
> Faced with the enormous evidence against their client, ... how could his defence team convince a jury their client was not guilty?
>
> Step number one: combine race and religion. It was a strategy led by defence counsel Donald Watkins, a black civil rights lawyer turned energy tycoon and banker, ...
>
> As part of the defence strategy, Scrushy, who is white, "left his suburban evangelical church and joined a black congregation in a blue-collar neighborhood," reported the *Washington Post.* The Guiding Light congregation was the recipient of a $1-million donation from Scrushy. "He bought a half-hour of local TV for a morning prayer show featuring himself and his wife, and frequent guest spots by black ministers. He had a prayer group praying for him every day of the trial." Also during the trial, Scrushy's son-in-law bought a small TV station and began broadcasting daily reports bolstering the defendant's case, says *USA Today.* Many members of Guiding Light turned up at Scrushy's trial and sat directly behind him....
>
> At the same time ... his defence team successfully manoeuvred to have seven blacks on the jury and five whites, all from working class backgrounds.
>
> Faced with five former CFOs testifying to Scrushy's guilt, his defence team decided to impugn their credibility, ... all negotiated lenient sentences prior to testifying ... characterized one witness as looking clean as a "Winn-Dixie chitlin" ... portrayed prosecution star witness William Owens, ... as a rat "who squeals 'trust me, believe me.'" ... "A witness was ridiculed because he used antidepressants." ... "Another witness was accused of faking tears on the stand." Yet another was forced to admit that he often cheated on his wife and lied about it.... The defence

[10] "The Strange Acquittal of Richard Scrushy," *Report on Fraud*, Navigant Consulting, the Canadian Institute of Chartered Accountants, and the American Institute of Certified Public Accountants, vol. 8, no. 2 (September 2005): 4–7.

> team's goal ... was to treat the group of CFOs as one ... comprised [of] a group of liars and cheats ... a bold move, but it worked, according to jurors.

Several jurors speaking after the trial said they wanted to see fingerprints on any of the evidence documents or a smoking gun that would tie Scrushy directly to the fraud. Two poorly made audiotapes were not sufficient, and "defence lawyers argued that Scrushy never employed words such as 'fraud' or 'illegal' and no documents or e-mails produced during the trial implicated their client."[11] It took twenty-one days for the jury to reach a verdict. Originally, seven jurors wanted acquittal, but the number grew to ten. One of the jurors who wanted a guilty verdict was replaced due to recurring migraine headaches, and since the replacement juror wanted an acquittal, only one holdout remained. She was finally convinced to vote for acquittal.

The issue of credibility—who to believe—seemed to be paramount. The words of one juror and one author probably captured the essence of the trial best:

> There were five CFOs who testified against Scrushy and they all seemed to have some reason to lie.... Based on that conclusion, he said, he had to vote to acquit.[12]
>
> [Scrushy] never took the stand. He chose, instead, to preach at his new congregation during the trial, although his pastor said he didn't attend the service following his acquittal.[13]

Expert observers do not view this verdict as a problem for the future enforcement of SOX. They view it as "a defeat for these particular prosecutors in this particular case."[14]

Questions

1. What were the major flaws in HealthSouth's governance?
2. What should HealthSouth's auditors, Ernst & Young, have done if they had perceived these flaws?
3. How—in accounting terms—did the manipulation of HealthSouth's financial statements take place?
4. Why did all the people who knew about the manipulation keep quiet?
5. What is the auditor's responsibility in a case of fraud?
6. What are the proper audit procedures to ensure existence of assets in the

HealthSouth Case Postscript—2009

In June 2009, the verdict in Richard Scrushy's civil lawsuit launched by angered investors was announced by a federal judge in Alabama. Unlike his criminal trial, which is reported on in the case above, Scrushy was found guilty and ordered to pay $2.9 billion to the company's shareholders.[1] According to the judge, the fraud ran for seven years and totaled $2.7 billion, and Scrushy was its "orchestrator.. It is important to note that in a criminal trial, conviction depends on a finding of guilt beyond a reasonable doubt, whereas in a civil trial, guilt depends on a preponderance of evidence (i.e., a reasonable probability of guilt), which is a much lower standard.

[1] Jack Healy, "Ex-Chief of HealthSouth Loses Civil Suit," New York Times, June 18, 2009, accessed January 1, 2014, at http://www.nytimes.com/2009/06/19/business/19scrushy.html?_r=0.

[11] Ibid.

[12] Ibid.

[13] Ibid.

[14] Ibid.

financial statements? What are the proper audit procedures to validate estimates?

7. What areas of risk can you identify in HealthSouth's control environment before 2003?
8. What areas of risk can you identify in HealthSouth's strategy before 2002?
9. What changes could be made in HealthSouth's control system and corporate governance structure to mitigate the risk of accounting fraud in future years?
10. Was Scrushy's defense ethical?

Note: Assistance in the preparation of this case is greatly appreciated from Miguel Minutti Meza, Catherine Hancharek, Lily Ding, Lei Guo, Joanna Qin, Crystal Wu, and Michelle Wu, all of whom were students in the Master of Management & Professional Accounting Program of the Rotman School of Management at the University of Toronto.

ETHICS CASE

Royal Ahold—A Dutch Company with U.S.-Style Incentives

According to the Royal Ahold company profile,

> Ahold is a global family of local food retail and foodservice operators that operate under their own brand names. Our operations are located primarily in the United States and Europe. Our retail business consists of retail chain sales, sales to franchise stores and sales to associated stores. The store format that we primarily use is the supermarket. Through our foodservice operations we distribute food, and offer services and expertise to restaurants and hotels, health care institutions, government facilities, universities, sports stadiums and caterers.
>
> In 2003, our consolidated net sales were Euro 56.1 billion, our retail trade and foodservice businesses representing approximately 70% and 30% of this total, respectively. At the end of 2003, Ahold's average number of employees in full-time equivalents totaled 256,649 worldwide.[1]

The company is listed on the Dutch and U.S.[2] stock markets. Ahold was one of the first large Dutch or European companies to implement U.S.-style large stock option compensation schemes for its managers, and that may have led to its downfall in late 2002 and early 2003.[3]

In 2002, Ahold claimed to be the world's third-largest retail group. However, due to unfavorable market conditions, the company had lower-than-expected U.S. sales. For years, the company outperformed its peers, expanding aggressively, but the expansion left Ahold with $12 billion in debt, one of the largest in the sector. In July, the company revised its full-year EPS growth target to 5% to 8%. The company's figures revealed a 6% fall in its core food service business in the United States and a 10% fall in the value of Ahold shares. In October, some investors suggested that Ahold's chief executive, Cees van der Hoeven, leaked the sales numbers to certain analysts and the share price suffered a first drop.

In February 2003, the company announced that net earnings and earnings per share would be significantly lower than previously indicated for fiscal 2002. In the same month, the company disclosed that its financial statements for fiscal 2000 and fiscal 2001 would be restated. A press release indicated that the restatements related primarily to overstatements of income related to vendor promotional allowance programs at its subsidiary, U.S. Foodservice. Managers of the subsidiary booked much higher promotional allowances

[1] From the Ahold website at http://www.ahold.com/index.asp?id52 (accessed January 24, 2005).

[2] As KONINKLIJKE AHOLD NV (AHODF.PK) on the PNK Exchange and as Koninklijke Ahold NV American Depositary Shares (each representing one Ordinary Share) (AHO) on the NYSE.

[3] Stephen Taub, "Royal Ahold in Dutch," CFO, February 25, 200, accessed January 24, 2005, at http://ww2.cfo.com/2003/02/royal-ahold-in-dutch.

(provided by vendors to promote their merchandise) than the company was to actually receive. Ahold estimated the amount of the overstatement to be close to $500 million.

Other irregularities under investigation were the legality and accounting treatment of questionable transactions at the Argentine subsidiary, Disco. Certain joint ventures were consolidated based on misrepresentations to Ahold's auditors. CEO Cees van der Hoeven and CFO Michiel Meurs resigned immediately. The SEC and the Dutch stock exchange Euronext investigated the irregularities, requiring Ahold to present documentation from 1999 to 2003. The company said the irregularities only began in 2001.

In May 2003, Ahold named a new CEO, former executive of Ikea, Anders Moberg.[4] While waiting for the results of the investigations, the company started a restructuring program that involved divesting Indonesian and South American operations. The company also entered into an emergent credit facility from a syndicate of banks.

In May 2003, a forensic report from PricewaterhouseCoopers (PwC) indicated a total overstatement of pretax earnings of approximately U.S.$880 million.[5] Offsetting the bad news of the report, Ahold said that no evidence of fraud was found at other operations. Later in the same month, Jim Miller, president and CEO of U.S. Foodservice, resigned from his position. Ahold considered that he was not implicated. In July 2003, the regulator's inquiry ended, and Ahold disclosed additional $84.4 million in accounting irregularities, bringing the total overstatement to $1.1 billion. The company declined to reveal when or where the latest accounting irregularities occurred.[6]

Ahold's auditors, Deloitte & Touche, insisted that they warned the firm about problems in its U.S. unit. The auditors also pointed out that Ahold did not supply them with full information. These problems were never disclosed to the public. Deloitte said during the inquiries that they identified the problems during the 2002 audit and gave the details to Ahold's board immediately before the audit was concluded in 2003.

In January 2005, nine executives were charged by the Securities Exchange Commission (SEC)[7] with participating in a scheme of accounting fraud at U.S. Foodservice. All executives were accused of approving documents that claimed U.S. Foodservice was owed millions of dollars more in promotional allowances than was actually the case. Former U.S. Foodservice chief marketing officer Mark P. Kaiser faced charges of conspiracy and fraud, along with former CFO Michael Resnick. Executives Timothy J. Lee and William F. Carter pleaded guilty to similar charges in 2004. All the executives have been named in a civil case involving John Nettle, former vice president of General Mills; Mark Bailin, former president of Rymer International Seafood; and Peter Marion, president of Maritime Seafood Processors. Nettle confirmed to the auditors false amounts owed by his company to U.S. Foodservice in 2001. Bailin and Marion benefited by buying U.S. Foodservice stock in 2000, ahead of the company's announcement that Royal Ahold was acquiring it.

According to SEC Litigation Release No. 18929, dated October 13, 2004,[8] the misdeeds were described as follows:

---

[4] "Ahold Turns to IKEA's Ex-Boss," May 2, 2003, accessed January 1, 2005, at http://news.bbc.co.uk/l/hi/business/2995135.stm.

[5] "Ahold Profits Inflated by $880m," May 8, 2003, accessed January 1, 2005, at http://news.bbc.co.uk/l/hi/business/3011103.stm.

[6] Gregory Crouch, "Royal Ahold's Inquiry Ends, Finding $1.1 Billion in Errors," July 2, 2003, C2, accessed January 21, 2005,at http://select.nytimes.com/gst/abstract.html?res5 F60A11F7395E0C718CDDAE0894DB404482.

[7] U.S. Securities and Exchange Commission, "Nine Individuals Charges by the SEC with Aiding and Abetting Financial Fraud at Royal Ahold's U.S. Subsidiary for Signing and Returning False Audit Confirmations. One Also Charged with Insider Trading," January 13, 2005, accessed January 26, 2005, at http://www.sec.gov/litigation/litreleases/lr19034.htm.

[8] U.S. Securities and Exchange Commission, "SEC Charges Royal Ahold and Three Former Top Executives with Fraud: Former Audit Committee Member Charged with Causing Violations of the Securities Laws," October 13, 2004, accessed January 26, 2005, at http://www.sec.gov/litigation/litreleases/lr18929.htm.

The Earnings Fraud at U.S. Foodservice

With respect to the fraud at U.S. Foodservice ("USF"), Ahold's wholly-owned subsidiary based in Columbia, Maryland, the Commission's complaint against Ahold alleges as follows:

- A significant portion of USF's operating income was based on vendor payments known as promotional allowances. USF executives materially inflated the amount of promotional allowances recorded by USF and reflected in operating income on USF's financial statements, which were included in Ahold's Commission filings and other public statements.
- USF executives also provided, or assisted in providing, Ahold's independent auditors with false and misleading information by, for example, persuading personnel at many of USF's major vendors to falsely confirm overstated promotional allowances to the auditors in connection with year-end audits.
- The overstated promotional allowances aggregated at least $700 million for fiscal years 2001 and 2002 and caused Ahold to report materially false operating and net income for those and other periods.

The Joint Venture Sales and Operating Income Fraud Ahold and the Top Officers

With respect to the fraudulent consolidation of joint ventures, the commission's complaints against Ahold, van der Hoeven, Meurs, and Andreae allege as follows:

> Ahold fully consolidated several joint ventures in its financial statements despite owning no more than fifty percent of the voting shares and despite shareholders' agreements that clearly provided for joint control by Ahold and its joint venture partners. To justify full consolidation of certain joint ventures, Ahold gave its independent auditors side letters to the joint venture agreements, signed by Ahold and its joint venture partners, which stated, in effect, that Ahold controlled the joint ventures ("control letters").
>
> However, at the time or soon after executing the control letters, Ahold and its joint venture partners executed side letters that rescinded the control letters—and thus the basis for full consolidation (the "rescinding letters").
>
> Meurs signed all but one of the control and rescinding letters on behalf of Ahold. He also knew that Ahold's auditors were relying on the control letters and were unaware of the existence of the rescinding letters.
>
> Van der Hoeven cosigned one of the rescinding letters and he was at least reckless in not knowing that the auditors were unaware of its existence.
>
> Andreae participated in the fraud by signing the control and rescinding letters for ICA, Ahold's Scandinavian joint venture, and by knowingly or recklessly concealing the existence of the ICA rescinding letter from the auditors.
>
> As a result of the fraud, Ahold materially overstated net sales by approximately EUR 4.8 billion ($5.1 billion) for fiscal year 1999, EUR 10.6 billion ($9.8 billion) for fiscal year 2000, and EUR 12.2 billion ($10.9 billion) for fiscal year 2001. Ahold materially overstated operating income by approximately EUR 222 million ($236 million) for fiscal year 1999, EUR 448 million ($413 million) for fiscal year 2000, and EUR 485 million ($434) for fiscal year 2001.

In February 2004, Ahold announced its plans with regard to the recommendations of the Dutch Tabaksblat Committee on Corporate Governance.[9] In order to restore

[9] From Ahold's company history at http://www.ahold.com/index.asp?id514 (accessed January 24, 2005).

trust in its governance processes, thirty-nine executives and managers were terminated, and an additional sixty employees faced disciplinary actions of different degrees. Members of the Corporate Executive Board will serve for a predetermined period, in which continuity and succession have been taken into account. According to the company, these measures will result in significant improvement in transparency and a far-reaching increase in the power of its shareholders.

The company is also replacing a decentralized system of internal controls with a one-company system with central reporting lines. The most important control, however, is making clear to Ahold's people what the company expects of them going forward. As a first step in this process, they initiated a company-wide financial integrity program. This is aimed at 15,000 managers, the entire middle and top ranks of the organization. The goal of the program is to underscore the importance of integrity and to help guide Ahold's people to apply its corporate business principles.

Questions

1. A vendor may offer a customer a rebate of a specified amount of cash or other consideration that is payable only if the customer completes a specified cumulative level of purchases or remains a customer for a specified period of time. When should the rebate be recognized as revenue? At what value should the rebate be recorded as revenue?
2. The SEC investigation found the individuals involved in the fraud "aided and abetted the fraud by signing and sending to the company's independent auditors confirmation letters that they knew materially overstated the amounts of promotional allowance income paid or owed to U.S. Foodservice." Is the confirmation procedure enough to validate the vendor's allowance amount in the financial statements?
3. The SEC investigation also revealed that "a significant portion of U.S. Foodservice operating income was based on vendor payments known as promotional allowances." How might irregularities have been discovered through specific external audit procedures?
4. Royal Ahold made several changes in its corporate governance structure. Discuss how those changes will mitigate the risk of accounting fraud in future years.

The Ethics of Bankruptcy: Jetsgo Corporation

ETHICS CASE

The discount airline Jetsgo Corporation began operations in June 2002. Within two and a half years, it grew to become Canada's third-largest airline, moving approximately 17,000 passengers per day on its fleet of twenty-nine airplanes, fifteen of which were company-owned Fokker F100s. With 1,200 employees, the company serviced twenty locations in Canada, a dozen in the Caribbean, and ten in the United States.

Jetsgo was a private company owned by Michel Leblanc. Leblanc had lived his life around airplanes. His father owned a flight school; he learned to fly at age sixteen. In his twenties, he was an aircraft salesman; in 1978, he co-owned an eleven-airplane forest-spraying business. From 1985 to 1990, he was a partner in Intair a regional airline in Quebec. In 1991, he and a new partner started Royal Aviation Inc., which he sold in 2001 for $84 million in stock to Canada 3000. Although he was subsequently sued by Canada 3000 for providing inaccurate financial information, the case was never tried because Canada 3000 went into bankruptcy protection in November 2001.

In June 2002, he launched Jetsgo. On Friday March 11, 2005, just before the busy spring-break travel week, Jetsgo entered bankruptcy protection, stranding thousands of passengers who could not return home and annoying those who could not leave on their spring-break holiday.

Throughout its short life, Jetsgo was plagued with both financial and maintenance problems. Leblanc kept operating costs low by doing the following:

- Paying low wages
- Making pilots pay for their own training
- Leasing old aircraft
- Minimizing spare parts inventory by flying only two types of airplanes: the McDonald Douglas MD-83 and the Fokker F100
- Promoting ticket sales through the Internet

Despite these cost saving moves, the company still had financial and maintenance problems. From 2002 to 2005, it filed a total of sixty incident reports with Transportation Canada. These included the following:

- Three months after it began operations, a plane had to make an emergency landing in Toronto because of a hydraulic fuel leak.
- In January 2004, smoke filled the passenger cabin of one plane due to a hydraulic fuel leak.
- In April 2004, a plane made an emergency landing in Winnipeg because of a clogged engine oil filter.
- In December 2004, a plane heading to Mexico had to return to Toronto after flames were seen coming out of an engine.
- In January 2005, a plane, landing in poor weather, slid off the runway in Calgary, hitting a runway sign before taking off again.
- In March 2005, a plane made an emergency landing in Columbia, South Carolina, because of incorrect oil pressure in an engine. It was the second such emergency landing for the plane due to oil pressures problems.

In November 2002, Transport Canada inspectors found twenty-three nonconformance items with the airline. In February 2005, Transportation Canada placed restrictions on Jetsgo and on March 8 said that operations would be suspended on April 9 if the maintenance problems were not fixed. Three days later, on March 11, the company ceased operations.

The company also had financial and cash flow problems. In the first three months of 2005, it lost $22 million. It fell behind in its payment to NAV Canada, which operates Canada's air traffic control system. On March 7, 2005, Jetsgo had to write a certified check to NAV Canada for $1.25 million—a "hostage payment" according to Leblanc—to forestall NAV Canada from seizing some of the company's planes. After it declared bankruptcy, Jetsgo was sued by NAV Canada for an additional $1.6 million for unpaid navigation services and $5.5 million by the Greater Toronto Airport Authority for unpaid airport improvement fees, landing fees, terminal fees, and parking fees. Eight of the company's leased aircraft were left in Toronto on March 11, while all of the company-owned Fokkers were flown to Quebec City and parked in a company-leased hangar.

Leblanc decided to close down operations commencing at midnight on Thursday, March 10, but would not make a public announcement until Friday. Meanwhile, he left the online booking system open. Also, on Thursday, supervisors told thirteen pilots to fly their Fokker airplanes to Quebec City for maintenance checks. Leblanc subsequently said that the "white lie" told to the pilots was justified so that all the company-owned aircraft could be kept safely in Quebec City. Leblanc felt it was better to have all the planes in one place, where they could be guarded, rather than be left at various airports across the country. "It was a white lie, but a necessary lie. You can't tell them, or the job won't get done. Half of them would have refused. The objective would not have been fulfilled and we would have had airplanes all over the damn place today and the estate of Jetsgo would not be protected." The other two company-owned Fokkers were later moved to Quebec City.

The pilots and other employees were then phoned on Friday beginning at 12:30 a.m., waking many from their sleep, and told that the company was bankrupt and that they should stay away from the airports. Customers who arrived at the airports on Friday were abruptly told that operations had been shut down. Although he expressed regret that people's travel plans had been ruined, especially before the popular spring break, and that there were many stranded passengers across North America, Leblanc was pleased that there was no unruly behavior. "Okay, on Friday morning, there were people who didn't fly," he said. "But did you see any airport riots? Did you see 2,000 people in the terminal punching Jetsgo employees? No." Afterward, Leblanc blamed NAV Canada and unfair competition from WestJet Airlines for causing him to close down his airline.

The stranded passengers had to make alternative arrangements to get home; some had to buy tickets on other airlines. WestJet Airlines offered $35 standby fares to the stranded pilots, flight attendants, and maintenance personnel. Some travel agencies provided refunds to their clients, and the Royal Bank said that anyone who booked a ticket online using a Royal Bank Visa card would be reimbursed by the bank. Nevertheless, critics have said that it was callous of Leblanc to have left the online reservation system open on Thursday when he knew that the reservations made that day would never be honored.

Questions

1. For many organizations, bankruptcy protection is just another operational and financial strategy. Discuss the ethical aspects of intentionally remaining silent, collecting money, and then suddenly announcing that the company is bankrupt.
2. Do you accept that the little "white lie" told to the pilots was justifiable?
3. Was it operationally wise for Jetsgo to keep the online reservation system open until the company officially declared bankruptcy? Was it an ethically correct or incorrect decision?
4. Should Leblanc have waited until the busy spring-break holiday period was over to then close down operations?

Sources: CBC News, "Creditors Seek to Seize Jetsgo Aircraft," March 23, 2005, http://origin.www.cbc.ca/money/story/2005/03/23/jetsgo-050323.html.

CBC News, "Jetsgo's Michel Leblanc," September 5, 2006, http://www.cbc.ca/news/background/airlines/leblanc_michel.html.

Robert Cribb, Fred Vallance-Jones, and Tamsin McMahon, "Jetsgo Problems Ignored," *Toronto Star*, June 16, 2006, http://www.thestar.com/News/article/144218.

Brent Jang, "Leblanc on Sorrow, Remorse and His Little 'White Lie': Admits He Misled Pilots to Protect Planes," *The Globe and Mail*, March 18, 2005, http://www.theglobeandmail.com/servlet/Page/document/v5/content/subscribe?user_URL5http://www.theglobeandmail.com%2Fservlet%2FArticleNews%2FTPStory%2FLAC%2F20050318%2FRJETSGO18%2FTPBusiness%2F&ord570437229&brand5theglobeandmail&force_login5true.

Stock Market Cases

Société Générale's Rogue Trader

ETHICS CASE

Jérôme Kerviel joined the French bank, Société Générale (SocGen), in 2000 at the age of twenty-three as part of its systems personnel in its back office. In 2005, he became a junior derivatives trader with an annual limit of €20 million, which is just under U.S.$30 million. However, in November 2007, exchange officials questioned SocGen about why he had traded more than U.S.$74 billion worth of stock-index futures contracts. Kerviel was allowed to continue trading until mid-January 2008, when SocGen liquidated his trading positions and realized a loss of U.S.$7.62 billion (€4.9 billion). How did this happen? Who should be blamed? Was he different than other rogue traders?

Société Générale began operations in France in 1864 and is one of the main European financial institutions. It is the sixth-largest French company and the third-largest bank in the Eurozone. By the mid-2000s, it had developed a risk culture. In 2007, for example, trading-related activities represented 35% of the bank's revenue, up from 29% in 2004. Traders were well rewarded, and it was not uncommon for them to briefly exceed trading limits.

Kerviel began working for the bank in its back office recording and reconciling trading activity. In 2005, he became a trader in the bank's arbitrage department, trading European stock futures. He took unauthorized positions in equities and futures and used his knowledge of the bank's control procedures to conceal his trading positions. Because he knew the timing of the nightly reconciliation of daily trades, he was able to delete and reenter his trades or enter fictitious offsetting trades. Although the bank's risk control department monitored the bank's overall position, it did not verify individual transactions, so his trades went undetected.

In November 2007, officials at Eurex, a derivatives exchange owned by the Deutsche Böerse, questioned SocGen about Kerviel's huge trading activity and position. But Kerviel "produced a faked document to justify the risk cover," according to prosecutor Jean-Claude Marin,[1] and he continued to trade.

By the end of 2007, his positions had generated a paper profit of €1.4 billion.[2] But because this was generated with positions well over his authorized limit, he used his knowledge of the bank's systems and controls to hide most of his success. At the time, Kerviel was making a salary and bonus of not more than €100,000 (approximately U.S.$145,000),[3] and no evidence indicated that he benefited other than through salary and bonus from his trades. Later, Kerviel did tell investigators that he had been promised a bonus of €300,000 for his efforts in 2007.[4]

On January 18, 2008, the bank's risk control department started an investigation after a week of his suspicious trades reached a position on €49 billion. His unauthorized trades were identified, and on January 21. the bank began to unwind his future positions. It took three days and represented 8% of all the trading activity on the Eurostoxx, DAX, and FTSE future indices. After it reversed all his unauthorized trading positions, the bank lost €4.9 billion. Although the bank received permission from French authorities to do this, they did not tell the public until after the positions had been fully unwound. When asked, the bank's CEO, Daniel Bouton, stated that "it didn't want to cause even more losses."[5] Interestingly, the losses could have been much less if the markets had not turned so negative on the three days of liquidation.

Apparently, Kerviel circumvented six levels of control.[6] Later, a special committee of the Board of Directors revealed numerous weaknesses in the bank's internal controls, including the following:

- There was a large increase in the volume of transactions within the equities department, but there was not an increase in the corresponding support services, including the information system.

---

[1] "Bank Warned on Trades: Prosecutor," Andrew Hurst and Thierry Leveque, *Toronto Star*, B1, B4.
[2] Ibid., B4.
[3] John Leicester, "Rogue Trader's Fall Stuns Old Friends, Neighbors," *Toronto Star*, January 26, 2008, B5.
[4] Ibid., B4.
[5] Paul Waldie, "Tough Questions Engulf SocGen," *The Globe and Mail*, January 26, 2008, B2.
[6] Molly Moore, "Trader Used Inside Knowledge," *Toronto Star*, January 25, 2008, B1, B4.

- The nominal value of trades, by traders, was not controlled.
- Duties were not clearly defined, reports were not centralized, and there was no feedback to the appropriate hierarchical level.
- Priority was given to the execution of trades, without an adequate degree of sensitivity to fraud risks.
- Internal audit bodies were insufficiently responsive.

According to a judicial official, Kerviel claimed that his "bank bosses were aware of his massive risk-taking on markets but turned a blind eye as long as he earned money."[7] He said, "I can't believe that my superiors were not aware of the amounts I was committing, it is impossible to generate such profits with small positions."[8]

Although Kerviel was initially accused of fraud, that charge was thrown out by an investigating judge, and he was put under investigation for breach of trust, computer abuse, and falsification.[9] He was later released on bail in March 2008 after the police and internal investigators highlighted the lack of internal controls at Société Générale.

Banks have been bedeviled by rogue traders on several occasions.[10] Kerviel was not the only rogue trader to use a lack of controls to cause huge losses. For example, due to a lack of proper internal controls at Barings Bank, which had been in business for 230 years, Nick Leeson bankrupted the English bank in 1995 after he lost £360 million (U.S.$1.38 billion) on Asian futures markets.

Questions

1. Did Jérôme Kerviel perpetrate a fraud? Why or why not?
2. When such mammoth unauthorized trades occur and the bank is bankrupted or severely damaged financially, should the Board of Directors, who have the ultimate responsibility for the bank's activities, or its executives, whose job it is to protect the bank, go to jail rather than the rogue trader?
3. Were the bank's actions in liquidating Kerviel's positions ethical?
4. Did the French officials who authorized the liquidation behave ethically?
5. There is considerable debate about whether better controls can ever stop a rogue trader. What is your opinion, and why?
6. If enhanced controls really cannot stop all rogue traders, how are companies to be protected from them?

[7] Angela Boland, "Trader Points Finger at Bosses," *Toronto Star*, January 30, 2008, B3.

[8] Ibid.

[9] Bank Warned on Trades," B1.

[10] Leicester, "Rogue Trader's Fall Stuns Old Friends, Neighbors," B5. Other rogue traders have included Brian Hunter, who lost U.S.$6.6 billion on natural gas futures in 2006; Yasuo Hamanaka, who lost U.S.$2.6 billion dealing in copper futures in 1996; and John Rusnak, who lost U.S.$691 million trading in currency options in 2002.

ETHICS CASE

Galleon's Insider Trading Network

Billionaire Raj Rajaratnam was arrested for insider trading on October 15, 2009, and marched in handcuffs from his New York apartment.[1] Up to that point, he had enjoyed fame and fortune for founding the $7 billion Galleon Group of hedge funds and its enviable record of securities trading. But instead of being the astute

[1] "Billionaire Galleon Founder Arrested for Insider Trading," October 16, 2009, accessed December 19, 2010, at http://wallstreetpit.com/11276-billionaire-galleon-group-founder-arrested-for-insider-trading.

investor everyone thought him to be, it appears that his success was based on using inside information from tipsters, not astute independent analysis of corporate performance. According to the enforcement chief of the Securities Exchange Commission (SEC), Rajaratnam was "not the master of the universe, rather [he was] a master of the rolodex."[2] He used his contacts to profit from tips on advance information on the performance of IBM, Google, Hilton Hotels, Intel, Polycom, Clearwire, AMD, Akamai, and Sun Microsystems, to name a few.[3]

The Galleon founder's inside information network came to light when Mark Lenowitz, a defendant in a 2007 insider trading case, agreed to assist investigators as part of his plea bargain. His assistance led to the prosecution of David Slaine, one of his colleagues at the hedge fund Chelsey Capital. In turn, Slaine fingered Zvi Goffer, a Galleon trader, and the ensuing investigation led to wiretap and other evidence against Rajaratnam and several others at Galleon.[4] The inside information network that had brought so much personal success to Rajaratnam (and others at Galleon) ended up working against them. Further investigations into other network connections are ongoing.

Some of the wiretap evidence reveals how interested Rajaratnam was in obtaining inside information. One of the SEC's witnesses spoke of how Rajaratnam first asked him about his sources of insider information when he applied for a job at Galleon in 2005. Rajaratnam asked him to "name companies where he had an 'edge'—access to inside information [according to prosecutors]"[5] Although the witness was not hired, he began to share and swap information with Rajaratnam.

The witness also agreed to tape calls between Rajaratnam and other hedge fund managers and friends that led to charges against Danielle Chiesi and Mark Kurland of New Castle Partners; Robert Moffat, a senior IBM vice president; Anil Kumar, a McKinsey director; and Rajiv Goel, a managing director at Intel. The transcript of some of these calls makes fascinating reading about the mind-sets of the participants.[6]

Ultimately, Chiesi and apparently Rajaratnam began to worry about being caught by a tipster or a caller wearing a wire. Then in October 2008, the economic downturn of the subprime lending crisis began to depress the stock markets, and the value of inside information about corporate fundamentals ceased to be useful. On October 15, the SEC investigator learned from a colleague on another investigation that Rajaratnam had bought a ticket to fly to London on the October 16. At 6:00 a.m. on the October 16, Rajaratnam was arrested.[7]

According to the SEC complaint,[8] advance information from tipsters was used to make profits for Galleon or for their tipsters or for a company related to them. Sometimes numerous trades were involved over a period of stock price volatility, enabling profits to be made when prices rose and losses to be avoided when prices fell. The transactions reported in the complaint included the following.

---

[2] John Helyar, "Galleon Insider-Trading Case Opens Window on Secret Hedge Funds," *Bloomberg*, October 19, 2009, accessed December 19, 2010, at http://www.bloomberg.com/apps/news?pid5newsarchive&sid5a01GJ_ry Etms.

[3] U.S. Securities and Exchange Commission, *Complaint against Galleon Management, LP*, et al, October 16, 2010, accessed December 17, 2010, at http://www.sec.gov/litigation/complaints/2010/comp21397.pdf.

[4] Grant McCool, "Insider Trading Case of 2007 Led to Galleon," Reuters, February 4, 2010, accessed December 19, 2010, at http://www.reuters.com/article/idUSTRE6134BO20100204.

[5] Helyar, "Galleon Insider-Trading Case Opens Window on Secret Hedge Funds."

[6] Ibid.

[7] Ibid.

[8] U.S. Securities and Exchange Commission, *Complaint against Galleon Management.*

TRANSACTION	INFORMATION ABOUT	PROFIT (AT LEAST)	LOSSES AVOIDED
Polycom call options	Q4 2005	$330,000	
Polycom shares	Q4 2005	570,000	
Polycom shares	Q1 2006	165,000	
Hilton shares	Going private, July 2007	4,000,000	
Google puts and calls	Q2 2007	9,300,000	
Intel shares	Q4 2006	1,000,000	$1,400,000
Intel short sales, purchases	Q1 2007	1,300,000	917,000
Intel shares	Q3 2007	690,000	
Clearwire three share trades	Joint venture	780,000	
PeopleSupport shares	Activities	Traded for a tipster (R.Goel), in 2008	
Akamai short sales & covers	Q2 2008	3,200,000	
Sun Microsystems	Q2 2009	Profit for New Castle (D.Chiesi) not Galleon	
AMD shares	Split off, June-Oct. 2008	9,500,000	

Rajaratnam and Chiesi pled not guilty to the indictment.[9] But the Galleon Funds were wound down in late 2009 after Rajaratnam was indicted, as investors pulled out their money.

In May 2010, Rajaratnam tried to have the wiretap evidence ruled inadmissible, but in late November 2010, the verdict went against him.[10] This will be the first time in which wiretap evidence will be used in a criminal insider case, and as such it represents a significant upgrade in the techniques available to investigators.[11] No longer will the white-collar criminals who misuse inside information be able to keep their phone conversations secret. They will be subject to wiretaps just like the mafia.

Video: "Horwitz Says Galleon 'Broke the Mould' on Insider Trading," *Bloomberg*, November 24, 2010, http://www.bloomberg.com/news/2010–11-24/horwitz-says-galleon-broke-the-mold-on-insider-trading-video.html.

Questions

1. Should inside traders who are non-violent, white-collar criminals be subject to Mafia-style investigation tools?
2. How can a stock trader know when he or she is receiving inside information that would be illegal to act on?
3. How can a stock trader avoid using insider information?
4. Would a private investor be subject to the same rules against using insider information as a stock trader?
5. Should a person giving a tip (the tipper) be subject to the same penalties as the user (the tippee)?

[9] Zachery Kouwe, "Galleon Founder and Hedge Fund Manager Plead Not Guilty in Insider Case," *New York Times*, December 21, 2009, accessed December 19, 2010, at http://www.nytimes.com/2009/12/22/business/22insider.html.

[10] Kenneth Herzinger, Amy M. Ross, and Katherine C. Lubin Orrick, "Court Allows Use of Wiretap Evidence in Galleon Insider Trading Case," November 29, 2010, accessed December 19, 2010, at http://www.orrick.com/publications/item.asp?action5article&articleID53153.

[11] See Horwitz video noted above.

ETHICS CASE

Conflicts of Interest on Wall Street

On December 20, 2002, New York's attorney general, Eliot Spitzer, announced a $1.4 billion settlement ending a multiregulator probe of ten brokerages that alleged that "investors were duped into buying over-hyped stocks during the 90s bull market."[1] But the settlement may represent only the tip of the iceberg as aggrieved investors review the findings and sue the brokerages for redress of their personal losses estimated to be $7 trillion since 2000.[2] Nonetheless, it promises an overdue start on the reform of Wall Street's[3] flawed conflict-of-interest practices. As such, the revisions ultimately adopted will provide a template for investment advisors around the world.

The story behind the probe is also an interesting one. It shows the capacity of a state's Attorney-General to force the Securities Exchange Commission (SEC), which has regulatory authority over U.S. capital markets, to act when they appeared reluctant to take on Wall Street in a direct, public, and serious manner. In fact, Spitzer was able to bring together his office, the SEC, the National Association of Securities Dealers, the New York Stock Exchange, and a group of state regulators, as well as the major brokerages involved, to arrange a settlement.

The accepted settlement, while indicating the complicity of the ten firms involved, will probably do more to restore lost confidence in the capital markets than to weaken it. Regulators have been seen to act, brokerages are on notice that the old practices will no longer be tolerated, and the right of investors to have unbiased advice is reinforced. The resulting sharpening of ethics awareness on the part of advisors, their firms, and the regulators, together with the emergence of more ethical practices, should assist in the restoration of investor trust in the capital markets.

The Settlement

Ten firms have agreed "to pay $1.435 billion, including $900 million in penalties, $450 million for research over the next five years and $85 million for investor education."[4] The list of payments, in millions, is shown in Table 1. Two other firms that had been part of the settlement talks did not participate in the announced settlement.

Some observers hailed the settlement and resulting changes to be "the dawn of a new day for Wall Street."[5] Others felt that the fines were a drop in the bucket. "Citicorp, for example, averaged about $65 million in profit each business day in the third quarter, meaning one good week would cover its payment."[6] If the payments turn out to be tax deductible, the impact would certainly be minor in size but would possess a significant signaling value.

What Caused Concern?

Conflicts of interest have been common practice in the brokerage business since its inception. For example, most brokerages (and brokers) have investments on which they take speculative positions and on which they make investment recommendations to investors. In the case of the brokerages, they are usually required to disclose to prospective investors when they are selling shares as a principal, but the presumption of unsuspecting investors has

[1] "Wall Street Firms to Pay Fines of $1.4 Billion U.S.," *Toronto Star*, December 21, 2002, D3.

[2] Alex Berenson and Andrew Ross Sorkin, "How Wall Street Was Tamed," *New York Times*, December 22, 2003.

[3] Wall Street is used in this case to signify the U.S. investment advisory/brokerage community, which is centered on Wall Street in New York City.

[4] Randall Smith, "Ten Firms Must Pay $1.4 Billion over Misleading Stock Research," *Wall Street Journal*, December 23, 2002.

[5] Ibid.

[6] "Wall Street Firms to Pay Fines of $1.4 Billion U.S.," D3.

TABLE 1 Wall Street Brokers Settlement Payments*

FIRM	FINES	INDEPENDENT INVESTOR RESEARCH	EDUCATION	TOTAL
Saloman Smith Barney				
Parent, Citigroup Inc.	$300	$75	$25	$400
Credit Suisse First Boston	150	50	0	200
Merrill Lynch	100*	75	25	200
Morgan Stanley	50	75	0	125
Goldman Sachs	50	50	10	110
Bear Stearns	50	25	5	80
Deutsche Bank	50	25	5	80
J. P. Morgan Chase	50	25	5	80
Lehman Brothers	50	25	5	80
UBS Warburg	50	25	5	80
Total	$900	$450	$85	$1,435

*Merrill Lynch agreed to pay an additional $100 million seven months earlier in response to Spitzer's original charges.[7]

been that brokerage employees—analysts and investment advisers—were acting in the best interest of the investors they were advising. How wrong they were!

According to Forbes.com, Spitzer's office found e-mails showing "Merrill Lynch analysts with their guard down, privately trashing the stocks they publicly recommended."[8] In addition, "there is the widespread phenomenon of research departments commencing coverage of companies their (investment) banks recently took public. This coverage is always positive."[9] Moreover, "analysts almost never say 'sell.' According to Thomson Financial/First Call, fewer than 2% of all financial analysts are 'sell' or 'strong sell.'… Third, there are cases like Enron that are not recent initial public offerings but companies that do massive and repeat business with Wall Street. The analysts can say they are not swayed by their firm's interests, and they can claim they were defrauded, but how do they explain the uniformity of their recommendations."[10]

Brokerages have long relied on the notion of the Chinese wall or a firewall that they claim can stop information known to investment bank personnel who develop and price independent public offerings from reaching stock analysts or brokers serving retail clients. However, there are those who doubt that Chinese walls are fully effective. According to Richard Epstein, a law professor at the University of Chicago, "The only thing [the analyst] needs to know [about the investment banking client] if he is inclined to swing his recommendation is that it is a client."[11] Since analysts have been remunerated partly on the basis of underwriting revenues and/or on the basis of retail commissions or total brokerage revenues, there is built-in remuneration motivation for promoting the stock of known or potential underwriting clients.

On other occasions, the attempts to influence analysts have been quite direct. "Perhaps the most startling example came

[7] Smith, "Ten Firms Must Pay $1.4 Billion over Misleading Stock Research."
[8] Ibid
[9] "Wall Street Firms to Pay Fines of $1.4 Billion U.S.," D3.
[10] Dan Ackman, "Everyone Wants a Shot at the Analysts," *Forbes.com*, May 1, 2002.
[11] Ibid.

in mid-November, when Citigroup chief executive Sanford Weill said he told Jack Grubman to re-examine his rating of AT&T and admitted that he helped Grubman's children gain admission to a prestigious Manhattan nursery school."[12]

In addition to providing investment advice that lacked integrity, Wall Street firms have been playing favorites. They have been offering shares of hot public offerings to the executives of companies regarded as good prospects for investment banking deals. This is known as "spinning," and due to the pent-up demand for the new offerings, a profit is virtually assured.

Proposed Structural Reforms

In order to help ensure that "stock recommendations are not tainted by efforts to obtain investment banking fees"[13,14,15] and other benefits, the settlement proposes several changes in the way investment business is done, including the following:

- "Each firm's research unit will reside in a unit separate from the investment banking unit, with its own legal and compliance staff, and which doesn't report to investment banking....
- Decisions to terminate [analyst] coverage must be made by research and not investment bankers, and can't substitute for a rating downgrade....
- Analysts can't be compensated based on investment banking work or input from bankers, and should be paid based partly on the accuracy of their stock picks."

Some problems still exist, and further framework changes will emerge, but a start has been made on cleaning up some of the conflicts of interest facing investors and the brokerage community.

On April, 2003, a Joint Release was issued and lodged on the SEC Press website by the five regulatory agencies involved, which had the following headlines:

> Ten of Nation's Top Investment Firms Settle Enforcement Actions Involving Conflicts of Interest Between Research and Investment Banking
>
> Historic Settlement Requires Payments of Penalties of $487.5 Million, Disgorgement of $387.5 Million to Fund Investor Education and Mandates Sweeping Structural Reforms

Questions

1. Identify and explain the conflicts of interest referred to in this case.
2. What additional rules should the SEC make?
3. What should be included in the investor education that the settlement funds are earmarked for?
4. Was it appropriate for the New York Attorney General's Office to have become involved in securities regulation, or should this have been left to securities regulators?

[12] Ibid.
[13] Ibid.
[14] "Wall Street Firms to Pay Fines of $1.4 Billion U.S.," D3.
[15] Smith, "Ten Firms Must Pay $1.4 Billion over Misleading Stock Research."

ETHICS CASE

Loyalty, but to Whom?

Glen Grossmith is an outstanding family man, a frequent coach for his children's teams, and a dedicated athlete who enjoys individual and team sports. One day, his boss at UBS Securities Canada Inc., Zoltan Horcsok, asked him to do a favor for a colleague, Mark Webb, with whom they had done business for a while. Glen did the favor without asking why it was needed. Here is the story of what happened:

> "At about 2:30 P.M." on February 4, 2004, "Mr. Webb called Mr. Horcsok. "I need your help with something badly right away," Mr. Webb told the Toronto trader. The two spoke soon after, working out a way to call one another without being taped. Mr. Webb, according to Mr. Horcsok, then told him: "You need to find a buyer for 10,000 Phelps Dodge. I may have a problem … you've got to be quick."
>
> Mr. Horcsok then told Mr. Grossmith he needed a Canadian buyer for the Phelps Dodge shares.
>
> Without knowing the details behind Mr. Webb's request, Mr. Grossmith got in touch with a client and asked the client to buy the shares. The client agreed.
>
> Mr. Horcsok then spoke to about a dozen traders in the Toronto office, trying to find a trade ticket stamped at about 2:15 P.M. "Webb is in trouble," he told his traders, according to the settlement documents.
>
> Eventually, a ticket time-stamped 9:43 A.M. was found. Mr. Grossmith, with Mr. Horcsok's knowledge, crossed out the stock trade that the ticket recorded and changed it to the Phelps Dodge symbol. Client information was also changed to reflect the Canadian buyer of the Phelps Dodge stock.
>
> He also sent "fabricated" trade information to Mr. Webb, the settlement document states. Mr. Grossmith also created an electronic ticket reflecting the Phelps Dodge trade, while Mr. Horcsok later destroyed the altered paper trade ticket, according to the settlement.[1]

Unfortunately, for Glen and Zoltan, their activities were investigated and discovered by their employer. It turned out that Mark Webb needed the trade covered up because he was retaliating against a client and the client complained to UBS, and the U.S. Regulators in the Market Regulation Services Inc. (RS) from the Ontario Securities Commission picked up the trail and subsequently claimed that

> "Mark Webb, a trader who worked at UBS's office in Stamford, Conn., received an order from a client to buy 120,000 shares of Phelps Dodge Corp. However, once 6,000 shares were bought at about 2:18 P.M., the client cancelled the rest and moved it to another investment dealer.
>
> Mr. Webb became angry and bought 10,000 Phelps shares for UBS's principal account in what RS alleges was "retaliation." After the client complained to UBS, Mr. Webb—who was fired along with Messrs. Horcsok and Grossmith in February—claimed the shares had been bought for a Canadian client, "when in fact they were not," RS said.[2]

Unfortunately for Horcsok and Grossmith, they were fired by UBS in late February over conduct that occurred earlier that month and were denied their 2004 bonus by the investment dealer. The two brokers have sued UBS, with Grossmith seeking $1,053,000 and Horcsok seeking $1,750,000, which they claim is owed to them as bonus. Both claim they are owed the money because the conduct over which they were fired took place in 2005, not in 2004:

---

[1] Wojtek Dabrowski, "Former UBS Brokers Fined $75,000 and $100,000: Cover-Up Allegations," *Financial Post*, July 19, 2005, FP1, FP2.

[2] Ibid.

> Additional court documents filed by Mr. Grossmith say UBS's reputation was "in tatters" by early 2005, following its settlement of unrelated allegations with RS in late 2004. He also claims UBS is improperly using him "as an example to try to enhance its reputation with the regulators."
>
> But UBS spokesman Graeme Harris said yesterday the two men did not receive 2004 bonuses because of "misconduct, breach of UBS's policies and code of conduct and jeopardizing of UBS's reputation and business."
>
> They were fired before the bonus payout date, and were therefore not entitled to one, Mr. Harris said.
>
> Furthermore, the figures the two are claiming aren't the sums that would have been awarded to them even if they had received a bonus from UBS, Mr. Harris said.[3]

Ultimately, on July 18, 2005, the two brokers

> settled regulators' allegations that they falsified information and records to cover up a trade made by an angry U.S. colleague retaliating against one of his clients. Glen Grossmith, a former sales trader at UBS, and Zoltan Horcsok, his supervisor and former head of equity sales trading at the brokerage, have been fined $75,000 and $100,000 respectively. Each man will also pay $25,000 in costs to Market Regulation Services Inc. (RS) as part of the settlement deal approved yesterday.
>
> "What we see here are two traders who falsified information and falsified trades to cover up the wilful action of a colleague and that's not acceptable," Maureen Jensen, RS's Eastern Region vice-president of market regulation, told reporters yesterday. "They need to bear the consequences."
>
> Both senior traders have been suspended from trading on Canadian equity markets for the next three months, after which they must be strictly supervised for six months. Mr. Horcsok is also prohibited from acting as a supervisor for a year following his three-month trading ban.
>
> Lawyers for the two men said yesterday that both regret their actions. Mr. Horcsok had not been disciplined in the past. In 2000, Mr. Grossmith was fined $35,000 and suspended for a month by the Toronto Stock Exchange for several high-close trades he executed.[4]
>
> After over a year out of work, "Grossmith and Horcsok found employment at Scotia Capital Inc. following their ousters from UBS, but were fired last month, also in relation to the allegations settled yesterday."[5]

Questions

1. Loyalty is a highly desirable ethical value, and disloyalty is a serious unethical and often illegal activity. Explain how and to whom Grossmith, Horcsok, and Webb were disloyal.
2. Although Grossmith's actions did not negatively affect the wealth of any client, why did UBS fire him?
3. How should an employer like UBS encourage employee loyalty?

[3] Ibid.

[4] Ibid.

[5] Ibid.

ETHICS CASE

Bankers Trust: Learning from Derivatives*

Bankers Trust (BT) was one of the most powerful and profitable banks in the world in the early 1990s. Under the stewardship of chairman Charles Sanford Jr., it had transformed itself from a staid commercial bank into "a highly-tuned manufacturer of high-margin, creative financial products—the envy of wholesale bankers."[1] BT prided itself on its innovative trading strategies, which used derivatives to manage risks; its performance-driven culture; and its profits: the bank made a profit of over U.S. $1 billion in 1993.[2]

Key to BT's success was the dominance of its business in derivatives—contracts in which companies make payments to each other based on some underlying asset, such as a commodity, a financial instrument, or an index.[3] The value of the payments—and thus the contract—is derived from those assets. Companies can use derivatives to lower financing costs, manage risk, or speculate on interest and currency rates. It is estimated that almost $400 million of BT's 1993 profits came from its leveraged derivatives business.

Derivatives, with their high margins, held a preeminent position with BT management, with their fervent focus on the bottom line. At BT, each product and each trader was given a value that was based on what income the product or trader could bring the firm.[4] The bank's intense focus on the bottom line decreased attention on products and services that had low margins but that fostered and nurtured client relationships. BT was known for courting customers only insofar as they would buy high-margin products.[5] In 1990, Charles Hill, former cohead of merchant banking, left with thirty members of his department because he saw no room at BT for offering clients impartial financial advice and deal structuring. One source within the company explained, "We got rid of the nurturers and builders—the defensive guys—and kept the offensive guys."[6] Those who remained describe a firm driven by intense internal rivalry, endless politicking, and discussions about profit and losses. They describe a "coliseum" mentality at the top level: "we look on while the guys are out there fighting the lions."[7] What remained was a bank where the customer's interests appeared to come second to the bank's.

It was within this context that BT, once one of the most powerful banks in the world, was disgraced by a series of highly publicized lawsuits brought forth by several of its clients in 1994 and 1995 over losses they incurred as a result of derivative products sold to them by BT. The clients contended that BT sold them the derivatives without giving them adequate warning and information regarding their potential risks. BT countered that these derivative deals were agreements between the bank and sophisticated clients who were now trying to escape from their loss-making contracts by crying foul.[8] At issue was whether the clients were naive and should have known

---

*Prepared by L. J. Brooks, with assistance from student papers of Linda Rutledge, Deryk Angstenderger, Kelly Kang, Nilou Makarechian, Roman Masley, Khalid Rashid, and Chao Xu.

[1] Y. D. Shirreff, "Can Anybody Fix Bankers Trust?," *Euromoney*, April 1995, 34–40.

[2] "Bankers Trust Blurred Vision," *The Economist*, April 8, 1995, 67–68.

[3] G. A. Edwards and G. E. Eller, "Overview of Derivatives Disclosures by Major US Banks," *Federal Reserve Bulletin*, September 1995, 817–31.

[4] Shirreff, "Can Anybody Fix Bankers Trust?"

[5] Ibid.

[6] Ibid.

[7] Ibid.

[8] "Bankers Trust Blurred Vision,"

what they were getting into or whether BT deliberately deceived them (p. 110).[9]

There were more than half a dozen companies that suffered losses as a result of derivatives due to BT's allegedly fraudulent sales practices (see table below), but the Procter & Gamble (P&G) case is representative of the other cases.

Companies That Procter & Gamble Says Lost Money on Derivatives Due to Bankers Trust's Allegedly Fraudulent Sales Practices

COMPANY	LOSS ($U.S. MILLION)
Procter & Gamble	195.5
Air Products	105.8
Sandoz	78.5
P.T. Adimitra Rayapratama	50.0
Federal Paper Board	47.0
Gibson Greetings	23.0
Equity Group Holdings	11.2
Sequa	7.5
Jefferson Smurfit	over 2.4

Source: *Business Week*, October 16, 1995.

The relationship between P&G and BT's derivatives unit was established in January 1993 when the company set up a broad agreement with the bank for derivatives contracts. In November 1993, P&G agreed to buy a leveraged derivative product; P&G would make large profits if interest rates decreased and would lose money if interest rates increased. Leveraged derivatives products are a complex type of derivative, and their value can fluctuate to a greater degree than ordinary derivatives. The derivative worked fine at first, and P&G was sufficiently satisfied to agree to a second leveraged derivative contract in February 1994. However, interest rates began to rise that same month, significantly increasing P&G's payments to BT.

It is unclear whether P&G knew the cost of getting out of the contract, and P&G has since acknowledged that its internal procedures were not followed when it agreed to this derivative. P&G claimed that Bankers fraudulently induced it to buy complex derivatives, misrepresented their value, and then induced P&G to buy more for alleged gains or to staunch losses. However, P&G appeared to be an active market player. It had $5 billion in long-term debt, and its treasury managed a large, sophisticated portfolio of derivatives. P&G has acknowledged that its internal procedures were not followed when it entered into the derivatives contracts in November 1993. Ed Artzt, P&G's CEO, said the executives who bought the derivatives ignored policies against such speculation and were "like farm boys at a country carnival." His treasurer, Ray Mains, did not read the contract he signed, did not ask the right Questions, and did not assess risk by seeking outside help. Artzt also said Mains "failed to tell his boss when he knew he had a problem, … delayed while losses piled up, … and misled his boss into believing the loss was much smaller than it was."[10] P&G's CFO, Erik Nelson, relied on Mains instead of getting outside advice and did not inform Artzt or the board of the problems with the deal.

P&G's court filings include taped conversations that took place at Bankers Trust. In November 1993, Kevin Hudson, a managing director and salesman on the P&G deal, told his fiancée that the transaction would bring BT a profit of $7.6 million. She asked, "Do they understand that? What they did?" He replied, "No. They understand what they did but they don't understand the leverage." She warned Hudson that the deal would blow up on him. He replied, "I'll be looking for a new opportunity at the bank by then anyways." When

[9] Kelly Holland, Linda Himelstein, and Zachary Schiller, "The Bankers Trust Tapes," *BusinessWeek*, October 16, 1995, 106–11.

[10] C. J. Loomis, "Bankers Trust Times—More Dirt about Derivatives," *Fortune Magazine*, November 27, 1995, 34.

the Fed raised interest rates in February 1994, P&G lost $157 million, and when asked if "they were dying," Hudson replied, "They don't know." He was even then trying to sell P&G a second leveraged derivative and said, "Let me just get the deutsche mark trade done first; then they can ask." By April 12 that year, P&G announced a $157 million derivatives bath. Hudson's bonus for 1993 was $1.3 million. (He and his fiancée were married on November 5, 1994; live in London; and are still working for BT.[11])

P&G contended that, when it asked for an explanation of the costs, it learned that the bank was using a proprietary model to calculate the costs that it would not share with P&G.[12] P&G alleged that, in April, BT gave the company charts that showed that it would have had to pay a penalty to get out of its November contract almost from the day it was initiated.

Further evidence points to taped conversations between BT employees in which a BT salesman, discussing P&G's decision to enter into the November contract, says "we set 'em up."[13] P&G finally locked in interest rates on both the derivatives; however, it claimed that by the time it finished doing so, its financing costs were $195.5 million higher than they should have been (p. 110).[14]

P&G asserted that BT employees were trying to deceive it from the day the derivatives contract was initiated. As evidence, P&G points to a taped conversation between Bankers employees about the November contract where one asks, "Do they [P&G] understand that? What they did?"[15] The other employee replies, "No. They understand what they did but they don't understand the leverage, no."[16] The first employee then says, "But I mean… how much do you tell them. What is your obligation to them?"[17] The second employee responds, "To tell them if it goes wrong, what does it mean in a payout formula."[18] P&G sued BT in October 1994, alleging that the bank "deliberately misled and deceived it, keeping the company in the dark about key aspects of the derivatives the bank was selling (p. 106)."[19]

BT countered that P&G was an active and sophisticated player in the financial markets and knew how its derivatives would perform. In court filings, BT described P&G as "sophisticated, experienced, and knowledgeable about the use of interest-rate derivative contracts and the risks presented by those contracts (p. 109)."[20] It added, "Although P&G would like this court to believe that it is a naive and unsophisticated user of derivatives transactions, the fact is that as part of its regular course of business and with authorization from top management, P&G's Treasury Department managed a large and sophisticated portfolio of derivative transactions (p. 109)."[21] BT asserted that P&G knew how the derivatives would perform and had included a taped conversation in its court filings in which a BT employee shows a P&G treasury employee how to calculate its rate on the November derivative.[22] BT also produced evidence in court filings that P&G top executives blamed their own personnel for the investments. "Rather than

[11] Ibid.
[12] Holland et al., "The Bankers Trust Tapes."
[13] Ibid.
[14] Ibid.
[15] Ibid.
[16] Ibid.
[17] Ibid.
[18] Ibid.
[19] Ibid.
[20] Ibid.
[21] Ibid.
[22] Ibid.

putting its own house in order, and accepting its losses, P&G chose instead to bring this lawsuit (p. 111)."[23]

On September 1, 1995, P&G filed a motion in U.S. District Court that was approved to add RICO (Racketeer-Influenced and Corrupt Organization) charges to the allegations against BT. A company found guilty of RICO charges is liable for three times the damages and plaintiff's legal costs. Banker's counterfiling called this "blackmail," saying P&G was hoping to vilify BT by the sheer number of its charges.

The lawsuit was settled out of court in May 1996.

Questions

1. What do you think the basis of settlement should have been?
2. Did BT have a duty to disclose all the information it had regarding the transactions to P&G, including pricing, mark to market value, and risk, or should P&G, a multi-billion-dollar company, have ensured that it knew and understood these figures and risks prior to engaging in the transactions?
3. Did BT have an ethical duty to ascertain the suitability of these products for P&G, or did its responsibilities end with providing its client with the product it demanded?
4. Was the maxim of "buyer beware" more appropriate than "seller beware"?
5. What other ethical issues are raised by the case?

[23] Ibid.

ETHICS CASE

Barings Bank: Rogue Trader

It was early on a Friday morning in London—7:15 a.m. on February 24, 1995, to be exact—that the phone call came for Peter Baring from Peter Norris. Baring's family had been in banking since 1763. They enjoyed the patronage of the Queen of England and had financed the Napoleonic Wars and the transcontinental railway in Canada. Barings, London's oldest merchant bank, would soon be owned by foreign interests because of Norris's news.

Early on the previous day, Norris, the head of investment banking, had been summoned to Singapore by James Bax, the regional managing director of Baring Securities. Its star trader, Nick Leeson, had not been seen since Wednesday afternoon Singapore time, and it appeared that he had left major unhedged securities positions that Barings might not be able to cover. If not, Barings would be bankrupt or owned by others who could pay off what was owed when the uncovered commitments came due.

At the beginning, Barings officials were not sure what had happened or the extent of the potential losses and commitments. When they did discover the nature of their obligations, they realized that the securities contracts were still open so that the upper limit of their losses would not be known until the closing date of the contracts. If the markets involved sank further by that time, Barings' losses would grow. This was a complete shock because Leeson was supposed to deal in fully hedged positions only, making his money on short-term price changes with virtually no chance of losing a significant amount of money. What had happened?

Norris found confirmation of what Bax had told him. Essentially, Leeson had built up two huge securities positions. He had arranged futures contracts committing Barings to buy U.S.$7 billion worth of Japanese equities and U.S.$20 billion or more of interest rate futures at future dates. Unfortunately, due to the Kobe earthquake in Japan, the Japanese stock market was falling, so the equity contracts were worth less than he had paid, and the projected losses were growing but not yet at their maximum. In fact, it was estimated that every 1% decline in the stock market raised the losses by U.S.$70 million.

When Peter Baring, the chairman of the bank, advised the Bank of England on Friday at noon that his bank had a potential problem, he estimated the combined losses at £433 million (U.S.$650 million), a figure that was close to the shareholders' equity of £541 million. The governor of the Bank of England, Eddie George, was recalled from his skiing holiday in France, and his deputy, Rupert Pennant-Rea, called other British bankers to meet at the Bank of England to pledge funds to help meet Barings' problem. Prospective purchasers were canvassed throughout Saturday, but the loss estimate rose to £650 million with no cap in sight. On Sunday, several options were pursued, including contacting the world's richest man, the Sultan of Brunei. The British bankers met again at the bank at 10 a.m., and by 2 p.m. they had agreed to provide £600 million. The question of what their return would be for advancing the money was being debated, but the issue of someone providing an upper cap to the losses remained. An offer arrived from the sultan to do so, which included the taking over of Barings. Unfortunately, this offer was withdrawn before a deal was consummated, and Eddie George had to sign an Administration Order that essentially put Barings under the administration of the Bank of England. At 10:10 p.m., the Bank of England announced that Barings had failed. Two hundred thirty-three years of stewardship by the Barings family was over.

One of the prospective buyers, ING, the second-largest insurance firm in the Netherlands, was still interested and had sent a squad of at least thirty people to complete due diligence examinations. ING was particularly interested in assessing the degree of risk of other losses and of the complicity of personnel in the London and Singapore offices in the Leeson problems. And Jacobs, the chairman of ING, agreed to buy Barings for £1 two hours before the Japanese market opened on Tuesday, February 28. As part of the deal, he agreed to keep the Barings name on the bank. In addition, he subsequently agreed to pay out most of the £105 million in bonuses that the Barings management had agreed to give its staff two days prior to the famous phone call.

How did this debacle happen? Bits and pieces of the puzzle came out slowly until the Report of the Bank of England's Board of Banking Supervision emerged. On Tuesday, February 28, Nick Leeson still had not been found, and he would not be detained until he and his wife arrived in Frankfurt on Thursday, March 2, having spent time in Kuala Lumpur and Kota Kinabalu, Malaysia. He would ultimately make a deal to assist investigators but would still be sent back to Singapore to stand trial.

Nick Leeson had gone to Singapore as the head of a unit that traded in futures, and he had prospered. He made money by buying and selling futures contracts for baskets of Japanese stocks known as Nikkei 225 futures. These Nikkei 225 futures contracts were traded on both the Osaka stock exchange and the SIMEX, Singapore's financial futures exchange. Since the prices on each exchange were slightly different, a sharp-eyed trader could buy on one and sell on the other exchange, making money on the spread. This was relatively safe since for every purchase, there was an immediate sale—if not, Barings would be exposed to very large risks since the transactions were highly leveraged. In 1992, his unit made £1.18 million; in 1993, it made £8.83 million; and in the first seven months of 1994, it made a total of £19.6 million, or more than one-third of the total profit for the whole group. Nick was a star.

Barings did send out its internal auditors to see that all was well. Although the twenty-four-page report condemned the lack of controls and particularly having one man in charge of both the front (investing) and the back (record-keeping) offices, it was not acted on for fear that Leeson would be aggravated and leave for a job at another broker. Leeson's profits, after all, provided bonuses for everyone. Even though Leeson's behavior was getting somewhat bizarre, no action was taken. For example, five months before, he was fined $200 (Singapore) for dropping his pants in a pub and daring a group of women to use his cell phone to call the police.

It appears that his ego and the pressure to make more and more profits pushed him in the direction of more risky investments, and he began to make unhedged transactions in which there was no immediate sale or purchase to offset the initial transaction. As a result, since the market was declining, his transactions required funds to meet margin calls. Since he reported not to Bax but rather directly to the head office in London, he contacted the head office, and £454 million was sent in late January and early February.

Somehow, he had convinced them that his operations were safe—but how? It seems that his ability to control the back office provided him the opportunity to do so. Earlier, when he began to trade heavily, the back office was swamped with transactions that included lots of errors made in the trading pits at the stock exchanges. He had been allegedly advised by Gordon Bowser, former derivatives trading chief, to set up a fictitious account, Error Account No. 88888, to put trading problems through and not to send reports to London so that the auditors would not be aroused. Instead, Leeson used the account as the hiding place for his losses—which totaled £2 million in 1992, £23 million in 1993, £208 million by the end of 1994, and £827 million by February 27—after Barings went into receivership. When the computer reports came off the printer for the fake account, Leeson destroyed them.

By happenstance, Anthony Hawes, the treasurer of Barings, visited Singapore. Over a sumptuous lunch on Wednesday, March 22, he told Leeson that he was to get a bonus of at least $2 million (Singapore) on Friday, March 24. In addition, he told Leeson that the bank had a new policy of control and that he wanted to review the backroom operation and check the accounting operation. Pleading that his wife was having a miscarriage and needed him, Leeson rushed from a meeting with Hawes on Thursday and left for Kuala Lumpur. He had evidently realized that the jig was about to be up and he would be caught.

Later, after he was caught, Leeson's wife revealed that the pressure for profits had become too much and that he had begun to take more risks. At the end, he was just trying to make back the losses. Before he was caught, Leeson reportedly phoned a friend from his Malaysian hotel and said, "People senior to me knew exactly the risks I was taking. Lots of people knew.... But it went wrong and now they're trying to lump all the blame on me."[1] Will we ever really know for sure?

Questions

1. How would you deal with a star trader who would be extremely sensitive to additional controls that implied he or she was not trusted or would generate more time on paperwork and explanations?
2. What ethical and accounting controls would you advise ING to institute at Barings?
3. Who was more at fault—top management or Nick Leeson?

Sources: "Leeson Expected to Receive a Light Sentence," *Financial Post*, December 2, 1995, 12.

"Police Hunt Rogue Trader Who Torpedoed Barings," *Financial Post*, February 28, 1995, 3.

"Buyers Circle Barings' Corpse," *Financial Post*, March 1, 1995, 5.

"Death Came Sudden and Swift for Barings," *Financial Post*, March 4, 1995, 6, 7.

"Leeson Says Barings Told Him to Set Up a Secret Account," *Financial Post*, February 14, 1996, 10.

"Ex-Barings Directors Sued by Auditors," *Financial Post*, November 30, 1996, 15.

"Barings Bank Goes Bust in 17 Bn Scam," *Manchester Guardian Weekly*, week ending March 5, 1995, 1.

"Busting the Bank," *The Observer*, March 5, 1995, 23–25.

"Barings' Dutch Master," *The Observer*, March 12, 1995, 8.

"Leeson's Resignation," *Toronto Star*, March 7, 1995, D1.

"Barings Loss Expands 50% as Take-Over Approved," *Toronto Star*, March 7, 1995, D6.

"Barings Saved, but City Faces Inquiry," *Manchester Guardian Weekly*, March 12, 1995, 1.

"Norris Was a Director in Singapore," *The Observer*, March 12, 1995, 1.

[1] "Busting the Bank," *The Observer*, March 5, 1995, 25.

Cases on Product Safety

ETHICS CASE

Dow Corning Silicone Breast Implants

On January 6, 1992, the "growing controversy over the safety factor led the U.S. Food and Drug Administration to call for a moratorium on breast implants."[1] As January wore on, the crisis deepened until, on January 30, the Toronto *Globe and Mail* carried a New York Times Service report titled "Dow Corning Fumbles in Damage Control." Among other critical points, the article stated,

> Regardless of whether Dow Corning Inc. ever convinces regulators its silicone-gel breast implants are safe, the company seems likely to be branded as bungling in its handling of the problem, say public relations and crisis management experts.
>
> "It's a textbook case of crisis management," … "it looks like the lawyers are in charge, trying to limit their liability." "But the damage is much worse to the corporation if they lose in the court of public opinion than if they lose in the court of law."
>
> Consultants concede that, because Dow Corning argues there is little evidence supporting many of the injury claims, it is difficult for the company to act sympathetically without appearing to undermine its legal strategy. (p. B1)

The controversy escalated until, on March 20, one month after the U.S. authorities called for sharply restricted use and their Canadian counterparts opted for a moratorium, Dow Corning canceled its breast implant line. The company also offered up to $1,200 each to women in the United States not covered by private insurance who needed to have their implants removed. In addition, $10 million was to be spent by the company on research into breast implants.[2]

Among the issues raised by this unfortunate controversy is how faulty breast implants could come to be sold by Dow Corning, a company that had been lionized for almost a decade in three Harvard cases for its outstanding ethics program. The basic details of this program[3] are as follows:

> Six managers serve three-year stints on a Business Conduct Committee; each member devotes up to six weeks a year on committee work.

Two members audit every business operation every three years; the panel reviews up to thirty-five locations annually:

> Three-hour reviews are held with up to 35 employees. Committee members use a code of ethics as a framework and encourage employees to raise ethical issues.

Results of audits are reported to a three-member Audit and Social Responsibility Committee of the Board of Directors:[4]

> Interestingly, although the silicone breast implant operation had been audited four times since 1983, and the ethics audit approach had failed to uncover any signs of problems, Jere Marciniak, an area vice president who is chairman of the Conduct

[1] Barnaby Feder, "Dow Corning Fumbles in Damage Control," *The Globe and Mail*, January 30, 1992, 3.

[2] Rob McKenzie, "Dow Cancels Implant Line," *Financial Post*, March 20, 1992, 3.

[3] Further details of the program are described in "Dow Corning Corporation: Business Conduct and Global Values (A)," Harvard Business School case #9-385-018. See also the article by P. E. Murphy, which is a reading in this chapter.

[4] John A. Byrne, "The Best Laid Ethics Programs," *BusinessWeek*, March 9, 1992, 67–69.

Dow Cancels Implant Line

Rob McKenzie

Financial Post, March 20, 1992

Beseiged Dow Corning Corp quit the breast implant business yesterday, offering money to some women in the U.S. who need their implants removed, but leaving Canadian taxpayers to fund any medical costs here.

Bert Miller, president of subsidiary Dow Corning Canada Inc., said the number of medically necessary removals will not be as high as critics expect.

"I honestly don't think it's a huge amount," he said.

Dow Corning insisted its gel-filled sacs are no health hazard.

"Our reasons for not resuming production and sales, therefore, are not related to issues of science or safety, but to the existing condition of the marketplace," Dow Corning chairman and chief executive Keith McKennon said in a statement.

Miller told reporters in Toronto he was "personally quite convinced that there's been no unnecessary risk that wasn't worth the benefit."

He added: "We at Dow Corning stand by our product."

Many women say the company's silicone-gel implants maimed them or caused other health problems, either by leaking or bursting.

On Feb. 20, a panel of the U.S. Food and Drug Administration recommended use of the implants be sharply restricted. In Canada the Department of Health and Welfare has imposed a moratorium on their use.

Dow Corning, a Michigan-based joint venture of Dow Chemical Co. and Corning Inc., sold more than 600,000 breast implants, including an estimated 27,000 in Canada.

Besides ceasing production and sales, the company said it will spend US$10 million on research into breast implants. In the U.S., it will offer up to US$1,200 each to women who for medical reasons need their implants excised, but are not covered by private health insurance.

Miller said such surgery in Canada is covered by health-care programs.

Women who fear their implants will harm them, but as yet show no ill effects, are not eligible for aid.

"If she has no physical manifestation and the implant is not giving any problems, she should be calmed," Miller said.

Bryan Groulx, a manager of business development for the Canadian unit, added: "We're not here to provide unnecessary surgery."

One of Dow Corning's strongest critics, Ottawa consultant and breast-implant expert Dr. Pierre Blais, said yesterday's announcement was "a courageous and an appropriate decision."

Breast implants account for about 1% of Dow Corning's sales.

Committee, has stated that "he has no plans to touch … the ethics program.… 'It will still aid and guide us through this difficult time.'"

Questions

1. Why did the Dow Corning ethics audit program not reveal any concerns about the silicone-gel breast implant line?
2. What are the critical factors necessary to make such an ethics audit program work effectively?
3. Was the announcement on March 20 well advised and ethical?
4. Are there any other ethical dilemmas raised by the case?

Source: "Dow Cancels Implant Line," *Financial Post*, March 20, 1992.

ETHICS CASE

Ford/Firestone Tire Recall

On August 9, 2000, 6.5 million Firestone tires were recalled in the United States.[1] One thousand five hundred and ninety-nine ATX, ATXII, and Wilderness AT tires installed on Ford Explorers were to be replaced at company cost due to evident defects, public outcry, government investigation, and earlier recalls in Venezuela, Malaysia, Thailand, Colombia, Ecuador, and Saudi Arabia. Early estimates of costs of the recall were in the range of $300 to $600 million,[2] but these did not include loss of future revenues due to loss of consumer confidence or costs of future litigation. Further recalls followed.[3] As of September 2001, an estimated 192 deaths and over 500 injuries had been attributed to these tires.[4]

As the prospect of having to recall faulty tires increased, Firestone and Ford had a falling out. Firestone, or Bridgestone/Firestone as it became known, alleged that the Ford Explorer suspension accounted for at least part of the problem. Ford charged that Firestone had failed to advise them of potential problems and provide their data for analysis. Ultimately, both companies were "invited" to face questioning and testify before U.S. Congress and Senate Subcommittees.

Déjà vu, All Over Again

Firestone and Ford had been in recall debacles before.

Firestone had to recall tires in 1977, 1978, and 1980. The 1978 recall was so large (14.5 million units) that it threatened the financial viability of the company. In fact, Bridgestone, a Japanese company and the number3 tire maker in the world, had to rescue Firestone, then the number 2 tire maker, from financial collapse in May 1988. Consequently, although most design and operating decisions preceded the takeover, much of the decision making with regard to the recall in 2000 was under the Bridgestone/Firestone regime. Many Firestone people, however, continued to be involved.

Ford had suffered significantly during the Pinto fires fiasco.[5] Introduced in 1970, the small Pinto would burst into flames when struck from the rear at a speed of twenty-one miles per hour. This was due to a design flaw that permitted the rupturing of the Pinto's gas tank. Many lawsuits persisted until the late 1970s.

Multiple failures of Ford and Firestone people—and of government regulators at the National Highway Traffic Safety Administration (NHTSA) to recognize such problems early and to deal with them effectively—raise interesting questions, including these: Why did the companies get involved in yet another recall debacle? Did the companies and the NHTSA know about the need to investigate and recall the Wilderness tires much earlier

[1] 14.4 million tires were produced, but at the recall date, only 6.5 million were estimated to still be on the road.

[2] Virginia Trial Lawyers Association, "Ford/Firestone Tire Recall Time Line."

[3] Statement of Michael P. Jackson, deputy secretary of transportation, before the Subcommittees on Telecommunications, Trade and Consumer Protection and Oversight and Investigation of the Committee on Energy and Commerce U.S. House of Representatives, June 19, 2001, **http://www.cengagebrain.com**. Jackson advises of the recall details as follows: On August 9, 2000, Firestone recalled all of its ATX and ATX II tires of the P235/75R15 size manufactured since 1991. It also recalled Wilderness AT tires of that size made at its Decatur plant, for a total of 14.4 million tires. On May 22, 2001, Ford announced a tire replacement program that includes all other Firestone Wilderness tires on certain Ford, Mercury, and Mazda sport-utility vehicles and light trucks. This replacement action totals approximately 13 million tires.

[4] National Highway Traffic Safety Administration, "Engineering Analysis Report and Initial Decision Regarding EA00-023: Firestone Wilderness AT Tires," **http://www.cengagebrain.com**.

[5] See the Ford Pinto case in this book for additional information.

than their official investigations began? If not, why not? Did the companies deal with the recall ethically? What lessons can be learned about crisis management?

The key events of the recall are summarized in the accompanying table.

The Safety Problems: Firestone Tire Tread Separation and Ford Explorer Design

The tread separation problem and the related NHTSA findings were summarized in the Executive Summary of NHTSA's Engineering Analysis Report and Initial Decision[6] as follows:

> Belt-leaving-belt tread separations, whether or not accompanied by a loss of air from the tire, reduce the ability of a driver to control the vehicle, particularly when the failure occurs on a rear tire and at high speeds. Such a loss of control can lead to a crash. The likelihood of a crash, and of injuries or fatalities from such a crash, is far greater when the tread separation occurs on a SUV than when it occurs on a pickup truck.
>
> Tread separation claims included in the Firestone claims database involving the recalled and focus tires have been associated with numerous crashes that have led to 74 deaths and over 350 injuries (as of March 2001). Tread separation complaints from all sources included in the ODI consumer complaint database (including the Firestone claims data) that can be identified as involving these tires have reportedly led to 192 deaths and over 500 injuries (as of September 2001).

Ford/Firestone Tire Recall Time Line

November 1978: Firestone recalled 14.5 million of the Firestone 500 series tires after reports of accidents and deaths due to tread separation on steel-belted radial tires.

May 1988: Bridgestone, the world's number 3 tire maker, acquired Firestone, the number 2 tire maker. The takeover rescued Firestone from potential financial collapse due to the 1978 recall.

February 1989: Arvin/Calspan Tire Research Facility of Alexandria, Virginia, an independent research lab hired by Ford, measured the performance of seventeen Firestone tires. The lab reported three belt-edge separation failures of the seventeen tires tested.

March 1990: The Explorer was introduced as a 1991 model. The Explorer was redesigned to its current chassis design in 1995.

1991: Bridgestone/Firestone ATX, ATX II, and Wilderness AT tires became original equipment for the Ford Explorer (1991–2000), Ford Ranger (1991–2000), F-150 truck (1991–1994), Mercury Mountaineer (1996–2000), Mazda Navajo (1991–1994) and B Series pickup truck (1994–2000). Eventually, over 14.4 million tires would be manufactured.

1992: Bridgestone/Firestone began investigating allegations of safety problems with its tires. Ford began receiving complaints regarding Firestone tires on its light-truck models.

1994–1996: The workers at Firestone's Decatur, Illinois, plant went out on strike. Firestone used replacement workers during this period to continue production.

July 1998: State Farm Insurance research analyst Sam Boyden sent an e-mail to the NHTSA reporting twenty-one tread separation cases involving the Firestone ATX tire. Boyden continued to send e-mails to the NHTSA about subsequent Firestone tread separation accidents.

October 1998: Ford noted tread separation problems on Ford Explorers in Venezuela and sent samples to Bridgestone/Firestone for analysis. A Ford-affiliated dealer in Saudi Arabia wrote to Ford Motor Company complaining of problems with Firestone tires.

[6] "Engineering Analysis Report."

Ford/Firestone Tire Recall Time Line *(continued)*

March 12, 1999: A Ford memorandum noted that Ford and Bridgestone/Firestone executives discussed notifying U.S. safety authorities about a planned tire recall in Saudi Arabia. Ford decided to replace the tires overseas without telling federal regulators.

April 1999: The NHTSA's Uniform Tire Grading Report gave Firestone ATX II and Wilderness AT tires the lowest grade on stress test temperature. The overwhelming majority of comparable tires received higher grades. It is believed that overheated tires lead to tread separation.

August 1999: Ford began replacing Firestone tires on Explorers sold in Saudi Arabia after reports of tread separation problems. Ford did not report the safety concerns but called the replacement program a "customer notification enhancement action."

January 19, 2000: Internal documents showed that Firestone executives knew about rising warranty costs due to accidents caused by the ATX, ATX II, and the Wilderness AT tires.

February 2000: Houston, Texas, TV station KHOU does a story on tread separation of Firestone tires used on Ford Explorers. The TV station gives the NHTSA's 800 telephone number for consumers to report complaints. Consumers start calling in with reports of tread separations of Firestone tires.

March 6, 2000: Based on the information the NHTSA received, primarily from complaints stemming from the Houston, Texas, TV story, the agency begins its initial evaluation of Firestone Tires.

May 2000: Ford changed Explorer's standard equipment to Goodyear tires in Venezuela while waiting for Firestone to come to a resolution regarding the tire separation problems. Ford recalled Firestone tires in Malaysia, Thailand, Colombia, and Ecuador. The entire overseas recall reached 46,912 sport-utility vehicles.

May 2/8, 2000: The NHTSA launched a formal investigation (PE-0020) into the tread separation cases involving the Firestone ATX and Wilderness tires.

May 10, 2000: The NHTSA sends letters to Ford and Firestone requesting information in connection with PE-0020.

June 8, 2000: Ford requests that Firestone provide all information that they gave to the NHTSA relating to PE-0020. This information includes the claims data that will demonstrate the high accident rate of the tires.

July 28, 2000: Ford receives Firestone's information, and begins an analysis.

August 4, 2000: Ford found a pattern in the data pointing to the fifteen-inch ATX, ATX II, and Wilderness AT tires made at the Decatur, Illinois, plant and called in the Firestone experts. They found that older tires produced late in each production year from 1994 to 1996 had a higher failure rate.

August 9, 2000: Bridgestone/Firestone announced a region-by-region recall of more than 6.5 million AT, ATX II, and Wilderness AT tires. Approximately 2 million Ford Explorers were named as subjects to the recall. The cost estimate for the recall ranged from $300 million to $600 million. The hot-weather regions were scheduled for tire replacement first, with other regions to follow. The NHTSA reports that Firestone tire separations were responsible for forty-six deaths.

August 10, 2000: Plaintiff attorneys involved with Firestone litigation over the past decade note they know of 107 related tire cases, with ninety of those having a direct link to the recalled tires.

August 10, 2000: Ford claimed it became aware of the tire separation problem one year ago from anecdotal reports from Saudi Arabia.

August 16, 2000: The NHTSA increased the number of deaths connected to the Firestone tread separations to sixty-two.

September 1, 2000: The NHTSA announced another twenty-four Firestone tire models showed rates of tread separation exceeding those of the recalled tires. The NHTSA also increased the estimate of deaths attributed to Firestone tires from sixty-two to eighty-eight. Venezuelan authorities report that at least forty-seven people died because of the Firestone tires.

"Ford/Firestone Tire Recall Time Line," Virginia Trial @ Lawyers Association, **http://www.cengagebrain.com**; "Firestone Tire Recall Timeline," Democratic Staff of the Commerce Committee, **http://www.cengagebrain.com**.

The belt-leaving-belt tread separations in the recalled and focus tires generally occur only after several years of operation. Thus, since the focus tires have not been on the road as long as the recalled ATX tires, the absolute number of failures of those tires, and the unadjusted failure rate of those tires, are less than those of comparable ATX tires. Claims in the Firestone claims database involving the focus tires have been associated with 17 deaths and 41 injuries, with additional crashes and casualties reported in the ODI complaint database, including reports of six additional fatalities. However, on a plant-by-plant basis, the focus tires manufactured at the Wilson and Joliette plants have exhibited tread separation failure trends that are similar to those experienced by the recalled ATX tires at similar service intervals.

These failure trends indicate that it is likely that, if they are not removed from service, the focus tires—at least those manufactured before May 1998—will experience a similar increase in tread separation failures over the next few years, leading to a substantial number of future crashes, injuries, and deaths. The tread separation failure experience of the focus tires is far worse than that of their peers, especially that of the Goodyear Wrangler RT/S tires used as original equipment on many Ford Explorers.

The belt-leaving-belt tread separations that have occurred and are continuing to occur in the recalled and focus tires begin as belt-edge separation at the edge of the second, or top, belt. This is the area of highest strain in a steel belted radial tire and is a region with relatively poor cord-to-rubber adhesion because bare steel is exposed at the cut ends of the cords. Once belt-edge separations have initiated, they can grow circumferentially and laterally along the edge of the second belt and develop into cracks between the belts. If they grow large enough, they can result in catastrophic tread detachment, particularly at high speeds, when the centrifugal forces acting on the tire are greatest.

ODI conducted a non-destructive analysis of numerous randomly collected focus tires and peer tires from southern states, where most of the failures have occurred, using shearography, which can detect separations inside a tire. This shearography analysis demonstrated that the patterns and levels of cracks and separations between the belts were far more severe in the focus tires than in peer tires.

Many of the focus tires that were examined were in the later stages of failure progression prior to complete separation of the upper belt. The shearography results for tires manufactured at Wilson were similar to those manufactured at Joliette.

A critical design feature used by tire manufacturers to suppress the initiation and growth of belt-edge cracks is the "belt wedge," a strip of rubber located between the two belts near the belt edges on each side of the tire. The belt wedge thickness, or gauge, in the ATX tires and the Wilderness AT tires produced prior to May 1998 is generally narrower than the wedge gauge in peer tires, and the wedge gauge in cured tires was often less than Firestone's target for this dimension. The tires with this wedge did not adequately resist the initiation and propagation of belt-edge cracks between the steel belts. During March and April 1998, Firestone changed the material composition and increased the gauge of the wedge in its Wilderness AT tires (and some other tire models).

Another important feature of radial tires related to the prevention of belt-leaving-belt separations is the gauge of the rubber between the two steel belts, or "inter-belt gauge." The inter-belt gauge initially specified by Firestone for the focus tires is generally narrower than the inter-belt gauges in peer tires and is narrower than Firestone's original specification for the ATX tires in the early 1990s. Moreover, the actual measured gauge under the tread grooves in several of the focus tires measured by ODI was far less than Firestone's minimum design specification. Since an inadequate inter-belt gauge reduces the tire's resistance to crack growth and its belt adhesion capabilities, this narrow inter-belt gauge may be partially responsible for the relatively low peel adhesion properties of the focus tires compared to peer tires. In August 1999, after becoming concerned about the adequacy of the inter-belt gauge in the cured Wilderness AT tires, especially in the regions directly under the tread grooves, Firestone changed the inter-belt gauge specification back to the original dimension.

Another relevant feature is the design of the shoulder pocket of the focus tires, which can cause higher stresses at the belt edge and lead to a narrowing, or "pinching," of the wedge gauge at the pocket. The focus tires exhibit a series of weak spots around the tire's circumference, leading to the initiation and growth of cracks earlier than in competitor tires and in other Firestone tires produced for light trucks and SUVs. In addition, many of the focus tires exhibited shoulder pocket cracking similar to that which Firestone identified as a significant contributor to the risk of tread detachment in the recalled ATX tires.

Because the tread separations at issue in this investigation occur only after several years of exposure, almost all of the failures on which ODI's analysis of field experience was based involved tires manufactured before May 1998, when Firestone increased the dimensions and improved the material of the belt wedge. In theory, these modifications to the wedge would tend to inhibit the initiation and propagation of the belt-edge cracks that lead to tread separations. If these modifications actually improved the resistance of the focus tires to belt-edge separations, the historical failure trends described above may not predict the future performance of the newer tires. However, because tread separation failures rarely occur in the focus tires until at least three years of use, it is not now possible to ascertain from field experience whether their actual performance has improved significantly.

The rate of tread separation failures on Ranger pickups is lower than the rate of such failures on Explorers for a variety of reasons, including the fact that the Explorer generally carries higher loads and is a more demanding application, and the tires on the Explorer had a significantly lower recommended inflation pressure (especially on the rear wheels). The risk of such a separation on Rangers remains a cause for possible concern. Nevertheless, because the likelihood of a crash due to a tread separation, and of deaths and injuries resulting from such a crash, is substantially lower when the separation occurs on a pickup than on a SUV, NHTSA's initial defect decision does not apply to focus tires installed on pickup trucks.

Under the National Traffic and Motor Vehicle Safety Act, in order to compel a manufacturer to conduct a recall, NHTSA has the burden of proving that a safety-related defect

> exists in the manufacturer's products. The record of this investigation supports a determination that a safety-related defect exists in the focus tires manufactured by Firestone prior to its 1998 modifications to the belt wedge that are installed on SUVs. Although the agency has concerns about the possibility of future tread separations in focus tires manufactured after the wedge change, the available evidence at this time does not clearly demonstrate that a safety-related defect exists in those focus tires. NHTSA will, however, continue to closely monitor the performance of these tires.
>
> Therefore, on the basis of the information developed during the ODI investigation, NHTSA has made an initial decision that a safety-related defect exists in Firestone Wilderness AT P235/75R15 and P255/70R16 tires manufactured to the Ford specifications prior to May 1998 that are installed on SUVs. These tires were manufactured primarily at Wilson and Joliette and, to a lesser extent, at Oklahoma City. The initial decision does not apply to the P255/70R16 tires produced at Decatur or any of the Wilderness AT tires produced at Aiken, since these tires were all manufactured after May 1998.

At the request of Bridgestone/Firestone's chairman, the NHTSA also investigated the claims that the Ford Explorer had a design defect, probably in its suspension, that contributed to the tread separation in Wilderness tires. In his Statement to the U.S. congressional committees, the NHTSA's deputy secretary, Michael P. Jackson, commented that "NHTSA has had no credible evidence that the Ford Explorer's design is in any way responsible for *causing* tread separation or other such catastrophic tire failure."[7]

When Did the Companies Know of Problems, and What Did They Do About Them?

According to the time line information, both Ford and Firestone received information about tire tread separations as early as 1992. These investigations may have been limited in some way, perhaps focused on or influenced by legal liability considerations. In any event, they do not appear to have raised "red flags" for Ford or Firestone such that either company was actively following up looking for further evidence.

Actually, Ford had received an earlier warning in February 1989, when an independent testing lab it hired found that three of seventeen tires tested had tread separations. Again, this information does not appear to have been carried forward as part of an ongoing formal risk assessment program.

Interestingly, in 1992, Ford chose the P235 tires, which were later recalled, over the smaller P225 tires, which had tested better in turning (a prelude to rollover) tests. A memo shows that Ford management was aware of the potential risk. Moreover, in order to improve the stability of the Explorer, Ford lowered the recommended tire pressure to 26 p.s.i. from the normal 30–35 p.s.i. that Firestone usually recommended. Firestone later insisted that this low pressure recommendation increased tire heat and caused the tire separations. At the time, however, Firestone went along; when Ford found that the mushier tires worsened fuel economy and asked for a fix, Firestone reduced the tire weight by about 3%.[8]

Unlike General Motors, which has their own in-house tire safety and research unit,[9]

---

[7] Statement of Michael P. Jackson.

[8] John Greenwald, "Inside the Ford/Firestone Fight," *Time Online Edition*, May 29, 2001, **http://www.cengagebrain.com**.

[9] Information from a student.

neither Ford nor Firestone had an ongoing tire safety, testing, and database analysis program. Perhaps, if they had, they would have been aware of and following the work of Sam Boyden, the State Farm insurance analyst who began to e-mail the NHTSA and have person-to-person conversations with the NHTSA about Firestone tire problems in July 1998. Unfortunately, these e-mails and conversations do not appear to have been followed up until May 2, 2000, when the official investigation started. Even the NHTSA has admitted that they did not have an ongoing database project. Ford had to wait for Firestone to send them data, and Firestone initially had only cursory warranty data and needed to build a more comprehensive and useful data set. The NHTSA had to assemble data from various sources, including the companies, as well. Neither of the companies nor the NHTSA were putting together a complete picture on an ongoing basis—they were all reacting, focused on short-term concerns, and using makeshift resources.

Ford and Firestone became aware of tire failures in warm climates in October 1998. The companies discussed the problems and Ford proposed a recall in Saudi Arabia. According to an internal Ford memo dated March 12, 1999, Firestone had asked Ford to handle it on a case-by-case basis so that the U.S. Department of Transportation would not have to be notified and so that the Saudi government would not overreact.[10] Ford had apparently told Firestone that the recall should be reported since the tires were also sold in the United States but ultimately did not do so. Later, Ford maintained that it was not obligated to report the foreign recalls to U.S. regulators.[11]

Ford asked Firestone to do some tests in November 1999. These tests, which became known as the "Southwest Study," were completed in April 2000, but no evidence of a problem was discovered.[12]

Ultimately, when facing inflamed public reactions in specific locales to mounting accidents and deaths, Ford recalled Firestone tires in Saudi Arabia, Venezuela, and four other countries between June 1999 and May 2000. Firestone continued to advise Ford that there were no problems with the tires and that recalls were unwarranted. Note that these recalls were undertaken before recalling the same tires in North America—a fact not lost on consumers and commentators when the salient facts began to surface.

A TV station in Houston, Texas, KHOU, aired a 10-minute story on the tread separations on tires on Ford Explorers in February 2000. They gave the 800 telephone number for the NHTSA, and complaints started to roll in. The news secrecy bubble had finally burst in the United States, and on March 6, the NHTSA began its initial evaluation of Firestone tires.[13] Subsequent analysis of Firestone warranty claims and other data showed a high accident rate for the tires and led to the recall on August 9. Again, actions were in response to public pressure.

Findings were ultimately identified, in part, from Firestone warranty data that could have been assessed much earlier. Whose responsibility should that have been? Who would have benefited? On Friday, July 28, 2000, Ford engineers picked up the Firestone warranty data and then set up a "war room" at Ford headquarters in Dearborn, Michigan.[14] Working with

[10] Stephen Power, "Tire Check: The Recall Rolls On: Bridgestone Fretted about Replacements," *Wall Street Journal*, September 6, 2000.

[11] Ibid.

[12] Democratic Staff of the Commerce Committee, "Firestone Tire Recall Timeline," **http://www.cengagebrain.com**.

[13] Ibid.

[14] Robert L. Simison et al., "Blowout: How the Tire Problem Turned into a Crisis for Firestone and Ford—Lack of a Database Masked the Pattern That Led to Yesterday's Big Recall—The Heat and the Pressure," *Wall Street Journal*, August 10, 2000.

Firestone personnel, after ten long days the investigators decided that "the problem tires appear[ed] to have come from the plant in Decatur, Ill., during specific periods of production. The bulk of the tire-separation incidents had occurred in hot states: Arizona, California, Florida and Texas. This correlated with information from overseas."[15]

"The rate of warranty claims on tires for Explorers surged in the mid-1990s, and the bulk of them involved tires made at Decatur. For the three years from 1994 through 1996, tread-separation claims attributed to ATX tires produced at the Decatur plant came in at rates ranging from roughly 350 to more than 600 tires per million. During the same years, tires of the same model produced at all other Firestone plants had claim rates of 100 per million tires."[16]

At least two factors may have contributed to these higher tread separation rates at Decatur. First, in preparation for a product liability suit in Florida, a retired worker has sworn that he saw inspectors pass tires without inspecting them on a daily basis in 1993 and 1994.[17] Second, Firestone used 2,300 scab or replacement workers when United Rubber Workers local 713 went on strike from 1994 to 1996. After the very acrimonious strike was settled, Firestone made the scab workers permanent hires.[18] An interesting question remains: Did Firestone fully appreciate and manage these risks effectively?

Misunderstanding the Risks

Perhaps the tread separation problems were found earlier and actions were suppressed in the United States due to concerns over potential legal ramifications and ensuing costs. Unfortunately, this is probably a correct line of reasoning, and it reflects an erroneous understanding of the significant risks of delay in dealing with a product safety matter.

Specifically, delay in dealing with a product safety matter can lead to a serious erosion of reputation and confidence among customers and result in a loss of future revenues and profits. Frequently, the cost of opportunities lost is the largest item to be taken into account in a cost–benefit analysis of the decision to recall a product. Moreover, failing to remedy a problem at the earliest point of recognition can lead to an inflation of the number of claims and the cost of satisfying them. If the executives had seen the cost–benefit analysis in the accompanying table, they would have seen the logic in speeding up their analysis and recognition of the tread separation problem.

Using an Ethical Decision-Making Framework

Had Ford and Firestone executives used an ethical decision-making framework such as those discussed in Chapter 5, they would have recognized the risks allowing legal defense strategy to dominate their thinking. Moreover, they might have considered the application of alternative remedies, such as the use of a nylon cap or safety layer between the steel belts and tread to keep the ends of the belts from chafing the tread rubber and contributing to tread separation. The nylon cap was apparently used in late-production Firestone tires in Venezuela at a cost of $1 per tire. According to engineers, the

[15] Ibid.

[16] Timothy Aeppel et al., "Road Signs: How Ford, Firestone Let The Warnings Slide by as Debacle Developed—Their Separate Goals, Gaps in Communication Gave Rise to Risky Situation—Bucking the Bronco Legacy," *Wall Street Journal*, September 6, 2000.

[17] Ibid.

[18] James R. Healey and Sara Nathan, "Could $1 Worth of Nylon Have Saved People's Lives? Experts: Caps on Steel Belts May Have Stopped Shredded Tires," *USA Today*, August 9, 2000.

extra cost was the only reason not to use them widely.[19] Bridgestone does use them on some tire lines, as does Pirelli on nearly all of its U.S.-market tires.[20]

The Aftermath

Not surprisingly, the sales of Ford Explorers dropped, as did Firestone's sales. In Venezuela, for example, Ford

Bridgestone's Stock Chart

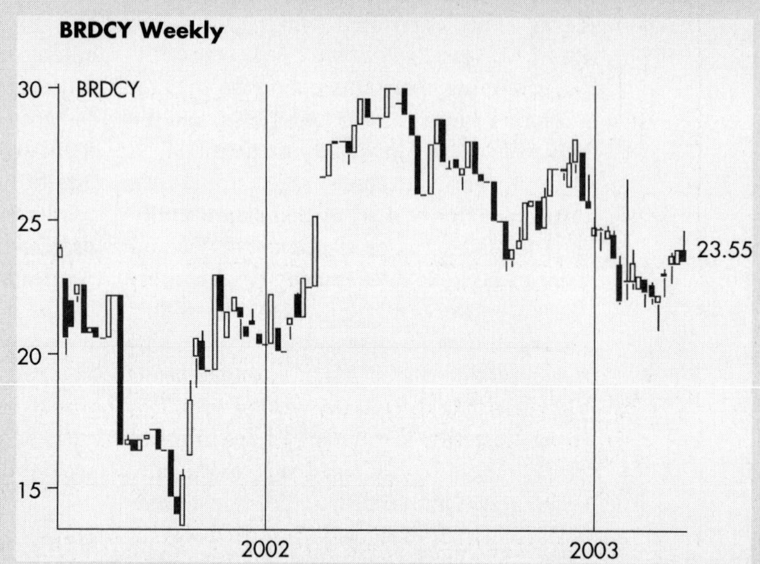

Ford's Stock Chart

[19] Ibid.

[20] Ibid.

Cost-Benefit Analysis of Decision to Use a Nylon Cap Safety Layer

	BENEFITS	
SAVINGS	**UNIT COST**	**TOTAL**
203 deaths[1]	$977,000	$198,331,000
700 injuries[2]	$327,925	229,547,500
Avoid legal fees & settlements		
Avoid recalling tires		
Avoid damage to reputation[3]		1,272,121,500
Total Benefits		$1,700,000,000
	COSTS	
COST	**UNIT COST**	**TOTAL**
Nylon Safety Cap for 10,000,000 recalled tires[4]	$1	10,000,000
Total Costs		$10,000,000

[1]The unit cost of death was obtained from an NHTSA study in 2000 on "The Economic Impact of Motor Vehicle Crashes" (see **http://www.cengagebrain.com**).
[2]The unit cost of injury was determined by applying the percentage cost of injury/death in 1971 from the Ford Pinto case ($67,000/$200,000 = 33.5%) to the unit cost of death estimated by the NHTSA survey from 2000: $977,000 × 33.5% = $327,295.
[3]The investment banking firm of UBS Warburg estimated that the tire problems could cost Firestone and Ford between $719 million and $2.7 billion. We assumed the total cost to be $1.7 billion (a number in the middle). Therefore, since we know the total cost to Ford & Firestone is $1.7 billion, we can calculate the residual amount to be allocated to the avoidance of legal fees, settlement fees, cost of recalling tires, and the cost of the loss of reputation: $1,700,000,000 − $427,878,500 = $1,272,121,500 (see **http://www.cengagebrain.com**).
[4]An article written in *USA Today* on August 9, 2000, by James R. Healey & Sara Nathan, proposed that a nylon safety cap could have prevented the tread separation problem. The article states that a nylon safety layer between the steel belts and the tread would keep the ends of the belts from chafing the tread rubber and contributing to tread separation. The article also cited that affidavits from tire engineers said that cost is the only reason not to use them. The estimated cost was $1 per tire to cover the radial piles with a nylon cap. We determined the number of tires affected as follows:

August 9, 2000	6.5 million tires were recalled
September 4, 2000	3.5 million additional tires were recalled
Total recalled	10.0 million

Source: Master of Management & Professional Accounting (MMPA) degree students at the Rotman School of Management, University of Toronto: Meghan Davis, Theresa Yim, Paul Spitzen, Michael Krofchick, and Katy Yeung. Group project, Fall 2002.

Explorer sales dropped 37% in 2000. In December 2000, Saudi Arabia banned new and used vehicles with Firestone tires. Firestone announced that it believed the ban was unjustified.

Both the U.S. Congress and Senate held hearings, and a new act was passed on October 11, 2000, called the *Transportation Recall Enhancement, Accountability, and Documentation Act*. The act does the following:

- Strengthens the reporting requirements for manufacturers of motor vehicles and motor vehicle equipment (including the reporting of defects first discovered in a foreign country)
- Increases the civil penalties for violations of safety regulations (e.g., fines for certain violations of Title 49 were raised from $1,000 to $5,000 for each violation, and the maximum penalty for a related series of violations was raised from $800,000 to $15,000,000)
- Provides additional criminal penalties (e.g., for any knowing and willful false statement that was intended to mislead NHTSA with respect to a defect that

causes death or grievous bodily harm, the possible prison term was raised from five years to 15)

- Requires NHTSA to revise and update its safety standards for tires
- Increases the number of years that a defect must be remedied without charge to the owner (from three years to five for tires)
- Increases the authorization for funding the NHTSA
- Requires the secretary of transportation to report to Congress within a year on the criteria, procedures, and methods that the NHTSA uses in determining whether to open an investigation of a possible defect
- Contains other safety-related provisions[21]

Questions

1. Why didn't Ford and Firestone learn from their past recall debacles?
2. Why did Ford, Firestone, and the NHTSA not discover the nature and seriousness of the tread-separation, product-liability problem earlier?
3. Why did Ford or Firestone not report the problem to U.S. authorities earlier?
4. Ultimately, which was the largest cost to Ford and Firestone: fines, lawsuit settlements, or the loss of reputation leading to loss of future revenue and profits?
5. What errors should be corrected in the cost–benefit analysis presented?
6. What were the ethical risks, if any, involved in this tire recall situation?
7. If you were advising Ford and Bridgestone, what should each include in their risk management program?

[21] United States Republican Policy Committee, "Lawyer's Silence and Highway Deaths," July 9, 2001, **http://www.cengagebrain.com.**

Alternative Governance Theories APPENDIX A

A Traditional Governance Model—Agency Theory

Agency theory is an attempt to explain organizational behavior and, in particular, corporate governance structures based on the premise that there is an inherent conflict of interest between principals (who own the firm) and agents (who manage the firm). From this principle of a conflict of interest, it develops a comprehensive theory that addresses the importance of contracts, both formal and informal and both written and tacit, that are used in monitoring, controlling, and motivating managerial behavior. It also explains the importance of financial reporting.

Agency theory is grounded on the concept of self-interest; this is not the cooperative self-interest of Thomas Hobbes and Adam Smith that leads to civil society and economic prosperity.[1] Rather, it is self-interest in a noncooperative fashion where the interest of the managers of the firm are not always aligned with the interest of the owners of the firm. Both investors and managers are interested in maximizing their personal utility. Investors want a reasonable return on their investment either in terms of stock price appreciation resulting in a capital gain or in terms of cash distributions from the firm through dividends. Management, by contrast, is interested in compensation. Managers are motivated through self-interest to do a good job and learn new managerial skills so that they can either receive more pay or move to another job where they can receive higher compensation. Agency theory makes the simplifying assumption that managers are motivated only by extrinsic tangible monetary-based rewards, such as direct cash compensation through regular pay and bonuses and indirect compensation through fringe benefits, such as pension plans, medical care, and stock options.

In a sole proprietorship, the owner of the business is also its manager. They are one in the same. However, in corporations, especially in large publicly traded companies, there is clear separation of ownership from control. The owners (called principals) have no desire to operate the firm; they simply want to earn a reasonable return on their investment. So, they hire and then delegate to management (the agent) the responsibility for operating the firm on the investors' behalf. Because they control the daily operations of the firm, management knows or has access to all the information about the firm. The investors, on the other hand, only know what they are told by management, normally through periodic financial statements and the annual report. As such, there is a huge information asymmetry problem. Although they are the owners of the firm, they really do not know what is happening at their firm. This gives rise to two potential problems: adverse selection and moral hazard. Both of these problems occur because agency theory assumes that the manager will always act opportunistically; that is, when valid options are available, the manager will choose the option that is in the best interest of management, even when that option might not be in the best interest of the investors.

Adverse selection occurs because management has better or more complete information about the firm than the investors. As such, management can make investment and credit decisions that may be profitable to managers but not to investors. A prime example is insider trading. Before management releases a piece of bad news that will negatively affect the price of the firm's stock, management might short the

[1] For the ethical theories of Hobbes and Smith, see Chapter 3.

stock and then buy the stock after the price falls. Management profits through a capital gain based on insider knowledge. This is why there are laws to prevent insider trading.

Moral hazard occurs because managerial behavior cannot be observed. All the investors see the consequences of the decisions of management. As such, managers can shirk. They can avoid putting in effort without being detected by the investors. For example, all other things being equal, investors would prefer to see high net income rather than low net income. However, management, who choose and implement the accounting policies of the firm, can artificially increase income by judiciously selecting specific income-increasing accounting policies. For example, straight-line amortization of long-life assets tends to show a lower expense in the early years of the assets' lives than double-declining balance. So, although neither policy has an impact on the cash flows of the firm, the straight-line method reports a lower expense and therefore a higher net income than the double-declining method. Management can also adjust discretionary accruals in order to manage reported earnings. Any accounting estimate that is determined by management, such as the allowance for doubtful accounts, inventory obsolescence, and the provision for warranty expense, can be selected opportunistically in order to manipulate the reported earnings of the firm without altering the firm's actual cash flows. These discretionary accruals are not separately disclosed in the firm's set of financial statements, so this form of managerial opportunism is not readily apparent to investors. Their manipulations cannot readily be observed by the investors.

In order to minimize the problems associated with moral hazard and adverse selection, investors implement various control mechanisms. The two most common are monitoring and bonding. Monitoring can occur by having the internal auditors check to ensure that the firm's control structures are operating efficiently and effectively. External accountants are hired by the investor to review and report on the financial statements that are prepared by management. But it is the board of directors that act as the key monitoring mechanism in most firms. The board represents all the investors. The board is to ensure that the decisions of management are in the best long-term interests of the firm and its owners. It does this by monitoring management and in particular by selecting and overseeing the CEO. However, monitoring can be costly and not always effective. Enron had a blue-ribbon board of directors, yet they failed to oversee and govern correctly.[2]

Bonding occurs through management compensation contracts. The idea is that a contract can be written to align the interest of management with those of the investor. For example, the investor is interested in a high net income. So, if the managers are given a share of the reported earnings, then they might be motivated to work very hard on the investors' behalf to increase reported earnings. Another contract might be to give management stock options. If management owns a piece of the firm, then their interests as investors of the firm should be the same as the other investors of the firm. Because their interests are now aligned, managers will make decisions that are in the best interests of the investors.

There are obvious problems with this line of reasoning. First, management can increase net income without expending any effort by simply changing the accounting policies. Second, stock options can be abused and be quite costly to the other shareholders. After they exercise their options, managers rarely continue to hold their firm's stock. They prefer to obtain a capital gain and then use the proceeds

[2] See Chapter 2 for a richer analysis of the failure of the Board of Directors to govern Enron adequately and the inability of Arthur Anderson to objectively assess Enron's financial statements.

to purchase a diversified portfolio, thereby mitigating their investment risk. Furthermore, prior to stock options being required to be reported as an expense in 2005, generous stock options were granted to employees on the basis that they were costless. In December 1997, Michael Eisner, then CEO of Disney Corporation, exercised stock options for $570 million. This was not recorded as an expense for Disney, but it was a cost to the other shareholders in terms of the dilution of their ownership by the amount of the options given to Eisner. This was not a costless transaction for the owners of Disney stock.

The primary weakness of agency theory is that it has a very narrow focus concerning human behavior. It views business activity as being conducted between atomistic principals and agents operating outside of a social context. Yet business is also a social activity conducted in a cooperative yet competitive manner as explained by Adam Smith.[3] People find satisfaction in work and an opportunity to utilize the skills and talents in a productive manner that contributes to their own well-being and, through the invisible hand, to the betterment of society. Stewardship Theory captures the social and cooperative aspects of work. The differences between Agency Theory and Stewardship Theory are identified in Table 5.24.

A More Holistic Approach to Governance—Stewardship Theory

Stewardship theory assumes no inherent conflict between principals and agents, between employees and investors, or between subordinates and their supervisors. There is no trade-off between personal needs and organizational needs. Stewards identify with the goals of the firm and strive to make sure those goals are achieved. The steward's interests are aligned with those of the investor, so the steward is less apt to engage in self-serving behaviors and actions that transfer wealth from the investor to the

TABLE 5.24 Comparison of Agency Theory & Stewardship Theory

	AGENCY THEORY	STEWARDSHIP THEORY
View of the individual	Economic agent	Complex and modern
Behavioral assumptions	Opportunistic wealth maximizer	Holistic and rounded view of human nature
Behavioral characteristics	• self-serving—employees will choose the options that are in their own best interests • Risk-averse—there is an increasing disutility for wealth • Effort-averse—employees will shirk	• Want to contribute • Will choose to do right • Strive to achieve • Like to innovate • Want to do competent work • Interested in a work—life balance
Management philosophy	Control-oriented	Involvement-oriented
Motivation	Extrinsic rewards	More intrinsic than extrinsic rewards
Organizational identification	Low value commitment	High Commitment
Trust	Low—employees are work-averse and so they will shirk	High—stewards have an inherent preference for honesty

Sources: James H. Davis, F. David Schoorman, and Lex Donaldson, "Toward a Stewardship Theory of Management," *Academy of Management Review* 22, no. 1 (1997): 20–47; Steven E. Salterio and Alan Webb, "Honesty in Accounting and Control: A Discussion of 'The Effect of Information Systems on Honesty in Managerial Reporting: A Behavioral Perspective,'" *Contemporary Accounting Research* 23, no. 4 (2006): 919–32.

[3] See Chapter 3 for a discussion of the importance of cooperation in economics, as per Adam Smith.

steward. As such, there is a lower need for monitoring and control mechanisms. Instead, in a stewardship environment, there is more emphasis placed on empowerment and structures that facilitate cooperative activities in a nonadversarial fashion.

Stewardship theory recognizes that there is often a very strong relationship between the success of the firm and the personal needs of the employees. Stewards take pride and satisfaction in working for the firm and share vicariously in the success and failures of the firm as well as the steward's coworkers. Employees proudly wear their firm's company logo on their clothing, while saying, "We just landed this great contract with a new supplier" even though they had no part in the contract negotiations.

Managers, under agency theory, are motivated by extrinsic monetary rewards. Stewards are motivated by both intrinsic and extrinsic rewards. Intrinsic rewards include recognition, advancement, growth, and the opportunity to learn and to become self-actualized. However, stewards normally want more intrinsic rewards than extrinsic ones. A survey of public accountants in Canada revealed that most were interested in interesting work that is intellectually challenging.[4] The number one workplace priority for those surveyed was interesting work, followed by intellectual challenge and then a good corporate culture. Of the top twelve priorities, high compensation (number four) and job security (number eight) were the only extrinsic rewards mentioned as being a priority. Canadian public accountants appear to be more aligned with stewardship than agency theory.

Most people acknowledge that there is an interdependent and interpenetrating relationship between business and society. Each influences and in turn is influenced by the other. The activities of business influence public policy, which in turn influences business. For example, the Enron and WorldCom debacles lead to Congress passing SOX in the United States. The rules and restrictions of SOX have, in turn, influenced business behavior, as mentioned in Chapter 2.

Stewardship theory acknowledges this interpenetrating relationship and sees an interconnectedness among the individual, his or her work, and society. It has a more holistic concept of the individual and the individual's place in business and society. Stewards want to contribute to the success and well-being of their firm. They also want to contribute to the success and well-being of society. They see no separation between these two activities. This may be why so many people want to work for socially responsible firms. An online survey in 2006 by Care2[5] of nearly 1,600 people revealed the following:

- 73% said that working for a socially responsible company was very important.
- 48% said that they would work for less pay if they could work for a socially responsible company.
- 40% said that they would work longer hours if they worked for a socially responsible company.

These are all aspects of a stewardship perspective that contends that that employees want to contribute to the success of their employer's business while at the same time contributing to the well-being of society.

The natural extension of this stewardship perspective into corporate governance was originally incorporated into the laissez-faire type of approach known as the original Carver model[6] of board governance, which was based on boards of directors

---

[4] See "What CAs Want," *CAMagazine*, August 2007, http://www.camagazine.com/index.cfm/ci_id/38627/la_id/1.

[5] See "Socially Responsible Companies Rank High with Job Seekers," January 31, 2006, press release by Care2, http://www.care2.com/aboutus/080206.html.

[6] See John Carver, *Boards That Make a Difference*, 2nd ed. (San Francisco: Jossey-Bass, 1997), or visit http://www.carvergovernance.com.

hiring the CEO and approving organizational policy but essentially delegating ongoing monitoring to the CEO. However, many of those who subscribed to this approach found that the ethics and operational risks of "governance by policy"—of divorcing the board from ongoing monitoring—were too high, and a revised Carver model was developed.

It is evident that the agency model—of top-down control that monitors opportunistic agents—still has a role to play today. The examples of unbridled greed and abuses of managerial power by unaccountable executives at Enron, WorldCom, Adelphia Communications, and Parmalat SpA illustrate the need for improved corporate governance structures. But the existence of rogue managers should not be used to stifle the creativity of other managers who have a stewardship perspective.

New governance structures are needed that balance the need for control with the need to create an innovative environment where talented managers can increase firm value in an ethically and socially responsible manner. This means that perspectives must be broadened. The firm is more than simply investors and managers. There are a variety of other stakeholders who have an interest, or stake, in the firm, and their interests cannot be ignored. The lessons of the last few years have shown that corporations are strategically accountable to numerous stakeholder groups, not only to shareholders. New perspectives on governance and accountability are required to meet this challenge.

6

Professional Accounting in the Public Interest

PURPOSE OF THE CHAPTER

Professional accounting has been challenged frequently by specific incidents to demonstrate that it is providing the fiduciary services that investors and the public expect. On several occasions, these challenges or expectations gaps have resulted in a crisis of credibility that caused the profession or regulating authorities to resolve by requiring more stringent ethical guidance. When the Enron, Arthur Andersen, and WorldCom debacles triggered the U.S. *Sarbanes-Oxley Act of 2002* (SOX), a new era of stakeholder expectations was crystallized for the business world and particularly for the professional accountants that serve in it. The drift away from the professional accountant's role as a fiduciary to that of a businessperson was called into question and reversed. The principles that the new expectations spawned and renewed resulted in changes in how the professional accountants are to behave, what services are to be offered, and what performance standards are to be met. These standards have been embedded in a new governance structure and in guidance mechanisms, which have domestic and international components.

In addition, the drive toward globalized standards was also an effort to eliminate the credibility gap and to restore the reputation of professional accountants worldwide. Looking forward, the influence of the International Accounting Standards Board (IASB) and the International Federation of Accountants (IFAC) will be as important as that of SOX in the long run because professional accounting bodies governing CPAs and CAs around the world are harmonizing their standards and codes of ethics to IASB and IFAC pronouncements.

This chapter examines each of these developments and provides insights into important areas of current and future practice. Building on the understanding of the new stakeholder accountability framework facing clients and employers developed in earlier chapters, this chapter explores public expectations for the role of the professional accountant and the principles that should be observed in discharging that role. This leads to consideration of the implications for services to be offered and of the key "value added" or competitive edge that accountants should focus their attention on to maintain their reputation, legitimacy, and vitality. Sources of ethical governance and guidance, including the IFAC, the American Institute of Certified Public Accountants (AICPA), and the Chartered Professional Accountants of Ontario (CPA Ontario or CPAO) codes of conduct, are also discussed.

PROFESSIONAL ACCOUNTING'S TRADITIONAL ROLE

Traditionally, a professional accountant has been expected to be an expert in the preparation, analysis, interpretation, and use of financial statements. But *professionalism involves much more than knowing how to work with financial data.* Since financial statements involve many estimates and choices between alternative values, procedures, and disclosures, *a professional accountant must apply professional judgment in making those choices in order to increase the credibility of the financial statements and protect the interests of the public. Professional judgment, in turn, depends on an understanding of professional thinking on right and wrong behavior as described in professional standards and embodied in professional practices.*

Professional behavior, as a result, depends on an understanding of what is expected, plus having the courage to choose alternatives based on how they lend credibility to financial data and its use and on the utility with which they serve the interest of the public. These choices are often made on the basis of the personal values of the decision maker, such as honesty, integrity, and independence. Choices should also be made so that clear interpretations can be made by all stakeholder groups, including current and future shareholders, government agencies, and those nonshareholder groups with a continuing or future interest.

Given this reliance on personal values and on fair treatment of current and future interests, it is not surprising that professional pronouncements provide insights into correct values for professional accountants and for ensuring fair disclosure of information and treatment of clients. The remainder of this chapter explores the insights that a professional accountant should be familiar with to ensure appropriate professional behavior. If too many professional accountants fail to behave appropriately, then the credibility of entire profession will be undermined and will lose the trust of the public.

HISTORIC SHORTFALLS IN MEETING PROFESSIONAL EXPECTATIONS

History shows that professional accountants have frequently failed to live up to stakeholder expectations, and the results have been tragic for investors and many others affected by the disappearance of a company or the weakening of an economy. When financial reports do not present credible portrayals of reality, many people can be misled, and the result can generate a crisis of confidence in financial reporting and corporate governance that will lead to economic hardship and a diminishment of the reputation of professional accountants both individually and as a profession.

In the past, the accounting profession has attempted to rectify shortfalls in meeting professional expectations by improving ethical guidance in the form of stricter codes of conduct (or interpretations thereof) or introducing more prescriptive practices. More recently, because of the outrage of the public, self-correction has not been deemed to be sufficient, so new regulations have been prescribed by government or the authorities who serve as overseers to the profession. Will these new rules be sufficient to restore and maintain the public trust in professional accountants? Time will tell.

The current era of professional accounting professional expectations is a result of many factors. First, as discussed in Chapter 1, there has been an increase in concern and sensitivity by traditional stakeholders concerning the subpar behavior in corporations or the accounting profession. This increasing sensitivity and an awareness of the globalization of corporate activities and investment, as well as early financial scandals discussed in Chapter 2, stimulated the internationalization of professional accounting standards and practices. For example, the founding of IFAC in 1977, now representing almost 3 million accountants through more than 175 members and associates in 130 countries and jurisdictions,[1] has led to the generation of guidance, such as ethical codes and standards for adoption by member associations around the world.

Specific scandals, also discussed in Chapter 2, have triggered the introduction of new laws and regulations governing the accounting profession. The impact of the Enron, Arthur Andersen, and WorldCom debacles gave rise to a crisis of credibility for the business community, for its reports and capital markets, and for professional accountants who were seen as part of the problem. The public was outraged and looking for a return to credibility founded on values such as trust, integrity, transparency of reports, and so on and a rededication to the public interest. In response, the U.S. government-enacted SOX, which required the Securities and Exchange Commission (SEC) to create regulations bringing governance reforms for both corporations and the accounting profession, provided much of the answer. These reforms forced change on those U.S. and foreign corporations (known as SEC registrants) and their auditors that wished to access U.S. capital markets. Enron-induced SOX reforms also triggered or reinforced the need for similar governance changes for corporations and professional accountants around the world.

Enron and other financial scandals also reinforced the need for the development of more transparent worldwide standards of disclosure and motivated support for IFAC to create and release accounting standards that could be adopted fully or in modified form in all jurisdictions. In 2001, IFAC released the initial version of the *IFAC Code of Ethics* with the intention that professional accountants in member countries would come to observe them. IFAC, through its associate, the International Ethics Standards Board for Accountants (IESBA), has since issued several revisions and now offers the *2015 Code of Ethics for Professional Accountants*.[2] The member organizations of IFAC—the professional accounting bodies around the world, such as the AICPA, the Institutes of Chartered Accountants, Chartered Professional Accountants of Canada, and others—agreed to bring their own codes of ethics into substantial agreement with the IFAC Code, which states,

> A distinguishing mark of the accountancy profession is its acceptance of the responsibility to act in the public interest.[3]

SOX and IFAC reforms have called for business to be more openly accountable to the investing public and for professional accountants to remember that they are professionals who are expected to protect the interests of investors and other stakeholders. Professional accountants are not expected to be involved in misrepresentations in order to assist management or to avoid risk of losing audit revenues—or their jobs if they are employees.

At the same time, the concerns of noninvestor stakeholders, such as customers, employees, or environmentalists, were becoming serious barriers to the achievement of corporate objectives. Damage to reputation caused by ethical problems was recognized as so significant as to be potentially fatal, as in the case of Arthur Andersen, which was once one of the world's largest and most respected auditing firms.

Consequently, both business and professional accountants have recognized that their future success depended on meeting new governance regulations, more transparent

---

[1] IFAC website at https://www.ifac.org/about-ifac, accessed May 13, 2016.

[2] IFAC appoints the members of the IESBA. The *2015 Code of Ethics for Professional Accountants* is downloadable from https://www.ifac.org/ethics.

[3] Ibid., Section 100.1.

reporting standards, and the ethical expectations of stakeholders. Governance mechanisms for both business and the accounting profession now, more than ever, need to ensure that these expectations will be met. History shows, however, that these are lessons that need to be relearned repeatedly.

PROFESSIONAL ACCOUNTING AND THE PUBLIC INTEREST

Public Expectations Control Reputation

Service in the public interest has long been the hallmark of highly regarded professions. So meeting the public's expectations of how a professional should behave and what services and how services should be performed is vital to the reputation of the professional and the profession.

The Enron, Arthur Andersen, WorldCom, and other recent financial and management debacles have confirmed that professional accountants owe their primary loyalty to the public interest, not to their clients or their management or to themselves. Unless professional accountants clearly and properly understand their roles, they cannot consistently answer important questions in an ethically responsible way and as a result will probably offer questionable advice and make decisions that leave them and their profession exposed to criticism or worse. For example, a clear understanding of their roles is essential to respond appropriately to questions about ethical trade-offs encountered as well as proper services to offer and at what levels, such as the following:

- Who really is my client—the company, the management, current shareholders, future shareholders, the public?
- In the event I have to make a decision with ethical ramifications, do I owe primary loyalty to my employer, my client, my boss, my profession, the public, or myself?
- Am I, as a professional accountant, bound by professional standards even when acting as an employee?
- Is professional accounting a profession or a business? Can it be both?
- When should I not offer a service?
- Can I serve two clients with competing interests at the same time?
- Is there any occasion when breaking the profession's guideline against revealing confidences is warranted?

PUBLIC EXPECTATIONS OF A PROFESSIONAL ACCOUNTANT There is little doubt that the public has different expectations of behavior for a member of a profession, such as a doctor or lawyer, than they do of a nonprofessional, such as a sales or personnel manager. Why is this? The answer seems to have to do with the fact that professionals often work with something of real value where trust in how competently they will function or how responsibly they will conduct themselves is particularly important. Ultimately, *the public's regard for a particular profession will govern the rights it enjoys*: to practice, frequently with a monopoly on the services offered; to control entry to the profession; to earn a relatively high income; and to self-regulation or to be judged by one's peers rather than government officials. If a profession loses credibility in the eyes of the public, the consequences can be quite severe and not only for the offending professional.

What makes a profession? In the final analysis, it is a combination of features, duties, and rights all framed within a set of common professional values—values that determine how decisions are made and actions are taken.

TABLE 6.1 What Makes a Profession

Essential Features (Bayles)

- Extensive training
- Provision of important services to society
- Training and skills largely intellectual in character

Typical Features

- Generally licensed or certified
- Represented by organizations, associations, or institutes
- Autonomy

Foundation of Ethical Values (Behrman)

- Significantly delineated by and founded on ethical considerations rather than techniques or tools

The thoughts of Bayles (1981) and Behrman (1988), which are summarized in Table 6.1, are useful in focusing on the important features. Professions are established primarily to serve society. The services provided to society are so important that high levels of expertise are required, which, in turn, call for extensive educational programs focused primarily on intellectual rather than mechanical or other training and skills. Almost always, the most highly regarded professions are licensed to practice on the public, and the degree of autonomy accorded a profession from government regulation, with its red tape, is evident by the degree of control exerted over the education and licensing programs by the organization representing the profession.

The importance of autonomy to a profession is worth noting. Autonomy, or freedom from government regulations and regulators, allows members of a profession to be judged by their informed, objective peers rather than by politically appointed regulators and for sanctions to be meted out without raising the attention of the public. This allows a profession to manage its affairs efficiently and discreetly so that the public has the impression that the profession is responsible and able to discharge its duties to members of the public properly. If, however, the public becomes concerned that these processes are not fair or objective or that the public's interest is not being protected, the government will step in to ensure that protection. Here, as it is in dealings with clients, the maintenance of the credibility of the profession is extremely important.

This lack of credibility caused by financial scandals was responsible for the introduction in 2002 of the Public Company Accounting Oversight Board (PCAOB)[4] by the SEC in the United States and the Canadian Public Accountability Board (CPAB)[5] by the Canadian Securities Administrators. The PCAOB oversees professional accountants who wish to audit SEC registrant companies—those from anywhere in the world whose stock is traded on U.S. stock exchanges or that wish to raise funds from U.S. public sources. This means that PCAOB oversight affects the practice of large professional accounting firms worldwide—and the generally accepted accounting policies that are applied to those companies' accounts. CPAB, the auditor of auditors in Canada, promotes high-quality audits. It inspects, reports on, and sanctions auditing firms that audit Canadian securities-issuing companies; it refers problems to regulators; and it makes recommendations on auditing and accounting standards.

[4] See PCAOB website, http://www.pcaobus.org.

[5] See CPAB website, http://www.cpab-ccrc.ca.

The services provided by a profession are so important to society that society is prepared to grant the profession the rights previously outlined, but it also watches closely to see that the corresponding duties expected of the profession are discharged properly. In general terms, the duties expected of a profession are the maintenance of the following:

- *Competence* in the field of expertise
- *Objectivity* in the offering of service
- *Integrity* in client dealings
- *Confidentiality* with regard to client matters
- *Discipline* over members who do not discharge these duties according to the standards expected

These duties are vital to the quality of service provided, a condition made more significant because of the fiduciary relationship a professional has with his or her clients. A fiduciary relationship exists when service provided is extremely important to the client and where there is a significant difference in the level of expertise between the professional and the client such that the client has to trust or rely on the judgment and expertise of the professional. The maintenance of the trust inherent in the fiduciary relationship is fundamental to the role of a professional—so fundamental that professionals have traditionally been expected to make personal sacrifices if the welfare of their client or the public is at stake.

In the past, some have argued that to be a true professional, the individual had to offer services to the public—that a person serving as an employee in an organization therefore did not qualify and could be excused from following the ethical code of the profession involved. It was presumed that the need to serve the employer should be dominant. Unfortunately, the failings of this limited perspective were exposed in cases where buildings and other structures collapsed due to cheap construction and, as with Enron, the disclosure of financial results was favorable to current management instead of current and future shareholders. In both instances, the professions involved—engineering and accounting—lost credibility in the eyes of the public. As a result, prior to Enron, some engineering and accounting professions had decided to make their primary responsibility to the public explicit in their code of conduct.

The U.S. Senate, SOX, the SEC, and IFAC (and therefore its worldwide member professional accounting bodies) have made it clear that service to the public interest is paramount. The concept of *loyal agency* only to an employer has been refuted and is clearly out of step with the current expectations of the public. The conditions of a *fiduciary relationship—the necessity to trust or rely on the judgment and expertise of a professional*—are as applicable to professionals who serve within organizations as employees as to those who offer services directly to the public. The public considers the provision of services within organizations as indirectly for the public's benefit in any event.

In order to support this combination of features, duties, and rights, it is essential that the profession in question develops a set of values or fundamental principles to guide its members and that each professional possess personal values that dovetail with these. Normally, desired personal values would include honesty, integrity, objectivity, discretion, courage to pursue one's convictions, and strength of character to resist tempting opportunities to serve themselves or others rather than the client. Without these values, the necessary trust required to support the fiduciary relationship cannot be maintained, so efforts are usually made by the profession to assess whether these values are possessed by candidates for the profession and by its members. Such screening is usually undertaken during the prequalification or articling period as well as by a discipline committee of the profession. Generally, criminal activity is considered cause for expulsion, and failure to follow the standards of the profession that are expressed in its code of conduct can bring remedial measures, fines, suspension of rights, or expulsion.

A professional accountant, whether engaged in auditing or management or as an employee or a consultant, is expected to be both an accountant and a professional. *A professional accountant is expected to have special technical expertise associated with accounting and a higher understanding than a layperson of related fields, such as management control, taxation, or information systems. In addition, he or she is expected to adhere to the general professional duties and values described above and also to adhere to those specific standards laid out by the professional body to which he or she belongs.* A deviation from these expected norms can produce a lack of credibility for or confidence in the whole profession. For example, when an individual or a profession puts their own interests before those of the client or the public, a lack of confidence can develop that can trigger public inquiries into the affairs of the profession in general. Such was the case with the Treadway Commission (1987) in the United States or the Macdonald Commission (1988) in Canada. Later crises of confidence and credibility, such as those with Enron, Arthur Andersen, and WorldCom, were met with new statutes and regulations, such as SOX and the related SEC regulations, or with intermediary agencies, such as the PCAOB, which now oversees "the audits of public companies in order to protect the interests of investors and further the public interest in the preparation of informative, accurate, and independent audit reports."[6]

Not surprisingly, professional accounting conforms quite well to the combination of features, duties, and rights in a framework of values as previously described for professions in general. These have been summarized specifically for professional accounting in Table 6.2.

DOMINANCE OF ETHICAL VALUES RATHER THAN ACCOUNTING OR AUDIT TECHNIQUES

Many accountants (and most nonaccountants) hold the view that mastery of accounting and/or audit technique is the sine qua non of the accounting profession. But relatively few financial scandals are actually caused by methodological errors in the application of technique—most are caused by *errors in judgment* about the appropriate use of a technique or the disclosure related to it. Some of these errors in judgment stem from misinterpretation of the problem as a result of its complexity, whereas others are a result of lack of attention to the ethical values of honesty, integrity, objectivity, due care, confidentiality, and the commitment to the interests of others before those of oneself.

Examples of placing too much faith in technical feasibility rather than proper exercise of ethical values or judgment are readily available. For example, a conceptually brilliant accounting treatment will lack utility if it is biased or sloppily prepared. Suppression of proper disclosure of uncollectible accounts or loans receivable prior to bankruptcy is often not a question of competence but one of biased judgment or misplaced loyalty to management, a client, or oneself rather than to the public, who might invest in the bank or savings and loan company.

It should be noted, however, that sometimes a disclosure problem is so complex or the trade-offs are so difficult that suppression of disclosure seems a reasonable interpretation at the time the decision is made. For example, accountants are often confronted with the decision of when and how much to disclose about a company's poor financial

[6] The PCAOB's mission statement can be accessed at https://pcaobus.org/About/History/Pages/default.aspx. A similar agency, the CPAB, has been created in Canada to audit Canadian auditors.

TABLE 6.2 Features, Duties, Rights, & Values of the Accounting Profession

Features

- Provision of important fiduciary services to society
- Extensive knowledge and skill are required
- Training and skills required are largely intellectual in character
- Overseen by self-regulating membership organizations
- Accountable to governmental authority

Duties essential to a fiduciary relationship

- Continuing attention to the needs of clients and other stakeholders
- Development and maintenance of required knowledge and skills, including professional skepticism
- Maintenance of the trust inherent in a fiduciary relationship by behavior exhibiting responsible values
- Maintenance of an acceptable personal reputation
- Maintenance of a credible reputation as a profession

Rights permitted in most jurisdictions

- Ability to hold oneself out as a designated professional to render important fiduciary services
- Ability to set entrance standards and examine candidates
- Self-regulation and discipline based on codes of conduct
- Participation in the development of accounting and audit practice
- Access to some or all fields of accounting and audit endeavor

Values necessary to discharge duties and maintain rights

- Honesty
- Integrity
- Objectivity, based on independent judgment
- Desire to exercise due care and professional skepticism
- Competence
- Confidentiality
- Commitment to place the needs of the public, the client, the profession, and the employer or firm before the professional's own self-interest

condition. It is possible that the corporation may work out of its problem if sufficient time is allowed, but to disclose the weakness may trigger bankruptcy proceedings.

Particularly in these situations of uncertainty, accountants must take care that their decisions are not tainted by failing to observe proper ethical values. At the very least, ethical values must be considered on a par with technical competence—both qualify as sine qua non. However, the edge in dominance may be awarded to ethical values on the grounds that, when a professional finds a problem that exceeds his or her current competence, it is ethical values that will compel the professional to recognize and disclose that fact. *Without ethical values, the trust necessary for a fiduciary relationship cannot be sustained, and the credibility accorded and rights allowed the accounting profession will be limited*—probably reducing the effectiveness an independent profession can bring to society.

From time to time, other members of other professions have made the mistake of doing something because it is technically possible without regard to the ethical consequences of doing so. Genetic cloning may be an example of this practice, which is referred to as the *technological imperative*—meaning if something can be done, it should be done. When this arises in accounting, it is usually because existing accounting standards do not prohibit the practice, and it is therefore presumed to be permitted. However, there are many examples of practices that were employed, such as pooling of interests or renegotiation of overdue mortgage loans that were then disclosed as current, only to be reversed, constrained, or changed when they were found not to satisfy the public interest fairly and objectively. In other words, they were not in accord with fundamental ethical principles. Consequently, even though technical feasibility may govern the short-term decisions of some accountants, in the longer term, ethical considerations are dominant. Whether the interest of the profession is well served by adopting technical methods without thoroughly exploring their potential consequences is a question worth examining. Conceivably, the problems associated with pooling-of-interest merger consolidations or the 3%-outside investee special purpose entities (SPEs) of Enron fame could have been foreseen and constraints devised if an "ethical screen" had been explicitly in place.

PRIORITY OF DUTY, LOYALTY, & TRUST IN A FIDUCIARY Who should be the real or most important client of a professional accountant? Because the primary role of the professional accountant is to offer important fiduciary services to society, the performance of those services often involves choices that favor the interests of one of the following at the expense of the others: the person paying your fee/salary, the current shareholder/owner of the organization; potential future shareholder/owners, and other stakeholders, including employees, governments, lenders, and so on. A decision will have differing impacts in the short and long terms depending on the interest and situation of each stakeholder, and each should be examined carefully where a significant impact is anticipated. The intricacies of stakeholder impact analysis are discussed in depth in Chapters 3 and 4, but several general observations are worthy of mention for auditors and accountants.

A professional accountant is given the right to provide important fiduciary services to society because he or she undertakes to maintain the trust inherent in the fiduciary relationship. Not only must the professional accountant have expertise, but he or she must also apply that expertise with courage, honesty, integrity, objectivity, due care and professional skepticism, competence, confidentiality, and avoidance of misrepresentation in order to ensure that those relying on the expertise can trust that proper care is taken of their interests.

History has shown, however, that these values, characteristics, and principles are not enough, on their own, to ensure predictability and best practice in the choice of accounting treatments or audit approach. Consequently, in order to narrow the range of acceptable choices of accounting treatment or auditing practice, professional accountants are expected to adhere to Generally Accepted Accounting Principles (GAAP) and Generally Accepted Auditing Standards (GAAS). These generally accepted principles and standards have been created so that the choices made according to them will be fair to the multiplicity of users of the resulting financial reports and audits (i.e., *fair to the public interest*). This means, for example, that audited financial statements are intended to be fairly presented from the perspectives of all of the current shareholders, future shareholders, lenders, management, government, and so on. If audited financial statements are biased in favor of one user group over another, the trust fundamental to that fiduciary relationship will have been broken. The professional accountant involved will not be worthy of the trust placed in him or her and will bring his or her fellow professionals into disrepute, thus affecting the reputation and credibility of the profession.

The need to adhere to the ethical values previously articulated and to GAAP is as important for professional accountants working in management, as employees, or as consultants as it is for those who are auditing financial reports. The difference between a skilled manipulator of numbers and a professional accountant is that a user can rely on or have trust in the integrity of the professional's work. Any involvement with misrepresentations, biased reports, or unethical activities will break the trust required in a professional's fiduciary relationships and will bring other members of the profession into disrepute.

If a person wants to be a professional accountant, he or she must be prepared to act with integrity always, not just sometimes. He or she should not, for example, be involved with misrepresentations or illegalities caused by a misguided sense of loyalty to an immediate client or employer. *Loyalty is owed first to the public interest and then to the accounting profession* through the observance of the principles articulated in its code of conduct and its standards.

Auditors are specifically appointed by shareholders or owners as their agents to examine the activities of an organization and to report on the soundness of its financial systems and the reasonableness of its annual statements. This is done to protect the interests of the shareholders/owners from a number of problems, including the unscrupulous conduct of management. Audited financial reports are used and relied on both by existing and prospective shareholders and creditors and by governments and others. This reliance is therefore critical to the effective running of commerce in general. The choice of accounting or disclosure treatment that maximizes current income at the expense of future income could breach the trust required for the fiduciary arrangement with the public—an outcome that could lead to charges of misrepresentation and loss of reputation for the auditor and the profession as a whole. Accordingly, *an auditor's loyalty to the public should be primary and should not be less than the loyalty to existing shareholders/owners. Loyalty to the management of the organization should rank below the public, existing shareholders, the accounting profession, and the audit firm.*

In the case of accountants employed by organizations or by audit firms, there is no statutory or contractual duty to shareholders or the public. However, in the performance of their duties to their employers, professional accountants are expected to exercise the values of honesty, integrity, objectivity, and due care. These values prohibit a professional accountant from being associated with a misrepresentation, so improper acts by an employer should cause professional accountants to consider their responsibility to other stakeholders, including those who would be disadvantaged by the act, and their professional colleagues whose reputation would be tarnished by association. From this perspective, the paramount duty of professional accountant employees is really to ensure the accuracy and reliability of their work for the benefit of the end user—the public. It is not surprising that professional codes of ethics or conduct require disassociation from misleading information and misrepresentations. Unfortunately, some current codes do this with the requirement of silence or confidentiality, thus leaving unsuspecting stakeholders to their fate. Logic would dictate that maintenance of the trust required in specific fiduciary relationships is based on the broader trust between the public and the profession as a whole; in the long term, codes should clearly require the protection of the public at large rather than a specific stakeholder.

In summary, confidence in and support for the accounting profession would be eroded if the interest of the public were not the prime motivator of actions by both professional accountants in public practice and those who are employees and the codes of conduct of the profession were seen to permit and reinforce this. Government pressure would be brought to bear to reform the profession or to create a new group of professionals free of bias and loyal to the public's interest. As discussed in Chapter 2, the lack of credibility precipitated by the Enron, Arthur Andersen, and WorldCom disasters gave rise to the SOX reforms that brought new governance regulation and reinforced an IFAC-led rededication of the accounting profession to the public interest.

Sometimes, clients or employers are confused in their thinking that a professional accountant has a real or an implied contract with them and must act only in the best interest of the client or employer. It is imperative to note, however, that the contract is one where the professional is understood to be answerable to the ethical codes of the profession, so it is unreasonable to expect absolute loyalty to the client or employer rather than the profession and ultimately to the public. By contrast, it is reasonable for the client/employer to expect that a professional accountant will place the client/employer interest before that of the professional's self-interest. To do otherwise would undermine the trust required for a fiduciary arrangement to work. Legitimate confidences about business problems would not be shared for fear that the interest of the client/employer would be subverted or obviated by premature release or misused for personal gain so that the professional accountant would not be able to work effectively or on sensitive matters. As a result, the scope of an audit could be constrained to the detriment of the auditor, the profession, and the public. To prevent the release of client/employer confidences, most codes of conduct require confidences not to be divulged except in a court of law or when required by the discipline process of the profession.

In the final analysis, a professional accountant facing a difficult choice should make that choice so as to preserve the trust inherent in the fiduciary relationships, first with the public, then with the profession, then with the client/employer, and finally with the individual professional. Placing the client/employer's interests first is valid only if those interests will be overridden by the interests of the public and the profession in circumstances where a proposed treatment would not be in the public interest or profession's interest, either legally or ethically. Any doubt about the primacy of the public interest should be erased by remembering that the once-revered, mighty, 85,000-strong Arthur Andersen disappeared within a year of being discovered violating the public's trust with regard to Enron.

CONFIDENTIALITY: STRICT OR ASSISTED The previous analysis places the professional accountant in the unenviable position of having to keep confidential those aspects of his or her client/employer that he or she might not agree with but that may not impact on the financial activities of the company sufficiently to be of concern to the public. If, for example, the professional is dismissed for refusing to misrepresent the receivables as current, he or she would have to seek other employment but could not discuss the reason for leaving the former employer. He or she should discuss client/employer problems only with persons bound by a code of confidentiality (i.e., someone in the accounting firm or a lawyer hired specifically for the purpose). Unless the professional society has an ethics advisor who could be called on, as many now have, this leaves the professional accountant in a disadvantaged position from many perspectives. It also gives unscrupulous client/employers an opportunity to get away with wrongdoing.

Professional societies have begun to recognize that this strict level of confidentiality is not in the interest of several stakeholders, including the public, and have introduced a limited, confidential consultation service to ensure that the professional has cost-free help to make the right decision, to call for a response from the client/employer and perhaps resolve the problem, and to reassure prospective employers. In its 2015 Ethics Code, IFAC stresses the need for a professional accountant to resolve situations where there is a conflict between fundamental principles, which in this case could be between confidentiality and the public interest. The Code suggests, among other things,[7] that the professional accountant consider obtaining "professional advice from the relevant professional body or legal advisors, and thereby obtain guidance on ethical issues without breaching confidentiality."[8] This recommendation will be applied around the world as the codes of professional accounting bodies are harmonized to the IFAC Code.

It is also noteworthy that, generally speaking, professional accountants are not yet expected to report problematic accounting treatments to securities regulators, taxation authorities, or their professional societies. It will be interesting to see if such a reporting responsibility emerges further. It has already done so in Canada, where all Chartered Professional Accountants must report apparent breaches of their rules of conduct and for auditors of financial institutions who must report viability problems to the Superintendent of Financial Institutions. Also, in England and Wales, Chartered Accountants are required to report money laundering for drugs and terrorists. Professional accountants in doubt about such responsibilities should check with their respective societies.

Implications for Services Offered

ASSURANCE & OTHER SERVICES Professional accountants have developed fiduciary services in the following traditional areas:

- Accounting and reporting principles, practices, and systems
- Auditing of accounting records, systems, and financial statements
- Financial projections: preparation, analysis, and audit
- Taxation: preparation of tax returns and advice
- Bankruptcy: trustee's duties and advice
- Financial planning: advice
- Decision making: facilitation through analysis and approach
- Management control: advice and design of systems
- Corporate and commercial affairs: general advice

All these services are bounded by the professional accountant's primary area of competence: accounting. However, as the needs of management changed, it was recognized that accounting expertise in the measurement, disclosure, and interpretation of data could be applied to provide services outside of the traditional area of accounting. For example, nonfinancial indicators of quality have become an important part of control systems and can be far more timely and helpful than traditional financial reports.

More important, when examining the future vision of CPAs in the United States and Canada, it was realized that there were many so-called *assurance services* that could be offered *where the professional accountant could add value by adding credibility or assurance to a report or process.*[9] In particular, the proper discharge of these services relies on the understanding possessed by professional accountants of fiduciary responsibilities, evidence-gathering and evaluation skills, skepticism, objectivity, independence and

[7] See 2015 IFAC Code, Sections 100.19–100.23.

[8] Ibid., Section 100.24.

[9] See, for example, AICPA Assurance Services Executive Committee, "A White Paper for Providers and Users of Business Information," 2013, 2, http://www.aicpa.org/InterestAreas/FRC/AssuranceAdvisoryServices/DownloadableDocuments/ASEC_WP_Providers_Users_BI.PDF.

integrity, and reporting skills. In 1997, the AICPA Special Committee on Assurance Services estimated that whereas traditional audit services would generate approximately $7 billion per annum, new assurance services would generate $21 billion. This study, while dated, identifies an ongoing problem that traditional audit services continue to shrink and no longer dominate the revenue of professional accounting firms. The Special Committee developed a list of over 200 possible new assurance services and then winnowed it down to assurance services concerning the following:

- Risk assessment
- Business performance measurement
- Information systems reliability
- Electronic commerce (website seal of approval)
- Health care performance measurement
- Elder care

Not surprisingly, both the AICPA and the IFAC have subsequently developed guidance to assist professional accountants in discharging these assurance services. For example, IFAC supports the International Auditing and Assurance Standards Board,[10] and the AICPA website offers advice.[11]

SEC & IFAC INDEPENDENCE RULES What the AICPA Special Committee on Assurance Services did not anticipate at first was the inability of its members to manage the inherent conflict of interest situations that arise when audit and other services are offered to the same client. This failure was partly responsible for the Enron, Arthur Andersen, and WorldCom disasters, and the remedial reaction in SOX, as discussed in Chapter 2, has set limits on the services that could be offered by SEC auditors to their SEC registrant clients. Conflict of interest management was discussed in Chapter 5 and continues in this section.

The limitations introduced by SOX and ordered by the SEC restrict the auditor of an SEC registrant corporation from auditing his or her own work or assuming an advocacy position for the client. This is to avoid situations where the independent judgment that must be employed by an auditor to fairly judge the positions taken by an audit client is likely to be impaired or swayed from protecting the public interest. For example, when auditing an information system installed by the audit firm, an auditor's self-interest (pride or wishing to retain the audit client revenue) may prevent him or her from pointing out an error or the result of an error. In addition, advocating a client position may sway an auditor's judgment with regard to disclosure in accordance with GAAP to further the interests of current shareholders or management. Although most auditors have been managing most of these conflict situations successfully for decades, the Enron, WorldCom, and other disasters illustrate the serious consequences that can come from failing to properly manage the risks involved.

To avoid these conflict of interest risks in large company audits and thereby protect the public interest, SOX required the SEC to ban the following nonaudit services from being offered by auditors to their SEC registrants because it was thought likely that they could impair or bias the audit firm's independent judgment:

- Bookkeeping or other services related to the accounting records or financial statements of the audit client

[10] See http://www.ifac.org/auditing-assurance.

[11] See http://www.aicpa.org/INTERESTAREAS/FRC/ASSURANCEADVISORYSERVICES/Pages/AssuranceAdvisoryServices.aspx.

- Financial information systems design and implementation
- Appraisal or valuation services, fairness opinions, or contribution-in-kind reports
- Actuarial services
- Internal audit outsourcing services
- Management functions or human resources
- Broker or dealer, investment advisor, or investment banking services
- Legal services and expert services unrelated to the audit

The SEC's principles of independence with respect to services provided by auditors are predicated largely on three basic principles, violations of which would impair the auditor's independence: (1) an auditor cannot function in the role of management, (2) an auditor cannot audit his or her own work, and (3) an auditor cannot serve in an advocacy role for his or her client.[12]

The SEC also adopted other measures beyond limiting the specific services offered that will do the following:

- Require that certain partners on the audit engagement team rotate after no more than five or seven consecutive years, depending on the partner's involvement in the audit, except that certain small accounting firms may be exempt from this requirement.
- Establish rules that an accounting firm would not be independent if certain members of management of that issuer had been members of the accounting firm's audit engagement team within the one-year period preceding the commencement of audit procedures.
- Establish rules that an accountant would not be independent from an audit client if any "audit partner" received compensation based on the partner procuring engagements with that client for services other than audit, review, and attest services.
- Require the auditor to report certain matters to the issuer's audit committee, including "critical" accounting policies used by the issuer.
- Require the issuer's audit committee to preapprove all audit and nonaudit services provided to the issuer by the auditor; and
- Require disclosures to investors of information related to audit and non-audit services provided by and fees paid to the auditor.[13]

These SOX/SEC limitations, as well as those subsequently approved,[14] apply only to services offered to SEC registrants around the world. All services could continue to be offered to non-SEC registrant audit clients and to audit clients of other firms. Moreover, the vast majority of professional accounting firms around the world do not service large SEC registrant companies or those trading securities on exchanges or in countries that will emulate the SOX/SEC position. The same criticism can be made of other governance regulations or guidelines around the world.

Fortunately, the standards of independence embedded in professional codes of ethics or conduct are in the process of being revised to apply these and other similar

[12] U.S. Securities and Exchange Commission, *Final Rule: Strengthening the Commission's Requirements Regarding Auditor Independence*, February 6, 2003, http://www.sec.gov/rules/final/33-8183.htm.

[13] U.S. Securities and Exchange Commission, *Commission Adopts Rules Strengthening Auditor Independence*, January 22, 2003, http://www.sec.gov/news/press/2003-9.htm.

[14] See, for example, those related to provision of tax services and contingent fees per PCAOB Release 2005-014, July 26, 2005.

independence principles to all professional accountants. In this regard, the ethics codes for virtually all professional accountants are being harmonized to the IFAC Code.

Nevertheless, *because the SEC and IFAC pronouncements are not perfectly specific, professional accountants will still have to use their best judgment to interpret them about which assurance service to offer, how to conduct them, and how to manage the conflict of interest risks involved.*

CRITICAL VALUE ADDED BY A PROFESSIONAL ACCOUNTANT A professional accountant's judgment about what services to offer and how to do so should be based, in part, on an understanding of the critical value added by a professional accountant. *Credibility* is the critical value added by professional accountants in the newer assurance services as well as the traditional ones. This has become much more apparent during the recent visioning exercises.

Competence is, of course, a fundamental factor, and high levels of competence can and do provide a competitive advantage. But it is apparent that high competence can be acquired by nonprofessionals and is therefore not, by itself, the critical value added by a professional accountant. *Credibility to the immediate client/employer and to the public at large depends on the reputation of the entire profession, and reputation stems from the professional values adhered to and the expectations those create in the people being served.* In particular, the critical value added by a professional accountant lies in the expectation that whatever services are offered will be based on integrity and objectivity, and these values, in addition to an ensured minimum standard of competence, lend credibility or assurance to the report or activity. These individual ethical values, reinforced by the standards of the profession, provide a competitive advantage to professional accountants and ensure that their services are in demand. In the words of Stanton Cook, president of the (Chicago) Tribune Company, accountants, entrepreneurs, manufacturers, salespeople, and even lawyers all say, "The product we are ultimately selling is credibility" (Priest 1991).

STANDARDS EXPECTED FOR BEHAVIOR The public and particularly a client expect that a professional accountant will perform fiduciary services with competence, integrity, and objectivity. Although not obvious, *integrity* is important because it ensures that whatever the service, it will be performed fairly and thoroughly. No detail will be omitted, understated, or misstated that would cloud the truth, nor would an analysis be put forward that misleads users. *Honesty*, or accuracy or truthfulness, is implied in all aspects of data gathering, measurement, reporting, and interpretation. Similarly, *objectivity* implies freedom from bias in the selection of measurement bases and disclosure so as not to mislead those served. Objectivity cannot be maintained unless the professional accountant is *independent* minded, or free from undue influence from one stakeholder or another. Independence is an issue developed at greater length in the conflict of interest discussion that follows.

Integrity, honesty, and objectivity are essential to the proper discharge of fiduciary duties. They are, with competence, so important to the critical value added from belonging to a profession that they must be protected by the profession in order to ensure its future. Consequently, professional accounting organizations take pains to investigate and discipline members whose conduct is questionable with regard to these ethical values.

Judgment & Values

IMPORTANCE TO VALUE ADDED The proper discharge of the ethical values of competence, integrity, honesty, and objectivity relies substantially, if not primarily, on the personal ethical values of the professional accountant involved. If the profession itself has high standards, the individual professional can choose to ignore them. Often, however, a professional is simply not sufficiently aware of potential ethical dilemmas or the appropriate values to properly discharge his or her duties. Additionally, a professional may err in her or his judgment about the potential outcome of an ethical dilemma or about the seriousness of the outcome for those who must bear the impact. *The credibility of the profession, therefore, rests on the values it espouses, the personal and professional ethical values of each individual member, and the quality of judgment exercised.*

DEVELOPMENT OF JUDGMENT & VALUES How do professional accountants develop the judgment they must apply to ethical dilemmas? In the past, trial and error has been the established mode—experienced largely when growing up, on the job, or by learning from others who have problems or pass on their own experience. But the limitations of trial and error are obvious, as significant costs may be borne by the learner, the client, society, and the profession. In addition, an orderly framework for thinking about future problems may never be developed, nor may the level attained by a professional be adequate to safeguard the profession's stakeholders, including the professionals themselves.

Trial and error can never be entirely supplanted by organized training or educational experiences, but many of the deficiencies previously noted can be remedied by a well-ordered, stimulating learning program that deals with the major issues to be faced and that suggests practical, ethical approaches to their resolution. In this regard, it is helpful to consider how far a student's ethical reasoning capacity has progressed and how to advance that capacity. A model developed by Lawrence Kohlberg is helpful in this regard (Kohlberg 1981, 1984; see also Colby and Kohlberg 1987).

Kohlberg argues that individuals pass through the six progressive stages of moral development, which are described in articles on accountants by Ponemon (1992); Ponemon and Gabhart (1993); Etherington and Schulting (1995); Cohen, Pant, and Sharp (1995); and Thorne and Magnan (1998). These six stages and the motivation that leads individuals to make decisions at each can be helpful, as is pointed out by W. Shenkir (1990), in designing an educational program to expose students to the six levels. Such exposure can enable students to develop their awareness, knowledge, and skills for dealing with ethical problems and may, through understanding the motivations involved, shift their moral reasoning to higher stages. The motivations that influence people at each of Kohlberg's stages of moral reasoning are identified in Table 6.3.

TABLE 6.3 Motives Influencing People at Kohlberg's Six Stages of Moral Reasoning

STAGE DESCRIPTION	MOTIVE FOR DOING RIGHT
Preconventional	***Self-interest***
1. Obedience	Fear of punishment and authorities
2. Egotism—instrumental and social exchange	Self-gratification, concern only for oneself "Let's make a deal"
Conventional	***Conformity***
3. Interpersonal concordance	Role expectation or approval from others
4. Law and duty (social order)	Adherence to moral codes or to codes of law and order
Postconventional, Autonomous, or Principled	***Interests of Others***
5. General individual rights and standards agreed on by society	Concern for others and broader social welfare
6. Self-chosen principles	Concern for moral or ethical principle

Researchers have found that students in business facing ethical decisions are largely in cognitive stages 2 or 3, so there is quite a bit of growth that is possible and desirable (Weber and Green 1991). Other researchers have found that business students believe that their success is more dependent on questionable ethical practices than do nonbusiness students, so orderly ethics education would appear desirable lest these attitudes pervade the students who enter the ranks of professional accounting (Lane and Schaup 1989). Leaving the cognitive development of students for the accounting profession and graduate accountants to trial and error rather than significant thought and formal training could, in itself, be unethical. Exposure to ethics education material and linked traditional course work, particularly featuring realistic cases, should provide students and graduate practitioners with a better understanding of the ethical issues, dilemmas, approaches to their resolution, and the values necessary to make good ethical judgments than would the vicissitudes of trial and error. For further thinking on ethical cognitive development, useful references may be made to the IFAC Education Committee's International Educational Standards (IES) Nos. 3 and 4[15] and to the *Ethics Education Committee Report* of 2004 by the Association to Advance Collegiate Schools of Business (AACSB).[16]

Sources of Ethical Guidance

There are several sources of guidance available to professional accountants. The codes of conduct or ethics of their professional body and of their firm or employer rank as important reference points. However, many other inputs should also be taken into account when appropriate because professional accountants must respond to a body of expectations and standards created by various professional accounting organizations in their own country and offshore together with standard setters, regulators, the courts, politicians, financial markets, and the public.

Expectations for behavior of professional accountants are and will be embodied in the following:

- Standard setters (IFAC, PCAOB, the Financial Accounting Standards Board [FASB], IASB, CPA Canada, the Institute of Chartered Accountants of England and Wales, etc.)
  - GAAP
  - GAAS
- Commonly understood standards of practice
- Research studies and articles
- Regulator's guidelines (SEC, PCAOB, the Ontario Securities Commission [OSC], the New York Stock Exchange, the Toronto Stock Exchange, etc.)
- Court decisions
- Codes of conduct from the following:
  - Employer (i.e., corporation or accounting firm)
  - Local professional accounting bodies
  - IFAC

No one organization has a monopoly on the creation of the environment of expectations or standards that a professional accountant in the United States, Canada, or elsewhere should meet. For example, as noted in Tables 6.4 and 6.5, there are several

[15] Downloadable at **http://www.cengagebrain.com**.
[16] Downloadable at **http://www.cengagebrain.com**.

TABLE 6.4 National & International Accounting Organizations Operating in North America

NAME	DESIGNATION	PRIME MANDATE(S)	LOCATION
American Institute of Certified Public Accountants (AICPA)	CPA	Auditing, management accounting	United States
Institute of Management Accountants (IMA)	CMA	Management accounting	United States
Chartered Professional Accountants of Canada (CPAC)	CPA	Auditing, management accounting	Canada
Association of Chartered Certified Accountants (ACCA)	ACCA	Accounting education	International

TABLE 6.5 Contributions to the North American Regulatory Framework for Professional Accountants

ORGANIZATION	CONTRIBUTION GOVERNING ORGANIZATION'S MEMBERS/USERS
American Institute of Certified Public Accountants (AICPA)	CPA designation, statements of Auditing Standards (SAS), research studies, journal articles, code of conduct
Association of Accountants and Financial Professionals in Business (IMA)	CMA designation, statements of accounting practice, research studies, journal articles, code of conduct
Financial Accounting Standards Board (FASB)	Financial Accounting Standards (FAS)
Chartered Professional Accountants of Canada (CPAC)	CPA designation, accounting and auditing standards in Canada, research studies, journal articles, code of conduct
U.S. Securities and Exchange Commission (SEC)	Regulations related to U.S. public securities markets including corporate disclosure and governance, GAAP, GAAS, behavior of auditors and other professionals practicing before the SEC. Regulation in respect to disclosure for companies raising funds in the USA. Standards of independence for CPAs auditing SEC companies.
Ontario Securities Commission (OSC)	Regulations related to financial disclosure in Canada's principal securities market (Ontario), whose regulations are accepted by the SEC.
U.S. and Canadian courts	Common law decisions affecting legal liability
International Federation of Accountants (IFAC):	Promotes global harmonization of standards
International Ethics Standards Board for Accountants (IESBA)	International Code of Ethics
International Auditing and Assurance Board (IAASB)	Auditing Standards (ISA)
International Accounting Standards Board (IASB)	Accounting and auditing standards (IAS)
International Financial Reporting Standards Foundation (IFRS)	IFRs, IFRIC, SIC
Public Accounting Oversight Boards	Oversight in the U.S. (PCAOB) and Canada (CPAB)
PCAOB	Issues Auditing Standards (U.S.), inspections, sanctions
CPAB	Inspection reports, sanctions

national and international professional accounting organizations operating in North America, plus their subsets in each U.S. state or Canadian province (e.g., the CPAO or a state society of Certified Public Accountants) plus several regulatory units that are contributing to the North American regulatory framework. This multiplicity contributes to a strong desire for some global convergence, making it likely the IASB and IFAC pronouncements will become increasingly more important sources of guidance, with the IFAC code emerging as the dominant ethics framework.

It is important to note that although a national body can develop a code of conduct, in North America the local state or provincial subset organization controls its own members by enacting its own code of conduct (using the national code as a guide but not always adopting all its provisions) and policing and disciplining its members. Consequently, the standard of ethical expectation varies somewhat from jurisdiction to jurisdiction and from organization to organization. Fortunately, basic principles of ethical conduct apply to all organizations, and the convergence toward global ethics principles, accounting, and auditing standards holds considerable promise for promoting a common standard of performance.

Professional Codes of Conduct

PURPOSE & FRAMEWORK Professional codes of conduct are designed to provide guidance about the conduct expected of members in order that the services offered will be of acceptable quality and the reputation of the profession will not be sullied. If that reputation is sullied, some aspect of a fiduciary relationship has been breached, and a service has not been performed in a professional manner. Alternatively, it may mean that a member has offended the rules of society in some way so as to bring the profession's name into disrepute and thereby damage the public trust required for its members to serve other clients effectively.

To be effective, codes of conduct need to blend fundamental principles with a limited number of specific rules. If a code were drafted to cover all possible problems, it would be extremely voluminous—probably so voluminous that few members would spend the time required to become familiar with it and to stay abreast of the constant flow of additions. With practicality in mind, most professional codes have evolved to the framework outlined in Table 6.6.

FUNDAMENTAL PRINCIPLES & STANDARDS The fundamental principles and standards described in Table 6.7 are found in most codes. IFAC, in its 2001 version of its Code of Ethics for Professional Accountants, articulated why professional accountants should *serve the public interest* when it stated,

> A distinguishing mark of a profession is acceptance of its responsibility to the public. The accountancy profession's public consists of clients, credit grantors, governments, employers, employees, investors, the business and financial community, and others who rely on the objectivity and integrity of professional accountants to maintain the orderly functioning of commerce. This reliance imposes a public interest responsibility on the accountancy profession. The public interest is defined as the collective well-being of the community of people and institutions the professional accountant serves.... A professional accountant's responsibility is not exclusively to satisfy the needs of an individual client

TABLE 6.6 Typical Framework for a Code of Conduct for Professional Accountants

Introduction and purpose
Fundamental principles, standards, and risk assessment approach
General rules applicable in public practice and in business
Specific rules applicable in public practice and in business
Discipline
Interpretations of rules

TABLE 6.7 Fundamental Principles in Codes of Conduct for Professional Accountants

Members should

- act in the public interest,
- at all times maintain the good reputation of the profession and its ability to serve the public interest,
- perform with
  - integrity
  - objectivity and independence
  - professional competence, due care, and professional skepticism
  - confidentiality,
- not be associated with any misleading information or misrepresentation, and
- continually assess the risk of failing to observe these principles.

> or employer. The standards of the accountancy profession are heavily determined by the public interest.[17]

This rationale underpins the current assertion in the 2015 IFAC and other codes, that "a distinguishing mark of the accountably profession is its acceptance of the responsibility to act in the public interest."[18] IFAC left unsaid but implied that other professional groups would be granted standing to serve the public if any group of professional accountants were proven to be unreliable in discharging this mandate.

The maintenance of the *good reputation* of the profession is fundamental to the ability of the profession to continue to enjoy its current rights and privileges, including autonomy in the discipline of its members, the setting of accounting and/or auditing standards, and the recognition by the public and government that new competing professional organizations need not be created to serve the *public interest* more effectively. The phrase *at all times* is significant because the public will view any serious transgression of a professional accountant, including those outside business or professional activity, as a black mark against the profession as a whole. Consequently, if a professional accountant is convicted of a criminal offense or fraud, his or her certification is usually revoked.

Maintenance of standards of care is also imperative for the proper service to clients and the public interest. *Integrity*, *objectivity*, and *honesty* in the preparation of reports, choice of accounting options, and interpretation of accounting data will ensure that the neither the client nor the public will be misled. Sometimes, reports or opinions can lack integrity if the professional involved has failed to maintain *independence* from one of the persons likely to benefit or be harmed by the report and this causes the professional to bias the report, decisions, or interpretations toward the favored party.

Charges of bias are very hard to refute, so professionals are often admonished to avoid any situation or relationship that might lead to the *perception of bias*. This is why, even though in the past many professionals have served successfully as bookkeeper, auditor, shareholder, and director of an organization, modern codes of conduct recommend against situations involving such apparent conflicts of interest. The prospect of an auditor misstating a report for his or her own gain or that of his or her fellow

[17] IFAC 2001 Code of Ethics for Professional Accountants, Sections 9 and 10.

[18] Section 100.1.

shareholders was judged to be too tempting a prospect to allow. Similar reasoning has led to the introduction of the separation of duties within an organization and, wherever possible, between the bookkeeping and audit functions. In simplistic terms, from the profession's viewpoint, why leave freshly baked cookies on the counter to cool if the temptation presented may lead someone to sneak one? It is interesting to speculate as to whom is more at fault: the person leaving the cookies in a vulnerable position or the person succumbing to temptation.

It would be impossible for a professional accountant to offer services at the level a client or an employer has the right to expect if the professional has failed to maintain his or her *competence* with regard to current standards of disclosure, accounting treatment, and business practice. However, beyond understanding and developing facility with current standards, a professional accountant must act with due care.

The exercise of *due care* involves an understanding of the appropriate levels and limits of care expected of a professional accountant in different circumstances. For example, a professional accountant is not expected to be all-knowing and all-seeing with regard to incidents of fraud that occur at a client or an employer. However, if the professional becomes aware of these (and there are now limited expectations for auditors to search out fraud), there are expectations for follow-up and reporting that need to be observed. Similarly, audit procedures need not specifically cover 100% of an organization's transactions; judgment sampling and statistical sampling may be applied to reduce specific coverage to a level deemed appropriate according to professional judgment. That level will be set with reference to what other professionals regard as providing sufficient evidence for the forming of an opinion based on due care. In a court of law, expert witnesses will be called to testify as to what levels of judgment represent the exercise of due care.

An important aspect of the exercise of due care is the *professional skepticism* demonstrated. A professional accountant is not expected to accept everything she or he is told or shown as being accurate or true. The exercise of proper professional skepticism would involve the continuous comparison of representations and/or information received to what would be considered reasonable and/or in line with other representations or information at hand or readily available. In addition, there should be a continuous questioning of whether the fact, decision, or action being considered is in the best interest of the client and is ethical, particularly with regard to the public interest. As evidenced by the actions of many accountants in recent financial scandals, without the continuous exercise of professional skepticism as described, an accountant will not be able to serve a client, society, profession, or himself or herself at the level of a trusted professional.

Confidentiality is fundamental to fiduciary relationships from several perspectives. First, these relationships are very important to the well-being of the client or employer. They usually involve personal information or information that is critical to the activities of the organization and that would result in some loss of privacy or of competitive advantage if it were disclosed to specific individuals or to the public. Advice, for example, about a business transaction, could be used in bargaining if known by the other party to the transaction. Second, it is not beyond the realm of possibility that such information could be used for the professional's own purposes for profit or to gain some other advantage. Finally, if it were suspected that a professional accountant was not going to maintain a client's or an employer's information in confidence, it is unlikely that full information would be shared. This would put an audit and other services on a faulty foundation, which could lead to substandard and potentially misleading opinions and reports.

Keeping information confidential should not, however, lead to illegal behavior. For example, codes of conduct usually specify that a professional accountant *should not be associated with any misrepresentations*. If the professional cannot induce revision by persuasion, then the professional is usually required by his or her code to disassociate from the misrepresentation by resignation. Professional accountants are also usually prohibited from disclosing the misrepresentation, except subject to a disciplinary hearing or in a court of law or to a legal advisor or an advisor from a professional accounting body.

To ensure that a constant vigilance is maintained against failing to observe these fundamental principles, professional accountants are expected to perform a continual *risk assessment process*. They must assess risks by considering the threats and safeguards, identifying what must be done to avoid or mediate these risks. Further discussion of possible threats and safeguards appears below.

For reference, the fundamental principles section of the IFAC 2015 Code of Ethics for Professional Accountants and the Conceptual Risk Management Framework are reproduced as Table 6.8.

DISCIPLINE Customarily, codes of conduct provide information about the operation of the discipline process of the professional association. Members should know how and to whom to report a concern over conduct, what the process is for investigation of the concern, what the hearing process entails, how decisions will be made, what fines and other penalties are possible, how results will be reported, and how appeals will be considered. Unless these facts are known, together with some examples of sanctions levied, a professional is likely to misjudge how important the ethical conduct of its members is to the profession and to society.

Sanctions for unethical behavior can include any of the items listed in Table 6.9. It should be noted, however, that the sanctions identified are not all levied by every professional accounting body or regulatory agency.

TABLE 6.8 IFAC 2015 Code of Ethics for Professional Accountants: Fundamental Principles & Conceptual Risk Management Framework

Fundamental Principles (Section 100.5)

A professional accountant shall comply with the following fundamental principles:

(a) *Integrity*—to be straightforward and honest in all professional and business relationships.

(b) *Objectivity*—to not allow bias, conflict of interest or undue influence of others to override professional or business judgments.

(c) *Professional Competence and Due Care*—to maintain professional knowledge and skill at the level required to ensure that a client or employer receives competent professional service based on current developments in practice, legislation and techniques, act diligently and in accordance with applicable technical and professional standards.

(d) *Confidentiality*—to respect the confidentiality of information acquired as a result of professional and business relationships and should not disclose any such information to third parties without proper and specific authority unless there is a legal or professional right or duty to disclose, nor use for the personal advantage of the professional accountant or third parties.

(e) *Professional Behavior*—to comply with relevant laws and regulations and avoid any action that discredits the profession.

Conceptual Risk Management Framework (Sections 100.17–.25)

The IFAC Code also establishes a *conceptual risk management framework* and requires professional accountants to "identify, evaluate, and address threats to compliance with the fundamentals." (Sec. 100.6) In so doing, the professional accountant must take into account any *safeguards* created by the profession, legislation, regulation or in the work environment. (Sec. 100.13) The 2015 IFAC Code also identifies *conflicts of interest* as a major threat to be considered, and specifies conflict resolution and reporting steps.

TABLE 6.9 Possible Sanctions for Unethical Behavior under Professional Accounting Codes of Conduct & Regulatory Authorities

	LEVIABLE ON THE	
	PROFESSIONAL	ACCOUNTING FIRM
Caution	Yes	Yes
Reprimand	Yes	Yes
Review by peer	Yes	Yes
Requirement to complete courses	Yes	No
Suspension:		
• for a specified period	Yes	No/Yes*
• for an indefinite period	Yes	No
• until specific requirements are completed	Yes	No
• from appearing before regulatory agencies (SEC, OSC)	Yes	Yes
• from auditing SEC or OSC registrant companies	Yes	Yes
Expulsion from membership	Yes	No
Compensation for damage	Yes	Yes
Fine	Yes	Yes
Costs of hearing	Yes	Yes
Ancillary orders		
• for community work	Yes	No
• financial support, etc.	Yes	Yes

*The SEC has suspended a firm's ability to audit SEC registrants and/or take on new clients.

Source: Distillation of discipline cases from North American jurisdictions.

Usually, the discipline process begins with a complaint being lodged at the professional organization about the ethical conduct of a member or firm. Alternately, conviction on a legal charge of consequence (fraud, etc.) may also trigger the discipline process. The complaint or legal charge is investigated by staff, and a decision is made to lay a charge or not. Laying a charge necessitates a hearing to determine guilt or innocence, and the hearing process can be quite cumbersome. It can be held in camera or in public. It can involve lawyers for plaintiff (the staff of the professional body) and defendant and a tribunal or panel to hear the case, which often includes an outside layperson to ensure that proper procedures are followed and the public interest is served.

The cost of the hearing can be substantial in terms of out-of-pocket costs and also lost work time, which otherwise could be billed to clients. In the end, the largest cost involved is the lost reputation of the guilty accountant—in the audit world, credibility is what professionals strive to protect the most since it is evidence of the value of their audit opinion. Without it, their audit services would be without demand.

When a professional accountant or firm is found guilty, the details of the case are made public, usually in the newsletter of the professional organization. It is essential that full details be published to warn other members of ethical problems and the sanctions they might encounter and to preserve the profession's upstanding image as a profession worthy of policing itself (i.e., worthy of the trust of the public).

A guilty professional should anticipate more than one sanction. For example, he or she might receive a reprimand, a fine, and the bill for costs of the lawyers and hearing. Alternatively, the penalty might be a suspension from membership until a set of required courses are completed plus compensation for damages and costs. If the professional appears to need supervision for a while, the penalty might include the review of all work by a peer.

Fines can range in size from less than $1,000 to more than the damage done to the injured party. The amounts are growing over time, and in the United States, fines in the millions have been levied, particularly against Arthur Andersen and some of its partners, as was outlined in Chapter 2. If the penalty involves the prohibition from practice or appearance before the securities commissions, the lost revenue can be very large indeed. The inability to appear before the SEC or PCAOB appears to be a most powerful sanction to use against accounting firms, perhaps because of the potential for loss or suspension of the ability to audit SEC registrant companies and/or the attendant notoriety and loss of reputation. It should be noted, however, that although Arthur Andersen was destroyed by the actions of the SEC, it is not as likely that this will happen again due to the public's perception that it would be fair if only the guilty few individuals were punished, not the whole firm.[19]

INTERPRETATIONS OF RULES When the profession finds that a concern arises in the profession as a result of a debate over the proper application of a rule, a clarification is issued in the form of an interpretation. These interpretations are often an addendum or appendix to the code, which can be added to as circumstances require.

SCANDALS & EXPECTATIONS MOTIVATE CHANGES IN PROFESSIONAL CODES The motivation for changes in professional codes has been surprisingly similar and cyclical over the years. An article by J. Michael Cook, "The AICPA at 100: Public Trust and Professional Pride" (May 1987), summarizes early professional pressures and developments. Usually, roughly every decade, pressure has come on the accounting profession due to a financial or accounting scandal that has eroded the credibility of the profession.[20] An *Expectations Gap* is the difference "between what the public expects or needs and the auditors can reasonably expect to accomplish" (Macdonald 1988, iii). In response to this credibility crisis, several investigations and commissions were created, including the Metcalf investigation,[21] the Treadway Investigation (1987), and the MacDonald Commission (1988), to investigate *how the members of the AICPA and the CICA (now CPA Canada) were serving the public interest.* In response to the Treadway Commission's *Report of the National Commission on Fraudulent Public Reporting*, a committee of the AICPA was struck under the chairmanship of W. Anderson, which redesigned the *AICPA Professional Standards: Ethics and Bylaws* (Anderson 1985, 1987). Paramount in the revisions proposed to the U.S. and Canadian codes by both the Anderson Committee and the Macdonald Commission was the desire for restoration of the public's faith that the profession was serving the public interest.

Although there were some specific problems that triggered these early studies, concern over the credibility of financial reporting was essentially responsible—for strikingly similar reasons—to those that became apparent in 2002 in the Enron and WorldCom financial scandals. There is little doubt that professional accountants forgot important ethics lessons and need to be reminded of their importance.

[19] For an example of professional discipline case, see the ethics case "Wanda Liczyk's Conflict of Interest" at the end of this chapter.

[20] Presentation of Mary Beth Armstrong, February 2, 2003 at the American Accounting Association Accounting Programs Leadership Group Conference, New Orleans.

[21] "Why Everybody's Jumping on the Accountants These Days," *Forbes*, March 15, 1977, http://www.forbes.com/forbes/1977/0315/037_print.html.

Generally, the pressure has been greatest when the North American economy has been weak, and this weakness caused companies and individuals to engage in fraud, misstatement of financial results, or the use of loopholes to take unfair advantage. In reaction, professional codes have been revised to provide more and stronger guidance to avoid such problems in the future.

Two factors were different with the motivations at the start of the new millennium. First, the Enron, Arthur Andersen, and WorldCom debacles occurred in good economic times—even though they gave rise to an erosion of credibility that drove confidence down and, in turn, the economy. This change suggests that ethics challenges can and will play a more serious and significant role than earlier imagined. Second, the desire for global convergence or harmonization of standards to facilitate global business and capital flows is providing a driver of change beyond the previously normal, domestically dominated political and corporate lobbying influences. As such, convergence may yield stronger standards and more rapid continuous changes than heretofore possible. Time will tell, however, if the needed companion regulatory compliance and enforcement framework, best exemplified by the SEC and the OSC, will be replicated in Europe and around the world to realize the possible improvement fully. In fact, global convergence has given rise to IFAC, whose members are the professional accounting organizations, securities regulators, and similar groups from 130 different countries. In turn, IFAC has created other boards that have created global standards and an internationally endorsed *IFAC Code of Ethics* to serve as a universal core of ethical behavior.

AICPA, CPAO, & IFAC CODES OF PROFESSIONAL CONDUCT In response, the current codes of professional accountants in the major industrial nations of the world—which resulted from the concerns, investigations, commissions, and committees of the late 1980s—are converging on the principles and practices embedded in the *IFAC Code of Ethics*. However, since there is no obligation to replicate the IFAC Code exactly, particularly if there are cultural or regulatory differences, it is worthwhile to study relevant country codes carefully and in comparison to the IFAC Code. For reference purposes, the IFAC Code Table of Contents is provided in Table 6.10.

The two most important codes of conduct in North America, based on numbers of CPA members covered, are the *AICPA Code of Professional Conduct* and the *Code of Professional Conduct of the CPA Ontario (CPAO)*. For reference purposes, summaries of the current AICPA and CPAO codes are included below. Discussions of the key provisions are also included below and elsewhere in this book. For example, discussion of the need to keep client information confidential is included in this chapter and in Chapter 5.

Recently, both the AICPA and the CPAO codes have been revised significantly (December 2015 and February 2016, respectively) to harmonize with features in the IFAC Code (see Table 6.10). They now include the following:

- Specification that the primary duty of the CPA is to serve the public interest.
- Adoption of a similar set of fundamental principles and a similar organization for sections dealing with general, professional accountants in public practice, and professional accountants in business.
- Mandatory use of a *Framework* for assessing, acting on, and documenting the risk and impacts of threats (and safeguards) that CPAs face in discharging the fundamental principles underpinning their role of serving the public interest and maintaining the good reputation of the profession. The AICPA Code discusses the application of the *Conceptual Framework* to assess problem issues or practices in general, ethical conflicts, independence, and conflict of interest concerns. The

TABLE 6.10 IFAC 2015 Code of Ethics for Professional Accountants Table of Contents

CPAO Code is similar, particularly in matters related to independence and conflicts of interests.

- Requirement for extensive analysis of independence and conflicts of interest issues. The risk assessment framework proposed by IFAC, AICPA, and the CPAO is discussed in the sections on conflicts of interest below.
- Consideration of conflict resolution processes when appropriate.
- Extensive, helpful guidance on difficult areas to interpret, including, in some cases, useful flowcharts as in the CPAO Code on pages 47 and 140.

SHORTFALLS WITH AND IN PROFESSIONAL CODES In the past, most professional accountants have tended to view their codes as being less relevant than the technical challenges they were required to deal with. In some cases, lack of awareness of the

AICPA Code

Summary of the AICPA Code of Professional Conduct*

Effective December 15, 2015, updated though December 10, 2015

Preface Overview, Structure & Application, Principles, Definitions

0.300	Principles of Professional Conduct *Members should:*
	Responsibilities principle—exercise sensitive professional and moral judgments in all their activities.
	Public Interest principle—act in a way that will serve the public interest, honor the public trust, and demonstrate a commitment to professionalism.
	Integrity principle—perform all professional responsibilities with the highest sense of integrity to maintain and broaden public confidence.
	Objectivity and independence principle—should maintain objectivity and be free of conflicts of interest in discharging professional responsibilities. A *member* in public practice should be independent in fact and appearance when providing auditing and other attestation services.
	Due care principle—observe the profession's technical and ethical standards, strive continually to improve competence and the quality of services, and discharge professional responsibility to the best of the *member's* ability.
	Scope and nature of services principle—observe the Principles of the Code of Professional Conduct in determining the scope and nature of services to be provided.
Part 1 Members in Public Practice *should:*	
1.000.010	***Conceptual Framework***—evaluate whether a relationship or circumstance would lead a reasonable and informed third party who is aware of the relevant information to conclude that there is a *threat* to the *member's* compliance with the rules that is not at an *acceptable level*, after taking into account *safeguards* present. Definitions of acceptable level, safeguards and threat are provided.
	Conceptual Framework Approach—identify threats, evaluate their significance, identify and apply safeguards: Are threats reduced to an acceptable level? If not, determine whether to decline or discontinue the professional service.
	Types of Threats discussed—*Adverse interest, Advocacy, Familiarity, Management participation, Self-interest, Self-review, undue influence.*
	Types of Safeguards discussed—created by the profession, legislation, or regulation; implemented by the client; implemented by the firm
1.000.020	***Ethical Conflicts***—arise when a *member* encounters one or both of the following: (a) Obstacles to following an appropriate course of action due to internal or external pressures, (b) Conflicts in applying relevant professional standards or legal standards. Assessment and course of action discussed.
1.100	***Integrity and Objectivity Rule***—In the performance of any *professional service*, a *member* shall maintain objectivity and integrity, shall be free of conflicts of interest, and shall not knowingly misrepresent facts or subordinate his or her judgment to others.
1.110	***Conflicts of Interest***—A *member* or his or her *firm* may be faced with a conflict of interest when performing a *professional service*. In determining whether a *professional service*, relationship or matter would result in a conflict of interest, a *member* should use professional judgment, taking into account whether a reasonable and informed third party who is aware of the relevant information would conclude that a conflict of interest exists. Examples, identification, evaluation, disclosure and consent are discussed. Reference is made to the *Independence Rule*, the *Integrity and Objectivity Rule, and the Confidential Client Information Rule*. Director positions are also discussed.
1.120	***Gifts and Entertainment***—conditions for consideration, giving and receiving.
1.130	***Misrepresentations***—are prohibited based on *Integrity and Objectivity Rule*, conditions are discussed.
1.140	***Client advocacy***—is considered to be a threat to integrity, objectivity, and independence.
1.150	***Use of a Third-Party Service Provider***—disclosure to client is discussed.
1.200	***Independence Rule***—A *member* in public practice shall be independent in the performance of *professional services* as required by standards promulgated by bodies designated by *Council*.

AICPA Code *(continued)*

	Conceptual Framework for Independence—use, definitions, approach including threats, safeguards, and impairment are discussed.
1.200	***Network Firms, Alternative Practice Structures, Mergers, etc.***—rules for firms involved
	Various practice matters
1.300	***General Standards Rule***—a member is to comply with standards and interpretations regarding professional competence, due professional care, planning and supervision, and sufficient relevant data. The conceptual framework is to be applied to assess threats and safeguards to such performance.
	Competence—the *member* or *member's* staff possess the appropriate technical qualifications to perform *professional services* and that the *member*, as required, supervises and evaluates the quality of work performed. Competence encompasses knowledge of the profession's standards, the techniques and technical subject matter involved, and the ability to exercise sound judgment in applying such knowledge in the performance of *professional services.*
1.310	***Compliance with Standards Rule***—A *member* who performs auditing, review, compilation, management consulting, tax, or other *professional services* shall comply with standards promulgated by bodies designated by *Council.*
1.320	***Accounting Principles Rule***—no misrepresentations about conformity with GAAP; application of conceptual framework to assess risks; clarification that when a GAAP choice yields misleading results, an alternative choice should be made that doesn't.
1.400	***Acts Discreditable Rule***—A *member* shall not commit an act discreditable to the profession. Apply conceptual framework to assess risks; discreditable acts include: discrimination and/or harassment, disclosure of CPA Exam questions and answers, failure to file a tax return or pay a tax liability, negligence in the preparation of financial statements or records,...
	Confidential Information—no disclosure of information obtained from employment or volunteer activities.
	No False, Misleading or Deceptive Acts in Promoting or Marketing professional Services or
	Misuse of CPA Credential
	Dealing with Records
1.500	***Fees and Other Types of Remuneration***—no contingent fees, except under limited circumstances
1.600	***Advertising and Other Forms of Solicitation***—no use of false, misleading or deceptive forms; conceptual framework to be applied to assess risks; use of CPA honors and credentials.
1.700	***Confidential Information***
	Confidential Client Information Rule—A *member* in *public practice* shall not disclose any *confidential client information* without the specific consent of the client; conceptual framework to be applied; exception for new auditor seeking information and some others, and in regard to some aspects of litigation.
1.800	***Form of Organization and Name Rule***—must conform to resolutions of the Council.
Part 2 Members in Business *should, to assess threats to compliance with rules, apply*	
2.000.010	***Conceptual Framework for Members in Business***—similar to section 1.000.010 for members in practice, but with examples relevant to employment for threats and safeguards.
2.000.020	***Ethical Conflicts***—similar to section 1.000.020 for members in practice.
	The following sections are similar to the sections above for members in practice
2.100	***Integrity and Objectivity Rule***
2.110	***Conflicts of Interest***
2.120	***Gifts and Entertainment***
2.130	***Misrepresentations***—as above, plus must be candid to external accountant
2.160	***Educational Services***—are to be considered professional services
2.300	***General Standards Rule & Competence***—similar to members in practice

AICPA Code *(continued)*

2.310	***Compliance with Standards Rule***
2.320	***Accounting Principles Rule***
2.400	***Acts Discreditable Rule***
	Confidential Information
	No False, Misleading or Deceptive Acts in Promoting or Marketing professional Services or
	Misuse of CPA Credential
Part 3 Other Members—members not in public practice or in business	
3.400	***Acts Discreditable Rule***—similar to above
	Confidential Information—similar to above, modified for employment
	No False, Misleading or Deceptive Acts in Promoting or Marketing professional Services or
	Misuse of CPA Credential—similar to above
Appendices A, B, C and D	

*Downloaded May 16, 2016, from http://pub.aicpa.org/codeofconduct/Ethics.aspx.

CPAO Code

Summary of CPAO Code of Professional Conduct*

Adopted February 26, 2016.

PREAMBLE

Characteristics of a Profession	Fundamental Characteristics: • Mastery of a particular intellectual skill, acquired by lengthy training and education; • Traditional foundation rests in public practice—the application of the acquired skill to the affairs of others for a fee; • The calling centers on personal services rather than entrepreneurial dealing in goods; • Objectivity; • Acceptance by the practitioners of a responsibility to subordinate personal interests to those of the public good; • A developed, independent society or institute, comprising the members of the calling, which sets and maintains standards of qualification, attests to the competence of the individual practitioner and safeguards and develops the skills and standards of the calling; • A specialized code of ethical conduct, laid down and enforced by that society or institute, designed principally for the protection of the public; • A belief, on the part of those engaged in the calling, in the virtue of interchange of views, and in a duty to contribute to the development of their calling, adding to its knowledge and sharing advances in knowledge and technique with their fellow members.
Fundamental Principles Governing Conduct	Derived from the professional's fundamental responsibility to act in the public interest, and the public's reliance on sound and fair financial reporting, and competent advice on business affairs: • *Professional behaviour*—conduct that at all times will maintain the profession's good reputation and its "ability to serve the public interest"

CPAO Code ***(continued)***

- *Integrity and due care*—standard of performance, sustain professional competence, comply with *Rules*
- *Objectivity*—no influences, conflicts of interest or relationships which would impair or bias professional or business judgment or objectivity, or appear to do so to a reasonable observer
- *Professional Competence*—maintenance of professional skills and competence by keeping informed of, and complying with, developments in professional standards.
- *Confidentiality*—duty of confidence, no exploitative use, in respect information acquired as a result of professional, employment and business relationships, not disclosure without permission, legal requirement, or professional duty.
- *Personal Character & Ethical Conduct*—CPAO Rules of Conduct are a minimum standard, compliance is based on personal character, high level of achievement is desirable.
- *Ethical Conflict Resolution*—consideration of all facts, role of and duty to directors and designated officers, seeking guidance from CPAO ethics advisers and lawyers, reporting within entity, disassociation if all else fails.
- *Principles Governing the Responsibilities of Firms*—principles and rules apply to all firms and firms will be held accountable for actions and for faulty guidance.

RULES:	ISSUES COVERED:	IMPORTANT INTERPRETATIONS:
General		
101	Compliance with legislation, bylaws, regulations, CPA Code	• is mandatory for members and firms.
102	Matters to be reported to CPAO, others	• conviction of criminal or similar offenses such as fraud, theft, money laundering, securities fraud, dishonesty on tax matters
103	No false or misleading applications to CPAO	• on a letter, report, statement, or representation
104	Must reply promptly in writing to CPAO correspondence, and attend when required	
105	No hindrance, inappropriate influence or intimidation related to CPAO processes	
Public Protection (Standards Affecting the Public Interest)		
201	Maintenance of the good reputation of the profession & its ability to serve the public interest	• at all times, both members and firms • conviction in other Canadian jurisdictions results in charges by the CPAO • guidance on criticism of work of other professionals, resignation/termination of auditors,
202.1	Integrity and due care	• mandatory for all members, students, and firms • imperative to proper fiduciary duty in a fiduciary relationship
202.2	Objectivity	• not allow professional or business judgment to be compromised by bias, conflict of interest or the undue influence of others. • Does not preclude advocacy • "Objectivity is a state of mind. Independence is not only a state of mind; it also includes the appearance of independence, in the view of a reasonable observer. It is the reasonable observer test that distinguishes 'independence' from 'objectivity' and that gives the public the necessary confidence that the member or firm can express a conclusion without bias, conflict of interest or the undue influence of others." (Guidance—Rule 202, 12, p. 23)

CPAO Code *(continued)*

		• Flowchart: *Overview of Independence Standard for Assurance Engagement*, p. 47.
203	Professional competence	• mandatory for members to maintain
204	Independence	• must apply *Framework to identify and assess threats to independence and safeguards* and if threats are not reduced to an acceptable level, the activity, interest or relationship should not be undertaken. Threats and safeguards are described.
		• Specific prohibitions listed—financial interests, loans, guarantees, close business relationships, family & personal relationships, employment, office or director, long association, services without approval of client audit committee, performance management functions; valuation, internal audit, IT, litigation support, legal services to audit or review client, some other services (HR, Corporate Finance, tax planning or tax advisory, non-assurance prior to audit or review) to audit or review client;
		• Fee and remuneration concerns
		• Gifts and hospitality prohibited unless insignificant to member, student, or firm
		• Client mergers and acquisitions concerns
		• must be written disclosure (specified) of any threat that is not clearly insignificant
		• Members or students must disclose prohibited interests and relationships (204.7)
		• firms must ensure compliance
		• member or firm must disclose impaired independence
		• those members, firms, or members of firms who give opinions on financial statements or are undertaking an insolvency engagement must be free of any influence, interest or relationship which, in the view of a reasonable observer, would impair professional judgment or objectivity, or has the appearance of doing so.
205	False or misleading documents or oral representations	• member or firm must have no association even where a disclaimer is given
		• covers letters reports, representations, financial statements, written or oral
206	Compliance with professional standards	• with GAAP and GAAS as set out in the *CPA Canada Handbook* or as identified in/by authoritative sources
		• applies to auditor, preparer, approver or member of an audit committee or board of directors, provider of professional services.
207	No unauthorized benefits	• from client or employer
208	Confidentiality of information	• no disclosure unless client, former client, employer, or former employer has knowledge and consent, or pursuant to the proceedings of lawful authority, Council, or the Professional Conduct Committee or subcommittees
		• no improper use for personal advantage, or of the firm, or of a third party, or to disadvantage the client
		• member or firm must take measures & obtain written agreement to protect
209	Borrowing from clients	• not generally allowed
210	Conflict of interest	• responsibility to detect before accepting engagement
		• no acceptance of a conflicted (self/firm vs. client, client vs. client, client/employer vs. third party) engagement by a member or firm unless they are able to rely upon conflict management techniques, and all affected parties are advised and consent

CPAO Code *(continued)*

		• documentation is required of the conflict, the resolution technique used, rationale for the choice of technique, and the disclosure made to each of the affected parties • where consent to continue service is implied, documentation must be kept of the proof that the affected parties had knowledge, and or their agreement to continue • guidance offers: (a) examples of conflicts of interest in employment, public accounting or related business or practice, professional service area, (b) the process for dealing with conflicts of interest: 1. Identify, 2. Assess, 3. Develop approach & Choose management techniques, Provide disclosure & obtain consent, 4. Assess effectiveness of conflict management plan, 5. Re-evaluate the plan during engagement; (c) documentation, (4) other considerations • *Conflicts of Interest Management Decision Chart* is provided on page 140
211	Duty to report apparent breaches of CPA Code	• of any information raising doubt as to competency, integrity, or capacity to practise • unless specific exemption or would breach statutory duty, solicitor-client privilege, etc • delay in reporting where engaged in criminal or civil investigation
212	Handling of trust funds and other property	• in accord with trust terms and trust law, including holding funds in separate trust account, and appropriate record keeping • handle with due care
213	No unlawful activity	• no association with any activity that is known or should be known to be unlawful
214	Fee quotations & billings	• provide only after obtaining adequate information about the assignment • render on fair & reasonable basis, provide such explanations as are necessary to understand
215	Contingent fees	• none allowed, except if there will be no real or apparent conflict of interest (Rule 204) and where the client consents in writing, or such fee would not influence the result of a compilation engagement or an income tax return prepared for the same client.
216	Payment or receipt of commissions	• if engaged in public accounting, none allowed, except in sale or purchase of an accounting practice. • If not engaged in public accounting, can pay or receive, provided compliance to Rule 207 incl. disclosure and consent
217	Advertising, solicitation and endorsements	• advertising cannot be false or misleading, reflect unfavorably on competence or integrity, include unsubstantiated statements, or brings disrepute on the profession • no solicitation is permitted if persistent, coercive or harassing • endorsements are possible under strict conditions, after suitable investigation
218	Retention of documentation & working papers	• for a reasonable time period
Relations with Professional Colleagues		
302	Communication with predecessor	• Acceptance of appointment where there is an incumbent auditor is not allowed without asking outgoing auditor if there are circumstances which should be taken into account • response is required from incumbent, confidentiality concerns must be considered & advice sought, presence of confidential matters must be reported but not specifics

CPAO Code *(continued)*

303	Provision of client information	• timely response required if written request received from successor • necessary client information is to be supplied, and co-operation given
304	Joint appointments	• carry joint and several liability • must advise other accountant of activities
305	Communication of special assignments to incumbent	• must communicate with incumbent unless client makes such a request in writing before the engagement is begun, or unless the services are outside the practice of public accounting.
306	Responsibilities owed to an incumbent	• no action to impair the position of the other accountant • no services beyond original referral terms, except with consent of referring member
Public Accounting Practices		
401	Practice names	• in good taste, approved by institute, not misleading or self-laudatory
402	Descriptive styles	• must use "Chartered Professional Accountant(s)" or "public accountant(s)" unless part of firm name • cannot use "Chartered Professional Accountant(s)" if a non-CA shares a proprietary interest.
403	Association with firms	• restricted association with firms practicing as "chartered professional accountant(s)" if some partners are not CPAs
404	Access to members practicing public accounting	• offices must be under the charge of a CPA normally in attendance • no part-time offices except per regulations
405	Office by representation	• not allowed if only represented by another public accountant
406	Responsibility for non-member	• public accountants are responsible for the failure of non-members associated with the practice or other related businesses to abide by the *CPA Code*
408	Association with non-member in public practice	• Cannot associate unless maintains good reputation of profession, and adheres to CPO governing legislation, regulations & the *CPA Code*, but cannot use any style, presentation or communication that implies the non-member is a member. • Can associate in a related business
409	Practice of public accounting in a corporate form	• prohibited except under in accord with CPAO legislation and bylaws such as through a properly incorporated professional corporation in Ontario or in another province
Firms		
501	Policies and procedures for compliance with professional standards	• Establish, maintain & uphold policies and procedures necessary for compliance with professional standards in accord with generally accepted standards of practice of the profession and the standards of the particular business or practice, provided that the standards of the particular business or practice are not lower than or inconsistent with those of the profession.
502	Policies and procedures for the conduct of a practice	• those necessary for compliance with expected competence and conduct of members, and any other persons contracted with
503	Association with Firms	• only if the other firm meets the ownership requirements per Rule 403

*Downloaded May 17, 2016, from http://www.cpaontario.ca/Resources/Membershandbook/1011page20931.pdf.

significance of the code was at the root of the problem, whereas in other instances, inability to interpret the general principles and rules was responsible. As our ethics environment has changed and ethical shortfalls have become recognized as serious threats to professional practice, there have been numerous calls for renewed interest, understanding, and commitment on the part of professionals themselves.

Ethics education is an official requirement of the formal education of professional accountants according to the AACSB,[22] and some professional bodies have introduced mandatory ethics education prior to attempting professional examinations. As a result, among professional accountants there is a growing awareness of ethical issues and the provisions of ethics codes, and some progress has been made on introducing ethical analysis into accounting curricula. However, more emphasis is required on ethical analysis because simple awareness of issues and of professional codes of conduct cannot solve all the problems professional accountants face. Fortunately, the AICPA, CPAO, and IFAC codes of conduct all require additional analysis of threats and safeguards on specific issues and documentation of it. What is needed in addition, however, is an appreciation of practical ethical decision making and techniques so that professional accountants can fully appreciate, identify, and quantify ethical threats and safeguards for professional services and consult clients or employers effectively on their business decisions.

It is becoming customary for codes of conduct to encourage professional accountants to seek counsel on ethical issues through their professional association or from outside legal counsel. While this is a progressive step, caution should be raised about the legalistic mind-set of outside counsel, which may lead to ignoring important stakeholder concerns, particularly of a longer term nature, that could affect adversely reputation and revenue streams.

Finally, codes of conduct do not provide a clear understanding of the sanctions to be expected from errant actions. Therefore, it is important to seek out the current record of sanctions that have been levied by professional accounting bodies and to project what might be the penalty for behavioral shortcomings that offend the codes.

ISSUES NOT USUALLY RESOLVED IN CORPORATE CODES OF CONDUCT Having examined the nature, content, and shortcomings of both corporate and professional accounting codes of conduct, it is appropriate to turn to the overlap between them. Several issues are often not resolved in codes of conduct that could be faced by employees, including professional accountants. Accordingly, some thought should be given to the following matters when a corporate code is being set up or revised:

1. *Conflicts between codes*
   Occasionally, a professional or some other employee will be subject to the company/employer's code and also another code, such as a professional code for engineers or accountants. To avoid placing the person in an ethical dilemma of debating which code to follow, at the very least, consultation with an ethics officer/ombudsman should be advised.
2. *Conflicts between competing interests or corporate stakeholders*
   Sometimes the priority of competing interests can be made clear in training sessions. If not, then protected routes for consultation should be available. This subject is discussed at length in this chapter and in Chapter 5.

[22] See the AACSB *Ethics Education Committee Report*, 2004, **http://www.cengagebrain.com**.

3. *When should a professional blow the whistle, and to whom?*
   A protected, internal route for discussion and reporting should be available for professional accountants. An employer should realize that every professional accountant has a professional duty to uphold, which could supersede loyalty to the employer. It would be helpful if the professional's accounting society were to provide consultation to the professional on a confidential basis to assist in these decisions, as is the case in the United Kingdom and some other jurisdictions.
4. *Adequate protection of whistleblowers*
   The most successful arrangements for whistleblowing involve reporting, in confidence, to an autonomous individual of high rank or to someone who reports to a person of very high rank in the organization, such as an ombudsperson who will follow up on concerns without revealing the informant's name or exposing the informant and who reports, without informant names, directly to the chairperson of the organization. With this level of apparent support, investigations can be undertaken without interference. The ombudsperson should report back to the informant.
5. *Service decisions involving judgment*
   Codes of conduct should be fashioned so as not to rule out the exercise of a professional's values when those are required for the judgments they must make. In the final analysis, it is the exercise of these values and the judgments based on these that could save the individual, the firm or employer, the profession, and the public from ethical problems. The challenge is to develop codes and cultures that do not force the abandonment of personal values but rather foster the development and exercise of values and judgment processes that will credit the stakeholders when they really need it.

Conceptual Framework for Assessing Threats to Compliance

Codes of conduct for professional accountants begin by providing the fundamental principles that must be met for ethical behavior to be maintained in order for professional accountants to serve the public interest. A conceptual framework is then provided for identifying and assessing threats to compliance with those principles, as are requirements for documentation of the assessment. Safeguards must also be considered to arrive at an overall conclusion that the threats to compliance are at or have been reduced to an acceptable level or, if not, that appropriate action is taken to nullify the threat or avoid the service involved. Figure 6.1 provides a representation of this approach that has been adopted in many other country codes, including in the AICPA and CPAO codes.

The conceptual framework approach requires professional accountants to continuously assess the threats they face in complying with all the fundamental principles, taking into account the safeguards that are relevant to the situations involved. The normal threats and safeguards that professional accountants should be aware of and assessing are identified in Tables 6.11 and 6.12.

The objective of this assessment process is for the professional accountant to come to a judgement, based on quantitative and nonquantitative threats and safeguards, that the risk of noncompliance with the fundamental principles of her or his code due to a specific course of action is low enough to be acceptable (or not). The analysis underlying this decision should be documented and the documentation retained.

If the overall assessment, after consideration of the safeguards that could reduce the impact of the threats, is that the threats identified are likely to cause a breach of the code, then the professional accountant should consider mitigating the threats, introducing

FIGURE 6.1 IFAC 2015 code of Ethics Conceptual Framework Approach

Source: *IFAC Code of Ethics for Professional Accountants,* April 15, 2016 (Section number).

additional safeguards, or not undertaking the proposed action. Consultation should be sought with colleagues, ethics counselors, and legal advisors if the professional is in doubt.

The following section illustrates the application of this conceptual risk assessment framework on matters related to independence and conflicts of interest.

Conflict of Interest Threats to Independence

One of the most bedeviling aspects of a professional accountant's life is the recognition, avoidance, and/or management of conflict of interest situations. This is because *conflict of interest situations threaten to undermine the reason for having an accounting profession—to provide assurance that the work of a professional accountant will be governed by independent judgment focused to protect the public interest.* For this reason, the independence standards that the accounting profession must live by are fundamental to the continued success of the profession, its members, and their firms.

A professional accountant is called on in his or her professional code to *"hold himself or herself free from any influence, interest or relationship in respect of his or her client's affairs, which impairs his or her professional judgment or objectivity or which, in the view of a reasonable observer would impair the member's professional judgment or objectivity."*[23] Consequently, there are two distinct aspects to be kept in mind: *the reality* of having a conflict of interests and *the appearance* that one might be present. Therefore, the traditional definition—*a conflict of interest is any influence, interest, or relationship that could cause a professional accountant's judgment to deviate from applying the profession's standards to client matters*—covers only part of the conflict of interest risk faced by a professional accountant.

[23] Institute of Chartered Accountants of Ontario, *Rules of Professional Conduct and Council Interpretations,* 1997, foreword, p. 505, updated continuously.

TABLE 6.11 Threats to Noncompliance—AICPA Code Sections 1.000.010.10—.16

Compliance with fundamental principles may be threatened by a broad range of circumstances. Many threats fall into the following categories:

Adverse interest threat: that a *member* will not act with objectivity because the *member's* interests are opposed to the *client's* interests.

Self-interest threat: that a *member* could benefit, financially or otherwise, from an interest in, or relationship with, a *client* or persons associated with the *client.*

Self-review threats: that a *member* will not appropriately evaluate the results of a previous judgment made or service performed or supervised by the *member* or an individual in the *member's firm* and that the *member* will rely on that service in forming a judgment as part of another.

Management participation threat: that a *member* will take on the role of *client* management or otherwise assume management responsibilities, such may occur during an engagement to provide nonattest services.

Advocacy threat: that a *member* will promote a *client's* interests or position to the point that his or her objectivity or *independence* is compromised.

Familiarity threat: that, due to a long or close relationship with a *client*, a *member* will become too sympathetic to the *client's* interests or too accepting of the *client's* work or product.

Intimidation threats/Undue influence threat: that a *member* will subordinate his or her judgment to an individual associated with a *client* or any relevant third party due to that individual's reputation or expertise, aggressive or dominant personality, or attempts to coerce or exercise excessive influence over the *member.*

IFAC 2015 Code of Ethics for Professional Accountants, Section 100.12
AICPA 2015 Code of Professional Conduct, Sections 1.000.010.08–.16
CPAO 2015 Code of Professional Conduct, Section 204.3

With one notable exception, a professional accountant's view of conflict of interest situations is very similar to that of a director, executive, or other employee, as discussed in Chapter 5. Consequently, the discussion in Chapter 5 covering *basic concepts, terms, causes,* (Figures 5.6 and 5.7 and Table 5.6) should be reviewed because they are applicable to professional accountants and the environment they face.

The notable exception is that a professional accountant is a fiduciary for the public. A professional accountant must protect his or her client or employer, but not at any cost and not if the public interest will suffer. *A professional accountant must adhere to a set of rules aimed at neutrality among stakeholder interests and at protecting the public interest—he or she should not go to absolutely any lengths to serve a specific client's interests, unless the public interest is also served.* The services rendered by a fiduciary must be able to be trusted, and the professional accountant's independence of judgment is essential to that trust.

ASSESSING CONFLICT OF INTEREST THREATS USING THE CONCEPTUAL FRAMEWORK APPROACH The IFAC Code's discussion of threats to compliance with fundamental principles amplifies the need for a professional accountant to maintain independence so that the integrity and objectivity of service to the public and clients are not compromised. It is concerned not only with performance but also with the wholesome appearance of that performance, which might lessen the effective transmission of information and lower the reputation of the profession. This requires continued vigilance about the actual state of mind of the professional accountant as well as about the appearance of independence. As Section 290.6 of the 2015 Code states,

> Independence requires:
>
> *Independence of Mind*
>
> The state of mind that permits the expression of a conclusion without being affected by influences that compromise professional judgment,

TABLE 6.12 Safeguards Reducing the Risk of Conflict of Interest Situations

Safeguards Created by the Profession, Legislation, or Regulation *AICPA Code Sec 1.000.010 & IFAC Code S 100.14*

(a) Education, training, experience requirement for entry

(b) Continuing education

(c) Professional standards, monitoring, and disciplinary processes

(d) External review by a legally empowered third party of reports, returns, communications or information produced by a professional accountant.

(e) External review of firm's quality control system

(f) Legislation governing independence requirements of the firm

(g) Competency and experience requirements for professional licensure

(h) Professional resources, such as hotlines, for consultation on ethical issues

Safeguards implemented by a *Client* *AICPA Code Sec 1.000.010 & IFAC Code 200.15*

(a) The *client* has personnel with suitable skill, knowledge, or experience who make managerial decisions about the delivery of *professional services* and makes use of third-party resources for consultation as needed.

(b) The tone at the top emphasizes the *client's* commitment to fair financial reporting and compliance with the applicable laws, rules, regulations, and corporate governance policies.

(c) Policies and procedures are in place to achieve fair financial reporting and compliance with the applicable laws, rules, regulations, and corporate governance policies.

(d) Policies and procedures are in place to address ethical conduct.

(e) A governance structure, such as an active audit committee, is in place to ensure appropriate decision making, oversight, and communications regarding a *firm's* services.

(f) Policies are in place that bar the entity from hiring a *firm* to provide services that do not serve the public interest or that would cause the *firm's independence* or objectivity to be considered *impaired.*

Safeguards Implemented by a *Firm* *AICPA Code Sec 1.000.010 & IFAC Code, Parts B & C*

(a) *Firm* leadership stresses the importance of complying with the rules and the expectation that engagement teams will act in the public interest.

(b) Policies and procedures that are designed to implement and monitor engagement quality control.

(c) Documented policies regarding the identification of *threats* to compliance with the rules, the evaluation of the significance of those *threats*, and the identification and application of *safeguards* that can eliminate identified *threats* or reduce them to an *acceptable level.*

(d) Internal policies and procedures that are designed to monitor compliance with the *firm's* policies and procedures.

(e) Policies and procedures designed to identify interests or relationships between the *firm* or its *partners and* professional staff and the *firm's clients.*

(f) The use of different *partners, partner equivalents*, and engagement teams from different offices or that report to different supervisors.

(g) Training on, and timely communication of, a *firm's* policies and procedures and any changes to them for all *partners* and professional staff.

(h) Policies and procedures that are designed to monitor the *firm's, partner's*, or *partner equivalent's* reliance on revenue from a single *client* and that, if necessary, trigger action to address excessive reliance

(i) 18 additional safeguards are listed—see AICPA Code S 0.100.010.23

thereby allowing an individual to act with integrity, and exercise objectivity and professional skepticism.

Independence in Appearance

The avoidance of facts and circumstances that are so significant that a reasonable and informed third party would be likely to conclude, weighing all the specific facts and circumstances that a firm's, or a member of the audit team's, integrity, objectivity or professional skepticism has been compromised.

Diagrammatically, these components and relevance of proper judgment are represented in Figure 6.2.

Professional accountants must be alert to conflict of interest problems because they have the potential to erode independence. As noted in Table 6.11, the AICPA Code lists *seven categories of threats or conflicts that could sway the professional accountant from acting in the public interest: adverse interest; self-interest; review of one's own work; management participation; advocating a client's position; familiarity with the management, directors, or owners of the client corporation; and intimidation or undue influence by management, directors, or owners.* Specifically, these categories involve the following:

- Adverse interest, when the professional accountant's interests are opposed to a client's, can become problematic if work is to be performed for two or more clients who are competitors. Deciding if one was disadvantaged in court proceedings can be very difficult.
- Self-interest, or the desire to protect or enhance one's position, certainly has been known to influence a professional accountant's judgment. Arthur Andersen provides a glaring example of this, as they wanted to retain the audit revenue from several clients, including Enron, WorldCom, Waste Management, and Sunbeam.
- Auditing one's own work is a variant of the self-interest problem wherein auditors are reluctant to criticize themselves and lose face with client management.
- Participation as part of management raises the possibility that a professional accountant will become so immersed in management activity, incentives, and strategies that

FIGURE 6.2 IFAC Code's Framework for Independent Judgment

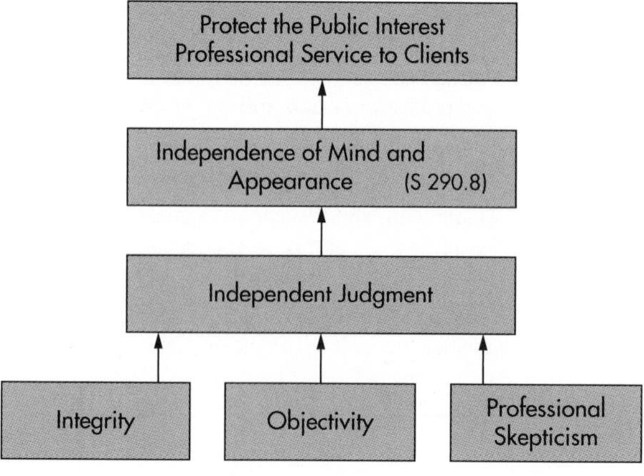

Source: *IFAC Code of Ethics for Professional Accountants,* 2005, S 290.8 & Independence Definition.

the accountant will no longer be seen as able to demonstrate the integrity, objectivity, and professional skepticism expected of a professional.

- Advocacy of client's positions to a third party occasionally puts a professional accountant in a poor position to argue a different and better position with regard to GAAP or disclosure with the client.
- Familiarity with client personnel, directors, or owners may create interpersonal bonds that leave a professional accountant not wanting to disappoint or offend the friends or close associates that familiarity has created.
- Intimidation or undue influence occurs in many cases where the senior management of a corporation has intimidated or used undue influence on professional accountants working for the corporation, thereby forcing them into misrepresentations, illegalities, and/or poor accounting choices. This problem is vividly illustrated in the WorldCom case in Chapter 2 and the *Livent—When Maria, When?* case later in this chapter.

Identification of any of these potential conflict of interest situations should be followed by their avoidance, elimination, or reduction of their risk through the application of safeguards. The AICPA and IFAC codes suggest that safeguards can be (1) found in techniques and approaches detailed in professional guidelines, legislation, regulation, (2) implemented by clients, or (3) implemented by professional accounting firms. Examples of safeguards provided in the AICPA and IFAC codes are listed in Table 6.13.

TABLE 6.13 Conflicts of Interest Examples—2015 AICPA Code Section 1.110.010.04

a. Providing corporate finance services to a *client* seeking to acquire an audit *client* of the *firm*, when the *firm* has obtained confidential information during the course of the audit that may be relevant to the transaction
b. Advising two *clients* at the same time who are competing to acquire the same company when the advice might be relevant to the parties' competitive positions
c. Providing services to both a vendor and a purchaser who are *clients* of the *firm* in relation to the same transaction
d. Preparing valuations of assets for two *clients* who are in an adversarial position with respect to the same assets
e. Representing two *clients* at the same time regarding the same matter who are in a legal dispute with each other, such as during divorce proceedings or the dissolution of a partnership
f. Providing a report for a licensor on royalties due under a license agreement while at the same time advising the licensee of the correctness of the amounts payable under the same license agreement
g. Advising a *client* to invest in a business in which, for example, the *immediate family* member of the *member* has a *financial interest* in the business
h. Providing strategic advice to a *client* on its competitive position while having a joint venture or similar interest with a competitor of the *client*
i. Advising a *client* on the acquisition of a business which the *firm* is also interested in acquiring
j. Advising a *client* on the purchase of a product or service while having a royalty or commission agreement with one of the potential vendors of that product or service
k. Providing forensic investigation services to a *client* for the purpose of evaluating or supporting contemplated litigation against another *client* of the *firm*
l. Providing tax or personal financial planning services for several members of a family whom the *member* knows to have opposing interests
m. Referring a personal financial planning or tax *client* to an insurance broker or other service provider, which refers *clients* to the *member* under an exclusive arrangement

Due to the importance of recognizing conflicts of interest, the AICPA Code puts forward the list of examples reproduced in Table 6.13. An extended discussion of conflicts of interest follows.

Most professional accountants take the proper handling of conflict of interest situations very seriously because that is fundamental to the maintenance of fiduciary relationships. Many professional accounting firms, including the largest, have additional codes of conduct or practice that offer the firm's guidance. Members of a multioffice or network firm often sign a document in which they promise not to discuss the affairs of—or trade in securities of—clients of any office in their firm, and a restricted list of clients' names is maintained for reference. Members of the firm are told that, even if they do not personally possess information on a client's activities, they may be presumed to do so by the interested public. Care must be taken to avoid the appearance of conflict as much as the reality. Reputation is too hard—and too costly—to restore. Consequently, most firms employ several techniques in the management of conflicts of interest to minimize potential harm, including the following:

- Firm codes, in addition to augment those of professional bodies
- Training sessions and reinforcing memos
- Client lists from all locales for reference and sign-off procedures signifying noninvestment
- Scrutiny of securities trading, particularly related to new issues
- Information barriers (also known as firewalls) to prevent information flows within firms
- Reporting and consultation with senior officers
- Avoidance
- Rules for serving clients with potentially conflicting interests
- Rules for taking on new clients or providing new services and for termination of client relations

CONFLICTS OF INTEREST: A STAKEHOLDER IMPACT ANALYSIS With the foregoing background, it is useful to consider what the most common conflicts of interest are for accountants. These can be grouped into four categories as to their stakeholder impact:

1. Self-interest of the professional conflicts with the interests of the other stakeholders
2. Self-interest of the professional and some other stakeholders and conflicts with some other stakeholders
3. Interests of one client favored over the interests of another client
4. Interests of one or more stakeholders favored over the interests of one or more other stakeholders

The first category pits the professional accountant against the other stakeholders in several spheres of activity. The undermined independent judgment of the professional can be evident in the services offered, the improper use of influence, and the misuse of information. The second category, where the professional sides with some stakeholders to the disadvantage of others, also offers opportunities for poor judgment in terms of the services offered, as does the third category, which refers specifically to clients. The fourth category, which involves stakeholder groups but where self-interest may not come into play except sometimes on the disadvantaged side, focuses primarily on the proper use of information and particularly on issues of confidentiality. These

TABLE 6.14 **Conflicts of Interest for Professional Accountants: A Stakeholder Impact Analysis**

STAKEHOLDER CATEGORY	SPHERE OF ACTIVITY AFFECTED	EXAMPLES
Self vs. others	Services offered Improper use of influence Misuse of information	Conflicting services, shaving quality Improper purchases of client goods Improper investments by relatives
Self and others vs. others	Services offered	Overinvolvement with management or directors erodes objectivity
Client vs. client Employer vs. employer	Services offered	Serving competing clients or competing employers at the same time
Stakeholder vs. stakeholder	Misuse of information (confidentiality)	Whistleblowing, reporting to government or regulators

relationships are summarized in Table 6.14, and a discussion follows of how judgment can be undermined in each of these spheres of activity.

CONFLICTS OF INTEREST AFFECTING SERVICES OFFERED Self-interest is a very powerful motivator that can disadvantage clients, the public, and other stakeholders through a degradation of the services offered by a professional accountant, whether the professional is in the role of auditor or management accountant. Many of the temptations auditors succumb to arise because the auditor's "business" side dominates his or her "professional" side, and the drive for profit or personal gain dominates the values that are needed to maintain the trust expected in a fiduciary relationship. When the needed trust breaks down, it does so because one or more of the essential aspects of professional service expected are not delivered in a manner that protects or furthers the interests that the professional should be serving before the professional's own interest.

For example, the desire for profit can lead to services being performed at *substandard levels of quality*. Because of the pressures of rising costs or in an effort to increase profit, services may be performed at substandard levels of quality. This may happen through the use of junior or unskilled staff or if staff are not adequately supervised by senior and more costly personnel. It may lead to pressures on staff to increase their working hours beyond reasonable levels or to encourage staff to work long hours but not to charge the clients for the total time spent. In either of these cases, the fatigue factor that results not only is unfair to staff but also can result in diminished capacity to detect errors on the audit. Although diminished services clearly affect clients and the public, these working conditions also present the staff involved with the very real ethical problem of how to react: should they complain, and, if so, how much and to whom? These issues will be addressed later in this chapter.

The quality of services provided can suffer for other reasons as well. A professional may be tempted to *lowball fee quotations* to clients in an effort to gain new business or retain old clients. Later, the reality of the low fee may present the dilemma of having to meet audit budgets that are too tight, which can again lead to substandard service quality and/or pressures on staff to bury or forget about time spent beyond budget allowances. Lowballing is occasionally rationalized on the basis of anticipated future price increases for audit services or the garnering of additional high-margin work in tax or consulting services. This hope is not always incorporated into audit planning, so budgets are occasionally set too tight. Moreover, the anticipated high-margin revenue sources may not materialize in any event. These exigencies have been understood for a long time and were the major reason why many professional societies prohibited the quotation of *fixed fees*. When something unexpected occurs, in a fixed or lowballed fee situation the cost of additional time spent comes right out of the auditor's pocket—giving rise to an obvious conflict of interest. Fees set on the basis of hourly rates per level of staff employed allow the need for quality service to be incorporated in the total fee even where unexpected problems arise during an audit.

Self-interest can also lead to the offer of services in situations leading to conflicts of interest with other stakeholders. For example, an auditor is in an excellent position to offer *management advisory services* or *assurance services* because the audit has developed a thorough knowledge of the client's affairs and personnel. On the other hand, if an auditor accepts an engagement to install an internal control system, there may be a reluctance to acknowledge its flaws when these become clear during a subsequent audit. Such reluctance can arise even where nonaudit personnel from the same firm are used. Unfortunately, living with a faulty system of internal control is like living with a time bomb, with the enhanced risk being borne by the client and the public. Another example that presents itself frequently involves a partner who is negotiating with a client's CFO on the adequacy of a provision for bad debts, knowing that next week the CFO will be making a decision on whether to award his or her firm or a competitor a very large consulting assignment. The threat to objectivity is obvious and overwhelming, yet the partner is expected to be objective nonetheless.

What are the remedies for such situations involving so-called *conflicting services* that involve self-criticism? Refusal to provide such services is one option, but it could lead to the client incurring unnecessary costs and the professional losing revenue. The long-established position of the accounting profession has been to rely on the personal integrity of the professionals involved to be able to criticize themselves in the event that they or their associates perform conflicting services. However, this reliance, which depends on the values, strength of character, and ethical awareness of the professionals involved, has been eliminated for the auditors of SEC registrant companies[24] by SOX regulations.

The self-interest of professional accountants can cause the professional to want to side with certain stakeholder groups to the detriment of others. Professional accountants can easily and inadvertently become overinvolved with clients or suppliers or other stakeholders. Sometimes this *overinvolvement* can make the professional's judgment susceptible to bias in favor of his or her newfound friends or compatriots. Gifts can create pressures for continuance. Involvement in management friendships and decisions can create the desire not to be critical, as can the continued, close involvement of an auditor with a Board of Directors. To borrow from the hierarchy of human needs developed by Maslow (1954), professionals can be subject to influence attempts directed at their ego, their social needs, or even their basic financial needs because of overinvolvement with other stakeholders, threatening the professional's independence. Frequently, overinvolvement begins very innocuously and builds imperceptibly to a condition that the professional does not expect (the slippery-slope problem noted earlier). Constant vigilance is required to stay out of the difficulty of putting the interests of management and directors ahead of shareholders and the public.

Sometimes a professional accountant develops a mutuality of interest with a client or becomes overinvolved with senior management at a client to the extent that the professional's skepticism and critical perspective are suspended. Friendship, partnerships, the desire to protect existing revenue streams or garner more, and the prospect of social interaction or admiration may all impact on the professional's independence of judgment to the detriment of the public interest. Care must be taken to ensure that a professional

[24] See discussion section on SEC and IFAC Independence Rules on p. 394.

accountant or his or her firm does not become so dependent on the revenue from one client that decisions contrary to the public interest become difficult to make. This appears to have happened, as noted in Chapter 2, in the case of Arthur Andersen and several of its audit clients, including Enron, WorldCom, and Waste Management.

Concern over the impact of consulting and other services on the independence of professional accountants alarmed the accounting profession and its regulators, particularly in the United States prior to the demise of Arthur Andersen. In 1998, PricewaterhouseCoopers (PwC) discovered[25] in a postmerger review that its predecessor firms (Price Waterhouse and Coopers & Lybrand) had failed to properly supervise their consulting and audit partners and personnel and that almost 50% of PwC's U.S. partners held improperly sanitized[26] investments in the firm's audit clients—thereby violating PwC and SEC conflict of interest guidelines. This led, in part, to the issuance of a proposed revision of the SEC's Auditor Independence Requirements[27] for auditors of companies that file SEC documentation in the United States. Among other guidance provided, the revised rule sought to clarify those services that an auditor of SEC registrant companies can and cannot engage in to preserve independence of judgment in fact as well as the perception of independence. It should be noted that the matters dealt with in the proposed revision were overtaken by the SOX reforms and the resulting SEC pronouncements[28] discussed earlier in this chapter.

Although embarrassed by the initial publicity of the PwC violations, PwC, the accounting profession, and regulators such as the SEC have not required complete separation between audit or assurance services and consulting services. As previously noted, SOX has required the SEC to specify those services that can be offered to audit clients. However, even though some large firms have sold off service lines, they continue to operate multidisciplinary consulting practices offering services to nonaudit clients.

The continuation in nonattest activity requires a strong set of guidelines and organizational culture to prevent the erosion of independent judgment and professional skepticism. Professional accountants have to continue to resist the temptation of focusing on the development of high-profit services to the detriment of low-margin audit services. An instance of this might be a new perversion of risk management in tax matters where the client is advised to take a questionable action based on the probability that government tax auditors are unlikely to appear because of other time demands, not because the tax treatment is in doubt. An additional aspect of a multidisciplinary firm that could cause difficulties is the potential conflict between the professional codes and practices of accountants, lawyers, and engineers. For example, accountants are not generally expected to blow the whistle on clients, but engineers are required to report any endangerment to life from a dangerous process or poorly maintained building.[29] Which profession's rules should prevail in the firm? Similarly, lawyers have a different standard of confidentiality that prevents them from advising competing clients, whereas

[25] SEC independent consultant, *Report of the Internal Investigation of Independence Issues at PricewaterhouseCoopers LLP*, January 6, 2000, http://www.sec.gov/news/press/pressarchive/2000press.shtml.

[26] Investment where PwC had precleared that no conflict of interests had or would occur.

[27] For the *Proposed Rule: Revision of the Commission's Auditor Independence Requirements*, July 17, 2000, see http://www.sec.gov/rules/proposed/34-42994.htm, 109. A final rule was released in January 2003.

[28] For *Final Rule: Strengthening the Commission's Requirements regarding Auditor Independence*, February 6, 2003, see http://www.sec.gov/rules/final/33-8183.htm; for *Commission Adopts Rules Strengthening Auditor Independence*, January 22, 2003, see http://www.sec.gov/news/press/2003-9.htm.

[29] Presumably, this difference in treatment is due to the higher priority attached by society (and therefore by engineers) to physical well-being as opposed to financial well-being. Society is willing to endorse the reporting of one but not yet the other.

professional accountants do so frequently provided that adequate safeguards are in place. We are also seeing some assurance services downgraded to the status of a nonaudit review or consulting services to lessen the legal liability involved in an effort to bolster profits. Increased attention to ethical principles for managing such conflicts of interest will be essential to the maintenance of the accounting profession's reputation in the future as well as the reputations of the other professions involved.

The examples of overindulged self-interest cited in Table 6.14 put the professional's reputation at risk because the interest of the client, employer, or public may not be considered before the professional's self-interest as is expected in a fiduciary relationship. The lure of personal profit from investment positions in clients may lead to the manipulation of accounting disclosure or the choice of accounting principles, which do not communicate the real state of affairs to shareholders because the stock price gains for the investor/professional accountant are too alluring to pass up. Fortunately, such investment has been barred for years in most professional codes. Similarly, skimping on quality of service, particularly of audit service, has proven difficult to resist in the past. As competition on the basis of price of services becomes more intense, professionals would be well advised to consider the longer-term possibilities of loss of reputation, fines, and higher insurance premiums.

It is possible—but very risky—for a professional accountant and his or her clients to *represent more than one client in a transaction*. Even if a professional is very knowledgeable about the matter, such as would be the case if an audit client were being sold, and the buyer and seller are good friends, it is very difficult to do your best for one except at the expense of the other. Later, if the buyer or seller becomes disenchanted, he or she may suspect that his or her interest has been shortchanged and launch a lawsuit. Therefore, even if more than one client who is party to a transaction wants a professional accountant to act on their behalf, the clients should at least be warned that each should have independent representation. Sometimes, it will be advisable to select and serve only one of the clients, even if they are insistent. Whenever more than one client is served in a transaction, the professional accountant must be able to show that all reasonable precautions were taken to avoid failing to act in the best interests of all parties.

For the accountant in management, it is similarly risky to consider *serving two or more employers*. Serving two or more masters has, over the years, proven to be very difficult because of the real, latent, and imaginary conflicts of interest that inevitably arise even where the employers are not competitors. Where the employers are competitors, it is sheer folly. A variant of this ethical problem surfaces when an accountant in management *invests in a competitor*. Care must be taken to ensure that conflicting interests do not influence judgment or work performance adversely for the employer.

Blind self-interest can prove to be the undoing of professional accountants, just as blind ambition has proven to be the bane of many managers. Frequently, however, professional accountants do not suffer from blind or rabid self-interest but do lose sight of *whether they are in a profession or in business*. They would do well to remember that few businesses are accorded the privilege of engaging in fiduciary relationships. A balance is called for that involves placing the interest of the public, the client, the profession, and the firm or employer before the professional's own self-interest.

CONFLICTS OF INTEREST INVOLVING IMPROPER USE OF INFLUENCE The desire to improve the professional's own lot can lead to the improper use of influence such that the independent judgment of the professional can be undermined. For example, a professional accountant employed by a corporation might be successful in arranging for a friend to be hired by the company. In so doing, however, the professional may put him- or herself in a position to be approached by management who want a *favor in return*, which may take the form of nondisclosure of a financial matter, the delay of such disclosure, or the minimization of the disclosure. The public, shareholders, other management, and the auditors can be misled in the process.

An auditor may also be unsuspectingly trapped by the use of his or her own influence. From time to time, auditors will want—and be encouraged by clients—to *purchase goods or services from the client* at substantial discounts beyond those available to the public. The risk is that the desire to do this or the satisfaction experienced will create a desire to subjugate public interests in favor of the interests of the management who control this privilege. Similarly, a professional employed by a corporation may wish to *buy goods or services from a supplier* at a discount. Is this a reasonable thing to do? The answer depends on the circumstances.

Alternatively, a professional in audit practice or employed by a corporation can be offered a *gift, a meal, entertainment, a trip, or preferential treatment* by a client or a supplier. Is it ethical to accept such a gift? Again, the answer depends on the circumstances. Fortunately, the guidelines outlined in Table 5.8 can be used to avoid the real or potential conflicts of interest that could develop when the giver expects a favor in return.

CONFLICTS OF INTEREST INVOLVING USE OR MISUSE OF INFORMATION (CONFIDENTIALITY) The misuse of information by a professional accountant can be detrimental to other stakeholders of the client or company involved. For example, the use of information by the professional before others have the right to use such information is unfair and considered unethical. This is the basic problem for anyone who is privy to *inside information* about a company by virtue of being the auditor or an employee—that is, an "insider"—to use that information personally or indirectly for *insider trading*. In order to ensure the basic fairness of stock markets so that the public and other noninsiders will wish to enter the market, regulatory bodies such as the SEC or the OSC require management insiders to wait until the information is released to the public before allowing insiders to trade, and then they must disclose these trades so that the public will know what has happened. The prospect of a "rigged game" in which insiders have an unfair advantage would not be in the public interest or in the interest of the corporations using the market for fund-raising in the long run. Insider trading rules also apply to the families of the insider, extending to those who are not part of the immediate family but for whom the insider has an obvious ability to influence. Some individuals with high-profile jobs in the public service go even further to avoid such conflicts of interest. In order to be seen as entirely ethical, some politicians have gone so far as to place their holdings and those of their dependents into so-called blind trusts, which are managed by someone else with instructions not to discuss trades or holdings with the politician.

The situation for auditors is somewhat different in that the ownership of shares or financial instruments of a client is forbidden based on the real or potential conflict of interest that would be created, as discussed in earlier segments of this book. Most auditing firms extend this ban in two ways. First, the ban is applied to the auditor's family and persons who would be considered significant dependents or subject to influence. Second, the ban may also apply for any client of the firm, even if that client is serviced through a wholly separate office (for international firms, even in another country) with which the individual does not have contact on a normally occurring basis. Where the ban is relaxed on trading in shares of the firm's clients for employees not directly involved in the client's affairs, extreme care should be taken through information barriers/firewalls and reporting/scrutiny mechanisms to manage the conflict of interest created. The extent of attention to the prevention of insider trading and the perception of it is indicative of the alarm with which most firms view its prospect.

Confidentiality is the term used to describe keeping confidential information that is proprietary to a client or employer. The release of such information to the public or to competitors would have a detrimental effect on the interests of the client, and it would be contrary to the expectations of trust of a fiduciary relationship. In the case of an auditor, this expectation of trust and privacy is vital to the client's willingness to discuss difficult issues, which are quite germane to the audit, to get the opinion of the auditor on how they might be dealt with in the financial statements and notes. How frank would the discussion of a contentious contingent liability be if there were a possibility the auditor would reveal the confidence? How could a contentious tax treatment be discussed thoroughly if there was the possibility of voluntary disclosure to the tax collection authorities? It is therefore argued that the maintenance of client confidences is essential to the proper exercise of the audit function and to the provision of the best advice based on full discussion of the possibilities.

There are, however, limits to privacy that some professions have enshrined in their codes of conduct or where these limits are spelled out in regulating frameworks. Engineers, for example, must disclose to appropriate public officials when they believe a structure or mechanism is likely to be harmful to the users, as in the potential collapse of a building due to violations of the building code. In Canada, the bankruptcy of two chartered banks resulted in the requirement to report lack of client-bank viability directly to the Federal Office of the Superintendent of Financial Institutions. In the United Kingdom, money laundering for drugs and terrorism must be reported. There appears to be an increasing focus on the public responsibility of auditors and an increasing expectation of action rather than silence.

This trade-off between the interests of client, management, public, regulators, the profession, and management promises to be a growing conundrum for accountants in the future. One issue that is not well understood is the consequences of a professional accountant observing *strict confidentiality* about the malfeasance of his or her employer and being directed by the professional code to resign if the employer cannot be convinced to change their behavior. This would follow from the codes of conduct that require no disclosure of client/employer confidences except in a court of law or subject to a disciplinary hearing and at the same time requiring resignation in order to avoid association with a misrepresentation. In the event of a resignation in silence, the ethical misdeed goes unrecognized by all stakeholders except the perpetrators and the silent professional. How does this protect the interests of the public, the shareholders, or the profession? A discussion of this issue earlier in the book gave rise to an argument for the modification of the strict confidentiality of codes and the introduction of *assisted confidentiality* involving consultations with officials of the relevant professional institute. Perhaps through such consultations, a means can be found to better judge what needs to be kept confidential, when and how disclosure ought to be made, and how the professional's and public's interests can be protected. For an auditor, the situation is different. When an auditor is discharged or replaced, the incoming auditor has the right to ask the outgoing auditor (and the client) what the circumstances were that led to the dismissal or resignation. In some jurisdictions, the removed auditor even has the right to address the shareholders at their annual meeting or by mail at the expense of the corporation involved.

One of the first items that ought to be examined is what action should be taken when a professional accountant realizes that a client or employer is engaging in *tax evasion*. Tax evasion involves the misrepresentation of facts to the taxation authorities, resulting in the commission of a fraud and the cheating of the public treasury. At present, the established practice is not to be involved in the misrepresentation, to counsel against it, but not to report the problem to the authorities. As a result, the perpetrators need not fear their misdeed will be reported by a *whistleblower* to the tax authorities or the public. Consequently, the interests of the public and, when the deed is found out, the shareholders and the profession will suffer. Hopefully, the corporation will recognize the large cost of not encouraging whistleblowers to come forward through protected internal channels so that unknown problems can be corrected and public disgrace and fines can be avoided.

Looking the other way when confronted with tax evasion does not appear to make ethical sense. In some cases, the professional involved may believe that the interpretation involved is debatable so that the problem is one of "avoision," and its borderline nature is worthy of support until the authorities find and rule on the problem. Avoidance of taxes is, of course, quite legal; avoision reflects borderline practices, and evasion is both illegal and unethical (Lynch 1987). The boundaries are blurred, so access to confidential consultation on these matters is essential to proper ethical action.

Enron's use of tax avoidance strategies that is reported in Chapter 2 offer an interesting case of avoidance and probably qualifies as avoision, according to the U.S. Senate Committee on Finance report.[30] The reaction to Enron's tax avoidance transactions added to the trends of (1) closing loopholes, such as using accommodation parties; (2) increased scrutiny of the business purpose of transactions; and (3) increased sanctions for extra-aggressive interpretations. The resulting publicity, potential loss of reputation, and potential for lawsuits have caused responsible advisors to consider ethical guidelines for limiting involvement with and the ethics risks inherent in such activities. This represents a significant change in thinking for many professionals engaged in tax practice.

Another tax practice, that of *risk management*, is worthy of comment here. If the risk management relates to a tax matter that is in doubt, that is an issue of avoision and worthy of estimation of the risks and support. However, if the risk management involves estimating whether a known illegality will be found because tax auditors are few and far between, then the practice would appear to represent support for an evasion of tax.

QUESTIONABLE TAX SERVICES AND PRACTICES In addition to the practices of avoision and evasion mentioned above, several tax practices/services have proven to be areas in which professional accountants have been shown to be vulnerable to costly conflicts of interest that brought serious financial and reputational consequences for their firm and themselves. In addition, corporations and the accounting profession should consider carefully those practices that may further harm to reputations. Professional accountants should be well aware of the potential of the following:

- Marketing overly aggressive tax shelters
- Unfair reduction of taxes:
  - Transfer pricing
  - Reverse takeovers

These questionable practices are discussed below.

[30] U.S. Senate Committee on Finance, *Report of the Investigation of Enron Corporation and Related Entities regarding Federal Tax and Compensation Issues, and Policy Recommendations, Volume 1: Report*, February 22, 2003, **http://www.cengagebrain.com**.

MARKETING AGGRESSIVE TAX SHELTERS: GOING TOO FAR In the 1935 tax case of *Gregory v. Helvering*, the U.S. Supreme Court ruled that a taxpayer can engage in any legal activity to reduce the amount of tax that is owed to the government. "The legal right of a taxpayer to decrease the amount of what otherwise would be his taxes, or altogether avoid them, by means which the law permits, cannot be doubted."[31] A similar ruling occurred in Great Britain in 1936 when Lord Tomlin ruled in favor of a tax avoidance scheme perpetrated by the Duke of Westminster that had been appealed to the House of Lords.

Over the intervening years, taxpayers and tax practitioners have devised a number of tax shelters to reduce taxes. Unfortunately, not all of them have been legal.

The advantage of tax shelters, from the tax practitioner's point of view, is that the costs are normally incurred in developing the shelter. Afterward, the more times the shelter can be sold, the larger the return on the practitioner's investment. In the 1990s, Ernst & Young (E&Y) designed four tax shelters that would effectively delay the paying of tax on stock options for up to thirty years. The complicated schemes were sold only to the richest of E&Y's clients. Two such clients were William Esrey and Ronald LeMay, the two senior executives at Sprint Corporation, an E&Y audit client. Each had received stock options of about $300 million, which, when excised from 1998 to 2000, generated taxes payable of $159 million and $60 million, respectively. However, because they had bought tax shelters from E&Y, they each paid no tax. The Internal Revenue Service (IRS) rejected the tax shelters, and each man had to pay the tax on the stock options as well as fines and penalties. E&Y paid a $15 million settlement to the IRS on July 2, 2003.

From 1996 to 2003, KPMG was also selling tax shelters to their wealthy clients. These tax shelters were targeted only at individuals who paid tax of $10 million to $20 million. Through a complicated series of transactions involving offshore bank accounts, joint ventures, and foreign currency purchases, the taxpayer would invest $1.4 million and then be able to declare a $20 million loss for tax purposes. These plans generated $11 billion of artificial tax losses for KPMG clients that cost the government over $2.5 billion in lost taxes.

In January 2004, KMPG announced that it was being investigated by the government concerning the sale of its tax shelters. KPMG chairman Eugene O'Kelly decided not to settle with the government. After O'Kelly retired for health reasons, Timothy Flynn became chairman. He was in a dilemma. If KPMG went to court and lost, then KPMG might go out of business. In 2002, Arthur Andersen was convicted of obstruction of justice with respect to the Enron audit. Andersen's reputation was so damaged by its association with Enron, the resulting provisional suspension by the SEC as an auditor of SEC registrant companies, and the criminal charge that, by the time the firm was eventually convicted, it had lost most of its clients and staff. Andersen ceased to exist. The same fate might happen to KPMG if it lost the court case. So, in August 2005, Flynn settled with the government. Instead of being put out of business, KPMG paid a $456 million fine, the largest penalty ever imposed on an accounting firm, and agreed to be monitored for three years. "Eight former partners and a lawyer who provided advice to KPMG were charged with tax-shelter fraud."[32] KPMG also put Jeffrey Eischeid, the former partner in charge of this area of service, on administrative leave some time after he had testified that

> the tax strategies being discussed represent an earlier time at KPMG and a far different regulatory and marketplace environment.... None of the

[31] U.S. Supreme Court, *Gregory v. Helvering*, 293 U.S. 454 (1935), http://supreme.justia.com/us/293/465/case.html.

[32] Peter Morton, "KPMG Pays US$456 Million to Settle Fraud Allegations," *Financial Post*, August 30, 2005, FP1.

strategies—nor anything like these tax strategies—is currently being offered by KPMG.[33]

It was argued that KPMG "scrambled" to avoid criminal prosecution as a firm because conviction could have caused the same fate of collapse and bankruptcy that Arthur Andersen suffered. Other major accounting firms were also fined and settled out of court for similar tax service problems. The ethics case "Marketing Aggressive Tax Shelters," located at the end of this chapter, is about these issues.

The government also contended that KPMG had issued fraudulent opinion letters. The firm had made false claims about the legitimacy of the tax shelters. They had said that the purpose of the shelters was to diversify their clients' portfolios when in reality they were sham transactions. Nor did KPMG disclose that they were not independent—that the firm had designed and implemented and were marketing the shelters. KPMG admitted to criminal wrongdoing and paid the fine.

Then, in 2007, four E&Y partners pled guilty to tax fraud. They had been selling a different set of tax shelters to some of their wealthy clients. These shelters involved foreign currency options, partnerships, and shell corporations. From 1999 to 2001, these shelters were sold to about 400 individuals, generating fees of $121 million for E&Y. The government claimed the shelters were bogus and disallowed the tax deductions. The E&Y partners involved in the scheme were fired from the partnership and bought up on charges by the IRS. Although the partnership itself was not prosecuted, E&Y's reputation was once again harmed by its association with fraudulent tax planning schemes.

In 2012, BDO USA paid a $50 million fine as a result of designing, promoting, and implementing illegal tax shelters that cost the U.S. government $1.5 billion. Two years later, the last of three partners of BDO was fined and sent to prison for his role in devising these illegal tax shelters that benefited only the accounting firm's wealthy clients.

Professional accountants are required to serve or uphold the public interest. This is a nonnegotiable requirement. Accounting firms are expected to be profitable while not compromising this fundamental tenant. BDO, E&Y, and KMPG put the profit motive ahead of the public interest. (So, too, had Arthur Andersen, which contributed to its demise.) These firms were reaping large commissions from selling tax shelters. In addition, the tax shelters themselves were only for the benefit of a select group of super-rich individuals who were able to reduce their tax liability to zero. Because the accounting profession would not police itself, the IRS issued *Circular 230.*

CIRCULAR 230: TAX ACCOUNTANTS NEED TO ACT PROFESSIONALLY The tax shelter settlements indicated to the government that tax practitioners were not being responsible. So, in September 2007, the IRS issued *Circular 230*,[34] which imposes professional conduct standards on anyone, including tax accountants and lawyers, who prepares tax returns or provides U.S. tax advice for compensation. In general, tax preparers and advisors must exercise due diligence in preparing tax returns and providing tax advice, especially by assessing the correctness of the information provided by the client.

---

[33] Robert Schmidt, "Tax-Shelter Pressure Sparks KPMG Shakeup?" *Financial Post*, January 13, 2001, FP4.

[34] Treasury Department Circular No. 230 (Rev. 4—2008), "Regulations Governing the Practice of Attorneys, Certified Public Accountants, Enrolled Agents, Enrolled Actuaries, Enrolled Retirement Plan Agents, and Appraisers before the Internal Revenue Service," http://www.irs.gov/pub/irs-utl/circular_230.pdf.

Circular 230 lists a set of best practices. The tax accountant must do the following:

- Provide the highest level of quality professional care, acting fairly, and with integrity.
- Communicate clearly with the client so that the client's needs and expectations are understood.
- Establish the facts of the tax situation and then draw a conclusion that is consistent with the facts and the applicable tax laws.
- Advise the client about the consequences of the conclusions reached and any potential penalties.
- Not advise the client to take a patently improper or frivolous position.

Furthermore, the accountant must do the following:

- Not charge "unconscionable" fees or charge contingency fees, except in a few restricted circumstances.
- Avoid conflicts of interests when representing more than one client.
- Not engage in false or misleading advertising or solicitation.
- Not cash IRS checks on behalf of clients.

Overall, the accountant must ensure that the tax returns and the tax advice are based on realistic assessments. If challenged, the returns and the advice should be able to be sustained on their merits. In other words, the returns and advice cannot be frivolous.

Circular 230 also addresses tax shelters, called "covered opinions." The accountant cannot provide advice that has tax avoidance or evasion as its principal purpose. However, a "reliance opinion" can be issued that provides tax advice that the accountant believes would probably be decided in the client's favor if challenged by the IRS. Once again, the accountant is not to advise the client to act frivolously. Instead, the accountant is to ascertain the facts, make reasonable assumptions, and then draw a conclusion that is consistent with the tax laws and where the outcome has a probable likelihood (i.e., better than a 50% chance) of success. The conclusion, called a "marketed opinion," must be written to support the marketing of the proposed tax strategy.

A consequence of *Circular 230* is that tax accountants and tax lawyers are adding standard disclaimers to all their written communications, including email. The disclaimer often says, in part, that "we are required to advise you that any tax advice contained herein is not intended or written to be used for the purpose of avoiding tax penalties that may be imposed by the IRS." Rather than performing the required due diligence when providing tax advice, they are opting to be more cautious. They are now choosing to error on the side of avoiding any potentially costly ramifications when they are providing advice that they are being paid to provide.

TAX HAVENS & ETHICAL RESPONSIBILITIES: THE PANAMA PAPERS In April 2016, an anonymous hacker named John Doe provided the German newspaper *Süddeutsche Zeitung* with over 11.5 million files from the database of the Panama-based law firm Mossack Fonseca. The information, now known as the Panama Papers, revealed the existence of hundreds of thousands of offshore shell companies used by the wealthy of the world to avoid paying taxes. Among the wealthy mentioned in the Panama papers were African despots, drug lords, friends of Russian Premier Vladimir Putin, as well as international businesspeople and politicians. Within one week of the release of these documents, the prime minister of Iceland, Sigmundur Gunnlaugsson, resigned over allegations that his family hid millions in offshore tax havens. Similarly, British Prime Minister David

Cameron came under severe criticism when it was discovered that his late father had invested in these offshore tax shelters.[35]

Members of the accounting profession design, promote, and sell tax shelters to their wealthy clients. Occasionally, the accounting firms go too far and create illegal shelters, as was the case with E&Y in 2003, KPMG in 2005, and BDO USA in 2012. Not only have the accounting firms pleaded guilty to engaging in tax fraud and paid fines of $15 million, $456 million, and $50 million, respectively, but tax partners from E&Y and BDO USA have been sent to jail. Clearly, professional accountants are not to engage in illegal activities. But what about tax schemes that are legal but perceived to be socially unacceptable?

The accounting profession operates as a self-governing body whose purpose is to promote the best interests of society, even at the personal expense of the professional accountant. Public accountants must always put the public's interests first. The *AICPA Code of Professional Conduct* states that when a conflict of interest arises, if public accountants fulfill their obligations to protect the public interest, then the interests of all members of society are best served. Are tax shelters that are designed for the richest 1% of the world's population in the public's best interests?

Tax accountants are obligated to encourage their clients to invest in legally authorized tax shelters, such as 401(k)s and individual retirement accounts in the United States, registered retirement savings plans in Canada, and private pension contributions in Great Britain. These tax shelters are specifically sanctioned under the law. Should tax accountants also spend an inordinate amount of time, trouble, and effort poring through the *Income Tax Act*, looking for the smallest flaw or unintentional ambiguity in the law, in order to minimize the taxes paid by the wealthiest?

Many accountants argue that they are doing nothing illegal in putting their clients into questionable tax shelters. The problem with this argument is that professional accountants must always obey the law. The law is the minimum standard of acceptable behavior. But accountants are required under their professional codes of conduct to hold themselves to a higher standard than simply obeying the law. They have ethical and professional obligations to act in the best interests of society, even at their own or their clients' expense.

This illustrates the ongoing dilemma for tax accountants: how do they serve their clients best interests while promoting the public interest? Their clients want tax minimization. Society, on the other hand, sees questionable tax shelters, designed by clever tax accountants to minimize the taxes of the wealthiest members of society, to not be in the public's best interest.[36] Tax accountants must think long and hard about this ethical dilemma and how to best balance these conflicting interests. (See the ethics case *KPMG's Questionable Tax Shelters* at the end of this chapter.)

TRANSFER PRICING TO ARTIFICIALLY REDUCE TAX Multinational corporations (MNCs) can use transfer pricing to shift or move profits to jurisdictions with low or no tax. Is this ethical? Is it legal? Professional judgment is definitely required to ensure responsible outcomes.

MNCs need to account for activities among their subsidiaries that are located in different countries around the world. The final product or services may be the result of a number of different activities and procurements that have occurred among the MNCs global operations. Each of these operations is normally conducted by a subsidiary

[35] J. Garside, L. Harding, H. Watt, D. Pegg, H. Bengtsson, S. Bowers, O. Gibson, and N. Hopkins, "Mossack Fonseca: Inside the Firm That Helps the Super-Rich Hide Their Money," *The Guardian*, April 8, 2016.

[36] For a longer discussion of this point, see P. Dunn, "Accounting Profession: Heal Thy Self," *The Globe and Mail,* May 16, 2016, B4

company of the MNC that is incorporated as a legal entity in a foreign jurisdiction. Transfer pricing is a mechanism to allocate a fraction of the overall profits of the MNC to the legally independent subsidiary companies that helped to generate the ultimate profit. But how should those profits be allocated among the subsidiaries?

The choice of transfer pricing approach can make a big difference to the taxes payable to countries in the supply chain—so much so that the Organization for Economic Cooperation and Development (OECD) developed a set of guidelines to help companies determine the appropriate transfer price and avoid charges and fines for misallocation. The three different measurement approaches identified by the OECD, each of which requires a high degree of professional judgment to apply, are the following:

- *Comparable uncontrolled price.* This is the most popular method according to an E&Y report. It uses as the transfer price: the price that would be in effect if the transaction was between two parties dealing at arm's length. The presumption is that two parties dealing at arm's length represents an uncontrolled price. For example, if raw sugar is sold by one subsidiary to another subsidiary, then the transfer price should be the comparable price that would have been in effect if the subsidiary had sold the raw sugar to an independent third party.
- *Resale price method.* This approach adjusts for any gross margin that would have been included in a sale to an independent third party. For example, assume that two distributors sell the same product but one distributor includes a warranty and the other does not. In that case, the transfer price should be adjusted for the warranty.
- *Cost-plus method.* This approach adds a markup to the cost of the product. This method is normally used when semifinished goods are transferred among subsidiary companies.

Because cross-border transactions among related companies are taxed according to unilateral tax laws (i.e., each country has its own) and bilateral tax treaties (countries may agree to respect each other's tax treatments), an accountant can adjust the transfer price of products so as to shift profits from high-taxation countries to those with low-tax regimes.

MNCs can use transfer pricing to artificially shift profits from one jurisdiction to another, normally from high-tax countries to countries with low tax rates. These tax-haven countries include Ireland, Bermuda, Lichtenstein, the Isle of Man, the Bailiwicks of Jersey and Guernsey, and the Cayman Islands. Through of the use of transfer pricing, MNCs can legally, albeit questionably, reduce the corporate taxes that they pay. (See the ethics case *Multinationals and Tax Planning* at the end of this chapter.) Various suggestions have been made to minimize this problem:

- Develop a common tax base for companies and divide that among the various countries in which the MNC has its operations. This would result in no tax advantage of shifting profits to a low-tax regime. However, it could be almost impossible to reach an agreement among sharing countries.
- Allocate taxes based on a number of operational factors, such as gross sales, the number of employees, and invested capital. This would limit having tax-haven countries generate disproportionately large percentages of the company's pretax profits.

Accountants working in industry should always consider all the relevant stakeholder groups and not only the shareholders. Shareholders may benefit from a reduced tax expense for the firm, but society may not be better off. Businesses enjoy the benefits of being in society, and in return they should demonstrate their financial responsibility to society. Taxes help fund the social services that businesses enjoy. Without an adequate tax base, businesses will not have the infrastructure that makes for an efficient and effective flow of goods and services. These services are not free, so everyone should pay their share. Unless all governments agree to a standardized system, the problem will continue.

Transfer pricing schemes that accountants design and use have significant financial as well as social implications. Transfer prices should approximate a fair representation of the costs and benefits that flow from one subsidiary to another subsidiary. The transfer price should not be adjusted to reduce a business's tax liability. Tax planning is a legitimate accounting goal, but artificially minimizing taxes through questionable, albeit legal, transfer prices is ethically questionable. When transfer prices do not result in a fair distribution of profit among countries, the result becomes *tax avoidance*, and significant fines and recovery of profits are increasingly likely, in addition to loss of corporate and personal reputation. Determining what is to be a fair distribution of profit requires a finely tuned sense of professional judgment. Errors in that judgment will result in serious loss of reputation and large fines in the future.

Transfer Pricing by Apple Inc.

Substantially all of Apple's hardware is manufactured in Asia, and the final assembly occurs in Ireland. From Ireland, the final products are then shipped to its stores around the world for sales to Apple customers. According to its 2012 annual report, net sales were as follows:

	Billions	Percent
Americas	$ 57.5	36.7
Asia	43.9	28.1
Europe	36.3	23.2
Retail	18.8	12.0
Total sales	$ 156.5	100.0

But 65% of Apple's net income was shifted to and reported as being earned in Ireland, where no tax was paid. The highest region of sales and the place where product ideas came from was the United States, but comparatively lower profits were reported there, so low taxes were paid. To many Americans, it appeared that Apple was not paying its fair share of tax in the United States.

In response to a public outcry, in May 2013, Tim Cook, the CEO of Apple Inc., was questioned by a panel of U.S. senators on its offshore tax practices. The senators said that Apple's transfer pricing policies were "convoluted," "pernicious," and "harmful." Cook's response was that Apple paid all the taxes that were required by law.

Transfer pricing allowed Apple to move $30 billion in profits from 2009 to 2011 to its Irish subsidiary, Apple Operations International, which paid no corporate income taxes on those profits. Another Irish subsidiary, Apple Sales International, earned $22 billion in pretax profits on its sales of products in Europe, Asia, the Middle East, and Africa. Apple Sales International paid only $10 million in taxes, for an effective tax rate of 0.05%. Tim Cook was correct. None of these transactions were illegal, but they are ethically questionable because they do not appear to be fair.[37]

[37] J. Slater and B. Curry, "U.S. Grills Apple on Offshore Tax Practices," *The Globe and Mail*, May 22, 2013, B1, B8.

UNITED STATES CLOSING DOWN THE INVERSION RULE Corporate tax rates are not uniform throughout the world. The United States, for example, has a high corporate rate at approximately 39%, whereas Ireland and Liechtenstein have low corporate rates of approximately 12.5%. There is, therefore, an economic incentive for American multinationals to be domiciled in countries with low tax rates.

One strategy for American multinational corporations is to engage in a reverse-takeover merger whereby a larger (American) company essentially buys or merges with a smaller (foreign) company and then moves the corporate headquarters of the newly merged company from the United States to the foreign jurisdiction. Burger King, an American company based out of Miami, did this when it merged with Tim Hortons, a Canadian company, and moved the corporate headquarters of the newly merged company to Canada. The American pharmaceutical company Pfizer wanted to merger with the Irish company Allergan and have the new company's headquarters be located in Ireland. Why do these mergers? Because the corporate tax rates in Canada and in Ireland are less than those in the United States. (See the feature *Tax Inversions: Deal and No Deal* reproduced on page 437.)

In the United States, foreign profits are taxed only when the profits are repatriated into the United States. Some companies have adopted the following strategy to get around the tax involved. A multinational American company buys or incorporates a subsidiary company in a foreign country that has a corporate tax rate lower than the U.S. rate. The American company then ensures that the profits of the multinational corporation are "earned" in the low-tax-rate foreign country. Then the American company borrows funds (i.e., the earned profits) from the foreign company, so the money comes back to the United States but no tax is paid. Actually, the interest paid on the borrowed funds is tax deductible in the United States, at the high tax rate, and is taxed as income, at the low tax rate, in the foreign jurisdiction. This is referred to as earnings stripping.[38]

During the 2016 presidential election campaigns, both Hillary Clinton and Bernie Sanders objected to American companies using these strategies to avoid paying their fair share of taxes. Donald Trump said, "We have so many companies leaving, it is disgraceful." On April 4, 2016, the U.S. Treasury Department announced changes to the tax rules concerning tax inversion. It said that it would make it more difficult for American companies to engage in earnings stripping. It also said that the new tax rules would make it harder for American companies to artificially move their corporate headquarters to foreign jurisdictions after a reverse-takeover merger.[39]

All of these tax strategies are quite legal now. The question is, Is there anything ethically incorrect about these tax planning strategies? Certainly, the corporation is benefiting, as are the shareholders. It is also a means of increasing tax revenues for the low-tax-rate jurisdiction. But this comes at a cost to the high-tax jurisdiction. It raises the question, Should professional accountants, who are obligated to uphold the public interest, engage in legal tax planning schemes that lower the taxes for (e.g., American) multinational corporations while increasing the tax burden for the rest of American society? While facilitating such transactions now is legal, will it become illegal soon, and should the accounting profession wait until that occurs or stop before public opinion turns against it?

---

[38] V. Houlder, "Tax Inversions: What the New Rules Mean," *Financial Times*, April 5, 2016.

[39] C. Humer and R. Pierson, "Obama's Inversion Curbs Kill Pfizer's $160 Billion Allergan Deal," *Reuters*, April 6, 2016.

Tax Inversions: Deal and No Deal

In December 2014, Burger King and Tim Hortons merged to become Restaurant Brands International, with its corporate headquarters located in Oakville, Ontario. This $12 billion merger created the third-largest fast-food chain in the world, with 18,000 locations in ninety-eight countries and global sales of $23 billion. After the merger, the two restaurant chains continued to operate as independent entities; Burger King, with its 13,667 restaurants, still had its headquarters in Miami, Florida, and Tim Hortons, with its 4,546 restaurants, still had its headquarters in Oakville. No formal explanation was provided as to why corporate headquarters was located in Ontario with operating headquarters in Miami and Oakville. However, prior to the merger, Burger King's tax rate in the United States was approximately 35%, while Tim Hortons's tax rate in Canada was about 26%.

In November 2015, the two giant pharmaceutical companies Pfizer and Allergan announced a $160 billion merger that would create the world's largest pharmaceutical company by sales. Pfizer's shareholders would have a 56% interest in the new combined company; Allergan's shareholders would own the remaining 44%. Pfizer is an American company with its headquarters in New York City; Allergan is Irish with its headquarters in Dublin. It was announced that the new company would have its operational headquarters in New York City, but its corporate headquarters would be in Dublin. The announcement also said that the new company's effective corporate tax rate would be between 17% and 18%. Pfizer's tax rate at the time of the announcement was approximately 25%, and the tax savings by engaging in the merger were estimated to be approximately $1 billion annually.

On Monday April 4, 2016, the U.S. government announced new rules that would limit tax inversions. The following day, Pfizer announced that it was canceling its merger with Allergan.

Source: T. Kiladze, "Explainer: What Is Tax Inversion and What Does It Have to Do with Donuts?," *The Globe and Mail*, August 25, 2014; C. Humer and R. Pierson, "Obama's Inversion Curbs Kill Pfizer's $160 Billion Allergan Deal," *Reuters*, April 6, 2016.

LAWS & JURISPRUDENCE

Professional accountants can also refer to legal cases and lawyers for interpretations of their legal liability and potential defenses. To assist the reader, an analysis of trends and a synopsis of important legal decisions is included in digital resources archive for this chapter, "Trends in the Legal Liability of Accountants and Auditors and Legal Defenses Available." It documents an early trend to a broadening of liability from strict "privity of contract" with existing shareholders to "foreseeable parties" who might use the financial statements. Partly to counteract the trend to very excessive liability, more recent cases, such as *Hercules Managements Ltd. et al. v. Ernst & Young* (1997), have been decided in favor of very limited liability for auditors. Since this case was defended on the rather bizarre basis that financial statements should not be used for investment decision purposes and therefore that an auditor has no legal liability to shareholders and investors, most observers believe that it is a temporary diversion in a progression toward greater auditor liability. In fact, the U.S. Senate Permanent Subcommittee on Investigations stated in its *Report on the Collapse of Enron* that financial statements and an auditor's independent opinions thereon were essential to the public investment process and its credibility.

To counter the trend to greater auditor liability, safe-harbor or limited liability arrangements are emerging for auditors. As noted in the later discussion of limited liability partnerships (LLP), these limit the dollar value of legal damages each partner has to bear from each lawsuit. LLPs, however, will not stop lawsuits.

Caution should be exercised in the application of legal standards to ethical problems, however, for three reasons. First, the law appears to offer timeless wisdom when in reality it is continuously changing as it tries to catch up to the positions society believes are reasonable. In other words, the law generally lags what society views as ethically desirable.

Second, and more important, *what is legal is not always ethical.* According to former U.S. Supreme Court Justice Potter Stewart, ethics is "knowing the difference between what you have the right to do and what is right to do." There are plenty of examples of this difference between legal standards, moral standards, and ethical standards. For example, a company may be able to pollute in a way that is harmful to the health of its workers in a developing country because the local standards are less stringent than at home in North America. Sometimes the legal standard is clear, such as in tax matters or bribery, but large portions of society do not adhere to it, so the mores or norms expected are different. What behavior is right? Legal, moral, and ethical standards are different and should be recognized as such.[40]

The third reason for caution in placing too much reliance on legal interpretations and remedies is that they appear not to be highly relevant to the launching of or final disposition of lawsuits, particularly in the United States. Of 800 allegations of audit failure during the period 1960–1990 against the fifteen largest audit firms in the United States, only sixty-four were tried to a verdict (Palmrose 1991, 154). Although some cases were still under way, less than 10% were submitted to judge or jury, a rate that drops to 2.1% for the 1985–1989 period.

By far, the highest percentage of cases cited in the Palmrose study were settled for practical reasons rather than legal precedent. Usually, audit firms found it cheaper to settle than to fight in court. The cost to their pocketbooks in legal fees and lost billable time, particularly to their reputation, rarely made recourse to the courts a sensible option, even where lawsuits were without legal foundation. This trend toward settlement has accelerated and shows no sign of reversal.

The reasons for this bizarre situation are outlined in a position statement authored by the Big 6 audit firms in August 1992 titled *The Liability Crisis in the United States: Impact on the Accounting Profession.* This statement, which is included as a chapter reading, indicates that several quirks that have developed in the legal framework and process are responsible for an intolerable level of liability for audit professionals—a level that has resulted in individuals who have been offered partnerships hesitating or declining the offer and in the bankruptcy in 1990 of one of the largest audit firms, Laventhol & Horwath. As the heads of the Big 6 said, "To restore equity and sanity to the liability system and to provide reasonable assurance that the public accounting profession will be able to continue to meet its public obligations requires substantial reform of both federal and state liability laws." Several reforms were suggested in the statement, but they have been slow to appear because of the multiple jurisdictions involved and the entrenchment of the practice of contingent legal fees and of the principle of joint and several liability.

[40] For a fuller description of the differences between legal, moral, and ethical standards, see Chapter 3.

Two developments are worthy of comment. In December 1995, the U.S. Congress enacted the *Private Securities Reform Act*, which changes auditor liability from having to share equally with his or her partners to having to bear a portion allocated by the jury involved (Andrews & Simonette 1996, 54). Secondly, the organizational form of the accounting firm was allowed to be altered to an LLP in many jurisdictions to provide limited liability for nonculpable partners of the firm. Historically, accounting firms were required to be partnerships where, if the firm was sued, each partner was "jointly and severally liable" and was required to pay the full loss from their investment in the firm (plus any additional, if required) from their personal assets. Afterward, they could sue other partners who were also liable for recovery of their fortunes if these other people had resources left. This meant that partners could lose their investment in their firm and their personal assets as well, even though someone else was at fault. This was draconian, but it was considered an appropriate way to ensure that professional accountants were very focused on providing competent service. The LLP changed this by providing that a negligent partner would be required to settle up using his or her investment in the firm *plus*, if needed, his or her personal assets, whereas the "innocent" partners could only lose from the assets they had invested in the firm. The personal assets of an "innocent" partner were protected. E&Y became the first LLP in New York on August 1, 1994. Many other jurisdictions have enacted similar legislation.

Given this scenario, in which the legal "cure" for a problem is still unpalatable—where a lawsuit can bankrupt a firm, although most of the partner's personal assets are untouched—"preventive medicine," or not to get into the dilemma in the first place, is preferred if at all possible. Instilling high standards of professional ethics into the values and culture of accounting professionals and their organizations can prove to be a significant safeguard against getting into practice dilemmas. Even in legal jurisdictions such as Canada or the United Kingdom, where the liability crisis is not quite as alarming, high ethical standards and skilled judgment in their application can eliminate or reduce professional exposure.

"A Lawyer's Perspective on an Accountant's Professional Obligations," which is included in the digital resources archive for this book, has been written by David Debenham, a lawyer qualified in forensic accounting and a partner in McMillan LLP, to develop the legal aspects underlying accountant's professional liability and the arguments for statutory changes in it. His comments raise issues that will enhance the reader's understanding of the role of professional codes, GAAP and GAAS, engagement letters, and judgment; the use of experts; range of payouts; strategies for and against inclusion of codefendants; fiduciary duty, negligence, and the duty of care; the six rules underlying integrity; professional obligations to society; and the relationship between professional and personal ethics. Most of these issues are usually dealt with by accounting or auditing professionals or ethicists, but the perspective of a practicing lawyer provides an interesting and needed anchoring of the very relevant professional obligation issues.

MORAL COURAGE IS VITAL TO PROFESSIONAL ACCOUNTING: GLOBALIZATION HEIGHTENS THE REQUIREMENT

In order to serve their primary duty to society, professional accountants must not only recognize ethical and practical problems but also have the moral courage to deal with them effectively. Usually that means having the courage to say no to a client or third party and explaining why or reporting a problem or potential problem to employers, clients, or their audit committees. Sometimes reports have to be made to professional accounting bodies and/or regulators. Whistleblowing if the professional is an employee or resignation from an audit or other assignment if the professional is a public accountant must always be options that are considered seriously.

Professional accountants often face choices requiring moral courage. Pressures from clients and friends and the professional's own perceived self-interest will be difficult to resist. But the reputation of the professional and of the profession ultimately depends on that resistance, whether the challenges come from conflicts of interests or from limitations on scope or capacity.

For example, a professional accountant must resist giving a clean audit opinion when he or she encounters significant auditor problems. These problems may be even more acute when they occur in a foreign jurisdiction. The courage to disclose such problems or take suitable alternative measures must be considered and actions taken. Sometimes the valuation on assets in a precarious locale may have to be reduced to zero. Some of the situations that would require the exercise of moral courage could include the following:

- Jurisdictions around the globe where
  - the rule of law is nonexistent or is applied so capriciously that ownership of assets and liability for breaching local convention may be in significant doubt,
  - the safety of audit personnel would be too endangered to visit the site of significant assets or operations, and
  - bribery dominates integrity.
- Records are destroyed deliberately or by natural disaster.
- Knowledgeable management personnel are not available to support the audit.
- Audit evidence is lost and is not recoverable.

Sometimes a professional accountant does not recognize an ethical or practice issue as one that should require moral courage. More frequently, the problem is recognized, but the strength of character needed to demonstrate moral courage and act in the best interest of society is lacking.

The future is clear. The move toward globalization of professional accounting will surely increase the uncertainties and challenges that demand moral courage.

WHEN CODES & LAWS DO NOT HELP

Frequently, professional accountants find themselves facing situations that are not covered explicitly in codes of conduct or that are not sufficiently close to jurisprudence to benefit from those sources of guidance. A professional accounting body may provide its member with consultation services through an on-staff ethics advisor. Most often, however, the professional accountant will be left to his or her own devices. He or she may hire his or her own advisor from the ranks of legal or ethical experts, but ultimately the accountant will have to rely on his or her own knowledge, values, and judgment to decide what is right. If such advisors are fortunate enough, they will have an understanding of the frameworks discussed in Chapters 3 and 4 to facilitate ethical decision making.

BROADENING ROLE FOR PROFESSIONAL ACCOUNTANTS

The need for integrity, independent judgment, expertise, and savvy in the preparation and presentation of financial analyses and reports is not abating; rather, it is increasing.

The move toward principles-based, international accounting and reporting standards will surely reinforce this trend.

In addition to this traditional fiduciary role, professional accountants are best suited to play the dominant or supporting roles in *design, preparation, and management* of the following that are *vital to good governance* in the era of stakeholder accountability:

- Stakeholder interests assessment
- Stakeholder-focused performance indicators and incentive systems
- Stakeholder-oriented reports for management, board, and public
- Ethical corporate culture
- Corporate codes of conduct
- Ethics compliance mechanisms and reporting to the board
- Ethical decision-making guidance frameworks
- Ethics risk management systems

Professional accountants understand the problems that caused the Enron, WorldCom, Arthur Andersen, subprime lending, and other recent fiascos and understand the potential contribution of an organization's internal control system as well as the pitfalls of an unethical culture. While the professional accountant's focus has been on financial reporting, there is a need to refocus on future performance and how to guide and manage it to help ensure that ethics are built into strategic plans, board compliance reviews, and corporate incentive systems.

Boards of directors have been struggling to consider and deal with these new necessities. Inability and lack of awareness resulted in the Enron problem and many others. Professional accountants can assist boards greatly in the new, ethics-sensitive era if they are ready to broaden their horizons.

CONCLUSION

Events such as the Enron, Arthur Andersen, and WorldCom disasters, as well as the subprime lending fiasco, have rededicated the focus of professional accountants on their expected role as fiduciaries for the public interest. The reputation and future standing of the profession has suffered, and its distinction and success depend on this rededication.

The professional accountant must develop judgment, values, and character traits that embrace the public's expectations, which are inherent in the emerging stakeholder-oriented accountability and governance framework. Codes of ethics are being refined to better guide professional accountants and ensure that unrestrained self-interest, bias, and/or misunderstanding do not cloud the professional's independent state of mind or give rise to an appearance that independence may be lacking.

Globalization is influencing the development of codes and harmonization to IFAC standards and will surely continue. Stakeholders have become a dominant force in the governance mechanism for corporations, which have outgrown domestic jurisdiction and boundaries, and stakeholders around the world will become more important in determining the performance standards for professional accountants. These professionals will increasingly serve global capital markets and global corporations, and their success will require the respect of employees and partners drawn from a much wider set than in the past.

Given their knowledge and skills, it will be interesting to see if professional accountants can seize the opportunities that present themselves for broadening their role. They are particularly well placed to assist in the further development of those mechanisms that will provide and ensure ethical guidance for organizations. They know that codes do not cover every possible challenge, nor are they sufficient on their own. Developing an understanding of the ethical decision-making frameworks developed in Chapters 3 and 4 and the special issues covered in Chapter 7 will assist those who choose to make the most of future opportunities.

Questions

1. Answer the seven questions in the opening section of this chapter.
2. What is meant by the term "fiduciary relationship"?
3. Why are most of the ethical decisions that accountants face complex rather than straightforward?
4. When should an accountant place his or her duty to the public ahead of his or her duty to a client or employer?
5. Which would you choose as the key idea for ethical behavior in the accounting profession: "Protect the public interest" or "Protect the credibility of the profession"? Why?
6. Why is maintaining the confidentiality of client or employer matters essential to the effectiveness of the audit or accountant relationship?
7. What is the difference between exercising "due care" and "exercising professional skepticism"?
8. Why did the SEC ban certain nonaudit services from being offered to SEC registrant audit clients even though it has been possible to effectively manage such conflict of interest situations?
9. Where on the Kohlberg framework would you place your own usual motivation for making decisions?
10. Why do more professional accountants not report ethical wrongdoing? Consider their awareness and understanding of ethical issues as well as their motivation and courage for doing so.
11. Which type of conflict of interest should be of greater concern to a professional accountant: actual or apparent?
12. An auditor naturally wishes his or her activity to be as profitable as possible, but when, if ever, should the drive for profit be tempered?
13. If the provision of management advisory services can create conflicts of interest, why are audit firms still offering them?
14. If you were an auditor, would you buy a new car at a dealership you audited for 17% off list price?
15. If you were a management accountant, would you buy a product from a supplier for personal use at 25% off list?
16. If you were a professional accountant and you discovered your superior was inflating his or her expense reports, what would you do?
17. Can a professional accountant serve two clients whose interests conflict? Explain.

18. If an auditor's fee is paid from the client company, is there not a conflict of interests that may lead to a lack of objectivity? Why doesn't it?
19. Why does the IFAC Code consider the appearance of a conflict of interests to be as important as a real but nonapparent influence that might sway the independence of mind of a professional accountant?
20. What is the most important contribution of a professional or corporate code of conduct?
21. Are one or more of the fundamental principles found in codes of conduct more important than the rest? Why?
22. Was the "expectations gap" that triggered the Treadway and Macdonald commissions the fault of the users of financial statements, the management who prepared them, the auditors, or the standard setters who decided what the disclosure standards should be?
23. Why should codes focus on principles rather than specific detailed rules?
24. Is having an ethical culture important to having an effective system of internal control? Why or why not?
25. What should an auditor do if he or she believes that the ethical culture of a client is unsatisfactory?
26. Are the governing partners of accounting firms subject to a "due diligence" requirement similar to that for corporation executives in building an ethical culture? Can a firm and/or its governors be sanctioned for the misdeeds of its members?
27. An engineer employed by a large multidisciplinary accounting firm has spotted a condition in a client's plant that is seriously jeopardizing the safety of the client's workers. The engineer believes that the professional engineering code requires that this condition be reported to the authorities, but professional accounting codes do not. How should the head of the firm resolve this issue?
28. Transfer pricing can be used to shift profits to jurisdictions with low or no tax to reduce the taxes payable for multinational companies. If such profit shifting is legal, is it ethical? Was Apple well advised to shift $30 billion in profits to its Irish subsidiary, where it paid no corporate income taxes on those profits? Why or why not?
29. Many professional accountants know of questionable transactions but fail to speak out against them. Can this lack of moral courage be corrected? How?
30. Why do codes of conduct or existing jurisprudence not provide sufficient guidance for accountants in ethical matters?

Reading Insights

The reading *The Liability Crisis in the United States: Impact on the Accounting Profession—A Statement of Position* is offered in the digital resources at **http://www.cengagebrain.com** to illustrate the nature and longevity of professional liability concerns.

Case Insights

The following cases have been selected to expose situations that shed light on the role of auditors and management accountants as they discharge their fiduciary duties. Specifically, the issues covered are as follows:

Famous Cases

- *Arthur Andersen*, *Enron*, and *WorldCom*. See Chapter 2.
- *Tyco*, *HealthSouth*, and *Royal Ahold*. See Chapter 5.
- *The Lehman Brothers Repo 105 Manipulation*. See Chapter 8.

- *Waste Management, Inc.* and *Sunbeam Corporation and Chainsaw Al*. See digital resources archive for this book at **www.cengagebrain.com**.
- *Parmalat—Europe's Enron* details how the world's seventh-largest supplier of dairy products and Italy's seventh-largest company—with 146 plants in thirty countries, employing 36,000 people worldwide—came to be placed under administration and declared insolvent in late December 2003. Because of its size and its involvement with SPEs, off-balance-sheet, and sham transactions, many regard it as Europe's Enron. Lack of good governance, executive dominance, and sloppy auditing were again to blame.

Professional & Fiduciary Duty

- *KPMG Partner Shares Confidential Information with a Friend* describes why a senior professional, thinking he was helping a friend in a small way, ruined his own career, damaged his firm's reputation, and caused his firm to resign from two major audits.
- *Livent—When Maria, When?* reveals pressures that are often brought to bear on professional accountants who discover manipulation and fraud and who must decide what they should do and when they should blow the whistle.
- *The Lang Michener Affair* shows how legal professionals can take to the slippery slopes of shady deals, conflicts of interest, self-interest, passing the buck, and failing to step forward when they should to protect themselves, their firm, and their profession. It also illustrates the frustrations of a whistleblower and the workings of a self-regulating profession.
- *Wanda Liczyk's Conflicts of Interest* deals with questionable conduct with suppliers and raises the issue of whether the accounting profession should be disciplining its own members.
- *Strategic Roles* are presented that are beyond traditional financial preparation. Professional accountants must decide what their appropriate roles should be when facing these in the future.
- *Locker Room Talk* presents a fascinating case on confidentiality and its strange treatment in professional accounting codes.
- *Advice for Sam and Ruby*. Frequently, professional accountants are asked to get involved in activities that initially do not appear to be questionable or illegal or where they are trying to help out a friend and do not even take a fee. Facing the urgent real-life issues for Sam and Ruby will enable professional accountants to better understand the "red flags" involved and consider appropriate actions to take if they find themselves already involved in a mess.
- *Biker Nightmare* involves a professional accountant, a single-parent mom, who has been involved with some questionable activities and must decide what to do.
- *Budget Conflict* recounts how a professional accountant attends a board meeting at which a strategically attractive but overly aggressive proposal is about to be accepted even though she has privately advised the president against it. What should she do?

- *An Exotic Professional Accountant?* Is this something a professional accountant should be doing?
- *Freebie Services for Staff* presents a potential conflict of interest situation and asks if the professional accountant involved should stop providing the free services to their coworkers.
- *Summer Camp Holdback* portrays a professional accountant faced with a questionable instruction from the Executive Committee and must decide what the best option is for dealing with it.
- *Theft Reimbursement Twice* presents the case of a clerk who alters checks and steals the funds. When the theft is discovered, two reimbursements arrive: one from the bank and one from the check protector service company's insurance firm. What should a professional accountant do, and when?

Accounting & Auditing Dilemmas

- *Sino-Forest Fraud—Audit Challenges in China* provides an outline of how difficult it can be to audit in China and how important it is to adhere to established audit standards when auditing foreign operations. The case also shows how opportunists can use a reverse-takeover technique to gain easy access to establish capital markets and co-opt many knowledgeable people into supporting their endeavors.
- *Massive Acquisition Write-Downs in the Mining Industry* identifies several massive write-downs of recently made investments in mining companies and raises the questions of who is responsible, if anyone, and what is the appropriate treatment of the original valuation and investment decision makers.
- *Accounting Rule Changes Increase Apple Computer's Revenue* describes Apple's objection to subscription accounting. When the accounting rule was changed, Apple's income and stock price rose. But does this change result in fair financial reporting? Should the stock price have risen?
- *The Impact of International GAAP on Earnings* describes a situation where a retailer's net income decreased because it was forced to use International Financial Reporting Standards. If the cash flows of the company remain the same, does the revenue recognition policy matter?
- *Auditor's Dilemma* portrays a young auditor who underreports his time to look good to his superior and then wrestles with the consequences that result.
- *Management Choice* focuses on Sue, a management accountant who has a choice of accounting policy and practice to make. She can probably get away with it. Should she?
- *To Qualify or Not?* introduces the real-life dilemma of wanting to qualify an audit opinion but realizing that doing so might cause the company to become insolvent.
- *Team Player Problems* deals with the situation faced by a professional accountant who is to be part of a team but not the leader of it when he or she disagrees with the use and presentation of data in the report. What would you advise?
- *Minimal Disclosure* investigates how an audit partner would deal with a client who wanted to avoid disclosing the amount of income made from derivative securities, details of a lawsuit, and the financial situation in a consolidated subsidiary.

- *Opinion Shopping* looks at some reasons for seeking a new auditor and at the responsibility of an auditor likely to lose an audit to another accounting firm that is willing to be more lenient in deciding on the acceptability of some accounting practices.
- *Lowballing a Fee Quotation* is a common temptation. Are there reasons why it is appropriate?

Fundamental Accounting & Auditing Issues

- *Societal Concerns* asks the reader to consider how realistic and shortsighted our traditional financial statements and reports are. Can accountants go beyond this traditional framework to take on environmental and other issues? Should they?
- In *Economic Realities or GAAP*, Stan Jones is asking penetrating questions about the fundamental utility of traditional financial reports and the role of the auditor.
- *Multidisciplinary Practices—Ethical Challenges* asks real questions about managing the new assurance service and expanded practices. If we do not get the answers right, the accounting profession could be in for a black eye.

Tax & Regulatory Cases

- *Multinationals and Tax Planning* offers a description why and how transfer pricing is used to shift profits to low-tax-rate jurisdictions and how prevalent the practice is as well as the results of current court cases for transfers that were not justifiable.
- *KPMG's Questionable Tax Shelters* raises questions on whether tax accountants serve or endanger the public interest in what they do and whether they should change their practices before public opinion seriously erodes the reputation of the accounting profession, particularly since the Panama Papers have recently shone a spotlight on suspected tax cheats.
- *Italian Tax Mores* provides a priceless glimpse of the facilitating payments, bribery, and regulatory problems faced by businesses operating in foreign jurisdictions.
- *Tax Return Complications* introduces the prospect of "bending the rules" to keep the client happy as well as having to decide to admit an error or attempt to hide it. This case provides a very good illustration of the slippery-slope problem.
- *Marketing Aggressive Tax Shelters* has been done for years by some professional accounting firms. As the case recounts, both E&Y and KPMG were in hot water for the very aggressive shelters they were marketing, so it is worth considering what distinguishes an acceptable from an unacceptable tax product or service and why.
- *Tax Advice* requires the consideration of some of the public policy and ethics issues associated with giving tax advice and the conflicts of interest involved.
- *Risk Management of Taxes Payable—Is It Ethical?* spotlights a new practice that can get the accountant into trouble if he or she is not careful.

References

Anderson, G. D. 1985. "A Fresh Look at Standards of Professional Conduct." *Journal of Accountancy*, September, 93–106.

Anderson, G. D. 1987. "The Anderson Committee: Restructuring Professional Standards." *Journal of Accountancy*, May, 77.

Andrews, A. R. and G. Simonette Jr. 1996. "Tort Reform Revolution." *Journal of Accountancy*, September, 54.

Arthur Andersen & Co., Coopers & Lybrand, Deloitte & Touche, Ernst & Young, KPMG Peat Marwick, and Price Waterhouse. 1992. *The Liability Crisis in the United States: Impact on the Accounting Profession.*

Bayles, M. D. 1981. *Professional Ethics*. Belmont, CA: Wadsworth.

Behrman, J. N. 1988. *Essays on Ethics in Business and the Professions*. Englewood Cliffs, NJ: Prentice Hall.

Brooks, L. J. 1989. "Ethical Codes of Conduct: Deficient in Guidance for the Canadian Accounting Profession." *Journal of Business Ethics* 8, no. 5 (May): 325–36.

Brooks, L. J. 1993. "No More Trial and Error: It's Time We Moved Ethics Out of the Clouds and into the Classroom." *CAmagazine*, March, 43–45.

Brooks, L. J. 2000. "Codes of Conduct: Trust, Innovation, Commitment and Productivity: A Strategic-Cultural Perspective." *Global Outlook: An International Journal of Business, Economics, and Public Policy* 12, no. 2, 1–11.

Brooks, L. J. and V. Fortunato. 1991. "Discipline at the Institute of Chartered Accountants of Ontario." *CAmagazine*, May, 40–43.

Cohen, J., L. Pant, and D. Sharp. 1995. "An Exploratory Examination of International Differences in Auditor's Ethical Perceptions." *Behavioral Research in Accounting* 7: 37–64.

Colby, A. and L. Kohlberg. 1987. *The Measurement of Moral Judgment: Theoretical Foundations and Research Validations, and Standard Scoring Manual.* Vols. 1 and 2. New York: Cambridge University Press.

Cook, J. M. 1987. "The AICPA at 100: Public Trust and Professional Pride." *Journal of Accountancy*, May, 307–79.

Dunn, P. 2016. "Accounting Profession: Heal Thyself." *The Globe and Mail*, May 16, B4.

Etherington, L. D., and L. Schulting. 1995. "Ethical Development of Accountants: The Case of Canadian Certified Management Accountants." *Research in Accounting Ethics* 1: 235–51.

Final Rule: Strengthening the Commission's Requirements Regarding Auditor Independence, U.S. Securities and Exchange Commission, http://www.sec.gov/rules/final/33-8183.htm modified February 6, 2003, and *Commission Adopts Rules Strengthening Auditor Independence,* U.S. Securities and Exchange Commission, http://www.sec.gov/news/press/2003-9.htm, January 22, 2003.

Gunning, K. S. 1989. "Completely at Sea." *CAmagazine*, April, 24–37.

International Ethics Standards Board for Accountants and International Federation of Accountants. 2006. *IFAC Code of Ethics for Professional Accountants, Section 290 (Revised).* New York: International Ethics Standards Board for Accountants and International Federation of Accountants, http://www.ifac.org/Store/Category.tmpl?Category=Ethics&Cart=1215563035160178; **http://www.cengagebrain.com**.

International Federation for Accountants. 2001. *IFAC Code of Ethics for Professional Accountants.* London: International Federation for Accountants. **http://www.cengagebrain.com**.

International Federation for Accountants Ethics Committee. 2005. *IFAC Code of Ethics for Professional Accountants.* New York: International Federation for Accountants Ethics Committee, http://www.ifac.org/Store/Category.tmpl?Category=Ethics&Cart=1215563035160178; **http://www.cengagebrain.com**.

Kohlberg, L. 1981. *Essays on Moral Development. Volume I: The Philosophy of Moral Development.* San Francisco: Harper & Row.

Kohlberg, L. 1984. *Essays on Moral Development. Volume II: The Psychology of Moral Development.* New York: Harper & Row.

Lane, M. S. and D. Schaup. 1989. "Ethics in Education: A Comparative Study." *Journal of Business Ethics* 8, no. 12 (December): 58–69.

Lynch, T. 1987. "Ethics in Taxation Practice." *The Accountant's Magazine*, November, 27–28.

Macdonald Commission. 1987. See Canadian Institute of Chartered Accountants. 1988. *The Report of the Commission to Study the Public's Expectations of Audits.* Toronto: Canadian Institute of Chartered Accountants.

O'Malley, S. F. 1993. "Legal Liability is Having a Chilling Effect on the Auditor's Role." *Accounting Horizons* 7, no. 2 (June): 82–87.

Palmrose, Z. V. 1992. "Trials of Legal Disputes Involving Independent Auditors: Some Empirical Evidence." *Journal of Accounting Research* 29, supplement: 149–85.

Ponemon, L. A. 1992. "Ethical Reasoning and Selection—Socialization in Accounting." *Accounting, Organizations and Society* 17, no. 3/4: 239–58, esp. 239–44.

Ponemon, L. A. and D. R. L. Gabhart. 1993. *Ethical Reasoning in Accounting and Auditing,* Vancouver, BC: CGA-Canada Research Foundation.

Priest, S. 1991. "Perspective: The Credibility Crisis." In *Ethics in the Marketplace*, 2. Chicago: Center for Ethics and Corporate Policy.

SEC's Independent Consultant's Report of the Internal Investigation of Independence Issues at PricewaterhouseCoopers LLP. 2000, http://www.sec.gov/news/press/2000-4.txt; http://www.sec.gov/news/press/pressarchive/2000press.shtml.

Shenkir, W. G. 1990. "A Perspective from Education: Business Ethics." *Management Accounting*, June 1990, 30–3.

Thorne, L. and M. Magnan. 1998. "The Generic Moral Reasoning Development and Domain Specific Moral Reasoning of Canadian Public Accountants." Unpublished manuscript. For a copy, contact lthorne@bus.yorku.ca.

Treadway Commission. 1987. See American Institute of Certified Public Accountants, *Report of the National Commission on Fraudulent Public Reporting*. Washington, DC: American Institute of Certified Public Accountants.

United States Sentencing Commission. 1991. *U.S. Sentencing Guidelines*. Washington, DC: United States Sentencing Commission.

Weber, J. and S. Green. 1991. "Principled Moral Reasoning: Is It a Viable Approach to Promote Ethical Integrity?" *Journal of Business Ethics* 10, no. 5 (May): 325–33.

Famous Cases

ETHICS CASE

Parmalat–Europe's Enron[1]

Parmalat Finanziaria S.p.A. and its subsidiaries manufacture food and drinks worldwide. Parmalat is one of the leading firms in the long-life milk, yogurt, and juices market. The company became the world's seventh-largest supplier of dairy products and Italy's seventh-largest company, with 146 plants in thirty countries, employing 36,000 people worldwide. In 2002, the company reported €7.6 billion in annual sales. In late December 2003, however, Parmalat was placed under administration and declared insolvent.

Because of its size and its involvement with Special Purpose Entities (SPEs), off-balance-sheet, and sham transactions, many regard it as Europe's Enron. In January 2004, it was reported that the company "had net debts of 14.3 billion euros (US$23.47 billion) shortly before its crisis erupted... almost eight times the figure given by former managers."[2] PricewaterhouseCoopers also found that earnings for the nine months ended September 30, 2003, were only one-fifth of what had been reported, and bondholders were expected to recover under 7% of their capital. Parmalat's failure is expected to have a stimulative effect on corporate governance reform in Europe for decades.

The company started in Parma, Italy, in 1961. By the 1970s, it had expanded to Brazil and later diversified into the pasta sauces and soups markets. In the 1990s, Parmalat's need for cash made the company go public and sell 49% of its shares to be traded on the Milan Stock Exchange. Calisto Tanzi, Parmalat's founder, kept effective control of the company, and Tanzi family members held several key positions in Parmalat and its subsidiaries.

Parmalat's series of acquisitions in the 1990s left the company with a reported $7.3 billion of debt. The company acquired subsidiaries in Asia, southern Africa, and Australia as well as adding to its North and South American holdings and moving into eastern Europe. The acquisitions were

[1] Much of this case was developed as a group assignment by the author's students in the Master of Management and Professional Accounting Program at the Rotman School of Management of the University of Toronto. The students included Sandy Egberts, Shivani Anand, Amanda Soder, Dave Scotland, Ramandeep Shergill, Fiona Li, and Tamer Alibux.

[2] W. Schomberg and G. Wynn, "Parmalat Debt Rises to €14.3 B," *Financial Post*, January 27, 2004, FP9.

done without planning. The company did not go through a process of consolidation. Many investments were done to support the Tanzi family in areas unrelated to Parmalat's core business, such as the acquisition of the soccer team Parma, A.C.; investments in travel agencies and hotels; and sponsorship of Formula 1 racing teams.

Over the course of more than a decade, Parmalat Finanziaria S.p.A. misrepresented its financial statements by billions of dollars. The company's founder and former CEO, Tanzi, now stands accused of market rigging, false auditing, and misleading investors and stock market regulators.[3] Tanzi established a series of overseas companies to transfer money among and to conceal liabilities in order to give the illusion of financial liquidity within the Parmalat. The scheme was eventually uncovered when the company was unable to make a bond payment and was forced to admit to having fraudulent assets on its accounts. The case raises a number of ethical issues that impact all stakeholders. The rights of shareholders were violated, and the expectations of stakeholders, with respect to the integrity of company management, were not met.

On December 9, 2003, Parmalat defaulted on a €150 million (U.S.$184 million) payment to bondholders. Rumors began to circulate that the company's liquidity had been overstated, and the credit rating agency Standard & Poor's downgraded Parmalat's bonds to "junk" status. As a result of the downgrade, the company's stock fell by 40%. On December 17, 2003, the Bank of America announced that a U.S.$5 billion account that Parmalat claimed to have had with it in the Cayman Islands did not exist. In a little more than a week, trading in the company's shares was suspended, and it was taken under administration and declared insolvent.

The company initially claimed that the missed payment to bondholders had been as a result of a late payment from Epicurum, a customer that was not paying its bills. Parmalat was eventually forced to concede, under pressure from its auditor Deloitte & Touche, that Epicurum was in fact simply a holding company of Parmalat's, located in the Cayman Islands. Furthermore, it could not access the funds from Epicurum that were required.

Parmalat had begun a period of rapid expansion in 1997, deciding to expand its operations globally and reposition itself in the marketplace. Those expanded operations, however, did not prove to be as profitable as Parmalat had hoped, and the company incurred losses. As a result of those losses, Parmalat began to invest more of its operations into derivatives and other risky financial ventures. The company expanded into tourism with a company called Parmatour and also invested in a soccer club, both of which generated further losses for the company.

As the company's expansion continued, its need for more funds, in the form of debt financing, grew. To give the appearance of greater liquidity to its bankers and other investors, the company created a series of fictitious offshore companies that were used to conceal Parmalat's losses. Parmalat disassociated itself with the companies by selling them to American citizens with Italian surnames, only to repurchase them later. The phony liquidity generated by these actions gave investors the assurance they needed to continue purchasing bonds from the company and enabled Parmalat to continue to issue debt to the public.

In a classic example of the type of fraudulent action that Parmalat perpetrated, one such company, Bonlat, alleged that it was owed $767 million by a Cuban firm that had ordered 300,000 tons of powdered milk. This money was then alleged to be owed to Parmalat. The entire transaction,

[3] "Q&A Parmalat's Collapse and Recovery," *BBC*, 2005, accessed November 16, 2005, at http://news.bbc.co.uk/1/hi/business/3340641.stm.

however, did not exist and was created to maintain the illusion of liquidity in Parmalat.[4]

Auditors failed to properly determine that roughly 200 companies created by Parmalat, such as Bonlat, did not exist. The fraud was perpetrated by, among others, CFO Fausto Tonna, who produced fake documents that he faxed to the auditors in order to falsify the existence of the subsidiaries.[5]

Calisto Tanzi admitted to having falsified Parmalat's accounts for over a decade and to having stolen at least $600 million from the publicly traded company and funneling it into family businesses. The Parmalat Board of Directors, which consisted mostly of family members of Tanzi and controlled 51% of Parmalat, did not raise any questions regarding how the company was run.

By 2003, some shareholders began lobbying Tanzi for an independent member, chosen by the minority shareholders, to be put on the company's Audit Committee. Even though it was their legal right, Tanzi refused this request, and the issue was dropped. This led some to become more suspicious of Tanzi. Many bankers, however, had been suspicious of Parmalat since the mid-1980s because of the company's practice of continuously issuing debt despite an abundance of cash. At the time of the Parmalat disaster, members of the Audit Committee of an Italian company were elected by the board in such a way[6] that the controlling shareholder could determine who was successful. They did not have to be either independent or a director of the company, and in fact, in Parmalat's case, they were neither.

In March 2003, Tanzi sent a thirty-four-page complaint to Consob, the Italian regulatory agency, claiming that he was being slandered by Lehman Brothers, Inc., who had issued a report that cast doubt on Parmalat's financial status. Tanzi stated that Lehman Brothers were doing this to deflate the price of Parmalat's shares in order to buy them at a cheaper price. The stir led to the publication of a series of articles critical of Parmalat and its management, which in turn had forced Parmalat to cancel a $384 million bond issue in February 2003.

Despite this, some banks, including Deutsche Bank and Citibank, were still optimistic about Parmalat and were willing to buy more debt and promote their bonds as sound financial assets. The actions of the banks raises questions about possible collusion between them and the management at Parmalat and the nature of the fiduciary duty of the banks.

After the critical December 9 default to bondholders, Tanzi appointed a turnaround specialist named Enrico Bondi. It was Bondi who decided to liquidate the U.S.$5 billion Bank of America account, which was revealed to be fictitious and which eventually led to the bankruptcy of the company.

Tanzi was accused of dealing in fraudulent complex financial deals and bond deals, creating nonexistent offshore accounts to hide losses, and false bookkeeping. He misled investors and stock market regulators into believing that Parmalat was not in crisis. By doing so, he ensured financing from individuals who believed that Parmalat was a sound company. Tanzi claimed, in his defense, that he was too far up the hierarchy to have known what top executives were doing, whom he blames for all Parmalat's problems.[7]

The story of Parmalat reveals many weaknesses in governance at both the corporate and the professional accounting

---

[4] David McHugh, "Parmalat's Scandal Not Very Clever," *Seattle Times*, January 20, 2004, accessed November 16, 2005, at http://seattletimes.nwsource.com/html/businesstechnology/2001839930_parmalat200.html.

[5] Ibid.

[6] Michael Gray, "ITALY: Corporate Governance Lessons from Europe's Enron," accessed April 11, 2005, at http://www.corpwatch.org.

[7] "Q&A Parmalat's Collapse and Recovery."

levels. One major weakness in corporate governance was a lack of oversight on the part of the Board of Directors. Despite the many suspicious aspects of Parmalat's business, the Board of Directors never demanded answers to any questions that they may have had, nor did they ever worry about the close relationship between management and its original auditors. By placing too much faith in the integrity of the Parmalat's managers and the competence of its auditors, the company became susceptible to fraud.

In several instances, flaws were also exposed in the accounting governance of the company. In 1999, Parmalat was required to change auditors (and did so but only partially) from Grant Thornton to Deloitte. This was due to a new Italian law—the "Draghi" law, passed in 1998 to improve corporate governance[8]—whereby a public company is required to change auditors every nine years. At the time of the auditor switch, Tanzi moved a series of offshore companies that he had created during the 1990s from the Dutch Antilles to the Cayman Islands. By effectively shutting down and reopening those companies in the new location, Tanzi was able to retain Grant Thornton as his auditor for seventeen offshore companies, including Bonlat,[9] and not require any new eyes to view the transactions of them. Furthermore, the Grant Thornton audit managers who had been auditing Parmalat since 1990 had been auditing the company for six years prior to that as managers with another auditing firm.

The testing procedures that the auditors used while auditing Parmalat were inadequate. Many of the company's assets were overstated and its liabilities understated, which had not been noticed by the company's auditors. For example, when Deloitte sent a confirmation to the Bank of America in regard to the fabricated \$5 billion account, they sent it through the Parmalat internal mail service. It was intercepted, and a favorable response was forged by the CFO Fausto Tonna (or persons under his direction) on scanned Bank of America letterhead.[10] Another example involved Deliotte's apparent inability to locate and/or audit what is referred to as Account 999, which held a debit of £8 billion (U.S.\$12.83 billion) representing the "'trash bin' for all faked revenues, assets and profits that Parmalat had accumulated over the years. To cover up the fake transactions, the entries were transformed into intercompany loans and credits."[11] In December 2003, executives "took a hammer to a computer at headquarters" in an attempt to destroy Account 999—but a printout survived.[12]

Parmalat sponsored an American Depositary Receipts (ADR) Program to raise funds in the United States and therefore came under the scrutiny of the U.S. Securities and Exchange Commission (SEC). The SEC charged Parmalat with securities fraud on December 30, 2003, and filed amended charges on July 28, 2004, covering the following:

- Parmalat Finanziaria consistently overstated its level of cash and marketable securities. For example, at year end 2002, Parmalat Finanziaria overstated its cash and marketable securities by at least €2.4 billion. As of year-end 2003, Parmalat Finanziaria had overstated its assets by at least £3.95 billion (approximately \$4.9 billion).
- As of September 30, 2003, Parmalat Finanziaria had understated its reported debt of £6.4 billion by at least £7.9

[8] In 1999, Italian companies were also asked to *voluntarily* comply with a new noncomprehensive set of governance rules known as the "Preda Code."

[9] Navigant Consulting, Canadian Institute of Chartered Accountants, and the American Institute of Certified Public Accountants, "Milk Gone Bad," *Report on Fraud* 6, no. 5–6 (March 2004).

[10] Ibid.

[11] F. Kapner, "Parmalat's Account 999 Points a Finger at Deloitte," *Financial Post*, April 12, 2004, FP16.

[12] Ibid.

billion. Parmalat Finanziaria used various tactics to understate its debt, including (1) eliminating approximately £3.3 billion of debt held by one of its nominee entities; (2) recording approximately £1 billion of debt as equity through fictitious loan participation agreements; (3) removing approximately £500 million of liabilities by falsely describing the sale of certain receivables as nonrecourse when in fact the company retained an obligation to ensure that the receivables were ultimately paid; (4) improperly eliminating approximately £300 million of debt associated with a Brazilian subsidiary during the sale of the subsidiary; (5) mischaracterizing approximately £300 million of bank debt as intercompany debt, thereby inappropriately eliminating it in consolidation; (6) eliminating approximately £200 million of Parmalat S.p.A. payables as though they had been paid when, in fact, they had not; and (7) not recording a liability of approximately £400 million associated with a put option.

- Between 1997 and 2003, Parmalat S.p.A. transferred approximately £350 million to various businesses owned and operated by Tanzi family members.
- Parmalat Finanziaria transferred uncollectible and impaired receivables to "nominee" entities, where their diminished or nonexistent value was hidden. As a result, Parmalat Finanziaria carried assets at inflated values and avoided the negative impact on its income statement that would have been associated with a proper reserve or write-off of bad debt.
- Parmalat Finanziaria used these same nominee entities to fabricate nonexistent financial operations intended to offset losses of its operating subsidiaries. For example, if a subsidiary experienced losses due to exchange rate fluctuations, the nominee entity would fabricate foreign exchange contracts to offset the losses. Similarly, if a subsidiary had exposure due to interest rate fluctuations, the nominee entity would fabricate interest rate swaps to curb the exposure.
- Parmalat Finanziaria used the nominee entities to disguise intercompany loans from one subsidiary to another subsidiary that was experiencing operating losses. Specifically, a loan from one subsidiary would be made to another subsidiary operating at a loss. The recipient then improperly applied the loan proceeds to offset its expenses and thereby increase the appearance of profitability. As a result, rather than have a neutral effect on the consolidated financials, the loan transaction served to inflate both assets and net income.
- Parmalat Finanziaria recorded fictional revenue through sales by its subsidiaries to controlled nominee entities at inflated or entirely fictitious amounts. In order to avoid unwanted scrutiny due to the aging of the receivables associated with these fictitious or overstated sales, the related receivables would be transferred or sold to nominee entities.[13]

On January 29, 2004, PricewaterhouseCoopers took over as the auditor of Parmalat. They discovered that cash had been misstated by billions of euros and that Parmalat's debt was eight times what was claimed. Further reinforcing suspicions that the company had been altering its financial statements since the 1980s, an independent auditor for the prosecutor in Milan found that Parmalat had been profitable for only one year between 1990 and 2002. Parmalat had claimed to be profitable all of those years. This material misstatement had not been noticed by either Grant Thornton or Deloitte. It was also found that there were many instances where Deloitte's Italian office did not apply aggressive enough audit procedures

[13] U.S. Securities and Exchange Commission, "SEC Alleges Additional Violations by Parmalat Finanziaria S.p.A.," *Litigation Release No. 18803*, July 28, 2003, accessed March 11, 2005, at http://www.sec.gov/litigation/litreleases/lr18803.htm.

despite being informed of irregularities with Parmalat, uncovered by other Deloitte offices around the world.[14]

It appears that at least some of Parmalat's auditors were in collusion with the company's managers to keep the fraud under wraps. By March 2004, eleven people from Grant Thornton had been arrested, and more arrests may follow.[15]

A number of large banks were also complicit in the fraud, according to Enrico Bondi, who was appointed as Parmalat's government-appointed administrator. His report stated,

> that banks facilitated the inflow of resources that hid Parmalat's deteriorated financial condition through the use of bonds placed in tax havens.[16]

Bondi went on to estimate that Parmalat obtained

> £13.2 billion from banks between Dec. 31, 1998 and Dec. 31, 2003. International banks supplied 80% of the funding, with the rest from Italian lenders. By contrast, Parmalat generated only £1 billion in gross cashflow.
>
> Mr Bondi calculates Parmalat spent about £5.4 billion on acquisitions and other investments, £2.8 billion on commissions and fees to banks, £3.5 billion on payments to bondholders, £900 million on taxes and £300 million on dividends. The remaining £2.3 billion was apparently siphoned off for other purposes....
>
> The Bondi Report suggests that, as early as 1997, there was sufficient information available about Parmalat's true condition for the financial community to have realized the company was in trouble.... As a result, while Parmalat might still have collapsed in 1997–98, the scandal would have cost investors less money.[17]

Under Italian law, banks and financial institutions can be sued for damage caused by and recovery of improper transactions. It is noteworthy that "Citigroup... had been instrumental in setting up the insolently named 'Buco Nero' ('black hole') as an offshore account for Parmalat"[18] and has found "itself under investigation by the SEC and the subject of a class action lawsuit."[19]

Questions

1. What conditions appear to have allowed the Parmalat situation to get out of control?
2. What specific audit procedures might have uncovered the Parmalat fraud earlier?
3. What audit steps should Deloitte have taken with regard to the seventeen offshore subsidiaries that continued to be audited by Grant Thornton?
4. What impact will the Parmalat fraud have on Grant Thornton and on Deloitte & Touche?
5. How did the following areas of risk in Parmalat's control environment contribute to the fraud: integrity and ethics, commitment, audit committee participation, management philosophy, structure, and authority?
6. How did the following areas of risk in Parmalat's strategy contribute to the fraud: changes in operating environment, new people and systems, growth, technology, new business, restructurings, and foreign operations?

[14] Y. Richard Roberts. P. Richard Swanson, and Jill Dinneen, "Spilt Milk: Parmalat and Sarbanes-Oxley Internal Controls Reporting," *International Journal of Disclosure and Governance* 1, no. 3 (June 2004): 215–26.

[15] Morgan O'Rourke. "Parmalat's Scandal Highlights Fraud Concerns. Risk Management," *New York* 51, no. 3 (March 2004): 44.

[16] T. Barber. "Parmalat Chief Slams Big Banks," *Financial Post*, July 23, 2004, FP12.

[17] Ibid.

[18] Navigant Consulting, "Milk Gone Bad."

[19] Ibid.

7. Should the banks and other creditors be legally responsible for so-called irresponsible lending that contributes to higher than necessary losses? If so, how can they protect themselves when dealing with clients whose viability is in doubt?
8. Do you think that applying bankruptcy projection models should be a regular tool used by auditors, creditors, and regulators to assess the reasonability of a company's financial statements?
9. Is independence important in corporate governance? What are the most recent rules on corporate governance for public firms?
10. Discuss which changes could be made to the Parmalat's control system and corporate governance structure to mitigate the risk of accounting and business fraud in future years.

Helpful References

BBC News. October 2003–January 2005. Parmalat. BBC News Archive. http://www.bbcnews.com.

BBC. 2005. "Parmalat: Timeline to Turmoil." September 28. http://news.bbc.co.uk/1/hi/business/3369079.stm (accessed November 17, 2005).

Celani, Claudio. 2004. "The Story behind Parmalat's Bankruptcy." *Executive Intelligence Review*. January 16. http://www.larouchepub.com/other/2004/3102parmalat_invest.html (accessed November 16, 2005).

CNN. 2003. "Parmalat Chief 'a Broken Man.'" December 31. http://www.cnn.com/2003/WORLD/europe/12/31/parmalat.arrests/index.html?iref=allsearch (accessed March 15, 2011).

CNN. 2003. "Tanzi 'Admits False Accounting.'" December 29. http://www.cnn.com/2003/WORLD/europe/12/29/parmalat.tanzi/index.html (accessed November 16, 2005).

CNN. 2005. "Timeline: Parmalat Fraud Case." September 28. http://www.cnn.com/2005/BUSINESS/09/28/parmalat.timeline/index.html (accessed November 16, 2005).

Cohn, Laura, and Gail Edmondson. 2010. "How Parmalat Went Sour." *BusinessWeek Online*. January 12. http://www.businessweek.com/magazine/content/04_02/b3865053_mz054.htm (accessed November 16, 2005).

Edmondson, Gail, David Fairlamb, and Nanette Byrnes. 2004. "The Milk Just Keeps on Spilling at Parmalat." *BusinessWeek Online*. January 26. http://www.businessweek.com/magazine/content/04_04/b3867074_mz054.htm (accessed November 16, 2005).

Knox, Noelle. 2003. "Parmalat Founder Might Face More Charges." *USA Today*. December 29. http://www.usatoday.com/money/world/2003-12-29-parmalat-int_x.htm (accessed November 16, 2005).

New York Times. October 2002–January 2005. Parmalat. New York Times News Archive. http://www.nytimes.com.

The Economist. 2004. "Special Report Europe's Corporate Governance." January 17, 59–61.

U.S. Securities and Exchange Commission. *Litigation Releases 18527, 18803*. http://www.sec.gov/litigation/litreleases.shtml.

Professional & Fiduciary Duty Cases

KPMG Partner Shares Confidential Information with a Friend

ETHICS CASE

On July 1, 2013, Scott London, a former KPMG audit partner, pleaded guilty to securities fraud. He had been passing information to his friend, Bryan Shaw, over a two-year period ending in 2012.

He told his friend about earnings announcements by Herbalife Ltd and Skecher USA Inc. as well as the planned merger of RCS Holdings with United Rentals and the takeover of Pacific Capital

Bankcorp by Union Bank. Overall, Shaw was tipped fourteen times and used that information to make approximately $1.3 million in trading profits.

Why would a senior partner knowingly break the rule of confidentiality? Confidentiality is a value at the heart of the accounting profession. London argued that he was merely helping a friend whose jewelry business was in financial trouble. London had advised him that it was unlikely that he would be caught. Regulators are not looking for "small fish," he advised his friend. Furthermore, Shaw thought that his golf partner was making small profits on the various tips that he had been given. He speculated that they were around $200,000 and was shocked when he learned that they were over $1 million. He said that he "about threw up" when he learned the size of Shaw's profits.

London contended that he never asked to share in any of the trading profits, although he did receive $60,000 in cash and a $12,000 Rolex watch from Shaw. Part of the cash payment was captured by a surveillance photo of Shaw and London in a parking lot. But London claimed that these were small gifts from a friend, and the amounts were immaterial relative to London's remuneration as the KPMG audit partner in charge of the Pacific Southwest region.

The negative consequences of this insider trading were both direct and indirect. London, who could have been sent to prison for 20 years, was sentenced to 14 months in April 2014.[1] Although KPMG was not involved in any wrongdoing, KPMG resigned as the auditor of both Herbalife and Skechers. London had been the partner in charge of both of these audits. KPMG said that they were reviewing their internal controls and procedures against the release of confidential information. They announced that their controls were "safe and effective" but that nevertheless they would be increasing their monitoring and training.

This event renewed the debate concerning the prohibition on insider trading. Those in favor of no prohibition argue that the stock market is made more efficient more quickly, but, as indicated in the text on page 427, insider trading is not a victimless crime. KPMG would certainly agree.

Questions

1. Should an accounting firm have to resign as the auditor of a company when the partner in charge of the audit is convicted of releasing confidential information about that audit client?
2. How can accounting firms ensure that their partners and staff do not release confidential information?

Sources: Alexandra Berzon, and Michael Rapoport, "Guilty Plea in KPGM Case," *Wall Street Journal*, July 2, 2013, C2.

Emily Flitter, "KPMG Auditor Charged for Disclosing Tips," *The Globe and Mail*, April 12, 2013, B7.

[1] Tamara Audi, "Former KPMG Partner Scott London Gets 14 Months for Insider Trading," *Wall Street Journal*, April 24, 2014, http://www.wsj.com/articles/SB10001424052702303380004579521870879321240.

ETHICS CASE

Livent—When Maria, When?

Livent, once the world's premier live entertainment companies, was sold in 1998 to buyers who soon found that the value they had paid for was an illusion. Livent had thrilled audiences with performances of *Phantom of the Opera*, *Ragtime*, *Kiss of the Spider Woman*, *Sunset Boulevard*, *Showboat*, *Joseph and the Technicolor Dreamcoat*, *Fosse*, *Candide*, and *Barrymore*. Needless to say, Garth Drabinsky and Myron Gottlieb, the creators of Livent, were suspected of fraud, but justice was slow in coming in Canada.

Whereas the U.S. Securities and Exchange Commission pursued fraud charges in 1999,[1] it was not until May 2008, over ten years after their alleged manipulation of earnings, that Drabinsky and Gottlieb finally went on trial in Toronto for two counts of fraud and one of forgery. The manipulations occurred from 1993 to 1998 and were reported to be significant. For example, according to the testimony of Gordon Eckstein, Livent's senior vice president of finance, an internal document showed a loss of $41 million for the third quarter of 1997 that was reported publicly as a $13.4 million profit after adjustments were made by accounting staff.[2] Eckstein also reported, "Just before Livent was sold, its managers wrote down the value of its assets to 'clean up the books' and declared a loss of $44 million for 1997."[3]

Maria Messina, Livent's CFO, had joined Livent in May 1996 after having been a partner at Deloitte & Touche, Livent's auditors. Messina had worked on the audit but testified that she did not become aware of the manipulation until July 1997, "when she saw a set of internal statements showing a loss of about $20 million for the first six months of 1997, then later saw a subsequent set showing an $8 million profit."[4] Interestingly, she never revealed the fraud to her former colleagues at Deloitte. In fact, she did not disclose Drabinsky's manipulative influence to any outsider until July 1998, when she met the new owner's CFO, Roy Furman. She then revealed the fraudulent behavior on August 6, 1998, when she met with Robert Webster, the new executive vice president, who had asked for a report on construction costs, the area affected by many of the manipulations.

Why did Maria delay so long? At first, she was shocked and numbed. She questioned her manager, Gordon Eckstein, who replied, "it's just income smoothing. Everybody does it."[5] She was so shocked that she panicked and was "completely immobilized by fear... didn't know how to get out of the situation and didn't have the courage to expose the fraud and 'take on' Mr. Drabinsky and Mr. Gottlieb."[6] Drabinsky, in particular, was somewhat famous and had a reputation for being frighteningly intimidating. "Instead she settled on a campaign of 'baby steps,' and tried to persuade Mr. Eckstein to stop the fraud."[7] During this period, she did work on manipulated financial statements. Eckstein's proposal was presented at an executive meeting in February 1998, but it was not accepted. In April 1998, she wrote a memo to Drabinsky and Gottlieb, indicating that proposed adjustments were not in accord with GAAP and that she would not support them. This worked: the manipulations were abandoned, and some of the accumulated fraud was written down.[8] However, on June 30, when she met with Drabinsky to show him an estimate of second-quarter earnings indicating a loss of $13 million, he said, "these numbers are all f—— up. You don't know what the f—— you are doing. You can't show these to anyone." Drabinsky then demanded that second-quarter earnings be boosted from a loss of $13 million to just $200,000.[9] This was the situation that she disclosed to Roy Furman, but she did not tell him about the earlier

[1] Release 99-3 SEC Sues Livent and Nine Former Livent Officials for Extensive Accounting Fraud; U.S. Attorney Files Criminal Charges Washington, https://www.sec.gov/news/press/pressarchive/1999/99-3.txt.

[2] Peter Small, "Livent Hid Large Losses, Court Told," *Toronto Star*, May 21, 2008, A7.

[3] Ibid.

[4] Janet McFarland, "Former Livent CFO 'Numb' over Extent of Fraud," *The Globe and Mail*, June 10, 2008, B3.

[5] Ibid.

[6] Ibid.

[7] Ibid.

[8] Janet McFarland, "Ex- Livent Executive Says She Blew the Whistle," *The Globe and Mail*, June 11, B3.

[9] Ibid.

fraud. When asked why not, she replied, "How do you tell somebody that, when you are a chartered accountant? I was also obviously going to be destroying my own life. It just took me several weeks to find the courage to do it."[10] She paid a high price. On January 7, 1999, she pleaded guilty to a federal felony charge and as a "36-year-old single mother of a 10-year-old girl faced up to five years in jail and fines as high as $250,000."[11] In addition, she lost her chartered accountant designation.

Questions

1. Did Maria blow the whistle at the right time? Why or why not?
2. Was her planned response appropriate? Why or why not?
3. How would you suggest she should have dealt with the problem?
4. Should whistleblowing be encouraged? Why or why not?

[10] Ibid.

[11] "Is Fraud the Thing?," *BusinessWeek*, February 15, 1999, 104.

ETHICS CASE

The Lang Michener Affair

Martin Pilzmaker was a young, aggressive lawyer from Montreal who was invited in 1985 to join the law firm Lang Michener in Toronto. It was expected that his immigration law practice "could enrich the (firm's) coffers by $1 million a year catering to the needs of Hong Kong Chinese already starting to panic over the crown colony's 1997 return to China's control."

Although rumors of Pilzmaker's questionable practices began to surface and were reported to the firm's executive committee in December, it was not until early February 1986 that a senior colleague, Tom Douglas, "drew aside Ament and Wiseman (Pilzmaker's junior colleagues) and grilled them on their boss's activities. They told him that Pilzmaker not only smuggled regularly but that he was running a double-passport operation.... The scam involved the false reporting of lost Hong Kong passports by his clients, which, in fact, would be kept by Pilzmaker in Canada. On their replacement passports, the clients could travel in and out of the country at will. When the time came to apply for citizenship—which requires three years' residence—they could supply the original 'lost' passports to show few if any absences from Canada."

Douglas told the executive committee of this activity, by memo, on February 10. The executive committee "speculated that Pilzmaker's admissions may have constituted only knowledge of wrongdoing on the part of certain clients and not active complicity. The committee decided to send (two members) Don Wright and Donald Plumley back to Pilzmaker to ask him, in the words of Farquharson's instructing memo, 'if he would be willing to agree' not to participate in any client violation of the *Immigration Act*."

Early in June 1986, angered that Pilzmaker had not been expelled, Tom Douglas sought advice from Burke Doran, "a colleague he regarded as a personal friend but moreover, one who was a bencher, or governor, of the Law Society. Doran went on to advise him to keep his head down and his mouth shut—a caution Doran later said he had no recollection of giving."

While mulling over this advice and some from another lawyer, Brendon O'Brien, a foremost authority on professional conduct, Douglas discovered a further problem. "This was a proposal by Pilzmaker to Brian McIntomny, a young associate lawyer, who was in the market to buy a house. The idea was that McIntomny would put up $50,000 for a $200,000 house, the balance supplied by a Pilzmaker client in Hong Kong. The client would officially own the house, have the phone and utilities registered in his name, while McIntomny lived in it and held a secret deed. After three years, he would pay the client the interest-free $150,000, register the deed to place title in his own name and benefit from the accrued increase in value. The client, meanwhile, would have 'proof' of having resided in Canada for the three years required for citizenship." Douglas arranged for Bruce McDonald, a member of the firm's new executive committee, now consisting of McDonald, Don Wright, Albert Gnat, Donald Plumley, and Bruce McKenna, to be informed.

An investigation was begun, and "at a July 28th Executive Committee meeting, a vote was taken on whether or not to expel Pilzmaker." The vote was three to two in favor of his staying. Douglas was allowed to address the meeting only after the vote was finalized, and he was enraged.

"On August 6, the night before McKenna's report was submitted but in partial knowledge of what it would likely contain, Douglas had dinner with Burke Doran again, this time in the company of a mutual colleague, Bruce Drake. Drake and Douglas subsequently claimed that when he was asked whether the firm had an obligation to report at least Pilzmaker's double-passport scam to the Law Society, Doran said no, 'because no white men have been hurt.' (Neither man took this as a racist remark but as meaning it was a victimless crime, with the clients knowingly involved.) The following morning at the office, Drake said he asked Doran if his remarks of the night before could be taken as official advice from the chairman of the Law Society. Doran said yes."

Doran has always denied that, confining his explanation to the dinner and not the morning after: "It's far-fetched to say I was sitting at a social dinner in my capacity as chairman of discipline." Don Wright would later testify, however, that it was Doran's view throughout the period "that we did not have any obligation to report to the Society."

On August 7, McKenna filed a scathing fifteen-page report to the executive committee, listing fifteen breaches of unethical behavior both inside and outside the firm by Pilzmaker, noting that "I am not aware of any material statement of fact made by him to me that I have checked out and has proven to be true." Furthermore, "I am concerned that I now have a personal responsibility, as a member of the Law Society and an officer of the court, to report the situation. If each of you review the facts closely, you will have similar concerns about your own obligations." "On August 20, the executive committee did finally decide Pilzmaker had to go, subject to confirmation by the entire partnership."

After this, events proceeded at a faster pace:

September 4: Brendon O'Brien, hired to counsel the firm, advised that "they couldn't afford not to report to the Society."

September 5: A general meeting of the firm's partners is called to review the matter.

September 18: The requisite two-thirds of the 200 votes were obtained to force expulsion.

September 26: Pilzmaker's files were secured at the firm.

October 1: The Executive Committee debated the impact on the reputation of the firm and of high-profile partners "such as Jean Chretien (who became the Prime Minister of Canada) and Burke Doran."

November 6: Douglas wrote Don Wright, urging the firm to report to the society.

November 18: Pilzmaker's lawyer filed suit to have Pilzmaker's files transferred to him.

November 21: The Law Society received a report from O'Brien "that (a) Pilzmaker had been expelled, (b) that he had been wrongly billing into the general, not trust, account and (c) that there was more than $300,000 in

> unpaid fees where Pilzmaker had either not done the work or had not even been retained in the first place." The society's investigator, Stephen Sherriff, began his investigation and subsequently called for a fuller report from the firm.
>
> December 5: Pilzmaker's request for his files was granted by Justice Archibald Campbell, who "was given no hint that the files contained evidence that at some point might need to be looked at by the Law Society."
>
> December 8: A fuller report is presented to the Law Society.

Twenty-five months later, "in January, 1989, Sherriff filed a lacerating 138-page confidential report that recommended a professional misconduct charge be laid against Burke Doran for placing himself in a conflict of interest situation in which he chose the interests of the firm over his responsibility as the Society's then chairman of discipline. Separate charges of professional misconduct were recommended against eight others in the firm. Sherriff contended that (a) they had failed to inform clients that Pilzmaker had likely given them unethical advice and to seek independent counsel and (b) they had failed to report in a timely manner what they knew about his behavior, indeed they reported only when Pilzmaker's lawsuit gave them no alternative."

An Ottawa lawyer, David Scott, was retained to help the society by analyzing what to do about Sherriff's recommendations. His report of March 2, 1989, was presented to Paul Lamek, the new chair of discipline for the society. "The ball was now in Lamek's court. He says he saw his job as twofold: To define who Scott meant by 'Managing partners and/or group' and to decide whether a charge could be made against Doran on a basis different from Sherriff's—namely, that as a bencher and chair of discipline, Doran had a 'higher duty' to report than did his colleagues. Although it wouldn't be officially disclosed until this spring, Lamek initially did opt to charge all eight, subject to clarifying just who exactly was on the executive committee from the crucial time on—a period Lamek pinned at June, 1986. That clarification consequently dropped several senior people out of the picture. As for Doran, 'after agonizing analysis' Lamek concluded that no complaint of any kind should be issued."

What was the outcome of these charges/events?

> In the Spring of 1989, when it became obvious that Douglas would have to testify against his colleagues that fall, he finally did resign—three years after he'd first threatened to.
>
> On October 31, without waiting for the panel's ruling, a disillusioned Sherriff resigned from his job: "What could have been a testament to the integrity of the Society had ended up sullying it. I had no choice but to quit." His departure, coupled with growing media speculation that there might be a "whitewash of a cover-up" in process, had many other members of the Society adding to the chorus of concern.
>
> At a convocation meeting of the benchers last September [1989], lawyer Clayton Ruby, who'd been given a copy of the investigation report by Sherriff, presented a motion that Lamek's decision be set aside and the original recommendations adopted. Ferrier ruled the motion out of order. "Douglas and Sherriff are right-wingish, not my kind of guys," [said] the notoriously left-leaning Ruby. "But I really felt that Lamek's decision to charge only five made it look as if we (the Society) were covering something up."
>
> At a general members meeting the following month, former bencher Paul Copeland tried to table a motion demanding simply an explanation for

> why only five had been charged. He says he too was "cut off" by Ferrier.
>
> On January 5 of this year [1990], the five who'd been charged were found guilty of professional misconduct for not reporting their concerns about Pilzmaker three months earlier than they did, specifically at the time McKenna made his damning report. The panel, however, found that the same concerns had not "imposed a duty on them" to inform clients that Pilzmaker had been expelled or that he might have given them unethical advice or that they should get independent legal advice.

Due to the ensuing controversy, on February 7, "the Society hired retired Manitoba former Chief Justice Archibald Dewar to review its handling of the entire affair." But his findings did not please everyone. "Dewar did not find any evidence of impropriety or favouritism in Lamek's charges. The Doran decision was a judgment call, he wrote, and while debatable, to proceed with a charge now would only satisfy critics but 'Not be seen as adding lustre to the discipline process.'"

What he did find, however, was a catalog of complaints against Sherriff. Sherriff was incensed. "The big deal, first," says Sherriff, "is that the real bad guy (Pilzmaker) almost went free. The big deal, second, is that the self-governing ability of this profession was compromised. 'Lawyers have special privileges, therefore, special responsibilities. Protecting the public is chief among them. That's the big deal. If you're a man of principle, you won't walk away from it.'"[1]

Questions

1. Are professionals bound to meet a higher standard of ethical behavior than nonprofessionals? If so, why?
2. In what respects were the actions of the lawyers involved in the Lang Michener affair not up to the ethical standard you would expect? Consider
   a. Pilzmaker's conduct;
   b. the conduct of members of the executive committee at Lang Michener—in particular, Burke Doran; and
   c. the investigation and proceedings by the Law Society.

   What obligations did each owe to clients, the legal profession, the Law Society, and the public?
3. Do the same considerations apply to other professionals as to lawyers?
4. Is the self-regulation of a profession on ethical matters effective from the perspective of
   a. the members of the profession?
   b. the public?
   c. clients?
5. Would you agree with the argument, which was used to exonerate members of the management team, that "when a professional makes a serious mistake, the error is of no consequence, if it is honestly made"? (Bud Jorgensen, *The Globe and Mail*, February 5, 1990, B9).

[1] Martin Pilzmaker was disbarred by the Law Society of Upper Canada in January 1990. Five other partners of his firm—Lang, Michener, Lash, and Johnston—were also found guilty and reprimanded. But the scandal refused to die, culminating in a major article in the "Insight" section of the *Toronto Star* on Sunday, July 22, 1990. The quotations in the case are from that article. Postscript: Martin Pilzmaker committed suicide.

ETHICS CASE

Wanda Liczyk's Conflicts of Interest

In 1984, twenty-three-year-old Wanda Liczyk received her designation as a chartered accountant. The following year, she left Coopers & Lybrand (now part of PricewaterhouseCoopers) to become a budget analyst for the City of North York. By 1991, she had become the city's treasurer and protégé of the mayor, Mel Lastman. In 1998, when North York was amalgamated into the City of Toronto, forming a megacity, Wanda became Toronto's CFO and treasurer, responsible for overseeing an operating budget of $6.5 billion.

Prior to the amalgamation of the cities, the City of North York awarded a computer contract to a company run by Michael Saunders. He was to develop a property tax management and collection system (TMACS). Liczyk was one of the three people on the committee that awarded Saunders the contract. However, she did not disclose to the other members of the committee that she had been having a sexual affair with the married Saunders. Although the affair ended in 1991, they remained friends, and Liczyk continued to give Saunders over $3 million in contracts. Furthermore, she convinced Mayor Lastman to select TMACS for the amalgamated City of Toronto even though a locally developed system, TMX, was already in place in other parts of the city. All of this became known only as a result of a formal public inquiry into a subsequent computer leasing scandal.

Shortly after the amalgamation, the City of Toronto signed a contract with MFP Financial Services to provide $43 million of computer equipment on a three-year lease. But the contract was not carefully monitored. After the payments almost doubled to $85 million, a lengthy public inquiry was conducted by Madam Justice Denise Bellamy. Her 2005 report revealed corruption, cronyism, and bribery. Former hairdresser Dash Domi became a salesman for MFP, earning a $1.2 million commission. Dash used his notoriety as the brother of National Hockey League player Tie Domi to wine, dine, and entertain various civic politicians and bureaucrats, including Tom Jakobek, the budget supervisor for the city, and Wanda Liczyk, the CFO of the city. Justice Bellamy found "credible evidence" that Dash made a $25,000 payoff to Jakobek. She also faulted Liczyk for not controlling the costs associated with the MFP leasing contract, for not reporting the overspending to city council on a timely basis, and for violating civic conflict of interest policies in her dealings with Saunders, even though Saunders had nothing to do with the MFP contract. Although the Bellamy Report is a scathing indictment of numerous civic officials, a subsequent investigation by the Ontario Provincial Police concluded that there was not enough evidence to press charges. No one was tried in a court of law, but Liczyk was charged and ultimately sanctioned by the Institute of Chartered Accountants of Ontario (ICAO).

As a result of the Bellamy Report, the professional conduct committee of the ICAO began an investigation in 2005 into the conduct of Liczyk, a member of the ICAO. After a closed in-camera session, the ICAO decided not to press charges against her. This led to a public outcry of protest. Doug Elliot, a Toronto resident, along with the City of Toronto, formally complained to the ICAO. Elliott argued that "the more sunshine that is shone on this secretive ICAO process, the greater the likelihood that justice will be seen to be done in the public interest."[1] The ICAO responded by hiring lawyer Richard Steinecke to review the professional conduct committee's decision. The new City of Toronto mayor, David Miller, said, "I'm very pleased with this decision. We called for the Institute to reconsider and it appears that they've taken the public interest very seriously."[2]

[1] Ken Mark, "Look at Decision Again, Reviewer Tells ICAO Panel," *The Bottom Line*, 2007.

[2] Ibid.

Steinecke's investigation concluded that the conduct committee gave few reasons for its decision, giving the impression that the case had not been taken seriously. Furthermore, a significant minority of the committee wanted the case to go to the disciplinary committee. As a result of his report, the ICAO reopened the investigation.

In a one-day disciplinary committee hearing in April 2007, a previously agreed statement of facts was read out. Liczyk pleaded guilty to three charges of violating Rule 201 of the Rules of Professional Conduct. She did not "maintain the good reputation of the profession" when she was providing contract work to Saunders, with whom she had a conflict of interest. Although she did not profit personally from any of the contracts that she sent to Saunders, she had compromised her independence and professional integrity. According to ICAO lawyer Paul Farley, "Time and time again Ms. Liczyk was deciding to approve proposals that resulted in city work going to her friend. She could have come to her senses but she didn't."[3] Liczyk was suspended as a chartered accountant for six months and ordered to pay a $15,000 fine and $7,000 of court costs.

Despite the Bellamy Report that severely criticized Liczyk for her involvement in the MFP leasing debacle, the ICAO initially wanted to take no action against her. Only after there was a public outcry did the ICAO reopen the case, but then it chose to prosecute Liczyk, not with respect to her involvement with the MFP scandal but rather for her involvement with Saunders.

The result of the ICAO trial was not to everyone's satisfaction. Doug Elliott, who had initially complained to the ICAO about its decision not to investigate Liczyk, called the verdict "a whitewash" and the fine "a slap on the wrist."[4] The Toronto city councilor, Michael Walker, had wanted Liczyk to lose her chartered accountant designation. Nor was he comfortable with the accounting profession policing itself. "If professional associations cannot take care of it [the disciplinary process] scrupulously and ruthlessly, then governments should take it over because the people would have more faith in it," Walker argued.[5]

Questions

1. If Wanda Liczyk did not benefit financially, did she really have a conflict of interest? Should she have been disciplined by the ICAO? Why or why not?
2. Should the accounting profession be allowed to police itself, or should an independent third party, such as the government, enforce professional codes of conduct?
3. Do you agree with Doug Elliott's complaint that closed-door trials of accountants by the accounting profession is not in the public interest?
4. By not prosecuting Liczyk after the Bellamy Report was published, did the ICAO give the appearance that it was protecting its own, and not wanting to publicly acknowledge that some chartered accountants actually violate the rules of professional conduct?
5. Should Liczyk, as the chief financial officer of the city, have been prosecuted by the ICAO on the more serious charge of failing to provide the required financial oversight, competence, and necessary due care associated with monitoring the MFP lease? Why or why not?

Sources: The factual information in this case has been drawn from various publications, including Shanti Fernando, "Ethics and Good Urban Governance," *Canadian Public Administration* 50, no. 3 (2007): 437–48.

Rob Kelly, "Settlement Is Looming for Liczyk," *The Bottom Line*, 2007.

Paul McLauglin, "The Importance of Being Ethical," *CAmagazine*, August 2008.

"Mega-Tasks in a Megacity," *CAmagazine*, April 1998.

David Rider, "Toronto Leasing Scandal Won't End in Charges: OPP," *The Record*, 2005.

[3] Rob Kelly, "CA Ticket Jerked for Six Months," *The Bottom Line*, 2007.

[4] Ibid.

[5] Mark, "Look at Decision Again, Reviewer Tells ICAO Panel."

ETHICS CASE

Strategic Roles

Assume that you are a professional accountant who is CFO of a medium-sized manufacturing company that plans to do the following:

- Misrepresent products that come from environmentally irresponsible sources as environmentally friendly.
- Bribe officials of a foreign government.
- Use analyses and/or decision techniques that you know are faulty or unethical.
- Encourage an unethical corporate culture.
- Mislead the audit committee.
- Ignore important internal controls.

Question

1. What is your responsibility in each of these situations?

ETHICS CASE

Locker Room Talk

Albert Gable is a partner in a CPA firm located in a small midwestern city that has a population of approximately 65,000. Mr. Gable's practice is primarily in the area of personal financial planning; however, he also performs an annual audit on the city's largest bank.

Recently, Mr. Gable was engaged by Larry and Susan Wilson to prepare a comprehensive personal financial plan. While preparing the plan, Mr. Gable became personal friends of the Wilsons. They confided to him that they have had a somewhat rocky marriage and, on several occasions, seriously discussed divorce. Preparation of the comprehensive personal financial plan, which is nearing completion, has taken six months. During this period, Mr. Gable also performed the annual audit for the bank.

The audit test sample selected at random from the bank's loan file included the personal loan files of Larry and Susan Wilson. Because certain information in the loan files did not agree with facts personally known to Mr. Gable, he became somewhat concerned. Although he did not disclose his client relationship with the Wilsons, he did discuss their loan in detail with a loan officer. The loan officer is very familiar with the situation because he and Larry Wilson were college classmates, and now they play golf together weekly.

The loan officer mentioned to Mr. Gable that he believed Larry Wilson was "setting his wife up for a divorce." In other words, he was arranging his business affairs over a period of time so that he would be able to "leave his wife penniless." The loan officer indicated that this was just "locker room talk" and that Mr. Gable should keep it confidential.

Mr. Gable's compensation from his firm is based on annual billings for services. If Mr. Gable resigns as CPA for the Wilsons, it would result in his losing a bonus constituting a substantial amount in annual personal compensation. Mr. Gable is counting on the bonus to contribute to support tuition and expenses for his youngest daughter, who will be starting as a freshman in college next fall.

Questions

1. What are the ethical issues?
2. What should Albert Gable do?

Source: Prepared by Paul Breazeale, Breazeale, Saunders & O'Neil Ltd, Jackson, Mississippi. Drawn from the Ethics Case Collection of the American Accounting Association.

ETHICS CASE

Advice for Sam and Ruby

Dear John:

I really appreciate your willingness to give me your opinion as a fellow professional accountant on what I should do and on what I should advise the minority owner to do. Given that I was asked to help out Ruby, a family friend, and have found myself in the following situation, your advice is welcomed. Please take into account that I am not (and have not been) retained, nor am I being compensated in any manner related to the situation; I have not been providing accounting services in any shape or form related to the situation, and I have ensured that Ruby did seek out accounting advice from another party as events unfolded.

Approximately three years ago, Jimmy, an owner of a small auto body shop, approached Ruby to give her a 10% equity stake in the shop and asked her to provide day-to-day management functions for the entity. Jimmy wanted Ruby to allow certain cash receipts to bypass the books of the shop, and in return Ruby would directly receive a commission on these transactions. We do not know if these amounts were claimed as taxable income by Jimmy, but it is possible. This cash bypass requirement was incorporated into the shareholders' agreement, signed by both parties, and witnessed. I informed Ruby and her accountant that these amounts must be tracked and reported on Ruby's tax returns as taxable income without deduction.

Ruby was lax and followed Jimmy's advice in completing certain paperwork, so the incorporation documents and subsequent filings still reflect her as the sole director of the company, even though she merely set up the new company formed at the time of the initial transaction. Now, Jimmy has approached her to buy her out.

During the course of the negotiations, which I attended, Jimmy's accountant disclosed he was aware that the "off-book" revenue was occurring, but I am still unaware of how it was treated for tax purposes. There is a high likelihood of premeditated tax evasion on Jimmy's part. Jimmy has had—and continues to have—various taxation "issues," including one for approximately $80,000 that caused him to approach Ruby in the first place. Jimmy was apparently attempting to hide assets from the tax authorities and used the then-unaware Ruby to effectively be a shield for him.

By the way, Jimmy's accountant has indicated that he is a professional accountant, and the negotiations for the sale of the minority shares have now been transferred to Ruby's lawyer. I am still providing some help through her lawyer.

I am looking forward to receiving your advice.

Sincerely,

Sam

Questions

1. Keeping in mind that no compensation or accounting services, were ever received or provided, has Sam stepped "out of bounds"?
2. What is your advice for Sam?
3. What is your advice for Ruby?
4. Given the alleged disclosure by Jimmy's accountant, has he crossed any boundaries? If so, does Sam have to take any actions, and what would these actions be?

ETHICS CASE

Biker Nightmare

I need your advice on an anonymous basis. I am a professional accountant employed by a company that imports bikes from China. Before I get into the issue, I wish to advise you that I really need this job, as I am a single mother of two teenagers, and jobs like the one I have are hard to come by in the area where I live.

The company deceptively avoids paying the mandatory import duty on the bikes it imports. Last week, the president of the company asked me to prepare and provide him with a statement of the duty avoided on the purchase of these bikes for the past three years. He also asked that I sign off on this statement. The statement that I prepared and presented to him showed that $200,000 in customs duties has been avoided by the company in the period covered.

Since I prepared that statement, I am having trouble sleeping at night.

Questions

1. What does our professional code say about this?
2. If this issue is uncovered by the government regulatory authorities, will I be implicated?
3. Should I quit my job and then go and report this situation to the regulatory authorities?

ETHICS CASE

Budget Conflict

I have a question that I need a bit of help on, but I am not sure where to turn, and I hope you may be able to help me out.

I am the CFO of a charitable organization, it is a paid position and I am a professional accountant. We are currently presenting our budget to the Board of Directors, which is a volunteer board. There is a chance they may pass a budget that is not fiscally possible; that is, we do not have the cash flow to execute it. It is not the budget we are recommending, but they may have us spend to levels of 25% growth (stretch budgeting).

Both our treasurer and I have tried on numerous occasions to explain this to our president, but she and other board members are not financially astute.

Our treasurer has stated that he will go on the record to advise against any such spending and budget and may even resign over it.

Questions

1. What should the CFO do?
2. Beyond resigning, how can the CFO protect him- or herself?

ETHICS CASE

An Exotic Professional Accountant?

Excuse me, we are both professional accountants, and I need some advice. I have a full-time management position with a company. I was wondering if I would be in violation of our Professional Code of Ethics if I took on the role of an exotic dancer at night in order to fund my husband through university?

Question

1. What advice would you give?

ETHICS CASE

Freebie Services for Staff

I am a professional accountant and hold the position of financial analyst, capital projects, with the Town of Pinecrest. In my position, I deal with, among others, developers and their lawyers with respect to development agreements, cost-sharing agreements, and financial agreements.

In the past, during lunch hours and after hours, I have provided informal financial advice to a fellow municipal employee with respect to her marriage separation, including a review of her ex-husband's personal tax returns (which included self-employment income). No issue arose in this regard. Currently, during lunch hours and after hours, I am providing informal financial advice to another fellow municipal employee with respect to her common-law separation.

A verbal "complaint" or "allegation" has been made to the town manager that I have a "conflict of interest" by being a municipal employee carrying out my duties as a public servant as paid for by the town and by helping a fellow municipal employee who is currently facing a common-law separation. The town does not have an internal "conflict of interest" policy for staff. I know of no basis for such a "complaint" or "allegation" except that the lawyer for a group of developers is also the lawyer for the ex-common-law spouse.

As there is no actual "complaint" or "allegation" to respond to, only rumors and innuendo, I am seeking your general advice at this time. In due course, as a municipal employee, I will be providing a written response to the town manager.

Question

1. What advice would you give to this professional accountant?

ETHICS CASE

Summer Camp Holdback

I think I have a problem. I am a professional accountant and work for a not-for-profit organization that operates a summer camp. We have obtained a legal opinion stating that a portion of our camp fees could be considered a charitable donation with respect to religious education costs for the 2007 summer and subsequent years.

When we originally invoiced parents for the 2007 summer (in January 2007), we billed the amounts as fees fully subject to sales tax and collected and remitted the tax to the government authorities. As a charitable donation, no sales tax needs to be collected, so we have since adjusted the 2007 invoices to reflect the amounts of taxes charged in error and are in the process of recovering these funds from the governments involved.

The issue that arises is that, as we are acting as an agent for the governments with respect to collection of taxes and therefore these funds are considered a "deemed trust," it is my opinion that these recovered taxes rightfully belong to the parents who originally paid them and should be refunded. Our Executive Committee believes that we can simply keep these funds and issue donation receipts without ever telling the parents that they are entitled to this money. I strongly believe that their view is unethical and have indicated as such, but they are intent on doing it regardless.

This leaves me in a difficult position in that I do not want to do anything that I feel is unethical, but I cannot afford to lose my employment by refusing their demands. Any guidance or advice you could give me would be most appreciated.

Question

1. What is your advice?

ETHICS CASE

Theft Reimbursement, Twice

I am the assistant controller at a medium-sized, not-for-profit organization. I hired a new accounts-payable clerk three months ago—let's call her Mary, which is not her real name—and then I fired her last week because she stole $16,583 from us by altering six checks. Mary's primary duties were to key in all the accounts-payable information and then, after the checks were printed, to match all the supporting documentation to each check. She then took the checks to the signing officers. After they were signed, she mailed the checks and filed the yellow copy with all the supporting documentation in the paid-invoices filing cabinet.

We pay each member of our board of directors a $2,000 honorarium. I prepare the list of the directors and how much to pay each director, which I give to Mary for inputting into the computer. Each honorarium check simply has the name of the director and no address or other information. We normally hand them to the directors during the meeting. Similarly, our expense report reimbursement checks only have the names of the individuals and no address or other information on the checks. We send those to our employees through the interoffice mail.

Well, after they were signed, Mary took four honorarium checks and two expense report checks and changed the names on the checks to her name. All of our checks are printed on light green paper. Well, Mary used White Out to alter the names, but she wasn't very smart. It was obvious that the names had been changed from the White Out used, and her name wasn't even the same font as the typing on the rest of the check. She took the checks across the street to an ATM machine and deposited them into her bank account. She then transferred the money to her family, who live in another country.

I discovered the false checks last week when I was doing the bank reconciliation. She admitted what she did, and we've had the police charge her with theft. Our bank was very apologetic and immediately reimbursed us the full $16,583. Our bankers admitted that the checks were so obviously falsified that they never should have cleared the bank in the first place.

Well, my problem is that, after I discovered the theft and before the bank reimbursed us, I decided to claim on our insurance policies. One of those policies is a check-protector service. Well, today we received a check for $16,583 from them. So I took the check to my boss, the controller, and I was laughing saying that we've been reimbursed twice and that I was going to send the check back to the insurance company. Well, he said, "No." He told me to deposit the check into a high-interest savings account. "We'll return the $16,583 to the insurance company after the court case is settled. In the meantime we'll earn interest on the money, and since we're a nonprofit organization, we won't even have to pay tax on the interest."

He said the interest represents the aggravation we're going through. Well, there has been a lot of aggravation. The other accounting clerks felt terrible about Mary. They felt violated and abused because they had trusted her. We will also have to spend a lot of time with the lawyers and time in court at Mary's trial. My boss's attitude is that the interest on the extra $16,583 will cover all of these additional costs associated with the Mary fiasco. He also said that the bank deserves to pay the interest to us since they should never have cashed those doctored checks in the first place.

Well, I don't think that this is right. But I don't want to challenge him since I was the one who hired Mary. So, like, what do you think I should do?

Questions

1. How would you answer the assistant controller?
2. What advice would you give to the controller?
3. What aspects of the organization's governance process and/or internal controls were flawed?
4. Should the directors be told about the fraud and/or any other matters?

Accounting & Auditing Dilemmas

ETHICS CASE

Sino-Forest Fraud? Audit Challenges in China

In mid-2011, Sino-Forest Corporation was a company with timber operations in China, including tree plantation (holding of timber for appreciation and/or harvesting), log and wood products trading, and manufacturing of wood products. Its shares were traded on the Toronto Stock Exchange (TSE) under the TRE symbol, with a total market capitalization in U.S. dollars of $4.2 billion at a share price of $ 18.21. However, in a research report dated June 2, 2011, Carson Block, the director of research of Muddy Waters, LLC, alleged that Sino-Forest Corporation was a reverse-takeover (RTO) fraud,[1] "a multi-billion-dollar Ponzi scheme... accompanied by substantial theft", and estimated the real value of a share to be less than $1.[2] Sino-Forest share prices plummeted; the Ontario Securities Commission (OSC) investigated the company's auditor, Ernst & Young, who subsequently settled a class action lawsuit with Sino-Forest's shareholders for $117 million; PricewaterhouseCoopers was called in by Sino-Forest to substantiate its assets, but the company went bankrupt. Muddy Waters was sued for $4 billion for defamation in 2012, but the lawsuit has not proceeded.

The Muddy Waters Research Report

In the Introduction and Executive Summary of *Research Report*,[3] Carson Block makes the following allegations:

- Sino-Forest Corp (traded on the TSE as TRE since 2010) has always been a fraud since it reported excellent results from early joint ventures even though the joint ventures never went into operation.
- TRE's sales transactions for standing timber were fabricated. For example, reported sales in Yunnan province exceeded "the applicable harvesting quotas by six times," and "transporting the harvested logs would have required over 50,000 trucks driving on two-lane roads winding through the mountains from this remote region, which is beyond belief (and likely road capacity)."
- "TRE massively exaggerates its assets." Purchases of trees for planting have been overstated, few legitimate agents have been used, and "the other agents appear to have been laundering money for TRE—moving large amounts of money to an undisclosed subsidiary of TRE and a trading company that TRE does business with. We also see clear evidence that TRE has falsified its books."
- In order to raise funds, TRE engaged Jakko Pöyry, a valuations company, to provide credible valuation reports on growing trees. However, TRE has been "all the while giving Pöyry manipulated data and restricting the scope of its work." According to the Research Report, Pöyry has been allowed to inspect "only 0.3% of [TRE's] purported holdings."
- TRE was using offshore companies, including "at least 20 British Virgin

[1] In a reverse takeover, a deal is made wherein a private company causes a public company (whose shares are traded on a stock exchange) to take over the private company so that its owners receive shares in the public company and can thereby gain access to capital markets to raise funds through public share offerings from the public company. In effect, the owners of the private company obtain a stock exchange listing by a reverse takeover without going through the scrutiny or effort required for an initial public listing and share offering.

[2] Muddy Waters Research Report, June 2, 2011, http://www.muddywatersresearch.com /research/tre/initiating -coverage-treto.

[3] Ibid., 1–3.

Island entities" that obscure the transparency of company operations.

- Forged documents were being used and were not detected by the auditors.
- TRE's Board of Directors, Audit Committee, and auditors were not sufficiently familiar with the politics, industry practice, language, and culture of the People's Republic of China.

The Reaction

Not surprisingly, Sino-Forest rejected these allegations, but the company's share price plunged 82% during July before rallying somewhat.[4] In addition, on June 6, 2011, Sino-Forest announced that an independent committee (IC) had been set up to review the Muddy Waters allegations. PricewaterhouseCoopers (PwC) was hired to conduct an independent investigation.[5] On August 15, it was announced that the PwC report would be delayed to the end of the year, and on August 26, the OSC suspended trading of TRE, stating that the company "appears to have engaged in significant non-arm's-length transactions which may have been contrary to Ontario securities laws and the public interest."[6]

On November 15, 2011, the IC issued an interim report that stated that PwC, whose report was due out by the end of December, had confirmed most of the cash balances expected in Hong Kong and in the rest of China. The IC had confirmed a total of 293 cash accounts in Hong Kong, "representing 100% of the expected cash position" in that city, and had confirmed twenty-eight of the 267 accounts elsewhere in China, "representing approximately 81% of the expected cash position in China."[7] However, there were "significant challenges in verifying the company's timberland holdings" particularly since, in some areas of China, a plantation rights certificate (PRC), which reflects landownership in a computerized land titles system, had not yet been issued.[8] "The [interim] report [also] noted that there was incomplete or inadequate record creation and retention practices, no integrated accounting system and employees conducted company business from time to time using personal devices and non-corporate email addresses."[9] The Board of Directors also concluded that they could not release the company's third-quarter results that were due on November 14, 2011, until outstanding issues had been resolved.[10]

Not surprisingly, the interim report did not stabilize the situation, which quickly degenerated. On January 10, 2012, Sino-Forest announced in a press release "that it still [could not] release the third quarter financial statements because it [had not] been able to determine the nature of certain relationships between the company and its

---

[4] Christopher Donville and Matt Walcoff, "Sino-Forest Shares Surge after Wellington Management Discloses 11.5% Stake," *Bloomberg*, July 5, 2011, accessed July 2, 2013, at http://www.bloomberg.com/news/2011-07-04/wellington-controls-11-5-of-sino-forest-as-timber-producer-s-stock-drops.html.

[5] "Sino-Forest Corporation Announcement: SINO-Forest Independent Committee Appoints Pricewaterhouse Coopers," June 6, 2011, accessed July 2, 2013, at http://www.kmlaw.ca/site_documents/A-125%20-%20-Sino%20Press%20Release%20-%20June%206,%202011%20-%20SF%20Independent%20Committee%20Appoints%20Pricewaterhousecoopers.pdf.

[6] OSC Alleges Fraud at Sino-Forest, *CBC News*, August 26, 2011, accessed July 2, 2013, at http://www.cbc.ca/news/business/story/2011/08/26/sino-forest-ceased-trading.html.

[7] ""Sino-Forest Announced Findings of the Independent Committee," CNW Canada Newswire, November 15, 2011, accessed July 2, 2013, at http://www.newswire.ca/en/story/877567/sino-forest-announces-findings-of-the-independent-committee.

[8] Ibid.

[9] "Sino-Forest Report Disputes Fraud Allegations," *CBC News*, November 15, 2011, accessed July 2, 2013, at http://www.cbc.ca/news/business/story/2011/11/15/sino-forest-fraud-report.html.

[10] "Sino-Forest Announced Findings of the Independent Committee."

business partners."[11] Moreover, "the circumstances that could cause the company to be unable to release the Q3 results could impact the company's historic financial statements. *For this reason, the company cautions that the company's historic financial statements and related audit reports should not be relied upon.*"[12] As a result, the company began "scrambling to convince a majority of holders of two of its bond issues not to tip the company into default. It needs a majority to agree to grant the company waivers from default after it failed to release its financial results and skipped a $9.8-million interest payment in December."[13]

On March 30, 2012, Sino-Forest filed for bankruptcy protection in Canada to give it time under court supervision to make a deal with creditors.[14] On the same date, Sino-Forest sued Muddy Waters and Carson Block for $4 billion ($3.5 billion for defamation, punitive damages of $400 million, and another $100 million for the cost of investigative "the tortious false allegations").[15] "The suit alleges that Muddy Waters, along with 100 unnamed hedge funds, set up short positions in Chinese companies with listings on Western stock exchanges. The suit then alleges the group would put out "what is popularly described as a 'bear attack' on the companies" in the form of a report with a "veneer of truth" that would create a "cataclysmic effect on the stock price,"[16] which would allow Muddy Waters and other hedge funds to profit by filling their short positions at depressed stock prices.

On December 3, 2012, a hearing was held by the OSC into allegations against the company auditors, Ernst & Young.

On December 10, 2012, the Ontario Superior Court approved a transaction whereby the assets of Sino-Forest Corp. were transferred to the company's bondholders,[17] and on January 30, 2013, a new company, Emerald Plantation Holdings Limited, was formed to receive those assets.[18]

OSC Allegations Against Ernst & Young LLP

According to the Statement of Allegations presented at the December 3, 2012, hearing, the OSC alleged that Ernst & Young did the following:

- Failed to perform sufficient audit work to verify Sino-Forest's ownership of its most significant assets.
- Failed to perform sufficient audit work to verify the existence of Sino-Forest's most significant assets.
- Failed to undertake their audit work on the Sino-Forest engagement with a sufficient level of professional skepticism.

Moreover, Ernst & Young failed to comply with Canadian generally accepted accounting standards (GAAS) although the firm had filed a number of documents

[11] Andy Hoffman, "Sino-Forest Warns Historic Financial Documents Should Not Be Relied Upon," *The Globe and Mail*, January 10, 2012, accessed July 3, 2013, at http://www.theglobeandmail.com/globe-investor/sino-forest-warns-historic-financial-documents-should-not-be-relied-upon/article1358189.

[12] Ibid., emphasis added.

[13] Ibid.

[14] "Sino-Forest Files for Bankruptcy Protection," *BBC News*, accessed July 2, 2103, at http://www.bbc.co.uk/news/business-17569840.

[15] Republished with permission of David Benoit, "Dow Jones Company from Sino-Forest Sues Muddy Waters for $4 Billion," *Wall Street Journal*, March 30, 2012; permission conveyed through Copyright Clearance Center, Inc.

[16] Ibid.

[17] Peter Koven, "Judge Approves Sino-Forest Restructuring despite Opposition from Funds," *Financial Post*, December 12, 2011, accessed July 2, 2013, at http://business.financialpost.com/2012/12/11/judge-approves-sino-forest-restructuring-despite-opposition-from-funds.

[18] See http:// www.emeraldplantationholdings.com, accessed July 3, 2013.

with the OSC representing that they had done so.[19]

The discussion contained in the Statement of Allegations is very informative, particularly in regard to the following audit requirements:

Generally Accepted Auditing Standards

28. As set out in GAAS, an auditor's objective is to identify and assess the risks of material misstatement, whether due to fraud or error, in an entity's financial statements. An auditor can achieve this objective by understanding the entity and its environment, including the entity's internal controls. This understanding provides the auditor with a basis for designing and implementing responses to the assessed risks.

(a) Sufficient Audit Evidence Required

29. GAAS requires auditors to obtain reasonable assurance that the entity's financial statements are free from material misstatements. Reasonable assurance is a high level of assurance. It is achieved when the auditor has obtained sufficient appropriate audit evidence to reduce audit risk to a low level and to provide a reasonable basis to support the content of the audit report. The sufficiency of the audit evidence gathered by the auditor is influenced by the level of materiality set for the audit and the level of risk associated with the audit.

30. The sufficiency and the appropriateness of the audit evidence gathered by the auditor are interrelated. Sufficiency is the measure of the quantity of the audit evidence. The quantity of the audit evidence needed is affected by the auditor's assessment of the risks of misstatement. That is, the higher the assessed risks, the more audit evidence is likely to be required. The quantity of audit evidence needed is also affected by the quality of the audit evidence. That is, the higher the quality of the audit evidence, the less audit evidence may be required.

31. Obtaining more audit evidence, however, may not compensate for its poor quality. Appropriateness is the measure of the quality of the audit evidence; that is its relevance and its reliability in providing support for the conclusions on which the auditor's opinion is based. The reliability of the audit evidence is influenced by its source and by its nature, and is dependent on the circumstances in which it is obtained.

(b) Professional Skepticism Required

32. GAAS requires auditors to plan and perform their audits using professional skepticism, recognizing that circumstances may exist that cause the financial statements to be materially misstated. Professional skepticism requires a questioning attitude which is alert to conditions which may indicate possible misstatement due to error or fraud. Professional skepticism requires an auditor to conduct a critical assessment of the audit evidence.

33. Professional skepticism requires the auditor to be alert to, amongst other things:

a. audit evidence that contradicts other audit evidence obtained;
b. information that brings into question the reliability of documents and responses to inquiries;
c. conditions that may indicate possible fraud; and
d. circumstances that suggest the need for additional audit procedures in addition to those required by minimum written professional standards.[20]

[19] *Statement of Allegations*, OSC Hearing, In the Matter of the Securities Act, R.S.O. 1990, c. S.5 as Amended—and—in the Matter of Ernst & Young LLP, December 3, 2012, Sections 2–4, accessed July 2, 2013, at http://www.osc.gov.on.ca/en/Proceedings_soa_20121203_ernst-young.htm.

[20] Ibid.

The SOA goes on to detail how, in the OSC's opinion, Ernst & Young did the following:

- Failed to adequately address ownership of timber:
  - Due to flawed purchase contracts: failure to collect all relevant documents, and to note that locations of timber were not specific. (SOA Sections 40–41); and failure to note that the same survey firm prepared all timber surveys throughout the PRC.
  - Due to an insufficient understanding of the company's legal claim to its Purported Assets (Section 44), and to appreciate the limits of a legal opinion (the Jingtian Opinion) discussing the legal regime relating to forestry assets (Section 46); and so did not follow up when and in such ways as appropriate.
- Failed to adequately address the existence of timber and the audit risks inherent in that the company did not make cash payments for the acquisition of Purported Assets as evidenced by
  - limited and ineffectual site visits (Section 52) and
  - inappropriate reliance on periodic valuations prepared by Pöyry Forest Industry Ltd. Relative to GAAS requirements (Sections 54–58)
- Failed to conduct its audits with a sufficient level of skepticism (Sections 59–60).
- Failed to properly structure the audit team so that Chinese speaking personnel were represented at all levels rather than relying on translated documents from which some important information was missing (Sections 61–63).[21]

Ernst & Young has denied the OSC allegations.

The Aftermath

On December 5, 2013, the OSC announced that its hearing to determine the veracity of its allegations of fraud against Sino-Forest and its executives, originally scheduled for June 2013, would be further delayed until September 2, 2014.[22]

On a separate but related matter, Ernst & Young was the subject of a $9.18 billion class-action lawsuit launched by Sino-Forest shareholders who charged audit negligence. Ultimately, Ernst & Young made a $117 million deal to settle the lawsuit. Some shareholders were unhappy with the settlement, which blocked further lawsuits, but the Ontario Court of Appeal rejected a challenge to this settlement on June 26, 2013.[23]

Muddy Waters continues to investigate and reveal fraudulent activity in other companies. It lists its track record of uncovering business fraud, accounting fraud, and fundamental problems, including important Sino-Forest events, on its Web page at http://www.muddywatersresearch.com/track-record. It will continue to be an important force as it fulfills its stated purpose as follows:

> **"Speaking Truth to Power**
>
> In the face of egregious market inefficiencies, Muddy Waters refuses to be deterred by the financial marketplace's insider titans. We speak truth to power, even when the message is unpopular or threatening to the status quo, and often when nobody else is willing to do so."[24]

[21] Ibid. See sections noted in the OSC Statement of Allegations.

[22] Barbara Shecter, "OSC Hearing to Test Fraud Allegations against Sino-Forest Delayed," *Financial Post*, December 5, 2013, accessed December 30, 2103, at http://business.financialpost.com/news/fp-street/osc-hearing-to-test-fraud-allegations-against-sino-forest-delayed.

[23] Jeff Gray, "Auditors' Sino-Forest Settlement Stands," *The Globe and Mail*, June 27, 2013, B7, http://www.theglobeandmail.com/report-on-business/industry-news/the-law-page/ontario-court-approves-117-million-settlement-with-sino-forest-auditors/article10044252.

[24] See Muddy Waters website, accessed December 30, 2013, at http://www.muddywatersresearch.com.

Questions

1. Describe the fraud that allegedly occurred through Sino-Forest Corporation Inc. Who benefited, and how?
2. Why did regulators not prevent this fraud from occurring? What were they relying on?
3. Why did the directors of Sino-Forest not prevent this fraud from occurring? What should they have done to discover the problems that were subsequently uncovered?
4. Why did shareholders not foresee this fraud? What were they relying on?
5. Why did Carson Block author the Muddy Waters Research Report? Was he altruistic or self-interested? What did his company stand to gain?
6. What basic assumptions were erroneously made by Ernst & Young that contributed to the audit problems of concern to the OSC?
7. What audit risks become important when auditing in unfamiliar cultures?
8. If you had been on the audit team of Sino-Forest, how would you have avoided allegations of a lack of adequate professional skepticism?
9. If the Chinese system of recording property rights were known to be incomplete, how would you have performed the audit of Sino-Forest's assets?
10. What audit problem was caused by the Sino-Forest practice of selling timber without receiving cash payments, and how would you have resolved it?
11. What would you do if you were a company director or auditor and you were advised that your company had incomplete or inadequate record creation and retention practices and no integrated accounting system and that employees conducted company business from time to time using personal devices and non-corporate email addresses?

ETHICS CASE

Massive Acquisition Write-Downs in the Mining Industry

Mergers and acquisitions (M&A) are strategies that help companies to grow in size rapidly. However, some incredibly questionable M&A decisions were reported in the mining industry in 2012 and 2013, including the following:

- The Canadian gold mining company Kinross Gold Corp. acquired some African mines when it purchased Red Back Mining Inc. for $7.1 billion in 2010. In 2012, Kinross wrote off $2.5 billion of its investment in Red Back and an additional $3.2 billion in 2013 as the costs of developing these African mines increased.
- In December 2012, Vale SA, the Brazilian metal and mining company, wrote down the value of a mine in northern Brazil by $2.85 billion as operating costs soared. The book value of the investment as of September 30 was $3.78 billion.
- In May 2013, Glencore, the Swiss mining giant, paid $44.6 billion to merge with Xstrata. Three months later, in August, the company wrote down its investment in Xstrata by $8.8 billion as a result of a decrease in commodity prices.
- The $14 billion write-down taken in January 2013 by the British-Australian multinational mining giant Rio Tinto is described below.

In January 2013, Rio Tinto recorded a $14 billion write-down of its assets, including a $10 billion write-off of its $38 billion investment in Alcan and a $3 billion write-off of its $3.7 billion investment in Riverside Mining. The company also announced that Tom Albanese, who had been CEO since 2007, would be stepping down, as would Doug Ritchie, head of the energy division, who had overseen the purchase of Riverside Mining.

In 2007, when aluminum was trading at its peak of $1.20 per pound, Rio Tinto paid $38 billion to acquire Alcan, a Canadian aluminum company. At the time of its acquisition, Albanese said that Alcan would have a competitive advantage because of its low-cost hydroelectric energy. He also predicted that China would be a net importer of aluminum. Instead, low-cost producers using cheap thermal coal sprung up within China, and China became self-sufficient in aluminum, which contributed to the price of aluminum falling to as low as $0.76 per pound. It subsequently rebounded to $0.91 per pound.

The 2013 write-down was the second time Rio Tinto had reduced its investment in Alcan, bringing its investment in the aluminum company down to $18 billion. In 2011, Rio Tinto bought a majority interest in Riverside Mining Ltd, which that operates coal mines in Mozambique. Its mines have been plagued with transportation and logistical problems. Rio Tinto has now written down that investment from $3.7 billion to $700 million.

Along with the announcement of the write-downs, the company also said that neither Doug Ritchie nor Tom Albanese, who had been with the company for thirty years, would be receiving any performance bonuses. Albanese does, however, get to keep £10.7 million of stock options that were awarded to him from 2003 to 2007.

Questions

1. Should the CEOs of these mining companies be held accountable for commodity prices that have dropped precipitously while operating costs have soared?
2. Should Albanese be held responsible for the fact that the Chinese market did not open as he predicted and that the price of aluminum drop precipitously? If not Albanese, then who should be held responsible?
3. Because of the $14 billion write-down, should Albanese be forced to forfeit his lucrative stock options?
4. Alcan was purchased in 2007, and there were two subsequent write-downs, reducing its value by more than half of its original purchase price. But Albanese did not resign until 2013. Was this resignation too late? When should a board of directors fire a CEO who has made a significant mistake?
5. The Rio Tinto executives made massive errors in judgment that cost the company billions. Were they treated too gently?
6. Since several companies have written off massive amounts paid for their acquisitions, were each of their managements wrong for specific reasons, or were there common factors affecting them all? If so, what were they?

Sources: P. Jordan and J. McNish, "Tom Albanese Out at Rio Tinto as Alcan Bet Goes Awry," *The Globe and Mail*, January 17, 2013.

P. Jordan, "Kinross Takes $3.2-billion Hit on African Mines," *The Globe and Mail*, February 13, 2013.

E. Reguly, "Glencore takes $7.7-Billion Writedown as Mining Industry Woes Continue," *The Globe and Mail*, August 20, 2013.

E. Rowley, "Rio Tinto CEO Tom Albanese Out over $14bn Write-Down," *The Telegraph*, January 17, 2013.

"Vale Takes Hefty Write-Down," *The Northern Miner*, December 21, 2012.

ETHICS CASE

Accounting Rule Changes Increase Apple Computer's Revenue

Numerous firms, including computer and communication companies, sell products that have multiple deliverables. For example, a telephone company may sell a customer a phone and a two-year unlimited long-distance telephone call package for a lump sum. How should the company account for the lump sum that it receives? Accounting rules required that the vendor allocate the lump sum between the two deliverables, separating the revenue from the sale of the hardware from the revenue from the sale of the service. Referred to as "subscription accounting," it required the phone company to immediately record the revenue from the sale of the hardware but defer and recognize the revenue from the long-distance telephone package over the two-year period.

Many high-tech companies objected to this accounting rule, including Apple Computer. Under subscription accounting, Apple was recording substantial amounts of deferred revenue associated with the sale of its iPhone and Apple TV products. Steve Jobs was a particularly vociferous opponent, arguing that subscription accounting obscured the real earnings growth of the company. "Because by its nature subscription accounting spreads the impact of iPhone's contribution to Apple's overall sales, gross margin, and net income over two years, it can make it more difficult for the average Apple manager or the average investor to evaluate the company's overall performance." So, Apple began to report both GAAP and non-GAAP results side by side. The non-GAAP earnings included the full revenue from the sale of its products and services.

In October 2009, the Financial Accounting Standards Board (FASB) issued *Accounting Standards Update No. 2009-13*, which addressed the issue of revenue recognition when there are multiple deliverables. The new standard allows companies, such as Apple, to recognize the revenue on multiple deliverables in the current period rather than over time. Apple no longer had to use subscription accounting. In an amended 10-K filing with the Securities and Exchange Commission, Apple noted,

> Under subscription accounting, revenue and associated product cost of sales for iPhone and Apple TV were deferred at the time of sale and recognized on a straight-line basis over each product's estimated economic life. This resulted in the deferral of significant amounts of revenue and cost of sales related to iPhone and Apple TV.... As of September 26, 2009, based on the historical accounting principles, total accumulated deferred revenue and deferred costs associated with past iPhone and Apple TV sales were $12.1 billion and $5.2 billion, respectively.... The new accounting principles result in the recognition of substantially all of the revenue and product costs from the sales of iPhone and Apple TV at the time of sale.... The adoption of the new accounting principles increased the Company's net sales by $6.4 billion, $5.0 billion, and $572 million for 2009, 2008, and 2007, respectively. As of September 26, 2009, the revised total accumulated deferred revenue associated with iPhone and Apple TV sales to date was $483 million; revised accumulated deferred costs for such sales were zero.

For the last quarter of 2009, Apple reported $15.6 billion of revenue, compared to $2.2 billion for the same quarter in the previous year. The increase in revenue was attributed to two factors: increased sales during the holiday shopping season and the change in its revenue recognition accounting policy. However, management would not say how much of the increased revenue was related to the change in accounting policy. The earnings were higher than analysts' expectations. Apple's share price rose $5.33 (2.7%) to close at $203.08.

Does recording substantially all the revenue in the current period result in fair reporting? Wilcox argues that this policy masks the fact that Apple has an ongoing relationship with its customers. "The iPhone is a work in progress, as evidenced by two full software upgrades and ongoing updates." Recording deferred revenue, on the other hand, would highlight Apple's obligation to its buyers.

Questions

1. Do you think that Apple's new accounting policy, which is consistent with the 2009 FASB statement, results in fair financial reporting?
2. Do you think that Apple's share price should have gone up as a result of increased revenue due to a change in an accounting policy?

Sources: Daniel Eran Dilger, "Inside Apple's iPhone Subscription Accounting Changes," *Roughly Drafted Magazine*, October 21, 2009, http://www.roughlydrafted.com/2009/10/21/inside-apples-iphone-subscription-accounting-changes.

Omar El Akkad, "Apple Rides iPhone, Mac to Record Profit," *The Globe and Mail*, January 26, 2010, B1, B6.

Financial Accounting Standards Board, "Revenue Recognition (Topic 605): Multiple- Multiple-Deliverable Revenue Arrangements—A Consensus of the FASB Emerging Issues Task Force," *Accounting Standards Update No. 2009-13*, October 2009, http://www.fasb.org/cs/BlobServer?blobcol=urldata&blobtable=MungoBlobs&blobkey=id& blobwhere=1175819938544&blobheader=application%2Fpdf.

U.S. Securities and Exchange Commission, "Amendment No. 1 to Form 10-K," Apple, Inc., January 25, 2010, http://www.sec.gov/Archives/edgar/data/320193/000119312510012091/d10ka.htm.

Joe Wilcox, "Accounting Rules Shouldn't Change to Benefit Apple, Other High-Tech Companies," *Beta News*, September 22, 2009, http://www.betanews.com/joewilcox/article/Accounting-rules-shouldnt-change-to-benefit-Apple-other-hightech-companies/1253649045.

The Impact of International GAAP on Earnings

ETHICS CASE

Following the pattern of many other countries, Canada converted from domestic generally accepted accounting principles to International Financial Reporting Standards (IFRS). The changeover occurred on January 1, 2011. As a result of the conversion to IFRS, the revenue recognition policies of many Canadian retail operators that offered customer reward programs had to change. Previously, there were no clear guidelines concerning loyalty programs, so many retailers recorded their sales at gross value rather than at net. For example, assume a customer makes purchases of \$200 and earns \$2 of reward points that can be redeemed at a later date. The retailer would record revenue of \$200 when the sale occurs and a further \$2 of sales when the points are redeemed. Total revenue recorded would be \$202. Under IFRS, this would not be an acceptable accounting policy. IFRS views the initial purchase as consisting of two elements: the customer is buying both the goods and the rewards. So, under IFRS, the retailer would record revenue of \$198 at the time of the sale and \$2 of deferred revenue for the associated points. The deferred revenue would be realized when the \$2 of points are redeemed. Total revenue would be \$200.

In 2010, stock analyst Kathleen Wong at Veritas Investment Research Corp. argued that this change in revenue recognition would have a negative effect on the earnings of Shoppers Drug Mart, which offers its customers the Shoppers Optimum Program, one of the largest loyalty programs in Canada. Shoppers Drug Mart does not reveal the impact of its reward program, but Wong speculates that the Optimum Program was adding 1% to 3% to the company's revenue. David Milstead contends that companies that chose the gross method were distorting their earnings. "They opted for a method that pushed a shiny sales growth figure to the forefront, rather than one that would more accurately portray their real revenue picture."

Questions

1. Do you think that the gross value method distorts earnings because it overstates revenue?
2. The total cash that the company receives is the same regardless of the method the company uses to report revenue. So, is one revenue recognition method just as good as any other?

Source: David Milstead, "A Close Inspection of Shoppers' Revenue Accounting," *The Globe and Mail*, May 17, 2010, B8.

ETHICS CASE

Auditor's Dilemma

Arthur sat back in his chair and looked at the other accountants who were working on their laptops. How had he gotten himself into this situation?

It began last year when he was hired by Castor Gotlieb LLP, the largest of the mid-size accounting firms in the country. Arthur graduated at the top of his class with a bachelor's degree in accounting. He had been recruited by all the major accounting firms, but he chose CG, as it was called, because he liked the "vibe." During the interview, Arthur and the recruiter had talked at length about honesty and personal integrity. These were the values that Arthur prized the most, and he was assured that honesty and integrity were consistent with the values and mission statement of CG.

At the first client that Arthur was sent to, he conducted the basic aspects of the audit. But he showed competence and an insight into potential audit problems, so on the next job he was given more complex aspects of the audit. He accomplished those on time and was given a very positive evaluation by his audit senior, Jonathan Lee.

Arthur enjoyed the work but not necessarily the long hours, especially during tax season. It was difficult to work from nine until five at the client's office and then return to CG's office, where he completed tax returns until eleven at night, only to repeat the entire routine the next day and each day after that. He only had one day off each week.

"Don't worry," he was advised by his manager, Stella Reese. "We book this time and then take time off during the summer, when there's less work to be done."

In the second week of March, Arthur was sent work on the audit of the Pine Crest Furniture Company. Pine Crest manufactured and sold contemporary living room and dining room furniture through two stores that were located at either end of town. Arthur was responsible for the inventory section of the file. He had a budget of forty hours to complete that part of the audit because the junior had spent forty hours on inventory section last year. The audit of the inventory was straightforward, and Arthur was confident that he would be able to complete that section of the file under budget.

On the second evening of the audit, while he was back in the office calculating the taxable capital gain for a wealthy client, Arthur realized that there might be an internal transfer pricing problem at Pine Crest with respect to one model of dining room furniture that had been moved from one store to the other store. For the next two days, Arthur spent an extra amount of time examining the internal transferring price scheme of the company. He carefully documented all his findings. After spending nearly fifty hours on the inventory section, Arthur concluded that there was no problem with the inventory. Arthur had been mistaken and was embarrassed that he had spent so much time on the inventory. He felt that if he had just followed standard audit procedures, he could have completed the section within the budget. Consequently, he reported that he had spent only forty hours when he had really spent fifty.

Arthur was reluctant to falsify his time report, but he justified his action on the basis that he was new and inexperienced. He also said that the extra ten hours was a learning experience. Also, no one would know that he had completed the time report incorrectly since Arthur had a reputation for having high integrity.

At the conclusion of the Pine Crest audit, Arthur received a glowing assessment from Jonathan Lee, the audit senior, as well as Stella Reese. Arthur's performance on the next two jobs was also of a high caliber, and he was promoted to intermediate staff accountant at the end of the year. Ms. Johnson, the senior partner at CG, had gone out of her way to congratulate Arthur on his work ethic and say how pleased she was that he was part of the CG family.

The following February, Arthur was called into a meeting to discuss the upcoming Pine Crest Furniture audit to be conducted next month. In the meeting were Jonathan Lee, Stella Reese, and the three other staff accountants who had been on the Pine Crest audit last year.

"As a result of the economic downturn," Stella said, "sales at Pine Crest are off this year. Their controller said they can't afford to pay the same amount this year for the audit. We're under a lot of pressure to keep the fee as low as possible, and so Ms. Johnson has agreed to lower the fee a bit, but she wants us to complete the audit in record time."

"What does that mean?" Jonathan asked.

"It means that the audit time budget has been cut by 10% this year across the board. Whatever the budget for the section was last year, it's 10% less this year."

"That's not fair'" Jonathan protested.

"Yes it is. We've got the same audit team working on the client this year as last year. We all know the client's operations and activities. There's no learning curve here, so it can be done. And I don't want to hear any protests."

No one said anything.

"That's all," Stella said.

As everyone filed out of the manager's office, Stella said, "Arthur, can you stay for another minute, please."

Arthur sat back down.

"I wanted to say that normally I consider the inventory at Pine Crest to be something a junior can do. But I want you to do the inventory section again because you did such a good job last year. I hadn't realized that there could be an inventory transferring pricing issue. Not until I read what you wrote last year. That was very insightful. I admired the way you honestly presented the issue. You did not bias your analysis. That's what we like about you Arthur; you're honest and you have integrity. That was part of the reason why we gave you that promotion last year.

"Last year you managed to complete the inventory section of the audit and do that pricing analysis all within the forty-hour budget. I want you to be just as thorough this year. But because you're aware of the transfer pricing issue, you should be able to breeze through the inventory section." She smiled. "Keep up the good work Arthur."

Arthur went back to the bullpen, where all the audit staff sat.

Oh no, he thought. A 10% reduction. That means that I'll have thirty-six hours to complete the inventory section this year. It took me fifty hours last year! So that means it's a—oh no! That's a 28% reduction. I can't possibly do the entire section in thirty-six hours when I spent fifty hours last year. Not if she wants me to do the same level of analysis as I did last year. What am I going to do?

The other staff accountants were working on their laptops. They didn't seem to care that the audit time budget had been cut by 10%. Perhaps they had not lied on their time reports, and so the time reduction didn't matter to them.

Arthur started to list his options on a piece of paper:

Tell Stella the truth—that he lied on last year's time report. Would he be fired because he had not shown honesty and integrity?

Complete the inventory audit and report thirty-six hours, regardless of how long it takes. Would this mean lying again on his time report? Would this be fair to whoever has to do the inventory section next year?

Complain to Ms. Johnson and say that an arbitrary 10% reduction in audit time is unfair. How would Jonathan and Stella react if he went over their heads to the audit partner?

Look for a job at another accounting firm. Why would he say that he was quitting?

Question

1. What should Arthur do? Why?

ETHICS CASE

Management Choice

Anne Distagne was the CEO of Linkage Construction Inc., which served as the general contractor for the construction of the air ducts for large shopping malls and other buildings. She prided herself on being able to manage her company effectively and in an orderly manner. For years, there had been a steady 22%–25% growth in sales, profits, and earnings per share that she wanted to continue because it facilitated dealing with banks to raise expansion capital. Unfortunately for Sue Fault, the CFO, the situation has changed.

"Sue, we've got a problem. You know my policy of steady growth—well, we've done too well this year. Our profit is too high: it's up to a 35% gain over last year. What we've got to do is bring it down this year and save a little for next year. Otherwise, it will look like we're off our well-managed path. I will look like I didn't have a handle on our activity. Who knows, we may attract a takeover artist. Or we may come up short on profit next year."

"What can we do to get back on track? I've heard we could declare that some of our construction jobs are not as far along as we originally thought, so we would only have to include a lower percentage of expected profits on each job in our profit this year. Also, let's take the $124,000 in R&D costs we incurred to fabricate a more flexible ducting system for jobs A305 and B244 out of the job costs in inventory and expense them right away."

"Now listen, Sue, don't give me any static about being a qualified accountant and subject to the rules of your profession. You are employed by Linkage Construction, and I am your boss, so get on with it. Let me know what the revised figures are as soon as possible."

Questions

1. Who are the stakeholders involved in this decision?
2. What are the ethical issues involved?
3. What should Sue do?

ETHICS CASE

To Qualify or Not?

Jane[1] Ashley was a staff accountant at Viccio & Martin, an accounting firm located in Windsor, Ontario. Jane had been a co-op student while in college, and during her first work term with the firm, she had the privilege of being on several audits of various medium-sized companies in the Windsor area, where she picked up some valuable audit experience. Fresh out of her final academic term, she felt ready to put her scholastic knowledge to work and show the seniors and partners of Viccio & Martin her stuff.

In her first assignment, Jane was placed on an audit team consisting of herself and a senior. This senior, Frankie Small, had been a qualified accountant for five years and had been on staff for over ten. He was well respected within the company and was known for his ability to continually bring engagements in under budget.

The client, Models Inc., which was Viccio & Martin's largest, was a private corporation which made its business in the distribution of self-assembly, replica models, toys, and other gaming products. It operated from a central warehouse in Windsor but also distributed from a small warehouse in Toronto and had a drop-off point in Michigan as it purchased merchandise from companies in the United States. Its year end was April 30. Since Jane had joined the firm on May 15, she had not been present for the year-end

[1]This case was adapted from an assignment submitted by Phil Reynolds, an MBA (accounting) student at the University of Toronto, in the summer of 1994.

inventory count, which was taken on the year-end date. Frankie S. was present, along with another co-op student, who, incidentally, had returned for her final academic term on May 11. Jane asked Frankie how just two people could simultaneously be present for an inventory count at three locations. Frankie responded by telling her that since the inventory balances at the Toronto warehouse and Michigan drop-off sites were of immaterial amounts (based on representations by management, company records, and audits in prior years), audit staff had only been present at the Windsor warehouse count. Models Inc. was on a periodic inventory system.

Since she had not been on this engagement before, the evening before her first day of fieldwork, Jane stayed at work late to review the previous year's audit files, this year's audit programs, and the notes on this year's inventory count so she could gain a knowledge of the client's business. After an hour or so of reviewing the information, Jane gained a knowledge of the client, but she could not quite understand what was happening with the inventory section because the working papers were messy and disorganized. On reviewing the inventory sheets from this year's count, she found that many of the items were unfamiliar and were referenced only by general product names; there were no serial numbers, no order numbers.

The first day of fieldwork arrived, and Jane was given the responsibility of accounts-payable cutoff. On tracing invoices to the master accounts-payable ledger, Jane found that she was having a hard time locating many of them. She brought this matter to the attention of the accounts-payable clerk, who provided the explanation that invoices received after the year-end date were not yet entered in the current year but should have been. Jane was provided with this list and traced it to the journal entry made to pick up the extra payables. Jane then performed audit procedures on this extra list. She again found that it was incomplete. The total cutoff problem was, in her estimation (of sample to population figures), in excess of $400,000. She also noted that many of the invoices received had invoice dates after April 30, but title to these goods had changed hands (F.O.B. shipping point) prior to April 30.

The financial statements originally provided by management showed healthy profits of $150,000. The current accounts-payable (trade) balance was $1.4 million, which was up over a half a million from last year. The current receivables balance was $800,000, which was up about $100,000 from the previous year. Sales had jumped from $8 million in 1988 to $10 million this year. The company had an operating (demand) line of credit with a lending institution of $1 million. The company owned its two warehouses, which had a net equity of approximately $1,600,000 at fair market.

Jane brought the cutoff problem to the attention of Frankie, who was perplexed and surprised by the whole issue. The two returned to the office that evening, and Jane was asked to prepare a memorandum explaining her findings. It was reviewed by the partner in charge, Mr. Viccio, who contacted the appropriate level of management of Models Inc. to explain the discrepancy.

The accounts-payable clerk recorded the transactions Jane had found left out, and the audit testing was again performed on the accounts-payable cutoff and the rest of the accounts-payable section to the satisfaction of the auditors with respect to all financial statement assertions. The total corrections made to accounts payable were in the order of $350,000. The impact of the adjustments was partially to inventory, where traceable, and partly to cost of goods sold. The total effect on the profit figure was $300,000. The financial statements showed a loss of $150,000.

The head manager and 50% shareholder of the corporation, Mrs. Hyst, was astonished and panic stricken by the entire situation. She was sure something was wrong and that this problem would be rectified at some point throughout the remainder of the audit.

No problems were encountered throughout the remainder of the audit fieldwork; however, Jane did notice, when she was in the accounts-payable clerk's office, that the clerk spent a great deal of time on the phone with suppliers, discussing how Models Inc. could pay down its over-ninety-day payables such that the company would not be cut off from purchasing further goods.

Toward the finalization of the audit, Mrs. Hyst came to the auditors and told them that there was most likely inventory that had been left out of the count. She provided a listing that amounted to approximately $200,000. In this listing were material amounts of inventory in the Toronto warehouse, the Michigan drop-off point, goods in transit, and goods stored at other locations.

The auditors, who were surprised by the list, decided to perform tests on it and found that it was very difficult and often impossible to track the inventory, given the poor system used by the company. Jane telephoned all of the companies that appeared on the list under "goods stored at other locations" and, in all cases, found that no inventory was being kept on behalf of Models Inc. Suppliers in the United States were telephoned for exact shipment dates, and based on the evidence of how long it usually takes to bring goods across the border, it was determined that those goods were included in the year-end inventory count. As for the "extra" inventory stored in the Toronto and Michigan sites, there was no reliable evidence that anything not already accounted for was there. However, there was no way to tell for sure. From the items on this extra list, $50,000 was accounted for as either already counted in inventory as of the year-end date or included in cost of goods sold. The whereabouts of the other $150,000 was not determinable.

Mrs. Hyst was asked to discuss this listing. At the meeting, Mr. Viccio, Frankie, and Jane were all present. Mrs. Hyst stated that if she showed these sorts of losses, the bank would surely call the company's operating loan of $1 million, and it would "go under." Mr. Viccio asked the client whether there was any way of determining where the other $150,000 was. She explained that it was hard, given their inadequate inventory system, but she was pretty sure that it was not counted in the year-end inventory count.

After the meeting, Mr. Viccio explained that there was no reason to doubt management's good faith and that the $150,000 most likely should be added to inventory and taken out of cost of goods sold. Frankie went along with this. Jane, however, was astonished. She felt that since there was no evidence backing up the claims made by the client, the firm should be conservative. She also related her experience to the other two concerning the problems the company was having with keeping up with its trade payables.

Mr. Viccio explained to her that the $150,000 should be added back to inventory and that, even if it was the cost of goods sold, the client will most likely recover in the near future anyway. "In these situations, we must help the client; we cannot be responsible for its downfall. Who are we to say that there isn't an extra $150,000 in inventory—we're just guessing." Frankie added to this by saying that if the loan were called, there would be plenty of equity in the buildings of the company to pay it off.

Jane went home that day very distraught. She felt that Mr. Viccio's decision was based on audit fees and that a poor picture on the financial statements would result in the loan being called and Mr. Viccio would not get his fees. Jane was also disappointed with the level of responsibility shown by Frankie, the senior. Jane could not believe what was happening given the fact that the original reason for the audit was because the bank had requested it several years ago as the operating loan was increasing. Jane was also aware that

Model Inc.'s major suppliers were requesting the year-end statements as well and, based on them, would make a decision whether to extend the company any more credit.

The next day, Jane expressed her opinion in a morning meeting held in Mr. Viccio's office. Frankie was also present. She was told that the $150,000 would be added back to inventory.

Question

1. What should Jane do? Why?

Team Player Problems

ETHICS CASE

"John, I have questions about that job you want me to do next week—the one where I am supposed to go and be part of that multidisciplinary team to study how the hospitals in Denver ought to be restructured for maximum efficiency and how they should be reporting that efficiency in the future. As you know, I am a professional accountant, but I'm not going to be the study leader. What happens if I disagree with the study's findings or recommendations? What do I do if I think they haven't used accounting data correctly and have recommended that a hospital be shut down when I don't think it should be? Do I go along? Do I blow the whistle?"

Question

1. Answer the questions put to John.

Minimal Disclosure

ETHICS CASE

Ted was the manager and Carl the partner on the audit of Smart Investments Limited, an investment company whose shares were traded on the NASDAQ exchange. They were discussing the issues to be debated at the upcoming Audit Committee meeting to finalize the financial statements and audit for the current year.

"As I see it, Carl, we have three problems that are going to be difficult because it's not in the interests of the CEO, CFO, and some directors to go along with us. Remember that all those stock options that may be exercised next month at $7.50 per share and with the stock trading at $9.50 now—well, they aren't about to upset the price with negative news.

"Anyway, the rules call for segmented disclosure of significant lines of business, and this year the company has made 55% of its profit through the trading of derivative securities. It's awfully high risk, and I'm not sure they can keep it up, so I think they ought to add a derivative securities disclosure column to their segmented disclosure information. They are going to argue that they are uncertain how much profit relates to derivative securities trading by itself and how much was realized because the derivative securities were part of hedging transactions to protect foreign currency positions.

"The second issue concerns their reluctance to reveal the potential lawsuit by their client, Bonvest Mutual Funds, for messing up the timing and placement of orders for several mining securities. I believe it should be mentioned in the Contingent Liabilities note, but they may be dragging their feet on calculating the size of the problem. They don't want to disclose an amount, anyway, because they argue that Bonvest will set that figure as the lower bound for its claim.

"Finally, as you know, the statements we are auditing are consolidated and include the accounts of the parent and four subsidiaries. One of these subs, Caribbean Securities Limited, is in tough shape, and I think they may let it go broke. That's the sub which is audited by the Bahamian firm of Dodds & Co., not our own affiliate there. There is no qualification on the

Dodds & Co. audit opinion, though, but I know how these guys at Smart think.

"I realize that a lot of this is speculative, but each of these issues is potentially material. How do you want to play each of them?"

Question

1. What should Carl, the partner, plan to do?

ETHICS CASE

Opinion Shopping

"We have had Paige & Gentry as our auditors for many years, haven't we, Jane? They have been here since I became president two years ago."

"Yes, Bob, I have been the CFO for seven years, and they were here before I came. Why do you ask?"

"Well, they were really tough on us during the recent discussions when we were finalizing our year-end audited statements—not at all like I was used to at my last company. When we asked for a little latitude, our auditors were usually pretty obliging. Frankly, I'm a little worried."

"Why, Bob, we had nothing to hide?"

"That's true, Jane, but let's look ahead. We're going to have difficulty making our forecast this year, and our bonuses are on the line. Remember, we renegotiated our salary/bonus package to give us a chance at higher incentives, and we have to be careful."

"Looking ahead, we've got a problem with obsolete inventory that's sure to come to require discussion for a second year in a row. We've got the warranty problem with the electrical harness on the mid-range machine, which is going to cost us a bundle, but we want to spread the impact over the next three years when the customers discover the problem and we have to fix it up. And don't forget the contaminated waste spill we just had—how much is that going to cost to clean up, if we ever get caught?"

"These are potentially big ticket items. Bill Paige, the guy who is in charge of our audit, is not going to let these go by. He said the inventory problem was almost material this year, and we had to argue really hard. You are a qualified accountant; how can we handle this?"

"Well, Bob, we could have some informal discussions with other auditors—maybe even the ones at your old company—to see how they would handle issues like these. The word will get around to Bill, and he may be more accommodating in the future and will probably shave his proposed audit fee for next year when he meets with our Audit Committee next month. If you really wanted to play hardball, we could talk the Audit Committee into calling for tenders from new auditors. After all this time, it's logical to check out the market anyway. We would have advance discussions during which we would sound them out on how they would assess materiality in our company's case. Our audit fee in getting pretty large—almost $50,000 this year—so some big firms will be really interested."

"Jane, let's play hardball. Get a list of audit firms together for the tender process, and I will approach the Audit Committee. Be sure to list some small firms, including Webster & Co., the firm auditing my old company."

Questions

1. Who are the major stakeholders involved in this situation?
2. What are the ethical issues involved?
3. Is this situation unethical? Why and why not?
4. What should Jane do if Webster & Co. looks like the choice the Audit Committee will make and recommend to the board of directors?

ETHICS CASE

Lowballing a Fee Quotation

"Look, Tim, I've been told that the competition for the audit of Diamond Health Services is really competitive, and you know what it would mean to the both of us to bring this one in. You would be a sure bet for the Executive Committee, and I would take over some new audit responsibility as your backup partner. Let's quote the job really competitively and get it."

"I'm not sure, Anne. After all, we have to make a reasonable profit or we're not pulling our weight. Anyway, you don't know what problems we may meet, so you should build in a cushion on the front end of the job."

"But, Tim, if we quote this job the usual way—on an hourly rate and estimated total time basis—we are going to miss it! The CFO as much as told me we would have to be lower than the current auditor, and we would have to guaranty the fee for two years. Now, are we in or not? I plan to put our best staff on the job. Don't worry; they won't blow it. What's the matter? Don't you think I can get the job done?"

"Well, Anne, I suppose there would be some overall saving to our firm because this audit is the only one of six companies in the Diamond Group that we don't audit. We certainly don't want any other auditors getting a foothold in the Diamond Group, do we? What are you proposing, anyway: a fee that's at a lower margin than normal or one that's below the projected cost for this job? Either way, it's unethical, isn't it?"

Question

1. Answer the question posed to Tim.

Fundamental Accounting and Auditing Issues Cases

ETHICS CASE

Societal Concerns

Two accounting students, Joan and Miguel, were studying for their final university accounting exam.

"Miguel, what if they ask us whether the accounting profession should speak out about the shortcomings in financial statements?"

"Like what, Joan? We know they don't show the value of employees or the impact of inflation, or the economic reality or market value of many transactions—is that what you mean?"

"No, I mean the advocacy of disclosures which will lead to a better world for all of us. For example, if we could only get companies to start disclosing their impacts on society, and particularly our environment, they would be induced to set targets and perform better the next year. We know that lots of externalities, like pollution costs, are not included in the financial statements, but we could speak out for supplementary disclosures."

"Joan, you go right ahead if you like. But I'm going to stick to the traditional role of accountants—to the preparation and audit of financial statements. It got us this far, didn't it?"

"Yes, but do medical doctors refrain from commenting on health concerns, or do lawyers refrain from creating laws that govern our future? Why should we shy away from speaking out on issues that we know something about that mean a lot to our future?"

Question

1. Is Joan or Miguel right? Why?

ETHICS CASE

Economic Realities or GAAP

Stan Jones was an investor who had recently lost money on his investment in Fine Line Hotels, Inc., and he was anxious to discuss the problem with Janet Todd, a qualified accountant who was his friend and occasional advisor.

"How can they justify this, Janet? This company owns 19.9% of a subsidiary, Far East Hotels, which has apparently sustained some large losses. But these consolidated statements don't show any of these losses, and the investment in Far East hasn't been written down to reflect the loss either. I bought my shares in Fine Line just after its last audited statements were made available but just before the papers reported that the statements didn't reflect any of the losses. What should I do in the future—wait until the papers report the true economic picture? If I can't rely on audited figures, what's the sense of having an audit? And don't tell me that, if the ownership percentage had been 20%, the consolidated statements would have reported the loss. That's just outrageous."

Question

1. How should Janet Todd respond?

ETHICS CASE

Multidisciplinary Practices—Ethical Challenges

Multidisciplinary practices are probably an inevitable development. Clients want "one-stop shopping," at a professional firm where they can go for all their needs, and where the partner responsible for their work can keep them briefed on new services that might be worth using. New services offered currently include the following:

- Legal services
- Actuarial services
- Engineering services
- Investment services
- Risk assessment services
- Ethics and integrity services

These new services, particularly in the area of legal services, have raised a high degree of controversy among existing accounting partners. Trevor, an older partner, and Dhana, a new and younger partner, were deep in discussion about the problems and benefits the new organization would bring.

"Trev, I don't really see what your problem is. We're going to be more helpful to our clients—that's the bottom line, isn't it?"

"I suppose so, D, but all these new services bring their own professionals. Are lawyers or engineers going to set aside their codes of conduct to live by ours? Whom do they report to—I don't have enough legal expertise or engineering expertise to supervise them, so how can I ensure they live up to our accounting standards of service and quality? Aren't I going to be holding myself out as their supervisor on false pretenses? If anything goes wrong, won't we be sued?

"Another thing, D, as the proportion of our operations from these new services grows, won't the entire firm take on a client focus just like any other business? As professional accountants, we are supposed to be serving the public—that's what keeps us from fudging the figures and our audit reports to benefit current management and current shareholders. Do you think that all these new professionals will buy into a 'public' focus rather than a 'client' focus where the bottom line drives decisions? How would we go about keeping them on the straight and narrow, even if we got them on it in the first place?"

"Trev, you sure do have a lot of worries. How close are you to retirement? Well, I just had a call from our CEO, Hajjad. He wants me to think about taking over our Ethics and Integrity practice. Say—you don't have anything I could read up on in that area, do you?"

Question

1. What are your answers to the questions raised in the case?

Tax and Regulatory Cases

Multinationals and Tax Planning

ETHICS CASE

Multinationals are headquartered in one country but have operations worldwide. Generally, each multinational pays income taxes in the jurisdiction in which it generates its profits. For example, a German company with operations in the United States and Switzerland would pay income taxes to the U.S. government on the profits that its American subsidiary earned in the United States, and its Swiss subsidiary would pay taxes to the Swiss government for the profits it earned in Switzerland.

However, tax rates are not uniform throughout the world, and some jurisdictions lower their taxes rates to encourage businesses to operate or invest in that jurisdiction. For example, in the United States, Nevada and Wyoming charge no corporate income taxes. Similarly, the Cayman Islands does not impose corporate income taxes on any business that is incorporated in the Cayman Islands. Both the Isle of Man, located in the Irish Sea, and the Bailiwicks of Jersey and Guernsey, located in the English Channel, use zero-10 corporate tax rate systems, whereby financial institutions pay 10% tax on their profits while all other businesses pay no corporate taxes.

Many of the world's largest economies (e.g., Australia, Canada, and Germany) have a corporate tax rate of approximately 30%, while the rate in the United Kingdom is less, at approximately 25%, and the rate in the United States is more, at approximately 39%. (All of these are general tax rates because there are countless exemptions and incentives in each of these countries that affect the actual rate that any one business would pay.)

Because multinationals operate in countries with high and low tax rates, they can strategically arrange their business affairs so as to shift profits from a high-tax regime to a low-tax jurisdiction. They can accomplish this through transfer pricing, whereby one subsidiary of a multinational sells items to another subsidiary of the same multinational. The sale or transfer price is set so as to shift or move the profits on the sale to the low-tax jurisdiction, thereby reducing the company's overall tax burden. In an attempt to close this tax loophole, many countries, as well as the Organisation for Economic Cooperation and Development, established transfer pricing guidelines that require that sales between controlled or related companies be at arm's-length prices. An arm's-length price is the price that would be charged in the marketplace between a willing seller and a willing buyer that are dealing without coercion.

However, transfer pricing is subject to an enormous amount of professional judgment, especially if the item being transferred does not sell in a competitive market. Also, not all countries use the arm's-length principle. This means that multinationals can strategically move their profits around the world so as to minimize the taxes that they pay. Consider the following examples:

- The British unit of Amazon.com Inc. had sales of $6.5 billion but paid only $ 3.7 million in taxes because it was transferring a substantial portion of its profits through a related company in Luxembourg, where the corporate tax rate is quite low.

- Apple Inc. has been accused of setting up two Irish subsidiaries in order to minimize its taxes; one subsidiary generated $30 billion in profits but paid no taxes, while the other had profits of $22 billion and paid only $10 million in taxes.
- GlaxoSmithKline PLC was assessed $51 million in back taxes as a result of transferring revenue from its Canadian subsidiary to a Swiss subsidiary.
- Google. Inc. shifted $9.8 billion to a subsidiary in Bermuda, thereby managing to avoid paying $2 billion in taxes.
- By moving $21 billion of revenue to subsidiaries in Ireland, Puerto Rico, and Singapore, Microsoft Corp. reduced its taxes by approximately $4.5 billion.
- Starbucks Corp. voluntarily paid $15 million in extra taxes to the British government after the company was accused of abusive transfer pricing policies.

Nonuniform worldwide tax rates encourage multinationals to strategically move their profits to minimize their taxes. Aggressive transfer pricing is illegal, and companies have been penalized for engaging in such practices. However, many tax practitioners argue that as long as the price falls within the general guidelines of the arm's-length principle, then transfer pricing makes good business sense. It reduces tax expense and therefore means that there is more money available for distribution to the shareholders in the form of dividends. Others argue that transfer price manipulation is available only to multinationals. Nonmultinationals cannot shift profit overseas. They pay their fair share of taxes based on the profits that they earn within that jurisdiction, while the multinationals, operating in the same tax jurisdiction, avoid paying taxes on the profits that they earned because of an artificial transfer pricing system.

Questions

1. Do you consider transfer pricing to be an ethical means of reducing a business's tax liability? Why, and why not?
2. At what level would a transfer price cease to become reasonable and become unethical and probably illegal?
3. Does transfer pricing impose an ethically unfair tax burden on nonmultinationals that cannot engage in such a scheme because they do not have international operations?
4. Do governments have an ethical responsibility to harmonize tax rates around the world?

Sources: J. Slater and B. Curry, "U.S. Grills Apple on Offshore Tax Practices," *The Globe and Mail*, May 22, 2013, B1, B8.

PricewaterhouseCoopers CI LLP, *Update on* the *0/10 Corporate Tax Regimes*, 2012–2013.

ETHICS CASE

KPMG's Questionable Tax Shelters

The leak of the Panama Papers in 2016 revealed the existence of hundreds of thousands of offshore shell companies used by the world's wealthy to avoid paying taxes, raised the public's awareness of advantaged treatment of the wealthy, and led to renewed concerns about unfair tax practices. But the Panama Papers revelations were not the start of such concerns.

Earlier, KPMG admitted that for an average fee of $10,000. it put twenty-seven wealthy Canadians into tax avoidance shelters on the Isle of Man that cost the Canadian government millions of dollars. Moreover, KPMG fought a court order requesting the names of these investors. As a result, on May 1, 2015, the Canada Revenue Agency (CRA) offered a tax amnesty to those tax dodgers if they paid the taxes that they avoided by investing in the Isle of Man tax shelters. There would be no fines or penalties imposed on those who used this amnesty program.

It was later revealed that, since 2010, CRA executives and officials had been wined and dined at various events sponsored by the tax policy committees of the Canadian accounting profession. In 2014 and 2015, the CRA officials who were offering the tax amnesty packages to the KPMG clients were entertained at the prestigious Rideau Club in Ottawa, along with personnel from KPMG.

KPMG was criticized on two different levels. Some were outraged at the optics of having KPMG entertain the government officials who are responsible for tax collection. Duff Conacher of Democracy Watch suggested that there was a conflict of interest having CRA enforcement personnel attend a private reception sponsored and paid for by the accountants who CRA are responsible for regulating, auditing, and, if need be, penalizing. CRA assistant commissioner Ted Gallivan defended having his staff attend these functions on the basis that "We... are trying to be responsive to the citizens that we serve, which includes large accounting firms. I don't think it's a problem." KPMG partner Gregory Wiebe doubted that CRA officials could be influenced so easily. "I've been in this business for over thirty years and I've met a lot of people from CRA, and I can't imagine that a beer and a piece of cheese would impact their integrity in one way whatsoever."

Others argue that having tax accountants intentionally look for inadvertent gaps and ambiguities in the *Income Tax Act* is inconsistent with the objective of the profession to promote the public interest, especially when tax accountants, better than most people, understand why the government writes laws to prohibit tax havens. The argument is that tax accountants are violating the spirit of the law when they purposefully look for loopholes in the laws prohibiting tax havens in order to have their wealthy clients invest in those tax havens, and that this does not promote the public interest. In response to this line of criticism, KPMG partner Wiebe's defense, before a Canadian parliamentary hearing on tax evasion and avoidance, was that the accounting firm did nothing wrong because these tax shelters, although socially unacceptable like smoking in restaurants, were not technically illegal.

Questions

1. Are offshore tax havens that are technically legal but socially unacceptable in the public interest?
2. Are tax accountants promoting the public interest when they design, promote, and sell tax shelters that reduce or eliminate paying taxes by the wealthiest members of society?
3. Is there a difference between tax planning strategies that use legally sanctioned shelters, such as retirement savings accounts, different from tax planning strategies that use questionable offshore tax havens?
4. Do you think that government tax enforcement officers should or should not socialize with tax policy committees of the accounting profession and/or directly with practitioners?

Sources: H. Cashore, K. Ivany, K. Pedersen, and F. Zalac, "CRA Exec Treated to Soirees at Private Club amid KPMG Probe," *CBC News*, April 18, 2016, http://www.cbc.ca/news/canada/kpmg-canada-revenue-agency-receptions-conferences-1.3540285.

B. Curry, "Tax-Avoidance Schemes Becoming Taboo, Finance Committee Hears," *The Globe and Mail*, May 3, 2016, B.

P. Dunn, "Accounting Profession: Heal Thy Self," *Globe and Mail*, May 16, 2016, B4, http://www.theglobeandmail.com/report-on-business/rob-commentary/panama-papers-leak-reveals-the-dark-side-of-the-accounting-profession/article30027339.

International Consortium of Investigative Journalists, *Giant Leak of Offshore Financial Records Exposes Global Array of Crime and Corruption, Overview of the Panama Papers*, April 3, 2016, accessed May 29, 2016, at http://www.webcitation.org/6gVXG3LvI.

ETHICS CASE

Italian Tax Mores

The Italian federal corporate tax system has an official, legal tax structure and tax rates just as the U.S. system does. However, all similarity between the two systems ends there.

The Italian tax authorities assume that no Italian corporation would ever submit a tax return that shows its true profits but rather would submit a return that understates actual profits by anywhere between 30% and 70%; their assumption is essentially correct. Therefore, about six months after the annual deadline for filing corporate tax returns, the tax authorities issue to each corporation an "invitation to discuss" its tax return. The purpose of this notice is to arrange a personal meeting between them and representatives of the corporation. At this meeting, the Italian revenue service states the amount of corporate income tax that it believes is due. Its position is developed from both prior years' taxes actually paid and the current year's return; the amount that the tax authorities claim is due is generally several times that shown on the corporation's return for the current year. In short, the corporation's tax return and the revenue service's stated position are the operating offers for the several rounds of bargaining that will follow.

The Italian corporation is typically represented in such negotiations by its *commercialista*, a function that exists in Italian society for the primary purpose of negotiating corporate (and individual) tax payments with the Italian tax authorities; thus, the management of an Italian corporation seldom, if ever, has to meet directly with the Italian revenue service and probably has a minimum awareness of the details of the negotiation other than the final settlement.

Both the final settlement and the negotiation are extremely important to the corporation, the tax authorities, and the *commercialista*. Since the tax authorities assume that a corporation *always* earned more money this year than last year and *never* has a loss, the amount of the final settlement, that is, corporate taxes that will actually be paid, becomes, for all practical purposes, the floor for the start of next year's negotiations. The final settlement also represents the amount of revenue the Italian government will collect in taxes to help finance the cost of running the country. However, since large amounts of money are involved and two individuals having vested personal interests are conducting the negotiations, the amount of *bustarella*—typically a substantial cash payment "requested" by the Italian revenue agent from the *commercialista*—usually determines whether the final settlement is closer to the corporation's original tax return or to the fiscal authority's original negotiating position.

Whatever *bustarella* is a paid during the negotiation is usually included by the *commercialista* in his lump-sum fee "for services rendered" to his corporate client. If the final settlement is favorable to the corporation, and it is the *commercialista*'s job to see that it is, then the corporation is not likely to complain about the amount of its *commercialist*'s fee, nor will it ever know how much of that fee was represented by *bustarella* and how much remained for the *commercialista* as payment for his negotiating services. In any case, the tax authorities will recognize the full amount of the fee as a tax-deductible expense on the corporation's tax return for the following year.

About ten years ago, a leading American bank opened a banking subsidiary in a major Italian city. At the end of its first year of operation, the bank was advised by its local lawyers and tax accountants, both from branches of U.S. companies, to file its tax return "Italian style," that is, to understate its actual profits by a significant amount. The American general manager of the bank, who was on his first overseas assignment, refused to do so both because he considered it dishonest and because it was inconsistent with the practices of his parent company in the United States.

About six months after filing its "American-style" tax return, the bank received an "invitation to discuss" notice from the Italian tax authorities. The bank's general manager consulted with his lawyers and tax accountants who suggested they hire a *commercialista*. He rejected this advice and instead wrote a letter to the Italian revenue service not only stating that his firm's corporate return was correct as filed but also requesting that they inform him of any specific items about which they had questions. His letter was never answered.

About sixty days after receiving the initial "invitation to discuss" notice, the bank received a formal tax assessment notice calling for a tax of approximately three times that shown on the bank's corporate tax return; the tax authorities simply assumed that the bank's original return had been based on generally accepted Italian practices, and they reacted accordingly. The bank's general manager again consulted with his lawyers and tax accountants who again suggested he hire a *commercialista* who knew how to handle these matters. On learning that the *commercialista* would probably have to pay *bustarella* to his revenue service counterpart in order to reach a settlement, the general manager again chose to ignore his advisors. Instead, he responded by sending the Italian revenue service a check for the full amount of taxes due according to the bank's American-style tax return even though the due date for the payment was almost six months hence; he made no reference to the amount of corporate taxes shown on the formal tax assessment notice.

Ninety days after paying its taxes, the bank received a third notice from the fiscal authorities. This one contained the statement: "We have reviewed your corporate tax return for 19____ and have determined the [the lira equivalent of] $6,000,000 of interest paid on deposits is not an allowable expense for federal purposes. Accordingly, the total tax due for 19____ is lira ____." Since interest paid on deposits is any bank's largest single expense item, the new tax assessment was for an amount many times larger than that shown in the initial tax assessment notice and almost fifteen times larger than the taxes that the bank had actually paid.

The bank's general manager was understandably very upset. He immediately arranged an appointment to meet personally with the manager of the Italian revenue service's local office. Shortly after the start of their meeting, the conversation went something like this:

> General Manager: "You can't really be serious about disallowing interest paid on deposits as a tax deductible expense."
>
> Italian Revenue Service: "Perhaps. However, we thought it would get your attention. Now that you're here, shall we begin our negotiations?"

Questions

1. Should the Italian bank's general manager hire a *commercialista* and pay *bustarella*?
2. Should the general manager phone the bank's American CEO in New York and ask for advice?
3. If you were the bank's American CEO, would you want to receive the phone call for advice?

This case, which is based on an actual occurrence, was prepared by Arthur L. Kelly. The author is the Managing Partner of KEL Enterprises L.P., a private investment partnership. He has been actively involved in international business for more than forty years and has served as a member of the Boards of Directors of corporations in the United States and Europe. These currently include BASF Aktiengesellshaft and Bayerische Motoren Werke (BMW) A.G. in Germany as well as Deere & Company, Northern Trust Corporation, and Snap-on Incorporated in the United States.

ETHICS CASE

Tax Return Complications

As Bill Adams packed his briefcase on Friday, March 15, he could never remember being so glad to see a weekend. As a senior tax manager with a major accounting firm, Hay & Hay, on the fast track for partnership, he was worried that the events of the week could prove to be detrimental to his career.

Six months ago, the senior partners had rewarded Bill by asking him to be the tax manager on Zentor Inc., a very important client of the firm in terms of both prestige and fees. Bill had worked hard since then ensuring that his client received impeccable service, and he had managed to build a good working relationship with Dan, the CEO of Zentor Inc. In fact, Dan was so impressed with Bill that he recommended him to his brother, Dr. Rim, a general medical practitioner. As a favor to Dan, Bill agreed that Hay & Hay would prepare Dr. Rim's tax return.

This week a junior tax person had prepared Dr. Rim's tax return. When it came across Bill's desk for review today, he was surprised to find that, although Dr. Rim's gross billings were $480,000, his net income for tax purposes from his medical practice was only $27,000. He discussed this with the tax junior, who said he had noted this also but was not concerned, as every tax return prepared by the firm is stamped with the disclaimer "We have prepared the return from information provided to us by the client. We have not audited or otherwise attempted to verify its accuracy."

On closer review, Bill discovered that the following items, among others, had been deducted by Dr. Rim in arriving at net income:

- $15,000 for meals and entertainment. Bill felt that this was excessive and probably had not been incurred to earn income, given the nature of Dr. Rim's practice.
- Dry-cleaning bills for shirts, suits, dresses, sweaters, and so on. Bill believed these to be family dry-cleaning bills that were being paid by the practice.
- Wages of $100 per week paid to Dr. Rim's twelve-year-old son.

Bill telephoned Dr. Rim and had his suspicions confirmed. When Bill asked Dr. Rim to review the expenses and remove all that were personal, Dr. Rim became very defensive. He told Bill that he had been deducting these items for years and his previous accountant had not objected. In fact, it was his previous accountant who had suggested he pay his son a salary as an income-splitting measure. The telephone conversation ended abruptly when Dr. Rim was paged for an emergency but not before he threatened to inform his brother that the accounting firm he thought so highly of was behind the times on the latest tax planning techniques.

Bill was annoyed with himself for having agreed to prepare Dr. Rim's tax return in the first place. He was afraid of pushing Dr. Rim too far and losing Zentor Inc. as a client as a result. He could not anticipate what Dan's reaction to the situation would be. Bill was glad to have the weekend to think this over.

Just as Bill was leaving the office, the tax senior on the Zentor Inc. account informed him that the deadline had been missed for objecting to a reassessment, requiring Zentor Inc. to pay an additional $1,200,000 in taxes. The deadline was Wednesday, March 13. The senior said he was able to contact a friend of his at the Tax Department, and the friend had agreed that if the Notice of Objection was dated March 13, properly signed, and appeared on his desk Monday, March 18, he would process it. Bill left his office with some major decisions to make over the weekend.

Questions

1. Identify the ethical issues Bill Adams should address.
2. What would you do about these issues if you were Bill?

Source: Prepared by Joan Kitunen, University of Toronto, 1994.

ETHICS CASE

Marketing Aggressive Tax Shelters

Before 2002, accounting firms would provide multiple services to the same firm. Hired by the shareholders, they would audit the financial statements that were prepared by management while also providing consulting services to those same managers. Some would provide tax advice to the managers of audit clients. However, the *Sarbanes-Oxley Act* (SOX) of 2002 restricted the type and the intensity of consulting services that could be provided to the management of audit clients because it might compromise the objectivity of the auditor when auditing the financial statements prepared by management on behalf of the shareholders. Nevertheless, both before and after the passage of SOX, Ernst & Young (E&Y) and KPMG were offering very aggressive tax shelters to wealthy taxpayers as well as to the senior managers of audit clients.

E&Y

In the 1990s, E&Y had created four tax shelters that they were selling to wealthy individuals. One of them, called E.C.S., for Equity Compensation Strategy, resulted in little or no tax liability for the taxpayer. The complicated tax plan was a means of delaying, for up to thirty years, paying taxes on the profits from exercising employee stock options that would otherwise be payable in the year in which the stock options were exercised. E&Y charged a fee of 3% of the amount that the taxpayer invested in the tax shelter, plus $50,000 to a law firm for a legal opinion that said that it was "more likely than not" that the shelter would survive a tax audit.

E&Y had long been the auditor for Sprint Corporation. They also took on as clients William Esrey and Ronald LeMay, the top executives at Sprint. In 2000, E&Y received the following:

- $2.5 million for the audit of Sprint
- $2.6 million for other services related to the audit
- $63.8 million for information technology and other consulting services
- $5.8 million from Esrey and LeMay for tax advice

In 1999, Esrey announced a planned merger of Sprint with WorldCom that potentially would have made the combined organization the largest telecommunications company in the world. The deal was not consummated because it failed to obtain regulatory approval. Nevertheless, Esrey and LeMay were awarded stock options worth about $311 million.

E&Y sold an E.C.S. to each of Esrey and LeMay. In the three years from 1998 to 2000, the options profits for Esrey were $159 million and the tax that would have been payable had he not bought the tax shelter amounted to about $63 million. The options profits for LeMay were $152.2 million and the tax thereon about $60.3 million.

Subsequently, the Internal Revenue Service (IRS) rejected the tax shelter of each man. Sprint then asked the two executives to resign, which they did. Sprint also dismissed E&Y as the company's auditor.

On July 2, 2003, E&Y reached a $15 million settlement with the IRS regarding their aggressive marketing of tax shelters. Then, in 2007, four E&Y partners were charged with tax fraud. These four partners worked for an E&Y unit called VIPER, "value ideas produce extraordinary results," later renamed SISG, "strategic individual solutions group." Its purpose was to aggressively market tax shelters, known as Cobra, Pico, CDS, and CDS Add-Ons, to wealthy individuals, many of whom acquired their fortunes in technology-related businesses. These four products were sold to about

400 wealthy taxpayers from 1999 to 2001 and generated fees of approximately $121 million. The government claims that the tax shelters were bogus and taxpayers were reassessed for taxes owing as well as penalties and interest.

KPMG

On August 26, 2005, KPMG agreed to pay a fine of $456 million for selling tax shelters from 1996 through 2003 that fraudulently generated $11 billion in fictitious tax losses that cost the government at least $2.5 billion in lost taxes. The four tax shelters went by the acronyms FLIP, OPIS, BLIPS, and SOS. Under the Bond Linked Premium Issue Structure (BLIPS), for example, the taxpayer would borrow money from an offshore bank and invest in a joint venture that would buy foreign currencies from that same offshore bank. About two months later, the joint venture would then sell the foreign currency back to the bank, creating a tax loss. The taxpayer would then declare a loss for tax purposes on the BLIPS investment. The way that the BLIPS were structured, the taxpayer had to pay only $1.4 million in order to declare a $20 million loss for tax purposes. They were targeted at wealthy executives who would normally pay between $10 million and $20 million in taxes. Buying a BLIPS, however, effectively reduced the investor's taxable income to zero. They were sold to 186 wealthy individuals and generated at least $5 billion in tax losses. The FLIP and OPIS involved investment swaps through the Cayman Islands, and SOS was a currency swap similar to the BLIPS. The government contended that these were sham transactions since the loans and investments were risk free. Their sole purpose was to artificially reduce taxes.

Some argued that the KPMG tax shelters were so egregious that the accounting firm should be put out of business. However, Arthur Andersen had collapsed in 2002, and if KPMG failed, then there would be only three large accounting firms remaining: Deloitte, PricewaterhouseCoopers, and E&Y. KPMG Chairman, Timothy Flynn, said "the firm regretted taking part in the deals and sent a message to employees calling the conduct 'inexcusable.'"[1] KPMG remains in business, but the firm was fined almost a half billion dollars.

Questions

1. What differentiates very aggressive tax shelters from reasonable tax shelters?
2. As a result of the E&Y and KPMG tax fiascos, the large accounting firms have become wary of marketing very aggressive tax shelters. Now, most shelters are being sold by tax "boutiques" that operate on a much smaller scale and so are less likely to be investigated by the IRS. Is it right that accountants market aggressive tax shelter plans? Are tax shelter plans in the public interest?

Sources: L. Browning, "Four Charged in Tax Shelter Case," *New York Times*, May 31, 2007.

H. Gleckman, A. Borus, and M. McNamee, "Inside the KPMG Mess," *BusinessWeek*, September 12, 2005.

Internal Revenue Service, *KPMG to Pay $456 Million for Criminal Violations*, IR-2005-83, August 29, 2005.

D. Johnston and J. Glater, "Tax Shelter Is Worrying Sprint's Chief," *New York Times*, February 6, 2003.

[1] Carrie Johnson, "9 Charged over Tax Shelters In KPMG Case: Accounting Firm Agrees to Pay as More Indictments Expected," *Washington Post*, August 30, 2005, A01.

ETHICS CASE

Providing Tax Advice

Sophia and Maya were having a quiet after-work drink at the Purple Pheasant around the corner from their office. Both are professional accountants in their late twenties and were talking about their futures in public accounting.

"I want to concentrate on the not-for-profit sector," said Sophia putting her glass of Chardonnay down on the table. "I really enjoyed the two months I spent at Save-a-Tree Foundation. And there's a huge demand for providing consulting advice to environmental groups and agencies."

"There's no money in that," said Maya. "They can't afford to pay you the big bucks. Not me. I like tax. That's where the money is; providing advice to wealthy clients who can easily afford to pay." She sat back in the booth sipping her Manhattan. "Do you know what my current billing rate is? It's outrageous, is what it is! But I've got a 94% recovery so I'm looking at being made a partner next year."

"It's not about money, it's about helping people. We're supposed to be upholding the public interest, not the interests of some fat cat executives." Sophia was leaning forward to make her point.

"Hey. I don't make the rules. I just follow them. The *Income Tax Act* is a rule book. I would never advise a client to break the law. But there's lots that's not covered. When the law doesn't prohibit something or when it's ambiguous, that's when we can advise them and come up with a plan. We always tell them there's a risk that the deduction might be disallowed. We cover our ass, and leave the ultimate decision up to them."

"But they're following your advice because you're the expert. They'd never come up with these schemes on their own. You're the one who found the loophole."

"We don't look for loopholes. We plan and offer sound advice that fits with the client's business objectives. Loopholes are outside the law."

"Whatever! You're the one who came up with the plan and how to implement it. You're telling them that it'll save them some money. They're not going to say no to that. They're like children, doing whatever mommy says."

"Yeah." Maya shrugged and smiled. "Occasionally they do ask for a second or third opinion."

Sophia was leaning forward again. "For many of them, tax is emotional. They don't want to pay anything and so they'd do anything to save a buck. They'd gladly pay you $350,000 in consulting fees if you could save them a million in tax."

"Yeah." Maya shrugged again and sipped her drink.

"But is that right? A million dollars that could have gone to the government for the good of society is now being siphoned off and 35% of it is being given to you. That can't possibly be in the public interest."

"Hey, the partners will pay tax on that three hundred and fifty, and the client will reinvest the remaining $650,000 in the business. Anyway many of my clients think that the government's wasteful. They don't want the government squandering their money."

"What the government does with the money is irrelevant." Sophia realized her voice was rising, so she settled back in the booth and had another sip of her wine. It was still early but the bar was beginning to fill up with the regular Friday night crowd.

"Tax is a redistribution system that is supposed to help everyone in society. And you're draining money out of that system, even if the partners are paying some tax on the money that should have gone to the government in the first place."

"Just a minute, Sophia." Maya was now leaning forward. "The poor are covered by tax relief and they're not my concern. As a tax specialist my first responsibility is to my clients. I'm being hired to save them money. That's what I'm supposed to do!"

"No, your first responsibility is to maintain the public interest; your second responsibility is to your clients. Anyway, why don't you look for tax loopholes for the poor?"

"First, the public interest doesn't pay me. And, second, poor people can't afford my billing rate. And third, we don't look for loopholes! We come up with tax plans that have a more likely than not chance of surviving a tax audit."

"Yeah. Whatever!"

Maya finished the last of her Manhattan. "What do you think I should do when I find a tax 'loophole'? Not advise my clients? What happens if some other tax specialist finds the same thing and comes up with a similar plan? If I remain silent, then they might steal my clients away by providing the tax advice that I should have been providing to them."

"If you find a loophole," Sophia was excited and talking very quickly, "then why don't you inform the government, and have them change the law to close the loophole?"

"Not a chance! You may be a do-gooder, Sophia, but this is my livelihood. I'm talented and professional. I charge top dollar to provide sound advice. That's how I make my living. I'm honest and candid with my clients. I'm straightforward when I explain the risks to them. I've got nothing to be ashamed about or to apologize for. So, let's order another round of drinks and talk about investment strategies instead."

Questions

1. Is there a basic conflict of interest between upholding the public interest and providing tax advice that reduces the amount of money taxpayers pay to the government? Why or why not?
2. How can professional accountants maintain the support of the public while giving tax advice? Is providing tax advice that only benefits the wealthy, who can afford to pay for tax advice, in the public interest? Is this fair? Is providing highly specialized tax advice to naive clients being paternalistic?
3. If a tax specialist spends only one hour devising a tax plan that saves a client $1 million, is it ethically acceptable for the tax specialist to charge that client more than the one-hour billing rate?
4. Is it ethically correct for a corporation to pay $350,000 to tax consultants so that the corporation can save a million in taxes?

ETHICS CASE

Risk Management of Taxes Payable—Is It Ethical?

"At the firm, we've got a new way of looking at tax issues. It's called 'risk management,' and, in your case, John, it means that we can be more aggressive than in the past. In the past, when there was an issue open to interpretation, we advised you to adopt a practice that was relatively safe, so that you would not get into trouble with the tax department. The thinking was that it would be better not to attract attention because that would lead to more audits and more difficult negotiations of questionable issues. We noticed, however, that there are fewer tax auditors now than in the past, particularly in remote areas, so it makes sense to take more chances than in the past—if you are audited, you can always pay up, anyway. It just makes good business sense to take advantage of all the possibilities open to your competitors. More and more of our clients are moving into this area of risk management, and you should think about it too."

Question

1. Is this new practice of risk management ethical?

7

Managing Ethics Risks & Opportunities

PURPOSE OF THE CHAPTER

Earlier chapters provided an understanding of the changing ethical expectations for business and professional accountants; the new frameworks of stakeholder accountability and governance stimulated by ethics, governance, and business scandals; and how to provide adequate guidance for ethical behavior in the future. Looking ahead, there are several areas that are worthy of specific discussion because of their current and potential significance to the successful future of corporations, directors, executives, and professional accountants. These areas hold risks and opportunities that modern businesspeople and professionals must consider in order to secure and maintain the support of their stakeholders.

This chapter develops an understanding of how to identify, assess, and manage *ethics risks* and opportunities effectively. Topics covered include the following:

- Ethics risk and opportunity identification, assessment, and management
- Enterprise risk management
- Effective stakeholder relations
- Sustainability/corporate social responsibility reporting
- Workplace ethics
- Whistleblower programs and ethics inquiry services
- Fraud and white-collar crime
- Bribery and international operations
- Crisis management

ETHICS RISK & OPPORTUNITY IDENTIFICATION & ASSESSMENT

Enterprise Risk Management Must Include Ethics Risks & Opportunities

ETHICS RISKS & OPPORTUNITIES The recognition of the need for corporate accountability to stakeholders has brought a corollary recognition that modern governance systems need to reflect the importance of satisfying the interests of stakeholders. Stakeholder satisfaction, in turn, is based on the respect a corporation shows for the interests of each stakeholder group from whom the corporation wants and needs support to reach its strategic objectives. Within this context, attention to ethics risks and opportunities—*since the risks of not meeting stakeholder expectations can lead to a potential loss of support for a corporation's objectives, and exceeding expectations can lead to opportunities to garner support*—is critical to avoid potential loss of support for a corporation's objectives and to discover opportunities of greater support.

This requires a much broader framework and mindset focus for risk assessment than most corporations have employed in traditional enterprise risk management (ERM) approaches because these have usually proceeded from a shareholder perspective rather than a more inclusive stakeholder viewpoint. *Without a stakeholder interests or support perspective, an investigator may not recognize risks that could lead to loss of support or opportunities for the creation of support based on competitive advantage or attention to other stakeholder interests.* To facilitate the stakeholder perspective, a new definition of an ethics risk—a risk that stems from the failure to apply ethical values to the level expected by stakeholders—and a new risk identification approach are developed below to facilitate an examination for ethics risks based on stakeholders' interests.

Risk management has been a commonly used concept since the late 1990s, when major stock exchanges listed it as one of those matters that directors needed to oversee.[1] However, risk management, as normally practiced, rarely involves a full examination of ethics risks and opportunities. There is a growing focus on fraud-related matters, but this does not go far enough to prevent loss of reputation and stakeholder support. Very recent changes to ERM protocols offer promise in this regard, and the discussion that follows of ethics and cultural risks will augment that promise.

LIMITATIONS WITH TRADITIONAL ERM APPROACHES During the 1990s, leading-edge corporations had employed some form of risk management, but most other corporations had not. The *Sarbanes-Oxley Act of 2002* (SOX) effectively made risk management an integral part of good governance when it brought governance reform to U.S. Securities and Exchange Commission (SEC) registrant companies around the world and spawned similar developments in many other jurisdictions. Section 404 of SOX, for example, which is aimed at risk assessment and prevention, requires each company to examine the effectiveness of its internal control systems with regard to financial reporting, and the CEO, CFO, and auditors must report on and certify that effectiveness.

As noted in Chapter 5, the mandatory review of internal control involves comparison of the corporation's systems with an accepted internal control framework such as that developed for ERM by the Committee of Sponsoring Organizations (COSO) of the Treadway Commission. Further information on the COSO approach is available in auditing texts or on the COSO website.[2] The traditional COSO ERM framework, developed in 2004,[3] assesses how an entity achieves its risk management objectives on four functional dimensions: strategy setting, operations, reporting, and compliance. Within each of these dimensions or categories, the ERM framework involves assessment of risk possibilities in eight interrelated aspects of the way an enterprise is managed (i.e., creating an internal environment, objective setting, and monitoring activities).

[1] The Toronto Stock Exchange identified risk management as a matter requiring oversight by directors in 1995.

[2] See, for example, Committee of Sponsoring Organizations (COSO) of the Treadway Commission, *Enterprise Risk Management—Integrated Framework: Executive Summary*, September 2004, http://www.coso.org/documents/COSO_ERM_ExecutiveSummary.pdf.

[3] Committee of Sponsoring Organizations of the Treadway Commission, *Enterprise Risk Management—Integrated Framework: Executive Summary*, September 2004, 5.

Ethics and an ethical corporate culture, which were explored in Chapter 5, are seen to play a vital role in setting an organization's control environment and thereby creating an effective ERM-oriented internal control system and influencing the behavior that results. Consequently, a traditional 2004 COSO ERM-oriented review will examine the tone at the top, codes of conduct, employee awareness, pressures to meet unrealistic or inappropriate goals, management's willingness to override established controls, code adherence in performance appraisals, monitoring of internal control system effectiveness, whistleblowing programs, and remedial actions in response to code violations.[4] But it will not explore deeply for the ethics risks and opportunities referred to in this chapter.

NEW 2016 ERM EXPOSURE DRAFT REVISION In June 2016, COSO released an Exposure Draft, *Enterprise Risk Management: Aligning Risk with Strategy and Performance*,[5] putting forward a significant revision of the ERM framework for comment. Based on comments received, COSO will deliberate and release a new ERM framework that will likely be ready for application in 2017.

The proposed ERM framework focuses on how risks and opportunities might impact on the achievement of strategic goals and on the creation, preservation, realization or erosion of value. ERM is defined as:

> *"The culture, capabilities, and practices, integrated with strategy-setting and its execution, that organizations rely on to manage risk in creating, preserving, and realizing value."*[6]

where

"...enterprise risk management emphasizes its focus on managing risk through:

- Recognizing culture and capabilities.
- Applying practices.
- Integrating with strategy-setting and its execution.
- Managing risk to strategy and business objectives.
- Linking to creating, preserving, and realizing value."[7]

The new ERM framework goes further to include consideration of impacts on the organization's culture with specific reference to the organization's mission, vision, and core values, when it says:

> "When enterprise risk management and strategy-setting are integrated, an organization is better positioned to understand:
>
> - How mission, vision, and core values form the initial expression of acceptable types and amount of risk for consideration when setting strategy.
> - The possibility of strategies and business objectives not aligning with the mission, vision, and core values.
> - The types and amount of risk the organization potentially exposes itself to from the strategy that has been chosen.

---

[4] Principal source: KPMG Forensic, *Integrity Survey 2005–2006*, 2005.

[5] *Enterprise Risk Management: Aligning Risk with Strategy and Performance*, June 2016 Edition, Committee of Sponsoring Organizations,of the Treadway Commission, http://erm.coso.org/Pages/viewexposuredraft.aspx.

[6] Ibid., p. 10, Section 27.

[7] Ibid., Section 28.

- The types and amount of risk to executing its strategy and achieving business objectives."[8]

The proposed ERM framework proceeds to develop 23 *Principles* that identify roles, responsibilities, considerations, approaches, and techniques that represent considerable advances over the 2004 framework. Comments provided below regarding the identification and assessment of ethics risks and opportunities fit well with the new framework and expand usefully upon it.

ETHICS RISKS GO UNDISCOVERED Few corporations approach risk management within the full ethics risk management framework necessary to support the new era of stakeholder accountability and governance. Depending on the organization, *traditional risk management has focused on issues from the perspective of their financial impacts on shareholders and does not incorporate ethics risks that spring from financial or nonfinancial impacts on stakeholders.* For example, financial institutions have tended to focus on financial risks, such as the bankruptcy of borrowers, or the risk of loss on loans and derivative investments. Other corporations have focused on broad business risks, such as those covered in studies by the Institute of Internal Auditors[9] or in the jointly published study by the American Institute of Certified Public Accountants (AICPA) and Canadian Institute of Chartered Accountants (now CPA Canada).[10] Table 7.1 provides

TABLE 7.1 Identification of Business Risks

RISK FOCUS/CATEGORIES		AICPA/ CICA*	INSTITUTE OF INTERNAL AUDITORS
Company Objectives		X	
Areas of Impact:	Reputation	X	
	Assets, Revenues, Costs	X	
	Performance	X	
	Stakeholders	X	
Sources of Risk:	Environmental	X	
	Strategic	X	X
	Operational	X	X
	Informational	X	
	Financial		X
Specific Hazards or Perils:	Lawsuits		X
	Fire	X	
	Theft	X	
	Earthquakes/Natural Disasters	X	X
Degree of Control over the Risk:	Little, Some, Great	X	
Documentation		X	

*CICA became CPA Canada (CPAC) in January 2013.

[8] Ibid, p. 12, Section 40.

[9] Tillinghast-Towers Perrin and the Institute of Internal Auditors Research Foundation, *Enterprise Risk Management: Trends and Emerging Practices* (Altamonte Springs, FL: Institute of Internal Auditors, 2001).

[10] American Institute of Certified Public Accountants and the Canadian Institute of Chartered Accountants, *Managing Risk in the New Economy* (New York: American Institute of Certified Public Accountants and the Canadian Institute of Chartered Accountants, 2001).

a summary of the business risks identified in the two studies. Because of their focuses, traditional ERM approaches have generally been limited in scope with regard to many issues of direct interest to stakeholders and therefore indirect interest to shareholders.

Specifically, because traditional ERM is not stakeholder focused, it fails to do the job expected for the following reasons:

- It does not specifically search for *ethics risks* or values-related risks including the following:
  - *Cultural support risks*—that exist when the organization's culture fails to provide sufficient support and guidance to ensure a culture of integrity.
  - *Mindset risks*—that exist when decision makers, employees, and agents
    - are improperly motivated or
    - use ethically unsound rationales for their decisions.
  - *Systemic ethics risks*—that exist over and above specific outcome-oriented risks.
- It is somewhat misdirected at identifying, assessing, and remedying specific risk outcomes associated with events rather than examining for ethics-related causality.
- It is often undertaken as a perfunctory compliance exercise.

In summary, while the traditional ERM approach can uncover some ethics-related risks, it does not examine thoroughly for all the ethics risks and the underlying ethics-related causes of other risks. Both shortcomings render prevention efforts ineffective and unnecessarily consign companies to have to remedy costly problems.

MISGUIDED ERM RELIANCE ON AUDITORS In addition, even within the traditional, financial impacts-focused ERM approach, there has been a mistaken reliance on external auditors. Some directors and executives have presumed that their external auditors, who were reviewing for risks, would bring any risks found to the attention of management and/or directors. This reliance, however, was and is misplaced.

Although, as part of their audit external auditors review a corporation's internal controls and sometimes some of the business risks, the normal external audit mandate requires concern only if risks found would have resulted in a material misstatement of the results of operations or financial position of the company. Moreover, because external auditors are only testing, they are not expected to find every reporting problem or fraud. It is noteworthy, however, that there never has been a requirement for external auditors to search for and report any ethics risks or opportunities.

The Statement of Auditing Standards (SAS 99),[11] released by the AICPA in response to the Enron and WorldCom disasters and SOX, illustrates how external auditors have been redirected toward greater fraud awareness, examination, and reporting thereon. Specifically, SAS 99 requires the following:

- Mandatory discussion and brainstorming among the audit team of and about the potential and causes for material misstatement in the financial statements due to fraud before and during the audit[12]
- Guidance to be followed about data gathering and audit procedures to identify the risks of fraud[13]

[11] "SAS 99," Official Releases column in the *Journal of Accountancy*, January 2003, 105–20.

[12] "Auditor's Responsibility for Fraud Detection," *Journal of Accountancy*, January 2003, 28–36.

[13] Ibid., 30–32.

- Mandatory assessment of the risks of fraud based on the risk factors found and under revised assumptions of management innocence to guilt[14] as follows:
  - Presume ordinarily that there is a risk of manipulation of revenues due to fraud and investigate.
  - Always identify and assess the risks that management could override controls as a fraud risk.
- Increased standards for examination, documentation, and reporting on audit steps taken to ensure that manipulation did not occur.
- Other measures, including the following:
  - Support of research on fraud
  - Development of antifraud criteria and controls
  - Allocation of 10% of CPE credits to fraud study
  - Development of fraud training programs for the public
  - Encouraging antifraud education at universities as well as appropriate materials[15]

Even after the adoption of SOX reforms, external auditors look for fraud and/or flaws in controls that will give rise to material misstatements of the financial statements. They are not normally be expected to pursue immaterial or other nonfinancial risks or opportunities. In other words, *they will not normally be expected to raise all ethical risks or opportunities* with management or the audit committee or any other committee or the board. Consequently, directors and executives, who are responsible for monitoring *all* ethics risks, must design in-house audit or review processes or specifically contract with designated outsiders to perform those reviews.

Ethics Risk Review or Audit—A Comprehensive Approach

Ethics risks in general (and systemic ethics risks) can best be identified by an *ethics risk review or audit of the values and practices underlying an organization's activities and of the activities on which it relies.* This review can be a demanding task.

After the values underpinning the company's activities are identified, a very reflective approach is required to project how these values are going to affect stakeholders in the short, medium, and longer terms. A series of questions need to be asked, including the following:

- Do/will the values employed affect any stakeholder negatively?
- Are the values employed justifiable and sustainable?
- Are there alternative values that would be optimal and sustainable?

Needless to say, although it is a demanding task, the executives and investors caught on the downside of the 2008 subprime lending crisis would be glad to enjoy the benefits of such a values audit if given a second chance to avoid the losses they suffered.

A comprehensive ethics risk and opportunity identification and assessment can be undertaken in several ways, but the three-phase approach presented in Figure 7.1 and discussed below offers a comprehensive approach.

Phase 1 of a sound ethics risk identification and assessment process should begin with the identification of the corporation's major stakeholders and their interests using the techniques discussed in Chapter 4. Investigators should then rank stakeholder

[14] Ibid., 32.

[15] Ibid., 36.

FIGURE 7.1 Ethics Risk and Opportunity Identification and Assessment

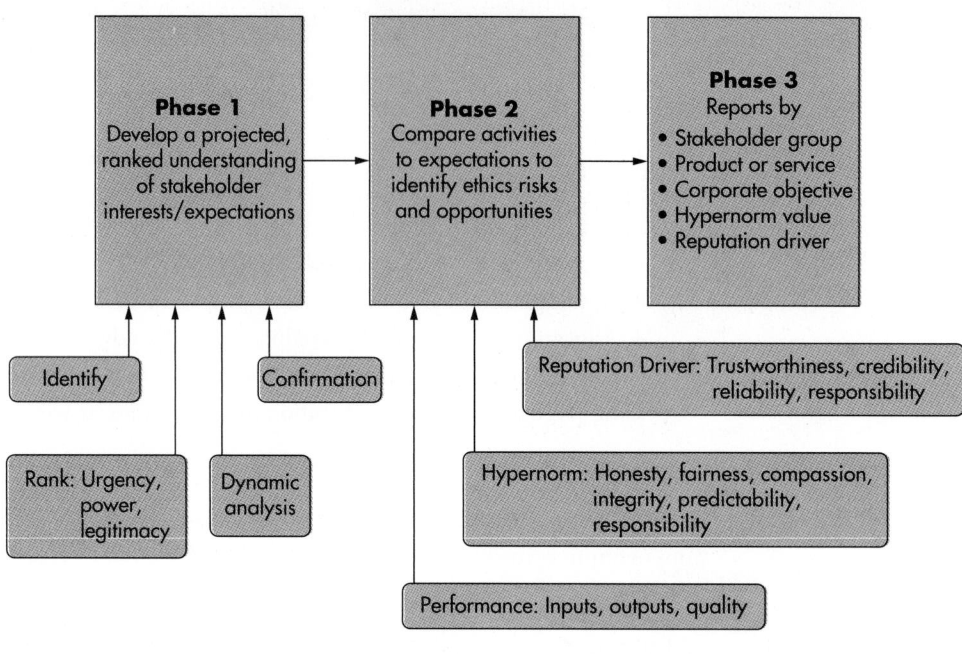

interests in importance using the urgency, legitimacy, and power framework[16] and dynamic influence analysis[17] also developed in Chapter 4. After completion of these steps, investigators should have a projected understanding of which stakeholder interest issues are sensitive and important and why.

Next, the investigator should confirm these projections by interacting with a representative stakeholder panel and with important stakeholder groups. This will show concern for their interests and open a dialog that should build trust that could be helpful if unfortunate problems arise later. At the end of this process of stakeholder consultation, a confirmed grid of important stakeholder expectations for performance should emerge.

In phase 2, against this mosaic of important stakeholder expectations, investigators should consider their corporation's activities and assess the risks of not meeting or the opportunities of exceeding expectations. When considering whether expectations have been met, comparisons should be made of relevant input, output, quality, and other performance variables.

In addition, comparison should be made of company activities and stakeholder expectations using the *six hypernorm values* identified in Chapter 1 that are universally respected in most cultures: *honesty*, *fairness*, *compassion*, *integrity*, *predictability*, and

[16] R. K. Mitchell, B. R. Agle, and D. J. Wood, "Toward a Theory of Stakeholder Identification and Salience: Defining the Principle of Who and What Really Counts," *Academy of Management Review* 22, no. 4 (1997): 853–86.

[17] T. Rowley, "Moving beyond Dyadic Ties: A Network Theory of Stakeholder Influences," *Academy of Management Review* 22, no. 4 (1997): 887–910.

responsibility.[18] If corporate activities respect these values, there is a good chance that those activities will also respect the expectations of the corporation's important stakeholders, domestic and foreign, now and in the near future.

Finally, the comparison of corporate activities and expectations should be reassessed from the perspective of potential impacts on the corporation's reputation. Charles Fombrun's model,[19] also developed in Chapter 1, where *reputation depends on four factors—trustworthiness, credibility, reliability, and responsibility*—can be a helpful framework to organize the comparison needed.

Phase 3 involves preparation of the reports generated by the process. Specific corporate needs should dictate the nature of the reports presented, but consideration should be given to at least the following reports of ethics risks and opportunities:

- By stakeholder group
- By product or service
- By corporate objective
- By hypernorm value
- By reputation driver

This set will provide data that will allow directors and executives to monitor ethics risks and opportunities, to plan to avoid and mitigate risks, and to strategically take advantage of opportunities.

A significant company official, such as the corporate ethics officer or corporate social responsibility officer, should be charged with the ongoing responsibility for monitoring the assumptions and inputs to the ethics risk and opportunity identification and assessment model and for reporting to the relevant subcommittee of the board on a periodic basis. Letting down the corporate guard on this continuing oversight could have very serious consequences, as corporations such as General Motors, Ford, and Chrysler have discovered relative to Toyota in the area of environmentally sustainable products, such as hybrid gas/electric cars.

Searching for Specific Ethics Risks

As noted above, traditional ERM often ignores situations when the ethical expectations of stakeholders are not met—defined as *ethics risks*—resulting in a loss of reputation and stakeholder support, thus preventing full and/or efficient achievement of strategic objectives. In other words, traditional ERM often ignores important ethical or value shortfalls that could lead to ethics risks in general as well as those specifically related to organizational culture, inappropriate mindsets, or systemic risks. Ethics risks and three important specific risks are identified in Table 7.2 and can be addressed as noted below.

ORGANIZATIONAL CULTURE RISKS One of the most common types of ethics risks occurs when *an organization's culture fails to provide sufficient support and guidance to ensure a culture of integrity*. In Chapter 5, the argument was made that an organization would be well advised to develop a culture of integrity to provide guidance for employees and agents to apply ethical policies. However, sometimes organizational cultures do not

[18] Ronald E. Berenbeim, director of the Working Group on Global Business Ethics Principles, discovered in research for the Working Group's Report, *Global Corporate Ethics Practices: A Developing Consensus* (New York: The Conference Board, May 1999).

[19] C. J. Fombrun, *Reputation: Realizing Value from the Corporate Image* (Boston: Harvard Business School Press, 1996).

TABLE 7.2 Ethics Risks

Ethics Risks exist when the ethical expectations of stakeholders are not met:
- Resulting in loss of reputation and stakeholder support.
- Preventing full and/or efficient achievement of strategic objectives.

Important Ethics Risks:

- ***Organizational culture risks*** exist when an organization's culture fails to provide sufficient support and guidance to ensure a culture of integrity.
- ***Mindset risks*** exist when decision makers, employees, and agents are:
  - improperly motivated, or
  - use ethically unsound rationales for their decisions.
- ***Systemic risks*** often originate outside an organization and affect an entire system of activity.

prove to be effective, and ethical problems arise. For example, risk that ethical malfeasance will take place will increase under the following conditions:

- There is an ethics code but no commitment to it.
- There is no one responsible for the culture.
- Organizational values encourage profit at any cost.
- Reward systems encourage maximization of short-term profit (or some other measure, such as revenue or new clients) by any means regardless of the consequences.

These are cultural red flags that are indicators of cultural risks. They and others like them can be identified and then assessed if there is a review of the following important aspects of a culture of integrity:

- Values guidance: code, tone at the top, reinforcement
- Structural support: code, chief ethics officer, ethics programs (training, monitoring, rewarding, or punishing)
- Procedural observance:
  - Ethical decision making on daily matters, major decisions, and crises
  - Ethics inquiry service
  - Strong internal controls to protect against wrongdoers
- Failsafe mechanisms:
  - Whistleblower encouragement and protection programs reporting to the Board of Directors
  - Periodic ethics audit
  - Periodic review of the organization's core values and their application

MINDSET RISKS A second critically important area where failure to use ethical values can lead to serious ethics risks but that traditional ERM does not search thoroughly is *the set of risks caused when the mindsets of decision makers, employees, and/or agents are improperly motivated or their decisions and actions are anchored in unethical rationales.*

Most investigative and forensic accountants subscribe to the following logic regarding a fraudster:

- He or she has to have the opportunity to act improperly.

FIGURE 7.2 **Fraud Triangle**

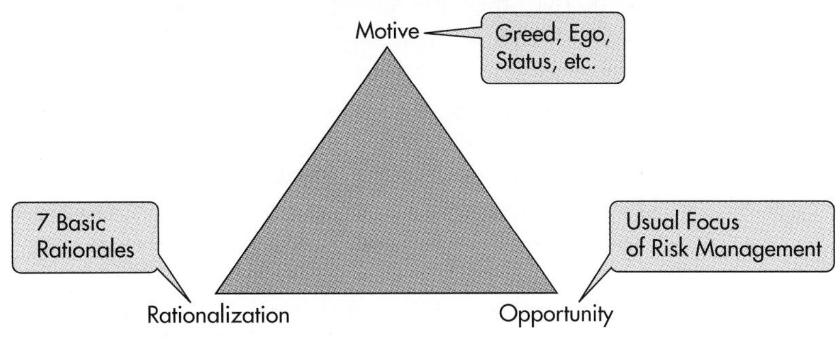

Source: D. L. Crumbley et al., 2005, 3.

- He or she has to be motivated by an unbalanced self-interest based on greed, ego or status, and/or the need to pay for drugs or offset losses.
- He or she has to use a faulty or unethical rationale for his or her decision.

These dimensions have been organized into the *Fraud Triangle*, which is pictured in Figure 7.2.

It has been known for a long time that decisions made on behalf of an organization can be affected by the self-interest or bias (greed, ego needs, status, discrimination, and so on) of the decision makers. These influences represent conflicts of interest that may produce decisions that are not in keeping with their organization's long-term objectives and may bias or undermine an organization's ethical treatment of its stakeholders.

In addition, a list of seven common unethical rationales (see Table 7.3) published by Joseph Heath provides a useful set of highly risky rationales to search for among decision makers, employees, and/or agents.

Some of these rationalizations are encountered frequently. How often have we heard that individuals realized something was going wrong but felt that it was not their responsibility to speak up or intervene? How often have we heard the remark that, although an action was questionable, the action was against a company that had a lot of money, and so the company really was not injured significantly? How often have we heard that an action was ethically reasonable because there really was no a victim because it was against the government or some other institution? Similarly, many people who act improperly often believe their actions to be justified because those who were criticizing

TABLE 7.3 **Seven Common Rationalizations of Immoral Decisions**

- Denial of responsibility
- Denial of injury
- Denial of the victim
- Condemnation of the condemners
- Appeal to higher loyalties
- Everyone else is doing it
- Entitlement

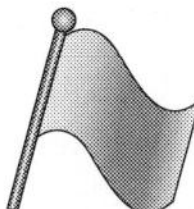

Red Flags

Source: Joseph Heath, "Business Ethics and Moral Motivation: A Criminological Perspective," *Journal of Business Ethics* 83 (2008): 595–614.

the action as unethical or illegal had committed questionable acts themselves and therefore lacked the moral right to object. Other wrongdoers justify their actions because they think that they are doing good for others and that the good outweighs the harm caused—such as justifying misleading investors in order to save a company from bankruptcy so that employees can continue to have jobs. Frequently, we hear the comments that cheating on your income tax or expense account is justified because everyone is doing it or that taking company resources is okay because you are entitled to them since they do not pay you what you are worth or that you built the company so that it is yours anyway. Most of these rationales are kind to the interests of the decision maker and harmful to other stakeholders and therefore very possibly unethical.

Mindset risks can be found by a review for abnormal instances of greed, ego satisfaction, status seeking, and/or personal indulgences or for the use of any of the seven justifications for taking an immoral decision.[20] Employees and managers can be trained in ethical decision making and made aware that they should be on the lookout for abnormal instances that bear reporting. Reports can be gathered annually by questionnaire or interview from managers and heads of units to ensure that they remain aware and vigilant on mindset issues. In addition, analysis of past problems, whistleblower reports, and brainstorming sessions can provide insights into problem procedures and trigger alteration of policies and training or the remediation of problem individuals. Perhaps in time, psychological tests will be available to identify employee's propensities for improper motivators or rationalizations.

Not to be overlooked is the need for boards of directors to continually assess the motivation and mindsets of board members, particularly the organization's senior management. Flawed leadership can quickly take organizations in the wrong direction.

SYSTEMIC ETHICS RISKS *A systemic ethics risk is one that often originates outside an organization and affects an entire system of activity*, including more than one organization. For example, in the case of the 2008 subprime lending crisis, the undermining of the values underpinning the U.S. housing market led to the undermining of the financial markets around the world and the best work of all those involved in them. There was a systemic risk that undermined the housing finance system, and it went on to present a systemic risk to financial markets and their participants.

Normally, a traditional risk management system focuses on events or outcomes that can impede an organization's progress toward its strategic goals. While this type of assessment often does look at significant external influences to determine if there are currency exchange risks, political risks, or new regulation risks, *it does not look for or assess the risk potential of the values or ethical principles underlying transactions or the raison d'être of an organization or a service being offered.* For example, the risk management practices in place before the subprime lending fiasco did not, in most instances, contemplate the unethical ramifications of offering unsustainable mortgages to uninformed people, buying unwarranted investment ratings on securitized mortgages to mislead investors, selling essentially uncollectible securitized mortgages to unsuspecting investors, undermining the market price of previously sold securities against the interest of client, and so on. Instead, the risk management practices in place were either ignored, overlooked, short-circuited, or used to assess for normal business risks. The risk management practices used were not designed to search for unethical values within each organization or for those associated with a major dimension of the worldwide financial markets. In this case, when the unethical asset valuations and practices used proved to

[20] See further discussion in the discussion of fraud and white-collar crime later in this chapter.

be unsustainable, the systemic ethics risk to the world's financial markets became evident, and a crash ensued. Only a few companies avoided the crash. Some did so because they understood that there were ethical weaknesses or risks to be avoided, as did the TD Bank, or they understood the precarious nature of the market caused by ethics risks. Further comment is provided in Chapter 8 on the subprime lending crisis.

ETHICS RISK & OPPORTUNITY MANAGEMENT

Once the organization's ethics risks and opportunities have been identified and assessed, strategies will need to be developed and tactics employed to best manage them to mitigate problems and to align activities with stakeholder interests. Discussions follow covering tools and techniques to employ and how to approach significant problem areas facing directors, executives, and professional accountants.

EFFECTIVE STAKEHOLDER RELATIONS

Strategies and tactics can be developed for dealing with each stakeholder or group, based on an assessment of stakeholder interests and possible changes in them. One approach originated by Savage et al. (1991) focuses on the potential for stakeholders to pose threats to the organization or to cooperate with it. Stakeholders can be susceptible to invitations to collaborate or become co-supporters, or, if they are not amenable to the company's position, consideration may be given to their need for monitoring or when a defense is needed against them. Figure 7.3 presents a useful model for considering such decisions.

The model suggests that the most desirable stakeholder group (called type 1) is likely to pose a low threat to an organization's objectives and a high degree of cooperation with them. If possible, it makes sense to *involve* this group more closely with the organization because they are likely to be *supportive*. A stakeholder group that is ranked high on cooperation and high as a potential threat holds some promise (i.e., is a *mixed blessing*),

FIGURE 7.3 **Diagnostic Typology of Organizational Stakeholders**

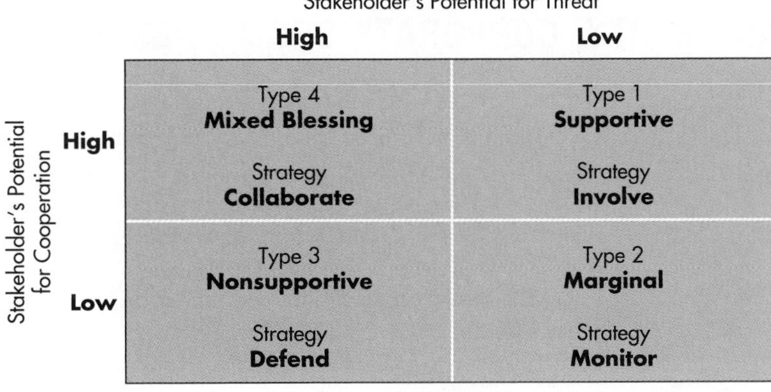

Source: G. Savage et al., "Strategies for Assessing and Managing Organizational Shareholders," *The Executive* 5, no. 2 (May 1991): 65.

and it is probably wise to try to *collaborate* with them to keep them as supporters. Where a stakeholder group is ranked as a high threat and a low cooperator, they are considered *nonsupportive* and should be *defended* against. A group low in potential to threaten and low in potential to cooperate is *marginal* to the development of support for company objectives, but it may be wise to *monitor* their expectations in the event that conditions change.

It should be noted that this is a somewhat static analysis. Consequently, any strategy for improving the support of stakeholders should be confirmed through periodic reanalysis that considers possible alliances of stakeholder groups through the use of the urgency, power, legitimacy framework, and particularly the position of and trends in media coverage. Surprise embarrassment can erode support very quickly. Where possible, advance communication with supporters is attractive in maintaining their support. Of course, the creation of rapport and trust will assist in providing an opportunity to explain problems or tactics if necessary.

It is also worth considering how stakeholders in one cell of the model can be moved to a more supportive position. Even if one group is being defended against, continuing to consider how to convert the group to supporters is very worthwhile. The interests of all stakeholder groups should regularly be reconsidered as input to the development of strategies for improved support.

This regular or continuous reconsideration of stakeholder interests and potential gaps from corporate behavior could be part of the organization's *environmental scanning or issues management programs* and could provide input into its *business-government relations program*. Although issues management programs have been in place for decades, their focus has not traditionally been organized on a comprehensive stakeholder interests gap analysis framework.

The same is true for business-government relations programs where the focus has been on specific issues and only recently has turned to the creation and maintenance of overall support from which the management of specific issues is facilitated. Additionally, there has been a change in the framing of successful proposals to government—to stress the proposed impact on the public interest (i.e., all stakeholders) rather than on a select group—perhaps because of a greater awareness of lobbyist scandals or a more mature awareness of the need for government to protect the public interest. Without doubt, *stakeholder gap analysis* can be of great utility in both framing proposals and creating and maintaining overall stakeholder support.

SUSTAINABILITY, CORPORATE SOCIAL RESPONSIBILITY, & CORPORATE CITIZENSHIP

Corporations have been thought to be legally accountable only to shareholders or owners, but in reality they are also strategically accountable to a broader range of stakeholders if they wish to garner the support necessary for achievement of strategic objectives. *To this extent, a paradigm shift is evident—from accountability to shareholders to accountability to stakeholders.*

As a result, organizations are increasingly interested in what stakeholders expect of them and how they are performing and perceived as performing against those expectations in order to enhance stakeholder support. There are also investors, directors, executives, and employees who, from an altruistic perspective, are interested in their organization's performance on nonfinancial matters. Both groups—those from an instrumental perspective and those from an altruistic perspective—are interested in the organization's *corporate social responsibility* (CSR) or *sustainability*[21] plans and performance or, as some prefer to describe it, as a *corporate citizen.*

While many companies continue to provide CSR reports, increasing numbers are disclosing sustainability reports as advocated by organizations such as the Global Reporting Initiative (GRI), the Corporate Register, and the UN Global Compact (UNGC). On June 24, 2016, the websites for those organizations provided access to the following reports:

- *GRI—23,586 GRI Reports for 9,182 organizations[22]
- *UNGC—over 28,000 Communications on Progress (COP) for 8,700 organizations[23]
- *Corporate Register—76,688 Corporate Responsibility Reports for 3,369 organization

Regardless of which label—CSR, sustainability, or corporate citizenship—is chosen, all refer to the degree to which an organization takes the interests of stakeholders into account and takes actions which respect those interests. High praise is no longer just for high profit; it depends how the profit is earned and how stakeholder interests are respected in the process. The key questions are, How does our organization want to be known? and How do we plan for it and make it happen?

Consequently, there is a growing interest in assessing stakeholder interests, planning for their integration into corporate governance, decision and action processes, and the measurement, reporting, and audit of corporate impacts on stakeholders. To effectively manage ethics risks and opportunities, organizations need to decide which elements are important and how they are to be incorporated, measured, and reported internally and externally. The precise nature and degree of action and CSR/sustainability disclosure will determine the image of corporate citizenship that the corporation will take on.

ORGANIZATIONAL OBJECTIVES & SUSTAINABILITY/CSR FRAMEWORKS To develop a comprehensive plan or framework for CSR, an organization should consider its strategic goals—both as an operation and how it wishes to appear as a corporate citizen, the cultures its operations will encounter, and the interests of its stakeholders—in both domestic and foreign theaters. These considerations, with an understanding of available measures of CSR, will allow the architect of the corporation's systems to match its aspirations with measures that will allow monitoring and reinforcement. Perhaps of equal or greater importance, they will also enable the organization's strategic planners to formulate objectives that are ethical and respectful of the interests of the stakeholders and cultures to be dealt with.

Several organizations provide overviews or reviews of the status of sustainability and CSR reporting. For example, *Currents of Change: The KPMG Survey of Corporate Social Responsibility Reporting 2015* provides worthwhile insights into (1) accounting for carbon, (2) quality of CSR reporting among the world's largest companies, and (3) global trends.[24] It states that the current rate of CSR reporting by the world's largest 250 firms is over 90%.

Framework initiatives have been developed to assist with the involvement of stakeholders in corporate planning and decisions, organize corporate activities and report on them, and audit what the corporation is doing and reporting. Three of these frameworks,

---

[21] With the advent of the GRI, many organizations are adopting the GRI sustainability approach and CSR definition.

[22] See http://database.globalreporting.org.

[23] https://www.unglobalcompact.org/participation/report/cop.

[24] Downloadable from https://assets.kpmg.com/content/dam/kpmg/pdf/2016/02/kpmg-international-survey-of-corporate-responsibility-reporting-2015.pdf.

involving accountability for sustainability and CSR more broadly, are discussed below, including the following:

- GRI G4
- UNGC
- ISO 26000 Guidance on Social Responsibility

GRI G4 REPORTING INITIATIVE The Sustainability Reporting Guidelines developed by the GRI—a cooperative venture of many stakeholders, including professional accounting bodies—provides a comprehensive framework for CSR/sustainability planning, performance assessment, and reporting.[25] The GRI provides learning and networking opportunities, report registration, and viewing databases, and has become a dominant hub for CSR reporting.

The fourth version of the GRI sustainability disclosure framework, the G4 Guidelines, is outlined in Table 7.4. Each company is to make a series of General Standard Disclosures to provide background on the entity and its sustainability and disclosure intentions. In addition, each entity is to make a series of Specific Standard (indicator) Disclosures to allow monitoring of its performance and benchmarking against other entities. Details on these disclosures can be found on the GRI website. GRI and AccountAbility have formed a strategic alliance in which AccountAbility provides information on stakeholder engagement and GRI on the aspects to be considered in the managed and reportable set. Companies that report using the GRI framework are able to benchmark or compare their activities to other enterprises or targets.

In order to prepare the G4 report, a number of decisions have to be made, that are represented in Figure 7.4. First, a decision has to be made as to whether the organization will report on a limited or "core" basis, or on a full or "comprehensive" basis. Then there needs to be agreement on the principles that will underlay the measurements of factors disclosed. Finally, the measurements are made and disclosures crystalized.

Table 7.5 shows the reporting principles to be considered before making the measurements required. Several relate to the boundaries of the report coverage, including the stakeholder interests to be covered or excluded, the sustainability context that the entity sees itself to be part of (i.e., how it aims to contribute in the future), the size and/or impact (i.e., materiality) that an event must exceed to be reported on, and how

TABLE 7.4 GRI G4 DISCLOSURES

GENERAL STANDARD DISCLOSURES	SPECIFIC STANDARD DISCLOSURES
Strategy and Analysis	Management Approach Indicators
Organizational Profile	Economic
Material Aspects and Boundaries	Environmental
Stakeholder Engagement	Social
Report Profile	Labor Practices and Decent Work
Governance	Human Rights
Ethics and Integrity	Society
	Product Responsibility

[25] GRI G4 Guidelines can be viewed at https://www.globalreporting.org/standards/g4/Pages/default.aspx

FIGURE 7.4 **GRI G4 DECISION PROCESS**

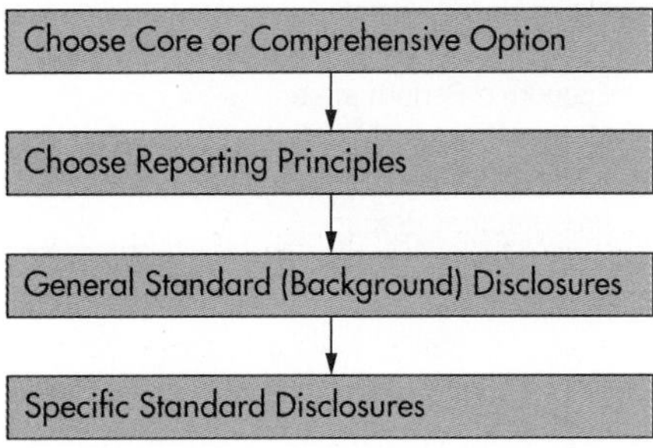

TABLE 7.5 **GRI G4 BOUNDARY & QUALITY DECISIONS**

PRINCIPLES FOR DEFINING	
REPORT CONTENT	**REPORT QUALITY**
Stakeholder Inclusiveness	Balance
Sustainability Context	Comparability
Materiality	Accuracy
Completeness	Timeliness
	Clarity
	Reliability

complete the report will be (i.e., whether are there any exclusions). Decisions also have to be made about the factors shown in Table 7.5 that are related to the underlying quality of the measurements in the report. A discussion of these principles and the choices necessary is found in Section 4 of the *GRI G4 Sustainability Reporting Guidelines: Reporting Principles and Standard Disclosures, Part 1.*[26]

Following these decisions, the General Standard Disclosures and Specific Standard Disclosures can be prepared and the GRI Report finalized. Table 7.6 shows the nature of the categories of disclosure and the specific indicators expected. These items are discussed in Section 5 of the GRI G4 Part 1 Guidelines.

UNGC The UNGC declares itself to be "the world's largest corporate sustainability initiative" and that it provides a "call to companies to align strategies and operations with universal principles on human rights, labour, environment and anti-corruption, and take actions that advance societal goals."[27] Its mission is to encourage "business to be a force for good.... by committing to sustainability [and] taking a shared responsibility for achieving a better world." Specifically, the Compact believes that

> it's possible to create a sustainable and inclusive global economy that delivers lasting benefits to people, communities and markets. To make this happen, the UN Global Compact supports companies to:

[26] Available for download from https://www.globalreporting.org/resourcelibrary/GRIG4-Part1-Reporting-Principles-and-Standard-Disclosures.pdf.
[27] https://www.unglobalcompact.org/what-is-gc.

TABLE 7.6 GRI G4 CATEGORIES & ASPECTS IN THE GUIDELINES

CATEGORY	ECONOMIC	ENVIRONMENTAL
Aspects	Economic Performance Market Presence Indirect Economic Impacts Procurement Practices	Materials Energy Water Biodiversity Emissions Effluents and Waste Products and Services Compliance Transport Overall Supplier Environmental Assessment Environmental Grievance Mechanisms

CATEGORY	SOCIAL			
SUB-CATEGORIES	LABOR PRACTICES & DECENT WORK	HUMAN RIGHTS	SOCIETY	PRODUCT RESPONSIBILITY
Aspects	Employment Labor/Management Relations Occupational Health and Safety Training and Education Diversity and Equal Opportunity Equal Remuneration for Women and Men Supplier Assessment for Labor Practices Labor Practices Grievance Mechanisms	Investment Non-discrimination Freedom of Association and Collective Bargaining Child Labor Forced or Compulsory Labor Security Practices Indigenous Rights Assessment Supplier Human Rights Assessment Human Rights Grievance Mechanisms	Local Communities Anti-corruption Public Policy Anti-competitive Behavior Compliance Supplier Assessment for Impacts on Society Grievance Mechanisms for Impacts on Society	Customer Health and Safety Product and Service Labeling Marketing Communications Customer Privacy Compliance

Source: GRI G4 Table 5, p. 44

1. Do business responsibly by aligning their strategies and operations with Ten Principles on human rights, labor, environment, and anti-corruption; and
2. Take strategic actions to advance broader societal goals, such as the UN Sustainable Development Goals, with an emphasis on collaboration and innovation.[28]

The Compact's Ten Principles are identified in Table 7.7, and the UNGC's website offers several guides for understanding corporate sustainability, implementing a sustainability program, and developing a report, a COP, or Communication on Progress, designed to show the corporation's progress or achievement toward their goals related to the ten principles. These COPs are to be submitted to the UNGC, where they are classified as Advanced, Active, or Learner and made available to the public via the UNGC website at https://www.unglobalcompact.org/participation/report/cop.

[28] https://www.unglobalcompact.org/what-is-gc/mission.

TABLE 7.7 UN GLOBAL COMPACT'S TEN PRINCIPLES

Human Rights

1. Businesses should support and respect the protection of internationally proclaimed human rights; and
2. Make sure that they are not complicit in human rights abuses.

Labor

3. Businesses should uphold the freedom of association and the effective recognition of the right to collective bargaining;
4. The elimination of all forms of forced and compulsory labor;
5. The effective abolition of child labor; and
6. The elimination of discrimination in respect of employment and occupation.

Environment

7. Businesses should support a precautionary approach to environmental challenges;
8. Undertake initiatives to promote greater environmental responsibility; and
9. Encourage the development and diffusion of environmentally friendly technologies.

Anti-Corruption

10. Businesses should work against corruption in all its forms, including extortion and bribery.

Source: https://www.unglobalcompact.org/what-is-gc/mission/principles.

ISO 26000 GUIDELINES ON SOCIAL RESPONSIBILITY A CSR framework can also be developed from *ISO 26000 Guidance on Social Responsibility*,[29] which was issued by the International Organization for Standardization (ISO) on November 1, 2010. Whereas the GRI G4 guideline focuses on a reporting model, ISO 26000 focuses on the nature of CSR and on how an organization can prepare itself to contribute to sustainable development, which the ISO posits as the overall objective of CSR. According to the Introduction of ISO 26000:

> This International Standard provides guidance on the underlying principles of social responsibility, recognizing social responsibility and engaging stakeholders, the core subjects and issues pertaining to social responsibility… and on ways to integrate socially responsible behaviour into the organization…. This International Standard emphasizes the importance of results and improvements in performance on social responsibility.[30]

Table 7.8 presents an overview of the topics covered in ISO 26000. The standard itself can be downloaded from the ISO website.

Schematically, ISO 26000 is organized into Clauses 1, 2, 3, and 4 as shown in ISO Figure 7.5.

It is noteworthy that the examples included in ISO 26000's Annex A of voluntary initiatives and tools represent an outstanding overview of significant studies and/or pronouncements by most intergovernmental, multi-stakeholder, single stakeholder, and even sectoral organizations. Plans are underway already to revise ISO 26000, so constant scrutiny of the ISO website would be well-advised.

When creating a CSR framework for a particular organization, it is essential that the framework respond to the actual stakeholder interests likely to be encountered. These could be developed using stakeholder survey, analysis, and focus group techniques developed in Chapter 5 in connection with the design of codes of conduct, ethical decision making, and corporate culture.

---

[29] International Organization for Standardization, *ISO 26000 Guidance on Social Responsibility*, accessed December 31, 2010, at http://www.iso.org.

[30] Ibid., vi.

TABLE 7.8 ***ISO 26000* Guidance on Social Responsibility—Overview**

CLAUSE/TOPIC	CLAUSE/TOPIC
1. Scope 2. Terms, definitions 3. Understanding Social Responsibility 4. Principles of Social Responsibility • Accountability • Transparency • Ethical behavior Respect for: • Stakeholder interests • The rule of law • International norms of behavior • Human rights 5. Fundamental Practices of Social Responsibility • Recognizing social responsibility • Stakeholder identification and engagement	6. Social Responsibility Core Subjects • Organizational governance • Human rights • Labor practices • Environment—rationale, core issues • Fair operating practices • Consumer issues • Community involvement and development 7. Integrating Social Responsibility (SR) throughout an organization • Understanding organization's SR • Voluntary initiatives for SR • Enhancing credibility re SR • Reviewing and improving actions and practices re SR • Communication on SR • Relationship of organization's characteristics to SR

Source: ISO 26000 *Guidance on Social Responsibility*, First Edition 2010-11-01, Figure 1, www.iso.org.

FIGURE 7.5 **Schematic Overview of *ISO 26000*: Guidance on social responsibility**[31]

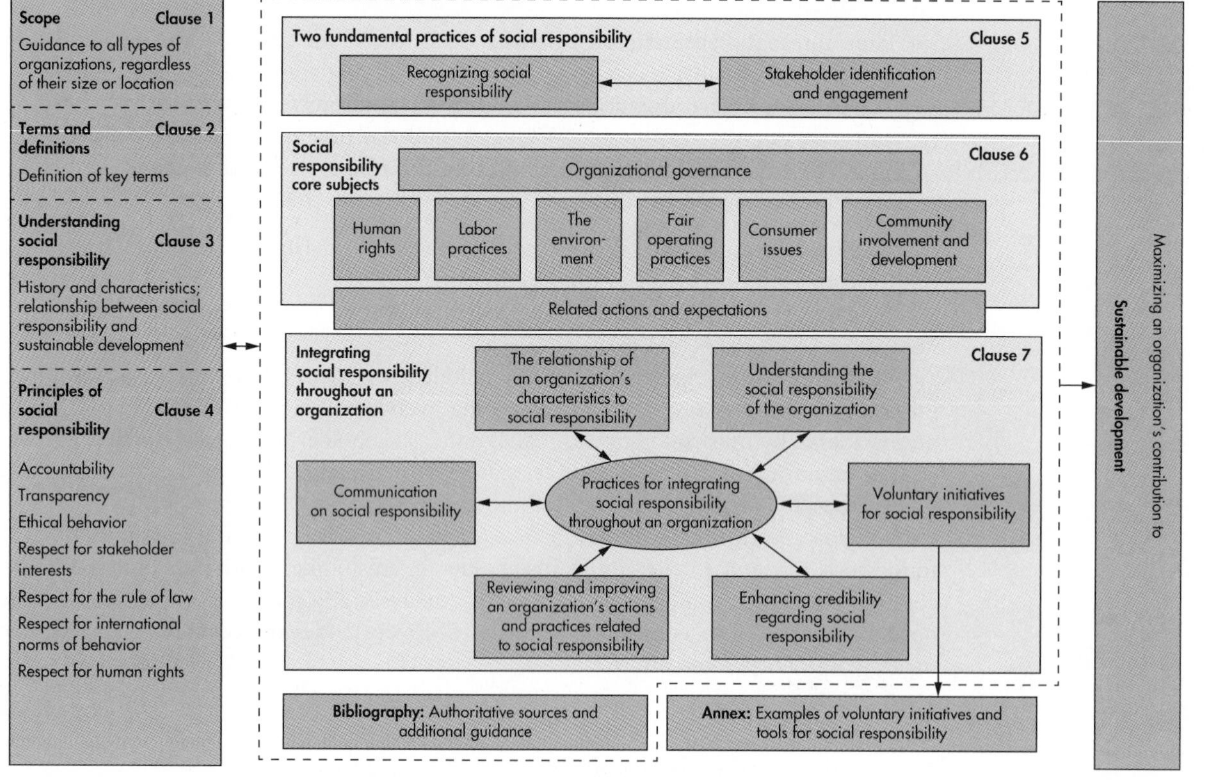

[31] Ibid., ix, reproduced with permission.

MEASUREMENT OF SUSTAINABILITY/CSR PERFORMANCE Specific measurements chosen for sustainability/CSR should highlight key factors that will contribute to the strategic objectives of the corporation. This will involve defining strategic objectives, and what they require in terms of the support needed from both domestic and foreign stakeholders. In addition, CSR measurements should be chosen to facilitate reports for customers, such as government purchasers, that may require CSR details such as the percent of women and minorities on staff or details of loans to minorities, for bids or assurance of CSR processes. Finally, as noted above, several organizations are developing guidance on standardized CSR reports, or audit protocols, and their efforts should be reviewed before finalizing a corporation's CSR measurement and reporting protocol.

Measurements or indicators of CSR can take many forms. There are a number of organizations[32] that rate the CSR of many companies, and their list of criteria can be used as a guide in establishing a set of appropriate measures. For example, indicators of historical fact, based on voluntary surveys sent to senior corporate officers, have been used by EthicScan Canada, first in their Corporate Ethics Monitor[33] and later in company profiles, including the following:

- Existence of statements of guidance, their currency, and reinforcement
- Employment record, including total staff as well as the number of women and minority group members on the Board of Directors or in management positions
- Amount of charitable donations in relation to other companies in the sector and allowing comparison to profits as a means of assessing relative generosity
- Existence and nature of community relations programs
- Labor relations and health and safety
- Environmental management indicators
- Environmental performance indicators
- Ethical sourcing and trading policies

There are other measures that may be useful in revealing attitudes of managers and employees toward ethical issues. These may be useful in capturing information about actions that are about to happen or about changes in attitude due to certain signals sent voluntarily or involuntarily by management or read into circumstances by employees. Examples of such *anticipatory measures* are the following:

- Employee attitude surveys such as those undertaken by Walker Information[34]
- Customer or other stakeholder surveys
- Evaluation by paid shoppers or solicited customer comments
- Media commentary assessment

Other measures concentrate on the operational merit of the organization's support mechanisms for ethical behavior. This could include quality assessments of the following:

- Codes of conduct
- Training programs

---

[32] See, for example, United States, KLD Research and Analytics, Inc., http://www.kld.com; in Canada, EthicScan Canada, http://www.ethicscan.ca, and Sustainalytics, http://www.sustainalytics.com; in the United Kingdom, Ethics Investment Research Service (EIRIS), ethics@eiris.win.uk.net.

[33] The *Corporate Ethics Monitor* is published by EthicScan Canada: http://www.ethicscan.ca.

[34] Walker Information's website is http://www.walkerinfo.com.

- Reinforcement mechanisms, including
  - newsletters and correspondence,
  - pay and reward systems, and
  - promotion
- Whistleblowing atmosphere/protection
  - protection for whistleblowers
  - follow-up on reported problems
  - speed of response
  - fairness of investigation and hearing and of penalty assigned

Measures are also available to indicate the following:

- The level of understanding that employees have of ethical issues[35]
- The principal motivator for an employee's ethical behavior[36]
- Whether an employee is disposed to raise ethical concerns due to his or her perception of his or her ability to affect the outcome of such debates (locus of control tests[37])
- The degree of inclusion of ethical concerns in "the development of plans, setting of goals, search of opportunities, allocation of resources, gathering and communication of information, measurement of performance, and promotion and advancement of personnel"[38]

A further source for the design of a measurement scheme can be found in the New York–based Social Accountability International SA8000 standard for working conditions. It can be accessed on this book's website at **www.cengagebrain.com**.

Table 7.9 is provided to show how the measures discussed can be related to the attribute or process involved in maintaining an ethical corporate culture.

MONITORING SUSTAINABILITY/CSR PERFORMANCE After the CSR measurements have been identified, the data have been gathered, and the report has been fashioned, the next step is monitoring how the corporation is doing. As with most measurement schemes, comparison can be helpful with the following:

- Strategic objective key success factors
- Similar organizations
- Best-practice alternatives for benchmarking
- Published standards such as those described earlier
- Industry statistics and averages

---

[35] See, for example, the Defining Issues Test (DIT) as discussed in James R. Rest, *Development in Judging Moral Issues* (Minneapolis: University of Minnesota Press, 1979).

[36] According to the subject's stage of moral reasoning per the schema developed by L. Kohlberg in *Essays in Moral Development, Volumes I and II: The Psychology of Moral Development* (San Francisco: Harper & Row, 1981 and 1984).

[37] "Locus of control is a self-regulatory aspect of character that captures individuals' tendency to feel that control of their lives rests in their own hands (internal locus of control) or in the hands of others (external locus of control). Those who are 'internals' take responsibility for their actions, and are therefore more likely to act upon their ethical judgment. 'Externals' are less likely to take responsibility for their actions and, therefore, are more susceptible to the pressures of the situation, feeling somewhat powerless." From Joanne Jones, Dawn W. Massey, and Linda Thorne, "Auditors' Ethical Reasoning: Insights from Past Research And Implications for the Future," *Journal of Accounting Literature*, 2003.

[38] Lynn Sharp Paine, "Managing for Organizational Integrity," *Harvard Business Review*, March–April 1994, 112.

TABLE 7.9 Techniques for the Measurement of Ethical Processes & Performance

Written objectives
- Existence - broad, specific by function
- Content – comprehensive set of values, clarity of coverage, relevance
- Date of most recent revision

Annual sign off – yes/no, minimal, involving reporting responsibility

Guidance given to directors, management, employees
- Process - training sessions, workshops, and employees
- Consultation with ombudsperson, others
- Comprehensiveness of coverage (e.g., new employees)
- Frequency, currency – board review, dissemination

Understanding of issues
- Rating developed by persons responsible for ethics program for each level of employee
- Tests are available (e.g., defining issues, stage of moral reasoning)

Inclusion of ethical concerns
- Evaluation by management in decision making
- In "the development of plans, setting of goals, search of opportunities, allocation of resources, gathering and communication of information, measurement of performance, and promotion and advancement of personnel"
- Frequency of coverage as agenda item

Commitment by all levels to the organization's ethical values
- Rating by ombudsperson
- Reports of ethical problems - fraud, customer and employee complaints
- Visible encouragement by top management

Achievement of ethical objectives
- Combination of - existence, stage of completion of plans, number of events, dollars spent, numbers experienced
- Monitoring and continuous improvement
- Identification of person(s) responsible
- Adequacy of resources allocated
- Periodic reports to senior management and Board
- Evident action based on feedback

Effectiveness of reporting
- Existence - internal, external
- Impact analysis on employees and external stakeholders
- Effectiveness analysis by researchers
- Favourable/unfavourable mentions in the media

- Management by objective targets
- Results obtained in earlier periods

Ethical performance could also be selectively monitored by reference to external studies, to books or publications on "best" or "award-winning" companies, or to industry or sector reports available for the GRI, the UNGC, or Corporate Register websites. Books such as *The 50 Best Ethical Stocks for…*[39] or industry studies may also be useful, as may several annual studies such as the "100 Best Corporate Citizens" in *Corporate Responsibility Magazine.*[40] Annual Business Ethics Awards are also offered that identify companies judged as outstanding performers.[41] Even general business publications such as *The Economist* offer useful and sometimes skeptical information in surveys and editorials. Organizations also exist, such as Toronto's Social Investment Organization (SIO), that provide information derived from CSR matters. On a specific company level, it is possible to obtain a specific report on the CSR performance of a company from research organizations, such as Jantzi Sustainalytics or EthicScan Canada, that are providing these to the corporate and investment community. Hiring a consultant specializing in ethical performance measurement may also be beneficial, especially if the consultant

---

[39] Deb Abbey and Michael C. Jantzi, *2001 Edition* (Toronto: Macmillan Canada, 2000).

[40] See CR's 100 Best 2011, http://www.thecro.com/content/corporate-responsibility-magazine's-"100-best-corporate-citizens-list" (accessed March 23, 2011).

[41] For example, an awards program providing similar sources of best practice is organized by *Corporate Knights Magazine*. The Best 50 Corporate Citizens in Canada Annual Survey can be found at http://www.corporateknights.ca/reports.

has extensive experience with ethical processes in other organizations that can be of use, on a confidential basis, for benchmarking purposes.

Reports will be most useful when reviewed and analyzed on a continuing basis. The chief ethics officer and other individuals carrying out the review and analysis should be familiar with the ethical performance process and should be committed to its improvement. They should be formally charged with and known throughout the organization to have the responsibility for improving the process and should also have the responsibility to report to senior levels of management and/or a subset of the Board of Directors. These individuals may be part of or report to an ethics advisory committee with ongoing responsibility and authority to revise the company's ethics program and/or to a subcommittee of the Board of Directors.

Chief ethics officers can remain up to date on measurement and review techniques through organizations such as the Ethics and Compliance Officers Association (http://www.theecoa.org) or the EthicsCentre (http://www.ethicscentre.ca). It should be noted that corporations that join the UNGC and then fail to report are identified on the UNGC website.

PUBLIC REPORTING The corporation that embarks on a CSR measurement program must consider how it will report on performance and whether the report will be internal only or available to the public. Internal reports can take on any form but should be focused on the program's performance objectives.

As noted above, several organizations have created and published guidelines for aspects of CSR and sustainability reports as well as their audit. They are continually testing and refining their creations and will be modifying them further. Consequently, it would be wise to maintain a watching brief on the following:

- The GRI, which is discussed above, involves the comprehensive G4 sustainability /CSR reporting framework covering economic, environmental, and social performance that has been developed by a global group, including noted stakeholder environmentalists, accountants, and others—see http://www.database.globalreporting.org. On June 11, 2016, this website held in its Sustainability Disclosure Database a total of 33,542 sustainability reports and 23,512 GRI reports.
- The UNGC encourages reporting of corporate progress in regard to the Ten Principles noted above, and its database, at https://www.unglobalcompact.org/participation/report/cop, held over 28,000 reports in June 2016 that are available for public review.
- The Corporate Register also provides a database, at http://www.corporateregister.com, of CR reports that held over 76,000 reports in June 2016.
- AccountAbility, a U.K. group, has developed the AA1000 sustainability reporting principles that provide guidance on how to "establish systematic accountability processes and how to assure how the underlying systems, processes and competencies live up to the AA1000 Assurance Standard" (see Table 7.10)—see http://www.accountability.org.uk.
- Social Accountability International (SAI) has developed SA8000, a "comprehensive and flexible system for managing ethical workplace conditions throughout global supply chains," and SAI, a system for auditing SA8000 performance as well as an auditor certification system—see http://www.sa-intl.org.

TABLE 7.10 AA1000 Accountability Assurance Standard Summary

Purpose, Sustainability Reporting and Assurance:

- The AA1000 Assurance Standard is a generally applicable standard for assessing, attesting to, and strengthening the credibility and quality of a reporting organizations' sustainability reporting, and its underlying processes, systems and competencies. It provides guidance on key elements of the assurance process (is a standard guiding the audit of sustainability reporting).
- The AA1000 Assurance Standard is primarily intended for use by assurance providers in guiding the manner in which their assurance assignments are designed and implemented.
- Assurance should provide confidence in the report's underlying information to the reporting organization's stakeholders, particularly the direct users of the report.

Assurance of sustainability reporting prepared in accordance with generally accepted standards:

- The AA1000 Assurance Standard supports assurance (whether made public or not) of reporting that adheres to specific standards and guidelines, and is customised by the reporting organization. It is specifically designed to be consistent with, and to enhance, the Global Reporting Initiative Sustainability Reporting Guidelines, as well as other related standards.

Commitment by reporting organizations:

- Reporting organizations commit to (1) identify and understand their environment, (2) respond to their stakeholders' aspirations, and (3) provide an account to their stakeholders regarding the organization's decisions, actions and impacts.

Assurance principles:

- Materiality: the assurance provider must evaluate if the report contain all the important information about the reporting organization's sustainability performance required by the organization's stakeholders for making informed judgements, decisions and actions.
- Completeness: the assurance provider must evaluate the extent to which the reporting organization has not omitted any material aspects of its performance.
- Responsiveness: the assurance provider must evaluate whether the reporting organization has responded to stakeholders' concerns, policies, and relevant standards; and adequately communicated these responses in the report.

Evidence (supporting the reported figures and disclosures):

- The assurance provider must evaluate whether the reporting organization has provided adequate evidence to support the information contained in the report.

Assurance statement (i.e., auditor's opinion):

- The assurance statement should address the credibility of the report and the underlying systems, processes, and competencies that deliver the relevant information, and underpin the reporting organization's performance.
- Elements of the assurance statement (i.e., auditor's report): statement on use of AA1000; description of work performed; conclusion on the quality of the report and; underlying organizational processes, systems, and competencies; Additional comments if necessary.

Assurance provider standards (i.e., auditor's independence and competencies):

- The credibility of a report's assurance relies on the assurance provider's competencies, independence, and impartiality.
  - The assurance provider should be independent of the reporting organization and impartial with respect to the organization's stakeholders. Any interests that detract from this independence and impartiality need to be transparently declared by the assurance provider.
  - The assurance provider must be impartial in its dealings with the reporting organization's stakeholders.
  - Assurance providers and the reporting organization must ensure that the individuals involved in any specific assurance process are demonstrably competent.
  - The organizations through which individuals provide assurance must be able to demonstrate adequate institutional competencies.

Source: A full version of the AA1000 Assurance Standard, 2008, is downloadable from http://www.accountability.org/images/content/0/5/056/AA1000AS%202008.pdf.

The G4, UN Compact, and AA1000 are particularly promising frameworks.

Public reports are becoming more common. Reporting ethical performance can do the following:

- Heighten awareness of ethical issues within an organization
- Provide encouragement for employees to adhere to ethical objectives

- Inform external stakeholders
- Enhance the image of the company

Internal reporting of ethical performance can take several forms. Newsletters can provide full or partial reports. They can also recognize exemplary behavior by employees. Other internal reporting systems could include charts or progress reports on bulletin boards, partial or full reports as stand-alone documents, and verbal or video reports by senior management. Written reports can be prepared by internal staff and certified by external agents, such as auditors, professors, or editors of ethics publications. Alternatively, reports can be prepared entirely by individuals independent of the corporation. Several organizations, including the Council on Economic Priorities Accreditation Agency (CEPAA) in New York and EthicScan Canada in Toronto, train auditors to review CSR/CEP activity, and large public accounting firms offer related services, including Ethics and Integrity (KPMG), Reputational Assurance (PricewaterhouseCoopers), Sustainability Services (EY), and Sustainability (Deloitte). Details are available on each organization's website.

Large corporations are releasing ethical performance reports to the public with greater frequency on a continuing basis. Such reports may be a few paragraphs in the annual report and may or may not be specifically identified as ethical performance reports or, more recently, as sustainability reports. For example, when Apple Inc., along with other computer and cellphone manufacturers, was questioned about whether raw materials in its components were "conflict-free,"[42] Apple submitted itself to an independent audit by the Fair Labor Association (FLA)[43]—the first technology company to do so. Apple now conducts its own audits of its suppliers (640 in 2015), which were reported on in the *Apple Supplier Responsibility: 2016 Progress Report*.[44]

Additional examples of interesting, useful reports include the following:

- Microsoft 2015 Corporate Citizenship Report; https://www.microsoft.com/about/csr/transparencyhub/citizenship-reporting
- Suncor—2015 Report on Sustainability; http://sustainability.suncor.com/2015/en/default.aspx
- Philips—2015 Report on Sustainability; https://www.annualreport.philips.com/#!/sustainability-statements
- Telus—2015 Sustainability Report, formerly the CSR Report, now follows the GRI definition of CSR; https://sustainability.telus.com/en

It is worth noting that senior management may not support public reporting, especially if the results to be reported are unfavorable or if the possibility of legal action is significant. This is, however, an evolving area. Stakeholders are becoming increasingly interested in ethical performance, and leading companies are responding. Organizations are recognizing that it can be to their benefit to report even when the results are unfavorable. Even if unfavorable results are not initially reported (which may be considered unethical), the motivation of improvement remains as a reason for corrective action to be taken because favorable results can then be reported in the future. *Environmental performance* reports, it should be noted, are mandatory disclosures in Europe.

---

[42] "Conflict minerals" are refined to become gold, tungsten, and tantalum but are mined under militia control in the Democratic Republic of Congo and neighboring countries. See, for example, Nicholas D. Kristof, "Death by Gadget," *New York Times*, June 26, 2010, accessed June 15, 2012, at http://www.nytimes.com/2010/06/27/opinion/27kristof.html?_r=1.

[43] Fair Labor Association, http://www.fairlabor.org.

[44] *Apple Supplier Responsibility: 2012 Progress Report*, http://www.apple.com/ca/supplier-responsibility/progress-report.

Finally, it is very important to recognize that *Integrated Reporting* is the newest area of development in Sustainability/CSR reporting and is well worth continuing attention. Born of the view that the multiplicity of reports for a single company was becoming too voluminous for investors and other stakeholders to analyze and understand, several groups from around the world (including regulators, investors, companies, standard setters, the accounting profession. nongovernmental organizations, and the GRI), joined forces to form the International Integrated Reporting Council (IIRC),[45] and designed a framework for an integrated or capstone report. That framework, the International Integrated Reporting Framework, was released in December 2013.[46] An integrated report is expected to contain key indicators of performance from detailed reports in the areas of financial, environmental, and social matters. It is expected not to remove the need for the detailed subject area reports but rather to provide a bird's-eye view of a corporation's performance and impacts on society. Details on the plans and assistance available through the IIRC can be found on the IIRC website at http://integratedreporting.org. Organizations are beginning to issue integrated reports, including some online, such as provided by PotashCorp's online *Integrated Reporting Centre.*[47]

RATINGS OF SUSTAINABILITY & CSR REPORTS There are many organizations that seek to rate or investigate specific issues and corporate sustainability or CSR reports,[48] and the time that management spends with each can be excessive. In order to make these interactions more manageable and to improve reports, the Global Initiative for Sustainability Ratings (CISR)[49] has been created with the mission

> to drive transparency and excellence in ESG research, ratings and indices to improve business performance and investment decision-making. GISR's strategy for advancing this mission is built on a four-pronged Center of Ratings Excellence (CORE) program.
>
> The GISR CORE encompasses four components:
>
> - **Framework**: including GISR's Principles for ratings excellence, and an associated Accreditation program to encourage transparency, rigor and usability,
> - **Hub**: A searchable online database of ESG ratings products enabling investors to make informed decisions on the ESG ratings and research best suited to their needs,
> - **Labs**: Cutting-edge research and development activities that create new knowledge and enhance the theory and practice of ratings, and
> - **Convenings**: In-person and online events to foster shared learning and dissemination of best practices among raters, investors, companies and other stakeholders.

The GISR's 12 principles involve both process and content issues as shown on the GISR website at http://ratesustainability.org/wp-content/uploads/2015/07/GISR_CORE_-Framework12Principles.pdf.

---

[45] Information on the IIRC can be found at http://integratedreporting.org/the-iirc-2.

[46] The International Integrated Reporting Framework can be downloaded from the IIRC website at http://integratedreporting.org/resource/international-ir-framework.

[47] PotashCorp's GRI *2012 Online Integrated Report*, http://www.potashcorp.com/irc/company/overview/ceo-letter.

[48] See, for example, CSRwire, http://www.csrwire.com/members.

[49] GISR website: http://ratesustainability.org/core.

Ratings of corporate performance can be performed for investors and corporations by investment research companies, including the following:

- EIRIS (http://www.eiris.org)
- GMI Ratings (http://www3.gmiratings.com)
- RobecoSAM (http://www.robecosam.com)
- Sustainalytics (http://www.sustainalytics.com)
- Vigeo (http://www.vigeo.com/csr-rating-agency/en/1-2-qui-sommes-nous-2)

There are also sustainability or CSR indices that are used by investors to aid in their investment decisions or to qualify companies to permit their shares to trade on specific stock exchanges, such as the following:

- **Jantzi Social Index**—a benchmarking stock index made up of sixty Canadian companies rated on environmental, social, and governance (ESG) criteria. Companies in the JSI are chosen by the Sustainalytics by criteria to meet broad ESG criteria, and *exclusionary* criteria—related to military weapons, nuclear power, and tobacco—that make associated companies ineligible for inclusion in the index.[50] Two companies have created mutual funds that include, with some alterations, the sixty companies that make up the index. These are Meritas Mutual Funds[51] in the Meritas Jantzi Social Index Fund and iShares (http://www.ishares.ca) in its iShares Jantzi Social Index® Fund, an Exchange Traded Fund.[52]
- **FTSE4Good Index Series**—benchmark and tradable indices of companies meeting "globally recognized corporate responsibility standards" (http://www.ftse.com/Indices/FTSE4Good_Index_Series/index.jsp). FTSE[53] traded companies that pass FTSE4-Good criteria[54]—corporate-responsibility criteria researched by the Ethical Investment Research Service (EIRIS) and partners—are grouped in eleven regional indices for "ESG investors."
- **Dow Jones Sustainability Indices**—benchmark indices for "best-in-class" companies chosen using economic, environmental, and social criteria across all industries (http://www.sustainability-indices.com/index.jsp). The objectives of the **Dow Jones Sustainability World Index**—one of several Dow Jones Sustainability Indexes—are to include "global sustainability leaders" based on a corporate sustainability assessment by RobecoSAM, a company whose focus is "sustainability investing." "The index represents the top 10% of the largest 2,500 companies in the S&P Global BMI based on long-term economic, environmental and social criteria."[55]
- **MSCI KLD 400 Social Index**—began as one of the first Social Reporting Indexes in 1990 as the Domini 400 Social Index. It rates the companies on several dimensions

[50] See Sustainalytics, *Jantzi Social Index Methodology Update*, 2012, http://www.sustainalytics.com/sites/default/files/jantzisocialindexmethodology-updatedseptember2012_revised2.pdf.

[51] Meritas Mutual Funds, now a part of OceanRock Investments Inc. See http://www.qtrade.ca/oceanrock/aboutus/about_meritas.jsp.

[52] Named iShares Jantzi Social Index Fund; see http://ca.ishares.com/product_info/fund/overview/XEN.htm.

[53] FTSE Group, originally formed by the Financial Times and the London Stock Exchange, is a registered company whose name, FTSE, is licensed by the London Stock Exchange to the FTSE Group.

[54] FTSE, "FTSE4Good Index Inclusion Criteria: Thematic Criteria and Scoring Framework," 2013, accessed November 27, 2013, at http://www.ftse.com/Indices/FTSE4Good_Index_Series/Downloads/FTSE4Good_Inclusion_all_copy_Aug2013.pdf.

[55] S&P Dow Jones Indices, McGraw-Hill Financial, *Fact Sheet*. "Dow Jones Sustainability World Index," October 2013, accessed November 27, 2013, at http://www.djindexes.com/mdsidx/downloads/fact_info/Dow_Jones_Sustainability_World_Index_Fact_Sheet.pdf.

of ESG performance, and the best-rated companies are used by investors to select their investments. In addition, several investment funds have been created by companies such as Blackrock (i.e., iShares MSCI KLD 400 Social ETF) to provide aggregations of the best-rated companies to invest in as mutual funds. For further information, see https://www.msci.com/resources/factsheets/index_fact_sheet/msci-kld-400-social-index.pdf.

Awards programs are another type of rating mechanism. There are several programs that announce the "best" sustainability or CSR performance annually or periodically, including the following:

- **Corporate Register Reporting Awards**—see http://www.corporateregister.com/crra
- **Chartered Professional Accountants of Canada**—see https://www.cpacanada.ca/en/connecting-and-news/awards/awards-of-excellence-in-corporate-reporting/winners/2015-winners/cpa-canada-honours-top-tier-corporate-reporting
- **Corporate Knights**—for an annual ranking of the 100 most sustainable companies in the world, see http://www.corporateknights.com/reports/global-100
- **Guardian Sustainable Business Awards**, an extensive annual award program, see https://www.theguardian.com/sustainable-business/gsb-awards
- **European CSR Awards,** offered by the Eurpoean Business Network for Corporate Social Responsibility, see http://www.csreurope.org/european-csr-awards

AUDIT ASSURANCE FOR SUSTAINABILITY & CSR REPORTS The spread of so-called audits of sustainability and CSR reports has been growing, particularly in Europe. European initiatives in environmental protection and through the ISO have had a driving influence on corporate behavior and have required public disclosure of environmental performance. As a result, many individuals and some large public accounting and other firms have become involved in attesting to the reports issued, as the following examples show:

- The Philips 2015 Report on Sustainability, mentioned above, was audited by KPMG NV in accordance with the Dutch Standard 3810N: "Assurance engagements relating to sustainability reports," which is a specified standard under the International Standard on Assurance Engagements (ISAE) 3000: "Assurance Engagements other than Audits or Reviews of Historical Financial Information." The KPMG audit report is available at https://www.annualreport.philips.com/#!/independent-assurance-report.
- Cisco has published a 2014 CSR Report in which it utilizes internal and external auditors to provide assurance on reported findings for its supply chain as it states on its website at http://www.cisco.com/assets/csr/pdf/CSR_Report_2014.pdf.
- The Telus Sustainability Report 2015 was audited by Deloitte LLP and the Assurance letter is available at https://sustainability.telus.com/en/about/assurance/. It concludes that:

  "Based on our work described in the Scope of Our Work section above, nothing has come to our attention that causes us to believe that the subject matter are not presented fairly, in all material respects, in accordance with the relevant criteria."

Independent audits of labor practices in undeveloped and developing countries have become rather common for retailers and their manufacturers whose products come significantly from such sources, such as Nike, Adidas, and Umbro. Organizations such as the FLA also follow and report on the labor practices of supply chains for these companies[56] and provide certifications when called on.[57] Care should be taken when relying on certifications because auditing standards have not yet become generally accepted for this kind of reporting and may provide comment on adherence to reporting principles (i.e., from AA1000) rather on the specific quality of the disclosure. Increasingly, however, national and international accounting bodies, such as the International Federation of Accountants,[58] and other organizations, such as CEPAA and AccountAbility, are focusing on the need for appropriate auditing standards, including standards for the content of audit reports and certifications. In addition, the next phase of ISO guidance may well push currently registered firms beyond documentation of systems to the reporting and audit levels.

It is possible for a corporation to have company personnel audit CSR reports. Internal audit staff may be used, as may managers from other divisions of a company. This managerial audit approach was used by Dow Corning and was lionized in Harvard Business School cases prior to the unfortunate breast implant scandal. It should be pointed out that the chairman of the Conduct Committee of Dow Corning remained convinced of the worth of the company's ethics audit program but acknowledged that audit improvements were warranted.[59]

CONCLUDING THOUGHTS The strategic accountability of corporations to stakeholders has become so evident and accepted that it would be shortsighted for an organization not to develop an effective concept of corporate citizenship and an effective program of corporate social responsibility. They will greatly facilitate better management of an organization's ethical culture and performance and the degree of support garnered from stakeholder groups. More important, providing guidance to employees and others about the corporation's intended CSR or corporate citizenship expectations will reduce the ethics risks and enable the taking of ethics opportunities in an orderly way.[60]

WORKPLACE ETHICS

OVERVIEW—BALANCE OF INTERESTS & TRENDS Expectations for ethical behavior in workplaces have changed on several dimensions. For example, actions taken can no longer satisfy just the business owners' interests—actions must not only consider employees' interests but also generally rank employees' interests as high as or higher than the employers'. The balance of consideration has definitely moved from an employer-interest-only model to an employee-and-employer-interest model. Employers can no longer do whatever they want in employee matters.

---

[56] See, for example, http://www.fairlabor.org/affiliate/adidas-group.

[57] See, for example, http://www.fairlabor.org/affiliate/nike-inc.

[58] International Federation of Accountants, *Investor Demand for Environmental, Social, and Governance Disclosures: Implications for Professional Accountants in Business*, February 6, 2012, accessed June 3, 2012, at http://www.ifac.org/publications-resources/investor-demand-environmental-social-and-governance-disclosures.

[59] See, for example, the quotation of the chairman of the Conduct Committee of Dow Corning in the ethics case "Dow Corning Silicone Breast Implants Case" in Chapter 5.

[60] Parts of this segment on CSR and corporate citizenship are reprinted with permission from L. J. Brooks and D. Selley, *Ethics and Governance: Developing and Maintaining an Ethical Corporate Culture*, 3rd ed. (Toronto: Canadian Centre for Ethics and Corporate Policy, 2008).

As will be discussed below, consider the following:

- Employees cannot be fired based on an emotional whim or personal bias—the reason must be specifically related to the individual's inability to do the job.
- Employees cannot be hired based or even questioned on family status, religion, sexual preference, and several other legally protected subjects—they must be hired based on their ability to do the jobs in question.
- Sexual discrimination cases are usually decided based on what the person receiving the unwanted attention believes to be the case rather than on what the person (often a manager or owner) providing the unwanted attention believes should be reasonable. Furthermore, the employer is held responsible for failing to provide a harassment-free workplace.
- Employers are expected to observe legal statutes or regulations that provide protection for employees from several frequently encountered situations, including lack of privacy and civility.

Changes in workplace ethics expectations have come about because of public sensitivity and stakeholder pressure on employers and regulators for more responsible corporate behavior. Regulations have changed, and companies have introduced governance procedures including codes of conduct to comply or go beyond legal requirements to moderate risks involved in misbehavior and/or to be and appear to be as responsible as or more so than their competitors. Frequently their reputations—the key to recruiting and retaining excellent workers—depend on how responsive they are to employee rights and concerns. It is also said the employees often believe the way a company treats them is their cue to how ethical the company is and how they should treat other stakeholders, thus determining how ethical the company is overall.

During this process on change, several employee interests or rights have strengthened relative to employers rights, including the following:

- Ability to exercise one's conscience—for example, not to pollute, not to risk an employee's health or safety or that of others, and to speak out when the truth is being distorted
- Respect for employee privacy and dignity, including the provision of a civil work environment
- Fair treatment
- Healthy and safe work environment
- Civil work environment

While executives and managers generally may be aware of these changes, they may not be fully cognizant of the degree or extent of change or of specific issues involved. Consequently, prudent risk management requires continuous training and reinforcement through governance mechanisms to ensure appropriate treatment of employees and the protection or enhancement of the firm's reputation.

Specifically, it is appropriate for businesspeople to have an appreciation of the major ethical themes and issues that have emerged or are emerging in regard to the conduct of employees in North American workplaces. The comments that follow are not intended to provide an exhaustive review, but they will raise awareness of the issues involved and provide some guidance, including when to seek more informed advice.

EMPLOYEE RIGHTS Since the early 1970s, there has been an increasing awareness that the rights of individual workers were worthy of more respect relative to the rights of the employer than had been the case before. For example, the rights of an employer have changed; the employer can no longer order his or her employees to pollute, risk their health or safety or that of others, or say nothing when the truth was being distorted. Some of the changed rights have become protected by legislation, whereas others have been influenced by common law cases, union contracts, and corporate practices that have been sensitive to stakeholder pressures.

Table 7.11 identifies those employee themes in North America that have led to new expectations by employees.

PRIVACY & DIGNITY INCLUDING THE PROVISION OF A CIVIL WORK ENVIRONMENT The right of an employer to search the person of a North American employee, to access any personal information desired, or to search any property has become significantly curtailed. North American society now endorses the position that an *individual's personal rights are more important than those of an employer, unless it can be shown that, in a particular circumstance, the employer's interest is reasonable, legitimate, and morally acceptable.* For example, in most locales, it is not acceptable to place a surveillance camera in a washroom unless there is a threat to life and health, such as through violent attacks or drug dealing. Even in these cases, outside legal authorities should be consulted before the surveillance, and in some cases notification of the intent to use a camera may be called for.

It should be noted, however, that simply notifying workers should not be taken to imply that they had consented to the procedure. Specific conditions must be met before the courts will agree that proper procedures have been followed. In fact, workers must be allowed what is called *informed consent*, wherein they have time to deliberate, have a free choice among reasonable alternatives, and have adequate information to understand the

TABLE 7.11 Employee Rights Themes in North America

Privacy and dignity of person, personal information and property:

- Boundaries of personal rights, employers rights and right of the public
- Proper procedures: notification and consent
- Testing for substance abuse
- Harassment, sexual and otherwise
- Civil work environment

Fair treatment:

- Discrimination: age, race, sex, employment, pay
- Fair policies
- Is equal treatment fair?

Healthy and safe work environment

- Expectations: reasonability right to know, stress, family life, productivity
- Quality-of-life concerns: smoking, health
- Family-friendly workplaces

Ability to exercise conscience

- Blind loyalty
- Whistleblowing

Trust—the key to leadership, innovation, loyalty, and performance—depends on ethics

- Operations: downsizing, contingent workforce

problem and options. In addition, the choice must be one that the courts consider possible to agree to make. An employee, for example, cannot bargain away his or her right to life or to take on extremely serious health risks. Legal advice is vital before action is taken.

Testing for substance abuse is a related area in which North American society has been reluctant to accept invasion of privacy without compelling reason, usually involving the life and health of coworkers or others. In fact, absent those safety concerns, random drug testing is illegal in many jurisdictions. In the case of airplane pilots, for example, random drug testing has long been accepted; it was approved by the U.S. Supreme Court in the late 1990s.

In addition, drug testing has been considered relatively inaccurate when measured against the potential harm done to the falsely accused so that discrete, repeat testing is desirable if an initial test is positive before any accusations are made. Confidentiality should be maintained throughout this time period if at all possible. There have been some testing programs for office workers, but several have been struck down by the courts as being unreasonable. For example, the Exxon program of random testing (started in response to the *Exxon Valdez* shipwreck; see the ethics case "The *Exxon Valdez*" at the end of this chapter) was considered to be too unreasonable because it resulted in a reassignment/suspension from the employee's position for up to seven years. The Toronto-Dominion Bank program for new recruits—if offered a job, a positive mandatory substance abuse test would lead to a required remediation program from which a cured person could have the job—was considered not to be sufficiently justified by the bank's desire to make sure that its employees would protect customer's assets properly to warrant allowing the personal intrusion involved.

It appears, however, that the stigma associated with drug and alcohol testing programs can be circumvented. Some trucking companies achieve the same ends (protection of the public and their assets) by requiring their drivers to score well on computer games (which feature hand–eye coordination) before they will be given their truck keys. Society does not regard such testing as sufficient invasion of privacy to object to its use. This is very important because drug testing is relatively poor at measuring current impairment quickly due to the lag in diagnosis and individual impact differentials, so impaired high-risk operators, such as truckers, are much more likely to be prevented from doing harm by failing scores on computer games.

Harassment is, of course, objectionable not only on grounds of dignity and privacy but also on grounds of fairness. Definitions of harassment vary depending on the locale, but the trend is toward more stringent tests than most businesspeople or professionals initially contemplate. *Harassment can be defined as any improper behavior directed at you that you find offensive and that the other person knew or ought reasonably to have known would be unwelcome.* Note that the test is not what the person doing the harassment thought about the act—the important test is what the offended party thought and whether the local authorities think it is reasonable behavior. Usually, they side with the offended person. It is therefore imperative if an employee alleges harassment that the claim be investigated immediately and discreetly. If the claim is justified, then the perpetrator should be warned (or dismissed if already warned) and dismissed subject to the due process rules of the company involved. If prompt action is not taken, the manager receiving the complaint and the company can be subject to legal proceedings for failing to provide a harassment-free workplace. In fact, if a traveling salesperson or visiting auditor is harassed, his or her organization must contact the management of the offending company and see that appropriate action is taken; otherwise, the manager and company of the complainant can be subject to legal proceedings. In addition to the need for quick action in the case of harassment and workplace violence, direct liability may follow for directors and management if the company does not have adequate training and compliance programs in place.

Leading-edge firms have begun to document the need to extend respect for privacy and dignity to the provision of a civil work environment. "Civil conduct includes:

- Treating others with dignity, courtesy, respect, politeness, and consideration.
- Speaking in tones of voice that are appropriate for the circumstances.
- Being respectful of others' right to express their views, even if you disagree.
- Managing conflict with others in a respectful way rather than a confrontational way."[61]

Organizations are more concerned with a pattern of uncivil behavior rather than an isolated act or two. Behavior that is considered uncivil would include the following:

- Shouting
- Profanity, abusive, aggressive, or violent language directed at an individual or individuals
- Using props suggestive of violence
- Slamming doors
- Throwing objects
- Humiliating, degrading, demeaning, belittling, insulting, frightening, or intimidating another person
- Distributing comments about an individual, whether verbally or in writing, including online, that are unjustified and are likely to have a negative impact on the individual if he or she were to see them
- Telling inappropriate jokes[62]

FAIR TREATMENT Discrimination is considered to be unethical and is considered illegal if it involves age, race, gender, and sexual preference. In addition, it is generally held that there should be equal opportunity for employment and equal pay for equal work, particularly for women and minorities. Many leading-edge companies strive to hire sufficient representation into their workforce so that it reflects the population that they are operating in. "Breaking the glass ceiling" is a phrase that is used to describe overcoming the barrier women face to promotion within their organizations, and some firms have found a competitive advantage by removing barriers and creating a level playing field for women and men. The Bank of Montreal, for example, found that many outstanding women managers applied for jobs when the bank did so, thus leaving the rest of the Canadian banks facing a dearth of promotable women.

Workers in North America believe that they are entitled to fair policies. These would include fair wages, fair hours, fair consideration for promotion, downsizing, and a fair hearing on all matters. If dismissal is required, then employees expect that it will be according to appropriate or due process, including adequate notice or pay in lieu of notice. Unjust dismissals are those that do not follow fair due processes, and reinstatement, remedial payments, and/or fines can result.

---

[61] See University of Toronto, *Human Resources Guideline on Civil Conduct*, http://www.hrandequity.utoronto.ca/Asset952.aspx?method=1.

[62] Ibid.

It should be noted that people with disabilities are frequently accorded more than an equal chance for employment. This treatment is more than fair, and it is considered ethical in view of their disabilities.[63]

In regard to hiring and firing decisions, the key principle is that decisions must be based on a person's ability to do the job. *Any other questions may produce lawsuits for discrimination even if they were innocently intended.* Consequently, when hiring, questions that are not related to a person's ability to do the job should be avoided, including those on the following:

- Marital status
- National origin and race
- Age
- Religion
- Disabilities (unless one is evident or disclosed, and then it is appropriate to ask how he or she could perform certain duties inherent in the job)
- Arrests, unless there is a demonstrated business necessity involved
- Financial condition, unless there is direct relevance to the job
- Personal questions[64]

HEALTHY & SAFE WORK ENVIRONMENT The balance between the rights of workers and owners has shifted to the point that it is considered ethical for workers to expect that their health and safety will not be unreasonably compromised. They must know what the risks are in advance, and many jurisdictions have created right-to-know laws to ensure that organizations make information on hazardous substances, processes, and related treatments readily accessible.

Concern is presently being expressed over extending these arguments to the less tangible areas of excessive stress in terms of hours of overtime expected, extreme levels of productivity, and degradation of family life. No guidelines have emerged as yet, but the pressure for them in these areas will grow, so a watch should be kept for future developments in this regard.

It is apparent that responsible companies are showing respect for the preferences of their workers before they are forced to do so by changing regulations. Smoke-free workplace areas are a case in point. In addition, other companies are recognizing the need for fitness and recreation by establishing centers for theses on-site. The desire to improve the family friendliness of workplaces has led to the provision of on-site day care for children of employees, the institution of flexible work hours, and other similar arrangements.

A survey of professional accountants who were thirty-five years and younger revealed that after interesting work, the most important factor in attracting and retaining employees is offering them a work/life balance. Not only must employers give employees the opportunity to take advantage of a work/life balance, but they must also make a shift in their organizational culture. They should not make employees feel guilty about not working excessive hours or penalize them through their performance evaluations.[65]

---

[63] A discussion of justice as fairness is also provided in Chapter 3.

[64] For an excellent elaboration on these issues, see, for example, Shawn Smith, "Illegal Job Interview Questions," http://www.sideroad.com/Human_Resources/illegal-job-interview_questions.html.

[65] "The Price of Happiness," *CAmagazine*, September 2006, http://www.camagazine.com/archives/print-edition/2006/sept/upfront/camagazine8265.aspx.

ABILITY TO EXERCISE ONE'S CONSCIENCE As noted elsewhere, the argument that a worker just did what he or she was ordered to do (i.e., acted with *blind loyalty*) will no longer provide the worker with protection in many jurisdictions, so the worker should exercise his or her own conscience. The concept of blind loyalty is not one that many employees would be comfortable with, in any case. They would prefer to bring their concerns forward and speak out against pollution or other misdeeds, but they are frequently prevented from doing so by their caution in exposing themselves to the wrath of their coworkers or managers.

Whistleblowing, although it could contribute to a more ethical organization, is nonetheless something most North Americans were taught not to do when they were growing up, and a stigma continues to be attached to it. To encourage whistleblowers to come forward within the organization rather than have them report their concerns outside the enterprise, many corporations are creating a whistleblower protection program. In these programs, an inquiry or allegation is handled by an individual who has credibility with employees to undertake a speedy, fair investigation without revealing the name of the inquirer. If it becomes necessary for the inquirer to testify against the accused, then the inquirer is asked to do so and may decline. Reports of inquiries received are made on an aggregate basis, without revealing the names of the whistleblowers. Some companies are calling these services ethics inquiry services rather than more pejorative terms, such as a "hotline" or "whistleblowing" service.

There are also a growing number of statutes that seek to protect whistleblowers. Therefore, and because secrets almost always become public, it would be wise for organizations to facilitate the exercise of employee conscience within the organization, where appropriate action can be taken without ruining the company's reputation. In order to facilitate corporate whistleblowing programs, many law firms, specialized consultancies, and corporations are now offering telephone and/or email hotlines. Details on whistleblower programs are available from KPMG's Integrity Survey.[66]

TRUST & ITS IMPORTANCE Only recently have researchers begun to document what farsighted owners and managers have known for some time. As noted earlier, the ethics of an organization are directly related to how leaders are perceived, to whether there is sufficient trust for people to share ideas without fear of losing jobs or the respect of their coworkers and managers, and to whether they believe that the organization is worthy of loyalty and hard work (Brooks 2000). In our current North American workplaces, it is increasingly unlikely that employees and managers will be willing to follow the instructions of an untrustworthy or unethical leader if they have any choice. Workers are not willing to contribute to innovation if they fear retribution or erosion of their position in some form, and they may not take the initiative on behalf of the company. Therefore, the organization will find that it may fall behind competitors whose employees trust the company and its leaders.

If employees have sufficient trust in their situation, they will participate wholeheartedly in restructuring sessions (this has been called a process of *ethical renewal*) that even involve downsizing and may accept the necessity of shared work assignments or part-time work contracts with greater understanding (this creates what is called a *contingent workforce*). To maintain the trust necessary for these steps, an organization would have to be prepared to make trustable commitments to recall employees to full-time status when possible or to provide fair termination or contracting arrangements. Continuation of benefits could be one such way of maintaining trust with a contingent workforce.

---

[66] KPMG Forensic, *Integrity Survey*.

OVERALL BENEFIT Many experts and successful practitioners subscribe to the belief that *the way employees view their own treatment by the company determines what the employees think about their company's ethics program.* Consequently, if an organization wants employees to employ a set of corporate ethical values, the workers must be convinced that the organization really means what it says, and there must be a level of trust that permits this belief to flourish. Treating employees properly is not only ethical; it is essential to them carrying out the organization's ethics program and to achieving its strategic objectives.

WHISTLEBLOWER PROGRAMS & ETHICS INQUIRY SERVICES

Whistleblower encouragement and protection programs, and ethics inquiry services are usually combined because they often service the same people. Whether they are called an "ethics hotline" or an "ethics inquiry service" or some other name, they are essential in modern organizations for several reasons. First, these programs make it possible for employees to be able to exercise their conscience as described in the previous section. Second, these programs reinforce an organization's ethics objectives and provide a necessary element of the code and ethics program put in place to provide appropriate guidance to executives, managers, employees, and agents. Third, because member of boards of directors, executives, and managers cannot be constantly in contact with all employees and agents, they must rely on information systems to bring them information on current performance and problems. Whistleblower programs and ethics inquiry services, properly installed, can act as "fail-safe" information systems to protect the directors, personnel, and the company from reputational and functional damage from unethical acts.

It is very easy to undermine an ethics program by failing to provide a mechanism for inquiry or consultation. The concepts included in a code of ethics or conduct are frequently complex and unfamiliar. Employees therefore often have questions about their applicability and need someone to consult. If answers are not available, ethics problems will probably remain unreported.

Unfortunately, employees may realize that something is wrong but are afraid to ask about it or to bring the wrongdoing to the notice of company officials. In many cultures, it is not considered appropriate to tell or to snitch on someone. Consequences of doing so can involve hostility from fellow employees and retribution from the person reported on or managers who are caught up in the process who may have known about the problem but took no action or who are friends of the accused. In any of these cases, the fallout for the person making the inquiry or report can be quite unpleasant, involving loss of merit, promotion, and often their jobs.

This negative reaction to doing what is right and raising issues an ethical company would want to know about is simply not in the interest of the individuals or the company (or particularly the Board of Directors) involved. Waiting until the company's culture changes to support ethical inquiries is not a sound prospect. Consequently, leading corporations are setting up ethics inquiry services in which inquiries are encouraged and kept confidential. When unethical acts are reported, they are quickly and fairly investigated. The reporter's name is kept confidential unless and until the matter has to go to court. Even then, the reporting individual is asked if he or she will permit his or her name to be used. Quarterly or annual reports of inquiries and follow-ups are made to very senior officers and to a subcommittee of the Board of Directors without revealing the names of the reporting individuals. These practices are essential to allay the often well-founded fears of the inquirers and reporters and the nightmares of senior officers and directors.

The findings of the Ethics Resource Center's 2011 National Business Ethics Survey, *Workplace Ethics in Transition*,[67] reinforce these comments and provide interesting support for the development of ethical corporate cultures and reporting mechanisms. The U.S. survey reports the following:

- The percentage of employees who witnessed misconduct at work fell to a new low of 45%. That compares to 49% in 2009 and is well down from the record high of 55% in 2007.
- Those who reported the bad behavior they saw reached a record high of 65%, up from 63% two years earlier and twelve percentage points higher than the record low of 53% in 2005.
- Retaliation against employee whistleblowers rose sharply. More than one in five employees (22%) who reported misconduct say they experienced some form of retaliation in return. That compares to 12% who experienced retaliation in 2007 and 15% in 2009.
- The percentage of employees who perceived pressure to compromise standards in order to do their jobs climbed five points to 13%, just shy of the all-time high of 14% in 2000.
- The share of companies with weak ethics cultures also climbed to near-record levels at 42%, up from 35% two years ago.

These ethics inquiry systems and protected whistleblower programs are often under the jurisdiction of the organization's ethics officer, ombudsperson, human resources office, or internal audit or legal department. Care should be taken not to send signals that would turn away employees from using the service. In this regard, locating the service within an internal audit department or legal department is not as attractive as locating it within a human resources department or as a stand-alone unit. A hotline to an undisclosed or third-party destination may also be suspect depending on the perception of its efficacy, trustworthiness, and credibility. Over 50% of the inquiries received by existing services are seeking information on personnel policies and practices, so basing the inquiry system in a human resource related or stand-alone unit that specializes in these matters is recommended.[68] While this may give rise to conflicts of interests in regard to poor human resource activities or policies, experience has shown this to be relatively rare compared to the volume of information-seeking calls.

Modern organizations cannot develop and maintain a successful ethics program without introducing some form of ethics inquiry service and a whistleblower encouragement and protection program. Without these essential services, organizations and their executives and boards of directors will continue to be exposed to significant ethical and operational risks.

FRAUD & WHITE-COLLAR CRIME

One of the challenges facing all organizations is the prospect of unethical employees who commit acts of fraud and white-collar crime. Executives are expected to ensure that they

---

[67] Page 12 of the Executive Summary report is downloadable from http://www.ethics.org/nbes.

[68] For further information, see, for example, Leonard J. Brooks, "Whistleblowers—Learn to Love Them!," *Canadian Business Review*, Summer 1993, 19–21.

take all reasonable steps to guide, influence, and control employees who might be inclined to become involved, and external auditors are expected to be alert for potential problems. Experience has suggested that an understanding of the circumstances leading to and enabling fraud and white-collar crime—and the motivation for it—provides a useful foundation for preventive measures. In order to provide that understanding, an analysis is offered of the motivation of a white-collar fraudster, Walt Pavlo, who was a star at MCI and a key enabler of a $6 million fraud at MCI. His story is told in the ethics case "Manipulation of MCI's Allowance for Doubtful Accounts" at the end of Chapter 5 and in the ethics case "Walt Pavlo's MCI Scams/Frauds" at the end of this chapter.

WALT PAVLO'S MOTIVATION & RATIONALE FOR FRAUD AS MCI'S STAR[69] Investigative and forensic accountants use a helpful framework—The Fraud Triangle[70] and its extension, The Fraud Diamond[71]—to identify potential fraudsters and situations that have potential for fraud. As shown in Figure 7.2, potential for fraud is said to be a function of the presence of three factors: *need*—financial or otherwise; *opportunity*—poor controls or overaggressive culture; and the willingness and ability to *rationalize* the fraudulent act. The Fraud Diamond adds a fourth factor, *capability* or *knowledge*.

Analysis of these factors can be facilitated by using the additional frameworks of Maslow's Hierarchy of Needs[72] and Heath's Seven Rationalizations of Unethical Behavior,[73] which are discussed later. The facts are gleaned from Walt Pavlo's book *Stolen without a Gun*[74] about his frauds on MCI and its customers.

WALT PAVLO STORY—BRIEF VERSION Walt Pavlo joined MCI in 1992 when MCI was a large U.S. telecommunications company (MCI is now a subsidiary of Verizon Communications, Inc.) and rapidly became second in command at the company's finance or long-distance collections unit. Walt left MCI in 1996 and ultimately resigned in early 1997. During the four years and just afterward, he participated in several frauds on MCI and on customers who were dealing with MCI. These frauds are detailed in the two cases noted earlier.

Walt was found out and, in January 2001, pleaded guilty to obstruction of justice, money laundering, and wire fraud. He was sentenced to forty-one months in prison and ordered to pay over $5.7 million in restitution to MCI, AT&T, and BTI. In addition, the banks won a $5.5 million judgment against him. Walt ultimately served twenty-four months in a federal prison and was released in 2003. The outcome was particularly hard on his two sons and his wife, who divorced him in 2003.

Walt was a great-looking blonde, athletic, and an MBA graduate and had a young wife and two young sons. He had the capacity to become a star at MCI. So what happened? What motivated Walt to become involved in fraudulent behavior, and how did he rationalize the actions he took?

---

[69] All details used in this case are taken from Walter Pavlo Jr. and Neil Weinberg, *Stolen without a Gun: Confessions from Inside History's Biggest Accounting Fraud—The Collapse of MCI WorldCom* (Tampa, FL: Etika Books LLC, 2007).

[70] Fraud Triangle—see CICA Handbook Section 5135 or the new CAS 240; see also W. S. Albrecht, C. C. Albrecht, and C. O. Albrecht, *Fraud Examination*, 2nd ed. (Mason, OH: Thomson South-Western, 2006), 31.

[71] David T. Wells and Dana R. Hermanson, "The Fraud Diamond," *The CPA Journal*, December 2004, 38–42.

[72] "The Hierarchy of Needs," from A. H. Maslow, "A Theory of Human Motivation," *Psychological Review* 50 (1943): 394–95, as reprinted in Deborah C. Stephens, ed., *The Maslow Business Reader* (New York: Wiley, 2000), 3–4.

[73] Joseph Heath, "7 Neutralization/Rationalization Techniques," speech at the Centre for Ethics at the University of Toronto, April 9, 2007.

[74] Ibid.

UNDERSTANDING FRAUDSTER MOTIVATION—MASLOW'S HIERARCHY OF NEEDS Like many newly graduated MBAs, Walt had a super strong drive to succeed. He wanted to fulfill his dreams:

- To prove himself to his mother and father and to his wife and her well-off family
- To earn enough remuneration to live comfortably and have enough for some indulgences
- To be recognized for his contributions at work, and be paid what he thought he was worth and have job security
- To be respected by and friendly with his boss, Ralph McCumber, a former military man

These desires led Walt to behave in ways he thought would lead to his success, including the following:

- Obeying orders unquestioningly, as if he was in a military culture,[75] such as by "making his numbers" by any means possible, including misrepresentation of the condition of bad debts through lapping and worse.
- Behaving ultra-aggressively and, even though some actions were distasteful, come in the next day ready to "bite the heads off chickens."
- Setting aside company policy, such as the "zero-tolerance" policy for allowing customer credit positions to deteriorate, to which company executives paid lip service.
- Creating apparently helpful mechanisms without the knowledge of his boss and for which he did not disclose the risks. An example of this is the Rapid Advance "factoring" program to speed up collections, where Walt signed an unauthorized guaranty of bank loans on behalf of his company.
- Consorting with shady individuals to rip off his company and its customers.
- Emulating his boss in terms of approaches for encouraging his subordinates and in encouraging them "not to worry about…"
- Once on the slippery slope,[76] ultimately succumbing to the "blinding powers of desperation and greed."

Walt's desires fit neatly into Maslow's Hierarchy of Needs,[77] which is shown in Figure 7.6. Maslow asserted that an individual's needs could be categorized and would be responded to in priority from the bottom of the pyramid. Later researchers[78] disagreed with this bottom-up priority sequence, citing many instances where needs at the top of the pyramid exerted a stronger influence than those at the bottom. Nonetheless, Maslow's categorization is widely respected and useful for understanding human needs and can be applied to the understanding the motivation of white-collar criminals and fraudsters.

---

[75] At one point when Ralph and Walt were discussing how to "whitewash" a $55 million debt, McCumber barked, "Don't tell me what I can and can't do! Orders are orders. You've got yours." *Stolen without a Gun*, 92.

[76] The term "slippery slope" refers to a situation in which a person starts by doing something slightly unethical but follows with a subsequent acts of growing significance, only to find that he or she must continue on to more highly unethical acts to cover up the earlier ones or because someone else who knows of the earlier transgressions threatens to reveal them in order to coerce further unethical or illegal acts.

[77] Maslow, "The Hierarchy of Needs."

[78] See discussion in A. Wahba and L. Bridgewell, "Maslow Reconsidered: A Review of Research on the Need Hierarchy Theory," *Organizational Behavior and Human Performance* 15: 212–40.

FIGURE 7.6 Maslow's Hierarchy of Needs

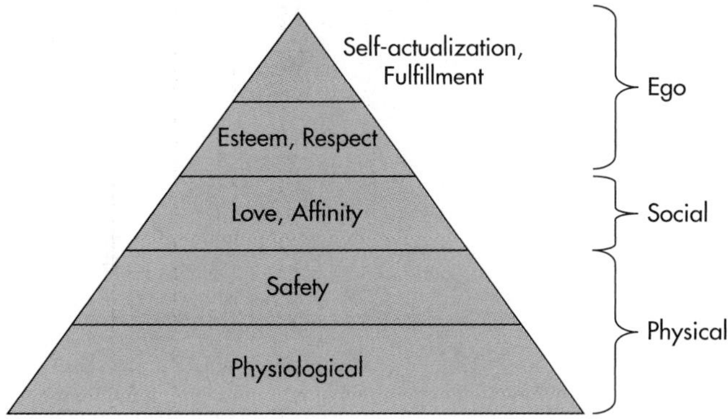

Walt's desires show that he was motivated by the need for money to maintain his family (a *physiological need*), and by job security (a *safety need*). In addition, he wanted to earn the respect of his boss and other MCI employees and higher-ups. When it came time to create the Rapid Advance factoring program, he signed a guaranty for the financing bank without advising his superiors because he wanted to feel like he was really contributing—he wanted to feel the joy of *fulfillment or self-actualization.* His bosses certainly played on Walt's need for *affinity*—to be seen as a worthy employee, one who was "making his numbers" or "biting the heads off chickens." Walt was subject to the influence of needs at all levels. Only he can say which category or which level—*ego*, *social*, or *physical needs*—played the dominant role. It is safe to say, however, that modern management can and will use all levels to motivate employees and that both management and the individual employee should understand the vulnerabilities involved.

UNDERSTANDING THE RATIONALIZATION OF FRAUD—HEATH'S SEVEN RATIONALIZATIONS According to Joseph Heath, the seven rationalizations identified in Table 7.12 are customarily used to justify unethical behavior.

Walt Pavlo's behavior conforms to Heath's set of seven rationalizations. In his book, Walt explains that he is just taking orders for the accounting chicanery he leads and that someone else at a higher pay grade is responsible for determining whether the actions involved are ethical. Similarly, when considering the monies he siphons off, he states that "you can't steal, what they're not going to get," indicating that he does not believe that there is any real injury caused by his action. Moreover, Walt takes the position that by hiding the true state of MCI's bad debts, he is supporting a pending buyout, thus helping the executives and current shareholders get a good price for their shares rather than making them victims of his crime.[79] He also views the money he helps skim from MCI's shyster customers (the ones he considers unethical) is a "victimless hustle" because it is stealing from crooks and scammers.

Walt begins to realize that he is not being recognized for his good work and that he has been taken advantage of because he has to hire staff who report to him for more than he is being paid. By demanding that he "make his numbers" in terms of hiding the real state of the bad debts, Walt believes he is being asked to do the impossible.

[79] A senior manager, who joined MCI relatively late in Walt Pavlo's tenure, has argued that MCI's most senior management wanted him to sort out the bad-debt problems and that he had their support in doing so.

TABLE 7.12 Heath's Seven Rationalizations of Unethical Actions

- Denial of responsibility.
- Denial of injury.
- Denial of the victim.
- Condemnation of the condemners.
- Appeal to higher loyalties.
- Everyone else is doing it.
- Entitlement.

Source: "7 Neutralization/Rationalization Techniques," a speech by Joseph Heath at the Centre for Ethics at the University of Toronto, April 9, 2007, later published as "Business Ethics and Moral Motivation: A Criminological Perspective," *Journal of Business Ethics*, 83 (2008): 595–614.

Consequently, he condemns the senior executives and the company in general. He feels that the company owes him and that he is entitled to help himself by engaging in fraud. He takes the view that many senior executives know what is going on and are turning a blind eye to the hiding of the size of the bad-debt problems. He believes they know that the accounting and reporting systems are a mess—a veritable black hole—and are taking advantage of it. He reasons that everyone else is doing it, so why shouldn't he?

Walt justifies some of his behavior by his loyalty to his family. He arranges for his father to buy a company and for his family to have a higher lifestyle that they would not otherwise have. His loyalty to family takes precedence over loyalty to MCI.

OPPORTUNITY & CAPACITY TO COMMIT FRAUD Even though there may be a need to commit fraud and the action can be rationalized, there must also be opportunities and the capacity or knowledge to commit fraud with acceptable levels of risk of getting caught and punished severely.

In Walt's case, he views the MCI accounting system as a veritable black hole—an "absolute shambles," as someone later described it. Reports are inaccurate, and no one seems to mind. There are no apparent controls over the accuracy of payment postings to the correct accounts. No one other than Walt has taken the time to understand the fundamental nature and economic substance of the Rapid Advancement and other schemes that are being put in place. Ultimately, the economic value falsely created in MCI's financial statements is removed in a huge write-off attributed to other problems. Clearly, senior management were not performing their oversight role properly, the organizational culture did not support whistleblowers and they were not encouraged to come forward, and internal audit functions were not effective.

These failings provided the opportunity that Walt was looking for and the belief that he would not get caught. He was particularly susceptible when one of his bosses or one of his co-fraudsters told him "not to worry about it right now." Perhaps it was also his belief that he could control the situation so that he would not be found out. Ultimately, he realized that he could not control his greedy colleagues, and he lost sight of the fact that he had ripped off a bank, not only scammers. Both misjudgments came back to haunt him.

In the end, for Walt the slippery slope proved uncontrollable. Walt would have been wise to be more suspicious at the start when he heard, "I'll make it worth your while." He should have listened to Ralph McCumber, his first boss whom he idolized, who had a keen "bullshit detector" and was fond of saying, "Don't make any promises you can't keep."

LESSONS LEARNED When executives and auditors engage in a process of considering where fraud and white-collar crime might emerge, they would do well to use the Fraud

Triangle or Fraud Diamond, Maslow's Hierarchy of Needs, and Heath's Seven Rationalizations of Unethical Acts as frameworks to spot red-flag problems before they cause or allow significant harm. Such a process of consideration might be part of an annual or periodic brainstorming session as is now required of auditors in some jurisdictions. These frameworks should also be considered when planning for or instituting new incentive and reward systems because they present opportunities for introduction of dysfunctional pressures. Similarly, when assessing the performance of supervisory staff, it would be useful to consider using the frameworks to assess if the motivational methods used, while productive in the short run, were potentially harmful in the longer term. Finally, in order to ensure adequate awareness and knowledge of the frameworks, their use should be discussed in supervisory training sessions. A sensitized supervisor, for example, should be able to red flag and correct potentially harmful rationalizations used by employees.

The analysis presented here shows how vulnerable accounting systems are to employees who are intent on taking advantage. It is also apparent that several people in addition to Walt suspected that something was not right, but they did not question or report their concerns. This was because MCI's corporate culture did not encourage such inquiries or whistleblowing. In fact, it accepted and even encouraged a culture of manipulation rather than ethical behavior. There is a definite advantage to installing an ethical corporate culture with a whistleblowing mechanism and instilling expectations of compliance with an ethical corporate culture from the beginning of employment as well as reinforcing these expectations periodically.

In addition, there was a military-like microculture in which employees were expected to follow orders rather than exercise their own conscience. Although this looks attractive in the short run, it prevents longer-term benefits from surfacing and raises risk for the enterprise as a whole.

Finally, the analysis of Walt's activities underscores the need to embed ethics concerns in the strategic and operational aspects of a company and have a senior corporate official designated to champion the ethics portfolio in a company as well as in each significant division of that company. Monitoring these concerns should be an important ongoing function of a committee of the Board of Directors. Only by integrating ethics concerns into the governance structure of a company can ethics risks and opportunities be managed effectively.

BRIBERY & INTERNATIONAL OPERATIONS

When any corporation operates outside of its domestic market, the normal guidance offered to employees must be reconsidered as to the following:

- How their usual operating practices will impact on the local economy and culture;
- Whether different local foreign practices, such as widespread gift giving or even bribery, should be endorsed or banned;
- The reaction to these changes by domestic stakeholders and particularly by primary stakeholders, including major customers and capital markets.

IMPACTS ON LOCAL ECONOMIES & THEIR CULTURES Multinational corporations may have a significant impact on local cultures that they would not have domestically. They must be careful not to have unfavorable local impacts on the following:

- Labor markets: wage rates and availability of supply
- Raw material and other input markets

- Political and legal processes
- Religious and social customs

If, for example, a multinational corporation decides to ignore local religious and/or social customs, it and its workers may be accused of *cultural imperialism* and may find it difficult to obtain cooperation for future activities. Similarly, by virtue of its size, a multinational may so dominate the locale that there may be an unintended domination of local governments, courts, or elections that, again, may produce a backlash at some point.

CONFLICTS BETWEEN DOMESTIC & FOREIGN CULTURES Perhaps the most difficult problems arise when the values of the primary corporate stakeholders differ from those in the local foreign country. Differences noted in the media in recent years have included the following:

- Approval of bribery
- Use of child labor
- Use of slave labor
- Unhealthy labor conditions
- Treatment of women
- Support of repressive regimes through location of operations
- Lack of freedom of association
- Respect for environment
- Dealings with family members are expected, not avoided

Often corporations locate operations in a country just because they want access to cheap labor, lower environmental protection costs, or less governmental red tape, and they are invited to come by the local politicians who do what they can by way of inducements. Why, then, should businesspeople worry about taking advantage of these opportunities when they find them? The reason lies in the new broader and global accountability the stakeholders expect and demand of corporations. Putting it simply, influential stakeholder groups have made it very difficult for corporations caught offending the values of the group anywhere in the world. Examples include the following:

- Boycott of clothing made in offensive labor situations:
  - As highlighted in the Rana Plaza garment factory collapse in Bangladesh in 2013
  - Nike, Reebok, Adidas, and other shoe manufacturers
- Frustration of the intended scuttling of Shell's Brent Spar oil storage vessel in the depths of the North Sea (see the ethics case "Brent Spar Decommissioning Disaster" at the end of this chapter) and the boycott of Shell products in Europe
- Worldwide boycott of Nestlé products for distributing powdered baby food to mothers in South Africa, who mixed the powder with contaminated water and harmed their babies
- Activist investors in North America pursuing many mining companies for their poor environmental protection practices elsewhere
- Boycott of beef grown on land cleared in the Amazon rain forest

In addition, environmental and personal disasters, such as that at Bhopal, have resulted in lawsuits launched by the same foreign politicians that invited the companies in and even entreated them to stay in adverse circumstances. Lawsuits have also arisen in these cases in domestic jurisdictions where the offending company's stock has been traded because of investors' and/or foreigners' claims that management was negligent and should have issued warnings of heightened risk caused by reduced safeguards. Although it seems that some customers want cheap goods and some investors rejoice in high profits, there are others who care about how these are produced and/or are willing to sue if an opportunity presents itself.

More important than the costs of a trial in terms of time lost, fines, and legal fees paid, companies should realize that the damage to their reputation is usually the most significant impact they suffer. The impact of lost reputation may not be seen for a while, but there is no doubt that it translates into lost future revenues of a very large magnitude.

Finally, there is an impact on the morale of domestic employees to be considered from engaging in practices not considered worthy. The desire of employees to be productive and to produce at high levels of quality may be undermined with serious consequences.

BRIBERY & FACILITATING PAYMENTS In their foreign operations, multinational corporations are likely to be asked for facilitating payments or bribes. A *facilitating payment* is usually nominal in value and made to speed up a result that would have happened anyway given enough time. For example, a small payment made to a customs official that all importers pay to facilitate movement of goods usually provides no competitive advantage. A bribe, on the other hand, is usually a larger payment than nominal and is paid to gain a competitive advantage and without which the desired result would not occur. Both payments are intended to influence outcomes, but some observers believe that a facilitating payment is of lesser ethical consequence than a bribe. Others do not make this distinction.

> **Bribery by Lockheed Corporation Spawns the U.S. FCPA**
>
> *In 1976, a subcommittee of the U.S. Senate decided that Lockheed Corporation had paid various government officials millions of dollars to guarantee purchases of planes. These included officials: in Japan for the F-104 Starfighter and the L-1011, in West Germany for the F-104 Starfighter, in Italy for the C-130, and in the Netherlands for the F-104 Starfighter. The company also paid $106 million in commissions to arms dealers to secure plane sales to Saudi Arabia. The resulting public outcry and investigation gave rise to the* U.S. Foreign Corrupt Practices Act *(FCPA) of 1977 prohibiting the corruption of foreign officials.*

Most business leaders understand that bribing government officials is illegal in the country where the bribe is paid. Yet at the same time, they know that bribery has been the normal way of doing business in some regions, and laws have been enforced only sporadically or not at all.

However, this lax enforcement regime is now changing. Because of the instigation of a multinational group, Transparency International, the United States and other leading Organization for Economic Development (OECD)[80] member countries decided to agree to an OECD Anti-Bribery Convention[81] whereby each signatory country would enact legislation similar to the FCPA[82] during late 1998 and early 1999. Once the international mechanisms are in place, these acts will allow a corporation that believes that its foreign competitor is

[80] See http://www.oecd.org.

[81] OECD Convention on Combating Bribery of Foreign Public Officials in International Business Transactions, http://www.oecd.org/daf/anti-bribery/oecdantibriberyconvention.htm.

[82] Enacted in 1977, in response to the Lockheed bribery scandal.

bribing officials in a third country to pursue the offending corporation through the domestic legal systems. For example, a U.S. corporation that suspected that a German company was bribing the officials in a South American country could apply to the U.S. legal system, which would, in turn, contact German authorities, who would search the German company's records for proof of the alleged transactions to be put forward in court. This initiative will make it much more risky to make payments to officials of foreign governments. It is a dramatic change from earlier positions where, for example, Germany considered a bribe outside of the country to be ethical and tax deductible but a bribe inside Germany to be unethical and illegal.

By May 2014, forty-one countries[83] had adopted the Anti-Bribery Convention and had enacted legislation making it illegal to pay a bribe to a foreign government official. In the United States, the FCPA is widely known because it has been on the books since 1977, when it was triggered by the Lockheed bribery scandal outlined in the insert box below. The FCPA is enforced by the SEC, which is imposing increasingly serious penalties, including fines and jail, such as in the Daimler AG and Siemens AG cases.[84] However, there still are many businesspeople who are unaware that other countries have enacted almost exactly identical laws and are beginning to enforce them. In some countries, local employees caught paying or receiving bribes may be severely punished, such as in China.[85]

More important, since 2010, the FCPA has been enforced globally, not only for actions in the United States, and in 2010, the U.K. government followed suit on an even broader scale by passing the *Bribery Act*. The *Bribery Act* applies to any company—and indeed any nonprofit organization—with a presence in the United Kingdom (i.e., even if not headquartered there) *for the bribery of business people or government officials*, not only the latter. Moreover, there are *penalties for the company or person giving a bribe as well as the company failing to guard adequately against the receipt of a bribe*. In addition, *the FCPA's allowance of facilitating payments is not available under the* Bribery Act, although reasonable expenses (which will require continuous scrutiny and interpretation) will apparently not give rise to charges. Finally, the *Bribery Act* introduces *unlimited fines and imprisonment up to 10 years*. As a result, businesses now face serious fines with jail time for executives for actions taken anywhere in the world with regard to bribery in business dealings as well as corruption of government officials. Even Canada is beginning to prosecute companies. In short, companies, nonprofit organizations, and their executives are now facing an entirely new, more stringent antibribery regime.

These antibribery developments are summarized in Figure 7.7 and in highlights provided in the Lockheed, Daimler, and Niko Resources cases.

Niko Resources—Canada's First Significant Bribery Prosecution

In June 2011, Niko Resources pleaded guilty to bribing an official of the government of Bangladesh by giving him a $190,000 vehicle, among other inducements, such as travel, to levy a low penalty for faulty and negligent drilling operations that resulted in unsafe conditions and an explosion. The company agreed to pay a fine of $9.5 million for the bribery. This was the second Canadian prosecution under the Corruption of Foreign Public Officials Act. *The first involved the bribing of a U.S. customs inspector for $28,299 by officials of Hydro Kleen Group Inc. Hydro Kleen was fined $25,000 in 2005.*

[83] OECD Anti-Bribery Convention, Ratification Status as of May 31, 2014, http://www.oecd.org/daf/anti-bribery/WGBRatificationStatus.pdf.

[84] See the ethics cases "Daimler's Settles U.S. Bribery Case for $185 Million" and "Siemens' Bribery Scandal," both in Chapter 5.

[85] See the ethics case "Rio Tinto's Bribes in China" in Chapter 5.

FIGURE 7.7 Antibribery Developments: 1975–2016

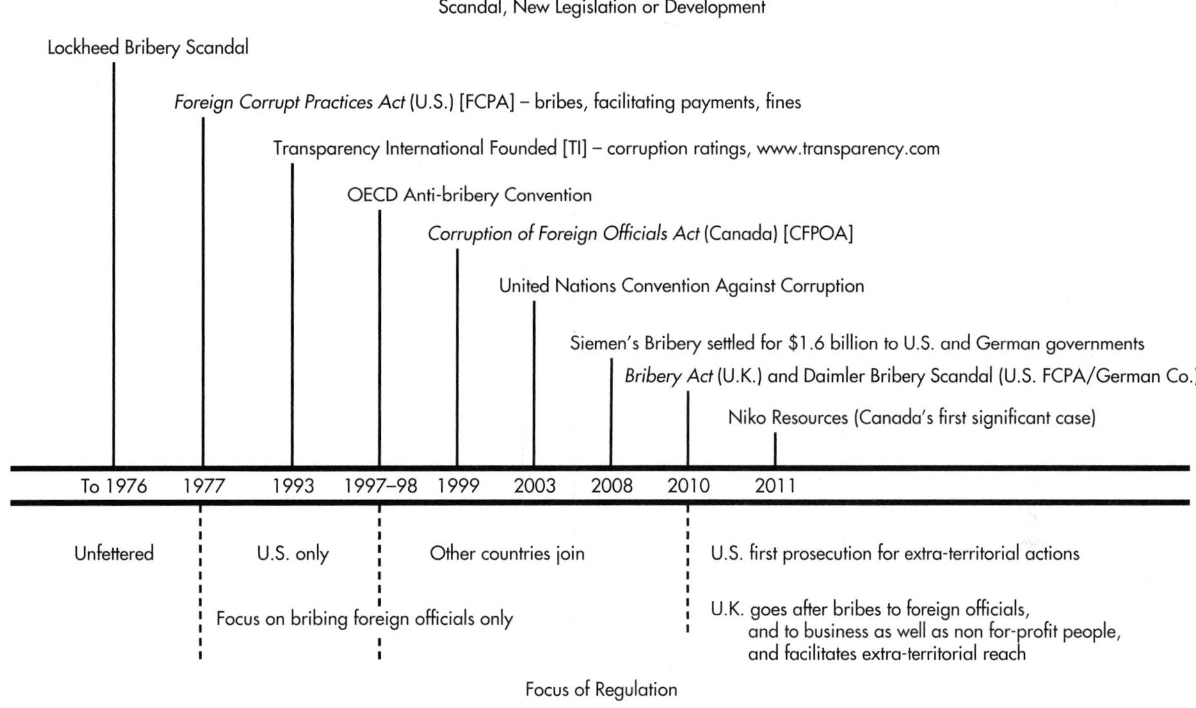

Transparency International (TI) has been one of the major driving forces of increased bribery awareness and the stimulation of governments to enact antibribery statutes and increased regulation. Founded in 1993 in Germany to do just that, TI has developed chapters in many countries around the world. Their websites are significant sources of information (see also Table 7.13, which compares the U.S. FCPA to the U.K. *Bribery Act*).

Faced with a much more comprehensive and high-risk environment, companies need to build antibribery risk identification and management techniques into their strategic planning, training, assessment, and incentive systems. A number of anti-corruption tools are available, including the *TI-Canada Anti-Corruption Compliance Checklist*, First Edition (Revised), 2011, which is downloadable from http://www.transparency.ca/New/Files/TI-Canada_Anti-Corruption_Checklist_2011R1.pdf. It provides a comprehensive overview of the subject with practical suggestions, background on major developments, and references to additional resources.

TI, along with its national chapters, is the primary source for authoritative information on international bribery and corruption. TI's research, which is available on its website http://www.transparency.org/research, includes studies such as a *Corruption Perceptions Index*, predictions, national assessments, help desks, business surveys, a *Bribe Payers Index*, and reports by country.

On a periodic basis, TI publishes its *Bribe Payers Index* (*BPI*), which ranks the likelihood for companies from twenty-eight countries to bribe,[86] and every year it publishes

[86] See the TI *2011 Bribe Payers Index*, http://bpi.transparency.org.

TABLE 7.13 Comparison of U.S. FCPA & U.K. *Bribery Act*

PROVISION	FCPA	*BRIBERY ACT*
Who is being bribed	Only bribes ("anything of value") paid or offered to a "foreign official" are prohibited.	Prohibits bribes paid to *any person* to induce them to act "improperly" (not limited to foreign officials).
Nature of advantage obtained	Payment must be "to obtain or retain business.	Focus is on improper action rather than business nexus (except in case of strict corporate liability).
"Active offense" vs. "passive offense"	Only the act of payment rather than the receipt/ acceptance of payment is prohibited.	Creates two offenses: (1) offense of bribing another ("active offense") and (2) offense of being bribed ("passive offense").
Corporate strict liability	Strict liability only under accounting provisions for public companies (failure to maintain adequate systems of internal controls).	Creates a new strict liability corporate offense for the failure of a commercial organization to prevent bribery (subject to defense of having "adequate procedures" in place designed to prevent bribery).
Jurisdiction	U.S. companies and citizens, foreign companies listed on U.S. stock exchange, or any person acting while in the United States.	Individuals who are U.K. nationals or are ordinarily resident in the United Kingdom and organizations that are either established in the United Kingdom or conduct some part of their business in the United Kingdom.
Business promotion expenditures	Affirmative defense for reasonable and bona fide expenditure directly related to the business promotion or contract performance.	No similar defense (but arguably such expenditures are not "improper" and therefore not a *Bribery Act* violation).
Allowable under local law	Affirmative defense if payment is lawful underwritten laws/regulations of foreign country.	No violation if permissible under written laws of foreign country (applies only in case of bribery of foreign public official; otherwise, a factor to be considered).
Facilitating payments	Exception for payment to a foreign official to expedite or secure the performance of a routine (nondiscretionary) government action.	No facilitating payments exception, although guidance is likely to provide that payments of small amounts of money are unlikely to be prosecuted.
Civil/criminal enforcement	Both civil and criminal proceedings can be brought by the Department of Justice and the SEC.	Criminal enforcement only by the U.K. Serious Fraud Office.
Potential penalties	Bribery: for individuals, up to five years' imprisonment and fines of up to $250,000; for entities, fines of up to $2 million. Books and records/ internal control violations: for individuals, up to twenty years' imprisonment and fines of up $5 million; for entities, fines of up to $25 million.	For individuals, up to ten years' imprisonment and potentially unlimited fines; for entities, potentially unlimited fines.

Source: http://www.transparency-usa.org/documents/FCPAvsBriberyAct.pdf. Reprinted with permission.

its *Corruption Perceptions Index* (*CPI*), which ranks the perceived levels of public sector corruption in 167 countries.[87] In 2011, according to the *BPI*, companies from the Netherlands and Switzerland tied at 8.8 out of 10 for the least bribery out of the twenty-eight countries, whereas Russian companies were worst at 6.1, followed by Chinese companies at 6.5 out of 10. In 2015, the lowest perceived incidence of bribery (in the *CPI*) of government officials was considered to be in Denmark, at 91 out of 100, while the worst scores were for Afghanistan, Somalia, and North Korea at 8 out of 100. In 2015, Canadian and U.S. companies were ranked at sixth and tenth in the *BPI*, respectively, and in 2015 their perceived incidence of corruption at ninth and sixteenth in the *CPI*,

[87] See the TI *2011 Corruption Perception Index*, http://www.transparency.org/cpi2015#results-table.

respectively. The *BPI* and *CPI* rankings are available on all TI websites and can be valuable tools for companies in assessing their operational risks in foreign countries, particularly in countries near the bottom of the list. The following TI websites are gold mines of information and guidance:

http://www.transparency.org—the worldwide site, based in Berlin

http://www.transparency-usa.org—the U.S. site

http://www.transparency.ca—the Canadian site

Of course, bribery and corruption are also bad on purely ethical grounds. They can have a devastating effect on development and create injustices for those not in a position to benefit or who have to pay the bribes. They are also damaging to reputations, as was discovered by Acres,[88] a major Canadian engineering consulting firm that was convicted in Lesotho of paying bribes. Even though Acres had denied guilt, it was essentially forced out of business. SNC-Lavalin was convicted of paying bribes in Libya and almost lost the right to bid on contracts with the Canadian government. In April 2013, the World Bank banned "an SNC subsidiary from bidding on World Bank projects for 10 years because of misconduct in projects in Bangladesh and Cambodia."[89] Daimler and Siemens are recent examples of companies that have taken a reputational hit. These bribery cases are located in Chapter 5.

Rather than leaving employees to make up their own minds as to when payment is appropriate, the corporation should have a policy concerning the nonpayment of bribes and conditions under which facilitating payments might be paid. For example, it may not be sufficient to simply say that no bribes shall be paid; it is important to provide guidelines to employees concerning what to do if they are asked. If a company permits facilitating payments, it needs to have very strict and clear policies surrounding their payment. The payments should be defined, there should be limits and approval processes, and they should be properly recorded in the accounts.

It should be clear that facilitating payments or bribes are problematic for reasons other than illegality, including the following:

- Adding to the cost of the operation, good, or service
- Undermining the practice of purchasing based on merit in a country or firm
- Risking possible negative consequences from stakeholder groups should they find out
- Impossibility of enforcing performance or obtaining a contract after bribes are paid
- Impossibility of assessing sales force effectiveness
- Indicating to employees elsewhere in the organization that bribes are permitted in spite of what codes of conduct say
- Indicating to seekers of bribes elsewhere that bribes are possible if they ask for them
- Risk to local employees and expatriate personnel should the bribes come to light
- The risk that a change in political control, particularly by revolution, could bring past practices to light and have serious consequences for the company and local employees

[88] "Corruption in Lesotho: Small Place, Big Wave," *The Economist*, September 19, 2002, accessed November 24, 2013, at http://www.economist.com/node/1338833.

[89] "SNC-Lavalin Face Charges of Fraud and Corruption in Libyan Business Dealings," CTV News Montreal, February 19, 2015, accessed June 13, 2016, at http://montreal.ctvnews.ca/snc-lavalin-face-charges-of-fraud-and-corruption-in-libyan-business-dealings-1.2243475.

- Undermining internal control (Usually, bribes paid are untraceable [e.g., frequently in cash], and management cannot know for sure that the real beneficiary was as reported. The recipient may in fact be an employee of the company who pretended that a bribe needed to be paid to an outsider.)

Some multinationals have banned the giving of bribes or facilitating payments and have continued to operate profitably in the countries concerned. On the other hand, some claim they have lost business to companies who do not have similar scruples. Because of their lower economic power and influence, smaller companies may find it more difficult to resist pressure. The OECD Convention and resulting legislation help to level the playing field, but it remains to be seen how helpful this will be to small companies.

In some cultures, particularly in Southeast Asia, China, and Japan, there is a long tradition of gift giving to cultivate long-term relationships that facilitate business dealings. In these situations, corporations may be best advised to have a permissive policy where employees would be required to consult a corporate ethics officer to make sure that cultural niceties are observed without breaking laws at home or abroad. Gift giving might cover such items as an iPad but would certainly not stretch to a Mercedes.

This is a good example of an issue that has moved from being a business aggravation to an ethical issue to a legal issue. But it is still an ethical issue. It needs to be covered in corporate codes of conduct and business policies and practices when a company is in a position to be asked for a bribe. Policies, especially for decision makers in the field, need to be clear and unequivocal. Management will not be saved by ignoring the issue or taking steps to ensure they do not know what goes on locally in high-risk countries. In particular, employing an agent to deal with business abroad does not get management off the hook. They are responsible for providing appropriate instructions to agents not to pay bribes and to monitor their expenditures to be alert for those that might indicate that bribes have been paid. An excellent article on this issue is "Not Seeing is no Defence" by James Miklotz.[90] Additional articles that provide useful background information about the fine line between gifts and bribes include "What is a Bribe in 2011?" by Matthew McClearn[91] and "A Gift for Mr. Hossain" by Greg McArthur.[92]

Boards, audit committees, and the management of companies operating in high-risk parts of the world should expect their auditors to be aware of the associated risk that illegal bribes may have been paid and to take the risk into account in their audits.[93]

Daimlerchrysler Subject to Bribery U.S. Laws

The first Foreign Corrupt Practices Act *(FCPA) extraterritorial bribery case involved the Germany automotive company DaimlerChrysler. Although Germany had outlawed bribery of foreign officials in 1999, David Bazzetta learned at a corporate audit executive committee in 2001 in Stuttgart, Germany, that units of*

[90] James Miklotz, "Not Seeing Is No Defence", *CAmagazine*, October 2006, http://www.camagazine.com/3/3/9/9/2/index1.shtml.

[91] Matthew McClearn, "What Is a Bribe in 2011?," *Canadian Business*, October 19, 2011, and November 7, 2011, http://www.canadianbusiness.com/article/51851--what-is-a-bribe-in-2011.

[92] Greg McArthur, "A Gift for Mr. Hossain," *Report on Business*, September 2011 [Niko Resources bribery], https://secure.globeadvisor.com/servlet/ArticleNews/story/gam/20110826/ROBMAG_SEPT2011_P38_39_40_41_42_43_44.

[93] This is a requirement of Canadian, U.S., and international auditing standards (CICA Handbook Section 5136, AICPA Au 317 and ISA 250, respectively).

DaimlerChrysler continued to do so and that the company was conspiring to continue. Since the company raised funds in the United States, it was an SEC registrant in the United States and was therefore subject to FCPA legislation and regulation. Mr. Bazzetta blew the whistle as is possible under the FCPA, which led in early April 2010 to guilty pleas in the United States to charges of bribery by German and Russian business units and to the failure to maintain books and records and of internal controls as required under the FCPA. The investigation of the whistleblower's allegations focused on only fifty-one transactions but revealed that bribes had been given in twenty-two countries. Daimler settled the case in 2010 by paying the SEC $91.4 million as disgorgement of profits and $93.6 million to the U.S. Department of Justice for related criminal charges for a total of $185 million for bribes made outside the United States.

APPARENT CULTURAL CONFLICTS WITH BANNING GIFTS, BRIBES, OR FACILITATING PAYMENTS As mentioned, in some cultures, particularly in Southeast Asia, China, and Japan, there is a long tradition of gift giving to cultivate long-term relationships that facilitate business dealings. In addition, it has been popularly believed that a corporation cannot do business in some countries unless payments are made to officials. Consequently, it has been said that if a corporation wants to do business in certain markets, bribery or facilitating payments is necessary. In fact, however, some corporations have found that they have been able to do business without such payments, primarily because their products or services are excellent. Allis Chalmers and Citibank are examples of such corporations.

***GUANXI* IN CHINA & ASIA** *Guanxi* is a social networking practice, prevalent in China and other Asian countries, that needs to be understood to avoid ethical difficulties. Essentially, *guanxi* involves drawing on personal connections for favors, but it is aimed at long-term, reciprocal relationships, not the kind of short-term, quick profit favors that are the usual focus of bribery attempts. In Chinese culture, according to Yadong Luo,[94] individuals should adhere to moral principles that respect social harmony, interdependence, and reciprocity as well as several other values.[95] If an individual does not follow the expected moral principles, then she or he will be seen to offend social etiquette and will lose face (reputation) and probably trustworthiness and/or credibility. Since these are foundational to building an individual's *guanxi*, failure to maintain or enhance them will prevent the building of *guanxi* by the offender. He or she will be seen to be a poor prospect for lasting reciprocal relationships within the expected moral bounds of Chinese society. In this context, gift giving in an open and transparent manner is important to building trust in a long-term relationship. Bribery, however, which is done in secret and is usually designed to illicit a short-term favor, does not usually build trust, or *guanxi*. Bribery would be seen to be detrimental to the building of long-term relationships based on traditional Chinese moral values.[96]

There is a social bonding aspect to networking in China that may have a relationship to building *guanxi*. For some relationships, the sharing of personal experiences—dinner, drinks, and karaoke—could be expected that go far beyond the normal ethical behavior and spending guidelines of Western corporations. These expectations should

[94] Yadong Luo, *Guanxi and Business*, 2nd ed. (Singapore: World Scientific Publishing, 2007).

[95] Ibid. In Confucian philosophy, social interaction is governed by eight moral principles: loyalty, respect, kindness, love, trust, justice, harmony, and peace.

[96] Research notes from Michael Shaunessy were used in preparing the comments on *guanxi*. Michael is a student in the University of Toronto's MMPA Program, which the author directs.

be recognized in advance and appropriate policy guidance given to employees and agents. However, when forming that policy guidance, it should be recognized that such social activities may be helpful for each party to develop a correct understanding about the expectations and capabilities of the other. Failure to understand those expectations and capabilities could lead to loss of face and trustworthiness. Since it often takes considerable amount of time and effort to build *guanxi* (i.e., to understand each other's expectations and capability), dining and other informal social activities are common in Asian business practices.[97]

MORAL IMAGINATION In other corporations, managers have used their *moral imagination* to devise alternatives that answered needs in the host culture but conformed to North American norms for acceptable behavior (see the ethics case "Bribery or Opportunity in China" at the end of Chapter 4). A manager in China refused to pay officials of a potential host city, citing company policy. When the officials insisted repeatedly, the manager sought and received approval for a corporate contribution toward the establishment of a community center in a local park that would offer services to senior citizens. This appealed to Chinese cultural values and was in line with the corporation's North American policy of community support. It was differentiated from a bribe in that no payment was made to an individual for personal benefit and all payments were made in public rather than in secret.

GUIDELINES FOR ETHICAL PRACTICE Two authors have made an extensive study of the ethics of foreign operations and have written excellent books on the subject. Tom Donaldson and Richard DeGeorge have each put forward useful guidelines for corporations with multinational operations.

Donaldson[98] argued that multinational corporations and their agents operating in foreign cultures should adopt, as a minimum standard of behavior, the protection of the following fundamental human rights:

- Freedom of physical movement
- Ownership of property
- Freedom from torture
- Fair trial
- Nondiscriminatory treatment
- Physical security
- Freedom of speech and association
- Minimal education
- Political participation
- Subsistence

Observing these fundamental rights, he said, would protect a corporation's moral right to—exist.[99] This is a condition affecting reputation, which is now recognized as far more important to ongoing success than a legal right.

DeGeorge[100] suggested seven practical, action-oriented principles to guide the activities of multinational corporations that would be useful in providing a sound "basis for

[97] A useful reference on guanxi can be found at http://en.wikipedia.org/wiki/Guanxi.

[98] Tom Donaldson, *The Ethics of International Business* (Oxford: Oxford University Press, 1989), 81.

[99] Ibid., 62.

[100] Richard T. De George, *Competing with Integrity in International Business* (Oxford: Oxford University Press, 1993), 45–56.

evaluating and responding to charges of unethical behavior."[101] These principles include the following:

1. Do no intentional direct harm.
2. Produce more good than harm for host country.
3. Contribute by their activity to the host country's development.
4. Respect human rights of their employees.
5. Provided that local culture does not violate ethical norms, respect and work with that culture, not against it.
6. Pay their fair share of taxes.
7. Cooperate with local government in developing and enforcing just background institutions.

Several other groups have also developed codes of ethics or guidelines to be used by multinationals in their development of appropriate policies and practices, including the following:

- UNGC (updated 2011)—ten principles related to human rights, labor, the environment and anticorruption: http://www.unglobalcompact.org/AboutTheGC/TheTenPrinciples/index.html
- Caux Round Table Principles for Business (updated 2010)—seven principles focusing on respect for stakeholder rights and laws and for building trust beyond the letter of the law and several related stakeholder management guidelines: http://www.cauxroundtable.org/index.cfm?menuid=8
- OECD Guidelines for Multinationals (2008)—a set of policies, disclosures, and implementation guidelines to be addressed by OECD member countries to multinational corporations covering stakeholder rights, good governance, and support for local cultures and governments: http://www.oecd.org/dataoecd/56/36/1922428.pdf
- The International Labour Organization—a set of fundamental principles created in 1997 to protect workers' rights: http://actrav.itcilo.org/actrav-english/telearn/global/ilo/guide/main.htm

These and other frameworks have been synthesized by Timo Herold and Christopher Stehr,[102] who developed a series of hypernorms for corporate codes of conduct to guide multinationals. They begin by considering whether the correct perspective should be the superiority of the home culture (ethnocentric view) or the local culture (relativistic view) or whether behavior should be universal across all cultures. They conclude with a series of hypernorms covering the corporation's responsibilities to employees, customers, suppliers, the environment, and society in general.

CONSULTATION BEFORE ACTION The presumption that an organization is best served by a monolithic and rigid ethical culture may not be correct. Dunn (2006) and Dunn and Shome (2009) show that cultural differences contribute to Chinese and Canadian business students holding different attitudes toward the appropriate action to take when confronted with questionable accounting and business situations. Leaving employees to

[101] Weber Shandwick, "Crisis Management Is Number One Success Factor for Global Chief Communications Officers, According to Annual Survey," press release, June 26, 2012, http://www.webershandwick.com/news/article/crisis-management-is-number-one-success-factor-for-global-chief-communicati.
[102] Ibid.

figure out how to deal with the various cultures encountered in international operations is a high-risk strategy. All organizations with international operations should sensitize their employees to cultural differences and equip them with an understanding of how the organization wants them to deal with the major issues likely to come up. At the very least, there should be an avenue for consultation with home office officials and a clear understanding of when to use it.

CRISIS MANAGEMENT

Crises are pervasive in the current business environment. In the *1997 Crisis Management Survey of Fortune 1000 Companies*, 71% of the respondents companies had a crisis management plan and/or program in place, and almost a further 12% indicated that one was in development. Even so, according to the 2012 Annual Survey of Global Chief Communications Officers, more than 70% report that their companies experienced a threat to their reputations in the prior two years, and crisis management is the number one success factor for global chief communications officers.[103]

A crisis has the potential to have a very significant impact of a crisis on the reputation of the company and its officers, on the company's ability to reach its objectives, and on its ability to survive.[104] According to the 2012 Annual Survey of Global Chief Communications Officers, "Crisis comes at a high cost to organizations that deal with them—most CEOs (74 percent) spend time on the resolution. It takes approximately 15 months to get past the problem and such crises beget a host of other issues, such as more media scrutiny (60 percent), more governmental scrutiny (51 percent) and reduced employee morale (42 percent)."[105] As a result, executives have learned that crises are to be avoided and that, if avoidance is not possible, the crisis is to be managed so as to minimize harm. Directors have learned that crisis assessment, planning, and management must be part of a modern risk management program.

Unfortunately, the urgent nature of a crisis causes a focus on survival, and ethical niceties are largely forgotten. According to Lerbinger, a crisis "*is an event that brings, or has the potential for bringing, an organization into disrepute and imperils its future profitability, growth, and, possibly its very survival.*"[106] Effective management of such events involves minimization of all harmful impacts. In reality, crisis-driven reactions rarely approach this objective unless advance planning is extensive and is based on a good understanding of crisis management techniques, including the importance of maintaining reputation based on ethical behavior.

If ethical behavior is considered to be of great importance by a corporation in its normal activities, ethical considerations should be even more important in crisis situations since crisis resolution decisions usually define the company's future reputation. Not only are crisis decisions among the most significant made in terms of potential impact on reputation, but opportunities may also be lost if ethical behavior is not a definite part of the crisis management process. For example, avoidance of crises may be easier if employees are ethically sensitized to stakeholder needs, phases of the crisis may be shortened if

---

103 Ibid., 45.

104 Timo Herald and Christopher Stehr, "Developing Hypernorms for Corporate Codes of Ethics," *Journal of Global Strategic Management* 7 (June 2010), http://www.isma.info/dosyalar/100-111_developing_hypernorms_for__corporate_codes_of_ethics.pdf.

105 O. Lerbinger, *The Crisis Manager: Facing Risk and Responsibility* (Mahwah, NJ: Lawrence Erlbaum Associates, 1997), 4.

106 Ibid.

FIGURE 7.8 **Phases of a Crisis**

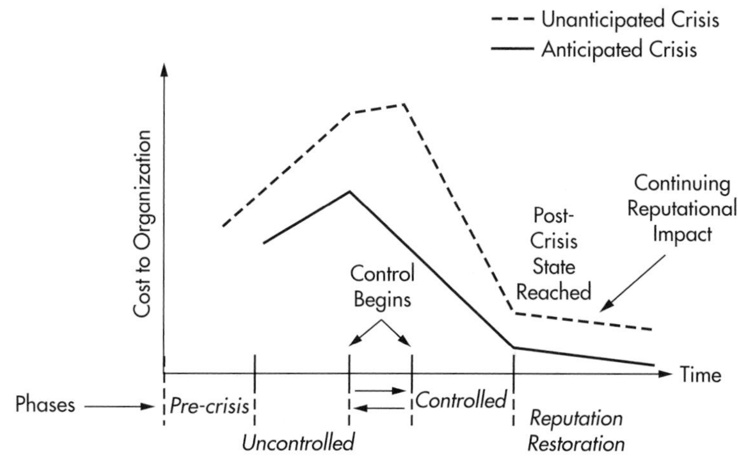

ethical behavior is expected of employees, and/or damage to reputations may be minimized if the public expects ethical performance based on past corporate actions. Moreover, the degree of trust that ethical concern instills in a corporate culture will ensure that no information or option will be suppressed and not given to the decision maker. Finally, constant concern for ethical principles should ensure that important issues are identified and the best alternatives canvassed to produce the optimal decision for the company.

Fundamental to the proper management of a crisis is an understanding of four phases of a crisis: precrisis, uncontrolled, controlled, and reputation restoration. These are outlined in Figure 7.8. The main goal of crisis management should be to avoid crises. If this is not possible, then the impacts should be minimized. This can be done by anticipating crises or recognizing early warning signs as soon as possible and responding to soften or minimize the impact and shorten the time during which the crisis is uncontrolled. These goals can best be achieved by proper advance planning, by continued monitoring, and by speedy, effective decision making during the crisis. Figure 7.8 shows two cost curves, where the lower one reflects the benefits of earlier control being applied, thus minimizing the overall cost and the ongoing damage to reputation.

Advance planning for a crisis should be part of a modern enterprise risk assessment and contingency management program because of the growing recognition of the potential negative impact of an unanticipated crisis. It can be done effectively by brainstorming for potential problem areas, assessing those identified, and devising contingency plans for effective action. Second, red flags or warning indicators can be picked out that will identify what is developing so that the earliest action can be taken to minimize cost. In the 1997 Crisis Survey noted earlier, 73% of the companies reporting had a senior-level management and corporate-level crisis management team that would focus on the crisis, and 76% had a crisis communication plan that could include notification of the public, employees, government, and the media.

The process of brainstorming to identify crises should address problems that could arise from the seven types identified by Lerbinger:[107]

1. Natural disasters
2. Technological disasters
3. Differences of expectations between individuals, groups, and corporations leading to confrontations
4. Malevolent acts by terrorists, extremists, governments, and individuals
5. Management values that do not keep pace with environmental and social requirements and obligations
6. Management deception
7. Management misconduct

Managing the crisis effectively once it has happened is vital to the achievement of crisis management goals. Quick identification and assessment of a crisis can be instrumental in influencing the outcome efficiently and effectively. One of the key characteristics of a crisis is that it will degenerate if no action is taken,[108] so delay in identification and action can have serious consequences.

Of the Fortune 1000 companies responding to the survey, 73% indicated that internal training was part of preparing for crisis awareness, identification, and management, and 48% used outside contract trainers. Major factors listed by respondents as needing improvement in crisis management included internal awareness (51%), communication (46%), drills/training (38%), vulnerability/risk assessment (36%), information technology (33%), planning/coordinating (32%), and business continuity (25%).

Undivided attention to the crisis and avoidance of other problems that can befuddle decision makers will result in better decisions, just as will the making of plans on a contingency basis and the integration of ethics into the decision-making process.

One of the most important aspects to keep in mind during the assessment of crises and the avoidance or minimization of their impact is the immediate and ongoing impact on the organization's reputation. By reflecting on how the organization's response to the crisis will affect the perception by stakeholders of it trustworthiness, responsibility, reliability, and credibility, decision makers can make choices that benefit all stakeholders and often *enhance* the organization's reputational capital or shorten the period of diminishment.

Ethics can be integrated into the decision-making process for crisis management in many ways. Specific instances involving prevention and warning, inclusion in an analytical approach, focusing a decision, and framing communications are outlined in Table 7.14.

Ethics also may be helpful in the communication aspects of the restoration phase of a crisis. As social media usage becomes more pervasive, it can provide a very fast and accurate means for corporations to communicate directly with stakeholders rather than through media that can put a biased spin on the message. However, a corporation known for unethical activities and misleading communications cannot consider its use of social media to be without immediate challenge by skeptics and cautious reception by stakeholders. Ultimately, reputation will be judged on the underlying ethical values

[107] Ibid., 10–14.

[108] C. F. Hermann, "Some Consequences of Crisis Which Limit the Viability of Organizations," *Administrative Sciences Quarterly* 8, no. 1 (1963): 62–82.

TABLE 7.14 How to Incorporate Ethics into Crisis Management

Prevention and warning:

- Code of conduct: identify values, adopt, emphasize, and make effective
- Identify potential ethics problems and warning indicators, and pre-plan responses, as part of an ongoing enterprise risk management and contingency planning program
- Ethical "red flags" or warning indicators:
  - Training to emphasize how to identify and what to do about them
  - Check as part of an ongoing enterprise risk management system
- Encourage by publicizing good examples, and awarding paper medals

Analytical approach:

- Apply a stakeholder-analysis framework as discussed in Chapter 5
- External ethics consultant
- Checklist or specific time to consider
  - ethics issues, alternatives and opportunities

Decision itself:

- Ethics/company's values: integrate into the decision making:
  - Consider how the crisis or its impact can be influenced ethically—timing, cost, mitigation?
  - Specific consideration of how to improve the organization's reputation drivers including—trustworthiness, responsibility, reliability, and credibility
  - Specific ethical communications objectives
  - Assign ethics watch dog responsibility
  - Use a checklist or template with specific ethics objectives
  - Apply moral imagination as discussed in Chapter 5

Communications on ethical intent to:

- Media, employees, customers, government, public & other stakeholders

that the organization lives by, and social media can put those under a spotlight for better or worse.

CONCLUSION

Modern corporations and other organizations are successful because they create, sustain, or improve on value. Ultimately, success depends on the support they engender from their stakeholders, and that depends on the respect shown for stakeholder expectations. Appropriate or ethical behavior is therefore circumscribed by the expectations of stakeholders, and care should be shown for the creation of guidance and other means for encouraging employees to "do what is right."

In this new era of stakeholder accountability, organizations would do well to observe the six hypernorms: honesty, fairness, compassion, integrity, predictability, and responsibility. These values should be built into governance, risk management, strategy, operations, ethical decision making, disclosure, and crisis management. Reputation and success depend on it whether you are a director, executive, or professional accountant.

Questions

1. In what ways do ethics risk and opportunity management, as described in this chapter, go beyond the scope of traditional risk management?
2. If a corporation's governance process does not involve ethics risk management, what unfortunate consequences might befall that corporation?
3. How will the U.S. external auditor's mindset change in order to discharge the duties contemplated by SAS 99 on finding fraud?
4. How could a corporation utilize stakeholder analysis to formulate strategies?
5. Descriptive commentary about corporate social responsibility performance is sometimes included in annual reports. Is this indicative of good performance, or is it just window dressing? How can the credibility of such commentary be enhanced?
6. Why should a corporation make use of a comprehensive framework for considering, managing, and reporting corporate social responsibility performance? How should they do so?
7. Do professional accountants have the expertise to audit corporate social performance reports?
8. What would you list as the five most important ethical guidelines for dealing with North American employees?
9. Is trust really important—can't employees work effectively for someone they are afraid of or at least where there is some "creative tension"?
10. Should a North American corporation operating abroad respect each foreign culture encountered or insist that all employees and agents follow only one corporate culture?
11. What should a North American company do in a foreign country where women are regarded as secondary to men and are not allowed to negotiate contracts or undertake senior corporate positions?
12. How would you advise your company's personnel to act with regard to expectations of *guanxi* in China?
13. What would you advise that corporations do to recognize the new worldwide reach of antibribery enforcement related to the FCPA and the U.K. *Bribery Act*?
14. Why should ethical decision making be incorporated into crisis management?

Case Insights

The cases provided to illuminate the issues developed in this chapter are surprisingly realistic and engage the reader quickly. The specific scenarios, with notation of the chapter section to which they primarily apply, are as follows:

CSR Cases—Environmental Issues

- *Harry Potter and the Green Brigade* examines how Harry Potter books came to be printed on recycled paper and identifies the significant environmental savings involved. The environmentally friendly roles of the author, J. K. Rowling, Rainforest Books, and the Rainforest Alliance are identified.
- *The Carbon Footprint of British Airways* examines whether it is ethical for an airline to fly thirty-two passengers across the Atlantic Ocean in an airplane that normally holds 100 passengers.

- *Pollution Caused by Cruise Ships* examines the dilemma of whether cruise ships that sail through two countries should dump their "gray water" in the country that has the more relaxed pollution standards.

Workplace Ethics Cases—Discrimination & Abusive Behavior

- *Texaco's Jelly Beans* is the story of how Texaco's discrimination against black workers ended up costing a $300 million fine and lost respect. Why did it happen?
- *Gender Discrimination at Dell Inc.* describes a $9.1 million class action settlement the company had to pay because it systematically discriminated against promoting women.
- *Novartis $250+ Million Gender Discrimination Case* tells how women at Novartis were systematically mistreated, what they did about it, and what Novartis had to do to settle the case.
- *Downsize or Bonus Allocation Decisions* confronts the reader with realistic, tough choices among staff, thus forcing decisions about what values the decision maker holds and which values ought to be communicated to the work team.
- Additional abuse cases located in Chapter 1:
  - *Pedophile Priests in the Catholic Church*
  - *Sexual Abuse by a Penn State Football Coach*

Workplace Ethics Case—White-Collar Crime

- *Walt Pavlo's MCI Scams and Frauds* explains how a young junior executive at MCI managed to defraud his employer of $6 million that he then transferred to the Cayman Islands.

Whistleblower/Ethics Inquiry Case

- *Hospital Governance Challenges* located in Chapter 5. Hospitals are primarily interested in providing the best health care possible, not in maximizing profit. The dominant hospital stakeholder group is the doctors, who work on trust and are motivated by duty. Expectations are for everyone to do the same—so hospitals are not looking for misdeeds. But frauds and mistakes happen, and effective whistleblower protection programs might help reveal them.

Bribery & International Operations Cases

- *Jail and a German Subcontractor* is a real story about a U.S. executive who went to Germany to supervise a project, only to be jailed due to the actions of a German subcontractor.
- *AIDS Medication in South Africa* causes students to face the reality that corporations face when they deal in a country that has a low standard of living and disposable income and where the local government sets aside property/patent rights and forces low prices or arranges for generic drugs, thus impacting negatively on corporate profits.
- Additional bribery cases located in Chapter 5:
  - *Siemens' Bribery Scandal*
  - *Wal-Mart Bribery in Mexico*
  - *SNC Lavalin Missing Funds Topples CEO and Triggers Bribery Investigation*
  - *Rio Tinto's Bribes in China*
  - *Daimler Settles U.S. Bribery Case for $185 Million*
  - *Bribery for Russian Contract with Anti-Bribery Prosecutor's Office*

Risk & Crisis Management Cases

- *BP's Gulf Oil Spill Risk Management* documents how BP, their consultants, and suppliers mismanaged the risks leading to the extremely tragic 2010 Deep Horizon/Macondo oil spill. Videos are referenced.
- *BP's Corporate Culture* examines allegations that BP's corporate culture was flawed and therefore responsible for the Deep Horizon Gulf oil well blowout or at least the way in which senior officials responded. A video provides interesting insights that companies should understand and risks to be managed.
- *Toyota's Recall Problems* explores how company officials handled the crisis of several deaths reportedly due to jammed accelerators. At the start, officials seemed to stumble, and Toyota's reputation suffered. Could they have handled the crisis better?
- *Digoxin Overdose—The Need for Skepticism, Courage, and Persistence* involves the death of a child that could have been avoided if only one of the many people involved had demonstrated sufficient skepticism, courage, and persistence. These deficiencies of character are frequently responsible for business and professional crises and scandal.
- *The Exxon Valdez* reviews the event of the shipwreck and oil spill that galvanized the public and environmental activists to pressure companies for better environmental protection. It is an exceptional lesson of what can go wrong to lead to a crisis and during the crisis.
- *The Brent Spar Decommissioning Disaster* deals with the crisis management fiasco that Shell faced when dealing with the outrage created by Greenpeace to stop a questionable environmental practice.
- *Wind River Energy Inc.* is a relatively small firm where the majority owner and CEO face multiple crises critical to the financial and physical well-being of the company's stakeholders. What would you do if you were the CEO?

Reading Insights

Appendix A: Ethics Audit Program Annual Questions provides useful insights for ethics risk management and control.

References

Albrecht, W. S., C. C. Albrecht, and C. O. Albrecht. 2006. *Fraud Examination*. 2nd ed. Mason, OH: Thomson South-Western.

American Institute of Certified Public Accountants and the Canadian Institute of Chartered Accountants. 2001. *Managing Risk in the New Economy*. American Institute of Certified Public Accountants and the Canadian Institute of Chartered Accountants.

Berenbeim, R. E. 1999. *The Conference Board, Director, Working Group on Global Business Ethics Principles*.

Brooks, L. J. 1990. "A Partial Preliminary Report on a Survey on the Effectiveness/Compliance of Corporate Codes of Conduct in Canada." Unpublished manuscript.

———. 2000. "Codes of Conduct, Trust, Innovation, Commitment, and Productivity: A Strategic-Cultural Perspective." *Global Focus* 12, no. 2: 1– 11.

Brooks, L. J., and D. Selley. 2008. *Ethics and Governance: Developing and Maintaining an Ethical Corporate Culture*. 3rd ed. Toronto: Canadian Centre for Ethics and Corporate Policy.

Corporate Ethics Monitor. Toronto: EthicScan Canada.

Crisis Management Survey of Fortune 1000 Companies. Conducted by the George Washington University Institute for Crisis, Disaster, and Risk Management and the Corporate Response Group.

De George, R. T. 1993. *Competing with Integrity in International Business*. New York: Oxford University Press.

Donaldson, T. 1989. *The Ethics of International Business*. New York: Oxford University Press.

———. 1996. "Values in Tension: Ethics Away from Home." *Harvard Business Review*, September–October, 48–62.

Dunn, P. 2006. "The Role of Culture and Accounting Education in Resolving Ethical Business Dilemmas by Chinese and Canadians." *Accounting and the Public Interest* 6, no. 1: 116–34.

Dunn, P., and A. Shome. 2006. "Cultural Crossvergence and Social Desirability Bias: Ethical Evaluations by Chinese and Canadian Business Students." *Journal of Business Ethics* 85, no. 4: 527–43.

Fombrun, C. J. 1996. *Reputation: Realizing Value from the Corporate Image*. Boston: Harvard Business School Press.

Gellerman, S. W. 1986. "Why Good Managers Make Bad Choices." *Harvard Business Review* 64, no. 4: 85–90.

Global Reporting Initiative. 2013. *G4 Sustainability Reporting Guidelines*, https://www.globalreporting.org/standards/g4/Pages/default.aspx.

Heath, Joseph. 2007. "7 Neutralization/Rationalization Techniques." Speech at the Centre for Ethics at the University of Toronto, April 9, 2007. Later published as "Business Ethics and Moral Motivation: A Criminological Perspective," *Journal of Business Ethics* 83 (2008): 595–614.

Hermann, Charles F. 1963. "Some Consequences of Crisis Which Limit the Viability of Organizations." *Administrative Sciences Quarterly* 8, no. 1: 62–82.

Institute of Social and Ethical Accountability. *AccountAbility*. http://www.accountability.org.uk.

International Organization for Standardization. 2010. *ISO 26000 Guidance on Social Responsibility*. http://www.iso.org (accessed December 31, 2010).

Jones, Joanne, Dawn W. Massey, and Linda Thorne. 2003. "Auditors' Ethical Reasoning: Insights from Past Research and Implications for the Future." *Journal of Accounting Literature* 22: 45–103.

KPMG Forensic. 2005. *Integrity Survey 2005–2006*. New York: KPMG Forensic.

Lerbinger, Otto. 1997. *The Crisis Manager: Facing Risk and Responsibility*. Mahwah, NJ: Lawrence Erlbaum Associates.

Luo, Yadong. 2007. *Guanxi and Business*. 2nd ed. Singapore: World Scientific Publishing.

Maslow, A. H. 1943. "A Theory of Human Motivation." *Psychological Review* 50: 394–95. Reprinted in Deborah C. Stephens, ed., *The Maslow Business Reader* (New York: Wiley, 2000), 3–4.

———. 1954. *Motivation and Personality*. New York: Harper and Row.

Michael Ramos. "Auditor's Responsibility for Fraud Detection." 2003. *Journal of Accountancy*. January, 28–36. Available online at http://www.journalofaccountancy.com/issues/2003/jan/auditorsresponsibilityforfrauddetection.html

Mitchell, R. K., B. R. Agle, and D. J. Wood. 1997. "Toward a Theory of Stakeholder Identification and Salience: Defining the Principle of Who and What Really Counts." *Academy of Management Review* 22, no. 4: 853–86.

Mitroff, I. I., P. Shrivastava, and F. E. Udwadia. 1987. "Effective Crisis Management." *Academy of Management Executive* 1, no. 3: 283–92.

Nitkin, D., and L. J. Brooks. 1998. "Sustainability Auditing and Reporting: The Canadian Experience." *Journal of Business Ethics* 17: 1499–507.

Nudell, Mayer, and Norman Antokol. 1988. *The Handbook for Effective Emergency and Crisis Management*. Lexington, MA: Lexington Books.

Paine, Lynne Sharp. 1994. "Managing for Organizational Integrity." *Harvard Business Review*, March–April, 112.

Pavlo, Walter, Jr., and N. Weinberg. 2007. *Stolen without a Gun: Confessions from Inside History's Biggest Accounting Fraud—The Collapse of MCI WorldCom*. Tampa, FL: Etika Books LLC.

Pellizzari, P. 2002. *Conscious Consumption: Corporate Social Responsibility and Canada's Grocery Giants*. Toronto: EthicScan Canada.

Rest, James R. 1979. *Development in Judging Moral Issues*. Minneapolis: University of Minnesota Press.

Roth, N. L., T. Hunt, M. Stravropoulos, and K. Babik. 1996. "Can't We All Just Get Along: Cultural Variables in Codes of Ethics." *Public Relations Review* 22, no. 2 (Summer): 151–61.

Rowley, T. 1997. "Moving beyond Dyadic Ties: A Network Theory of Stakeholder Influences." *Academy of Management Review* 22, no. 4: 887–910.

"SAS 99." Official Releases column in the *Journal of Accountancy*, January 2003, 105–20.

Sethi, S. P. 1999. "Codes of Conduct for Global Business: Prospects and Challenges of Implementation." In *Principles of Stakeholder Management*. Toronto: Clarkson Centre for Business Ethics, Rotman School of Management, University of Toronto, 9–20.

Smith, Shawn. "Illegal Job Interview Questions." http://www.sideroad.com/Human_Resources/illegal-job-interview_questions.html.

Social Accountability International. 1997. *SA8000: Guideline for Social Accountability*. New York: Social Accountability International.

"The Price of Happiness." 2006. *CAmagazine*, September, http://www.camagazine.com/archives/print-edition/2006/sept/upfront/camagazine8265.aspx.

Tillinghast-Towers Perrin and the Institute of Internal Auditors Research Foundation. 2001. *Enterprise Risk Management: Trends and Emerging Practices*. Altamonte Springs, FL: Institute of Internal Auditors.

U.K. Bribery Act. 2010. http://www.justice.gov.uk/publications/bribery-bill.htm.

University of Toronto. 2010. *Human Resources Guideline on Civil Conduct*. http://www.hrandequity.utoronto.ca/Asset952.aspx?method=1.

U.S. Securities and Exchange Commission. *Complaint, United Sates Securities and Exchange Commission v. Daimler AG*, United Sates District Court for the District of Columbia, Case: 1:10- cv-00473. http://www.sec.gov/litigation/complaints/2010/comp-pr2010-51.pdf (accessed November 26, 2010).

Wartick, S. L., and P. L. Cochran. 1985. "The Evolution of the Corporate Social Performance Model." *Academy of Management Review* 10, no. 4: 758–69.

Wolfe, D. T., and D. R. Hermanson. 2004. "The Fraud Diamond: Considering the Four Elements of Fraud." *The CPA Review*, December, 38–42.

CSR Cases—Environmental Issues

Harry Potter and the Green Brigade

ETHICS CASE

Harry Potter is known to tens of millions of readers as a figment of J. K. Rowling's imagination. One of the good guys, he is a gifted apprentice magician and budding wizard. Harry and his pals have bested evil wizards in tale after tale and many movies, including the following:

- *Harry Potter and the Philosopher's Stone*
- *Harry Potter and the Chamber of Secrets*
- *Harry Potter and the Prisoner of Azkaban*
- *Harry Potter and the Goblet of Fire*
- *Harry Potter and the Order of the Phoenix*
- *Harry Potter and the Half-Blood Prince*
- *Harry Potter and the Deathly Hallows*

But the story that most do not know is how Harry Potter dealt with the green brigade and, with a wave of his real wand, made a very tangible difference to society.

In 2003, the so-called green brigade—a collection of environmental groups and tree huggers, including Greenpeace and others—declared success in getting Harry Potter's U.K. publisher, Bloomsbury, to print *Harry Potter and the Order of the Phoenix* "on paper made from 10% post consumer waste recycled paper, and the adult version of the book on 20% recycled paper."[1] Their objective was stated as follows: "Greenpeace wants to see books in the marketplace with much more recycled content and with any virgin fibre used in the paper coming from well managed forests, certified to the standards of the Forest Stewardship Council."[2]

The Canadian hardcover edition, copublished by Raincoast Books and Bloomsbury was printed on 100% post-consumer, chlorine-free paper, resulting in the following ecological savings:

- 39,320 trees
- 64,435,801 liters of water (water to fill forty-two Olympic-sized swimming pools)

[1] Greenpeace UK, "Harry Potter Goes on Part Recycled Paper," July 17, 2004, accessed November 20, 2010, at http://www.greenpeace.org.uk/media/press-releases/harry-potter-goes-on-part-recycled-paper.

[2] Ibid.

- 854,988 kilograms of solid waste
- Electricity to power the average home for 262 years
- Greenhouse gases equivalent to driving a car 5.3 million kilometers[3]

Finding enough recycled paper was not easy, and it finally was sourced from Wisconsin. According to Rainforest Alliance spokesperson Tessa Vanderkop,

> Using the so-called Ancient Forest Friendly Paper, which is 100 percent post-consumer recycled, chlorine-free paper and fibre, costs about an additional three percent per book. On the Potter project, that worked out to an extra cost of $200,000 for Raincoast,…
>
> "We've completed this huge first run on the paper," she said Wednesday. "We're hoping the high profile of the Harry Potter books will raise awareness get other publishers on board. That would help drive the price down and make it more affordable."[4]

J. K. Rowling was pleased and urged other publishers to do what Raincoast had done. Even so, the pressure was kept up. In 2005, Greenpeace and the National Wildlife Federation called for a boycott of the U.S. edition of *Harry Potter and the Half-Blood Prince*, which was being published by Scholastic Inc. Instead, they encouraged people to purchase the Raincoast edition that used 100% postconsumer waste.[5]

The big breakthrough came in 2007, when Scholastic Inc. made the following announcement about *Harry Potter and the Deathly Hallows*:

> In agreement with the Rainforest Alliance, *Deathly Hallows* pages will contain a minimum of 30% post consumer waste fiber. In addition, 2/3 of the paper will be approved by the Forest Stewardship Council. In their news statement, Scholastic claimed that, "This historic commitment is the largest purchase of FSC-certified paper to be used in the printing of a single book title."
>
> Scholastic also announced that there will be a special deluxe edition of the book that will be printed entirely on 100% recycled paper.[6]

When *Harry Potter and the Deathly Hallows* came out in July 2007, it sold 11 million copies in the United States and United Kingdom on the first day.[7] No wonder one conservationist remarked, "If we get *Harry Potter* and the *Bible*, that pretty much covers the best sellers."[8]

Questions

1. If the cost of printing Harry Potter books on recycled paper added 3% to the cost, was the publishing company really serving the interest of its shareholders given that the demand for Potter books was so high that all copies would probably have been sold in spite of any boycott? Explain why and why not, and come to a conclusion.
2. There is the possibility of huge environmental savings by shifting to

---

[3] Ibid.

[4] "Harry Potter Author Runs Out of Paper," *Harry Potter Daily Prophet News*, April 8, 2006, accessed November 21, 2010, at http://www.harrypotter.ca/news-detail.php?ID=58.

[5] Alisa Elizabeth King Terry, "Harry Potter and the Deathly Hallows Goes Green," *Associated Content*, March 27, 2007, accessed November 20, 2010, at http://www.associatedcontent.com/article/193973/harry_potter_and_the_deathly_hallows.html?cat=38.

[6] Ibid.

[7] "Harry Potter Finale Sales Hit 11m," *BBC News*, July 23, 2007, accessed November 25, 2010, at http://news.bbc.co.uk/2/hi/entertainment/6912529.stm.

[8] "Harry Potter and the Deathly Hallows Goes Green."

recycled paper. Would the savings be even greater if books were published in digital format? Should publishers move to the 100% digital mode immediately? Why and why not?

3. What do you think would be a reasonable environmental strategy to recommend to authors and publishers for books to be published in the next five years?

ETHICS CASE

The Carbon Footprint of British Airways

Society is quite concerned about the level of greenhouse gases that are being emitted by various businesses. Many firms are responding by becoming more candid about the effects that their operations are having on the planet. Some are reporting this information through formal reports that follow the Global Reporting Initiative guidelines. Others are simply posting more environmental information on their websites.

British Airways (BA), the flag-carrier airline of the United Kingdom, adopted a One Destination policy in 1984. The overall objective is to act responsibly with respect to air travel. The company's website lists four areas in which BA will act responsibly: environment, community, marketplace, and workplace. Environment includes reducing carbon waste and noise and improving air quality, community involves supporting charities and community, marketplace involves encouraging customers and suppliers to be responsible, and workplace involves creating an environment that motivates, engages, supports, and develops the company's employees.

One of BA's environmental goals is to ensure that the airline reduces its carbon dioxide emissions. It is doing this, in part, by buying more fuel-efficient airplanes that are also quieter. The company is replacing its fleet of Boeing 767-300 and Boeing 747-400 aircraft with a mixture of Airbus A380s and Boeing 787s. According to the BA website, "The Airbus A380 has 17% lower fuel burn per seat than the Boeing 747 [and] the A380 emits about 10% less NOx per aircraft than the Boeing 747–400." Overall, BA is trying to do its part in reducing its carbon footprint.

In September 2009, BA was accused of hypocrisy when it announced that it was launching "Club World London City," a luxury service between London and New York. Customers would pay £1,901 to £5,000 for a return ticket to travel on a customized Airbus A318, a plane that is smaller than the A380. The A318, which normally holds 100 people, would seat just thirty-two passengers. The environmental group Plane Stupid protested the maiden flight. Greenpeace said that the service was "another example of BA saying one thing, and doing another. Only last week, Willie Walsh [BA's CEO] announced that the industry is committed to playing its part in the fight against climate change. But it is blindingly obvious that the aviation industry doesn't intend to cut emissions at all. Rather airlines, like BA, want to pay other countries and sectors to make those cuts so that the industry can carry on with business as usual."

BA's main source of revenue is the yield on premium seats, the seats that are often occupied with business people. However, these yields had recently fallen by 10% as passengers traded down to economy seats. The Club World London City flights, designed for business-class travelers, fly out of the Dockland's airport, close to London's financial district.

Questions

1. Do you think that British Airways is being hypocritical?
2. British Airways is attempting to reduce its carbon footprint by flying more fuel- efficient airplanes, such as the A318. The carbon footprint per passenger is lower if 100 people

occupy the A318 rather than only 32 people. Does the airline also have a responsibility to reduce each passenger's carbon footprint?

3. The passengers who fly on the Club World London City flight pay a substantial premium for the luxury accommodation. Do you think that the increased premium they pay offsets the increased carbon footprint of having only 32 passengers in the airplane?

4. Is it socially responsible for British Airways to fly 32 passengers in an aircraft that can normally hold 100 passengers?

Sources: British Airways, "Environment—Our Future Fleet," http://www.britishairways.com/travel/csr-new-aircraft/public/en_gb, and "One Destination," http://www.britishairways.com/travel/csr-corporate-responsibility/public/en_gb.

David Teather, "British Airways Launches Luxury Service to New York," *The Guardian*, September 29, 2009, http://www.guardian.co.uk/business/2009/sep/28/theairlineindus try-britishairways.

ETHICS CASE

The Pollution Caused by Cruise Ships

In essence, cruise ships are floating small towns. They carry thousands of passengers on ships that often stand thirteen decks tall. The cruise ship industry that travels from Washington State to Alaska contributes billions of dollars into the economies of many American and Canadian port cities. Each time a ship docks at Seattle, it pumps $1.7 million into the local economy, $2 million into the greater Vancouver economy, and $1 billion annually into Victoria's tourism sector.

The cruise line industry spends millions of dollars annually promoting trips with photos and videos of travel through pristine waters and of passengers observing aquatic wildlife in its natural habitat while enjoying the scenic beauty of the shorelines of the Pacific Northwest. However, cruise ships, which normally carry 3,000 passengers and crew, generate enormous amounts of both water pollution and air pollution.

A typical cruise ship produces approximately 170,000 gallons of gray water (the water from showers, sinks, swimming pools, dishwashing, and laundry), 21,000 gallons of sewage, 6,400 gallons of bilge water, and 1 ton of solid waste per day. However, there are no consistent regulations concerning water pollution caused by cruise ships. For example, the states of Washington and Alaska have rules about discharging gray water, but the province of British Columbia does not. Therefore, cruise ships tend to release their untreated gray water as they pass through the Straits of Juan de Fuca separating Vancouver Island from the mainland of Canada and the United States. According to Beatrice Olivastri, CEO of Friends of the Earth Canada, "Cruise ship companies are taking advantage of Canada's weaker laws on sewage discharge to save money. It is bizarre that B.C. residents should bear the burden of cruise ship pollution from well-heeled tourists."[1]

The sulfur content of heavy bunker oil is 2,000 times more than the sulfur content of diesel fuel that is burned by smaller ships. The estimated daily air pollution generated by a 3,000-passenger ship burning bunker fuel is the equivalent of 12,000 cars. The U.S. Environmental Protection Agency (EPA) estimated that the pollution from these Alaska-bound cruise ships can travel over 4,000 kilometers, across British Columbia and Alberta, to as far away as North Dakota in the United States. In order to reduce air pollution, some cities, including Juneau, Vancouver, and Seattle, allow cruise ships to connect to the local power grid when in port.

Prior to 2012, the sulfur content of the bunker fuel that was burned by cruise ships sailing from Seattle to Alaska

[1] "Cruise Ships Turn B.C. into 'Toilet Bowl of North America' Critics Say," *Postmedia News*, August 20, 2010.

averaged 1.5% to 1.8%. In 2012, new laws enacted in both the United States and Canada forced container ships, oil tankers, and large cruise ships to reduce their bunker fuel air pollution. The allowable level was to be 1% in 2012, dropping to 0.1% by 2015. When the new rules were enacted, the EPA estimated that the improved air quality resulting from these new regulations would save as many as 14,000 lives each year. They said that this was the same as eliminating the sulfur dioxide emissions of 12.7 million cars per day.

Pollution rules only apply to cruise ships sailing within the 200-mile limit of Canada and the United States. Ships outside the limit can burn heavy bunker fuel and discharge their gray water and sewage without violating any international environmental laws or regulations. However, the International Maritime Organization, a UN agency, has proposed a worldwide limit of 0.5% sulfur content on all marine vessels by 2020.

Complying with pollution standards can be costly. The EPA estimated that the cost of following the 2012 rules would be an additional charge of $7 per day for a cruise line ticket. The industry estimated the cost to be $19.46 per day, or over $133 per passenger charge for a seven-day cruise. By way of comparison, a $50 head tax imposed by Alaska was blamed for a decrease of 142,000 passengers traveling in 2010.

In 2013, Carnival Corp. announced that it was spending more than $180 million to install filtration and air pollution control equipment, called scrubbers, on thirty-two of its cruise ships in order to comply with the 2015 standard of 0.1% sulfur pollution. Tom Dow, the vice president of public affairs, said, "It means that we're going to burn more economical fuel with a better environmental impact. The outcome's better, the cost is less."[2]

The cruise line industry has not always complied with the prevailing pollution laws and regulations. From 2010 to 2014, the U.S. government levied 129 wastewater violations and forty-nine air pollution violations against numerous cruise ship companies. These included the following:

- Ten violations against the Norwegian Cruise Line
- Fifteen violations against the Holland American Line
- Twenty-six wastewater violations against Princess Cruises in 2013 alone

In 2015, the Alaskan government charged Royal Caribbean International and Celebrity Cruises with environmental violations that spanned a period of five years. Fines and penalties are not new. In 2000, Royal Caribbean International paid $3.5 million to the Alaskan government for polluting the state's water.

Questions

1. If the pollution laws are lax in one country but strict in another, do cruise ship companies have an obligation to follow the stricter pollution laws even when they are temporarily sailing through the waters of the country with the more lax pollution regulations?
2. Many cruise ships travel outside the 200-mile limits set by the United States and Canada. Do these ships have any environmental responsibilities when they are sailing in international waters?
3. Should port cities compromise on pollution standards in order to generate tourism business?
4. Based on the facts presented in this case, is the cruise ship industry ethical? Explain why and why not.

Sources: James Brooks, "DEC Alleges Cruise Lines Broke Rules," *Juneau Empire*, August 9, 2015.

Carmen Chai, 2010. Juliet Eilperin, "Cruise Ship Lines, Alaska Officials Question New Air Pollution Limits," *Washington Post*, July 22, 2012.

[2] "Carnival Investing $180 Million in Clean-Air Technology," *Miami Herald*, September 5, 2013.

Andrew Sheivachman, "These Cruise Ships Got Caught Polluting in Alaska," *Skift.com*, August 18, 2015.

Hannah Sampson, 2013. Wendy Stuek, "Clean-Air Rules Prompt Warning from Cruise Line," *The Globe and Mail*, July 9, 2010.

Lee Van der Voo, "Big Cruise Ships Pollute Big Time and Can Sail Away from Regulation," *Investigate West*, August 16, 2010.

Carla Wilson, "Cruise Ships Experts Watch New Emission Rules," *Postmedia News*, July 22, 2010.

Workplace Ethics Cases—Discrimination and Abuse

ETHICS CASE

Texaco's Jelly Beans

In[1] March 1994, six African Americans employed at Texaco Inc. filed a class action lawsuit on behalf of 1,400 current and former African American employees. They alleged that Texaco had systematically discriminated against them in terms of promotions and had fostered a hostile corporate environment for minority employees.[2]

Richard Lundwall was the senior coordinator of personnel services in the Finance Department at Texaco's office in Harrison, New York. During an August 5, 1994, deposition,[3] he testified that he and other officials in Texaco's Finance Department retained records relating to the promotion of minority employees. He was asked to produce these documents. On August 14, 1994, Lundwall attended a meeting with other members of the Texaco Finance Department to discuss the production of these requested documents. Among the officers attending this meeting were Robert Ulrich, treasurer; David Keough, senior assistant treasurer; and various division heads, such as Peter Meade, Brian Ashley, Pete Wissel, and Steve Carlson.[4] Prior to entering the meeting, Lundwall placed a small tape recorder in his pocket and turned it on. When later asked why he had taken such action, he stated that "over the years I've seen a number of people thrown to the wolves when something went wrong, and I didn't want to be fodder for the wolves."[5] On a more practical level, however, Lundwall was also in charge of taking minutes of the meeting and found that recording the meetings ensured the accuracy of the minutes.[6] He stated that after the meeting, he placed the tapes in his desk and forgot about them.[7]

In the spring of 1996, Lundwall was informed that he was being downsized out of his job and had to leave Texaco by the end of August 1996. After thirty-one years of loyal service to Texaco, he expected more; he had seen other employees being pushed out when they reached fifty-five years of age and realized that the same thing was now happening to him.[8] It was not until he was in the hospital recovering from surgery in March 1996 that he remembered the tapes and had time to listen to them.[9] Lundwall maintains, on an interview on *60 Minutes*, that he had only to mention his possession of the tapes to a senior executive, and his job would have been secure. When asked why he did not take such an action, he responded,

[1] Prepared from a case submission by students Sudha Kutty, Philip Malin, Yasmina Miller, Shelley Pancham-Candler, and David Wong.

[2] *Roberts et al. v. Texaco Inc.*, 94 Civ. 2015.

[3] U.S. attorney, Southern District of New York, press release, November 19, 1996.

[4] Affidavit of Cyrus Mehri, sworn October 28, 1996, citing deposition of R. Lundwall.

[5] *60 Minutes* interview, transcript, 2.

[6] Affidavit of Cyrus Mehri, 6.

[7] *60 Minutes.*

[8] Ibid.

[9] Ibid., 3.

"It's not the right thing to do. That's called extortion and that's illegal. And ... the world's a crummy enough place without adding to it."[10]

By July 1996, Lundwall realized that there would be no job at Texaco. On his last day of work, he approached one of the employees who had launched the suit and informed her that "depending on how my situation turns out, you might have an ally."[11] Lundwall's reasoning was that, if a job did surface, then he would not have been able to come forward with the tapes, not for a while, anyway.[12] On August 1, 1996, Lundwall contacted Cyrus Mehri at the law firm of Cohen, Milstein, Hausfield, and Toll, lawyers for the plaintiffs. He informed Mehri that he had in his possession information that would be useful in the lawsuit against Texaco. In subsequent conversations, Lundwall informed Mehri that such information included tape recordings. On August 12, 1996, Lundwall met with Mehri and informed him that the tape recordings, created after the litigation began, revealed himself and other senior officials in the Finance Department discussing the destruction of documents relevant to the plaintiffs' case.[13] After this meeting, Lundwall retained a lawyer and in September 1996 handed over copies of two tapes to attorneys for the plaintiffs. On October 25, 1996, Lundwall met again with Mehri and listened to the tapes. He confirmed that the tapes were the same ones he had provided to his counsel to hand over.[14] He admitted that one of the purposes for the meeting of August 14, 1994, was to review the materials requested by the plaintiffs after the deposition and to hide documents from the plaintiffs. He admitted that he and others had shredded portions of the requested evidence, that handwritten comments were deleted from certain documents, and that certain finance officials were told to say that they did not retain their own copies of such information.[15] In one part of the tape, the following was revealed:

> ***Ulrich:*** You know, there is no point in even keeping the restricted version any more. All it could do is to get us in trouble. That's the way I feel. I would not keep anything.
>
> ***Lundwall:*** Let me shred this thing and any other restricted version like it.

In another segment:

> ***Keough:*** They'll find it when they look through it.
>
> ***Lundwall:*** Not if I take it out they won't.

Matters did not end here. The tape recording of the August 14, 1994, meeting contained other interesting bits of conversation. The initial transcript of the recordings, which hit the *New York Times* on November 4, 1996, indicated the use of expletives and racist terms, such as *niggers* and *black jelly beans*. According to the *Times*, at one point in the tape the treasurer states, "It's this diversity thing. You know how black jelly beans agree...," to which Lundwall responds, "That's funny. All the black jelly beans seem to be glued to the bottom of the bag." At another point in the tape, Lundwall states, "I'm still having trouble with Hanukkah. Now we have Kwanzaa. These f——ing niggers, they s—— all over us with this."[16]

Texaco was quick to act over the revelation of these tapes. At a news conference

---

[10] Ibid.

[11] Ibid.

[12] Ibid.

[13] Affidavit of Joseph Magan, special agent with the FBI, sworn November 19, 1996.

[14] Ibid.

[15] Ibid.

[16] *Court TV* Library, *Texaco Suit—Order to Show Cause*, transcript. Kwanzaa is an African American cultural festival.

held on November 4, 1996, Texaco chairman Peter Bijur apologized for the remarks on the tape, stating that such remarks represent not only a profound contempt for the law but also a contempt for Texaco's values and policies. Bijur indicated that the company was taking six steps to reinforce company policy and its code of conduct. Such measures included visits by senior executives to company locations to apologize to employees, the expansion of Texaco's "diversity learning experience," and a renewed emphasis on the company's core values. Two current employees were suspended with pay, and the benefits of Lundwall and former treasurer Robert Ulrich (who had retired in March 1995) were cut off. Texaco retained the services of Peter Armstrong, former assistant U.S. attorney for the Southern District of New York, to conduct an independent investigation into the matter. In his report released November 11, 1996, Mr. Armstrong notes that by using digital processing techniques, he was able to obtain a clearer version of the recording.[17] After listening to this version, he concluded that the word *nigger* was never used, as initially alleged in the plaintiffs' transcript:

> ***Ulrich:*** "I've heard that diversity thing, we don't have black jelly beans or green…"
>
> ***Lundwall:*** "… that's funny, all the black jelly beans seem to be glued to the bottom of the bag."

Through his attorney, Mr. Ulrich indicated that the term *jelly bean* was not meant to be pejorative and actually was a reference from a speech given by a gentleman later identified as Doctor R. Roosevelt Thomas Jr., who uses a jelly bean analogy as a means of describing diversity.[18]

Armstrong's conclusion was that the terms *f——ing nigger* were never used and that the references to jelly beans do not appear to have been intended as a racial slur. Bijur was quick to indicate that these preliminary findings merely correctly identified what words were actually spoken in the conversation but by no means changed the unacceptable context or tone of the conversation. The report's findings were published in the *New York Times* on November 11, 1996. Civil rights leaders interviewed on November 12, 1996, felt that the distinction in the transcript made little difference, as the tone of the conversation indicated a clear disdain for both Hanukkah and Kwanzaa and revealed intolerant overtures.[19] Bijur spent most of the day meeting with civil rights leaders, such as Kweisi Mfume of the National Association for the Advancement of Colored People and Reverend Jesse Jackson, many of whom called for a national boycott of Texaco.

On November 15, 1996, Texaco announced it had reached an Agreement in Principle to settle the *Roberts et al. v. Texaco* lawsuit. The terms of the settlement were as follows:

- Provide payment to the plaintiff class in the amount of $ 115 million, in addition to a one-time salary increase of approximately 11% for current employees of the plaintiff class effective January 1, 1997[20]
- Create an Equality and Tolerance Task Force, which will be charged with

[17] Peter Armstrong, "Interim Report of Independent Counsel," November 11, 1996, 2. This report was prepared for Texaco. See http://articles.philly.com/1996-11-12/living/25647258_1_jelly-beans-texaco-chairman-peter-bijur-texaco-case.

[18] Ibid.

[19] Kurt Eichenwald, "Civil Rights Leaders Issue Call for a National Boycott of Texaco," November 13, 1996, http://www.nytimes.com/1996/11/13/business/calls-issued-for-boycott-of-texaco.html.

[20] For the sake of accuracy, it should be noted that the plaintiff class had yet to be certified as a class and was to appear before the court on December 6, 1996, for a hearing regarding class certification. In the Agreement in Principle, the parties agree for the sake of the settlement to the certification of a class consisting of all African Americans employed in a salaried position in the United States by Texaco or its subsidiaries at any time from March 23, 1991, to November 16, 1996 (Agreement in Principle, November 15, 1996).

determining potential improvements to Texaco's human resources programs and monitor the progress of such programs

- Adopt and implement company-wide diversity and sensitivity, mentoring and ombudsperson programs
- Consider nationwide job posting of more senior positions
- Monitor its performance on the programs and initiatives provided for in the settlement agreement

The total cost of the agreement was said to be $176.1 million, making it the largest settlement for a race discrimination suit in history.[21] Texaco's problems, however, are far from over. On November 13, 1996, two Texaco shareholders launched a shareholder's derivative action lawsuit, stating that Texaco's directors and officers breached fiduciary duty and damaged Texaco's name.

Some would say that it was about time Texaco was finally caught. In 1991, Texaco paid a record $17.7 million in compensatory and punitive damages to an employee who sued for sex discrimination after the company denied her a promised promotion and gave her job to a man.[22] Others say that Texaco was forced to settle the case not on its legal merits but due to the inaccurate transcript published by the *New York Times*.[23] Some have argued that what the Texaco case proves is that "if you can create enough bad publicity, depicting a company as hopelessly racist, you can win without ever going to trial."[24] This may not be entirely correct. Had this matter gone to trial, damages in the Roberts action were estimated at $71 million in back pay and damages for each plaintiff in the amount of $300,000, resulting in a total liability of $491 million.[25] Furthermore, in June 1996, Spencer Lewis Jr., a district director of the Equal Employment Opportunity Commission (EEOC) for the New York City District, found against Texaco for failing to promote blacks and pursuing a companywide pattern of racial bias.[26] Lewis held that Texaco used an evaluation system to promote employees that did not comply with EEOC guidelines. Questions about Texaco's corporate culture exist. In a company whose core values state that "each person deserves to be treated with respect and dignity"[27] and where it is within the corporate conduct guidelines to report known or suspected violations of company policy to supervisors, some say that such a conversation could not have arisen if it were not prevalent for such written policies to be undermined by the actions of senior executives.

When Lundwall was questioned as to why he turned over the tapes, he indicated that it was not to get back at Texaco but, rather, to maintain a job.[28] In retrospect, he admits that he was naive bordering on stupid to think that handing over the tapes would help his cause. If anything, handing over the tapes apparently hurt his cause. On November 19, 1996, Robert Lundwall was arrested and charged with obstruction of justice in that, from July 1994 to August 1994, he corruptibly destroyed, concealed, and withheld documents requested by attorneys for the plaintiffs. As of December 17, 1996, Lundwall was involved in discussions with the prosecuting attorneys

[21] *60 Minutes*, 1.

[22] Jack E. White. "Texaco's White Collar Bigots," *Internet Bulletin* 148, no. 123 (November 18, 1996).

[23] John Leo, "Jelly Bean: The Sequel," *US News Online*, reproduced in *Incorrect Thoughts: Notes on Our Wayward Culture*, by John Leo, 129; see https://books.google.ca/books?id=DvDWFqwH1K8C&pg=PA129&dq=John+Leo+Jelly+Bean&hl=en&sa=X&ved=0ahUKEwjH0Nq6gt3OAhUJuBoKHRfUC1QQ6AEIJjAA#v=onepage&q=John%20Leo%20Jelly%20Bean&f=false.

[24] Ibid.

[25] Derivative Action Complaint filed November 13, 1996, 7.

[26] Cohen, Milstein, Hausfeld, and Toll, *Texaco Discrimination Lawsuit Sparks National Dialog on Racism in Corporate America*, November 1996, **http://www.cengagebrain.com**.

[27] "Texaco Apologizes for Racist Remarks of Senior Executives but Questions about Culture Remain."

[28] *60 Minutes*, 4.

to possibly resolve the charge without going to trial by either pleading to a lesser charge or offering help in exchange for immunity.[29] As a result of Lundwall's criminal subpoena before the grand jury, further questionable actions on the part of Texaco's executives have come to light. In addition to the documents pertaining to the promotion of minority employees, the grand jury records included a draft memo dated June 24, 1994, summarizing the results of an employee survey in Texaco's Finance Department. The results were distinctly unfavorable toward the criteria for promotions of employees. The draft results were forwarded by Lundwall to a lawyer in Texaco's Legal Department on June 30, 1994, requesting advice on publication of the survey results. A handwritten reply on Lundwall's covering memo from the lawyer dated July 26, 1994, advised delaying publication of the survey results to avoid its becoming part of the discovery process in the class action suit.[30] While Texaco lawyers state that this draft memorandum was not subject to discovery, the plaintiffs' lawyers claim that it did fall within the time frame.

When asked why it appears on certain portions of the tape that he took the initiative to shred documents, Lundwall would not comment.[31] His attorney indicates that the transcripts of the tape make it clear that Lundwall was directed to shred and destroy the evidence.[32]

When asked what he would do if he had to do it all over again, Lundwall stated that he would "slip quietly into the night with my benefits and let the system stay as screwed up as it is."[33]

Questions

1. In a company as progressive as Texaco, what permitted such discrimination to occur?
2. How could such discrimination have been prevented?
3. Is whistleblowing ethical?
4. Could a protected whistleblowing mechanism or conscientious ombudsperson have helped?

Sources: Cohen, Milstein, Hausfeld, and Toll, *Texaco Discrimination Lawsuit Sparks National Dialog on Racism in Corporate America*, November 1996, http://www.cengagebrain.com.

Court TV Library, *The Texaco Suit*, 1996, http:// www.cengagebrain.com.

K. Eichenwald, *Texaco Lawyers Reportedly Tried to Conceal Damaging Documents*, November 15, 1996, http://www.cengagebrain.com.

J. Leo, *Jelly Bean: The Sequel*, http://www.cengagebrain.com.

60 Minutes, *The Texaco Tapes* (Livingston, NJ: Burrelle's Transcripts, April 13, 1997).

Stepshow, *Ex-Texaco Exec May Avoid Trial*, December 17, 1996.

Kurt Eichenwald, "U.S. Negotiating with Ex-Official in Texaco Case," *New York Times*, December 18, 1996.

J. B. White, "Texaco's White Collar Bigots," *Internet Bulletin* 148, no. 123 (November 18, 1996).

[29] Stepshow, *Ex-Texaco Exec May Avoid Trial*, December 17, 1996, http://www.cengagebrain.com.

[30] K. Eichenwald, *Texaco Lawyers Reportedly Tried to Conceal Damaging Documents*, November 15, 1996, http://www.cengagebrain.com.

[31] *60 Minutes*, 5.

[32] Ibid.

[33] Ibid., 6.

ETHICS CASE

Gender Discrimination at Dell Inc.

In October 2008, Jill Hubley, a former senior strategist in the Dell Americas human resource group, a Dell Inc. division located in Texas, filed a lawsuit against the world's second-largest maker of personal computers. She alleged that Dell had systematically discriminated against female employees with respect to compensation and promotion. Her contention was that the men at Dell were paid higher wages for equal work and that women were not promoted to senior management positions.[1] The company denied the accusation even though there were no women on the top management team at Dell despite the fact that employed approximately 80,000 people worldwide. Ms. Hubley's lawsuit became a class action suit after four other women filed similar discrimination suits against the company.

In July 2009, Dell settled the class action suit with a $9.1 million payment: $4.5 million in back pay, $1.1 million for plaintiff legal costs, and $3.5 million to establish a pay-equity fund designed to adjust certain job grades for current management and nonmanagement personnel. Dell also agreed to establish a panel to ensure internal compliance with the settlement. Furthermore, the company announced it would hire an expert psychologist and a labor economist to review and make recommendations about the company's employment and compensation practices.

Questions

1. What factors contribute to a firm engaging in sexual discrimination?
2. What factors should the Board of Directors consider if there is an internal complaint of sex discrimination on the basis of pay and promotion?
3. What other costs might Dell incur because of its practice of discrimination?
4. How can a firm ensure that it does not engage in sexual discrimination?

Sources: Kirk Ladendorf, "Dell Settles Austin Discrimination Case for $9.1 Million," *Statesman.com*, July 24, http://www.statesman.com/business/content/business/stories/technology/2009/07/24/0724dell.html.

Joel Rosenblatt, "Dell Will Pay $9.1 Million to Settle Gender Discrimination Suit," *Bloomberg*, July 25, 2009, http://www.bloomberg.com/apps/news?pid=newsarchive&sid=aZtD.RbF.pjY.

CBS News, "Dell Slapped with New Discrimination Suit," October 31, 2008, http://www.cbsnews.com/stories/2008/10/31/business/main4560135.shtml.

[1]Joel Rosenblatt, "Dell Will Pay $9.1 Million to Settle Gender Discrimination Suit," *Bloomberg*, July 25, 2009, http://www.bloomberg.com/apps/news?pid=newsarchive&sid=aZtD.RbF.pjY.

ETHICS CASE

Novartis' $250+ Million Gender Discrimination Case

On May 17, 2010, a federal jury in New York decided that Novartis, a Swiss-headquartered drug company, was guilty of discriminating against women and should pay the twelve women plaintiffs who testified in the trial $3.37 million in *compensatory damages*.[1] Since there were 5,600 women in the class the plaintiffs were arguing on behalf of in the class action lawsuit, the total compensatory damages could have reached $1 billion if two-thirds of the plaintiffs had gone to New York and to state their case.[2]

On May 19, 2010, after further deliberations the jury awarded punitive damages of $250 million, or about $44,000 for each of the 5,600 women represented in the class action.[3] This was the largest award of *punitive damages* for any discrimination case in the United States. The amount equals 2.6% of the $9.5 billion revenue Novartis reported in 2009. The plaintiff's lawyers had asked for an award of between 2% and 3% of Novartis's revenue.[4]

According to the jury of five women and four men, Novartis "engaged in

[1] Chad Bray, "Women Awarded $250-Million in Bias Case against Novartis," *The Globe and Mail*, May 20, 2010, B13.

[2] David Glovin and Patricia Hurtado, "Novartis Must Pay $250 Million in Gender Bias Lawsuit (Update 5)," *Bloomberg Businessweek*, May 19, 2010, accessed November 26, 2010, at http://www.businessweek.com/news/2010-05-19/novartis-must-pay-250-million-in-gender-bias-lawsuit-update5-.html.

[3] Ibid.

[4] Ibid.

discrimination against pregnant women, with respect to the terms and conditions of their employment [and] in a pattern or practice of discrimination against the female sales representatives in pay and promotions."[5] Specific instances of discrimination cited at the trial included the following:

- One district manager "showed women pornographic images and invited them to sit on his lap,"[6] and the company's lawyer later indicated that "he wasn't that bad a manager. He was just terrible with women."[7] Later, the plaintiff's lawyer commented to the jury that Novartis "just doesn't get it. You can't be a good management if you're terrible with women."[8]
- One woman testified she was told by a male manager to get an abortion.
- Another said she was excluded from professional and social gatherings, including outings on which male colleagues took doctors to strip clubs."[9]
- "... women claimed that doctors groped them and made inappropriate comments. The company had a corporate culture that expected its female employees to be 'available and amenable to sexual advances from the doctors they call on' and 'looked the other way' when female representatives complained about inappropriate doctors. In one case, a doctor allegedly stuck his tongue in a saleswoman's ear. Novartis' response, according to the women, was to say the doctors were good customers, and not to overreact. Novartis said the women were lying."[10]
- "The suit also claimed that the women were paid less, not promoted into management, and punished if they became pregnant."[11]

After the verdict, Novartis indicated they would appeal, and on July 14, 2010, a $152.5 million settlement was announced subject to verification by a judge. The settlement included the following:

- $22.5 million over three years to improve its personnel policies
- $40.1 million in attorney's fees for the plaintiff's lawyers
- $60 million for back pay
- $40 million in compensatory damages for women who held sales positions from July 15, 2002, to July 14, 2010
- Additional payments to named plaintiffs and those who testified[12]

Novartis did not admit that there was systematic discrimination. Instead, its CEO stated that "some of our associates had experiences influenced by managerial behavior inconsistent with our values."[13] The company did agree, however, "to revise its sexual harassment policies and training, strengthen its employee complaint process, hire an outside specialist to help it identify gender pay disparities

---

[5] Bray, "Women Awarded $250-Million in Bias Case against Novartis."

[6] Larry Neumeister, "Novartis Hit with $250M Gender Bias Damages," *MSNBC.com*, from http://www.msnbc.msn.com/id/37233213/ns/business-us_business# (accessed November 28, 2010).

[7] Ibid.

[8] Ibid.

[9] Patricia Hurtado and David Glovin, "Novartis Must Pay Punitive Damages in Sex-Bias Case, Jury Rules," *Bloomberg Business Week*, May 18, 2010, accessed November 26, 2010, at http://www.businessweek.com/news/2010-05-18/novartis-must-pay-punitive-damages-in-sex-bias-case-jury-rules.html.

[10] Courtney Rubin, Inc., "Novartis Verdict Opens Door for More Gender Bias Lawsuits," May 20, 2010, laccessed November 28, 2010, at http://www.inc.com/news/articles/2010/05/novartis-gender-bias-case-opens-door-for-more-lawsuits.html.

[11] Ibid.

[12] "Novartis Reaches $152.5 Million Sex-Bias Settlement," *Bloomberg Businessweek*, July 14, 2010, accessed November 28, 2010, at http://www.businessweek.com/news/2010-07-14/novartis-reaches-152–5-million-sex-bias-settlement.html.

[13] Ibid.

in the company, and revise its performance management process."[14]

Questions

1. Was the verdict fair?
2. Will this verdict cause other companies to review for and remedy any systematic discrimination uncovered?
3. How should systemic discrimination be prevented?
4. Were the lawyer's fees fair?
5. Could this case have been successfully prosecuted if it were not a class action?

[14] Ibid.

ETHICS CASE

Downsize or Bonus Allocation Decisions

Assume that you have just been placed in charge of the Claims Investigation Unit of a small insurance company based in Minneapolis. Your personnel department has provided the following details on your personnel. However, because your insurance company is in the midst of takeover discussions, you have been asked to decide whom you would terminate if you were called on to downsize by one person and, alternatively, how you would allocate a bonus of $20,000 if no one were to be dismissed. You really want your team to function well after the decision is made because your future depends on it.

Question

1. What would your answers be, and what would your reasoning be for each?

Personnel Characteristics of Claims Investigation Unit

NAME	SALARY	TITLE	YEARS OF SENIORITY	PERFORMANCE	PERSONAL
Carol	$84,000	Analyst	5	Acceptable, misses deadlines	Married, many dependents
Gord	$72,000	Analyst	2	Outstanding, pushy suggestions	Single, no dependents
Jane	$68,000	Junior	8	Consistent, excellent, dependable	Married to successful architect
Ralph	$86,000	Senior	15	Acceptable, plodder	Married, two children in University
Hilary	$64,000	Junior	6	Acceptable, costly mistakes	Single, dependable, chronically ill mother

Workplace Ethics Cases—White-Collar Crime

ETHICS CASE

Walt Pavlo's MCI Scams/Frauds

Walt[1] Pavlo joined MCI in 1992 and rapidly became second in command at the company's finance or long-distance collections unit, as is documented in the ethics case "Manipulation of MCI's Allowance for Doubtful Accounts" in Chapter 5. Walt left MCI in 1996 and ultimately resigned in early 1997. During the four years and just afterward, he participated in several frauds on MCI and on customers who were dealing with MCI. The frauds against MCI are detailed in the case noted earlier, and the frauds he perpetrated against others are detailed here. Walt's motivation, opportunity for, and rationalization of these frauds are analyzed in the illustration in Figure 7.3.

Walt initially became caught up in an attempt to cover up the fact that many of the accounts receivable from companies that resold MCI's telephone connection time to consumers were far past due and collection ultimately unlikely. Senior executives at MCI were reluctant to show the true state of MCI's bad debts[2] because they wanted to isolate the company's earnings and assets in order to attract a favorable takeover bid buyout of shares that would make them rich. Consequently, although total bad debts approached $120 million, upper management encouraged MCI finance staff to use a number of techniques to minimize the visibility of the problem and limit the annual write-off of bad debts to only $15 million. The minimization techniques included the following:

- Restructuring a $55 million account receivable into the form of a promissory note—but one without collateral—so that the amount would not appear old in an aging analysis.
- Restructuring other bad debts into notes in a similar fashion.
- Lapping—applying checks from one creditor to the account of another to make it appear that bad accounts were being paid. The accounting system was notorious for its delays and inaccuracies, so if a customer complained about his account, it was "fixed" by a transfer from another customer's account with only a few accounting staff knowing what was going on.
- Disappearing an account—an extension of lapping where the balance on an account is eliminated by spreading it into the accounts of others through lapping.
- Recording "cash in transit" and using it to reduce problem accounts receivable—large payments of $50 million to $60 million per month from WorldCom, for example, were picked up by a clerk, faxed in, and recorded as a debt to cash in transit with the credit to a problem account. When the real check arrived, the entries would be reversed and proper entries made, but the interval of a few days allowed some "management" of accounts receivable.
- Misapplying vagabond payments—millions of dollars per month were

[1] All details used in this case are taken from Walter Pavlo Jr. and Neil Weinberg, *Stolen without a Gun: Confessions from Inside History's Biggest Accounting Fraud—The Collapse of MCI WorldCom* (Tampa, FL: Etika Books LLC, 2007).

[2] This mindset of MCI during senior executives has been challenged by a senior executive, who joined MCI during the fraudulent behavior and was asked by senior executives at MCI to investigate and clean up the area. He stated that most of MCI's bad debts were written off, so a large bad-debt allowance was not necessary.

sent in, and MCI's inefficient accounting system could not figure out which account the money belonged.

Walt was encouraged to "make his bad debt aging numbers," as he says in his own words: "Instead of gaming the system, MCI Finance had turned the system into a game, going so far as to send around a monthly internal report, grading departments on how well they did in sticking to their 'aging' numbers. Pavlo got a hearty pat on the back from his superiors, and he passed on the favor by praising his staff for their heroism in battle."[3] Walt was seen—and saw himself—as a "solutions provider" for MCI in managing the exposure to and of its bad debts.

One of Walt's customers, Harold Mann, introduced him to Mark Benveniste, the owner of a company called Manatee Capital, who had a proposal for "factoring" MCI's accounts receivable—paying MCI up front for a portion of certain receivables and collecting the entire receivable when it was paid. MCI would get their money much faster in return for a factoring discount or fee. It sounded great except that Manatee would not do the deal unless MCI guaranteed any accounts that proved to be uncollectible.[4] In Walt's terms, Manatee would, in effect, advance or loan money to MCA's clients to allow them to pay early, provided that MCI guaranteed these loans—and Walt was sure that MCI would not do so.[5]

Nonetheless, as time went on, Walt was under increasing pressure to "make his numbers" in terms of collections, which meant hiding overdue accounts receivable. Hoping a solution would emerge, Walt agreed to meet with Manatee's bankers from the National Bank of Canada. The meeting went well. Walt felt great—in charge—and he continued discussions with Benveniste over the coming months until the day came to sign off the legal documents. Although he had not discussed the Manatee arrangements with anyone at MCI and he knew that only company officers were authorized to sign such documents, he went ahead anyway and signed the bank documents committing MCI to guaranty up to $40 million if Manatee could not collect.[6] The bank took Walt at his word after checking with a switchboard operator that he was employed at MCI. Walt's bosses did not find out until it was too late, and by then they were on the hook for millions.

Needless to say, Walt took the factoring scheme forward within MCI under the banner of the Rapid Advancement Program for financing sales. It made him extremely popular with both the sales and collections people. Walt was a hero, and no one investigated how it worked sufficiently to question the economics involved or uncover the MCI guaranty.

During one of his meetings with Harold Mann, Walt told Harold that Robert Hilby, whose shady MCI reseller operation, Simple Access, had offered Walt a job, and that he was considering it. Not wanting to lose Walt as a potential co-operator within MCI, Mann proposed that Walt play "hardball" with Hilby by threatening to cut him off from the network (essentially stopping his business) unless he came up with a $2 million payment to eliminate his overdue account. Mann further suggested that Walt tell Hilby that Mann would help him raise the money for a fee. Mann had earlier told Walt that he would make their relationship "worth his while," so Walt told Hilby that the MCI's new zero-tolerance policy would require him to pay up and that he should talk to Mann. Hilby did call Mann, who told him that Mann would take over Hilby's company's $2 million debt in return

[3] Ibid., 103.

[4] This is known as factoring "with recourse" because the risk of loss stays with the account owner, MCI.

[5] Pavlo and Weinberg, *Stolen without a Gun*, 97.

[6] Ibid., 110.

for an up-front payment of $300,000, plus monthly payments to Mann until the $2 million was fully paid. Walt questioned Mann about where the money was actually going to go, and Mann proposed that if Walt would write off or "disappear" the $2 million account, he and Walt could split the money. Mann rationalized this saying, "If we don't pay MCI, it's not really out anything. I mean, you can't steal money MCI wasn't going to get anyway, right?"[7] Walt protested, but Mann countered: "You guys're cooking the books over there and you know it. Everybody cheats. That's the way the world works."[8]

Walt decided to think about it. It "was no worse than what MCI customers were doing to MCI, or what MCI was doing to its shareholders. Embezzlement was the legal term for Mann's proposal. But it wasn't like he was going to trick old ladies out of their savings or bash anyone over the head. It was victimless embezzlement—unless you counted hustlers as victims."[9] In the end, Walt decided to go for it.

Walt went on to play hardball with other MCI customers. They would pay Mann and his company, Walt would make the amount owing MCI disappear, and he and Mann would split the money. At least that was how it should have worked. Ultimately, Walt found that Mann was taking more than his share. In addition, Walt had to work through others in MCI Finance, who became accomplices. Unfortunately for Walt, one of these decided to deal with Mann directly, and Walt lost control of the operation. Ultimately, between the bilked clients and the National Bank wanting its guaranty, the house of cards that Walt built came tumbling down.

[7] Ibid., 118.
[8] Ibid., 120.
[9] Ibid., 120.

Questions

1. What aspects of the schemes described in this case were
   a. unethical?
   b. illegal?
   c. fraudulent?
2. When would a healthy skepticism by senior management or professional skepticism by an accounting or legal professional have been useful in combating the opportunities faced by Walt?
3. Was the Hilby caper a victimless crime and therefore okay?
4. What ethical issues should have occurred to Walt and MCI in regard to the schemes described?
5. What governance measures might have protected MCI if they had been in place and enforced?
6. What is the role of internal auditors in regard to such schemes?

Bribery & International Operations Cases

Jail and a German Subcontractor (names are fictitious)

ETHICS CASE

Harold Johns found himself in jail in Germany. He was a vice president of Baranca Industries Inc., a U.S. firm that constructs and installs factory equipment. Unfortunately, he was the highest-ranking Baranca official in Germany while he was in Germany overseeing the installation of some equipment. Much to his surprise, there was a problem with the way a subcontractor paid his workers. Apparently, the way the subcontractor calculated the pay was illegal. In Germany, when a subcontractor does something illegal, it is assumed that the company hiring the subcontractor had knowledge and was also guilty. In addition, the highest-ranking officials with the subcontractor and the firms who hired him are held legally responsible. Therefore, Harold and the head of the subcontractor were arrested—as was the head of the enterprise that owned the factory.

Questions

1. Is this a fair law?
2. If you were Harold Johns, how would you ensure that Baranca executives and Baranca itself would never be vulnerable to such problems again?

ETHICS CASE

AIDS Medication in South Africa

"South Africa and the drug companies have changed forever," say David Pilling and Nicol degli Innocenti.[1]

South Africa is to the drug pharmaceutical industry what Vietnam was to the U.S. military. Nothing will be quite the same again.

That, at least, is the view of Oxfam, the U.K. charity that has mounted a campaign for affordable medicines in poor countries. With other activist groups, it has championed the cause of the South African government, which has been in a three-year legal tussle with the drug industry about national legislation making it easier to override patents.

Yesterday, the drug industry, exhausted by the vitriol that has been heaped upon it, threw in the towel.

In return, they appear to have won certain assurances from the government that it will respect the World Trade Organization's Agreement on Trade Related Intellectual Property Rights (TRIPS),... [which they had earlier argued] allows the health minister to ignore patents without due process.

The threat of such wholesale disregard for patents—the lifeblood of the research-based drug industry—has prompted it to take some extraordinary steps. Several companies,... have offered to sell AIDS medicines to the developing world at manufacturing cost, slashing the price of triple therapy from at least $10,000 in the West for an annual supply to about $600.

[This differential price strategy] carries several risks. Drugs may flow back into Western markets. The scheme also exposes the companies to political pressures in Western markets, where consumers may start asking for similar discounts... [whereas the drug companies will]... "need some markets in which to recoup our development costs."

The article went on to raise questions about the way in which the government of South Africa was not waging an all-out war on AIDS, as follows. "The government doesn't have a good record with HIV," says Glenda Gray, an HIV specialist in Soweto's enormous Barawanath hospital. "We have a president who questions whether HIV causes AIDS... and a program that raises awareness but can't get condoms to people. It's difficult to see how winning this court case would be translated into treatment."

Questions

1. Is it legal, moral, or ethical for South Africa to override AIDS medication patents?
2. Is it legal, moral, or ethical for drug patent holders to resist?
3. If you were a senior executive in an affected drug patent holder, what solution would you suggest?

[1] "A Crack in the Resolve of an Industry," *Financial Times*, April 19, 2001, 15.

Risk & Crisis Management Cases

ETHICS CASE

BP's Gulf Oil Spill Risk Management

In its own *Internal Investigation*,[1] released on September 8, 2010, BP provided its analysis of why the Deepwater Horizon oil rig exploded, precipitating one of the largest oil spills the world has ever seen. Eleven oil rig crew members were killed and seventeen injured, the ecological base for the region's economy was dramatically compromised, and BP's financial viability was brought into question.

Problems developed after the initial drilling had been completed during the temporary abandonment process prior to the preparation of the well for oil production. Essentially, the temporary abandonment process involved making the wellhead and well bore secure from potential leakage from the oil reservoir under the seafloor to the sea. Usually, cement is forced into areas of the pipe casing and wellhead to provide a friction or mechanical seal so that oil flows only up a pipe attached to the wellhead. Tests are performed at various stages to assess the effectiveness or integrity of the pipe casing and the cement seal. In the case of the Macondo deep water well, BP, its partners, and suppliers botched the sealing process as well as the follow-up actions.

Although the Deepwater Horizon rig and the Macondo well are referred to as BP's, it is important to note that the oil drilling rig was owned and operated by Transocean,[2] the cement seal was designed and arranged for by Halliburton,[3] and BP had two partners: Anadarko Petroleum (25%) and Japan's Mitsui (10%). All have some culpability in the disaster.

In the Executive Summary[4] of its Internal Investigation released on November 8, 2010, BP lists the following reasons for the disaster and provides the reference diagram, reproduced as Figure 1.

1. *The annulus cement barrier did not isolate the hydrocarbons.* The day before the accident, cement had been pumped down the production casing and up into the well bore annulus to prevent hydrocarbons from entering the well bore from the reservoir. The annulus cement that was placed across the main hydrocarbon zone was a light, nitrified foam cement slurry. This annulus cement probably experienced nitrogen breakout and migration, allowing hydrocarbons to enter the well bore annulus. *The investigation team concluded that there were weaknesses in cement design and testing, quality assurance, and risk assessment.*
2. *The shoe track barriers did not isolate the hydrocarbons.* Having entered the well bore annulus, hydrocarbons passed down the wellbore and entered the 9 7/8 × 7-inch production casing through the shoe track, installed in the

[1] BP, *BP Deepwater Horizon Accident Investigation Report*, September 8, 2010, accessed December 11, 2010, at http://www.bp.com/liveassets/bp_internet/globalbp/globalbp_uk_english/incident_response/STAGING/local_assets/downloads_pdfs/Deepwater_Horizon_Accident_Investigation_Report.pdf.

[2] Transocean corporate website, http://www.deepwater.com.

[3] Halliburton corporate website, http://www.halliburton.com.

[4] *BP Deepwater Horizon Accident Investigation Report, Executive Summary*, September 8, 2010, accessed December 11, 2010, at http://www.bp.com/liveassets/bp_internet/globalbp/globalbp_uk_english/incident_response/STAGING/local_assets/downloads_pdfs/Deepwater_Horizon_Accident_Investigation_Report_Executive_summary.pdf. These reasons are generally echoed by the White House Oil Spill Commission's report of preliminary findings; see "Factbox: Oil Spill Commission Findings," Reuters, November 8, 2010, accessed December 12, 2010, at http://www.reuters.com/article/idUSTRE6A74FH20101108.

FIGURE 1 The Macondo Well

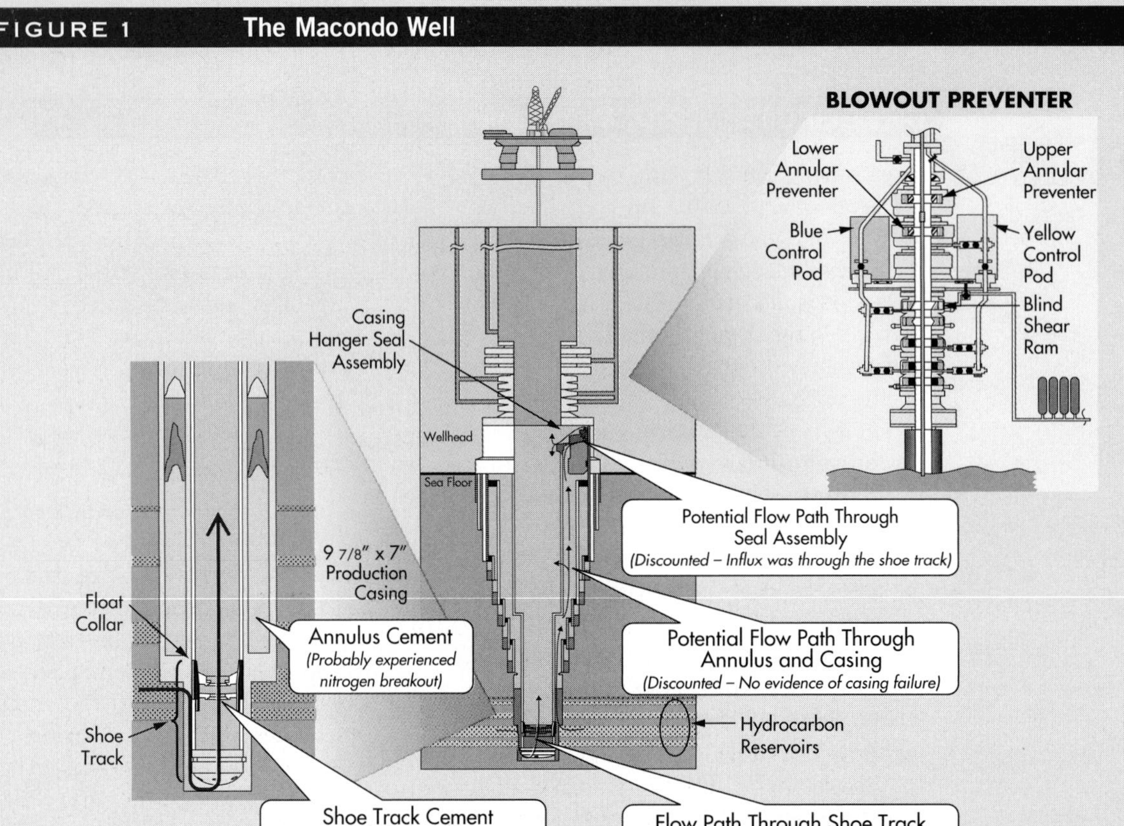

bottom of the casing. Flow entered into the casing rather than the casing annulus. For this to happen, both barriers in the shoe track must have failed to prevent hydrocarbon entry into the production casing. The first barrier was the cement in the shoe track, and the second was the float collar, a device at the top of the shoe track designed to prevent fluid ingress into the casing. *The investigation team concluded that hydrocarbon ingress was through the shoe track rather than through a failure in the production casing itself or up the well bore annulus and through the casing hanger seal assembly. The investigation team has identified potential failure modes that could explain how the shoe track cement and the float collar allowed hydrocarbon ingress into the production casing.*

3. *The negative-pressure test was accepted, although well integrity had not been established.* Prior to temporarily abandoning the well, a negative-pressure test was conducted to verify the integrity of the mechanical barriers (the shoe track, production casing, and casing hanger seal assembly). The test involved replacing heavy drilling mud with lighter seawater to place the well in a controlled underbalanced condition. In retrospect, pressure readings and volume bled at the time of the negative-pressure test were indications of flow-path communication with the reservoir, signifying that the integrity of these barriers had not been achieved. *The Transocean rig crew and BP well site leaders reached the incorrect view that the test was successful and that well integrity had been established.*

4. *Influx was not recognized until hydrocarbons were in the riser.* With the negative-pressure test having been accepted, the well was returned to an overbalanced condition, preventing further influx into the well bore. Later, as part of normal operations to temporarily abandon the well, heavy drilling mud was again replaced with seawater, underbalancing the well. Over time, this allowed hydrocarbons to flow up through the production casing and passed the BOP (blowout preventer; see Figure 1). Indications of influx with an increase in drill pipe pressure are discernible in real-time data from approximately forty minutes before the rig crew took action to control the well. The rig crew's first apparent well control actions occurred after hydrocarbons were rapidly flowing to the surface. *The rig crew did not recognize the influx and did not act to control the well until hydrocarbons had passed through the BOP and into the riser.*
5. *Well control response actions failed to regain control of the well.* The first well control actions were to close the BOP and diverter, routing the fluids exiting the riser to the Deepwater Horizon mud gas separator (MGS) system rather than to the overboard diverter line. *If fluids had been diverted overboard rather than to the MGS, there may have been more time to respond, and the consequences of the accident may have been reduced.*
6. *Diversion to the mud gas separator resulted in gas venting onto the rig.* Once diverted to the MGS, hydrocarbons were vented directly onto the rig through the twelve-inch goosenecked vent exiting the MGS, and other flow lines also directed gas onto the rig. This increased the potential for the gas to reach an ignition source. *The design of the MGS system allowed diversion of the riser contents to the MGS vessel, although the well was in a high-flow condition. This overwhelmed the MGS system.*
7. *The fire and gas system did not prevent hydrocarbon ignition.* Hydrocarbons migrated beyond areas on Deepwater Horizon that were electrically classified to areas where the potential for ignition was higher. *The heating, ventilation, and air-conditioning system probably transferred a gas-rich mixture into the engine rooms, causing at least one engine to overspeed, creating a potential source of ignition.*
8. *The BOP emergency mode did not seal the well.* Three methods for operating the BOP in the emergency mode were unsuccessful in sealing the well:
   - The explosions and fire very likely disabled the emergency disconnect sequence, the primary emergency method available to the rig personnel, which was designed to seal the well bore and disconnect the marine riser from the well.
   - The condition of critical components in the yellow and blue control pods on the BOP very likely prevented activation of another emergency method of well control, the automatic mode function (AMF), which was designed to seal the well without rig personnel intervention on loss of hydraulic pressure, electric power, and communications from the rig to the BOP control pods. An examination of the BOP control pods following the accident revealed that there was a fault in a critical solenoid valve in the yellow control pod and that the blue control pod AMF batteries had insufficient charge; these faults likely existed at the time of the accident.
   - Remotely operated vehicle intervention to initiate the autoshear function, another emergency method of operating the BOP,

likely resulted in closing the BOP's blind shear ram (BSR) thirty-three hours after the explosions, but the BSR failed to seal the well.

Through a review of rig audit findings and maintenance records, the investigation team found indications of potential weaknesses in the testing regime and maintenance management system for the BOP.

The team did not identify any single action or inaction that caused this accident. Rather, a complex and interlinked series of mechanical failures, human judgments, engineering design, operational implementation, and team interfaces came together to allow the initiation and escalation of the accident. Multiple companies, work teams, and circumstances were involved over time.

Based on BP's own analysis, the key faults or failures giving rise to the Macondo Gulf oil spill include the following:

- Related to the drilling rig and equipment:
  - Faulty design of MGS system (Executive Summary reasons 6 and 7)
  - Poor operations (Items 4 and 5)
  - Failure to keep BOP properly maintained (Reasons 2, 5, 8, and others)
- Related to the cement plug:
  - Poor design by consultant (Reason 1)
  - Poor mix by supplier (Reason 1)
  - Poor testing (Reason 1)
- Related to the mistake in interpreting test of well integrity:
  - Lack of technical expertise (Reason 3)
  - Lack of due diligence (Reason 3)

These faults or failures implicate not only the rig owner and crew (Transocean), the cement consultant (Halliburton), the cement supplier, and BP's onsite personnel but also BP's risk management program and practices. BP acted as the project operator and therefore had an overall responsibility for ensuring that all the other parties fulfilled their duties in a satisfactory manner. Since the oil spill occurred, it is evident that BP failed its oversight responsibility.

Videos

http://channel.nationalgeographic.com/epi sode /gulf-oil-spill-5488/Overview http://video.pbs.org/video/1625293496

Questions

1. Why did BP fail its oversight and decision capabilities?
2. Describe your vision of a good risk management process that BP should have been following.
3. What aspects of a good risk management process does BP not appear to have been using?
4. Has BP had other ecological disasters since 2000 that should have alerted the company to improve its risk management process?

ETHICS CASE

BP's Corporate Culture

BP has had a record of mishaps affecting life, the environment, and the property of the company and other stakeholders. On October 26, 2010, the Public Broadcasting System (PBS) in the United States aired a fifty-three-minute TV documentary titled *The Spill*, which covered BP's problems at its Texas City refinery, its Thunder Horse oil platform, its pipeline in Alaska, and the Gulf oil spill.

Questions

Review the PBS documentary *The Spill* at http://video.pbs.org/video/1625293496 and answer the following questions:

1. Analyze whether BP's corporate culture was ethical?
2. Why has BP's culture developed as it has?
3. How you would suggest changing its culture?

4. What roles should the CEO and the Board of Directors play in making this change?
5. How could this change in culture be measured?

ETHICS CASE

Toyota's Recall Problems

In 2000,[1] Toyota had a strong and growing reputation for quality. Its engineering excellence was peaking with the worldwide introduction of the first successful commercially available hybrid, the Prius, in 2001. But by 2010, over 10 million individual recalls[2]—including multiple recalls of some models—had left Toyota's reputation in tatters, allowing other manufacturers to regain their momentum and even the leadership in sales. Ultimately, Akio Toyoda, the president of Toyota Motor Corporation, journeyed from Japan to testify before the U.S. House Oversight and Government Reform Committee on February 24, 2010. How this change of fortune transpired is a complex and interesting story.

Toyota's own website reports seventeen specific recalls beginning in 2000 and ending in 2010.[3] These recalls were all related to floor mat interference with the accelerator pedal or with accelerator malfunctions from other causes. Numerous accidents were reported where the installation of a winter floor mat over the regular summer floor mat caused the accelerator to jam at high speeds so that the car would race uncontrollably and sometimes crash. To remedy this, Toyota contacted current owners and explained the problem. They told customers that two mats were not to be installed on top of one another. The company also shortened the accelerator pedal so that two mats could not jam the pedal. The second set of reported problems related to a suspected flaw in the accelerator linkage, or the acceleration control software, that also caused the car to accelerate suddenly and race uncontrollably. The remedy for this problem was to install a small metal chip in the pedal linkage to remove the possibility that the mechanism would stick. Toyota maintained that the braking system in the car would bring it to a stop in either case, but it installed a brake override system in some cars to further facilitate this.

Toyota's recall problems were exacerbated by several sensational news stories about runaway cars where drivers reportedly could only hang on and hope for salvation. In California, a Prius driver had to stand on his brake pedal and, as directed by a highway patrol policeman who caught up and drove alongside, pull on the emergency brake to get the car to slow down.[4] One 911 call from a driver of a Lexus whose accelerator was reportedly jammed was broadcast on some media outlets right up to the crash that killed all four members of his family.[5] Other interviews were aired on TV stations with individuals who claimed that jammed accelerator pedals led to similar incidents. Pressure mounted dramatically as Toyota seemed to be facing a wall of criticism.

---

[1] This case benefited from an analysis prepared by the following students in Professor Brooks's 2010 Business and Professional Ethics course (MGT 1102) in the Master of Management and Professional Accounting Program at the University of Toronto: Jaclyn Chiang, Leon Sun, Tina Sun, and Neal Yang.

[2] "2009–2010 Toyota Vehicle Recalls," Recall Timeline, *Wikipedia*, http://en.wikipedia.org/wiki/Toyota_recalls (accessed January 23, 2010).

[3] Toyota, "Toyota Recall Update," http://www.toyota.com/toyotaSearch/search?keyword=recalls&locale=en (accessed January 23, 2011),

[4] For a video of the driver telling is story, see "Runaway Prius in California," Reuters, March 9, 2010, http://www.reuters.com/news/video?videoId=54378733.

[5] For a partial replay of the audio tape, see "CHP Releases 911 Call in Officer's Fiery Crash," *Metacafe*, October 1, 2009, accessed January 23, 2011, at http://www.metacafe.com/watch/3474726/chp_releases_911_call_in_officers_fiery_crash. The crash took place in California on August 28, 2009.

To many observers, Toyota was slow to react empathetically to what seemed to be evident problems. In addition, there were charges that the company knew of the problems long before any recalls were initiated or information was shared with car owners. There were also claims that Toyota was unconcerned about or ignored the problems in an effort to reduce expected legal costs. Toyota was later fined $16.4 million because the company did not report potential difficulties on a timely basis. The company knew about the sticking pedals on September 29, 2009, but did not report this until January 2010 even though the National Highway Traffic Safety Association (NHTSA) required reporting this problem within five days.[6]

The cost to Toyota was significant. "More than 20 percent of those who said they were considering a Toyota prior to the recall now say they no longer are considering the brand for their next vehicle purchase. In addition, Toyota's overall brand consideration dropped to third-place and now trails its domestic rivals, first- place Ford and second- place Chevrolet."[7] Toyota's stock price declined approximately 16% from January 1, 2010, to October 22, 2010, on the New York Stock Exchange, and as a result Zacks Equity Research ranked the stock as a "strong sell" for investors.[8] Estimates of the cost of the recalls reached as high as $2 billion, including warranty payments and lost sales. The number of class action suits was growing daily.[9]

The pressure mounted on Toyota to be accountable, and the Japanese parent company president, Akio Toyoda, was called to testify in Washington in public on February 24, 2010. During his testimony, he stated,

- In the past few months, our customers have started to feel uncertain about the safety of Toyota's vehicles, and I take full responsibility for that…
- Toyota has, for the past few years, been expanding its business rapidly. Quite frankly, I fear the pace at which we have grown may have been too quick. I would like to point out here that Toyota's priority has traditionally been the following: First; Safety, Second; Quality, and Third; Volume. These priorities became confused, and we were not able to stop, think, and make improvements as much as we were able to before, and our basic stance to listen to customers' voices to make better products has weakened somewhat. We pursued growth over the speed at which we were able to develop our people and our organization, and we should sincerely be mindful of that. I regret that this has resulted in the safety issues described in the recalls we face today, and I am deeply sorry for any accidents that Toyota drivers have experienced.
- Especially, I would like to extend my condolences to the members of the Saylor family, for the accident in San Diego. I would like to send my prayers again, and I will do everything in my power to ensure that such a tragedy never happens again.

---

[6] Ken Thomas, "Toyota to Pay Record $16.4 Million Recall Fine," Associated Press, April 19, 2010, accessed January 25, 2011, at http://www.msnbc.msn.com/id/36634661/ns/business-autos. A video is embedded in the article.

[7] Kelley Blue Book, "Kbb.com Study: Toyota Brand Consideration, Vehicle Interest Dramatically Drops Following Recall," February 3, 2010, accessed January 25, 2011, at http://www.prnewswire.com/news-releases/kbbcom-study-toyota-brand-consideration-vehicle-interest-dramatically-drops-following-recall-83425457.html.

[8] Zacks Equity Research, "Total Recall Rerun," October 22, 2010, accessed January 25, 2011, at http://finance.yahoo.com/news/Toyota-Recall-zacks-2538726313.html?x=0&.v=l.

[9] Margaret Cronin Fisk, "Toyota Recall Cost to Exceed $2 Billion, Lawyers Say (Update 2)," *Bloomberg Businessweek*, February 9, 2010, accessed January 25, 2011, at http://www.businessweek.com/news/2010-02-09/toyota-recall-cost-to-exceed-2-billion-lawyers-say-update2-.html.

- Since last June, when I first took office, I have personally placed the highest priority on improving quality over quantity, and I have shared that direction with our stakeholders. As you well know, I am the grandson of the founder, and all the Toyota vehicles bear my name. For me, when the cars are damaged, it is as though I am as well. I, more than anyone, wish for Toyota's cars to be safe, and for our customers to feel safe when they use our vehicles. Under my leadership, I would like to reaffirm our values of placing safety and quality the highest on our list of priorities, which we have held to firmly from the time we were founded. I will also strive to devise a system in which we can surely execute what we value…
- I would like to discuss how we plan to manage quality control as we go forward. Up to now, any decisions on conducting recalls have been made by the Customer Quality Engineering Division at Toyota Motor Corporation in Japan. This division confirms whether there are technical problems and makes a decision on the necessity of a recall. However, reflecting on the issues today, what we lacked was the customers' perspective.
- To make improvements on this, we will make the following changes to the recall decision-making process. When recall decisions are made, a step will be added in the process to ensure that management will make a responsible decision from the perspective of "customer safety first." To do that, we will devise a system in which customers' voices around the world will reach our management in a timely manner, and also a system in which each region will be able to make decisions as necessary. Further, we will form a quality advisory group composed of respected outside experts from North America and around the world to ensure that we do not make a misguided decision. Finally, we will invest heavily in quality in the United States, through the establishment of an Automotive Center of Quality Excellence, the introduction of a new position—Product Safety Executive, and the sharing of more information and responsibility within the company for product quality decisions, including defects and recalls.
- Even more importantly, I will ensure that members of the management team actually drive the cars, and that they check for themselves where the problem lies as well as its severity. I myself am a trained test driver. As a professional, I am able to check on problems in a car, and can understand how severe the safety concern is in a car. I drove the vehicles in the accelerator pedal recall as well as the Prius, comparing the vehicles before and after the remedy in various environmental settings. I believe that only by examining the problems on-site, can one make decisions from the customer perspective. One cannot rely on reports or data in a meeting room.
- Through the measures I have just discussed, and with whatever results we obtain from the investigations we are conducting in cooperation with NHTSA, I intend to further improve on the quality of Toyota vehicles and fulfill our principle of putting the customer first.
- My name is on every car. You have my personal commitment that Toyota will work vigorously and unceasingly to restore the trust of our customers.[10]

Reaction to Mr. Toyoda's testimony was generally favorable, even though

[10] Akio Toyoda, *Prepared Testimony of Akio Toyoda, President, Toyota Motor Corporation*, February 24, 2010, accessed January 25, 2011, at https://oversight.house.gov/wp-content/uploads/2012/01/20100224Toyoda.pdf. The complete transcript is downloadable from **www.cengagebrain.com**.

rumors about cost cutting and misguided leadership[11] continued to affect consumer assessment of Toyota quality. For example, two former company presidents, Katsuaki Watanabe and Hiroshi Okuda, took the view that the troubles were "less a quality crisis and more a management and public-relations crisis of Mr. Toyoda's making."[12] Others have speculated that the governance mechanism of Toyota was partly to blame since Toyota had taken advantage of a "home-country exemption" from SOX regulations. Furthermore, its directors may have lacked independence and have been less loyal to shareholders. This may have fostered "a culture of stonewalling and secrecy."[13]

Throughout the period, the U.S. media continued to stir the pot with one sensational story after another. Some observers wondered if some stories were slanted to damage the reputation of Toyota cars relative to North American car manufacturers, which had suffered through bankruptcy and bailout and had lost sales to Toyota in major markets. To some degree, Toyota's delay in responding strongly to such stories may have allowed reputational damage that could have been avoided.

In fairness to Toyota, there may have been more smoke than fire in the news stories. Although it was not known publicly until mid-July 2010, when seventy-five fatal accidents attributed to sudden acceleration due to jammed or sticking gas pedals were investigated by the NHTSA using "black boxes" from the cars involved, it was found that "the throttles were wide open and the brakes were not being depressed." This result suggested that driver error was the cause since "drivers were mistakenly standing on the gas pedal when they thought they were standing on the brakes." None of the throttle linkages were at fault. In only one case was the gas pedal jammed, and that was due to an all-weather floor mat from another automobile being installed over the Toyota mat.[14]

Questions

1. Did Toyota handle its recalls ethically? Why and why not?
2. What changes would you recommend to Toyota's crisis management approach? Why?
3. Do you think that Mr. Toyoda's testimony on February 24, 2010, was effective? How might it be improved?
4. Toyota did not immediately disclose that each car carried an airplane-style "black box" that recorded details on how the car was functioning. Was this timing appropriate?
5. What possible reasons could account for Toyota's delay in advising the NHTSA of the problems known on September 29, 2009?
6. Can Toyota recover from these recall problems? If so, how long will that take? What would Toyota have to do to recover fully?

---

[11] Steve Tobak, "Inside Toyota: Leadership Conflict Turns Destructive," BNET, April 20, 2010, accessed January 25, 2011, at http://www.bnet.com/blog/ceo/inside-toyota-leadership-conflict-turns-destructive/%204421.

[12] Ibid.

[13] Michael W. Stocker and Yoko Goto, "A Recall for Toyota's Corporate Governance?," *Pensions and Investments*, April 5, 2010, accessed January 25, 2011, at http://www.pionline.com/article/20100405/PRINTSUB/304059981.

[14] Scott Evans, "DOT Report: Driver Error, Not Defects to Blame in Toyota Sudden Acceleration," *Wall Street Journal*, July 14, 2010, reprinted in *Automobile*, accessed January 25, 2011, at http://rumors.automobilemag.com/dot-report-driver-error-not-defects-to-blame-in-toyota-sudden-acceleration-3942.html.

ETHICS CASE

Digoxin Overdose—The Need for Skepticism, Courage, and Persistence

A two-month-old child was accidentally given a drug overdose at a Texas hospital despite the fact that seven health care professionals reviewed the prescription order before the drug was given to the baby. The following excerpts from a *New York Times* article[1] illustrate how important it is that individuals continually question actions and their outcomes rather than assume that others have gotten it right. Although the setting is health care, most businesspeople and professionals have found themselves (or will find themselves) in situations in which skepticism, courage, and persistence are vital. All too often in business and professional situations, and particularly in those that escalate into crises, individuals suspect there is something that is not right, but they do not do anything (or enough) about it. As a result, the problem or crisis gets worse:

> On a Friday afternoon last summer, tiny Jose Eric Martinez was brought to the outpatient clinic of Hermann Hospital in Houston for a checkup. The 2-month-old looked healthy to his parents, and he was growing well, so they were rattled by the news that the infant had a ventricular septal defect, best described as a hole between the pumping chambers of his heart.
>
> He was showing the early signs of congestive heart failure, the doctors said, and those symptoms would need to be brought under control by a drug, Digoxin, which would be given intravenously during a several-day stay. The child's long-term prognosis was good, the doctors explained.
>
> Time would most likely close the hole, and if it did not, routine surgery in a year or so would fix things. The Digoxin was a bridge between here and there. There was nothing to worry about.
>
> On the Friday afternoon that the boy was admitted… the attending doctor discussed the Digoxin order in detail with the resident. First, the appropriate dose was determined in micrograms, based on the baby's weight, then the micrograms were converted to milligrams. They did those calculations together, double-checked them and determined that the correct dose was.09 milligrams, to be injected into an intravenous line.
>
> They went on to discuss a number of tests that also needed to be done, and the resident left to write the resulting list of orders on the baby's chart. With a slip of the pen that would prove fatal, the resident ordered 0.9 milligrams of Digoxin rather than.09.
>
> The list complete, the resident went back to the attending doctor and asked, "Is there anything else I need to add on here?" The attending scanned the list, and said no, there was nothing to add. The error went unnoticed.
>
> A copy of the order was faxed to the pharmacy, and a follow-up original copy was sent by messenger. The pharmacist on duty read the fax and thought that the amount of Digoxin was too high. The pharmacist paged the resident, and then put the order on top of the pharmacy's coffeepot, site of the unofficial "important" pile. What the pharmacist did not know was that the resident had left for the day and did not receive the page.
>
> Sometime later, the backup copy of the as-yet-unfilled order arrived at the pharmacy. This time a technician looked at it and filled a

[1] Lisa Belkin, "How Can We Save the Next Victim?," *New York Times*, June 15, 1997.

vial with 0.9 milligrams of Digoxin. The technician then set the order and the vial together on the counter so that the pharmacist could double-check the work.

The pharmacist verified that the dosage on the prescription matched the dosage in the vial, and did not remember questioning the dosage in the first place. The order of the digoxin was sent up to the pediatric floor.

A nurse there took the vial, read its dosage, and worried that it was wrong. She approached a resident who was on call but had not personally gone over the drug calculation with the attending.

"Would you check this order?" she asked. Or maybe she said, "Is this what you want me to give?"

The resident took out a calculator, redid the math, and came up with.09, the correct dose. Looking from the calculator to the vial, the resident saw a "0" and "9" on both and did not notice the difference in the decimal point.

There was one remaining step. Following procedure, the first nurse asked a second nurse to verify that the order in the chart was the same as the label on the vial. She did, and it was.

At 9:35 p.m., a troubled nurse gave Jose Martinez a dose of Digoxin that was 10 times what was intended. It took 20 minutes for the entire dose to drip through his IV tube. At 10 p.m., the baby began to vomit while drinking a bottle, the first sign of a drug overdose.

Digoxin works by changing the flux of ions in the heart, altering the cell membranes. Too much allows the heart to flood with calcium, so it cannot contract. There is an antidote, called Digibind, and the nurse, her fears confirmed, called for it immediately. But even immediately was too late.

"They killed my son," the boy's father, Jose Leonel Martinez, sobbed on the local TV news. "Those people who work there are not professional and they shouldn't be there." A restaurant worker who had moved his family from Mexico a few years earlier, Martinez was shocked that the world's best health care system could make such a mistake.

"When I asked the doctor if the medicine they were going to put in him was strong, the doctor said no, that it was normal," he said through an interpreter. "That it was just so the child would function better."

The residents and the nurse were "given some time off" during the investigation, Walts [the hospital CEO] says; no one was fired. "It sobered us to realize that we've always dealt with errors as a discipline problem, yet we're not eliminating errors by firing people," she adds.

All those in the chain of error are back at work, and all are still haunted by the death of Jose Martinez. When the system fails, the patient is not the only victim. "It was an absolutely devastating thing," the attending doctor says. "The loss to the parents was indescribable. There are no words.… The only thing that made it possible for me to struggle through was my concern for these young people"—meaning the two residents. "I had to make them understand that this did not mean they were bad doctors."

Questions

1. What should the individuals involved have done?
2. How can the Hermann Hospital ensure that individuals do what they should?

3. Should the doctor, residents, pharmacist, and nurses involved in this tragedy be fired? If not, should they be sanctioned, and, if so, how?
4. Should such health care failures be made public?

ETHICS CASE

The *Exxon Valdez*

Shortly after midnight on March 24, 1989, the oil tanker *Exxon Valdez* ran aground on Bligh Reef in Alaska's Prince William Sound, spilling 11 million gallons of crude oil. Ecological systems were threatened, and the lives and livelihood of area residents were severely disrupted. For the tanker's owner, New York–based Exxon Corporation, the effects were profound.

How did such a tragedy occur? Opinions vary considerably. One oil company executive put it this way: "It's simple. A boat hit a rock." On the other hand, the evidence shows a much more complex picture of human and technical errors.

At the time of the grounding, the vessel had departed from normal shipping lanes to avoid ice in the water and had failed to make a corrective turn in time to avoid the submerged reef. The ship was piloted by third mate Gregory Cousins, who did not hold a required license; the captain, Joseph Hazelwood, was in his quarters. Hazelwood, whose driver's license was at the time suspended for driving while intoxicated, later failed a sobriety test. When the Trans-Alaska pipeline was originally opened, strict traffic lanes were established in the Sound to guarantee safe tanker passage. But, in recent years, disintegration of the Columbia Glacier had filled the lanes with ice. To avoid slowing down to dodge icebergs—thereby delaying the oil's delivery to market—tanker captains routinely moved out of the shipping lanes.

Onshore, no one was keeping watch. Although the U.S. Coast Guard was charged with monitoring vessels through Prince William Sound, in fact its outdated radar system did not reliably track vessels as far out as Bligh Reef. An earlier proposal to upgrade the radar system had been rejected as too expensive. And the Coast Guard's oversight, to say the least, was lax: at the time of the *Valdez* grounding, the only radar man on duty had stepped out for a cup of coffee.

Other corners had also been cut. The Coast Guard had reduced the use of specially trained harbor pilots to guide tankers out of the Sound and had withdrawn a proposal for tugboat escorts. Rules, such as those governing the number of crew members on the bridge, were not enforced.

The response to the accident was also fraught with difficulties. Alyeska, the consortium of oil companies that built and operate the Trans-Alaska pipeline, is responsible for cleaning up oil spills that occur in Prince William Sound. At the time of the accident, Alyeska's contingency plan promised to reach a stricken vessel within five and a half hours and to recover half of a 200,000-barrel spill within seventy-two hours, yet when the event occurred, Alyeska's plan was revealed, as Alaska's commissioner for energy conservation later put it, as "the greatest work of maritime fiction since *Moby Dick*." The cleanup crew had no instructions, the barge was in dry dock for repairs, needed boom and skimmers were buried under tons of other equipment in a warehouse, and lightering supplies were lost under a snowdrift.

Alyeska did not even reach the *Valdez* until almost twelve hours after the accident and in the first three days was able to pick up only 3,000 barrels of oil—2% of what it had promised. Incredibly, a group of local fishermen, later dubbed the "mosquito fleet," managed to retrieve more oil with their fishing boats and five-gallon buckets than did Alyeska with all its money and equipment.

When Alyeska's cleanup collapsed, a response effort had to be hastily jury-rigged by Exxon and the federal and state governments. Federal law called for an inter-agency team effort in which Exxon was responsible for cleaning up the oil, and different federal agencies were responsible variously for providing scientific advice, protecting the parks, and safeguarding birds and animals. The Coast Guard and Alaska's Department of Environmental Conservation were supposed to supervise the whole effort, yet no established procedures existed for bringing these organizations together into a working crisis management team under unified leadership. The result was a response effort "paralyzed by indecision, a struggle over authority, and vastly different and conflicting expectations as to which measures would work."

The debate over the use of dispersants, detergent-like chemicals that break up oil into droplets that descend below the water's surface, illustrates the costs for this paralysis. Exxon wanted to use dispersants and immediately flew in planes and chemicals. But under Alaskan guidelines, dispersants would be used in an oil spill only if less harmful to the environment than the crude itself. Since no one knew whether they were, the Coast Guard ordered tests, which were inconclusive. After two days of indecision, the government finally approved the dispersants—but that night the weather turned, and a spring blizzard whipped the oil into an impervious, frothy mousse. The opportunity had been lost.

The reaction of the public was predictable. A complete cleanup was demanded, which cost Exxon a reported $2 billion in 1989 and a further $200 million in 1990, with more out-of-pocket costs to come. More than 150 civil lawsuits were filed, not including those on behalf of the state and federal governments. The state and federal claims may be settled for a reported $1.2 billion.

Not surprisingly, Exxon's profits and stock price have remained flat since the accident. Shareholder groups have, however, been very active, particularly the institutional investors who as a group own 35% of Exxon's shares. With the support of the administrators of the New York City pension funds (which own 6 million Exxon shares), the Coalition for Environmentally Responsible Economies (CERES) brought pressure to bear on the company during 1990 to accept and endorse a code of conduct known as the Valdez Principles (see below) for dealing with the corporation's environmental behavior.

The company resisted accepting the Valdez Principles on several grounds, including that the principles were not sufficiently developed to be workable, that they went too far, and that further study was needed. In 1990, Exxon did, however, appoint an outside environmentalist to the Board of Directors and placed a senior officer in charge of environmental matters. The tanker was rechristened the *Exxon Mediterranean* and will operate henceforth in the Pacific Ocean. It was not refitted with a double hull, which would have cost about $20 million. Observers have also reported that Exxon has bought back substantial amounts of its stock: a move possibly made to support the stock price and pressure investors.

The Valdez (CERES) Principles

Leading environmental organizations—including the Sierra Club, the National Audubon Society, and the National Wildlife Federation—joined with the Social Investment Forum to form the Coalition for Environmentally Responsible Economics (CERES), whose first act was to draft the Valdez Principles for corporations to sign. The idea is to make the Valdez Principles a litmus test of corporate behavior. Companies are being pressured to abide by the following prescripts:

1. Protection of the Biosphere

We will minimize the release of any pollutant that may cause environmental damage to the air, water, or earth. We will safeguard habitats in rivers, lakes, wetlands, coastal zones, and oceans and will minimize contributing to the greenhouse effect, depletion of the ozone layer, acid rain, or smog.

2. Sustainable Use of Natural Resources

We will make sustainable use of renewable natural resources, such as water, soils and forests. We will conserve nonrenewable natural resources through efficient use and careful planning. We will protect wildlife habitat, open spaces, and wilderness, while preserving biodiversity.

3. Reduction and Disposal of Waste

We will minimize waste, especially hazardous waste, and wherever possible recycle materials. We will dispose of all wastes through safe and responsible methods.

4. Wise Use of Energy

We will make every effort to use environmentally safe and sustainable energy sources to meet our needs. We will invest in improved energy efficiency and conservation in our operations. We will maximize the energy efficiency of products we produce or sell.

5. Risk Reduction

We will minimize the environmental, health, and safety risks to our employees and the communities in which we operate by employing safe technologies and operating procedures and by being constantly prepared for emergencies.

6. Marketing of Safe Products and Services

We will sell products or services that minimize adverse environmental impacts and that are safe as consumers commonly use them. We will inform consumers of the environmental impacts of our products or services.

7. Damage Compensation

We will take responsibility for any harm we cause to the environment by making every effort to fully restore the environment and to compensate those persons who are adversely affected.

8. Disclosure

We will disclose to our employees and to the public incidents relating to our operations that cause environmental harm or pose health or safety hazards. We will disclose potential environmental, health, or safety hazards posed by our operations and we will not take any retaliatory personnel action against any employees who report on any condition that creates a danger to the environment or poses health or safety hazards.

9. Environmental Directors and Managers

At least one member of the Board of Directors will be a person qualified to represent environmental interests. We will commit management resources to implement these Principles, including the funding of an office of vice president for environmental affairs or an equivalent executive position, reporting directly to the CEO, to monitor and report on our implementation efforts.

10. Assessment and Annual Audit

We will conduct and make public an annual self-evaluation of our progress in implementing these Principles and in complying with all applicable laws and regulations throughout our worldwide operations. We will work toward the timely creation of independent environmental audit procedures which we will complete annually and make available to the public.

For more information, visit **http://www.cengagebrain.com**.

Questions

1. Who was responsible for the accident?
2. What were the responsibilities of the company, the government authorities, and the employees of the company, that were not properly discharged?
3. Should Exxon abide by the Valdez Principles?
4. Could a better code of conduct have prevented this accident?
5. If Exxon had known, before the accident, about the captain's alcohol problem, what actions should have been taken, if any?

Sources: J. W. Barnard, "Exxon Collides with 'Valdez Principles,'" *Business and Society Review*, Fall 1990, 32–35.

R. Gehani, "Will Oil Spills Sink Exxon's Bottom Line?," *Business and Society Review*, Fall 1990, 80–83.

"Lawsuits Proliferate from Grounding of the Exxon Valdez," *The Globe and Mail*, November 29, 1989, B2.

A. T. Lawrence, "An Accident Waiting to Happen," *Business and Society Review*, (Fall 1990, 93–95.

"Shareholders' Suggestions Get Exxon Nod." *The Globe and Mail*, May 12, 1989, B2.

"Exxon Looking at Offer to Settle Oil Spill Suits," *Financial Post*, February 8, 1991, 7.

ETHICS CASE

The Brent Spar Decommissioning Disaster

According to the Greenpeace Web page,

> On 16 February last year (1995), Greenpeace learned that the U.K. government had granted permission for Shell Oil to dump a huge, heavily contaminated oil installation, the 14,500 tonne Brent Spar, into the North Atlantic despite it being loaded with toxic and radioactive sludge. Dumping operations, just west of Ireland and Scotland, were expected to begin in May. Greenpeace went into action with plans to take over and occupy the rig to prevent the dumping. More than two dozen activists from six North Sea countries pulled operations together. Video and photo staff were called upon to document the Brent Spar platform and the occupation. The Moby Dick delivered activists to the platform (on April 30) and remained in the area to provide back up…
>
> Greenpeace believes that if this platform were to be dumped at sea, with some 400 others at work in the North Sea alone, this would have set a dangerous precedent.[1]

Without doubt, this act of piracy caused serious consternation at the headquarters of Shell UK and at the parent company's head office in the Netherlands.

Shell UK had been studying options for decommissioning the oil storage and tanker loading platform since 1991, but no perfect option had emerged. The Brent Spar was 140 meters in length, with 109 below the water level, so tearing it apart would be likely to cause leakage of hazardous substances. Consequently, for reasons of cost as well as environmental safety, Shell had chosen to apply to the U.K. government for a permit to sink the platform in the deep ocean. This decision was based on extensive assessments of the following options:

- Horizontal dismantling (and onshore disposal)
- Vertical dismantling (and onshore disposal)
- In-field disposal
- Deep-water disposal
- Refurbishment and reuse
- Continued maintenance

[1] Greenpeace, "Greenpeace Brent Spar Protest in the North Sea," http://www.greenpeace.org/%7Ecomms/brent/brent.html (accessed October 14, 1996).

Structure of Brent Spar

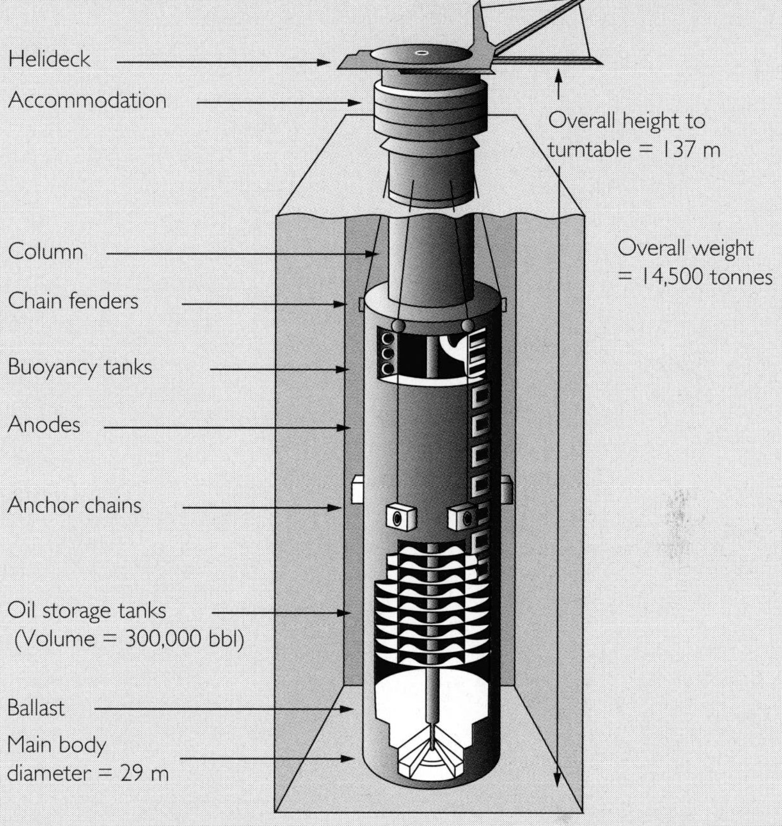

Deep-water disposal (at roughly $60 million)[2] was expected to be between 5% and 40% cheaper than other options, and, since the structure would not leak for 1,000 years, it was expected to be so buried by silt at that point as to be harmless.

The problem faced by Shell UK was what to do? The U.K. government was expected to issue a dumping permit momentarily. The Fourth North Sea Conference was scheduled to debate the issue of deep-sea disposal on June 8–9, and rumor had it that eleven of the thirteen countries involved could call for a moratorium on such dumping.

The following events transpired on or just after April 30, 1995:

- April 30: Greenpeace charged that large amounts of hazardous and radioactive oil were stored on the Brent Spar.
- May 5: The U.K. government issued deep sea disposal permit.
- May 13: Shell failed to evict Greenpeace from oil platform.
- May 19: Shell failed to obtain court consent to evict Greenpeace.
- May 22: Shell failed to evict Greenpeace.
- May 23: Shell removed activists from Brent Spar.
- June 7: Greenpeace reboarded and occupied a tow tug.

[2] Arkady Ostrovsky and Tim Burt, "Shell to Break Up Oil Platform to Make Quay," *Financial Times*, January 30, 1998, 8.

- June 9: Greenpeace revealed leaked document about cheap land option.
- June 10: Greenpeace battled to prevent tow to dump site.
- June 11: Shell postponed tow due to bad weather, tangled wire.
- June 12: Shell begins tow.
- June 14: Protesters in Germany threatened to damage 200 Shell service stations—50 were subsequently damaged, two were firebombed, and one was raked with bullets—unrest continued until June 20.
- June 15: Protesters in continental northern Europe strongly opposed—Chancellor Kohl protested deep water disposal at G7 Summit from June 15 to the 17.
- June 16: Greenpeace reoccupied Brent Spar.
- June 20: Several governments opposed.
- June 20: Shell UK aborted deep-water proposal and sought onshore disposal.
- June 21: Shell UK apologized to Prime Minister Major for any embarrassment.
- Late June: Support grew for Shell's early scientific approach.
- July 7: Permission granted to moor in Erford, Norway, temporarily.
- August 26: U.K. television executives admitted to lack of objectivity and balance in their coverage using dramatic film footage supplied by Greenpeace.
- September 5: Greenpeace apologizes to Shell UK for sampling errors and inaccurate claims that Spar contained 5,500 tonnes of oil in three of six tanks and so on.[3]

Questions

1. What would you have done if you were calling the shots at Shell UK? When?
2. What would you have done if you were calling the shots at the parent Shell head office?

[3] Chronology derived from Greenpeace website cited above and Shell UK Exploration and Production home page, http://ellexpro.brentspar.com/sites/brentspar/index.html (accessed October 14, 1996).

ETHICS CASE

Crisis at Wind River Energy Inc.

Lynn James was in the vortex of a set of crises. Lynn, an entrepreneur and the president, CEO, and 75% owner of Wind River Energy Inc., was one week away from closing a deal to secure much-needed financing for existing and new operations via an independent public offering (IPO) on NASDAQ under the sponsorship of prominent stockbrokers in New York and Toronto. All Lynn had worked for was in danger of going up in smoke, and there was grave risk to the lives of innocent workers and citizens. What on earth could and should Lynn do?

Over the last nine years, Lynn had been very successful. Initially, Lynn had been intrigued by the possibility of developing small, freestanding energy installations that fed their power into regional electrical grids or provided power to small, isolated towns. It had been possible to acquire and refurbish several small hydroelectric generating stations that had been mothballed by large northeastern energy producers or the small cities that still owned them. Due to the rise in the cost of fossil and nuclear fuels, these waterfall plants made a rate of return on invested capital of roughly 22%. Over the years, Lynn and various associates had bought and refurbished five plants, sold two, and continued to operate three in Ontario and Vermont. Based on successful operations in the East, Lynn had arranged for the incorporation of Wind River Energy Inc., into which energy holdings were transferred to provide collateral for bank loans and vendor mortgage financing.

During the last six years, Lynn became interested in the generation of energy using windmills. After visiting "wind farms" in California and off the shore of Denmark, Lynn realized that the wind conditions were exceptionally favorable just east of portions of the Rocky Mountains. He began to investigate providing energy needs to small, isolated towns in that area. Four years ago, a ten-windmill installation was developed outside of Freeman, Alberta, which initially contributed to the town's energy needs. The town owned an old hydroelectric plant on the local river and had a backup oil generator system for emergencies. Two years ago, Wind River acquired the town's energy generation systems and became the sole source of energy for Freeman. Four years ago, Freeman was a town of 2,000 homes that was using all the energy it could produce, so it welcomed the windmill installation. Since that time, 750 more homes were built to house the workers at two new mines in the area, and the town's hospital was enlarged. Further investment was now needed to provide additional generating capacity.

Based on favorable operations in Freeman, Wind River Energy had developed a reputation for reliability. The company took pride in keeping its commitments—a fact that attracted the attention of the mayor and leaders of West Fork, a neighboring town to Freeman. They approached Wind River, and Lynn signed a contract to provide energy to West Fork on the same basis as for Freeman. Part of the anticipated financing was to provide funds for the purchase of West Fork's electrical generating capacity.

Disaster struck during the last week. On Monday, the Wind River manager in Freeman, Ben Trent, called Lynn in Toronto to say that something had gotten stuck in one of the water input pipes to the hydrostation, and he wanted to know what to do. Summer was just starting, and air-conditioning needs would go beyond Wind River's capacity. Wind River's chief engineer was away on holiday, but Lynn checked with his assistant, who suggested that if the input door could be closed, someone could enter the clean-out pipe that intersected the input pipe. When this was relayed to Ben, he said that he did not think that the input door had ever been shut and might not work, nor had the clean-out pipe been used during the forty years the plant had been in service. He would check on them and call back. On Tuesday, Lynn received a notification from the Province of Ontario stipulating that Wind River's Ontario hydrostation would have to be shut down no later than Thursday. The court order stated that the stagnant water at the edges of the pond where the water intake pipe was located was likely to allow the breeding of mosquitoes that would spread the West Nile virus. The stagnant water situation would have to be remedied before the plant could restart, and Wind River would be liable to any persons from the local community who were diagnosed with West Nile virus from Tuesday to five days after the stagnant water problem was remedied. When Lynn went to consult the chief engineer's assistant (the only other real engineer on staff), he found that the man had just gone home sick with a SARS-like attack of the flu. Unfortunately, the chief engineer was in the middle of a backpacking trip in the Rockies and would be unreachable unless he activated the satellite phone that Lynn had insisted he take.

Ben called back on Wednesday to say that they had finally closed the input door and had just sent a small, thin man into the clean-out pipe to crawl up the intake pipe and clear the obstruction. Because the fellow was so keen, Ben told him to crawl all the way up to the intake door and try to grease the hinges on the inside.

On Thursday morning, Ben called to say that the fellow had done a great job of clearing the input pipe and had examined the hinges on the inside of the input door. He had just gone back in to try to remove the hinge pins, replace the bushings around the pins, and grease the bushings and pins. The mayor was pleased because the fellow was his brother-in-law, who had never really done anything else very well.

At about noon on Thursday, Lynn's lawyer called to remind him of the meeting on the following Tuesday during which Lynn, the CFO, and the chief engineer would have to sign off documents attesting to the excellent status of the company so that the IPO could go ahead. Any delay would jeopardize the financing deal. Lynn did not know what to say. He just thanked his lawyer and hung up.

In the early afternoon, Ben called to say that the fellow had gotten out of the pipe all right but had jammed one of the hinge pins when reinserting it and did not think the input door would open to allow water into the generating equipment. Someone bigger and stronger would have to go into the pipe to fix the hinge. Ben did not know what to do. He was not a real engineer, having been promoted to be manager on the basis of long service and personal connections with the city council, and he wanted Wind River's chief engineer to take responsibility and tell him what to do.

In addition, Ben said that the transformer station regulating the power from the company's windmills had been hit about a month ago by lightning and was operating only partially on an intermittent basis. The mayor of Freeman was getting calls about the intermittent "brownouts" of electricity and was putting pressure on Ben. Ben was really fed up. He also had a call from the mayor of West Fork, but he had not returned it yet.

Question

1. What would you do if you were Lynn?

Ethics Audit Program Annual Audit Questions APPENDIX A

Questions to Be Asked at Each Business Unit

Responsibility

- Is there a person at the business unit who is responsible for answering questions on and administering the *Code*? Who is this?
- Do the employees know of this person's responsibility with regard to the *Code*?

Awareness and Commitment

- Has the *Code* been distributed to all employees and managers?
- Have all managers signed the Representation Letter confirming that "during the past year, [they] and, to the best of their knowledge after due inquiry, [their] immediate subordinates who hold management responsibilities have complied with the *Code* and have taken appropriate actions to ensure compliance by other employees (who are [their] subordinates) and by contractors and consultants (who [they] have engaged or are responsible for)?
- Have all employees signed off during the past year that they have observed the *Code* and will continue to do so, and that they know of no unreported breaches of the *Code*?
- Are all new employees signing off when they join the company?
- Do all suppliers, contractors, and consultants receive a written notification that it is understood they will abide by the *Code* or specific provisions of it such as those on gifts or inducements, conflicts of interest, health and safety, or environmental protection?

Training

- Do new employees receive training on the *Code* when they join before they sign the *Code* sign-off?
- Have existing employees received training on the *Code* during the past year? What is the nature of this training?
- Do suppliers, contractors, and consultants receive a briefing on the *Code* and their need to observe it?

Commitment and Support Provided by Management

- Has management above the business unit shown personal commitment and support for the *Code* and the values on which it is based? How? (Speeches, memos, news articles, etc.)
- Has the management of the business unit shown personal commitment and support for the *Code* and the values on which it is based? How? (speeches, memos, use in screening merit and promotion decisions, etc.)
- Has there been reinforcing publicity in newsletters or through publicity of good or bad examples of behavior?

Operations

Regarding the business unit's systems for answering ethics inquiries, bringing ethics concerns forward for investigation, and investigation and sanction:

- Do employees and managers have confidence in these systems?
- Survey 10 employees and five managers.
- What are the annual usage statistics of each system?
- Were any significant ethical problems not handled appropriately?
- Were actions taken on a timely and appropriate basis?
- Do any items or issues require clarification to avoid further problems?
- Are there any suggestions for improvement of the *Code* or the processes involved?

- Do timely periodic reports to division management exist covering the activities of these systems?
- Are all items reported?

Questions to Be Asked of Each Division Operation, Assessment, and Continuous Improvement

- Are there personnel assigned (specify who) and systems in place to monitor and ensure the following?
  - Compliance with the *Code* in each business unit and at the division level
  - Effectiveness of the procedures for complying with the *Code* in such matters as training, sign-off, inquiry, investigation, and sanction
  - Assessment of operations and risks
  - Reinforcement and support
- Are necessary actions taken on timely and appropriate bases?
- Are timely reports prepared for and reviewed by division management?
- Are objectives related to the *Code* built into the divisional and business unit yearly operating objective statements?
- Are appropriate actions taken/reinforced by division management?
- Is there appropriate feed-forward reporting to head office to allow remedial action and solutions to be shared across the company?
- Does head office react and respond to feed-forward or requests for clarification?
- Has management above the division shown personal commitment and support for the *Code* and the values on which it is based? How? (speeches, memos, news articles, etc.)
- Are there any issues needing further clarification and/or suggestion?
- Are there any issues that should be reported to the board for information or action?

---

[1] See GISR website, http://ratesustainability.org/about/frequently-asked-questions.

[2] See GISR Partners website, http://ratesustainability.org/partners.

[3] Ibid., adapted from GISR website: *About GISR: Frequently Asked Questions*, "How Does GISR Differ from the Many Other Sustainability Initiatives?," accessed November 28, 2013, at http://ratesustainability.org/about/frequently-asked-questions.

[4] Ibid.

[5] KPMG, *KPMG International Survey of Corporate Responsibility Reporting 2011*, 6, http://www.kpmg.com/Global/en/IssuesAndInsights/ArticlesPublications/corporate-responsibility/Documents/2011-survey.pdf.

8

Subprime Lending Fiasco—Ethics Issues

PURPOSE OF THE CHAPTER

The subprime lending crisis began to be felt in earnest in 2008. As the number of mortgage foreclosures and walkaways grew, huge investor losses followed that threatened the vitality of financial institutions, intermediary companies, investors, and many individuals. Questions about how this situation developed, who was to blame, and what could be done to avoid similar occurrences in the future gave way to questions about the ethics (or lack of ethics) that underlay the actions causing so much distress. This chapter explores those questions and proposes lessons to be learned to help protect the future from similar fiascos.

THE ECONOMIC TRAIN WRECK—A GLOBAL DISASTER

The subprime lending fiasco brought the United States and world financial markets to their knees by precipitating a liquidity crisis and economic downturn so severe that major financial corporations had to be rescued from insolvency by governments and private investors. Stock prices in the United States declined in excess of 40% amid extreme volatility. The International Monetary Fund (IMF) helped to bail out Iceland's three major banks and save that country from financial ruin. Several countries, including Hungary and Ukraine, applied to the IMF, the lender of last resort for countries, for financial assistance, raising concerns that the IMF's capitalization of U.S.$250 billion might not be sufficient to meet the demand. European governments also pumped funds into several of their banks to keep them afloat. The European Economic Union provided funds and loan guaranties for the debt issued by Greece and other European countries.

All of this turmoil arose principally[1] because financial institutions, pension funds, corporations, and private investors purchased mortgage-backed securities that ultimately turned out to be worth much less than anyone ever imagined possible. The decline in value of these investments, and an inability to accurately estimate their worth, undermined the liquid funds or capital available to do business, to make loans, or to settle commitments. A "credit crunch" or liquidity crisis ensued that caught many overleveraged financial institutions by surprise, threatened their existence, and forced some into bankruptcy, such as Lehman Brothers. Reasonably leveraged financial institutions were unable to borrow, and it became very difficult for financial institutions to get and give

[1] An additional but related cause was that derivative securities such as credit default protections/swaps grew significantly, based largely on computer-generated valuation models that incorporated unsound risk projection /calculations.

normal overnight loans, even at very high rates of interest. More important, it became difficult or next to impossible for their customers to obtain financing as a result of the loss of trust. Because of the lack of liquidity of normal financial sources and the lack of desire by others to lend in uncertain times, borrowing became very difficult for individuals and businesses.

After much debate, the United States and other governments announced their desire to buy the depressed securities with the intent to hold them until their values recovered and to inject liquid funds through loans, equity investments, or other means to keep the banks and other enterprises afloat. Some major financial corporations, however, were allowed to go bankrupt or were taken over by stronger companies in forced, 11th-hour fire-sale transactions. General Motors, for example, declared bankruptcy in June of 2009 and sought financial assistance from the U.S. government.

The impact of this liquidity crisis on individuals was brutal. Many lost their homes or saw their houses, their major assets, fall in value when they needed them to remain high to support their retirements, lifestyles, or other borrowings. Entrepreneurs, businesses, car purchasers, and others who needed credit were unable to secure financing, so business activity declined with the inevitable result of reducing employment. Inevitably, the lack of credit slowed economies worldwide, causing layoffs of workers who, in turn, were unable to pay their credit cards and other debts, ultimately forcing banks and other lenders to incur and disclose increased credit losses.

The economic engine of society was sputtering not only in the United States but also around the world. European leaders agreed "to provide capital for banks caught short of funds because of frozen money markets and to ensure or buy into new debt issues."[2] From their perspective, the "root cause of the crisis was a U.S. housing boom that went bust, and with it a market in mortgage-related debt, and derivatives that turned toxic with the downturn. That marked the start of a credit squeeze that snowballed worldwide."[3] According to the then French President and European Union President Nicolas Sarkozy, the crisis was so grave that "[it needed] concrete measures and unity—none of our countries acting alone could end this crisis."[4]

STAGES OF THE SUBPRIME LENDING FIASCO

The subprime lending fiasco developed gradually as a result of many decisions that appeared to make some sense at the time but that contributed to a super-inflated housing price bubble that burst, leading to a huge financial catastrophe. Other decisions, which again appeared to be sensible when taken, led to an inability of financial institutions and investors to understand the impending risks and to withstand the losses that occurred. In retrospect, many of these decisions benefited the self-interest of financial intermediaries while raising the potential risk to investors and innocent bystanders. Ultimately, governments that had failed to see the economic train wreck coming and regulate effectively against it had to bail out many banks and corporations to try to mitigate against a 1930s-style depression and then belatedly introduce new regulations to try to prevent reoccurrences.

The many decisions and resulting actions underlying the housing bubble fiasco can be divided into the four stages identified in Figure 8.1: enabling, building, bursting, and aftermath.

---

[2] "European Leaders Pledge Aid for Banks in Crisis," *Toronto Star*, October 13, 2008, B1, B4.

[3] Ibid.

[4] Ibid.

FIGURE 8.1 Subprime Lending Fiasco—Stages

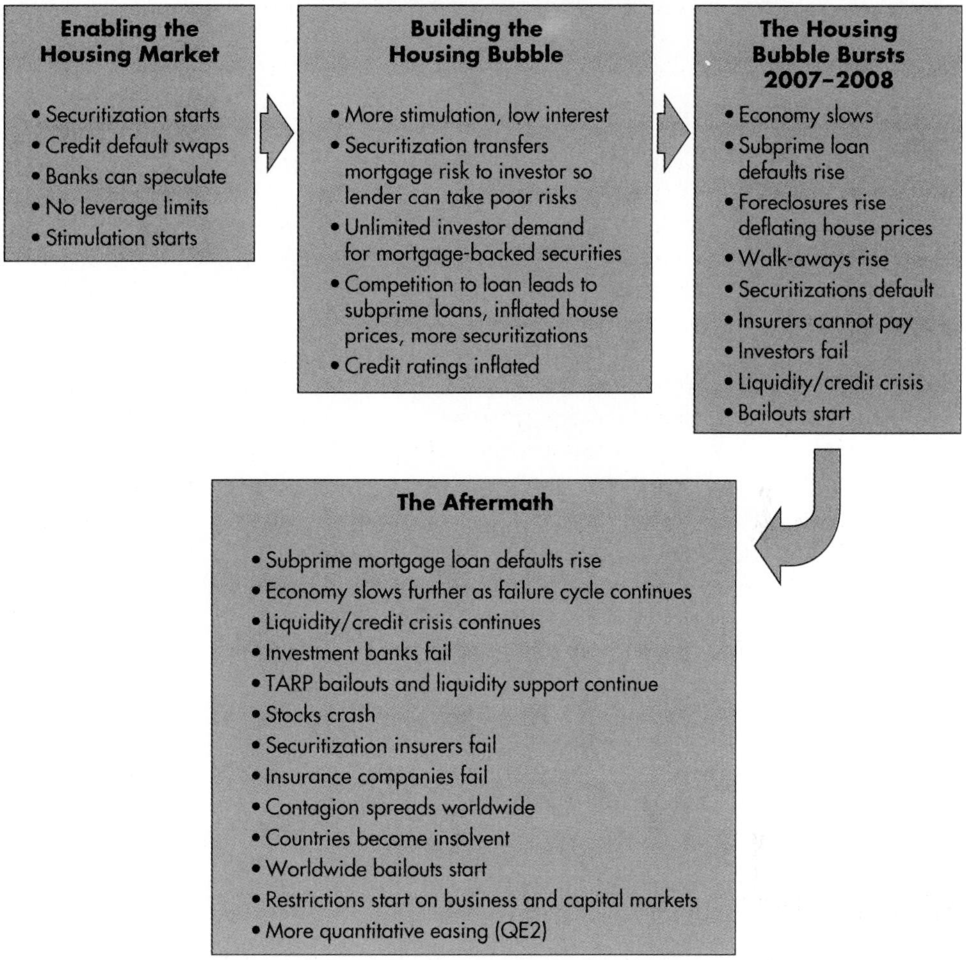

The key events involved in four stages of the subprime lending fiasco that are discussed in the rest of the chapter are presented in Figure 8.2.

HOW DID THE SUBPRIME LENDING CRISIS HAPPEN?

Opinions differ on the root causes of the creation and bursting of the U.S. mortgage bubble that led to the worldwide economic crisis. Some observers claim that the U.S. Federal Reserve Board's (the Fed) policy of very "deep cuts in interest rates earlier in this decade, together with its lack of regulation on subprime mortgages—ultimately estimated to total 33% of the total U.S. mortgage market—fueled the housing and credit bubbles."[5]

[5] David Parkinson, "A Train Wreck? Greenspan Says He Didn't See It Coming," *The Globe and Mail*, November 8, 2008, B2.

FIGURE 8.2 Subprime Lending Fiasco—Key Events

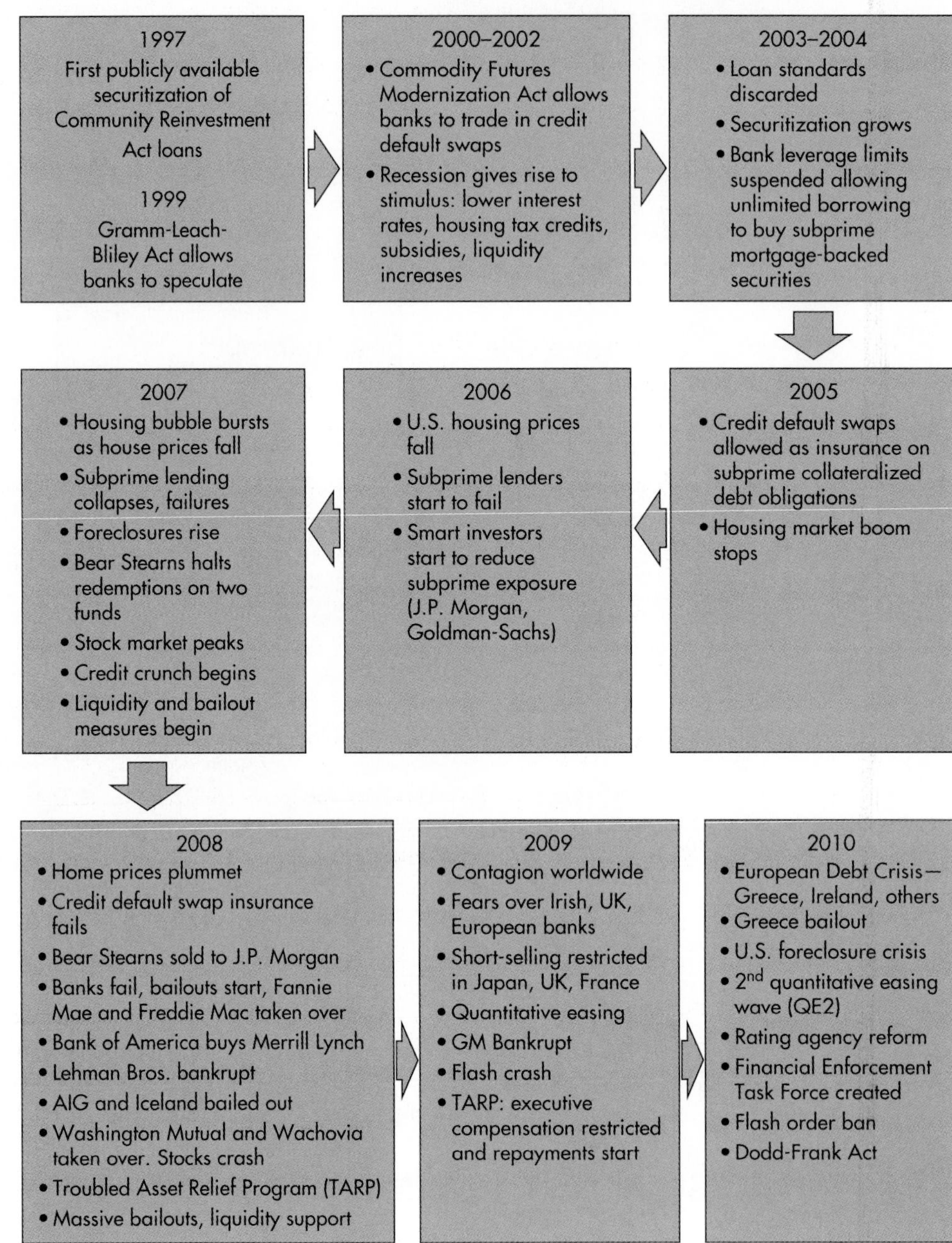

Source: Federal Reserve Bank of New York.

In response, former Federal Reserve Chairman Alan Greenspan stated that the situation was "being driven by global forces …" and that "[t]here's really nothing we could have done about it."[6] He said that

[6] Ibid.

the Fed cut interest rates to stave off a deflation threat, but once it started raising short-term interest rates again, the long-term rates didn't follow suit. He said the globalization of debt markets and a glut of savings from booming emerging economies undermined the Fed's efforts.

He said the Fed first became concerned about the subprime lending market around 2000, but adopted a "wait-and-see" approach as the market remained healthy for the next five years. It was only when global demand for U.S. mortgage-backed instruments began to boom in 2005 did the quality of mortgage products deteriorate,...

"We hadn't the slightest inclination at the time that the securitization problems would become so large."[7,8]

Subprime Lending Developments

Regardless of where the blame for the creation of a U.S. housing bubble lies—overstimulation as a result of very low interest rates or excessive foreign savings or both—the main vehicle involved in the financial and economic train wreck was the securitization and resale of U.S. mortgage-backed securities to investors, which lost value when house prices plummeted and home owners walked away without obligation to repay the mortgage loans. It is also the case that U.S. regulations were insufficient to prevent the creation of highly risky mortgages and the transfer of this risk to unsuspecting investors.[9]

Moreover, the conditions that allowed the subprime lending fiasco started to develop before the period identified by Alan Greenspan. For example, banks and other financial intermediaries that were central to the creation and transfer process played an active role in encouraging the modification of preventive regulation as early as 1999.

Bankers are usually very careful. They want to ensure that their loans are protected, so they assess the prospects for repayment based on the financial strength of the borrower through earnings and other investments or—if the borrower cannot repay—the bank's ability to recover its loss from the value of the underlying collateral (the value of the house), which could be sold for enough to cover the loan. Why were U.S. bankers not prudent with the subprime mortgages that fueled the current crisis? Frankly, the securitization of mortgage investments and related insurance arrangements *allowed lenders and bankers to transfer mortgage risks to other investors*, or so they thought. Consequently, they did not look carefully at the lending practices used in subprime lending.

The breakdown in prudent lending practices actually started with the repeal in 1999 of the 1933 *Glass-Steagall Act* (GSA). The GSA had originally been put in place to force banks to choose between commercial and investment bank activities. The act was to protect depositors' funds from the more speculative risks of securities underwriting, except for government bonds, by limiting the income derived from underwriting to 10% of total bank income. In other words, the U.S. banks' participation in mortgage lending was restricted. This GSA protection concept was extended in 1956 (by the passage of the

---

[7] Ibid.

[8] It was subsequently learned that Greenspan, the Congress, the Fed, and the Treasury Department had been warned earlier of potential problems with derivatives and a largely unregulated derivative and CDO market by Brooksley Born, who was the chairperson of the Commodities Futures Trading Commission from 1996 to 1999. He and other financial leaders in Washington rejected her and stigmatized her warnings. See *The Warning*, a PBS *Frontline* documentary, October 20, 2009, http://www.pbs.org/wgbh/pages/frontline/warning/view.

[9] Other derivatives were also to blame, including credit default swaps, in which executives relied on faulty risk valuation tools and flawed rating agency judgments.

Bank Holding Company Act) to preclude banks from underwriting insurance, although they were permitted to sell insurance products underwritten by others. In 1999, however, the *Gramm-Leach-Bliley Act* was passed, allowing banks to become heavily involved in investment bank activities. It permitted banks to underwrite, trade, and invest in mortgage-backed securities and collateralized debt obligations and to develop structured investment vehicles (SIVs) to facilitate this. Then, in October 2004, the U.S. Securities and Exchange Commission (SEC) effectively suspended the capital requirements limits for investment bankers Goldman Sachs, Merrill Lynch, Lehman Brothers, Bear Stearns, and Morgan Stanley.[10] This freed these firms to borrow and invest as much as forty times their ownership capital, but this left a cushion of capital of only a 2.5% (40/1) to withstand losses from investments. This meant that if a bank's investment portfolio fell by over 2.5%, then, all other things being equal, the bank would be bankrupt. In hindsight, this cushion proved to be too small.

These developments spurred competition in the mortgage markets and stimulated the creation of investment vehicles that allowed the transfer of mortgage risks from the issuer to the ultimate investors in these SIVs. This freed the initial mortgagees (and the banks and other financial intermediaries that bundled mortgages up in the securitization process and resold them) from the normal risks of credit collection losses. At the same time, low interest rates were set by the Fed to stimulate housing starts, and huge pools of foreign savings increased the demand for securitized mortgage-backed investments. These two factors kept rates low and stimulated housing prices. *In order to fill the investment demand, super-competitive lending practices were unleashed that had not been seen before, such as lending to mortgagors without any deposit, without proper documentation, and without proper concern for their ability to pay:*

- Mortgagees were advancing 100% of the purchase price instead of requiring a deposit of 10% to 25% of the purchase price, which would have required the borrower to have some capital at risk to prevent walkaways when repayment became difficult. Often, a borrower could obtain a low-rate or subprime mortgage for 90% to 95% of the house value and a second mortgage for the remaining 5% to 10%. These loans were sometimes referred to as *teaser loans* because the combination of no deposit and low interest lured many borrowers into arrangements that contemplated higher interest rates on renewal that were to be met from increased salaries or increased borrowing as house prices rose—two prospects that did not materialize.
- *No document* or *liar loans* attracted people with poor credit histories.
- *Ninja loans* were common, in which the mortgagee had no income, no job, and no assets.

These practices initially made it far easier to obtain mortgage financing, and the housing market boomed as house prices soared, but ultimately the ticking time bomb blew up. When it came time to renew the teaser mortgages, many individuals could not meet the higher interest and payment costs. Because house prices had not gone up as expected, they chose to walk away from their mortgage obligations—creating the term "jingle mail" when the homeowner mailed the keys to the house to the mortgagee—and let the mortgagee/bank foreclose and sell the house. In the United States, turning over the house to the lender extinguishes house mortgage commitments by the mortgagor. However, as the number of foreclosures grew, the selling value of homes declined past

[10] Steven Labaton, "The Reckoning: Agency's '04 Rule Let Banks Pile Up New Debt," *New York Times*, October 2, 2008, accessed December 27, 2010, at http://www.nytimes.com/2008/10/03/business/03sec.html?_r=1.

the point where lenders could recoup their capital. In a sense, these subprime lending practices were unfair and predatory[11] to borrowers who got into mortgages that were more difficult than they expected, if not impossible, to repay.

Transfer of Risk & the Liquidity Freeze

Many lenders bundled their mortgage loans and sold them to second-party consolidators, such as investment banks and other financial institutions, such as Fannie Mae and Freddie Mac.[12] The mortgages would be pooled into a special investment vehicle (SIV) where the consolidator might or might not guarantee collections on the mortgages. The pooled mortgages in the SIV became the security for the investment that would be issued to companies, pension plans, and individual investors. In other words, *the risk of noncollection of the mortgage loans was passed from the original lender to a counterparty and then to investors* who thought they were getting very sound, high-yield investments for their portfolios. In fact, the increasing number of walkaways and falling house prices meant that foreclosure, repossession, and resale did not recoup the original principal, and the insurance-like guarantee of the counterparties—known as a credit-default swap[13] or CDS—was often worthless, so the ultimate investors had to face the fact that their investments had fallen dramatically in value.

In the case of banks and other publicly owned investors who were complying with mark-to-market (M2M) accounting standards, this decrease in value of their investments had to be reflected in the company's financial statements as a provision for a significant loss. To complicate this scenario, the speed of the fall in value and the uncertainty created meant that even the reduced values were very difficult to estimate. Investor company share prices naturally fell, adding further to the financial unrest. Faced with large losses and uncertainty, most lenders became unwilling to lend to anyone until matters settled down, and *a worldwide liquidity or credit freeze* occurred leading to job losses, takeovers, bankruptcies, and bailouts.

Figure 8.3 provides a schematic representation of some of the factors already discussed that led to the U.S. housing bubble.

Contributions of Fannie Mae & Freddie Mac

The culpability and fate of the Federal National Mortgage Association (called Fannie Mae) and the Federal Home Loan Mortgage Corporation (called Freddie Mac) are also worth understanding. They were the two giant purchasers and resellers of home loans prior to and during the housing bubble.[14] As such, based on misapplied expansionist government policy, they contributed significantly to the overall development of the

[11] Predatory lending practices are traditionally taken to mean practices that unknowingly place the borrower at a disadvantage so that repayment becomes harder and renewal very difficult so that the lender can take the asset back and resell it at a profit with the borrower losing at least some of the investment. Sometimes lenders would promise a low rate of interest but switch to a higher rate just before the final signoff. Adjustable-rate mortgages could also be used so that investors might face higher rates than they could repay.

[12] Fannie Mae is the Federal National Mortgage Association, and Freddie Mac is the Federal Home Loan Mortgage Corporation.

[13] A credit-default swap (CDS) is a contract in which one party agrees to accept the risk of default on a mortgage-backed security in return for a payment from the investor. If the investment defaults, the investor will receive payment from the issuer of the CDS provided that the issuer has enough funds to pay.

[14] Fannie Mae and Freddie Mac were originally created by the U.S. government to expand the secondary market for mortgages (i.e., provide more funds for mortgages). Both firms issued shares that became publicly traded.

FIGURE 8.3 Subprime Lending Fiasco—U.S. Housing Bubble

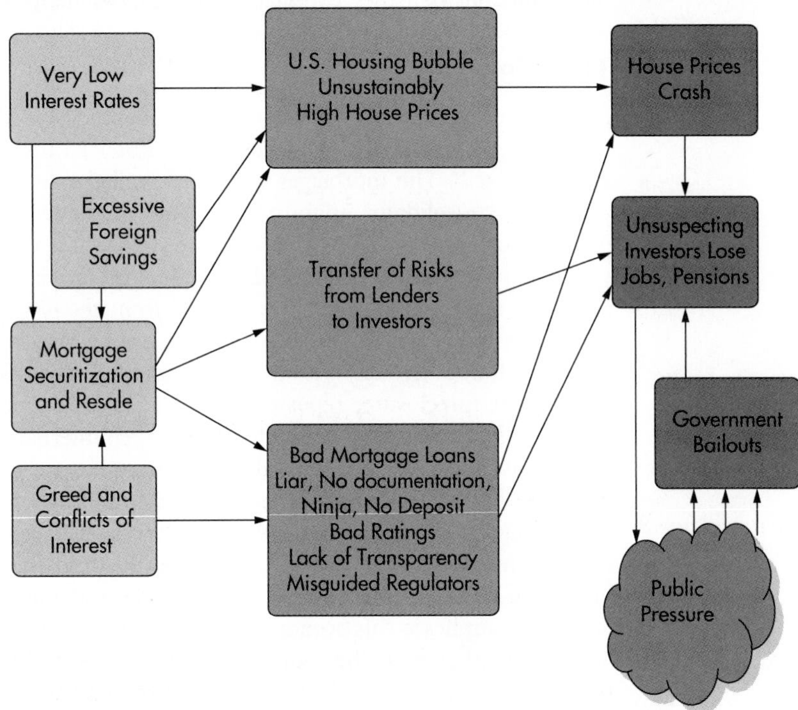

bubble and the systemic risk[15] it involved. As a result of the loss of value of the homes mortgaged and guaranteed, they also suffered huge losses, to the point where they were unable to continue to buy mortgages. Rather than allow this inability to freeze the mortgage market, in early September 2008 the U.S. government essentially took over both publicly traded firms and injected as much as $200 billion to keep the mortgage markets flowing.[16]

The CEOs of both firms were replaced, but they agreed to continue to assist and were allowed to keep significant severance packages. Fannie Mae's Daniel Mudd and Freddie Mac's Richard Syron left with $7.3 million and $6.3 million, after earning $11.6 million and $18.3 million, respectively, in the previous year. The severance payments raised the ire of many, including then-Senator Barack Obama, who wrote to Treasury Secretary Henry Paulson, saying, "Under no circumstances should the executives of these institutions earn a windfall at a time when the U.S. Treasury has taken unprecedented steps to rescue these companies with taxpayer resources."[17] The ousted CEOs'

[15] Carol D. Leonnig, "How HUD Mortgage Policy Fed the Crisis," *Washington Post*, June 10, 2008, accessed December 27, 2010, at http://www.washingtonpost.com/wp-dyn/content/article/2008/06/09/AR2008060902626.html.

[16] David Ellis, "U.S. Seizes Fannie and Freddie," CNNMoney.com, September 7, 2008, accessed November 9, 2008, at http://money.cnn.com/2008/09/07/news/companies/fannie_freddie/index.htm?postversion=2008090720.

[17] William Heisel, "Fannie Mae and Freddie Mac CEOs to Get Golden Parachutes," *Los Angeles Times*, September 8, 2008.

records speak for themselves. When Mudd took over as CEO of Fannie Mae in December 2004, its stock was trading at about $70, but it closed at 73 cents on September 8, 2008. Syron took over as CEO of Freddie Mac in December 2003, when its shares sold at about $55, later sinking to 88 cents on September 8, 2008.[18] More important, if these two men had had the foresight and/or moral courage to speak out and act against the subprime lending characteristics that ultimately led to the fiasco rather than attempting to take advantage of it, the fiasco might have been avoided, and their companies might have been able to continue to serve their purpose without government intervention. Did these men not understand the risks and unethical processes involved in the subprime lending chain even as their companies were becoming less profitable and losing their vitality? Even if these CEOs could be excused for focusing only on short-term profit, which they cannot, it is definitely the role of their boards of directors to be concerned with strategy—a concern that should involve both the long term and ethics.

The Conflicted Credit-Rating Sham

Banks, mortgage companies, and other financial intermediaries were not the only ones complicit in this transfer of explosive risk onto unsuspecting investors. The credit-rating agencies (Moody's Corp., Standard & Poor's [S&P], and Fitch Ratings) also played a major role[19] because they, at least initially,[20] bestowed sound investment grade ratings on the collateralized debt obligations (CDOs) and mortgage-backed securities (MBSs) bought by reliant investors even though some personnel knew and others should have known their ratings did not capture and signal all the risk involved. Emails and transcripts released in October 2008 by a U.S. House of Representatives panel[21] are illustrative:

- From a series of S&P structured finance division employees about to rate a structured deal: "That deal is ridiculous,… I know right… [our rating] model does not capture half of the [risk]…. We should not be rating it… We rate every deal. It could be structured by cows and we would rate it."[22]
- From an S&P employee: "Let's hope we are all wealthy and retired by the time this house of cards falters."[23]
- Raymond McDaniel, chair and chief executive of Moody's, described the slippery slope of events. "What happened in '04 and '05 with respect to subordinated tranches is that our competition, Fitch and S & P, went nuts. Everything was investment grade. We tried to alert the market. We said we're not rating it. This stuff isn't investment grade. No one cared because the machine just kept going."[24]
- When Mr. McDaniel was queried over potential conflicts of interest involved in the process of rating—rating agencies are paid by investment firms who create the

[18] Ibid.

[19] Curtis C. Verschoor, "Who Should Be Blamed the Most for the Subprime Loan Scandal?," *Strategic Finance*, December, 2007, 11, 12, 59.

[20] Moody's and the S&P stopped rating SIVs and MBSs as the crisis deepened.

[21] See the website of the Committee on Oversight and Governance Reform of the U.S. House of Representatives for references to a hearing titled "Credit Rating Agencies and the Financial Crisis," October 22, 2008, at http://house.resource.org/110/gov.house.ogr.20081022_hrs01RFM2154.1.pdf search for e-mail.

[22] Paul Waldie, "Rating Agencies Face the Music," *The Globe and Mail*, October 23, 2008, B10.

[23] Lorraine Woellert and Dawn Kopecki, "Debt Raters Ripped for 'Colossal Failure'," *Toronto Star*, October 23, 2008, B3.

[24] Ibid.

securities and then use the ratings to sell the securities—he said: "Our ratings are not influenced by commercial considerations,… that is a conflict that has to be identified, managed properly and controlled."[25]

- But a Moody's employee said: It "seems to me that we had blinders on and never questioned the information we were given. It is our job to think of the worst-case scenarios and model them. Combined, these errors make us look either incompetent at credit analysis, or like we sold our sole [*sic*] to the devil for revenue."[26]
- When he briefed his Board of Directors in 2007, Mr. McDaniel told directors that the agencies are pushed to provide high ratings to clients in order to win business and generate fees. "It turns out that ratings quality has surprisingly few friends: Issuers want high ratings; investors don't want rating downgrades."[27]

Regulators Looked in the Wrong Direction

It is also noteworthy that several "watchdog" regulators tried to blow the whistle and were thwarted. According to *Businessweek*, in April 2003 the attorneys general for North Carolina and Iowa went to Washington to warn officials about "predatory real estate financing" and seek help in limiting the practices involved.[28] Instead, the Office of the Comptroller of the Currency (OCC) and the Office of Thrift Supervision "sided with lenders." The OCC then argued that, in accord with the Preemption Doctrine, federal regulation dominates or preempts state legislation when the two conflict. This led to banks being outside state regulation and saw "state-chartered mortgage firms sell themselves to national banks and then declare that they [were]…sheltered from state oversight." States were then unable even to examine the records of mortgage lenders operating in their state that were subsidiaries of a national bank. National regulations and regulators were comparatively quite lax, and irresponsible lending practices continued unchecked and developed into a lending frenzy. As events turned out, the OCC and other national officials were not acting in the public interest—they were contributing to the crisis.

Special Purpose Vehicles—Key to the Crisis

Investment banks would set up and sell to unsuspecting investors, investments known as special purposes vehicles (SPVs), in which the investment bank retained low or no equity interests. These SPVs were incredibly risky investments given the collapse of the U.S. housing prices in 2007 and 2008, but this risk was not understood by the vast majority of investors. They thought that the investment banks, rating agencies, and others in the investment approval chain were acting in the investors' interest. How wrong they were.

To create an SPV, the investment bank would buy mortgage loans from retail banks and use those mortgages as security for a mortgage backed security (MBS) that would be issued as the SPV. The SPV contract would then cause the cash received from the mortgagors to pay the interest and eventually the principal on the security. The security was referred to as a collateralized debt obligation (CDO) because the cash flow from the

[25] Ibid.

[26] Ibid.

[27] Ibid., B6.

[28] Robert Berner and Brian Grow, "They Warned Us: The Watchdogs Who Saw the Subprime Disaster Coming—And How They Were Thwarted by the Banks and Washington," *Businessweek*, October 20, 2008, 36–42.

pooled mortgages was used to guarantee the cash flow to the purchaser of the security. Unlike a bond that has periodic interest payments and principal at maturity, the owner of an MBS would receive a blended interest and principal payment, similar to the blended interest and principal payment that the mortgagee was paying to the bank each month.

The CDO was broken into tranches, or slices, and the cash flow from the pooled mortgages was used to service the security, first to the senior or lowest-risk tranche, then to the next group (called mezzanine tranches), and then to all the other tranches in order of ascending risk. Because the senior tranche would receive the cash first, it had a low rate of return. The mezzanine would receive its cash after the senior tranche was paid, so this second-tiered tranche had a higher level of risk and therefore a higher rate of return. This proceeded down through all the tranches, to the lowest one, which had the highest risk because this tranche was the last to be paid and therefore had the highest rate of return.

Because the senior tranche was considered the least risky, the rating agencies, such as Moody's, Fitch Ratings, and S&P, usually rated these tranches AAA, which is equivalent to a government-risk grade. They rated the mezzanine tranches also as investment grade, varying from AA to BBB. The lowest tranches were rated as non–investment-grade securities. Unfortunately, in addition to instances of willful misrating reported above, the rating agencies made two fundamental errors in their evaluation of these CDOs. The first was that they relied on computer-generated valuation models that incorporated unsound risk projection calculations. More important, they assumed that each of the tranches represented a stochastically independent risk. That is, they assumed that the riskiness of the AAA tranche was independent of the riskiness of all the other tranches. The reality was that interdependency existed because all the tranches were dependent on the home owners continuing to make their regular monthly payments on their mortgages. Such interdependency is referred to as systemic risk.[29]

The interdependency of the tranches in a mortgage-backed security can be illustrated by the interdependency of first, second, and third mortgages on a house. Second and third mortgages are much riskier than first mortgages because a second mortgagor cannot foreclose on a property unless the first mortgagor also forecloses. Furthermore, if a home owner pays the first mortgage but makes no payments on the second mortgage, then the second mortgagor cannot foreclose on the property as a means of recouping the initial amount that was lent to the home owner. A third mortgagor has even higher risk because the third mortgagor receives a payout on foreclosure only after the debts of the first and second mortgagor are satisfied.

Any CDO that was backed by second or third mortgages had a very high degree of risk, but investors were hard pressed to understand the underlying riskiness. Most buyers relied on the underwriter (the investment bank) and the rating agency (Moody's or S&P) to do their due diligence and examine the CDO agreement and its tranches to determine what could go wrong and build risk into the ratings. Some investors might examine SEC filings and/or the prospectus. The prospectus is a legal document, used to market the investment, that could be in excess of 300 difficult-to-read pages that warned of every conceivable risk in the same way that medical advertisements warn of every possible side effect while promoting their drugs on TV. Other investors might want to go further and review the original documents or check out the mortgage and the home owner, but in many cases there was no easy access to these original documents or even obtain the

[29] For a more thorough analysis of the systemic risk associated with subprime mortgage securities see: Sinn, Hans-Werner. 2010. *Casino Capitalism.* Oxford University Press.

names of the home owners and the amounts of their mortgages. So there was no real alternative but to rely on the underwriter and the credit-rating agency.[30]

When the housing market collapsed in 2008, the cash flow from the pooled mortgages was not enough to pay the interest or service the CDOs, so the value of the bonds fell. As the value of CDOs fell, investors began to quickly sell their CDOs, which provided an excess of supply thereby causing the price of all CDOs to fall even further. Eventually, the entire CDO market collapsed. In retrospect, investors should have realized that CDOs that were dependent on a stable housing and mortgage market were risky investments, especially if the CDO was backed by second or third mortgages. Finally, the bond-rating agencies have a lot to answer for. They should have been able to determine the risk of the CDOs and then disclose that level of risk to potential investors. The rating agencies failed to do so.

A Subprime Mortgage-Backed Security Gone Awry

In 2006, Goldman Sachs created the securitization vehicle Goldman Sachs' Alternative Mortgage Products (GSAMP) Trust 2006-S3. It issued a $494 million collateral debt bond backed by 8,274 second-mortgage loans. One-third of these mortgages were on homes in California and were high risk no-documentation loans or low-documentation loans. The average ownership interest in these homes was less than 1%.

Goldman Sachs packaged this securitized investment into thirteen tranches: three senior tranches worth $336 million, seven mezzanine tranches worth $123 million, and three other tranches worth $35 million. The bond was then rated by Moody's and S&P. Because the owners of the senior tranches would be paid first, these three tranches, called A-1, A-2, and A-3, were rated AAA grade. Owners of the mezzanine tranches would be paid after the AAA payments, so these tranches were rated from AA to BBB. The remaining three tranches were not rated as investment grade because they were very risky. This meant that 93% of the bond was rated as investment grade, and 63% (the AAA rating) was evaluated as the equivalent to a government bond, even though it was backed by ultra-risky second-mortgage loans.

When the housing market collapsed, especially in California, the value of these mortgage-backed securities plummeted. By July 2008, the ten tranches that were rated below AAA had defaulted, and investors were no longer receiving interest payments. At this point, 28% of the A-1 tranche was still outstanding in addition to 98% of the A-2 and A-3 tranches. Together, these bonds had a face value of $159.9 million but were supported by only $79.6 million of mortgages. In other words, 50% of the bonds had no financial backing. By October 2009, the A-1 tranche had lost 25% of its value, while the other two tranches had lost 90% of their value.

At the same time that Goldman Sachs was promoting the mortgage-backed securities issued by GSAMP, the investment bank was also short selling an index of mortgage-backed securities. In other words, Goldman Sachs sold the GSAMP securities to investors and then, in order to make a profit for the firm, sold short these same investments,[31] *thus causing their value to decrease. Apparently, Goldman Sachs did not consider that being loyal to their investor clients was to be their highest priority.*

Sources: Alan Sloan, "Junk Mortgages under the Microscope," *Fortune*, October 16, 2007; Alan Sloan, "Once upon a Time in Mortgage Land," *Washington Post*, November 28, 2009.

[30] For an example of the lack of candor by investment banks in their disclosure documents see: Sloan, Alan. 2007. Junk mortgages under the microscope. *Fortune* (October 16).

[31] When a security is sold short, the seller hopes the security declines in value so that the seller can buy the security at a lower price in time to deliver the security. The seller makes a profit by selling at a high price and then buying at a lower price.

Unlimited Toxic Risk—Credit Default Swaps, Naked & Otherwise

Prior to the subprime lending crisis, very well-informed financiers, investors, bankers, and insurers understood how incredibly risky and destructive credit default swaps (CDSs) could be, but many others were unable to resist the high levels of fees and the potential profits involved. CDSs are negotiable instruments and can be extremely complex. They took on a life of their own and eventually traded in enormous volumes (reportedly over $26 trillion in 2010—many times greater than any underlying debt and way beyond the ability of the issuers/insurers to pay out if the original debt defaulted).

Credit default swaps are financial instruments that were originally intended to manage the risk of default that arises from holding debt. A bank, for example, may hedge its risk that a borrower may default on a loan by entering into a CDS contract as the buyer of protection. If the loan goes into default, for the bank, the proceeds from the CDS contract cancel out the losses on the underlying debt. For the issuer, there would be a loss. By buying a CDS, a lender, such as a bank, can lay off default risk while still keeping the loan in its portfolio. The downside to this hedge is that without default risk, a bank may have no motivation to actively monitor the loan, and the counterparty has no relationship to the borrower.

A "naked" CDS (NCDS) is essentially a CDS issued by an institution that does not own or have an insurable interest in the loan that is insured. Therefore, an almost unlimited volume of insurance can be written on a single loan, which, if it goes into default, can cause financial havoc if the issuing/insuring party cannot pay all the claims. That is what happened in 2008 and why American International Group (AIG) failed and needed to be taken over.

Trading in NCDSs was high-risk gambling. The winners, memorialized in the movie *The Big Short* (2015), won big—the losers lost the same. The financier George Soros famously called for an outright ban on them, viewing them as "toxic" and allowing speculators to bet against companies or countries.

CDSs were a major contributing factor in the 2008 financial crisis and subsequent government bailout because the issuing parties (notably AIG) were unable to pay out on the insurance losses incurred. This caused a liquidity crisis that affected banks and other financial institutions around the world.

Crisis, Bankruptcy, Bailouts, & New Regulations

As subprime lending losses became apparent, normal banks as well as *shadow banks*[32] refused to lend, and the credit crunch turned into a liquidity crisis. Meetings were held of the heads of the major banks, investment banks, and officials of the U.S. Treasury Department, as well as the Federal Reserve Bank, but they could not find a solution.

During the meetings, John Thain, the CEO of Merrill Lynch, a large investment broker and investment bank, realized his firm was overextended and vulnerable. He approached the CEO of the Bank of America on the weekend, and they worked out a deal for the bank to buy Merrill at a low price, which they announced on Sunday, September 14, 2008.[33] Repercussions were immediate.

---

[32] Shadow bank sources refers to unregulated financial intermediaries involved in the creation of credit (hedge funds, other funds, and lenders) and unregulated activities of regulated institutions (unlisted derivatives, credit default swaps, and so on). According to *Investopedia*, the unregulated financial intermediaries escaped regulation because they did not take deposits. See http://www.investopedia.com/terms/s/shadow-banking-system.asp.

[33] Charlie Gasparino, "Bank of America to Buy Merrill Lynch for $50 Billion," CNBC, September 14, 2008, accessed December 28, 2010, at http://www.cnbc.com/id/26708319/Bank_of_America_to_Buy_Merrill_Lynch_for_50_Billion.

The next day, Lehman Brothers, once a very respected and venerable investment banking firm, filed for bankruptcy. Lehman Brothers reported record revenues of almost $60 billion and record earnings in excess of $4 billion for the fiscal year ended November 30, 2007, but only ten months later, on September 15, 2008, their bankruptcy proceeding became the largest ever filed.[34] (An in-depth analysis of Lehman's bankruptcy is provided at the end of this chapter in the ethics case "Lehman Brothers Repo 105 Manipulation.") The brief explanation for the demise of Lehman Brothers is that the investment bank attempted to carry investments of roughly $700 billion, with a capital cushion for losses of just $25 billion or 3.6% (28/1).[35] That cushion proved insufficient to induce lenders to extend loans or the Fed to extend emergency financing during the liquidity crisis caused by uncertainty in the financial markets during September 2008. In fact, Lehman Brothers had been told by the secretary of the Treasury that it had to raise more capital than the $6 billion it had raised in June 2008, or face the consequences. Prior to raising the new $6 billion, its capital cushion was only about 2.7%. In other words, it had $37 of debt for every $1 of invested capital. Obviously, Lehman did not have a sufficient capital cushion or sufficient CDS protection from viable insurers, nor could the firm attract sufficient backers to stave off bankruptcy.

Panic prevailed. Governments were forced to step in to save large companies from becoming insolvent and to inject liquidity capital to restart the lending process. According to one account of the peak of the crisis,

> This is what a credit crisis looks like. It's not like a stock market crisis, where the scary plunge of stocks is obvious to all. The credit crisis has played out in places most people can't see. It's banks refusing to lend to other banks—even though that is one of the most essential functions of the banking system. It's a loss of confidence in seemingly healthy institutions like Morgan Stanley and Goldman—both of which reported profits even as the pressure was mounting. It is panicked hedge funds pulling out cash. It is frightened investors protecting themselves by buying credit-default swaps—a financial insurance policy against potential bankruptcy—at prices 30 times what they normally would pay.
>
> It was this 36-hour period two weeks ago—from the morning of Wednesday, Sept. 17, to the afternoon of Thursday, Sept. 18—that spooked policy makers by opening fissures in the worldwide financial system.
>
> In their rush to do something, and do it fast, the Federal Reserve chairman, Ben S. Bernanke, and Treasury Secretary Henry M. Paulson Jr. concluded the time had come to use the "break the glass" rescue plan they had been developing. But in their urgency, they bypassed a crucial step in Washington and fashioned their $700 billion bailout without political spadework, which led to a resounding rejection this past Monday in the House of Representatives.
>
> That Thursday evening, however, time was of the essence. In a hastily convened meeting in the conference room of the House speaker, Nancy Pelosi, the two men presented, in the starkest terms imaginable, the outline of the $700 billion plan to Congressional leaders. "If we don't do this," Mr. Bernanke

[34] Anton R. Valukas, *Report of Anton R. Valukas, Examiner, Lehman Brothers Holdings Inc.*, Chapter 11 Case No. 08-13555(JMP) (Jointly Administered), United States Bankruptcy Court, Southern District of New York, March 11, 2010, accessed at http://lehmanreport.jenner.com; see also www.cengage.com/accounting/brooks.
[35] Ibid., 4.

said, according to several participants, "we may not have an economy on Monday."[36]

On October 3, 2008, the U.S. Senate and Congress voted for a $700 billion–plus rescue package, known as the *Troubled Asset Relief Plan* (TARP), and then the Treasury Department under Secretary Henry Paulson and the Federal Reserve Bank under Chairman Ben Bernanke bailed out essentially insolvent companies, such as Fannie Mae, Freddie Mac,[37] and AIG,[38] forced buyouts of others, such as Merrill Lynch & Co.,[39] and provided billions to buy up distressed mortgage investments that the Fed could hold until housing prices recovered. An excellent ongoing summary of TARP programs, bailouts, investments, and repayments can be found at CNNMoney.com's bailout tracker.[40]

By itself, TARP did not prove to be sufficient to restore confidence and relieve the liquidity crisis. What no one could determine accurately in October and November 2008 was the full extent of the impact of the subprime lending fiasco on the world economy and of the ensuing cascade of impacts that a general economic downturn would create and what the mitigating affect would be of the massive economic stimulus packages subsequently put in place. A narrow snapshot provided in late January 2009 puts into perspective one aspect of the credit cascade—the projected percentage of defaults of adjustable-rate mortgages (ARMs) relative to subprime mortgages. Close to $750 billion of ARMs were issued from 2004 to 2007 to higher-credit-score customers than subprime mortgages but with some of the same documentation difficulties. ARMs allowed borrowers options as to how much they paid each month with the minimum payment being less than the monthly interest due, thus necessitating that the interest shortfall be added to the carrying value of the loan. As housing prices declined, the market value of many houses fell short of the related loan values. With loss of jobs due to the general economic downturn, many ARM holders defaulted, which created the significant impact described in the following quote:

> The nearly $750-billion of options ARMs issued from 2004 to 2007 compares with roughly $1.9-trillion each of subprime and jumbo mortgages in that period.
>
> Nearly 61% of option ARMs originated in 2007 will eventually default, according to a recent analysis by Goldman Sachs, which assumed a further 10 per cent decline in home prices. That compares with a 63 per cent default rate for subprime loans originated in 2007. Goldman estimates more than half of all option ARMs outstanding will default.[41]

Cascade impacts such as that of the ARMs and the poor financial health of credit-squeezed and revenue-diminished corporations in general set the stage for truly huge rejuvenation measures. In particular, the U.S. government also embarked on a program

[36] Joe Nocera, "The Reckoning: As Crisis Spiraled, Alarm Led to Action," *New York Times*, October 1, 2009, accessed December 27, 2010, at http://www.nytimes.com/2008/10/02/business/02crisis.html?_r=1&hp=&pagewanted=all.

[37] David Ellis, "U.S. Seizes Fannie and Freddie," *CNN Money*, September 7, 2008, http://money.cnn.com/2008/09/07/news/companies/fannie_freddie.

[38] See also the two ethics cases on AIG at the end of this chapter, "M2M Accounting and the Demise of AIG" and "The Ethics of AIG's Commission Sales."

[39] C. Mollenkamp, S. Craig, S. Ng, and A Lucchetti, "Lehman Files for Bankruptcy, Merrill Sold AIG Seeks Cash," *Wall Street Journal*, September 16, 2008, accessed November 9, 2008, athttp://online.wsj.com/article/SB122145492097035549.html.

[40] See http://money.cnn.com/news/storysupplement/economy/bailouttracker/index.html.

[41] Ruth Simon, "Falling Home Prices Create Rival for Subprime," reprinted on the *Wall Street Journal* page (B8) of *The Globe and Mail*, January 30, 2009. Original article is from "Option ARMs See Rising Defaults," http://online.wsj.com/article/SB123327627377631359.html.

of monetary or quantitative easing where funds were injected directly into banks. Foreign governments, the European Economic Community, and the IMF also advanced funds or guaranteed the borrowing of foreign countries. Slowly, the world economy strengthened, and although some of the TARP funding was repaid, in 2010 a second round of quantitative easing (QE2) was initiated by the U.S. government.

In addition, the *Dodd-Frank Wall Street Reform and Consumer Protection Act*[42] was passed in the United States on July 21, 2010, to provide tighter regulation of investment banking and afford consumers increased protection. New initiatives included the following:

> **Consumer Protections with Authority and Independence:** Creates a new independent watchdog, housed at the Federal Reserve, with the authority to ensure American consumers get the clear, accurate information they need to shop for mortgages, credit cards, and other financial products, and protect them from hidden fees, abusive terms, and deceptive practices.
>
> **Ends Too Big to Fail Bailouts:** Ends the possibility that taxpayers will be asked to write a check to bail out financial firms that threaten the economy by: creating a safe way to liquidate failed financial firms; imposing tough new capital and leverage requirements that make it undesirable to get too big; updating the Fed's authority to allow system-wide support but no longer prop up individual firms; and establishing rigorous standards and supervision to protect the economy and American consumers, investors, and businesses.
>
> **Advance Warning System:** Creates a council to identify and address systemic risks posed by large, complex companies, products, and activities before they threaten the stability of the economy.
>
> **Transparency and Accountability for Exotic Instruments:** Eliminates loopholes that allow risky and abusive practices to go on unnoticed and unregulated—including loopholes for over-the-counter derivatives, asset-backed securities, hedge funds, mortgage brokers, and payday lenders.
>
> **Executive Compensation and Corporate Governance:** Provides shareholders with a say on pay and corporate affairs with a nonbinding vote on executive compensation and golden parachutes.
>
> **Protects Investors:** Provides tough new rules for transparency and accountability for credit-rating agencies to protect investors and businesses.
>
> **Enforces Regulations on the Books:** Strengthens oversight and empowers regulators to aggressively pursue financial fraud, conflicts of interest, and manipulation of the system that benefits special interests at the expense of American families and businesses.[43]

The future will doubtless see the introduction of additional regional or worldwide regulatory regimes and perhaps worldwide enforcement programs.

Worldwide Contagion

The analysis presented in this chapter is focused on developments in the United States, but the subprime lending crisis led to a contagion that spread quickly to European capital markets and throughout the world. Almost no one understood the cascade impact triggered and the high degree of connectivity of borrowing and lending of equity and

---

[42] The *Dodd-Frank Wall Street Reform and Consumer Protection Act* became law on July 21, 2010.

[43] *Brief Summary of the Dodd-Frank Wall Street Reform and Consumer Protection Act*, U.S. Senate Banking Committee, July 1, 2010, accessed December 28, 2010, at http://banking.senate.gov/public/_files/070110_Dodd_Frank_Wall_Street_Reform_comprehensive_summary_Final.pdf.

debt investment and of economies around the world. The recession and liquidity problems in the United States were soon replicated in Europe and elsewhere and depressed worldwide economic activity for most of a decade. The resulting recognition of this interconnectivity generated more coordinated worldwide thinking about systemic risks and their regulation, about banking and securities regulation in general, and about the need to watch markets carefully rather than presume that market participants, guided by their own self-interest, will act in the best interests of society.

In response, new regulatory bodies and regulations have been put in place. On January 1, 2011, the European Union established the European Banking Authority to harmonize rules for the European Union banking system. Other banking regulations were passed in the United Kingdom as a result of the final report of the Independent Commission on Banking in September 2011.

Investment Bankers in the Movies

Investment bankers had been the fodder for films from the evil Mr. Potter in It's a Wonderful Life *(1946) to the greedy Gordon Gekko in* Wall Street *(1987) to the redeemed Ebenezer Scrooge in* A Christmas Carol *(1951). With the rare exception of George Bailey, investment bankers are normally portrayed as greedy, self-indulgent men. It is rare to see a woman investment banker in the movies. As a result of the 2008 financial crisis, Hollywood produced a spate of movies about the crisis, in which, once again, investment bankers are not portrayed in a favorable light.*

The documentaries Inside Job *(2010) and* Capitalism: A Love Story *(2009) are highly critical analyses of the economic crisis that began in 2008. The former, an Academy Award–winning film, is a biting condemnation of the entire financial industry, while the latter, also an award-winning film, studies the effect that the crisis had on the lives of average Americans. The documentary* Money for Nothing: Inside the Federal Reserve *(2013) examines the history of the Fed and its actions and inactions during the financial crisis.* Too Big to Fail *(2011) is a television drama that provides an inside look at how Treasury Secretary Henry Paulson made the decision to let the investment firm of Lehman Brothers collapse. The Academy Award–winning movie* The Big Short *(2015), based on the Michael Lewis book of the same name, follows three groups of investors who decided to bet against the overheated housing bubble by shorting mortgage-backed securities. But of all the movies produced so far, the most realistic portrayal of the dilemma faced by banking executives when they know that the financial systems of mortgage-backed securities is about to collapse is* Margin Call *(2011). This movie displays the ethical debates that these executives faced and the choices that they made.*

Subsequent Events

A record and ongoing update of aftermath developments can be found at the *Financial Turmoil Timeline*[44] and the *International Responses to the Crisis Timeline*,[45] both of which are published by the Federal Reserve Bank of New York.

---

[44] Federal Reserve Bank of New York, "Financial Turmoil Timeline," http://data.newyorkfed.org/research/global_economy/Crisis_Timeline.pdf.

[45] Federal Reserve Bank of New York, "International Responses to the Crisis Timeline," http://www.ny.frb.org/research/global_economy/IRCTimelinePublic.pdf.

JP MORGAN CHASE FINES & SETTLEMENTS Part of the *Dodd-Frank Act* eschews investment banks from engaging in high-risk investing and trading activities. Even though JP Morgan Chase & Co. lost billions in the subprime mortgage debacle, the bank continued to trade in derivatives. Unfortunately, it did not always invest wisely. In 2012, the bank's London office lost $6.2 billion in trades associated with CDSs. In September 2013, JP Morgan was fined $920 million because of its poor risk management controls, inadequate governance structures, and poor internal controls that allowed the bank's traders to initially hide the investment losses. The fines were the following:

- $300 million to the OCC
- $200 million to the Federal Reserve
- $200 million to the SEC
- $219.7 (£137.6) million to the United Kingdom's Financial Conduct Authority

Initially, JP Morgan's chairman and CEO, Jamie Dimon, said that the criticisms of the bank's London office were "a tempest in a teapot." Afterward, he apologized for that remark and admitted the bank's error. "We have accepted responsibility and acknowledged our mistakes from the start, and we have learned from them and worked to fix them. Since these losses occurred, we have made numerous changes that have made us stronger, smarter, better company."[46]

The irony in this episode is that it was the investors who lost twice: first with the huge trading losses and then with the fines. As for accepting responsibility, the bank's chief investment officer, Ina Drew, who oversaw the London traders, took early retirement. After a thirty-year career with the bank, she retired with $21.5 million settlement. Mr. Dimon, on the other hand, remained as chairman and CEO of the investment bank, although the Board of Directors did cut his bonus in half. He was paid "only" $10.5 million in 2012 because of the London office trading fiasco. However, his compensation was increased to $20 million in 2014.

But the September 2013 fines were not the end of the bank's dealings with government. In November 2013, JP Morgan agreed to a $13 billion settlement with the U.S. government over its involvement in the 2007–2008 financial crisis. The amount of the settlement is approximately equal to the profits that the investment bank earned during 2013 up until November. The payment included the following:

- $2 billion as a civil penalty
- $7 billion to be paid to investors who bought mortgage-backed securities from JP Morgan Chase
- $4 billion that will be paid to assist home owners who are still suffering as a result of the financial crisis

This is the largest sum ever paid to the government as the result of corporate impropriety. The other investment banks have also been fined by the government. As Jamie Dimon said, "You have to ask them [the government] why they picked us first, but it could have been somebody else.... There was going to be a first."[47]

The other significant aspect is that, to date, no senior executive has been held accountable for the financial crisis. Various traders have been investigated, but few have been jailed. However, many employees lost their jobs when the various investment banks

---

[46] D. Rushe, "London Whale Scandal to Cost JP Morgan $920m in Penalties," *The Guardian*, September 19, 2013.

[47] J. Slater, "JP Morgan Wraps Up $13-Billion Deal," *The Globe and Mail*, November 20, 2013, 10.

collapsed or shrunk in size. But no CEO has been charged with inappropriate behavior or gross negligence as a result of the subprime mortgage financial disaster. True accountability would require both the firm and those who manage the firm to be responsible for the activities of the firm and the consequences of those actions. We await the government's next steps and hope that it involves charging both the firms and their managers with the consequences of inappropriate and unethical business behavior.

FINES & PENALTIES BY OTHER INVESTMENT BANKS All the other investment banks were fined. In July 2014, Citigroup paid $7 billion, and in August 2014, Bank of America paid $16.7 billion. In February 2015, Morgan Stanley paid $2.6 billion, and in January 2016, Goldman Sachs reached a $5.1 billion settlement. The top twenty European banks paid fines and penalties of about $125 billion. As a result of these fines, the investment banks increased the costs of their internal compliance. For example, Bank of America spends $15 billion per year and JPMorgan over $8 billion[48] to ensure that a similar crisis does not reoccur.

The Big 4 accounting firms were also penalized for conducting shabby audits of the investment banking firms. In October 2008, PricewaterhouseCoopers paid a $97.5 million fine for its poor audit of AIG. In August 2011, KPMG paid a $44.7 million fine for the audit of New Century Financial and that same month a $37 million fine for the audit of Wachovia. In June 2012, Deloitte & Touche paid $19.9 million for the failed audit of Bear Sterns. Finally, in November 2013, Ernst & Young reached a $99 million settlement with the government over its audit of Lehman Brothers.

Who received the cash from these fines and penalties? The *Wall Street Journal* analyzed more than thirty settlements from the six largest banks and found that of the following of the $110 billion that had been collected:

- $49 billion went to the Treasury Department.
- $45 billion went for consumer relief in the form of helping borrowers and community housing groups.
- $10 billion went to other government agencies, including federal housing agencies.
- $5.3 billion went to various state governments and agencies.
- $447 million went to the Justice Department.[49]

How Much Were the Investment Bankers Paid during the Crisis?

Throughout the financial crisis and its subsequent bailout, each of the CEOs of the major investment banks was paid tens of millions of dollars in annual compensation in the form of salary, bonuses, and stock options. Meanwhile, the companies they were in charge of spiraled into financial ruin, received billion-dollar bailouts, and paid huge fines:

- *Stan O'Neal, the CEO of Merrill Lynch, received compensation of $48 million in 2006. In October 2007, Merrill Lynch recorded a $2.2 billion quarterly loss. Shortly thereafter, O'Neal stepped down as CEO. His severance pay was $160 million.*
- *In January 2008, O'Neal was replaced by John Thain, who received a $15 million signing bonus. Thain oversaw the financial demise and eventual sale of Merrill Lynch to Bank of America in September 2008. Thain then joined*

[48] Noonan, Laura. 2015. Bank litigation costs hit $260bn – with $65bn to come. *Financial Times* (August 23).

[49] Rexrode, Christina and Glazer, Emily. 2016. Big banks paid $100 billion in mortgage-related fines. Where did the money go? *The Wall Street Journal* (March 9).

the financial holding company CIT Group, where he was given $8 million and stock options worth $16 million.

- *Ken Lewis, who retired as CEO of Bank of America in 2009, was given $83 million in pension, stock, and other retirement benefits. Bank of America also paid his $10 million fine as well as its own $15 million fine for criminal misrepresentation when Bank of America bought Merrill Lynch.*
- *In 2014, the two senior executives of Goldman Sachs, Lloyd Blankfein and Gary Cohen, received $24 million and $22 million, respectively. Goldman also received a government bailout of $12.9 billion to keep the company afloat.*
- *In 2014, JPMorgan Chase increased the compensation paid to its CEO, Jim Dimon, from $11.5 million to $20 million. That same year, JPMorgan Chase paid fines of $35.2 billion because of its contribution to the financial crisis.*
- *However, the poster boy of Wall Street greed was Richard (Dick) Fuld Jr. As CEO of Lehman Brothers, he was paid $484 million from 2000 to 2007. Fuld was in charge of the company as it slid into bankruptcy. Lehman Brothers is the largest bankruptcy in American history.*

No bank executives have returned any of the compensations received during the financial crisis. No bank executives or members of the boards of directors of all investment banks have gone to jail for their involvement in the global financial crisis.

Source: William D. Cohan, "Wall Street Executives from the Financial Crisis of 2008: Where Are They Now?," *Vanity Fair*, March 18, 2015.

FINANCIAL CRISIS INQUIRY COMMISSION In 1990, the famous economist John Kenneth Galbraith analyzed financial bubbles in his book *A Short History of Financial Euphoria*. He argued that all financial crises have five common factors:

- A new kind of financial instrument
- The mistaken belief that money and intelligence are linked
- Too much leverage
- The assignment of blame to everybody else
- The market systems themselves

His analysis of boom-and-bust phenomena such as the dot-com bubble of the 1980s, the stock market crash of the 1920s, and the Tulip bubble in the Netherlands in the 1630s all had these five common factors. These five factors also help to explain the subprime mortgage crisis.

Unfortunately, as Galbraith points out, people's memories are notoriously short. We do not seem to learn from past errors, so we are doomed to repeat them over and over again.

The subprime mortgage debacle led to the Great Recession that began in 2008. In May 2009, the U.S. Congress established the Financial Crisis Inquiry Commission to examine the causes of the 2007–2008 financial crisis. The ten-member panel interviewed more than 700 witnesses, read thousands of documents, and issued a 566-page report.

Overall, the commission "found dramatic breakdowns of corporate governance, profound lapses in regulatory oversight, and near fatal flaws in our financial system. We also found that a series of choices and actions led us toward a catastrophe for which we were ill prepared."[50] The following is a summary of the nine observations drawn by the Financial Crisis Inquiry Commission:

[50] "Conclusions of the Financial Crisis Inquiry Commission," xxvii–xxviii. The full report of the commission is available at http://fcic.law.stanford.edu.

- **The financial crisis could have been avoided.** Managers failed to heed warning signs. These warning signs included the following: risky and often predatory mortgage-lending practices, unsustainable increase in mortgage debt, unreasonable expectation that housing prices would continue to increase, securitization of mortgage loans, an unregulated derivative market, as well as failure to follow prudent lending practices.
- **There was a failure of financial regulation and supervision.** Key safeguards had been removed as the financial industry became more and more deregulated. Meanwhile, regulatory agencies, such as the SEC and the Federal Reserve Bank of New York, that had the power to regulate, monitor, and control the financial marketplace chose not to do so.
- **There was a failure of corporate governance and risk management.** The banks became too big to manage as they took on more and more risky trading activities. They replaced prudent judgment with mathematical models, while their compensation schemes rewarded short-term rather than long-term performance.
- **There was excessive borrowing, risky investments, and lack of transparency.** The investment banks were undercapitalized, with leverage ratios as high as forty to one. This meant that a 3% decrease in the asset values of any one of these overleveraged firms could bankrupt the firm and did so in the case of Lehman Brothers. Through overnight and "repo" loans, the banks were financing their operations with short-term money. With over-the-counter derivatives, many of these loans were not being recorded on the bank's books. Meanwhile, consumer mortgage debt rose 63% while salaries remained stagnant. Many home owners took out loans with payments so low that their mortgage debt rose each month.
- **The government was ill prepared and inconsistent in its response.** Because of a lack of transparency, regulators failed to fully understand the risks and interconnections within the financial marketplace as the contagion spread. They mistakenly thought that the bankruptcy of Bear Sterns in March of 2008 was "relatively unique." This was followed with an inconsistent response to the crisis: the U.S. government rescued Bear Sterns, let Lehman Brothers collapse, and then saved AIG.
- **There was a systematic breakdown in accountability and ethics.** Consumers took out mortgages that they knew they could not repay. Lenders lent mortgage money to consumers who the banks knew would be unable to repay the loans. Investment banks knowingly packaged and sold mortgage-backed securities that failed to satisfy their own underwriting standards.
- **Poor mortgage-lending standards spread the flame of contagion.** The commercial banks had been making very risky mortgage loans. These loans were then securitized and used to support mortgage-backed securities. Consequently, when the borrowers stopped paying their mortgages, the losses, amplified by derivatives, spread rapidly through the financial marketplace.
- **Derivatives contributed to the crisis.** Derivatives, especially CDSs, fueled the housing bubble and CDOs, which were synthetic bets on the performance of mortgage-backed securities, amplified the losses when the housing bubble burst.
- **Failure by the credit-rating agencies.** The credit-rating agencies, especially Moody's, overrated the quality of the mortgage-backed securities; 83% of the AAA securities were subsequently downgraded.

The most telling conclusion of the commission was that the crisis was created by people, not computer programs. Home owners, bankers, investors, and regulators were all culpable in creating a financial crisis that could have been avoided if everyone had followed prudent business practices, adhered to high ethical standards, and not focused on the short-term. Greed, incompetence, dishonesty, conflicts of interest, nontransparency, lack of moral courage, and poor risk management all contributed to a financial and economic crisis that need not have occurred.

ETHICS ISSUES—THE SUBPRIME LENDING FIASCO

Greed, Incompetence, Dishonesty, Conflicts of Interest, Non-transparency, Lack of Moral Courage, & Poor Risk Management

Why did *sophisticated and experienced* lenders such as banks and large pension funds invest in subprime mortgages when the prospect for renewal was so unlikely and the underlying property value was so vulnerable? To be fair, some lenders understood the risks and decided not to invest at all. The TD Bank is one example of this.[51] However, most of the lenders simply put too low a probability on the risk of default and too low an estimate of loss. They might have been misled into thinking that the counterparties who guaranteed the mortgages through CDSs may have been robust enough to cover the losses, but this proved not to be the case. In some instances, these poor aspects of risk management were honest mistakes or the result of the non-transparency of the risks, but in most instances lenders really did not do a good enough review to identify the underlying inadequacies. In other cases, investors knew the risks but decided to take the chance because of the possibility of high returns—they were greedy.

In either case, because AAA investment yields were very low, many institutional investors and individuals "chased yield" and blinded themselves to risk because of their desperation to achieve what they considered reasonable or attractive returns. To do otherwise would have risked dismissal. Fund managers, who opted for the safest, or best-understood, investments, would have had lower returns that would have led, in turn, to lost market share. It would have taken a farsighted board of directors to put up with such apparently suboptimal behavior.

In the case of the original lenders, some may have believed in the possibility of the renewal of teaser or liar loans, but most would have understood the risks. Those who understood the risks were part of the chain of those who aided and abetted transferring those risks onto ill-informed or unsuspecting investors. That chain included many investment advisors and others who pocketed very large gains from bonuses and stock options and holdings based on overstated earnings.

The investment advisors and executives involved were supposed to be acting in the best interest of others—investors or shareholders—but did they act only in their own interest? Were these facilitators dishonest? Did they understand and guard against harmful effects of conflicts of interest? Did they do something illegal? Should they be punished? How?

From a governance perspective, it is apparent that no one—including the mortgage-lending units, the banks, and the intermediaries that legitimized the process and pipeline for selling the SIVs, MBSs, and CDOs to the ultimate investors or the executives who pocketed large bonuses and stock option gains—bore any significant risk until the subprime lending scandal erupted. For example, U.S. banks were not required to retain any

[51] See the ethics case "Moral Courage: Toronto-Dominion Bank CEO Refuses to Invest in High-Risk Asset-Based Commercial Paper" at the end of this chapter.

risk (as they are to a limited extent in Canada[52]), and therefore the U.S. executives involved could afford to be reckless without fear of reprisal, and they were. There simply was insufficient regulation—governmental or self-interest—to offset or contain the unbridled greed let loose on the public.

Corporate Psychopaths—Potential Role in the Subprime Lending Crisis

An interesting theory has been proposed about the potential role of senior financial directors (i.e., executives) in the global financial crisis. Clive Boddy[53] argues that psychopaths working in financial corporations played a major role in causing the crisis. He identifies significant ways in which they caused havoc.

Boddy questions how traditional financial institutions with decades-long sterling reputations end up with leaders who appear devoid of ethical values and who demonstrate poor leadership that enables unethical and high-risk conduct by management employees. This, he argues, can occur when the primary motivating force within an organization is bonus maximization, even at the expense of the interests of long-standing clients. The following quotes provide an introduction to the behavior of people whom Boddy labels as corporate psychopaths:

> In watching these events unfold it often appears that the senior directors involved walk away with a clean conscience and huge amounts of money. Further, they seem to be unaffected by the corporate collapses they have created. They present themselves as glibly unbothered by the chaos around them, unconcerned about those who have lost their jobs, savings, and investments, and as lacking any regrets about what they have done. They cheerfully lie about their involvement in events, are very persuasive in blaming others for what has happened and have no doubts about their own continued worth and value. They are happy to walk away from the economic disaster that they have managed to bring about, with huge payoffs and with new roles advising governments how to prevent such economic disasters.
>
> Many of these people display several of the characteristics of psychopaths and some of them are undoubtedly true psychopaths. Psychopaths are the 1% of people who have no conscience or empathy and who do not care for anyone other than themselves. Some psychopaths are violent and end up in jail, others forge careers in corporations.

Members of the latter group are called Corporate Psychopaths and, it is argued, are highly attracted to financial institutions.

> Expert commentators on the rise of Corporate Psychopaths within modern corporations have also hypothesized that they are more likely to be found at the top of current organizations than at the bottom. Further, that if this is the case, then this phenomenon will have dire consequences for the organisations concerned and for the societies in which those organisations are based.
>
> There is also some evidence that they may tend to join some types of organisations rather than others and that, for example, large financial organisations

[52] Guideline D3: Accounting for NHA Mortgage Backed Securities gives the accounting treatment for securitization, which requires that, on sale, the net present value of the future spread is set up as a balance sheet asset.
[53] Clive R. Boddy, "The Corporate Psychopaths Theory of the Global Financial Crisis," *Journal of Business Ethics* 102 (Spring 2011): 255–259, 256.

may be attractive to them because of the potential rewards on offer in these organisations.[54]

The Corporate Psychopaths Theory of the Global Financial Crisis suggests that Corporate Psychopaths' "single-minded pursuit of their own self-enrichment and self-aggrandizement to the exclusion of all other considerations has led to an abandonment of the old-fashioned concept of noblesse oblige, equality, fairness, or any real notion of corporate social responsibility."[55] The theory argues that "changes in the way people are employed have facilitated the rise of corporate psychopaths to senior positions and their personal greed in those positions has created the crisis."[56]

To the extent that this theory holds true (and there are those who do not agree with it), the only solutions would appear to be to vigilantly monitor such people or to keep them out of senior management positions. They should not be allowed to manage other people's money, nor should they be allowed to cause severe damage to an economy through excessive risk taking. Obviously, the most effective way of achieving this is to not hire them in the first place. Therefore, directors and hiring committees need to be aware of this issue and take steps to assess the moral character of applicants, perhaps employing experts to help in the assessment. Another deterrent is to establish reward mechanisms that do not encourage psychopaths. For example, bonuses should do the following:

- Discourage excessive risk taking
- Focus on long-term success
- Be able to be clawed back if those already paid, payable, or accrued can be linked to inappropriate conduct
- Link bonuses to success for all key stakeholders, not just the bottom (or, even worse, the top) line

Also, so-called golden parachutes should not be payable when an employee is terminated for cause or resigns. In fact, it may be prudent for companies to eschew such parachutes altogether.

If all else fails and corporate psychopaths are already entrenched, directors and senior management should have the means to identify them and fire them or at least keep them on a very short leash (at which point they might well leave of their own accord). All these steps are made more difficult by the fact that these people are likely charming and very persuasive.

In summary, directors and senior management should be on the lookout for key individuals in any organization who appear to have no moral compass at all. At present, it is unlikely that this vigilance is happening except rarely and episodically.

Lack of Regulation & Sound Decision Making

In September 2008, Hilary Clinton, appearing on CNN during the Obama–McCain presidential election campaign, was asked if the Democratic Party did not bear some blame for the subprime fiasco because her husband had signed the *Gramm-Leach-Bliley (GLB) Act*, which replaced the *Glass-Steagall Act*, into law when he was president. She answered that although he had signed the bill into law, there had always been a planned second

[54] Clive R. Boddy, "Corporate Psychopaths Theory of the Global Financial Crisis," *Journal of Business Ethics* 102 (Spring 2011): 255–59, 257.

[55] Ibid.

[56] Ibid.

phase of stronger regulation in mind but that no one had an appetite for it after the *GLB Act* was signed. Unfortunately, the extra level of robust regulation never came into being. Was this because of greed, ignorance, lack of moral fiber, or lack of courage to stand up to corporate interests and argue that unbridled markets are too poor or slow at self-regulation to protect the public interest?

Others argue that U.S. regulators at the Federal Reserve, the OCC, and the SEC had the mandate to protect the public interest and failed to do so. Although this is literally true, it has not been a popular philosophy, politically speaking, to argue for increased regulation when stock and housing markets appear to be healthy. The problem with this line of thinking is that it focuses on the short term and not on the risks, costs, and benefits of the longer term—a flawed perspective that produces many bad ethical decisions. Moral courage is a rare commodity and should be appreciated for its true worth.

It is also evident that there should be promptly enforced and effective regulation. The subprime lending crisis illustrates that the ultimate free-market adjustment—a meltdown—comes too late to protect many from loss and has been judged too horrific to be allowed to happen. As we have seen, governments have stepped in to bail out the system rather than allow the ultimate free-market sanction to operate fully. Moreover, the principle of allowing the market to operate on self-interest *alone* is under question. Even Alan Greenspan has stated that "I made a mistake in presuming that the self-interests of organizations, specifically banks and others, were such that they were capable of protecting their own shareholders and their equity of the firms."[57] Perhaps, given the problems noted, it is time to integrate ethical thinking—to introduce the consideration of interests beyond the short-term interests of current shareholders and executives—into corporate decision-making processes that are normally based on profit, shareholder returns such as dividends, and legal considerations. Because some legal jurisdictions preclude such consideration, a first step would be to make it permissible, at least, for boards of directors to specifically include ethics in their financial decision making. This would allow them to broaden their considerations beyond the short-term interest of current shareholders and executives.

Are Mark-to-Market (M2M) Accounting Standards to Blame?

As the subprime mortgage meltdown escalated, financial institutions were required to record more and more losses on their income statement as they wrote down the value of their mortgage-backed derivative assets because of M2M accounting. The accounting rule, FAS 157 on fair value measurements, issued by the Financial Accounting Standards Board (FASB), required that, effective November 15, 2007, financial assets, such as derivatives, were to be revalued each reporting period at their current market or best-estimate values. In the case of financial institutions, this meant that every three months, when the financial institution issued its quarterly financial statements, it was required to revalue its investment portfolio, including the derivatives it owned. If the market had risen, then unrealized gains were to be reported on the income statement, thereby increasing the firm's net income. However, if the market value of the portfolio had fallen during that three-month period, then the institution was to record an unrealized loss, which reduced net income. In the case of the financial institutions during the subprime meltdown, adhering to FAS 157 increased the losses reported on their income statements.

[57] Barrie McKenna, "Greenspan Admits 'Mistake' on Bank Regulation; Ex-U.S. Fed Chief Wrongly Thought That Self-Interest Would Mitigate Risk," *The Globe and Mail*, October 24, 2008, 1, 16.

Not only did falling investment values negatively affect profits but also the valuation of the company's investment assets declined, which reduced the overall assets of the bank. For many, this meant that they were in jeopardy of falling below the capital requirements needed to meet bank protection limits or to fund operations. Banks chose to restrict new loans to conserve their capital, thus contributing to the credit freeze. Stock brokers and insurance companies such as Merrill Lynch,[58] Bear Stearns,[59] Wachovia,[60] and AIG[61] were taken over at fire-sale prices. Lehman Brothers went bankrupt.[62]

Many affected executives and investors called for a change to this accounting rule. On September 29, 2008, at the Manulife Financial's Investors Day, Domenic D'Alessandro, the longtime and well-respected CEO of Manulife, Canada's largest insurance company, launched into an impromptu five-minute tirade on fair value accounting. He said that the M2M accounting rules "are wrong theoretically. They're wrong operationally. They make no sense for anybody."[63] A chartered accountant himself, he contended that the rule exaggerated the tendency toward greed and short-term thinking. Similar sentiments were expressed in the United States and Europe.

On September 30, 2008, the SEC issued a joint statement with FASB, saying that if there was no ready market for a firm's derivative portfolio, then instead of using the M2M rule, management could estimate the value of its portfolio.[64] A few days later, the International Accounting Standards Board (IASB) said that firms could reclassify their damaged financial assets (to signal their condition) so that fair value changes would not have to be recognized immediately in net income.[65] On October 17, the Canadian Institute of Chartered Accountants announced that it was rushing through new accounting rules, similar to the IASB rules, for Canadian firms.[66]

The accounting profession was quick to change the rules after stubbornly insisting that M2M were good accounting rules. What happened? Did the accounting rules contribute to the subprime mortgage problem? Did they exacerbate the problem, as D'Alessandro contended? The answer depends on whether you are looking at financial statements from the investor's point of view or from the perspective of management. These two viewpoints are not always the same.

The objective of financial reporting is to provide information that is useful to investors and creditors in helping them make their investment and credit decisions. In particular, they want to be able to assess the amount, timing, and uncertainty of the future cash flows of the firm. M2M was introduced to speed up the signaling of potentially lower future cash flows by reflecting them as a current loss or reduction in profits. Assets have long been valued conservatively by using the lower of cost or market value rule,

---

[58] Mollenkamp et al., "Lehman Files for Bankruptcy, Merrill Sold, AIG Seeks Cash." Wall Street Journal, September 16, 2008, accessed November 9, 2008 at http://online.wsj.com/article/SB122145492097035549.html.

[59] J. P. Morgan acquired Bear Stearns in September 2008 for a fraction of its earlier worth.

[60] Wells Fargo acquired Wachovia in October 2008 at a fraction of its earlier value.

[61] M. Karnitschnig, D. Solomon, L. Pleven, and J. Hilsenrath, "U.S. to Take Over AIG in $85 Billion Bailout; Central Banks Inject Case as Credit Dries Up," *Wall Street Journal*, September 17, 2008, accessed November 10, 2008, at http://online.wsj.com/article/SB122165238916347677.html.

[62] Mollenkamp et al., "Lehman Files for Bankruptcy, Merrill Sold AIG Seeks Cash."

[63] Domenic D'Alessandro, "Mark-to-Market Madness," *National Post*, October 3, 2008, FP 13.

[64] SEC Office of the Chief Accountant and FASB Staff, "Clarifications on Fair Value Accounting," September 30, 2008, accessed November 10, 2008, at http://www.sec.gov/news/press/2008/2008–234.htm.

[65] International Accounting Standards Board, Press Release, October 17, 2008, http://www.iasb.org/NR/rdonlyres/7AF46D80–6867-4D58–9A12–92B931638528/0/PRreclassifications.pdf.

[66] Canadian Institute of Chartered Accountants, Media Release, "Canada Announces Important Changes in the Accounting for Financial Assets," http://www.acsbcanada.org/media-releases/item18398.pdf,

forcing the recognition of losses when they are thought to be permanent but allowing for some judgment and permitting some delay. M2M accounting was more stringent, requiring the *immediate recognition* of those losses and the expectation of lower cash flows on the ultimate sale or liquidation of the assets.

It is interesting to note that M2M required the relatively immediate recognition of gains on investments as well as losses. Not surprisingly, many executives who did not complain about the recognition of gains that gave rise to performance bonuses and rising share prices were upset over the recognition of losses.[67] Executives' self-interest of this nature, however, was not reason enough to cause M2M accounting to be set aside in favor of other means of disclosure.

The more important objection to M2M accounting was that the depressed valuations of mortgage-backed securities were believed to be temporary, so the estimated losses were expected to be reversed and probably eliminated in the longer term when housing prices recovered. Because it was also very difficult to accurately estimate the current fair value of the depressed assets in question, it was argued that forcing losses to be recognized immediately would be misleading. Hence, M2M accounting was set aside in favor of separate, specific disclosure of the doubtfully collectible assets in question.

It should be clear that there is no perfect method of disclosure of the risks inherent in the mortgage-backed securities when the reality of ultimate collection was extremely uncertain. At the same time, M2M essentially sped up the recognition of losses that would have been required under the conservative lower of cost or market approach. The wisdom of delaying recognition of worst-case bad news was questionable and could ultimately have led to a different kind of misrepresentation.

From a sophisticated investor perspective, it should also be noted that M2M treatment of projected potential losses on mortgage-backed securities was not expected to have much influence on short-term cash flows, except for the potential tax impact involved and the triggering of management bonuses or of clients/depositors withdrawing their money. This was because the direct cash flows involved took place when the assets were bought and sold, not when the losses were estimated. These estimates gave rise to noncash charges that affected profits but not direct cash flows.

However, from the perspective of management, M2M treatment could affect management performance assessments and corresponding bonuses. If net income rose, management was presumed to have done a good job, and they expected to be rewarded. Unfortunately, as noted previously, adoption of M2M during the subprime lending crisis usually required recording estimated losses, thereby reducing net income and bonuses even though the losses might never be incurred.

In summary, M2M accounting was not responsible for the subprime lending fiasco. It provided more immediate information to investors about the firm's probable future cash flows, but the information may not have been accurate. Management, however, favored M2M accounting during boom times when prices were rising and unrealized gains were reported on the income statement, but, in contrast, management was loath to report unrealized losses that would adversely affect how their stewardship was assessed, and that might have a negative effect on their bonuses based on reported earnings.

Did M2M accounting contribute to the subprime lending problem and ensuing credit freeze? The answer was that it might have sped up the recognition of the magnitude of the problem and thereby contributed to its solution. The meltdown in the

[67] Harry Koza, "Mark-to-Market: Great on the Way Up, Very Painful on the Way Down," *The Globe and Mail*, November 7, 2008, B12.

marketplace was caused by irresponsible lending and the passing on of the risks to naive, unsuspecting, or unprepared investors, with the inevitable huge losses leading to a credit freeze.

For some, M2M accounting was a distraction. As D'Alessandro said with respect to his own firm, "We've been able to run our business constantly with the view as to what is the best economic decision; not what is the best accounting decision."[68] This is the best decision-making perspective. However, the subprime lending crisis was caused by poor business decisions, not by poor accounting policies. M2M accounting provided useful information that simply highlighted the fact that financial institutions were holding onto investments that were rapidly losing their value. The real problems were greed and poor risk management.

The Ultimate Risk Bearers

So often when greed, lack of transparency about risks, and flawed focus on the short term are poorly regulated and allowed to foment into financial fiascos, governments have to step in to prevent unreasonable harm to the public. As a result, the ultimate bearers of the risk are not those who made the early returns or bonuses or stock gains—rather, it is the public, the taxpayer, those workers who lose their job, and so on who have to pay to pick up the pieces and put them back together. It is too bad that those who made money unethically cannot be made to pay restitution or give up their ill-gotten gains. It is too bad that those regulators who failed in their duties cannot be held accountable. It is too bad that the politicians who failed to consider and act in the long-term interest of the public cannot be identified. Although the damage done can never be repaired perfectly, identifying bad decisions and those who made them would give others reason to consider such decisions differently.

ETHICS LESSONS

In order to prevent a repeat of the tragedy, important ethics lessons must be identified, kept in mind, and acted on in the future. Key lessons to consider include the following:

- *Actions should be based on realistic expectations and responsible behavior:*
  - Potential home owners must remember that taking on debt is realistic only if they can afford to make the monthly mortgage payments. Because owning a home and having a mortgage are the largest asset and liability that most people will have, they should make these purchases based on their current, realistic financial prospects. Home ownership should not be based on speculation that the debt can be repaid only if house prices increase.
  - Lenders should be prudent in their lending practices, not talking naive home owners into taking on more debt than they can reasonably afford. Because there was little or no down payment requirement, those home owners had insufficient equity interest in their homes to motivate them to continue to make mortgage payments when their mortgage loans were to be refinanced at higher interest rates. It was easier for them to walk away from their homes and their debt. To avoid this *adverse selection problem*, lenders have a responsibility to verify the suitability of people to take on sizable home ownership debts.

[68] Domenic D'Alessandro, "Mark-to-Market Madness," National Post, October 3, 2008, FP 13.

- *Full risk assessment, due diligence, and virtues are expected.* Investors must always *consider fully the risks* associated with their investments. Because these mortgage-backed securities were supposedly insured, investors had little motivation to monitor their investments. Because the securities had been repackaged so often, it was difficult for investors to identify, investigate fully, and monitor the initial borrower/home owner. Investors expected that the original lenders and financial intermediaries had done their *due diligence* in this regard. The tragedy is that they had not, and investors forgot that they must take personal responsibility for understanding their investment vehicles and the risks associated with those investments.
- *Ethics risks, including conflicts of interest, are ever present and require constant vigilance, especially in boom times.* It is wise to understand that it is not only how much profit you make; it is equally important how you make it. Too often decision makers at all levels of business and the professions face *moral hazards* unknowingly and make the wrong decisions.
- Simply acting within *existing laws and regulations may not be a good guide for decisions because these can be shortsighted and manipulative,* which does not effectively serve the public interest—their ultimate purpose. Ethical assessments refocusing attention on key long-run issues are critical.
- Risk management assessment of subprime lending techniques failed to consider the fundamental *unfairness* involved for the mortgagees, the ultimate investors, and the public.
- Insufficient consideration was given to the *virtues expected* by executives and firms in the lending market, by the credit-rating agencies, and by regulators. They probably had no understanding of virtue ethics and mistakenly believed that maximizing profit in the short term was sufficient.
- Corporations have been known to take advantage of unsuspecting nations with low environmental standards, but in the case of the subprime lending crisis, they took advantage of unsuspecting mortgagees and investors in supposedly sophisticated markets. Don't the unsuspecting have the right to transparent disclosure of the risks involved in corporate activities?
- *Compensation schemes should be based on a balance between financial incentives on one side and financial*[69] *and ethical considerations and risks on the other. In addition, full details of compensation schemes should be disclosed to the public.* Such schemes should not just be based on profit earned at any cost.
- *Moral courage*—to speak up against unethical acts—is a rare and much-needed virtue.
- *Corporate governance systems have again proven to be inadequate to contain self-interest and short-term thinking and to focus on the medium and longer term with the view to producing lasting value for the public.*

In conclusion, it is clear that the decision-making processes of the executives involved in the subprime lending fiasco would have benefited from the ethics and governance frameworks discussed in earlier chapters. There has been an evident lack of consideration for the full consequences of subprime lending activities, particularly on investors and other stakeholders, including the public. In addition, there was little regard for the rights of investors as well as the fiduciary duty and fairness owed them. Finally, the ethical expectations or virtues expected from the investment community were hopelessly submerged by its self-interest. What options are there to remedy this fiasco—self-regulation involving the institution of ethical cultures, increased external regulation

[69] "Jarislowsky Blames Financial Mess on Lax Governance Rules," *The Globe and Mail*, October 24, 2008, B12.

mandating greater attention to the public interest, or both? As with the Enron disaster, the subprime lending fiasco has caused society to raise its expectations for business and professional governance and for personal ethics. Time will tell if the lessons of the subprime lending fiasco have been learned and how well.

Ultimately the lessons learned need to be applied on a global basis because business is done, and, as we learned with Enron and the subprime lending scandal, investment is made on a worldwide basis. The accounting profession has led the way by attempting to harmonize accounting and disclosure standards globally, and headway is evident. Corporate governance standards have also improved, but these are slower to change. Fortunately, the rigorous enforcement of antibribery and anticorruption laws on a worldwide basis, the prosecution of LIBOR scandal banks, and the huge fines levied and lost profits suffered by BP for its oil spill and VW for its cheating on air quality tests have triggered new ethical decision making at many multinational companies.

Incongruous as it may seem, the future of business and professional ethics has probably never been brighter.

Questions

1. How much and in which ways did unbridled self-interest contribute to the subprime lending crisis?
2. How could increased regulation improve the exercise of unbridled self-interest in decision making?
3. How could ethical considerations improve unbridled self-interest in ethical decision making?
4. Identify and explain five examples where executives or directors faced moral hazards and did not deal with them ethically.
5. How much should the exiting CEOs of Fannie Mae and Freddie Mac have received when they were replaced in September 2008?
6. The government bailout of the financial community included taking an equity interest in publicly traded companies such as AIG. Is it right for the government to become an investor in publicly traded companies?
7. Should CEOs who made large bonuses by having their firms invest in mortgage-backed securities in the early years have to repay those bonuses in the later years when the firm records losses on those same securities?
8. Should the CEOs who refused to have their firms invest in mortgage-backed securities in the early years because the risks were too great receive bonuses in the latter years because their firms did not incur any mortgage-backed security losses? How would you determine the size of these bonuses?
9. Should organizations that have a risk-taking culture, such as the one developed by Stan O'Neil at Merrill Lynch, enjoy the gains and suffer the losses, without recourse to government bailouts?
10. Are the criticisms that M2M accounting rules contributed to the economic crisis valid?
11. The global economic crisis was caused by the meltdown in the U.S. housing market. Should the U.S. government bear some of the responsibility of bailing out the economies of all countries that were harmed by this crisis?

12. Given that the marketplace for securities is global and that the risks involved can affect people worldwide, should there be a global regulatory regime to protect investors? If so, should it be based on the regulations of one country? Should enforcement be global or by country?
13. Should members and executives in investment firms be forced to be members of a profession with entrance exams and with adherence to a professional code such as is the case for professional accountants or lawyers?
14. Does the *Dodd-Frank Act* go far enough, or are some important issues not addressed?
15. What were the three most important ethical failures that contributed to the subprime lending fiasco?

Case Insights

The cases that follow capture important aspects of the subprime lending fiasco that businesspeople and professionals should be alert to identify and avoid in the future, including a culture of integrity, the impact of accounting rules, appropriate risk-taking and reward systems, and astute risk management and moral courage:

- *Questionable Values Produce Resignation at Goldman Sachs* allows the reader to reflect on Goldman's culture, the impact of not having a culture of integrity during and after the subprime lending crisis.
- *Naked Short Selling—Overstock.com Lawsuit against Goldman Sachs & Merrill Lynch* provides details of how the two investment advisors counseled clients to undermine the value of Overstock's shares and misused their brokerage functions to assist in this endeavor.
- *Lehman Brothers Repo 105 Manipulation* documents how Lehman Brothers, a famous investment bank that went bankrupt due to excessive leverage and lack of liquidity, actually hid up to $50 billion in borrowings. Ernst & Young's commentary as auditor is included.
- *Goldman Sachs's Conflicts: Guilty or Not?* exposes Goldman Sachs's roles in regard to the ABACUS deal, where very uncreditworthy subprime mortgages were securitized and sold to poorly informed investors, insured unwisely by AIG, bet against by Goldman traders, and ultimately partly responsible for a TARP bailout of AIG. Did Goldman act appropriately?
- *M2M Accounting and the Demise of AIG* is a case in which the CEO of AIG argues that the mark-to-market accounting rule contributed to the collapse of the company. Do you agree?
- *Subprime Lending—Greed, Faith, & Disaster* presents the story of a CEO who changed the corporate culture at Merrill Lynch to an aggressive risk-taking institution and how the purchase of subprime mortgage-backed securities led to huge losses for the brokerage house but a large termination payment for the CEO, Stan O'Neil.
- *Moral Courage: Toronto-Dominion Bank CEO Refuses to Invest in High-Risk Asset-Based Commercial Paper* explains how the CEO of a major Canadian bank refused to invest in subprime mortgage derivatives when all other banks were doing so, on the basis that the instruments were too risky.

- *The Ethics of AIG's Commission Sales* describes how huge commissions and bonuses were paid to Joe Cassano for work that was ultimately responsible for the unprecedented losses incurred by AIG and its eventual bailout by the Federal Reserve.

Useful References

Many individuals and organizations have contributed to the current debate and have offered useful comments and recommendations, including the following:

- Caux Round Table. "Global Prosperity at Risk: The Current Crisis and the Responsible Way Forward." cauxroundtable@aol.com. Draft cited.
- Johnson, Lewis D., and Edwin H. Neave. 2008. "The Subprime Mortgage Market: Familiar Lessons in a Next Context." *Management Research News* 31, no. 1: 12–26.
- Rotman School of Management. 2008. *The Finance Crisis and Rescue*. Toronto: University of Toronto Press.

- Consult **www.cengagebrain.com** for further references.

As Johnson and Neave indicate in their essay, the lessons to be learned have been evident in the past. Will they be learned well enough this time? Those who are alert to ethics issues should have a better chance at long-run success.

Useful Videos & Films

- *The Love of Money*—PBS series with three parts, first showing July 12, 2010: http://www.tvo.org/TVOsites/WebObjects/TvoMicrosite.woa?political_literacy_the_love_of_money.
- *The Warning*—PBS *Front Line* documentary, aired on October 20, 2009: http://www.pbs.org/wgbh/pages/frontline/warning/view. This documentary outlines events and the warning by Brooksley Born that the federal government had prior to 2000 of the potential subprime lending crisis.
- *Inside Job* (2010)—the Academy Award–winning documentary provides a detailed and easy-to-understand analysis of the subprime mortgage crisis.
- The film *Wall Street: Money Never Sleeps* (2010) realistically portrays the crisis meetings that led to TARP and the bankruptcy of a firm like Lehman Brothers.
- *Margin Call* (2011) is a fictional portrayal of an investment bank (such as Goldman Sachs) that attempts to reduce its portfolio of toxic investments before any of the buyers realize that the investments are toxic and the ethical dilemma about adopting such a strategy.
- Also, all the movies mentioned in the section, *Investment Bankers in the Movies*.

References

Berner, R., and B. Grow. 2008. "They Warned Us: The Watchdogs Who Saw the Subprime Disaster Coming—And How They Were Thwarted by the Banks and Washington." *Businessweek*, October 20, 36–42.

Biktimirov, E. N., and D Cyr. 2013. "Using *Inside Job* to Teach Business Ethics." *Journal of Business Ethics* 117: 209–19.

Canadian Institute of Chartered Accountants. 2008. "Canada Announces Important Changes in the Accounting for Financial Assets." Media release. http://www.iasb.org/NR/rdonlyres/7AF46D80-6867-4D58-9A12-92B931638528/0/PRreclassifications.pdf.

Caux Round Table. "Global Prosperity at Risk: The Current Crisis and the Responsible Way Forward." cauxroundtable@aol.com.

CNNMoney.com. "Bailout Tracker." http://money.cnn.com/news/storysupplement/economy/bailouttracker/index.html.

Committee on Oversight and Governance Reform of the U.S. House of Representatives. 2008. "Credit Rating Agencies and the Financial Crisis," October 22. http://house.resource.org/110/gov.house.ogr.20081022_hrs01RFM2154.1.pdf (Search for e-mail Crisis Timeline, http://data.newyorkfed.org/research/global_economy/Crisis_Timeline.pdf).

D'Alessandro, D. 2008. "Mark-to-Market Madness." *National Post*, October 3, FP 13.

Ellis, D. 2008. "U.S. Seizes Fannie and Freddie." *CNNMoney.com*, September 7. Accessed November 9, 2008, at http://money.cnn.com/2008/09/07/news/companies/fannie_freddie/index.htm?postversion=2008090720.

Emergency Economic Stabilization Act of 2008. http://en.wikipedia.org/wiki/Emergency_Economic_Stabilization_Act_of_2008.

"European Leaders Pledge Aid for Banks in Crisis." *Toronto Star*, October 13, B1, B4.

Federal Reserve Bank of New York. "Financial Turmoil Timeline." http://data.newyorkfed.org/research/global_economy/Crisis_Timeline.pdf.

———. "International Responses to the Crisis Timeline." http://www.ny.frb.org/research/global_economy/IRCTimelinePublic.pdf.

"Financial Crisis 2007–Present." *Wikipedia*, http://en.wikipedia.org/wiki/Financial_crisis_of_2007%E2%80%932010.

Galbraith, J. K. 1990. *A Short History of Financial Euphoria*. New York: Penguin Books.

Gasparino, C. 2008. "Bank of America to Buy Merrill Lynch for $50 Billion," September 14. Accessed December 28, 2010, at http://www.cnbc.com/id/26708319/Bank_of_America_to_Buy_Merrill_Lynch_for_50_Billion.

Heisel, W. 2008. "Fannie Mae and Freddie Mac CEOs to Get Golden Parachutes." *Los Angeles Times*, September 8.

International Accounting Standards Board. 2008. Press release, October 17. http://www.iasb.org/NR/rdonlyres/7AF46D80-6867-4D58-9A12-92B931638528/0/PRreclassifications.pdf.

Investopedia. 2010. "Shadow Banking System." Accessed December 28, 2010, at http://www.investopedia.com/terms/s/shadow-banking-system.asp.

"Jarislowsky Blames Financial Mess on Lax Governance Rules." 2008. *The Globe and Mail*, October 24, B12.

Johnson, L. D., and E. H. Neave. 2008. "The Subprime Mortgage Market: Familiar Lessons in a Next Context." *Management Research News* 31, no. 1: 12–26.

Karnitschnig, M., D. Solomon, L. Pleven, and J. Hilsenrath. 2008. "U.S. to Take Over AIG in $85 Billion Bailout; Central Banks Inject Cash as Credit Dries Up." *Wall Street Journal*, September 17. Accessed November 10, 2008, at http://online.wsj.com/article/SB122165238916347677.html.

Koza, H. 2008. "Mark-to-Market: Great on the Way Up, Very Painful on the Way Down." *The Globe and Mail*, November 7, B12.

Labaton, S. 2008. "The Reckoning: Agency's '04 Rule Let Banks Pile Up New Debt." *New York Times*, October 2.

Leonnig, C. D. 2008. "How HUD Mortgage Policy Fed the Crisis." *Washington Post*, June 10.

McKenna, B. 2008. "Greenspan Admits 'Mistake' on Bank Regulation; Ex-U.S. Fed Chief Wrongly Thought That Self-Interest Would Mitigate Risk." *The Globe and Mail*, October 24, 1, 16.

Mollenkamp, C., S. Craig, S. Ng, and A. Lucchetti. 2008. "Lehman Files for Bankruptcy, Merrill Sold, AIG Seeks Cash." *Wall Street Journal*, September 16. Accessed November 9, 2008, at http://online.wsj.com/article/SB122145492097035549.html.

Nocera, J. 2009. "The Reckoning: As Credit Crisis Spiraled, Alarm Led to Action." *New York Times*, October 1. Accessed December 27, 2010, at http://www.nytimes.com/2008/10/02/business/02crisis.html?_r=1&hp=&pagewanted=all.

Parkinson, D. 2008. "A Train Wreck? Greenspan Says He Didn't See It Coming." *The Globe and Mail*, November 8, B2.

Rotman School of Management. 2008. *The Finance Crisis and Rescue*. Toronto: University of Toronto Press.

SEC Office of the Chief Accountant and FASB Staff. 2008. "Clarifications on Fair Value Accounting," September 30. Accessed November 10, 2008, at http://www.sec.gov/news/press/2008/2008-234.htm.

Simon, R. 2009. "Falling Home Prices Create Rival for Subprime." Reprinted on the *Wall Street Journal* page (B8) of *The Globe and Mail*, January 30. Original article is from "Option ARMs See Rising

Defaults," http://online.wsj.com/article/SB123327627377631359.html.

Sinn, H.-W. 2010. *Casino Capitalism*. Oxford: Oxford University Press.

Sloan, A. 2007. "House of Junk." *Fortune*, October 29, 2007, 117–18, 120, 122, 124.

"The Love of Money." 2010. PBS series with three parts, first showing July 12. http://www.tvo.org/TVOsites/WebObjects/TvoMicrosite.woa?political_literacy_the_love_of_money.

U.S. Senate Banking Committee. 2010. *Brief Summary of the Dodd-Frank Wall Street Reform and Consumer Protection Act*, July 1. Accessed December 28, 2010, at http://banking.senate.gov/public/_files/070110_Dodd_Frank_Wall_Street_Reform_comprehensive_summary_Final.pdf.

Valukas, A. R. 2010. *Report of Anton R. Valukas, Examiner, Lehman Brothers Holdings Inc.*, Chapter 11 Case No. 08–13555 (JMP) (Jointly Administered), United States Bankruptcy Court, Southern District of New York, March 11, 4. http://lehmanreport.jenner.com. See also www.cen gage.com/accounting/brooks.

Verschoor, C. C. 2007. "Who Should Be Blamed the Most for the Subprime Loan Scandal?" *Strategic Finance*, December, 11, 12, 59.

Waldie, P. 2008. "Rating Agencies Face the Music." *The Globe and Mail*, October 23, B10.

Wall Street: Money Never Sleeps. 2010. Directed by Oliver Stone, 20th Century Fox.

Wikipedia. "Subprime Mortgage Crisis." http://en.wikipedia.org/wiki/Subprime_mortgage_crisis.

———."Timeline of United States Housing Bubble."http://en.wikipedia.org/wiki/Timeline_of_the_United_States_housing_bubble.

Woellert, L., and D. Kopecki. 2008. "Debt Raters Ripped for 'Colossal Failure.'" *Toronto Star*, October 23, B3, B6.

ETHICS CASE

Questionable Values Produce Resignation at Goldman Sachs

Allegations of serious impropriety and perhaps illegality surrounding Goldman Sachs's contribution to the 2008 financial crisis have been well publicized. Allegations included trading for their own benefit directly against the interests of its clients (e.g., the ABACUS deal involved deliberately stuffing collateralized debt obligations with inferior mortgage assets, selling them to clients, and then short selling them for their own account) and abusive practices generally.[1] These allegations and a description of the ABACUS deal are the subject of the ethics case "Goldman Sachs's Conflicts: Guilty or Not?" which begins on page 640.

The underlying values associated with this kind of activity were obviously troubling. This was further illustrated in 2012 when Greg Smith, head of Goldman's U.S. equity derivatives business in Europe, Africa, and the Middle East, wrote an op-ed piece in the *New York Times* about his resignation[2] in response to the appalling deterioration of the firm's culture. Goldman's old culture had previously been recognized for its ethicality that he describes as revolving around "teamwork, integrity, a spirit of humility, and always doing right by your clients." The modern culture he describes as "toxic" and "destructive."

The following are some quotes from his article:

> To put the problem in the simplest terms, the interests of the client continue to be sidelined in the way the firm operates and thinks about making money.
>
> Leadership (in Goldman) used to be about ideas, setting an example and doing the right thing. Today, if you make enough money for the

[1] See, for example, the BBC News report "Goldman Sachs Accused Of Misleading Investors," April 14, 2011, a report based on testimony at the U.S. Senate Permanent Committee on Investigations, http://www.bbc.co.uk/news/business-13077509.

[2] Greg Smith, "Why I Am Leaving Goldman Sachs," *New York Times*, March 14, 2012, accessed March 30, 2012, at http://www.nytimes.com/2012/03/14/opinion/why-i-am-leaving-goldman-sachs.html?pagewanted=all.

> firm… you will be promoted into a position of influence.
>
> It makes me ill how callously people talk about ripping their clients off. Over the last 12 months I have seen five different managing directors refer to their own clients as "muppets."

He comments on what he believes to be the three quick ways to become a leader at Goldman:

a) Persuade your clients to invest in stocks or other products that Goldman was trying to get rid of because they were not seen as being sufficiently profitable (described as the firm's "axes").
b) "Hunt elephants," that is, persuade your clients to buy the products that are the most profitable for Goldman rather than what is best for the client.
c) Trade "any illiquid, opaque product with a three letter acronym."

Of course, Goldman disputes this view of its practice, but Smith's interpretation intuitively explains how it—and other firms with similar cultures—got so far off the rails during the subprime lending crisis.

Questions

According to Greg Smith, the culture he describes existed in 2012, long after the 2008 financial crisis and subsequent fall-out, suggesting that the lessons have not been learned and that the problems are at least as bad as they were before the crisis.

1. How could the culture described be changed?
2. Who will need to cause this culture to change?
3. What will have to happen to cause this change?
4. Is it likely that Goldman Sachs will be able to hire the best and brightest recruits unless they change the culture described? Why and why not?
5. Corporate psychopaths would likely be attracted to a firm with Goldman's modern culture. How would Goldman ensure that they are not hired?

ETHICS CASE

Naked Short Selling—Overstock.com Lawsuit against Goldman Sachs & Merrill Lynch

Short selling occurs when a seller borrows shares from a brokerage house and then sells those shares. At a later date, the seller buys the shares and delivers them to the brokerage house. If the price falls during the shorting period, then the short seller makes a profit and generates a loss if the stock price rises. In theory, short selling is supposed to be done when the seller has made arrangements to deliver shares in order that the total shares sold should not exceed the number of borrowable shares.

Naked short selling occurs when the seller sells shares that he or she does not own and has not borrowed. When the seller does not purchase the shares that it has shorted within a required time frame, then the seller has "failed to deliver" the securities. Naked short selling permits the number of shares sold to expand to any level, thus driving down prices abnormally, to the great disadvantage of the existing shareholders. Unfortunately, it can be used aggressively to intentionally decrease a stock price.

Overstock.com, also known as O Co., is an online retailer of overstocked merchandise. In May 2007, O Co. successfully sued various brokers and hedge funds for colluding to damage its stock through short selling. These were followed by lawsuits against Goldman Sachs and Merrill Lynch. O Co. alleges that these two brokerage houses collusively urged their clients to take out naked short sales on

O Co., thereby driving down its stock price. Although much of the evidence presented by the defense was under a publication ban, an error by legal representatives released some into the public domain in May 2012, as reported in *The Economist* and elsewhere. Much of the released evidence was in the form of emails that provided evidence of appalling ethical values, if not illegalities, at these two brokerage houses.

Email excerpts showed that stock deliveries on short sales were intentionally failed by the two brokerage houses, even though both houses had millions of shares available. By permitting failure to deliver, the expected purchases to cover the short sales were never consummated, and therefore the market price sank lower than it should have. Merrill's internal compliance officers described some of this conduct as totally unacceptable. However, their warnings were ignored by Merrill's traders. One senior executive suggested that Merrill "might want to consider allowing… customers to *fail*." Another said, "F___k the compliance area—procedures, schmecedures."[1]

In June 2015, a California court found that it did not have jurisdiction over Goldman Sachs, but in January 2016, Overstock reached a settlement with Merrill Lynch for $20 million.

Questions

1. Should short selling be outlawed?
2. Should naked short selling be outlawed?
3. How would you describe the ethical cultures at Goldman Sachs and Merrill Lynch with respect to failed trades?
4. Short of wholesale firings, fines, and jail terms, can you suggest ways that the ethical cultures at Goldman Sachs and Merrill Lynch could be corrected?

[1] "An Enlightening Mistake," *The Economist*, May 15, 2012, accessed May 22, 2012, at http://www.eco nomist .com/node/21555472.

ETHICS CASE

Lehman Brothers Repo 105 Manipulation

On September 15, 2008, Lehman Brothers Holdings Inc., one of the world's most respected and profitable investment banks, filed for Chapter 11 bankruptcy protection in the United States Bankruptcy Court in the Southern District of New York.[1] Although Lehman Brothers (LB) had reported record revenues of almost $60 billion and record earnings in excess of $4 billion for the fiscal year ended November 30, 2007, only ten months later, their bankruptcy proceeding became the largest ever filed.[2] How and why this happened is a complex story, part of which involves financial statement manipulation using a technique that has come to be known as Lehman's Repo 105 to modify information provided to investors and regulators about the extent to which LB was using other investors' funds to leverage their own.

Banks generate revenue and profit principally by investing funds borrowed from other investors, such as depositors or lenders. Although some of the funds they invest are their own, banks can increase their activity by attracting and using other investors' funds—an approach that is known as "leverage" because it is using the bank's own capital to attract investments from others to increase or lever revenue- and profit-generation

[1] Voluntary Petition (Chapter 11), Docket No. 1, *Lehman Brothers Holdings Inc.*, No. 08-13555 (Bankr. S.D.N.Y. Sept. 15, 2008).
[2] Valukas, *Report of Anton R. Valukas, Examiner, Lehman Brothers Holdings Inc.*

investments beyond the capacity of the bank's own limited resources. A bank's profit from lending activities is generated by "the spread"—the higher rate of return at which a bank lends funds than it pays outside depositors and investors for the use of their funds. However, outside investors or depositors will invest with a bank only if they are convinced that the bank's own capital is sufficient to provide an adequate cushion against loss of their investment in the event that the bank suffers losses. Consequently, outside investors want accurate information on the extent of leverage employed by the bank, which is usually provided as a ratio as follows:

$$\text{Leverage Ratio} = \frac{\text{Total Assets}}{\text{Shareholders' Equity (the bank's own capital)}}$$

In its simplest form, the Repo 105 mechanism—a multiple-step technique[3] combined with the failure to disclosure promises to reacquire assets—was used by LB to reduce the reported total assets and net assets included in the leverage ratio, *thus showing a lower ratio or more conservative use of leverage than was actually the case*. Consequently, bank investors were misled about LB's ability to cushion losses with its own equity compared to banks that did not artificially depress their leverage ratios.

Each of the steps in the Repo 105 technique represented a transaction undertaken near the end of a reporting period designed to reduce the leverage ratio, but the impact of this was essentially reversed just after the beginning of the next reporting period. This reduction and reversal process was repeated each quarterly reporting period from 2001 to 2008. Because most of these periods (those up to November 30, 2007) were subject to audit by Ernst & Young (E&Y), questions have been raised about what E&Y knew and thought about the Repo 105 technique and its impact and what they should have done and did do during their audit process. In addition, the role and responsibility of LB's management and the Board of Directors has come into question.

Why Did Lehman Brothers Fail?

According to the Bankruptcy Examiner's Report[4] by Anton Valukas, LB failed for several reasons, including the following:

- The poor economic climate caused by the subprime lending crisis leading to a degeneration of confidence and therefore a disenchantment and devaluation of asset-backed commercial paper and other financial instruments in which LB and others had invested.
- A very highly leveraged position prior to the onset of the subprime lending crisis—LB "maintained approximately \$700 billion of assets… on capital of approximately \$25 billion,"[5] a ratio of 28:1.
- Decisions involving excessive risk taking by LB executives. For example, as the subprime lending crisis unfolded, LB management decided to invest more or "double down"[6] in depressed assets hoping for a quick gain when values rebounded. LB's aggressive decisions resulted in it exceeding its own risk limits and controls.[7]
- A mismatch between longer-term assets and the shorter-term liabilities used to

[3] A repo is a repurchase agreement whereby one party sells a security to another party on the understanding that the first party will repurchase the security at a later date. In LB's case, it would sell securities just before its financial statements were issued and use the proceeds from the sale to pay down its debt. After the financial statements were issued, LB would borrow money and use the borrowed money to repurchase the securities.

[4] Ibid., 2.

[5] Ibid., 3.

[6] Ibid., 4.

[7] Ibid.

finance them, thus making LB vulnerable to shifts in the preferences of creditors or the cost of the credit needed to finance the assets. Because the assets were of a longer-term nature, they were not maturing in time to pay off creditors who were making reinvestment decisions on a much shorter time scale. LB had to have creditors who had sufficient confidence in LB to be willing to invest daily so that LB could be sustained.

- A masking of the extent to which LB was leveraged through the use of repurchase transactions—otherwise known as *repo transactions*—including ordinary repo transactions, Repo 105 transactions, and Repo 108 transactions. (Repo transactions are explained more fully in the next section.) This masking prevented creditors and investors from understanding how leveraged LB was, thus permitting LB to expand.
- In March 2008, Bear Stearns, a rival investment house, began to falter and nearly collapsed, putting the spotlight on LB, which was considered the next most vulnerable.
- Investor confidence was further eroded when Lehman announced its first-ever loss of $2.8 billion for its second quarter of 2008. At this time, the SEC and the Federal Reserve Bank of New York sent personnel to take up residence on-site to monitor LB's liquidity.
- In fact, LB had masked approximately $50 billion in leverage in the first and second quarters of 2008, so their condition was worse than disclosed. Although LB raised $6 billion of new capital on June 12, 2008, "[U.S.] Treasury Secretary Henry M. Paulson, Jr., privately told [LB CEO] Fuld that if Lehman was forced to report further losses in the third quarter without having a buyer or a definitive survival plan in place, Lehman's existence would be in jeopardy. On September 10, 2008 Lehman announced that it was projecting a $3.9 billion loss for the third quarter of 2008."[8]
- On September 15, 2008, LB's bankruptcy filing proved Paulson to be correct.

The Repo 105 Mechanism and Impact

There are three kinds of repo transactions: (1) ordinary, (2) Repo 105, and (3) Repo 108. All three are illustrated along with their impact on the balance sheet and leverage ratio in volume 3 of the Examiner's Report.[9] Most investment banks used ordinary repo transactions to borrow funds using securities as collateral, which they shortly repaid for a 2% fee (interest charge), or "haircut" as it became known. Because the cash received as well as the assets used as collateral and the liability for repurchase are all shown on the balance sheet, it and the leverage ratios are accurately stated.[10] Schematically, an ordinary repo transaction sequence can be represented as follows:[11]

A Repo 105 transaction sequence is different in that prior to the reporting date, (1) the initial transaction is treated as a sale, not a borrowing; (2) the cash received is used to pay off liabilities; and then, after the reporting date, (3) LB borrows funds elsewhere to repurchase the securities sold including a 5% interest charge.[12] The

[8] Ibid., 10.

[9] Ibid., 752–67.

[10] Ibid., see illustration 2, vol. 3, 753.

[11] Ibid., 768.

[12] There is a fourth difference in that Lehman Brothers International (Europe) (LBIE) created a $5 Derivative Asset that represented the requirement to pay a 5% fee to repurchase the sold securities. This derivative asset is left off of the flow diagrams for simplicity of presentation. See Valukas, *Report of Anton R. Valukas, Examiner, Lehman Brothers Holdings Inc.*, 781, 790.

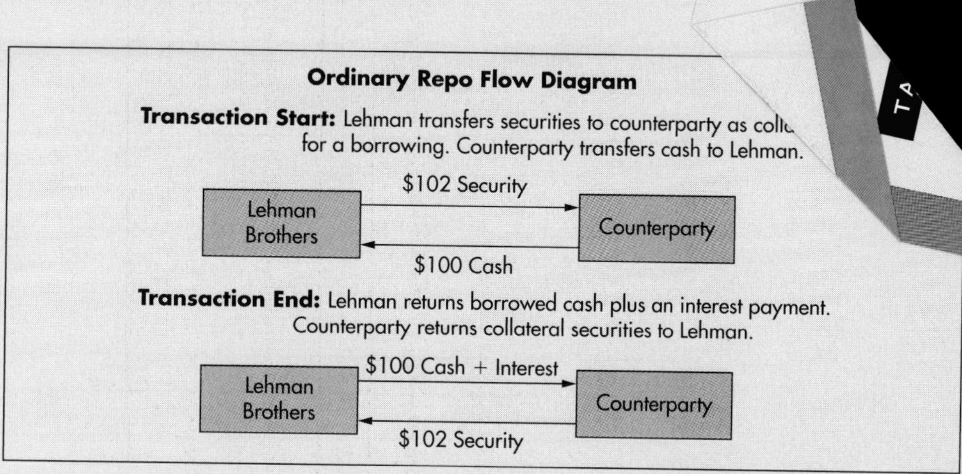

overall impact is to reduce the assets and the liabilities on the balance sheet at the reporting date, thus reducing the leverage ratio because the numerator and the denominator of that ratio are reduced by the same amount.

The balance sheet and leverage impacts of ordinary repo transactions as well as Repo 105 or 108 transactions are shown in the following sequence of illustrations.[13,14,15,16,17]

Balance Sheet and Leverage Impacts of Lehman Repo Transactions

In order to make the initial sale transaction credible, LB needed a letter from a law firm specifying that it constituted a "true sale." Interestingly, LB could not obtain such an opinion under U.S. law from U.S. lawyers, but Lehman Brothers International (Europe) (LBIE), based in London, did obtain one from Linklaters, a U.K. firm.[18] Consequently, when Repo 105 and Repo 108 transactions were needed, they were done via transfers to and from LBIE in London. Repo 105 transactions were used with highly liquid securities, whereas Repo 108 transactions involved nonliquid or equity securities. To make sure these transactions went according to protocol, LB created an Accounting Policy Manual Repo 105 and 108 to guide their personnel.[19]

LB employed ordinary repo transactions as well as Repo 105 and Repo 108 transactions. The interest charges or fees involved were 2%, 5%, and 8%, respectively. The higher interest rate charges on the Repo 105 and 108 transactions were to compensate for their higher level of risk. But, because ordinary repo transactions could have been used to raise cash[20] at a cost of 2%, it has been argued that LB used the higher-cost Repo 105 and 108 transactions only because they provided a way to manage LB's balance sheet and leverage ratio. This was confirmed by LB employees who commented as follows:

> "A senior member of Lehman's Finance Group considered Lehman's Repo 105 program to be balance

[13] Ibid., 752.
[14] Ibid., 753.
[15] Ibid., 754.
[16] Ibid., 758.
[17] Ibid., 760.
[18] Ibid., 784.
[19] Ibid., 776.
[20] Although this is correct, there would have been some limit at which ordinary repo transactions would have raised risk such that Repo 105 and Repo 108 transactions would have been inhibited.

[T]ABLE 1 Assume This Simplified Balance Sheet for Lehman

ASSETS (IN MILLIONS)		LIABILITIES	
Cash	7,500	Short-term borrowings	200,000
Financial instruments	350,000	Collateralized financings	325,000
Collateralized agreements	350,000	Long-term borrowings	150,000
Receivables	20,000	Payables	98,000
Other	72,500	Stockholders' equity	27,000
Total	800,000		800,000
Gross Leverage[1]	30		
Net Leverage[2]	17		

Note: The footnotes on page 752 of the Examiner's Report are:

[1]Gross leverage, *for illustrative purposes in this set of examples only*, is calculated as total assets divided by stockholders' equity and

[2]*For illustrative purposes in this set of examples only*, a simplified definition of net leverage is used: net leverage = (total assets – collateralized agreements) divided by stockholders' equity.

TABLE 2 Ordinary Repo of $50 Billion—Leverage Ratio Rises

ASSETS (IN MILLIONS)		LIABILITIES	
Cash	***57,500***	Short-term borrowings	200,000
Financial instruments	350,000	Collateralized financings	***375,000***
Collateralized agreements	350,000	Long-term borrowings	150,000
Receivables	20,000	Payables	98,000
Other	72,500	Stockholders' equity	27,000
Total	***850,000***		***850,000***
Gross Leverage	***31***		
Net Leverage	***19***		

TABLE 3 $50 Billion Is Used to Pay Off Current Liabilities—Leverage Ratio Is Reduced to Normal

ASSETS (IN MILLIONS)		LIABILITIES	
Cash	7,500	Short-term borrowings	200,000
Financial instruments	350,000	Collateralized financings	***325,000***
Collateralized agreements	350,000	Long-term borrowings	150,000
Receivables	20,000	Payables	98,000
Other	72,500	Stockholders' equity	27,000
Total	800,000		***800,000***
Gross Leverage	30		
Net Leverage	17		

TABLE 4 **$50 Billion Repo 105 Transaction Characterized as a Sale—Leverage Ratio Should Be Higher (19:1 as Indicated by Illustration 2) but Agreement to Repurchase Is Not Disclosed Causing Misstatement.**

ASSETS (IN MILLIONS)		LIABILITIES	
Cash	***57,500***	Short-term borrowings	200,000
Financial instruments	***300,000***	Collateralized financings	325,000
Collateralized agreements	350,000	Long-term borrowings	150,000
Receivables	20,000	Payables	98,000
Other	72,500	Stockholders' equity	27,000
Total	800,000		800,000
Gross Leverage	30		
Net Leverage	17		

TABLE 5 **$50 Billion Repo 105 Transaction Funds Used to Reduce Collateralized Financings—Further Lowering Leverage Ratio to 15:1, Whereas It Should Be 19:1 per Illustration 2**

ASSETS (IN MILLIONS)		LIABILITIES	
Cash	7,500	Short-term borrowings	200,000
Financial instruments	***300,000***	Collateralized financings	***275,000***
Collateralized agreements	350,000	Long-term borrowings	150,000
Receivables	20,000	Payables	98,000
Other	72,500	Stockholders' equity	27,000
Total	***750,000***		***750,000***
Gross Leverage	***28***		
Net Leverage	***15***		

sheet "window-dressing" that was "based on legal technicalities."[21]

Other former Lehman employees characterized Repo 105 transactions as an "accounting gimmick" and a "lazy way of managing the balance sheet."[22]

When queried about meeting internal leverage targets for the second quarter, an employee responded by email saying: "V[ery] close… anything that moves is getting 105'd."[23]

The reduction in leverage ratios achieved through the use of Repo 105 and 108 transactions are shown below:[24]

[21] Ibid., 742.
[22] Ibid., 743.
[23] Ibid., 748; for detailed computations, see 889.
[24] Ibid., 889.

DATE	REPO 105 USAGE (BILLIONS)	REPORTED NET LEVERAGE USING REPO 105	LEVERAGE WITHOUT REPO 105	REDUCTION IN NET LEVERAGE
Q4 2007	$38.6	16.1	17.8	1.7
Q1 2008	$49.1	15.4	17.3	1.9
Q2 2008	$50.38	12.1	13.9	1.8

According to the Bankruptcy Examiner, E&Y noted that LB's threshold for determining material items requiring reopening a closed balance sheet for correction was "any item individually, or in the aggregate, that moves net leverage by 0.1 or more (typically $1.8 billion)."[25] Consequently, the usage of Repo 105 transactions noted previously resulted in changes that were many times greater than LB's standard of materiality, which should have been a red-flag indicator to management and the auditors.

Ratings agencies, on whose ratings LB's credibility with lenders depended, were queried as to what they knew of the Repo 105 usage and materiality of the impact involved. According to the Examiner's Report,

> Eileen Fahey, an analyst at Fitch, said that she had never heard of repo transactions being accounted for as true sales on the basis of a true sale opinion letter or repo transactions known as Repo 105 transactions. Fahey stated that a transfer of $40 billion or $50 billion of securities inventory—*regardless of the liquidity of that inventory*—from Lehman's balance sheet at quarter-end would be "material" in Fitch's view, and upon having a standard Repo 105 transaction described, Fahey remarked that such a transaction "sounded like fraud."[26]
>
> Fahey likened this "manipulation" to an investment bank telling regulators that it did not own any mortgage-backed securities when, in fact, it owned them but had temporarily transferred them to a counterparty and was obligated to repurchase them shortly thereafter.[27]

the usage Enron made with its special purpose entities.)

The timing of the use of Repo 105 transactions corroborates that the intention was to manipulate LB's end-of-quarter balance sheets, as is shown in the following graph:[28]

At the end of each quarter, LB's assets are significantly higher than at the end of the two previous months. Thus, as a result of these transactions, LB's end-of-quarter balance sheet shows significantly less assets than would have been reported at any other time during the quarter.

LB's Accounting Analysis

LB's Repo 105 transactions were undertaken under paragraph 9 of the FASB's Statement of Financial Accounting Standards (SFAS) 140, which reads as follows:

Accounting for Transfers and Servicing of Financial Assets

A transfer of financial assets (or all or a portion of a financial asset) in which the transferor surrenders control over those financial assets shall be accounted for as a

[25] Ibid., 889.

[26] Ibid., 905.

[27] Ibid., 907.

[28] Ibid., 875.

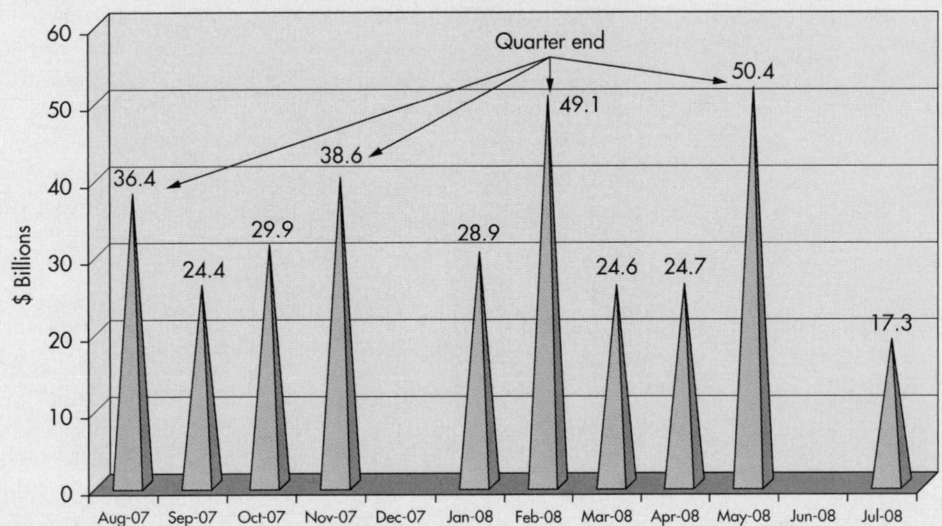

sale to the extent that consideration other than **beneficial interests** in the transferred assets is received in exchange. The transferor has surrendered control over transferred assets if and only if *all of the following conditions* are met:

a. The transferred assets have been isolated from the transferor—put presumptively beyond the reach of the transferor and its creditors, even in bankruptcy or other receivership (paragraphs 27 and 28).

b. Each transferee (or, if the transferee is a qualifying special purpose entity (paragraph 35), each holder of its beneficial interests) has the right to pledge or exchange the assets (or beneficial interests) it received, and no condition both constrains the transferee (or holder) from taking advantage of its right to pledge or exchange and provides more than a trivial benefit to the transferor (paragraphs 29–34).

c. The transferor does not maintain effective control over the transferred assets through either (1) an agreement that both entitles and obligates the transferor to repurchase or redeem them before their maturity (paragraphs 47–49) or (2) the ability to unilaterally cause the holder to return specific assets, other than through a **cleanup call** (paragraphs 50–54).[29]

SFAS 140 comments further in paragraph 218 that control over the assets transferred is maintained (thus breaking condition b above) if repurchase arrangements cover as much as 98% collateralization or as little as 102% overcollateralization. LB interpreted this to mean that because the "haircut" or fee charged in Repo 105 transactions was 5% and therefore greater than the 2% collateralization limit, control could be considered to have been surrendered, thus allowing the transfer to be considered a sale. Essentially, based on

[29] Financial Accounting Standards Board, *Statement of Financial Accounting Standards No. 140,* Accounting for Transfers and Servicing of Financial Assets and Extinguishments of Liabilities, Norwalk, CT, September 2000, para. 9, p. 9, http://www.gasb.org/cs/BlobServer?blobcol=urldata&blobtable=MungoBlobs&blobkey=id&blobwhere=1175820919404&blobheader=application%2Fpdf.

the percentages, LB took the position that they did not have the funds available to fund substantially all of the repurchase cost.[30]

To further bolster the position that the transfer of assets was a sale, LB obtained a letter from a U.K. law firm, Linklaters of London, that the transaction was a "true sale."[31] Such an opinion was possible under U.K. law but not under U.S. law, but the opinion was addressed to LBIE, thus necessitating transfers to LBIE so that the transactions would qualify as sales under U.K. law. LB, however, did not observe this need for transfer entirely.[32]

According to the Examiner, LB had this treatment as a sale vetted by outside auditors (E&Y) and lawyers.[33] However, on May 16, 2008, Matthew Lee, former LB senior vice president, Finance Division, who was in charge of Global Balance Sheet and Legal Entity Accounting, sent a whistleblower letter to senior LB management expressing concerns about possible LB Ethics Code violations[34] about the balance sheet irregularities related to the $50 billion in Repo 105 transactions then under way. According to the examiner,

> Lee's letter contained the following six allegations: (1) on the last day of each month, Lehman's books and records contained approximately $5 billion of net assets in excess of what was managed on the last day of the month, thereby suggesting that the firm's senior management was not in control of its assets to be able to present full, fair, and accurate financial statements to the public; (2) Lehman had "tens of billions of dollars of unsubstantiated balances, which may or may not be 'bad' or non-performing assets or real liabilities"; (3) Lehman had tens of billions of dollars of illiquid inventory and did not value its inventory in a "fully realistic or reasonable" way; (4) given Lehman's rapid growth and increased number of accounts and entities, it had not invested sufficiently in financial systems and personnel to cope with the balance sheet; (5) the India Finance office lacked sufficient knowledgeable management, resulting in the real possibility of potential misstatements of material facts being distributed by that office; and (6) certain senior level audit personnel were not qualified to "properly exercise the audit functions they are entrusted to manage."[35]

Lee was interviewed by E&Y representatives about his concerns on June 12, 2008.[36]

E&Y's Reaction

E&Y faced questions from the business press and their clients as soon as the Examiner's Report was made public. In response, a letter was quickly issued to clients, which apparently found its way into the public domain by being published on the Web. That letter was originally published without the opening and closing paragraphs by Francine McKenna[37] on

[30] See Valukas, *Report of Anton R. Valukas, Examiner, Lehman Brothers Holdings Inc.*, 778–80.

[31] Ibid., 784–86.

[32] Ibid., 786.

[33] Ibid., 914.

[34] Ibid., 956, fn. 3700

[35] Ibid.

[36] Ibid., 957.

[37] Francine McKenna, "An Ernst & Young Response: Dear Audit Committee Member…," March 20, 2010, http://retheauditors.com/2010/03/20/an-ernst-young-response-dear-audit-committee-member.

March 20, 2010, at http://www.retheauditors.com. E&Y's letter, which is shown below,[38] was published in its entirety on March 23, 2010, on the Contrarian Pundit website at http://www.contrarianpundit.com.

[38] The E&Y letter was downloaded on June 18, 2010, from the following websites: http://www.contrarianpundit.com/wp-content/uploads/2010/03/EYLetter1.pdf and http://www.contrarianpundit.com/wp-content/uploads/2010/03/EYLetter2.pdf.

ERNST & YOUNG

23 March 2010

To:

Recently, there have been extensive media reports about the release of the Bankruptcy Examiner's Report relating to the September 2008 bankruptcy of Lehman Brothers. As you may have read, Ernst & Young was Lehman Brothers' independent auditors.

The concept of an examiner's report is a feature of US bankruptcy law. It does not represent the views of a court or a regulatory body, nor is the Report the result of a legal process. Instead, an examiner's report is intended to identify potential claims that, if pursued, may result in a recovery for the bankrupt company or its creditors. EY is confident we will prevail should any of the potential claims identified against us be pursued.

We wanted to provide you with EY's perspective on some of the potential claims in the Examiner's Report. We also wanted to address certain media coverage and commentary on the Examiner's Report that has at times been inaccurate, if not misleading.

A few key points are set out below.

General Comments

- EY's last audit was for the year ended November 30, 2007. Our opinion stated that Lehman's financial statements for 2007 were fairly presented in accordance with US GAAP, and we remain of that view. We reviewed but did not audit the interim periods for Lehman's first and second quarters of fiscal 2008.
- Lehman's bankruptcy was the result of a series of unprecedented adverse events in the financial markets. The months leading up to Lehman's bankruptcy were among the most turbulent periods in our economic history. Lehman's bankruptcy was caused by a collapse in its liquidity, which was in turn caused by declining asset values and loss of market confidence in Lehman. It was not caused by accounting issues or disclosure issues.
- The Examiner identified no potential claims that the assets and liabilities reported on Lehman's financial statements (approximately $691 billion and $669 billion, respectively, at November 30, 2007) were improperly valued or accounted for incorrectly.

Accounting and Disclosure Issues Relating to Repo 105 Transactions

- There has been significant media attention about potential claims identified by the Examiner related to what Lehman referred to as "Repo 105" transactions. What has not been reported in the media is that the Examiner did not challenge Lehman's accounting for its Repo 105 transactions.

- As recognized by the Examiner, all investment banks used repo transactions extensively to fund their operations on a daily basis; these banks all operated in a high-risk, high-leverage business model. Most repo transactions are accounted for as financings; some (the Repo 105 transactions) are accounted for as sales if they meet the requirements of SFAS 140.
- The Repo 105 transactions involved the sale by Lehman of high quality liquid assets (generally government-backed securities), in return for which Lehman received cash. The media reports that these were "sham transactions" designed to off-load Lehman's "bad assets" are inaccurate.
- Because effective control of the securities was surrendered to the counterparty in the Repo 105 arrangements, the accounting literature (SFAS 140) *required* Lehman to account for Repo 105 transactions as sales rather than financings.
- The potential claims against EY arise solely from the Examiner's conclusion that these transactions ($38.6 billion at November 30, 2007) should have been specifically disclosed in the footnotes to Lehman's financial statements, and that Lehman should have disclosed in its MD&A the impact these transactions would have had on its leverage ratios if they had been recorded as financing transactions.
- While no specific disclosures around Repo 105 transactions were reflected in Lehman's financial statement footnotes, the 2007 audited financial statements were presented in accordance with US GAAP, and clearly portrayed Lehman as a leveraged entity operating in a risky and volatile industry. Lehman's 2007 audited financial statements included footnote disclosure of off balance sheet commitments of almost $1 trillion.
- Lehman's leverage ratios are not a GAAP financial measure; they were included in Lehman's MD&A, not its audited financial statements. Lehman concluded no further MD&A disclosures were required; EY did not take exception to that judgment.
- If the Repo 105 transactions were treated as if they were on the balance sheet for leverage ratio purposes, as the Examiner suggests, Lehman's reported gross leverage would have been 32.4 instead of 30.7 at November 30, 2007. Also, contrary to media reports, the decline in Lehman's reported leverage from its first to second quarters of 2008 was not a result of an increased use of Repo 105 transactions. Lehman's Repo 105 transaction volumes were comparable at the end of its first and second quarters.

Handling of the Whistleblower's Issues

- The media has inaccurately reported that EY concealed a May 2008 whistleblower letter from Lehman's Audit Committee. The whistleblower letter, which raised various significant potential concerns about Lehman's financial controls and reporting *but did not mention Repo 105*, was directed to Lehman's management. When we learned of the letter, our lead partner promptly called the Audit Committee Chair; we also insisted that Lehman's management inform the Securities & Exchange Commission and the Federal Reserve Bank of the letter. EY's lead partner discussed the whistleblower letter with the Lehman Audit Committee on at least three occasions during June and July 2008.
- In the investigations that ensued, the writer of the letter did briefly reference Repo 105 transactions in an interview with EY partners. He also confirmed to EY that he was unaware of any material financial reporting errors. Lehman's senior executives did not advise us of any reservations they had about the company's Repo 105 transactions.
- Lehman's September 2008 bankruptcy prevented EY from completing its assessment of the whistleblower's allegations. The allegations would have been the subject of significant attention had EY completed its third quarter review and 2008 year-end audit.

Should any of the potential claims be pursued, we are confident we will prevail.

Thank you for your support in this matter. Please feel free to call me at anytime at

With best regards,

Lehman's Risk Management

LB was a major player in a field that involved many varieties of risk and had specifically identified that their risk appetite for Repo 105 transactions in July 2006 was "1x leverage… or $17 billion, [and] $5 billion for Repo 108 transactions."[39] Consequently, LB's internal cap on repo transactions was breached by significant amounts beginning in 2007.[40] Recognizing that the levels of $40 billion to 50 billion were unsustainable, LB made efforts to obtain outside financing to be used to cut the level of repo transactions in 2008. Unfortunately, that effort was too little, too late. On September 15, 2008, LB declared bankruptcy.

Questions

1. What was the most important reason for the LB failure?
2. What is leverage and why is it so important?
3. Prepare the journal entries for a Repo 105 transaction sequence for $1 million in securities.
4. In your opinion, how large should a Repo 105 transaction be to be considered material and why?
5. Was LB's interpretation of SFAS 140—Repo 105 transactions could be treated as sales—correct? Provide your reasons.
6. If, as the Examiner's Report states,[41] LB continued to collect the revenue from the securities involved in the Repo 105 transactions, how could LB say that they had given up ownership?
7. An emerging issue Interpretation Bulletin[42] accompanying FAS 140 gives examples indicating that Repo 102 transactions would not qualify as sales but that Repo 110 would. Why do you think this Bulletin was issued? See Q&A 140—A Guide to Implementation of Statement 140 on Accounting for Transfers and Servicing of Financial Assets and Extinguishments of Liabilities at http://www.fasb.org/cs/ContentServer?c=Document_C&pagename=FASB%2FDocument_C%2FDocumentPage&cid=1175801856780 (accessed March 27, 2011).
8. Knowing that LB could not obtain a "true sale" opinion from a U.S. lawyer under U.S. law, should LB have tried to obtain the opinion from a U.K. law firm? Why and why not?
9. Do the Repo 105 arrangements constitute fraud? Why and why not?
10. What is the auditor's responsibility if a fraud is suspected or discovered? What professional standards are most important in such cases and why?
11. If you were the audit partner in charge in the United States, what would you have required be done in regard to the Linklater "true sale" letter?
12. Should consolidated financial statements of a U.S. parent company include (i.e., consolidate) foreign subsidiary accounts prepared on a basis not considered appropriate U.S. GAAP?

---

[39] Ibid., 741.

[40] In fact, there were also two other "loosely known" rules established to control total Repo 105 usage and "to make sure there was a legitimate business purpose" involved: (1) the "80/20" or "continual use rule" and (2) the "120%" rule. Ibid., 743.

[41] See Valukas, *Report of Anton R. Valukas, Examiner, Lehman Brothers Holdings Inc.*, 757, fn. 2930. Question suggested by Francine McKenna.

[42] See "Q&A 140—A Guide to Implementation of Statement 140 on Accounting for Transfers and Servicing of Financial Assets and Extinguishments of Liabilities," http://www.fasb.org/cs/ContentServer?cDocument_C&pagenameFASB%2FDocument_C%2FDocumentPage&cid1175801856780 (accessed March 27, 2011).

13. Would the adoption of IFRS have prevented the Repo 105 misrepresentations?
14. What should the following have done on learning of Matthew Lee's whistleblower's letter—LB's management, Board of Directors, and the external auditors, E&Y?
15. Arthur Andersen tried to keep its Enron audit problems quiet, whereas E&Y spoke out in its own defense. Was it a good idea for E&Y to send a letter, such as the one reproduced previously, to their clients? Why and why not?
16. Based on the letter, should E&Y be in the clear of any wrongdoing related to the Repo 105 and 108 transactions and reporting? Provide your reasons for and against.
17. If an auditor explains a problem to the chair of an audit committee, is there any further obligation on the part of the auditor to ensure that the full board has been notified and why?
18. Organizations who use the Enterprise Risk Management (ERM) framework[43] should work through the following stages: review on the internal environment, identification of the organization's risk appetite or objectives, risk identification and measurement, risk assessment, risk response, providing risk information and communications, and risk monitoring. In which of these did LB fail? Who was to blame for the failure?
19. How should the U.S. Bankruptcy Examiner's Report be regarded—as a neutral set of findings or as a signpost intended to point creditors in the direction of potential recoveries? What are the implications of each?
20. After the Enron and WorldCom fiascos, regulators sought to avoid future misrepresentation by enacting the *Sarbanes-Oxley Act* (SOX) in 2002. Why did SOX not prevent Lehman's use of Repo 105 and 108 misrepresentations? Does that mean that SOX is a failure?

[43] See, for example, Committee of Sponsoring Organizations of the Treadway Commission, *Enterprise Risk Management—Integrated Framework: Executive Summary*, September 2004, http://www.coso.org/documents/COSO_ERM_ExecutiveSummary.pdf.

ETHICS CASE

Goldman Sachs Conflicts: Guilty or Not?

During the depths of the subprime lending crisis in 2008, a major U.S. investment banking firm, Goldman Sachs, required a $10 billion bailout from the U.S. government's Troubled Asset Relief Program (TARP) to stay afloat. But in 2009, Goldman's fortunes reversed as the firm earned $13.4 billion profit, repaid the $10 billion to TARP, and paid its employees over $16 billion.[1]

The firm's nickname, "Golden Socks," appears to be well earned. But is this spectacular reversal just too good to be true—or at least the result of unethical, if not illegal, practices? Did Goldman profit unfairly by somehow taking advantage of unsuspecting clients or by undermining a floundering U.S. or even world economy? In fact, serious allegations have been raised about Goldman's role in the financial crisis, including the following:

1. Duping American International Group, Inc. (AIG) into insuring poor-quality mortgage securities and then
   a. triggering insurance payments to Goldman by setting artificially low securities valuations, thereby
   b. precipitating a $130 billion–plus bailout of AIG and a transfer of 79.9% equity ownership to the U.S. Federal Reserve Bank and

[1] Roben Farzad and Paula Dwyer "Goldman Sachs: Don't Blame Us,", *Bloomberg Businessweek*, April 12, 2010, 30–38, http://www.businessweek.com/magazine/content/10_15/b4173030234603.htm.

   c. causing the U.S. government to pay $52.5 million to Goldman in settlement of credit default swaps in which AIG had insured mortgage securities.[2]
2. Betting against clients by taking "short positions on collateralized debt obligations [CDOs] that it had created and sold to clients."[3]
3. Stuffing "these CDOs with inferior mortgage assets that ensured their collapse."[4]

The ABACUS Deal: Goldman Engineered, Paulson & Co. Influenced

The spotlight fell on one of Goldman's transactions, known as ABACUS 2007-AC1, when the SEC filed securities fraud charges on April 16, 2010, against Goldman and one of its employees, Fabrice Tourre, who vainly dubbed himself the "fabulous Fab" for creating the deal.[5] According to the SEC's allegations, Goldman created and marketed a synthetic CDO to customers without disclosing to investors that the underlying subprime residential mortgage-backed securities (RMBS) had been selected, in part, by a hedge fund, Paulson & Co. Inc.,[6] which immediately bet that ABACUS 207-AC1 would fail by buying CDSs from Goldman (GS&Co) that effectively insured against losses related to that failure.[7] According to the SEC,

> The deal closed on April 26, 2007. Paulson paid GS&Co approximately $15 million for structuring and marketing ABACUS 2007-AC1. By October 24, 2007, 83% of the RMBS in the ABACUS 2007-AC1 portfolio had been downgraded and 17% was on negative watch. By January 29, 2008, 99% of the portfolio had allegedly been downgraded. Investors in the liabilities of ABACUS 2007-AC1 are alleged to have lost over $1 billion. Paulson's opposite CDS positions yielded a profit of approximately $1 billion.[8]

On July 15, 2010, the SEC announced that Goldman had paid $550 million, the highest penalty ever paid to settle the case, and agreed to remedial actions but did not admit or deny the allegations. Two hundred and fifty million was to be returned to investors, and $300 million was paid to the U.S. Treasury. In court papers filed, Goldman acknowledged that

> the marketing materials for the ABACUS 2007-AC1 transaction contained incomplete information. In particular, it was a mistake for the Goldman marketing materials to state that the reference portfolio was "selected by" ACA Management LLC without disclosing the role of Paulson & Co. Inc. in the portfolio selection process and that Paulson's economic interests were adverse to CDO investors. Goldman regrets that the marketing materials did not contain that disclosure.[9]

---

[2] Ibid., 33, and http://en.wikipedia.org/wiki/American_International_Group.

[3] Ibid.

[4] Ibid.

[5] Jonathan Weil, "Goldman Slapped," *Bloomberg Businessweek*, April 26–May 2, 2010, 13–14.

[6] Owned by billionaire John Paulson.

[7] "The SEC Charges Goldman Sachs with Fraud in Connection with the Structuring and Marketing of a Synthetic CDO," Litigation Release No. 21489, April 16, 2010, *Securities and Exchange Commission v. Goldman, Sachs & Co. and Fabrice Tourre*, 10 Civ. 3229 (BJ) (S.D.N.Y. filed April 16, 2010) (accessed September 19, 2010).

[8] Ibid.

[9] Goldman Sachs to Pay Record $550 Million to Settle SEC Charges Related to Subprime Mortgage CDO, U.S. Securities and Exchange Commission, Litigation Release No. 21592, July 15, 2010, *Securities and Exchange Commission v. Goldman, Sachs & Co. and Fabrice Tourre*, Civil Action No. 10 Civ. 3229 (S.D.N.Y. filed April 16, 2010) (accessed September 19, 2010).

Deals with AIG

AIG, once the world's largest insurer, began to insure portions of subprime mortgage deals in 2003.[10] Many observers came to believe that the company "was reckless during the mortgage mania," and as it turned out, AIG "had written far more insurance than it could possibly have paid off if a national mortgage debacle occurred—as, in fact, it did."[11] This was the underlying reason why the federal government had to step in September 2008 and ultimately bail out AIG by providing $180 billion and taking over the company.[12]

Reports have indicated that Goldman received $7 billion from AIG before the rescue and $12.9 billion after the rescue, plus "a portion of $11 billion in taxpayer money that went to Société Générale, a French bank that traded with AIG, was subsequently transferred to Goldman under a deal the two banks had struck."[13] Since Goldman knew that AIG was insuring other companies' deals as well, should Goldman not have known that AIG was being stretched, in a risk of default sense, to or beyond that company's reasonable limit?

It is possible that the Black Swan[14] phenomenon was at work. AIG and many other insurers and investors put such a low probability on a national mortgage default that they discounted the overall impact far too much and did not have a clear view of the risk limits of AIG and other market participants. But it has been reported that Goldman was betting significant capital that the mortgage market would decline or crash as early as 2006.[15] Moreover, Goldman was pressing AIG to recognize Goldman's abnormally low market valuations on the mortgages insured so that AIG would have to pay off on their insurance. These valuations were so low that AIG objected strenuously, but Goldman would not submit them to outside adjudication.[16]

Betting against the Market and Clients: A Shift in Focus and Culture

Goldman's significant bets in 2006 and later against the stability of the national mortgage raise other concerns. Throughout this period, Goldman was actively structuring deals like ABACUS and marketing these to their investor clients. But Goldman was being disingenuous. They were marketing mortgage-backed securities to their clients while at the same time investing Goldman's own resources in ways that would pay off if mortgage securities sank in value (e.g., short positions). In addition, Goldman's proprietary trading would be undermining the market price of the mortgage-backed securities being sold to others. It is worth noting that the financial market reforms introduced in September 2010 crystallized the

---

[10] Gretchen Morgenson and Louise Story, "Testy Conflict with Goldman Helped Push A.I.G. to Edge," *New York Times*, February 6, 2010, accessed September 21, 2010, at http://www.nytimes.com/2010/02/07/business/07goldman.html?_r=1&pagewanted=1&ref=business.

[11] Ibid.

[12] See, for example, Matthew Karnitschnig, Deborah Solomon, Liam Pleven and Jon Hilsenrath, "U.S. to Take Over AIG in $85 Billion Bailout; Central Banks Inject Cash as Credit Dries Up," *Wall Street Journal*, September 16, 2008.

[13] Morgenson and Story, "Testy Conflict with Goldman Helped Push A.I.G. to Edge."

[14] The black swan phenomenon refers to a very rare event—like finding a black swan. However, a black swan event, even though it is rare, can have an incredibly large impact or cost, such as the economic disruption of the subprime lending crisis. Many investors were thinking only of the low probability of a subprime lending crisis and overlooked the huge cost of the failure. They focused on the low probability of the event rather than the expected value of it (expected value = probability of event × cost or payoff amount).

[15] Morgenson and Story, "Testy Conflict with Goldman Helped Push A.I.G. to Edge."

[16] Ibid.

so-called Volker Rule,[17] which placed restrictions on proprietary trading by investment banks based on conflict-of-interest concerns.[18]

Goldman's culture and revenue had changed significantly since the 1990s toward a heavy reliance on proprietary trading and special situation investing and away from the traditional investment bank services of "getting to know companies and their executives inside out, while advising them on mergers, acquisitions, and stock offerings."[19] Once the dominant activity, traditional investment banking services were increasingly dwarfed by proprietary trading until in 2009 proprietary trading "accounted for three-quarters of the firm's $45 billion (U.S.) in revenues,"[20] whereas investment banking accounted for only a tenth.

Although both activities are intended to generate profit, the "time frame and approach—executives wooed over years of lunches and dinners, not rapid-fire trades during the course of a day—are poles apart."[21] "On the investment banking side, you protected your clients and your market share,"[22] both of which involved long-term thinking and stewardship. "On the trading side, it was all about making money."[23]

This shift in thinking was articulated in what has become known as the "fork in the road speech" given in 2005 by Lloyd Blankfein, who was then the chief operating officer. "He argued Goldman had to combine its roles as an adviser, financier, and investor, or risk irrelevance. By focusing more on putting its own money to work, new conflicts would arise, but Goldman was skilled at managing them, he said."[24]

Goldman Sachs's Response: ". . . Not Guilty. Not One Little Bit."

According to Goldman's senior executives, as might be expected, the firm is "not guilty. Not one little bit."[25] In the firm's Letter to Shareholders[26] accompanying its 2009 Annual Report, these executives provide Goldman's official response, as follows:

Our Relationship with AIG

Over the last year, there has been a lot of focus on Goldman Sachs' relationship with AIG, particularly our credit exposure to the company and the direct effect the U.S. government's decision to support AIG had or didn't have on our firm. Here are the facts:

Since the mid-1990s, Goldman Sachs has had a trading relationship with AIG. Our business with them spanned a number of their entities, including many of their insurance subsidiaries. And it included multiple activities, such as stock lending, foreign exchange, fixed income, futures and mortgage trading.

AIG was a AAA-rated company, one of the largest and considered one of the most sophisticated trading counterparts in the world. We established credit terms with them commensurate with those extended to other major counterparts, including a willingness to do substantial trading volumes but subject to collateral arrangements that were tightly managed.

---

[17] Paul Volker, former secretary of the U.S. Treasury, first suggested it.

[18] See, for example, Donald Kilpatrick, Michael Oimette, and Anthony D. Foti, Pillsbury, Winthrop, Shaw, Pitman LLP, "Dodd-Frank Act: The Volcker Rule," July 21, 2010, accessed May 29, 2011, at http://www.pillsburylaw.com/siteFiles/Publications/CorpSec_Alert_Volcker%20Rule_07-21-10_secure.pdf.

[19] Joanna Slater, "How Goldman Changed," *The Globe and Mail*, April 24, 2010, B5.

[20] Ibid.

[21] Ibid.

[22] Ibid.

[23] Ibid.

[24] Ibid.

[25] Farzad and Dwyer "Goldman Sachs," 31.

[26] Letter to shareholders, in *Goldman Sachs 2009 Annual Report*, 2–9, accessed September 1, 2010, at http://www2.goldmansachs.com/our-firm/investors/financials/current/annual-reports/2009-complete-annual.pdf.

As we do with most other counterparty relationships, we limited our overall credit exposure to AIG through a combination of collateral and market hedges in order to protect ourselves against the potential inability of AIG to make good on its commitments.

We established a pre-determined hedging program, which provided that if aggregate exposure moved above a certain threshold, credit default swaps (CDS) and other credit hedges would be obtained. This hedging was designed to keep our overall risk to manageable levels.

As part of our trading with AIG, we purchased from them protection on super-senior collateralized debt obligation (CDO) risk. This protection was designed to hedge equivalent transactions executed with clients taking the other side of the same trades. In so doing, we served as an intermediary in assisting our clients to express a defined view on the market. The net risk we were exposed to was consistent with our role as a market intermediary rather than a proprietary market participant.

In July 2007, as the market deteriorated, we began to significantly mark down the value of our super-senior CDO positions. Our rigorous commitment to fair value accounting, coupled with our daily transactions as a market maker in these securities, prompted us to reduce our valuations on a real-time basis which we believe we did earlier than other institutions. This resulted in collateral disputes with AIG. We believe that subsequent events in the housing market proved our marks to be correct—they reflected the realistic values markets were placing on these securities.

Over the ensuing weeks and months, we continued to make collateral calls, which were based on market values, consistent with our agreements with AIG. While we collected collateral, there still remained gaps between what we received and what we believed we were owed. These gaps were hedged in full by the purchase of CDS and other risk mitigants from third parties, such that we had no material residual risk if AIG defaulted on its obligations to us.

In mid-September 2008, prior to the government's action to save AIG, a majority of Goldman Sachs' exposure to AIG was collateralized and the rest was covered through various risk mitigants. Our total exposure on the securities on which we bought protection was roughly $10 billion. Against this, we held roughly $7.5 billion in collateral. The remainder was fully covered through hedges we purchased, primarily through CDS for which we received collateral from our market counterparties. Thus, if AIG had failed, we would have had the collateral from AIG and the proceeds from the CDS protection we purchased and, therefore, would not have incurred any material economic loss.

In this regard, a list of AIG's cash flows to counterparties indicates little about each bank's credit exposure to the company. The figure of $12.9 billion that AIG paid to Goldman Sachs post the government's decision to support AIG is made up as follows:

> $4.8 billion for highly marketable U.S. Government Agency securities that AIG had pledged to us in return for a loan of $4.8 billion. They gave us the cash, we gave them back the securities. If AIG hadn't repaid the loan, we would simply have sold the securities and received the $4.8 billion of value in that way.
>
> An additional $2.5 billion that AIG owed us in collateral from September 16, 2008 (just after the government's action) through December 31, 2008. This represented the additional collateral that was called as markets continued to deteriorate and was consistent with the existing agreements that we had with AIG.
>
> $5.6 billion associated with a financing entity called Maiden Lane

III, which was established in mid-November 2008 by the Federal Reserve to purchase the securities underlying certain CDS contracts and to cancel those contracts between AIG and its counterparties. The Federal Reserve required that the counterparties deliver the cash bonds to Maiden Lane III in order to settle the CDS contracts and avoid any further collateral calls. Consequently, the cash flow of $5.6 billion between Maiden Lane III and Goldman Sachs reflected the Federal Reserve paying Goldman Sachs the face value of the securities (approximately $14 billion) less the collateral (approximately $8.4 billion) we already held on those securities. Goldman Sachs then spent the vast majority of the money we received to buy the cash bonds from our counterparties in order to complete the settlement as required by the Federal Reserve.

While our direct economic exposure to AIG was minimal, the financial markets, and, as a result, Goldman Sachs and every other financial institution and company, benefited from the continued viability of AIG. Although it is difficult to determine what the exact systemic implications would have been had AIG failed, it would have been extremely disruptive to the world's already turbulent financial markets.

Our Activities in the Mortgage Securitization Market

Another issue that has attracted attention and speculation has been how we managed the risk we assumed as a market maker and underwriter in the mortgage securitization market. Again, we want to provide you with the facts.

As a market maker, we execute a variety of transactions each day with clients and other market participants, buying and selling financial instruments, which may result in long or short risk exposures to thousands of different instruments at any given time. This does not mean that we know or even think that prices will fall every time we sell or are short, or rise when we buy or are long.

In these cases, we are executing transactions in connection with our role of providing liquidity to markets. Clients come to us as a market maker because of our willingness and ability to commit our capital and to assume market risk. We are responding to our clients' desire either to establish, or to increase or decrease, their exposure to a position on their own investment views. We are not "betting against" them.

As a market maker, we assume risk created through client purchases and sales. This is fundamental to our role as a financial intermediary. As part of facilitating client transactions, we generally carry an "inventory" of securities. This inventory comprises long and short positions. Its composition reflects the accumulation of customer trades and our judgments about supply and demand or market direction. If a client asks us to transact in an instrument we hold in inventory, we may be able to give the client a better price than it could find elsewhere in the market and to execute the order without potential delay and price movement. This inventory represents a risk position that we manage continuously.

In so doing, we must also manage the size of our inventory and keep exposures in line with risk limits. We believe that risk limits are an important tool in managing our firm. They are established by senior management, and scaled to be in line with our financial resources (capital, liquidity, etc.). They help ensure that regardless of the opinions of an individual or business unit about market direction, our risk must remain within prescribed levels. In addition to selling positions, we use other techniques to manage risk. These include establishing offsetting positions ("hedges") through the same or other instruments, which serve to reduce the firm's overall exposure.

In this way, we are able to serve our clients and to maintain a robust client franchise while prudently limiting overall risk consistent with our financial resources.

Through the end of 2006, Goldman Sachs generally was long in exposure to residential mortgages and mortgage-related products, such as residential mortgage-backed securities (RMBS), CDOs backed by residential mortgages and credit default swaps referencing residential mortgage products. In late 2006, we began to experience losses in our daily residential mortgage-related products P&L as we marked down the value of our inventory of various residential mortgage-related products to reflect lower market prices.

In response to those losses, we decided to reduce our overall exposure to the residential housing market, consistent with our risk protocols—given the uncertainty of the future direction of prices in the housing market and the increased market volatility. The firm did not generate enormous net revenues or profits by betting against residential mortgage-related products, as some have speculated; rather, our relatively early risk reduction resulted in our losing less money than we otherwise would have when the residential housing market began to deteriorate rapidly.

The markets for residential mortgage-related products, and subprime mortgage securities in particular, were volatile and unpredictable in the first half of 2007. Investors in these markets held very different views of the future direction of the U.S. housing market based on their outlook on factors that were equally available to all market participants, including housing prices, interest rates and personal income and indebtedness data. Some investors developed aggressively negative views on the residential mortgage market. Others believed that any weakness in the residential housing markets would be relatively mild and temporary. Investors with both sets of views came to Goldman Sachs and other financial intermediaries to establish long and short exposures to the residential housing market through RMBS, CDOs, CDS and other types of instruments or transactions.

The investors who transacted with Goldman Sachs in CDOs in 2007, as in prior years, were primarily large, global financial institutions, insurance companies and hedge funds (no pension funds invested in these products, with one exception: a corporate-related pension fund that had long been active in this area made a purchase of less than $5 million). These investors had significant resources, relationships with multiple financial intermediaries and access to extensive information and research flow, performed their own analysis of the data, formed their own views about trends, and many actively negotiated at arm's length the structure and terms of transactions.

We certainly did not know the future of the residential housing market in the first half of 2007 any more than we can predict the future of markets today. We also did not know whether the value of the instruments we sold would increase or decrease. It was well known that housing prices were weakening in early 2007, but no one—including Goldman Sachs—knew whether they would continue to fall or to stabilize at levels where purchasers of residential mortgage-related securities would have received their full interest and principal payments.

Although Goldman Sachs held various positions in residential mortgage-related products in 2007, our short positions were not a "bet against our clients." Rather, they served to offset our long positions. Our goal was, and is, to be in a position to make markets for our clients while managing our risk within prescribed limits.[27]

[27] Ibid., 7–9.

In their *Bloomberg Businessweek* article on April 12, 2010, Robert Farzad and Paula Dwyer[28] investigated the positions taken by Goldman's senior executives. In conclusion, the authors state,

> Business is booming, but Goldman, which once prided itself on avoiding the ostentations and on making money for the long haul, is a different firm, with a perception problem that mere explanation can't solve. In committing to market-making at all costs, the firm has opened itself up to forces beyond its control. The Question is: Has Goldman Sachs shorted itself?[29]

Questions

1. Based on the conflicts of interest raised in the case, has Goldman Sachs, in effect, shorted itself? Explain why and why not.
2. How should Goldman Sachs have handled each conflict of interest?
3. If Goldman Sachs really is innocent of all conflicts, why has the firm's reputation suffered?
4. Referring to the outrage over the apparent abuse of AIG, Farzad and Dwyer ask the question, "If the firm could just write a multibillion-dollar check to erase the outrage—deserved or not—over the AIG payout and be done with the public agony, wouldn't it just do it?"[30] What would your answer be? Provide your reasoning for and against.
5. Is it appropriate for Goldman Sachs to "bet against their clients" through their investment activities?
6. One of Goldman's main arguments in their defense is that their intentions were good—they did what they did in response to client requests, thus facilitating markets and making the world a better place.
   a. Is the "good intention" argument sufficient to claim actions following from it are ethical? Why and why not? Remember the saying, "The road to hell is paved with good intentions."
   b. Is there something in addition to good intentions that Goldman Sachs would have been wise to consider in its decision making?
7. How would you have advised Goldman Sachs's executives to have handled this crisis better?
8. What would an appropriate level of bonus payments be for Goldman Sachs as a whole?
9. Would bonuses paid in Goldman Sachs stock be more appropriate than those paid in cash?

[28] Ibid., dated April 1, 2010, on the Web but published in the April 12, 2010, edition of *Bloomberg Businessweek*.

[29] Ibid., 38.

[30] Ibid.

ETHICS CASE

Mark-to-Market (M2M) Accounting and the Demise of AIG

American International Group, Inc. (AIG) was the world's largest insurance company with major offices in New York, London, Paris, and Hong Kong. From 2005 to 2008, the company had a series of accounting problems. First, it was convicted of fraudulent financial reporting and then of reporting mammoth unrealized losses that led to the company being taken over by the government. Throughout this period, it went through four CEOs.

On June 6, 2005, the SEC laid charges against executives at AIG and General Re alleging that they committed securities fraud by engaging in two reinsurance sham transactions that artificially increased the loss reserves of AIG by $500 million, thereby making the financial results of AIG look better than they were in the fourth quarter of 2000 and the first quarter of 2001. According to the SEC, "The transactions were initiated by AIG to quell criticism by analysts concerning a reduction in the company's loss reserves in the third quarter of 2000."[1] Billionaire Warren Buffet, who owned General Re, was not involved in the SEC suit, but Maurice Greenberg, the then CEO of AIG, was identified as an unindicted coconspirator who was aware of the sham transactions.[2] Afterward, Greenberg was pressured to leave the company.

In February 2006, AIG agreed to pay a $1.6 billion fine,[3] and two years later five former executives of General Re and AIG were found guilty of securities fraud.[4] Meanwhile, AIG began replacing its CEO. In 2005, Greenberg was replaced by Martin Sullivan, who was replaced in June 2008 by Robert Willumstad after AIG recorded mammoth losses and its stock price plummeted. Willumstad was replaced three months later by Edward Liddy, after the government took over AIG.

Although its primary business was selling insurance, in 1987 AIG began to sell financial products through its subsidiary, AIG Financial Products Corp. One of its major products was a credit default swap (CDS) contract designed to protect investors against defaults on fixed-income investments such as mortgage-backed securities and other mortgage-backed derivatives. However, internal controls at the subsidiary were weak. In late November 2007, AIG's auditors Pricewaterhouse-Coopers raised concern with Sullivan about material weaknesses in the risk management areas. In March 2008, the Office of Thrift Supervision said, "We are concerned that the corporate oversight of AIG Financial Products…lacks critical elements of independence, transparency, and granularity."[5]

Nevertheless, the subsidiary continued to sell its financial products, including CDS contracts on $441 billion of asset-backed securities, $57.8 billion of which related to mortgage-backed securities. When the subprime mortgage meltdown occurred in 2007, AIG began to record losses on these CDSs as result of FASB 157. The FASB issued Statement No. 157 on Fair Value Measurements in 2006 that became effective in 2007. The fair value measurement rule, referred to as the "mark-to-market" (M2M) rule, required that financial assets and liabilities be revalued to their market values each reporting period. In the case of a financial instrument, this would be at the quoted price of the instrument in an active market. As the market for subprime mortgages deteriorated, so, too, did the market for financial instruments that were backed by those mortgages.

In February 2008, the unrealized losses were $4.8 billion, which were increased to $11 billion by the end of the month. In June, Sullivan resigned as CEO but was given a $15 million "golden parachute."[6] On September 16, AIG reported losses of $13.2 billion for the first six months of

[1] Securities and Exchange Commission, "SEC Charges Gen Re Executive for Aiding in AIG Securities Fraud," June 6, 2005, http://www.sec.gov/news/press/2005-85.htm.

[2] David Voreacos and Jane Mills, "Former AIG, General Re Officials Convicted of Fraud," February 26, 2008, http://www.washingtonpost.com/wp-dyn/content/article/2008/02/25/AR2008022502722.html.

[3] Brooke Masters, "AIG Agrees to $1.6 Billion Fine to Settle Fraud, Bid-Rigging Case," *Seattle Times*, February 10, 2006.

[4] Voreacos and Mills, "Former AIG, General Re Officials Convicted of Fraud."

[5] Brian Ross and Tom Shine, "After Bailout, AIG Exec Heads to California Resort," *ABC News Internet Ventures*, October 7, 2008.

[6] Ibid.

2008. Its shares were trading at $3.14, down more than 90% from its peak of $190 billion market value at the end of 2006.[7] The federal government decided that AIG, one of the five largest financial companies in the world, was "too big to fail," so it announced a bailout for the company. The government provided a credit-liquidity facility of $85 billion, which was later increased, in return for receiving warrants. In essence, the warrants gave the government a 79.9% equity interest in AIG. On September 17, AIG drew down $28 billion of the credit-liquidity facility. By October 24, it had drawn down $90.3 billion of the $122.8 billion bailout.

In testimony before the House of Representatives Committee on Oversight and Government Reform on October 7, 2008, Willumstad laid part of the blame for the company's failure on the accounting rules that forced AIG to record unrealized losses on its CDSs:

> However, when the market for the underlying bonds froze toward the end of 2007, accounting rules required AIG to "mark to market" the value of its swaps. But the market was not functioning. The way the accounting rules were applied in this unprecedented situation forced AIG to recognize tens of billions of dollars in accounting losses in the fourth quarter of 2007 and the first two quarters of 2008, even though, as far as I am aware, AIG has made very few payments on any of the credit default swaps it wrote and the vast majority of the securities underlying the swaps are still rated investment grade or better by the rating agencies.[8]

So, according to Willumstad, the collapse of AIG and the subsequent bail out were the result of M2M accounting. In a speech the next day, Lynn Turner, the former chief accountant of the SEC, said, "AIG is blaming its downfall on accounting rules which require it to disclose losses to its investors. That's like blaming the thermometer, folks, for a fever."[9] On October 10, 2008, FASB loosened the M2M accounting rule, permitting companies to forgo writing down their securities if there is no ready market for them, provided that the existence and nature of the securities is disclosed.

Questions

1. The argument is that M2M accounting caused AIG to record huge unrealized losses. These losses led to a downgrade in the quality of AIG stock. The downgrade and frozen credit markets led to eventual bailout. So, do you agree that the accounting rules contributed to AIG's demise?
2. The government said that AIG was "too big to fail." It was concerned that if AIG declared bankruptcy, then individuals holding personal insurance as well as other investments would have no insurance and would be in danger as the financial and liquidity crisis deepened. But many felt that the federal government should not be investing in publicly traded companies. There is risk in the marketplace, and one such risk is that occasionally businesses go bankrupt. Should the federal government have bailed out AIG, especially when it had not rescued Lehman Brothers and had let Merrill Lynch be taken over by Bank of America?

---

[7] Hugh Son, "AIG Plunges as Downgrades Threaten Quest for Capital," *Bloomberg.com*, September 16, 2008, http://www.bloomberg.com/apps/news?pid=20601087&sid=amuMN6feT0kE&refer=home.

[8] *Statement of Robert B. Willumstad before the United States House of Representatives Committee on Oversight and Government Reform*, October 7, 2008, http://oversight.house.gov/documents/20081007101054.pdf.

[9] Michael de la Merced and Sharon Otterman, "AIG's Spending Scorned," *San Diego Union-Tribune*, October 8, 2008, http://www.signonsandiego.com/uniontrib/20081008/news_1b8aig.html.

ETHICS CASE

Subprime Lending—Greed, Faith, and Disaster

In December 2002, Stan O'Neal became CEO of Merrill Lynch & Co. Inc., the world's largest brokerage house. Known as "Mother Merrill" to insiders, the firm had a nurturing environment that accepted lower profit margins so that veteran employees could remain with the firm. O'Neal changed that culture. He laid off one-third of the workforce—24,000 employees—and fired nineteen senior executives while eliminating senior management perks. He put in a new young management team, expanded the firm's overseas activities, and made Merrill a more aggressive, risk-friendly organization. In 2006, for example, the firm made $7 billion in trading securities, compared with $2.2 billion in 2002. Under O'Neal's leadership, Merrill became the most profitable investment bank in America, making more money per broker than any of its competitors. O'Neal was rewarded well—in 2007, he became one of Wall Street's best-paid executives, earning $48 million in salary and bonuses.

He pushed the company into new lines of business, including investing in collateralized debt obligations (CDOs). Merrill led the industry in its exposure to CDOs. Over an eighteen-month period to the summer of 2007, its investment in these subprime mortgage-backed CDO pools rose from $1 billion to more than $40 billion. Then the subprime mortgage bubble burst.

The term "subprime" refers not to the interest rate changed on the mortgage but rather to the risk associated with the borrower. Subprime mortgages are given to high-risk customers who are charged an interest rate that is greater than prime. These mortgages are typically given to people who would not normally qualify for a mortgage from a conventional lender, such as a bank. From the lender's point of view, as long as house prices increase, the risk of a loss on the mortgage is low. As such, the mortgages became low-risk, high-yield investments. The lenders of these subprime mortgages would then package these mortgages as bundles of asset-backed synthetic securities, such as CDOs, which were sold to third parties, including individuals, corporations, pension funds, banks, insurance companies, and brokerage houses.

The subprime mortgage bubble bust when house prices in the United States began to fall. People could no longer refinance their homes or pay off their mortgages by selling their homes. By late 2006, one in eight subprime mortgages was in default. Throughout 2007, nearly 1.5 million American home owners lost their homes. As the housing market imploded, mortgage payment defaults increased, and the value of subprime mortgages fell, as did the value of the subprime mortgage-backed CDOs. By the summer of 2007, subprime-related losses were being reported by all the major financial institutions.

In the third quarter of 2007, Merrill announced a loss of $2.3 billion, compared with a profit of $3.05 billion for the third quarter in 2006. It also announced a $7.9 billion provision for losses on mortgage-related investments, larger than the warning of a possible $5 billion write-down that it had made a month earlier. Within a week of reporting the largest quarterly loss in the company's ninety-three-year history, O'Neal resigned as chairman and CEO of Merrill Lynch. Although he did not receive any severance, O'Neal did receive $161 million in stock and retirement benefits.

Questions

1. Subprime mortgages targeted lower-income Americans, new immigrants, and people who had a poor credit history. The customers were told that because house prices had been rising, the borrower would be able to refinance the loan at a later date with the increased equity in the house. Was this an ethically correct sales

pitch? Were the lenders taking advantage of financially naïve customers?

2. O'Neal transformed Merrill Lynch from a conservative bank into an aggressive risk-taking institution. Risk taking means that there is the potential for high rewards as well as large losses. From 2002, when O'Neal became CEO, Merrill's share rose 53%. Should the investors now be upset that, as a result of the subprime mortgage meltdown, Merrill's stock price fell by about 30% in 2007?
3. As a result of the subprime mortgage debacle, the CEOs at Merrill Lynch, Citigroup, Bear Stearns, and Morgan Stanley all resigned or were fired. Their departure packages were $161 million, $68 million, $40 million, and $18 million, respectively. Are these settlements unreasonably high given the huge financial losses and write-downs that their companies recorded?

Sources: Janet McFarland, "Amid Billions in Write-downs and Plunging Stocks, Attention Turns to Executive Paycheques," *The Globe and Mail*, March 21, 2008, B1.

"Merrill Lynch Chief Set to Resign," *Seattle Post-Intelligencer*, October 28, 2007, http://seattlepi.nwsource.com/business/337204_merrill29.html.

Steve Rosenbush, "Merrill Lynch's O'Neil Takes the Hit," *Businessweek*. October 24, 2007, http://www.businessweek.com/bwdaily/dnflash/content/oct2007/db20071024_830456.htm.

"The U.S. Subprime Mortgage Meltdown," *CBC News*, August 31, 2007, http://www.cbc.ca/news/background/personalfinance/mortgage-meltdown.html.

Eric Weiner, "Stan O'Neal: The Rise and Fall of a Numbers Guy," *NPR.org*, October 29, 2007, http://www.npr.org/templates/story/story.php?storyId515768986.

ETHICS CASE

Moral Courage: Toronto-Dominion Bank CEO Refuses to Invest in High-Risk Asset-Backed Commercial Paper

Although the Canadian banks did not suffer as much as other financial institutions around the world, they were not immune from the economic consequences of the subprime mortgage meltdown. In Canada, the earliest crisis concerned the liquidity of asset-backed commercial paper (ABCP) that was affected by the precipitous decline of U.S. housing prices and the related mortgage-backed securities on which those prices were based.

ABCP were short-term debt obligations, generally issued by a special purpose entity or trust and secured by a bundle of assets such as mortgages and other types of consumer loans. The repayment and maturity of these ABCPs was dependent on the cash flow of the underlying assets. The ABCPs were issued to investors by trusts that were sponsored or managed by either banks or nonbank financial institutions. The nonbank-sponsored portion of the Canadian market was approximately $35 billion.

In July 2007, as the U.S. subprime mortgage market began to deteriorate, the Canadian issuers began to fear that they, too, could face a liquidity crisis that would prevent the recovery of capital or refinancing of borrowings when they came due. As such, in August, a number of nonbank ABCP sponsors agreed to a sixty-day standstill period, called the Montreal Accord, during which the holders (those who had invested in the ABCP) promised not to roll over or redeem their paper at maturity, and the issuers agreed not to make any collateral calls. A committee, chaired by Toronto lawyer Purdy Crawford, then began to work out a deal whereby the short-term ABCP could be converted into long-term floating-rate debt that would have a much greater likelihood of recovery or refinance because the underlying assets would eventually recover their value.

The agreement required the support of the five major banks in Canada. They were each to pay $500 million in order to shore up the country's debt market. However, Canada's third-largest bank, the Toronto-Dominion Bank (TD), balked at the suggestion on the basis that, three years earlier, the bank intentionally had moved to eliminate its exposure in the nonbank ABCP market.

In May 2005, Edmund Clark, CEO of the TD, announced that the bank would exit the structured loans products market, including interest rate derivatives and collateralized debt obligations such as ABCPs. The bank decided that it would focus on consumer banking rather than the securities business. Clark, who had a Ph.D. in economics from Harvard, contended that the securities business was too risky. He had been briefed by experts who traded these securities on the nature of credit and equity products and concluded that the risk was too great. "The whole thing didn't make sense to me. You're going to get all your money back, or you're going to get none of your money back. I said 'wow!' if this ever went against us, we could take some serious losses here." The TD generated 80% of its profit from consumer lending and money management. "I'm an old school banker. I don't think you should do something you don't understand, hoping there's somebody at the bottom of the organization who does."[1]

Meanwhile, all of the other major Canadian banks invested in the ABCP market. They collectively controlled two-thirds of the ABCP market.[2] The yields were high, and everyone was on the bandwagon. It took great courage for Clark to go against the tide. As David Baskin of Baskin Financial Services said, "He's absolutely to be commended for not getting caught up in the subprime frenzy."[3] And Clark was right. When the ABCP market collapsed, the other banks reported large write-downs on their securities, estimated to be in excess of $2 billion.[4]

As the commercial credit market began to collapse, the Montreal Accord was extended. The liquidity of the ABCP market was drying up, and only the major chartered banks could help solve the problem. TD was under a lot of pressure to help participate in the repair of the credit market, but Clark's attitude was "that it would not be in the best interest of TD shareholders to assume incremental risk for activities in which we were not involved."[5] TD was not part of the problem, so he thought it should not be part of the solution. Finally, the federal government, through its agency the Bank of Canada, weighed in, saying that it wanted the problem solved and that it was in both the public interest and the interest of the financial marketplace that all the banks participate in restructuring the commercial paper segment of the market. Since TD was part of the financial community, although it had not created the problem, it had a moral and financial obligation to help.

TD could have held out, but as one analyst said, "It's like protesting going to your mother-in-law's house for Christmas. Despite your protest, you know you're going because it's been determined that it's in your best interest to do so. In my view, the Bank of Canada will win the argument."[6] On March 13, 2008, the five major Canadian banks, including TD, said that they would provide $950 million to

[1] Sean Pasternak, "Toronto-Dominion Avoids Subprime as Banks Costs Rise," *Bloomberg.com.*, May 26, 2008, http://www.bloomberg.com/apps/news?pid=newsarchive&sid=aeAsOI6GUU1Y.

[2] "Credit Crunch Could be 'Quite Ugly' for Months: TD CEO," *CBC News*, September 11, 2007, http://www.cbc.ca/money/story/2007/09/11/credit.html?ref=rss.

[3] Pasternak, "Toronto-Dominion Avoids Subprime as Banks Costs Rise."

[4] "TD Bank Will Consider Montreal Accord Proposals on ABCP but Won't Take Risks," *The Canadian Press*, December 17, 2007.

[5] Nicole Mordant, "TD Bank Throws Wrench into Canada ABCP Repair," Reuters, December 17, 2007.

[6] Barry Critchley, "TD May Join ABCP Bailout," *Financial Post*, December 19, 2007.

support the newly restructured credit market, in which $32 billion of short-term commercial paper would be swapped for long-term notes.[7]

Questions

1. Because the TD was neither a manufacturer nor a distributor of ABCP products, did the bank have a moral responsibility to assist in the restructuring of the commercial paper market?
2. If you were Edmund Clark, how would you explain to the Board of Directors that you were having the bank exit a market in which your competitors were making a lot of money?
3. The banks in Canada are highly regulated by the federal government. If the banks could not come to a voluntary agreement, should the federal government have forced the banks through legislation to providing $950 million financial support to help solve the ABCP liquidity crisis?

[7] Doug Alexander and Sean Pasternak, "Canada Commercial Paper Group Gets Credit Protection," *Bloomberg.com*, March 17, 2008, http://www.bloomberg.com/apps/news?pid=newsarchive&sid=aO.ysqLVjxUc.

ETHICS CASE

The Ethics of AIG's Commission Sales

The advantage of commission sales is that if the salesperson puts in effort and makes a sale, then both the company and the salesperson benefit. The salesperson receives a commission, and the company receives the proceeds of the sale, net of the commission. Referred to as a first-best contract, its purpose is to align the interests of both the company and its sales force. In addition, companies often reward their leading salespeople with expensive trips and holidays. They are considered thank-you gifts for generating so much revenue for the company. But commissions and holidays can be problematic. Consider the case of AIG.

American International Group, Inc. (AIG) was among the five largest financial companies in the world.[1] A diversified company, its primary business was selling both personal and corporate insurance, but it was also involved in businesses, such as lease financing, real estate, and selling financial products. With respect to insurance, AIG did not have agents but, rather, sold insurance through independent brokers. In this way, AIG had to pay a commission only if the broker was successful at selling one of AIG's products. If the independent broker was unsuccessful at making a sale, then there was no cost to AIG. Only successful sales were rewarded with a commission.

In 1987, the company formed a subsidiary, AIG Financial Products Corp., to sell a variety of financial products, including credit default swap (CDS) contracts. These products were designed to protect investors against defaults on fixed-income investments.[2] This business flourished under the leadership of Joe Cassano. At one point, it had sold protection on $441 billion of asset-backed securities, including $57.8 billion that were related to subprime mortgages.[3] Cassano and his team were paid a commission of 30% on every dollar of business generated. As the market for these CDSs increased, the sales

[1] Hugh Son, "AIG Plunges as Downgrades Threaten Quest for Capital," *Bloomberg.com*, September 16, 2008.
[2] Karnitschnig et al., "U.S. to Take Over AIG in $85 Billion Bailout."
[3] Son, "AIG Plunges as Downgrades Threaten Quest for Capital."

staff received more and more commissions. In the eight-year period from 2000, Cassano was paid $280 million.[4]

In 2007, the subprime mortgage market turned as the housing crisis in the United States deepened. As a result, losses in the Financial Products subsidiary on CDSs began to increase. In February 2008, AIG said that the swaps lost $4.8 billion in October and November 2007. By the end of February, the losses had reached $11 billion, and Cassano was replaced as CEO of the division. He collected his bonuses of $34 million and was then hired back as a consultant at $1 million per month to oversee winding down the CDS business.[5] But the losses generated by Financial Products kept increasing. On September 16, AIG reported losses of $13.2 billion for the first six months of 2008. That same day, the government announced that it was prepared to pay $85 billion to bail out the company.

Meanwhile, at the beginning of October, as the company was being supported by the government to forestall bankruptcy, AIG paid $444,000 for a California holiday for its senior sales personnel. Although relatively small, the optics of this was questionable. The cost of their weeklong retreat at the St. Regis Resort, a luxury resort and spa, was $200,000 for rooms, $150,000 for meals, $23,000 in the spa, $7,000 in greens fees, $1,400 in the salon, and $10,000 in the bar.[6] Congressional leaders were appalled. "This is unbridled greed. It's an insensitivity to how people are spending our dollars," said Congressman Mark Souder. "They're getting pedicures and their manicures and the American people are paying for that," said Congressman Elijah Cummings.[7] When asked why Cassano, who had been responsible for the losses incurred by the Financial Products subsidiary, had been hired back as a consultant after he had been fired, Martin Sullivan, the former CEO of AIG, said, "I wanted to retain the twenty-year knowledge of the transactions."[8]

Questions

1. Commission salespeople are paid their commission after they write successful insurance policies or consummate the sale of financial products. Should their commissions be recovered if the company subsequently suffers a loss as a result of the business written by the sales staff? Should there be an upper limit placed on commissions so that no one employee receives $280 million in commissions over an eight-year period? How could such an upper limit be selected if a company wished to establish one?
2. Is it right that perks such as holidays at luxury resorts are provided only to senior executives and the sales staff but not to the other employees of the firm?
3. Should senior officers who have extensive firm-specific knowledge be hired back as consultants to help rectify their mistakes?

---

[4] Frank Ahrens, "Joe Cassano: The Man Who Brought Down AIG?," *Washingtonpost.com*, October 7, 2008.

[5] Henry Champ, "Lawmakers Fume at Excess of Failed Firm's Execs," *Washington File*, October 8, 2008.

[6] Ibid.

[7] Ross and Shine, "After Bailout, AIG Exec Heads to California Resort."

[8] Ahrens, "Joe Cassano."

INDEX

Page numbers followed by *f* indicate figures; and those followed by *t* indicate tables.

A

B

F